Making America

A History of the United States

Making America

A History of the United States
Volume II: Since 1865

Third Edition

Carol Berkin
Baruch College, City University of New York

Christopher L. Miller
The University of Texas—Pan American

Robert W. Cherny
San Francisco State University

James L. Gormly
Washington and Jefferson College

Houghton Mifflin Company

Boston   New York

Editor-in-Chief: Jean L. Woy
Sponsoring Editor: Mary Dougherty
Development Editor: Leah Strauss
Senior Project Editor: Carol Newman
Editorial Assistant: Reba Frederics
Senior Production/Design Coordinator: Jill Haber
Senior Manufacturing Coordinator: Priscilla Bailey
Senior Marketing Manager: Sandra McGuire

Cover image: Barse Miller, *Factory Town*, 1946, oil on canvas;
Toledo Museum of Art, Toledo, Ohio (Museum Purchase Fund,
acc. no. 1948.70)

Text Credits
p. 506: Excerpt from Part 2 [Moloch], from "Chicago" in *Chicago Poems* by Carl Sandburg, copyright © 1916 by Holt, Rinehart and Winston, Inc. and renewed 1944 by Carl Sandburg. Reprinted by permission of Harcourt Brace & Company; pp. 596–597: From Luther Standing Bear, *Land of the Spotted Eagle*, 1933, pp. 189–191. Reprinted with permission from Geoffrey M. Standing Bear; p. 722: From *Collected Poems*, HarperCollins. Copyright 1922, 1950 by Edna St. Vincent Millay; p. 880: From "Howl," from *Collected Poems 1947–1980* by Allen Ginsberg. Copyright © 1955 by Allen Ginsberg. Reprinted with permission of HarperCollins Publishers; pp. 910–911: Reprinted from *The Massachusetts Review*, © 1966 The Massachusetts Review, Inc.; p. 944: Text from *El Malcraido*. Used by permission of United Farm Workers of America, AFL-CIO; p. 999, Figure 34.1: "Expansion and Recession," *The New York Times*, Nov. 27, 2001, p. C1. Copyright © by The New York Times Company. Reprinted by permission.

Printed in the U.S.A.

Library of Congress Catalog Number: 2001133225

ISBN: 0-618-19068-6

4 5 6 7 8 9-VH-06 05 04 03

BRIEF CONTENTS

CONTENTS

FEATURES

Tables

Authors of textbooks may dream of cheering audiences and mountains of fan mail, but this is rarely their reality. Yet, there are occasional moments of glory. A colleague drops by our office to tell us she has been using our text and the students seem more prepared and more interested in class. A former student, now teaching, sends an e-mail, saying he has used our book as a basis for his first set of class lectures and discussions. Or, a freshman in a survey class adds a note at the end of her exam, saying, "thanks for writing a text that isn't boring." Maybe none of this adds up to an academy award or a photo on the cover of *People* magazine, but comments like these do assure us that the book we envisioned a decade ago is, if not perfect, at least on the right track. And, the improvements we have made in this third edition of *Making America*, make us even more confident.

From the beginning, our goal has been to create a different kind of textbook, one that meets the real needs of the modern college student. Every history classroom reflects the rich cultural diversity of today's world, with its mixture of native-born Americans and recent immigrants, and its significant number of serious-minded men and women whose formal skills lag behind their interest and enthusiasm for learning. As professors in large public universities located on three of the nation's borders—the Pacific Ocean, the Atlantic, and the Rio Grande—we know the basic elements both the professor and the students need in the survey text for that classroom: a historical narrative that does not demand a lot of prior knowledge about the American past; information organized sequentially, or chronologically, so that students are not confused by too many topical digressions; and a full array of integrated and supportive learning aids to help students at every level of preparedness comprehend and retain what they read.

The first edition of *Making America* was an account of the American past firmly anchored by a political chronology framing the many centuries under discussion. In it, people and places were brought to life not only through words but also with maps, paintings, and photos. We made a genuine effort to communicate with students rather than to impress them. And *Making America* presented history as a dynamic process shaped by human expectations, difficult choices, and often surprising consequences. With this focus on history as a process, *Making America* encouraged students to think historically and to develop into citizens who value the past.

Yet, as veteran teachers, we the authors of *Making America* knew that any history project, no matter how good, could be improved. Having scrawled "Revise" across the top of student papers for several decades, we decided to impose the same demands on ourselves. For this third edition, we subjected our text to the same critical reappraisal. We eliminated features that professors and students told us did not work as well as we had hoped; we added features that we believed would be more effective; and we tested our skills as storytellers and biographers more rigorously this time around. The result is a book more vibrant with individual historical figures whose lives—and whose words—provide a window onto the eras in which they lived.

THE APPROACH

Professors and students who have used the previous editions of *Making America* will recognize immediately that we have preserved many of its central features. We have again set the nation's complex story within an explicitly political chronology, relying on a basic and familiar structure that is nevertheless broad enough to accommodate generous attention to social, economic, and diplomatic aspects of our national history. We remain confident that this political framework allows us to integrate the experiences of all Americans into a meaningful and effective narrative of our nation's development. Because our own scholarly research often focuses on the experiences of women, African Americans, and Native Americans, we would not have been content with a framework that excluded or marginalized their history. *Making America* continues to be built on the premise that all Americans are historically active figures, playing significant roles in creating the history that we and other authors narrate. We have also continued what is now a tradition in

Making America, that is, providing pedagogical tools for students that allow them to master complex material and enable them to develop analytical skills.

THEMES

This edition continues to thread five central themes through the narrative of *Making America*. The first of these themes, the political development of the nation, is evident in the text's coverage of the creation and revision of the federal and local governments, the contests waged over domestic and diplomatic policies, the internal and external crises faced by the United States and its political institutions, and the history of political parties.

The second theme is the diversity of a national citizenry created by immigrants. To do justice to this theme, *Making America* explores not only English and European immigration but immigrant communities from Paleolithic times to the present. The text attends to the tensions and conflicts that arise in a diverse population, but it also examines the shared values and aspirations that define middle-class American lives.

Making America's third theme is the significance of regional economies and cultures. This regional theme is developed for society before European colonization and for the colonial settlements of the seventeenth and eighteenth centuries. It is evident in our attention to the striking social and cultural divergences that existed between the American Southwest and the Atlantic coastal regions as well as between the antebellum South and North.

A fourth theme is the rise and impact of large social movements, from the Great Awakening in the 1740s to the rise of youth cultures in the post–World War II generations, movements prompted by changing material conditions or by new ideas challenging the status quo.

The fifth theme is the relationship of the United States to other nations. In *Making America* we explore in depth the causes and consequences of this nation's role in world conflict and diplomacy, whether in the era of colonization of the Americas, the eighteenth-century independence movement, the removal of Indian nations from their traditional lands, the impact of the rhetoric of manifest destiny, American policies of isolationism and interventionism, or in the modern role of the United States as a dominant player in world affairs.

LEARNING FEATURES

The chapters in *Making America* follow a format that provides students essential study aids for mastering the historical material. Each chapter begins with a map and timeline that set the scene for the most significant events and developments in the narrative that follows. While the opening timeline sets significant events in a broader time frame, a chronological chart in the interior of the chapter outlines more fully the events of the given time period. On the chapter-opening page, there is a topical outline of the material students will encounter in the chapter. Then, to help students focus on the broad questions and themes, we provide critical thinking, or focus, questions at the beginning of each major chapter section. Each chapter ends with a summary that reinforces the most important themes and information the student has read.

To ensure that students have full access to the material in each chapter, we provide a page-by-page glossary, defining terms and explaining their historically specific usage the first time they appear in the narrative. The glossary also provides brief identifications of the major historical events, people, or documents discussed on the page. This running glossary will help students build their vocabularies and review for tests. The glossary reflects our concern about communicating fully with student readers without sacrificing the complexity of the history we are relating.

The illustrations in each chapter provide a visual connection to the past, and their captions analyze the subject of the painting, photograph, or artifact and comment on its significance. For this edition we have selected many new illustrations to reinforce or illustrate the themes of the narrative.

NEW TO THE THIRD EDITION

In this new edition we have preserved what our colleagues and their students considered the best and most useful aspects of *Making America*. We also have replaced what was less successful, revised what could be improved, and added new elements to strengthen the book—and, miraculously, we have achieved these goals without increasing the length of the text.

Each chapter now begins with the "Individual Choices" feature that is a brief biography of a man or woman whose life reflects or illustrates the central themes of the chapter. Some of the figures the student will encounter are familiar, famous historical characters while others are ordinary folk, yet all of these individuals invite the students to enter the past. In telling their stories, we introduce the student to the impact that key events had on the people of the era and the role those people played in shaping the era's events. Through their stories, the student will be introduced to the central conflicts, the common assumptions, and the changing views of an historical period.

Each chapter now ends with a new feature called "Individual Voices," which provides a primary source and a series of thought-provoking questions about that source. In this feature, we let the men and women of the past speak directly to the student of today, without the historian's intervention. The feature also allows the students hands-on experience in working with the "stuff" of history, the sources that we work with every day in order to reconstruct the past.

We have made important changes in the text itself. These changes reflect our commitment to incorporating the newest scholarship in American history so that it is available even to the newest students of the field. Changes in the organization of chapters reflect our commitment to producing a coherent narrative rather than an oversimplified one.

Chapter 1 acknowledges the recent reconceptualization of America's early history as part of a history of the transatlantic world. Setting the pre-Columbian eras in the context of this broader, transatlantic world, we have expanded the discussions of developments in Africa and reexamined the role of Native American trading networks in shaping European colonization and commerce. In Chapter 3, greater attention has been paid to the society and culture of the Powhatan Indians and the interaction between the English colonists at Jamestown and the Powhatan confederacy, while Chapter 4 expands the coverage of conflicts among the English colonists. The newest scholarship on the legal, political, and economic development of the United States during the early national period has been integrated into Chapters 7, 8, and 9. Chapter 10 provides an extended discussion of Indian affairs and the relationship of American expansionism and the breakdown of diplomacy between the United States and Great Britain. Greater attention to American expansionism, westward migration, and the cultures displaced by that expansionism is evident in Chapter 13. And, the discussion of the Civil War, like the dis-

cussion earlier of the American Revolution, pays closer attention to the impact of the war on the civil population.

The many significant developments of the post-Civil War era have always presented the most serious organizational challenge in a textbook. While most texts handle this material in thematic or topical chapters, in the third edition of *Making America*, we have succeeded in providing fundamentally chronological coverage that does justice to all the major events, movements and broad developments of this critical era. Chapter 16 covers Reconstruction. Chapter 17 narrates the emergence of an industrial order, while Chapter 18 describes and analyses the development of an urban, industrialized society. Chapter 19 covers the transformation of the American west from 1865 to 1902, while Chapters 20 to 23 provide chronological accounts of economic crash and social upheaval between 1890 and 1900, the Progressive era of 1900 to 1917, America and the world, 1913 to 1920, and the "Roaring Twenties," 1920 to 1929. Foreign relations are interwoven into these chapters, as are the experiences of ethnic, racial, and gender groups. Thus, for example, African Americans do not vanish from the text after the chapter on Reconstruction.

Readers familiar with *Making America* will note that the discussion of the New Deal, once covered in two chapters, is now contained in a new Chapter 24. This reorganization promotes continuity and provides full coverage of the causes of the Depression, Hoover's response, and Roosevelt's New Deal, as well as popular reaction to the Depression and the government programs it engendered. Chapter 25 now offers a new emphasis on Roosevelt's direction of U.S. foreign policy and the steps toward World War II. Chapter 30 provides a reassessment of Presidents Carter and Reagan, with an increased emphasis on the impact of the economy on politics and society. It includes new material on women and on minorities. Chapter 31 carries the narrative of American history up to the election of President George W. Bush and the tragic events of September 11, 2001.

NAMING IN *MAKING AMERICA*

We have thought carefully about the names by which we have identified ethnic groups. As a general rule, we have tried to use terms that were in use among members of that group at the time under consideration. At times, however, this would have distracted readers from the topic to the terminology, and we wanted to avoid that. In such instances, we have tried to use the terms in general use today among members of that group.

Thus, we have used *African American* and *black* relatively interchangeably. The same applies to the terms *American Indian* and *Native American*. If we are writing about a particular Indian group, we have tried to use the most familiar names by which those groups prefer to be identified, e.g., *Lakota* rather than *Sioux*.

Sometimes the names by which groups are identified are controversial within the group itself. Thus, in identifying people from Latin America, some prefer *Latino* and others *Hispanic*. Our usage in this regard often reflects our own regional perspective— Bob Cherny has tended to use *Latino* as that term is more widely used in California, and Chris Miller has often used *Hispanic* because that term is more widely used in Texas. In other places, we have used more specific terms; for example, we have used *Mexican* or *Mexican American* to identify groups that migrated to the United States from Mexico and because that is the usage most common among scholars who have studied those migrants in recent years.

Finally, in a few instances when we have discussed nondominant groups, we have indicated the names that such groups used for dominant groups. In some discussions of the Southwest, for example, you will encounter the term *Anglo* to indicate those people who spoke English rather than Spanish, although we are well aware that many who were (and are) called *Anglo* are not of English (or Anglo-Saxon) descent. *Anglo* has to do with language usage, from the perspective of those who spoke Spanish, rather than having to do with those English-speakers' own sense of ethnicity. Similarly, we sometimes use the term *haole* in our discussions of Hawai'i, to indicate those people whom the indigenous Hawai'ians considered to be outsiders.

We the authors of *Making America* believe that this new edition will be effective in the history classroom. Please let us know what you think by sending us your views through Houghton Mifflin's web site, located at **http://college.hmco.com**.

STUDY AND TEACHING AIDS

A number of useful learning and teaching aids accompany the third edition of *Making America*. They are designed to help students get the most from the course and to provide instructors with some useful teaching tools. Supplements available with *Making America* include the following:

For Students:

- **Study E-pack; printed Study Guide in two volumes, with access to premium Textbook Companion Web Site** provides students with many review exercises and tips on how to study and take tests effectively. Prepared by Kelly Woestman of Pittsburg State University, each chapter of the study guide includes learning objectives, an annotated outline of the chapter, key terms; multiple-choice questions with rejoinders; and essay questions with answer guidelines. The companion web site has self-quizzes, interactive activities that connect to material in the text, and other resources that can help students to succeed in the course.

- **Student's Textbook Companion Web Site** features ACE self-quizzes; online primary sources with activities; annotated web links; and suggestions for further reading organized by chapter.

- **American History GeoQuest CD-ROM** contains thirty interactive historical maps.

- **The *Making America* @history CD-ROM— student's version** contains over 1,000 searchable primary sources, sources (text and graphic), video, and audio, many of which are accompanied by introductory headnotes, writing activities and questions.

- **Rand McNally Atlas of American History**

For Instructors:

- **Test Items**, prepared by Norman Caulfield of Fort Hays State University, provide twenty key terms and definitions, forty to fifty multiple-choice questions, five to ten essay questions with answer guidelines, and an analytical exercise to test critical thinking skills.

- **HM ClassPrep CD-ROM with HM Testing** is a complete electronic resource for instructors that features the text's maps and graphics in Power-Point for presentations, and other documents in Word, such as lecture outlines. Also included is **HM Testing** for Macintosh and Windows. This computerized version of the printed Test Items file allows instructors to create customized tests by editing and adding questions. Most electronic resources can be customized to complement the way you teach your course.

- **Instructor's Resource Manual**, prepared by Kelly Woestman of Pittsburg State University, includes for every chapter instructional objectives that are drawn from the textbook's critical thinking questions, chapter summary and annotated outline, lecture topics that include resource material and references to the text; discussion questions; answers to the critical thinking questions that follow each major heading in the text; cooperative and individual learning activities; map activities; ideas for paper topics; and a list of audiovisual resources.

- **Instructor's Textbook Companion Web Site** features online primary sources with instructor's notes, suggested lecture topics, and annotated web links.

- **American History Map Transparencies, Volumes I and II** is a set of over 150 full-color maps.

- **The** *Making America* **@history CD-ROM—instructor's version** contains over 1,000 searchable primary sources, sources (text and graphic), video, and audio, many of which are accompanied by introductory headnotes, writing activities and questions that can be used to analyze, interpret, and discuss primary sources; to enhance collaborative learning; and to create multimedia lecture presentations.

Please visit us on the web at **http://college.hmco.com** or contact your local Houghton Mifflin representative for more information about the ancillary items or to obtain desk copies.

ACKNOWLEDGMENTS

The authors of *Making America* have benefited greatly from the critical reading of this edition of the book by instructors from across the country. We would like to thank these scholars and teachers: Michael Bertrand, University of Mississippi; Mary Ann Bodayla, Shelby State Community College; Norman Caulfield, Fort Hays State University; Ron Cox, Jr., University of South Carolina; Linda J. Cross, Tyler Junior College; Patrica Norred Derr, Kutztown University; David A. Gerber, SUNY—Buffalo; Daniel K. Gibran, Tennessee State University; Kim M. Gruenwald, Kent State University; Thomas Humphrey, Cleveland State University; Virginia G. Jelatis, Western Illinois University; Troy R. Johnson, California State University; Kimberly R. Kellison, Baylor University; Sean C. Madden, California University of Pennsylvania; Scott C. Martin, Bowling Green State University; J. Kent McGaughy, Houston Community College; Nora E. McMillan, San Antonio College; Susan Roig, Rio Hondo College; William R. Sutton, University of Texas—San Antonio; Daniel B. Thorp, Virginia Tech; Jonathan Wilson, Cuesta College; and Kelly Woestman, Pittsburg State University.

Carol Berkin, who is responsible for Chapters 3 through 7, would like to thank the following historians, teachers, and students: Mary-Jo Kline, Leslie Horowitz, Roberta McCutcheon, Angelo Angelis, Cindy Lobel, and Kathy Feeley for their willingness to suggest new sources and to discuss the significance of new scholarship in early American history. She also thanks the librarians at Baruch College and The Graduate Center for their always able assistance and her colleagues in both history departments for their ongoing, stimulating discussions of history and historical methods of inquiry. Finally, she thanks her children, Hannah and Matthew, for providing an anchor to the present in the midst of her frequent forays into the past.

Christopher L. Miller, who is responsible for Chapters 1 and 2 and 8 through 15, is indebted to his students at the University of Texas—Pan American for providing the constant inspiration to innovate. Provost Rodolfo Arevalo assisted also through awarding him with the annual Teaching With Technology Award, which afforded resources for additional innovation. Thanks, too, are due to the University of Texas TeleCampus, the fully online component of Texas's state university system, for release time and capital equipment that eased the task of revising this volume and bringing it more fully into a form that will be useable in many different teaching contexts. His colleagues on various H-NET discussion lists as always were extremely generous with advice, guidance, and often abstruse points of information. His co-authors also proved again to be the ideal partners in an often frustrating and difficult task. Finally, personal thanks are due to Lisa J. Travis, who assisted in a thousand ways—both personal and professional—and without whom this task could not have been completed.

Robert W. Cherny, who is responsible for Chapters 16 through 23, wishes to thank his students who, over the years, have provided the testing ground for much that is included in these chapters, and especially to thank his research assistants who have helped with the first, second, or third edition: Randolf Arguelles, Marie Bolton, Katherine Davis, Beth Haigin, Michelle Kleehammer, Cynthia Taylor, and David Winn. The staff of the Leonard Library at San Francisco State has always been most helpful; the staff of the Kansas State Historical Society was also very helpful with locating the material on Annie Diggs in Chapter 20. Among his colleagues at San Francisco State, Jerry Combs, Tony D'Agostino, Bill Issel, Paul Longmore, Barbara Loomis, Abdiel Oñate, and Jules Tygiel have provided valuable advice on particular sections. Rebecca Marshall Cherny, Sarah Cherny, and Lena Hobbs Kracht Cherny have been unfailing in their encouragement, inspiration, and support.

James L. Gormly, who is responsible for Chapters 24 through 31, would like to acknowledge the support and encouragement he received from Washington and Jefferson College. He wants to gives a special thanks to Sharon Gormly, whose support, ideas, advice, and critical eye have helped to shape and refine his chapters.

As always, this book is a collaborative effort between authors and the editorial staff of Houghton Mifflin. We would like to thank Jean Woy, editor in chief; Colleen Kyle and Leah Strauss, who guided the book from beginning to completion; Pembroke Herbert, who helped us fill this edition with remarkable illustrations, portraits, and photographs; and Carol Newman, whose keen eye caught every error large and small before the final copy went to press. These talented, committed members of the publishing world encouraged us and generously assisted us every step of the way.

Dear Student:

History is about people—brilliant and insane, brave and treacherous, loveable and hateful, murderers and princesses, daredevils and visionaries, rule breakers and rule makers. It has exciting events, major crises, turning points, battles, and scientific breakthroughs. We, the authors of *Making America*, believe that knowing about the past is critical for anyone who hopes to understand the present and chart the future. In this book, we want to tell you the story of America from its earliest settlement to the present and to tell it in a language and format that helps you enjoy learning that history.

This book is organized and designed to help you master your American history course. The narrative is chronological, telling the story as it happened, decade by decade or era by era. We have developed special tools to help you learn. In the next couple of pages, we'll introduce you to the unique features of this book that will help you to understand the complex and fascinating story of American history.

At the back of the book, you will find some additional resources. In the Appendix, you will find a bibliography listing the books on which we relied in writing the chapters. You will also find reprinted several of the most important documents in American history: the Declaration of Independence, the Articles of Confederation, and the Constitution. Here, too, are tables that give you quick access to important data on the presidents and their cabinets. Finally, you will see the index, which will help you locate a subject quickly if you want to read about it.

In addition, the Study E-pack provides you with many review exercises and tips on how to study and take tests effectively. Ask your bookstore for a copy of this study guide that grants you special access to a premium web site. On the book's companion web site, you'll also find other resources that can help you to succeed in the course. In addition to multiple-choice questions that serve as a tutorial, you'll find suggestions for further reading on the subjects covered in the text, so that you can explore other viewpoints or look in depth at subjects that interest you.

We hope that our textbook conveys to you our own fascination with the American past and sparks your curiosity about the nation's history. We invite you to share your feedback on the book: you can reach us through Houghton Mifflin's American history web site, which is located at http://college.hmco.com.

Carol Berkin, Chris Miller, Bob Cherny, and Jim Gormly

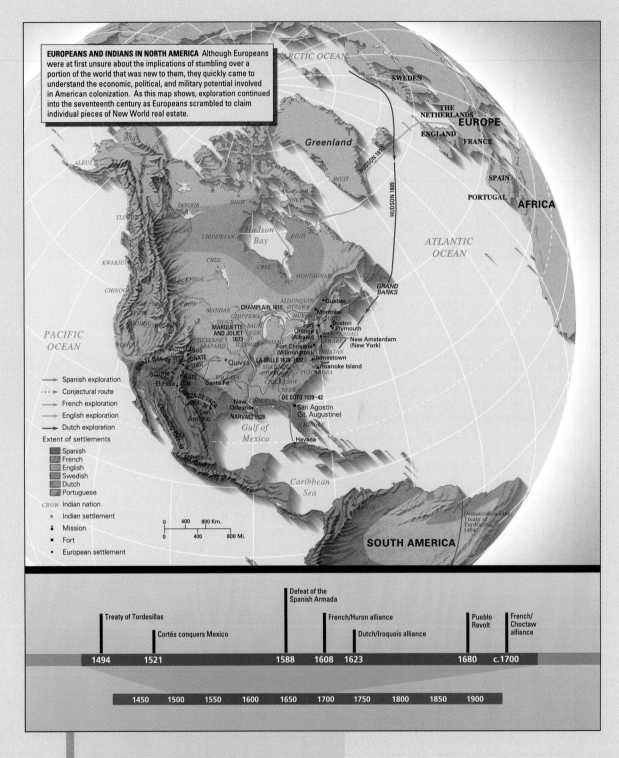

EUROPEANS AND INDIANS IN NORTH AMERICA Although Europeans were at first unsure about the implications of stumbling over a portion of the world that was new to them, they quickly came to understand the economic, political, and military potential involved in American colonization. As this map shows, exploration continued into the seventeenth century as Europeans scrambled to claim individual pieces of New World real estate.

→ Spanish exploration
--→ Conjectural route
→ French exploration
→ English exploration
→ Dutch exploration

Extent of settlements
- Spanish
- French
- English
- Swedish
- Dutch
- Portuguese

CROW   Indian nation
▪   Indian settlement
⚑   Mission
▪   Fort
●   European settlement

0   400   800 Km.
0   400   800 Mi.

Timeline:

Treaty of Tordesillas — 1494
Cortés conquers Mexico — 1521
Defeat of the Spanish Armada — 1588
French/Huron alliance — 1608
Dutch/Iroquois alliance — 1623
Pueblo Revolt — 1680
French/Choctaw alliance — c.1700

1494   1521   1588   1608   1623   1680   c.1700

1450   1500   1550   1600   1650   1700   1750   1800   1850   1900

At the beginning of each chapter, you will find a **Map** and **Timeline,** which set the scene for the most significant events and developments in the chapter narrative.

INDIVIDUAL CHOICES

Bartolomé de Las Casas

In 1550 Spanish church officials ordered a council of learned theologians to assemble in the city of Valladolid to moderate a debate over an issue so important that it challenged the entire underpinning of Spain's New World empire. At issue was the question of whether Native American Indians were human beings. Arguing that they were not was the well-respected scholar Juan Ginés de Sepúlveda. Arguing on the Indians' behalf was a former conquistador and encomendero named Bartolomé de Las Casas.

Born in 1474, Las Casas was the son of a small merchant in Seville. Although we have no evidence that his family was particularly prominent or wealthy, they obviously were comfortable: young Bartolomé had both the access and the leisure to study at the academy attached to Seville's cathedral. Like many of his contemporaries, Las Casas decided to pursue a military career, going to Granada as a soldier in 1497. Then in 1502 he embarked to the West Indies to seek his fortune in the conquest of the Americas.

Apparently Las Casas was successful as a conquistador: within a few years he had earned an imperial land grant with a full complement of Indian laborers. Meeting the demands of both church and king, he taught them Catholicism while he exploited their labor. Eventually, however, the former came to outweigh the latter and Las Casas's religious devotion grew in proportion. After a decade

BARTOLOMÉ DE LAS CASAS

Himself a former conquistador, Bartolomé de Las Casas was ordained as a Catholic priest in 1512 and later became one of the most vocal opponents of Spain's brutal exploitation of Native American people. He petitioned the King in 1540 and won major reforms in the way Spaniards were

Chapter-opening feature **Individual Choices** provides a portrait of one individual whose life illustrates a central theme in the chapter. Some of the individuals are famous historical figures, while others are ordinary people who played a role in shaping the events of their era. This feature dramatizes the theme that historical events are not inevitable but are the result of real people making real choices.

INDIVIDUAL VOICES

Examining a Primary Source

Bartolomé de Las Casas Argues for the American Indians

In his debate with Juan Ginés de Sepúlveda before the Council of Valladolid in 1550 and 1551, Bartolomé de Las Casas repeatedly stressed the many remarkable accomplishments made by Indians, both in creating advanced civilizations of their own and in adapting to Spanish civilization. Many witnesses (most of whom had never been to America) disputed these claims, but more damaging was the argument that such accomplishments were irrelevant. Though perhaps clever, Sepúlveda argued, Indians lacked souls and therefore could never become truly civilized Christians. Like animals, then, they could be exploited but never embraced. Las Casas thought otherwise, and drew on Church doctrine to refute this claim. In the end, Las Casas's argument won the day and became the official position for the Catholic church and the Spanish Crown.

● What, exactly, is Las Casas asserting in this sentence? How does this proposition set up the rest of his argument?

Who, therefore, except one who is irreverent toward God and contemptuous of nature, has dared to write that countless numbers of natives across the ocean are barbarous, savage, uncivilized, and slow witted when, if they are evaluated by an accurate judgment, they completely outnumber all other men? ● *This is consistent with what Saint Thomas writes: "The good which is proportionate to the common state of nature is to be found in most men and is lacking only in a few. . . . Thus it is clear that the majority of men have sufficient knowledge to guide their lives, and the few who do not have this knowledge are said to be half-witted or fools." Therefore, since barbarians of that kind, as Saint Thomas says, lack that good of the intellect which is knowledge of the truth, a good*

● What does the reference to writings by Saint Thomas

Chapter-ending feature **Individual Voices** presents a primary source document in an accessible way, allowing you to explore a primary source as a historian would. Each document is written by or is closely connected to the person in the Individual Choices feature. The primary source documents include personal letters, poems, speeches, political statements, and newspaper articles. Brief introductions set the context for the primary sources, and color-coded **Exploration Points** in the margin pose provocative questions and provide interesting facts about what the document reveals.

chronology

New World Colonies and Native Americans

1494	Treaty of Tordesillas
1512	Creation of the *encomienda* system
1519–1521	Hernando Cortés invades Mexico
1551	Council of Valladolid rules that American Indians are human beings with souls
1558	Elizabeth I becomes queen of England
1565	Spanish found St. Augustine in present-day Florida
1588	English defeat Spanish Armada
1598	Don Juan de Oñate destroys Ácoma pueblo
1608	French-Huron alliance
1609	Henry Hudson sails up Hudson River Spanish found Santa Fe in present-day New Mexico
1623	Beginning of Dutch-Iroquois alliance
1627	Creation of Company of New France
1645	Dutch West India Company reorganized under Peter Stuyvesant
1680	Pueblo Revolt
1683	La Salle expedition down the Mississippi River to the Gulf of Mexico
c. 1700	Beginning of French/Choctaw alliance

The **Chronology** is a box that lists the significant events that we discuss in the chapter. You can refer to this chart while reading the chapter, and afterward you can use it to review the major events of the period.

THE NEW EUROPE AND THE ATLANTIC WORLD

- Why did European rulers promote exploration and colonization in North America?
- What political and religious rivalries influenced the ways in which each European power approached New World colonization?

Expansion into the New World and the subsequent economic and political pressures of colonization aggravated the crisis of authority in Europe. Eager to enlist political allies against Protestant dissenters,

Focus Questions begin major sections of the chapter and increase comprehension by guiding you to the most important themes in the section. These critical thinking questions help you prioritize and understand events and developments in their context.

The **Page-by-Page Glossary,** found in the lower-right-hand corner of each page, defines key terms, concepts, and vocabulary on the same page where the term is first used in the narrative. The glossary serves as a convenient review tool, and is of special benefit to non-native speakers of English and students who need help with vocabulary.

gentry The class of English landowners ranking just below the nobility.

Sir Walter Raleigh English courtier, soldier, and adventurer who attempted to establish the Virginia Colony.

Roanoke Island Island off North Carolina that Raleigh sought to colonize, beginning in 1585.

inflation Rising prices that occur when the supply of currency or credit grows faster than the available supply of goods and services.

Carol Berkin

Born in Mobile, Alabama, Carol Berkin received her undergraduate degree from Barnard College and her Ph.D. from Columbia University. Her dissertation won the Bancroft Award. She is now professor of history at Baruch College and the Graduate Center of City University of New York, where she serves as deputy chair of the Ph.D. program in history. She has written *Jonathan Sewall: Odyssey of an American Loyalist* (1974) and *First Generations: Women in Colonial America* (1996). She has edited *Women of America: A History* (with Mary Beth Norton, 1979), *Women, War and Revolution* (with Clara M. Lovett, 1980), and *Women's Voices, Women's Lives: Documents in Early American History* (with Leslie Horowitz, 1998). She was contributing editor on southern women for *The Encyclopedia of Southern Culture* and has appeared in the PBS series *Liberty! The American Revolution* and The Learning Channel series *The American Revolution*. Professor Berkin chaired the Dunning Beveridge Prize Committee for the American Historical Association, the Columbia University Seminar in Early American History, and the Taylor Prize Committee of the Southern Association of Women Historians, and she served on the program committees for both the Society for the History of the Early American Republic and the Organization of American Historians. In addition, she has been a historical consultant for the National Parks Commission and served on the Planning Committee for the U.S. Department of Education's National Assessment of Educational Progress.

Christopher L. Miller

Born and raised in Portland, Oregon, Christopher L. Miller received a Bachelor of Science from Lewis and Clark College and his Ph.D. from the University of California, Santa Barbara. He is currently associate professor of history at the University of Texas—Pan American. He is the author of *Prophetic Worlds: Indians and Whites on the Columbia Plateau* (1985), and his articles and reviews have appeared in numerous scholarly journals. Dr. Miller is also active in contemporary Indian affairs, having served, for example, as a participant in the American Indian Civics Project through Humboldt State University and as a member of the National Advisory Council for the Brothertown Indian Nation of New York. Professor Miller has also been active in projects designed to improve history teaching, including programs funded by the Meadows Foundation, the U.S. Department of Education, and other agencies.

Robert W. Cherny

Born in Marysville, Kansas, and raised in Beatrice, Nebraska, Robert W. Cherny received his B.A. from the University of Nebraska and his M.A. and Ph.D. from Columbia University. He is professor of history at San Francisco State University. His books include *American Politics in the Gilded Age, 1868–1900* (1997), *San Francisco, 1865–1932: Politics, Power, and Urban Development* (with William Issel, 1986), *A Righteous Cause: The Life of William Jennings Bryan* (1985, 1994), and *Populism, Progressivism, and the Transformation of Nebraska Politics, 1885–1915* (1981). His articles on politics and labor in the late nineteenth and early twentieth centuries have appeared in journals, anthologies, and historical dictionaries and encyclopedias. In 2000, he and Ellen Du Bois co-edited a special issue of the *Pacific Historical Review* that surveyed woman suffrage movements in nine locations around the Pacific Rim. He has been an NEH Fellow, Distinguished Fulbright Lecturer at Moscow State University (Russia), and Visiting Research Scholar at the University of Melbourne (Australia). He has served as president of the Society for Historians of the Gilded Age and Progressive Era and of the Southwest Labor Studies Association and a member of the council of the American Historical Association, Pacific Coast Branch. He helped to found and continues to edit e-mail discussion lists for historians on the Gilded Age and Progressive Era (H-SHGAPE) and the history of California (H-California), both parts of H-Net, and he has served as a member of the council of H-Net (an association of more than one hundred electronic networks for scholars in the humanities and social sciences). He has also served several terms on the Academic Senate of the California State University system and has been a member of that body's executive committee.

James L. Gormly

Born in Riverside, California, James L. Gormly received a B.A. from the University of Arizona and his M.A. and Ph.D. from the University of Connecticut. He is now professor of history and chair of the history department at Washington and Jefferson College. He has written *The Collapse of the Grand Alliance* (1970) and *From Potsdam to the Cold War* (1979). His articles and reviews have appeared in *Diplomatic History, The Journal of American History, The American Historical Review, The Historian, The History Teacher,* and *The Journal of Interdisciplinary History.*

Making America

A History of the United States

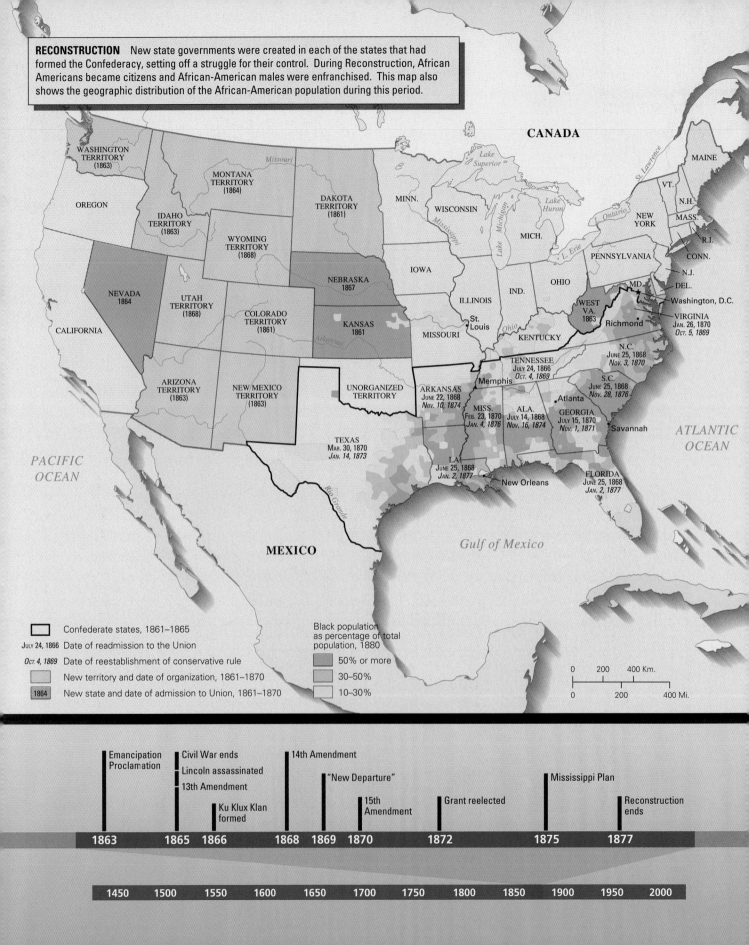

RECONSTRUCTION New state governments were created in each of the states that had formed the Confederacy, setting off a struggle for their control. During Reconstruction, African Americans became citizens and African-American males were enfranchised. This map also shows the geographic distribution of the African-American population during this period.

CANADA

WASHINGTON TERRITORY (1863)

OREGON

MONTANA TERRITORY (1864)

IDAHO TERRITORY (1863)

DAKOTA TERRITORY (1861)

Missouri

MINN.

WISCONSIN

Lake Superior

Lake Huron

MAINE

VT.

N.H.

MASS.

NEW YORK

R.I.

WYOMING TERRITORY (1868)

Mississippi

MICH.

Lake Michigan

Ontario

L. Erie

PENNSYLVANIA

CONN.

N.J.

NEVADA 1864

UTAH TERRITORY (1868)

NEBRASKA 1867

IOWA

OHIO

IND.

MD.

DEL.

Washington, D.C.

CALIFORNIA

COLORADO TERRITORY (1861)

KANSAS 1861

Arkansas

ILLINOIS

St. Louis

MISSOURI

Ohio

KENTUCKY

WEST VA. 1863

Richmond

VIRGINIA JAN. 26, 1870 OCT. 5, 1869

ARIZONA TERRITORY (1863)

NEW MEXICO TERRITORY (1863)

UNORGANIZED TERRITORY

ARKANSAS JUNE 22, 1868 NOV. 10, 1874

Memphis

TENNESSEE JULY 24, 1866 OCT. 4, 1869

N.C. JUNE 25, 1868 NOV. 3, 1870

S.C. JUNE 25, 1868 NOV. 28, 1876

MISS. FEB. 23, 1870 JAN. 4, 1876

ALA. JULY 14, 1868 NOV. 16, 1874

Atlanta

GEORGIA JULY 15, 1870 NOV. 1, 1871

Savannah

TEXAS MAR. 30, 1870 JAN. 14, 1873

LA. JUNE 25, 1868 JAN. 2, 1877

New Orleans

FLORIDA JUNE 25, 1868 JAN. 2, 1877

ATLANTIC OCEAN

PACIFIC OCEAN

Rio Grande

MEXICO

Gulf of Mexico

Confederate states, 1861–1865

JULY 24, 1866 Date of readmission to the Union

OCT. 4, 1869 Date of reestablishment of conservative rule

New territory and date of organization, 1861–1870

1864 New state and date of admission to Union, 1861–1870

Black population as percentage of total population, 1880

50% or more

30–50%

10–30%

0   200   400 Km.

0   200   400 Mi.

Emancipation Proclamation

Civil War ends

Lincoln assassinated

13th Amendment

Ku Klux Klan formed

14th Amendment

"New Departure"

15th Amendment

Grant reelected

Mississippi Plan

Reconstruction ends

| 1863 | 1865 | 1866 | 1868 | 1869 | 1870 | 1872 | 1875 | 1877 |

| 1450 | 1500 | 1550 | 1600 | 1650 | 1700 | 1750 | 1800 | 1850 | 1900 | 1950 | 2000 |

Reconstruction: High Hopes and Shattered Dreams, 1865–1877

16

Andy Anderson

Andy Anderson was born into slavery in east Texas in 1843. In 1937, when he was 94 years old, he told an interviewer about the day when he made the decision to be free. The interview was one of more than two thousand conversations with former slaves that the Federal Writers Project (a New Deal agency for unemployed professionals) collected between 1936 and 1938. Interviewers were instructed to record the interviews exactly, word for word.

Anderson explained that he had been born on the plantation of Jack Haley. Anderson remembered Haley as "kind to his cullud folks" and "kind to ever'body." Haley had rarely whipped his slaves, Anderson recalled, and he had been "reasonable" when he did apply the lash. Anderson remembered that Haley treated his slaves so well that neighboring whites called them "petted niggers." With the coming of the Civil War, however, conditions changed. Haley sold Anderson to W. T. House, whom Anderson remembered as a man that "hell am too good fo'," and who whipped Anderson for a minor accident with a wagon.

De overseer ties me to de stake an' ever' ha'f hour, fo' four hours, deys lay 10 lashes on my back. Aftah I's stood dat fo' a couple of hours, I's could not feel de pain so much an' w'en dey took me loose, I's jus' ha'f dead. I's could not feel de lash 'cause my body am numb, an' my mind am numb. De last thing I's 'membahs am dat I's wishin' fo' death. I's laid in the de bunk fo' two days gittin' over dat whuppin'. Dat is, gitting' over it in de body but not in de heart. No Sar! I's have dat in de heart 'til dis day.

Soon after the whipping, Anderson was sold again, to House's brother John, who, to Anderson's knowledge, had never struck a slave.

As the Civil War was winding down to its end, Anderson remembered the day when House called his slaves together and told them that they were free and that the official order would soon be given. He offered any who wished to stay the choice to work for wages or work the land as sharecroppers, and he urged the freed people to "stay with me." Anderson was standing near House and said to himself, not expecting anyone to hear, "Lak hell I's will." He meant only that he intended to take his freedom, but House heard him, took it as a challenge, and promised that he would "tend to yous later." Anderson recalled that he was sure to keep his lips closed when he thought, "I's won't be heah."

Toward sundown, Anderson left the House plantation for good. He traveled at night to avoid the patrollers, who were always on the lookout for African Americans on the road without passes, and hid in the brush during the day. Though he was 21 years old, he'd never been farther from home than a neighbor's house, and he was uncertain of his way. Nonetheless he managed to locate the Haley plantation and to find his father, who hid Anderson. Haley permitted Anderson to stay on his place until the final proclamation of freedom.

ANDY ANDERSON

Andy Anderson was 94 years old when he was interviewed in 1937. Unfortunately, no photo of him has been found. This photo depicts an African-American family from east Texas, the area where Anderson was born and grew up and where he began to farm. The photo shows what Anderson's home may have looked like in the 1840s. *East Texas Research Center, Stephen F. Austin State University.*

Sheldon Cauthier of the Federal Writers Project interviewed Andy Anderson on September 16, 1937, and Anderson gave him this account of his taking of his freedom. By then, Anderson was living in Fort Worth, Texas. Anderson provided only limited information on his later life. He left Haley's farm soon after emancipation to work on another farm for $2 a month plus clothing and food, and he continued to do farm work until his old age. He married in 1883, when he was about 40, an indication, perhaps, that his labor did not provide enough income to support a family until then. He and his first wife had two children but both children and his wife died. He married again in 1885, and he and second his wife had six children, of whom four were still living in 1937. His second wife died in 1934, and he married a third time in 1936. He joked with the interviewer that "Dere am no chilluns yet f'om my third mai'age." Though we know little of what Anderson experienced during the years of Reconstruction, we do have his dramatic account of how he claimed his freedom.

INTRODUCTION

Andy Anderson was not the only African American who claimed freedom while the war was raging. Anderson's experience was repeated time and time again, with many variations, all across the South. Those decisions were made legal by the Emancipation Proclamation, the presence of Union armies, and later the Thirteenth Amendment to the Constitution. The **freed people** now faced a wide range of new decisions—where to live, where to work, how to create their own communities.

The war was a momentous event for nearly all Americans. By 1865, when the war ended, some 2.6 million men—and a few hundred women—had served in the Union or Confederate armies, equal to almost 40 percent of all the men aged 15 to 40 in the United States in 1860. More than a half-million had died—more deaths than in any other American war—and many others were permanently disabled. By 1865, the war had touched the lives of nearly every person living in the nation.

Nearly all the major battles occurred in the South or in the border states. Toward the end of the war, Union armies swept across the South, leaving havoc behind them: burned and shelled buildings, ravaged fields, twisted railroad tracks. This destruction, and the collapse of the region's financial system, devastated the southern economy.

More distressing for many white southerners than the ravaged countryside was the **emancipation** of 4 million slaves. In 1861 fears for the future of

slavery under Republicans had caused the South to attempt to **secede** from the Union. With the end of the war, fears became reality. The end of slavery forced southerners of both races to develop new social, economic, and political patterns.

Historians identify the years between 1865 and 1877 as **Reconstruction**. Although the period was a time of physical rebuilding throughout the South, Reconstruction refers primarily to the rebuilding of the federal Union and to the political, economic, and social changes that came to the South as it was restored to the nation. Reconstruction involved some of the most momentous questions in American history. How was the defeated South to be treated? What was to be the future of the 4 million former slaves? Should key decisions be made by the federal

---

freed people   Former slaves; *freed people* is the term used by historians to refer to former slaves, whether male or female.

emancipation   Release from slavery.

secede   To withdraw from membership in an organization; in this case, refers to the attempted withdrawal of eleven southern states from the United States in 1860–1861, giving rise to the Civil War.

Reconstruction   Term applied by historians to the years 1865–1877, when the Union was restored from the Civil War, important changes were made to the federal Constitution, and social, economic, and political relations between the races were transformed in the South.

government or in state capitols and county court-houses throughout the South? Which branch of the government was to establish policies?

As the dominant Republicans turned their attention from waging war to reconstructing the Union, they wrote into law and the Constitution new definitions of the Union itself. They also defined the rights of the former slaves and the terms on which the South might rejoin the Union. And they permanently changed the definition of American citizenship.

Most white southerners disliked the new rules emerging from the federal government, and some resisted. Disagreement over the future of the South and the status of the former slaves led to conflict between the president and Congress. A temporary result of this conflict was a more powerful Congress and a less powerful executive. A lasting outcome of these events was a significant increase in the power of the federal government and new limits on local and state governments.

Reconstruction significantly changed many aspects of southern life. In the end, however, Reconstruction failed to fulfill many African Americans' hopes for their lives as free people.

PRESIDENTIAL RECONSTRUCTION

• What did Presidents Lincoln and Johnson seek to accomplish through their Reconstruction policies? How did their purposes differ? In what ways were their policies similar?

• How did white southerners respond to the Reconstruction efforts of Lincoln and Johnson? What does this suggest about the expectations of white southerners?

On New Year's Day 1863, the Emancipation Proclamation took effect. More than four years earlier, Abraham Lincoln had insisted that "this government cannot endure permanently half slave and half free. . . . It will become all one thing, or all the other." With the Emancipation Proclamation, President Lincoln began the legal process by which the nation became all free. At the time, however, the Proclamation did not affect any slave because it abolished slavery only in territory under Confederate control, where it was unenforceable. But every advance of a Union army after January 1, 1863, brought the law of the land—and emancipation—to the Confederacy.

Republican War Aims

For Lincoln and the Republican Party, freedom for the slaves became a central concern partly because

This engraving celebrating the Emancipation Proclamation first appeared in 1863. While it places a white Union soldier in the center, it also portrays the important role of African-American troops and emphasizes the importance of education and literacy. *The Library Company of Philadelphia.*

abolitionists were influential party constituents. The Republican Party had promised only to prohibit slavery in the territories during their 1860 electoral campaign, and Lincoln initially defined the war only as one to maintain the Union. Some leading Republicans, however, favored abolition of slavery everywhere in the Union. As Union troops moved into the South, some slaves took matters into their hands by walking away from their owners and seeking safety with the advancing army. Within a year, former slaves had become an important part of the Union army's work force. Abolitionists throughout the North—including Frederick Douglass, an escaped slave and an important leader of the abolition movement—began to argue that emancipation

abolitionist An individual who condemns slavery as morally wrong and seeks to abolish (eliminate) slavery.

chronology

Reconstruction

1863	Emancipation Proclamation The Ten-Percent Plan
1864	Abraham Lincoln reelected
1865	Freedmen's Bureau created Civil War ends Lincoln assassinated Andrew Johnson becomes president Thirteenth Amendment (abolishing slavery) ratified
1866	Ku Klux Klan formed Congress begins to assert control over Reconstruction Civil Rights Act of 1866 Riots by whites in Memphis and New Orleans
1867	Military Reconstruction Act Command of the Army Act Tenure of Office Act
1868	Impeachment of President Johnson Fourteenth Amendment (defining citizenship) ratified Ulysses S. Grant elected president
1869–1870	Victories of "New Departure" Democrats in some southern states
1870	Fifteenth Amendment (guaranteeing voting rights) ratified
1870–1871	Ku Klux Klan Acts
1872	Grant reelected
1875	Civil Rights Act of 1875 Mississippi Plan ends Reconstruction in Mississippi
1876	Disputed presidential election: Hayes versus Tilden
1877	Compromise of 1877 Rutherford B. Hayes becomes president End of Reconstruction

would be meaningless unless the government guaranteed the civil and political rights of the former slaves. Thus some Republicans expanded their definition of war objectives to include not just preserving the Union but also abolishing slavery, extending citizenship for the former slaves, and guaranteeing the equality of all citizens before the law. At the time, these were extreme views on abolition and equal rights, and the people who held them were called **Radical Republicans** or simply Radicals.

Thaddeus Stevens, 73 years old in 1865 and perhaps the leading Radical in the House of Representatives, had made a successful career as a Pennsylvania iron manufacturer before he won election to Congress in 1858. Born with a clubfoot, he always seemed to identify with those outside the social mainstream. He became a compelling spokesman for abolition and an uncompromising advocate of equal rights for African Americans. A masterful parliamentarian, he was known for his honesty and his sarcastic wit. From the beginning of the war, Stevens urged that the slaves be not only freed but also armed, to fight the Confederacy. By the end of the war, some 180,000 African Americans, the great majority of them freedmen, had served in the Union army and a few thousand in the Union navy. Many more worked for the army as laborers.

Charles Sumner of Massachusetts, a prominent Radical in the Senate, had argued for **racial integration** of Massachusetts schools in 1849 and won

Radical Republicans A group within the Republican Party during the Civil War and Reconstruction that advocated abolition of slavery, citizenship for the former slaves, and sweeping alteration of the South.

racial integration Equal opportunities to participate in a society or organization by people of different racial groups; the absence of race-based barriers to full and equal participation.

Radical Republicans initially hoped that Andrew Johnson would be their ally. Instead he proved to be unsympathetic to most Radical goals. His self-righteous and uncompromising personality led to conflict that eventually produced an unsuccessful effort to remove him from office in 1868. *Library of Congress.*

election to the U.S. Senate in 1851. Immediately establishing himself as the Senate's foremost champion of abolition, he became a martyr to the cause after a severe beating he suffered in 1856 because of an antislavery speech. After emancipation, Sumner, like Stevens, fought for full political and civil rights for the freed people.

Stevens, Sumner, and other Radicals demanded a drastic restructuring not only of the South's political system but also of its economy. They opposed slavery not only on moral grounds but also because they believed free labor was more productive. Slaves worked to escape punishment, they argued, but free workers worked to benefit themselves. Eliminating slavery and instituting a free-labor system in its place, they claimed, would benefit everyone by increasing the nation's total production. Free labor

not only contributed centrally to the dynamism of the North's economy, they argued, but was crucial to democracy itself. "The middling classes who own the soil, and work it with their own hands," Stevens once proclaimed, "are the main support of every free government." For the South to be fully democratic, the Radicals concluded, it had to elevate free labor to a position of honor.

Not all Republicans agreed with the Radicals. All Republicans had objected to slavery, but not all Republicans were abolitionists. Similarly, not all Republicans wanted to extend full citizenship rights to the former slaves. Some favored rapid restoration of the South to the Union so that the federal government could concentrate on stimulating the nation's economy and developing the West. Republicans who did not immediately endorse severe punishment for the South or citizenship for the freed people are usually referred to as **moderates**.

Lincoln's Approach to Reconstruction: "With Malice Toward None"

After the Emancipation Proclamation, President Lincoln and the congressional Radicals agreed that the abolition of slavery had to be a condition for the return of the South to the Union. Major differences soon appeared, however, over other terms for reunion and the roles of the president and Congress in establishing those terms. In his second inaugural address, a month before his death, Lincoln defined the task facing the nation:

> *With malice toward none; with charity for all; with firmness in the right, as God gives us to see the right, let us strive on to finish the work we are in: to bind up the nation's wounds; to care for him who shall have borne the battle, and for his widow and orphan, to do all which may achieve and cherish a just and lasting peace among ourselves, and with all nations.*

Lincoln began to rebuild the Union on the basis of these principles. He hoped to hasten the end of the

---

moderates People whose views are midway between two more extreme positions; in this case, Republicans who favored some reforms but not all the Radicals' proposals.

war by encouraging southerners to renounce the Confederacy and to accept emancipation. As soon as Union armies occupied portions of southern states, he appointed temporary military governors for those regions and tried to restore civil government as quickly as possible.

Drawing on the president's constitutional power to issue **pardons** (Article II, Section 2), Lincoln issued a Proclamation of **Amnesty** and Reconstruction in December 1863. Often called the "Ten-Percent Plan," it promised a full pardon and restoration of rights to those who swore their loyalty to the Union and accepted the abolition of slavery. Only high-ranking Confederate leaders were not eligible. Once those who had taken the oath in a state amounted to 10 percent of the number of votes cast by that state in the 1860 presidential election, the pardoned voters were to write a new state constitution that abolished slavery, elect state officials, and resume self-government. Some congressional Radicals disagreed with Lincoln's lenient approach. When they tried to set more stringent standards, however, Lincoln blocked them, fearing their plan would slow the restoration of civil government and perhaps even lengthen the war.

Under Lincoln's Ten-Percent Plan, new state governments were established in Arkansas, Louisiana, and Tennessee during 1864 and early 1865. In Louisiana, the new government denied voting rights to men who were one-quarter or more black. Radicals complained, but Lincoln urged patience, suggesting the reconstructed government in Louisiana was "as the egg to the fowl, and we shall sooner have the fowl by hatching the egg than by smashing it." Events in Louisiana and elsewhere convinced Radicals that freed people were unlikely to receive equitable treatment from state governments formed under the Ten-Percent Plan. Some moderates agreed and moved toward the Radicals' position that only **suffrage** could protect the freedmen's rights and that only federal action could secure black suffrage.

Abolishing Slavery Forever: The Thirteenth Amendment

Amid questions about the rights of freed people, congressional Republicans prepared the final destruction of slavery. The Emancipation Proclamation had been a wartime measure, justified partly by military necessity, and it never applied in Union states.

State legislatures or conventions abolished slavery in West Virginia, Maryland, Missouri, and the reconstructed state of Tennessee. In early 1865, however, slavery remained legal in Delaware and Kentucky, and old, prewar state laws—which might or might not be valid—still permitted slavery in the states that had seceded. To destroy slavery forever, Congress in January 1865 approved the **Thirteenth Amendment**, which read simply, "Neither slavery nor involuntary servitude, except as a punishment for crime whereof the party shall have been duly convicted, shall exist within the United States, or any place subject to their jurisdiction."

The Constitution requires any amendment to be ratified by three-fourths of the states—then 27 of 36. By December 1865, only 19 of the 25 Union states had ratified the amendment. The measure passed, however, when eight of the reconstructed southern states approved it. In the end, therefore, the abolition of slavery hinged on action by reconstructed state governments in the South.

Andrew Johnson and Reconstruction

After the assassination of Lincoln in mid-April 1865, Vice President Andrew Johnson became president. Born in North Carolina, he never had the opportunity to attend school and spent his early life in a continual struggle against poverty. As a young man in Tennessee, he worked as a tailor and then turned to politics. After he married, his wife, Eliza McCardle Johnson, tutored him in reading, writing, and arithmetic. A Democrat, Johnson relied on his oratorical skills to win several terms in the Tennessee legislature. He was elected to Congress and afterward served as governor before winning election to the U.S. Senate in 1857. His political support came

---

pardon A governmental directive canceling punishment for a person or people who have committed a crime.

amnesty A general pardon granted by a government, especially for political offenses.

suffrage The right to vote.

Thirteenth Amendment Constitutional amendment, ratified in 1865, that abolished slavery in the United States and its territories.

primarily from small-scale farmers and working people. The state's elite of plantation owners usually opposed him. Johnson, in turn, resented their wealth and power and blamed them for secession and the Civil War.

Johnson was the only southern senator who rejected the Confederacy. Early in the war, Union forces captured Nashville, capital of Tennessee, and Lincoln appointed Johnson as military governor. Johnson dealt harshly with Tennessee secessionists, especially wealthy planters. Radical Republicans thought that Johnson's severe treatment of former Confederates was exactly what the South needed. Johnson was elected vice president in 1864, receiving the nomination for vice president in part because Lincoln wanted to appeal to Democrats and to Unionists in border states.

When Johnson became president, Radicals hoped he would join their efforts to transform the South. Johnson, however, soon made clear that he was strongly committed to states' rights and opposed the Radicals' objective of a powerful federal government. "White men alone must manage the South," Johnson told one visitor, although he recommended limited political roles for the freedmen. Self-righteous and uncompromising, Johnson saw the major task of Reconstruction as **empowering** the region's white middle class and excluding the wealthy planters from power.

Johnson's approach to Reconstruction differed little from Lincoln's. Like Lincoln, he relied on the president's constitutional power to grant pardons. His desire for a quick restoration of the southern states to the Union apparently overcame his bitterness toward the southern elite, and he granted amnesty to most former Confederates who pledged loyalty to the Union and support for emancipation. In one of his last actions as president, he granted full pardon and amnesty to all southern rebels, although after 1868 the Fourteenth Amendment prevented him from restoring their right to hold office.

Johnson appointed **provisional** civilian governors for the southern states not already reconstructed. He instructed them to reconstitute functioning state administrations and to call constitutional conventions of delegates elected by pardoned voters. Some provisional governors, however, appointed former Confederates to state and local offices, outraging those who expected Reconstruction to bring to power loyal Unionists committed to a new southern society.

The Southern Response: Minimal Compliance

Johnson expected the state constitutional conventions to abolish slavery within each state, ratify the Thirteenth Amendment, renounce secession, and **repudiate** the state's war debts. The states were then to hold elections and resume their places in the Union. State conventions during the summer of 1865 usually complied with these provisions, though some did so grudgingly. Johnson had specified nothing about the rights of the freed people, and every state rejected black suffrage.

By April 1866, a year after the close of the war, all the southern states had fulfilled Johnson's requirements for rejoining the Union and had elected legislators, governors, and members of Congress. Their choices troubled Johnson. He had hoped for the emergence of new political leaders in the South and was dismayed at the number of rich planters and former Confederate officials who won state contests.

Most white southerners, however, viewed Johnson as their protector, standing between them and the Radicals. His support for **states' rights** and his opposition to federal determination of voting rights led white southerners to expect that they would shape the transition from slavery to freedom—that they, and not Congress, would define the status of the former slaves.

FREEDOM AND THE LEGACY OF SLAVERY

• How did the freed people respond to freedom? What seem to have been the leading objectives among freed people as they explored their new opportunities?

• How did southern whites respond to the end of slavery?

• How do the differing responses of freed people and southern whites show different understandings of the significance of emancipation?

---

empower To increase the power or authority of some person or group.

provisional Temporary.

repudiate To refuse to acknowledge or pay.

states' rights A political position favoring limitation of the federal government's power and the greatest possible self-government by the individual states.

Before Emancipation, slaves typically made their own simple and rough clothing or they received the cast-off clothing of their owners and overseers. With Emancipation, those freed people who had an income could afford to dress more fashionably. The Harry Stephens family probably put on their best clothes for a visit to the photographer G. Gable in 1866. *Gilman Paper Company, New York.*

As state conventions wrote new constitutions and politicians argued in Washington, African Americans throughout the South set about creating new, free lives for themselves. In the antebellum South, all slaves and most free African Americans had led lives tightly constrained by law and custom. They were permitted few social organizations of their own. Eric Foner, in his comprehensive study *Reconstruction* (1988), described the central theme of the black response to emancipation as "a desire for independence from white control, for autonomy both as individuals and as members of a community." The prospect of **autonomy** touched every aspect of life—family, churches, schools, newspapers, and a host of other social institutions. From this ferment of freedom came new black institutions that provided the basis for southern African-American communities. At the same time, the economic life of the South had been shattered by the Civil War and was being transformed by emancipation. Thus white southerners also faced drastic economic and social change.

Defining the Meaning of Freedom

At the most basic level, freedom came every time an individual slave stopped working for a master and claimed the right to be free. Thus freedom did not come to all slaves at the same time or in the same way. For some, freedom came before the Emancipa-

tion Proclamation, when they walked away from their owners, crossed into Union-held territory, and asserted their liberty. Toward the end of the war, as civil authority broke down throughout much of the South, many slaves declared their freedom and left the lands they had worked in bondage. Some left for good, but many remained nearby, though with a new understanding of their relationship to their former masters. For some, freedom did not come until ratification of the Thirteenth Amendment.

Across the South, the approach of Yankee troops set off a joyous celebration—called a Jubilee—among those who knew that their enslavement was ending. As one Virginia woman remembered, "Such rejoicing and shouting you never heard in your life." A man recalled that, with the appearance of the Union soldiers, "We was all walking on golden clouds. Hallelujah!" Once the celebrating was over, however, the freed people had to decide how best to use their freedom.

The freed people expressed their new status in many ways. Some chose new names to symbolize their new beginning. Andy Anderson (see Individual Choices, page 458), for example, had been called Andy Haley, after the last name of his owner. On

---

autonomy   Control of one's own affairs; self-government.

claiming his freedom, he changed his name to Anderson, the last name of his father. Many freed people changed their style of dress, discarding the cheap clothing provided to slaves. Some acquired guns. A significant benefit of freedom was the ability to travel without a pass and without being checked by the **patrollers** who had enforced the **pass system**. Many freed people took advantage of this new opportunity to travel. Indeed, some felt they had to leave the site of their enslavement to experience full freedom. Andy Anderson refused to work for his last owner, not because he had anything against him but because he wanted "to take my freedom." One freed woman said, "If I stay here I'll never know I'm free." Most did not move, however. Those who did mostly traveled only short distances, usually to find work or land to farm, to seek family members separated from them by slavery, or for other well-defined reasons.

The towns and cities of the South attracted some freed people. The presence of Union troops and officials promised protection from the random violence against freed people that occurred in many rural areas. A new federal program, the **Freedmen's Bureau**, offered assistance with finding work and necessities. Cities and towns also offered black churches, schools (which before the war had usually operated in secret), and other social institutions begun by free blacks before the war. Many African Americans also came to towns and cities looking for work. With little housing available, however, most crowded into hastily built shanties. Sanitation was poor and disease a common scourge. In September 1866, for example, more than a hundred people died of **cholera** in Vicksburg, Mississippi. Such conditions improved only very slowly.

Creating Communities

During Reconstruction, African Americans created their own communities with their own social institutions, beginning with family ties. Joyful families were reunited after years of separation caused by the sale of a spouse or children. Some people spent years searching for lost family members.

The new freedom to conduct religious services without white supervision was especially important. Churches quickly became the most prominent social organizations in African-American communities. Churches were, in fact, among the very first social institutions that African Americans fully controlled. During Reconstruction, black denominations, including the African Methodist Episcopal,

Churches were the first institutions in America to be completely controlled by African Americans, and ministers were highly influential figures in the African-American communities that emerged during Reconstruction. This photograph shows the Reverend John Qualls at the pulpit of his church in New Orleans in the 1880s. *Historic New Orleans Collection.*

African Methodist Episcopal Zion, and several Baptist groups (all founded well before the Civil War) grew rapidly in the South. Black ministers helped to lead congregation members as they adjusted to the changes that freedom brought, and many ministers became key leaders within developing African-American communities.

---

patrollers During the era of slavery, white guards who made the rounds of rural roads to make certain that slaves were not moving about the countryside without written permission from their masters.

pass system Laws that forbade slaves from traveling without written authorization from their owners.

Freedmen's Bureau Agency established in 1865 to aid former slaves in their transition to freedom, especially by administering relief and sponsoring education.

cholera Infectious and often fatal disease associated with poor sanitation.

During Reconstruction, the freed people gave a high priority to the establishment of schools, often with the assistance of the Freedmen's Bureau and northern missionary societies. This photograph of a newly established school was taken around 1870, showing both the barefoot students and the teacher. *Library of Congress.*

Throughout the cities and towns of the South, African Americans—especially ministers and church members—worked to create schools. Setting up a school, said one, was "the first proof" of independence. Many new schools were for both children and adults, whose literacy and learning had been restricted by state laws prohibiting education for slaves. The desire to learn was widespread and intense. One freedman in Georgia wrote to a friend: "The Lord has sent books and teachers. We must not hesitate a moment, but go on and learn all we can."

Before the war, free public education had been rudimentary in much of the South, and wholly absent in many places. When African Americans set up schools, they faced severe shortages of teachers, books, and schoolrooms—everything but students. As abolitionists and northern reformers tried to assist the transition from slavery to freedom, many of them focused first on education.

In March 1865, Congress created the Freedmen's Bureau to assist the freed people in their transition to freedom. It played an important role in organizing and equipping schools. Freedmen's Aid Societies also sprang up in most northern cities and, along with northern churches, collected funds and supplies for the freed people. Teachers—mostly white women, often from New England and often acting on religious impulses—came from the North. Northern aid societies and church organizations, together with the Freedmen's Bureau, established

schools to train black teachers. Some of those schools evolved into black colleges. By 1870, the Freedmen's Bureau supervised more than 4,000 schools, with more than 9,000 teachers and 247,000 students. Still, in 1870, the schools had room for only one black child in ten of school age.

In addition to churches and schools, other African-American social institutions emerged and grew, including **fraternal orders**, **benevolent societies**, and newspapers. By 1866, the South had ten black newspapers led by the *New Orleans Tribune*, and black newspapers played important roles in shaping African-American communities.

In politics, African Americans' first objective was recognition of their equal rights as citizens. Spokesman Frederick Douglass insisted, "Slavery is not abolished until the black man has the ballot." Political conventions of African Americans attracted hundreds of leaders of the emerging black communities. They called for equality and voting rights and pointed to black contributions in the American Revolution and the Civil War as evidence of patriotism

fraternal order An organization of men, often with a ceremonial initiation, that typically provided rudimentary life insurance; many fraternal orders also had auxiliaries for the female relatives of members.

benevolent society Group of people associated for some charitable purpose.

and devotion. They also appealed to the nation's republican traditions, in particular the Declaration of Independence and its dictum that "all men are created equal."

Land and Labor

Former slaveowners reacted to emancipation in many ways. Some tried to keep their slaves from learning of their freedom. A very few white southerners welcomed the end of slavery—Mary Chesnut, for example, a plantation mistress from South Carolina, believed that the power of male slaveholders over female slaves led to sexual coercion and adultery and she was glad to see the end of slavery. Few former slaveowners provided any compensation to assist their former slaves. One freedman later recalled, "I do know some of dem old slave owners to be nice enough to start der slaves off in freedom wid somethin' to live on . . . but dey wasn't in droves, I tell you."

Many freed people looked to Union troops for assistance. When General William T. Sherman led his victorious army through Georgia in the closing months of the war, thousands of African-American men, women, and children claimed their freedom and followed in the Yankees' wake. Their leaders told Sherman that what they wanted most was to "reap the fruit of our own labor." In January 1865, Sherman issued Special Field Order No. 15, setting aside the Sea Islands and land along the South Carolina coast for freed families. Each family, he specified, was to receive 40 acres and the loan of an army mule. By June, the area had filled with forty thousand freed people settled on 400,000 acres of "Sherman land."

Sherman's action encouraged many African Americans to expect that the federal government would redistribute land throughout the South. "Forty acres and a mule" became a rallying cry. Only land, Thaddeus Stevens proclaimed, would give the freed people control of their own labor. "If we do not furnish them with homesteads," Stevens said, "we had better left them in bondage."

By the end of the war, the Freedmen's Bureau controlled some 850,000 acres of land abandoned by former owners or confiscated from Confederate leaders. In July 1865, General Oliver O. Howard, head of the bureau, directed that this land be divided into 40-acre plots to be given to freed people. However, President Johnson ordered Howard to halt **land redistribution** and to reclaim land already handed over and return it to its former own-

ers. Johnson's order displaced thousands of African Americans who had already taken their 40 acres. They and others who had hoped for land felt disappointed and betrayed. One later recalled that they had expected "a heap from freedom dey didn't git."

The congressional act that created the Freedmen's Bureau also authorized it to assist white refugees. In a few places, white recipients of aid outnumbered the freed blacks. The vast majority of southern whites had never owned slaves, and some opposed secession, but the outcome of the war meant that some lost their livelihood, and many feared that they would now have to compete with the freed people for farmland or wage labor. Like the freed people, many southern whites lacked the means to farm on their own. With the collapse of the Confederate government, Confederate money—badly devalued by rampant inflation—became worthless. This currency fiasco, together with the failure of southern banks and the devastation of the southern economy, meant that even many whites with large landholdings lacked the cash to hire farm workers.

Sharecropping slowly emerged across much of the South as an alternative both to land redistribution and to wage labor on the plantations. Sharecropping derived directly from the central realities of southern agriculture. Much of the land was in large holdings, but the landowners had no one to work it. Many families, black and white, wanted to raise their own crops with their own labor but had no land, no supplies, and no money. The entire region was short of **capital**. Under sharecropping, an individual—usually a family head—signed a contract with a landowner to rent land as home and farm. The tenant—the sharecropper—was to pay, as rent, a share of the harvest. The share might amount to half or more of the crop if the landlord provided mules, tools, seed, and fertilizer as well as land. Many landowners thought that sharecropping encouraged tenants to be productive, to get as much value as possible from their shares of the crop. The rental contract often allowed the landlord to specify what crop would be planted, and most landlords

---

land redistribution   The division of land held by large landowners into small plots that are turned over to people without property.

sharecropping   An agricultural lease system in which tenant farmers give landlords a share of their crops, rather than cash, as rent.

capital   Money, especially the money invested in a commercial enterprise.

Sharecropping gave the African Americans more control over their labor than did labor contracts. But sharecropping also contributed to the South's dependence on one-crop agriculture and helped to perpetuate widespread rural poverty. Notice that the child standing on the right is holding her kitten, probably to be certain it is included in this family photograph. *Library of Congress.*

chose cotton so that their tenants would not hold back any of the harvest for personal consumption. Thus, sharecropping helped to perpetuate the dependency of the South on cotton.

Southern farmers—black or white, sharecroppers or owners of small plots—often found themselves in debt to a local merchant who advanced supplies on credit. In return for credit, the merchant required a lien (a legal claim) on the growing crop. Many landlords ran stores that they required their tenants to patronize. Often the share paid as rent and the debt owed the store exceeded the value of the entire harvest. Furthermore, many rental contracts and **crop liens** automatically renewed if all debts were not paid at the end of a year. Thus, in spite of their efforts to achieve greater control over their lives and labor, many southern farm families, black and white alike, found themselves trapped by sharecropping and debt. Still, sharecropping gave freed people more control over their daily lives than had slavery.

Landlords often exercised political as well as economic power over their tenants. Until the 1890s, the act of casting a ballot on election day was an open process, and any observer could see how an individual voted (see page 475). Thus, when a landlord or merchant advocated a particular candidate, the unspoken message was often an implicit threat to cut off credit at the store or to evict a sharecropper if he did not vote accordingly. Such forms of economic **coercion** had the potential to undercut voting rights.

The White South: Confronting Change

The Civil War and the end of slavery transformed the lives of white southerners as well as black southerners. For some, the changes were nearly as profound as for the freed people. Savings vanished. Some homes and other buildings were destroyed. Thousands left the South.

Before the war, few white southerners had owned slaves, and even fewer owned large numbers. Distrust or even hostility had always existed between the privileged planter families and the many whites who farmed small plots by themselves. Some regions populated by small-scale farmers had resisted secession, and some of them welcomed the Union victory and supported the Republicans during Reconstruction. Some southerners also welcomed the prospect of the economic transformation that northern capital might bring.

Most white southerners, however, shared what one North Carolinian described in 1866 as "the bitterest hatred toward the North." Even people with no attachment to slavery detested the Yankees who so profoundly changed their lives. For many white southerners, the "lost cause" of the Confederacy came to symbolize their defense of their prewar lives, not an attempt to break up the nation or protect slavery. During the early phases of Reconstruction, most white southerners apparently expected that, except for slavery, things would soon be put back much as they had been before the war.

As civil governments began to function in late 1865 and 1866, state legislatures passed **black codes** defining the new legal status of African Americans.

---

crop lien   A legal claim to a farmer's crop, similar to a mortgage, based on the use of crops as collateral for extension of credit by a merchant.

coercion   Use of threats or force to compel action.

black codes   Laws passed by the southern states after the Civil War to define the status of freed people as subordinate to whites.

These regulations varied from state to state, but every state placed significant restraints on black people. Various black codes required African Americans to have an annual employment contract, limited them to agricultural work, forbade them from moving about the countryside without permission, restricted their ownership of land, and provided for forced labor by those found guilty of **vagrancy**—which usually meant anyone without a job. Some codes originated in prewar restrictions on slaves and free blacks. Some reflected efforts to ensure that farm workers would be on hand for planting, cultivating, and harvesting. Taken together, however, the black codes represented an effort by white southerners to define a legally subordinate place for African Americans.

Some white southerners also used violence to coerce freed people into accepting a subordinate status within the new southern society. Clara Barton, who had organized women as nurses for the Union army, visited the South from 1866 to 1870 and observed "a condition of lawlessness toward the blacks" and "a disposition . . . to injure or kill them on slight or no provocation."

Violence and terror became closely associated with the **Ku Klux Klan**, a secret organization formed in 1866 and led by a former Confederate general. Most Klan members were small-scale farmers and workers, but the leaders were often prominent within their own communities. As one Freedmen's Bureau agent observed, "The most respectable citizens are engaged in it." Klan groups existed throughout the South, but operated with little central control. Their major goals were to restore **white supremacy** and to destroy the Republican Party. Other, similar organizations also formed and adopted terrorist tactics.

Klan members were called ghouls. Officers included cyclops, night-hawks, and grand dragons, and the national leader was called the grand wizard. Klan members covered their faces with hoods, wore white robes, and rode horses draped in white as they set out to intimidate black Republicans and their Radical white allies. Klan members also attacked less politically prominent people, whipping African Americans accused of not showing sufficient deference to whites. Nightriders also burned black churches and schools. By such tactics, the Klan devastated Republican organizations in many communities.

In 1866 two events dramatized the violence that some white southerners were inflicting on African Americans. In early May, in Memphis, Tennessee,

In this picture, the artist has portrayed a group of bizarrely dressed Klansmen contemplating the murder of a white Republican. *Library of Congress.*

black veterans of the Union army came to the assistance of a black man being arrested by white police, setting off a three-day riot in which whites, including police, indiscriminately attacked African Americans. Forty-five blacks and three whites died. In late July, in New Orleans, some forty people died, most of them African Americans, in an altercation between police and a largely black prosuffrage group. General Philip Sheridan, the military commander of the district, called it "an absolute massacre by the police." Memphis and New Orleans were unusual only in the numbers of casualties. Local authorities often seemed uninterested in stopping such violence, and federal troops were not always available when they were needed.

vagrancy   The legal condition of having no fixed place of residence or means of support.

Ku Klux Klan   A secret society organized in the South after the Civil War to resurrect white supremacy by means of violence and intimidation.

white supremacy   The racist belief that whites are inherently superior to all other races and are therefore entitled to rule over them.

CONGRESSIONAL RECONSTRUCTION

• Why did congressional Republicans take control over Reconstruction policy? What did they seek to accomplish? How successful were they?

• How did the Fourteenth and Fifteenth Amendments change the nature of the federal Union?

The black codes, violence against freed people, and the failure of southern authorities to stem the violence turned northern opinion against President Johnson's lenient approach to Reconstruction. Increasing numbers of moderate Republicans accepted the Radicals' arguments that the freed people required greater federal protection, and congressional Republicans moved to take control of Reconstruction. When Johnson's stubborn and uncompromising personality ran up against the equally stubborn and uncompromising Thaddeus Stevens, the nation faced a constitutional crisis.

Challenging Presidential Reconstruction

In December 1865, the Thirty-ninth Congress (elected in 1864) met for the first time. Republicans outnumbered Democrats by more than three to one. The president's annual message proclaimed Reconstruction complete and the Union restored. Few Republicans agreed. Events in the South had convinced most moderate Republicans of the need to protect free labor in the South and to establish basic rights for the freed people. Most also agreed that Congress could withhold representation from the South until reconstructed state governments met these conditions.

On the first day of the Thirty-ninth Congress, moderate Republicans joined Radicals to exclude newly elected congressmen from the South. Citing Article I, Section 5, of the Constitution (which makes each house of Congress the judge of the qualifications of its members), Republicans set up a Joint Committee on Reconstruction to evaluate the qualifications of the excluded southerners and to determine whether the southern states were entitled to representation. Some committee members wanted to launch an investigation of presidential Reconstruction. In the meantime, the former Confederate states had no representation in Congress.

Congressional Republicans also moved to provide more assistance to the freed people. Moderates and Radicals approved a bill extending the Freedmen's Bureau and giving it more authority against racial discrimination. When Johnson vetoed it, Congress drafted a slightly revised version. Similar Republican unity produced a **civil rights** bill, a far-reaching measure that extended citizenship to African Americans and defined some of the rights guaranteed to all citizens. Johnson vetoed both the civil rights bill and the revised Freedmen's Bureau bill, but Congress passed both over his veto. With creation of the Joint Committee on Reconstruction and passage of the Civil Rights and Freedmen's Bureau Acts, Congress took control of Reconstruction.

The Civil Rights Act of 1866

The Civil Rights Act of 1866 defined all persons born in the United States (except Indians not taxed) as citizens. It also listed certain rights of all citizens, including the right to testify in court, own property, make contracts, bring lawsuits, and enjoy "full and equal benefit of all laws and proceedings for the security of person and property." This was the first effort to define in law some of the rights of American citizenship. It placed significant restrictions on state actions on the grounds that the rights of national citizenship took precedence over the powers of state governments. The law expanded the power of the federal government in unprecedented ways and challenged traditional concepts of states' rights. Though the law applied to all citizens, its most immediate consequence was to benefit African Americans.

Much of the debate in Congress over the measure focused on the situation of the freed people. Some supporters saw the Civil Rights Act as a way to secure the freed people's basic rights. Some northern Republicans, for example, hoped the law would encourage freed people to stay in the South. For other Republicans, the bill carried broader implications because it empowered the federal government to force states to abide by the principle of equality before the law. They applauded its redefinition of federal-state relations. Senator Lot Morrill of Maine described it as "absolutely revolutionary" but added, "Are we not in the midst of a revolution?"

When President Johnson vetoed the bill, he argued that it violated states' rights. By defending states' rights and taking aim at the Radicals,

---

civil rights The rights, privileges, and protections that are a part of citizenship.

These white southerners are shown taking the oath of allegiance to the United States in 1865, as part of the process of restoring civil government in the South. The Union soldiers and officers are administering the oath. *Library of Congress.*

Johnson may have hoped to generate enough political support to elect a conservative Congress in 1866 and to win the presidency in 1868. He probably expected the veto to appeal to voters and to turn them against the Radicals. Instead, the veto led most moderate Republicans to give up all hope of cooperation with him. In April 1866, when Congress passed the Civil Rights Act over Johnson's veto, it was the first time ever that Congress had overridden a presidential veto of major legislation.

Defining Citizenship: The Fourteenth Amendment

Leading Republicans, though pleased that the Civil Rights Act was now law, worried that it could be amended or repealed by a later Congress or declared unconstitutional by the Supreme Court. Only a constitutional amendment, they concluded, could permanently safeguard the freed people's rights as citizens.

The **Fourteenth Amendment** began as a proposal made by Radicals seeking a constitutional guarantee of equality before the law. But the final wording—the longest of any amendment—resulted from many compromises. Section 1 of the amendment defined

> **Fourteenth Amendment** Constitutional amendment, ratified in 1868, defining American citizenship and placing restrictions on former Confederates.

American citizenship in much the same way as the Civil Rights Act of 1866, then specified that

> No State shall make or enforce any law which shall abridge the privileges or immunities of citizens of the United States; nor shall any State deprive any person of life, liberty, or property, without due process of law; nor deny to any person within its jurisdiction the equal protection of the laws.

The Constitution and Bill of Rights prohibit federal interference with basic civil rights. The Fourteenth Amendment extends this protection against action by state governments. Eventually, the Fourteenth Amendment became as important as the Bill of Rights in protecting the rights of American citizens.

The amendment was vague on some points. For example, it penalized states that did not **enfranchise** African Americans by reducing their congressional and electoral representation, but it did not specifically guarantee to African Americans the right to vote.

Some provisions of the amendment stemmed from Republicans' fears that a restored South, allied with northern Democrats, might try to undo the outcome of the war. One section barred from public office anyone who had sworn to uphold the federal Constitution and then "engaged in insurrection or rebellion against the same." Only a two-thirds vote of Congress could override this provision. (In 1872 Congress passed a blanket measure pardoning nearly all former Confederates.) The amendment also prohibited federal or state governments from assuming any of the Confederate debt or from paying any claim arising from emancipation.

Not everyone approved of the final wording. Charles Sumner condemned the provision that permitted a state to deny suffrage to male citizens if it accepted a penalty in congressional representation. Stevens wanted to bar former Confederates not just from holding office but also from voting. Woman-suffrage advocates, led by **Susan B. Anthony** and **Elizabeth Cady Stanton**, complained that the amendment, for the first time, introduced the word male into the Constitution in connection with voting rights.

Despite such concerns, Congress approved the Fourteenth Amendment by a straight party vote in June 1866 and sent it to the states for ratification. Johnson protested that Congress should not propose constitutional amendments until all representatives of the southern states had taken their seats. Tennessee promptly ratified the amendment, became the first reconstructed state government to be recog-

nized by Congress, and was exempted from most later Reconstruction legislation.

Although Congress adjourned in the summer of 1866, the nation's attention remained fixed on Reconstruction. In May and July, the bloody riots in Memphis and New Orleans turned more moderates against Johnson's Reconstruction policies. Some interpreted the congressional elections that fall as a referendum on Reconstruction and the Fourteenth Amendment, pitting Johnson against the Radicals. Johnson undertook a speaking tour to promote his views, but one of his own supporters calculated that Johnson's reckless tirades alienated a million voters. Republicans swept the 1866 elections, outnumbering Democrats 143 to 49 in the new House of Representatives, and 42 to 11 in the Senate. Lyman Trumbull, senator from Illinois and a leading moderate, voiced the consensus of congressional Republicans: Congress should now "hurl from power the disloyal element" in the South.

Radicals in Control: Impeachment of the President

As congressional Radicals struggled with Johnson over control of Reconstruction, it became clear that the Fourteenth Amendment might fall short of ratification. Rejection by ten states could prevent its acceptance. By March 1867, the amendment had been rejected by twelve states—Delaware, Kentucky, and all the former Confederate states except Tennessee. Moderate Republicans who had expected the Fourteenth Amendment to be the final Reconstruction measure now became more receptive to other proposals that the Radicals put forth.

The Military Reconstruction Act of 1867, passed on March 2 over Johnson's veto, divided the Confederate states (except Tennessee) into five military districts. Each district was to be governed by a military commander authorized by Congress to use military force to protect life and property. The ten states were to hold constitutional conventions, and all adult male citizens were to vote, except former Con-

---

enfranchise   To grant the right to vote to an individual or group.

Susan B. Anthony   Tireless campaigner for woman suffrage and close associate of Elizabeth Cady Stanton.

Elizabeth Cady Stanton   A founder and leader of the American woman suffrage movement from 1848, and the Seneca Falls Conference, until her death in 1902.

federates barred from office under the proposed Fourteenth Amendment. The constitutional conventions were to create new state governments that permitted black suffrage, and the new governments were to ratify the Fourteenth Amendment. Congress would then evaluate whether those state governments were to regain representation in Congress.

Congress had wrested a major degree of control over Reconstruction from the president, but it was not finished with him. On the same day, March 2, Congress further limited Johnson's powers. The Command of the Army Act specified that the president could issue military orders only through the General of the Army, then Ulysses S. Grant, considered an ally of Congress. It also specified that the General of the Army could not be removed without Senate permission. Congress thereby blocked Johnson from direct communication with military commanders in the South. The Tenure of Office Act specified that officials appointed with the Senate's consent were to remain in office until the Senate approved a successor, thereby preventing Johnson from removing federal officials who opposed his policies. Johnson understood both measures as invasions of presidential authority.

Early in 1867, some Radicals began to consider impeaching President Johnson. The Constitution (Article I, Sections 2 and 3) gives the House of Representatives exclusive power to **impeach** the president—that is, to charge the chief executive with misconduct. The Constitution specifies that the Senate shall hold trial on those charges, with the chief justice of the Supreme Court presiding. If found guilty by a two-thirds vote of the Senate, the president is removed from office.

In January 1867, the House Judiciary Committee investigated charges against Johnson but found no convincing evidence of misconduct. Johnson, however, challenged Congress over the Tenure of Office Act by removing Edwin Stanton as secretary of war. This provocation gave Johnson's opponents something resembling a violation of law by the president. Still, an effort to secure impeachment through the House Judiciary Committee failed. The Joint Committee on Reconstruction, led by Thaddeus Stevens, then took over and developed charges against Johnson. On February 24, 1868, the House adopted eleven articles, or charges, nearly all based on the Stanton affair. The actual reasons the Radicals wanted Johnson removed were clear to all: they disliked him and his actions.

To convict Johnson and remove him from the presidency required a two-thirds vote by the Senate.

Tickets such as these were in high demand, for they permitted the holder to watch the historic proceedings as the Radical leaders presented their evidence to justify removing Andrew Johnson from the presidency. *Collection of David J. and Janice L. Frent.*

Johnson's defenders argued that he had done nothing to warrant impeachment. The Radicals' legal case was weak, but they urged senators to vote on whether they wished Johnson to remain as president. Republican unity unraveled when some moderates, fearing a precedent of removing a president for such flimsy reasons, joined with Democrats to defeat the Radicals. The vote, on May 16 and 26, 1868, was 35 in favor of conviction and 19 against, one vote short of the required two-thirds. By this tiny margin, the Congress maintained the principle that it should not remove the president from office simply because they disagreed with or disliked each other.

Political Terrorism and the Election of 1868

The Radicals' failure to unseat Johnson left him with less than a year remaining in office. As the election approached, the Republicans nominated Ulysses S. Grant for president. A war hero, popular throughout the North, Grant had fully supported Lincoln and Congress in implementing emancipation. By 1868, he had committed himself to the congressional view of Reconstruction. The Democrats nominated Horatio Seymour, a former governor of New York, and focused their energies on denouncing Reconstruction.

---

impeach To charge a public official with improper, usually criminal, conduct.

This engraving appeared on the cover of *Harper's Weekly* in November of 1867. It shows black men lined up to cast their ballots in that fall's elections. Note that the artist has shown first an older black workingman, with his hammer in his pocket; and next a well-dressed young black man, probably a city dweller and perhaps a leader in the emerging black community; and next a black Union soldier. Note, too, the open process of voting. Voters received a ballot (a "party ticket") from a party campaigner and deposited that ballot in a ballot box, in full sight of all. Voting was not secret until much later. *Library of Congress.*

In the South, the campaign stirred up fierce activity by the Ku Klux Klan and similar groups. **Terrorists** assassinated an Arkansas congressman, three members of the South Carolina legislature, and several other Republican leaders. Throughout the South, mobs attacked Republican offices and meetings, and sometimes attacked any black person they could find. Such coercion had its intended effect at the ballot box. For example, as many as two hundred blacks were killed in St. Landry Parish, Louisiana, where the Republicans previously had a thousand-vote majority. On election day, not a single Republican vote was recorded from that parish.

Despite such violence, many Americans may have been anticipating a calmer political future. In June 1868 Congress had readmitted seven southern states that met the requirements of congressional Reconstruction. In July the secretary of state declared the Fourteenth Amendment ratified. In November Grant easily won the presidency, carrying twenty-six of the thirty-four states and 53 percent of the vote.

Voting Rights and Civil Rights

With Grant in the White House, Radical Republicans now considered pressing for voting rights for all African Americans. In 1867 Congress had removed racial barriers to voting in the District of Columbia and in the territories, but elsewhere the states still defined voting rights. Congress had required southern states to enfranchise black males as the price of readmission to the Union, but only seven northern states had taken that step by 1869. Further, any state that had enfranchised African Americans could change its law to reverse the policy. In addition to the principled arguments of Douglass and other Radicals, many Republicans concluded that they needed to guarantee black suffrage in the South if they were to continue to win presidential elections and enjoy majorities in Congress.

To secure suffrage rights for all African Americans, Congress approved the **Fifteenth Amendment** in February 1869. Widely considered to be the final step in Reconstruction, the amendment prohibited both federal and state governments from restricting a person's right to vote because of "race, color, or previous condition of servitude." Like the Fourteenth

terrorists   Those who use threats and violence to achieve ideological or political goals.

Fifteenth Amendment   Constitutional amendment, ratified in 1870, that prohibited states from denying the right to vote because of a person's race or because a person had been a slave.

Amendment, the Fifteenth marked a compromise between moderates and Radicals. Some African-American leaders argued for language guaranteeing voting rights to all male citizens because prohibiting some grounds for **disfranchisement** might imply the legitimacy of other grounds. Some Radicals tried, unsuccessfully, to add "**nativity**, property, education, or religious beliefs" to the prohibited grounds. Democrats condemned the Fifteenth Amendment as a "revolutionary" change in the rights of states to define voting rights.

Elizabeth Cady Stanton, Susan B. Anthony, and other advocates of woman suffrage opposed the amendment because it ignored restrictions based on sex. For nearly twenty years, the cause of women's rights and the cause of black rights had marched together. Once black male suffrage came under discussion, however, this alliance began to fracture. When one veteran abolitionist declared it to be "the Negro's hour" and called for black male suffrage, Anthony responded that she "would sooner cut off my right hand than ask the ballot for the black man and not for woman." The break between the women's movement and the black movement was eventually papered over, but the wounds never completely healed.

Despite such opposition, within thirteen months the proposed amendment received the approval of enough states to take effect. Success came in part because Republicans, who might otherwise have been reluctant to impose black suffrage in the North, concluded that the future success of their party required black suffrage in the South.

The Fifteenth Amendment did nothing to reduce the violence—especially at election time—that had become almost routine in the South after 1865. When Klan activity escalated in the elections of 1870, southern Republicans looked to Washington for support. In 1870 and 1871, Congress adopted several Enforcement Acts—often called the Ku Klux Klan Acts—to enforce the Fourteenth and Fifteenth Amendments.

Despite a limited budget and many obstacles, the prosecution of Klansmen began in 1871. Across the South many hundreds were indicted, and many were convicted. In South Carolina, President Grant declared martial law. By 1872, federal intervention had broken much of the strength of the Klan.

Congress eventually passed one final Reconstruction measure. Charles Sumner introduced a bill prohibiting **discrimination** in 1870 and in each subsequent session of Congress until his death in 1874. On his deathbed, Sumner urged his visitors to "take care of the civil-rights bill," begging them "Don't let it fail." Passed after Sumner's death, the **Civil Rights Act of 1875** prohibited racial discrimination in the selection of juries and in public transportation and **public accommodations**.

BLACK RECONSTRUCTION

● What major groups made up the Republican Party in the South during Reconstruction? Compare their reasons for being Republicans, their relative size, and their objectives.

● What were the most lasting results of the Republican state administrations?

Congressional Reconstruction set the stage for new developments at state and local levels throughout the South, as newly enfranchised black men organized for political action. African Americans never completely controlled any state government, but they did form a significant element in the governments of several states. The period when African Americans participated prominently in state and local politics is usually called **Black Reconstruction**. It began with efforts by African Americans to take part in politics as early as 1865 and lasted for more than a decade. A few African Americans continued to hold elective office in the South long after 1877, but they could do little to bring about significant political change.

The Republican Party in the South

Not surprisingly, nearly all African Americans who participated actively in politics did so as Republicans. African Americans formed the large majority

---

disfranchisement   To take away an individual's or group's right to vote.

nativity   Place of birth.

discrimination   Denial of equal treatment based on prejudice or bias.

Civil Rights Act of 1875   Law passed by Congress in 1875 prohibiting racial discrimination in selection of juries and in transportation and other businesses open to the general public.

public accommodations   Hotels, bars and restaurants, theaters, and other places set up to do business with anyone who can pay the price of admission.

Black Reconstruction   The period of Reconstruction when African Americans took an active role in state and local government.

This lithograph from 1883 depicts prominent African-American men, several of whom had leading roles in Black Reconstruction. *Library of Congress.*

of those who supported the Republican Party in the South. Nearly all black Republicans were new to politics, and they often braved considerable personal danger by participating in a party that many white southerners equated with the conquering Yankees. In the South, the Republican Party also included some southern whites along with a smaller number of transplanted northerners—both black and white.

Suffrage made politics a centrally important activity for African-American communities. The state constitutional conventions that met in 1868 included 265 black delegates. Only in Louisiana and South Carolina were half or more of the delegates black. With suffrage established, southern Republicans began to elect African Americans to public office. Between 1869 and 1877, fourteen black men served in the national House of Representatives, and Mississippi sent two African Americans to the U.S. Senate: Hiram R. Revels and Blanche K. Bruce.

Across the South, six African Americans served as lieutenant governors, and one of them, P. B. S.

Pinchback, succeeded to the governorship of Louisiana for forty-three days. More than six hundred black men served in southern state legislatures during Reconstruction, but only in South Carolina did African Americans ever have a majority in the state legislature. Elsewhere they formed part of a Republican majority but rarely held key legislative positions. Only in South Carolina and Mississippi did legislatures elect black presiding officers.

Although politically inexperienced, most African Americans who held office during Reconstruction had some education. Of the eighteen who served in statewide offices, all but three are known to have been born free. P. B. S. Pinchback, for example, was educated in Ohio and served in the army as a captain before entering politics in Louisiana. Most black politicians first achieved prominence through service with the army, the Freedmen's Bureau, the new schools, or the religious and civic organizations of black communities.

Throughout the South, Republicans gained power only by securing some support from white voters. These white Republicans are usually remembered by the names fastened on them by their political opponents: "carpetbaggers" and "scalawags." Both groups included idealists who hoped to create a new southern society, but both also included opportunists expecting to exploit politics for personal gain.

Southern Democrats applied the term *carpetbagger* to northern Republicans who came to the South after the war, regarding them as second-rate schemers—outsiders with their belongings packed in a cheap suitcase (see illustration of a carpet bag on the next page). In fact, most northerners who came south were well-educated men and women from middle-class backgrounds. Most men had served in the Union army and moved south before blacks could vote. Some were lawyers, businessmen, or newspaper editors. Whether as investors in agricultural land, teachers in the new schools, or agents of the Freedmen's Bureau, most hoped to transform the South by creating new institutions based on northern models, especially free labor and free public schools. Few in number compared with southerners, transplanted northerners nonetheless took leading roles in state constitutional conventions and

carpetbagger   Derogatory term for the northerners who came to the South after the Civil War to take part in Reconstruction.

Bags made of carpeting, like this one, were inexpensive luggage for traveling. Southern opponents of Reconstruction fastened the label "carpetbaggers" on northerners who came south to participate in Reconstruction, suggesting that they were cheap opportunists. *Collection of Antique Textile Resource, Nancy Gerwiz.*

Creating an Educational System and Fighting Discrimination

Free public education was perhaps the most permanent legacy of Black Reconstruction. Reconstruction constitutions throughout the South required tax-supported public schools. Implementation, however, was expensive and proceeded slowly. By the mid-1870s, only half of southern children attended public schools.

In creating public schools, Reconstruction state governments faced a central question: would white and black children attend the same schools? Many blacks favored racially integrated schools. On the other hand, southern white leaders, including many southern white Republicans, argued that integration would destroy the fledgling public school system by driving whites away. In consequence, no state required school integration. Similarly, southern states set up separate black normal schools (to train schoolteachers) and colleges.

On balance, most blacks probably agreed with Frederick Douglass that separate schools were "infinitely superior" to no public education at all. Some found other reasons to accept segregated schools: separate black schools gave a larger role to black parents, and they hired black teachers.

Funding for the new schools was rarely adequate. Creating and operating two educational systems, one white and one black, was costly. The division of limited funds posed an additional problem, and black schools almost always received less support per student than white schools. Despite their accomplishments, the segregated schools institutionalized discrimination.

Reconstruction state governments moved toward protection of equal rights in areas other than education. As Republicans gained control in the South, they often wrote into the new state constitutions prohibitions against discrimination and protections for civil rights. Some Reconstruction state governments enacted laws guaranteeing **equal access** to

state legislatures. Some were also prominent advocates of economic modernization.

Southern Democrats reserved their greatest contempt for those they called *scalawags,* slang for someone completely unscrupulous and worthless. Scalawags were white southerners who became Republicans. They included many southern Unionists, who had opposed secession, and others who thought the Republicans offered the best hope for economic recovery. Scalawags included merchants, artisans, and professionals who favored a modernized South. Others were small-scale farmers who saw Reconstruction as a way to end political domination by the plantation owners.

The freedmen, carpetbaggers, and scalawags who made up the Republican Party in the South hoped to inject new ideas into that region. They tried to modernize state and local governments and make the postwar South more like the North. They repealed outdated laws and established or expanded schools, hospitals, orphanages, and penitentiaries.

scalawag Derogatory term for white southerners who aligned themselves with the Republican Party during Reconstruction.

equal access The right of any group to use a public facility, such as streetcars, as freely as all other groups in the society.

The Hampton Normal and Agricultural Institute was founded in 1868 with financial assistance from the Freedmen's Bureau and the American Missionary Association. Its purpose was to provide education for African Americans to prepare males for jobs in agriculture or industry, and to prepare women as homemakers. As a normal school, it also trained teachers. One of Hampton's most prominent graduates was Booker T. Washington, who attended shortly after this picture was taken around 1870. *Archival and Museum Collection, Hampton University.*

public transportation and public accommodations. Elsewhere efforts to pass equal access laws foundered on the opposition of southern white Republicans, who often joined Democrats to favor **segregation**. Such conflicts pointed up the internal divisions within the southern Republican Party. Even when equal access laws were passed, they were often not enforced.

Railroad Development and Corruption

Across the nation, Republicans sought to use the power of government to encourage economic growth and development. Efforts to promote economic development—North, South, and West—often focused on encouraging railroad construction. In the South, as elsewhere in the nation, some state governments granted state lands to railroads, or lent them money, or committed the state's credit to **underwrite** bonds for construction. Sometimes they promoted railroads without adequate planning or determining whether companies were financially

sound. Some efforts to promote railroad construction failed as companies squandered funds without building rail lines. During the 1870s, only 7,000 miles of new track were laid in the South, compared with 45,000 miles elsewhere in the nation. Even that was a considerable accomplishment for the South, given its dismal economic situation.

Railroad companies sometimes sought favorable treatment by bribing public officials. All too many officeholders—North, South, and West—accepted their offers. Given the excessive favoritism that most public officials showed to railroads, revelations and allegations of corruption became common from New York City to Mississippi to California.

segregation Separation on account of race or class from the rest of society, such as the separation of blacks from whites in most southern school systems.

underwrite To assume financial responsibility for; in this case, to guarantee the purchase of bonds so that a project can go forward.

In the period after the Civil War, railroads were often equated with economic development and with prosperity. This photo shows locomotives involved in logging. *Stephen F. Austin State University.*

Conditions in the South were ripe for political corruption as government responsibilities expanded rapidly and created new opportunities for scoundrels. Many Reconstruction officials—white and black—had only modest holdings of their own and wanted more. One South Carolina legislator bluntly described his attitude toward electing a U.S. senator: "I was pretty hard up, and I did not care who the candidate was if I got two hundred dollars." Corruption was usually nonpartisan, but it seemed more prominent among Republicans because they held the most important offices. One Louisiana Republican claimed, "Corruption is the fashion." Charges of corruption became common everywhere in the nation as politicians sought to discredit their opponents.

THE END OF RECONSTRUCTION

• What major factors brought about the end of Reconstruction? Evaluate their relative significance.

• Many historians began to re-evaluate their interpretations of Reconstruction during the 1950s and 1960s. Why do you suppose that happened?

From the beginning, most white southerners resisted the new order that the conquering Yankees imposed on them. Initially, resistance took the form of black codes and the Klan. Later, some southern opponents of Reconstruction developed new strategies, but terror remained an important instrument of resistance.

The "New Departure"

By 1869, some leading southern Democrats had abandoned their last-ditch resistance to change, deciding instead to accept some Reconstruction measures and African-American suffrage. At the same time, they also tried to secure restoration of political rights for former Confederates. Behind this **New Departure** for southern Democrats lay the belief that continued resistance would only cause more regional turmoil and prolong federal intervention.

Sometimes southern Democrats supported conservative Republicans for state and local offices instead of members of their own party, hoping to defuse concern in Washington and dilute Radical influence in state government. This strategy was tried first in Virginia, the last southern state to hold an election under its new constitution. There William Mahone, a former Confederate general, railroad promoter, and leading Democrat, forged a broad political **coalition** that accepted black suffrage. In 1869 Mahone's organization elected as governor a northern-born banker and moderate Republican. In this way, Mahone got state support for his railroad plans, and Virginia successfully avoided Radical Republican rule.

Coalitions of Democrats and moderate Republicans won in Tennessee in 1869 and in Missouri in 1870. Elsewhere leading Democrats endorsed the New Departure, accepted black suffrage, and attacked Republicans more for raising taxes and increasing state spending than for their racial policies. And Democrats almost always charged Republicans with corruption. Such campaigns brought a positive response from many taxpayers because southern tax rates had risen drastically to support the new educational systems, railroad subsidies, and other modernizing programs. In 1870 Democrats won the governorship in Alabama and Georgia. For Georgia, it meant the end of Reconstruction.

The victories of so-called **Redeemers** and New Departure Democrats in the early 1870s coincided with renewed terrorist activity aimed at Republicans. The worst single incident occurred in 1873. A group of armed freedmen fortified the town of Colfax, Louisiana, to hold off Democrats who were planning to seize the county government. After a three-week siege, well-armed whites overcame the black defenders and killed 280 African Americans. Leading Democrats rarely endorsed such bloodshed, but they reaped political advantages from it.

The 1872 Presidential Election

The New Departure movement, at its peak in 1872, coincided with a division within the Republican Party in the North. The Liberal Republican movement grew out of several elements within the Republican Party. Some were moderates, concerned that the Radicals had gone too far, especially with the Enforcement Acts, and had endangered federalism. Others opposed Grant on issues unrelated to Reconstruction. All were appalled by growing evidence of corruption in Washington. Liberal Republicans found allies among Democrats by arguing against further Reconstruction measures.

Horace Greeley, editor of the *New York Tribune*, won the Liberal nomination for president. An opponent of slavery before the Civil War, Greeley had given strong support to the Fourteenth and Fifteenth Amendments. But he had sometimes taken puzzling positions, including a willingness to let the South secede. His unkempt appearance and whining voice conveyed little of a presidential image. One political observer described him as "honest, but . . . conceited, fussy, and foolish."

Greeley had long ripped the Democrats in his newspaper columns. Even so, the Democrats nominated him in an effort to defeat Grant. Many saw the Democrats' action as desperate opportunism, and Greeley alienated many northern Democrats by favoring restrictions on the sale of alcohol. Grant won convincingly, carrying 56 percent of the vote and winning every northern state and ten of the sixteen southern and border states (see Map 16.1).

New Departure   Strategy of cooperation with some Reconstruction measures adopted by some leading southern Democrats in the hope of winning compromises favorable to their party.

coalition   An alliance, especially a temporary one of different people or groups.

Redeemers   Southern Democrats who hoped to bring the Democratic Party back into power and to suppress Black Reconstruction.

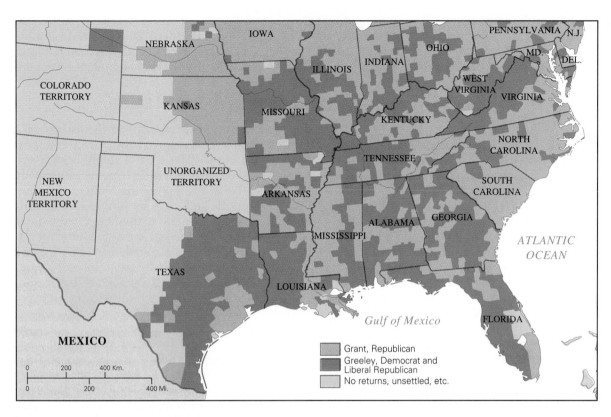

MAP 16.1 Popular Vote for President in the South, 1872 This map shows which candidate carried each county in the southeastern United States in 1872. Looking at both this map and the chapter-opening map, you can see the relation between Republican voting and African-American population in some areas, as well as where the southern Republican Party drew strong support from white voters.

The Politics of Terror: The "Mississippi Plan"

By the 1872 presidential race, nearly all southern whites had abandoned the Republicans, and Black Reconstruction ended in several states. African Americans, however, maintained their Republican loyalties. As Democrats worked to unite all southern whites behind their banner of white supremacy, the South polarized politically along racial lines. Elections in 1874 proved disastrous for Republicans: Democrats won more than two-thirds of the South's seats in the House of Representatives and "redeemed" Alabama, Arkansas, and Texas.

Terrorism against black Republicans and their remaining white allies played a role in some victories by Democrats in 1874. Where the Klan had once worn disguises and ridden at night, by 1874 in many places Democrats openly formed rifle companies, put on red-flannel shirts, and marched and drilled in public. In some areas, armed whites prevented African Americans from voting or terrorized prominent Republicans, especially African-American Republicans.

Republican candidates in 1874 also lost support in the North because of scandals within the Grant administration and because a major economic **depression** that had begun in 1873 was producing high unemployment. Before the 1874 elections, the House of Representatives included 194 Republicans

depression A period of economic contraction, characterized by decreasing business activity, falling prices, and high unemployment.

and 92 Democrats. After those elections, Democrats outnumbered Republicans by 169 to 109. Now southern Republicans could no longer look to Congress for assistance. Even though Republicans still controlled the Senate, the Democratic majority in the House of Representatives could block any new Reconstruction legislation.

During 1875 in Mississippi, political violence reached such levels that the use of terror to overthrow Reconstruction became known as the **Mississippi Plan**. Democratic rifle clubs broke up Republican meetings and attacked Republican leaders in broad daylight. One black Mississippian described the election of 1875 as "the most violent time we have ever seen." When Mississippi's carpetbagger governor, Adelbert Ames, requested federal help, President Grant declined, fearful that the southern Reconstruction governments had become so discredited that further federal military intervention might endanger the election prospects of Republican candidates in the North.

The Democrats swept the Mississippi elections, winning four-fifths of the state legislature. When the legislature convened, it impeached and removed from office Alexander Davis, the black Republican lieutenant governor, on grounds no more serious than those brought against Andrew Johnson. The legislature then brought similar impeachment charges against Governor Ames, who resigned and left the state. Ames had foreseen the result during the campaign when he wrote, "A revolution has taken place—by force of arms."

The Compromise of 1877

In 1876, on the centennial of American independence, the nation stumbled through a deeply troubled—and potentially dangerous—presidential election. As revelations of corruption multiplied, the issue of reform took center stage. The Democratic Party nominated Samuel J. Tilden, governor of New York, as its presidential candidate. A wealthy lawyer and businessman, Tilden had earned a reputation as a reformer by fighting political corruption in New York City. The Republicans selected **Rutherford B. Hayes**, a Civil War general and governor of Ohio, whose unblemished reputation proved to be his greatest asset. Not well known outside Ohio, he was a candidate nobody could object to. During the campaign in the South, intimidation of Republicans, both black and white, continued in many places.

First election reports indicated a victory for Tilden (see Map 16.2). In addition to the border

states and South, he also carried New York, New Jersey, and Indiana. Tilden received 51 percent of the popular vote versus 48 percent for Hayes. Leading Republicans quickly realized that their party still controlled the counting and reporting of ballots in South Carolina, Florida, and Louisiana, and that those three states could change the Electoral College majority from Tilden to Hayes. Charging **voting fraud**, Republican election boards in those states rejected enough ballots so that the official count gave Hayes narrow majorities and thus a one-vote margin of victory in the Electoral College. Crying fraud in return, Democratic officials in all three states submitted their own versions of the vote count.

Angry Democrats vowed to see Tilden inaugurated by force if necessary, and some Democratic newspapers ran headlines that read "Tilden or War." For the first time, Congress faced the problem of disputed electoral votes that could decide the outcome of an election. To resolve the challenges, Congress created a commission: five senators (chosen by the Senate, which had a Republican majority), five representatives (chosen by the House, which had a Democratic majority), and five Supreme Court justices (chosen by the justices). Initially, the balance was seven Republicans, seven Democrats, and one independent from the Supreme Court. The independent withdrew, however, and the remaining justices (all but one of whom had been appointed by Republican presidents) chose a Republican to replace him. The Republicans now had a one-vote majority on the commission.

This body needed to make its decision before the constitutionally mandated deadline of March 4. Some Democrats and Republicans worried over the potential for violence. However, as commission hearings droned on through January and into February 1877, informal discussions took place among leading Republicans and Democrats. The result was

Mississippi Plan   Use of threats, violence, and lynching by Mississippi Democrats in 1875 to intimidate Republicans and bring the Democratic Party to power.

Rutherford B. Hayes   Ohio governor and former Union general who won the Republican nomination in 1876 and became president of the United States in 1877.

voting fraud   Altering election results by illegal measures to bring about the victory of a particular candidate.

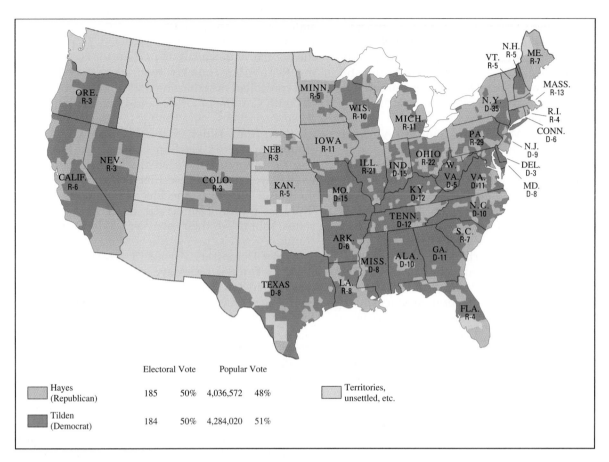

	Electoral Vote		Popular Vote	
Hayes (Republican)	185	50%	4,036,572	48%
Tilden (Democrat)	184	50%	4,284,020	51%
Territories, unsettled, etc.				

MAP 16.2 Election of 1876 The end of Black Reconstruction in most of the South combined with Democratic gains in the North to give a popular majority to Samuel Tilden, the Democratic candidate. The electoral vote was disputed, however, and was ultimately resolved in favor of Rutherford B. Hayes, the Republican.

often called the **Compromise of 1877**. Southern Democrats demanded an end to federal intervention in southern politics but insisted on federal subsidies for railroad construction and waterways in the South. And they wanted one of their own as postmaster general because that office held the key to most federal patronage. In return, southern Democrats seemed willing to abandon Tilden's claim to the White House.

Although the Compromise of 1877 was never set down in one place or agreed to by all parties, most of its conditions were met. By a straight party vote, the commission confirmed the election of Hayes. Soon after his peaceful inauguration, the new president ordered the last of the federal troops withdrawn from occupation duties in the South. The Radical era of a powerful federal government

pledged to protect "equality before the law" for all citizens was over. The last three Republican state governments fell in 1877. The Democrats, the self-described party of white supremacy, now held sway in every southern state. One Radical journal bitterly concluded that African Americans had been forced "to relinquish the artificial right to vote for the natural right to live." In parts of the South thereafter, election fraud and violence became routine. One Mississippi judge acknowledged in 1890 that "since

Compromise of 1877 Name applied by historians to the resolution of the disputed presidential election of 1876; it gave the presidency to the Republicans and made concessions to southern Democrats.

1875 . . . we have been preserving the ascendancy of the white people by . . . stuffing ballot boxes, committing perjury and here and there in the state carrying the elections by fraud and violence."

The Compromise of 1877 marked the end of Reconstruction. The Civil War was more than ten years in the past. Many moderate Republicans had hoped that the Fourteenth and Fifteenth Amendments and the Civil Rights Act would guarantee black rights without a continuing federal presence in the South. Southern Democrats tried hard to persuade northerners—on paltry evidence—that carpetbaggers and scalawags were all corrupt and self-serving, that they manipulated black voters to keep themselves in power, that African-American officeholders were ignorant and illiterate and could not participate in politics without guidance by whites, and that southern Democrats wanted only to establish honest self-government. The truth of the situation made little difference.

Northern Democrats had always opposed Reconstruction and readily adopted the southern Democrats' version of reality. Such portrayals found growing acceptance among other northerners too, for many had shown their own racial bias when they resisted black suffrage and kept their public schools segregated. In 1875, when Grant refused to use federal troops to protect black rights, he declared that "the whole public are tired out with these . . . outbreaks in the South." He was quoted widely and with approval throughout the North.

In addition, a major depression in the mid-1870s, unemployment and labor disputes, the growth of industry, the emergence of big business, and the development of the West focused the attention of many Americans, including many members of Congress, on economic issues.

Some Republicans, to be certain, kept the faith of their abolitionist and Radical forebears and hoped the federal government might again protect black rights. After 1877, however, though Republicans routinely condemned violations of black rights, few Republicans showed much interest in using federal power to prevent such outrages.

After Reconstruction

Southern Democrats read the events of 1877 as permission to establish new systems of politics and race relations. Most Redeemers worked to reduce taxes, dismantle Reconstruction legislation and agencies, and grab political influence away from black citizens. They also began the process of turning the South into a one-party region, a situation that reached its fullest development around 1900 and persisted until the 1950s and in some areas later.

Voting and officeholding by African Americans did not cease in 1877, but the context changed profoundly. Without federal enforcement of black rights, the threat of violence and the potential for economic retaliation by landlords and merchants sharply reduced meaningful political involvement by African Americans. Black political leaders soon understood that efforts to mobilize black voters posed dangers to candidates and voters, and they concluded that their political survival depended on favors from influential white Republicans or even from Democratic leaders. The public schools survived, segregated and underfunded, but presenting an important opportunity. Many Reconstruction-era laws remained on the books. Through much of the 1880s, many theaters, bars, restaurants, hotels, streetcars, and railroads continued to serve African Americans without discrimination.

Not until the 1890s did black disfranchisement and thoroughgoing racial segregation become widely embedded in southern law. From the mid-1870s to the late 1890s, African Americans exercised some constitutional rights. White supremacy had been established by force of arms, however, and blacks exercised their rights at the sufferance of the dominant whites. Such a situation bore the seeds of future conflict.

After 1877, Reconstruction was held up as a failure. Although far from accurate, the southern version of Reconstruction—that conniving carpetbaggers and scalawags had manipulated ignorant freedmen—appealed to many white Americans throughout the nation, and it gained widespread acceptance among many novelists, journalists, and historians. William A. Dunning, for example, endorsed that interpretation in his history of Reconstruction, published in 1907. Thomas Dixon's popular novel *The Clansman* (1905) inspired the highly influential film *The Birth of a Nation* (1915). Historically inaccurate and luridly racist, the book and the movie portrayed Ku Klux Klan members as heroes who rescued the white South, and especially white southern women, from domination and debauchery at the hands of depraved freedmen and carpetbaggers.

Against this pattern stood some of the first black historians, notably George Washington Williams, a Union army veteran whose two-volume history of African Americans appeared in 1882. *Black Recon-*

struction in America, by W. E. B. Du Bois, appeared in 1935. Both presented fully the role of African Americans in Reconstruction and pointed to the accomplishments of the Reconstruction state governments and black leaders. Not until the 1950s and 1960s, however, did large numbers of American historians begin to reconsider their interpretations of Reconstruction. Historians today recognize that Reconstruction was not the failure that had earlier been claimed. The creation of public schools was the most important of the changes in southern life produced by the Reconstruction state governments. At a fed-

eral level, the Fourteenth and Fifteenth Amendments eventually provided the constitutional leverage to restore the principle of equality before the law that so concerned the Radicals. Historians also recognize that Reconstruction collapsed partly because of internal flaws, partly because of divisions within the Republican Party, and partly because of the political terrorism unleashed in the South and the refusal of the North to commit the force required to protect the constitutional rights of African Americans.

INDIVIDUAL VOICES

Examining a Primary Source

A Freedman Offers His Former Master a Proposition

This letter appeared in the *New-York Daily Tribune* on August 22, 1865, with the notation that it was a "genuine document," reprinted from the *Cincinnati Commercial*. At that time, all newspapers had strong connections to political parties, and both of these papers were allied to the Republicans. By then, battle lines were being drawn between President Andrew Johnson and Republicans in Congress over the legal and political status of the freed people.

● How does the author indicate that the lives of these freed people have changed by leaving Tennessee for Ohio?

● Anderson's monthly wages of $25 in 1865 would be equivalent to about $265 in 2000. The amount he asks for as compensation for his slave labor, $11,680 in 1865 would be equivalent to nearly $125,000 in 2000.

DAYTON, Ohio, August 7, 1865
To my Old Master, Col. P. H. ANDERSON, Big Spring, Tennessee
SIR: *I got your letter and was glad to find that you had not forgotten Jordan, and that you wanted me to come back and live with you again, promising to do better for me than anybody else can. . . .*
I want to know particularly what the good chance is you propose to give me. I am doing tolerably well here; I get $25 a month, with victuals and clothing; have a comfortable home for Mandy (the folks here call her Mrs. Anderson), and the children, Milly[,] Jane and Grundy, go to school and are learning well. . . . Now, if you will write and say what wages you will give me, I will be better able to decide whether it would be to my advantage to move back again. ●
As to my freedom, which you say I can have, there is nothing to be gained on that score, as I got my free-papers in 1864 from the Provost-Marshal-General of the Department at Nashville. Mandy says she would be afraid to go back without some proof that you are sincerely disposed to treat us justly and kindly—and we have concluded to test your sincerity by asking you to send us our wages for the time we served you. This will make us forget and forgive old sores, and rely on your justice and friendship in the future. I served you faithfully for thirty-two years, and Mandy twenty years, at $25 a month for me and $2 a week for Mandy.
● *Our earnings would amount to $11,680. Add to this the interest for the time*

● How does the author use this letter to raise a wide range of issues about the nature of slavery and about the uneasiness of freed people about life in the South in 1865?

● Evaluate the likelihood that this letter was actually written by a former slave. What are the other possibilities? Why do you think this letter appeared in newspapers in August of 1865?

our wages has been kept back and deduct what you paid for our clothing and three doctor's visits to me, and pulling a tooth for Mandy, and the balance will show what we are in justice entitled to. . . . If you fail to pay us for faithful labors in the past we can have little faith in your promises in the future. We trust the good Maker has opened your eyes to the wrongs which you and your fathers have done to me and my fathers, in making us toil for you for generations without recompense. . . .

In answering this letter please state if there would be any safety for my Milly and Jane, who are now grown up and both good looking girls. You know how it was with poor Matilda and Catherine. I would rather stay here and starve and die if it had to come to that than have my girls brought to shame by the violence and wickedness of their young masters. You will also please state if there has been any schools opened for the colored children in your neighborhood, the great desire of my life now is to give my children an education, and have them form virtuous habits. ●

From your old servant, ● JOURDAN ANDERSON.
P.S.—Say howdy to George Carter, and thank him for taking the pistol from you when you were shooting at me.

SUMMARY

At the end of the Civil War, the nation faced difficult choices regarding the restoration of the defeated South and the future of the freed people. Committed to ending slavery, President Lincoln nevertheless chose a lenient approach to restoring states to the Union, partly to persuade southerners to accept emancipation and abandon the Confederacy. When Johnson became president, he continued Lincoln's approach.

The end of slavery brought new opportunities for African Americans, whether or not they had been slaves. Taking advantage of the opportunities that freedom opened, they tried to create independent lives for themselves, and they developed social institutions that helped to define black communities. Because few were able to acquire land of their own, most became either sharecroppers or wage laborers. White southerners also experienced economic dislocation, and many also became sharecroppers. Most white southerners expected to keep African Americans in a subordinate role and initially used black codes and violence toward that end.

In reaction against the black codes and violence, Congress took control of Reconstruction away from President Johnson and passed the Civil Rights Act of 1866, the Fourteenth Amendment, and the Reconstruction Acts of 1867. An attempt to remove Johnson from the presidency was unsuccessful. Additional federal Reconstruction measures included the Fifteenth Amendment, laws directed against the Ku Klux Klan, and the Civil Rights Act of 1875. Several of these measures strengthened the federal government at the expense of the states.

Enfranchised freedmen, white and black northerners who moved to the South, and some southern whites created a southern Republican Party that governed most southern states for a time. The most lasting contribution of these state governments was the creation of public school systems. Like government officials elsewhere in the nation, however, some southern politicians fell prey to corruption.

In the late 1860s, many southern Democrats chose a "New Departure": they grudgingly accepted some features of Reconstruction and sought to recapture control of state governments. By the mid-1870s, however, southern politics turned almost solely on race. The 1876 presidential election was very close and hotly disputed. Key Republicans and Democrats developed a compromise: Hayes took office and ended the final stages of Reconstruction. Without federal protection for their civil rights, African Americans faced terrorism, violence, and even death if they challenged their subordinate role. With the end of Reconstruction, the South entered an era of white supremacy in politics and government, the economy, and social relations.

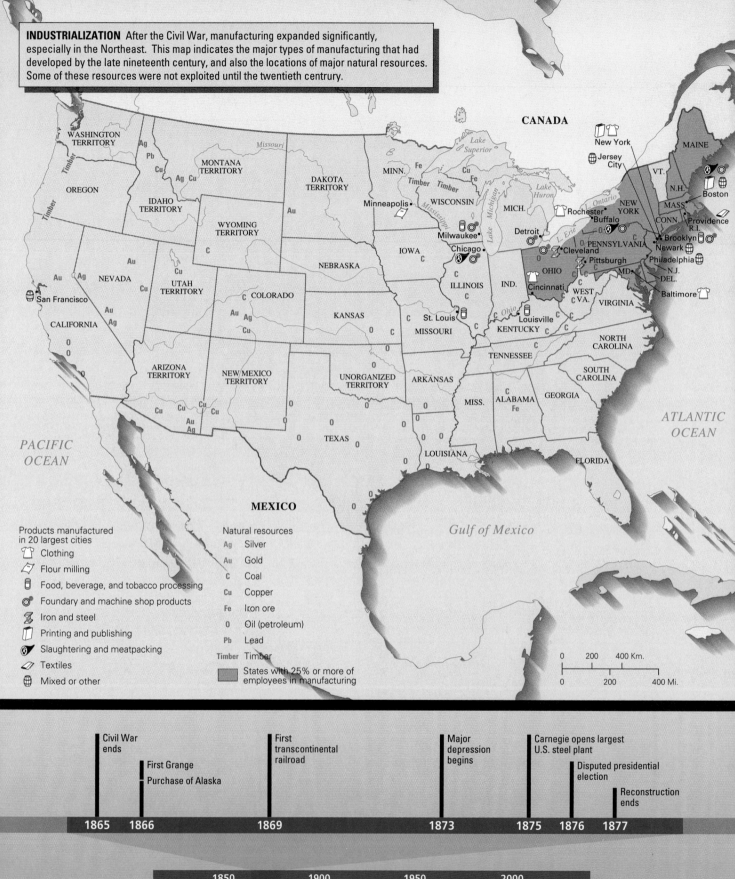

INDUSTRIALIZATION After the Civil War, manufacturing expanded significantly, especially in the Northeast. This map indicates the major types of manufacturing that had developed by the late nineteenth century, and also the locations of major natural resources. Some of these resources were not exploited until the twentieth century.

CANADA

WASHINGTON TERRITORY

OREGON

MONTANA TERRITORY

IDAHO TERRITORY

WYOMING TERRITORY

DAKOTA TERRITORY

MINN.

Minneapolis

WISCONSIN

Milwaukee

MICH.

Chicago

Detroit

Rochester

Buffalo

NEW YORK

New York

Jersey City

MAINE

VT.

N.H.

MASS.

Boston

CONN.

Providence R.I.

NEVADA

UTAH TERRITORY

COLORADO

NEBRASKA

IOWA

ILLINOIS

IND.

Cincinnati

OHIO

Cleveland

Pittsburgh

PENNSYLVANIA

Brooklyn

Newark

Philadelphia

N.J.

DEL.

MD.

Baltimore

San Francisco

CALIFORNIA

KANSAS

St. Louis

MISSOURI

KENTUCKY

Louisville

WEST VA.

VIRGINIA

NORTH CAROLINA

ARIZONA TERRITORY

NEW MEXICO TERRITORY

UNORGANIZED TERRITORY

ARKANSAS

TENNESSEE

SOUTH CAROLINA

GEORGIA

MISS.

ALABAMA

TEXAS

LOUISIANA

FLORIDA

MEXICO

PACIFIC OCEAN

ATLANTIC OCEAN

Gulf of Mexico

Lake Superior

Lake Michigan

Lake Huron

Lake Erie

L. Ontario

Missouri

Mississippi

Ohio

Products manufactured in 20 largest cities
- Clothing
- Flour milling
- Food, beverage, and tobacco processing
- Foundary and machine shop products
- Iron and steel
- Printing and publishing
- Slaughtering and meatpacking
- Textiles
- Mixed or other

Natural resources
- Ag   Silver
- Au   Gold
- C   Coal
- Cu   Copper
- Fe   Iron ore
- O   Oil (petroleum)
- Pb   Lead
- Timber   Timber
- States with 25% or more of employees in manufacturing

0   200   400 Km.

0   200   400 Mi.

| Civil War ends | First Grange | First transcontinental railroad | Major depression begins | Carnegie opens largest U.S. steel plant | Disputed presidential election | Reconstruction ends |

Purchase of Alaska

1865   **1866**   **1869**   **1873**   **1875**   **1876**   **1877**

1850   1900   1950   2000

Frank Roney

FRANK RONEY

This photograph of Frank Roney was probably taken in the 1880s when Roney was head of the San Francisco Trades Assembly, an umbrella organization for the city's trade unions. *University of California at Berkeley, Bancroft Library.*

Frank Roney arrived in New York from Ireland in 1868. Born in 1841, he had served a seven-year apprenticeship to become an iron molder. (Iron molders make objects of cast iron by heating iron until it melts and pouring it into molds.) His father was a skilled carpenter and an officer in the carpenters' union. Some of the skilled iron molders from whom Roney learned his trade also taught him about the Friendly Society of Iron Molders, the Irish trade union for molders. Both his father and his mentors, then, had a role in introducing him to organized labor. Around the age of 21, Roney completed his apprenticeship and qualified as a journeyman (skilled) iron molder. Soon he became involved with the struggle for Irish independence from England and was imprisoned. A sympathetic judge gave Roney the chance to go free if he would leave Ireland and go to America.

Roney found that many American foundry workers lacked the self-respect he associated with his craft. In Ireland, molders "worked rationally, intelligently, and well, and had some of their work remaining for the next day." By contrast, "American molders seemed desirous of doing all the work required as if it were the last day of their lives." Roney learned that many American workers were paid by the piece rather than by the day, so that the more work they did, the more they were paid. Wages, he discovered, "were periodically reduced" and "the more this was done and the greater the reduction the harder the men worked" to earn the same pay. Roney was appalled. For him, being a skilled iron molder was a mark of status, and he found the pace maintained by the American workers to be not only physically exhausting but personally degrading.

He worked for a time in Jersey City, New Jersey, and then sampled life in St. Louis and Chicago. Chicago foundries, he discovered, also "operated on the breakneck principle," and he lost his position there when he refused to work overtime without extra pay. Traveling to Omaha, he worked in the shops of the Union Pacific Railroad and quickly became an officer in Iron Molders Union No. 190. William Sylvis, the national president of the molders union, was also head of the National Labor Union, and Roney eagerly joined up, hoping the new organization and its associated political party might accomplish its goal of abolishing poverty. After the collapse of that party, he went to Salt Lake City for a time, and then pushed on to San Francisco, arriving in 1875.

In San Francisco, Roney secured work in the Union Iron Works, the largest foundry on the Pacific coast. He was again disgusted by the workers around him. "No foreman was needed to urge these men to work to the point of exhaustion. They labored hard of their volition and displayed an eagerness most discouraging to one who wished to see each of them [behave like] a man." Manliness, for Roney, involved dignity. He became active in the local molders' union and helped to form the Trades and Labor Assembly, a central body for trade unions. But a major concern remained—the work habits of his fellow molders. "Men who work

as hacks and drudges are not those from whom to expect high thoughts or ideas of social improvement," he wrote. "A slavish worker," he argued, "has a slavish mind." He set out, in the shop and in union meetings, to persuade his fellow workers by word and deed to recognize the evils of "rushing" and competing with each other. "A well-timed remark," he knew, was often more effective "than a long-winded dissertation." Gradually, he sensed some success, and with it came the growth of the union. Roney emerged as an officer and then became a leader of organized labor more generally in the city. Under his leadership, many San Francisco unions gained members and strength. Once again, however, union activism cost Roney his job.

INTRODUCTION

Frank Roney's experiences in the iron works and the union hall were tied to an economy that was being dramatically and profoundly transformed. At the end of the Civil War, in 1865, more than half of all American workers toiled in agriculture. Anyone contemplating the prospects for manufacturing would have been struck by the obstacles: a poorly developed transportation system, limited amounts of capital, an unsophisticated system for mobilizing funds, and an uncertain labor force. Some, however, would have pointed to the great potential evident in America's vast natural resources and skilled workers

A generation later, by 1900, much of that potential had been realized, and the United States stood as a major industrial power. The changes in the nation's economy far exceeded the wildest expectations of Americans living in 1865. Many then probably anticipated economic growth, but few could have imagined that steel production could increase a thousand times by 1900, or that railroads could operate nearly six times as many miles of track, or that farms could triple their harvests. These economic changes and many others were the result of decisions by many individuals—where to seek work, where to invest, whether to expand production, how to react to a business competitor, whom to trust. Like Roney, many Americans also had to make choices about competition and cooperation.

As the industrial economy took off, many people found themselves in a love-hate relationship with competition. Andrew Carnegie, a leader in the new steel industry, loved it, arguing that competition "insures the survival of the fittest" and "insures the future progress of the race" by producing the highest quality, largest quantity, and lowest prices. Other

entrepreneurs saw competition as the single most unpredictable factor they faced and a serious constraint on economic progress. Carnegie's zeal for competition was, in fact, unusual. Although many entrepreneurs publicly applauded the idea of the "survival of the fittest," most loved competition in the abstract but preferred to find alternatives to it in their own business affairs.

Other Americans also found themselves making choices regarding cooperation. Individualism was deeply entrenched in the American psyche, yet the increasing complexity of the economy presented repeated opportunities for cooperation. Railroad executives sometimes cooperated by dividing a market rather than competing in it. Like Frank Roney, wage earners sometimes joined with other workers in standing up to their employers and demanding better wages or working conditions. The result of these many decisions was the industrialization of the nation and the transformation of the economy.

FOUNDATION FOR INDUSTRIALIZATION

• What were the most important factors that encouraged economic growth and industrial development after the Civil War?

• What were the major changes in the U.S. economy from the Civil War to World War I?

By 1865, conditions in the United States were ripe for rapid industrialization. A wealth of natural resources, a capable work force, an agricultural base that produced enough food for a large urban population, and favorable government policies laid the foundation.

In the popular imagination of most Americans in the late nineteenth century, the West was a vast and unpopulated storehouse of riches—fertile agricultural land, timber waiting to be cut, minerals there for the taking. Such attitudes were encouraged by popular prints such as this lithograph by Currier and Ives, entitled "Across the Continent: Westward the Course of Empires Takes Its Way" (1868), depicting ambitious pioneers moving west. In such imaginative depictions, there was rarely any indication that, in fact, the West was already home to many American Indians and Mexican Americans. *Museum of the City of New York.*

Resources, Skills, and Capital

At the end of the Civil War, **entrepreneurs** could draw on vast and virtually untapped natural resources. Americans had long since plowed the fertile farmland of the Midwest (where corn and wheat dominated) and the South (where cotton was king). They had just begun to farm the rich soils of Minnesota, Nebraska, Kansas, Iowa, and the Dakotas, as well as the productive valleys of California. Through the central part of the nation stretched vast grasslands that received too little rain for farming but were well suited for grazing. The Pacific Northwest, the western Great Lakes region, and the South all held extensive forests untouched by the lumberman's saw.

The nation was also rich in mineral resources. Before the Civil War, the iron **industry** had become centered in Pennsylvania as a result of easy access to iron ore and coal. Pennsylvania was also the site of early efforts to tap underground pools of crude oil. The California gold rush, beginning in 1848, had drawn many people west, and some of them had found great riches. Reserves of other minerals

lay unused and, in many cases, undiscovered at the end of the war, including iron ore in Michigan, Minnesota, and Alabama; coal throughout the Ohio Valley and in Wyoming and Colorado; oil in the Midwest, Oklahoma, Texas, Louisiana, southern California, and Alaska; gold or silver in Nevada, Colorado, and Alaska; and copper in Michigan, Montana, Utah, and Arizona. Many of these natural resources were far from population centers, and their use awaited adequate transportation facilities. Exploitation of some of these resources also required new technologies.

---

entrepreneur   A person who takes on the risks of creating, organizing, and managing a business enterprise.

industry   A basic unit of business activity in which the various participants do similar activities; for example, the railroad industry consists of railroad companies and the firms and factories that supply their equipment.

chronology

The Growth of Industry

1823	Monroe Doctrine
1850s	Development of Bessemer and Kelly steel-making processes
1854	U.S. Navy opens trade with Japan
1861	Protective tariff
1862	Homestead Act Land-Grant College Act Pacific Railroad Act
1865	Civil War ends
1866	National Labor Union organized
1867	First Grange formed French troops leave Mexico; Maximilian executed Senate rejects purchase of Danish West Indies United States purchases Alaska from Russia
1868	Ulysses S. Grant elected president
1869	First transcontinental railroad completed
1870	Senate rejects annexation of Santo Domingo
1871	Boss Tweed indicted
1872	Crédit Mobilier scandal Grant reelected Montgomery Ward opens first U.S. mail-order business Arbitration of *Alabama* claims

1872–1874	Granger laws
1873	"Salary Grab" Act
1873–1878	Depression
mid-1870s	Grange membership peaks
1874	Republicans lose majority in House of Representatives
1875	Whiskey Ring scandal Andrew Carnegie opens nation's largest steel plant
1876	Secretary of War William Belknap resigns
1877	Disputed presidential election Rutherford B. Hayes becomes president Reconstruction ends Great Railway Strike *Munn v. Illinois*
1878	Bland-Allison Act Greenback Party peaks
1879	George, *Progress and Poverty*
1882	U.S. Navy opens trade with Korea

In addition to natural resources, a skilled and experienced work force was essential for economic growth. In the 1790s and early nineteenth century, New Englanders had developed manufacturing systems based on **interchangeable parts** (first used for manufacturing guns and clocks) and factories for producing cotton cloth. These accomplishments gave them a reputation for "Yankee ingenuity"—a talent for devising new tools and inventive methods. Such skills and problem-solving abilities, however, were not limited to New England—they were key ingredients in nearly all large-scale manufacturing because early factories usually relied on skilled **artisans** to direct less-skilled workers in assembling products. Some of the early artisans

interchangeable parts   Mechanical parts that are identical and can be substituted for one another.

artisan   A skilled worker, whether self-employed or working for wages.

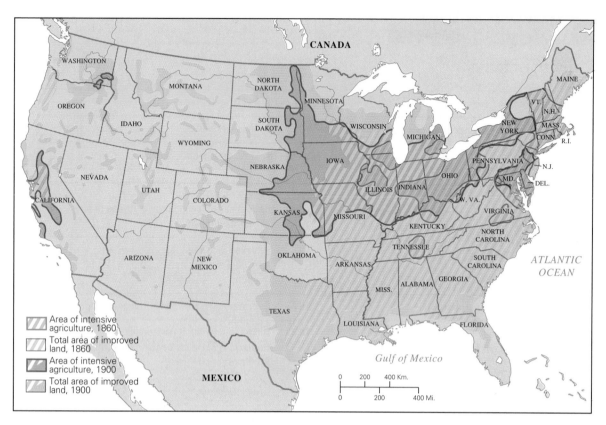

MAP 17.1 Expansion of Agriculture, 1860–1900 The amount of improved farmland more than doubled during these forty years. This map shows how agricultural expansion came in two ways—first, western lands were brought under cultivation; second, in other areas, especially the Midwest, land was cultivated much more intensely than before.

and factory owners came from Great Britain, where they had learned mechanical skills or honed entrepreneurial abilities in the world's first industrial nation.

Another crucial element for industrialization was capital, and institutions that could mobilize capital had developed and begun to thrive before the Civil War. During the years before the war, capital became centered in the seaport cities of the Northeast—Boston, New York, and Philadelphia, especially—where prosperous merchants had invested their profits in banks and factories. Banks were important instruments for mobilizing capital. Before the Civil War, some bankers had begun to specialize in arranging financing for large-scale enterprises, and some of these had opened permanent branch offices in Britain to tap sources of capital there. **Stock exchanges** had also developed long before the Civil War as important institutions for raising capital for new ventures.

The Transformation of Agriculture

The expanding economy of the nineteenth century rested on a productive agricultural base. Improved transportation—canals early in the nineteenth century and railroads later—speeded the expansion of agriculture by making it possible to move large amounts of agricultural produce over long distances. Up to the Civil War, farmers had developed 407 million acres into productive farmland. During the next thirty-five years, this figure more than doubled, to 841 million acres. Map 17.1 indicates where this growth occurred.

> **stock exchange** A place where people buy and sell stocks (shares in the ownership of companies); stockholders may participate in election of the company's directors and share in the company's profits.

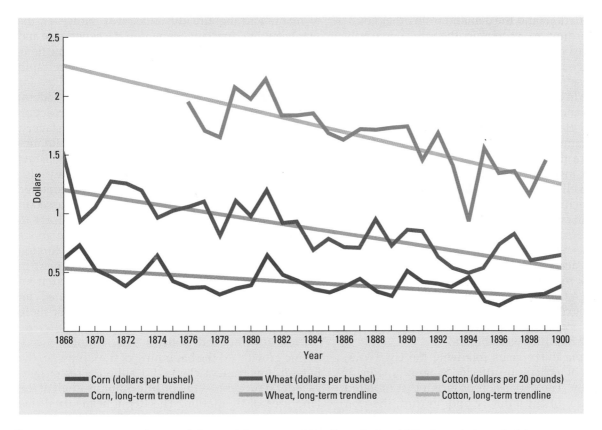

FIGURE 17.1 Corn, Wheat, and Cotton Prices, 1868–1900 From the late 1860s through the end of the century, prices for major crops fell. This graph shows both the year-to-year fluctuations (solid lines) and the long-term trends (broken lines). *Source*: U.S. Department of Commerce, Bureau of the Census, *Historical Statistics of the United States, Colonial Times to 1970*, Bicentennial edition, 2 vols. (Washington: Government Printing Office, 1975), I: 510–512, 517–518.

The federal government contributed to the rapid settlement of Kansas, Nebraska, the Dakotas, and Minnesota through the **Homestead Act** of 1862, a leading example of the Republican Party's commitment to using federal landholdings to speed economic development. Under this act, any person could receive free as much as 160 acres (a quarter of a square mile) of government land by building a house, living on the land for five years, and farming it. Between 1862 and 1890, 48 million acres passed from government ownership to private hands in this way. Other federally owned land could be purchased for as little as $1.25 per acre, and much more was obtained at this bargain price than was acquired free under the Homestead Act.

Production of leading commercial crops increased more rapidly than the overall expansion of farming. Though the total number of acres in farmland doubled between 1866 and 1900, the number of acres planted in corn, wheat, and cotton more than tripled. New farming methods increased harvests even more—corn by 264 percent, wheat by 252 percent, and cotton by 383 percent. Through these years, farm output grew more than twice as much as the population.

As production of major crops rose, prices for them fell. Figure 17.1 shows the prices and long-term price trends for wheat, corn, and cotton—the most significant commercial crops. Though several factors contributed to this decline in farm prices, the most obvious was that supply outpaced demand. Production increased more rapidly than both the population (which largely determined the demand

> **Homestead Act** Law passed by Congress in 1862 that offered ownership of 160 acres of designated public lands to any citizen who lived on and improved the land for five years.

within the nation) and the demand from other countries. According to economic theory, oversupply causes prices to fall, and falling prices lead producers to reduce their output. When American farmers received less for their crops, however, they usually raised *more* in an effort to maintain the same level of income. To increase their harvests, they bought fertilizers and elaborate machinery. Between 1870 and 1890, the amount of fertilizer consumed in the nation more than quadrupled. And the more they raised, the lower prices fell—and with them, the economic well-being of many farmers.

New machinery especially affected the production of grain crops, greatly increasing the amount of land one person could farm. A single farmer with a hand-held scythe and cradle, for example, could harvest 2 acres of wheat in a day. Using the McCormick reaper (first produced in 1849), a single farmer and a team of horses could harvest 2 acres in an hour. For other crops too, a person with modern machinery could farm two or three times as much land as a farmer fifty years before.

During the thirty years following the Civil War, the growth of agriculture affected other segments of the economy. The expansion of farming stimulated the farm equipment industry and, in turn, the iron and steel industry. The large volume of agricultural exports—cotton, tobacco, wheat, meat—spurred oceanic shipping and shipbuilding, and increased shipbuilding meant a greater demand for iron and steel. Railroads played a crucial role in the expansion and commercialization of agriculture by carrying farm products to distant markets and transporting fertilizer and machinery from factories (usually in distant cities) to farming regions.

The Impact of War and New Government Policies

In 1865 nearly three times as many Americans worked in agriculture as in manufacturing. Most manufacturing was small in scale and local in nature—a shop with a few workers who made barrels or assembled farm wagons, mostly for people nearby. Nonetheless, many conditions were ripe for the emergence of a manufacturing economy. The Civil War encouraged some entrepreneurs to deliver military supplies to distant parts of the nation, and some of them now sought to develop similar business patterns in peacetime. At the end of the war, too, some people found themselves looking for places to invest their wartime profits. By diverting labor and capital into war production, the Civil War may have slowed an expansion of manufacturing already under way. However, the war brought important changes in the experience and expectations of some entrepreneurs. At the same time, new government policies encouraged a more rapid rate of economic growth.

When Republicans took command of the federal government in 1861, the South seceded in reaction to the new administration's opposition to slavery, and secession led to the Civil War. While the Republicans made war against the Confederacy, abolished slavery, and undertook Reconstruction, they also forged new policies intended to stimulate economic growth. First came a new **protective tariff**, passed in 1861. The tariff increased the price of imports to equal or exceed the price of American-made goods in order to protect domestic products from foreign competition and thereby encourage investment in manufacturing. Though tariff rates changed from time to time, the protective tariff remained an important part of federal economic policy for more than a half-century.

New federal land policies also stimulated economic growth. At the beginning of the Civil War, the federal government claimed a billion acres of land as federal property—the **public domain**—half of the land area of the nation. The Republicans used this land to encourage economic development in a variety of ways, including free land for farmers, beginning with the Homestead Act (1862). Recognizing the importance of higher education, the **Land-Grant College Act** (1862)—often called the Morrill Act for its sponsor, Senator Justin Morrill of Vermont—gave federal land to each state (excluding those that had seceded) to sell or otherwise use to raise funds to establish a public university, which was required to provide education in engineering and agriculture and to train military officers. Also in 1862, Congress approved a land grant for the first transcontinental railroad, and more land grants to railroads followed.

---

protective tariff   A tax placed on imported goods for the purpose of raising the price of imports as high as or higher than the prices of the same item produced within the nation.

public domain   Land owned by the federal government.

Land-Grant College Act   Law passed by Congress in 1862 that gave states land to use to raise money to establish public universities that were to offer courses in engineering and agriculture and to train military officers.

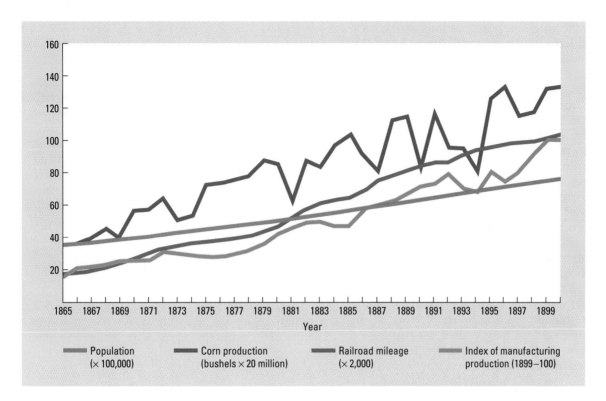

FIGURE 17.2 Measures of Growth, 1865–1900 Though many measures of economic productivity are related to population size, this graph shows how several measures of economic productivity grew at more rapid rates than did population size. *Source*: U.S. Department of Commerce, Bureau of the Census, *Historical Statistics of the United States, Colonial Times to 1970*, Bicentennial edition, 2 vols. (Washington: Government Printing Office, 1975), I: 8, 510–512; 2: 667, 727–731.

Overview: The Economy from the Civil War to World War I

Given the solid foundation for industrialization, the expansion of agriculture, and favorable governmental policies, the nation grew dramatically in the late nineteenth and early twentieth centuries. For example, between 1865 and 1920, the nation's population increased by nearly 200 percent, from 36 million to 106 million (the causes of this growth are discussed in the next chapter). During the same years, railroad mileage increased by more than 1,000 percent, from 35,000 miles to 407,000 miles. The output of manufacturing increased by a similar margin. Agricultural production grew far faster than the population. Perhaps most significantly, the total domestic product, per capita, in constant dollars, nearly tripled. (Figure 17.2 presents some of these patterns.)

Much of this growth was sporadic. Economic historians think of the economy as developing through a cycle in which periods of **expansion** (growth) alternate with times of **contraction** (**recession** or

depression, characterized by high unemployment and low productivity). Though this alternation between expansion and contraction is predictable, there is no predictability or regularity to the duration of any given up or down period. During the late nineteenth century, contractions were sometimes severe, producing widespread unemployment and distress. After 1865, a postwar recession lasted until

expansion In the economic cycle, a time when the economy is growing as indicated by increased production of goods and services and usually by low rates of unemployment.

contraction In the economic cycle, a time when the economy has ceased to grow, characterized by decreased production of goods and services and often by high rates of unemployment.

recession/depression A recession is an economic contraction of relatively short duration; a depression is an economic contraction of longer duration.

late 1867, reflecting sharp dislocations as the economy shifted from wartime production to other ventures. This was followed by several expansions and contractions of similar length. A major depression began in October 1873 and lasted until March 1879. The period from 1879 to 1893 was generally a period of expansion (105 months of growth), spurred in particular by railroad construction, but the growth was interrupted three times by contractions (totaling 61 months), two of them quite short. Another major depression began in January 1893 and lasted (despite a brief upswing) until June 1897 and was then followed by alternating periods of expansion and contraction of almost equal length, with the longest expansion in 1904–1907 (33 months) and the longest contraction in 1910–1912 (24 months).

During boom periods, companies advertised for labor and ran their operations at full capacity. When the demand for manufactured goods fell, companies reduced production, cutting hours of work or dismissing employees as they waited for business to pick up. Some businesses shut down temporarily; others closed permanently. Thus Americans living in the late nineteenth and early twentieth centuries came to expect that "hard times" were likely in the future, regardless of how prosperous life seemed at the moment. Federal intervention in the economy was limited largely to stimulating growth through the protective tariff and land distribution programs. Unemployed workers had little to fall back on besides their savings or the earnings of other family members. Some churches and private charity organizations gave out food, but state and federal governments provided no unemployment benefits. Families who failed to find work might go hungry or even become homeless. In a depression, jobs of any sort were scarce, and competition for every opening was intense. Most adult Americans therefore understood the wisdom of saving up for hard times, whether or not they were able to do so.

The depression that began in 1873 was both severe and long-lasting. Between 1873 and 1879, 355 banks closed down, a number equivalent to one bank in nine that existed in 1873. Nearly 54,000 businesses failed, also equivalent to one in nine operating in 1873. No reliable unemployment data exist, but evidence indicates that the contraction hit urban wage earners especially hard. Many lost their jobs or suffered a reduced workweek. Workers who kept their jobs saw their daily wages fall by 17–18 percent from 1873 to 1878 or 1879. For example, unskilled laborers' daily wages fell from an average of $1.52 in 1873 to a low of $1.26 in 1878, and blacksmiths' daily wages fell from $2.70 in 1873 to $2.21 in 1879. One Massachusetts worker described the consequences for his family in 1875:

> I have six children . . . Last year three of my children were promoted [to the next grade in school], and I was notified to furnish different books. [Schoolchildren then were responsible for providing their own textbooks.] I wrote a note to the school committee, stating that I was not able to do so. . . . I then received a note stating that, unless I furnished the books called for, I must keep my children at home. I then had to reduce the bread for my children and family, in order to get the required books to keep them at school. Every cent of my earnings is consumed in my family; and yet I have not been able to have a piece of meat on my table twice a month for the last eight months.

Thus, though long-term economic trends reflect dramatic growth, the short-run boom-and-bust nature of the economy repeatedly claimed its victims.

RAILROADS AND INDUSTRY

- What was the significance of the railroad and steel industries in the new industrial economy that emerged after the Civil War?
- What might account for the changes in historians' views of the industrial entrepreneurs of the post-Civil War period?

To many Americans of the late nineteenth century, nothing symbolized economic growth so effectively as a locomotive—a huge, powerful, noisy, smoke-belching machine barreling forward. Railroads set much of the pace for economic expansion after the Civil War. Growth of the rail network stimulated industries that supplied materials for railroad construction and operation—especially steel and coal—and industries that relied on railroads to connect them to the emerging national economy. Railroad companies also came to symbolize "big business"—companies of great size, employing thousands of workers, operating over large geographic areas—and some Americans began to fear their power.

Railroad Expansion

At the end of the Civil War, the nation lacked a comprehensive national transportation network. Before the Civil War, much of the nation's commerce moved on water—on rivers, canals, and coastal waterways.

In his novel *The Octopus* (1901), Frank Norris described not just the physical power of the railroad, but also its economic and political prowess: "The galloping terror of steam and steel, with its single eye, cyclopean, red, shooting from horizon to horizon, symbol of a vast power, huge and terrible; the leviathan with tentacles of steel, to oppose which meant to be ground to instant destruction beneath the clashing wheels." This Currier and Ives lithograph from 1863, entitled "The Lightning Express Trains: Leaving the Junction," captures some of that sense of power. *Museum of the City of New York.*

Railroads had only begun to challenge boats, and there was no national rail network until well after the war's end. Railroad companies operated on tracks of varying **gauges**, which made the transfer of railcars from one line to another impossible. Instead, freight had to be moved by hand or wagon from the cars of one line to those of another. Few railway bridges crossed major rivers. Until 1869, no railroad connected the eastern half of the country to the booming Pacific coast region. Every route between the Atlantic and Pacific coasts required more than a month and posed serious discomfort if not outright danger. The choices were equally intimidating: a sea voyage around the storm-tossed tip of South America; or a boat trip to Central America, then transit over mountains and through malaria-infested jungles to the Pacific, and then another boat trip up the Pacific coast; or a seemingly endless overland journey by riverboat and stagecoach.

By the mid-1880s, all the elements were finally in place for a national rail network. The first transcontinental rail line was completed in 1869, connecting California to Omaha, Nebraska (where Frank Roney briefly worked in the railroad's shops), and ultimately to eastern cities. (For more on the construction of this railroad, see page 584.) Within the next fifteen years, three more rail lines linked the Pacific coast to the eastern half of the nation, and a fourth was completed in 1893. Between 1865 and 1890, railroads grew from 35,000 miles of track to 167,000 miles (see Map 17.2). By the mid-1880s, most major rivers had been bridged. Companies had replaced many iron rails with steel ones, allowing them to haul heavier loads. New inventions increased the speed, carrying capacity, and efficiency of trains. In 1886 the last major lines converted to a standard gauge, making it possible to transfer railcars from one line to another simply by throwing a switch. This rail network encouraged entrepreneurs to think

gauge In this usage, the distance between the two rails making up railroad tracks.

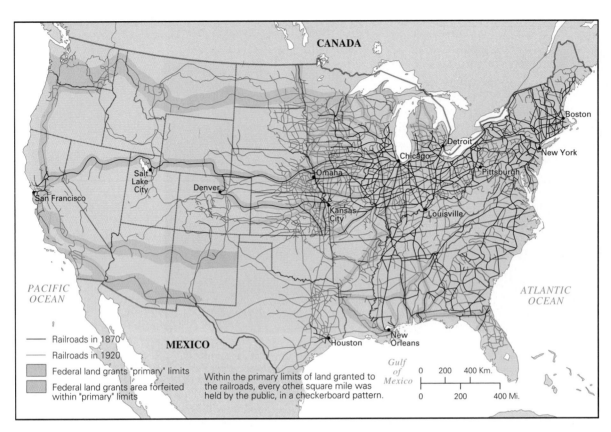

MAP 17.2 Railroad Expansion and Federal Land Grants Post–Civil War railroad expansion produced the transportation base for an industrial economy. In the West, federal land grants encouraged railroad construction. Within a grant, railroads received every other square mile. Land could be forfeited if construction did not meet the terms of the grant legislation.

in terms of a national economic system in which raw materials and finished products might move easily from one region to another.

Railroads, especially in the West, expanded with generous governmental assistance. The first transcontinental rail line was made possible by the **Pacific Railway Act** of 1862. Congress provided the Union Pacific and Central Pacific companies not only with sizable loans but also with 10 square miles of the public domain for every mile of track laid—an amount that was doubled in a subsequent act in 1864. By 1871, Congress had authorized some seventy railroad land grants, involving 128 million acres—more than one-tenth of the entire public domain, an area approximately equal to Colorado and Wyoming together—though not all companies proved able to claim their entire grants. Most railroads sold their land to raise capital for railroad operations. By encouraging farmers, businesses, or organizations to develop the land, railroad companies tried to build

up the economies along their tracks and thereby to boost the demand for their freight trains to haul supplies to new settlers and carry their products (wheat, cattle, lumber, ore) to market.

Railroads: Model for Big Business

The expansion of railroads created the potential for a nationwide market, stimulated the economic development of the West, and created a demand for iron, steel, locomotives, and similar products. Railroad companies also provided an organizational model for newly developing industrial enterprises.

> **Pacific Railway Act** Law passed by Congress in 1862 that gave loans and land to the Central Pacific and Union Pacific Railroad companies to subsidize construction of a rail line between Omaha and the Pacific coast.

Because they spanned such great distances and managed so many employees and so much equipment, railroads often encountered problems of scale that few companies had faced before but that other industrial entrepreneurs soon had to address. Not surprisingly, businesses that came along later often adopted solutions that railroads first developed.

Railroad companies required a much higher degree of coordination and long-range planning than most businesses up to that time. Earlier companies typically operated at a single location, but railroads functioned over long distances and in multiple sites of operation. They had to keep up numerous maintenance and repair facilities and maintain many stations to receive and discharge both freight and passengers. Financial transactions carried on over hundreds of miles by scores of employees required a centralized accounting office. One result was development of a company bureaucracy of clerks, accountants, managers, and agents. Railroads became training grounds for administrators, some of whom later entered other industries. Indeed, the experience of the railroads was central in defining the subject of business administration when it began to be taught in colleges at the turn of the century.

Railroads required far more capital than most manufacturing concerns. In 1875 the largest steel furnaces in the world cost $741,000; at the same time, the Pennsylvania Railroad was capitalized at $400 million. (One dollar in 1875 had the purchasing power of more than $14 today.) Even railroads that received government subsidies required large amounts of private capital—and Congress gave out the last federal land grant in 1871. Private capital and support from state and local governments underwrote the enormous railroad expansion of the 1880s. The railroads' huge appetite for capital made them the first American businesses to seek investors on a nationwide and international scale. Those who invested their money could choose to buy either stocks or **bonds**. Sales of railroad stocks provided the major activity for the New York Stock Exchange through the second half of the nineteenth century.

Railroads faced higher **fixed costs** than most previous companies. These costs included commitments to bondholders and the expense of maintaining and protecting far-flung equipment and property. To pay their fixed costs and keep profits high, railroad companies tried to operate at full capacity whenever possible. Doing so, however, sometimes proved difficult. Where two or more lines competed for the same traffic, one might choose to cut rates in an effort to lure business from the other.

But if the other company responded with cuts in its rates, neither stood to gain significantly more business, and both took in less income. Competition between railroad companies sometimes became so intense that no line could show a profit.

Cornelius Vanderbilt, called "Commodore" because of his earlier investments in steamships, controlled the New York Central Railroad (which ran along the Mohawk Valley in upstate New York) and various connecting lines to New York City and into Ohio, and he hoped to extend his holdings all the way to Chicago. The Erie Railroad, controlled by Daniel Drew, ran parallel to Vanderbilt's holdings in many places. Both Drew and Vanderbilt had reputations as hard-driving moguls, but no one could match Drew's reputation for deviousness. When Vanderbilt raised his freight rates, Drew undercut him by 20 percent. When Vanderbilt set out to buy enough rival stock to seize control of the Erie from Drew, Drew and his allies, James "Diamond Jim" Fisk and Jay Gould, issued more stock and even offered some of it for sale, keeping Vanderbilt from control and enriching themselves in the process. At one point, the battle shifted to the New York state legislature, where Gould tried to secure passage of a law that would legalize their dubious Erie stock issues. Stories circulated through Albany about shameless bidding for legislators' votes, and one subsequent investigation indicated that Gould spent a million dollars in Albany. Both sides also sought friendly judges. Finally Vanderbilt sent a simple message to Drew: "I'm sick of the whole damned business. Come and see me."

Some railroad operators chose to defuse such intense competition by forming a **pool**. In a pool, the railroads agreed to divide the existing business among themselves and not to compete on rates. The most famous was the Iowa Pool, made up of the railroads running between Chicago and Omaha, across Iowa. Formed in 1870, the Iowa Pool operated until 1874, and some pooling continued until the mid-1880s. Few pools lasted very long. Often one or

---

bond A certificate of debt issued by a government or corporation guaranteeing payment of the original investment plus interest at a specified future date.

fixed costs Costs that a company must pay even if it closes down all its operations—for example, interest on loans, dividends on bonds, and property taxes.

pool An agreement among businesses in the same industry to divide up the market and charge equal prices instead of competing.

This cartoon, published by Currier and Ives, was sold during the "Erie War," the struggle for control over the Erie Railroad. Vanderbilt is depicted "watering" (i.e., watering the stock of) the Hudson River Railroad, one of the connecting lines for his New York Central company, while Jim Fisk, in the distance, busily waters the Erie Railroad. *"Westward the Course of Empire Takes Its Way" 1868, Currier & Ives. Museum of the City of New York.*

more pool members tired of a restricted market share and broke the pool arrangement in an effort to expand, thereby setting off a new price war. When a pooling arrangement became known, it brought loud complaints from customers, who concluded that they paid higher rates because of the pool.

To compete more effectively, railroads adjusted their rates to attract companies that did a great deal of shipping. Favored customers sometimes received a **rebate**. Large shipments sent over long distances cost the railroad companies less per mile than small shipments sent over short distances, so companies developed different rate structures for long hauls and short hauls. Thus the largest shippers, with the power to secure rebates and low rates, could ship more cheaply than small businesses and individual farmers. Railroad companies defended the differences on the basis of differences in costs, but small shippers who paid high prices saw themselves as victims of rate discrimination.

Railroads viewed state and federal governments as sources of valuable subsidies. At the same time,

they constantly guarded against efforts by their customers to use government to restrict or regulate their enterprises—by outlawing rate discrimination, for example. Companies sometimes campaigned openly to secure the election of friendly representatives and senators and to defeat unfriendly candidates. They maintained well-organized operations to **lobby** public officials in Washington, D.C., and in state capitals. Most railroad companies issued free passes to public officials—a practice that reformers attacked as bribery. Some railroads won reputations as the most influential political power in entire states—the Southern Pacific in California, for example, or the Santa Fe in Kansas.

Stories of railroad officials bribing politicians became commonplace after the Civil War. The

---

rebate   The refund of part of a payment.
lobby   To try to influence the thinking of public officials for or against a specific cause.

BIRD'S-EYE VIEW OF THE BUSINESS DISTRICT OF CHICAGO

In this lithograph, the railroad metropolis is depicted from a spot high over Lake Michigan, looking south toward the financial and commercial center of the city. The many railroad tracks and plumes of smoke were important symbols of progress and prosperity. *Chicago Historical Society.*

Crédit Mobilier scandal touched some of the most influential members of Congress in the 1870s. A decade later, Collis P. Huntington of the Southern Pacific Railroad candidly explained his expectations regarding public officials: "If you have to pay money to have the right thing done, it is only just and fair to do it." For Huntington, "the right thing" meant favorable treatment for his company.

Chicago: Railroad Metropolis

The financing of railroads was centered in New York, but Chicago experienced the most dramatic change as a consequence of railroad construction. Between 1850 and 1880, railroads transformed Chicago from a town of 30,000 residents to the nation's fourth-largest city, with a half-million people. By 1890, it was second only to New York in size, and in 1900 its population stood at 1.7 million people. Thanks in part to tireless efforts by local promoters and in part to geography, Chicago emerged as the rail center not just of the Midwest but of much of the nation. By 1880, more than twenty railroad

lines and 15,000 miles of tracks connected Chicago with nearly all of the United States and much of Canada. The boom in railroad construction during the 1880s only reinforced the city's prominence. Entrepreneurs in manufacturing and commerce soon developed new enterprises based on Chicago's unrivaled location at the hub of a great transportation network.

Chicago's rail connections made it the logical center for the new business of **mail-order sales**, and the two pioneers in that field—Montgomery Ward, in 1872, and Sears, Roebuck and Co., in 1895—began business there (see pages 536–537). Central location and rail connections also made Chicago a major manufacturing center. By the 1880s, Chicago's factories produced more farm equipment than those of any other city, and its iron and steel production rivaled

> **mail-order sales** The business of selling goods using the mails; mail-order houses send out catalogs, customers submit orders, and the products are delivered all by mail.

that of Pittsburgh. Other leading Chicago industries produced railway cars and equipment, metal products, a wide variety of machinery, and clothing. At the same time, the city also claimed title as the world's largest grain market.

Location and rail lines made Chicago the nation's largest center for **meatpacking.** Livestock from across the Midwest and from as far as south Texas was unloaded in Chicago's Union Stockyards—over 400 acres of railroad sidings, chutes, and pens filled with cattle, hogs, and sheep. Huge slaughterhouses flanking the stockyards received a steady stream of live animals and disgorged an equally steady stream of fresh, canned, and processed meat. The development in the 1870s of refrigeration for railroad cars and ships permitted fresh meat to be sent throughout the nation and even to Europe.

Chicago's rapid growth and rising economic significance gave it an aura of energy and vitality that impressed nearly all visitors. Louis Sullivan, later a leading architect, remembered his first impressions of the city in 1873: "An intoxicating rawness; a sense of big things to be done. 'Biggest in the world' was the braggart phrase on every tongue." A French visitor called Chicago "the boldest" and "most American" of the cities of the United States. The poet Carl Sandburg celebrated this aspect of the city in his poem "Chicago" in 1914:

Hog Butcher for the World,
Tool Maker, Stacker of Wheat,
Player with Railroads and the Nation's Freight
*   Handler;*
Stormy, husky, brawling,
City of the Big Shoulders

Andrew Carnegie, as depicted by an unknown painter around 1901, when he sold his steel holdings to J.P. Morgan and transformed himself from a fiercely competitive entrepreneur into a generous philanthropist. *National Portrait Gallery.*

Andrew Carnegie and the Age of Steel

The new, industrial economy rode on a network of steel rails, propelled by locomotives made of steel. Steel plows broke the tough sod of the western prairies. Skyscrapers, the first of which appeared in Chicago in 1885, relied on steel frames as they boldly shaped urban skylines (see page 548). Steel, a relative latecomer to the industrial revolution, defined the age. Made by combining carbon and molten iron and then burning out impurities, steel has greater strength, resilience, and durability than iron. This superior metal was difficult and expensive to make until the 1850s, when Henry Bessemer in England and William Kelly in Kentucky independently discovered ways to make steel in large quantities at a reasonable cost. Even so, the first Bessemer or Kelly process plants did not begin production in the United States until 1864. In that year, the entire nation produced only 10,000 tons of steel.

In 1875, just south of Pittsburgh, Pennsylvania, **Andrew Carnegie** opened the nation's largest steel plant, employing 1,500 workers. From then until 1901 (when the plant had grown to more than eight thousand workers), Carnegie held central place in the steel industry. Born in Scotland in 1835, Carnegie and his penniless parents came to the

---

meatpacking   The business of slaughtering animals and preparing their meat for sale as food.

Andrew Carnegie   Scottish-born industrialist who made a fortune in steel and believed the rich had a duty to act for the public benefit.

United States in 1848. Young Andrew worked first in a textile mill, then became a messenger in a telegraph office, and soon was promoted to telegraph operator. His great skill at the telegraph key won him a position as personal telegrapher for a high official of the Pennsylvania Railroad. Carnegie rose rapidly within that company and became a superintendent (a high management position) at the age of 25. At the end of the Civil War, he devoted his full attention to the iron and steel industry, in which he had previously invested money. He quickly applied to his iron companies the management lessons he had learned with the railroad.

Carnegie's basic rule was "Cut the prices; scoop the market; run the mills full." An aggressive competitor, he took every opportunity to cut costs so that he might show a profit while charging less than his rivals. He occasionally participated in pools with other steel-making companies, but he usually chose to undersell competitors rather than cooperate with them. In 1864 steel rails sold for $126 per ton; by 1875, Carnegie was selling them for $69 per ton. Driven by improved technology and Carnegie's competitiveness, steel prices continued to fall, reaching $29 in 1885 and less than $20 in the late 1890s. By then, the nation produced nearly 10 million tons of steel each year.

Carnegie's company was larger and more complex than any manufacturing enterprise in pre-Civil War America. In its own day, however, it was by no means unique. Other companies operated plants that were as complex, and several challenged it in size. By 1880, five steel companies had more than 1,500 employees, as did an equal number of textile mills and a locomotive factory. The size of such operations continued to grow. In 1900 the three largest steel plants each employed 8–10,000 workers, and seventy other factories employed more than 2,000, producing everything from watches to locomotives, from cotton cloth to processed meat.

During the late nineteenth century, drawing in part on railroads' innovations in managing large-scale operations, Carnegie and other entrepreneurs transformed the organizational structure of manufacturing. They often joined a range of operations formerly conducted by separate businesses—acquisition of raw materials, processing, distribution of finished goods—into one company, achieving **vertical integration**. Companies usually developed vertical integration to ensure steady operations and to gain a competitive advantage. Control over the sources and transportation of raw materials, for example, guaranteed a reliable flow of crucial sup-

plies at predictable prices. Such control may also have denied materials to a competitor.

Steel plants stood at one end of a long chain of operations that Carnegie owned or controlled: iron ore mines in Michigan and Wisconsin, a fleet of ships that transported iron ore across the Great Lakes, hundreds of miles of railway lines, tens of thousands of acres of coal lands, ovens to produce coke (coal treated to burn at high temperatures), and plants for turning iron ore into bars of crude iron. Carnegie Steel was vertically integrated from the point where the raw materials came out of the ground through the delivery of steel rails and beams.

Survival of the Fittest or Robber Barons?

Many Americans were uneasy with the new economic powerhouses bred by industrialization. In a book published in 1889, economist David A. Wells remarked on the "wholly unprecedented" size of the new businesses, the "rapidity" with which they emerged, and their tendency to be "far more complex than what has been familiar." Such giant enterprises, he noted, "are regarded to some extent as evils." But, he added, "they are necessary, as there is apparently no other way in which the work of production and distribution . . . can be prosecuted."

The concentration of power and wealth during the late nineteenth century generated extensive comment and concern. One prominent view on the subject was known as **Social Darwinism**, reflecting its roots in Charles Darwin's work on evolution. In his book *On the Origin of Species* (published in 1859), Darwin had concluded that those creatures that survive in competition against other creatures and in the face of an often inhospitable environment are those that have best adapted to their surroundings. Such adaptation, he suggested, leads to the

---

vertical integration The process of bringing together into a single company several of the activities in the process of creating a manufactured product, such as the acquiring of raw materials, the manufacturing of products, and the marketing, selling, and distributing of finished goods.

Social Darwinism The philosophical argument, inspired by Charles Darwin's theory of evolution, that competition in human society produced "the survival of the fittest" and therefore benefited society as a whole; Social Darwinists opposed efforts to regulate competitive practices.

evolution of different species, each uniquely suited to a particular ecological niche.

Two philosophers, Herbert Spencer, writing in England in the 1870s and after, and William Graham Sumner, in the United States in the 1880s and after, put their own interpretations on Darwin's reasoning and applied it to the human situation, producing Social Darwinism (a philosophical perspective that bore little relation to Darwin's original work). Social Darwinists contended that competition among people produced "progress" through "survival of the fittest" and that competition provided the best possible route for improving humankind and advancing civilization. Further, they argued that efforts to ease the harsh impact of competition only protected the unfit and thereby worked to the long-term disadvantage of all. Some concluded that powerful entrepreneurs constituted "the fittest" and benefited all humankind by their accomplishments.

Andrew Carnegie enthusiastically embraced Spencer's arguments and endorsed individualism and self-reliance as the cornerstones of progress. "Civilization took its start from that day that the capable, industrious workman said to his incompetent and lazy fellow, 'If thou dost not sow, thou shalt not reap,'" Carnegie wrote. When applied to government, this notion became a form of laissez faire, the belief that the economy functions best when the government leaves it strictly on its own.

Carnegie, though, was inconsistent, also preaching what he called the **Gospel of Wealth**: the idea that the wealthy should return their riches to the community by creating parks, art museums, educational institutions. He spent his final eighteen years giving away his fortune: he funded 3,000 public library buildings and 4,100 church organs all across the nation, gifts to universities, Carnegie Hall in New York City, and several foundations. (One humorist, though, poked fun at Carnegie's libraries by suggesting that they would serve the community better if they contained a kitchen and beds so that the poor might eat and sleep in them.) Like Carnegie, other great entrepreneurs of the late nineteenth century gave away vast sums—even as some of them also built ostentatious mansions, threw extravagant parties, and otherwise flaunted their wealth. Duke University, Stanford University, Vanderbilt University, the Morgan Library in New York City, and the Huntington Library in southern California all carry the names of men who amassed fortunes in the new, industrial economy and donated part of their riches to promote learning and research.

Although many Americans subscribed to the vision of Social Darwinism propounded by Spencer and Sumner, many others did not. Entrepreneurs themselves often welcomed some forms of government intervention in the economy—from railroad land grants to the protective tariff to suppression of strikes—although most agreed with the Social Darwinists that government should not assist the poor and destitute.

Furthermore, many Americans disagreed with the Social Darwinists' equating of laissez faire with progress. Henry George, a San Francisco journalist, pointed out in *Progress and Poverty* (1879) that "amid the greatest accumulations of wealth, men die of starvation," and he concluded that "material progress does not merely fail to relieve poverty—it actually produces it." Lester Frank Ward, a sociologist, in 1886 posed a carefully reasoned refutation of Social Darwinism, suggesting that biological competition produced bare survival, not civilization. Civilization, he argued, represented "a triumph of mind" that derived not from "ceaseless and aimless competition" but from rationality and cooperation.

Americans also disagreed about whether the railroad magnates and powerful industrialists were heroes or villains. Some accepted them wholeheartedly as benefactors of the nation. Others sided with E. L. Godkin, a journalist who in 1869 compared Vanderbilt to a medieval robber baron—a feudal lord who stole from the travelers who dared pass through his domain. Those who have called the wealthy industrialists and bankers **robber barons** point out that they were unscrupulous, greedy, exploitative, and antisocial. Looking only at the deeds or misdeeds of individual entrepreneurs, however, hides more about the economy than it reveals. Understanding these men and the larger economic changes of the era requires more than an examination of individual behavior, whether despicable or praiseworthy.

Gospel of Wealth   Andrew Carnegie's idea that all possessors of great wealth have an obligation to spend or otherwise disburse their money to help people help themselves.

robber baron   In medieval times, a feudal aristocrat who laid exorbitant charges on all who crossed his territory; in the late nineteenth century, an insulting term applied to powerful industrial and financial figures, especially those who disregarded the public interest in their haste to make profits.

The McCormick plant in Chicago (left) produced farm equipment, and the Richmond, Virginia, factory (right) employed women to make cigars. In both factories, individual machines drew their power from a central source through a system of belts and shafts, and workers toiled under the watchful eye of the foreman, who could usually adjust the speed of the belts and shafts to speed up the machines of the individual workers. *(left) McCormick factory: State Historical Society of Wisconsin; (right) Valentine Museum.*

Thomas C. Cochran, a historian, has looked at the broad cultural context that affected not just prominent entrepreneurs but also most Americans. He identified three broadly shared "cultural themes" as central for understanding the period: (1) a belief that the economy operated according to self-correcting principles, especially the law of supply and demand; (2) the ideas of Social Darwinism; and (3) an assumption that people were motivated primarily by a desire for material gain. These themes shed light not only on the actions of the entrepreneurs of the late nineteenth century but also on those of the political leaders of the day and on the reception those actions received from other Americans.

WORKERS IN INDUSTRIAL AMERICA

• How did industrialization change the lives of those who came to work in the new industries?

• What was the basis for craft unionism? How does the nature of its organization help to explain both its successes and its shortcomings?

The rapid expansion of railroads, mining, and manufacturing created a demand for labor to lay the rails, dig the ore, tend the furnaces, operate the refineries, and carry out a thousand other tasks. America's new workers—men, women, and children from many ethnic groups—came from across the nation and around the world. Despite hopes for a rags-to-riches triumph such as Andrew Carnegie's, very few rose from the shop floor to the manager's office.

The Transformation of Work

Most adult industrial workers had been born into a rural society, either in the United States or in another part of the world. They found industrial work quite different from work they had done in the past. Farm families might toil from sunrise to sunset, but they did so at their own speed. They could take a break when they felt the need and adjust the pace of their work to avoid exhaustion. Self-employed blacksmiths, carpenters, dressmakers, and other skilled workers also controlled the speed and intensity of their work, although, like the farmer, they might work very long hours. Frank Roney considered this autonomy to be part of the dignity of labor. In many early factories, the most skilled workers, such as Roney, often set the pace of work around them. They also earned more than other workers and were difficult to replace.

By the late nineteenth century, the workday in most industries averaged ten or twelve hours, six days a week. People from rural settings expected to work long hours, but they found that industrial work controlled them, rather than the other way around. The speed of the machines set the pace of the work, and machine speeds were often controlled. If managers ordered a **speed-up**, workers worked faster but rarely received an increase in pay. Foremen, too, pushed workers to work faster and faster. Ten- or twelve-hour days at a constant, rapid pace drained the workers. A woman textile worker in 1882 said, "I get so exhausted that I can scarcely drag myself home when night comes." The pace of the work and the resulting exhaustion, together with inadequate safety precautions, contributed to a high rate of industrial accidents, injuries, and deaths, but careful records were not kept until much later.

Workers for Industry

After the Civil War, the labor force grew rapidly, almost doubling by 1890. The largest increases occurred in industries undergoing the greatest changes (see Figure 17.3). Agriculture continued to employ the largest share of the labor force, ranging downward from more than half in 1870 to two-fifths in 1900, but the proportional growth of those engaged in agriculture was the smallest of all major categories of workers.

Some workers for the rapidly expanding economy came from within the nation, especially from rural areas. Throughout rural parts of New England and the Middle Atlantic states, many people found it difficult to make a living from agriculture and moved to urban or industrial areas. In New England, some farms—usually small and unproductive—were abandoned when their owners chose to take a job in a factory town or to move west.

The expanding economy, however, needed more workers than the nation itself could supply. As a result, the years from the Civil War to World War I (1865–1914) witnessed the largest influx of immigrants in American history: more than 26 million people, equivalent to three-quarters of the nation's entire population in 1865. By 1910, immigrants and their children made up more than 35 percent of the total population.

Large-scale immigration contributed many adult males to the work force—especially in mining, manufacturing, and transportation. But the expanding economy also pulled women and children into the industrial work force. They had often contributed to the work on family farms or business, but now increasing numbers became industrial wage earners. By 1880, a million children (under the age of 16) worked for wages, the largest number in agriculture. Others worked as newsboys, bootblacks, or domestic

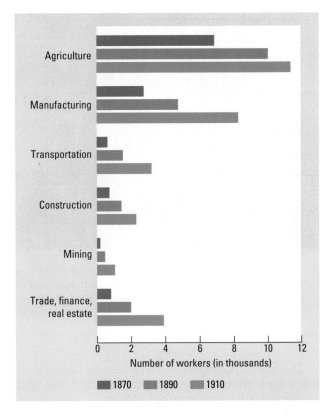

FIGURE 17.3 Industrial Distribution of the Work Force, 1870, 1890, 1910 The number of workers in every industry grew significantly after the Civil War. Though agriculture continued to employ more workers than any other industry, other industries were growing more rapidly than agriculture.

servants. Many children were employed in the textile industry, especially in the South. Mostly girls, they worked 70-hour weeks and earned 10 to 20 cents a day. Children worked in tobacco and cotton fields in the South, operated sewing machines in New York, and sorted vegetables in Delaware canneries. Other children worked at home, alongside their parents who brought home **piecework**. Most working children turned over all their wages to their parents.

Most of the women who found employment outside the home were unmarried. Data before 1890 are unreliable, but by 1890, 40 percent of all single women worked for wages, along with 30 percent of widowed

speed-up An effort to make employees produce more goods in the same time or for the same pay.

piecework Work for which the pay is based on the number of items turned out, rather than by the hour.

The coal mines of Pennsylvania employed more than ten thousand boys under the age of 16. Known as "breaker boys," they sorted coal. Such work was dangerous and sometimes fatal, as attested by this 1911 headline. *Library of Congress.*

tion from clerical worker to managerial status. For women, office work usually paid less than factory work but was considered safer and of higher status. Women and children workers almost always earned less than their male counterparts. In most industries, work was separated by age and gender, and adult males usually held the jobs requiring the most skill and commanding the best pay. Even when men and women did the same work, they rarely received the same pay (see Figure 17.4). This wage differential was often explained by the argument that a man had to support a family, whereas a woman worked to supplement the income of her husband or father.

Not all women earned money through working for wages. Some women were self-employed, for example, in making and selling women's hats or dresses. In factory towns or working-class neighborhoods of the cities, some married women rented a room to a boarder or charged to do other people's laundry or sewing. In rural areas, many married women kept chickens and sold eggs to supplement their family's income.

Despite rags-to-riches success stories like the Carnegie legend, such mobility was highly unusual. Nearly all successful business leaders, in fact, came from middle-class or upper-class families. Few workers moved more than a step or so up the economic scale. An unskilled laborer might become a semiskilled worker, or a skilled worker might become a foreman, but few wage earners moved

or divorced women. Among married women, only 5 percent did so. Black women were employed at much higher rates in all categories. Like child workers, most single young women who lived at home often turned over part or all of their wages to their parents.

A report of the Illinois Bureau of Labor Statistics for 1884 explained that some children and women worked for wages because of the "meager earnings of many [male] heads of families." A study in 1875 showed that the average male factory worker in Lawrence, Massachusetts, earned $500 per year. The study also showed that the average family in Lawrence required a minimum annual income of $600 to provide sufficient food, clothing, and shelter. In such circumstances, a family could not make ends meet without two or more incomes.

As more and more women entered the wage-earning work force, some occupations came to be filled mainly by women. By 1900, females—adults and children—made up more than 70 percent of the workers in clothing factories, knitting mills, and other textile operations. Women also dominated certain types of office work, accounting for more than 70 percent of the nation's secretaries and typists and 80 percent of telephone operators. However, as women moved into office work, displacing men, wage levels fell along with the likelihood of promo-

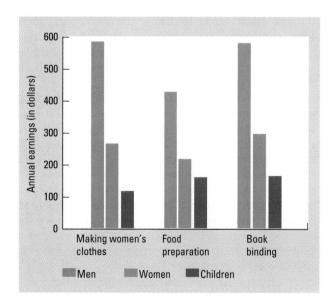

FIGURE 17.4 Average Annual Earnings for Men, Women, and Children, in Selected Industries, 1890

into the middle class. If they did, it was usually as the owner of a small and often struggling business.

Craft Unionism—and Its Limits

Just as the entrepreneurs of the late nineteenth century faced choices between competition and cooperation, so too did their employees. Like Frank Roney, some workers reacted to the far-reaching changes in the nature of work by joining with other workers in efforts to maintain or regain control over their working conditions.

Skilled workers remained indispensable in many fields. In construction, only an experienced carpenter could build stairs or hang doors properly. In publishing, only a skilled typesetter could quickly transform handwritten copy into lines of lead type. Only a skilled iron molder could set up the molds and know exactly when and how to pour the molten iron into them. Such workers took pride in the quality of their work and knew that their skill was crucial to their employer's success. One union leader was referring to such workers when he said, "The manager's brains are under the workman's cap."

Skilled workers formed the first unions, called **craft unions** or trade unions because membership was limited to skilled workers in a particular craft or trade. Before the Civil War, workers in most American cities created local trade unions in an attempt to regulate the quality of work, wages, hours, and working conditions within their craft. Local unions eventually formed national trade organizations—twenty-six of them by 1873, thirty-nine by 1880. They sometimes called themselves brotherhoods—for example, the United Brotherhood of Carpenters and Joiners, formed in 1881—and they drew on their craft traditions to forge bonds of unity.

The skills that defined craft unions' membership also provided the basis for their success. Skills that sometimes took years to develop made craft workers valuable to their employers and extremely difficult to replace. Such unions often limited their membership not just to workers with particular skills but to white males with those skills. If most craft workers within a city belonged to the local union, a strike could badly disrupt or shut down the affected businesses. The strike, therefore, was a powerful weapon in the efforts of skilled workers to define working conditions.

A strike most often succeeded in times of prosperity, when the employer wanted to continue operating and was best able financially to make concessions to workers. When the economy experi-

Local trade unions usually ordered elaborate banners, such as this one, which hung in their union hall during their meetings and which they carried in parades or displayed at funerals of members. Such organizations sometimes styled themselves brotherhoods, symbolizing not only the solidarity of the organization but also its masculine nature. © *Bettmann/Corbis.*

enced a serious downturn and employers sharply reduced work hours or laid off workers, craft unions usually disintegrated because they could not use the strike effectively. Only after the 1880s did local and national unions develop strategies that permitted them to survive depressions.

The craft union tradition served some skilled workers well but was of little help to most manufacturing workers. Unskilled or semiskilled workers—the majority of employees in many emerging industries—lacked the skills that gave the craft unions their bargaining power. Without such skills, they could be replaced easily if they chose to strike. The most effective unions, therefore, were groups of skilled workers—sometimes called the "aristocracy of labor."

---

craft union Labor union that organizes skilled workers engaged in a specific craft or trade; also called a trade union.

Shortly after the Civil War, in 1866, craft unionists representing a variety of local and national organizations joined with reformers to create the **National Labor Union** (NLU), headed by William Sylvis of the Iron Molders until his death in 1869. The NLU also included representatives of women's organizations and, after vigorous debate, decided to encourage the organization of black workers. The most important of the NLU objectives was to establish eight hours as the proper length for a day's work. In 1870 the NLU divided itself into a labor organization and a political party, the National Labor Reform Party, which Roney joined so hopefully when he was working in Omaha. In 1872 the political party nominated candidates for president and vice president, but the campaign was so unsuccessful and divisive that neither the NLU nor the party met again.

POLITICS: PARTIES, SPOILS, SCANDALS, AND STALEMATE

- What was the significance of political parties in the late nineteenth century?

- Compare the presidencies of Grant and Hayes. Which was the more successful?

At a time when the nation's economy was changing at a breakneck pace, politics seemed to change little if at all. Political parties dominated nearly every aspect of the political process from the 1830s until the early 1900s, more so than before or since. During those years, Americans expected that politics meant party politics and that all meaningful political choices came through the structure of parties. Men were expected to hold intense party loyalties—allegiances so strong they were even seen as part of a man's gender role. (All states barred women from voting as did nearly all the territories.) An understanding of politics, therefore, must begin with an analysis of political parties—what they were, what they did, what they stood for, and what choices they offered to voters.

Parties, Conventions, and Patronage

The two major parties—Democrats and Republicans—had similar organizations and purposes. Both nominated candidates, tried to elect them to office, and attempted to write and enact their objectives into law.

After the 1830s, nominations for political offices came from **party conventions**. The process of select-ing convention delegates began when neighborhood voters gathered in party **caucuses** to choose one or more delegates to represent them at local conventions. Conventions took place at county, state, and national levels and at the level of congressional districts and various state districts. At most conventions, the delegates listened to speech after speech glorifying their party and denouncing the opposition. They nominated candidates for elective offices or chose delegates to another convention further up the party hierarchy. And they adopted a **platform**, a written explanation of their positions on important issues and their promises for policy change. Party leaders worked to create compromises that satisfied major groups within their party, and such deal making sometimes occurred in informal settings—hotel rooms thick with cigar smoke and cluttered with whiskey bottles. Such behind-the-scenes bargaining reinforced the notion of political parties as all-male bastions into which no self-respecting women would venture.

After choosing their candidates, the parties conducted their campaigns. Party organizers tried to identify all their supporters and worked to get them to vote on election day. Such party organizing was often done in places such as saloons, where males congregated and women were barred. Nominees campaigned as party candidates, and campaigns were almost entirely focused on party identity. Nearly every newspaper identified itself with a political party. A party expected to subsidize sympathetic newspapers and, in return, expected both whole-hearted support for its candidates and officeholders and slashing criticism of the other party. During the month or so before an election, local

---

National Labor Union   Federation of trade unions and reform societies organized at Baltimore in 1866; it lasted only six years but helped push through a law limiting government employees to an eight-hour workday.

party convention   Party meeting to nominate candidates for elective offices and to adopt a political platform.

caucus   A gathering of people with a common political interest—for example, to choose delegates to a party convention or to seek consensus on party positions on issues.

platform   A formal statement of the principles, policies, and promises on which a political party bases its appeal to voters.

This cartoon depicts government patronage as "cake" and all party leaders as greedily clamoring for a piece, despite the president's efforts to maintain peace in his party. Such frantic scrambles eventually brought reform and the introduction of the merit system for appointing people to governmental positions. *Library of Congress.*

party organizations tried to whip up enthusiasm among the party's supporters and to attract new or undecided voters through parades by marching clubs, free barbecues with speeches for dessert, and rallies capped by oratory that lasted for hours.

On election day, each party tried to mobilize all its supporters and make certain that they voted. This form of political campaigning produced very high levels of voter participation. In 1876 more than 80 percent of the eligible voters cast their ballots. Turnout sometimes rose even higher, although exact percentages were affected by poor record keeping or fraud. At the polling places, party workers distributed lists or "tickets" of their party's candidates, which voters then used as ballots. Voting was not secret until the 1890s. Before then, everyone could see which party's ballot a voter deposited in the ballot box (see illustrations of voting on page 475 and 562). Such a system obviously discouraged voters from crossing party lines.

Once the votes were counted, the winners turned to appointing people to government jobs. In the nineteenth century, government positions not filled by elections were staffed through the **patronage system**—that is, newly elected presidents or governors or mayors appointed their loyal supporters to government jobs, widely considered an appropriate reward for hard work during a campaign. Everyone also understood that those appointed to such jobs were expected to return part of their salaries to the party. The use of patronage for party purposes was often called the spoils system after a statement by Senator William Marcy in 1831: "To the victor belong the spoils." Its defenders were labeled **spoilsmen**.

Party loyalists inevitably outnumbered the available patronage jobs, so competition for appointments was always fierce. When James A. Garfield became president in 1881, he was so overwhelmed with demands for jobs that he exclaimed in disgust, "My God! What is there in this place that a man should ever want to get into it?" The government jobs most in demand involved purchasing supplies or otherwise handling government contracts. Purchasing and contracts became another form of spoils, awarded to entrepreneurs who supported the party. This system invited corruption, and the invitation was all too often accepted. One Post Office Department official, for example, pressured **postmasters** across the country to buy clocks from one of his political associates. Business owners competing to receive government contracts sometimes paid bribes to the officials who made the decisions.

patronage system System of appointment to government jobs that lets the winner in an election distribute nearly all appointive government jobs to loyal party members; also called the spoils system.

spoilsmen Derogatory term for defenders of the patronage or spoils system.

postmaster An official appointed to oversee the operations of a post office.

Using an elephant to symbolize the Republicans and a donkey for the Democrats dates to the 1870s and the work of Thomas Nast, the most talented cartoonist of his age. At the time, Republicans often preferred an eagle or star and Democrats usually chose a rooster. *Library of Congress.*

Opportunities were limited only by the imagination of the spoilsmen.

Some critics found a more fundamental defect in the system, beyond its capacity for corruption. By concentrating so much on patronage, politics ignored principles and issues and revolved instead around greed for government employment. The spoils system had many defenders, however. One party loyalist explained, "You can't keep an organization together without patronage. Men ain't in politics for nothin'. They want to get somethin' out of it." This spoilsman was describing the reality that all local party activists faced: given the enormous numbers of party workers needed to identify supporters and mobilize voters, politics required some sort of reward system.

Republicans and Democrats

Beneath the hoopla, fireworks, and interminable speeches, important differences characterized the two major parties. Some of those differences appeared in the ways the parties described themselves in their platforms, newspapers, speeches, and other campaign appeals.

During the years after the Civil War, Republicans asserted a virtual monopoly on patriotism by pointing to their defense of the Union during the war and claiming that Democrats—especially southern Democrats—had proven themselves disloyal during the conflict. Trumpeting this accusation was often called "waving the bloody shirt," after an instance when a Republican displayed the bloodstained shirt of a northerner (and Republican) beaten by southern white supremacists (who were Democrats). "Every man that shot a Union soldier," Robert Ingersoll, a Republican orator, proclaimed, "was a Democrat." Republicans exploited the Civil War legacy in other ways too. Republicans in Congress voted to provide generous federal pensions to disabled Union army veterans and to the widows and orphans of those who died. Republican Party leaders carefully cultivated the **Grand Army of the Republic** (GAR), the organization of Union veterans, attending their meetings and urging them to "vote as you shot." Republican presidential candidates

Grand Army of the Republic Organization of Union army veterans.

were almost all Union veterans, as were many state and local officials throughout the North.

Prosperity was another persistent Republican campaign theme. Republicans pointed to the economic growth of the postwar era and insisted that it stemmed largely from their wise policies, especially the protective tariff. Many Republicans also claimed to be the party of decency and morality. Senator George Hoar of Massachusetts once boasted that all upright and virtuous citizens "commonly, and as a rule, by the natural law of their being, find their place in the Republican party." Republican campaigners delighted in portraying as typical Democrats "the old slave-owner and slave-driver, the saloon-keeper, the ballot-box-stuffer, the Kuklux [Klan], the criminal class of the great cities, the men who cannot read or write."

Where Republicans defined themselves in terms of what their party did and who they were, Democrats typically focused on what they opposed. Most leading Democrats stood firm against "governmental interference" in the economy, especially the protective tariff and land grants, equating government activism with privileges for a favored few. The protective tariff, they charged, protected manufacturers from international competition at the expense of consumers who paid higher prices. The public domain, they maintained, should provide farms for citizens, not subsidies for corporations. All in all, Democrats favored a strictly limited role for the government in the economy, a position much closer to **laissez faire** than that of the Republicans.

Just as the Democrats opposed governmental interference in the economy, so too did they oppose governmental interference in social relations and behavior. In the North, especially in Irish and German communities, they condemned **prohibition** (efforts to ban the sale of alcoholic beverages), which they called a violation of personal liberty. In the South, Democrats rejected federal enforcement of equal rights for African Americans, which they denounced as a violation of **states' rights**. There, Democrats called for **white supremacy**.

Most voters developed strong loyalties to one party or the other, often on the basis of **ethnicity**, race, or religion. Nearly all Catholics and many Irish, German, and other immigrants supported the Democrats. Poor voters in the cities usually supported the local party organization, whether Democratic or Republican—but far more were Democrats. Most southern whites supported the Democrats as the party of white supremacy. The Democrats'

opposition to the protective tariff attracted a few businessmen and professionals who favored more competition. The Democrats, all in all, comprised a very diverse **coalition**, one that held together primarily because its various components could unite to oppose government action on social or economic matters.

Outside the South, most **old-stock** Protestants voted Republican, as did most Scandinavian and British immigrants. Nearly all African Americans supported the Republicans too, as the party of emancipation, as did most veterans of the abolition movement. So many Union veterans supported the Republicans that someone suggested the initials GAR stood for "generally all Republicans." Republicans always did well among the voters of New England, Pennsylvania, and much of the Midwest. In California and New Mexico Territory, many Hispanics voted Republican. For the most part, the Republicans developed the more coherent political organization, united around a set of policies that involved federal government action to encourage economic growth and to protect blacks' rights. As one leading Republican put it, "The Republican party does things, the Democratic party criticizes." Neither party, however, advocated government action to regulate, restrict, or tax the newly developing industrial corporations.

---

laissez faire   The principle that the government should not interfere in the workings of the economy.

prohibition   A legal ban on the manufacture, sale, and use of alcoholic beverages.

states' rights   A political argument that states' rights, under the Constitution, permitted state governments to violate the civil rights of African Americans; sometimes also cited to justify state opposition to other federal actions.

white supremacy   The political argument that the white race should control politics and government and that people of other races should occupy an inferior position.

ethnicity   Having to do with common racial, cultural, religious, or linguistic characteristics; an ethnic group is one that has some shared racial, religious, linguistic, cultural, or national heritage.

coalition   An arrangement, often rather loose, by which different groups work together toward some common objective.

old-stock   People whose ancestors have lived in the United States for several generations.

During the Civil War and early years of Reconstruction, the dominant Republicans changed the very nature of the federal government. They significantly revised the nature of citizenship, relations between the federal government and the states, and the role of the federal government in the economy. Most of the economic policies established in the 1860s persisted with little change for more than a generation. The protective tariff and the use of the public domain to encourage rapid economic development both involved governmental action to stimulate economic development. Thus federal economic policy during these years should not be described as pure laissez faire, even though there was little regulation, restriction, or taxation of economic activity.

Grant's Troubled Presidency: Spoils and Scandals

Ulysses S. Grant's success as a general failed to prepare him for the presidency. During his two terms in office (elected in 1868 and re-elected in 1872), he rarely challenged congressional dominance of domestic policymaking. He often appointed friends or acquaintances to posts for which they possessed no particular qualifications. He proved unable to form a competent cabinet and faced constant turnover among his executive advisers. Many of his appointees seemed to view their positions as little more than the spoils of party victory, and Grant sometimes proved too willing to believe his appointees' denials of wrongdoing. He did choose a highly capable secretary of state, Hamilton Fish, and he eventually found in Benjamin Bristow a secretary of the treasury who vigorously combated corruption.

Congress supplied its full share of scandal. Visiting Washington in 1869, young Henry Adams (great-grandson of the second president and grandson of the sixth) was surprised to hear a member of the cabinet bellow, "You can't use tact with a Congressman! A Congressman is a hog! You must take a stick and hit him on the snout!" Too many members of Congress behaved in a way that confirmed such a cynical view. In 1868, before Grant became president, several prominent congressional leaders had become stockholders in the **Crédit Mobilier**, a construction company created by the chief shareholders in the Union Pacific Railroad. The Union Pacific officers awarded to Crédit Mobilier a generous contract to build the railroad. Thus the company's chief shareholders paid themselves handsomely for constructing their own railroad. To protect this arrangement from congressional scrutiny, the company sold shares at cut-rate prices to key members of Congress. Purchasers included some leading Republicans. Revelation of these arrangements in 1872 and 1873 scandalized the nation. No sooner did that furor pass than Congress voted itself a 50 percent pay raise and made the increase two years retroactive. Only after widespread public protest did Congress repeal its "salary grab."

Public disgrace was not limited to the federal government or to leading Republicans. In New York City, the so-called **Tweed Ring** supplied a seemingly endless string of scandals involving city and state officials. At the center was **William Marcy Tweed**, whose name became synonymous with urban political corruption. Tweed entered New York City politics in the 1850s and became head of the Tammany Hall organization in 1863. By 1868, this organization dominated the local Democratic Party and also controlled much of city and state government. Tweed and his associates built public support by spending tax funds on various charities, and they gave to the poor from their own pockets— pockets often lined with public funds or bribes. Under Tweed's direction, city government launched major construction projects: new public buildings, improvements in streets, parks, sewers, and docks. Much of the construction was riddled with corruption. Between 1868 and 1871, the Tweed Ring may have systematically plundered $200 million from the city, mostly by giving bloated construction contracts to businesses that returned a **kickback** to the Ring. In 1871 evidence of corruption led to Tweed's indictment and ultimately his conviction and imprisonment.

Crédit Mobilier   Company created to build the Union Pacific Railroad; in a scandalous deal uncovered in 1872–1873, it sold shares cheaply to congressmen who approved federal subsidies for railroad construction.

Tweed Ring   Name applied to the political organization of William Marcy Tweed, accused of using bribery, kickbacks, and padded accounts to steal money from New York City.

William Marcy Tweed   New York City political boss who used the Tammany organization to control city and state government from the 1860s until his downfall in 1871.

kickback   An illegal payment by a contractor to the official who awarded the contract.

Though Grant had been re-elected without difficulty in 1872 (see page 481), the midterm elections of 1874 were a different story. The congressional scandals alienated some voters. Moreover, the depression that began in 1873 gave Democrats in urban industrial areas a barbed response when Republicans claimed to be the party of prosperity. And throughout the South, political terrorism suppressed the Republican vote. All these factors combined to give Democrats widespread gains in the House of Representatives. Where Republicans previously had 194 seats to 92 for the Democrats, the Democrats now held 169 seats to the Republicans' 109. For the next twenty years, from 1874 until 1894, Democrats generally commanded a majority in the House of Representatives. Even though Republicans usually won the presidency, Democratic control of the House made it difficult or impossible for the Republicans to push through major legislation. The scandals, depression, and political terrorism in the South had cost the Republicans control of Congress.

More scandals were to come. In 1875 Treasury Secretary Bristow took the lead in fighting widespread corruption in the collection of whiskey taxes. A **Whiskey Ring** of federal officials and distillers, centered in St. Louis, had conspired to evade payment of taxes. The 230 men indicted included several of Grant's appointees and even his private secretary. The next year, William Belknap, Grant's secretary of war, resigned shortly before he was impeached for accepting bribes.

President Rutherford B. Hayes and the Politics of Stalemate

Rutherford B. Hayes became president after the contested election of 1876 (see page 483). His personal integrity and principled stand on issues helped to restore the reputation of the Republican Party after the humiliations of the Grant administration, but any hope he had for significant change ran up against the Democratic majority in the House of Representatives and significant opposition within his own party. His harshest Republican critic was Roscoe Conkling, a flamboyant senator from New York and the boss of that state's large and hungry Republican organization. He became especially hostile after Hayes refused to install Conkling supporters in key federal patronage positions.

Hayes promised to serve only one term and probably could not have secured a second nomination had he sought one. His handling of patronage

annoyed many Republicans, and he estranged reformers by not seeking a full-scale revision of the spoils system. When the White House stopped serving alcohol, Hayes's opponents blamed his wife, Lucy Webb Hayes, the first college-educated First Lady and a committed reformer, and dubbed her "Lemonade Lucy." By mid-1880, Hayes seemed to welcome the end of his presidency.

Challenges to Politics as Usual: Grangers, Greenbackers, and Silverites

Though political change seemed to move at a glacial pace, especially after 1874, at some times and in some places, groups emerged to challenge mainstream politics and to seek a variety of political changes. Given the large proportion of the work force that was still engaged in agriculture, it should not be surprising that farmers were prominent in several influential movements.

After the Civil War, farmers joined organizations that they hoped would provide relief from the scourges of falling prices and high railroad freight rates. Oliver H. Kelley formed the first in 1867. Kelley called it the Patrons of Husbandry and wrote for it a secret ritual modeled on the Masons'. Usually known as the **Grange**, the new organization extended full participation to women as well as men. Kelley hoped that the Grange would provide a social outlet for farm families and educate them in new methods of agriculture. Far exceeding his expectations, it soon led to political action.

The Grange grew rapidly, especially in the Midwest and the central South. In the 1870s, it became a leading proponent of cooperative buying and selling. Many local Grange organizations set up cooperative stores, and some even tried to sell their crops cooperatively. A **cooperative** store (or consumers'

Whiskey Ring Distillers and revenue officials in St. Louis who were revealed in 1875 to have defrauded the government of millions of dollars in whiskey taxes, with the collusion of federal officials.

Grange Organization of farmers that combined social activities with education about new methods of farming and cooperative economic efforts; formally called the Patrons of Husbandry.

cooperative A business enterprise in which workers and consumers share in ownership and take part in management.

This poster appeared in 1869, two years after the founding of the Grange. It depicts the farmer as a member of the producing class, laboring in the soil to produce value. It shows a military officer, railroad magnate, physician, politician, lawyer, merchant, and preacher as living off the farmer's labor. *Library of Congress.*

Parties," their most conspicuous demand was state legislation to prohibit railroad rate discrimination. Other groups, especially merchants, also sought such laws, but the role of the Grangers was so prominent that the resulting state laws, most of them dating to 1872–1874, were usually called **Granger laws**. When the constitutionality of such regulation was challenged, the Supreme Court ruled, in *Munn v. Illinois* (1877), that businesses with "a public interest," including warehouses and railroads, "must submit to be controlled by the public for the common good."

The Grange reached its zenith in the mid-1870s. Hastily organized cooperatives soon began to suffer financial problems, especially in the context of national depression, and the collapse of cooperatives often pulled down Grange organizations. Political activity brought some successes but also generated bitter disputes within the Granges. The organization lost many members, and after the late 1870s, the surviving Granges tended to avoid both cooperatives and politics.

With the decline of the Grange, some farmers looked to **monetary policy** for relief. After the Civil War, most prices fell (a situation called **deflation**) because of increased production, more efficient techniques in agriculture and manufacturing, and the failure of the money supply to grow as rapidly as the economy. Deflation has always injured debtors because it means that the money used to pay off a loan has greater purchasing power (and so is harder to come by) than the money of the original loan. The Greenback Party argued that printing more **greenbacks**, the paper money issued during the Civil War, would stabilize prices, and they

cooperative) was one set up by members, who agreed to shop there and then divided any profits realized among themselves. In cooperative selling (or a producers' cooperative), farmers hoped to hold their crops back from market and to negotiate over prices rather than simply accepting the buyers' offers. Two state Granges began manufacturing farm machinery, and Grangers laid ambitious plans for cooperative factories producing everything from wagons to sewing machines. Some Grangers formed mutual insurance companies, and a few experimented with cooperative banks.

The Grange defined itself as nonpartisan. However, as Grange membership rapidly climbed in the 1870s, its midwestern and western members began to delve into political action. New political parties emerged in eleven states. Usually called "Granger

Granger laws State laws establishing standard freight and passenger rates on railroads; they were passed in various states in the 1870s in response to lobbying by the Grange and other groups, including merchants.

monetary policy In the late nineteenth century, federal monetary policy was extremely limited, having to do primarily with the nature of the circulating currency (gold, silver, or paper) and with the relations between the types of currency.

deflation Falling prices, a situation in which the purchasing power of the dollar increases; the opposite of deflation is inflation, when prices go up and the purchasing power of the dollar declines.

greenbacks Paper money, not backed by gold, that the federal government issued during the Civil War.

The Grange tries to awaken the public to the approaching locomotive (a symbol of monopoly power) that is bringing consolidation (mergers), extortion (high prices), bribery, and other evils. *Culver Pictures.*

found a receptive audience among farmers who were in debt. Greenbackers were arguing for the quantity theory of money. According to this view, if the currency (money in circulation, whether of paper or precious metal) grew more rapidly than the economy, the result was inflation (rising prices), but if the currency failed to grow as rapidly as the economy, the outcome was deflation (falling prices). Greenbackers hoped to control the monetary supply in such a way as to stabilize prices.

In the congressional elections of 1878, the Greenback Party received nearly a million votes and elected fourteen congressmen. In the 1880 presidential election, the Greenback Party not only endorsed inflation but also tried to attract urban workers by supporting the eight-hour workday, legislation to protect workers, and the abolition of child labor. They also called for regulation of transportation and communication, a **graduated income tax** (on the grounds that it was the fairest form of taxation), and woman suffrage. For president, they nominated James B. Weaver of Iowa, a Greenback congressman and former Union army general. Weaver got only 3.3 percent of the vote. In 1884, with

a similar platform and the erratic Benjamin Butler as their presidential nominee, the Greenbackers fared even worse.

A similar monetary analysis motivated those who wanted the government to resume issuing silver dollars. Until 1873, federal law specified that federal mints would accept gold and silver and make them into coins as the easiest way to get money into circulation. Throughout the mid-nineteenth century, however, owners of silver made more money by selling it commercially than by taking it to the mints. Thus no silver dollars existed for many years. In 1873 Congress dropped the silver dollar from the list of approved coins, following the lead of Britain and Germany, which had specified that only gold was to serve as money. Some Americans believed that adhering to this **gold standard** was essential if American businesses were to compete effectively in international markets for capital and for the sale of goods. Soon after 1873, however, silver discoveries in the West drove down the commercial price of silver. Arguments for the coining of all available silver into dollars quickly found support not just among farmers but also among silver mining interests. Members of this farming-mining coalition were soon called "Silverites." In 1878, over Hayes's veto, Congress passed the **Bland-Allison Act** authorizing a limited amount of silver dollars, but the move failed to counteract deflation and neither side was satisfied. Silverites condemned the action as too feeble, and gold supporters denounced it for diluting the gold standard.

The Great Railway Strike of 1877 and the Federal Response

During Hayes's first year in the presidency, the nation witnessed for the first time the implications of widespread labor strife. In response to the

graduated income tax Percentage tax that is levied on income and varies with income, so that individuals with the lowest income pay taxes at the lowest rates.

gold standard A monetary system based on gold; under such a system, legal contracts typically called for the payment of all debts in gold, and paper money could be redeemed in gold at a bank.

Bland-Allison Act Law passed by Congress in 1878 providing for federal purchase of limited amounts of silver to be coined into silver dollars.

This engraving depicts striking railroad workers in Martinsburg, West Virginia, as they stopped a freight train on July 17, 1877, in the opening days of the great railway strike of that year. Engravings such as this, showing strikers to be heavily armed, may or may not have been accurate depictions of events. But the photography of that day could rarely capture live action, and the technology of the day could not reproduce photographs in newspapers, so the public's understanding of events such as the 1877 strike were formed through artists' depictions. *Library of Congress.*

depression that began in 1873, railroad companies reduced operating costs by repeatedly cutting wages. Railroad workers' pay fell by more than a third from 1873 to 1877. Union leaders talked of organizing a strike but failed to bring one off.

Without union leadership, railway workers took matters into their own hands when companies announced additional pay cuts. On July 16, 1877, a group of firemen and brakemen on the Baltimore & Ohio Railroad stopped work in Maryland. The next day, nearby in West Virginia, a group of railway workers refused to work until the company restored their wages. Some members of the local community supported the strikers. The governor of West Virginia sent in the state **militia**, but the strikers still prevented the trains from running. The governor then requested federal troops, and Hayes sent them.

Federal troops restored service on the Baltimore & Ohio, but the strike spread to other lines. Strikers shut down trains in Pittsburgh. When the local militia refused to act against the strikers, the governor of Pennsylvania sent militia units from Philadelphia. The troops killed twenty-six people. Strikers and their sympathizers then attacked the militia, forced the troops to retreat, and burned and looted railroad property throughout Pittsburgh.

Strikes erupted across Pennsylvania and New York and throughout the Midwest. Everywhere, the strikers drew support from their local communities. In various places, coal miners, factory workers,

owners of small businesses, farmers, black workers, and women demonstrated their solidarity with the workers. In St. Louis, local unions declared a **general strike** to secure the eight-hour workday and to end child labor. State militia, federal troops, and local police eventually broke up the strikes, but not before hundreds had lost their lives. By the strikes' end, railroad companies had suffered property damage worth $10 million, half of the losses in Pittsburgh.

The **Great Railway Strike of 1877** revealed widespread dislike for the new railroad companies and significant community support for striking workers. However, the strike alarmed many other Americans. Some considered the use of troops only a temporary expedient and, like Hayes, hoped for "education of

---

militia   A military force consisting of civilians who agree to be mobilized into service in times of emergency; organized by state governments during the nineteenth century but now superseded by the National Guard.

general strike   A strike by members of all unions in a particular region.

Great Railway Strike of 1877   A series of strikes in American cities triggered by railroad wage cuts; the strikes showed widespread support for the demands of workers.

the strikers," "judicious control of the capitalists," and some way to "remove the distress which afflicts laborers." Others saw in the strike a forecast of future labor unrest, and they called for better means to enforce law and order.

THE UNITED STATES AND THE WORLD, 1865–1880

• How did American policymakers define the role of the United States in North America during the period 1865 to 1880?

• How did they define the role of the United States in other parts of the world?

During much of the nineteenth century, the U.S. role in world affairs was slight, and most Americans expected that their nation would avoid foreign conflicts, in keeping with the advice of George Washington to "steer clear of permanent alliances with any portion of the foreign world." In fact, Americans had few worries about being pulled into European wars, for Europe remained relatively peaceful. The insulation imposed by the Atlantic and Pacific reinforced Americans' feeling of security, and the powerful British navy provided a protective umbrella for American commercial shipping. Thus world events posed few threats to American interests. During the years 1865–1880, American involvement in world affairs began to expand, but gradually and uncertainly. The effect of America's economic transformation on its foreign relations, as on its domestic politics, was slow in appearing.

Alaska, Canada, and the *Alabama* Claims

In 1866 the Russian minister to the United States hinted to Secretary of State **William H. Seward** that Tsar Alexander II might dispose of Russian holdings in North America if the price were right. Seward, one of the most capable secretaries of state in the nineteenth century, had often voiced his belief in America's destiny to expand across the North American continent. He made an offer, and in 1867 the two diplomats agreed on a price slightly over $7 million—less than 2 cents per acre. The deal was done, and the land that was to become the state of Alaska was in U.S. hands.

The Alaska treaty differed from earlier agreements acquiring territory in one significant way.

Previous treaties had specified that the inhabitants of the territories (except Indians) would immediately become American citizens and that the territories themselves would eventually become states. The Alaska treaty extended citizenship but carried no promise of eventual statehood. It therefore moved a half-step away from earlier patterns of territorial expansion and foreshadowed later patterns of colonial acquisition.

Some journalists derided the new purchase as a frozen, worthless wasteland and branded the bargain "Seward's Folly." The Senate, however, greeted the windfall with considerable enthusiasm. Charles Sumner, chairman of the **Senate Foreign Relations Committee**, looked on the purchase of Alaska as the first step toward the ultimate possession of Canada. Many others shared his hope.

Canada was on Sumner's mind as he considered claims against Great Britain arising out of the Civil War. Several Confederate warships, notably the *Alabama* and *Florida*, had badly disrupted northern shipping. British shipyards had built those ships for the Confederacy. British ports had also offered repairs and supplies to Confederate ships. The United States claimed that Britain had violated its neutrality by allowing these activities, but Britain refused to accept responsibility for the damage done by the Confederate cruisers. In 1869, however, as relations between Britain and Russia grew tense, the British began to fret that American shipyards might provide similar services for the Russians. Sumner argued that the damages caused by the Confederate navy included not just direct claims for shipping losses but many indirect claims as well, amounting, he insisted, to the entire cost of the last two years of the war. The total, by Sumner's calculations, was more than $2 billion—so much, he suggested, that Britain could best meet its obligation by ceding all its North American possessions, including Canada, to the United States.

Grant's secretary of state, Hamilton Fish, found Sumner's claims unrealistic and convinced Grant

---

William H. Seward U.S. secretary of state under Lincoln and Johnson, a former abolitionist who had expansionist views and arranged the purchase of Alaska from Russia.

Senate Foreign Relations Committee One of the standing (permanent) committees of the Senate; it deals with foreign affairs, and its chairman often wields considerable influence over foreign policy.

not to support them. Instead, in the Treaty of Washington (1871), the two countries agreed to **arbitration**. The 1872 arbitration decision held Britain responsible for the direct claims and set $15.5 million as damages to be paid to the United States.

The United States and Latin America

After the Civil War, American diplomats turned their attention to Latin America, partly because European powers were starting to exert influence in that direction and partly because some Americans wanted the United States to take a more prominent role in the region. In 1823 President James Monroe had announced that North and South America were not areas for colonial expansion by European powers, that the United States would consider any attempt by a European power to colonize in the Western Hemisphere a threat to the United States, and that the United States would not interfere with existing colonies nor become involved in European power politics. Though later a linchpin of American policy, the **Monroe Doctrine** was rarely mentioned by presidents over the next two-thirds of the nineteenth century.

In 1861, as the United States lurched into civil war, France, Spain, and Britain sent a joint force to Mexico to collect debts that Mexico could not pay. Spain and Britain soon withdrew, but French troops remained, occupying key areas despite resistance led by **Benito Juarez**, president of Mexico. Some of Juarez's political opponents cooperated with the French emperor, Napoleon III, to name Archduke **Maximilian** of Austria as emperor of Mexico. Maximilian, an idealistic young man, apparently believed that the Mexican people genuinely wanted him as their leader, and he hoped to serve them well. He antagonized some of his conservative supporters with talk of reform but failed to win other support. Resistance became war, and Maximilian held power only because the French army kept his enemies at bay.

As these events were unfolding, the United States was involved in its own civil war. The Union recognized Juarez as president of Mexico but could do little else. When the Civil War ended, Secretary of State Seward demanded that Napoleon III withdraw his troops. At that point, the United States possessed the most experienced, and perhaps the largest, army in the world. Seward underscored his demand when fifty thousand battle-hardened

troops moved to the Mexican border. Thus confronted, Napoleon III agreed to withdraw. The last French soldiers sailed home in early 1867, but Maximilian unwisely remained behind, where he was defeated in battle by Juarez and then executed. Though Seward did not cite the Monroe Doctrine at any point, the withdrawal of the French troops in the face of substantial American military force renewed respect in Europe for the role of the United States in Latin America.

Some Americans had long regarded the Caribbean and Central America as potential areas for expansion. One vision was a canal through Central America to shorten the coast-to-coast shipping route around South America. In addition, after the Civil War, both the Caribbean and the Pacific attracted attention as regions where the navy might need bases. In 1867, seeking suitable sites, Secretary of State Seward negotiated treaties to buy part of the **Danish West Indies** and to secure a base site in **Santo Domingo**, but both efforts failed to win congressional approval.

In 1870, with Grant in the White House, Hamilton Fish became secretary of state. Rather than pursuing annexation of territory, Secretary of State Fish sought expansion of trade with Latin America. When the dictator of Santo Domingo offered either to annex his entire country to the United States or to lease a major bay for a naval base, Fish objected. Nonetheless, urged on by Americans eager to invest

---

arbitration   Process by which parties to a dispute submit their case to the judgment of an impartial person or group (the arbiter) and agree to abide by the arbiter's decision.

Monroe Doctrine   Announcement by President James Monroe in 1823 that the Western Hemisphere was off-limits for future European colonial expansion.

Benito Juarez   Elected president of Mexico who led resistance to the French occupation of his country in 1864–1867; the first Mexican president of Indian ancestry.

Maximilian   Austrian archduke appointed by France to be emperor of Mexico in 1864; later executed by Mexican republicans.

Danish West Indies   Island group in the Caribbean, including St. Croix and St. Thomas, which the United States finally purchased from Denmark in 1917; now known as the U.S. Virgin Islands.

Santo Domingo   Nation in the Caribbean that shares the island of Hispaniola with Haiti; it became independent from Spain in 1865; now known as the Dominican Republic.

in the area, Grant asked the Senate to ratify a treaty of annexation. Approval required support of two-thirds of the Senate. With Sumner leading the opposition, the treaty failed by a vote of 28 to 28. Grant nevertheless proclaimed an extension, or **corollary**, of the Monroe Doctrine, specifying that no territory in the Western Hemisphere could ever be transferred to a European power.

Eastern Asia and the Pacific

Americans had long taken a strong commercial interest in eastern Asia. The China trade dated to 1784, and goods from Asia and the Pacific accounted for about 8 percent of all U.S. imports after the Civil War. Exports to that area were disappointing, however, less than 2 percent of the total, and some Americans dreamed of profits from selling to China's hundreds of millions of potential consumers. American missionaries began to preach in China in 1830. Although they counted few converts, their lectures back in the United States stimulated public interest in the Asian nation.

In 1839–1842, the British navy humiliated Chinese forces in a naval war. The Chinese government had long placed severe restrictions on foreign trade. The war began over Chinese efforts to prevent British merchants from importing and selling **opium** in China, but the British defined the issue as the right to engage in trade without restraints. In defeat, China granted trading privileges to Britain and subsequently to other nations that wished to sell goods there. The first treaty between China and the United States, in 1844, included a provision granting **most-favored-nation status** to the United States. Japan and Korea had also refused to engage in trade, their way of deflecting Western influences and avoiding European power rivalries. In 1854 an American naval force convinced the Japanese government to open its ports to foreign trade. A similar navy action opened Korea in 1882.

Growing trade prospects between eastern Asia and the United States fueled American interest in the Pacific. Whether in sailing ships or steamships, the American **merchant marine** needed ports in the Pacific for supplies and repairs. Interest focused especially on Hawai`i. Hawai`i had attracted Christian missionaries from New England as early as 1819, shortly after King Kamehameha the Great united the islands into one nation. The **missionaries** were first concerned with preaching the Gospel and convincing the unabashed Hawaiians to wear clothes, but later some missionaries and their descendants

King David Kalakaua of Hawai`i loved to pose in full military uniform, but he was, in fact, a weak monarch who yielded a good deal of power to haoles and outsiders. *Bishop Museum.*

came to exercise great influence over several Hawaiian monarchs.

The islands' location near the center of the Pacific made them an ideal place to stockpile supplies of fresh food and water for ships crossing the Pacific and for whaling vessels. After 1848, ships traveling from New York around South America to San Francisco also routinely stopped in Hawai`i for supplies. As early as 1842, President John Tyler

---

corollary   A proposition that follows logically and naturally from an already proven point.

opium   An addictive drug made from poppies.

most-favored-nation status   In a treaty between nation A and nation B, the provision that commercial privileges extended by A to other nations automatically become available to B.

merchant marine   Ships engaged in commerce.

stated that the United States would not allow the islands to pass under the control of another power, but Britain and France continued to take a keen interest in them.

David Kalakaua became king of Hawai`i in 1874. During his reign, relations with the United States became much closer. Kalakaua was the first reigning monarch ever to visit the United States, in 1874, and in 1875 he approved a treaty of reciprocity that gave Hawaiian sugar duty-free access to the United States. The outcome was a rapid expansion of the Hawaiian sugar industry as the sons and daughters of New England missionaries joined representatives of American sugar refiners in developing huge sugar plantations. Soon Hawaiian sugar spawned a vertically integrated industry that included American-owned sugar plantations, ships to carry raw sugar to the mainland, and sugar refineries in California—and the economies of the two nations became closely linked.

INDIVIDUAL VOICES

Examining a Primary Source

Andrew Carnegie Explains the Gospel of Wealth

Unlike the typical industrial magnate, Andrew Carnegie wrote extensively about his ideas on a wide range of topics, including competition and wealth. Carnegie's views, from the vantage point of the boardroom, contrast sharply with those of Frank Roney down on the shop floor, as quoted from his autobiography in the Individual Choices feature at the beginning of this chapter. This selection, from an article written by Carnegie that he entitled "Wealth," appeared in *The North American Review* in June 1889.

● How do you think Frank Roney would have responded to Carnegie's praise of competition?

The price which society pays for the law of competition, like the price it pays for cheap comforts and luxuries, is also great; but the advantages of this law are also greater still, for it is to this law that we owe our wonderful material development, which brings improved conditions in its train. . . . It is here; we cannot evade it; no substitutes for it have been found; and while the law may be sometimes hard for the individual, it is best for the race, because it insures the survival of the fittest in every department. We accept and welcome, therefore, as conditions to which we must accommodate ourselves, great inequality of environment, the concentration of business, industrial and commercial, in the hands of a few, and the law of competition between these, as being not only beneficial, but essential for the future progress of the race. . . . ●

This, then, is held to be the duty of the man of Wealth: First, to set an example of modest unostentatious living, shunning display or extravagance; to provide moderately for the legitimate wants of those dependent upon him; and after doing so to consider all surplus revenues which come to him simply as trust funds, which he is called upon to administer, and strictly bound as a matter of duty to administer in the manner which, in his judgment, is best calculated to produce the most beneficial results for the community. . . . The

● How does Carnegie's notion of the Gospel of Wealth compare with Social Darwinism?

● Is Carnegie being consistent in arguing for the benefits of competition and survival of the fittest, on the one hand, and insisting on the obligations of the wealthy, on the other?

best means of benefiting the community is to place within its reach the ladders upon which the aspiring can rise—parks, and means of recreation, by which men are helped in body and mind; works of art, certain to give pleasure and improve the public taste, and public institutions of various kinds, which will improve the general condition of the people. . . . Thus is the problem of the Rich and Poor to be solved. . . . Individualism will continue, but the millionaire will be but a trustee for the poor; intrusted for a season with a great part of the increased wealth of the community, but administering it for the community far better than it could or would have done for itself. . . . ●

The man who dies leaving behind him millions of available wealth, which was his to administer during life, will pass away "unwept, unhonored, and unsung," no matter to what uses he leaves the dross which he cannot take with him. Of such as these the public verdict will then be: "The man who dies thus rich dies disgraced." . . . Such, in my opinion, is the true Gospel concerning Wealth, obedience to which is destined some day to solve the problem of the Rich and the Poor, and to bring "Peace on earth, among men of Good-Will." ●

SUMMARY

After 1865, large-scale manufacturing developed quite quickly in the United States, built on a foundation of abundant natural resources, a pool of skilled workers, expanding harvests, and favorable government policies. The outcome was the transformation of the U.S. economy.

Entrepreneurs improved and extended railway lines, creating a national transportation network. Manufacturers and merchants now began to think in terms of a national market for raw materials and finished goods. Railroads were the first businesses to grapple with the many problems related to size, and they made choices that other businesses imitated. Steel was the crucial building material for much of industrial America, and Andrew Carnegie revolutionized the steel industry. He became one of the best known of many entrepreneurs who developed manufacturing operations of unprecedented size and complexity. Social Darwinists acclaimed unrestricted competition for producing progress and survival of the fittest. Others criticized the negative aspects of the era's economy. Some simply condemned the great entrepreneurs as robber barons, but more complex treatments place such figures within the cultural context of their own time.

Industrial workers had little control over the pace or hours of their work and often faced unpleasant or dangerous working conditions. Even so, workers in both the United States and other parts of the world chose to migrate to expanding industrial centers from rural areas. The new work force included not only adult males but also women and children. Some workers formed labor organizations to seek higher wages, shorter hours, and better conditions. Trade unions, based on craft skills, were the earliest and most successful of such organizations.

Americans in the late nineteenth century expected political parties to dominate politics. All elected public officials were nominated by party conventions and elected through the efforts of party campaigners. Most civil service employees were appointed in return for party loyalty. Republicans used government to promote rapid economic development, but Democrats argued that government works best when it governs least. Most voters divided between the major parties largely along the lines of region, ethnicity, and race. The presidency of Ulysses S. Grant was plagued by scandals. President Rutherford B. Hayes restored Republican integrity but faced stormy conflict between Republican factions. Grangers, Greenbackers, and Silverites all challenged the major parties, appealing most to debt-ridden farmers. The Great Railway Strike of 1877 was the first indication of what widespread industrial strife could do to the nation's new transportation network based on railroads, and public officials resorted to federal troops to suppress the strike.

From 1865 to 1889, few Americans expected their nation to take a major part in world affairs, at least outside North America. The United States did acquire Alaska and convince the French to withdraw from Mexico, and some Americans hoped that Canada might become U.S. territory. At the same time, the United States took actions to encourage trade with the nations of eastern Asia, and the kingdom of Hawai`i became closely integrated with the American economy.

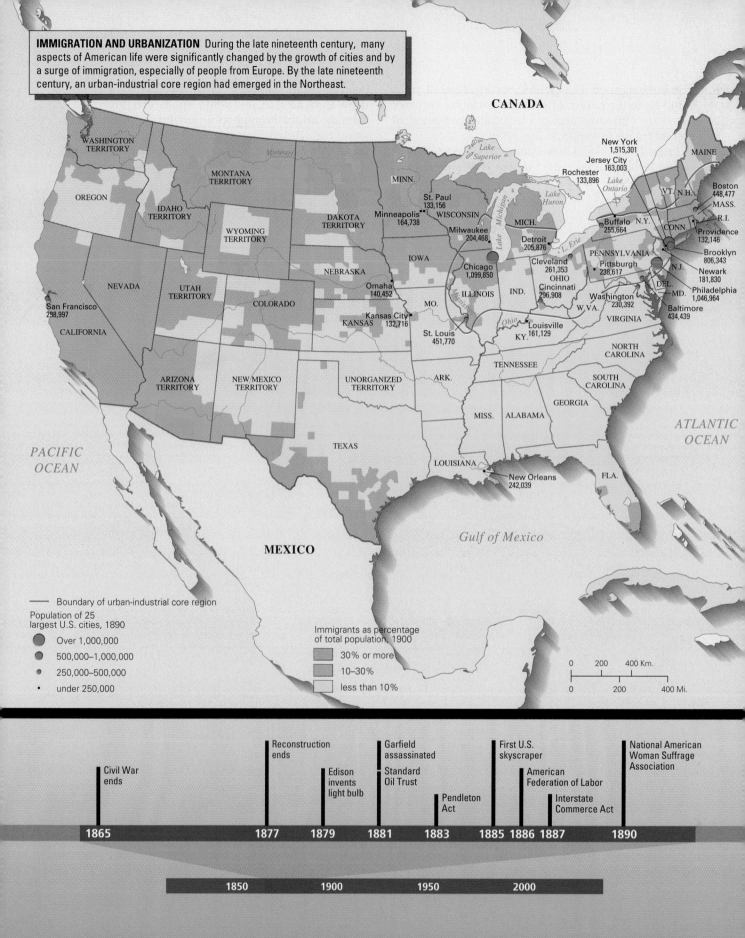

IMMIGRATION AND URBANIZATION During the late nineteenth century, many aspects of American life were significantly changed by the growth of cities and by a surge of immigration, especially of people from Europe. By the late nineteenth century, an urban-industrial core region had emerged in the Northeast.

CANADA

WASHINGTON
TERRITORY

OREGON

IDAHO
TERRITORY

MONTANA
TERRITORY

Missouri

MINN.

Lake Superior

New York
1,515,301

Jersey City
163,003

Rochester
133,896

MAINE

Lake Huron

Lake Ontario

VT. N.H.

Boston
448,477

MASS.

R.I.

St. Paul
133,156

Minneapolis
164,738

WISCONSIN

WYOMING
TERRITORY

DAKOTA
TERRITORY

Milwaukee
204,468

MICH.

Buffalo
255,664

N.Y.

CONN.

Providence
132,146

Detroit
205,876

L. Erie

PENNSYLVANIA

Brooklyn
806,343

NEVADA

UTAH
TERRITORY

COLORADO

NEBRASKA

IOWA

Chicago
1,099,850

ILLINOIS

IND.

Cleveland
261,353

OHIO

Cincinnati
296,908

Pittsburgh
238,617

N.J.

Newark
181,830

DEL.

Philadelphia
1,046,964

MD.

Baltimore
434,439

San Francisco
298,997

CALIFORNIA

Omaha
140,452

MO.

Kansas City
132,716

KANSAS

St. Louis
451,770

Mississippi

Ohio

Louisville
161,129

KY.

Washington
230,392

W. VA.

VIRGINIA

NORTH
CAROLINA

ARIZONA
TERRITORY

NEW MEXICO
TERRITORY

UNORGANIZED
TERRITORY

ARK.

TENNESSEE

SOUTH
CAROLINA

GEORGIA

PACIFIC
OCEAN

TEXAS

MISS.

ALABAMA

ATLANTIC
OCEAN

LOUISIANA

New Orleans
242,039

FLA.

MEXICO

Gulf of Mexico

— Boundary of urban-industrial core region

Population of 25
largest U.S. cities, 1890

⬤ Over 1,000,000

⬤ 500,000–1,000,000

• 250,000–500,000

· under 250,000

Immigrants as percentage
of total population, 1900

30% or more

10–30%

less than 10%

0   200   400 Km.

0   200   400 Mi.

Reconstruction
ends

Garfield
assassinated

First U.S.
skyscraper

National American
Woman Suffrage
Association

Civil War
ends

Edison
invents
light bulb

Standard
Oil Trust

American
Federation of Labor

Pendleton
Act

Interstate
Commerce Act

1865   **1877**   **1879**   **1881**   **1883**   **1885** **1886** **1887**   **1890**

1850   1900   1950   2000

Becoming an Urban Industrial Society, 1880–1890

FRANCES WILLARD

This very formal portrait of Frances Willard was probably taken in the 1880s, when she was not only the president of the WCTU, but also one of the best-known women in the world. *Library of Congress.*

Frances Willard

In 1874 Frances Willard faced a difficult decision: become head of a fashionable school for young women or accept a post in the newly organized Women's Christian Temperance Union (WCTU). She was 34 years old at the time, and all her previous experience pointed to the headmistress position. After a childhood in rural Wisconsin, she had attended the Evansville (Illinois) College for Ladies, graduated as valedictorian of her class, and became a professor and dean of women at the Women's College of Northwestern University. Guided by her devotion to the precepts of the Methodist Church and by her religious commitment to the salvation of individuals and society, Willard chose what one of her students later described as "the thorny path of the reformer." She rose rapidly in the WCTU and assumed the national presidency in 1879.

The WCTU was organized in 1874 by women who regarded alcohol as the chief reason for men's neglect and abuse of their families. WCTU members committed themselves to total abstinence from all alcohol, and they sought to protect the home and family by converting others to abstinence and the legal prohibition of alcohol. The organization typically operated through such old-stock Protestant churches as the Methodists, Presbyterians, Congregationalists, and Baptists.

From 1879 until her death in 1898, Willard was the driving force in the organization. Her personal motto was "Do everything," and she was untiring in her work for the cause of temperance. By the early 1890s, the WCTU claimed 150,000 members, making it the largest women's organization in the nation. Yet for Willard the organization remained very much within the traditional women's arena of family and home. She once offered a simple statement of purpose for the WCTU: "to make the whole world homelike." In 1883 she joined with Lady Henry (Isabel Cocks) Somerset, president of the British Women's Temperance Association, to organize the World's Women's Christian Temperance Union and served as its first president.

For many WCTU members, including Willard, their commitment to home and family led them into the public arena of politics, as they gathered signatures on petitions to prohibit the sale of alcohol, spoke at political rallies, and lobbied legislators in the corridors of state capitols. In 1882 the WCTU endorsed woman suffrage, the first support for that cause from a major women's organization other than those formed specifically to advocate woman suffrage. By the late 1880s, if not before, Willard had become, in the language of the day, a "broad-gauge" reformer, seeking alliances with a wide range of other reformers and embracing causes that complemented her concerns for protecting the home and family.

Drawing on the proselytizing traditions of Protestantism, the WCTU sent "round-the-world missionaries" to carry the message of prohibition and women's political rights to Hawai`i (then an independent kingdom), New Zealand, Australia, China, Japan, India, South Africa, and elsewhere. The crusade had its greatest immediate success when local recruits secured the adoption of woman suffrage in New Zealand in 1893 and in Australia in 1902. WCTU missionaries also made their presence felt in other parts of the world, helping to lay a basis for a women's movement in such places as Japan and India. At her death, admirers acclaimed Frances Willard as the second only to Queen Victoria of Great Britain among the most influential women of the world.

INTRODUCTION

Frances Willard's work with the WCTU took place during a time period that historians usually call the Gilded Age, after *The Gilded Age: A Tale of Today*, a novel by Samuel L. Clemens and Charles Dudley Warner, published in 1873. In the novel—the first for either writer—Clemens and Warner satirized the business and politics of their day. (Clemens went on to fame, under the pen name Mark Twain, as author of *Huckleberry Finn* and other classics.) Applying the term "the Gilded Age" to the years from the 1860s through the 1890s suggests both the gleam of a **gilded** surface and the cheap nature of the base metal underneath. The previous two chapters have portrayed some aspects of late-nineteenth-century life that might justify the label "gilded." The dramatic expansion of the economy, the extravagant wealth and great power of the new industrial entrepreneurs, and the rapid economic development of the West all provided the glitter. The grim realities of life for most industrial workers and the plight of racial and ethnic minorities lay just below that thin golden surface.

This chapter, centered on the 1880s, especially examines the new patterns of life in American urban and industrial society that developed in the decades after Reconstruction. Most of the changes were related to the great transforming experiences of the late nineteenth century—industrialization, urbanization, massive immigration from Europe, and the development of the West. Cities expanded so rapidly that municipal governments sometimes proved unable to meet all the demands placed on them—for example, should they use their limited resources to pave streets or build sewers? Women such as Frances Willard entered into the public sphere on a scale not previously seen. The expansion of the educational system presented many Americans with new opportunities. In the South, where industrialization and urbanization lagged, some tried to develop a more diverse economy. The expanding industrial economy and mushrooming cities attracted migrants from throughout Europe who came to America hoping to acquire free land or earn high wages.

EXPANSION OF THE INDUSTRIAL ECONOMY

- How did the industrial economy change from the 1870s to the 1880s?
- How and why did companies expand their operations and control within an industry?
- In what ways was the economy of the South distinctive?

The patterns of industry that emerged after the Civil War, especially railroad construction and expansion of the steel industry, continued to drive the economy in the 1880s, but important new developments emerged as well. John D. Rockefeller took the lead in bringing vertical and horizontal integration to the

gild To cover a cheaper metal with a very thin layer of gold.

production of kerosene and other petroleum products. Innovative technologies and the integrated railway network began to affect other parts of the economy, changing the ways that Americans shopped for goods from clothing to food to home lighting products.

Standard Oil: Model for Monopoly

Just as Carnegie provided a model for other steel companies and for heavy industry in general, **John D. Rockefeller** revolutionized the petroleum industry and provided a model for other consumer-goods industries. Rockefeller was born in upper New York State in 1839 and educated in Cleveland, Ohio. After working as a bookkeeper and clerk, he became a partner in a grain and livestock business in 1859 and earned large profits during the Civil War. At that time, Cleveland was the center for refining oil from northwestern Pennsylvania, then the nation's main source for crude oil. (The first oil well in the nation was drilled in 1859 near Titusville, Pennsylvania.) The major product of oil refining was kerosene, which transformed home lighting as kerosene lamps replaced candles and oil lamps. Rockefeller, in 1863, invested his hefty wartime profits in a **refinery**. After the war, he bought control of more refineries and incorporated them as Standard Oil in 1870.

The refining business was relatively easy to enter and highly competitive. Aggressive competition became a distinctive Standard Oil characteristic. Recognizing that technology could bring a competitive advantage, Rockefeller recruited experts to make Standard the most efficient refiner. He secured reduced rates or rebates from railroads by offering a heavy volume of traffic on a predictable basis. He usually sought to persuade his competitors to join the **cartel** he was creating. If they refused, he often tried to drive them out of business.

By 1881, following a strategy of **horizontal integration**, Rockefeller and his associates controlled some forty oil refineries, accounting for about 90 percent of the nation's refining capacity. In the 1880s, Standard also moved toward vertical integration by gaining control of oil fields, building transportation facilities (including pipelines and oceangoing tanker ships), and creating retail marketing operations (see Figure 18.1). By the early 1890s, Standard Oil had achieved almost complete vertical and horizontal integration of the American petroleum industry—a virtual **monopoly** over an entire industry.

John D. Rockefeller posed for this portrait in 1884, when he was 47 years old and one of the most powerful industrialists in the nation. *Rockefeller Archive Center.*

John D. Rockefeller American industrialist who amassed great wealth through the Standard Oil Company and donated much of his fortune to promote learning and research.

refinery An industrial plant that transforms raw materials into finished products by removing impurities or otherwise changing the material into something that can be sold; a petroleum refinery processes crude oil to produce a variety of products for use by consumers.

cartel A group of separate companies within an industry that cooperate to control the production, pricing, and marketing of goods within that industry; another name for a pool.

horizontal integration Merging one or more companies doing the same or similar activities as a way of limiting competition or enhancing stability and planning.

monopoly Exclusive control by an individual or company of the production or sale of a product.

chronology

Urban Industrial America

1865	Civil War ends 248,120 immigrants enter United States
1868	First medical school for women
1869	National Woman Suffrage Association and American Woman Suffrage Association formed Wyoming Territory adopts woman suffrage
1870	Utah Territory adopts woman suffrage Standard Oil incorporated 25 cities have populations exceeding 50,000
1871	Great Chicago Fire
1872	Samuel L. Clemens and Charles Dudley Warner name the Gilded Age
1874	Women's Christian Temperance Union founded
1876	Telephone invented
1877	Reconstruction ends
1879	Light bulb invented
1880s	Railroad expansion and consolidation
1880	James A. Garfield elected president
1881	Garfield assassinated Chester A. Arthur becomes president Standard Oil Trust organized 669,431 immigrants enter United States United Brotherhood of Carpenters and Joiners organized
1882–1885	Recession
1883	Pendleton Act
1884	Grover Cleveland elected president
1885	William LeBaron Jenney designs first U.S. skyscraper
1886	Last major railroad converts to standard gauge First Sears, Roebuck and Co. catalogue *Wabash Railway v. Illinois* Knights of Labor reaches peak membership Haymarket Square bombing American Federation of Labor founded
1887	American Sugar Refining Company formed American Protective Association founded Interstate Commerce Act Congress disfranchises women in Utah Territory
1888–1892	Australian ballot adopted
1888	First electric streetcar system Benjamin Harrison elected president
1890	58 cities have populations exceeding 50,000 Louis Sullivan designs Wainwright Building Idaho becomes a state
1889	North Dakota, South Dakota, Montana, and Washington become states
1890	National American Woman Suffrage Association formed Wyoming becomes a state, the first with woman suffrage
1893	Colorado voters (all male) adopt woman suffrage

Between 1879 and 1881, Rockefeller also centralized decision making among all his companies by creating the Standard Oil Trust. The **trust** was a new organizational form designed to get around state laws that prohibited one company from owning stock in another. To create the Standard Oil Trust, Rockefeller and others who held shares in the individual companies exchanged their stock for trust certificates issued by Standard Oil. Standard Oil

trust   A legal arrangement in which an individual (the trustor) gives fiduciary control of property to a person or institution (the trustee); in the late nineteenth century, a legal device to get around state laws prohibiting a company chartered in one state from operating in another state, and often synonymous in common use with *monopoly*; first used by John D. Rockefeller to consolidate Standard Oil.

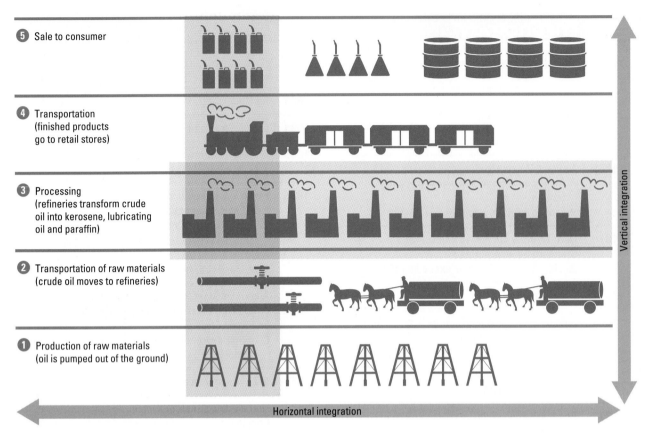

5 Sale to consumer

4 Transportation
(finished products
go to retail stores)

3 Processing
(refineries transform crude
oil into kerosene, lubricating
oil and paraffin)

2 Transportation of raw materials
(crude oil moves to refineries)

1 Production of raw materials
(oil is pumped out of the ground)

Vertical integration

Horizontal integration

● Steps in petroleum production/distribution

FIGURE 18.1 Vertical and Horizontal Integration of the Petroleum Industry This diagram represents the petroleum industry before Standard Oil achieved its dominance. The symbols represent different specialized companies, each engaged in a different step in the production of kerosene. Rockefeller entered the industry by investing in a refinery, and first expanded *horizontally* by absorbing several other refineries (indicated by the blue band). His Standard Oil Company then practiced *vertical integration* by acquiring oil leases, oil wells, pipelines, advantageous contracts with railroads, and eventually even retail stores (an example of vertical integration is indicated by the green band). For a time, Standard Oil controlled nearly 90 percent of the industry.

thus controlled all the individual companies, though technically it did not own them. Eventually, new laws in New Jersey made it legal for corporations chartered in New Jersey to own stock in other companies. So Rockefeller set up Standard Oil of New Jersey as a **holding company** for all the companies in the trust.

Once Rockefeller achieved his near-monopoly, Standard Oil consolidated its operations by closing many of its older refineries and building larger plants that incorporated the newest technology. These and other innovations reduced the cost of producing petroleum products by more than two-thirds, leading to a decline by more than half in the price paid by consumers of fuel and home-lighting

products. Standard also took a leading role in the world market, producing nearly all American petroleum products sold in Asia, Africa, and Latin America during the 1880s.

Rockefeller retired from active participation in business in the mid-1890s. Standard's petroleum monopoly was short-lived, however, because of the discovery of new rich oil fields in Texas and elsewhere at the turn of the century. New companies

holding company A company that exists to own other companies, usually through holding a controlling interest in their stocks.

emerged to tap those fields and quickly followed their own paths to vertical integration. Nonetheless, the "Rockefeller interests" (companies dominated by Rockefeller or his managers) steadily gained in power. They included the National City Bank of New York (an investment bank second only to the House of Morgan), railroads, mining, real estate, steel plants, steamship lines, and other industries.

Thomas Edison and the Power of Innovation

By the late nineteenth century, most American entrepreneurs had joined Rockefeller and Carnegie in viewing technology as a key competitive device. Railroads wanted more powerful locomotives, roomier freight cars, and stronger rails so they could carry more freight at a lower cost. Steel companies demanded larger and more efficient furnaces to make more steel more cheaply. Ordinary citizens as well as famous entrepreneurs seemed infatuated with technology. One invention followed another: an ice-making machine in 1865, the vacuum cleaner in 1869, the telephone in 1876, the phonograph in 1878, the electric light bulb in 1879, an electric welding machine in 1886, and the first American-made gasoline-engine automobile in 1895, to name only a few. By 1900, many Americans had come to expect a steady flow of ever-more-astounding creations.

Many new inventions relied on electricity, and in the field of electricity one person stood out: **Thomas A. Edison**. Born in 1847, he became a telegraph operator as a teenager. He began to experiment with electrical devices and in 1869 secured the first of his thousand-plus **patents**.

In 1876 Edison set up the first modern research laboratory, where he and his staff could work. He opened a new facility in 1887 that quickly became the world leader in research and development, especially for electricity. Edison promised "a minor invention every ten days and a big thing every six months," and he backed up his words with results. Sometimes building on the work of others, Edison's laboratories invented or significantly improved electrical lighting, electrical motors, the storage battery, the electric locomotive, the phonograph, the mimeograph, and many other products. Such research and development by Edison's laboratories and by others soon translated into production and sales. Nationwide, sales of electrical equipment were insignificant in 1870 but reached nearly $2 million ten years later and nearly $22 million in 1890.

This photograph from 1893 shows Thomas A. Edison in his laboratory, the world's leading research facility when it opened in 1876. By creating research teams, the Edison laboratories could pursue several projects at once. They developed a dazzling stream of new products, most based on electrical power. *Library of Congress.*

The sale of new electrical devices depended on the availability of electricity. Generating and distribution systems had to be constructed, and wires for carrying electrical current had to be installed along city streets and in homes. Early developers of electrical devices and electrical distribution systems realized quickly that they needed major financial assistance, and investment bankers came to play an important role in public utilities industries. General Electric, for example, came about through a series of **mergers** arranged by the New York banking firm of J. P. Morgan.

Thomas A. Edison   American inventor, especially of electrical devices, among them the microphone (1877), the phonograph (1878), and the light bulb (1879).

patent   A government grant that gives the creator of an invention the sole right to produce, use, or sell that invention for a set period of time.

merger   The joining together of two or more organizations.

Selling to the Nation

The expansion of manufacturing in the 1880s produced an acceleration of earlier trends toward a larger array of new and affordable consumer goods of many kinds, from household utensils to ready-made clothing and processed foodstuffs. Large, vertically integrated manufacturers of consumer products often produced items that differed little from each other and that cost virtually the same to produce. Often, such companies came to compete not on the basis of price but instead by advertising to differentiate their products.

Much of the advertising in the mid-nineteenth century was for **patent medicines** and books. By the late nineteenth century, however, large-scale advertising also promoted packaged foods, clothing, soap, and petroleum products. Advertisements in newspapers and magazines became larger and more complex. In some cases—notably for cigarettes—advertising actually created demand and greatly expanded the market for the product. After the federal Patent Office registered the first **trademark** in 1870, companies rushed to develop brands and logos that they hoped would distinguish their products from nearly identical rivals.

Accompanying advertising came new ways of selling goods to customers. Before this time, most people expected to purchase whatever they needed directly from artisans who made goods on order (shoes, clothes, furniture), or from door-to-door peddlers (pots and pans), or in small specialty stores (hardware, dry goods) or general stores. In urban areas during the Gilded Age, the first American **department stores** appeared and flourished, offering a wide range of choices in ready-made products—clothing, household furnishings, shoes, and much more. Department stores' products, unlike the wares in most previous retail outlets, not only had clearly marked prices but also could be returned or exchanged if the customer was dissatisfied. In the vanguard were R. H. Macy's in New York City, Wanamaker's in Philadelphia, Jordan Marsh in Boston, and Marshall Field in Chicago. Such stores relied heavily on newspaper advertising to attract large numbers of middle- and upper-class customers, especially women, from throughout the city and its suburbs.

The variety presented by department stores paled, however, when compared with the vast array of goods available through the new mail-order catalogues. Led by Montgomery Ward (which issued its first catalogue in 1872) and Sears, Roebuck and Co. (whose first catalogs appeared in the late 1880s)—

Mail-order companies led by Montgomery Ward and Sears, Roebuck and Co., both based in Chicago, issued advertising catalogs that brought the most remote farm family into contact with the latest fashions and the most recent developments in equipment. The cover for this 1899 catalog depicts a giant cornucopia, the traditional symbol of abundance, filled with consumer goods. *Granger Collection.*

both based in Chicago—mail-order houses aimed at rural America. They offered a wider range of choices than most rural-dwellers had ever before seen—everything from handkerchiefs to harnesses.

patent medicine   A medical preparation that is advertised by brand name and available without a physician's prescription.

trademark   A name or symbol that identifies a product and is officially registered and legally restricted for use by the owner or manufacturer.

department store   Type of retail establishment that developed in cities in the late nineteenth century and featured a wide variety of merchandise organized in separate departments.

Department stores and mail-order houses became feasible because manufacturers had begun to produce many types of consumer goods in huge volumes. Mail-order houses also depended on railroads and the U.S. mail to deliver their catalogues and products across great distances, and department stores relied on railroads to deliver consumer goods from distant factories. Together, advertising, mail-order catalogues (in rural areas), and the new department stores for consumer goods (in urban areas) began to change not only Americans' buying habits, but also their thinking about what they expected to buy ready-made.

Railroads, Investment Bankers, and "Morganization"

Railroads expanded significantly in the 1880s, laying over 75,000 miles of new track, but some new lines earned little profit. Some ran through sparsely populated areas of the West. Others spread into areas already saturated by rail service. In the 1880s, however, a few ambitious, talented, and occasionally unscrupulous railway executives maneuvered to produce great regional railway systems. The Santa Fe and the Southern Pacific, for example, came to dominate the Southwest, and the Great Northern and the Northern Pacific held sway in the Northwest. The Pennsylvania and the New York Central controlled much of the shipping in the Northeast. By consolidating many of the lines within a region, railway executives tried to create more efficient systems with less duplication, fewer price wars, and more dependable profits.

To raise the enormous amounts of capital necessary for construction and consolidation, railroad executives turned increasingly to **investment banks**. By the late 1880s, **John Pierpont Morgan** had emerged as the nation's leading investment banker. Born in Connecticut in 1837, he was the son of a successful merchant who turned to banking (and helped fund Andrew Carnegie's first big steel plant). After schooling in Switzerland and Germany, young Morgan began working in his father's bank in London. In 1857 he moved to New York, where his father had arranged a banking position for him.

Morgan's background and his growing stature in banking gave him access to capital within the United States and abroad, in London and Paris. His investors wanted to put their money where it would be safe and would give them a reliable **return**. Morgan therefore tried to stabilize the railroad business,

J. P. Morgan, Sr., was at the pinnacle of his power when this photograph was taken around 1900. In this photograph, as in others taken at that time, Morgan seems to exude both power and anger. The sense of anger may, in fact, reflect his anxiety over having his picture taken. Morgan was very sensitive about his appearance, especially his nose. He suffered from acne rosacea, which made his nose large and misshapen. He was so offended by one photograph, by the famous photographer Edward Steichen, that he tore it up when he first saw it. *New-York Historical Society.*

especially the cutthroat rate competition that often resulted when several companies served one market. Railroad companies that turned to Morgan for

investment bank   An institution that acts as an agent for corporations issuing stocks and bonds.

John Pierpont Morgan   The most prominent and powerful American investment banker in the late nineteenth century.

return   The yield on money that has been invested in an enterprise or product.

help in raising capital found strings attached to funding. Morgan regularly insisted that beneficiaries reorganize to simplify corporate structures and to combine small lines into larger, centrally controlled systems. He often demanded a seat on the board of directors as well, to guard against risky decisions in the future. Some began to refer to this process as "Morganization," and "Morganized" lines soon included some of the largest in the country. A few other investment bankers followed similar patterns.

Economic Concentration in Consumer-Goods Industries

Carnegie, Rockefeller, Edison, Morgan, and a few others helped to redefine the expectations of other entrepreneurs and provided models for their activities. In a number of industries, massive, complex companies—vertically integrated, sometimes horizontally integrated, often employing extensive advertising—appeared relatively suddenly in the 1880s. At first they were concentrated in consumer-goods industries.

The American Sugar Refining Company, created in 1887, imitated Rockefeller's organization to control three-quarters of the nation's sugar-refining capacity by the early 1890s. In the 1880s, James B. Duke used efficient machinery, extensive advertising, and vertical integration to become the largest manufacturer of cigarettes. In 1890 he merged with his four largest competitors to create the American Tobacco Company, which dominated the cigarette industry. Gustavus Swift in the early 1880s began to ship fresh meat from his slaughterhouse in Chicago to markets in the East, using his own refrigerated railcars. He eventually added refrigerated storage plants in each city, along with a sales and delivery staff. Other meatpacking companies followed Swift's lead. By 1890, half a dozen firms, all vertically integrated, dominated meatpacking. Such a market, in which a small number of firms dominate an industry, is called an **oligopoly**. Oligopolies were (and are) more typical than monopolies.

Some of the new manufacturing companies did not sell stock or use investment bankers to raise capital. Standard Oil, like Carnegie Steel, never "went public"—that is, they never sold stock on a stock exchange to raise capital. Rockefeller expanded either through mergers or by making purchases capitalized by the profits of the business itself. Rockefeller, like Carnegie, concentrated ownership and control in his own hands. So did many others among the new manufacturing companies. As late

as 1896, for example, the New York Stock Exchange sold stock in only twenty manufacturing concerns.

Gradually, however, with the passing of the first generation of industrial empire builders, ownership grew apart from management. Many new business executives were professional managers. Ownership rested with hundreds or thousands of stockholders, all of whom wanted a reliable return on their investment, even though the vast majority remained uninvolved with business operations. The huge size of the new companies also meant that most managers rarely saw or talked with most of their employees. Careful **cost analysis**, the desire for efficiency, and the need to pay shareholders regular **dividends** led many companies to treat most of their employees as expenses to be increased or cut as necessary, with little regard to the effect on individuals.

Laying an Economic Base for a New South

The term **New South** usually refers to efforts by some southerners to modernize their region during the years after Reconstruction. Some advocates of the New South promoted a more diverse economic base, with more manufacturing and less reliance on a few staple agricultural crops, as a way to strengthen the southern economy and integrate it more thoroughly into the national economy.

Foremost among proponents of the New South was **Henry Grady**, who built the *Atlanta Constitution*

---

oligopoly A market or industry dominated by a few firms (from Greek words meaning "few sellers"); compare *monopoly* (from Greek words meaning "one seller").

cost analysis Study of the cost of producing manufactured goods in order to find ways to cut expenses.

dividend A share of a company's profits received by a stockholder; companies customarily announce dividends every quarter (three months).

New South Late-nineteenth-century term used by some southerners to promote the idea that the South should become industrialized, have a more diverse agriculture, and be thoroughly integrated into the economy of the nation.

Henry Grady Prominent Atlanta newspaper publisher and leading proponent of the concept of a New South.

Much of the new southern textile industry was based on child labor. These children were photographed by Lewis Hines in 1908. *National Archives/ Lewis Hines.*

into a powerful regional newspaper in the 1880s. Like Chicago, Atlanta grew as a railroad center. Though destroyed by Sherman's troops in 1864, Atlanta developed quickly once the war was over. It became the capital of Georgia in 1877. Thanks in part to Grady's skillful journalism, Atlanta's population boomed in the 1880s by 75 percent, and the city emerged as a symbol of the New South—a center for transportation, industry, and finance.

The importance of railroads in spurring Atlanta's growth was no coincidence. After the Civil War, inadequate transportation, especially railroads, posed a critical limit on the South's economic growth. During the 1880s, however, southern railroads more than doubled their miles of track. In the 1890s, J. P. Morgan led in reorganizing southern railroads into three large systems, dominated by the Southern Railway. With the emergence of better rail transportation, some entrepreneurs began to consider introducing new industries.

Some southerners had long advocated that their cotton be manufactured into cloth in the South. Early efforts to establish textile manufacturing in the region had been stymied by the economic chaos of the Civil War and its aftermath. The southern cotton textile industry finally boomed, however, during the 1880s and 1890s as the number of textile

mills increased from 161 in 1880 to 400 in 1900. The new mills had more modern equipment and were larger and more productive than the mills of New England. Southern textile mills also had cheaper labor costs, partly because they relied extensively on child labor. An official of the American Cotton Manufacturers' Association estimated that 70 percent of southern cotton-mill workers were younger than 21, and another observer calculated that 75 percent of the cotton spinners in North Carolina were under the age of 14. Similar patterns characterized the emergence of cigarette manufacturing as a new southern industry. In the end, though, these enterprises did little to transform the regional economy. Most of the new companies paid low wages, and some located in the South specifically to take advantage of its cheap, unskilled, nonunion labor.

Other southerners tried to diversify the region's agriculture and to reduce its dependence on cotton and tobacco. Such efforts, however, ran up against the cotton textile and cigarette industries, both of which built factories in the South to be near their raw materials. Thus southern agriculture changed little: owners and sharecroppers farmed small plots, obligated by their rental contracts or crop liens to raise cotton or tobacco. In some parts of the South, farmers became even more dependent on cotton than they had been before the Civil War. Parts of Georgia, for example, produced almost 200 percent more cotton in 1880 than in 1860.

Fencing laws brought some long-term improvement to southern livestock raising. States adopted such laws to keep farmers from allowing their cattle and hogs to run free in unfenced wooded areas. Fencing permitted more prosperous farmers to introduce new breeds, control breeding, and thereby improve the stock. But the law placed at a disadvantage many small-scale farmers who now had to fence their grazing areas but could not afford to buy the new breeds.

Despite repeated backing for the idea of a New South by some southern leaders, and despite growth of some new industries in the South, the late nineteenth century was also the time when the myth of the **Old South** and the so-called **Lost Cause** pervaded nearly every aspect of southern life. Popular fiction and song, North and South, romanticized the pre-Civil War Old South as a place of gentility and gallantry, where "kindly" plantation owners cared for "loyal" slaves. The Lost Cause myth portrayed the Confederacy as a heroic, even noble, effort to retain the life and values of the Old South. Leading southerners—especially Democratic Party leaders—promoted the nostalgic notion of the Lost Cause, and many white southerners embraced it as justification for the dislocation and suffering that so many of them had experienced during and after the Civil War. Hundreds of statues of Confederate soldiers appeared on courthouse lawns, and gala commemorative events and organizations reflected devotion to the myth among many white southerners.

ORGANIZED LABOR IN THE 1880S

• How did the Knights of Labor differ from craft unions in membership and objectives?

• Which type of labor organization was more successful? Why?

The expansion of railroads and manufacturing and the growth of cities led to dramatic increases in the number of wage-earning workers. The Great Railway Strike of 1877 (see page 521) had suggested that working people could unite across lines of occupation, race, and gender, but no organization drew on that potential until the early 1880s, when the Knights of Labor emerged as an alternative to craft unions. Though the Knights scored some organizing successes, they failed to sustain their organization against a challenge from craft unions.

The Knights of Labor

The **Knights of Labor** grew out of an organization of Philadelphia garment workers that dated to 1869. Abandoning their craft union origins, they proclaimed that labor was "the only creator of values or capital," and they opened their ranks to all whom they defined as part of "the producing class"—those who, by their labor, created value. Anyone joining the Knights was required to have worked for wages at some time, but the organization specifically excluded only professional gamblers, stockbrokers, lawyers, bankers, and liquor dealers.

The Knights accepted African Americans as members, and some sixty thousand joined by 1886. In many cases, local organizations of black workers seem to have organized themselves and joined the Knights rather than waiting to be approached by an organizer. Nearly all African Americans were enrolled in separate, all-black, local organizations, though some integrated local assemblies did exist. After one organizer formed a local organization of women in 1881, the Knights officially opened their ranks to women and enrolled about fifty thousand by 1886. Some women and African Americans held leadership positions at local and regional levels, and the Knights briefly appointed a woman as a national organizer. Through their activities, the Knights provided both women and African Americans with experience in labor organizing.

Terence V. Powderly, a machinist, directed the Knights from 1879 to 1893. Under his leadership, they focused on organization, education, and cooperation as their chief objectives. Powderly generally opposed strikes. A lost strike, he argued, often destroyed the local organization and thereby

---

Old South   Term used in both South and North for the antebellum (pre-Civil War) South, suggesting that it was a place of gentility and gallantry.

Lost Cause   Term used to refer to the Confederate struggle in the Civil War as a noble but doomed effort to preserve a way of life.

Knights of Labor   Labor organization founded in 1869; membership, open to all workers, peaked in 1886.

Terence V. Powderly   Leader of the Knights of Labor who called for cooperative production instead of a wage system.

This cartoon shows Terence Powderly, in the center, advocating the position of the Knights of Labor on arbitration. The Knights urged that labor and management (identified here as "capital") should settle their differences this way, rather than by striking. Note how the cartoonist has depicted labor and management as of equal size, and given both of them a large weapon; management's club is labeled "monopoly" and labor's hammer is called "strikes." In fact, labor and management were rarely equally matched when it came to labor disputes in the late nineteenth century. *Puck, April 7, 1886.*

delayed the more important tasks of education and cooperation. The Knights favored political action to accomplish a range of labor reforms, including health and safety laws for workers, the eight-hour workday, prohibition of child labor, equal pay for equal work regardless of gender, and the graduated income tax. They also endorsed government ownership of the telephone, telegraph, and railroad systems. In 1878, 1880, and 1882, Powderly won election as mayor of Scranton, Pennsylvania, as the candidate of a labor party. Other local labor parties sometimes appeared in other cities where the Knights were strong.

The Knights' endorsement of cooperation was related to the argument that only labor produces value. A major objective of the Knights was "to secure to the workers the full enjoyment of the wealth they create." Toward that end, they commit-

ted themselves in their first national meeting in 1878 to introduce a system of producers' and consumers' **cooperatives**, which they hoped would "supersede the wage-system." They established some 135 cooperatives by the mid-1880s, but few lasted very long. Like the Grangers' cooperatives in the 1870s (see page 519), some of the Knights' cooperatives folded because of lack of capital, some because of opposition from rival businesses, and some because of poor organization.

Despite the lackluster record of their cooperatives, the Knights of Labor quickly grew to be the

> **cooperative** A business enterprise in which workers and consumers share in ownership and take part in management.

largest labor organization in the country, expanding from 9,000 members in 1879 to a high point of 703,000 in 1886. This meteoric growth suggested that many working people were seeking ways to respond to the emerging corporate behemoths or to regain some control over their own working lives. Although the Knights opposed striking, much of the increase in membership in the mid-1880s came because local Knights organizers played major roles in helping to win strikes against prominent railroads in 1884 and 1885. Although many members seem to have joined in order to unite against their employers, the national leadership played down such conflicts in the interests of long-term economic and political change.

1886: Turning Point for Labor?

The railway strike of 1877 and the rise of the Knights of Labor seemed to signal a growing sense of common purpose among many working people. After 1886, however, labor organizations often found themselves on the defensive and were divided between those trying to adjust to the new realities of industrial capitalism and those seeking to change it.

On May 1, 1886, some eighty thousand Chicagoans marched through the streets in support of an eight-hour workday, a cause that united a wide variety of unions and radical groups. Three days later, Chicago police killed several strikers at the McCormick Harvester Works. Hoping to build on the May Day unity, a group of **anarchists** called a protest meeting for the next day at Haymarket Square. When police tried to break up the rally, someone tossed a bomb at the officers. The police then opened fire on the crowd, and some protesters fired back. Eight policemen died, along with an unknown number of demonstrators, and a hundred people suffered injuries.

The Haymarket bombing sparked public anxiety and antiunion feelings. Employers who had opposed unions before now tried to discredit them by playing on fears of terrorism. Some people who had supported what they saw as legitimate union goals now shrank back in horror. In Chicago, amid widespread furor over the violence, eight leading anarchists stood trial for inciting the bombing and, on flimsy evidence, were convicted. Four were hanged, one committed suicide, and three remained in jail until a sympathetic governor, John Peter Altgeld, released them in 1893.

Uniting the Craft Unions: The American Federation of Labor

Two weeks after the Haymarket bombing, trade union leaders met in Philadelphia to discuss the inroads that the Knights of Labor were making among their members. They proposed an agreement between the trade unions and the Knights: trade unions would recruit skilled workers, and the Knights would limit themselves to unskilled workers. When the Knights refused, the trade unions organized the **American Federation of Labor** (AFL) to coordinate their struggles with the Knights for the loyalty of skilled workers. Membership in the AFL was limited to national trade unions. The combined membership of the thirteen founding unions amounted only to 140,000.

Samuel Gompers became the AFL's first president. Born in London in 1850 to Dutch Jewish parents, he learned the cigarmaker's trade before coming to the United States in 1863. He joined the Cigarmakers' Union in 1864 and became its president in 1877. Except for one year, Gompers continued as president of the AFL from 1886 until his death in 1924. A socialist in his youth, Gompers became more conservative as AFL president, opposing labor involvement with radicalism or politics. Instead, he and other AFL leaders came to favor what Gompers called "pure and simple" unionism: higher wages, shorter hours, and improved working conditions for their own members. Most AFL unions did not challenge capitalism, but they did use strikes to achieve their goals and sometimes engaged in long and bitter struggles with employers.

After the 1880s, the AFL suffered little competition from the Knights of Labor. The decline of the Knights came swiftly: 703,000 members in 1886, 260,000 in 1888, 100,000 in 1890. The failure of several strikes involving the Knights in the late 1880s cost them many supporters. Some who abandoned the Knights were probably disappointed when a "cooperative commonwealth" was not quickly

anarchist   A person who believes that all forms of government are oppressive and should be abolished.

American Federation of Labor   National organization of trade unions founded in 1886; it used strikes and boycotts to improve the lot of craft workers.

Samuel Gompers   First president of the American Federation of Labor; he sought to divorce labor organizing from politics and stressed practical demands involving wages and hours.

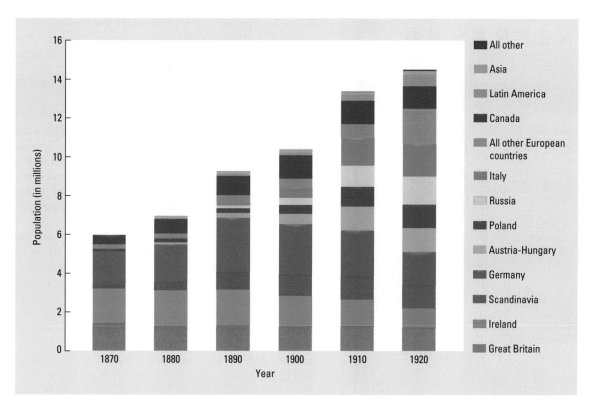

FIGURE 18.2 **Foreign-Born Population of the United States, 1870–1920** This graph shows the largest foreign-born groups living in the United States at the time of the census every ten years. Note that the total number of foreign-born increased dramatically during these fifty years, and also that the foreign-born were increasingly diverse by country of origin. *Source*: U.S. Department of Commerce, Bureau of the Census, *Historical Statistics of the United States, Colonial Times to 1970*, Bicentennial edition, 2 vols. (Washington: Government Printing Office, 1975), 1: 116–117.

achieved. Some units of the Knights were organized much like trade unions, and these groups preferred the very practical AFL, rather than the more visionary Powderly. The most prominent was the United Mine Workers of America, which switched from the Knights to the AFL in 1890 but retained some central principles of the Knights, including commitments to include both whites and African Americans and to reach all workers, rather than only the most skilled.

NEW AMERICANS FROM EUROPE

• What expectations did immigrants have upon coming to the United States?

• How did their expectations regarding assimilation compare with those of old-stock Americans?

Many of the members and leaders of both the Knights of Labor and the AFL craft unions were immigrants from Europe, reflecting the international flavor of the American work force in the Gilded Age. The United States has attracted large numbers of immigrants throughout its history, but it had never experienced a flood of immigrants like the one between the Civil War and World War I. Nearly all these immigrants came from Europe, and many settled in cities.

A Flood of Immigrants

The numbers of immigrants varied from year to year—higher in prosperous years, lower in depression years—but the trend was constantly upward. Nearly a quarter of a million arrived in 1865,

Railroad companies, seeking to sell their land grants, advertised in Europe for immigrants to buy farmland in the West. This poster, issued by the Burlington and Missouri railroad, probably in the 1880s, is in Czech, but the same poster was also issued in German and Swedish. The poster's sequence of drawings shows a six-year transition from bare prairie to prosperous farm. Such advertising helped to attract many European immigrants to the north central states (see the map at the beginning of the chapter). *Nebraska State Historical Society.*

of the foreign-born population for the census years from 1870 through 1920. Note especially how the foreign-born population became increasingly diverse after the 1890s.

Immigrants left their former homes for a variety of reasons, but most came to the United States because it was known everywhere as the "land of opportunity." They came, as one bluntly said, for "jobs" and, as another declared, "for money." Some were also attracted by the reputation of the United States for toleration of religious difference and commitment to democracy. In fact, the reasons for immigrating to America varied from person to person, country to country, and year to year.

In Ireland, for example, a fourfold population increase between 1750 and 1850 combined with changes in agriculture to push people off the land. Repeated failure of potato crops after 1845 produced widespread famine and starvation, greatly increasing migration for several years. Irish immigrants, many desperately poor, arrived in greatest numbers before the Civil War, but Irish immigration continued at high levels until the 1890s. They settled at first in the cities of the Northeast, composing a quarter of the population in New York City and Boston as early as 1860.

The chapter-opening map reveals concentrations of immigrants in the urban-industrial core region, or **manufacturing belt**, especially in urban areas, but distinctive immigrant communities were not limited to cities. Many of the immigrants who came in the 1870s and 1880s found that good farmland could still be acquired relatively easily in the north-central states, for there farmland was relatively cheap, or even free under the Homestead Act. Scandinavians, Dutch, Swiss, Czechs, and Germans were most likely to be farmers, but many other groups also formed rural farming settlements. One woman recalled that, in rural Nebraska in the 1880s, her family could attend Sunday church services in Norwegian, Danish, Swedish, French, Czech, or German, as well as English.

Scandinavia   The region of northern Europe consisting of Norway, Sweden, Denmark, and Iceland.

manufacturing belt   A region that includes most of the nation's factories; in the late nineteenth century, the U.S. manufacturing belt also included most of the nation's large cities and railroad lines and much of its mining.

---

two-thirds of a million in 1881, and a million in 1905. In the 1870s and 1880s, most immigrants came from Great Britain, Ireland, **Scandinavia**, Germany, and Canada, but during the 1890s and after, increasing numbers began to arrive from southern and eastern Europe. Figure 18.2 shows the place of birth

Thus patterns of immigrant settlement reflect the expectations immigrants had about America, as well as the opportunities they found when they arrived. After 1890, farmland was more difficult to obtain. The 1890s also marked a shift in the sources of immigration, with proportionately more coming from southern and eastern Europe and arriving with little or no capital. Newcomers after 1890 were more likely to find work in the rapidly expanding industrial sectors of the economy in mining, transportation, and manufacturing. Of course, individual variations on these patterns were many. Some immigrants coming after 1890 intended to become farmers and succeeded. Many who came before 1890 became industrial workers or took other urban jobs.

Hyphenated America

In the nineteenth century, most old-stock Americans assumed that immigrants should quickly learn English, become citizens, and restructure their lives and values to resemble those of long-time residents. Most immigrants, however, resisted rapid **assimilation**. For the majority, assimilation took place over a lifetime or even over generations. Most retained elements of their own cultures even as they embraced a new life in America. Their sense of identity drew on two elements—where they had come from and where they lived now—and they often came to think of themselves as hyphenated Americans: German-Americans, Irish-Americans, Norwegian-Americans.

On arriving in America, with its strange language and unfamiliar customs, many immigrants reacted by seeking others who shared their cultural values, practiced their religion, and, especially, spoke their language. Ethnic communities emerged throughout regions with large numbers of immigrants. These communities played a significant role in newcomers' transition from the old country to America. They gave immigrants a chance to learn about their new home with the assistance of those who had come before. At the same time, newcomers could, without apology or embarrassment, retain cultural values and behaviors from their homelands.

Hyphenated America developed a unique blend of ethnic institutions, often unlike anything in the old country but also unlike the institutions of old-stock America. Fraternal lodges based on ethnicity sprang up and provided not only social ties but sometimes also financial benefits in case of illness or death. Singing societies devoted to the music

The photographer Lewis Hine took this picture of a family from eastern Europe who arrived in the United States in 1905. After 1890, immigrants came ashore at Ellis Island and were processed by the Immigration Service. For millions of immigrants, Ellis Island was their portal to America. *Courtesy George Eastman House.*

of the old country flourished. Foreign-language newspapers were vital in developing a sense of identity that connected the old country to the new, for they provided news from the old country as well as from other similar communities in the United States.

For members of nearly every **ethnic group**, religious institutions provided the most important building blocks of ethnic group identity. In most of Europe, a state church was officially sanctioned to perform certain functions. Membership in a religious body was voluntary in America, but religious ties often became stronger here, partly because

---

assimilation The process of becoming like something else; among immigrants, the process of adapting to the new society in which they found themselves.

ethnic group A group that shares a certain racial, religious, linguistic, cultural, or national heritage.

religious organizations provided an important link among people with a similar language and cultural values. Protestant immigrant groups created new church organizations based on both theology and language. Catholic parishes in immigrant neighborhoods often took on the ethnic characteristics of the community. Their services were conducted in the native language, and special observances were transplanted from the old country. Jewish congregations, too, often differed according to the ethnic background of their members.

Nativism

Many Americans (including some only a generation removed from immigrant forebears themselves) expected immigrants to lay aside their previous identities, embrace the behavior and beliefs of old-stock Americans, and blend neatly into old-stock American culture. This view of immigrants eventually came to be identified with the image of the **melting pot** after the appearance of a play by that name in 1908. But the melting-pot metaphor rarely described the reality of immigrants' lives. Most immigrants changed in some ways, but most did so slowly, over lifetimes, gradually adopting new patterns of thinking and behavior or modifying previous beliefs and practices.

Few old-stock Americans appreciated or even understood the long-term nature of immigrants' adjustments to their new home. Instead of seeing the ways immigrants changed, many old-stock Americans saw only immigrants' efforts to retain their own culture. They fretted over the multiplication of newspapers published in German and Swedish, feared to go into communities where they rarely heard an English sentence, and shuddered at the sprouting of Catholic schools. Such fears and misgivings fostered the growth of **nativism**: the view that old-stock values and social patterns were preferable to those of immigrants. Nativists argued that only their values and institutions were genuinely American, and they feared that immigrants posed a threat to those traditions.

American nativism was often linked to anti-Catholicism. Irish and German immigrant groups, and later Italian and Polish groups, included large numbers of Catholics, and many old-stock Americans came to identify the Catholic Church as an immigrant church. The **American Protective Association**, founded in 1887, noisily proclaimed itself the voice of anti-Catholicism. Its members pledged

not to hire Catholics, not to vote for them, and not to strike with them.

Jews, too, faced religious antagonism. In the 1870s, increasing numbers of organizations and businesses began to discriminate against Jews. Some employers refused to hire Jews. After 1900, such discrimination intensified. Many social organizations barred Jews from membership, and **restrictive covenants** kept them from buying homes in certain neighborhoods.

THE NEW URBAN AMERICA

- What were the key factors in the transformation of American cities in the late nineteenth century?
- What were some of the results of that transformation?

By 1890, immigrants made up more than 40 percent of the population of New York, San Francisco, and Chicago, and more than a third of the population in several other major cities. But immigrants were not the only people who thronged to the cities. Others came from rural areas and small towns. Thus Americans in the 1880s witnessed a burgeoning of their cities as Chicago doubled in size to take second rank, behind New York. In just ten years, Brooklyn had grown by more than 40 percent, St. Louis by nearly 30 percent, and San Francisco by almost as much. Cities not only added more people, but also expanded upward and outward and became more complex, both socially and economically.

Surging Urban Growth

What Americans saw in their cities often fascinated them. Cities boasted the technological innovations

---

melting pot   A concept that American society is a place where immigrants set aside their distinctive cultural identities and are absorbed into a homogeneous culture.

nativism   The view that old-stock values and social patterns were preferable to those of immigrants.

American Protective Association   An anti-Catholic organization founded in Iowa in 1887 and active during the next decade.

restrictive covenant   Provision in a property title designed to restrict subsequent sale or use of the property, often specifying sale only to a white Christian.

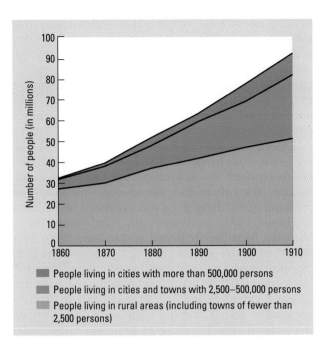

People living in cities with more than 500,000 persons

People living in cities and towns with 2,500–500,000 persons

People living in rural areas (including towns of fewer than 2,500 persons)

FIGURE 18.3 Urban and Rural Population of the United States, 1860–1910 Although much of the population increase between 1860 and 1910 came in urban areas, the number of people living in rural areas increased as well. Notice, too, that the largest increase was in towns and cities that had between 2,500 and 500,000 people. *Source:* U.S. Bureau of the Census, Department of Commerce, *Historical Statistics of the United States*, 2 vols. (Washington, D.C.: U.S. Government Printing Office, 1975), Series A-58, A-59, A-69, A-119.

that many equated with progress. But the lure of the city stemmed from far more than telephones, streetcars, and technological gadgetry. Samuel Lane Loomis in 1887 listed the many choices to be found in cities: "The churches and the schools, the theatres and concerts, the lectures, fairs, exhibitions, and galleries . . . and the mighty streams of human beings that forever flow up and down the thoroughfares."

Not every urban vista was so appealing. Some visitors were shocked and repulsed by the poverty, crime, and filth that cluttered the urban landscape. Guillermo Prieto, visiting San Francisco in 1877, was struck by the contrast of luxurious wealth and desperate poverty: "Behind the palaces run filthy alleys, or rather nasty dungheaps without sidewalks or illumination, whose loiterers smell of the gallows."

Filled with glamour and destitution, cities grew rapidly. Cities with more than 50,000 people were growing almost twice as fast as rural areas (see Figure 18.3). The nation had twenty-five cities that large in 1870, with a total population of 5 million. By 1890, fifty-eight cities had reached that size and held nearly 12 million people. Most of these cities were in the Northeast and near the Great Lakes. This growth came largely through migration from rural areas in the United States and Europe. The mechanization of American farms meant that agriculture required fewer workers per acre than ever before. Rural birth rates remained high, however, and rural death rates were lower than in the cities. America's farmlands contributed significantly to the growth of the cities, but many other new urban residents came from outside the United States, especially from Europe.

Jacob Riis, himself a Danish immigrant, provided this striking description of Manhattan in 1890:

A map of the city, colored to designate nationalities, would show more stripes than on the skin of a zebra, and more colors than any rainbow. The city on such a map would fall into two great halves, green for the Irish prevailing in the West Side tenement districts, and blue for the Germans on the East Side. But intermingled with these ground colors would be an odd variety of tints that would give the whole the appearance of an extraordinary crazy quilt.

Riis then pieced in some smaller parts of the ethnic patchwork by describing neighborhoods of Italians, African Americans, Jews, Chinese, Czechs, Arabs, Finns, Greeks, and Swiss.

The growth of manufacturing went hand in hand with urban expansion. By the late nineteenth century, the nation had developed a manufacturing belt. This region, which included nearly all the largest cities as well as the bulk of the nation's manufacturing and finance, may be thought of as constituting the nation's urban-industrial "core" (see the chapter-opening map). Some of the cities in this region— Boston, New York, Baltimore, Buffalo, and St. Louis, for example—had long been among the busiest ports in the nation. Now manufacturing also flourished there and came to be nearly as important as trade. In other cases, cities developed as industrial centers from their beginnings. Some cities became known for a particular product: iron and steel in Pittsburgh, clothing in New York City, meatpacking in Chicago, flour milling in Minneapolis. A few cities, especially New York, stood out as major centers for finance.

Louis Sullivan designed the Wainwright Building (1890) with the intention of creating a new way of thinking about height and about the relationship between form and function. The building was widely acclaimed and often imitated. *Missouri Historical Society/Emil Boehl.*

New Cities of Skyscrapers and Streetcars

As the urban population swelled and the urban economy grew more complex, cities expanded upward and outward. In the early 1800s, most cities measured only a few miles across, and most residents got around on foot. Historians call such places **"walking cities."** Buildings were low (anything higher than three stories was unusual) and rarely designed for a specific economic function. Small factories existed here and there among warehouses and commercial offices near the docks. In the late nineteenth century, new technologies for construction and transportation transformed the cities.

Until the 1880s, construction techniques restricted building height because the lower walls carried the structure's full weight. The higher a building, the thicker its lower walls had to be. William LeBaron Jenney usually receives credit for designing the first skyscraper—ten stories high, erected in Chicago in 1885. Chicago architects also took the lead in designing other tall buildings. They could do

so because of new construction technologies that allowed a metal frame to carry the weight of the walls. Jenney's building used an iron frame, but architects quickly turned to the greater strength of steel. Another crucial technological advance was the elevator, a necessity for multistory buildings. Economical and efficient, skyscrapers created unique city skylines.

Among the Chicago architects who developed high-rise structures, **Louis Sullivan** stands out. He recognized the skyscraper as the architectural form of the future and introduced a new way of thinking about height. In the Wainwright Building (St. Louis, 1890), Sullivan emphasized height, creating what he called a "proud and soaring thing." He also tried to design exteriors that reflected the interior functions, in keeping to his rule that "form follows function." Frank Lloyd Wright, perhaps the greatest American architect of the twentieth century, applauded the Wainwright Building as signifying the birth of "the 'skyscraper' as a new thing under the sun."

Just as steel-frame buildings allowed cities to grow upward, so new forms of transportation permitted cities to expand outward. In the 1850s, horses pulled the first streetcars over iron rails laid in city streets. Some cities also had **elevated rail lines** powered by steam locomotives, but the smoke and soot from the coal they burned made them unpopular in urban areas. By the 1870s and 1880s, some cities boasted streetcar lines powered by underground moving cables. Electricity, however, finally revolutionized urban transit. Frank Sprague, a protégé of Thomas Edison, designed a streetcar driven by an electric motor that drew its power from an overhead wire. Sprague's system was first installed in Richmond, Virginia, in 1888. Electric streetcars replaced nearly all horse cars and cable cars within a dozen years. In the early 1900s, some large cities,

walking city   Term that urban historians use to describe cities before changes in urban transportation permitted cities to expand beyond the distance that a person could easily cover on foot.

Louis Sullivan   American architect of the late nineteenth century whose designs reflected his theory that the outward form of a building should express its function.

elevated rail line   A train that runs on a steel framework above a street, leaving the roadway free for other traffic.

This photograph, from about 1900, shows Wabash Avenue in downtown Chicago, where the elevated trains thundered between recently built multistory commercial buildings, some of which, in the distance, may have been among the nation's first skyscrapers. Elevated trains and streetcars greatly increased the size of cities, and the use of steel frames permitted city buildings to rise to heights that were previously impractical. *From* Birth of a Century, *Kea Publishing Services, Ltd.*

choked with traffic, began to move their electrical streetcars above or below street level, thereby creating elevated trains and subways. Thus, elaborate networks of rails came to crisscross most large cities, connecting suburban neighborhoods to central business districts. Middle-class women wearing white gloves and stylish hats rode on streetcars to well-stocked downtown department stores. Skilled workers took other streetcar lines to and from their jobs. Other lines carried the typists, bookkeepers, and corporate executives who filled the banks and offices in the city's center.

New construction technologies also launched bridges spanning rivers and bays that had once limited urban growth. When the Brooklyn Bridge was completed in 1883, it was hailed as a new wonder of the world. Other great bridges soon followed.

As bridges and streetcar lines pushed outward from the city's center, the old walking city expanded by annexing suburban areas. In 1860 Chicago had occupied 17 square miles; only thirty years later, it took in 178 square miles. During the same years, Boston grew from 5 square miles to 39, and St. Louis from 14 square miles to 61.

As streetcars expanded the city beyond distances that residents could cover on foot, suburban railroad lines began to bring more distant villages within commuting distance of urban centers.

Wealthier urban residents who could afford the passenger fare now left the city at the end of the workday. As early as 1873, nearly a hundred suburban communities sent between five and six thousand commuters into Chicago each day, and by 1890 seventy thousand suburbanites were pouring in daily. At about the same time, commuter lines brought more than a hundred thousand workers daily into New York City just from its northern suburbs.

Building an Urban Infrastructure

Caught up in headlong growth, cities developed with only minimal planning. Local governments did little to regulate expansion or create building standards in the public interest, leaving to individual landowners, developers, and builders most decisions about land use and construction practices. Everywhere, builders and owners hoped to achieve a high return on their investment by producing the most square footage for the least cost. Such profit calculations rarely left room for such amenities as varied designs or open space. Most of the great urban parks that exist today, including Central Park in New York City, Prospect Park in Brooklyn, and Golden Gate Park in San Francisco, were established on the outskirts of their cities, before the surrounding areas were developed.

Given the rapid and largely unplanned nature of most urban growth, city governments usually found it difficult to meet all the demands for expanded municipal utilities and services—fire and police protection, schools, sewage disposal, street maintenance, water supply.

The quality and quantity of the water supply varied greatly from city to city. Some cities spent enormous sums to transport water over long distances, but water quality remained a problem in most locales. As city officials began to understand that germs caused diseases, cities introduced filtration and **chlorination** of their water. Even so, by the early twentieth century, only 6 percent of urban residents received filtered water.

City residents also faced major obstacles in disposing of sewage, cleaning streets (especially given the ever-present horse), and removing garbage. Even when cities built sewer lines, they usually emptied the untreated sewage into some nearby body of water. The disgusted mayor of Cleveland in 1881 called the Cuyahoga River "an open sewer through the center of the city," but similar situations existed in most large cities.

Few city streets were paved, and most became mud holes in the rain, threw up clouds of dust in dry weather, and froze into deep ruts in the winter. Chicago in 1890 included 2,048 miles of streets, but only 629 miles were paved—and typically with wooden blocks. Chicago was not unusual in the proportion of its paved streets or its choice of paving materials. Only in the late nineteenth century did cities begin using asphalt paving. Sometimes it was easier to pave streets than to maintain them: after clearing garbage from a street in the 1890s, one Chicagoan discovered pavement buried under 18 inches of trash.

Private companies, operating under **franchises** from the city, typically supplied such city utilities and services as gas, public transit, sometimes water, and later electricity and telephone service. Entrepreneurs eagerly competed for such franchises, sometimes bribing city officials to secure them. As a result, new residential areas sometimes had gas lines before sewers and streetcars before paved streets.

Everywhere, urban growth seemed at first to outstrip the abilities of city officials and residents to provide for its consequences. Nonetheless most city utilities and services improved significantly between 1870 and 1900. New York City created the first uniformed police force in 1845, and other cities

followed. By 1871, all major cities had switched from volunteer fire companies to paid professional firefighters, but the **Great Chicago Fire** of 1871 dramatically demonstrated that even the new system was inadequate. The fire devastated 3 square miles, including much of the downtown, killed more than 250 people, and left 18,000 homeless. Such disasters spurred efforts to improve fire protection. Pressured by citizens and fire insurance companies, many city officials worked to train and equip firefighters and to regulate construction so that buildings were more fire-resistant. By 1900, most American cities had impressive firefighting forces, especially compared with those in other parts of the world. Chicago had more firefighters and fire engines than London, a city three times its size.

The New Urban Geography

The new technologies that transformed the urban **infrastructure** interacted with the growth of manufacturing, commerce, and finance to change the geography of American cities. In the largest cities, areas became increasingly specialized by economic function.

Early manufacturing in port cities was often scattered among warehouses near the waterfront. Clothing factories sometimes began in buildings formerly used by sail makers or as warehouses. Other manufacturing firms required specially designed facilities. Iron and steel making, meatpacking, shipbuilding, and oil refining had to be established on the outskirts of a city. There, open land was plentiful and relatively cheap, freight transportation was convenient, and the city center suffered less from the noise, smoke, and odor of heavy industry.

Many manufacturing workers could not afford to ride the new streetcars, so they often had no

---

chlorination The treatment of water with the chemical chlorine to kill germs.

franchise Government authorization allowing a company to provide a public service in a certain area.

Great Chicago Fire A fire that destroyed much of Chicago in 1871 and spurred national efforts to improve fire protection.

infrastructure Basic facilities that a society needs to function, such as transportation systems, water and power lines, and public institutions such as schools, post offices, and prisons.

Sears, Roebuck and Company issued this catalog of building plans in 1911, extending its mail-order business to the developing suburbs. The cover depicts a model middle-class suburb of the period—large, square houses with spacious porches, surrounded by well-tended lawns, facing quiet, tree-lined streets. *Sears, Roebuck and Company.*

choice but to live within walking distance of their work. Construction of industrial plants outside cities, therefore, usually meant working-class residential neighborhoods nearby. Some companies established planned communities: a manufacturing plant surrounded by residences, stores, and even parks and schools. Such company towns were sometimes well intended, but few earned good reputations among their residents. Workers whose employer was also their landlord and storekeeper usually resented the ever-present authority of the company—and the lack of alternatives to the rents and prices it charged.

At the same time that heavy manufacturing moved to the outskirts of the cities, areas in the city centers tended to become more specialized. By 1900 or so, the center of a large city usually had developed distinct districts. A district of light manufacturing might include clothing and printing factories. Next to or overlapping light manufacturing was often a wholesale trade district with warehouses and offices of **wholesalers**. **Retail** shopping districts, anchored by department stores, emerged in a central location, where streetcar and railroad lines could bring middle-class and upper-class shoppers from outlying areas. In the largest cities, banks, insurance companies, and headquarters of large corporations clustered to form a financial district. A hotel and entertainment district often lay close to the financial and retail blocks. These areas together made up a **central business district**.

Just as specialized downtown areas emerged according to economic function, so too did residential areas develop according to economic status. New suburbs ranged outward from the city center in order of wealth. Those who could afford to travel the farthest could also afford the most expensive

---

wholesaler Person engaged in the sale of goods in large quantities, usually for resale by a retailer.

retail Related to the sale of goods directly to consumers.

central business district The part of a city that includes most of its commercial, financial, and manufacturing establishments.

homes. Those too poor to ride the new transportation lines lived in densely populated and deteriorating neighborhoods in the center of the city or clustered around industrial plants. Much of the burgeoning urban middle class lived between the two extremes, far enough from the central business district that many residents rode streetcars downtown to work or shop, but outside the least desirable ring of tenement neighborhoods.

NEW PATTERNS OF URBAN LIFE

- How did the middle class adjust to the changing demands and opportunities of the era?
- What important new social patterns emerged in urban areas in the late nineteenth century?

The decades following the Civil War brought far-reaching social changes to nearly all parts of the nation. The burgeoning cities presented new vistas of opportunity for some, especially the middle class. In the new urban environments, some women questioned traditionally defined gender roles, as did gays and lesbians.

The New Middle Class

The Gilded Age brought significant changes to the lives of many middle-class Americans, especially urban dwellers. The development of giant corporations and central business districts was accompanied by the appearance of an army of accountants, lawyers, secretaries, insurance agents, and middle-level managers, who staffed corporate headquarters and professional offices. The new department stores succeeded by appealing to the growing urban middle class. Streetcar lines allowed members of the middle class to live beyond walking distance of their work. Thus industrialization and urban expansion produced not only large neighborhoods of the industrial working class and enclaves of the very wealthy, but also an expansion of distinctively middle-class neighborhoods and suburbs.

Single-family houses set amid wide and carefully tended lawns were common in many new middle-class neighborhoods, or **suburbs**, in the late nineteenth century. Such developments accelerated the tendency of American urban and suburban areas to sprawl for miles and to have population densities much lower than those of expanding European cities of the same time. Acquiring land had long

been a cornerstone of the American dream. In the late nineteenth century, the single-family house became the realization of that dream for many middle-class families. Many members of the middle class found it especially attractive to acquire that house in a suburb, outside the city but connected to it by streetcar tracks or a commuter rail line. Moving to a leafy middle-class suburb allowed them to avoid the congestion of the slums, the violence of labor conflicts, and the higher property taxes that funded city governments.

In the new middle-class suburbs and urban neighborhoods, households followed social patterns somewhat different from those of working-class or farm families. Middle-class families often employed a domestic servant to assist with household chores, and many middle-class women participated in social organizations outside the home. Middle-class parents rarely expected their children to contribute to the family's finances, and they usually insisting on their being educated at least through high school.

Middle-class families provided the major market for an expansion of daily newspapers, which began to include sections designed to appeal to women—household hints, fashion advice, and news of women's organizations—along with sports sections aimed largely at men and comics for the children. Joseph Pulitzer's *New York World* pioneered such innovations, and others soon emulated them. Urban middle-class households were also likely to subscribe to family magazines such as the *Ladies' Home Journal* and *Saturday Evening Post,* which included household advice, fiction, and news. Much of the advertising (see page 536) in such publications was aimed at the middle class, fostering the emergence of a so-called **consumer culture** among middle-class women, who became responsible for nearly all their families' shopping. Such publications, through both their articles and their advertising, also helped to extend middle-class patterns to readers across the country.

---

suburb   A residential area lying outside the boundaries of a city; many of the residents of suburbs work and shop in the city even though they live outside it.

consumer culture   A consumer is an individual who buys products for personal use; a consumer culture emphasizes the values and attitudes that derive from the participants' roles as consumers.

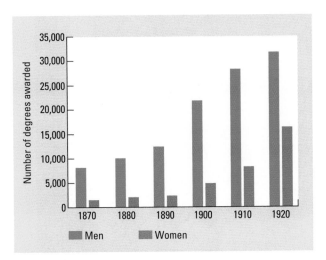

FIGURE 18.4 Number of First Degrees Awarded by Colleges and Universities, 1870–1920   This figure shows the change in the number of people receiving B.A., B.S., or other first college degrees, at ten-year intervals from 1870 to 1920. Notice that, after 1890, the number of women increased more rapidly than the number of men. *Source:* U.S. Department of Commerce, Bureau of the Census, *Historical Statistics of the United States, Colonial Times to 1970*, Bicentennial edition, 2 vols. (Washington: Government Printing Office, 1975), 1: 385–386.

Ferment in Education

Middle-class parents' concern for their children's education combined with other factors to produce important changes in American education, from **kindergarten** through university. The number of kindergartens—first created outside the public schools to provide childcare for working mothers—grew from two hundred in 1880 to three thousand in 1900. Kindergartens also began to be included in the public school system in some cities, beginning with St. Louis in 1873. Between 1870 and 1900, most northern and western states and territories established school attendance laws, requiring children between certain ages (usually 8 to 14) to attend school for a minimum number of weeks each year, typically twelve to sixteen. In the 1880s, New York City schools began to provide textbooks rather than requiring students to buy their own, and the practice expanded slowly. By 1898, ten states required school districts to provide textbooks to students without charge.

The largest increase in school attendance was at the secondary level. There were fewer than 800 high schools in the entire nation in 1878, but 5,500 by 1898. The proportion of high school graduates in the population tripled in the late nineteenth century. By 1890, high schools had extended to a fourth year (grades 9 through 12) everywhere but in the South. The high school curriculum also changed significantly, adding courses in the sciences, civics, business, home economics, and skills needed by industry, such as drafting, woodworking, and the mechanical trades. From 1870 onward, women outnumbered men among high school graduates. The growth of high schools, however, was largely an urban phenomenon. In rural areas, few students continued beyond the eighth grade.

College enrollments also grew, with the largest gains in the new state universities created under the Land-Grant College Act of 1862. Even so, college students came disproportionately from middle-class and upper-class families and rarely from farms. The college curriculum changed greatly, from a set of classical courses required of all students (mostly Latin, Greek, mathematics, rhetoric, and religion) to a system in which students focused on a major subject and chose courses from a list of electives. The Land-Grant College Act required its universities to provide instruction in engineering and agriculture. Other new college subjects included economics, political science, modern languages, and laboratory sciences. Many universities also began to offer courses in business administration and teaching. In 1870 the curricula in most colleges still resembled those of a century before. By 1900, curricula looked more like those of today.

Despite the growing female majority through the high school level, far fewer women than men marched in college graduation processions. Only one college graduate in seven was a woman in 1870, and this ratio improved only to one in four by 1900 (see Figure 18.4). In 1879 fewer than half of the nation's colleges admitted women, although most state universities did so. Twenty years later, four-fifths of all colleges, universities, and professional schools enrolled women.

Regardless of such impressive gains for coeducation, some colleges remained all-male enclaves,

kindergarten   German for "children's garden"; a preschool program developed in the late nineteenth century initially as childcare for working mothers; based on programs first developed in Germany.

Nannie Helen Burroughs, on the left, holding the banner, was a leader in the women's club movement and also in the Baptist church. By 1900, the women's auxiliary for black Baptist churches numbered more than a million members. *Library of Congress.*

especially prestigious private institutions such as Harvard, Princeton, and Yale. Colleges exclusively for women began to appear after the Civil War, partly because so many colleges still refused to admit women and partly in keeping with the notion that men and women should occupy "separate spheres." The first, founded in 1861, was **Vassar College**, whose faculty of eight men and twenty-two women included Maria Mitchell, a leading astronomer and the first female member of the American Academy of Arts and Sciences.

Redefining Gender Roles

Greater educational opportunities for women marked only one part of a major reconstruction of gender roles. Throughout the nineteenth century, most Americans had defined women's roles in domestic terms, as wife and mother and guardian of the family, responsible for its moral, spiritual, and physical well-being. This emphasis on **domesticity** also permitted women to take important roles in the church and the school. Business and politics, however, with their sometimes lax moral standards, were thought to pose a risk of corruption that might

> **Vassar College** The first collegiate institution for women, founded in Poughkeepsie, New York, in 1861.
>
> **domesticity** The notion common throughout much of the nineteenth century that women's activities were ideally rooted in domestic labor and the nurture of children.

endanger women's roles as their families' spiritual guardians. Domesticity, some argued, required women to occupy a so-called **separate sphere**, immune from such dangers. The Illinois Supreme Court even ruled, in 1870, that "God designed the sexes to occupy different spheres of action." Widely touted from the pulpits and in the journals of the day, the concepts of domesticity and separate spheres applied mostly to white middle-class and upper-class women in towns and cities. Farm women and working-class women (including most women of color) witnessed too much of the world to fit easily into the patterns of dainty innocence prescribed by advocates of separate spheres.

Domesticity and, especially, separate spheres came under increasing fire in the late nineteenth century. One challenge came through education, especially at colleges. As more and more women finished college, some entered the professions. An early breakthrough came in medicine. In 1849 Elizabeth Blackwell became the first woman to complete medical school, and she helped to open a medical school for women in 1868. By the 1880s, some twenty-five hundred women held medical degrees. By the end of the century, about 3 percent of all physicians were women, proportionately more than during most of the twentieth century. After 1900, however, medical schools imposed enrollment practices that sharply reduced the number of female medical students and hence physicians. Access to the legal profession proved even more difficult. Arabella Mansfield was the first woman to be admitted to the bar, in 1869, but the entire nation counted only sixty practicing women attorneys ten years later. Most law schools refused to admit women until the 1890s. Other professions also yielded very slowly to women seeking admission.

Professional careers attracted a few women, but many middle-class and upper-class women in towns and cities became involved in other women's activities. Women's clubs became popular among middle- and upper-class women in the late nineteenth century, claiming one hundred thousand members nationwide by the 1890s. Ida Wells, a crusader for black civil rights who, after marrying, was known as Ida Wells-Barnett, actively promoted the development of black women's clubs. Such clubs often began within the separate women's sphere as forums in which to discuss literature or art, but they sometimes led women out of their insulation and into reform activities. (Of course, women had publicly participated in reform before, especially in the movement to abolish slavery.) Women organized the **Women's Christian Temperance Union**, one of the most prominent women's reform organizations, in 1874. Female participation swelled the ranks and produced leaders for a variety of reform organizations, especially those linked to domesticity—**temperance**, opposition to prostitution, and abolition of child labor.

Women's church organizations, clubs, and reform societies all provided experience in working together toward a common cause and sometimes in seeking changes in public policy. Through them, women developed networks of working relationships and cultivated leadership skills. These experiences and contacts contributed to the growing effectiveness of women's efforts to establish their right to vote (see pages 562–563).

Just as women's gender roles were undergoing reconstruction in the late nineteenth century, so too were those of men. In the early nineteenth century, manliness was defined largely in terms of "character," which included courage, honor, independence, duty, and loyalty (including loyalty to a political party), along with providing a good home for a family. With the growth of the urban industrial society, fewer men were self-employed (and thus no longer "independent"), and fewer men had the opportunity to demonstrate courage or boldness. The rise of big-city political organizations dominated by saloonkeepers and working-class immigrants caused some middle- and upper-class males to question older notions of party loyalty.

In response, some middle-class men seem to have turned to organizations and activities that emphasized male bonding or masculinity. Fraternal organizations modeled on the Masons and Odd Fellows multiplied in the late nineteenth century, usually providing both a ritualistic retreat to a pre-industrial

---

separate sphere   The notion that men and women should engage in different activities: women were to focus on the family, church, and school, whereas men were to support the family financially and take part in politics, activities considered too competitive and corrupt for women.

Women's Christian Temperance Union   Women's organization founded in 1874 that opposed alcohol beverages and supported reforms such as woman suffrage.

temperance   Self-restraint in eating and drinking; in the U.S., 1850–1930, temperance also came to mean complete abstinence from alcohol.

era and meager insurance benefits for widows and orphans. Professional athletics, including baseball and boxing, began to attract large numbers of middle- and upper-class male spectators. The Young Men's Christian Association (YMCA) spread rapidly in American cities after the Civil War, emphasizing Christian values, physical fitness, and service. Wilderness camping and hunting—necessities for many Americans in earlier times—became a middle-class and upper-class male sport, a demonstration of masculinity. Theodore Roosevelt delighted in hunting big game, claiming that it promoted the manly virtues of "nerve control" and "cool-headedness." He specified that "the dweller in cities" had fewer opportunities "to keep his body sound and vigorous," but that "bodily vigor" was necessary for "vigor of the soul."

Emergence of a Gay and Lesbian Subculture

Urbanization and economic change contributed to the social redefinition of gender roles for middle-class women and men, but a quite different redefinition occurred at the same time, as burgeoning cities provided a setting for the development of gay and lesbian subcultures.

Homosexual behavior was illegal in all states and territories throughout the nineteenth and early twentieth centuries. At the same time, however, men and women engaged in a wide variety of socially acceptable same-sex relationships. The concept of separate spheres and the tendency for most schools and workplaces to be segregated by sex meant that many men and women spent much of their time with others of their own sex. Many occupations involved working closely with a partner, sometimes over long periods of time. Such partners—both male or both female—could speak of each other with deep affection without violating prevailing social norms. Same-sex relationships may not have involved physical contact, although kisses and hugs—and sleeping in the same bed—were common expressions of affection among young women. Participants in such same-sex relationships did not consider themselves to be committing what the laws called "an unnatural act," and most of them married partners of the opposite sex.

Same-sex relationships that involved genital contact, however, violated both the law and the expectations of society. In rural communities, where most people knew one another, people physically attracted to those of their own sex seem to have suppressed such tendencies or to have exercised them very discreetly. The record of convictions for **sodomy** indicates, however, that some failed to conceal their activities. A few men and somewhat more women changed their dress and behavior, passed for a member of the other sex, and married someone of their own sex.

In the late nineteenth century, in parts of the United States and Europe, burgeoning cities permitted an anonymity not possible in rural societies. Homosexuals and lesbians gravitated toward the largest cities and began to create distinctive **subcultures**. By the 1890s, one researcher reported "perverts of both sexes maintained a sort of social set-up in New York City, had their places of meeting, and [the] advantage of police protection." Reports of regular homosexual meeting places—clubs, restaurants, steam baths, parks, streets—also issued from Boston, Chicago, New Orleans, St. Louis, and San Francisco. Although most participants in these subcultures were secretive, some flaunted their sexuality. In a few places, "drag balls" featured cross-dressing, especially by men.

In the 1880s, physicians began to study members of these emerging subcultures and created medical names for them, including "homosexual," "lesbian," "invert," and "pervert." Earlier, law and religion had defined particular actions as illegal or immoral. The new, clinical definitions emphasized not the actions but instead the persons taking the actions. Some theorists in the 1880s and 1890s proposed that such behavior resulted from a mental disease, but others concluded that homosexuals and lesbians were born so.

New medical and legal definitions of homosexuality were accompanied by a similar delineation of heterosexuality. As medical and legal definitions shifted from actions to persons, the nature of same-sex relationships also changed. Once-acceptable behavior, including expressions of affection between heterosexuals of the same sex, became less common as individuals tried to avoid any suggestion that they were anything but heterosexual.

---

sodomy Varieties of sexual intercourse prohibited by law in the nineteenth century, typically including intercourse between two males.

subculture A group whose members differ from the dominant culture on the basis of some values or interests but who share most values and interests with the dominant culture.

THE POLITICS OF STALEMATE

• Compare the presidencies of Garfield, Arthur, and Cleveland. Which do you consider more successful? Why?

• What were some of the goals of the different reform groups, such as the Grangers and Greenbackers (discussed in Chapter 17), civil service reformers, prohibitionists, and supporters of woman suffrage? Why were some reformers able to accomplish more than others?

During the 1880s, as the nation's economy and social patterns changed with astonishing speed, American politics ironically seemed to be stalled at dead center. From the end of the Civil War to the mid-1870s, much of American politics had revolved around issues arising out of the war. By the late 1870s, other issues emerged as crucial, notably the economy and political corruption. After the mid-1870s, however, voters divided almost evenly between the two major political parties, beginning a long political **stalemate** during which neither party enacted significant new policies.

The Presidencies of Garfield and Arthur

As Rutherford B. Hayes neared the end of his term as president—a term made difficult by his conflicts with Roscoe Conkling and the railway strike of 1877 (see pages 521–522)—Republican leaders looked for a presidential candidate who could lead them to victory in 1880. James G. Blaine of Maine, a spellbinding orator who attracted loyal supporters and bitter enemies, sought the party's nomination. Conkling and his followers, calling themselves **Stalwarts**, tried to nominate former president Grant instead. Few major differences of policy separated Conkling from Blaine. Conkling showed more commitment to the spoils system and the defense of southern black voters, and Blaine took more interest in the protective tariff and economic policies, encouraging industrialization and western economic development. Conkling, however, dismissed Blaine and his supporters as **Half-Breeds**—not real Republicans.

After a frustrating convention deadlock, the Republicans compromised by nominating James A. Garfield, a congressman from Ohio. Born in a log cabin, Garfield had grown up in poverty. A minister, college president, and lawyer before the Civil War, he became the Union's youngest major general. For vice president, the delegates tried to placate the Stalwarts and secure New York's electoral votes by nominating Conkling's chief lieutenant, Chester A. Arthur.

The Democrats nominated Winfield Scott Hancock, a former Civil War general with little political experience. Both candidates worked at avoiding matters of substance during the campaign. Garfield won the popular vote by only half a percentage point. He won the electoral vote convincingly, however, even though he failed to carry a single southern state. Republicans, it appeared, could win the White House without the southern black vote.

Garfield brought to the presidency a solid understanding of Congress and a careful and studious approach to issues. Hoping to work cooperatively with both Stalwarts and Blaine supporters, he appointed Blaine as secretary of state, the most prestigious cabinet position. Discord soon threatened when Conkling demanded the right to name his supporters to key federal positions. In response, Garfield showed himself to be shrewder politically than any president since Lincoln. When Conkling acknowledged defeat by resigning from the Senate, Garfield scored a victory for a stronger presidency.

On July 2, 1881, four months after taking the oath of office, Garfield was shot while walking through a Washington railroad station. His assassin, Charles Guiteau, a mentally unstable religious fanatic, called himself "a Stalwart of the Stalwarts" and claimed he had acted to save the Republican Party. Two months later, Garfield died of the wound.

Chester A. Arthur became president. Long a close ally of Conkling, Arthur was probably best known as a capable administrator and a dapper dresser. However, as one of his former associates said, he soon showed that "He isn't 'Chet' Arthur any more; he's the President." In 1882 doctors diagnosed the president as suffering from Bright's disease, a kidney condition that produced fatigue, depression, and eventually death. Arthur kept the news

---

stalemate   A deadlock; a situation in which no one can move forward.

Stalwarts   Faction of the Republican Party led by Roscoe Conkling of New York; as the name implies, Stalwarts claimed to be the genuine Republicans.

Half-Breeds   Insulting name that Roscoe Conkling gave to his opponents (especially James Blaine) within the Republican Party to suggest that they were not fully committed to Republican ideals.

secret from all but his family and closest friends. Overcoming both political liabilities and his own physical limitations, Arthur proved a competent president.

Reforming the Spoils System

The Republicans had slim majorities in Congress after the 1880 election, but the Democrats recovered control over the House of Representatives in 1882. Acting quickly, before the newly elected Democrats took their seats, the Republicans enacted the first major tariff revision in eight years and the **Pendleton Act** reforming the civil service. Both measures had support from a few Democrats.

Named for its sponsor, Senator George Pendleton (an Ohio Democrat), the Pendleton Act had far-reaching consequences, for it brought into being a merit system for filling federal positions to replace the long-criticized spoils system. The new law designated certain federal positions, initially about 15 percent of the total, as "classified." **Classified civil service** positions were to be filled only through competitive examinations.

The law also authorized the president to add positions to the classified list. When an office was first classified, the patronage appointee then holding it was protected from removal for political reasons. Presidents could therefore use the law to entrench their own appointees. When those appointees retired, however, their replacements came through the merit system. Thus the law used patronage in the short run to bring the long-term demise of the patronage system. Within twenty years, the law applied to 44 percent of federal employees. Most state and local governments eventually adopted merit systems as well. Arthur's approval of the measure marked his final break with the Stalwarts.

The most persistent critics of the spoils systems—and those who most loudly claimed credit for the Pendleton Act—were a group known as **Mugwumps** to their contemporaries. Centered in Boston and New York, most of these reformers were Republicans of high social status. They traced many of the defects of politics to the spoils system, and they argued that eliminating patronage would drive out the machines and opportunists. Only then, they insisted, could corruption be eliminated and political decency restored. Instead of basing appointments on political loyalty, the Mugwumps advocated a merit system based on a job seeker's ability to pass a comprehensive examination. Educated, dedicated civil servants, they believed, would stand above party politics and provide capable and honest administration.

Cleveland and the Democrats

In the end, Arthur proved more capable than anyone might have predicted. Given his failing health, he exerted little effort to win his party's nomination in 1884. Blaine—charming and quick-witted—secured the Republican nomination. The Democrats nominated Grover Cleveland, who as governor of New York had earned a reputation for integrity and political courage, particularly by attacking **Tammany Hall**, the dominant Democratic Party organization in New York City. Many Irish voters, who made up a large component in Tammany, retaliated by supporting Blaine even though they were staunch Democrats.

The 1884 campaign quickly turned nasty. Many Mugwumps disliked Blaine and revealed an old letter of his urging a cover-up of allegations that he had profited from pro-railroad legislation. When the Mugwumps broke with their party, they drew the contempt of most party politicians. Blaine called them "conceited, foolish . . . pretentious but not powerful." Other party politicians questioned the Mugwumps' manhood, reflecting the extent to which being a loyal party member was closely tied to the male gender role in the minds of many.

Blaine supporters gleefully trumpeted that Cleveland had avoided military service during the Civil War and had fathered a child outside marriage. Democrats chanted, "Blaine, Blaine, James G. Blaine! The continental liar from the state of Maine." Republicans shouted back, "Ma! Ma! Where's my pa?"

Pendleton Act Law passed by Congress in 1883 that created the Civil Service Commission and instituted the merit system for federal hiring and jobs.

classified civil service Federal jobs filled through the merit system instead of by patronage.

Mugwumps Reformers, mostly Republicans, who opposed political corruption and campaigned for reform, especially reform of the civil service, in the 1880s and 1890s, sometimes crossing party boundaries to achieve their goals.

Tammany Hall A New York City political organization that dominated city and sometimes state politics by dominating the Democratic Party in New York City.

The election hinged on New York State, where Blaine expected to cut deeply into the usually Democratic Irish vote. A few days before the election, however, Blaine heard a preacher in New York City call the Democrats the party of "rum, Romanism [Catholicism], and rebellion." Blaine ignored this insult to his Irish Catholic supporters until newspapers blasted it the next day. By then the damage was done. Cleveland won New York by a tiny margin, and New York's electoral votes gave him the presidency.

Cleveland enjoyed support from many who opposed the spoils system, already being whittled away by the Pendleton Act. Though Cleveland did not dismantle the patronage system, he did insist on demonstrated ability in those he appointed to office. He was also deeply committed to minimal government and cutting federal spending. Between 1885 and 1889, Cleveland vetoed 414 bills—most of them granting pensions to individual Union veterans—twice as many vetoes as all previous presidents combined. Cleveland provided little leadership regarding legislation but did approve several important measures produced by the Democratic House and Republican Senate, including the Dawes Severalty Act (see Chapter 19) and the Interstate Commerce Act.

The Interstate Commerce Act grew out of political pressure from farmers and small businesses. In the early 1870s, several midwestern states passed laws regulating railroad freight rates (usually called Granger laws; see page 519). Though the Supreme Court, in *Munn v. Illinois*, had agreed that businesses with "a public interest" were subject to regulation, later, in *Wabash Railway v. Illinois* (1886), the court significantly limited states' power to regulate railroad rates involving interstate commerce.

In response to the *Wabash* decision and continuing protests over railroad rate discrimination, Congress passed the Interstate Commerce Act in 1887. The new law created the **Interstate Commerce Commission** (ICC), the first federal regulatory commission. The law also prohibited pools, rebates, and differential rates for short and long hauls, and it required that rates be "reasonable and just." The ICC had little real power, however, until the Hepburn Act strengthened it in 1906.

Cleveland considered the nation's greatest problem to be the federal budget surplus. After the Civil War, the tariff usually generated more income than the country needed to pay federal expenses (see Figure 18.5). Throughout the 1880s, the annual surplus often exceeded $100 million. Worried that the surplus encouraged wasteful spending, Cleveland demanded in 1887 that Congress cut tariff rates. He hoped not only to reduce federal income but also, by reducing prices on raw materials, to encourage companies to compete with recently developed monopolies.

Cleveland's action provoked a serious division within his own party. So long as Democrats did not have responsibility for the tariff, they could criticize Republican policies without restraint. Urged to take positive action by their own party chief, however, they failed. Cleveland exerted little leadership, leaving the initiative to congressional leaders. The Democratic majority in the House of Representatives created a bill with little resemblance to Cleveland's proposal but with ample benefits for the South, and the Republican majority in the Senate responded with amendments targeting southern economic interests. In the end, Congress adjourned without voting on the bill, and Cleveland's call for tariff reform came to nothing.

In the 1888 presidential election, the Democrats renominated Cleveland, but he backed off from the tariff issue and did little campaigning. The Republicans nominated Benjamin Harrison, senator from Indiana and a former Civil War general. Known as thoughtful and cautious, Harrison also impressed many as cool and distant. The Republicans launched a vigorous campaign focused on the virtues of the protective tariff. They raised unprecedented amounts of campaign money by systematically approaching business leaders on the tariff issue, and they issued more campaign materials than ever before. Harrison received fewer popular votes than Cleveland (47.9 percent to Cleveland's 48.7 percent), but he won in the Electoral College. As important for the Republicans as their narrow presidential victory, however, were the majorities they secured in both House and Senate. (For the Fifty-first Congress, see page 605.)

The Mixed Blessings of Urban Machine Politics

In most cities, politics meant something very different from what it meant in the corridors and salons of Washington. Throughout the late nineteenth century,

Interstate Commerce Commission The first federal regulatory commission, created to regulate railroads.

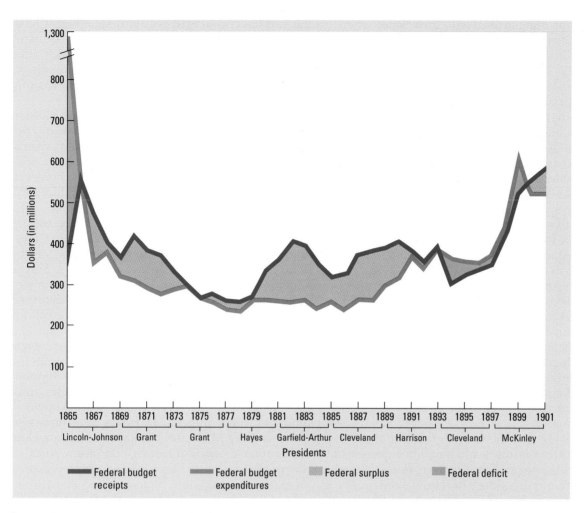

FIGURE 18.5 Federal Receipts and Expenditures, 1865–1901   The surplus usually shrank during economic downturns (the mid-1870s and mid-1890s) and grew in more prosperous periods (1880s). During the Harrison administration, however, the surplus virtually disappeared although the economy remained generally prosperous, reflecting efforts to reduce income and increase expenditures. *Source:* U.S. Department of Commerce, Bureau of the Census, *Historical Statistics of the United States, Colonial Times to 1970,* Bicentennial edition, 2 vols. (Washington, D.C.: U.S. Government Printing Office, 1975), 1: 1104.

big-city politicians built loyal followings in poor neighborhoods by addressing the residents' needs directly and personally. In return, they wanted political loyalty from the poor. Such urban political organizations flourished during the years 1880–1910, and some survived long after that.

In 1905 a newspaper reporter published a series of conversations with a long-time participant in New York City politics, George W. Plunkitt. Plunkitt's observations provide insights into the nature of urban politics and its relation to urban poverty. Born in a poor Irish neighborhood of New York City, Plunkitt left school at the age of 11. He

entered politics, eventually becoming a district leader of Tammany Hall, which dominated the city's Democratic Party. Between 1868 and 1904, he also served in a number of elected positions in state and city government. Plunkitt described to the reporter his formula for keeping the loyalty of the voters in his neighborhood.

Go right down among the poor families and help them in the different ways they need help. . . . It's philanthropy, but it's politics, too—mighty good politics. . . . The poor are the most grateful people in the world, and, let me tell you, they have more

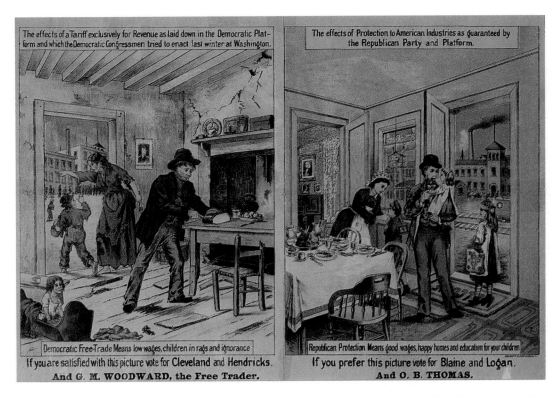

The effects of a Tariff exclusively for Revenue as laid down in the Democratic Platform and which the Democratic Congressmen tried to enact last winter at Washington.	The effects of Protection to American Industries as guaranteed by the Republican Party and Platform.

Democratic Free-Trade Means low wages, children in rags and ignorance

**If you are satisfied with this picture vote for Cleveland and Hendricks.
And G. M. WOODWARD, the Free Trader.**

Republican Protection Means good wages, happy homes and education for your children

**If you prefer this picture vote for Blaine and Logan.
And O. B. THOMAS.**

Republicans circulated this cartoon in 1884, claiming that the Democrats' proposed tariff reform would threaten wage levels and endanger little children, but Republicans' commitment to the protective tariff would protect wage levels and make families more secure. *Museum of American Political Life/photo by Steve Laschever.*

friends in their neighborhoods than the rich have in theirs. If there's a family in my district in want I know it before the charitable societies, and me and my men are first on the ground. . . . The consequence is that the poor look up to George W. Plunkitt as a father, come to him in trouble—and don't forget him on election day.

Plunkitt typified many big-city politicians across the country. Because neighborhood saloons sometimes served as social gathering places for working-class men, would-be politicians frequented saloons—in fact, they sometimes owned them—and tried to build a personal rapport with the voters at the bar. They responded to the needs of the urban poor by providing a bucket of coal on a cold day, or a basket of food at Thanksgiving, or a job in some city department. In return, they expected the people they assisted to follow their lead in politics. Political organizations based among working-class and poor voters, usually led by men of poor immigrant parentage, emerged in

nearly all large cities and experienced varying degrees of political success. Where they amassed great power, their rivals denounced the leader as a boss and the organization as a machine.

In every city, opponents of the machine charged corruption. Most bosses were cautious, but some accumulated sizable fortunes—sometimes through gifts or retainers from companies seeking franchises or city contracts (their critics called these bribes), sometimes through advance knowledge of city planning. Richard Croker, the boss of Tammany in the 1890s, accumulated an immense personal fortune, but he always insisted that he had never taken a dishonest dollar. Above all, the bosses centralized political decision making. A machine politician in Boston, for example, insisted, "There's got to be in every ward somebody that any bloke can come to—no matter what he's done—to get help." If a pushcart vender needed a permit to sell tinware, or a railroad president needed permission to build a bridge, or a saloonkeeper wanted to stay open on

This sketch of women voting in Cheyenne, Wyoming Territory, appeared in 1888. In 1869, Wyoming became the first state or territory to extend suffrage to women. This drawing appeared shortly before Wyoming requested statehood, a request made controversial by the issue of woman suffrage. *Library of Congress.*

part in reform efforts, even though they could not cast a ballot on election day, and a few even sought to take part in party activities. In the late nineteenth century, some women also pushed for full political participation through the right to vote.

The struggle for woman suffrage was of long standing. In 1848 Elizabeth Cady Stanton and four other women organized the world's first Women's Rights Convention, held at Seneca Falls, New York. The participants drafted a Declaration of Principles that announced, in part, "It is the duty of the women of this country to secure to themselves their sacred right to the elective franchise." Stanton became the most prominent leader in the struggle for women's rights, especially voting rights, from 1848 until her death in 1902. After 1851, Susan B. Anthony became her constant partner in these efforts. They achieved some success in convincing lawmakers to modify laws that discriminated against women but failed to change laws that limited voting to men. During the nineteenth century, however, women increasingly participated in public affairs: movements to abolish slavery, mobilize support for the Union, improve educational opportunities, end child labor, and more.

In 1866 Stanton and Anthony unsuccessfully opposed inclusion of the word *male* in the Fourteenth Amendment (see page 473). In 1869 they formed the **National Woman Suffrage Association** (NWSA), its membership open only to women. The NWSA sought an amendment to the federal Constitution as the only sure route to woman suffrage. It built alliances with other reform and radical organizations and worked to improve women's status. For example, members pressed for easier divorce laws and birth control (which Stanton called "self-sovereignty") and promoted women's trade unions. By contrast, the **American Woman Suffrage Association** (AWSA), organized by Lucy Stone and other suffrage advocates, also in 1869, concentrated strictly on winning the right to vote and avoided other issues. For twenty years, these two organizations led the suffrage cause,

Sunday in violation of the law, the machine could help them all—if they showed the proper gratitude in return. Always, the machine cultivated its base of support among poor and working-class voters.

Challenging the Male Bastion: Woman Suffrage

In the masculine political world of the Gilded Age, men expected one another to display strong loyalty to a political party, but they considered women— who could not vote—to stand outside the party system. The concepts of domesticity and separate spheres dictated that women avoid politics, especially party politics. In fact, some women did involve themselves in political struggles by taking

National Woman Suffrage Association   Women's suffrage organization led by Elizabeth Cady Stanton and Susan B. Anthony; it accepted only women as members and worked for related issues such as unionizing female workers.

American Woman Suffrage Association   Boston-based women's suffrage organization led by Lucy Stone, Julia Ward Howe, and others; it welcomed men and worked solely to win the vote for women.

disagreeing not on the goal but on the way to achieve it. They merged in 1890, under Stanton's leadership, to become the National American Woman Suffrage Association. Until the early twentieth century, however, their support came largely from middle-class women—and men—who were largely of old-stock American Protestant descent.

The first victories for suffrage came in the West. In 1869, in Wyoming Territory, the territorial legislature extended the **franchise** to women. At the time, Wyoming was home to about seven thousand men but only two thousand women. Wyoming women had forged a well-organized suffrage movement, and they may have persuaded some male legislators. At the same time, other legislators may have hoped that woman suffrage would attract more women to Wyoming. Thus, women in Wyoming Territory could—and did—vote, serve on juries, and hold elective office. In 1889, when Wyoming asked for statehood, some congressmen balked at admitting a state with woman suffrage. Wyoming legislators, however, bluntly stated, "We will remain out of the Union a hundred years rather than come in without the women." Finally Congress voted to approve Wyoming statehood—with woman suffrage—in 1890.

Utah Territory adopted woman suffrage in 1870. Mormon men formed the majority of Utah's voters, and Mormon women far outnumbered the relatively few non-Mormon women. By enfranchising women, Mormons strengthened their voting majority and may have hoped, at the same time, to silence the critics who claimed that **polygamy** degraded women. However, in an act aimed primarily at the Mormons, Congress outlawed polygamy in 1887 and simultaneously disfranchised the women in Utah. Not until Utah became a state, in 1896, did its women regain the vote.

In 1893 Colorado voters (all male) approved woman suffrage, making Colorado the first state to adopt woman suffrage through a popular vote. In addition to a well-organized campaign by Colorado women, their cause was assisted by support from the new Populist Party (see Chapter 20). In Idaho, where both Mormon and Populist influences were strong, male voters approved woman suffrage in 1896.

In addition, several states began to extend limited voting rights to women, especially on matters outside party politics, such as school board elections and school bond issues. These concessions perhaps reflected the widespread assumption that women's gender roles included child rearing. By 1890, women could vote in school elections in nineteen states and on bond and tax issues in three.

Structural Change and Policy Change

The Grangers, Greenbackers (see pages 519–520), local labor parties with ties to the Knights of Labor, the WCTU, Mugwumps, and advocates of woman suffrage all challenged basic features of the party-bound political system of the Gilded Age. They and other groups sought political changes that the major parties ignored: abolition of the spoils system, woman suffrage, prohibition, the **secret ballot**, regulation of business, an end to child labor, a monetary policy that did not disadvantage debtors, and more.

Most of these groups called themselves reformers, meaning that they wanted to change the form of politics. Most reforms fall into one of two categories—structural change and policy change. Structural change, or structural reform, modifies the *structure* of political decision making. Structural issues include the way in which public officials are chosen—for example, the convention system for making nominations, voting, and the appointment of government employees. Those seeking to eliminate the spoils system and substitute the merit system, therefore, addressed one element in the structure of politics. Eligibility to vote was another. Woman suffrage was therefore a structural change.

Policy issues, in contrast, have to do with the way that governmental power is used to accomplish particular objectives. The debate over federal economic policy in the Gilded Age provides an array of contrasting positions. Many Democrats favored a policy of laissez faire, believing that federal interference in the economy created a privileged class. Most Republicans favored a policy of distribution, meaning that they wanted to distribute benefits (land, tariff protection) to companies and individuals to encourage economic growth. Grangers favored regulation: they wanted the government to enforce basic rules governing economic activity—in this case, by prohibiting pools and rebates and setting

---

franchise   As used here, the right to vote; another word for suffrage.

polygamy   The practice of a man having more than one wife; Mormons refer to this practice, common to their religion, as plural marriage.

secret ballot   The practice of marking one's ballot in private; also called the Australian ballot because it originated there.

policy   A course of action adopted by a government, usually one that is pursued over a period of time and may involve several different laws and agencies.

maximum rates. Greenbackers wanted to use monetary policy to benefit debtors—or, as they would have put it, to replace a monetary policy that benefited lenders.

Groups seeking change may find they have little in common, or they may overlook differences to cooperate with other groups. Frances Willard of the WCTU, for example, embraced a wide range of reforms. One key distinction between the National Woman Suffrage Association and the American Woman Suffrage Association was that the NWSA often welcomed political alliances with groups such as the Greenbackers, who supported suffrage for all citizens in 1880. The AWSA, fearing that such alliances would lose more support for suffrage than they gained, chose a narrow focus on the suffrage issue.

Some groups combined structural and policy proposals. The tiny Prohibition Party, for example, wanted government to eliminate alcohol, but the Prohibitionists also favored woman suffrage because they assumed that most women voters would oppose alcohol. In this instance, they promoted a structural reform, woman suffrage, not just for its own sake but also to accomplish a policy reform, prohibition of alcohol. Advocates of woman suffrage also argued that enfranchising women would lead to a new approach to politics and to new policies.

One important structural change received widespread support from many political groups, and many states adopted it soon after its first appearance. The Australian ballot—printed and distributed by the government, not by political parties, listing all candidates of all parties, and marked in a private voting booth—was adopted by the first states in the late 1880s. The idea spread rapidly and was in use in most states by 1892. This reform carried important implications for political parties. No longer did voters find it difficult to cross party lines and vote a split ticket. No longer could party activists see which party's ballot a voter dropped into the ballot box. The switch to the Australian ballot and the Pendleton Act marked the first significant efforts to limit parties' power and influence.

The United States and the World, 1880–1889

Presidents Garfield, Arthur, and Cleveland spent little time on foreign relations and paid little attention to the army and navy. After the end of most conflicts with American Indians in the late 1870s and early 1880s (discussed in Chapter 19), the army was limited to a few garrisons, most of them near Indian reservations. The navy's wooden sailing vessels deteriorated to the point that some people ridiculed them as fit only for firewood. When a coal barge accidentally ran down a navy ship, one congressman joked that the worn-out navy was too slow even to get out of the way!

Whether from embarrassment or insight, Congress, in 1882, authorized construction of two steam-powered cruisers—the first new ships since the Civil War—and four more ships in 1883. Still, Secretary of the Navy William C. Whitney announced in 1885 that "we have nothing which deserves to be called a navy." Whitney persuaded Congress to fund several more cruisers and the first two modern battleships. Though Congress approved these ships, most federal decision makers still understood the role of the navy as limited to protecting American coasts.

Diplomacy was similarly routine. The most active American secretary of state also served the shortest term. James G. Blaine, Garfield's secretary of state, promoted closer relations with Latin America partly to encourage more trade among the nations of the Western Hemisphere—including more opportunities for the sale of products from the United States. He believed, too, that the United States should take a more active role among Latin American nations in resolving problems that might lead to war or European intervention. But when Garfield died, Arthur replaced Blaine at State, and Blaine's ambitious plans for hemispheric cooperation were scrapped.

Hawai`i continued to attract the attention of some American entrepreneurs and policymakers. Despite the economic ties between Hawai`i and the United States that had developed through the sugar trade and other connections, relations between King David Kalakaua and the *haole* business and planter community of Hawai`i were never comfortable. Kalakaua wanted to preserve political power for **indigenous** Hawaiians, but haoles charged that he was ignoring the needs of business and the sugar plantations and that he protected corrupt officials.

In 1887 the news broke that Kalakaua himself had profited from bribery related to licenses for selling opium. Leaders of the haole community quickly

---

haole Hawaiian word for persons not of native Hawaiian ancestry, especially whites.

indigenous Original to an area.

forced a constitution on Kalakaua, reducing him to little more than a figurehead. Haoles soon dominated much of the government. That same year, Kalakaua approved the extension of the reciprocity treaty of 1875, with an additional provision giving the U.S. Navy exclusive rights to use Pearl Harbor. (The secretary of the navy admitted at the time, though, that he had no ships to send there.) Among some members of the royal family, resentment festered over the new constitution, the Pearl Harbor provision, and especially the extent of haole control, resentments that boiled over after Kalakaua's death in 1891.

Samoa, in the South Pacific, likewise attracted attention from the United States, and also from Britain and Germany. When German activity suggested an attempt at annexation, President Cleveland vowed to maintain Samoan independence. All three nations dispatched warships to the vicinity in 1889, and conflict seemed likely until a typhoon scattered the ships. A conference in Berlin then produced a treaty that provided for Samoan independence under the protection of the three Western nations.

> **Samoa**   A group of volcanic and mountainous islands in the South Pacific.

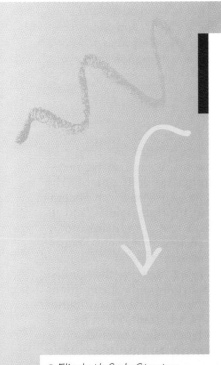

INDIVIDUAL VOICES

Examining a Primary Source

Frances Willard Proposes Making the Whole World Homelike

Frances Willard had been involved with the WCTU since 1874 and had been its president for the preceding twelve years. By 1891, when Willard gave the following speech to a gathering of women, the WCTU had become one of the largest and most influential lobbying organizations in the nation.

Beloved Friends and Comrades in a Sacred Cause:
"A difference of opinion on one question must not prevent us from working unitedly on those on which we can agree." . . .

The name of her who uttered words so harmonious is Elizabeth Cady Stanton, and it shall live forever in the annals of woman's heroic struggle up from sexhood into humanhood. Our friends have said that, as President of the National American Woman Suffrage Association, Mrs. Stanton leads the largest army of women outside, and I the largest one inside, the realm of a conservative theology. However this may be, I rejoice to see the day when, with distinctly avowed loyalty to my Methodist faith, and as distinctly avowed respect for the sincerity with which she holds to views quite different, I can clasp hands in loyal comradeship with one whose dauntless voice rang out over the Nation for "woman's rights" when I was but a romping girl upon a prairie farm. . . . ●

● *Elizabeth Cady Stanton was the best-known advocate of woman suffrage at that time. How does Willard signal her differences with Stanton?*

● The references to "gold-bug" and "silver pin" refer to the contemporary political dispute over the coining of silver versus the gold standard. "White slavery" was the term that reformers applied to prostitution. Why do you think Willard listed these particular locations for white slaves?

● How does this speech illustrate Willard's reputation as a "broad-gauge" reformer? What groups did she look to as allies?

● How do these comments reflect Willard's slogan, "Do everything," and her commitment "to make the whole world homelike"?

Every atom says to every other one, "Combine," and, doing so, they change chaos into order. When every woman shall say to every other, and every workman shall say to every other, "Combine," the war-dragon shall be slain, the poverty-viper shall be exterminated, the gold-bug transfixed by a silver pin, the saloon drowned out, and the last white slave liberated from the woods of Wisconsin and the bagnios [brothels] of Chicago and Washington. ●

For combination is "a game that two can play at"; the millionaires have taught us how, and the labor-tortoise is fast overtaking the capitalistic hare. . . .

Our expectation of justice is not in the lily-handed men of college, court, and cloister, but in the farmers whose "higher education" has been the Grange, and in the mechanics trained by trades-unions and the Knights of Labor. These are the men who have been known to go on strike because sewing women toiled at starving rates; who stand stoutly by their motto, "equal pay for equal work;" who declare in their platforms that we shall have the ballot, and who are the force that shall yet bring about an evenness between the eight-hour day of the husband and the sixteen-hour day of the wife! . . . ●

The whole rationale of women's place in finance and politics is set forth in the remark of a Knight of Labor, who, referring to an undesirable locality, said, "It's not a fit place for a woman," and the quick reply of a comrade, "Then it's time for women to go down there and make it fit." . . .

We hope to start upon their journey around the world a commission of women in charge of our great petition, which asks the governments of all nations to separate themselves from all legal complicity with the trade in opium and alcohol. . . . I have come with the world's petition against alcohol and opium; another, in which the signers agree not to wear as trimmings the bodies or plumage of birds, and a third, asking the Russian Government to show mercy to the exiles of Siberia. ●

SUMMARY

In the Gilded Age, as industrialization transformed the economy, urbanization and immigration challenged many established social patterns. John D. Rockefeller was one of the best known of many entrepreneurs who created manufacturing operations of unprecedented size and complexity, producing oligopoly and vertical integration in many industries. Technology and advertising emerged as important competitive devices. Investment bankers, notably J. P. Morgan, led in combining separate rail companies into larger and more profitable systems. Some southerners proclaimed the creation of a New South and promoted industrialization and a more diversified agricultural base. The outcome was mixed—the South did acquire significant industry, but the region's poverty was little reduced.

Espousing cooperatives and reform, the Knights of Labor chose to open their membership to the unskilled, to African Americans, and to women—groups usually not admitted to craft unions. The Knights died out after 1890. The American Federation of Labor was formed by craft unions, and its leaders rejected radicalism and sought instead to work within capitalism to improve wages, hours, and conditions for its members.

Many Europeans immigrated to the United States because of economic and political conditions in their homelands and their expectations of better opportunities in America. Immigrants often formed distinct communities, frequently centered on a church. The flood of immigrants, particularly from eastern and southern Europe, spawned nativist reactions among some old-stock Americans.

As rural Americans and European immigrants sought better lives in the cities, urban America changed dramatically. New technologies in construction, transportation, and communication produced a new urban geography with separate retail, wholesale, finance, and manufacturing areas and residential neighborhoods defined by economic status.

Urban growth brought a new urban middle class. Education underwent far-reaching changes, from kindergartens through universities. Socially defined gender roles began to change as some women chose professional careers and took active roles in reform. Some men responded by redefining masculinity through organizations and athletics. Urbanization offered new choices to gay men and lesbians by making possible the development of distinctive urban subcultures. In response, medical specialists tried to define homosexuality and lesbianism.

The closely balanced strengths of the two parties contributed to a long-term political stalemate. Presidents James A. Garfield and Chester A. Arthur faced stormy conflict between factions in their own Republican Party. Mugwumps argued for the merit system in the civil service, accomplished through the Pendleton Act of 1883. As president, Grover Cleveland approved the Interstate Commerce Act. The growth of cities encouraged a particular variety of party organization, based on poor neighborhoods, where politicians traded favors for political support. By the late nineteenth century, a well-organized woman suffrage movement had emerged. A wide range of reform groups sought both structural changes and policy changes. Presidents during the 1880s largely neglected foreign relations because the period was one of stability in world affairs, and presidents saw little reason for the United States to become involved in foreign situations.

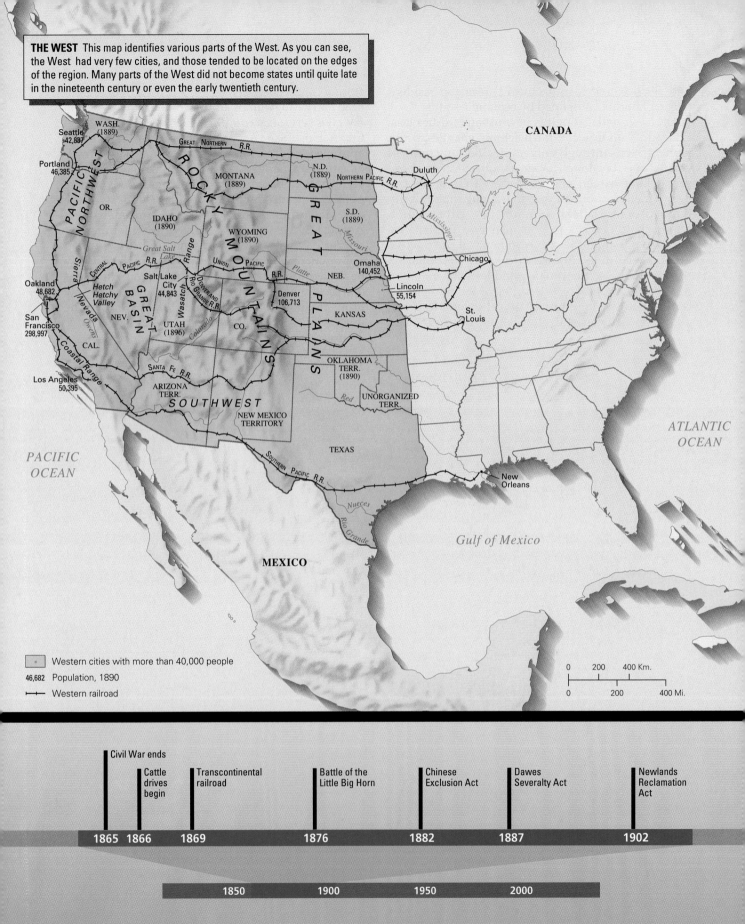

THE WEST This map identifies various parts of the West. As you can see, the West had very few cities, and those tended to be located on the edges of the region. Many parts of the West did not become states until quite late in the nineteenth century or even the early twentieth century.

CANADA

PACIFIC NORTHWEST

WASH. (1889)
Seattle 42,837
Portland 46,385
OR.
IDAHO (1890)

ROCKY MOUNTAINS

GREAT NORTHERN R.R.

MONTANA (1889)

N.D. (1889)
NORTHERN PACIFIC R.R.
Duluth

S.D. (1889)

WYOMING (1890)

Great Salt Lake

Sierra Nevada

Central Pacific R.R.

Oakland 48,682
San Francisco 298,997
CAL.
Coastal Range
Los Angeles 50,395

Hetch Hetchy Valley

GREAT BASIN

NEV.

Salt Lake City 44,843

Wasatch Range

UTAH (1896)

Denver and Rio Grande R.R.

Colorado

UNION PACIFIC R.R.

Platte

Omaha 140,452

NEB.

Lincoln 55,154

Denver 106,713

CO.

KANSAS

Owens

ARIZONA TERR.

NEW MEXICO TERRITORY

Santa Fe R.R.

SOUTHWEST

OKLAHOMA TERR. (1890)

Red

UNORGANIZED TERR.

TEXAS

Southern Pacific R.R.

Missouri

Mississippi

Chicago

St. Louis

New Orleans

PACIFIC OCEAN

Nueces

Rio Grande

MEXICO

Gulf of Mexico

ATLANTIC OCEAN

▪ Western cities with more than 40,000 people
46,682 Population, 1890
⊢—⊣ Western railroad

| 0 | 200 | 400 Km. |
| 0 | 200 | 400 Mi. |

Civil War ends

Cattle drives begin

Transcontinental railroad

Battle of the Little Big Horn

Chinese Exclusion Act

Dawes Severalty Act

Newlands Reclamation Act

| 1865 | 1866 | 1869 | 1876 | 1882 | 1887 | 1902 |

| 1850 | 1900 | 1950 | 2000 |

Conflict and Change in the West, 1865–1902

19

Sitting Bull

SITTING BULL

After Sitting Bull returned to the United States from Canada in 1881, he became a favorite subject for many photographers. This photo dates to the mid-1880s, when he was about fifty years old. *Denver Public Library.*

In 1868 Sitting Bull, a leader of the Hunkpapa Lakotas, refused to accept a treaty that was being presented to the Lakota and Cheyenne people of the northern Great Plains. The U.S. Army had invited the Lakota and Cheyenne to a great conference at Fort Laramie, Wyoming Territory. Federal officials hoped to end attacks along the Bozeman Trail, which ran through eastern Wyoming, and to persuade the Lakota and Cheyenne to live to the north of the major transportation routes that ran through the new state of Nebraska. At the conference, the army agreed to close the Bozeman Trail and to abandon the forts that guarded it, if the Lakotas and their allies agreed to live on a Great Sioux Reservation—the western half of what is now South Dakota.

Many of the Lakotas were willing to consider the army's proposal. Their battles against the forts along the Bozeman Trail included great victories but also serious losses. Red Cloud, an Oglala Lakota and leader of those struggles, was the most prominent of those who agreed to live on the reservation. Most of those who signed the treaty, however, probably had little idea of what they approved.

Sitting Bull refused to accept the treaty. Instead, he continued to follow the buffalo herd and to defend the territories that his people had wrested from their enemies, the Crows, against anyone—Indian or white—who invaded those regions. By rejecting the treaty, he declared his willingness to fight against army efforts to force the Hunkpapas onto a reservation. Sitting Bull soon became one of the most significant leaders of opposition to the treaty and to reservation life.

In 1868 Sitting Bull was in his mid-30s. He had counted his first coup at the age of 14, when he killed a Crow during a raid, and he earned the name Tatanka-Iotanka, Sitting Bull, a tribute to his fighting endurance. In 1857, when Sitting Bull was about 26 years old, the Hunkpapas named him one of the tribal war chiefs in recognition of his fearlessness in battle and his many victories over the Crows and other Native American enemies of the Lakotas. He also came to be considered a holy man, whose visions were messages from Wakantanka, the Great Mystery. To his people, Sitting Bull embodied the Lakota virtues of bravery, fortitude, generosity, and wisdom.

Perhaps one-third of the Lakotas, especially the Hunkpapas, joined Sitting Bull in rejecting the Fort Laramie Treaty. The Oglala Lakotas were divided, with many following Red Cloud to the reservation and some following Crazy Horse to the west of the reservation to live on "unceded lands" in northwestern Wyoming. In 1869 a group of Sitting Bull's supporters arranged a gathering of Lakotas and Cheyennes at which Sitting Bull was named to an unprecedented position: war chief of the Lakota nation. Given the fluidity of leadership among the Lakotas, the reservation Lakotas did not accept this action, nor did all those who had spurned the treaty. But it was a signal honor.

Over the next decade, Sitting Bull exercised greater leadership among the Lakota tribes than any previous leader had. In June 1876, many of the nonreservation Lakotas and Cheyennes gathered into a large village along the

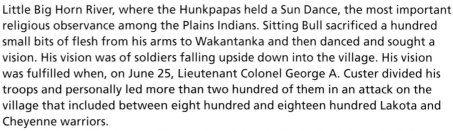

Little Big Horn River, where the Hunkpapas held a Sun Dance, the most important religious observance among the Plains Indians. Sitting Bull sacrificed a hundred small bits of flesh from his arms to Wakantanka and then danced and sought a vision. His vision was of soldiers falling upside down into the village. His vision was fulfilled when, on June 25, Lieutenant Colonel George A. Custer divided his troops and personally led more than two hundred of them in an attack on the village that included between eight hundred and eighteen hundred Lakota and Cheyenne warriors.

The defeat of Custer was the greatest victory by the Plains Indians in their many battles with the army, but it provoked strong counterattacks. As the army attacked and attacked again, Sitting Bull and his followers lost their tipis and their provisions. Finally they fled to Canada and remained there for several years. Soon, however, the last buffalo disappeared from the plains, ending the Hunkpapas' traditional way of life more effectively than the army had been able to do. Eventually they agreed to return south and live on a reservation. Sitting Bull spent a few years touring with William F. ("Buffalo Bill") Cody's Wild West Show and then retired to live in a log cabin on the reservation. There he died at the hands of Native American policemen, some from his own Hunkpapa tribe, in 1890.

INTRODUCTION

Sitting Bull and his allies were not alone in their resistance to the army. At the same time that eastern cities were burgeoning with immigrants from Europe and Andrew Carnegie and John D. Rockefeller were building industrial empires, the army was eliminating the last armed Indian resistance in the West. There, entrepreneurs had already begun building their own empires. Americans have shown a long-lasting interest in the West of the late nineteenth century. Popular fiction and drama have glorified the West as a land where rugged individualism held sway and pioneers overcame great odds. The reality of western life was more complex.

For years before the Civil War, the issue of slavery had blocked efforts to develop the West. The secession of the southern states permitted the Republicans who took over the federal government in 1861 to open the West to economic development and white settlement, through measures such as the Pacific Railroad Act and the Homestead Act, both passed in 1862.

As Americans faced west, their prior experience suggested the steady westward extension of family farms. American farmers had taken more than a half-century to fill the area between the Appalachian Mountains and the Mississippi River. Some thought it would take as long to extend cultivation to the Rocky Mountains. In 1827 a cabinet officer had predicted that the nation would take five hundred years to fill up the West. However, travelers to the West had described it as an area of vast deserts, forbidding mountains, and well-armed, mounted Indian warriors, suggesting that parts of the West might never be developed like the eastern half of the nation.

In most of the West, rainfall was markedly less than in the eastern United States, where sufficient water was simply taken for granted. In the West, the scarcity of water presented new questions. What sort of development was appropriate in a region with little rain? How could water be harnessed to support development? Who would control the water, and who would benefit from it?

Similarly, the ethnic and racial composition of the West differed significantly from patterns in the East and South. At the end of the Civil War, the northeastern and north-central United States was almost entirely of European descent. The South was a biracial society—white and black. Some American Indians lived east of the Mississippi, but larger numbers had been pushed westward and were sharing parts of the West with tribal groups who claimed it as their ancestral homeland. The Southwest was home to significant numbers of people who spoke Spanish, who were often of mixed white and Native American ancestry, and whose families had lived in the region for generations. Santa Fe, New Mexico, for example, had been founded by Spanish conquistadores before 1610, and the first Spanish settlements in California dated to 1769. By the time of the Civil War, the Pacific coast had attracted immigrants from Asia, especially China, who had crossed the Pacific going east in hopes of finding their fortune in America, much as European immigrants crossed the Atlantic going west. In the late nineteenth century, these concentrations of ethnic groups marked the West as a distinctive place.

As individual Americans began to shape the development of the West—from seeking free land under the Homestead Act to speculating in mining stock to adjusting to an unfamiliar environment—federal officials had to decide what to do about the American Indians who occupied much of the region. Given the realities of the West, development there proved sometimes to be quite different from previous experience. The result was the transformation of the American West.

WAR FOR THE WEST

• What did federal policymakers after the Civil War hope to accomplish regarding American Indians? How did western Indians respond?

• How can you explain the decisions of both federal policymakers and western Native Americans?

When Congress decided to use the public domain—western land—to encourage economic development, most white Americans considered the West to be largely vacant. In fact, American Indians lived throughout most of the West, and their understanding of their relationship to the land differed greatly from that of most white Americans. The most tragic outcome of the development of the West was certainly the experience of the American Indians who lived there.

The Plains Indians

By the time white Americans began to move west, the acquisition of horses and guns had already transformed the lives of many Native Americans. This transformation occurred most dramatically among the tribes living on or near the **Great Plains**—the vast, relatively flat, and treeless region that stretches from north to south across the center of the nation and that was the range land of huge herds of buffalo. The introduction of the horse to the Great Plains took place slowly, trickling northward from Spanish settlements in what is now New Mexico and eventually reaching the upper plains in the mid-eighteenth century. By the mid-eighteenth century, French and English traders working northeast of the plains had begun to provide guns to the Indians in return for furs. Together horses and guns transformed the culture of some Plains tribes.

The Native Americans of the plains followed two different ways of life: farming and hunting. The farmers lived most of the year in large permanent villages. Among this group were the Arikaras, Pawnees, and Wichitas (who spoke languages of the Caddoan family) and the Mandans, Hidatsas, Omahas, Otos, and Osages (who spoke Siouan languages). On the northern plains, their large, dome-shaped houses were typically made of logs and covered with dirt. In southern areas, their houses were often covered with grass. These Indians farmed the fertile river valleys, harvesting corn, squash, pumpkins, beans, sunflowers, and tobacco. They gathered wild fruit and vegetables and hunted and fished near their villages. Men hunted, fished, and cultivated tobacco. Women farmed, prepared, and preserved food crops. Before the arrival of horses, twice a year entire villages went, on foot, on extended hunting trips for buffalo—once in the early summer after their crops were planted, then again in the fall after the harvest. One favorite method of killing buffalo was to stampede an entire herd off a high cliff, causing large numbers to be killed or seriously injured. During these hunts, the people lived in **tipis**, cone-shaped tents of buffalo hide that were easy to move. Acquisition of horses changed the culture of these Indians only slightly.

The horse utterly revolutionized the lives of other Plains Indians. Because a hunter on horseback could

---

Great Plains   High grassland of western North America, stretching from roughly the 98th meridian to the Rocky Mountains; it is generally level, treeless, and fairly dry.

tipi   Conical tent made from buffalo hide and used as a portable dwelling by Indians on the Great Plains.

chronology

Transforming the West

1700s	Horse culture spreads throughout Great Plains
1847	First Mormon settlements near Great Salt Lake
1848	Treaty of Guadalupe Hidalgo California gold rush begins
1862	Homestead Act Pacific Railroad Act Land-Grant College Act
1865	Civil War ends
1866–1880	Cattle drives north from Texas
1867–1868	Treaties establish major western reservations
1868–1869	Army's winter campaign against southern Plains Indians
1869	First transcontinental railroad completed
Early 1870s	Cattle raising begins on northern plains
1870s	Destruction of buffalo herds Silver-mining boom in Nevada
1870s–1880s	Extension of farming to Great Plains
1871–1885	Anti-Chinese riots across West
1874	American Indian resistance ends on southern plains Patent issued for barbed wire Women's Christian Temperance Union founded
1875	Andrew Carnegie opens nation's largest steel plant
1876	Spring and summer campaign on northern plains Indian victory in Battle of Little Big Horn
1877	Reconstruction ends Army subdues last major Indian resistance on northern plains Surrender and death of Crazy Horse Chief Joseph and the Nez Perce flee Workingmen's Party of California attacks Chinese
1881	Surrender of Sitting Bull
1882	Chinese Exclusion Act
1883	Northern Pacific Railroad completed to Portland
1884	Federal court prohibits hydraulic mining
1885	First U.S. skyscraper
1886	Surrender of Geronimo *Yick Wo v. Hopkins*
1886–1887	Severe winter damages northern cattle business
1887	Dawes Severalty Act
Late 1880s	Reduced rainfall forces many homesteaders off western farms
1890	Sitting Bull killed Conflict at Wounded Knee Creek
1892	Sierra Club formed
1893	Great Northern Railway completed Frederick Jackson Turner presents his frontier thesis
1902	Reclamation Act

kill twice as many buffalo as one on foot, the horse substantially increased the number of people the plains could support. The horse also increased mobility, permitting a band to follow the buffalo as they moved across the grasslands. The buffalo provided most essentials: food (meat), clothing and shelter (made from hides), implements (made from bones and horns), and even fuel for fires (dried dung). Some groups abandoned farming and became nomadic, living in tipis year round and following the buffalo herds. The Cheyennes, for example, made this transition within a single generation

John Mix Stanley painted this buffalo hunt in 1845, dramatically illustrating how the horse increased the ability of Native American hunters to kill buffalo. Before the horse, a hunter could not safely have gone into the midst of a stampeding herd to drive a lance into a buffalo's heart. *Smithsonian American Art Museum, Washington, D.C./ Art Resource, N.Y.*

after 1770. By the early nineteenth century, the **horse culture** existed throughout the Great Plains. The largest groups practicing this lifestyle included—from north to south—the Blackfeet, Crows, **Lakotas**, **Cheyennes**, Arapahos, Kiowas, and Comanches.

The Lakotas, largest of all the groups, were the westernmost members of a large group of Native American peoples often called Sioux; the eastern Sioux were called Dakotas or Nakotas. The name *Sioux*, which means "enemy," may stem from their custom of considering all those who were not members of their **confederacy** to be their enemies. All the Lakotas shared a common language. Membership in the Lakota confederacy was not limited to those speaking a particular language, however, as the northern Cheyennes were generally considered members of the Lakota confederacy by the mid-nineteenth century.

Whether nomadic buffalo hunters or **sedentary** farming people, Indians living on the Great Plains and in other areas of North America understood the land differently from white settlers. From the time of the first European migrants to America, most white Americans had considered land to be a commodity to be bought and sold, owned and improved by individuals. According to Native American tradition, however, land was to be used but not individually owned. Horses, weapons, tipis, and clothing were all individually owned, but not land. Though

they did not practice individual ownership of land, tribes did claim specific territories.

Before the arrival of horses, young men derived status from raiding a neighboring tribe to seize agricultural produce, capture a member of that tribe as a slave, or seek revenge for a raid. With the development of the horse culture, wealth was measured in horses. Now raids were staged primarily to steal horses, retaliate, or both. A young man acquired status through demonstrations of daring and bravery in raids. Signs of success were the number of horses captured, the number of opponents defeated in battle,

---

horse culture   The nomadic way of life of those American Indians, mostly on the Great Plains, for whom the horse brought significant changes in their ability to hunt, travel, and make war.

Lakota   A confederation of Siouan Indian peoples who lived on the northern Great Plains.

Cheyenne   Indian people who became nomadic buffalo hunters after migrating to the Great Plains in the eighteenth century.

confederacy   An organization of separate groups who have allied for mutual support or joint action.

sedentary   Living year-round in fixed villages and engaging in farming; as opposed to nomadic, or moving from camp to camp throughout the year.

and success in returning home uninjured. An individual won special glory by **counting coup**—that is, by touching an enemy, either with one's hand or with a stick.

Historians and anthropologists once thought that conflict between and among Plains tribes was largely related to stealing horses and seeking honor by counting coup. More recently, scholars have pointed to serious contests for territory, for example, the wars between Lakotas and Crows in which Sitting Bull first emerged as a leader. Conflicts over territory often developed as tribes were pushed to the west as tribes to their east were also pushed west by expanding European settlements along the Atlantic coast. The Lakotas and Cheyennes, for example, once lived just east of the northern plains but were pushed onto the plains as the tribes to their east came under pressure.

Among most of the Plains Indians, acquisition of goods was not a pressing goal. A person achieved high social standing not by accumulating possessions but by sharing. Francis La Flesche, son of an Omaha leader, learned from his father that "the persecution of the poor, the sneer at their poverty is a wrong for which no punishment is too severe." His mother reinforced the lesson: "When you see a boy barefooted and lame, take off your moccasins and give them to him. When you see a boy hungry, bring him to your home and give him food."

The Plains Wars

In 1851 Congress approved a new policy intended to provide each tribe with a definite territory "of limited extent and well-defined boundaries," within which the tribe was to live. The government was to supply whatever needs the tribes could not meet themselves from the lands they were assigned. Federal officials first planned large reservations taking up much of the Great Plains. At a great conference held at Fort Laramie, they signed treaties that guaranteed extensive territory to the northern Plains tribes.

Before the 1851 policy, federal policymakers had considered the region west of Arkansas, Missouri, Iowa, and Minnesota and east of the Rocky Mountains to be a permanent Indian country. But farmers bound for Oregon and gold seekers on their way to California soon carved trails across the central plains, and some people began promoting a railroad to connect the Pacific coast to the East. The policy initiated in 1851 was designed in part to open the central plains as a route to the Pacific.

Far more easterners thronged westward than federal officials had anticipated, and conflicts some-

times erupted along the trails. Then thousands of prospectors poured into Colorado after discovery of gold there in 1858. Withdrawal of many federal troops with the outbreak of the Civil War in 1861 may have encouraged some Plains Indians to believe they could expel the invaders. A series of Cheyenne and Lakota raids in 1864 brought demands for reprisals. Late in November, at Sand Creek in Colorado, a territorial militia unit massacred a band of Cheyennes who had had no involvement in the raids. Soon after, the discovery of gold in Montana prompted construction of forts to protect a road, the **Bozeman Trail**, through Lakota territory. Cheyennes and Lakotas, led by **Red Cloud**, mounted a sustained war against the road.

In April 1868, many members of the northern Plains tribes met at Fort Laramie and agreed to a Great Sioux Reservation. They believed that they retained "unceded lands" for hunting in the Powder River country—present-day northeastern Wyoming and southeastern Montana. In return, the army abandoned its posts along the Bozeman Trail, a victory for the Lakotas and Cheyennes.

The creation of the new reservation was part of a larger plan. With the end of the Civil War in 1865, railroad construction crews prepared to build westward (see pages 502, 584). Federal policymakers tried to head off hostilities by carving out a few great western reservations. One was to be for northern Plains tribes, north of the new state of Nebraska. Another was to be for southern Plains tribes, south of Kansas. The third was to be for the tribes of the mountains and the Southwest, in the Southwest. The remainder of the West was to be opened for development—railroad building, mining, and farming. Native Americans on the reservations were to receive food and shelter and agents were to teach them how to farm and raise cattle.

The Fort Laramie Treaty of 1868 was one of several negotiated in 1867 and 1868 in fulfillment of the new policy. In 1867 a conference at Medicine Lodge Creek produced treaties by which the major southern Plains tribes accepted reservations in what is

---

counting coup   Among Plains Indians, to win glory in battle by touching an enemy; *coup* is French for "blow," and the term comes from the French fur traders who were the first Europeans to describe the practice.

Bozeman Trail   Trail that ran from Fort Laramie, Wyoming, to the gold fields of Montana.

Red Cloud   Lakota chief who led a successful fight to prevent the army from keeping forts along the Bozeman Trail.

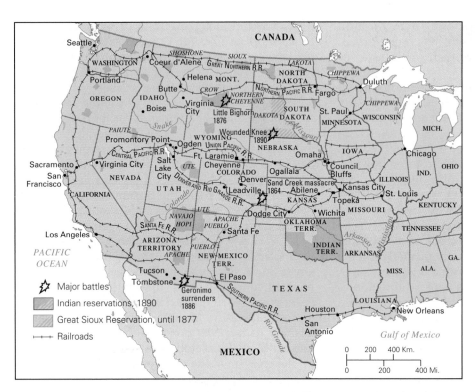

MAP 19.1 Indian Reservations   This map indicates the location of most western Indian reservations in 1890, as well as the Great Sioux Reservation before it was broken up and severely reduced in size. Note how the development of a few large reservations on the northern plains and others on the southern plains opened the central plains for railroad construction and agricultural development.

now western Oklahoma (see Map 19.1). In May 1868 the Crows agreed to a reservation in Montana. In June 1868 the Navajos accepted a large reservation in the Southwest. Given the highly fluid structure of authority among the Plains Indians, however, those who signed the treaties did not necessarily obligate those who did not.

As some federal officials were negotiating these treaties, other federal officials were permitting and even encouraging white buffalo hunters to kill the buffalo—for sport, for meat, for hides. Slaughter of the buffalo accelerated when **tanneries** in the East began to buy buffalo hides. In the mid-1870s, more than 10 million buffalo were killed and stripped of their hides, which sold for a dollar or more. The southern herd was wiped out by 1878, the northern herd by 1883. Only two thousand survived, the remnant of a species whose numbers once seemed as vast as the stars. Given the importance of the buffalo in the lives of the Plains Indians, their way of life was doomed once the slaughter began.

Some members of the southern Plains tribes refused to accept the terms of the Medicine Lodge Creek treaties and continued to live in their traditional territory. Resisting efforts to move them onto the reservations, they occasionally attacked stagecoach stations, ranches, travelers, and military units. General William Tecumseh Sherman, the Civil War general and now head of the army, planned military strategy on the plains. After a group of southern Cheyennes inflicted heavy losses on an army unit, Sherman decreed that all Native Americans not on reservations "are hostile and will remain so till killed off."

Sherman's response was the usual reaction of a conventional military force to guerrilla warfare: concentrate the friendly population in defined areas

> **tannery**   An establishment where animal skins and hides are made into leather.

(in this case, reservations) and then open fire on anyone outside those areas. In the winter of 1868–1869, the army launched a southern plains campaign under the command of General Philip Sheridan, another Union army veteran, who directed his men to "destroy their villages and ponies, to kill and hang all warriors, and bring back all women and children." The brutality that ensued convinced most southern Plains tribes to abandon further resistance.

In the early 1870s, however, sizable buffalo herds still roamed west and south of Indian Territory, in the Red River region of Texas. Though this was nonreservation land, the Medicine Lodge Creek treaties permitted Indians to hunt there. When white buffalo hunters began encroaching on the area in 1874, young men from the Kiowa, Comanche, and southern Cheyenne tribes attacked them. Sheridan responded with another **war of attrition**, destroying tipis, food, and animals. When winter came, the cold and hungry Indians surrendered to avoid starvation. Tribal war leaders were imprisoned in Florida, far from their families. Buffalo hunters then quickly exterminated the remaining buffalo on the southern plains.

Hunting grounds outside reservations were also a cause of conflict on the northern plains. Many Lakotas and some northern Cheyennes, led by **Crazy Horse** and Sitting Bull, lived on unceded hunting lands in the Powder River region. Complicating matters further, gold was discovered in the Black Hills, in the heart of the Great Sioux Reservation in 1874, touching off an invasion of Indian land by miners. As the Northern Pacific Railroad prepared to lay track in southern Montana, federal authorities determined to force all Lakota and Cheyenne people onto the reservation, triggering a conflict sometimes called the **Great Sioux War**.

Military operations in the Powder River region began in the spring of 1876. Sheridan ordered troops to enter the area from three directions and converge on the Lakota and Cheyenne. The offensive went dreadfully wrong when Lieutenant Colonel George A. Custer, without waiting for the other units, sent his Seventh Cavalry against a major village that his scouts had located. The encampment, on the **Little Big Horn River**, proved to be one of the largest ever on the northern plains. Custer unwisely divided his force, and more then two hundred men, including Custer, met their deaths.

That winter, U.S. soldiers unleashed another campaign of attrition on the northern plains. Troops defeated some bands. Hunger and cold drove others to surrender. Crazy Horse and his band held out until spring and surrendered only when told that

they could live in the Powder River region. A few months later, Crazy Horse was killed when he resisted being put into an army jail. Sitting Bull and his band escaped to Canada and remained there until 1881, when he finally surrendered. The government cut up the Great Sioux Reservation into several smaller units and took away the Powder River region, including the Black Hills (which the Lakotas considered sacred), and other lands.

The Last Indian Wars

After the Great Sioux War, no Native American group could muster the capacity for sustained resistance. Small groups occasionally left their reservations but were promptly tracked down by troops. In 1877 the Nez Perce, led by **Chief Joseph**, attempted to flee to Canada when the army tried to force them to leave their reservation in western Idaho. Between July and early October, they evaded the army as they traveled east and north through Montana. More than two hundred died along the way. Joseph surrendered on the specific condition that the Nez Perce be permitted to return to their previous home. His surrender speech is often quoted to illustrate the hopelessness of further resistance:

Our chiefs are killed. . . . The old men are dead. . . . It is cold and we have no blankets. The little children are freezing to death. . . . My heart is sick and sad. From where the sun now stands, I will fight no more forever!

---

war of attrition   A form of warfare based on deprivation of food, shelter, and other necessities; if successful, it drives opponents to surrender out of hunger or exposure.

Crazy Horse   Lakota leader who resisted white encroachment in the Black Hills and fought at the Little Big Horn River in 1876; he was killed by U.S. soldiers in 1877.

Great Sioux War   War between the tribes that took part in the Battle of Little Big Horn and the U.S. Army; it ended in 1881 with the surrender of Sitting Bull.

Little Big Horn River   River in Montana where in 1876 Lieutenant Colonel George Custer attacked a large Indian encampment; Custer and most of his force died in the battle.

Chief Joseph   Nez Perce chief who led his people in an attempt to escape to Canada in 1877; after a grueling journey they were forced to surrender and were exiled to Indian Territory.

Federal officials sent the Nez Perce not back to Idaho but to Indian Territory, where, in an unfamiliar climate, many soon died of disease.

The last sizable group to refuse to live on a reservation was Geronimo's band of Chiricahua Apaches, who long managed to elude the army in the mountains of the Southwest. They finally gave up in 1886, and the men were sent to prison in Florida.

The last major confrontation between the army and Native Americans came in 1890, in South Dakota. Some Lakotas had taken up a new religion, the **Ghost Dance**, which promised to return the land to the Indians, restore the buffalo, and sweep away the whites. Fearing an uprising as the Ghost Dance gained popularity, federal authorities ordered the Lakotas to stop the ritual. Concerned that Sitting Bull might encourage defiance, federal authorities ordered his arrest; he was killed in the ensuing scuffle. A small band of Lakotas, led by Big Foot, fled but was surrounded by the Seventh Cavalry near **Wounded Knee Creek**. When one Lakota refused to surrender his gun, both Indians and soldiers fired their weapons. The soldiers, with their vastly greater firepower, quickly prevailed. As many as 250 Native Americans died, as did 25 soldiers.

The events at Wounded Knee marked the symbolic end of armed conflict on the Great Plains. In fact, the end of the horse culture was written long before. Once the federal government began to encourage rapid economic development in the West, displacement of the Indians was probably inevitable. From the beginning, the Indians faced overwhelming odds—they had a superior knowledge of the terrain, superior horsemanship and mobility, and great courage, but the U.S. Army had superior numbers and superior technology. Then, too, the army was often able to find allies among Native American groups who were traditional enemies of the defiant tribes. The desperate nature of Indian resistance suggests that they clearly understood that they were facing the loss not only of their hunting grounds but also of their culture and even their lives.

TRANSFORMING THE WEST: MORMONS, COWBOYS, AND SODBUSTERS

• What did Mormons, cattle raisers, and farmers seek to accomplish in the West? How did they adapt their efforts to the western environment?

• What were the motivations of these three groups in seeking to develop the West?

This painting by Yellow Nose, a Ute, was done in 1891. It depicts the Ghost Dance, a religion that promised to restore the buffalo and banish the whites. The dancers' shirts were thought to make them immune to harm. The cult began in Nevada in the 1880s and gained support throughout the West until the Wounded Knee massacre. *Smithsonian Institution.*

Long before the last battles between the army and the Indians, the economic development of the West was well under way. Quite different groups sought to transform the West and make it suit their needs, among them, Mormons, cattle ranchers, and farmers.

Zion in the Great Basin

By the end of the Civil War, development of the Great Basin region (between the Rocky Mountains and the Sierra Nevada) was well advanced due to efforts by **Mormons**. Controversial because of their religious beliefs, which included **polygamy**, Mor-

---

Ghost Dance   Indian religion centered on a ritual dance; it held out the promise of an Indian messiah who would banish the whites, bring back the buffalo, and restore the land to the Indians.

Wounded Knee Creek   Site of a conflict in 1890 between a band of Lakotas and U.S. troops, sometimes characterized as a massacre because the Lakotas were so outnumbered and overpowered; the last major encounter between Indians and the army.

Mormons   Members of the Church of Jesus Christ of Latter-Day Saints, founded in New York in 1830.

polygamy   The practice of having more than one wife at a time; Mormons referred to this as "plural marriage."

mons had been hounded out of one eastern state after another. In 1847 they finally settled near the Great Salt Lake, then northern Mexico. Led by Brigham Young, they planned to build a great Mormon state, which they called Deseret, in a region so remote that no one would interfere with them. The Treaty of Guadalupe Hidalgo (1848), which ended the Mexican War, soon incorporated the region into the United States. Congress created Utah Territory in 1850, with boundaries much smaller than those Young had envisioned for Deseret.

Nevertheless, in the remoteness of the Great Basin—isolated by mountains and deserts from the rest of the nation—the Mormons created their Zion, organizing themselves into a *theocracy* (a society governed by church officials). Church authority extended to politics, as a church-sponsored political party dominated elections for local and territorial officials.

Meager rainfall and poor soil made farming difficult. Young decreed communal ownership of both land and streams. Ignoring eastern laws that limited property owners from removing water from streams running through their properties, Young devised a system for creating farms and irrigation projects based on diverting water for irrigation. The communal ownership of land ended after 1869, when the Homestead Act of 1862 was extended to the territory, but the new definitions for water diversion remained.

With development firmly controlled by the church, the settlement thrived. By 1865, more than twenty thousand people lived in Utah Territory. The church established a consumers' cooperative known as Zion's Cooperative Mercantile Institute, or ZCMI. In addition to selling a variety of goods, ZCMI manufactured some products, including sugar made from sugar beets. Such cooperative enterprises mirrored practices within the 20 to 40 percent of families who practiced polygamy. Church officials urged some of the women in such households to take up home industries (such as silk production) or outside professional employment (such as teaching).

Mormons eventually came under strong federal pressure to renounce polygamy. Proposals for Utah statehood were repeatedly blocked because of that issue. Though Republican leaders branded polygamy as sinful, many politicians were also concerned about the political power of the Mormon church. In 1890, to clear the way for statehood, church leaders dissolved their political party, encouraged Mormons to divide themselves among the national political parties, and disavowed polygamy. Utah became a state in 1896.

At some time in the 1870s, these cowboys put on good clothes and sat for a photographer's portrait before a painted background. They probably worked together and were friends. Most cowboys were young African Americans, Mexican Americans, or poor southern whites. *Collection of William Gladstone.*

Cattle Kingdom on the Plains

As the Mormons were building their centralized and cooperative society in the Great Basin, a more individualistic enterprise was emerging on the Great Plains. There, cattle came to dominate the economy.

The expanding cities of the eastern United States were hungry for beef. At the same time, cattle were wandering the ranges of south Texas. Cattle had first been brought into south Texas—then part of New Spain (Mexico)—in the eighteenth century. The environment encouraged the herds to multiply, and Mexican ranchers developed an **open-range** system. The cattle grazed on unfenced plains, and *vaqueros* (cowboys) herded the half-wild longhorns from horseback. Many practices that developed in south Texas were subsequently transferred

---

open range Unfenced grazing lands on which cattle ran freely and ownership was established through branding.

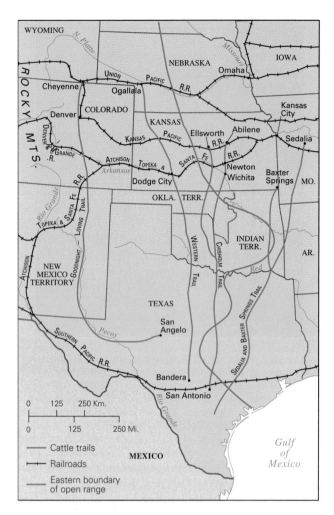

MAP 19.2 Western Cattle Trails and Railroads, 1865–1890 The demand for beef in northeastern cities encouraged Texans to drive cattle north to the railroads, which carried the cattle to eastern slaughterhouses. As railroad construction moved west, cattle trails did, too, creating a series of "cattle towns" where the trails met the tracks.

through Indian Territory (now Oklahoma) to the railroads being built westward (see Map 19.2). Half a dozen cowboys, a cook, and a foreman (the trail boss) could drive one or two thousand cattle. Not all the animals survived the drive, but enough did to yield a good profit. Between 1866 and 1880, some 4 million cattle plodded north from Texas.

As railroad construction crews pushed westward, cattle towns sprung up—notably Abilene and Dodge City, Kansas. In cattle towns, the trail boss sold his herd and paid off his cowboys, most of whom quickly headed for the cattle town's saloons, brothels, and gambling houses. Eastern journalists and writers of **dime novels** discovered and embroidered the exploits of town marshals like **James B. ("Wild Bill") Hickock** and **Wyatt Earp**, giving them national reputations—deserved or not—as "town-tamers" of heroic dimensions. In fact, the most important changes in any cattle town came when middle-class residents—especially women—organized churches and schools, and determined to create law-abiding communities like those from which they had come.

Although most Texas cattle were eventually loaded on east-bound trains, some continued north to northern ranges where cattlemen had virtually free access to vast lands still in the public domain. One result of these "long drives" was the extension of open-range cattle raising from Texas into the northern Great Plains. By the early 1870s, the profits in cattle raising on the northern plains attracted attention in the East. From the East, England, and elsewhere swarmed investors eager to make a fortune. Some brought in new breeds of cattle, which they bred with Texas longhorns, producing hardy range cattle that yielded more meat.

to the range-cattle industry, including **roundups** and **branding**.

Between 1836, when Texas separated from Mexico, and the Civil War, few changes occurred in south Texas. Texans occasionally drove cattle to distant markets, but cattle drives ended during the Civil War. At the end of the war, 5 million cattle ranged across Texas. And, in the slaughterhouses of Chicago, cattle brought ten times or more than their price in Texas.

To get cattle from south Texas to markets in the Midwest, Texans herded cattle north from Texas

roundup A spring event in which cowboys gathered together the cattle herds, branded newborn calves, and castrated most of the new young males.

branding To burn a distinctive mark into an animal's hide using a hot iron as a way to establish ownership.

dime novel A cheaply produced novel of the mid-to-late nineteenth century, often featuring the dramatized exploits of western gunfighters.

James B. ("Wild Bill") Hickock Western gambler and gunfighter who for a time was the town marshal (law enforcement officer) in Abilene, Kansas.

Wyatt Earp American frontier marshal and gunfighter involved in 1881 in a controversial shootout at the O.K. Corral in Tombstone, Arizona, in which several men were killed.

By the early 1880s so many cattle ranches were operating that beef prices began to fall. Then, in the severe winter of 1886–1887, uncounted thousands of cattle froze or starved to death on the northern plains. Many investors went bankrupt. Cattle raising lost some of its romantic aura and afterward became more of a business than an adventure. Surviving ranchers fenced their ranges and made certain that they could feed their herds during the winter.

Another important change, both on the northern plains and in the Southwest, was the rise of sheep raising. By 1900, Montana had more sheep than any other state, and the western states accounted for more than half of the sheep raised in the nation.

As the cattle industry grew, the cowboy became a popular **icon**. Fiction after the 1870s, and motion pictures later, created the cowboy image: a brave, white, clean-cut hero who spent his time outwitting rustlers and rescuing fair-haired white women from snarling villains. In fact, most real cowboys were young and unschooled; many were African Americans or of Mexican descent, and others were former Confederate soldiers. On a cattle drive, they worked long hours (up to twenty a day), faced serious danger if a herd stampeded, slept on the ground, and ate biscuits and beans. They earned about a dollar a day and spent much of their working time in the saddle with no human companionship. Some joined the Knights of Labor.

Plowing the Plains

Removal of the Native Americans and buffalo from most of the Great Plains facilitated railroad construction and expansion of the cattle industry. When farmers entered this region, however, they encountered an environment significantly different from that to the east. Nevertheless, many first tried eastern farming methods. Some adapted successfully, but others failed and left.

After the Civil War, the land most easily available for new farms stretched from what is now the northern boundary of North Dakota and Minnesota southward through the current state of Oklahoma. Mapmakers in the early nineteenth century had labeled this region the Great American Desert. It was not a desert, however, and some parts of it were very fertile. But west of the line of **aridity**—roughly the 98th or 100th **meridian** (see Map 19.3)—sparse rainfall limited farming. Farmers who followed traditional farming practices risked not only failing but also damaging an unexpectedly fragile **ecosystem**.

When the vast region was opened for development by the Kansas-Nebraska Act (1854), the first settlers stuck to eastern areas, where the terrain and climate were similar to those they knew. After the Civil War, farmers pressed steadily westward, spurred by the offer of free land under the Homestead Act or lured by railroad advertising that promised fertile and productive land at little cost.

Those who came to farm were as diverse as the nation itself. Thousands of African Americans left the South, seeking farms of their own. Immigrants from Europe—especially Scandinavia, Germany, **Bohemia**, and Russia—also flooded in. Most homesteaders, however, moved from areas a short distance to the east, where farmland had become too expensive for them to buy.

Single women could and did claim 160 acres of their own land. Sometimes the wife of a male homesteader did the same, claiming 160 acres in her own name next to the claim of her husband. By one estimate, one-third of all homestead claims in Dakota Territory were held by women in 1886. The prohibitive cost of farmland made such efforts almost impossible to the east. Some single women seem to have seen homesteading as a speculative venture, intending to sell the land and use the money for such purposes as starting a business, paying college tuition, or creating a nest egg for marriage.

The Homestead Act, together with cheap railroad land, brought many people west, but the Homestead Act had clear limits. The 160 acres that it provided were sufficient for a farm only east of the line of aridity. West of that line, it was possible to raise wheat in some places, but most of the land required irrigation or was suitable only for cattle raising, which required much more than 160 acres.

Federal officials were sometimes lax in enforcing the Homestead Act's requirements. Some cattle

---

icon   A symbol, usually one with virtues considered worthy of copying.

aridity   Dryness; lack of enough rainfall to support trees or woody plants.

meridian   Any of the imaginary lines representing degrees of longitude that pass through the North and South Poles and encircle the earth.

ecosystem   A community of animals, plants, and bacteria, considered together with the environment in which they live.

Bohemia   A region of Central Europe now part of the Czech Republic.

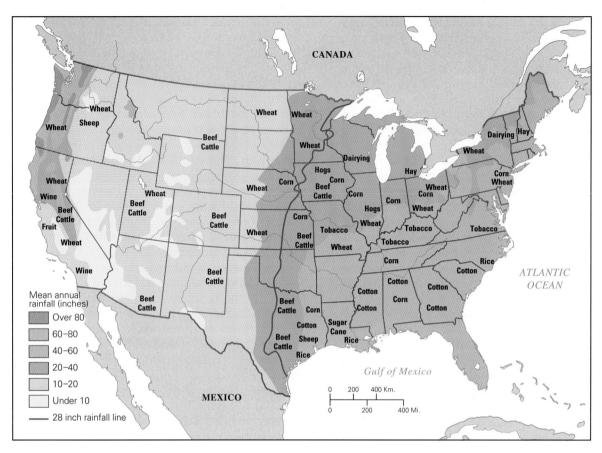

MAP 19.3 Rainfall and Agriculture, c. 1890 The agricultural produce of any given area depended upon the type of soil, the terrain, and the rainfall. Most of the western half of the nation received relatively little rainfall compared to the eastern half, and crops such as corn and cotton could not be raised in the West without irrigation. The line of aridity, beyond which most crops required irrigation, falls between twenty-eight inches and twenty inches of rain annually.

ranchers manipulated the law by having their cowboys file claims and then transfer the land to the rancher after they received title to it. Or ranchers claimed the land along both sides of streams, knowing that surrounding land was worthless without access to water, and thus they could control the whole watershed without establishing ownership.

Those who complied with the requirement to build a house and farm the land often faced an unfamiliar environment. The plains were virtually barren of trees. The new plains settlers, therefore, scavenged for substitutes for the construction material and fuel that eastern pioneers obtained without cost from the trees on their land.

Initially, many families carved homes out of the land itself. Some tunneled into the side of a low hill to make a cavelike dugout. Others cut the tough prairie **sod** into blocks from which they fashioned a

small house. Many combined dugout and sod construction. "Soddies" became common throughout the plains but seldom made satisfactory dwellings. Years later, women told their grandchildren of their horror when snakes dropped from the ceiling or slithered out of walls. For fuel to use in cooking or heating, women burned dried cow dung or sunflower stalks. Sod houses were usually so dark that many household tasks were done outside whenever the weather permitted.

---

sod A piece of earth on which grass is growing; if grass has grown there a long time, the grass roots, dead grass from previous growing seasons, and the growing grass will be dense, tough, and fibrous, and the soil hard-packed.

Omer M. Kem (standing, slicing ripe watermelon) posed for the photographer with his children and his aged father outside his sod house in Custer County, Nebraska, in 1886. Such houses were made of sod cut into blocks and laid like bricks to make walls. Four years later, Kem was elected to the U.S. House of Representatives as a Populist, representing the grievances of western farmers. The photographer, Solomon Butcher, compiled a valuable collection of pictures illustrating the nature of life on what one historian termed "the sod-house frontier." *Nebraska State Historical Society.*

Plains families looked to technology to meet many of their needs. Barbed wire, first patented in 1874, provided a cheap and easy alternative to wooden fences. The barbs effectively kept ranchers' cattle off farmland. Ranchers eventually used it too, to keep their herds from straying. Much of the plains had abundant ground water, but the **water table** was deeper than in the East. Windmills pumped water from great depths. Because the sod was so tough, special plows were developed to make the first cut through it. These plows were so expensive that most farmers hired a specialist (a "sodbuster") to break their sod.

The most serious problem for pioneers on the Great Plains was a much-reduced level of rainfall compared with eastern farming areas. During the late 1870s and into the 1880s, when the central plains were farmed for the first time, the area received unusually heavy rainfall. Then, in the late 1880s, rainfall fell below normal and crop failures drove many homesteaders off the plains. By one estimate, half of the population of western Kansas left between 1888 and 1892. Only after farmers learned better techniques of dry farming, secured improved strains of wheat (some brought by **Russian-German** immigrants), and began to practice irrigation did agriculture become viable. Even so, farming practices in some western areas failed to protect soil that had formerly been covered by natural vegetation. This exposed soil became subject to severe wind erosion in years of low rainfall.

TRANSFORMING THE WEST: RAILROADS, MINING, AGRIBUSINESS, LOGGING, AND FINANCE

- What difficulties confronted western entrepreneurs engaged in mining, agriculture, or logging? What steps did those entrepreneurs take to develop their industries?

- How did economic development in the West during the late nineteenth century compare with that taking place in the eastern United States at the same time?

At the end of the Civil War, most of the West was sparsely populated. (Many parts of it remain so at the beginning of the twenty-first century.) From 1865 onward, the West of the lone cowboy and solitary prospector was also a region in which most people lived in cities. In a region of great distances, few people, and widely scattered population centers, railroads were a necessity for economic development. Given the scarcity of water in much of the West, by 1900 many westerners had concluded that an adequate

> **water table**   The level at which the ground is completely saturated with water.
>
> **Russian-German**   Refers to people of German ancestry living in Russia; most had come to Russia in the eighteenth century at the invitation of the government to develop agricultural areas.

Only a few of the photographs of the construction of the first transcontinental railroad show the Chinese laborers who were responsible for some of the most dangerous construction on the Central Pacific route through the Sierra Nevada. This photograph was taken, apparently by a photographer for the Union Pacific, when the two lines joined near Promontory Summit, in Utah Territory. *Denver Public Library.*

supply of water was as important for economic development as was their network of steel rails.

Western Railroads

In the eastern United States, railroad construction usually meant connecting already established population centers. Eastern railroads moved through areas with developed economies, connected major cities, and hauled freight to and from the many towns along their lines. At the end of the Civil War, this scenario existed almost nowhere in the West.

Most western railroads were built first to connect the Pacific coast to the eastern half of the country. Only slowly did they begin to find business along their routes. Railroad promoters understood that building a transcontinental line was very expensive and that such a railway was unlikely at first to carry enough freight to justify the cost of construction. Thus they turned to the federal government for assistance with costs. The Pacific Railroad Act of 1862 provided loans and also 10 square miles (later increased to 20) of the public domain for every mile of track laid. Federal lawmakers promoted railroad construction to tie California and Nevada, with their rich deposits of gold and silver, to the Union and to stimulate the rapid economic development of other parts of the West.

Two companies received federal support for the first transcontinental railroad: the Union Pacific, which began laying tracks westward from Omaha, Nebraska, and the Central Pacific, which began build-

ing eastward from Sacramento, California. Construction began slowly, partly because crucial supplies—rails and locomotives—had to be brought to each starting point from the eastern United States, either by ship around South America to California or by riverboat to Omaha. Both lines experienced labor shortages. The Union Pacific solved its labor shortages only after the end of the Civil War, when former soldiers and construction workers flooded west. Many were Irish immigrants. The Central Pacific filled its rail gangs earlier by recruiting Chinese immigrants. By 1868, Central Pacific construction crews totaled six thousand workers, Union Pacific crews five thousand.

The Central Pacific laid only 18 miles of track during 1863, and the Union Pacific laid no track at all until mid-1864. The sheer cliffs and rocky ravines of the Sierra Nevada slowed construction of the Central Pacific. Chinese laborers sometimes dangled from ropes to create a roadbed by chiseling away the solid rock face of a mountain. Because the companies earned their federal subsidies by laying track, construction became a race in which each company tried to build faster than the other. In 1869, with the Sierra far behind, the Central Pacific boasted of laying 10 miles of track in a single day. The tracks of the two companies finally met at Promontory Summit, north of the Great Salt Lake (see Map 17.2, page 502), on May 10, 1869. Other lines followed during the next twenty years, bringing most of the West into the national market system.

Westerners greeted the arrival of a railroad in their communities with joyful celebrations, but some soon wondered if they had traded isolation for dependence on a greedy monopoly. The Southern Pacific, successor to the Central Pacific, became known as the "Octopus" because of its efforts to establish a monopoly over transportation throughout California. It had a reputation for charging the most that a customer could afford. James J. Hill of the Great Northern, by contrast, was called the "Empire Builder," for his efforts to build up the economy and prosperity of the region alongside his rails. Whether "Octopus" or "Empire Builder," railroads provided the crucial transportation network for the economic development of the West. In their wake, western mining, agriculture, and lumbering all expanded rapidly.

Western Mining

During the forty years following the California gold rush (which began in 1848), prospectors discovered gold or silver throughout much of the mountain West (see the chapter-opening map for Chapter 17). Any such discovery brought fortune seekers surging to the area, and boomtowns sprang up almost overnight. Stores that sold miners' supplies quickly appeared, along with boarding houses, saloons, gambling halls, and brothels. Once the valuable ore gave out, towns were sometimes abandoned. Discoveries of precious metals and valuable minerals in the mountainous regions of the West inevitably prompted the construction of rail lines to the sites of discovery, and the rail lines in turn permitted rapid exploitation of the mineral resources by bringing in supplies and heavy equipment.

Many of the first miners found gold by **placer mining**. The only equipment they needed was a pan, and even a frying pan would do. Miners "panning" for gold simply washed gravel that they hoped contained gold. Any gold sank to the bottom of the pan as the lighter gravel was washed away by the water.

After the early gold seekers had taken the most easily accessible ore, elaborate mining equipment became necessary. Gold-mining companies in California developed hydraulic systems that used great amounts of water under high pressure to demolish entire mountainsides. One **hydraulic** mining operation used sixteen giant water cannon to bombard hillsides with 40 million gallons of water a day—about the same amount of water used daily by the people of Baltimore. Hydraulic mining wreaked havoc downstream, filling rivers with sediment and causing serious flooding. It ended only when a fed-

eral court ruled in 1884 that the technique inevitably damaged the property of others and had to stop.

In most parts of the West, the exhaustion of surface deposits led to construction of underground shafts and tunnels. In Butte, Montana, for example, a gold discovery in 1864 led to discoveries of copper, silver, and zinc in what has been called the richest hill on earth. Mine shafts there reached depths of a mile and required 3,000 miles of underground rail lines.

Such operations required elaborate machinery to move men and equipment thousands of feet into the earth and keep the tunnels cool, dry, and safe. By the mid-1870s, some Nevada silver mines boasted the most advanced mining equipment in the world. There, temperatures soared to 120 degrees in shafts more than 2,200 feet deep. Mighty air pumps circulated air from the surface to the depths, and ice was used to reduce temperatures. Massive water pumps kept the shafts dry. Powerful drills speeded the removal of ore, and enormous ore-crushing machines operated day and night on the surface.

The mining industry changed rapidly. Solitary prospectors panning for gold in mountain streams gave way to gigantic companies whose operations were financed by banks in San Francisco and eastern cities. Mining companies became vertically integrated, operating mines, ore-crushing mills, railroads, and companies that supplied fuel and water for mining. Western miners organized too, forming strong unions. Beginning in Butte and spreading throughout the major mining regions of the West, miners' unions secured wages five-to-ten times higher than what miners in Britain or Germany earned.

The Birth of Western Agribusiness

Throughout the Northeast, the family farm was the typical agricultural unit. In the South after the Civil War, family-operated farms, whether run by owners or by sharecroppers, also became typical. Very large farming operations in the East and South tended to be exceptions. In California and other parts of the

---

placer mining   A form of gold mining that uses water to separate gold from gravel deposits; because gold is heavier, it settles to the bottom of a container filled with water and agitated.

hydraulic   Having to do with water moved in pipes; hydraulic mining uses water under great pressure to wash away soil from underlying mineral deposits.

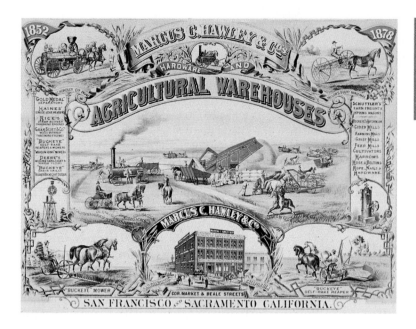

Mechanization greatly increased the amount of land that an individual could farm. This 1878 lithograph depicts a California crew setting a world's record for the amount of wheat harvested in a single day. *Department of Special Collections, F. Hal Higgins Library of Agricultural Technology, University of California, Davis.*

West, agriculture sometimes developed on a different scale, involving huge areas, the intensive use of heavy equipment, and wage labor. Today agriculture on such a large scale is known as **agribusiness**.

Wheat was the first major crop for which farming could be entirely mechanized. By 1880, in the Red River Valley of what is now North Dakota and in the San Joaquin Valley in central California, wheat farms were as large as 100 square miles. Such farming businesses required major capital investments in land, equipment, and livestock. One Dakota farm required 150 workers during spring planting and 250 or more at harvest time. By the late 1880s, some California wheat growers were using huge steam-powered tractors and **combines**.

Most of the great Dakota wheat farms had been broken into smaller units by the 1890s, but in some parts of California agriculture flourished on a scale unknown in most parts of the country. One California company, Miller and Lux, held more than a million acres, scattered through three states. Though California wheat raising declined in significance by 1900, large-scale agriculture employing many seasonal laborers became established for several other crops.

Growers of fruits and similar crops tended to operate small farms, but they still required a large work force at harvest time to pick the crops quickly so that they could be shipped to distant markets while still fresh. Fruit raising spread rapidly as California growers took advantage of refrigerated railroad cars

and ships. By 1892, fresh fruit from California was for sale in London.

At first, growers relied on Chinese immigrants for such seasonal labor needs. After the Exclusion Act of 1882 (discussed later in this chapter), the number of Chinese fell, and growers turned to other groups—Japanese, Sikhs from India, and eventually Mexicans.

Logging in the Pacific Northwest

The coastal areas of the Pacific Northwest (see chapter-opening map and Map 19.3) are very different from other parts of the West. There, heavy winter rains and cool, damp, summer fogs nurture thick stands of evergreens, especially tall Douglas firs and coastal redwoods.

The growth of California cities and towns required lumber, and it came first from the coastal redwoods of central and northern California. When the most accessible stands of timber had been cut, attention shifted north to Oregon and Washington. Seattle developed as a lumber town from the late 1850s on-

---

agribusiness A large-scale farming operation typically involving considerable land holdings, hired labor, and extensive use of machinery; may also involve processing and distribution as well as growing.

combine A large harvesting machine that both cuts and threshes grain.

San Francisco rapidly emerged as the metropolis of the western United States. This 1905 photograph shows a San Francisco policeman talking to a young girl at one of the city's busiest intersections. Note the cable car on the right. *San Francisco Maritime National Historic Park, Muhrman Collection AZZ.16.824N.*

ward, as companies in San Francisco helped to finance an industry geared to providing lumber for California cities. By the late nineteenth century, some companies had become vertically integrated, owning **lumber mills** along the northwest coast, a fleet of schooners that hauled rough lumber down the coast to California, and lumber yards in the San Francisco Bay area.

In 1883, the Northern Pacific Railroad reached Portland, Oregon, and was extended to the Puget Sound area a few years later. The Great Northern completed its line to Seattle in 1893 (see Map 19.1). Both railroads promoted the development of the lumber industry by offering cheap rates to ship logs. Lumber production in Oregon and Washington boomed, leaving behind treeless hillsides subject to severe erosion during heavy winter rains. Westerners committed to rapid economic development seldom thought about ecological damage, for the long-term cost of such practices was not immediately apparent.

Western Metropolis: San Francisco

Lumber companies, the Miller and Lux land company, major mining companies, and the Southern Pacific Railroad all located their headquarters in San Francisco. Between the end of the Civil War and 1900, that city emerged as the **metropolis** of the West and was long unchallenged as the commercial, financial, and manufacturing center for much of the region west of the Rockies.

From 1864 to 1875, the Bank of California, led by William Ralston, played a key role in the development in San Francisco. Like many western entrepreneurs, Ralston saw himself as a visionary leader bringing civilization into the wilderness, and he expected to profit from his efforts. He once argued that "what is for the good of the masses will in the end be of equal benefit to the bankers." Seeking to build a diversified California economy, Ralston channeled profits from Nevada's silver mines into railroad and steamboat lines and factories that turned out furniture, sugar, woolen goods, and more. Other entrepreneurs pursued similar endeavors. By the 1880s, San Francisco was home to foundries that produced locomotives, some of the world's most advanced mining equipment, agricultural implements for large-scale farming, and ships.

James Bryce, an English visitor, wrote in the 1880s that "California, more than any other part of the Union, is a country by itself, and San Francisco a capital." The city, he explained, "dwarfs" other western cities and is "more powerful over them than is any Eastern city over its neighbourhood." This

---

lumber mill   A factory or place where logs are sawed into rough boards.

metropolis   An urban center, especially one that is dominant within a region.

power of San Francisco over much of the West came partly because it had headquarters of many leading western corporations and partly because it was the western center for finance capitalism—the Pacific coast counterpart of Wall Street. By 1900, a few other western cities—Denver, Salt Lake City, Seattle, Portland, and especially Los Angeles—were challenging the economic dominance of San Francisco.

Water Wars

From the first efforts at western economic development, water was a central concern. Prospectors in the California gold rush needed water to separate worthless gravel from gold. On the Great Plains, a cattle rancher claimed grazing land by controlling a stream. Throughout much of the West, water was scarce, and competition for water sometimes produced conflict—usually in the form of courtroom battles.

Lack of water potentially posed stringent limits on western urban growth. Beginning in 1901, San Francisco sought federal permission to put a dam across the Hetch Hetchy Valley, on federal land adjacent to Yosemite National Park in the Sierra Nevada, in order to create a reservoir. Opposition came from the **Sierra Club**, formed in 1892 and dedicated to preserving Sierra Nevada wilderness. Congress finally approved the project in 1913, and the enormous construction project took another twenty-one years to complete. Los Angeles resolved its water problems in a similar way, by diverting the water of the Owens River to its use—even though Owens Valley residents tried to dynamite the **aqueduct** in resistance.

Throughout much of the West, irrigation was vital to the success of farming. As early as 1899, irrigated land in the eleven westernmost states produced $84 million in crops. Although individual entrepreneurs and companies undertook significant irrigation projects, the magnitude of the task led many westerners to look for federal assistance, just as they had sought federal assistance for railroad development. "When Uncle Sam puts his hand to a task, we know it will be done," wrote one irrigation proponent. "When he waves his hand toward the desert and says, 'Let there be water!' we know that the stream will obey his commands."

The National Irrigation Association, created in 1899, organized lobbying efforts, and Francis Newlands, member of Congress from Nevada, introduced legislation. The **Reclamation Act** of 1902 promised federal construction of irrigation facilities. The Reclamation Service, established by the law, eventually became a major power in the West as it sought to move the region's water to areas where it could be used for irrigation. Reclamation projects sometimes drew criticism, however, for disproportionately benefiting large landowners.

ETHNICITY AND RACE IN THE WEST

• Compare the experiences of American Indians, Mexican Americans, and Chinese Americans between the end of the Civil War (1865) and about 1900.

In its ethnic and racial composition, the West has always differed significantly from the rest of the nation. In 1900 the western half of the United States included more than 80 percent of all Native Americans, Chinese Americans or Japanese Americans, and Mexican Americans. The northeastern quarter of the nation remained predominantly white until World War I, and the South was largely a biracial society of whites and African Americans. The West has long had greater ethnic diversity. (These patterns can be seen in Figure 19.1.)

Immigrants to the Golden Mountain

Between 1854 and 1882, some three hundred thousand Chinese immigrants entered the United States. Most came from southern China, which in the 1840s and 1850s suffered from political instability, economic distress, and even **famine**. The fortune seekers who poured in from around the world as part of the California gold rush included significant numbers of Chinese. Among the early Chinese immigrants, California became known as "Land of the Golden Mountain."

Sierra Club Environmental organization formed in 1892 and now dedicated to preserving and expanding the world's parks, wildlife, and wilderness areas.

aqueduct A pipe or channel designed to transport water from a remote source, usually by gravity.

Reclamation Act Law passed by Congress in 1902 that provided funding for irrigation of western lands and created the Reclamation Service to oversee the process.

famine A serious and widespread shortage of food.

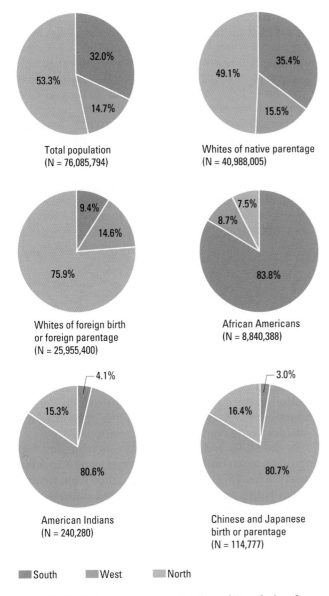

FIGURE 19.1 Regional Distribution of Population, by Race, 1900 These pie charts indicate the distinctiveness of the West with respect to race and ethnicity. Note that the West held about 15 percent of the nation's total population and about the same proportion of the nation's white population (including whites who were foreign-born or of foreign parentage), but included more than four-fifths of American Indians and those of Chinese and Japanese birth or parentage. *Source:* Data from *Twelfth Census of the United States: 1900* (Washington, D.C., 1901), Population Reports, vol. 1, p. 483, Table 9.

grants worked as agricultural laborers and farmers too, especially in California, throughout the late nineteenth century. Some of them made important contributions to crop development, especially fruit growing.

In San Francisco and elsewhere in the West, they established **Chinatowns**—relatively autonomous and largely self-contained Chinese communities. In San Francisco's Chinatown, immigrants formed kinship organizations and district associations (whose members had come from the same part of China) to assist and protect each other. A confederation of such associations, the Chinese Consolidated Benevolent Association (often called the "Six Companies"), eventually dominated the social and economic life of Chinese communities in much of the West. Such communities were largely male, partly because immigration officials permitted only a few Chinese women to enter the country, apparently to prevent an American-born generation. As was true in many largely male communities, gambling and prostitution flourished, giving Chinatowns reputations as centers for vice.

Almost from the beginning, Chinese immigrants encountered discrimination and violence. In 1854 the California Supreme Court prohibited Chinese (along with Native Americans and African Americans) from testifying in court against a white person. A state tax on foreign-born miners posed a significant burden on Chinese (and also Latino) gold seekers. During the depression of the 1870s, many white workers blamed the Chinese for driving wages down and unemployment up. In fact, different economic factors depressed wage levels and brought unemployment, but white workers seeking a scapegoat instigated anti-Chinese riots in Los Angeles in 1871 and in San Francisco in 1877. In 1885 anti-Chinese riots swept through much of the West. A mob of white miners burned the Chinatown in Rock Springs, Wyoming, and killed twenty-eight Chinese, mostly mine workers. This anti-Chinese violence prompted many Chinese to retreat to the largest Chinatowns, especially the one in San Francisco.

In these riots, the message was usually the same: "The Chinese Must Go." This slogan surfaced in San Francisco in 1877 as part of the appeal of the Workingmen's Party of California, a political organization that blamed unemployment and low wages on the Chinese and on the capitalists who hired them. In 1882 Congress responded to repeated pressures

Though many Chinese worked in mining, they also formed a major part of construction labor in the West, especially for railroad building. Chinese immi-

> **Chinatown** A section of a city inhabited chiefly by people of Chinese birth or ancestry.

This public letter writer in San Francisco represents an institution that Chinese immigrants brought with them to America. By the 1880s, the Chinatowns of large western cities had become places of refuge that provided immigrants with some degree of safety from anti-Chinese agitation. *California Historical Society, San Francisco E.N. Sewell FN-01003.*

from unions, especially Pacific coast unions, by passing the **Chinese Exclusion Act**, prohibiting entry to all Chinese people except teachers, students, merchants, tourists, and officials. The law also specified that Asian immigrants were not eligible to become naturalized citizens.

In some parts of the West, the Chinese were subjected to segregation similar to that imposed on blacks in the South, including residential and occupational segregation rooted in local custom rather than law. In 1871 the San Francisco school board barred Chinese students from that city's public schools. The ban lasted until 1885, when the parents of **Mamie Tape** convinced the courts to order the city to provide education for their daughter. The city then opened a segregated Chinese school. Segregated schools for Chinese-American children were also set up in a few other places, but most school segregation began to break down in the 1910s and 1920s.

Among Chinese immigrants, merchants often took the lead in establishing a strong economic base. Organizations based on kinship, region, or occupation were sometimes successful in fighting anti-Chinese legislation. When San Francisco passed a city law restricting Chinese laundry owners, they brought a court challenge. In the case of *Yick Wo v. Hopkins* (1886), the U.S. Supreme Court for the first time declared a licensing law unconstitutional because local authorities had used it to discriminate on the basis of race.

When other immigrants began to arrive from Asia, they too concentrated in the West. Significant numbers of Japanese immigrants started coming to the United States after 1890. From 1891 through 1907, nearly 150,000 arrived, most through the Pacific coast port cities. Whites in the West, especially organized labor, viewed Japanese immigrants in much the same way as they had earlier immigrants from China—with hostility and scorn. Pushed by western labor organizations, President Theodore Roosevelt in 1907 negotiated an agreement with Japan to halt immigration of Japanese laborers.

Forced Assimilation

As the headlines about the Great Sioux War, the Nez Perce, and Geronimo faded from the nation's newspapers, many Americans began to describe American Indians as a "vanishing race." But Indian people did not vanish. With the end of armed conflict, the relation between Native Americans and the rest of the nation entered a new phase, one appropriate to consider in the context of racial relations.

By the 1870s, federal policymakers were developing plans to **assimilate** Native Americans into white society. After 1871, federal policy shifted from treating Indian tribes as sovereign dependent nations, with whom federal officials negotiated treaties, to viewing them as wards of the federal government. Leading scholars, notably Lewis Henry Morgan of the Smithsonian Institution, viewed culture as an evolutionary process. Rather than seeing each culture as unique, they analyzed groups as being at one of three stages of development: savagery (hunters and gatherers), barbarism (those who practiced agriculture and made pottery), and civilization (those with a written language). All peoples, they thought, were evolving

Chinese Exclusion Act Law passed by Congress in 1882 that prohibited Chinese laborers from entering the United States; it was extended periodically until World War II.

Mamie Tape Chinese girl in San Francisco whose parents sued the city in 1885 to end the exclusion of Chinese students from the public schools.

assimilate To absorb immigrants or members of a culturally distinct group into the prevailing culture.

toward "higher" cultural types. Most white Americans probably agreed that western Europeans and their descendants throughout the world had reached the highest level of development.

Public support for a change in federal policy grew in response to speaking tours by American Indians and white reformers and to the publication of several exposés, notably Helen Hunt Jackson's *A Century of Dishonor* (1881) and *Ramona* (a novel, 1884). Soon federal policymakers accepted reformers' arguments for speeding up the evolutionary process for Native Americans. Apparently no reformers or federal policymakers understood that American Indians had complex cultures that were very different from—but not inferior to—the culture of Americans of European descent.

Education was an important element in the reformers' plans for "civilizing" the Indians. Federal officials worked with churches and philanthropic organizations to establish schools distant from the reservations, and many Native American children were sent to these institutions to live and study. The teachers' goal was to educate their students to become part of white society, and to that end they forbade the Indian students from speaking their languages, practicing their religions, or otherwise following their own cultural patterns. Other educational programs aimed to train adult Indian men to be farmers or mechanics. Federal officials also tried to prohibit some religious observances and traditional practices on reservations.

The **Dawes Severalty Act** (1887) was another important tool in the "civilizing" effort. Its objective was to make the Indians into self-sufficient, property-conscious, profit-oriented, individual farmers model citizens of nineteenth-century white America. The law created a governmental policy of severalty—that is, individual ownership of land by Native Americans. Reservations were to be divided into individual family farms of 160 acres. Once each family received its allotment, surplus reservation land was to be sold by the government and the proceeds used for Indian education projects. This policy therefore found enthusiastic support among reformers urging rapid assimilation and among westerners who coveted Indian lands.

Individual landownership, however, was at odds with traditional Native American views that land was for the use of all and that sharing was a major obligation. Some Indian leaders urged Congress to defeat the Dawes Act. D. W. Bushyhead, leader of the Cherokee Nation, joined with delegates from the Cherokee, Creek, and Choctaw Nations in a petition to Congress. "Our people have not asked for or authorized this," they stressed, and they explained,

Susan La Flesche was the first Indian woman to graduate from medical college. Her sister, Susette, was a prominent crusader for Indian rights and her brother, Francis, was a leading ethnologist. Well-educated, they chose to live in and mediate between two societies—the Omaha and the dominant whites. *Nebraska State Historical Society.*

"Our own laws regulate a system of land tenure suited to our condition."

Despite such protests, Congress approved the Dawes Act. The result bore out the warning of Senator Henry Teller of Colorado, who called it "a bill to despoil the Indians of their land." Once allotments to Indian families were made, about 70 percent of the land area of the reservations remained, and much of it was sold outright. In the end, the Dawes Act did not end the reservation system, nor did it reduce the Indians' dependence on the federal government. It did separate the Indians from a good deal of their land.

Native Americans responded to their situation in various ways. Some tried to cooperate with the

> **Dawes Severalty Act**   Law passed by Congress in 1887 intended to break up Indian reservations to create individual farms (holding land in severalty) rather than maintaining common ownership of the land; surplus lands were to be sold and the proceeds used to fund Indian education.

assimilation programs. Susan La Flesche, for example, daughter of an Omaha leader, graduated from medical college in 1889 at the head of her class. But she disappointed her teachers, who wanted her to abandon Indian culture completely, when she set up her medical practice near the Omaha reservation, treated both white and Omaha patients, took part in tribal affairs, and managed her land allotment and those of other family members. Dr. La Flesche also participated in the local white community through the temperance movement and sometimes by preaching in the local Presbyterian church.

Dr. La Flesche seems to have moved easily between two cultures. Some Native Americans preferred the old ways, hiding their children to keep them out of school and secretly practicing traditional religious ceremonies. Although Native American people's cultural patterns changed, it was not always in the way that federal officials anticipated. In Oklahoma, where many groups with different traditional cultures lived in close proximity, people began to borrow cultural practices from other groups. In some places, Indians became an important element in the wage-earning work force near their reservations, sometimes against the wishes of reservation officials. In the late nineteenth century, the **peyote cult**, based on the hallucinogenic properties of the peyote cactus, emerged as an alternative religion. It evolved into the Native American Church, combining elements of their traditional culture, Christianity, and peyote use.

In the late nineteenth and early twentieth centuries, Mexican Americans became a major part of the work force for constructing and maintaining railroads in the Southwest. This crew of Mexican-American linemen was working in south Texas when this photograph was taken in 1910. They may have been employed by a railroad to put up and maintain its communication lines or by a telegraph or telephone company. *Texas State Library and Archives Commission.*

Mexican Americans in the Southwest

The United States annexed Texas in 1845 and soon after acquired vast territories from Mexico at the end of the Mexican War. Living in those territories were large numbers of people who spoke Spanish, many of them **mestizos**—people of mixed Spanish and Native American ancestry. The treaties by which the United States acquired those territories specified that Mexican citizens living there automatically became American citizens.

Throughout the Southwest during the late nineteenth century, many Mexican Americans lost their land as the region attracted English-speaking whites (often called **Anglos** by those whose first language was Spanish). The Treaty of Guadalupe Hidalgo, which ended the war with Mexico, guaranteed Mexican Americans' landholdings, but the vagueness of Spanish and Mexican land grants encouraged legal

challenges. Sometimes Mexican Americans were cheated out of their land through fraud.

In California, some **Californios**—Spanish-speaking people born in California—had welcomed the break with Mexico. However the California gold rush attracted fortune seekers from around the world, including Mexico and other parts of Latin America.

---

peyote cult A religion that included ceremonial use of the hallucinogenic peyote cactus, native to Mexico and the Southwest.

mestizo A person of mixed Spanish and Indian ancestry.

Anglo A term applied in the Southwest to English-speaking whites.

Californios Spanish-speaking people born in California before California was acquired by the United States.

Leon Trousset, born in France, began to paint in California and the Southwest in the 1850s, when that region had just been acquired by the United States from Mexico. His paintings mix history and romance, depicting the old Southwest as a place of imposing missions, residents in Mexican dress, and tidy plazas. In this painting done in the mid-1880s, entitled *Old Mesilla Plaza* (showing Messilla, New Mexico Territory), Trousset shows the Church of San Albino as much larger than it actually was, and he presents the buildings lining the plaza as adobe (as they would have been in the 1850s), rather than the brick buildings of the 1880s. *Smithsonian American Art Museum, Washington, D.C./Art Resource, N.Y.*

Most came from the eastern United States and Europe. In northern California, a hundred thousand gold seekers inundated the few thousand Mexican Americans. Latinos (people from Latin America) who came to California as gold seekers were often driven from the mines by racist harassment and a tax on foreign miners. In southern California, however, there were fewer Anglos until late in the nineteenth century. There, Californios won election to local, and even state, office, notably Romualdo Pacheco, who served as state treasurer and lieutenant governor and who succeeded to the governorship in 1875.

By the 1870s, many of the **pueblos** (towns created under Mexican or Spanish governments) had become **barrios**—some rural, some in inner cities—centered on a Catholic church. In some ways, the barrios resembled the neighborhoods of European immigrants in the eastern United States at the same time. Both had mutual benefit societies, political associations, and newspapers published in the language of the community, and the cornerstone of both was often a church. There was an important difference, however. Neighborhoods of European immigrants consisted of people who had come to a new land where they anticipated making some changes in their own lives in order to adjust. The residents of the barrios, in contrast, lived in regions that had been home to Mexicans for generations but now found themselves surrounded by English-speaking Americans who hired them for cheap wages, sometimes sneered at their culture, and pressured them to assimilate.

In Texas, as in California, some of the **Tejanos** (Spanish-speaking people born in Texas) had welcomed the break with Mexico. For example, Lorenzo de Zavala served briefly as the first vice president of the Texas Republic. Like the Californios, some Tejanos

lost their lands through fraud or coercion. By 1900, much of the land in south Texas had passed out of the hands of Tejano families—sometimes legally, sometimes fraudulently—but the new, Anglo ranch owners usually maintained the social patterns characteristic of Tejano ranchers.

A large section of Texas—between the Nueces River and Rio Grande and west to El Paso—remained culturally Mexican, home to Tejanos and to two-thirds of all Mexican immigrants who came to the United States before 1900. In the 1890s, one journalist described the area as "an overlapping of Mexico into the United States." During the 1860s and 1870s, conflict broke out occasionally as some Mexican Americans challenged the political and economic power of Anglo newcomers. In social relations and in politics, all but a few wealthy Tejanos came to be subordinate to the Anglos who dominated the regional economy and the professions.

In New Mexico Territory, **Hispanos** (Spanish-speaking New Mexicans) were clearly the majority of the population and the voters throughout the nineteenth century. They consistently composed a majority in the territorial legislature and were frequently elected as territorial delegates to Congress (the only position elected by the entire territory). Republicans usually prevailed in territorial politics,

pueblo   Town created under Mexican or Spanish rules.
barrio   A Spanish-speaking community, often a part of a larger city.
Tejanos   Spanish-speaking people born in Texas before it was acquired by the United States.
Hispanos   Spanish-speaking New Mexicans.

Popular fiction and Hollywood movies have contributed much to the creation of the "winning of the West" myth, which depicted much of the West as empty wilderness waiting for the transforming hand of bold white settlers. This myth either ignored or minimized previous inhabitants of the West. *Collection of David J. and Janice L. Frent.*

their party led by wealthy Hispanos and Anglos who began to arrive in significant numbers after the entrance of the first railroad in 1879. Although Hispanos were the majority and could dominate elections, many who had small landholdings lost their land in ways similar to patterns in California and Texas—except that some who enriched themselves in New Mexico were wealthy Hispanos.

In the 1880s, a secretive organization emerged dedicated to protecting the property—and lives—of poor Mexican Americans. Calling themselves *las Gorras Blancas* (the White Caps), they used violence at times to protect Mexican-Americans' property or to fight the railroads. In 1889 three hundred Gorras Blancas destroyed extensive property belonging to the Santa Fe Railroad. Other Gorras Blancas aligned themselves with the Knights of Labor or tried to use electoral politics to accomplish their goals.

From 1856 to 1910 throughout the Southwest, the Latino population grew more slowly than the Anglo population. After 1910, however, that situation reversed itself as political and social upheavals in Mexico prompted massive migration to the United States. Probably a million people—equivalent to one-tenth of the entire population of Mexico in 1910—arrived over the next twenty years. More than half stayed in Texas, but significant numbers settled in southern California and throughout other parts of the Southwest. Inevitably, this new stream of immigrants changed some of the patterns of ethnic relations that had characterized the region since the mid-nineteenth century.

THE WEST IN AMERICAN THOUGHT

- How have historians' views of the West changed?
- How does the myth of the West compare with its reality?

The West has long fascinated Americans, and the "winning of the West" has become a national myth—one that has sometimes obscured or distorted the actual facts. Many Americans have thought of the West in terms of a frontier, an imaginary line marking the westward advance of mining, cattle raising, farming, commerce, and associated social patterns. According to this way of thinking, east of the frontier lay established society, and beyond it lay the wild, untamed West. Often this view was closely related to evolutionary notions of civilization like those put forth by Lewis Henry Morgan and the Social Darwinists. For those who thought about the West in this way, the frontier represented the dividing point between barbarism and civilization.

The West as Utopia and Myth

During the nineteenth and much of the twentieth century, the West seemed a potential **utopia** to some who thought of the frontier as dividing emptiness from civilization. Generations of Americans dreamed of a better life on "new land" in the West, though many never ventured forth. In the popular mind of the late nineteenth century, the West was vacant, waiting to be filled and formed. Out there, it seemed, nothing was predetermined. A person could make a fresh start. People who dreamed of creating communities based on new social values often looked to the West, especially to California.

The West appealed as well to Americans who sought to improve their social and economic standing. The presence of free or cheap land, the ability to start over, the idea of creating a place of one's own, all were part of the West's attraction. Of course, not all who tried to fulfill their dreams succeeded, but enough did to justify the image of the West as a land of promise.

utopia An ideally perfect place.

The West achieved mythical status in popular novels, movies, and later television. Stories about the "winning of the West" usually begin with the grandeur of wide grassy plains, towering craggy mountains, and vast silent deserts. In most versions, the western Indians face a tragic destiny. They usually appear as a proud, noble people whose tragic but unavoidable demise clears the way for the transformation of the vacated land by bold men and women of European descent. The starring roles in this drama are played by miners, ranchers, cowboys, farmers, and railroad builders who struggle to overcome both natural and human obstacles. These pioneers personify rugged individualism—the virtues of self-reliance and independence—as they triumph through hard work and personal integrity. Many of the human obstacles are villainous characters: brutal gunmen, greedy speculators, vicious cattle rustlers, unscrupulous moneylenders, selfish railroad barons. Some are only doubters, too timid or too skeptical of the promise of the West to risk all in the struggle to succeed.

The novelist **Willa Cather** presents a sophisticated—and woman-centered—version of many of these elements. In *O Pioneers!* (1913), the major character is Alexandra Bergson, daughter of Swedish immigrant homesteaders on the Great Plains. When her father dies, Alexandra struggles with the land, the climate, and the skepticism of her brothers to create a lush and productive farm. Cather's *My Ántonia* (1918) presents Ántonia Shimerda, daughter of Czech immigrants, who survives run-ins with a land speculator, grain buyer, and moneylender, only to become pregnant outside marriage by a railroad conductor. Dishonored, Ántonia regains the respect of the community through her hard work. She builds a thriving farm, marries, raises a large family, and becomes "a rich mine of life, like the founders of early races." *My Ántonia* explicitly presents another aspect of the myth. Jim Burden, the narrator of the story, grows up on the frontier with Ántonia but becomes a prosperous New York lawyer whose own marriage is childless. Ántonia, symbolizing western fecundity, is thus contrasted with eastern sterility.

The Frontier and the West

Starting in the 1870s, accounts of the winning of the West suggested to many Americans the existence of an America more attractive than the steel mills and urban slums of their own day, a place where people were more virtuous than the barons of industry and corrupt city politicians, where individual success was possible without labor strife or racial and ethnic discord. The myth has evolved and exerts a hold on Americans' imagination even today. From at least the 1920s onward, the cowboy has been the most prominent embodiment of the myth. The mythical cowboy is a brave and resourceful loner, riding across the West and dispelling trouble from his path and from the lives of others. He rarely does the actual work of a cowboy.

Like all myths, the myth of the winning of the West contains elements of truth but ignores others. The myth usually treats Indians as victims of progress. It rarely considers their fate after they meet defeat at the hands of the cavalry. Instead, they obligingly disappear. The myth rarely tempers its celebration of rugged individualism by acknowledging the fundamental role of government at every stage in the transformation of the West: dispossessing the Indians, subsidizing railroads, dispensing the public domain to promote economic development, and rerouting rivers to bring their precious water to both farmland and cities. The myth often overlooks the role of ethnic and racial minorities—from African-American and Mexican cowboys to Chinese railroad construction crews—and it especially overlooks the extent to which these people were exploited as sources of cheap labor. Women typically appear only in the role of helpless victim or noble helpmate. Finally, the myth generally ignores the extent to which the economic development of the West replicated economic conditions in the East, including monopolistic, vertically integrated corporations and labor unions. If such influences appear in the myth, they are usually as obstacles that the hardy pioneers overcame.

In 1893 **Frederick Jackson Turner**, a young historian, presented an influential essay called "The Significance of the Frontier in American History." In it, he challenged the prevailing idea that answers to questions about the nature of American institutions and values were to be found by studying the European societies to which white Americans traced their ancestry. Turner focused instead on the frontier as a uniquely defining factor. Turner argued that "American social development has been continually beginning over again on the frontier" and

---

Willa Cather   Early-twentieth-century writer, many of whose novels chronicle the lives of immigrants and others on the American frontier.

Frederick Jackson Turner   American historian who argued that the frontier and cheap, abundant land were dominant factors in creating American democracy and shaping national character.

that these experiences constituted "the forces dominating American character." The western frontier, he claimed, was the region of maximum opportunity and widest equality, where individualism and democracy most flourished.

Turner's view of the West and the importance of the frontier dominated the thinking of historians for many years. Today, however, historians focus on many elements missing from Turner's analysis: the importance of cultural conflicts among different groups of people; the experiences of American Indians (the original inhabitants of the West), and of the Spanish-speaking mestizo peoples of the Southwest, and of Asian Americans; gender issues and the experiences of women; the natural environment and ecological issues, especially those involving water; the growth and development of western cities; and the ways in which the western economy resembles and differs from the economy of the East. If western individualism and mobility have been formative to the American experience, as Turner suggested, so too have been these other elements in the history of the West.

INDIVIDUAL VOICES

Examining a Primary Source

Luther Standing Bear Tells of His Experience with Forced Assimilation

Luther Standing Bear was called Ota K'te when he was born in 1868, the son of Standing Bear, a chief of the Oglala Lakota, who fought against Custer at the Battle of the Little Big Horn. He attended the Carlisle Indian School in Pennsylvania, toured with a Wild West Show, became an actor, and belonged to the Actors' Guild (a union). By birth, he was also a hereditary chief of the Oglala Lakota. In the 1920s, Standing Bear began to write about his experiences and to record the history of his people, seeking to improve their lives and to change federal Indian policies. This selection from his book, *Land of the Spotted Eagle* (1933), describes his experience at Carlisle, in Pennsylvania, a leading Indian school, where he was sent in 1879 to be "civilized."

● How does Standing Bear characterize the process of rapid assimilation that was thrust upon him?

At the age of eleven years, ancestral life for me and my people was most abruptly ended without regard for our wishes, comforts, or rights in the matter. At once I was thrust into an alien world, into an environment as different from the one into which I had been born as it is possible to imagine, to remake myself, if I could, into the likeness of the invader. . . . At Carlisle the transforming, the 'civilizing' process began. It began with clothes. . . . Our accustomed dress was taken and replaced with clothes that felt cumbersome and awkward. . . . Leather boots caused actual suffering. . . . Red flannel undergarments were given to us for winter wear, and for me, at least, discomfort grew into actual torture. . . . Of course, our hair was cut. . . . In some mysterious way long hair stood in the path of our development. . . . ●

● At the time Standing Bear wrote this account, several Indian boarding schools were still in operation. What changes does Standing Bear advocate? Why?

● What factors in addition to those listed might have contributed to the high mortality rate among the schoolchildren?

● Despite Standing Bear's criticism of Carlisle, the education he received there permitted him to move between white and Lakota cultures, to have an acting career, and to be a force for change. Would that have been possible without the trauma of forced assimilation? Explain.

Almost immediately our names were changed to those in common use in the English language. . . . I was told to take a pointer and select a name for myself from the list written on the blackboard. I did, and since one was just as good as another, and as I could not distinguish any difference in them, I placed the pointer on the name Luther. . . . By this time we had been forbidden to speak our mother tongue, which is the rule at all boarding-schools. This rule is uncalled for, and today is not only robbing the Indian, but America of a rich heritage. The language of a people is part of their history. Today we should be perpetuating history instead of destroying it, and this can only be effectively done by allowing and encouraging the young to keep it alive. A language unused, embalmed, and reposing only in a book, is a dead language. . . . ●

Of all the changes we were forced to make, that of diet was doubtless the most injurious, for it was immediate and drastic. . . . Had we been allowed our own simple diet of meat, either boiled with soup or dried, and fruit, with perhaps a few vegetables, we should have thrived. But the change in clothing, housing, food, and confinement combined with lonesomeness was too much, and in three years nearly one half of the children from the Plains were dead and through with all earthly schools. ● *In the graveyard at Carlisle most of the graves are those of little ones.* ●

SUMMARY

The West underwent tremendous change during the thirty or forty years following the Civil War. Federal policymakers hoped for the rapid development of the region, and they often used the public domain to accomplish that purpose. Native Americans, especially those of the Great Plains, were initially seen as obstacles to development, but most were defeated by the army and relegated to reservations.

Patterns of development varied in different parts of the West. In the Great Basin, Mormons created a theocracy, organized cooperatives, and employed irrigation. A cattle kingdom emerged on the western Great Plains, as railroad construction made it possible to carry cattle east for slaughter and processing. As farming moved west, lack of water led to new crops and improved farming methods.

Throughout the West, railroad construction overcame the vast distances, making possible most forms of economic development. As western mining became highly mechanized, control shifted to large mining companies able to secure the necessary capital. In California especially, landowners transformed western agriculture into a large-scale commercial undertaking. The coniferous forests of the Pacific Northwest attracted lumbering companies. By the 1870s, San Francisco had become the center of much of the western economy. Water posed a significant constraint on economic development in many parts of the West, prompting efforts to reroute natural water sources.

The western population included immigrants from Asia, American Indians, and Latino peoples in substantial numbers, but each group had significantly different expectations and experiences. White westerners chose to use politics and, sometimes, violence to exclude and segregate Asian immigrants. Federal policy toward American Indians proceeded from the expectation that they could and should be rapidly assimilated and must shed their separate cultural identities, but such policies largely failed. Latinos—descendants of those living in the Southwest before it became part of the United States and those who came later from Mexico or elsewhere in Latin America—often found their lives and culture under challenge.

Americans have viewed the West both as a utopia and as the source of a national myth. But those views frequently romanticize or overlook important realities in the nature of western development and in the people who accomplished it.

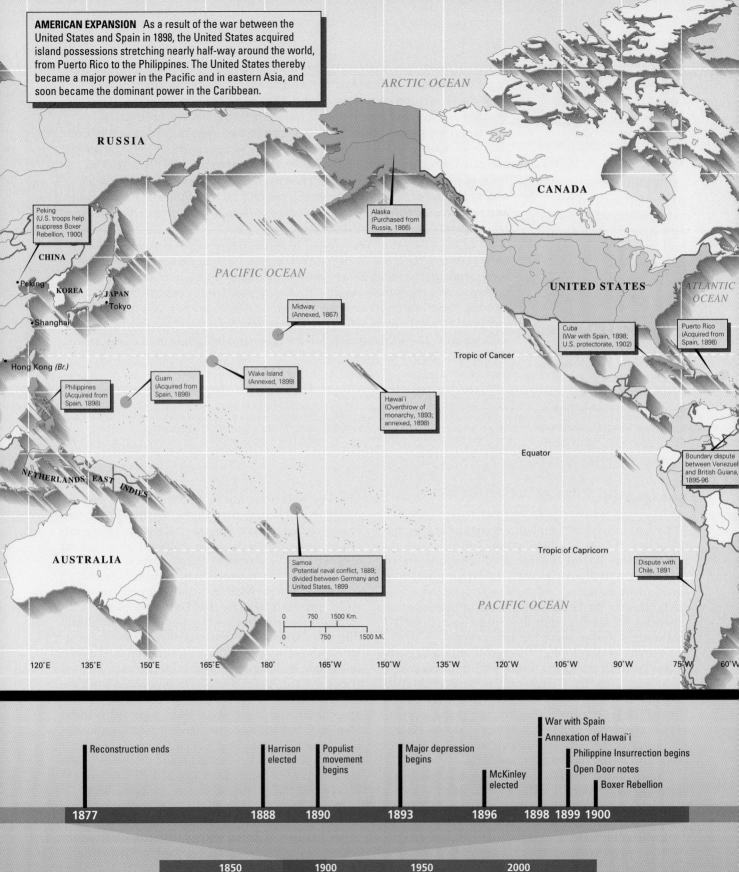

AMERICAN EXPANSION As a result of the war between the United States and Spain in 1898, the United States acquired island possessions stretching nearly half-way around the world, from Puerto Rico to the Philippines. The United States thereby became a major power in the Pacific and in eastern Asia, and soon became the dominant power in the Caribbean.

ARCTIC OCEAN

RUSSIA

CANADA

Peking
(U.S. troops help
suppress Boxer
Rebellion, 1900)

Alaska
(Purchased from
Russia, 1866)

CHINA

PACIFIC OCEAN

UNITED STATES

ATLANTIC
OCEAN

•Peking   KOREA   JAPAN
                  •Tokyo

Midway
(Annexed, 1867)

Cuba
(War with Spain, 1898;
U.S. protectorate, 1902)

Puerto Rico
(Acquired from
Spain, 1898)

•Shanghai

Tropic of Cancer

Hong Kong *(Br.)*

Philippines
(Acquired from
Spain, 1898)

Guam
(Acquired from
Spain, 1898)

Wake Island
(Annexed, 1899)

Hawai'i
(Overthrow of
monarchy, 1893;
annexed, 1898)

Equator

NETHERLANDS EAST INDIES

Boundary dispute
between Venezuel
and British Guiana,
1895-96

AUSTRALIA

Tropic of Capricorn

Dispute with
Chile, 1891

Samoa
(Potential naval conflict, 1889;
divided between Germany and
United States, 1899

PACIFIC OCEAN

0	750	1500 Km.
0	750	1500 Mi.

120°E   135°E   150°E   165°E   180°   165°W   150°W   135°W   120°W   105°W   90°W   75°W   60°W

War with Spain

Annexation of Hawai'i

Reconstruction ends

Harrison
elected

Populist
movement
begins

Major depression
begins

Philippine Insurrection begins

Open Door notes

McKinley
elected

Boxer Rebellion

1877	1888	1890	1893	1896	1898	1899	1900

1850	1900	1950	2000

Economic Crash and Political Upheaval, 1890–1900

ANNIE LE PORTE DIGGS

There are surprisingly few photographs of Annie Le Porte Diggs, given the prominent role that she played in Kansas politics in the 1890s. This one was probably taken in the mid-1890s. *Kansas State Historical Society.*

Annie Le Porte Diggs

In 1890 Annie Le Porte Diggs took a long step into party politics, though she may not have realized it at the time. Early that year, she was writing a weekly column for her local newspaper, the *Lawrence* [Kansas] *Journal*. Her column presented news from the Women's Christian Temperance Union (WCTU; see Individual Choices: Frances Willard, page 530), whose cause she had supported for a number of years. In mid-February, however, she told her editor that she wanted to change her column and devote it instead to the activities of the Farmers' Alliance, a new organization. Fueled by abysmally low prices for corn and fanned by farmers' outrage at the refusal of Republican and Democratic politicians to address the problems of farmers, the Alliance was spreading like wildfire across Kansas and other Great Plains states.

Annie L. Diggs was no stranger to controversy in 1890. Born in Ontario, Canada, in 1853, daughter of a French-Canadian father and a New Jersey-born mother, she came to Kansas at the age of 19, soon married, had three children, and became active in the Unitarian Church and the temperance movement (including the WCTU and the Prohibition Party). Her church and temperance work first led her into journalism. Soon after taking up the cause of the Farmers' Alliance, she became associate editor of the Kansas Alliance's state newspaper, the *Topeka Farmers Advocate*, and from there she moved into politics when the Farmers' Alliance sponsored the creation of the People's, or Populist, Party.

In her editorials for the *Advocate*, she ably promoted the ideals of the Populists, seeking to improve the situation of farmers and workers–producers through state and federal legislation. Her editorials also staunchly supported woman suffrage and prohibition, and condemned capital punishment. She soon became a leading Populist campaign orator as well—one of her speeches in 1890 ran from 4 P.M. until sundown, perhaps three hours. Though she weighed only a bit over 90 pounds and, as one of her admirers said, "stood shoulder high to only the shortest men," she became a powerful figure in Kansas politics.

She attended all party gatherings and gained a reputation as a mediator, able to smooth over the various petty disputes that arose among the men who made up the vast majority of convention delegates. As one observer explained, "Thus she built up a hold on the Populists that was never broken, nor was her sincerity in the cause of the underdog ever questioned."

Diggs was a strong proponent of the tactic of *fusion* in Kansas—that is, a coalition between the Populists and Democrats (who ran a dismal third in state elections after the appearance of the Populists). She supported cooperation between the two parties in Kansas, gave strong support to the campaign of William Jennings Bryan (who won both the Democratic and Populist nominations for president in 1896), and emerged as the moving

force in both the Democratic and Populist Parties of Kansas in the late 1890s. Along the way, she found time to serve as president of the Kansas Women's Free Silver League in 1896 and of the Kansas Equal Suffrage Association in 1899. In 1898 the Populist governor of Kansas (whom she had helped to elect) appointed her state librarian, the first woman to hold that position. In 1900 the *Kansas City Journal* said of her, "She has more political sagacity than the whole bunch of past party leaders put together. . . . In their day they tried to run things by dictating to the masses what they should do. She leads by first finding out what the common people of her party want and then going to the front to help them get it."

INTRODUCTION

In July 1892, a new political party, the People's Party, met in Omaha to choose its candidates for president and vice president. Born in protest against the economic and political events of the previous quarter-century, the new party—soon called the Populists—drafted a platform that boldly called for governmental action to aid the victims of industrialization. Most Americans, however, were unwilling to create a vastly more powerful federal government. Although most voters rejected the Populists' remedies, few doubted that industrialization, urbanization, immigration, and the development of the West had profoundly transformed the nation's social and economic life.

During the early 1890s, a number of other developments also affected the course of American politics. Urban poverty captured public attention, as did efforts to mitigate its worst features through settlement houses. Southern states approved new laws that disfranchised black voters and legitimized and extended racial segregation. Nativism took on political dimensions with efforts to limit immigration from Europe. A major contraction shook the economy, producing serious unemployment and deprivation. Eventually the Populists merged with the Democrats in support of the presidential candidacy of William Jennings Bryan in 1896. In 1896, however, voters chose William McKinley, the Republican candidate for president, thereby endorsing a more conservative approach to federal economic policy. The long-term outcome was a decisive shift in American politics.

During the 1890s, too, the United States emerged as a major world power, with a strong, modern navy. In war with Spain in 1898, the nation gained a colonial empire that stretched nearly halfway around the world, from Puerto Rico in the Caribbean to the Philippine Islands off the coast of eastern Asia. This, too, marked a major transformation of American politics, as henceforth foreign relations became an increasingly important part of the responsibility of federal policymakers.

POVERTY AND THE CITY

• What groups and movements arose to address urban poverty by the 1890s?

• What do their different approaches tell you about each group?

The dramatic growth of cities in the 1870s and 1880s was accompanied by an equally dramatic growth of urban poverty. The slums of New York City had worried thoughtful Americans since before the Civil War, but the huge influx of people to the cities after the war multiplied the misery. In the 1890s, journalists and reformers began to focus on urban poverty, and new ways of addressing it captured national attention.

"How the Other Half Lives"

In 1890 Jacob Riis shocked many Americans with the revelations in *How the Other Half Lives*. In a city of a million and a half inhabitants, Riis claimed, half a million (136,000 families) had begged for food at some time over the preceding eight years. Of these, more than half were unemployed, but only 6 percent were physically unable to work. Most of Riis's book described the appalling conditions of **tenements**— home, he claimed, to three-quarters of the city's population.

Strictly speaking, a tenement is an apartment house occupied by three or more families, but the term came to imply overcrowded and badly maintained housing that was hazardous to the health and safety of its residents. Riis described the typical, cramped New York tenement of his day as

> *a brick building from four to six stories high on the street, frequently with a store on the first floor. . . . Four families occupy each floor, and a set of rooms consists of one or two dark closets, used as bedrooms, with a living room twelve feet by ten. The staircase is too often a dark well in the center of the house . . . no direct through ventilation is possible.*

Such buildings, Riis insisted, "are the hotbeds of the epidemics that carry death to rich and poor alike; the nurseries of pauperism and crime that fill our jails and police courts. . . . Above all, they touch the family life with deadly moral contagion." He especially deplored the harmful influence of poverty and miserable housing conditions on children and families.

Crowded conditions in working-class sections of large cities developed in part because so many of the poor needed to live within walking distance of their work and of multiple sources of employment for various family members. By dividing buildings into small rental units, landlords packed in more tenants and collected more rent. To pay the rent, many tenants took in lodgers. Such practices produced shockingly high population densities in lower-income urban neighborhoods.

No other city was as densely populated as New York, but nearly all urban, working-class neighborhoods were crowded. Most Chicago stockyard workers, for example, lived in small row houses near the slaughterhouses. Many owned their own homes. A survey in 1911 revealed that three-quarters of the houses were subdivided into two or more living units, and that a small shanty often sat in the backyard. Half of all the living units had four rooms, a few had five, and none had more. More than half of all families took in lodgers, and lodgers who worked different shifts at the stockyards sometimes took turns sleeping in the same bed.

This photograph was either taken by Jacob Riis, or taken at his direction, in the early 1890s. It shows an interior court on the lower East Side of New York City, open to the sky above. As the photograph suggests, such busy places were often the playground for the children of the poor residents. On the far right is a water pump, perhaps the source of water for the residents of the building. Though the photographs in Riis's books were once attributed to him, it is now clear that most were taken by other people. Adding such powerful visual images to Riis's books— something made possible because of new printing technologies—greatly increased their effectiveness in mobilizing reform. *Museum of the City of New York.*

Few agreed on the causes of urban poverty, even fewer on its cure. Riis divided the blame, in New York City, among greedy landlords, corrupt officials, and the poor themselves. Henry George, a San Franciscan, in *Progress and Poverty*, pointed to the increase in the value of real estate due to urbanization and industrialization, which made it difficult or impossible for many to afford a home of their own. The Charity Organization Society (COS), by contrast, argued for individual responsibility. With chapters in a hundred cities by 1895, COS claimed that, in most cases, individual character defects produced poverty and that assistance for such people

tenement A multifamily apartment building, often unsafe, unsanitary, and overcrowded.

chronology

The United States in the 1890s

1886	First U.S. settlement house opens
1887	American Protective Association founded Florida segregates railroads
late 1880s	Farmers' Alliances spread
1888	Benjamin Harrison elected president
1888–1892	Australian ballot adopted in most states
1889–1891	Fifty-first Congress: McKinley Tariff, Sherman Anti-Trust Act, Sherman Silver Purchase Act, significant increase in naval appropriation; federal elections bill defeated
1889	North Dakota, South Dakota, Montana, and Washington become states Hull House opens First Samoa treaty
1890	Jacob Riis's *How the Other Half Lives* Alfred Thayer Mahan's *Influence of Sea Power upon History, 1660–1783* Second Mississippi Plan National American Woman Suffrage Association formed Idaho becomes a state Wyoming becomes a state, the first with woman suffrage Populist movement begins Wounded Knee
1891	Lili`uokalani becomes Hawaiian queen President Benjamin Harrison threatens war with Chile
1892	Homestead strike Cleveland elected president again
1893–1897	Depression
1893	Colorado men vote to adopt woman suffrage Sherman Silver Purchase Act repealed Queen Lili`uokalani overthrown

1894	Coxey's Army Pullman strike
1895–1896	Venezuelan boundary crisis
1895	Booker T. Washington delivers Atlanta Compromise J. P. Morgan stabilizes gold reserve
1896	Utah becomes a state, adopts woman suffrage Reconcentration policy in Cuba William Jennings Bryan's "Cross of Gold" speech William McKinley elected president Idaho adopts woman suffrage South Carolina adopts white primary *Plessy v. Ferguson*
1897	Dingley Tariff
1898	De Lôme letter published in the *New York Journal* U.S. warship *Maine* explodes War with Spain United States annexes Hawai`i by joint resolution Treaty of Paris signed
1899	Senate debates imperialism Treaty of Paris ratified Treaty of Berlin divides Samoa Open Door notes
1899–1902	Philippine insurrection suppressed
1900	Gold Standard Act Foraker Act McKinley reelected Boxer Rebellion
1901	United States Steel organized
1902	Insular cases Civil government in the Philippines Cuba becomes a protectorate

only rewarded immorality or laziness. Public or private help should be given only after careful investigation, COS insisted, and should be temporary, only until the person secured work. Moreover, COS officials expected the recipients of aid to be moral, thrifty, and hardworking.

This photo shows children from the Hull House kindergarten, probably from the 1890s. Kindergartens were first set up in Germany in the 1830s as a way to encourage learning through activities. In most American cities, settlement houses or other charitable organizations initially created kindergartens to provide day-care for children in poor and working-class neighborhoods. *The University of Illinois at Chicago, the university library, Jane Addams Memorial Collection, JAMC neg 109.*

Challenging Urban Poverty: The Settlement Houses

By the early 1890s, in several cities, young, college-educated men and women began to confront poverty differently from the Charity Organization Societies. These humanitarians tried to provide a range of assistance for the poor to deal with the problems they faced in housing, nutrition, and sanitation. The **settlement house** idea originated in England in 1884, at Toynbee Hall, a house in London's slums where idealistic university graduates lived among the poor and tried to help them. The concept spread to New York in 1886 with the opening of a settlement house staffed by young male college graduates. In 1889 several women who had graduated from Smith College (a women's college) opened another settlement house in New York.

Also in 1889, two women opened **Hull House**, the first settlement house in Chicago. For many Americans, its cofounder Jane Addams became synonymous with the settlement house movement. Born in 1860 in a small town in Illinois, the youngest daughter of a bank president, Addams attended college, then traveled in Europe. There she and Ellen Gates Starr, a friend from college, visited Toynbee

Hall and learned about its approach to helping the urban poor. Inspired by that example, the two set up Hull House in a working-class, immigrant neighborhood in Chicago. Addams lived at Hull House for the rest of her life, attracting a circle of impressive associates and making Hull House the best-known example of settlement work. Hull House offered a variety of services to the families of its neighborhood: a nursery, a kindergarten (childcare for preschool children), classes in child rearing, a playground, and a gymnasium. Addams and other Hull House activists also challenged the power of city bosses and lobbied state legislators, seeking cleaner streets, the abolition of child labor, health and safety regulations for factories, compulsory school attendance, and more. Her efforts brought national recognition.

---

settlement house   Community center operated by resident social reformers in a slum area in order to help poor people in their own neighborhoods.

Hull House   Settlement house founded by Jane Addams and Ellen Gates Starr in 1889 in Chicago.

Other settlement house workers across the country provided similar assistance to poor urban families: cooking and sewing classes, public baths, childcare facilities, instruction in English, housing for unmarried working women. Some settlement houses were church-sponsored, and others were secular. Nearly all tried to minimize class conflict because they agreed with Addams that "the dependence of classes on each other is reciprocal." Some historians have suggested that settlement house workers tried to bridge the gap between urban economic classes by imparting middle-class values to the poor and by persuading the wealthy to help mitigate poverty. Such a view suggests that their efforts reflected urban middle-class anxieties over growing extremes of wealth and poverty. Other historians have added that some settlement house workers drew on a notion of gender solidarity to appeal to upper- and middle class women for funds to assist working-class and poor women and children. Historians agree that, like Addams, many settlement house workers became forces for urban reform, promoting better education, improved public health and sanitation, and honest government.

Settlement houses spread rapidly, with some four hundred operating by 1910. By then, three-quarters of settlement workers were women, and settlement houses became the first institutions created and staffed primarily by college-educated women. They led to a new profession—social work. When universities began to offer study in social work (first at Columbia, in 1902), women tended to dominate that field too. Women college graduates thus created a new and uniquely urban profession at a time when many other careers remained closed to them.

Church-affiliated settlement houses often reflected the influence of the **Social Gospel**, a movement popularized by urban Protestant ministers who were concerned about the social and economic problems of the cities. One of the best known, Washington Gladden, of Columbus, Ohio, called for "Applied Christianity," by which he meant the application to business of Christ's injunctions to love one another and to treat others as you would have them treat you. Another minister, C. S. Sheldon, wrote *In His Steps* (1896), the story of a fictional local church whose members chose to live for one year in full compliance with the teachings of Jesus. The book suggested that if all Americans did the same, both unemployment and saloons—not to mention a host of other ills—would soon disappear. A similar strain of social activism appeared among some Catholics, especially those inspired by *Rerum Novarum* ("Of

New Things," 1891), a message from Pope Leo XIII urging greater attention by the church to the problems of the industrial working class.

POLITICAL UPHEAVAL, 1890–1892

- What groups and which issues led to the formation of the Populist Party?
- What accounts for the failure of the Republicans in the elections of 1890 and 1892?

Though urban poverty claimed the attention of many city-dwellers, it had little bearing on national politics. Benjamin Harrison had led the Republican Party to victory in the 1888 elections. When the new Congress convened late in 1889, the Republicans quickly set about writing their campaign promises into law. A torrent of new laws began to pour out of Washington. Simultaneously, new elements in politics were developing. Nativism took political forms through the American Protective Association and efforts to restrict immigration. And in 1890–1891 the People's Party, or Populists, emerged, offering a radical political alternative.

Harrison and the Fifty-first Congress

With Harrison in the White House and Republican majorities in both houses of Congress, the Republicans set out to do a lot and to do it quickly. When the fifty-first session of Congress opened late in 1889, Harrison worked more closely with congressional leaders of his own party than any other president in memory had done. Democrats in the House of Representatives tried to delay progress on the administration's agenda, but Speaker Thomas B. Reed—an enormous man renowned for his wit—announced new rules designed to speed up House business.

The Republicans' first major task was tariff revision—to cut the troublesome federal surplus (see pages 563–564) without reducing protection. Led by

---

Social Gospel A reform movement of the late nineteenth century led by Protestant clergy who drew attention to urban problems and advocated social justice for the poor.

Representative William McKinley of Ohio, the **House Ways and Means Committee** drafted a tariff bill that moved some items to the free list (notably sugar, a major source of tariff revenue) but raised tariff rates on other items, sometimes so high as to be prohibitive. The House passed the **McKinley Tariff** in May 1890 and sent it on to the Senate.

In July the House also approved a federal elections bill, intended to protect the voting rights of African Americans in the South. Its Democratic opponents called it the "force bill," to emphasize its potential for federal intervention in southern affairs. Proposed by Representative Henry Cabot Lodge of Massachusetts, the bill would have permitted federal supervision over congressional elections to prevent disfranchisement, fraud, or violence. The measure passed the House and went to the Senate, where approval by the Republican majority seemed likely.

The Senate, meanwhile, was laboring over two measures named for Senator John Sherman of Ohio: the **Sherman Anti-Trust Act** and the **Sherman Silver Purchase Act**. The Silver Purchase Act somewhat increased the amount of silver being coined into dollars but stopped short of approving the coinage of all available silver (see page 520). The Anti-Trust Act, the work of several Republican senators close to Harrison, was approved with only a single dissenting vote. Created in response to growing public concern about the new trusts and monopolies, the law declared that "every contract, combination in the form of trust or otherwise, or conspiracy, in restraint of trade or commerce among the several states, or with foreign nations, is hereby declared to be illegal." Republicans thereby tried to be responsive to concerns about monopoly power, and the United States became the first industrial nation to attempt to prevent monopolies. In fact, however, the law proved difficult to interpret or enforce, and it had little effect on companies for more than ten years.

The tariff and elections bills still awaited Senate approval. Harrison wanted them passed as a party package, but some Senate Republicans feared that a Democratic **filibuster** against the elections bill would prevent passage of both measures. Finally a compromise emerged—if Republicans would table the elections bill, the Democrats would not delay the tariff bill. Despite strong protests from a few New England Republicans, their party sacrificed African-Americans' voting rights to gain the revised tariff. (Some seventy more years passed before Congress finally acted to protect black voting rights in the South.) Harrison signed the McKinley Tariff on October 1, 1890, and the revised tariff soon produced the intended result: it reduced the surplus by cutting tariff income.

The McKinley Tariff and Sherman Anti-Trust Act were only the tip of the iceberg. In ten months the Republicans had passed what one Democrat called "a raging sea of ravenous legislation." Among the record number of new laws were a major increase in pension eligibility for disabled Union army veterans and their dependents, admission to statehood of Idaho and Wyoming, creation of territorial government in Oklahoma, and appropriations that laid the basis for a modern navy. Republicans hoped they had finally broken the political logjam that had clogged the capitol since 1875. However, as Congress labored in Washington, new and sometimes disturbing currents began to roil state and local politics.

The Politics of Nativism

During the 1890s, **nativism** (see page 546) became both more visible and more political. The **American Protective Association** (APA), the self-proclaimed

---

House Ways and Means Committee One of the most significant standing committees of the House of Representatives, responsible for initiating all taxation measures.

McKinley Tariff Tariff passed by Congress in 1890 that sought not only to protect established industries but by prohibitory duties to stimulate the creation of new industries; it soon became extremely unpopular.

Sherman Anti-Trust Act Law passed by Congress in 1890 authorizing the federal government to prosecute any "combination" "in restraint of trade"; because of adverse court rulings, at first it was ineffective as a weapon against monopolies.

Sherman Silver Purchase Act Law passed by Congress in 1890 requiring the federal government to increase its purchases of silver to be coined into silver dollars.

filibuster A long speech by a bill's opponents to delay legislative action; usually applies to extended speeches in the U.S. Senate, which has no time limit on speeches and where a minority may therefore try to "talk a bill to death" by holding up all other business.

nativism The view that old-stock American values and social patterns were superior to those of immigrants.

American Protective Association An anti-Catholic organization founded in Iowa in 1887 and active during the next decade.

voice of anti-Catholicism (see page 546) intensified its crusade against Catholics. They claimed a half million members by 1894. Sometimes, APA members fomented mob violence against Catholics. More often they tried to dominate the Republican Party, and they succeeded in several areas, especially in the Midwest, before they died out by the late 1890s.

In some parts of the Midwest in the early 1890s, nativists (not necessarily the APA) pushed through laws requiring schools to be taught only in English, a slap at German immigrants. The growth of prohibition sentiment was accompanied by unflattering nativist stereotypes of Irish saloonkeepers and German beer-brewers.

During the 1890s, a diverse political coalition emerged aimed at reducing immigration. Labor organizations began to look at immigration as a potential threat to jobs and wage levels. (Anti-Chinese grumblings among Pacific coast unions had contributed to passage of the Chinese Exclusion Act in 1882; see page 590). At the same time, a few employers began to connect immigrants with unions and radicalism and to charge that unions represented foreign, un-American influences. Foreign-born radicals and especially **anarchists** were a special target, as newspapers claimed that "there is no such thing as an American anarchist." In 1901 Leon Czolgosz, an American-born anarchist with a foreign-sounding name, assassinated President William McKinley, and Congress promptly passed a bill barring anarchists from immigrating to the United States.

During the 1890s, the sources of European immigration began to shift from northwestern Europe to southern and eastern Europe, bringing larger numbers of Italians, Poles and other Slavs, and eastern European Jews (see Figure 18.4, page 553). This also furthered nativism. Anti-Catholicism and anti-Semitism combined with cruel stereotypes of those from southern and eastern Europe to create a sense that these **"new immigrants"** were less desirable than **"old immigrants"** from northwestern Europe.

The arrival of significant numbers of "new immigrants" after 1890 coincided with a wave of sentiment that glorified Anglo-Saxons (ancestors of the English) and accomplishments by the English and English Americans. Relying on Social Darwinism and its argument for survival of the fittest, proponents of Anglo-Saxonism were alarmed by statistics that showed old-stock Americans having fewer children than did immigrants. Some voiced fears of "race suicide" in which Anglo-Saxons allowed themselves to be bred out of existence. With such anxi-

eties feeding their prejudices, some nativists became blatant racists.

By the 1890s, these economic, political, religious, and racist strains converged in demands that the federal government restrict immigration from Europe. Given stereotypes that immigrants were ignorant, advocates of restriction argued that immigrants should pass a literacy test before being admitted. In 1891 Henry Cabot Lodge (who had worked so hard to protect black voting rights) pushed the literacy test in Congress. The depression that began in 1893 apparently convinced the American Federation of Labor to endorse a literacy test to reduce immigration. Many business leaders, however, opposed restrictions on immigration for fear that limits would cut into their supply of labor. Congress passed literacy bills in 1897 and 1913, but both met presidential vetoes. In 1917 President Woodrow Wilson vetoed another effort, but Congress overrode his veto and enacted the measure into law. When it failed to reduce the numbers coming from Europe, more sweeping restrictions came in the 1920s.

The Origins of the People's Party

As some southern politicians loudly promoted white supremacy and some midwestern politicians flirted with nativism, a quite different political movement was developing in response to the economic problems of southern and western farmers. In 1890 this movement sponsored the first **Populist** Parties at a state level. Understanding Populism must begin with understanding the economic problems of farmers. During the 1870s and 1880s, farmers had become more and more dependent on the national railroad network, on national markets for

---

anarchists   Radicals who opposed all government, arguing that governments were created by the wealthy to protect their property.

"new immigrants"   Newcomers from southern and eastern Europe who began to arrive in the United States in significant numbers during the 1890s and after.

"old immigrants"   Newcomers from northern and western Europe who made up much of the immigration to the United States before the 1890s.

Populists   Members of the People's Party, who held their first presidential nominating convention in 1892 and called for federal action to reduce the power of big business and to assist farmers and workers.

grain and cotton, and on sources of credit in distant cities. At the same time, some of them felt increasingly apprehensive about the great concentrations of economic power that seemed to be dominating their lives. (For earlier farmers' organizations, see pages 518–520.)

Perhaps most troubling were the prices that farmers received for their crops. Crop prices fell steadily after the Civil War as production of wheat, corn, and cotton grew much faster than the population (see Figure 17.1 and page 497). Some farmers, however, denied that prices were falling solely because of overproduction, pointing to the hungry and ragged residents in the slums. Farmers also condemned the monopolistic practices of the **commodity markets** in Chicago and New York that determined prices for crops. Farmers knew that the bushel of corn that they sold for 10 or 20 cents in October brought three or four times that amount in New York in December. When they brought their crops to market, however, they had to accept the price that was offered because they needed cash to pay their debts and because most of them had no way to store their crops for later sale at a higher price.

Farmers had accomplished much of the post–Civil War agricultural expansion on borrowed money, and falling prices magnified their indebtedness. For example, suppose a farmer borrowed $1,000 for five years in 1881. With corn selling at 63 cents per bushel, the $1,000 would have been equivalent to 1,587 bushels of corn. In 1886, when the loan came due, corn sold for 36 cents per bushel, requiring 2,777 bushels to repay the $1,000. Because prices for crops sank lower and lower, farmers raised more and more just to pay their mortgages and buy necessities. Given the relation between supply and demand, the more they raised, the lower prices fell. One historian compared the farmers' plight to the character in *Alice in Wonderland* who had to run faster and faster just to stay in the same place.

The railroads also angered many farmers. The railroads, farmers insisted, were greedy monopolies that charged as much as possible to deliver supplies to rural America and carry their crops to market. It sometimes cost four times as much to ship freight in the West as to ship the same amount over the same distance in the East. Farmers also protested the railroads' involvement in politics, claiming that they dominated state nominating conventions and state legislatures and distributed free passes to politicians in return for favorable treatment. One North Carolina farm editor in 1888 bemoaned the railroads' power in his state: "Do they not own the newspapers? Are not all the politicians their dependents? Has not every Judge in the State a free pass in his pocket?"

Crop prices, debt, and railroad practices were only some of the farmers' complaints. They protested, too, that local bankers charged 8, 9, or 10 percent interest— or even more—in western and southern states, compared with 6 percent or less in the Northeast. They argued that federal monetary policies (see page 563) contributed to falling prices and thereby compounded their debts. Farmers complained that the giant corporations that made farm equipment and fertilizer overcharged them. Even local merchants drew farmers' reproach for exorbitant markups. In the South, all these problems combined with sharecropping and crop liens (see page 468).

The Grange, the Greenback Party, and the silver movement in the late 1870s had expressed farmers' grievances, but those movements faded during the relatively prosperous 1880s. By 1890, however, falling crop prices and widespread indebtedness brought renewed concern among farmers and farm organizations. The Republicans' Silver Purchase Act of 1890 tried to calm this rising concern by increasing the amount of silver to be coined. As had been the case with the Bland-Allison Act (page 520) before it, however, both silverites and advocates of the **gold standard** found the law unsatisfactory.

The People's Party

The Grange had demonstrated the possibility for united action, but its decline left an organizational vacuum among farmers, and the Greenback Party failed to fill it. In the 1880s, however, three new organizations emerged, all called **Farmers' Alliances**. One was centered in the north-central states. Another, the Southern Alliance, began in Texas in the late 1870s and spread eastward across

---

commodity market   Financial market in which brokers buy and sell agricultural products in large quantities, thus determining the prices paid to farmers for their harvests.

gold standard   A monetary system based on gold; under such a system, legal contracts typically called for the payment of all debts in gold, and paper money could be redeemed in gold at a bank.

Farmers' Alliances   Agricultural organizations of the 1880s and 1890s that carried forward agrarian causes after the decline of the Grange.

the South, absorbing similar local groups along its way. Because the Southern Alliance limited its membership to white farmers, a third group, the Colored Farmers' Alliance, was formed for black farmers. Like the Grange and Knights of Labor (see pages 518 and 540), the Alliances defined themselves as organizations of the "producing classes" and looked to cooperatives as a partial solution to their problems. Alliance stores were most common. The Texas Alliance also experimented with cooperative cotton selling, and some midwestern local Alliances built cooperative **grain elevators**.

Local Alliance meetings featured social and educational activities. By the late 1880s, a host of weekly newspapers across the South and West presented Alliance views. One Kansas woman described the outcome: "People commenced to think who had never thought before, and people talked who had seldom spoken. . . . Everyone was talking and everyone was thinking. . . . Thoughts and theories sprouted like weeds after a May shower."

The Alliances defined themselves as nonpartisan and expected their members to work for Alliance aims within the major parties. This was especially important in the South, where any white person who challenged the Democratic Party risked being condemned as a traitor to both race and region. Many midwestern Alliance leaders, however, came out of the Granger Party tradition, and some had been Greenbackers. Others had aligned themselves with the Knights of Labor and took pride in its role in fostering local labor parties. Not until the winter of 1889–1890, however, did widespread support materialize for independent political action in the Midwest. By then, corn prices had fallen so low that some farmers found it cheaper to burn their corn than to sell it and buy fuel.

Through the hot summer of 1890, as the Fifty-first Congress argued over the McKinley Tariff and the Lodge federal elections bill, members of the Farmers' Alliance in Kansas, Nebraska, the Dakotas, Minnesota, and surrounding states formed new political parties to contest state and local elections. One leader explained that the political battle they waged was "between the insatiable greed of organized wealth and the rights of the great plain people."

Women took a prominent part in Populist campaigning, especially in Kansas and Nebraska. Mary Elizabeth Lease of Kansas was among the most effective. She acquired lasting fame when newspapers quoted her as urging farmers to "Raise less corn and more hell!" Annie Diggs attracted less

When the Populists launched their new party, one cartoonist depicted them as a hot-air balloon of political malcontents. This cartoon may have inspired Frank Baum, author of *The Wizard of Oz*, whose wizard arrived in Oz in a hot-air balloon launched from Omaha, the site of the Populists' 1892 nominating convention. *Library of Congress.*

attention than Lease at first, but proved the more significant power within Kansas Populism.

Soon dubbed the People's Party, or Populists, the new party emphasized three elements in their campaigns: **antimonopolism**, government action on behalf of farmers and workers, and increased popular control of government. Their antimonopolism drew on their own unhappy experiences with railroads, grain buyers, and manufacturing companies, but it

---

grain elevator Storehouses for grain located near railroad tracks; such structures were equipped with mechanical lifting devices (elevators) that permitted the grain to be loaded into railcars.

antimonopolism Opposition to great concentrations of economic power such as trusts and giant corporations, as well as to actual monopolies.

also derived from a long American tradition of opposition to concentrated economic power. Populists quoted Thomas Jefferson on the need for equal rights for all, and they compared themselves to Andrew Jackson in his fight against the Bank of the United States.

"We believe the time has come," the Populists proclaimed in their 1892 platform, "when the railroad companies will either own the people or the people must own the railroads." The Populists' solution to the dangers of monopoly was government action on behalf of farmers and workers, including federal ownership of the railroads and the telegraph and telephone systems, and government alternatives to private banks. Some Populists also endorsed a scheme of the Southern Alliance called the Sub-Treasury Plan, under which crops stored in government warehouses might be collateral for low-interest loans to farmers. Populists also demanded currency inflation (through greenbacks, silver, or both) and a **graduated income tax**. Through such measures, they hoped, in the words of their 1892 platform, that "oppression, injustice, and poverty shall eventually cease in the land." They had some following within what remained of the Knights of Labor, and they hoped to gain broad support among other urban and industrial workers by calling for the eight-hour workday and for restrictions on companies' use of private armies in labor disputes.

Finally, the People's Party favored a series of structural changes to make government more responsive to the people, including expansion of the merit system for government employees, election of U.S. senators by the voters instead of by state legislatures, a one-term limit for the president, the secret ballot, and the **initiative** and **referendum**. Many of them also favored woman suffrage. In the South, the Populists not only opposed disfranchisement of black voters but also posed a serious challenge to the prevailing patterns of politics by seeking to forge a political alliance of the disadvantaged of both races.

Thus the Populists wanted to use government to control, even to own, the corporate behemoths that had evolved in their lifetimes. But they deeply distrusted the old parties and wanted to increase the influence of the individual voter in political decision making.

The Elections of 1890 and 1892

The issues in the 1890 elections for members of the House of Representatives and for state and local offices varied by region. In the West, the Populists

stood at the center of the campaign, lambasting both major parties for ignoring the needs of the people. In the South, Democrats held up Lodge's "force bill" as a warning of the potential dangers if Southern whites should bolt the party of white supremacy. There, members of the Southern Alliance worked within the Democratic Party to secure candidates committed to the farmers' cause. In the Northeast, Democrats attacked the McKinley Tariff for producing higher prices for consumers. In the Rocky Mountain region, nearly all candidates pledged their support for unlimited silver coinage. In parts of the Midwest, Democrats scourged Republicans for supporting prohibition and school laws unpopular with German Americans.

The new Populist Party scored several victories, marking it as the most successful new party since the appearance of the Republicans in the 1850s. Kansas Republican senator John J. Ingalls had dismissed Populists as "a sort of turnip crusade," but Populists silenced Ingalls by winning enough seats in the Kansas legislature to elect a Populist to replace him in the Senate. Elsewhere Populists elected state legislators, members of Congress, and one other U.S. senator. All across the South, where Alliance members had remained within the Democratic Party, the Alliance claimed that successful candidates owed their victories to Alliance voters.

Everywhere Republicans suffered defeat, losing to Populists in the West and to Democrats in the Midwest and Northeast. In the House of Representatives, the Republicans went from 166 seats in 1889 to only 88 in 1891. Many Republican candidates for state and local offices also lost. Republican disappointment in the results of the 1890 elections bred dissension within the party, and President Harrison could not maintain party unity.

For the 1892 presidential election, the Republicans renominated Harrison despite a lack of enthusiasm among many party leaders. The Democrats again chose Grover Cleveland as their candidate. Farmers'

---

graduated income tax Proportional tax levied on income so that individuals with the least income pay taxes at the lowest rate.

initiative Procedure allowing voters to petition to have a law placed on the ballot for consideration by the general electorate.

referendum Procedure whereby a bill or constitutional amendment is submitted to the voters for their approval after having been passed by a legislative body.

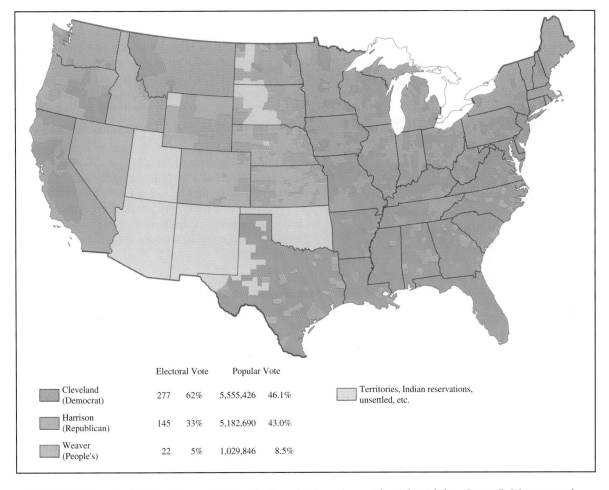

	Electoral Vote		Popular Vote	
Cleveland (Democrat)	277	62%	5,555,426	46.1%
Harrison (Republican)	145	33%	5,182,690	43.0%
Weaver (People's)	22	5%	1,029,846	8.5%

Territories, Indian reservations, unsettled, etc.

MAP 20.1 Popular Vote for Weaver, 1892   The Populist Party's presidential candidate, James B. Weaver, made a strong showing in 1892. This map indicates that his support was concentrated regionally in the West and South but that he had relatively little support in the northeastern states.

Alliance activists from the South joined western Populists to form a national People's Party and to nominate James Weaver, who had run for president as a Greenbacker twelve years earlier. Democrats and Populists scored the most impressive victories. Cleveland won with 46.1 percent of the popular vote, becoming the only president in American history to win two nonconsecutive terms. Harrison got 43 percent, and Weaver captured 8.5 percent. The Democrats kept control of the House of Representatives and won a majority in the Senate. Populists displayed particular strength in the West and South (see Map 20.1). The Democrats now found themselves where the Republicans had stood four years before: in control of the presidency and Congress and poised to translate their promises into law.

ECONOMIC COLLAPSE AND RESTRUCTURING

• What were the short-term and long-term effects of the depression that began in 1893?

• What conclusions might union leaders have drawn from Homestead and Pullman?

After the Democrats swept to power in the 1892 elections, they suddenly faced the collapse of the national economy. Labor organizations suffered major defeats in 1892 and 1894, putting unions on the defensive thereafter. As the nation began to recover from the depression, anxious entrepreneurs launched a merger movement intended to bolster economic stability that also brought much greater economic concentration.

Economic Collapse and Depression

Ten days before Cleveland took office, the Reading Railroad declared bankruptcy. A **financial panic** quickly set in. One business journal reported in August that "never before has there been such a sudden and striking cessation of industrial activity." Everywhere, industrial plants shut down in large numbers. More than fifteen thousand businesses failed in 1893, more proportionately than in any year since the depression of the 1870s.

At the time, no one really understood why the economy collapsed so suddenly and completely. In retrospect, the downturn seems to have resulted from both immediate events and underlying weaknesses. The collapse of a major English bank led some British investors to call back investments in the United States. This combined with the reduction in federal revenues caused by the McKinley Tariff to produce a sharp decline in federal **gold reserves**. This, in turn, combined with the bankruptcies of a few large companies to trigger a stock market crash in May–June 1893.

Beyond these immediate events, the most important underlying weaknesses included the slowing of agricultural expansion and railroad construction. Railroad building drove the industrial economy in the 1880s, but railroad construction first slowed and then fell by half between 1893 and 1895. The decline in railroad construction initiated a domino effect, toppling industries that supplied the railroads, especially steel. Production of steel rails fell by more than a third, and thirty-two steel companies closed their doors. (Figure 17.2, page 499, shows the drop in manufacturing in the mid-1890s.) In addition, some railway companies found they lacked sufficient traffic to pay their fixed costs, and several large lines declared bankruptcy, among them the Erie, Northern Pacific, Santa Fe, and Union Pacific. By 1894, almost one-fifth of the nation's railroad mileage had fallen into bankruptcy. Banks with investments in railroads and steel companies collapsed along with their client firms. Nearly five hundred banks failed in 1893 alone, and more than five hundred more closed by the end of 1897, equivalent to one bank out of every ten.

No agency kept careful national records on unemployment, but a third or more of the workers in manufacturing may have been out of work. During the winter of 1893–1894, Chicago counted one hundred thousand unemployed—roughly two workers out of five. Many who kept their jobs received smaller paychecks, as employers cut wages and hours. In 1892 the average nonfarm wage earner received $482 per year. By 1894, this sum had shrunk to $420.

The depression produced widespread suffering. Many who lost their jobs had little to fall back on except charity. Newspapers told of people who chose suicide when faced with the dire options of starving to death or stealing food. Susan Orcutt, a Kansas farm wife nearly nine months pregnant, saw the worst of both farm poverty and depression unemployment:

> I take my Pen In hand to let you know that we are Starving to death It is Pretty hard to do without any thing to Eat hear in this God for saken country we would have had Plenty to Eat if the hail hadent cut our rye down and ruined our corn and Potatoes . . . My Husband went a way to find work and came home last night and told me that we would have to Starve he has bin in ten countys and did not Get no work

Like Orcutt's husband, many men and some women left home desperate to find work, hoping to send money to their families as soon as they could. Some walked the roads, and others hopped on freight trains, riding in boxcars.

A dramatic demonstration against unemployment began in January 1894, when Jacob S. Coxey, an Ohio Populist, proposed that the government hire the unemployed to build or repair roads and other public works and to pay them with greenbacks, thereby inflating the currency. He called on the unemployed to join him in a march on Washington to push this program. The response electrified the nation—all across the country, men and women tried to join the march. In the West, given the vast distances, some groups hijacked trains (fifty in all) and headed east, pulling **boxcars** loaded with unemployed men. (None of the pirated trains traveled far before authorities stopped them and arrested the leaders.) Several thousand people took part in **Coxey's Army** in some

---

financial panic   Widespread anxiety about financial and commercial matters, prompting hasty measures to prevent losses, which often lead to financial disaster; for example, in a panic, investors may sell large amounts of stock to cut their own losses, only to drive prices much lower.

gold reserves   The stockpile of gold with which the federal government backed up the currency.

boxcar   An enclosed railroad car with sliding side doors, used to transport freight.

Coxey's Army   Unemployed workers led by Jacob S. Coxey, who marched to Washington to demand relief measures from Congress following the depression of 1893.

In 1894, Jacob Coxey, an Ohio Populist, led his "petition in boots" on a march from Ohio to Washington, D.C., demanding that Congress provide public-works jobs to the unemployed. *Library of Congress.*

way, but most never reached Washington or reached it too late.

When Coxey and several hundred followers arrived in Washington, police arrested Coxey and others for trespassing and dispersed the rest. Never before had so many voices urged federal officials to create jobs for the unemployed, nor had so many protesters ever marched on Washington.

Labor on the Defensive: Homestead and Pullman

In the 1890s, workers often found that even the largest unions could not withstand the power of the new industrial companies. A major demonstration of this came in 1892 in Homestead, Pennsylvania, at the giant Carnegie Steel plant that was managed by Henry Clay Frick, Carnegie's partner. The plant was a stronghold of the Amalgamated Association of Iron, Steel, and Tin Workers, the largest AFL union, which had a contract with Carnegie Steel. When Frick proposed major cuts in wages, the union balked. Frick then locked out the union members and prepared to bring in replacements.

Frick hired as guards three hundred agents of the Pinkerton detective agency. They came by riverboat, but ten thousand strikers and community supporters resisted when the private army tried to land. Shots rang out. In the ensuing gun battle, seven Pinkertons and nine strikers were killed and sixty people injured. The Pinkertons surrendered, leaving the strikers in control. Soon after, however, the governor of Pennsylvania sent in the state militia to patrol the city and incidentally to protect the strike-

breakers. The Amalgamated Association never recovered. This crushing defeat suggested that no union could stand up to America's industrial giants, especially when those companies could call on the government for assistance.

A similar fate befell the most ambitious organizing drive of the 1890s. In 1893, under the leadership of **Eugene V. Debs**, railway workers launched the American Railway Union (ARU). Born in Indiana in 1855, Debs had served as an officer of the locomotive firemen's union. Railway workers had organized separate unions for engineers, firemen, switchmen, and conductors, but Debs hoped to bring all railway workers together into one union. Instead of using skill as the qualification for membership, he proposed employment anywhere in the railway industry as the basis for membership, thereby creating an **industrial union**. Success came quickly. Within a year, the ARU claimed 150,000 members and became the largest single union in the nation.

The twenty-four railway companies whose lines entered Chicago had formed the General Managers Association (GMA) as a way of addressing their common problems. Alarmed at the rise of the ARU, they found an opportunity to challenge the new union in 1894. Striking workers at the Pullman

Eugene V. Debs   American Railway Union leader who was jailed for spearheading the Pullman strike; he later became a leading socialist and ran for president.

industrial union   Union that organizes all workers in an industry, whether skilled or unskilled, and regardless of occupation.

KING DEBS.

This famous cartoon about the Pullman strike, originally published in *Harper's Weekly* in 1894, shows Eugene Debs, head of the American Railway Union, sitting atop a railway bridge that has been turned to cut off all rail traffic. The railroad cars behind him are labeled "fresh vegetables," "beef," and "fruit," to emphasize the perishable nature of the products that could not be delivered, and others are identified as "U.S. Mail." In the background, factories have "closed" signs on them. This cartoon, and others like it, helped to mobilize opinion against the strikers. *Library of Congress.*

two grounds: that the strike prevented delivery of the mail and that it violated the recently approved Sherman Anti-Trust Act. Olney convinced President Cleveland to use thousands of **U.S. marshals** and federal troops to protect trains operated by strike-breakers. In response, mobs lashed out at railroad property, especially in Chicago, burning trains and buildings. ARU leaders condemned the violence, but a dozen people died before the strike finally ended. Union leaders, including Debs, were jailed, and the ARU was destroyed.

The depression that began in 1893 further weakened the unions. In 1894 Gompers acknowledged that nearly all AFL affiliates "had their resources greatly diminished and their efforts largely crippled" through lost strikes and unemployment. Nevertheless, the AFL hung on. By 1897, the organization claimed fifty-eight national unions with a combined membership of nearly 270,000.

The "Merger Movement"

As the economy revived in the late 1890s, Americans witnessed an astonishing number of mergers in manufacturing and mining—a "merger movement" that lasted from 1898 until 1902. The high point came in 1899, with 1,208 mergers involving $2.3 billion in capital. The merger movement resulted partly from economic weaknesses revealed by the depression, especially among railroad companies. The threat of vicious competition among reviving manufacturing companies prompted reorganization there too.

The most prominent of the new corporations was United States Steel. As the economy edged out of the depression, J. P. Morgan began combining separate steel-related companies to create a vertically integrated operation. Andrew Carnegie had never carried vertical integration to the point of manufacturing final steel products such as wire, barrels, or tubes. By vertically integrating to include that last step, Morgan threatened to close off a significant part of Carnegie's market. Faced with the formi-

Palace Car Company (a manufacturer of luxury railway cars) asked the ARU to boycott **Pullman cars**—to disconnect them from trains and proceed without them. When the ARU agreed, it found itself on a collision course with the GMA. The managers threatened to fire any worker who observed the boycott, but their real purpose, as expressed by the GMA chairman, was to eliminate the ARU and "to wipe him [Debs] out."

Within a short time, all 150,000 ARU members were on strike in support of members who were fired for boycotting Pullman cars. Rail traffic in and out of Chicago came to a halt, affecting railways from the Pacific coast to New York State. The companies, however, found an ally in U.S. Attorney General Richard Olney, a former railroad lawyer. Olney obtained an **injunction** against the strikers on

---

Pullman car A railroad passenger car with private compartments and sleeping berths.

injunction A court order requiring an individual or a group to do something or to refrain from doing something.

U.S. marshal A federal law-enforcement official.

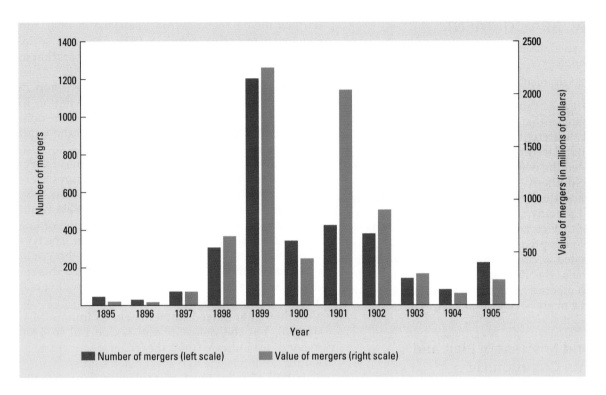

FIGURE 20.1 Recorded Mergers in Mining and Manufacturing, 1895–1905 The last few years of the 1890s and early 1900s witnessed the "merger movement," a restructuring of significant parts of corporate America. Note the influence on the graph of the creation of United States Steel in 1901, the first "billion-dollar corporation."

dable prospect of having to build his own manufacturing plants for finished products, Carnegie sold all his holdings to Morgan for $480 million. In 1901 Morgan combined Carnegie's company with his own to create United States Steel, the first corporation capitalized at over a billion dollars (see Figure 20.1).

As had been true with railroad reorganization in the 1880s, investment bankers usually sought two objectives in reorganizing an industry: first, to make the industry stable so that investments would yield predictable dividends, and second, to make the industry efficient and productive so that dividends would be high. Toward that end, investment bankers not only drove the mergers but also placed their representatives on the boards of directors of the newly created companies, to guarantee that those two objectives were top priority. By 1912, the three leading New York banking firms together occupied 341 directorships in 112 major companies. Investment bankers argued that benefits from their

activities extended far beyond the dividends that shareholders received. One of Morgan's associates claimed in 1901 that, as a result of mergers and restructuring, "production would become more regular, labor would be more steadily employed at better wages, and panics caused by over-production would become a thing of the past."

In fact, the new industrial combinations failed to produce long-term economic stability. The economy continued to alternate between expansion and contraction. After the severe depression of 1893–1897, for example, a period of general expansion was interrupted by downturns in 1903, 1907–1908, 1910–1911, and 1913–1914. Morgan's hopes for stability through centralized control failed to be realized, but his activities and those of his contemporaries created many of the characteristics of modern business. Many industries were oligopolistic, dominated by a few vertically integrated companies, and the stock market had moved beyond the sale of railroad securities to play an important role in raising capital for industry.

POLITICAL REALIGNMENT

- What main issues divided the candidates in the 1896 presidential election?
- What were the short-term and long-term results of the election?

During the 1890s, the nation underwent a series of political changes that, taken together, resulted in a significantly different political system. One set of changes took place in the South, where Mississippi Democrats led the way to disfranchisement and segregation of southern African Americans. Nationally, Cleveland and the Democrats failed to stabilize the collapsing economy. Their failure opened the door to Republican victories in 1894. When the Democrats in 1896 adopted some of the Populists' issues and nominated a candidate sympathetic to many Populist goals, the People's Party threw in its lot with the Democrats, but the rebounding Republicans scored a major victory that year.

The Second Mississippi Plan and the Atlanta Compromise

In the 1890s, politics in the South underwent a major shift, toward writing white supremacy into law. Although Reconstruction came to an end in 1877 (see page 485), the Civil Rights Act of 1875, at least in theory, protected African Americans against discrimination in public places (see page 476). Some state laws required racial separation—for example, many states prohibited racial intermarriage. State or local law, or sometimes local practice, had produced racially separate school systems, cemeteries, hospitals, churches, and other voluntary organizations. Segregation existed throughout the South, frequently driven by local custom and the ever-present threat of violence against any African American who dared to challenge it. Restrictions on black political participation were also extralegal, enforced through coercion or intimidation.

Then, in the **Civil Rights cases** (1883), the U.S. Supreme Court ruled the Civil Rights Act of 1875 unconstitutional. The Court said that the "equal protection" clause of the Fourteenth Amendment applied only to states and not to individuals and companies. Thus state governments were obligated to treat all citizens as equal before the law, but private businesses need not offer equal access to their facilities. Now southern lawmakers slowly began to require businesses to practice segregation. In 1887 the Florida legislature ordered separate accommodations on railroad trains. Mississippi passed a sim-

ilar law the next year, as did Louisiana in 1890, and four more states followed in 1891. Law and social custom began to specify greater racial separation in other ways too.

Mississippi whites took a more brazen step in 1890, holding a state constitutional convention to eliminate African Americans' participation in politics. The new provisions did not mention the word *race*. Instead, they imposed a **poll tax**, a literacy test, and assorted other requirements for voting. Everyone understood, though, that these measures were designed to disfranchise black voters. Men who failed the literacy test could vote if they could understand a section of the state constitution or law when a local (white) official read it to them. The typical result was that the only illiterates who could vote were white. Most of the South watched this so-called Second Mississippi Plan unfold with great interest (see page 483 for the first Mississippi Plan). No other state moved immediately to imitate Mississippi, but the defeat of the Lodge bill in 1890 seemed to indicate that the federal government would not intervene to protect black rights.

In 1895 a black educator signaled his apparent willingness to accept disfranchisement and segregation for the moment. Born into slavery in 1856, **Booker T. Washington** had worked as a janitor while studying at Hampton Institute, a school that combined preparation for elementary school teaching with vocational education in agriculture and industrial work. Washington soon returned to Hampton as a teacher. In 1881 the Alabama legislature authorized a black **normal school** at Tuskegee. Washington became its principal, and he made Tuskegee Normal and Industrial Institute into a leading black educational institution.

In 1895 Atlanta played host to the Cotton States and International Exposition. The exposition direc-

---

Civil Rights cases   A series of cases that came before the Supreme Court in 1883, in which the Court ruled that private companies could legally discriminate against individuals based on race.

poll tax   An annual tax imposed on each citizen; used in some southern states as a way to disfranchise black voters, as the only penalty for not paying the tax was the loss of the right to vote.

Booker T. Washington   Former slave who became an educator and founded Tuskegee Institute, a leading black educational institution; he urged southern African Americans to accept disfranchisement and segregation for the time being.

normal school   A school to train teachers.

This portrait of Booker T. Washington was taken shortly after his Atlanta speech. By the time of the photograph, he had already reached national fame as the leading black advocate for accommodation. *Tuskegee University Library.*

tors invited Washington to speak at the opening ceremonies, hoping he could reach out to the anticipated crowd of southern whites, southern blacks, and northern whites. Washington did not disappoint the directors. In his speech, he seemed to accept an inferior status for blacks, at least for the present: "No race can prosper till it learns that there is as much dignity in tilling a field as in writing a poem. It is at the bottom of life we must begin, and not at the top." He also seemed to condone segregation: "In all things that are purely social, we can be as separate as the fingers, yet one as the hand in all things essential to mutual progress. The wisest among my race understand that the agitation of questions of social equality is the extremest folly." Furthermore, he implied that equal rights had to be earned: "It is important and right that all privileges of the law be ours, but it is vastly more important that we be prepared for the exercise of these privileges."

The speech—dubbed the **Atlanta Compromise**—won great acclaim for Washington. Southern whites were pleased to hear a black educator urge his race

to accept segregation and disfranchisement. Northern whites too were receptive to the notion that the South would work out its thorny race relations by itself. Until his death in 1915, Washington was the most prominent black leader in the nation, at least among white Americans.

Among African Americans, Washington's message found a mixed reception. Some accepted his approach as the best that might be secured. Others criticized him for sacrificing black rights. Henry M. Turner, a bishop of the African Methodist Episcopal church in Atlanta, declared that Washington "will have to live a long time to undo the harm he has done our race." Privately, however, Washington never accepted disfranchisement and segregation as permanent fixtures in southern life.

Even as African Americans debated Washington's Atlanta speech, southern lawmakers were redefining the legal status of African Americans. The rise of southern Populism, with its support for a black and white political coalition of the poor, alarmed some southern conservatives. State after state followed the lead of Mississippi and disfranchised black voters. Louisiana, in 1898, added the infamous **grandfather clause**, which specified that men prevented from voting by the various new stipulations would be permitted to vote if their fathers or grandfathers had been eligible to vote in 1867 (before the Fourteenth Amendment extended the suffrage to African Americans). The rule reinstated poor or illiterate whites into the electorate but kept blacks out. Specific methods varied, but each southern state set up barriers to voting and then carved holes through which only whites could pass. Several southern states added an additional barrier in the form of the white primary, which specified that political parties had the right to limit participation in the process by which they chose their candidates. Southern Democrats, who had long

Atlanta Compromise   Name applied to Booker T. Washington's 1895 speech in which he urged African Americans to temporarily accept segregation and disfranchisement and to work for economic advancement as a way to recover their civil rights.

grandfather clause   Provision in Louisiana law that permitted a person to vote if his father or grandfather had been entitled to vote in 1867; designed to permit white men to vote who might otherwise be disfranchised by laws targeting blacks. Often applied to any law that permits some people to evade current legal provisions based on past practice.

proclaimed themselves to be the "white man's party" or the party of white supremacy, quickly restricted their primaries and conventions to whites only. South Carolina took this step first, in 1896, and other states soon followed. Even as southern states were removing African Americans from their political systems, some southern politicians sought to deflect the remaining attraction of Populism by arguing for the unity of all white voters in support of white supremacy.

Southern lawmakers also began to extend segregation by law. They were given a major assist by the decision of the U.S. Supreme Court in *Plessy v. Ferguson* (1896), a case that involved a Louisiana law requiring segregated railroad cars. When the Court ruled that "separate but equal" facilities did not violate the equal protection clause of the Fourteenth Amendment, southern legislators soon applied that reasoning to other areas of life, eventually requiring segregation of everything from prisons to telephone booths—and especially such public places as parks and restaurants.

Violence directed against blacks accompanied the new laws, providing an unmistakable lesson in the consequences of resistance. From 1885 to 1900, when the South was redefining relations between the races, the region witnessed more than twenty-five hundred deaths by lynching—about one every two days. The victims were almost all African Americans, and the largest numbers were in the states with the most black residents. Once the new order was in place, lynching deaths declined slightly.

The Failure of the Divided Democrats

While the South was eliminating African Americans from state and local politics, very different political changes were underway elsewhere. When Congress met in 1893, the majority Democrats faced several controversial issues, especially silver coinage and the tariff. The depression and unemployment also demanded attention. President Cleveland, holding staunchly to his party's traditional commitment to minimal government and laissez faire, opposed any federal assistance to those in need. And, in the midst of the nation's financial crisis, Cleveland suffered a personal crisis. Doctors detected cancer in his mouth. Fearing that news of his condition might lead to further financial panic, the president kept his surgery and recuperation secret.

Many business leaders argued that the Sherman Silver Purchase Act (1890, see page 606) had caused the gold drain that set off the depression, but many western and southern Democrats supported it as better than no silver coinage at all. Convinced that silver coinage had contributed to the economic collapse, Cleveland asked Congress to repeal the Sherman Silver Purchase Act. In the House of Representatives, most Republicans voted for repeal, but more than a third of the Democrats voted against. In the Senate, Republicans supported Cleveland by 2 to 1, but Democrats divided almost evenly. Cleveland won but divided his own party, pitting the Northeast against the West and much of the South.

The Democrats still faced the major challenge of the tariff. After their outspoken condemnation of the McKinley Tariff and commitment to cut tariff rates, they now had to demonstrate that they kept their word. The tariff bill produced by the House reduced duties, tried to balance sectional interests, and created an income tax to replace lost federal revenue. In the Senate, however, some Democrats tagged on so many amendments and compromises that Cleveland characterized the result as "party dishonor." He refused to sign it, and it became law without his signature. (The Supreme Court soon declared the income tax unconstitutional.)

Voters recorded their disgust with the disorganized Democrats in the 1894 elections. Democrats lost everywhere but in the Deep South, giving up 113 seats in the House of Representatives. Populists made few gains, and suffered losses in some of their previous strongholds. Republicans scored their biggest gain in Congress ever, adding 117 House seats. Not surprisingly, Republicans looked forward eagerly to the approaching 1896 presidential election.

Repeal of the Sherman Act failed to stop the flow of gold from the treasury as investors responded to economic uncertainties by converting their securities to gold. The gold reserve fell dangerously low, causing some to fear that the government might be unable to meet its obligations. In desperation, in 1895 Cleveland turned to J. P. Morgan for assistance in floating a bond issue to restore the gold reserve. Cleveland now came under renewed criticism, both for the price paid to Morgan and for going to Morgan—symbol of Wall Street and the trusts—in the first place.

Plessy v. Ferguson Supreme Court decision in 1896 that upheld a Louisiana law requiring the segregation of railroad facilities on the grounds that "separate but equal" facilities were constitutional under the Fourteenth Amendment.

In 1896, William Jennings Bryan (left), candidate for the Democratic, Populist, and Silver Republican parties, traveled some eighteen thousand miles in three months, speaking to about five million people. William McKinley (right), the Republican, stayed home in Canton, Ohio, greeting thousands of well-wishers. *Bryan: Nebraska State Historical Society; McKinley: Ohio Historical Society.*

The 1896 Election: Bryan Versus McKinley, Silver Versus Protection

Republicans confidently anticipated victory in the presidential election of 1896. They nominated William McKinley, a Union veteran who had risen to the rank of major. McKinley had served fourteen years in Congress (where he had specialized in the tariff) and two terms as governor of Ohio. Known as a calm and competent leader, McKinley billed himself as the "Advance Agent of Prosperity." The Republican platform pronounced in favor of the gold standard and against silver, but McKinley preferred to focus on the tariff. When the convention voted against silver, several western Republicans walked out of the convention and out of the party.

When the Democratic convention met, silverites held the majority but were split among several candidates. Then the platform committee chose **William Jennings Bryan** of Nebraska to speak in a convention debate on silver. Blessed with a commanding voice, Bryan had won election to the House of Representatives in 1890 and 1892 and gained national attention

for his eloquent defense of silver. His speech was masterful. Defining the issue as a conflict between "the producing masses" and "the idle holders of idle capital," he argued that the first priority of federal policy should be "to make the masses prosperous," rather than to benefit the rich in the hope that "their prosperity will leak through on those below." His closing rang defiant: "We will answer their demand for a gold standard by saying to them: You shall not press down upon the brow of labor this crown of thorns. You shall not crucify mankind upon a cross of gold." The speech provoked an enthusiastic half-hour demonstration in support of silver—and Bryan. Only 36 years old, Bryan soon won the presidential nomination.

The Populists and the defecting western Republicans, who were quickly dubbed Silver Republicans, held nominating conventions next, amid frustration

> **William Jennings Bryan**   Nebraska congressman who advocated free coinage of silver, opposed imperialism, and ran for president unsuccessfully three times on the Democratic ticket.

Political buttons with pins attached to the back were patented shortly before the 1896 presidential campaign, and they were in great abundance that year. The Bryan-Sewall button pictured shows a clock at 16 minutes to 1, a reference to the Democratic Party's commitment to increase the coinage of silver dollars, with a ratio of 16:1 between the weight of silver in a silver dollar to the weight of gold in a gold dollar. The McKinley campaign made a strenuous effort to reach all organized groups that might support their candidate and to appeal to their group's interest. This button celebrates support for McKinley by a wheelmen's club, that is, an organization of bicyclists. *Collection of Janice L. and David J. Frent.*

that the Democrats had stolen their thunder. Bryan favored silver, the income tax, and a broad range of reforms that Populists also favored, and he had worked closely with Populists. Populists felt compelled to give him their nomination too, and Silver Republicans did the same. Subsequently, a group of Cleveland supporters nominated a Gold Democratic candidate.

Bryan and McKinley fought all-out campaigns but used sharply contrasting tactics. Bryan, vigorous and young, knew that his speaking voice was his greatest campaign tool. He took his case directly to the voters in four grueling train journeys through twenty-six states and more than 250 cities. Speaking to perhaps 5 million people in all, he stressed over and over that the most important issue was silver and that other reforms would follow once it was settled. Large crowds of excited and enthusiastic supporters greeted him nearly everywhere.

McKinley stayed at home in Canton, Ohio, and campaigned from his front porch. The Republicans not only flooded the country with speakers, pamphlets, and campaign paraphernalia but also chartered trains and brought thousands of supporters to hear McKinley speak from his front porch. Many business leaders feared that Bryan and silver coinage would bring complete financial collapse, and they opposed Bryan's other proposals such as the income tax and lower tariff rates. McKinley's campaign manager, Marcus Hanna, played on such fears to secure a campaign fund more

than double the size of any previous effort, and many times what the Democrats were able to raise.

McKinley won by the largest margin of victory since 1872. As Map 20.2 shows, Bryan carried the South and nearly the entire West. McKinley's victory came in the urban, industrial Northeast (compare Map 20.2 with the Chapter 18 opening map on page 528). Of the twenty largest cities in the nation, only New Orleans went for Bryan. The crucial battleground was the Midwest, where McKinley carried not only the urban industrial regions but also many farming areas.

Bryan's defeat spelled the end of the Populist Party. Some populists moved into Bryan's Democratic Party, but a few tried to hold together the tattered remnants of Populism. Others joined the Socialist Party, some returned to the Republican Party, and a few simply ignored politics. The issues they had raised—control of huge corporations, the extension of democratic processes, a fair monetary system—lived on, to be addressed by others. Their influence remained especially prominent in Bryan's wing of the Democratic Party.

After 1896: The New Republican Majority

The presidential election of 1896 focused on economic issues, sharpened by the depression. Bryan's silver crusade appealed most to debt-ridden farmers, western miners, and traditional Democrats in the South and big cities. McKinley forged a broader appeal by emphasizing the gold standard and protective tariff as keys to economic recovery. For many urban residents—workers and the middle class alike—silver seemed to promise only higher prices, but the protective tariff meant manufacturing jobs. McKinley also won, in part, by restraining his party's nativist tendencies and denouncing the anti-Catholic American Protective Association, thereby gaining support among immigrants who approved of his stand on gold and the tariff.

McKinley's victory ushered in a generation of Republican dominance of national politics. The depression and the political campaigns of the 1890s caused some voters to re-evaluate their partisan commitments and to change parties. Republicans had majorities in the House of Representatives for twenty-eight of the thirty-six years after 1894, and in the Senate for thirty of those thirty-six years. Republicans also won seven of the nine presidential elections between 1896 and 1932. Similar patterns of Republican dominance appeared in state and local government, especially in the manufacturing belt.

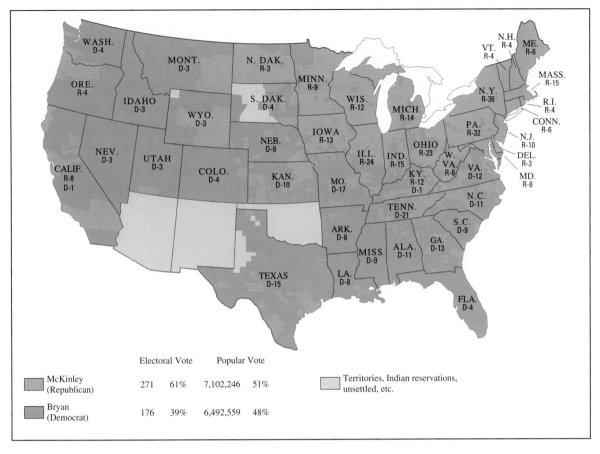

MAP 20.2 Election of 1896   Bryan could not win with just the votes of the South and West, for they had few electoral votes. Even if he had won all the West, South, and border states, he still would have needed one or more northeastern states. McKinley won in the urban, industrial core region and the more prosperous farming areas of the Midwest.

The events of the 1890s brought about drastic changes in the Democratic Party. As Bryan led the Democrats over much of the next sixteen years, he and his allies moved the party away from its commitment to minimal government and laissez faire. While retaining Democrats' traditional distrust of monopoly and opposition to government favoritism toward business, Bryan and other new Democratic leaders agreed with the Populists that the solution to the problems of economic concentration lay in a more active government that could limit monopoly power. "A private monopoly," Bryan never tired of repeating, "is indefensible and intolerable." Some traditional Democratic commitments persisted, however. The party clung to its version of states' rights that permitted southern Democrats to perpetuate white-supremacist regimes. And most northern Democrats continued to oppose nativism and such moral reforms as prohibition.

McKinley provided strong executive leadership and worked closely with leaders of his party in Congress to develop and implement new policies. In 1897 a revised protective tariff fulfilled that Republican campaign promise, driving tariff rates sharply higher and reducing the list of imports that could enter the nation without charge. The surplus disappeared as an issue partly because of large naval expenditures. In 1900 the **Gold Standard Act** wrote that Republican pledge into law.

Although the majority of American voters now considered themselves Republicans, many of them

---

Gold Standard Act   Law passed by Congress in 1900 that made gold the monetary standard for all currency issued.

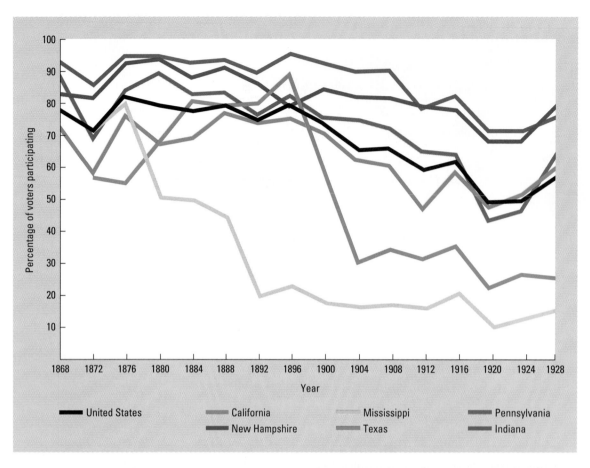

FIGURE 20.2 Voter Participation in Presidential Elections, 1868–1928, for the United States and for Selected States   On this graph, note both the general pattern of declining participation and also the variation among states. For Mississippi and Texas, note the sharp decline that accompanied the disfranchisement of black voters. *Source:* U.S. Department of Commerce, Bureau of the Census, *Historical Statistics of the United States, Colonial Times to 1970,* Bicentennial edition, 2 vols. (Washington: Government Printing Office, 1975), 2: 1071–72.

held their new party commitments less intensely than before. For most voters before 1890, ethnicity and party went hand in hand. Now voters sometimes felt pulled toward one party by their economic situation and toward the other party by their ethnicity. Such voters sometimes supported Republicans for some offices and Democrats for others, choices now much easier because of the Australian ballot.

Sometimes voters resolved their conflicts by not voting. As more and more government positions became subject to the merit system, fewer and fewer party workers could be rewarded with jobs, so there were no legions of volunteers laboring to get people to the polls on election day. For these reasons and others, voter participation began to decline, dropping from 79 percent in 1896 to 65 percent in 1908 to

59 percent in 1912. Figure 20.2 shows this decline for the United States as a whole and for selected states. Part of this decline was caused by the disfranchisement of African Americans in the South (note Mississippi and Texas) and, during the early twentieth century, the disfranchisement of some northern voters through a variety of new voting rules. Some part of the falling turnout rate, however, reflected eligible voters who neglected to vote.

The political role of newspapers also changed. In the 1890s, technological advances in paper manufacturing and printing, together with increasing numbers of literate adults, brought the emergence of mass circulation newspapers. Enterprising publishers, notably William Randolph Hearst and Joseph Pulitzer, transformed large urban newspapers, competing for readership through eye-catching headlines and sensational stories. As they focused on increasing their circulation and advertising, they also played down their ties to political parties. Some journalists began to develop the idea of providing balanced coverage of both parties.

American politics in 1888 looked much like American politics in 1876 or even 1844. But in the 1890s, American politics changed. In the early 1900s, the continued decline of political parties and partisan loyalties among voters combined with the emergence of organized interest groups to create even more change, producing the major structural features of American politics in the twentieth century.

STEPPING INTO WORLD AFFAIRS: HARRISON AND CLEVELAND

• How and why did some Americans' attitudes about the U.S. role in world affairs begin to change between 1889 and 1897?

• What were the policy implications of these changes?

During the 1890s, America's involvement in world affairs changed in important ways. One element revolved around a new role for the U.S. Navy and the commissioning of modern ships able to carry it out. Another related to the emergence and acceptance of new concepts of America's global status and foreign policy.

Building a Navy

Alfred Thayer Mahan played a key role in the development of a modern navy. President of the Naval War College, Captain Mahan exerted a powerful influence. In lectures to navy officers, in his book *The Influence of Sea Power upon History* (1890), and in articles in popular magazines and journals, Mahan argued that sea power had been the determining factor in the great European power struggles since the mid-seventeenth century. He also explored the significance of geography, population, and government as they related to establishing sea power, and he drew implications for his own day. He urged support for a strong merchant marine and advocated a large, modern navy centered on huge, powerful battleships capable of carrying American power to distant seas. He also stressed the need to extend American power beyond the national boundaries, to establish and control a canal through Central America, command the Caribbean, domi-

As late as 1880, the U.S. Navy specified that ship captains should only use steam power when "absolutely necessary" and otherwise should rely on sail. Alfred Thayer Mahan, pictured here, took the lead in revolutionizing American thinking about sea power. *The Mariner's Museum, Newport News, VA.*

nate strategic locations in the Pacific, and create naval bases at key points.

In 1889, with Harrison in the White House and Republican majorities in both houses of Congress, Secretary of the Navy Benjamin F. Tracy urged Congress to modernize the navy and to expand it significantly: eighteen more battleships (up from two), nearly fifty more cruisers, and more smaller vessels. Tracy's ambitious proposal might have eliminated the federal budget surplus all by itself! Congress did not give him all that he asked for but did vote to create a modern navy centered on battleships. When

Alfred Thayer Mahan Naval officer and specialist on naval history who stressed the importance of sea power in international politics and diplomacy.

construction was under way on three modern battleships, Tracy happily announced that "we shall rule [the sea] as certainly as the sun doth rise!"

A New American Mission?

Mahan's strategic arguments and Tracy's battleship launchings came as some Americans began, in Mahan's phrase, to "look outward." Appeals for change came from many sources: Protestant ministers, scholars, business figures, historians, politicians. Together they redefined the way American policymakers viewed the role of the nation in world affairs. Josiah Strong, for example, offered the perspective of a Protestant minister and missionary. His book *Our Country* (1885) argued that expansion of American Protestant ideals to the world constituted a Christian duty and was practically inevitable. "The world is to be Christianized and civilized," he predicted, adding that "commerce follows the missionary."

Lewis Henry Morgan's book, *Ancient Society* (1877), influenced not only federal Indian policy, but also thinking about other parts of the world. Theodore Roosevelt, writing two years before he became president, implicitly accepted Morgan's analysis when he argued that conflict was inevitable when "civilized" and "barbarian" peoples came into contact because barbarians were inherently warlike. In such a situation, Roosevelt argued, expansion by "a great civilized power" not only extended peace but also meant "a victory for law, order, and righteousness."

"Progress" and Social Darwinism (see page 507) merged with a belief in the superiority of the Anglo-Saxons—the people of England and their descendants. In the 1880s, popular books claimed that Anglo-Saxons had demonstrated a unique capacity for civilization and had a duty to enlighten and uplift other peoples. Albert Beveridge, a Republican senator from Indiana, blended some of these ideas with American nationalism when he proclaimed, "[God] has made us the master organizers of the world to establish system where chaos reigns." Rudyard Kipling, an English poet, expressed this feeling in 1899 when he urged the United States to "take up the white man's burden," a phrase that came to describe a self-imposed obligation to go into distant lands, bring the supposed blessings of Anglo-Saxon civilization to their peoples, Christianize them, and sell them Western products.

Today historians understand Anglo-Saxonism and the "white-man's-burden" as deeply tinged with racism. Such views assumed that some people, by virtue of race, possessed a superior capability for self-government and cultural accomplishment. This thinking elevated only one cultural pattern as "civilization," dismissing all others as inferior and ignoring their cultural accomplishments.

Revolution in Hawai`i

Belief in the "white man's burden," together with new understandings of the strategic significance of the Pacific, focused the attention of many Americans on Hawai`i when a revolution broke out there early in 1893. The most immediate causes of the revolution stemmed from changes in American tariff rates on sugar. In 1890, when the McKinley Tariff put sugar on the free list, all imported sugar entered the United States without paying a tariff. Previously only Hawaiian sugar had entered duty-free. Now it faced stiff competition in the American market, notably from Cuban sugar. The McKinley Tariff had also provided that sugar grown within the United States was to receive a subsidy of 2 cents per pound. Facing economic disaster, many Hawaiian planters began to talk of annexation to the United States.

In 1891 King Kalakaua died and was succeeded by his sister, **Lili`uokalani**, who hoped to restore Hawai`i to the indigenous Hawaiians and to return political power to the monarchy. Some *haole* entrepreneurs feared that they might lose both their political clout and their economic holdings. On January 17, 1893, a group of plotters proclaimed a republic and announced that they would seek annexation by the United States. John L. Stevens, the U.S. minister to Hawai`i, ordered the landing of 150 U.S. Marines. Lili`uokalani surrendered, as she put it, "to the superior force of the United States." Stevens immediately recognized the new republic, declared it a **protectorate** of the United States, and raised the American flag.

The Harrison administration **repudiated** Stevens's overzealous deeds but opened negotiations with representatives of the new republic. The Senate received a treaty of annexation shortly before Cleve-

---

**Lili`uokalani**   Last reigning queen of Hawai`i, whose desire to restore land to the Hawaiian people and perpetuate the monarchy prompted haole planters to remove her from power in 1893.

protectorate   A country partially controlled by a stronger power and dependent on that power for protection from foreign threats.

repudiate   To reject as invalid or unauthorized.

Queen Lili`uokalani came to the Hawaiian throne in 1891 and hoped to regain royal power that had been lost by her predecessor, King Kalakaua. Instead, in 1893, *haole* planters and businessmen overthrew the monarchy, aided by 150 U.S. Marines ordered ashore by the American minister to Hawai`i. *The Lili`uokalani Trust.*

land became president. Cleveland was willing to consider annexing Hawai`i if the Hawaiian people requested it, but he withdrew the annexation treaty to study it further. When he learned that the revolution could not have succeeded without the intervention of the marines, he asked the new officials to restore the queen. They refused, and Hawai`i continued as an independent republic, dominated by its haole business and planter community.

Crises in Latin America

Although Harrison and Cleveland acted at cross-purposes regarding Hawai`i, they moved in similar directions with regard to Latin America. Both presidents extended American involvement, and both threatened the use of force.

A rebellion in Chile in 1891 ended with victory for the rebels. Because the American minister to

Chile seemed to side against the rebels, anti-American feelings ran high. In October 1891, in Valparaiso, a mob set upon several American sailors on shore leave and beat them, injuring several and killing two. The Chilean government gave no sign of apologizing, so Harrison threatened "such action as may be necessary." Using language that Americans considered insulting, the Chilean government insinuated that Harrison was wrong. When Harrison responded with plans for a naval war and threats to cut off diplomatic relations, Chile gave in, apologized, and promised to pay damages and to meet other terms.

In 1895 and 1896, Cleveland also took the nation to the edge of war. At issue was a long-standing boundary dispute between Venezuela and British Guiana. Venezuela proposed arbitration, which Cleveland also favored, but Britain refused. Discovery of gold in the contested region intensified claims by both sides. In July 1895, Secretary of State Richard Olney demanded that Britain submit the issue to arbitration. Citing the Monroe Doctrine, he bombastically declared the United States to be pre-eminent throughout the Western Hemisphere. The British still refused. Cleveland then asked Congress for authority to determine the boundary and enforce it. Thus, Britain faced the possibility of conflict with the United States—and at a time when it was increasingly concerned about the rising power of Germany and was facing war in South Africa against the Boer republics. Britain agreed to arbitration.

In both instances, American presidents behaved more forcefully than had any of their predecessors for twenty years. Both times, the American response surprised the other nation. Harrison's action toward Chile was a heavy-handed assertion of American power unlikely to encourage closer relations with Latin America. Cleveland's major objective was to serve notice to European imperial powers that the Western Hemisphere was off-limits in the ongoing scramble for colonies.

Cleveland faced a very different situation in Cuba. Cuba and Puerto Rico were all that remained of the once mighty Spanish Empire in the Americas, and Cuba had rebelled against Spain repeatedly. In the early 1890s, when the McKinley Tariff permitted Cuban sugar to enter the United States without charge, the Cuban sugar industry boomed. By 1894, the United States was receiving nearly 90 percent of Cuba's exports, primarily sugar. That year, however, a new tariff law restored a high duty on Cuban sugar, removed the tariff on Hawaiian sugar, and caused a depression in Cuba. Fueled by economic distress, a new insurrection erupted against Spanish rule, and the advocates of *Cuba libre* ("a free Cuba") received support from sympathizers in the United States. In 1896, in response to the **insurgents' guerrilla warfare**, the Spanish commander, General Valeriano Weyler, established a **reconcentration** policy. The civilian population was ordered into fortified towns or camps. Everyone who remained outside these fortified areas was assumed to be an insurgent, subject to military action. Disease and starvation soon swept through the camps, killing many Cubans.

American newspapers—especially **Joseph Pulitzer's** *New York World* and **William Randolph Hearst's** *New York Journal*—vied in portraying Spanish atrocities. Papers sent their best reporters to Cuba and exaggerated the reports, a practice called **yellow journalism**. Sickened from the steady diet of such sensational stories, many Americans began clamoring for action to rescue the Cubans.

Cleveland reacted cautiously, intent on avoiding American involvement. He proclaimed American neutrality and warned Americans not to support the insurrection. When members of Congress pushed Cleveland to seek Cuban independence, he only urged Spain to grant some concessions to the insurgents. Cleveland doubted that the insurgents were capable of self-rule. Just as he had earlier opposed annexation of Samoa and Hawai`i, so now Cleveland resisted the notion of intervening in Cuba. He feared that such a move might lead to annexation regardless of the will of the Cuban people. Even so, by the time he left the presidency in early 1897, he had begun to warn Spain of possible American intervention.

STRIDING BOLDLY IN WORLD AFFAIRS: MCKINLEY, WAR, AND IMPERIALISM

• What events led the United States into war with Spain?

• What was the result of the war? Should Americans have been surprised about the outcome?

• What new attitudes about America's role in world affairs appeared in the debate over the acquisition of new possessions?

In 1898 the United States went to war with Spain over Cuba. Far from combat, John Hay, the American ambassador to Great Britain, celebrated the conflict as "a splendid little war," and the description stuck. Some who promoted American intervention

on behalf of the suffering Cubans envisioned a quick war to establish a Cuban republic. Others saw war with Spain as an opportunity to seize territory and acquire a colonial empire for the United States.

McKinley and War

William McKinley became president amid increasing demands for action regarding Cuba. He moved cautiously, however, gradually stepping up diplomatic efforts to resolve the crisis. Late that year Spain responded by softening the reconcentration policy and offering the Cubans limited self-government but not independence. In February 1898, however, two events scuttled progress toward a negotiated solution.

First, Cuban insurgents stole a letter written by **Enrique Dupuy de Lôme**, the Spanish minister to the United States, and released it to the *New York Journal*. In it, de Lôme criticized President McKinley as "weak and a bidder for the admiration of the crowd." The letter also implied that the Spanish government's commitment to reform in Cuba was not serious. Although de Lôme immediately resigned, the letter aroused intense anti-Spanish feeling among many Americans.

A few days later, on February 15, an explosion ripped open the American warship *Maine*, which

---

insurgents Rebels or revolutionaries.

guerrilla warfare An irregular form of war carried on by small bodies of men acting independently.

reconcentration Spanish policy in Cuba in 1896 that ordered the civilian population into fortified camps so as to isolate and annihilate the Cuban revolutionaries who remained outside the camps.

Joseph Pulitzer Hungarian-born newspaper publisher whose *New York World* printed sensational stories about Cuba that helped precipitate the Spanish-American War.

William Randolph Hearst Publisher and rival to Pulitzer whose newspaper, the *New York Journal*, sensationalized and distorted stories and actively promoted the war with Spain.

yellow journalism The use of sensational exposés, embellished reporting, and attention-grabbing headlines to sell newspapers.

Enrique Dupuy de Lôme Spanish minister to the United States whose private letter criticizing President McKinley was stolen and printed in the *New York Journal*, increasing anti-Spanish sentiment.

U.S.S. Maine American warship that exploded in Havana harbor in 1898, inspiring the motto "Remember the *Maine*!" which spurred the Spanish-American War.

On February 15, 1898, an explosion destroyed the American warship *Maine* as it lay at anchor in the harbor at Havana, Cuba. Some two hundred sixty Americans lost their lives. Many Americans blamed the Spanish government of Cuba, although there was no evidence to suggest who was responsible. *Library of Congress.*

was anchored in Havana harbor, and it sank, killing more than 260 Americans. The yellow press accused Spain of sabotage but could produce no evidence. An official inquiry blamed a submarine mine but could not determine whose it may have been. (Years later, an investigation indicated that the blast was probably of internal origin, resulting from a fire.) Regardless of how the explosion occurred, those advocating intervention now had a rallying cry: "Remember the *Maine*!"

McKinley extended his demands: an immediate end to the fighting, an end to reconcentration, measures to relieve the suffering, and **mediation** by McKinley himself. He also specified that one possible outcome of mediation might be Cuban independence. In reply, the Spanish government promised reforms, agreed to end reconcentration, and consented to cease fighting if the insurgents asked for an **armistice**. Spain was silent, though, on mediation by McKinley and independence for Cuba.

On April 11, McKinley sent a message to Congress stating that "the war in Cuba must stop" and asking for authority to act. Congress answered on April 19 with four resolutions: (1) declaring that Cuba was and should be independent, (2) demanding that Spain withdraw "at once," (3) authorizing the president to use force to accomplish Spanish withdrawal, and (4) disavowing any intention to annex the island. The first three resolutions

amounted to a declaration of war. The fourth is usually called the **Teller Amendment** for its sponsor, Senator Henry M. Teller, a Silver Republican from Colorado. In response, Spain declared war.

Most Americans wholeheartedly approved what they understood to be a war undertaken to bring independence and aid to the long-suffering Cubans. Some, however, distrusted the McKinley administration, fearing that a humanitarian war might become a struggle for the conquest of Cuba. In Congress, Democrats, Silver Republicans, and Populists sought recognition of the insurgents as the legitimate government of Cuba, but Republican congressional leaders squelched their efforts. The Teller Amendment also reflected a concern that the McKinley administration might try to make Cuba an American possession rather than granting it independence.

---

mediation   An attempt to bring about the peaceful settlement of a dispute through the intervention of a neutral party.

armistice   An agreement to halt fighting, at least temporarily.

Teller Amendment   Resolution approved by the U.S. Senate in 1898, by which the United States promised not to annex Cuba; introduced by Senator Henry Teller of Colorado.

Theodore Roosevelt's Rough Riders, on foot because there was not room aboard ship for their horses, are shown in the background of this artist's depiction of the battle for Kettle Hill, a part of the larger battle for San Juan Hill, overlooking the city of Santiago. The artist has put into the foreground members of the Ninth and Tenth Cavalry, both African-American units that also played a key role in that engagement, but one often overlooked because of the attention usually given Roosevelt and the Rough Riders. *Chicago Historical Society.*

The "Splendid Little War"

Since 1895, Americans' attention had been riveted on Cuba. Thus many were surprised that the first engagement in the war occurred in the **Philippine Islands**—nearly halfway around the world from Cuba. A Spanish colony for three hundred years, the Philippines had rebelled repeatedly, most recently in 1896.

Some Americans understood the islands' strategic location with regard to eastern Asia—including Assistant Secretary of the Navy **Theodore Roosevelt**. In February 1898, six weeks before McKinley's war message to Congress, Roosevelt cabled George Dewey, the American naval commander in the Pacific, to crush the Spanish fleet at Manila Bay if war broke out.

At sunrise on Sunday, May 1, Dewey's squadron of four cruisers and three smaller vessels steamed into the harbor and quickly destroyed or captured ten Spanish cruisers and gunboats. The Spanish lost 381 men, and the Americans lost one, a victim of heat prostration. Dewey instantly became a national hero. A few weeks later, on June 21, an American cruiser secured the surrender of Spanish forces on Guam.

Dewey's victory at Manila focused public attention on the Pacific and, for some, immediately raised the prospect of a permanent American presence there. This possibility, in turn, revived interest in the Hawaiian Islands—now seen as a crucial base

halfway to the Philippines. The McKinley administration had negotiated a treaty of annexation with the Hawaiian government in 1897, shortly after Cleveland left the White House, but anti-imperialist sentiment in the Senate made approval unlikely. Now, with Dewey's victory and the prospect of an American base in the Philippines, McKinley revived the joint-resolution precedent by which Texas had been annexed in 1844. Only a majority vote in both houses of Congress was required to adopt a joint resolution, rather than the two-thirds vote of the Senate needed to approve a treaty. Annexation of Hawai'i was accomplished on July 7.

Dewey's victory demonstrated that the American navy was clearly superior to Spain's. In contrast, the Spanish army in Cuba outnumbered the entire American army by more than five to one. The Spanish troops also had years of experience fighting in Cuba. When war was declared, McKinley called for

---

Philippine Islands   A group of islands in the Pacific Ocean southeast of China that came under U.S. control in 1898 after the Spanish-American War; they became an independent nation after World War II.

Theodore Roosevelt   American politician and writer who advocated war against Spain in 1898; McKinley's vice president in 1900, he became president in 1901 upon McKinley's assassination.

volunteers, and nearly a million men responded—five times as many as the army could enlist. The army now needed many weeks to train and supply the new recruits. Congress declared war in late April, but not until June did the first troop transports head for Cuba.

Sent to training camps in the South, the new soldiers found chaos and confusion. Food, uniforms, and equipment arrived at one location while the men for whom they were intended stood hungry and idle at another. Uniforms were often of heavy wool, totally unsuited for the climate and season. Disease raged through some camps, killing many men. Others died from tainted food, called "embalmed beef" by the troops. Some African-American soldiers refused to comply with racial segregation, and many white southerners objected to the presence in their communities of so many uniformed and armed black men.

Finally dispatched to Cuba, American forces tried to capture the port city of Santiago, where the Spanish fleet had taken refuge. Inexperienced, poorly equipped, and unfamiliar with the terrain, the Americans landed some distance from Santiago and then assaulted the fortified hills surrounding the city. Theodore Roosevelt had resigned as assistant secretary of the navy to organize a cavalry unit known as the **Rough Riders**. At Kettle Hill, he led a successful charge of Rough Riders and regular army units, including parts of the Ninth and Tenth Cavalry, made up of African Americans. All but Roosevelt were on foot because their horses had not yet arrived. Driving the Spanish from the crest of Kettle Hill cleared a serious impediment to the assault on nearby, and strategically more important, San Juan Heights and San Juan Hill. Roosevelt and his men were less prominent in that attack, but journalists loved Roosevelt—and newspapers all over the country declared Roosevelt the hero of the Battle of San Juan Hill.

Americans suffered heavy casualties during the first few days of the attack on Santiago. Nearly 10 percent of the troops were killed or wounded. Worsening the situation, the surgeon in charge of medical facilities refused assistance from Red Cross nurses because he thought field hospitals were not appropriate places for women. He was later overruled. Red Cross nurses also helped care for injured Cuban insurgents and civilians.

Once American troops secured control of the high ground around Santiago harbor, the Spanish fleet (four cruisers and two destroyers) tried to escape. A larger American fleet under Admiral William Samp-

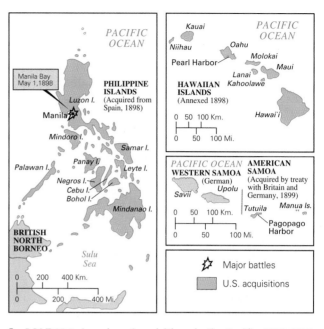

MAP 20.3 American Acquisitions in the Pacific, 1898–1899 In the 1890s, the United States became a major power in the Pacific. This map indicates major acquisitions in 1898 and 1899. In addition, the United States acquired Guam from Spain in 1898 and annexed Wake Island in 1899.

son and Commodore Winfield Schley met them and duplicated Dewey's rout at Manila—every Spanish ship was sunk or run aground. The Spanish suffered 323 deaths, the Americans one.

Their fleet destroyed, surrounded by American troops, the Spanish in Santiago finally surrendered on July 17. A week later American forces occupied Puerto Rico. Spanish land forces in the Philippines surrendered when the first American troops arrived in mid-August (see Map 20.3). The "splendid little war" lasted only sixteen weeks. More than 306,000 men served in the American forces. Only 385 of them died in battle, but more than 5,000 died of disease and other causes.

The Treaty of Paris

On August 12, the United States and Spain agreed to stop fighting and to hold a peace conference in

---

Rough Riders The First Volunteer Cavalry, a brigade recruited for action in the Spanish-American War by Theodore Roosevelt, who served first as its lieutenant colonel, then its colonel.

Paris. The major question for the conference centered on the Philippines. Finley Peter Dunne, a popular humorist, parodied the national debate on the Philippines in a discussion between his fictional characters, Mr. Dooley (a Chicago saloonkeeper) and a customer named Hennessy. Hennessy insists that McKinley should take the islands. Dooley responds that "it's not more than two months since you learned whether they were islands or canned goods," he sputters and then confesses his own indecision: "I can't annex them because I don't know where they are. I can't let go of them because someone else will take them if I do. . . . It would break my heart to think of giving people I've never seen or heard of back to other people I don't know. . . . I don't know what to do about the Philippines. And I'm all alone in the world. Everybody else has made up his mind."

McKinley voiced as many doubts as Mr. Dooley. At first, he seemed to favor only a naval base, leaving Spain in control elsewhere. However, Spanish authority collapsed throughout the islands by mid-August as Filipino insurgents took charge. Britain, Japan, and Germany watched carefully, and one or another of them seemed likely to step in if the United States withdrew. By then, McKinley and his advisers had apparently decided that defending a naval base on Manila Bay would require control of the entire island group. No one seems to have seriously considered the Filipinos' desire for independence.

McKinley was well aware of the political and strategic importance of the Philippines for eastern Asia. He invoked other reasons, however, when he explained his decision to a group of visiting Methodists. He repeatedly prayed for guidance on the Philippine question, he told them. Late one night, he said, it came to him that "there was nothing left for us to do but to take them all, and to educate the Filipinos, and uplift and civilize and Christianize them and by God's grace do the very best we could by them." In fact, most Filipinos had been Catholics for centuries, but no one ever expressed more clearly the concept of the "white man's burden."

Spain resisted giving up the Philippines, but McKinley remained adamant. The Treaty of Paris, signed in December 1898, required Spain to surrender all claim to Cuba, cede Puerto Rico and Guam to the United States, and sell the Philippines for $20 million. For the first time in American history, a treaty acquiring new territory failed to confer U.S. citizenship on the residents. Nor did the treaty mention future statehood. Thus these acquisitions repre-

sented a new kind of expansion—America had become a colonial power.

The terms of the **Treaty of Paris** dismayed Democrats, Populists, and some conservative Republicans. They immediately sparked a public debate over acquisition of the Philippines in particular and **imperialism** more generally. An anti-imperialist movement quickly formed, with William Jennings Bryan, Grover Cleveland, Andrew Carnegie, Mark Twain, and Jane Addams among its outspoken proponents. The treaty provisions, they argued, denied self-government for the newly acquired territories. For the United States to hold colonies, they claimed, threatened the very concept of democracy. "The Declaration of Independence," warned Carnegie, "will make every Filipino a thoroughly dissatisfied subject." Others worried over the perversion of American values. "God Almighty help the party that seeks to give civilization and Christianity hypodermically with 13-inch guns," prayed Senator William Morris of Illinois. Some anti-imperialists argued from a racist perspective that Filipinos were incapable of taking part in a Western-style democracy and that the United States would be corrupted by ruling people unable to govern themselves. Union leaders, fearing Filipino migration to the United States, repeated arguments once used to secure Chinese exclusion.

Those who defended acquisition of the Philippines echoed McKinley's lofty pronouncements about America's duty along with more mundane claims about economic benefits. Albert Beveridge, senator from Indiana after 1899, presented the commercial benefits: "We are raising more than we can consume, making more than we can use. Therefore we must find new markets for our produce." Such "new markets" were not limited to the Philippines or other new possessions. A strong naval and military presence in the Philippines would make the United States a leading power in eastern Asia. American business might therefore anticipate support for their continued access to markets in China.

Treaty of Paris   Treaty ending the Spanish-American War, under which Spain granted independence to Cuba, ceded Puerto Rico and Guam, and sold the Philippines to the United States for $20 million.

imperialism   The practice by which a nation acquires and holds colonies and other possessions, denies them self-government, and usually exploits them economically.

William Jennings Bryan, the Democratic presidential candidate in 1896, urged Senators to approve the treaty. That way, he reasoned, the United States alone could determine the future of the Philippines. Once the treaty was approved, he argued, the United States should immediately grant them independence. By a narrow margin, the Senate approved the treaty on February 6, 1899. Soon after, senators rejected a proposal for Philippine independence.

Republic or Empire: The Election of 1900

Bryan hoped to make independence for the Philippines the central issue in the 1900 presidential election. He easily won the Democratic nomination for a second time, and the Democrats' platform condemned the McKinley administration for its "imperialism." Bryan found, however, that many conservative anti-imperialists would not support his candidacy because he still insisted on silver coinage and attacked big business.

The Republicans renominated McKinley. For vice president, they chose Theodore Roosevelt, "hero of San Juan Hill." The McKinley re-election campaign seemed unstoppable. Republican campaigners pointed proudly to a short and highly successful war, legislation on the tariff and gold standard, and the return of prosperity. Bryan repeatedly attacked imperialism. McKinley and Roosevelt never used the term at all and instead took pride in expansion. Republican campaigners questioned the patriotism of anyone who proposed to pull down the flag where it had once been raised. McKinley easily won a second term with 51.7 percent of the vote, carrying not only the states that had given him his victory in 1896 but also many of the western states where Populism had once flourished.

Organizing an Insular Empire

The Teller Amendment specified that the United States would not annex Cuba, but the McKinley administration refused to recognize the insurgents as a legitimate government. Instead, the U.S. Army took control. Among other tasks, the army undertook sanitation projects intended to reduce disease, especially yellow fever. After two years of army rule, the McKinley administration permitted Cuban voters to hold a constitutional convention.

The convention met in 1900 and drafted a constitution modeled on that of the United States. Nowhere did it define relations between Cuba and the United States. In response, the McKinley administration drafted, and Congress adopted, terms for Cuba to adopt before the army would withdraw. Called the **Platt Amendment** for Senate Orville Platt, who introduced them as an amendment to an army appropriations bill, the terms specified that (1) Cuba was not to make any agreement with a foreign power that impaired the island's independence, (2) the United States could intervene in Cuba to preserve Cuban independence and maintain law and order, and (3) Cuba was to lease facilities to the United States for naval bases and coaling stations. Cubans reluctantly agreed, changed their constitution, and signed a treaty with the United States stating the Platt conditions. In 1902 Cuba thereby became a protectorate of the United States.

The Teller Amendment did not apply to Puerto Rico. There, the army provided a military government until 1900, when Congress approved the **Foraker Act**. That act made Puerto Ricans citizens of Puerto Rico but not citizens of the United States. Under its provisions Puerto Rican voters were to elect a legislature, but final authority was to rest with a governor and council appointed by the president of the United States. In 1901, in the **Insular cases**, the U.S. Supreme Court confirmed the colonial status of Puerto Rico and, by implication, the other new possessions. The Court ruled that they were not equivalent to earlier territorial acquisitions and that their people did not possess the constitutional rights of citizens.

Establishment of a civil government in the Philippines took longer. Between Dewey's victory and the arrival of the first American soldiers three months later, a Philippine independence movement led by **Emilio Aguinaldo** established a provisional

---

Platt Amendment An amendment to the Army Appropriations Act of 1901, sponsored by Senator Orville Platt, which set terms for the withdrawal of the U.S. Army from Cuba.

Foraker Act Law passed by Congress in 1900 that established civilian government in Puerto Rico; it provided for an elected legislature and a governor appointed by the U.S. president.

Insular cases Cases concerning Puerto Rico, in which the U.S. Supreme Court ruled in 1901 that people in new island territories did not automatically receive the constitutional rights of U.S. citizens.

Emilio Aguinaldo Leader of unsuccessful struggles for Philippine independence, first against Spain and then against the United States.

The Spanish banished Emilio Aguinaldo (on horseback) from the Philippines because of his efforts to end Spanish rule. American naval officials returned him to the islands. There he helped to establish an independent Filipino government and later led armed resistance to American authority, until he was captured in 1901. *Corbis/Bettmann Archives.*

government and took control everywhere but Manila. (Manila remained in Spanish hands until American troops arrived.) Aguinaldo and his government wanted independence. When the United States determined to keep the islands, the Filipinos resisted.

Quelling what American authorities called the "Philippine insurrection" required three years (1899–1902), took the lives of 4,200 American soldiers (more losses than in the Spanish-American War) and perhaps 20,000 Filipinos, and cost $400 million (twenty times the price of the islands). When some Filipinos resorted to guerilla warfare, U.S. troops adopted the same practices that Spain had used in Cuba. Both sides committed atrocities, and anti-imperialists pointed to brutish behavior by American troops as proof that a colonial policy was corrupting American values. American troops captured Aguinaldo in 1901, but resistance continued into mid-1902.

With defeat of Aguinaldo, Congress set up a government for the Philippines similar to that of Puerto Rico. Filipinos became citizens of the Philippine Islands, but not of the United States. The president of the United States appointed the governor. Filipino voters elected one house in the two-house legislature, and the governor appointed the other. Both the governor and the U.S. Congress could veto laws passed by the legislature. **William Howard Taft**, governor of the islands from 1901 to 1904, tried to build local support for American control, secured limited land reforms, and started to build public schools, hospitals, and sanitary facilities. However, when the first Philippine legislature met, in 1907, more than half of its members favored independence.

The Open Door and the Boxer Rebellion in China

Late in 1899, Britain, Germany, and the United States signed the Treaty of Berlin, which divided Samoa between Germany and the United States. The new Pacific acquisitions of the United States— Hawai`i, the Philippines, Guam, and Samoa—were all endowed with excellent harbors and suitable sites for naval bases. Combined with the modernized navy, these acquisitions greatly strengthened American ability to protect access to commercial markets in eastern Asia and to assert American

William Howard Taft Governor of the Philippines from 1901 to 1904; he was elected president of the United States in 1908 and became chief justice of the Supreme Court in 1921.

A FAIR FIELD AND NO FAVOR!
UNCLE SAM: "I'M OUT FOR COMMERCE, NOT CONQUEST!"

In this 1899 cartoon celebrating the Open Door policy, Uncle Sam insists that the nations of Europe must compete fairly for China's commerce and must not seize Chinese territory. In the background, John Bull (Britain) lifts his hat in approval. *Library of Congress.*

Japan, asking them to preserve some semblance of Chinese sovereignty within their spheres of influence and urging them not to discriminate against citizens of other nations who were engaged in commerce within their spheres. Hay wanted both to prevent the dismemberment of China and to maintain commercial access for American entrepreneurs throughout China. Some replies proved less than fully supportive, but Hay announced in a second letter that all had agreed to his so-called Open Door principles. Hay's letters have usually been called the **Open Door notes.**

The next year, in 1900, a Chinese secret society tried to expel all foreigners from China. Because the rebels used a clenched fist as their symbol, westerners called them Boxers. The Boxers laid siege to the section of Beijing, the Chinese capital, that housed foreign **legations**. Hay feared that the major powers might use the rebellion as a pretext to take control and divide China permanently. To block such a move, the United States took full part in an international military expedition to rescue the hostages and to crush the **Boxer Rebellion**.

Although China did not lose territory, the intervening nations required it to pay an **indemnity**. After compensating U.S. citizens for their losses, the United States government returned the remainder of its indemnity to China. To show its appreciation, the Chinese government used the money to send Chinese students to study in the United States.

power in the region. The United States now began to seek full participation in the east Asian **balance of power**.

Weakened by war with Japan in 1894-1895, the Chinese government could not resist European nations' demands for territory. By 1899, Britain, Germany, Russia, and France had all carved out **spheres of influence**—areas where they claimed special rights, usually a monopoly over trade. In keeping with the treaty of 1844, the United States claimed no such privileges in China and argued instead for the "Open Door"—a situation where citizens of all nations would have equal status in seeking trade. American diplomats, however, began to fear the breakup of China into separate European colonies and the subsequent exclusion of American commerce.

In 1899 Secretary of State John Hay circulated a letter to Germany, Russia, Britain, France, Italy, and

balance of power   In international politics, the notion that nations may restrict one another's actions because of the relative equality of their naval or military forces, either individually or through alliance systems.

sphere of influence   A territorial area where a foreign nation exerts significant authority.

Open Door notes   An exchange of diplomatic letters in 1899–1900 by which Secretary of State John Hay announced American support for Chinese autonomy and opposed efforts by other powers to carve China into exclusive spheres of influence.

legation   A diplomatic mission in a foreign country.

Boxer Rebellion   Uprising in China in 1900 directed against foreign powers who were attempting to dominate China; it was suppressed by an international army that included American participation.

indemnity   Payment for damage, loss, or injury.

INDIVIDUAL VOICES

Examining a Primary Source

Annie Diggs Sympathizes with Filipinos Seeking Independence

Annie L. Diggs, a leading Populist, wrote this poem in 1899. By then, the United States was using its army (armed with Krag-Jorgensen rifles) to suppress Aguinaldo's government in the Philippines, and the expression "Little brown brother" was in widespread use to designate the people of the Philippines.

● In one widely quoted newspaper story, an American had compared the Filipinos with jack-rabbits.

● What is Diggs's point here? Who is she trying to convince?

● Why does Diggs mention Valley Forge and Brandywine? What might she have in mind by wondering about Lafayette?

● In the Bible, Cain killed his brother Abel. What "mark of Cain" does Diggs refer to here?

Little Brown Brother
Little Brown Brothers across the sea
Running your race for liberty,
Here's to you,
We've been there ourselves.

Odd little Brown Men,
like "jack-rabbits" you run. ●
Bang the Krag-Jorgensen;
"Pick 'em off, it's great fun!"
Halt!
"Jack-rabbits" are they? . . .
Well, even sparrows fall not unheeded.

Halt! Who goes there?
Not jack-rabbits, not rebels, but Men.
Fighting for life, liberty, homes.
Homes? Bamboo huts.
Well, homes are homes, brown stone or bamboo. . . .

A Brown Man lies dead 'neath his own island sky;
A Brown Wife utters a strange wild cry,
The billowy deep brings the piteous sound
Hearts are the same God's sweet world round. ●

O little Brown Child whose father lies low,
Just when will your love and your loyalty flow . . .
To the Flag and the Nation that made you an orphan?

Little Brown Brothers across the blue sea,
Are your bare, brown feet all bleeding and torn?
So were ours.
Valley Forge! Brandywine!
Where's Lafayette? . . . ●

God made of one blood all nations on earth,
Brothers all,
Lord God of Nations, spare us Cain's mark. ●

● *What is Diggs's view on imperialism? What does she wish for the people of the Philippines?*

Little Brown Brothers across the blue sea,
Battling so bravely for liberty,
Here's to you.
We've been there ourselves—and won. ●

SUMMARY

The 1890s saw important and long-lasting changes in American politics. In 1889–1890, Republicans wrote most of their campaign promises into law, breaking the political logjam of the preceding fourteen years. Nativism began to take political form in the 1890s, in the short-lived American Protective Association and the more successful immigration restriction movement. A political upheaval began when western and southern farmers joined the Farmers' Alliances and then launched a new political party, the Populist Party. In 1892 voters rejected the Republicans in many areas, choosing either the new Populist Party or the Democrats.

The nation entered a major depression in 1893. Organized labor suffered defeat in two dramatic encounters, one at the Homestead steel plant in 1892 and the other over the Pullman car boycott in 1894. At the end of the 1890s, entrepreneurs and investment bankers launched a merger movement that lasted until 1902, producing among other massive new companies United States Steel.

President Grover Cleveland proved unable to meet the political challenges of the depression, and his party, the Democrats, lost badly in the 1894 congressional elections. Southern Democrats began to write white supremacy into law by disfranchising black voters and requiring segregation of the races. In 1896 the Democrats chose as their presidential candidate William Jennings Bryan, a critic of Cleveland and supporter of silver coinage. The Republicans nominated William McKinley, who favored the protective tariff. McKinley won, beginning a period of Republican dominance in national politics that lasted until 1930. Under Bryan's long-term leadership, the Democratic Party discarded its commitment to minimal government and instead adopted a willingness to use government against monopolies and other powerful economic interests.

During the 1890s, the United States took on a new role in foreign affairs. During the administration of Benjamin Harrison, Congress approved creation of a modern navy. Although a revolution presented the United States with an opportunity to annex Hawai`i, President Cleveland rejected that course. However, Cleveland threatened war with Great Britain over a disputed boundary between Venezuela and British Guiana, and Britain backed down.

A revolution in Cuba led the United States into a one-sided war with Spain in 1898. The immediate result was acquisition of an American colonial empire that included the Philippines, Guam, and Puerto Rico. Congress annexed Hawai`i in the midst of the war, and the United States acquired part of Samoa by treaty in 1899. Filipinos resisted American authority, leading to a three-year war that cost more lives than the Spanish-American War. With the Philippines and an improved navy, the United States took on a new prominence in eastern Asia, especially in China, where U.S. diplomatic and commercial interests promoted the Open Door and where American troops took part in suppressing the Boxer Rebellion.

ADOPTION OF PROGRESSIVE REFORMS BY 1915 This map shows the states that had adopted three progressive reforms before 1915. Woman suffrage, long advocated, finally moved toward national adoption during these years. Prohibition was the leading example of moral reform during the period, and the initiative and referendum became popular vehicles for voter expression in some states.

CANADA

WASHINGTON

MONTANA

NORTH DAKOTA

MINN.

OREGON

IDAHO

WISCONSIN

MICH.

MAINE

VT.

N.H.

NEW YORK

MASS.

R.I.

CONN.

WYOMING

SOUTH DAKOTA

IOWA

PENNSYLVANIA

N.J.

NEVADA

UTAH

COLORADO

NEBRASKA

ILLINIOS

IND.

OHIO

MD.

DEL.

W.VA.

VIRGINIA

CALIFORNIA

KANSAS

MISSOURI

KENTUCKY

NORTH CAROLINA

ARIZONA

NEW MEXICO

OKLAHOMA

ARKANSAS

TENN.

SOUTH CAROLINA

MISS.

ALABAMA

GEORGIA

PACIFIC OCEAN

TEXAS

LOUISIANNA

ATLANTIC OCEAN

FLA.

MEXICO

Gulf of Mexico

HAWAI'I TERRITORY

0   100 Km.

0   100 Mi.

PACIFIC OCEAN

RUSSIA

ALASKA TERRITORY

CANADA

0   250 500 Km.

0   250   500 Mi.

PACIFIC OCEAN

Full prohibition

Full woman suffrage

Initiative and referendum

Note: Maryland and New Mexico adopted the referendum only.

0   200   400 Km.

0   200   400 Mi.

Spanish-American War

Roosevelt becomes president

Hay-Bunau-Varilla Treaty

Hepburn Act

NAACP formed

Wilson elected

| 1898 | 1901 | 1904 | 1906 | 1910 | 1912 |

| 1850 | 1900 | 1950 | 2000 |

The Progressive Era, 1900–1917

THEODORE ROOSEVELT

President Theodore Roosevelt's distinctive face attracted photographers and cartoonists, and he was often shown with a big grin. He loved fun, and a friend of his once observed that "You must always remember that the President is about six." *Brown Brothers.*

Theodore Roosevelt

On September 7, 1901, President William McKinley was shaking the hands of well-wishers at an exposition in Buffalo, New York. Suddenly Leon Czolgosz, an American-born anarchist, opened fire with a small handgun. McKinley died a week later, and Theodore Roosevelt became president.

Roosevelt was only 42 years old, the youngest person ever to assume the presidency. He was unusual in other ways, too. His refined manners pointed to his distinguished family background, just as his thick spectacles hinted at his intellectual accomplishments. At a time when most presidents had been "practical men," Roosevelt had written more than a dozen books on history, natural history, and his own experiences as a rancher and hunter. Professors used his *Naval War of 1812* (1882) as a college textbook. His *Winning of the West* (4 vols., 1889–1896) had won wide acclaim. Though he wrote a book, on average, every two years, he had also made a career in Republican politics and captured the popular imagination as the "Hero of San Juan Hill" (see page 629).

Less than a year after assuming the presidency, Roosevelt faced a potential crisis, and he dealt with it quite differently from the approach of his predecessors. In June 1902, anthracite coal miners went on strike in Pennsylvania, seeking higher wages, an eight-hour workday, and union recognition. Mine owners refused to negotiate or even to meet with representatives of the United Mine Workers.

The railroads of the coal-mining region owned the mines, and the president of the Reading Railroad, George F. Baer, spoke for the mining companies. When urged to negotiate with the union, Baer replied,

> The rights and interests of the laboring men will be protected and cared for—not by the labor agitators, but by the Christian men to whom God in his infinite wisdom has given control of the property interests of this country.

Baer's claim to God-given control failed to impress the miners, much of the public, or Roosevelt.

As cold weather approached and coal prices edged upward, public concern grew because many people heated their homes with coal. Roosevelt knew that nothing in the Constitution or federal law required him to take action, but he did so nonetheless. In early October, Roosevelt called both sides to Washington, where he urged them to submit their differences to arbitration by a board that he would appoint. The owners haughtily refused and instead insisted that the army be used against the miners. After all, that was how Cleveland had broken the Pullman strike ten years before and Hayes had put down the railroad strike of 1877. Roosevelt, now angry, blasted them as "insolent" and so "obstinate" as to be both "utterly silly" and "well-nigh criminal."

Roosevelt, instead of pitting troops against the strikers, began to consider using the army to dispossess the mine owners and reopen the mines. Roosevelt sent his secretary of war, Elihu Root, to talk with J. P. Morgan, the prominent investment banker (see pages 614–615), who held a significant stake in the railroad companies. After talking with Root, Morgan convinced the companies to accept Roosevelt's offer of arbitration. The arbitration board granted the miners higher wages and a nine-hour workday but denied their other objectives. The companies were permitted to raise their prices to cover their additional costs.

No president had ever before intervened in a strike by treating a union as equal to the owners, let alone threatening to use the army on the side of labor. By taking bold action and asserting the power of the presidency, Roosevelt acted as what he called "the steward of the people," mediating a conflict between organized interest groups in an effort to advance the public interest. In this and other ways, Roosevelt significantly changed both the office of the presidency and the authority of the federal government.

INTRODUCTION

Roosevelt became president at a time that historians call the Progressive Era—a time when "reform was in the air," as one small-town journalist later recalled. In 1912 Walter Weyl, a former settlement house worker, described American politics this way:

We are in a period of clamor, of bewilderment, of an almost tremulous unrest. We are hastily revising all our social conceptions. We are hastily testing all our political ideals.

Weyl's characterization, overstated as it was, reflected the widespread popular expectation for change. Reform was "in the air" almost everywhere, and many individuals and groups joined the crusade, often with quite different expectations. The variety of competing organizations seeking to reform politics could—and did—produce nearly as much clamor and bewilderment as Weyl described.

At the dawn of the new century few Americans could have anticipated the extent of change that lay just ahead. Most probably expected a continuation of nineteenth-century political patterns, in which parties dominated politics, and the federal government did little in the economy other than to stimulate development through the tariff and land policies. At the same time, many Americans believed that something should be done to curb the power of the new industrial corporations and to resolve the problems of the cities. Some Americans also came to identify traditional political practices as an impediment to reform.

Progressivism took shape through many decisions by voters and political leaders. A basic question loomed behind many of those decisions: Should government play a larger role in the lives of Americans? This question lay behind debates over regulation of railroads in 1906 and regulation of banking in 1913, as well as behind proposals to prohibit alcoholic beverages and to limit working hours of women factory workers. Time after time, Americans chose a greater role for government. Often the consensus favoring government intervention was so broad that the only debate was over what form the intervention would take. As Americans gave government more power, they also sought to make it more responsive to ordinary citizens. They limited the roles of political parties and introduced ways for people to participate more directly in politics. Although progressives imposed new regulations on some businesses, traditional values of private property and individualism proved hardy. The political changes of the Progressive Era, following on the heels of the political realignment of the 1890s, fundamentally altered American politics and government in the twentieth century. The Progressive Era gave birth to many aspects of modern American politics.

ORGANIZING FOR CHANGE

- What important changes transformed American politics in the early twentieth century?
- What did women and African Americans seek to accomplish by creating new organizations devoted to political change?

During the early twentieth century, politics dramatically expanded to embrace wide-ranging concerns raised by a complex assortment of groups and individuals. In the swirl of proponents and proposals, politics more than ever before came to reflect the interaction of organized interest groups.

The Changing Face of Politics

As the United States entered the twentieth century, the lives of many Americans changed in important ways. The railroad, telegraph, and telephone had transformed concepts of time and space and fostered formation of new organizations. Executives of the new industrial corporations now thought in terms of regional or national markets. Union members allied with others of their trade in distant cities. Farmers in Kansas and Montana studied grain prices in Chicago and Liverpool. Physicians organized to establish nationwide standards for medical schools.

Manufacturers, farmers, merchants, carpenters, teachers, lawyers, physicians, and many others established or reorganized national associations to advance their economic or professional interests. Sometimes that meant seeking governmental assistance. As early as the 1870s, for example, associations of merchants, farmers, and oil producers had

pushed for laws to regulate railroad freight rates (see page 519).

Other forms of associative activity also developed. Some graduates emerged from the recently transformed universities (see page 553) with the conviction that their knowledge and skills could improve society, and they formed professional associations to advance those objectives. Long-established church organizations sometimes fostered the emergence of new associations devoted to moral reform, especially prohibition. Some people formed groups with humanitarian goals such as ending child labor. Members of ethnic and racial groups set up societies to further their groups' interests. Reformers organized to limit the power of corporations or to defeat party bosses. Overlapping with many of these new associations were the organizational activities of women, including middle-class women, new college graduates, and factory and clerical workers.

Sooner or later, many of the new associations sought changes in laws to help them reach their objectives. Increasing numbers of citizens related to politics through such organized **interest groups**, even as the traditional political parties found they could no longer count on the voter loyalty typical of the Gilded Age.

Many of these new groups optimistically believed that responsible citizens, acting together, assisted by technical know-how, and sometimes drawing on the power of government, could achieve social progress—improvement of the human situation. As early as the 1890s, some had begun to call themselves "progressive citizens." By 1910, many were simply calling themselves "progressives."

Historians use the term *progressivism* to signify three related developments during the early twentieth century: (1) the emergence of new concepts of the purposes and functions of government, (2) changes in government policies and institutions, and (3) the political agitation that produced those changes. A progressive, then, was a person involved in one or more of these activities. The many individuals and groups promoting their own visions of change made progressivism a complex phenomenon. There was

---

interest group A coalition of people identified with a particular cause, such as an industry or occupational group, a social group, or a policy objective.

chronology

The Progressive Era

1885	Mark Twain's *The Adventures of Huckleberry Finn*
1889	Hazen Pingree elected mayor of Detroit
1893	Stephen Crane's *Maggie: A Girl of the Streets* World's Columbian Exposition, Chicago
1895	Anti-Saloon League formed *United States v. E. C. Knight*
1898	South Dakota adopts initiative and referendum War with Spain
1899	Permanent Court of Arbitration created Scott Joplin's "Maple Leaf Rag"
1900	First city commission, in Galveston, Texas Robert M. La Follette elected governor of Wisconsin President William McKinley reelected
1901	Socialist Party of America formed McKinley assassinated; Theodore Roosevelt becomes president Formation of U.S. Steel by J.P. Morgan Frank Norris's *The Octopus*
1902	Muckraking journalism begins Oregon adopts initiative and referendum Antitrust action against Northern Securities Company Roosevelt intervenes in coal strike Reclamation Act
1903	Women's Trade Union League formed W. E. B. Du Bois's *Souls of Black Folk* First World Series Cuba becomes a protectorate
1904	Hay–Bunau-Varilla Treaty; construction begins on Panama Canal Roosevelt Corollary Lincoln Steffens's *The Shame of the Cities* Roosevelt elected president
1905	Niagara Movement formed Industrial Workers of the World organized Roosevelt mediates Russo-Japanese War

1906	Upton Sinclair's *The Jungle* Hepburn Act Meat Inspection Act
1907	Financial panic
1908	*Muller v. Oregon* Race riot in Springfield, Illinois First city-manager government, in Staunton, Virginia William Howard Taft elected president
1909	Payne-Aldrich Tariff
1910	State of Washington approves woman suffrage National Association for the Advancement of Colored People formed Revolt against Cannonism Mann Act Taft fires Pinchot Hiram W. Johnson elected governor of California
1911	Fire at Triangle Shirtwaist factory
1912	Progressive ("Bull Moose") Party formed Wilson elected president
1913	Sixteenth Amendment (federal income tax) ratified Seventeenth Amendment (direct election of U.S. senators) ratified Underwood Tariff Federal Reserve Act Armory Show introduces European abstract expressionism
1914	Clayton Antitrust Act Federal Trade Commission Act Panama Canal completed
1915	National Birth Control League formed
1916	Louis Brandeis appointed to the Supreme Court Montana elects Jeannette Rankin, the first woman, to Congress Wilson reelected
1917	United States enters World War I

no one progressive movement. To be sure, an organized **Progressive Party** emerged in 1912 and sputtered for a brief time after, but it failed to capture the allegiance of all those who called themselves progressives. Although there was no typical progressive, many aspects of progressivism reflected concerns of the urban middle class, especially urban middle-class women.

Progressivism appeared at every level of government—local, state, and federal. And progressives promoted a wide range of new government activities: regulation of business, moral revival, consumer protection, conservation of natural resources, educational improvement, tax reform, and more. Through all these avenues, they brought government more directly into the economy and more directly into the lives of most Americans.

Women and Reform

Organizations formed by or dominated by women burst onto politics during the **Progressive Era**. By 1900 or so, a new ideal for women had emerged from women's colleges and clubs and from discussions on national lecture circuits and in the press. The New Woman stood for self-determination rather than unthinking acceptance of roles prescribed by the concepts of domesticity and separate spheres. By 1910, this attitude, sometimes called **feminism**, was accelerating the transition from the nineteenth-century movement for suffrage to the twentieth-century struggle for equality and individualism.

Women's increasing control over one aspect of their lives is evident in the birth rate, which fell steadily throughout the nineteenth and early twentieth centuries as couples (or, perhaps, women alone) chose to have fewer children. Abortion was illegal, and state and federal laws banned the distribution of information about contraception. As a result, women or couples seeking to prevent conception often had little reliable guidance. In 1915 a group of women formed the National Birth Control League to seek the repeal of laws that barred contraceptive information. In 1916 **Margaret Sanger**, a nurse practicing among the poor in New York City, attracted wide attention when she went to jail for informing women about birth control.

Other women also formed organizations to advance specific causes. Some, like the settlement houses, were oriented to service. The National Consumers' League (founded in 1890) and the Women's Trade Union League (1903) tried to improve the lives of working women. Such efforts received a

tragic boost in 1911 when fire roared through the Triangle Shirtwaist Company's clothing factory in New York City, killing 146 workers—nearly all young women—who were trapped in a building with no outside fire escapes and locked exit doors. The public outcry produced a state investigation and, in 1914, a new state factory safety law.

Some states passed laws specifically to protect working women. In *Muller v. Oregon* (1908), the Supreme Court approved the constitutionality of one such law, limiting women's hours of work. Louis Brandeis, a lawyer working with the Consumers' Union, defended the law on the grounds that women needed special protection because of their social roles as mothers. Such arguments ran contrary to the New Woman's rejection of separate spheres and ultimately raised questions for women's drive for equality. At the time, however, the decision was widely hailed as a vital and necessary protection for women wage earners. By 1917, laws in thirty-nine states restricted women's working hours.

Though prominent in reform politics, most women could neither vote nor hold office. Support for suffrage grew, however, as more women recognized the need for political action to bring social change. By 1896, four western states had extended the vote to women (see page 562). No other state did so until 1910, when Washington approved female suffrage. Seven more western states followed over the next five years. In 1916 **Jeannette Rankin** of Montana—born on a ranch, educated as a social worker, experienced

---

Progressive Party   Political party formed in 1912 with Theodore Roosevelt as its candidate for president; it fell apart when Roosevelt returned to the Republicans in 1916.

Progressive Era   Period of reform in the late nineteenth and early twentieth centuries.

feminism   The conviction that women are and should be the social, political, and economic equals of men.

Margaret Sanger   Birth-control advocate who believed so strongly that information about birth control was essential to help women escape poverty that she disobeyed laws against its dissemination.

Muller v. Oregon   Supreme Court case in 1908, upholding an Oregon law that limited the hours of employment for women.

Jeannette Rankin   Montana reformer and pacifist who in 1916 became the first woman elected to Congress; she worked to pass the woman suffrage amendment and to protect women in the workplace.

Margaret Sanger is seen here in 1916, leaving court after being charged with distributing birth control information illegally. During the Progressive Era, women worked to remove legal barriers to obtaining information on preventing conception. *Smith College Collection, Smith College.*

as a suffrage campaigner—became the first woman elected to the House of Representatives. Suffrage scored few victories outside the West, however.

Convinced that only a federal constitutional amendment would gain the vote for all women, the **National American Woman Suffrage Association** (NAWSA), led by Carrie Chapman Catt and Anna Howard Shaw, developed a national organization geared to lobbying in Washington, D.C. Alice Paul advocated public demonstrations and civil disobedience, tactics she learned from suffragists in England, where she had been a settlement house worker from 1907 to 1910. In 1913 Paul and her followers formed the Congressional Union to pursue militant strategies. Some white suffragists tried to build an interracial movement for suffrage—NAWSA, for example, condemned lynching in 1917—but most feared that attention to other issues would weaken their position.

Although its leaders were predominantly white and middle-class, the cause of woman suffrage ignited a mass movement during the 1910s, mobilizing women of all ages and socioeconomic classes. Opponents of woman suffrage argued that voting would bring women into the male sphere, expose them to corrupting influences, and render them unsuitable as guardians of the moral order. Some suffrage advocates now turned that argument on its head, claiming that women would make politics more moral and family oriented. Others, especially feminists, argued that women should vote because they deserved full equality with men.

Moral Reform

Causes other than suffrage also stirred women to action. Moral reformers focused especially on banning alcohol, which they labeled Demon Rum. The temperance movement dated to at least the 1820s, but most early temperance advocates merely tried to persuade individuals to give up strong drink. By the late nineteenth century, however, they looked to government to prohibit the production, sale, or consumption of alcoholic beverages. Many saw prohibition as a progressive reform and expected government to safeguard what they saw as the public interest. Few reforms could claim as many women activists as prohibition.

The drive against alcohol developed a broad base during the Progressive Era. Some **old-stock** Protestant churches—notably the Methodists—termed alcohol one of the most significant obstacles to a better society. Most adherents of the Social Gospel (see page 605) viewed prohibition as urgently needed to save the victims of industrialization and urbanization. Others, appealing to concepts of domesticity, emphasized protecting the family and home from the destructive influence of alcohol on husbands and fathers. Scientists related alcohol to disease and publicized the **narcotic** and **depressive** qualities of the drug.

National American Woman Suffrage Association
  Organization formed in 1890 that united the two major women's suffrage groups of that time.

old-stock Characteristic of people whose families had been in the United States for several generations.

narcotic A drug that reduces pain and induces sleep or stupor.

depressive Tending to lower a person's spirits and to lessen activity.

THE AWAKENING

This cartoon, entitled "The Awakening," shows a western woman, draped in a golden robe, bringing the torch of woman suffrage from the western states that had adopted suffrage to enlighten the darkness of the eastern states that had not done so. In the dark eastern states, women eagerly reach toward the light from the West. Yellow had become closely associated with the suffrage movement, and western suffrage advocates often depicted suffrage as a woman in a golden robe. *Library of Congress.*

Sociologists demonstrated links between liquor and prostitution, sexually transmitted diseases, poverty, crime, and broken families. Other evidence pointed to alcohol as contributing to industrial accidents, absenteeism, and inefficiency on the job.

Earlier prohibitionists had organized into the Prohibition Party and the Women's Christian Temperance Union (see page 555). By the late 1890s, however, the **Anti-Saloon League** became the model for successful interest-group politics. Proudly describing itself as "the Church in action against the saloon," the Anti-Saloon League usually operated through mainstream old-stock Protestant churches. The League focused its antagonism on the saloon, attacking it as the least defensible element in the liquor industry. Reformers viewed saloons as corrupting not only individuals—men who neglected their families—but politics as well. Saloons, where political cronies struck deals and mingled with voters, had long been identified with big-city political machines.

The League endorsed only politicians who opposed Demon Rum, regardless of their party or their stands on other issues. As the prohibition cause demonstrated its growing political clout, more politicians lined up against the saloon. At the same time, the League promoted statewide referendums to ban alcohol. Between 1900 and 1917, voters adopted prohibition in nearly half of the states, including nearly all of the West and the South. Elsewhere, many towns and rural areas voted themselves "dry" under **local option laws**.

Anti-Saloon League   Political interest group advocating prohibition, founded in 1895; it organized through churches and endorsed only politicians who favored prohibition.

local option law   A state law that permitted the residents of a town or city to decide, by an election, whether to ban liquor sales in their community.

Opposition to prohibition came especially from immigrants—and their American-born descendants—from Ireland, Germany, and southern and eastern Europe. These groups did not regard the use of alcohol as inherently sinful. For them, beer or wine was an accepted part of social life, and they resisted prohibition as an effort by some to impose their moral views on others. Companies that produced alcohol, especially beer brewers, also organized to fight the prohibitionists and subsidized some associations, especially the German American Alliance, to build a political coalition against the "dry" crusade. "Personal liberty" became the slogan for these "wets."

The drive against alcohol, ultimately successful at the national level, was not the only target for moral reformers. Reformers—many of them women—tried to eliminate prostitution through state and federal legislation. Beginning in Iowa in 1909, states passed "red-light abatement" laws designed to close brothels. In 1910 Congress passed the **Mann Act**, making it illegal to take a woman across a state line for "immoral purposes." Other moral reform efforts—to ban gambling or make divorces more difficult, for example—also represented attempts to use government power to regulate individual behavior.

Racial Issues

During the Progressive Era, racial issues were generally less prominent than other reform causes. Only a few white progressives actively opposed disfranchisement and segregation in the South. Indeed, southern white progressives often took the lead in enacting discriminatory laws. Journalist Ray Stannard Baker was one of the few white progressives to examine the situation of African Americans. In his book *Following the Color Line* (1908), Baker asked, "Does democracy really include Negroes as well as white men?" For most white Americans, the answer appeared to be no.

Lynchings and violence continued as a fact of life for African Americans. Between 1900 and World War I, lynchings claimed more than eleven hundred victims, most in the South but many in the Midwest. During the same years, race riots wracked several cities. In 1906 Atlanta erupted into a riot as whites randomly attacked African Americans, killing four, injuring many more, and vandalizing property. In 1908, in Springfield, Illinois (where Abraham Lincoln had made his home), a mob of whites lynched two black men, injured others, and destroyed black-owned businesses. In North and South alike, little effort was spent to prosecute the mob leaders.

An unknown photographer captured this lynching on film and preserved all its brutality and depravity. Although there are many such photographic records of lynch mobs, local authorities nearly always claimed that they were unable to determine the identity of those responsible for the murder. *The Picture Cube.*

During the Progressive Era, some African Americans challenged the accommodationist leadership of Booker T. Washington. **W. E. B. Du Bois**, the first African American to receive a Ph.D. from Harvard, wrote some of the first scholarly studies of African Americans. He emphasized the contributions of black men and women, disproved racial stereotypes, and urged African Americans to take pride in their accomplishments. A professor at Atlanta University

Mann Act   Law passed by Congress in 1910, designed to suppress prostitution; it made transporting a woman across state lines for immoral purposes illegal.

W. E. B. Du Bois   African-American intellectual and civil rights leader, author of important works on black history and sociology, who helped to form and lead the NAACP.

A brilliant young intellectual, W. E. B. Du Bois had to choose between leading the life of a quiet college professor or challenging Booker T. Washington's claim to speak on behalf of all African Americans. *Schomburg Center for Research in Black Culture, New York Public Library, Astor, Lenox and Tilden Foundations.*

after 1897, Du Bois used his book *Souls of Black Folk* (1903) to criticize Washington and to exhort African Americans to struggle for their rights "unceasingly." "The hands of none of us are clean," he argued, speaking to both whites and blacks, "if we bend not our energies to a righting of these great wrongs."

African-American leaders organized in support of black rights. In 1905 Du Bois and others met in Canada, near Niagara Falls, and drafted demands for racial equality—including civil rights and equality in job opportunities and education—and an end to segregation. The Springfield riot so shocked some white progressives that in 1909 they called a biracial conference to seek ways to improve race relations. In 1910 delegates formed the **National Association for the Advancement of Colored People** (NAACP), which later provided important leadership in the fight for black equality. Du Bois served as the NAACP's director of publicity and research.

Other African Americans joined the struggle for equality and dignity in their own ways—**Ida B. Wells**, for example. Born in Mississippi in 1862,

Wells had attended a school set up by the Freedman's Bureau and worked as a rural teacher from 1884 to 1891. Then, in Memphis, Tennessee, she began to write for the black newspaper *Free Speech* and attacked lynching, arguing that several local victims had been targeted as a way of eliminating successful black businessmen. When a mob destroyed the newspaper office, she moved north. During the 1890s and early 1900s, Wells crusaded against lynching, speaking throughout the North and in England and writing *Southern Horrors* (1892) and *A Red Record* (1895). Her speeches and articles relentlessly challenged southern whites' justifications for lynching. Eventually she persuaded some white northerners to recognize and condemn the horror of lynching. She married in 1895, taking the name Ida Wells-Barnett, and lived in Chicago during the Progressive Era. There she promoted the development of black women's clubs and a black settlement house. Initially a supporter of the NAACP, she came to regard it as too cautious.

Challenging Capitalism: Socialists and Wobblies

Many progressive organizations reflected middle- and upper-class concerns, such as businesslike government, prohibition, and greater reliance on experts. Not so the **Socialist Party of America** (SPA), formed in 1901. Proclaiming themselves the political arm of workers and farmers, the Socialists argued that industrial capitalism had produced "an economic slavery which renders intellectual and political tyranny inevitable." They rejected most progressive proposals as inadequate to resolve the nation's problems and called instead for a cooperative commonwealth in which workers would control the means of production. Most looked to the political process and the ballot box as the means to accomplish this transformation.

National Association for the Advancement of Colored People   Racially integrated civil rights organization founded in New York City in 1910; it continues to work to end discrimination in the United States.

Ida B. Wells   Reformer and journalist who crusaded against lynching and advocated racial justice and woman suffrage; upon marrying in 1895, she became Ida Wells-Barnett.

Socialist Party of America   Political party formed in 1901 and committed to socialism—that is, government ownership of most industries.

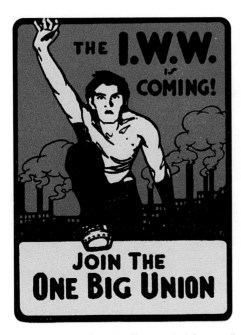

This design appeared originally on a "stickerette," a small poster (2½" × 3") with glue on the back. When the glue was moistened, the poster could be stuck on a fence post or inside a box car (where migratory workers often traveled). Wobblies sometimes called the stickerettes "silent agitators." *Courtesy Labor Archives and Research Center, San Francisco State University.*

sharecroppers, women workers, African Americans, and the "new immigrants" from southern and eastern Europe. Such workers were usually ignored by the American Federation of Labor, which instead emphasized skilled workers, most of them white males. The Wobblies' objective was simple: when the majority of workers across the country had joined the IWW, they would call a general strike, labor would refuse to work, and capitalism would collapse.

The IWW did organize a few dramatic strikes and demonstrations and even scored a handful of significant victories. Most AFL union leaders would have nothing to do with such radicals, however. The IWW often met brutal suppression by local authorities and made few lasting gains for their members.

The SPA counted considerably more victories than the Wobblies. Hundreds of cities and towns—ranging from Reading, Pennsylvania, to Milwaukee, Wisconsin to Berkeley, California—elected Socialist mayors or council members. Socialists won election to state legislatures in several states. Districts in New York City and Milwaukee sent Socialists to the U.S. House of Representatives. Most Americans, however, had no interest in eliminating private property. Most progressive reformers looked askance at the Socialists and sometimes tried to undercut their appeal with reforms that addressed some of their concerns but stopped short of challenging capitalism.

The Socialists' best-known national leader was Eugene V. Debs, leader of the Pullman strike (see pages 613–614) and virtually the only person able to unite the many socialist factions, ranging from theoretical **Marxists** completely opposed to capitalism to Christian Socialists, who drew their inspiration from religion rather than from Marx. Strong among immigrants, some of whom had become socialists in their native lands, the SPA also took in small numbers of trade unionists, municipal reformers, and intellectuals, including W. E. B. Du Bois, Margaret Sanger, and Upton Sinclair. The party also had pockets of supporters among farmers, especially in Oklahoma and Kansas, where they attracted some former Populists.

In 1905 a group of unionists and radicals organized the Industrial Workers of the World (IWW). IWW organizers boldly proclaimed, "We have been naught, we shall be all," as they set out to organize the unskilled and semiskilled workers at the bottom of the occupational ladder. They aimed their message at **sweatshop** workers in eastern cities, **migrant** farm workers who harvested western crops, southern

THE REFORM OF POLITICS, THE POLITICS OF REFORM

• What did the muckrakers and new professional groups contribute to reform?

• What were the characteristics of the reforms of city and state government?

• How did the rise of interest groups reflect new patterns of politics and government?

Progressivism emerged at all levels of government as cities elected reform-minded mayors and states swore in progressive governors. Some reformers

---

Marxist   A believer in the ideas of Karl Marx and Friedrich Engels, who opposed private ownership of property and looked to a future in which workers would control the economy.

sweatshop   A shop or factory in which employees worked long hours at low wages under poor conditions.

migrant   Traveling from one area to another.

A NAUSEATING JOB, BUT IT MUST BE DONE

(President Roosevelt takes hold of the investigating muck-rake himself in the packing-house scandal.)

U.S. INSP'D AND CONDEMNED

Upton Sinclair's novel, *The Jungle* (1906), prompted President Theodore Roosevelt to order an investigation of Sinclair's allegations about unsanitary practices. Roosevelt then used the results of that investigation to pressure Congress into approving new federal legislation to inspect meatpacking, including a stamp such as the one shown here for condemned meat. *Stamp: Chicago Historical Society; Cartoon: Utica Saturday Globe.*

hoped only to make government more honest and efficient. Others wanted to change the basic structure and function of government, to make it more responsive to the needs of an urban industrial society. In their quest for change, reformers sometimes found themselves in conflict with the entrenched leaders of political parties and sought to limit the power of those parties.

Exposing Corruption: The Muckrakers

Journalists played an important role in preparing the ground for reform. By the early 1900s, magazine publishers discovered that their sales boomed when they presented dramatic exposés of scandal—political corruption, corporate wrongdoing, and other scandalous offenses. Those who practiced this provocative journalism acquired the name **muckrakers** in 1906 when President Theodore Roosevelt compared them to "the Man with the Muck-rake," a character in John Bunyan's classic allegory *Pilgrim's*

Progress. Roosevelt intended the comparison as a rebuke, but journalists accepted the label with pride.

McClure's Magazine led the surge in muckraking journalism, especially after October 1902, when the magazine began a series by **Lincoln Steffens** on corruption in city governments. *McClure's* January 1903 issue featured Steffens's installment on Minneapolis, the first article in a series by **Ida Tarbell** on Stan-

muckrakers Progressive-era journalists who wrote articles exposing corruption in city government, business, and industry. In John Bunyan's *Pilgrim's Progress*, "The Man with the Muck-rake" is so preoccupied with raking through the filth at his feet that he didn't notice he was being offered a celestial crown in exchange for his rake.

Lincoln Steffens Muckraking journalist and managing editor of *McClure's Magazine*, best known for investigating political corruption in city governments.

Ida Tarbell Progressive-era journalist whose exposé revealed the ruthlessness of the Standard Oil Company.

dard Oil's sordid past, and a piece by Ray Stannard Baker revealing corruption and violence in labor unions. Sales of *McClure's* boomed, and other journals—including *Collier's* and *Cosmopolitan*—copied its style, publishing accounts of the defects of patent medicines, fraud in the insurance industry, the horrors of child labor, and more.

Muckraking soon extended from periodicals to books. Many muckraking books were simply reports on social problems. Both Steffens and Tarbell collected their articles and published them in book form (*The Shame of the Cities*, 1904; *The History of the Standard Oil Company*, 1904). The most famous muckraking book, however, was a novel: *The Jungle*, by **Upton Sinclair** (1906). In following the experiences of fictional immigrant laborers in Chicago, Sinclair exposed with disgusting accuracy the serious failings of the meatpacking industry. He described in chilling detail the afflictions of packing-house workers—severed fingers, tuberculosis, blood poisoning. The nation was shocked to read of men who "fell into the vats" and "would be overlooked for days, till all but the bones of them had gone out to the world as Durham's Pure Leaf Lard!" Sinclair, a Socialist, hoped readers would recognize that the offenses he portrayed were the results of industrial capitalism.

The Jungle horrified many Americans, and President Roosevelt appointed a commission to investigate its allegations. The report confirmed Sinclair's charges. Pressured by Roosevelt and the public, Congress passed the **Pure Food and Drug Act**, which banned impure and mislabeled food and drugs, and the **Meat Inspection Act**, which required federal inspection of meatpacking—a move the industry itself welcomed to reassure nauseated consumers. Sinclair, however, was disappointed because his revelations produced only regulation rather than converting readers to socialism. "I aimed at the public's heart," Sinclair later complained, "and by accident I hit it in the stomach."

Reforming City Government

In the early twentieth century, muckrakers, especially Lincoln Steffens, helped to focus public concern on city government. By the time of Steffens's first article (1902), advocates of **municipal reform** had already won office and brought changes to some cities, and municipal reformers soon appeared in many other cities.

Municipal reformers urged honest and efficient government, and many—perhaps most—also argued that corruption and inefficiency were inevitable with-

out major changes in the structure of city government. **City councils** usually consisted of members elected from **wards** corresponding roughly to neighborhoods. Most voters lived in middle-class and working-class wards, which therefore dominated most city councils. Reformers, however, condemned the ward system as producing city council members unable to see beyond the needs of their own narrow neighborhoods. Reformers pointed to support for political bosses and machines in poor immigrant neighborhoods and concluded that the ward leaders' devotion to voter needs kept the machine in power despite its corruption. They argued that citywide elections, in which all city voters chose from one list of candidates, would produce city council members who could better address the problems of the city as a whole—men with citywide business interests, for example—and that citywide elections would undercut the influence of ward bosses and machines.

James Phelan of San Francisco provides an example of an early structural reformer. Son of a pioneer banker, he was equally at home in the worlds of politics, business, and the arts. Phelan attacked corruption in city government and won election as mayor in 1896. He then spearheaded the adoption of a new charter that strengthened the office of mayor and required citywide election of supervisors (equivalent to city council members).

Some municipal reformers proposed more fundamental changes in the structure of city government, notably the **commission system** and the

---

Upton Sinclair Socialist writer and reformer whose novel *The Jungle* exposed unsanitary conditions in the meatpacking industry and advocated socialism.

Pure Food and Drug Act Law passed by Congress in 1906, forbidding the sale of impure and improperly labeled food and drugs.

Meat Inspection Act Law passed by Congress in 1906 requiring federal inspection of meatpacking.

municipal reform Political activity intended to bring about changes in the structure or function of city government.

city council A body of representatives elected to govern a city.

ward A division of a city or town, especially an electoral district, for administrative or representative purposes.

commission system System of city government in which all executive and legislative power is vested in a small elective board, each member of which supervises some aspect of city government.

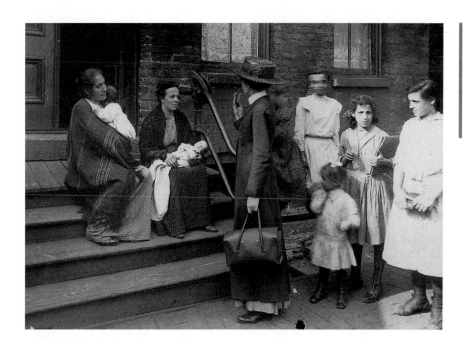

This visiting nurse from the Infant Welfare Society is visiting poor families in Chicago around 1900. Such visiting nurses provided advice on nutrition and child-rearing, and contributed to the emergence of the new field of public health during the Progressive Era.

city-manager plan. Both reflect prominent traits of progressivism: a distrust of political parties and a desire for expertise and efficiency. The commission system first developed in Galveston, Texas, after a devastating hurricane and tidal wave in 1900. The governor appointed five businessmen to run the city, and they garnered widespread publicity for their efficiency and effectiveness. Within two years, some two hundred communities had adopted a commission system. Typically all the city's voters elected the commissioners, and each commissioner then managed a specific city function. The city-manager plan—an application of the administrative structure of the corporation to city government—had similar objectives. It featured a professional city manager (similar to a corporate executive) who was appointed by an elected city council (similar to a corporate board of directors) to handle most municipal administration. Staunton, Virginia, tried such a system in 1908 but attracted little attention. In 1913 a serious flood prompted the citizens of Dayton, Ohio, to adopt a city-manager plan, and other cities then followed.

Most municipal reformers hoped to bring about honest, efficient, and effective city administration by changing the structure of city government. A few reformers went further to advocate social reforms. Hazen Pingree, a successful and socially prominent businessman, attracted national attention as mayor of Detroit. Elected in 1889 as an advocate of honest, efficient government, he soon began to criticize the city's gas, electric, and streetcar companies for overcharging customers and providing poor service. The depression of 1893 led him to address the needs of the unemployed with work projects and community vegetable gardens. A prosperous manufacturer, Samuel "Golden Rule" Jones, won election as mayor of Toledo, Ohio, in 1897. He boasted of running his factory in accordance with the Golden Rule—"Do unto others as you would have them do unto you"—and he brought the same standard to city government. Under his leadership, Toledo acquired free concerts, free public baths, kindergartens (childcare centers for working mothers), and the eight-hour workday for city employees. In addition, Phelan, Pingree, Jones, and a few others advocated city ownership of utilities—the gas, water, electricity, and streetcar systems.

The Progressive Era also saw early efforts at city planning. Throughout most of the nineteenth century, urban growth had been largely unplanned, driven primarily by the market economy. In the early twentieth century, city officials began to designate separate zones for residential, commercial, and industrial use (first in Los Angeles, in 1904–1908)

---

city-manager plan   System of city government in which a small council, chosen on a nonpartisan ballot, hires a city manager who exercises broad executive authority.

and to plan more efficient transportation systems. A few cities tried to improve substandard housing. In 1907 Hartford, Connecticut, set up one of the first city planning commissions, charged with planning on a continuing basis. The emergence of **city planning** represents an important transition in thinking about government and the economy, for it emphasized expertise and presumed greater government control over use of private property.

Saving the Future

The emergence of several new professions—especially public health, mental health, and social work—led to additional efforts to use government, especially local government, to solve some of the fundamental problems of an urban industrial society. Their objective was to use scientific and social scientific knowledge to control social forces and thereby to shape the future.

The public schools attracted a number of reformers. As university programs began graduating teachers and school administrators, these new professionals began to seek greater control over education, especially in the cities. Stressing the challenges of educating multiethnic urban students—many of whom did not speak English—and preparing them for life in a complex and technological society, professional educators pushed for greater centralization and professionalization in school administration. They particularly wanted to reduce the role of local, usually elected, **school boards** and to replace elected school superintendents with appointed professionals. Professional educators also began to rely on the recently developed intelligence tests as a way of identifying children unable to perform at average levels and to isolate them in special classes.

Advances in medical knowledge, together with efforts by the American Medical Association to raise the standards of medical colleges and to restrict access to the profession, improved the professional status of physicians. Professionals also worked to transform hospitals from charities that provided minimal care for the poor into centers for dispensing the most up-to-date treatment. New knowledge about disease and health, often developed in research universities, together with the facilities of modern hospitals, presented an opportunity to reduce disease on a significant scale. Physicians helped initiate public health programs to wipe out **hookworm** in the South, **tuberculosis** in the slums, and sexually transmitted diseases. Public health emerged as a new medical field, combining the knowledge of the medical doctor

with the insight of the social scientist and the skills of the corporate manager.

Other emerging professional fields with important implications for public policy included mental health and social work. Mental health professionals—psychiatrists and psychologists—tried to transform **insane asylums** (places to confine the mentally ill) into places where patients could be treated and perhaps cured. Social workers often found themselves allied with public health and mental health professionals in their efforts to extend government control over urban health and safety codes.

Reforming State Government

As reformers launched changes in many cities and as new professionals considered ways to improve society, **Robert M. La Follette** pushed Wisconsin to the forefront of reform. A Republican, he entered politics soon after graduating from the University of Wisconsin. He served three terms in Congress in the 1880s but found his political career blocked when he accused the leader of the state Republican organization of unethical behavior. He finally won election as governor in 1900 and by then was convinced of the need for reform.

Conservative legislators, many of them Republicans like La Follette, defeated his proposals to regulate railroad rates and replace nominating conventions with the **direct primary** (in which the voters affiliated

---

city planning The policy of planning urban development by regulating land use.

school board A local board of policymakers who oversee the public schools of a city or town.

hookworm A parasite, formerly common in the South, that causes loss of strength.

tuberculosis An infectious disease that attacks the lungs, causing coughing, fever, and weight loss; spread by unsanitary conditions and practices, such as spitting in public, it was common and often fatal in the nineteenth and early twentieth centuries and is reappearing today.

insane asylum In the nineteenth and early twentieth centuries, an institution for the incarceration of people with mental disorders.

Robert M. La Follette Governor of Wisconsin who instituted reforms such as direct primaries, tax reform, and anticorruption measures in Wisconsin.

direct primary A primary election in which voters who identify with a specific party choose that party's candidates to run in the general election against the candidates of other parties.

Robert La Follette enjoyed taking his campaigns to the voters. He is shown here in 1900, campaigning for election as governor of Wisconsin. When he went to the voters, he saw his speechmaking as a process of education, and he often spent an hour or more explaining the intricacies of policy issues. *Library of Congress.*

with a party chose that party's candidates through an election). La Follette threw himself into an energetic campaign to elect reformers to the state legislature. He earned the nickname "Fighting Bob" as he traveled the state and propounded his views wherever a crowd gathered. Most of his candidates won, and La Follette built a strong following among Wisconsin's farmers and urban wage earners, who returned him to the governor's mansion in 1902 and 1904.

La Follette secured legislation designed to limit both corporations and political parties. Acclaimed as a "laboratory of democracy," Wisconsin adopted the direct primary, set up a commission to regulate railroad rates, increased taxes on railroads and other corporations, enacted a merit system for state employees, and restricted lobbyists. In many of his efforts, La Follette drew on the expertise of faculty members at the University of Wisconsin. These reforms, along with reliance on experts, came to be called the **Wisconsin Idea**. La Follette won election to the U.S. Senate in 1905 and did his best to import the Wisconsin Idea to Capitol Hill until his death in 1925.

La Follette's success prompted imitation elsewhere. In 1901 Iowans elected Albert B. Cummins governor, and Cummins launched a campaign against railroad corporations that paralleled La Follette's. He too went on to the Senate. Reformers won office in other states as well, but only a few matched La Follette's legislative and political success.

Progressivism came to California relatively late. California reformers accused the Southern Pacific Railroad of running a powerful political machine that controlled the state by dominating the Republican Party. In 1906 and 1907 a highly publicized investigation revealed widespread bribery in San Francisco government. The ensuing trials made famous one of the prosecutors, **Hiram W. Johnson**. Reform-minded Republicans, organized as the Lincoln-Roosevelt Republican League, persuaded Johnson to run for governor in 1910. He conducted a vigorous campaign and won.

Once in power, California progressives produced a volume of reform that rivaled that of Wisconsin. Stubborn and principled, Johnson proved to be an uncompromising foe of corporate influence in politics. As governor, he pushed for regulation of railroads and public utilities, restrictions on political parties, protection for labor, and conservation. Progressives in the legislature sometimes went beyond Johnson's proposals, notably by sending a state constitutional amendment on woman suffrage to the voters. California voters approved the measure. Johnson showed more sympathy for labor than did most progressive reformers. He appointed union leaders to state positions and supported a variety of measures to benefit working people, including an eight-hour workday law for women, **workers' compensation**, and restric-

---

Wisconsin Idea The program of political reforms sponsored by Robert La Follette in Wisconsin and designed to decrease political corruption, foster direct democracy, and regulate corporations.

Hiram W. Johnson Governor of California who promoted a broad range of reforms, including regulation of railroads and measures to benefit labor.

workers' compensation Payments that employers are required by law to award to workers injured on the job.

tions on child labor. California progressives in both parties vied with each other, however, in the vehemence of their attacks on Asian immigrants and Asian Americans. In 1913 the progressive Republicans pushed through a law that prohibited Asian immigrants from owning land in California.

Like La Follette, Johnson moved on to national politics. In 1912 he was the vice-presidential candidate of the new Progressive Party. Re-elected governor in 1914, he won election to the U.S. Senate in 1916 and served there until his death in 1945.

The Decline of Parties and the Rise of Interest Groups

Like California, many other states moved to restrict political parties. City and state reformers charged that bosses and machines manipulated nominating conventions, managed public officials, and controlled law enforcement. They claimed that bosses, in return for payoffs, used their influence on behalf of powerful interests. Articles by muckrakers and a few highly publicized bribery trials convinced many voters that the reformers were correct. The mighty party organizations that had dominated politics during the nineteenth century now came under attack along a broad front.

Reforms intended to enhance the power of individual voters and to reduce the power of party organizations sprouted nearly everywhere. State after state adopted the direct primary, and many reformers sought to use the merit system to reduce the number of state positions filled through patronage. In many states, judgeships, school board seats, and educational offices were made nonpartisan.

A number of cities and states also adopted the initiative and referendum (see chapter-opening map). The **initiative** permitted voters to adopt a new law directly: if enough voters signed a petition, the proposed law would be voted on at the next election; if approved by the voters, it became law. The **referendum** permitted voters, through a petition, to have the final word on a law adopted by the legislature. Adopted first in South Dakota in 1898, the initiative and referendum gained national attention after Oregon voters adopted them in 1902. Oregon reformers led by William U'Ren, a former Populist turned progressive Republican, employed the initiative to create new laws. The Oregon reformers received so much attention that the initiative and referendum were sometimes called the **Oregon System**. Some states also adopted the **recall**, a procedure that permits voters through petitions to initiate a special

election to remove an elected official from office. The direct primary, initiative and referendum, and recall are known collectively as **direct democracy** because they remove intermediate steps between the voter and final political decisions.

One outcome of the switch to direct primaries and decline of party organizations was a new approach to campaigning for office. Candidates now appealed directly to voters rather than to party leaders and convention delegates. Individual candidates built up personal organizations (separate from party organizations) to win nomination and election. Formerly, the party leaders who managed nominating conventions had often insisted on informal **term limits**, but now voters sometimes returned the same individuals to office again and again. As campaigns focused more on individual candidates and less on parties, advertising supplanted the armies of party retainers who had mobilized voters in the nineteenth century (see page 513). At the same time, new voter registration laws and procedures disqualified some voters, especially transient workers. Voter turnout fell (see Figure 20.2, page 622). Ironically, the emergence of new channels for political participation created the illusion of a vast outpouring of public involvement in politics—but proportionally fewer voters actually cast ballots.

New avenues of political participation opened not only through direct democracy but also through organized interest groups. Such groups were often attracted to politics as the most direct way to advance their specialized concerns. Occasionally,

initiative   Provision in a state or other unit of government that permits voters to petition to place a proposed law on the ballot so that voters may accept or reject it; also called direct legislation.

referendum   Provision in a state or other political unit that permits voters, through petitions, to place a law that has been approved by the legislature on the ballot so that voters can accept or reject it.

Oregon System   Name given to the initiative and referendum, first used widely in state politics in Oregon after 1902.

recall   Provision in a state or other political unit that permits voters, through the petition process, to hold a special election to remove an elected official from office.

direct democracy   Provisions that permit voters to make political decisions directly, including the direct primary, initiative, referendum, and recall.

term limit   A limit on the number of times one person can be elected to the same political office.

groups cooperated when their political objectives coincided, as when merchants and farmers both favored regulation of railroad rates. Other times, they found themselves in conflict, perhaps over tariff policy. The many groups that advocated change sometimes fought among themselves over which reform goals were most important and how best to achieve them. More and more groups took up the tactics of the Anti-Saloon League—they ignored parties, pressured individual candidates to accept their group's position, and urged their members to vote only for candidates who did so. In 1904, for example, the National Association of Manufacturers (NAM) targeted and defeated two key pro-labor members of Congress, one in the House and one in the Senate. The American Federation of Labor (AFL) responded in 1906 with a similar strategy and managed to elect six union members to the House of Representatives.

Organized interest groups often focused their attention on the legislative process. When Congress was in session, they retained the services of full-time representatives, or **lobbyists**, in Washington. Lobbyists urged members of Congress to support their group's position on pending legislation, reminded senators and representatives of their group's electoral clout, and arranged campaign backing for those who supported their cause. Eventually many legislators became dependent on lobbyists for information about their **constituents** and sometimes relied on lobbyists to help draft legislation and raise campaign funds. Similar patterns developed in state legislatures.

Thus, as political parties receded from the dominant position they once occupied, organized interest groups moved in. Pushed one way by the AFL and the other by the NAM, under opposing pressure from the Anti-Saloon League and liquor interests, some elected officials came to see themselves less as loyal members of a political party and more as mediators among competing interest groups.

ROOSEVELT, TAFT, AND REPUBLICAN PROGRESSIVISM

• What did Theodore Roosevelt mean by a "Square Deal"? How do his accomplishments exemplify this description? Do any of his actions not fit this model?

• How did the role of the federal government in the economy and the power of the presidency change as a consequence of Theodore Roosevelt's activities in office?

When Theodore Roosevelt became president upon the death of William McKinley, his buoyant optimism and energy fascinated Americans—one visitor reported that the most exciting things he saw in the United States were "Niagara Falls and the President . . . both great wonders of nature!" "TR" quickly became recognizable everywhere, as cartoonists delighted in sketching his bristling mustache, pince-nez glasses, and toothy grin.

Roosevelt later wrote, "I cannot say that I entered the Presidency with any deliberately planned and far-reaching scheme of social betterment." Nonetheless, Americans soon saw Roosevelt as the embodiment of progressivism. In seven years, he changed the nation's domestic policies more than any president since Lincoln—and made himself a legend.

Roosevelt: Asserting the Power of the Presidency

Roosevelt was unlike most politicians of his day. He had inherited wealth, and he had added to it from the many books he had written. He saw politics as a duty he owed the nation rather than as an opportunity for personal advancement, and he defined his political views in terms of character, morality, hard work, and patriotism. Uncertain whether to call himself a "radical conservative" or a "conservative radical," he considered politics a tool for forging an ethical and socially stable society. Confident in his own personal principles, Roosevelt did not hesitate to wield to the fullest the powers of the presidency. He also used the office as what he called a "bully pulpit," to bring attention to his concerns.

In his first message to Congress, in December 1901, Roosevelt sounded a theme that he repeated throughout his political career: the growth of powerful corporations was "natural," but some of them exhibited "grave evils" that the law needed to penalize. As Roosevelt later explained, "When I became President, the question as to the method by which the United States Government was to control the corporations was not yet important. The absolutely vital question was whether the Government had power to control them at all." He set out to establish that power.

---

lobbyist   A person who tries to influence the opinions of legislators or other public officials for or against a specific cause.

constituents   Voters in the home district of a member of a legislature.

The chief obstacle to regulating the new corporations was the Supreme Court decision in *United States v. E. C. Knight* (1895), preventing the Sherman Anti-Trust Act from being used against manufacturing monopolies. Roosevelt soon found an opportunity to challenge the Knight decision. Some of the nation's most prominent business leaders—J. P. Morgan, the Rockefeller interests, and railroad magnates James J. Hill and Edward H. Harriman—had joined forces to create the Northern Securities Company, which combined several railroad lines to create a railroad monopoly in the Northwest. The *Knight* case had involved manufacturing; the Northern Securities Company, on the other hand, provided interstate transportation. If any industry could satisfy the Supreme Court that it fit the language of the Constitution authorizing Congress to regulate interstate commerce, Roosevelt believed, the railroads could.

In February 1902, Roosevelt advised Attorney General Philander C. Knox to seek dissolution of the Northern Securities Company for violating the Sherman Act. Wall Street leaders condemned Roosevelt's action, but most Americans responded positively. For the first time, the federal government was challenging a powerful corporation. In 1904 the Supreme Court agreed that the Sherman Act could be applied to the Northern Securities Company and ordered it dissolved.

Bolstered by this confirmation of federal power, Roosevelt launched additional antitrust suits and gloried in his reputation as a trustbuster. In all, he initiated more than forty antitrust actions, though not all were successful. He used **trustbusting** selectively, however. Large corporations, he thought, were natural, inevitable, and potentially beneficial. He thought regulation was preferable to breaking them up. Companies that met Roosevelt's standards of character and public service—and that acknowledged the power of the presidency—had no reason to fear antitrust action. Such nods to presidential power sometimes meant informal understandings between Roosevelt and corporate heads. In 1907, for example, in the midst of a financial panic, officials of United States Steel Corporation secured Roosevelt's consent before taking over the Tennessee Coal and Iron Company, arguing that the takeover would stabilize the industry.

Roosevelt's willingness to take bold action was not limited to trustbusting. In time of crisis, he felt, the president should "do whatever the needs of the people demand, unless the Constitution or the laws explicitly forbid him to do it." A year after he took office, he asserted new presidential powers to deal with a strike by coal miners (see Individual Choices, page 638). His bold action produced what he liked to call a **Square Deal**, fair treatment for all parties.

The Square Deal in Action: Creating Federal Economic Regulation

Roosevelt's trustbusting and handling of the coal strike brought him great popularity across the country. In 1903 Congress approved several measures he requested or endorsed: the Expedition Act, to speed up prosecution of antitrust suits; creation of a cabinet-level Department of Commerce and Labor, including a Bureau of Corporations to investigate corporate activities; and the **Elkins Act**, which amended the Interstate Commerce Act by setting penalties for railroads that paid rebates.

When Roosevelt sought election in 1904, he won by one of the largest margins up to that time, securing more than 56 percent of the popular vote. Conservatives had temporarily taken control of the Democratic Party and hoped to attract enough support from conservatives to defeat Roosevelt. But Alton B. Parker, their drab nominee, made one of the Democrats' worst showings ever. Elected in his own right, with a powerful demonstration of public approval, Roosevelt set out to secure meaningful regulation of the railroads, largest of the nation's big businesses.

Roosevelt and reformers in Congress wanted to regulate railroad rates—the prices they charged for hauling freight and carrying passengers. In Roosevelt's year-end message to Congress in 1905, he asked for legislation to regulate railroad rates, open the financial records of railroads to government inspection, and increase federal authority in strikes involving interstate commerce. At the same time, the attorney general filed suits against some of the nation's largest corporations. Muckrakers (some of them friends of Roosevelt) also fired off scathing exposés of railroads and attacks on Senate conservatives.

trustbusting   Use of antitrust laws to prosecute and dissolve big businesses ("trusts").

Square Deal   Theodore Roosevelt's term for his efforts to deal fairly with all.

Elkins Act   Law passed by Congress in 1903 that supplemented the Interstate Commerce Act of 1887 by penalizing railroads that paid rebates.

Although Roosevelt compromised with conservative Republicans on some issues, he got most of what he wanted. On June 29, 1906, Congress passed the **Hepburn Act**, allowing the Interstate Commerce Commission (ICC) to establish maximum railroad rates and extending ICC authority to other forms of transportation. The act also limited railroads' ability to issue free passes, a practice reformers had long considered bribery. The next day, on June 30, Congress approved the Pure Food and Drug Act and the Meat Inspection Act, as the aftermath to Sinclair's stomach-turning revelations. Congress also passed legislation defining employers' liability for workers injured on the job in the District of Columbia and on interstate railroads.

Regulating Natural Resources

An outspoken proponent of strenuous outdoor activities, Roosevelt took great pride in establishing five national parks and more than fifty wildlife preserves, to save what he called "beautiful and wonderful wild creatures whose existence was threatened by greed and wantonness." Preservationists, such as John Muir of the Sierra Club, applauded these actions and urged that wilderness areas be kept forever safe from developers. Setting aside parks and wildlife refuges, however, was only one element in Roosevelt's conservation agenda.

Roosevelt and **Gifford Pinchot**, the president's chief adviser on natural resources, believed conservation required not only preservation of wild and beautiful lands but also carefully planned use of resources. Trained in scientific forestry in Europe, Pinchot combined scientific and technical expertise with a managerial outlook. He and Roosevelt withdrew large tracts of federal timber and grazing land from public sale or use. By establishing close federal management of these lands, they hoped to provide for the needs of the present and still leave resources for the future. While president, Roosevelt removed nearly 230 million acres from public sale, more than quadrupling the land under federal protection.

Roosevelt strongly supported the Reclamation Act of 1902 (see page 588). The act set aside proceeds from the sale of federal land in sixteen western states to finance irrigation projects, and it established a commitment later expanded many times: the federal government had the responsibility for constructing western dams, canals, and other facilities that made agriculture possible in areas of scant rainfall. Thus water, perhaps the single most important resource in the arid West, was to be managed. Far from preserv-

In 1903, at Yosemite National Park, Theodore Roosevelt met with John Muir, a leading advocate for the preservation of wilderness. While Roosevelt made important contributions to the preservation of parks and wildlife refuges, he was more interested in the careful management of national resources, including federal lands. *Yosemite Museum.*

ing the western landscape, federal water projects profoundly transformed it, vividly illustrating the vast difference between the preservation of wilderness that Muir advocated and the careful management of resources that Pinchot sought.

Taft's Troubles

Soon after Roosevelt won the election of 1904, he announced that he would not seek reelection in

---

Hepburn Act Law passed by Congress in 1906 that authorized the Interstate Commerce Commission to set maximum railroad rates and to regulate other forms of transportation.

Gifford Pinchot Head of the Forestry Service from 1898 to 1910; he promoted conservation and urged careful planning in the use of natural resources.

This postcard depicts how President Theodore Roosevelt, in command of the Republican Party, persuaded his friend William Howard Taft to run for president in 1908. Taft was not eager for that office, but Roosevelt succeeded in convincing him to seek it. With Roosevelt's strong support, Taft was elected, but he proved a disappointment to Roosevelt. *Collection of Janice L. and David J. Frent.*

1908. By 1908, he may have regretted this statement, but he kept his word. He remained immensely popular, however, and virtually named his successor. Republicans nominated William Howard Taft. A graduate of Yale and former federal judge, Taft had served as governor of the Philippines before joining Roosevelt's cabinet as secretary of war in 1904.

William Jennings Bryan, leader of the progressive wing of the Democratic Party, won his party's nomination for the third time. Roosevelt's popularity and his strong endorsement of Taft overcame a lackluster Republican campaign. Taft won just under 52 percent of the vote, and Republicans kept control of the Senate and the House. After turning the presidency over to Taft, Roosevelt set off to hunt big game in Africa.

Roosevelt had been Taft's mentor in politics, but Taft was far more restrained than his predecessor. Unlike Roosevelt, Taft hated campaigning and disliked conflict. His legalistic approach often appeared timid when compared with Roosevelt's boldness. But Taft worked to demonstrate his support for Roosevelt's Square Deal. His attorney general initiated some ninety antitrust suits in four years, twice as many as during Roosevelt's seven years. And Taft approved legislation to strengthen regulatory agencies, as in 1910 when Congress extended the power of the Interstate Commerce Commission to cover most communication companies.

During the Taft administration, progressives amended the Constitution twice. Reformers had long considered an income tax to be the fairest means of raising federal revenues. With support from Taft, enough states ratified the **Sixteenth Amendment** (permitting a federal income tax) for it to take effect in 1913. By contrast, Taft took no position on the **Seventeenth Amendment**, proposed in 1912 and ratified shortly after he left office in 1913. It changed the method of electing U.S. senators from election by state legislatures to election by voters, another longtime goal of reformers, who claimed that corporate influence and even outright bribery had swayed state legislatures and shaped the Senate.

Roosevelt had handed Taft a Republican Party divided by battles over the Hepburn Act and similar issues. Divisions between conservatives and progressives continued, and Taft increasingly sided with the conservatives. In 1909, he called on Congress to reform the tariff. Though the resulting **Payne-Aldrich Tariff** retained high rates on most imports, Taft signed the bill. When Republican progressives protested, Taft became defensive, alienating them further by calling it "the best bill that the Republican party ever passed."

Sixteenth Amendment   Constitutional amendment ratified in 1913 that gives the federal government the authority to establish an income tax.

Seventeenth Amendment   Constitutional amendment ratified in 1913 that requires the election of U.S. senators directly by the voters of each state, rather than by state legislatures.

Payne-Aldrich Tariff   Tariff passed by Congress in 1909; the original bill was a Republican attempt to reduce tariffs, but the final version retained high tariffs on most imports.

The battle within the Republican Party intensified when Republican progressives attacked the high-handed exercise of power by Joseph Cannon, Speaker of the House of Representatives since 1902. Notorious for his profanity and poker playing, Cannon used the Speaker's power to support conservatives and stifle progressives. Taft first favored progressives' efforts to replace Cannon. He backed off, however, and he made his peace with Cannon, offending Republican progressives. In 1910 Nebraska representative George W. Norris led Republican progressives in a "revolt against Cannonism" that gained the support of the Democrats and permanently reduced the power of the Speaker.

A dispute over conservation further damaged Republican unity. Taft had kept Gifford Pinchot as head of the Forest Service. Pinchot soon charged that Taft's secretary of the interior, Richard A. Ballinger, had weakened the conservation program and favored corporate interests by opening reserved lands. Taft concluded, however, that Ballinger was reversing improper actions by Roosevelt's administration. Pinchot persisted, publicly airing charges against Ballinger. Taft now considered Pinchot "a radical and a crank" and fired him. An investigation by Congress cleared Ballinger, but the affair further estranged Taft from congressional progressives and undermined his generally strong record on conservation. By 1912, when Taft faced re-election, the Republican Party was in serious disarray, and he faced opposition from most progressive Republicans.

"CARRY A BIG STICK": ROOSEVELT, TAFT, AND WORLD AFFAIRS

- What were Theodore Roosevelt's objectives for the United States in world affairs? What did he do to realize those objectives?
- How did Roosevelt reshape America's foreign policy?

Theodore Roosevelt not only remolded the presidency and established new federal powers over the economy, he also significantly expanded America's role abroad. Few presidents have had so great an influence. He once expressed his fondness for what he referred to as a West African proverb, "Speak softly and carry a big stick; you will go far." As president, however, Roosevelt seldom spoke softly. Everything he did, it seemed, he did strenuously. Well read in history and current events, Roosevelt entered the presidency with definite ideas on the place of the

United States in world affairs. As he advised Congress in 1902, "The increasing interdependence and complexity of international political and economic relations render it incumbent on all civilized and orderly powers to insist on the proper policing of the world." The United States, Roosevelt made clear, stood ready to do its share of "proper policing."

Taking Panama

While McKinley was still president, American diplomats began efforts to create a canal through Central America. Many people had long shared the dream of such a passage between the Atlantic and Pacific Oceans. A French company actually began construction in the late 1870s (building on the success of the Suez Canal), but the task proved too great and the project was abandoned.

During the Spanish-American War, the battleship *Oregon* took well over two months to steam from the West Coast, around South America, to join the rest of the fleet off Cuba. A canal would have permitted the *Oregon* to reach Cuba in three weeks or less. McKinley pronounced an American-controlled canal "indispensable." In the Clayton-Bulwer Treaty of 1850, however, Britain and the United States had agreed that neither would exercise exclusive control over a canal. Between 1900 and 1901, Secretary of State John Hay negotiated new agreements with Britain, the **Hay-Pauncefote Treaties**, which yielded the canal project to the United States alone.

Experts identified two possible locations for a canal, Nicaragua and Panama (then part of Colombia). The Panama route was shorter, and the French company had completed some of the work. **Philippe Bunau-Varilla**—formerly the chief project engineer for the French effort, now a major stockholder and indefatigable lobbyist—did his utmost to sell the French company's interests to the United States. Building through Panama, however, meant overcoming formidable mountains and fever-ridden swamps. Previous studies had preferred Nicaragua. Its geography

---

Hay-Pauncefote Treaties Two separate treaties (1900 and 1901) signed by the United States and Britain that gave the United States the exclusive right to build, control, and fortify a canal through Central America.

Philippe Bunau-Varilla Chief engineer of the French company that attempted to build a canal through the Panamanian isthmus, chief planner of the Panamanian revolt against Colombia, and later minister to the United States from the new Republic of Panama.

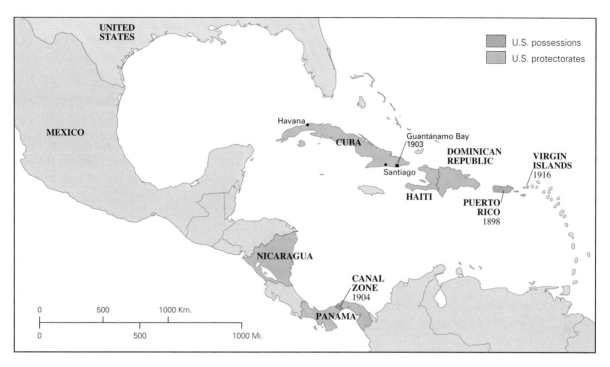

MAP 21.1 The United States and the Caribbean 1898–1917 Between 1898 and 1917, the United States expanded into the Caribbean by acquiring possessions and establishing protectorates. As a result, the United States was the dominant power in the region throughout this time period.

posed fewer natural obstacles, and much of the route lay through Lake Nicaragua.

In 1902, shortly before Congress was to vote on the two routes, a volcano erupted in the Caribbean. Bunau-Varilla quickly distributed to all senators a Nicaraguan postage stamp showing a smoldering volcano looming over a lake. Bunau-Varilla's lobbying—and his stamps—reinforced efforts by prominent Republican senators such as Mark Hanna. The Senate approved the route through the Colombian state of Panama.

Negotiations with Colombia bogged down over treaty language that limited Colombia's sovereignty. When American representatives applied pressure, the Colombian government offered to accept limitations on its sovereignty in return for more money. Outraged, Roosevelt called the offer "pure bandit morality." To break the impasse, Bunau-Varilla and his associates encouraged and financed a revolution in Panama. Aware of such a possibility, Roosevelt ordered U.S. warships to the area to prevent Colombian troops from crushing the uprising. The revolution quickly succeeded. Panama declared its independence, and the United States immediately extended diplomatic recogni-tion. Bunau-Varilla became Panama's minister to the United States and promptly signed a treaty that gave the United States much the same arrangement earlier rejected by Colombia.

The **Hay–Bunau-Varilla Treaty** (1904) granted the United States perpetual control over the Canal Zone, a strip of Panamanian territory ten miles wide, for a price of $10 million and annual rent of $250,000, and it made Panama the second American protectorate (Cuba was the first, see page 631; see also Map 21.1). The United States purchased the assets of the French company and began construction. Roosevelt considered the canal his crowning deed in foreign affairs. "When nobody else could or would exercise efficient authority, I exercised it," he wrote in his *Autobiography* (1913). He always denied that he took part in instigating the revolution, but he once bluntly claimed, "I took the canal zone."

> **Hay–Bunau-Varilla Treaty** Treaty with Panama that granted the United States sovereignty over the Canal Zone in return for a $10 million payment plus an annual rent.

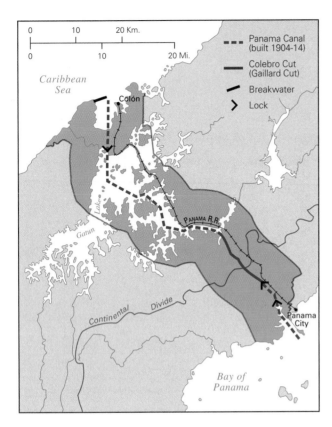

MAP 21.2 The Panama Canal The Panama Canal could take advantage of some natural waterways. The most difficult part of the construction, however, was devising some way to move ships over the mountains near the Pacific end of the canal (lower right). This was done through a combination of cutting a route through the mountains and constructing massive locks.

Construction proved difficult. Just over 40 miles long, the canal took ten years to build and cost nearly $400 million. Completed in 1914, just as World War I began, it was considered one of the world's great engineering feats (see Map 21.2).

Making the Caribbean an American Lake

Well before the canal was finished, American policymakers considered how to protect it. Roosevelt determined to establish American dominance in the Caribbean and Central America, where the many harbors might permit a foreign power to prepare for a strike against the canal or even the Gulf Coast of the United States. Acquisition of Puerto Rico, protectorates over Cuba and Panama, and naval facilities in all three locations as well as on the Gulf Coast made the United States a powerful presence.

The Caribbean and the area around it contained twelve independent nations. Britain, France, Denmark, and the Netherlands held nearly all the smaller islands and Britain had a coastal colony. Several Caribbean nations had borrowed large amounts of money from European bankers, raising the prospect of intervention to secure loan payments. In 1902, for example, Britain and Germany declared a blockade of Venezuela over debts owed their citizens. In 1904 several European nations hinted that they might intervene in the Dominican Republic. Roosevelt waved his "big stick" and presented to Congress what became known as the **Roosevelt Corollary** to the Monroe Doctrine. He warned European nations against any intervention in the Western Hemisphere, even if provoked by loan default or other action. If intervention by what he termed "some civilized nation" became necessary in the Caribbean or Central America in order to correct "chronic wrongdoing," Roosevelt insisted that the United States would handle it, acting as "an international police power."

Roosevelt acted forcefully to establish his new policy. In 1905 the Dominican Republic agreed to permit the United States to collect customs (the major source of governmental revenue) and supervise government expenditures, including debt repayment. Thus the island nation became the third U.S. protectorate. The Senate initially rejected this arrangement but approved an amended version in 1907. In the meantime, Roosevelt ordered the U.S. Navy to collect Dominican customs, claiming that he could do so under his presidential powers.

Roosevelt's successors, William Howard Taft and Woodrow Wilson, continued and expanded American domination in the Caribbean region. The Taft administration encouraged Americans to invest there. Taft hoped that diplomacy could open doors for American investments and that American investments would both block investment by other nations and stabilize and develop the Caribbean economies.

Roosevelt Corollary Extension of the Monroe Doctrine announced by Theodore Roosevelt in 1904, in which he proclaimed the right of the United States to police the Caribbean areas.

Theodore Roosevelt, in his 1904 Corollary to the Monroe Doctrine, asserted that the United States was dominant in the Caribbean. Here a cartoonist capitalized on Roosevelt's boyish nature, depicting the Caribbean as Roosevelt's pond. *Culver Pictures, Inc.*

Taft supported such **"dollar diplomacy"** throughout the region, especially in Nicaragua.

In 1912 Taft sent U.S. Marines to Nicaragua to suppress a rebellion against President Adolfo Días. They remained after the turmoil settled, ostensibly to guard the American legation but actually to prop up the Días government—making Nicaragua the fourth U.S. protectorate. A treaty was drafted giving the United States responsibility for collecting customs, but the Senate rejected it. At that point, the State Department, several American banks, and Nicaragua set up a **customs receivership** through the banks.

Roosevelt and Eastern Asia

In eastern Asia, Roosevelt built on the Open Door notes and American participation in the international force that suppressed the Boxer Rebellion. He was both concerned and optimistic about the rise of Japan as a major industrial and imperial power. Aware of Alfred Thayer Mahan's warnings of the potential danger that Japan posed to the United States in the Pacific, Roosevelt was also hopeful. He admired Japanese accomplishments and anticipated that Japan might exercise the same sort of international police power in its vicinity that the United States claimed under the Roosevelt Corollary.

In 1904 Russia and Japan went to war over **Manchuria**, part of northern China. Russia had pressured China to grant so many concessions in Manchuria that it seemed to be turning into a Russian colony. Russia seemed also to have designs on Korea, a nominally independent kingdom. Japan saw Russian expansion as a threat to its own interests and responded with force. The Japanese scored smashing naval and military victories over the Russians but had too few resources to sustain a long-term war.

dollar diplomacy   Name applied by critics to the Taft administration's policy of supporting U.S. investments abroad.

customs receivership   An agreement whereby one nation takes over the collection of customs (taxes on imported goods) of another nation and exercises some control over that nation's expenditures of customs receipts, thus limiting the autonomy of the nation in receivership.

Manchuria   A region of northeast China that the Russians and Japanese fought to control in the late nineteenth and early twentieth centuries.

This souvenir bandana celebrated Theodore Roosevelt's mediation of the Russo-Japanese War, for which he received the Nobel Peace Prize in 1906. The heart-shaped ribbon around Roosevelt's portrait contains the legend, "First in War, First in Peace, First in the Hearts of His Countrymen," a tribute first applied to George Washington. That statement explains why Roosevelt's war exploits (at the top) were linked with his peace making. *Collection of Janice L. and David J. Frent.*

Roosevelt concluded that American interests were best served by reducing Russian influence in the region so as to maintain a balance of power. Such a balance, he thought, would also be most likely to preserve nominal Chinese sovereignty in Manchuria. Early in the war, he indicated some support for Japan, and as its resources ran low, Japan asked Roosevelt to act as mediator. The president agreed, concerned by then that Japanese victories might be as dangerous as Russian expansion. The peace conference took place in Portsmouth, New Hampshire. The **Treaty of Portsmouth** (1905) recognized Japan's dominance in Korea and gave Japan the southern half of Sakhalin Island and Russian concessions in southern Manchuria. Russia kept its railroad in northern Manchuria. China remained responsible for civil authority in Manchuria. For his mediation, Roosevelt received the 1906 Nobel Peace Prize.

That same year, Roosevelt mediated another dispute. The San Francisco school board ordered students of Japanese parentage to attend the city's segregated Chinese school. The Japanese government protested what it considered an insult, and some Japanese newspapers even hinted at war. Roosevelt brought the school officials to Washington and convinced them to withdraw the order. He promised in return to try to curtail Japanese immigration. He soon negotiated a so-called **gentlemen's agreement** by which Japan agreed informally to limit the departure of laborers to the United States. In 1908 the American and Japanese governments further agreed to respect each other's territorial possessions (the Philippines and Hawai`i for the United States; Korea, Formosa, and southern Manchuria for Japan) and to honor as well "the independence and integrity of China" and the Open Door.

The Taft administration extended dollar diplomacy to China. Proponents sought Chinese permission for American citizens not only to trade with China but also to invest there, especially in railroad construction. Taft hoped that such investments could head off further Japanese expansion. The effort received Chinese government sanction, but little ever came of it.

The United States and the World, 1901–1913

Before the 1890s, the United States had few clear or consistent foreign-policy commitments or objectives. By 1905, its commitments were obvious to all. The Philippines, Guam, Hawai`i, Puerto Rico, eastern Samoa, and the Canal Zone were highly visible evidence that a new concept of America's role in world affairs had been born.

Central to that concept was a large, modern navy, without which every other commitment was merely a moral pronouncement. Roosevelt was so proud of the navy that in 1907 he dispatched sixteen battleships—painted white to signal their peaceful intent—on an around-the-world tour. He claimed

Treaty of Portsmouth Treaty in 1905, ending the Russo-Japanese War; negotiated at a conference in Portsmouth, New Hampshire, through Theodore Roosevelt's mediation.

gentlemen's agreement An agreement rather than a formal treaty; in this case, Japan agreed in 1907 to limit Japanese emigration to the United States.

"The Nations Pride"

This picture was issued as a penny postcard, expressing the nation's pride in the "White Fleet." The Post Office department gave its approval to penny postcards in 1902, and the period between 1905 and 1915 is sometimes considered the "golden age" for penny postcards in the United States. The one-penny price for postage made them highly affordable, and the wide variety of subjects available made them collectable. *Collection of Picture Research Consultants and Archives.*

that his primary purpose in sending the Great White Fleet "was to impress the American people." But Roosevelt was clearly interested in impressing other nations, especially Japan, and in demonstrating that the American navy was fully capable of moving quickly to distant parts of the globe.

Another aspect of America's new role in the world revolved around American control of the Panama Canal. The need to protect the canal led the United States to dominate the Caribbean and Central America to prevent any other major power from threatening the canal. The new American role also focused on the Pacific. As Mahan and other naval strategists pointed out, just as the Atlantic Ocean had been the theater of conflict among European nations in the eighteenth century, so the Pacific Ocean was likely to be the theater of twentieth-century conflict. Thus considerations of commercial enterprise, such as the China trade, coincided with naval strategy and led the United States to acquire possessions at key locations in the Pacific and off eastern Asia (the Philippines).

America's new vision of the world divided nations into broad categories. In one class were all the "civilized" nations. In the other were those nations that Theodore Roosevelt described, at various times, as "barbarous," "impotent," or simply unable to meet their obligations. With "civilized" countries—the European powers, Japan, the large, stable nations of Latin America, Canada, Australia, New Zealand—American diplomats focused on finding ways to realize mutual objectives, especially arbitration of disputes. In eastern Asia, McKinley, Roosevelt, and Taft looked to a balance of power among the contending "civilized" powers as most likely to realize the American objective of maintaining commercial access to markets in China.

The conviction that arbitration was the appropriate means to settle disputes among "civilized" countries was widespread. An international conference in 1899 created a Permanent Court of Arbitration in the Netherlands. Housed in a marble "peace palace" built through a donation from Andrew Carnegie, the **Hague Court** provided neutral arbitrators for international disputes. Both Roosevelt

Hague Court   Body of delegates from about fifty member nations, created in the Netherlands in 1899 for the purpose of peacefully resolving international conflicts; also known as the Permanent Court of Arbitration.

Political buttons continued to be ubiquitous in 1912. Roosevelt and his running mate, Hiram Johnson, the governor of California, are pictured with the Bull Moose that came to symbolize the Progressive Party after Roosevelt exclaimed that he felt as fit as a bull moose. Taft, the Republican candidate, and Wilson, the Democrat, are depicted with more traditional symbols of patriotism and party. *Collection of Janice L. and David J. Frent.*

and Taft tried to negotiate arbitration treaties with major powers, but the Senate refused to ratify them for fear that arbitration might diminish the Senate's role in approving agreements with other countries.

The United States and Britain repeatedly used arbitration to settle their disputes. Throughout the late nineteenth and early twentieth centuries, American relations with Great Britain improved steadily, mostly as a result of British decisions. As Germany expanded its army and navy, implicitly challenging Britain, British policymakers sought to improve relations with the United States, the only nation besides Britain with a navy comparable to Germany's. During the war with Spain, Britain alone among the major European powers sided with the United States and encouraged its acquisition of the Philippines. By signing the Hay-Pauncefote Treaties and reducing its naval forces in the Caribbean, Britain delivered a clear signal—it not only accepted American dominance there but now depended on the United States to protect its holdings in the region.

WILSON AND DEMOCRATIC PROGRESSIVISM

• What choices confronted American voters in the presidential election of 1912? What were the short-term and long-term outcomes of the election?

• How did Wilson's views on reform evolve from the 1912 election through 1916?

• How did the Wilson administration change the role of the federal government in the economy?

The presidential election of 1912 marks a moment when Americans actively and seriously debated their future. All three nominees were well educated and highly literate. Roosevelt and Wilson had written respected books on American history and politics. They approached politics with a sense of destiny and purpose, and they talked frankly to the American people about their ideas for the future.

Debating the Future: The Election of 1912

As Taft watched the Republican Party unravel, Theodore Roosevelt was traveling abroad, first hunting in Africa and then hobnobbing with European leaders. When he returned in 1910, he undertook a speaking tour and, without criticizing Taft, proposed a broad program of reform he labeled the **New Nationalism**. Roosevelt did not openly question Taft's re-election, but other Republican progressives began to do so. In the 1910 congressional elections, Republicans fared badly, plagued by divisions within their party and an economic downturn. For the first time since 1892, Democrats won a majority in the House of Representatives. Democrats, including Woodrow Wilson in New Jersey, also won a number of governorships.

New Nationalism   Program of labor and social reform that Theodore Roosevelt advocated before and during his unsuccessful bid to regain the presidency in 1912.

By early 1911, many Republican progressives were looking to Robert La Follette to wrest the Republican nomination from Taft. Though Roosevelt found La Follette too radical and irresponsible, the former president had lost confidence in Taft. He began to criticize Taft for failing to maintain Republican unity and for his conservation and antitrust policies. Finally, in February 1912, Roosevelt announced he would oppose Taft for the Republican presidential nomination.

Thirteen states had established direct primaries to select delegates to the national nominating convention. There Roosevelt won 278 delegates to 48 for Taft and 36 for La Follette. Elsewhere, however, Taft had all the advantages of an incumbent president in control of the party machinery. At the Republican nominating convention, many states sent rival delegations, one pledged to Taft and one to Roosevelt. Taft's supporters controlled the **credentials committee** and gave most contested seats to Taft delegates. Roosevelt's supporters stormed out, complaining that Taft was stealing the nomination. The remaining delegates nominated Taft on the first ballot. Roosevelt refused to accept defeat. "We stand at Armageddon," he thundered, invoking the biblical prophecy of a final battle between good and evil. "And," he continued, "we battle for the Lord." His supporters quickly formed the Progressive Party, nicknamed the **Bull Moose Party** after Roosevelt's boast that he was "as fit as a bull moose." The delegates sang "Onward, Christian Soldiers" and issued a platform based on the New Nationalism, including tariff reduction, regulation of corporations, a minimum wage, an end to child labor, woman suffrage, and the initiative, referendum, and recall. Women were prominent at the Progressive convention and helped draft the platform—especially the sections dealing with labor. Settlement house pioneer Jane Addams addressed the convention to second the nomination of Roosevelt.

Democrats were overjoyed, certain that the Republican split gave them their best chance at the presidency in twenty years. The nomination was hotly contested, and the convention took forty-six ballots to nominate Woodrow Wilson, the governor of New Jersey. Their platform attacked monopolies, favored limits on campaign contributions by corporations, and called for major tariff reductions. Wilson labeled his program the **New Freedom**.

Much of the campaign focused on Roosevelt and Wilson, ignoring Taft. Roosevelt continued to maintain that the behavior of corporations was the problem, not their size. After Wilson's nomination, he met with **Louis Brandeis**, a Boston attorney and leading critic of corporate consolidation. Brandeis convinced Wilson to center his campaign on the issue of big business and to offer a solution significantly different from the regulation promised by Roosevelt. Wilson depicted monopoly itself as the problem, not the misbehavior of individual corporations. Breaking up monopolies and restoring competition, he argued, would benefit consumers because competition would yield better products and lower prices. He also pointed to what he considered the most serious flaw in Roosevelt's proposals for regulation: as long as monopolies faced regulation, they would seek to control the regulator—the federal government. Only antitrust actions, Wilson argued, could protect democracy from this threat.

Though Roosevelt and Wilson presented quite different proposals for dealing with big business and attacked each other's right to claim the title "progressive," they agreed that Taft was not a progressive at all. Taft could claim a stronger record as a trustbuster than Roosevelt but was clearly the most conservative of the candidates. Eugene V. Debs, the Socialist candidate, rejected both regulation and antitrust actions and argued instead for government ownership of monopolies.

The real contest was between Roosevelt and Wilson. In the end, Wilson received most of the usual Democratic vote and won with 42 percent of the total. Democrats also won sizable majorities in both houses of Congress. Roosevelt and Taft split the traditional Republican vote, 27 percent for Roosevelt and 23 percent for Taft. Debs, with only 6 percent, placed first in a few counties and city precincts (see Map 21.3).

Wilson and Reform, 1913–1914

Born in Virginia in 1856, Woodrow Wilson grew up in the South during the Civil War and Reconstruction.

credentials committee Party convention committee that settles disputes arising when rival delegations from the same state demand to be seated.

Bull Moose Party Popular name given to the Progressive Party in 1912 as a tribute to its presidential candidate, Theodore Roosevelt.

New Freedom Program of reforms that Woodrow Wilson advocated during his 1912 presidential campaign, including reducing tariffs, revising the monetary system, and prosecuting trusts.

Louis Brandeis Lawyer and reformer who opposed monopolies and defended individual rights; in 1916 he became the first Jewish justice on the Supreme Court.

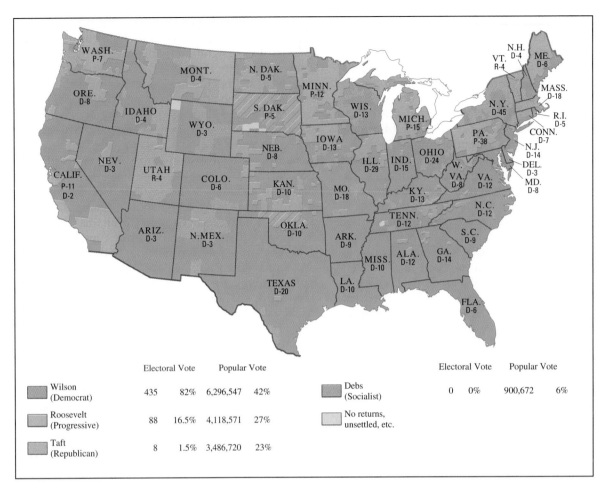

MAP 21.3 **Election of 1912, by Counties** The presidential election of 1912 was complicated by the campaign of former president Theodore Roosevelt running as a Progressive. Roosevelt's campaign split the usual Republican vote without taking away much of the usual Democratic vote. Woodrow Wilson, the Democratic candidate, carried many parts of the West and Northeast that Democratic candidates rarely won.

His father, a Presbyterian minister, impressed on him lessons in morality and responsibility that remained with him his entire life. Wilson earned a Ph.D. from Johns Hopkins University, and his first book, *Congressional Government*, analyzed federal law-making. A professor at Princeton University after 1890, he became president of Princeton in 1902 and introduced educational reforms that brought him wide attention.

In 1910 New Jersey Democrats needed a respectable candidate for governor. Party leaders picked Wilson because of his reputation as a conservative and a good public speaker. He won the election but shocked his party's conservative leaders by suddenly embracing reform. As governor, he led the legislature to adopt several progressive measures, including a direct primary and regulation of railroads and public utilities. His record won support from many Democratic progressives when he sought the 1912 presidential nomination.

Wilson firmly believed in party government and an active role for the president in policymaking. He set out to work closely with Democrats in Congress and succeeded to such an extent that, like Roosevelt, he changed the nature of the presidency itself. Confident in his oratorical skills, he became the first president since John Adams to address Congress in person.

Wilson first tackled tariff reform, arguing that high tariff rates fueled the creation of monopolies by reducing competition. Despite an outcry from manufacturers, Congress passed the **Underwood Tariff** in October 1913, establishing the most significant reductions since the Civil War. To offset federal revenue losses, the Underwood Act also implemented the income tax recently authorized by the Sixteenth Amendment.

The next matter facing Wilson and the Democrats was reform of banking. The national banking system dated to 1863, and periodic economic problems—most recently, a panic in 1907—had confirmed the system's major shortcomings: it had no real center to provide direction and no way to adjust the **money supply** to meet the needs of the economy. In 1913 a congressional investigation also revealed the concentration of a great power in the hands of the few investment bankers. Conservatives, led by Carter Glass of Virginia, joined with bankers in proposing a more centralized system with minimal federal regulation. Progressive Democrats, especially William Jennings Bryan (now Wilson's secretary of state) and Louis Brandeis, favored strong federal control.

The debate ended in compromise. In December 1913, Wilson approved the **Federal Reserve Act**, establishing twelve regional Federal Reserve Banks. These banks were "bankers' banks," institutions where commercial banks kept their reserves. All national banks were required to belong to the Federal Reserve System, and state banks were invited to join. The participating banks owned all the stock in their regional Federal Reserve Bank and named two-thirds of its board of directors; the president named the other third. The regional banks were to be regulated and supervised by the Federal Reserve Board, a new federal agency with members chosen by the president. The Federal Reserve Act stands as the most important domestic act of the Wilson administration, for it still provides the basic framework for the nation's banking and monetary system.

In 1914 Congress passed the **Clayton Antitrust Act**, which prohibited specified business practices, including **interlocking directorates** among large companies that could be proven to inhibit competition. It also exempted farmers' organizations and unions from antitrust prosecution under the Sherman Act. The antitrust sections in the final version of the Clayton Act, however, did little to break up big corporations. The weakening of the antitrust provisions in the Clayton Act partly reflected a change of course by Wilson. Instead of breaking up big business, Wilson now moved closer to Roosevelt's position favoring regulation. Wilson also supported passage of the **Federal Trade Commission Act** (1914), a regulatory measure intended to prevent unfair methods of competition.

More Reforms and the Election of 1916

Progressives generally applauded the Wilson administration for tariff reform, the Federal Reserve System, and the Clayton Act. But many progressives criticized his appointees to the Federal Trade Commission and the Federal Reserve Board for their sympathies with business and banking. Congress fulfilled a Democratic campaign promise by creating a separate cabinet-level Department of Labor. As secretary of labor Wilson appointed William Wilson (not a relative), a union member and labor advocate. President Wilson did little more, however, to appeal to social reformers. He considered federal action to outlaw child labor to be unconstitutional, and he questioned the need to amend the Constitution for woman suffrage.

During his first year in office, Wilson drew sharp criticism from some northern social reformers when his appointees initiated racial segregation in several federal agencies. A southerner by birth and heritage, Wilson undoubtedly believed in segregation even though he resisted the most extreme racists in his party. At a cabinet meeting shortly after Wilson took office, the postmaster general (a southerner) proposed racial segregation of all federal employees. No cabinet member objected, and several federal agencies began to segregate African Americans. Wilson was surprised at the swell of protest, not just from African Americans but also from some white progressives in the

---

Underwood Act   Law passed by Congress in 1913 that substantially reduced tariffs and made up for the lost revenue by providing for a small graduated income tax.

money supply   The amount of money in the economy, such as cash and the contents of checking accounts.

Federal Reserve Act   Law passed by Congress in 1913 establishing twelve regional Federal Reserve Banks to hold the cash reserves of commercial banks and a Federal Reserve Board to regulate aspects of banking.

Clayton Antitrust Act   Law passed by Congress in 1914 banning monopolistic business practices such as price fixing and interlocking directorates; it also exempted farmers' organizations and unions from prosecution under antitrust laws.

interlocking directorates   Situation in which the same individuals sit on the boards of directors of various companies in one industry.

Federal Trade Commission Act   Law passed by Congress in 1914 that outlawed unfair methods of competition in interstate commerce and created a commission appointed by the president to investigate illegal business practices.

North and Midwest. He never designated a change in policy, but the process of segregating federal facilities slowed significantly.

In 1912 Wilson had received less than half of the popular vote and had won the White House only because the Republicans split. As the 1916 election approached, he joined Democratic progressives in Congress—and social reformers outside Congress—in pushing measures intended to secure his claim as the true voice of progressivism and to capture the loyalty of all progressive voters.

In January 1916, Wilson nominated Louis Brandeis for the Supreme Court. Brandeis's reputation as a staunch progressive and critic of business aroused intense opposition from conservatives. He was the first Jewish nominee to the Court, and some dissent to his confirmation carried anti-Semitic overtones. The Senate vote on the nomination was close, but Brandeis was confirmed in June 1916 with support from a few progressive Republicans. Wilson followed up that slim victory with support for several reform measures—credit facilities for farmers, workers' compensation for federal employees, and the elimination of child labor. Under threat of a national railroad strike, Congress passed and Wilson signed the Adamson Act, securing an eight-hour workday for railroad employees.

The presidential election of 1916 was conducted against the background of the war that had been raging in Europe since 1914 (see Chapter 22). Wilson's shift toward social reform helped solidify his standing among progressives. His support for organized labor earned him strong backing among unionists, and labor's votes probably ensured his victory in a few states, especially California. In states where women could vote, many of them seem to have preferred Wilson, probably because he backed issues of interest to women, such as outlawing child labor and keeping the nation out of war. By 1916, Theodore Roosevelt had returned to the Republican Party, bringing many of his followers with him but losing some to Wilson, especially in the West. In a very close election, Wilson won with 49 percent of the popular vote to 46 percent for Charles Evans Hughes, a progressive Republican.

NEW PATTERNS IN CULTURAL EXPRESSION

• How would you compare the influence of developments in the United States with the influence of developments in Europe with regard to cultural expression in the late nineteenth century?

• How did social and technological changes contribute to new patterns in mass entertainment?

The changes sweeping American society also affected cultural expression. Shortly after 1900, the director of the nation's most prominent art museum, the Metropolitan Museum of New York, observed "a state of unrest" in art, literature, music, painting, and sculpture. "And," he added, "I dislike unrest." Unrest meant change, and Americans at that time witnessed dramatic changes in art, literature, and music—many of them directly influenced by the new urban industrial society, and some of them reflecting the concerns of the Progressive Era.

Realism, Impressionism, and Ragtime

At the turn of the century, American novelists increasingly turned to a realistic—and sometimes critical—portrayal of life, rejecting the romanticism characteristic of the pre-Civil War period. The towering figure of the era remained **Mark Twain** (pen name of Samuel L. Clemens), whose novel *The Adventures of Huckleberry Finn* (1885), may be read at many levels, ranging from a nostalgic account of boyhood adventures to profound social satire. In this masterpiece, Twain reproduced the everyday speech of unschooled whites and blacks, poked fun at social pretensions, scorned the Old South myth, and challenged prevailing, racially biased attitudes toward African Americans. Twain continued to be an important social commentator until his death in 1910. The novels of William Dean Howells and Henry James, by contrast, presented restrained, realistic portrayals of upper-class men and women, and Kate Chopin sounded feminist themes in *The Awakening* (1899), dealing with repression of a woman's desires. Stephen Crane, Theodore Dreiser, and Frank Norris showed the influence of Emile Zola, a prominent French novelist, as they sharpened the critical edge of fiction. Crane's *Maggie: A Girl of the Streets* (1893) depicted how urban squalor could turn a young woman to prostitution. Norris's *The Octopus* (1901) portrayed the abusive power that a railroad could wield over people.

As American literature moved toward realism and social criticism during these years, many American

---

Mark Twain Pen name of Samuel Clemens, prominent American author of the late nineteenth century; wrote *The Adventures of Huckleberry Finn* and many other American literary classics.

In this painting of 6th Avenue at 30th Street, done in 1906, John Sloan seems to glory in the diversity and excitement of life in New York City. He was a member of the Ash Can School of painters, who often focused on ordinary life in the cities, sometimes including unpleasant subjects. *"6th Avenue at 30th St., 1907" by John Sloan/Vivian and Meyer P. Potamkin Collection.*

painters were also experimenting with new modes of expression. One exception was Thomas Eakins, a realist and probably the most accomplished painter working in the United States during much of the Gilded Age. Although he received limited recognition at the time, he is now considered a leading American painter. By 1900, many American painters had abandoned realism in response to French **impressionism**, which emphasized less an exact reproduction of the world and more the artist's impression of it. Mary Cassatt was the only American—and one of only two women—to rank among the leaders of impressionism, but she lived and painted mostly in France. Among prominent impressionists working in the United States was Childe Hassam, who often depicted urban scenes. Attention to the city was also characteristic of work by Robert Henri, John Sloan, and others. Labeled the **Ash Can School** because of their preoccupation with everyday urban life and people, they produced the artistic counterpart to critical realism in literature.

In 1913 the most widely publicized art exhibit of the era permitted Americans to view examples of prominent innovative European painters of the day. Known as the Armory Show, for its opening in New York's National Guard Armory (it was later displayed in Chicago and Boston), the exhibit pre-

sented works by Pablo Picasso, Henri Matisse, Marcel Duchamp, Wassily Kandinsky, and others. Sophisticated critics and popular newspapers alike dismissed them as either insane or anarchists. One reviewer scornfully suggested that Duchamp's cubist painting, *Nude Descending a Staircase*, be retitled "explosion in a shingle factory." The abstract, modernist style, however, soon became firmly established.

As with painting, many aspects of American music derived from European models. John Philip Sousa, who produced well over a hundred works between the 1870s and his death in 1932, was the most popular American composer of the day, best known for his stirring patriotic marches. Perhaps more significant in the long run was the African-American composer Scott Joplin. Born in Texas, Joplin had formal instruction in the piano and then traveled through African-American communities from New Orleans to Chicago. En route, he encountered **ragtime** music and soon began to write his own. In 1899 he published "Maple Leaf Rag" and quickly soared to fame as the leading ragtime composer in the country. Though condemned by some at the time as vulgar, ragtime contributed significantly to the later development of jazz.

Mass Entertainment in the Early Twentieth Century

In the late nineteenth century, changes in transportation (the railroads) and communication (telegraph and telephone) combined with increased leisure time among the middle class and skilled workers to foster new forms of entertainment. Traveling dramatic and musical troupes had long entertained some Americans, but now booking agencies could schedule such groups into nearly every corner of the country. Traveling actors, singers, and other performers offered everything from Shakespeare to **slapstick**, from opera

impressionism A style of painting that developed in France in the 1870s and emphasized the artist's impression of a subject.

Ash Can School New York artists of varying styles who shared a focus on urban life.

ragtime Style of popular music characterized by a syncopated rhythm and a regularly accented beat; considered the immediate precursor of jazz.

slapstick A rowdy form of comedy marked by crude practical jokes and physical humor, such as falls.

Professional baseball developed a strong popular appeal in the years after the Civil War, as most major cities acquired one or more teams. Thomas Eakins, who depicted these ballplayers at work in 1875, was the most impressive realist painter in the country at the time. *"Baseball Players Practicing" by Thomas Eakins 1875/Museum of Art, Rhode Island School of Design, Jesse Metcalf and Walter H. Kimball Funds. Photo by Cathy Carver.*

to **melodrama**. By 1900, booking agencies had developed a star system: each traveling company had one or two popular performers who attracted the audience and helped to make up for the inadequacies of the other players. Other traveling spectacles also took advantage of improved transportation and communication to establish regular circuits, including circuses and Wild West shows. One of the most popular traveling shows was the **Chautauqua**, a blend of inspirational oratory, educational lectures, and entertainment. The programs, often a week or two in length, attracted hundreds, even thousands, of people from the surrounding countryside.

During the late nineteenth century, a quite different form of mass entertainment appeared—professional baseball. Teams traveled by train from city to city, and urban rivalries built loyalty among fans. In 1876 team owners (often drawn initially from the ranks of players) formed the National League, as a way to monopolize the industry by excluding rival clubs from their territories and controlling the movement of players from team to team. Because African Americans were barred from the National League, separate black clubs and Negro leagues emerged. In the 1880s and 1890s, the National League warded off challenges from rival leagues and defeated a players'

union. Not until 1901 did another league—the American League—successfully organize. In 1903 the two leagues merged into a new, stronger cartel and staged the first World Series—in which the Boston Red Sox beat the Pittsburgh Pirates. As other professional spectator sports developed, they often imitated the organization, labor relations, and racial discrimination first established in baseball.

Celebrating the New Age

In 1893, when the World's Columbian Exposition opened in Chicago, Hamlin Garland, a writer living there, wrote to his parents in South Dakota, "Sell the cook stove if necessary and come. . . . You must see this fair." Between 1876 and 1915, Americans repeatedly held great expositions, beginning with one in Philadelphia in 1876 that commemorated the centennial of independence and concluding with one in San Francisco in 1915 that celebrated the opening of the Panama Canal. Others took place in Atlanta, Buffalo, Omaha, Portland (Oregon), San Diego, and St. Louis. The most impressive and influential was the Columbian Exposition in Chicago, marking the four-hundredth anniversary of Columbus's voyage to the New World.

These expositions typically featured vast exhibition halls where companies demonstrated their latest technological marvels, artists displayed their creations, and farmers presented their most impressive produce. In other halls, states and foreign nations showcased their accomplishments. The exhibits nearly always expressed the conviction that technology and industry would inevitably improve the lives of all. After 1898, most also included demeaning exhibits of "savage" or "barbarian" people from the nation's new overseas possessions.

Behind the gleaming machines in the imitation marble palaces, however, lurked troubling questions that never appeared in the exhibits glorifying "Progress." What should be the working conditions of those whose labor created such technological marvels? Were democratic institutions compatible with the concentration of power and control in industry and finance or with the acquisition of colonies?

---

melodrama A sensational or romantic stage play with exaggerated conflicts and stereotyped characters.

Chautauqua A traveling show offering educational, religious, and recreational activities, part of a nationwide movement of adult education that began in the town of Chautauqua, New York.

At the center of the Columbian Exposition of 1893 was a great water-filled basin, with an elaborate sculpture representing Columbus at one end and this dramatic, 65-foot tall depiction of the republic at the opposite end. The sculptor, Daniel Chester French, represented the American republic with one hand on a pole with a liberty cap at its end and with the other hand holding a globe surmounted by an American eagle. Though this view shows the entire statue as golden, in fact the head and arms were an ivory color and the rest of the statue was gilded. The statue may still be seen in Chicago's Jackson Park. *Chicago Historical Society.*

PROGRESSIVISM IN PERSPECTIVE

- Was progressivism successful? How do you define success?
- How did progressivism affect modern American politics?

The Progressive Era began with efforts at municipal reform in the 1890s and sputtered to a close during World War I. Some politicians who called themselves progressives remained in prominent positions afterward, and progressive concepts of efficiency and expertise continued to guide government decision making. But the war, which the United States entered in 1917, diverted public attention from reform, and by the end of the war political concerns had changed. By the mid-1920s, many of the major leaders of progressivism had passed from the political stage.

The changes of the Progressive Era transformed American politics and government. Before the Hepburn Act and the Federal Reserve Act, the federal government's role in the economy consisted largely of distributing land grants and setting protective tariffs. After the Progressive Era, the federal government became a significant and permanent player in the economy, regulating a wide range of economic activity and enforcing laws to protect consumers and some workers. The income tax quickly became the most significant source of federal funds, without which it is impossible to imagine the many activities that the federal government has assumed since then—from vast military expenditures to social welfare to support for the arts. Since the 1930s, the income tax has also been a potential instrument of social policy, by which the federal government can redistribute income.

During the Progressive Era, political parties declined in significance, and political campaigns were increasingly focused on personality and driven by advertising. These patterns accelerated in the second half of the twentieth century under the influence of television and public opinion polling. Organized pressure groups have proliferated and become ever more important. Women's participation in politics has continued to increase, especially in the last third of the twentieth century.

The assertion of presidential authority by Roosevelt and Wilson reappeared in the presidency of Franklin D. Roosevelt (1933–1945). The two Roosevelts and Wilson transformed Americans' expectations regarding the office of the presidency itself. Throughout the nineteenth century, Congress had dominated the making of domestic policy. During the twentieth century, Americans came to expect domestic policy to flow from forceful executive leadership in the White House.

Finley Peter Dunne, the leading political humorist of the Progressive Era, voiced a cynical view of reform when he observed that "a man that would expect to train lobsters to fly in a year is called a lunatic; but a man that thinks men can be turned into angels by an election is called a reformer." However, Dunne also realized that change is an integral part of American politics. He compared reform to housecleaning, and he quoted this conversation between a woman who ran a boarding house and one of her lodgers:

"I don't know what to do," says she. "I'm worn out, and it seems impossible to keep this house clean. What is the trouble with it?"

"Madam," says my friend Gallagher, . . . "the trouble with this house is that it is occupied entirely by human beings. If it was a vacant house, it could easily be kept clean."

Thus, Dunne concluded about progressive reform, "The noise you hear is not the first gun of a revolution. It's only the people of the United States beating a carpet."

INDIVIDUAL VOICES

Examining a Primary Source

Theodore Roosevelt Asserts Presidential Powers

Theodore Roosevelt was one of the nation's most informed presidents. He read widely, especially in history and natural history, and he wrote extensively on those topics. Among his interests was the nature of executive power—a few years before he became president, he wrote a biography of Oliver Cromwell, who led the Puritan army that overthrew the British monarchy and who governed England in the mid-1600s. In Roosevelt's *Autobiography* (1913), he discussed some of his ideas about the nature of the presidency.

The most important factor in getting the right spirit in my Administration, next to the insistence upon courage, honesty, and a genuine democracy of desire to serve the plain people, was my insistence upon the theory that the executive power was limited only by specific restrictions and prohibitions appearing in the Constitution or imposed by the Congress under its Constitutional powers. . . . I declined to adopt the view that what was imperatively necessary for the Nation could not be done by the President unless he could find some specific authorization to do it. . . . I did and caused to be done many things not previously done by the President and the heads of the departments. ● *I did not usurp power, but I did greatly broaden the use of executive power. . . . I did not care a rap for the mere form and show of power; I cared immensely for the use that could be made of the substance. . . .*

● Which of Roosevelt's actions were "things not previously done by a President"?

There have long been two schools of political thought . . . The course I followed, of regarding the executive as subject only to the people, and, under the Constitution, bound to serve the people affirmatively in cases where the Constitution does not explicitly forbid him to render the service, was substantially the course followed by both Andrew Jackson and Abraham Lincoln. Other honorable and well-meaning Presidents, such as James Buchanan, took the opposite and, as it seems to me, narrowly legal view that the President is the servant of Congress rather than of the people, and can do nothing, no matter how necessary it be to act, unless the Constitution explicitly commands the action. ● *Most able lawyers who are past middle age take this view. . . .*

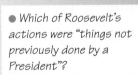

● What do you observe in the presidencies of Jackson, Lincoln, and Buchanan to support Roosevelt's views?

● *Can you find examples of such behavior in U.S. foreign affairs? in domestic policy? Can you find contrary examples? How successful was Roosevelt in meeting his own standard?*

● *What dangers might result from Roosevelt's views of sweeping presidential powers?*

In foreign affairs the principle from which we never deviated was to have the Nation behave toward other nations precisely as a strong, honorable, and upright man behaves in dealing with his fellow-men. . . . ●

In internal affairs I cannot say that I entered the Presidency with any deliberately planned and far-reaching scheme of social betterment. I had, however, certain strong convictions . . . I was bent upon making the Government the most efficient possible instrument in helping the people of the United States to better themselves in every way, politically, socially, and industrially. I believed with all my heart in real and thoroughgoing democracy, and I wished to make this democracy industrial as well as political. . . . I believed that the Constitution should be treated as the greatest document ever devised by the wit of man to aid a people in exercising every power for its own betterment, and not as a straitjacket cunningly fashioned to strangle growth. . . . ●

SUMMARY

Progressivism, a phenomenon of the late nineteenth and early twentieth centuries, refers to new concepts of government, to changes in government based on those concepts, and to the political process by which change occurred. Those years marked a time of political transformation, brought about by many groups and individuals who approached politics with often contradictory objectives. Organized interest groups became an important part of this process. Women broke through long-standing constraints to take a more prominent role in politics. The Anti-Saloon League was the most successful of several organizations that appealed to government to enforce morality. Some African Americans fought segregation and disfranchisement, notably W. E. B. Du Bois and the NAACP. Socialists and the Industrial Workers of the World saw capitalism as the source of many problems, but few Americans embraced their radical solutions.

Political reform took place at every level, from cities to states to the federal government. Muckraking journalists exposed wrongdoing and suffering. Municipal reformers introduced modern methods of city government in a quest for efficiency and effectiveness. Some tried to use government to remedy social problems by employing the expertise of new professions such as public health and social work. Reformers attacked the power of party bosses and machines by reducing the role of political parties.

At the federal level, Theodore Roosevelt set the pace for progressive reform. Relishing his reputation as a trustbuster, he challenged judicial constraints on federal authority over big business and promoted other forms of economic regulation, thereby increasing government's role in the economy. He also regulated the use of natural resources.

His successor, William Howard Taft, failed to maintain Republican Party unity and eventually sided with conservatives against progressives.

Roosevelt played an important role in defining America's status as a world power, as he secured rights to build a U.S.-controlled canal through Panama and established Panama as an American protectorate. The Roosevelt Corollary declared outright that the United States was the dominant power in the Caribbean and Central America. In eastern Asia, Roosevelt tried to bolster the Open Door policy by maintaining a balance of power. Roosevelt and others sought arbitration treaties with leading nations but failed because of Senate opposition. Faced with the rise of German military and naval power, Great Britain improved relations with the United States.

In 1912 Roosevelt led a new political party, the Progressives, making that year's presidential election a three-way contest. Roosevelt called for regulation of big business, but Wilson, the Democrat, favored breaking up monopolies through antitrust action. Wilson won the election but soon preferred regulation over antitrust actions. He helped to create the Federal Reserve System to regulate banking nationwide. As the 1916 election approached, Wilson also pushed for social reforms in an effort to unify all progressives behind his leadership.

The new urban, industrial, multiethnic society contributed to critical realism in literature, new patterns in painting, and ragtime music, although many creative artists continued to look to Europe for inspiration. Urbanization and changes in transportation and communication also fostered the emergence of a mass entertainment industry.

Progressive reforms made a profound impression on later American politics. In many ways, progressivism marked the origin of modern American politics.

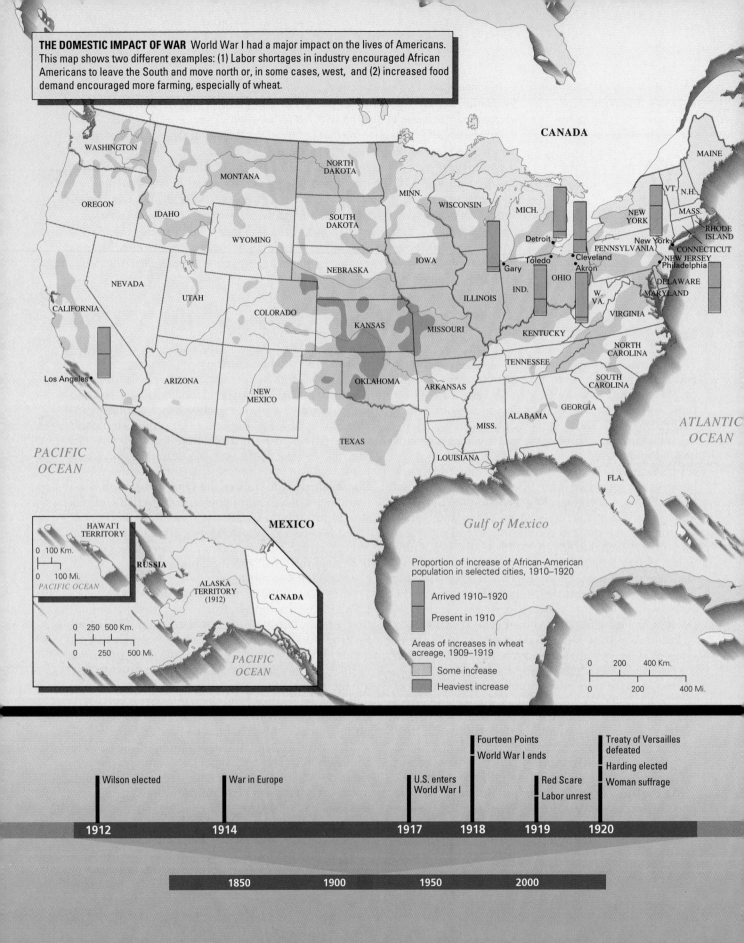

THE DOMESTIC IMPACT OF WAR World War I had a major impact on the lives of Americans. This map shows two different examples: (1) Labor shortages in industry encouraged African Americans to leave the South and move north or, in some cases, west, and (2) increased food demand encouraged more farming, especially of wheat.

CANADA

MAINE

WASHINGTON

OREGON

IDAHO

MONTANA

NORTH DAKOTA

MINN.

WISCONSIN

MICH.

VT. N.H.

NEW YORK

MASS.

RHODE ISLAND

New York

CONNECTICUT

NEW JERSEY

Philadelphia

DELAWARE

MARYLAND

Detroit

PENNSYLVANIA

Cleveland

Akron

W. VA.

VIRGINIA

Toledo

Gary

OHIO

IND.

ILLINOIS

KENTUCKY

NORTH CAROLINA

SOUTH CAROLINA

TENNESSEE

SOUTH DAKOTA

WYOMING

IOWA

NEBRASKA

NEVADA

UTAH

COLORADO

KANSAS

MISSOURI

CALIFORNIA

Los Angeles

ARIZONA

NEW MEXICO

OKLAHOMA

ARKANSAS

TEXAS

LOUISIANA

MISS.

ALABAMA

GEORGIA

FLA.

PACIFIC OCEAN

ATLANTIC OCEAN

Gulf of Mexico

HAWAI'I TERRITORY

0   100 Km.

0   100 Mi.

PACIFIC OCEAN

RUSSIA

ALASKA TERRITORY (1912)

CANADA

MEXICO

0   250   500 Km.

0   250   500 Mi.

PACIFIC OCEAN

Proportion of increase of African-American population in selected cities, 1910–1920

■ Arrived 1910–1920

■ Present in 1910

Areas of increases in wheat acreage, 1909–1919

□ Some increase

■ Heaviest increase

0   200   400 Km.

0   200   400 Mi.

Fourteen Points

World War I ends

Treaty of Versailles defeated

Harding elected

Woman suffrage

Wilson elected

War in Europe

U.S. enters World War I

Red Scare

Labor unrest

1912   **1914**   **1917**   **1918**   **1919**   **1920**

1850   1900   1950   2000

The United States in a World at War, 1913–1920

Alvin York

ALVIN YORK

Alvin York, a devout Christian, had to choose between his moral compunctions about killing and his sense of obligation to his country. This photograph was taken in 1919, the year York was promoted to sergeant and received the Congressional Medal of Honor, as well as similar awards from many of the Allies for his exploits in battle. *Brown Brothers.*

On June 28, 1914, a Serbian terrorist killed Archduke Franz Ferdinand, heir to the throne of Austria-Hungary, and his wife Sophie. The royal couple were visiting Sarajevo, in Bosnia-Herzegovina, which the Austrians had recently annexed against the wishes of the neighboring kingdom of Serbia. In response to the assassinations, Austria first consulted with its ally Germany and then made stringent demands on Serbia. Serbia sought help from Russia, which was allied with France. Tense diplomats invoked elaborate, interlocking alliances. Huge armies began to move. By August 4, most of Europe was at war.

Despite efforts to remain neutral, the United States entered the war in April 1917. Shortly after, Congress specified that all men aged 21 to 30 (later extended to 18 to 45) were subject to military service. Nearly 3 million men were drafted into service, among them, Alvin York.

Born in the Cumberland Mountains of Tennessee in 1887, York was raised in a backwoods community where people expected to secure some of the food on their tables through skill with their hunting rifles. He grew up with guns, remembering that his father "threatened to muss me up right smart if I failed to bring a squirrel down with the first shot or hit a [wild] turkey in the body instead of [shooting] its head off." From his youth, red-haired Alvin York was highly proficient with both rifle and pistol.

As a young man, York was known for his drinking, carousing, and recklessness. He put all that behind him when he became a born-again Christian in 1915 and joined a small fundamentalist church. He took his new faith seriously, and his commitment posed difficult choices for him when the war came:

> I loved and trusted old Uncle Sam and I have always believed he did the right thing. But I was worried clean through. I didn't want to go and kill. I believed in my Bible. And it distinctly said "thou shalt not kill." And yet old Uncle Sam wanted me. And he said he wanted me most awful bad. And I jest didn't know what to do. I worried and worried. I couldn't think of anything else. My thoughts just wouldn't stay a hitched.

York sought exemption from the draft as a conscientious objector but was refused.

Called to active duty, he made "good friends" with his new rifle and excelled at target practice. Still deeply troubled about the morality of war, he shared his concern with his battalion commander, Major Edward Buxton, who spent long hours discussing the Bible with York and trying to convince him that a good Christian might morally choose to go to war. Buxton recognized York's sincerity, however, and offered him the choice of noncombatant duty if he decided he could not kill on the battlefield. After struggling with his religious beliefs, York finally decided not only that he could fight in good conscience but that he was doing the Lord's work in helping to bring peace.

York's unit arrived on the front lines in France in June 1918 and took part in several major battles. On October 8, York—now a corporal—was part of a sixteen-man unit sent to take out some enemy machine guns in the Argonne Forest. They captured a small group of Germans, but a sudden burst of machine-gun fire killed or wounded nine of the Americans, including the sergeant, putting York in command. Leaving the surviving Americans to guard the prisoners, York coolly practiced his mountaineer sharpshooting, killing fourteen or so Germans as they trained machine-gun fire in his direction and tried to determine his position. When six Germans charged him with fixed bayonets, he dropped them all with his pistol. He then captured the German lieutenant in command and had him call on his men to surrender. York shot those who resisted. Prisoners in tow, York and other members of his unit then moved from position to position, using the German lieutenant to order each to surrender. Credited with killing twenty-five enemy soldiers and silencing thirty-five machine guns, York and the six other Americans marched 132 prisoners back to their astonished commanding officer.

The next day, York returned to the area searching for survivors. There he knelt and prayed for the souls of the dead, including those he had killed.

For his bravery and cool competence under fire, York received the Congressional Medal of Honor, the Croix de Guerre (France's highest decoration), and similar awards from other nations. Still, the blessings of his contemporaries were not enough to settle his conscience. Toward the end of his life, confined to bed, Alvin York pressed his son, a minister, for assurance that God would approve his deeds in the Argonne Forest.

INTRODUCTION

Before the events of August 1914, many Americans—including Theodore Roosevelt—had concluded that war had become unthinkable among what Roosevelt called the world's "civilized" nations. As president, Roosevelt had argued that the best way to preserve peace was by developing naval and military strength. Given the widely held expectation that war had become virtually obsolete, many Americans were shocked, saddened, and repelled in August 1914 when the leading "civilized" nations of the world—all of which had been busily accumulating arsenals—lurched into war.

When the nations of Europe went to war, the United States was no minor player on the international scene. Between 1898 and 1908, America acquired the Philippines and the Panama Canal, came to dominate the Caribbean and Central America, and actively participated in the balance of power in eastern Asia. The three presidents of the Progressive Era—Roosevelt, William Howard Taft, and Woodrow Wilson—agreed wholeheartedly that the United States should exercise a major role in world affairs.

INHERITED COMMITMENTS AND NEW DIRECTIONS

• Before the outbreak of war in Europe, how did Wilson conceive of America's role in dealing with other nations?

• In what new directions did Wilson steer U.S. foreign policy before the coming of war in Europe?

When Woodrow Wilson entered the White House in 1913, he expected to spend most of his time dealing with domestic issues. Though well read on international affairs, he had neither significant international experience nor carefully considered foreign policies. For secretary of state he chose William Jennings Bryan, who also had devoted most of his political career to domestic matters and had little experience that qualified him as the nation's foreign-policy chief. Both Wilson and Bryan were devout Presbyterians, sharing a confidence that God had a plan for humankind. Both hoped—idealistically and perhaps naively—that they might make the United States a model among nations for the peaceful settlement of international disputes. Wilson first fixed his attention on the three world regions of greatest American involvement: Latin America, the Pacific, and eastern Asia. There, he tried to balance the anti-imperialist principles of his Democratic Party against the expansionist practices of his Republican predecessors. He marked out some new directions, but in the end he actually extended many previous commitments.

Anti-Imperialism, Intervention, and Arbitration

Wilson's party had opposed many of the foreign policies of McKinley, Roosevelt, and Taft, especially imperialism. Secretary of State Bryan was a leading anti-imperialist who had criticized Roosevelt's "Big Stick" in foreign affairs. "The man who speaks softly does not need a big stick," Bryan said, adding, "If he yields to temptation and equips himself with one, the tone of his voice is very likely to change." Wilson shared Taft's support for American commercial expansion, but he faulted dollar diplomacy for using the State Department to advance the interests of particular companies.

During the Wilson administration, the Democrats' long-standing commitment to anti-imperialism produced two measures. In 1916 Congress established a bill of rights for residents of the Philippine Islands and promised them independence, though without specifying a date. The next year, Congress made Puerto Rico an American territory and extended American citizenship to its residents. Thus the Democrats wrote into law a limited version of the anti-imperialism they had proclaimed for some twenty years.

Democrats had criticized Roosevelt's actions in the Caribbean, but Wilson eventually intervened more in Central America and the Caribbean than did any other administration. In Nicaragua, Taft had used marines to prop up the rule of President Adolfo Días. Wilson now sought more authority for the United States within that country. Senate Democrats rejected his efforts, reminding him of their party's opposition to further protectorates. Even so, the **Bryan-Chamorro Treaty** of 1914 gave the United States significant concessions, including the right to build a canal through Nicaragua.

In Haiti, which owed a staggering debt to foreign bankers, the dictatorial president ordered many of his opponents put to death in 1915. When a mob tore him apart, Wilson sent in American marines. A treaty followed, making Haiti a protectorate in which American forces controlled most aspects of government until 1933. Wilson sent marines into the Dominican Republic in 1916, and U.S. naval officers took control there until 1924. In 1916, too, the United States agreed to buy the Virgin Islands from Denmark for $25 million.

Although Wilson made few changes in previous policies regarding the Caribbean, he enthusiastically encouraged Bryan to promote arbitration of international disputes. Roosevelt's and Taft's secretaries of state had sought arbitration treaties, but their efforts had foundered on the Senate's refusal to yield any of its role in foreign relations. Learning from those failures, Bryan drafted a model arbitration treaty and obtained approval of it from the Senate Foreign Relations Committee. The State Department then distributed the proposal—called "President Wilson's Peace Proposal"—to the forty nations that maintained diplomatic relations with the United States. Negotiations produced twenty-two ratified treaties, all of which featured a cooling-off period for disputes, typically a year, during which the nations agreed not to go to war and instead to seek arbitration. The treaties marked the beginning of a process by which Wilson sought to redefine international relations, substituting rational negotiations for raw power.

Wilson and the Mexican Revolution

In Mexico, Wilson attempted to influence internal politics but eventually found himself on the verge of war. **Porfirio Díaz** had ruled Mexico for a third of a

---

Bryan-Chamorro Treaty Treaty in 1914 in which Nicaragua received $3 million in return for granting the United States exclusive rights to a canal route and a naval base.

Porfirio Díaz Mexican soldier and politician who became president after a coup in 1876 and ruled Mexico until 1911.

chronology

The United States and World Affairs, 1913–1920

1912	Woodrow Wilson elected president
1913	Victoriano Huerta takes power in Mexico
	Wilson denies U.S. recognition to Huerta
	Secretary of State Bryan proposes cooling-off treaties
1914	U.S. Navy occupies Veracruz
	War breaks out in Europe
	United States declares neutrality
	Stalemate on the western front
	Bryan-Chamorro Treaty
1915	German U-boat sinks the *Lusitania*
	United States occupies Haiti
1915–1920	Great Migration
1916	U.S. troops pursue Pancho Villa into Mexico
	National Defense Act
	United States purchases Virgin Islands from Denmark; takes possession in 1917
	Sussex pledge
	United States occupies Dominican Republic
	Wilson reelected
1917	Wilson calls for "peace without victory"
	American troops leave Mexico
	Germany resumes submarine warfare
	Overthrow of tsar of Russia
	United States declares war on Germany
	Committee on Public Information
	War Industries Board
	Selective Service Act
	Espionage Act
	Race riot in East St. Louis
	Government crackdown on IWW
	Bolsheviks seize power in Russia
	Russia withdraws from the war
	Bolsheviks publish secret treaties
	Railroads placed under federal control

1917–1918	Union membership rises sharply
	Lynchings increase
1918	Wilson presents Fourteen Points to Congress
	Germans launch major offensive
	National War Labor Board
	Sedition Act
	U.S. troops in northern Russia and Siberia
	Successful Allied counteroffensive
	Republican majorities in Congress
	Armistice in Europe
1918–1919	Worldwide influenza epidemic
	Civil war in Russia
	Rampant U.S. inflation
1919	Versailles peace conference
	Prohibition approved
	General strike in Seattle
	Urban race riots
	Wilson suffers stroke
	Boston police strike
	Senate defeats Versailles treaty
1919–1920	Steel strike
	Red Scare
	Palmer raids
1920	Senate defeats Versailles treaty again
	Nineteenth Amendment (woman suffrage) approved
	Warren G. Harding elected president

century, supported by the great landholders, the church, and the military. During his rule, and with his encouragement, many American companies invested in the Mexican economy. By the early twentieth century, however, discontent was brewing among peasants, workers, and intellectuals. Rebellion broke out, and mobs took to the streets demanding that Díaz resign. He did so in 1911. Francisco Madero, a leading advocate of reform, assumed the presidency to great acclaim but proved

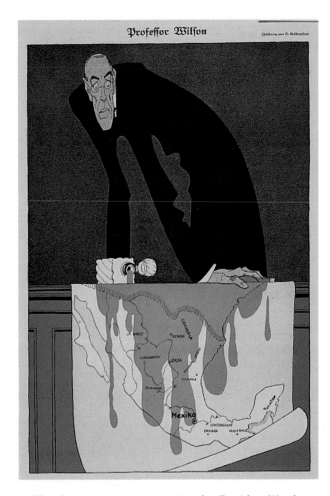

This dramatic cartoon suggesting that President Woodrow Wilson had erred in his intervention in Mexico appeared in the German magazine *Simplicissimus* in 1914, only a few months before Germany and the rest of Europe plunged into war themselves. *"Simplicissimus" May 11, 1914. The Bancroft Library, University of California, Berkeley.*

incapable of uniting the country. Discontent rolled across Mexico as peasant armies calling for *tierra y libertad* ("land and liberty") attacked the mansions of great landowners. Conservatives feared Madero as a reformer, but radicals dismissed him as too timid. Conservative forces launched an uprising in Mexico City in February 1913, working with the commander of the army, General **Victoriano Huerta**. Huerta took control of the government and had Madero executed.

Most European governments extended diplomatic recognition to Huerta because his government clearly held power in Mexico City. Taft—about to hand over the presidency—left that matter to his successor, so

Wilson faced that decision soon after his inauguration. American companies with investments in Mexico, especially mining and oil, urged recognition because they considered Huerta likely to protect their holdings. Wilson, however, considered Huerta a murderer and privately vowed "not to recognize a government of butchers." In public, Wilson announced that he was withholding recognition because Huerta's regime did not rest on the consent of the governed.

Wilson's addition of a moral dimension to diplomatic recognition constituted something new in American foreign policy. Previous American presidents had automatically extended diplomatic recognition to governments in power. Labeled "missionary diplomacy," Wilson's approach implied that the United States would discriminate between pure and impure governments. Telling one visitor, "I am going to teach the South American republics to elect good men," Wilson engaged in what he called "watchful waiting," seeking an opportunity to act against Huerta. In the meantime, anti-Huerta forces led by **Venustiano Carranza** began to make significant gains.

In April 1914, Wilson found an excuse to intervene when Mexican officials in Tampico arrested a few American sailors who had come ashore. The city's army commander immediately released them and apologized. Wilson, however, used the incident to justify ordering the U.S. Navy to occupy **Veracruz** (see Map 22.1). As the leading Mexican port, Veracruz was the major source of the Huerta government's revenue (from customs) and the landing point for most government military supplies. The occupation cut these off. It also cost more than a hundred Mexican lives and turned many Mexicans against Wilson for violating their national sovereignty over a petty dispute. Facing Carranza's armies and without munitions and customs revenues, Huerta fled the country in mid-July. Wilson withdrew the last American forces from Veracruz in November.

Victoriano Huerta Mexican general who overthrew President Francisco Madero in 1913 and established a military dictatorship until forced to resign in 1914.

Venustiana Carranza Mexican revolutionary leader who helped to lead armed opposition to Victoriano Huerta and who succeeded to the presidency in 1914; his government was overthrown in 1920.

Veracruz Major port city, located in east-central Mexico on the Gulf of Mexico; in 1914, Wilson ordered the U.S. Navy to occupy the port.

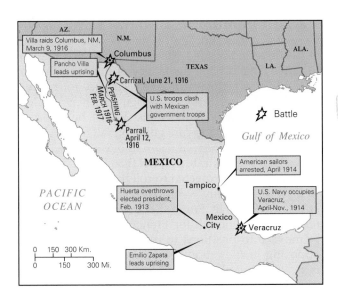

MAP 22.1 The United States and the Mexican Revolution This map identifies the key locations for understanding relations between the United States and Mexico during 1913–1917.

Carranza succeeded Huerta as president, and Wilson officially recognized his government. Carranza faced armed opposition, however, from **Francisco "Pancho" Villa** in northern Mexico and Emiliano Zapata in the south. When Villa suffered serious setbacks, he apparently decided to try to defeat Carranza by inciting a war with the United States. Villa's men murdered several Americans in Mexico and, in March 1916, raided across the border and killed several Americans in Columbus, New Mexico. After securing reluctant approval from Carranza, Wilson sent an expedition of nearly seven thousand men, commanded by General John Pershing, into Mexico to punish Villa. Villa deftly evaded the American troops, all the while drawing them ever deeper into Mexico.

Alarmed, Carranza protested the size of the American expedition and the distance it penetrated into Mexico. When a clash between Mexican government forces and American soldiers produced deaths on both sides, Carranza asked Wilson to withdraw the American troops. Wilson refused. Villa then doubled behind the American army and raided into Texas, killing more Americans. Wilson sent more men into Mexico, though Carranza insisted that all American forces be withdrawn. Wilson still refused. Only in early 1917, when Wilson began to anticipate that America might soon be at

war with Germany, did he order the troops to pull back, leaving behind a deep reservoir of Mexican resentment and suspicion toward the United States.

THE UNITED STATES IN A WORLD AT WAR, 1914–1917

- Why did Wilson proclaim American neutrality? What were the attitudes of the nation toward this objective?
- What forces outside the United States made neutrality difficult? What forces within the United States were pushing for the nation to enter the war?
- How did Wilson justify going to war?

At first, Americans paid only passing attention to the assassinations at Sarajevo. The nations of Europe, however, began methodically—sometimes regretfully, sometimes enthusiastically—to activate their intricate alliance networks. When Europe plunged into war, Wilson and all Americans faced difficult choices.

The Great War in Europe

Throughout much of the nineteenth and early twentieth centuries, most European governments had encouraged their citizens to identify strongly with their nation, thereby cultivating the intense patriotism known as **nationalism**. Within the ethnically diverse empires of Austria-Hungary, Russia, and Turkey, a different sort of nationalism fueled hopes for independence based on language and culture. Ethnic antagonisms and aspirations were especially powerful in the **Balkan Peninsula**, where the Ottoman (Turkish) Empire had lost territory as several groups had established their independence. Some of the new Balkan states, however, were weak, attracting the attention of the neighboring Austrian and Russian empires. As Austria-Hungary sought to

---

Francisco "Pancho" Villa Mexican bandit and revolutionary who led a raid into New Mexico in 1916, which prompted the U.S. government to send troops into Mexico in unsuccessful pursuit.

nationalism Intense patriotism, or a movement that favors a separate nation for an ethnic group that is part of a multiethnic state.

Balkan Peninsula Region of southeastern Europe; once ruled by the Ottoman Empire, it included a number of relatively new and sometimes unstable states in the early twentieth century.

annex new territories, Russia claimed the role of protector of other **Slavic** peoples.

During the same years, competition for world markets and territory spawned an unprecedented arms buildup. After the 1870s, Germany had the most powerful army in Europe and, in 1898, launched a naval construction program designed to make its navy as powerful as Britain's. By 1900, most European powers had a thoroughly professional corps of military and naval officers and had instituted **universal military service**. Technological advances produced powerful weapons including the machine gun, and designers quickly adapted automobiles and airplanes for combat.

The major powers of Europe had avoided armed conflict with one another since 1871, when Germany had humiliated France in the brief Franco-Prussian War, but they continued to prepare for war by lining up allies. Eventually European diplomats constructed two major alliance systems: the **Triple Entente** (Britain, France, and Russia; Britain was also allied with Japan) and the **Triple Alliance** (Germany, Austria-Hungary, and Italy).

Thus the events at Sarajevo occurred in the midst of an arms race between rival alliances. The assassinations themselves grew out of a territorial conflict between Austria-Hungary and Serbia. Austria-Hungary, whose empire included several restive Slavic groups, feared that Serbia might mold a strong Slavic state on its south. Russia, alarmed over Austrian expansion in the Balkans, presented itself as the protector of Serbia, which, like Russia and unlike Austria, was Orthodox in religion and used the Cyrillic alphabet. Called the "powder keg of Europe," the Balkans lived up to their explosive nickname in 1914.

Austria first assured itself of Germany's backing, then declared war on Serbia. In turn, Russia confirmed France's support, then **mobilized** its army in support of Serbia. Germany declared war on Russia on August 1 and on France soon after. German strategists planned to bypass French defenses along their border by advancing through neutral Belgium (see Map 22.2). When the Belgian government refused permission to cross its territory, Germany invaded Belgium. Britain entered the conflict in defense of Belgium. By August 4, much of Europe was at war. Eventually Germany and Austria-Hungary combined with Bulgaria and the Ottoman Empire to form the **Central Powers**. Italy abandoned its Triple Alliance partners and joined Britain, France, Russia, Romania, and Japan as the Allies.

At first, Secretary of State Bryan took a hopeful view of events in Europe. "It may be," he suggested, "that the world needed one more awful object lesson to prove conclusively the fallacy of the doctrine that preparedness for war can give assurance for peace." Sir Edward Grey, Britain's foreign minister, was less optimistic. At twilight on August 3, 1914, he mourned to a friend, "The lamps are going out all over Europe. We shall not see them lit again in our lifetime." Grey proved a more accurate prophet than Bryan.

The Germans expected to roll through Belgium, a small and militarily weak nation, and land a quick knockout blow to France. The Belgians, however, resisted long enough for French and British troops to move into positions to block the Germans. The opposing armies soon settled into lines across 475 miles of Belgian and French countryside, extending from the English Channel to the Alps (see Map 22.2). By the end of 1914, the **western front** consisted of elaborate networks of trenches separated from the enemy's entrenchments by a desolate **no man's land** filled with coils of barbed wire, where any movement brought a burst of machine-gun fire. As the war progressed, terrible new weapons—poison gas, aerial bombings, tanks—took thousands of lives but failed to break the deadlock.

Slavic   Relating to the Slavs, a linguistic group that includes the Poles, Czechs, Slovaks, Slovenes, Serbs, Croats, Bosnians, and Bulgarians of Central Europe, as well as Russians, Ukrainians, Belarussians, and other groups in eastern Europe.

universal military service   A governmental policy specifying that all adult males (or, rarely, all adults) are required to serve in the military for some period of time.

Triple Entente   Informal alliance that linked France, Great Britain, and Russia in the years before World War I.

Triple Alliance   Alliance that linked Germany, Italy, and Austria-Hungary in the years before World War I.

mobilize   To make ready for combat.

Central Powers   In World War I, the coalition of Germany, Austria-Hungary, Bulgaria, and the Ottoman Empire.

western front   The western line of battle between the Allies and Germany in World War I, located in French and Belgian territory; the eastern front was the line of battle between the Central Powers and Russia.

no man's land   The field of battle between the lines of two opposing, entrenched armies.

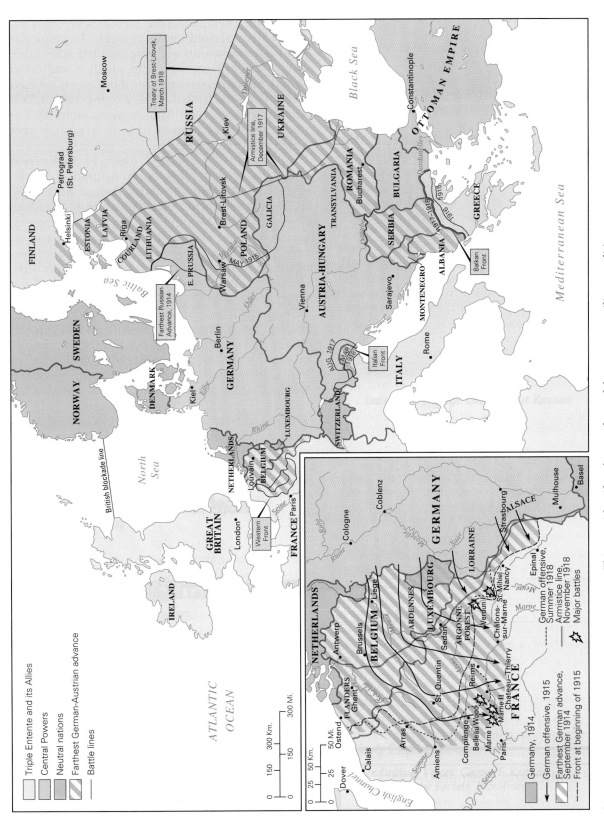

MAP 22.2 The War in Europe, 1914–1918 This map identifies the members of the two great military coalitions: the Central Powers and the Allies. Notice how much territory Russia lost by the Treaty of Brest-Litovsk as compared to the armistice line (the line between the two armies when Russia sought peace).

American Neutrality

Wilson's initial reaction to the European conflagration revealed his own deep religious beliefs—he wrote privately of his confidence that "Providence has deeper plans than we could possibly have laid for ourselves." On August 4, he announced that the United States was not committed to either side and was to be accorded all **neutral** rights. The death of his wife, Ellen, on August 6, briefly drew the grief-stricken Wilson away from public appearances. Later, on August 19, he spoke to the nation, urging Americans to be "neutral in fact as well as in name . . . impartial in thought as well as in action."

Wilson hoped not only that America would remain outside the conflict, but also that he might serve as the peacemaker. Such hopes proved unrealistic. Most of the warring nations wanted to gain territory, and only a decisive victory could deliver such a prize. The longer they fought, the more territory they coveted to satisfy their losses. So long as they saw a chance of winning, they had no interest in the appeals of Wilson or other would-be peacemakers.

Wilson's hope that Americans could remain impartial was also unrealistic. American socialists probably came the closest, as they condemned all the warring nations for seeking imperial spoils at the expense of the workers who filled the trenches. Most Americans probably sided with the Allies. England had cultivated American friendship for decades, and trade and finance united many members of their business communities. Memories of French assistance during the American Revolution fueled enthusiasm for France. And the martyrdom of Belgium aroused American sympathy. Allied propagandists worked hard to generate anti-German sentiment in America, publicizing—and sometimes exaggerating—German atrocities in Belgium and portraying the war as a conflict between civilized peoples and barbarian **Huns**.

Not all Americans sympathized with the Allies. Nearly 8 million of the 97 million people in the United States had one or both parents from Germany or Austria. Not surprisingly, many of them disputed depictions of their cousins as bloodthirsty barbarians. Many of the 5 million Irish Americans disliked England for ruling their ancestral homeland and held no sympathy for the English.

Neutral Rights and German U-Boats

Wilson and Bryan agreed on the need to keep American interests separate from those of either side in the European conflict, and both men believed that the United States should remain neutral. They took different approaches for carrying out that goal, however. Bryan proved willing to sacrifice traditional neutral rights if insistence on those rights seemed likely to pull the United States into the conflict. Wilson, in contrast, stood firm on maintaining all traditional rights of neutral nations, a posture that actually favored the Allies.

Bryan initially opposed loans to **belligerent** nations as incompatible with neutrality. Wilson agreed at first, hoping to starve the war financially. When Wilson realized that the ban hurt the Allies more, however, he modified it to permit buying goods on credit. Eventually, he dropped the ban on loans, partly because neutrals had always been permitted to lend to belligerents and partly, perhaps, because the freeze endangered the stability of the American economy.

Traditional neutral rights included freedom of the seas: neutrals could trade with all belligerents. However, Wilson soon found himself in conflict with both sides over the rights of neutral ships, as both sides turned to naval warfare to break the deadlock on the western front. Britain commanded the seas at the war's outset and began to redefine neutral rights by announcing a blockade both of German ports and of neutral ports from which goods could reach Germany. Britain also expanded traditional definitions of **contraband** to include anything that might give indirect aid to its enemy—even cotton and food. In addition, Britain extended the right to "visit and search," which enabled belligerent nations to stop and search neutral ships for contraband. Insisting that large, modern ships could not be carefully searched at sea, Britain escorted neutral ships to port, thus imposing costly delays.

---

neutral   A neutral nation is one not aligned with either side in a war; traditionally, a neutral nation had the right to engage in certain types of trade with nations that were at war.

Hun   Disparaging term used to describe Germans during World War I; the name came from a warlike tribe that invaded Europe in the fourth and fifth centuries.

belligerent   A nation formally at war.

contraband   Goods prohibited from being imported or exported; in time of war, contraband included materials of war.

Though New York newspapers carried warnings from the German embassy about the dangers of trans-Atlantic travel, the passengers who boarded the *Lusitania* on May 1, 1915, probably did not imagine themselves in serious danger from submarine attack. The ship was sunk on May 7. Of the 1,959 passengers and crewmembers, 1,198 died, including 128 Americans. *Warning: Cobb Heritage Centre, England, photo by Larry O. Nighswander/NGS; Sketch: Culver Pictures.*

Germany declared a blockade of the British Isles, to be enforced by its submarines, called **U-boats**. Because U-boats were relatively fragile, a lightly armed merchant ship might sink one that surfaced and ordered the merchant ship to stop in the traditional manner. Consequently, submarines struck from below the surface without issuing the warning called for by traditional rules of naval warfare. When Britain began disguising its ships by flying the flags of neutral countries, Germany specified that a neutral flag no longer guaranteed protection. Wilson had issued token protests over Britain's practices, but now he strongly denounced those of Germany. Because Germany's violations of neutrality produced loss of life, he considered them to be significantly different from Britain's, which caused only financial hardship.

On February 10, 1915, Wilson warned that the United States would hold Germany to "strict accountability" for its actions and would do everything necessary to "safeguard American lives and property and to secure to American citizens the full enjoyment of their acknowledged rights on the high seas." On May 7, 1915, a German U-boat torpedoed the British passenger ship *Lusitania*. More than a thousand people died, including 128 Americans.

Americans reacted with shock and horror. When Bryan learned that the *Lusitania* carried rifle cartridges and other contraband, he urged restraint in protesting to Germany. Wilson, however, sent a message that stopped just short of demanding an end to submarine warfare against unarmed merchant ships. When the German response was noncommittal, Wilson composed an even stronger protest. Bryan feared it would lead to war, and he resigned as secretary of state rather than sign it.

Robert Lansing, Bryan's successor, strongly favored the Allies. Where Bryan had counseled restraint, Lansing urged a show of strength. U-boat attacks continued, and Wilson sent more protests, but he knew that most Americans opposed going to war over that issue. The sinking of the unarmed

U-boat A German submarine (in German, *Unterseeboot*).

Lusitania British passenger liner torpedoed by a German submarine in 1915; more than one thousand drowned, including 128 Americans, creating a diplomatic crisis between the United States and Germany.

French ship *Sussex* in March 1916, which injured several Americans, led Wilson to warn Germany that if unrestricted submarine warfare did not stop, "the United States can have no choice" but to sever diplomatic relations—usually the last step before declaring war. Germany responded with the *Sussex* **pledge**, promising that U-boats would no longer strike noncombatant vessels without warning, provided the United States convinced the Allies to obey "international law." Wilson accepted the pledge but did little to persuade the British to change their tactics.

The war strengthened America's economic ties to the Allies. Exports to Britain and France grew dramatically, from $756 million in 1914 to $2.7 billion in 1916. American companies exported $6 million worth of explosives in 1914 and $467 million in 1916. Even more significant was the transformation of the United States from a debtor to a **creditor nation**. By April 1917, American bankers had loaned more than $2 billion to the Allied governments. At the same time, the British blockade stifled Americans' trade with the Central Powers, which fell from around $170 million in 1914 to almost nothing two years later.

Convinced that the best way to keep the United States neutral was to end the war, Wilson sent his closest confidant, Edward M. House, to London and Berlin early in 1916. Wilson directed House to present proposals for peace, **disarmament**, and a league of nations to maintain peace in the future. House received no encouragement from either side and concluded that they were not interested in negotiations.

Soon after, increasing numbers of Americans demanded "preparedness"—a military buildup. In the summer of 1916, Congress doubled the size of the army and appropriated the largest naval expenditures in the country's peacetime history. Wilson accepted both measures.

The Election of 1916

By embracing preparedness, Wilson took control of an issue that otherwise might have helped the Republicans in the 1916 presidential campaign. The Democrats nominated Wilson for a second term, and they campaigned on their progressive domestic accomplishments and preparedness programs, frequently repeating the slogan, "He kept us out of war."

Republicans nominated Charles Evans Hughes, a Supreme Court justice and former governor of New York with a reputation as a progressive. Hughes avoided taking a clear position on preparedness and neutrality, hoping for support both from German Americans upset with Wilson's harshness toward Germany and from those who wanted maximum assistance for the Allies. As a result, he failed to present a compelling alternative to Wilson. Hughes made other errors—in California, he slighted unions and Senator Hiram Johnson, both powerful forces, and Wilson narrowly carried California.

The contest was very close. Most voters identified themselves as Republicans, and Wilson needed support from at least some of them. First election reports—from eastern and midwestern states—gave Hughes such an edge that some Democrats conceded defeat. But Wilson won by uniting the always-Democratic South with the West, much of which was progressive. Wilson also received significant backing from unions, socialists, and women in states where women could vote. In the end, Wilson received 49.4 percent of the vote to 46.2 percent for Hughes.

The Decision for War

After the election, in January 1917, Wilson spoke to the Senate on the need to achieve and preserve peace. The galleries were packed as he eloquently called for a league of nations to keep peace in the future and to replace the old balance-of-power concept with "a community of power." He urged that the only lasting peace would be a "peace without victory" and a "peace among equals" in which neither side exacted gains from the other. He called for government by consent of the governed, freedom of the seas, and reductions in armaments. Wilson admitted privately that he had really aimed his speech toward "the people of the countries now at war," hoping to build public pressure on the governments to seek peace. He won praise from **left-wing** opposition parties in several countries, but the

---

Sussex **pledge**   German promise in 1916 to stop sinking merchant ships without warning if the United States would compel the Allies to obey "international law."

creditor nation   A nation whose citizens or government have loaned more money to the citizens or governments of other nations than the total amount that they have borrowed from the citizens or governments of other nations.

disarmament   The reduction or dismantling of a nation's military forces or weaponry.

left-wing   Not conservative; usually implies socialist or otherwise radical leanings.

British, French, and German governments had no interest in "peace without victory."

In Germany, the initiative now passed to those who wanted to resume unrestricted submarine warfare. They expected that this would bring the United States into the war but gambled on being able to defeat the British and French before American troops could arrive in Europe. When Germany announced it was resuming unrestricted submarine warfare, Wilson broke off diplomatic relations. German U-boats began immediately to take a devastating toll on Atlantic shipping.

A few weeks later, on March 1, Wilson released a decoded message from the German foreign minister, **Arthur Zimmermann**, to the German minister in Mexico. Writing on January 16, Zimmermann proposed that, if the United States went to war with Germany, Mexico should ally itself with Germany and attack the United States. Zimmermann went on to pledge that, if Germany and Mexico won, Mexico would recover its "lost provinces" of Texas, Arizona, and New Mexico. Zimmermann also proposed that Mexico should encourage Japan to enter the war against the United States. The British had intercepted the message and, on February 24, gave it to American representatives. Zimmermann's suggestions outraged Americans, increasing public support for Wilson's proposal to arm American merchant ships for protection against the U-boats. A few senators, mostly progressives, blocked the measure, arguing that it was safer to bar merchant ships from the war zone. Wilson then acted on his own and authorized merchant ships to be armed.

Between February 3 and March 21, German U-boats sank six American ships. Wilson could now avoid war only by backing down from his previous insistence on "strict accountability." He did not retreat. On April 2, 1917, Wilson asked Congress to declare war on Germany. Wilson apparently thought that the nation was unlikely to go to war solely to protect American commerce with the Allies, and he himself probably felt the need to justify war in more noble terms. In fact, his major objective in going to war seems to have been to put the United States, and himself, in a position to demand the sort of peace he had outlined in January. Thus, in asking for war, Wilson tried to unite Americans in a righteous, progressive crusade. He condemned German U-boat attacks as "warfare against mankind." "The world must be made safe for democracy," he proclaimed, and he promised that the United States would fight for self-government, "the rights and liberties of small nations," and a league of nations to "bring peace and safety to all nations and make the world itself at last free."

Not all members of Congress agreed that war was necessary, and not all were ready to join Wilson's crusade to transform the world. During the four days of debate that ensued, Senator George W. Norris, a progressive Republican from Nebraska, best voiced the arguments of the opposition. The nation, he claimed, was going to war "upon the command of gold" to "preserve the commercial right of American citizens to deliver munitions of war to belligerent nations." In the Senate, Norris, Robert La Follette, and four others voted no, but eighty-two senators voted for war. Jeannette Rankin of Montana, the first woman to serve in the House of Representatives, was among those who said no when the House voted 373 to 50 for war. In December, Congress also declared war against Austria-Hungary.

THE HOME FRONT

- What steps did the federal government take to mobilize the economy and society in support of the war? How successful was the mobilization effort?

- How did the war affect Americans, especially women, African Americans, and opponents of war?

Historians call World War I the first "total war" because it was the first war to demand mobilization of an entire society and economy. The war altered nearly every aspect of the economy, as the progressive emphasis on expertise and efficiency produced unprecedented centralization of economic decision making. Mobilization extended beyond war production to the people themselves, especially their attitudes toward the America's involvement.

Mobilizing the Economy

The ability to wage war effectively depended on a fully engaged industrial economy. Thus warring nations sought to direct economic activities toward

---

Arthur Zimmermann   German foreign minister who proposed in 1917 that if the United States declared war on Germany, Mexico should become a German ally and win back Texas, Arizona, and New Mexico and should try to persuade Japan to go to war with the United States.

supplying their war machines. In the United States, shortages, railway transportation snarls, and delays in manufacturing led to increased federal direction over manufacturing, food and fuel production, and transportation. This was not unusual among the nations at war and in fact was probably less extreme than in other nations because the United States entered the war later. Even so, the extent of direct federal control over so much of the economy has never been matched since World War I.

Though unprecedented, much of the government intervention was also voluntary. Business enlisted as a partner with government and supplied its cooperation and expertise. Some prominent entrepreneurs volunteered their full-time services for a dollar a year. Much of the wartime centralization of economic decision making came through new agencies composed of government officials, business leaders, and prominent citizens.

The **War Industries Board** (WIB) was established in 1917 to supervise production of war materials. At first, it had only limited success in increasing industrial productivity. Then, in early 1918, Wilson appointed Bernard Baruch, a Wall Street financier, to head the board. By pleading, bargaining, and sometimes threatening, Baruch usually managed to persuade companies to set and meet production quotas, allocate raw materials, develop new industries, and streamline their operations. Though Baruch once threatened steel company executives with a government takeover, he accomplished most goals without coercion. And industrial production increased by 20 percent.

Efforts to conserve fuel included the first use of **daylight saving time**. To improve rail transportation, the federal government consolidated the country's railroads in 1917 and ran them as a single system for the duration of the war. The government also took over the telegraph and telephone system and launched a huge shipbuilding program to expand the merchant marine.

The **National War Labor Board**, created in 1918, endorsed **collective bargaining** to resolve labor disputes and thereby facilitate production. The board also gave some support for an eight-hour workday in return for a no-strike pledge from unions. Many unions secured contracts with significant wage increases, and union membership boomed from 2.7 million in 1916 to more than 4 million by 1919. Most union leaders fully supported the war. Samuel Gompers, president of the AFL, called it "the most wonderful crusade ever entered upon in the whole history of the world."

In 1918, this poster by James Montgomery Flagg appealed to American women to contribute to victory by conserving food through raising and preserving food for their families. The woman is shown sowing seeds (in the way that grain was planted before the development of agricultural machinery for that task), garbed in a dress made from an American flag, and wearing a red Liberty cap, a symbol that originated in the French Revolution. *Ohio Historical Society.*

War Industries Board   Federal agency headed by Bernard Baruch that coordinated American production during World War I.

daylight saving time   Setting of clocks ahead by one hour to provide more daylight at the end of the day during late spring, summer, and early fall.

National War Labor Board   Federal agency created in 1918 to resolve wartime labor disputes.

collective bargaining   Negotiation between the representatives of organized workers and their employer to determine wages, hours, and working conditions.

REMEMBER · BELGIUM ·

**Buy Bonds
Fourth
Liberty
Loan**

This poster encouraged Americans to buy Liberty bonds (that is, loan money to the government) by emphasizing the image of the vicious and brutal Hun. This was part of a larger process of demonizing the people of the Central Powers that extended to condemning the music of Beethoven and the writings of Goethe. *Collection of Robert Cherny.*

One crucial American contribution to the Allies was food, for the war had severely disrupted European agriculture. Wilson appointed **Herbert Hoover** as Food Administrator. A prominent mining engineer, Hoover had won wide praise for directing the relief program in Belgium. He now promoted conservation and increased production of food, urging families to conserve food through Meatless Mondays and Wheatless Wednesdays and to plant "war gardens" to raise vegetables. Farmers brought large areas under cultivation for the first time. (The chapter-opening map indicates the expansion of wheat growing.) Food shipments to the Allies tripled.

Some progressives urged that the Wilson administration pay for the war solely by taxing the war-time profits and earnings of corporations. That did not happen, but taxes—especially the relatively new income tax—did account for almost half of the $33 billion that the United States spent on the war between April 1917 and June 1920. The government borrowed the rest, most of it through **Liberty Loan** drives. Rallies, parades, and posters pushed all Americans to buy "Liberty bonds." Groups such as the Red Cross and the YMCA urged people to donate time and energy in support of American soldiers.

Mobilizing Public Opinion

Not all Americans supported the war. Some German Americans were reluctant to see their sons sent to war against their cousins. Some Irish Americans took even less interest in saving Britain after the English brutally suppressed an attempt at Irish independence in 1916. When the Socialist Party determined to oppose the war, Socialist candidates greatly increased their share of the vote in several cities in 1917—to 22 percent in New York City and 34 percent in Chicago—suggesting that their antiwar stance attracted many voters.

To mobilize public opinion in support of the war, Wilson in 1917 created the Committee on Public Information, headed by George Creel. Once a muckraking journalist, Creel set out to sell the war to the American people. The **Creel Committee** eventually counted 150,000 lecturers, writers, artists, actors, and scholars championing the cause and whipping up hatred of the "Huns." Social clubs, movie theaters, and churches all joined what Creel called "the world's greatest adventure in advertising." "Four-Minute Men"—volunteers ready to make a four-minute patriotic speech anytime and anywhere a crowd gathered—made 755,190 speeches in 5,000 towns.

Wartime patriotism, fanned at times by the Creel Committee, sparked extreme measures against those considered "slackers" or pro-German. "Woe to the

Herbert Hoover   U.S. food administrator during World War I, known for his proficient handling of relief efforts; he later served as secretary of commerce (1921–1928) and president (1929–1933).

Liberty Loan   One of a series of four bond issues floated by the U.S. Treasury Department from 1917 to 1919 to help finance World War I.

Creel Committee   The U.S. Committee on Public Information (1917–1919), headed by journalist and editor George Creel; it used films, posters, pamphlets, and news releases to mobilize American public opinion in favor of World War I.

man or group of men that seeks to stand in our way," warned Wilson. "He who is not with us, absolutely and without reserve of any kind," echoed former president Theodore Roosevelt, "is against us, and should be treated as an alien enemy." Zealots everywhere took up the cry. "Americanization" drives promoted rapid assimilation among immigrants. Some states prohibited the use of foreign languages in public. Officials removed German books from libraries and sometimes publicly burned them. Some communities banned the music of Bach and Beethoven, and some dropped German classes from their schools. Even certain words became objectionable: sauerkraut, for example, became "liberty cabbage." Sometimes mobs hounded people with German names and occasionally attacked or even lynched people suspected of antiwar sentiments.

Civil Liberties in Time of War

German Americans suffered the most from the wartime hysteria, but pacifists, socialists, and other radicals also became targets for government repression and **vigilante** action. Congress passed the **Espionage Act** in 1917 and the **Sedition Act** in 1918, prohibiting interference with the draft and outlawing criticism of the government, the armed forces, or the war effort. Violators faced large fines and long prison terms. Officials arrested some fifteen hundred people for violating the Espionage and Sedition Acts, including Eugene V. Debs, leader of the Socialist Party. The Espionage Act permitted the postmaster general to decide what could pass through the nation's mails. By the war's end, the Post Office Department had denied mailing privileges to some four hundred periodicals, including, at least temporarily, the *New York Times* and other mainstream publications.

Dissenters found they could not rely on the courts for protection. When opponents of the war challenged the Espionage Act as unconstitutional, the Supreme Court ruled that freedom of speech was never absolute. Just as no one has the right to falsely shout "Fire!" in a theater and create panic, said Justice Oliver Wendell Holmes, Jr., so in time of war no one has a constitutional right to say anything that might endanger the security of the nation. The Court also upheld the Sedition Act in 1919, by a vote of 7 to 2.

Although the Industrial Workers of the World (IWW) made no public pronouncement against the war, most Wobblies probably opposed it. IWW members and leaders quickly came under relentless attack from employers, government officials, and patriotic vigilantes, most of whom had disliked the IWW before the war. In September 1917, Justice Department agents raided IWW offices nationwide and arrested the union's leaders, who were sentenced to jail terms of up to twenty-five years and to fines totaling millions of dollars. Deprived of most of its leaders and virtually bankrupted, the IWW never recovered.

A few Americans protested the abridgment of civil liberties. One group formed the Civil Liberties Bureau—forerunner of the American Civil Liberties Union, or ACLU—under the leadership of Roger Baldwin. Most Americans, however, did not object to the repression, and many who did kept silent.

Changes in the Workplace

Intense activism and remarkable productivity characterized American labor's wartime experience. Union membership almost doubled, and a significant number of women were among the surge of new cardholders. In addition, unions benefited from the encouragement that the National War Labor Board gave to collective bargaining between unions and companies as the most effective way to keep labor peace. The board also stepped in and helped to settle labor disputes. Never before had a federal agency interceded this way. Nevertheless, many workers felt that their purchasing power was not keeping pace with increases in prices.

Demands for increased production at a time when millions of men were marching off to war opened opportunities for women in many fields. Employment of women in factory, office, and retail jobs had increased before the war, and the war accelerated those trends. At the war's end, many women's wartime jobs returned to male hands, but in office work and some retail positions women continued to predominate after the war.

---

vigilante A person who takes law enforcement into his or her own hands, usually on the grounds that normal law enforcement has broken down.

Espionage Act Law passed by Congress in 1917, mandating severe penalties for anyone found guilty of interfering with the draft or encouraging disloyalty to the United States.

Sedition Act Law passed by Congress in 1918 to supplement the Espionage Act by extending the penalty to anyone deemed to have abused the government in writing.

Labor shortages attracted new people into the labor market and opened up some jobs to women and members of racial minorities. In May 1918, these women worked in the Union Pacific Railroad freight yard in Cheyenne, Wyoming. Most of them seem delighted to have their picture taken in their work clothes. *Wyoming State Museum.*

Most women who worked outside the home were young and single. Some middle-class women who now entered the paid labor force gave up not only their homebound roles but also their parents' standards of morality and behavior. Some adopted instead the less-restricted lifestyles that had long been experienced by many wage-earning, working-class women, taking control over their income and using it to establish autonomy from familial controls.

The Great Migration and White Reactions

The war had a great impact on African-American communities. Until the war, about 90 percent of all African Americans lived in the South, 75 percent in rural areas. By 1920, perhaps as many as a half-million had moved north in what has been called the **Great Migration**.

The largest increases in the African-American population came in the industrial cities of the Midwest. Gary, Indiana, showed one of the greatest gains—1,284 percent between 1910 and 1920. Outside the Midwest, New York City, Philadelphia, and Los Angeles also attracted many blacks (see the chapter-opening map). Several factors combined to produce this migration, but the most important were the brutality of southern life and the economic opportunities in the cities of the North. "Every time a lynching takes place in a community down South," said T. Arnold Hill of Chicago's Urban League, "colored people will arrive in Chicago within two weeks." Southern agricultural hardships provided further incentive to leave. In 1915 and 1916, southern farmers alternately battled drought and severe rains and fought the **boll weevil**.

Perhaps the most significant factor in the Great Migration was American industry's desperate need for workers at the same that European immigration declined sharply. The wartime labor needs of northern cities attracted hundreds of thousands of African Americans seeking better jobs and higher pay. In the North, one could earn almost as much in a day as in a week in the South—for example, industrial jobs often paid $3 a day, compared with 50 cents for picking cotton. The impact on some southern cities was

Great Migration Movement of about a half-million black people from the rural South to the urban North during World War I.

boll weevil Small beetle that infests cotton plants and damages the cotton bolls, which contain the cotton fibers.

Labor shortages and high wages drew African Americans from the South to the North. This family, including members of three generations, posed for a photographer upon their arrival in Chicago from the South, as part of the Great Migration during World War I. *Schomburg Center for Research in Black Culture, New York Public Library.*

striking. Jackson, Mississippi, for example, was estimated to have lost half of all working-class African Americans and between a quarter and a third of black business owners and professionals.

Severe wartime racial conflicts erupted in several cities at the northern end of the Great Migration trail. One of America's worst race riots swept through the industrial city of East St. Louis, Illinois, on July 2, 1917. Thousands of African-American laborers, most from the South, had settled in the city during the previous two years. A least thirty-nine of them perished in the riot, and six thousand found themselves homeless. Incensed that such brutality could occur just weeks after the nation's moralistic entrance into the war, W. E. B. Du Bois charged, "No land that loves to lynch 'niggers' can lead the hosts of Almighty God," and the NAACP led a silent protest parade of ten thousand people through **Harlem**.

AMERICANS "OVER THERE"

- What role did American ships and troops play in ending the war?

- In what ways did Wilson try to keep America's participation in the war separate from the Allies? Why?

With the declaration of war, the United States needed to mobilize quickly for combat in a distant part of the world. The navy was already large and powerful after nearly three decades of shipbuilding, and preparedness measures in 1916 further strengthened it. The army, however, was tiny compared to the armies contesting in Europe. Millions of men and thousands of women had to be inducted, trained, and transported to Europe.

Mobilizing for Battle

Almost immediately the navy began to strike back at the German fleet. The American and British navies' convoy technique, in which several ships traveled together under the protection of destroyers, helped to cut shipping losses in half by late 1917. By spring 1918, U-boats ceased to pose a significant danger.

Harlem   A section of New York City in the northern part of Manhattan; it became one of the largest black communities in the United States.

About 10,000 American Indians enlisted or were drafted into the army during World War I, including John Miller (left) and Charlie Wolf, members of the Omaha tribe. In some cases, the Indians who went to war first underwent tribal ceremonies, long unpracticed, for preparing warriors for battle, and thus may have contributed to the preservation of traditional customs. Indians' participation in the war led to increased demands for full citizenship and enfranchisement for all American Indians, a step that came in 1924. *Nebraska State Historical Society.*

In April 1917, however, the combined strength of the U.S. Army and National Guard stood at only 372,000 men. Many men volunteered but not enough. In May, therefore, Congress passed the **Selective Service Act**, requiring men aged 21 to 30 (later extended to 18 to 45) to register with local boards to determine who would be called to duty. Some, including members of Congress, objected that conscription (usually called "the draft") was undemocratic. The law exempted those who opposed war on religious grounds, but such **conscientious objectors** were sometimes badly treated.

Few people demonstrated against the draft, and most seemed to accept it as efficient and fair. Like Alvin York, 24 million men registered and 2.8 million were drafted—about 72 percent of the entire army. By the end of the war, the combined army, navy, and marine corps counted 4.8 million members.

No women were drafted, but almost 13,000 joined the navy and marines, most serving in clerical capacities. For the first time, women held full naval and marine rank and status. The army, however, refused to enlist women, considering it a "most radical departure." Nearly 18,000 women served in the Army Corps of Nurses, but without army rank, pay, or benefits. At least 5,000 civilian women served in various capacities in France, sometimes near the front lines. The largest number served through the Red Cross, which helped to staff hospitals and rest facilities.

Nearly 400,000 African Americans served during World War I. Almost 200,000 served overseas, nearly 30,000 on the front lines. Emmett J. Scott, an African American and former secretary to Booker T. Washington, became special assistant to the secretary of war, responsible for the uniform application of the draft and the morale of African Americans. Nevertheless, black soldiers were often treated as second-class citizens. They served in segregated **Jim Crow** units in the army, were limited to food service in the navy, and were excluded altogether from the marines. More than 600 African Americans earned commissions as officers, but the army was reluctant to commission more. White officers commanded most black troops.

"Over There"

By mid-1918, it seemed that Allied troops all along the western front had taken up a tune by the popular American composer George M. Cohan:

Over there, over there,
Send the word, send the word over there,
The Yanks are coming, the Yanks are coming,
And we won't come back 'til it's over over there.

Selective Service Act   Law passed by Congress in 1917 establishing compulsory military service for men aged 21 to 30.
conscientious objector   Person who refuses to bear arms or participate in military service because of religious beliefs or moral principles.
Jim Crow   Refers to laws or practices that discriminate against black people; probably derived from a minstrel-show character named Jim Crow.

This is a stereoscope photograph. Such photographs were taken by a special camera with two lenses a short distance apart. When viewed through a stereoscope (a device found in most middle-class homes in the early twentieth century), the two photographs produced a three-dimensional image. The caption of this photo is "Our Answer to the Kaiser—3,000 of America's Millions Eager to Fight for Democracy." Such photographs were popular, both reflecting popular attitudes and helping to shape them. *Collection of George Kimball.*

A few Yanks—troops in the **American Expeditionary Force** (AEF)—arrived in France in June 1917, commanded by General John J. Pershing, recently returned from Mexico. Most American troops, however, were still to be inducted, supplied, trained, and transported across the Atlantic.

Throughout the war, Wilson held the United States apart from the Allies, referring to the United States as an Associated Power, rather than one of the Allies, and trying as much as possible to keep American troops separate. This distinction stemmed partly from his distrust of Allied war aims but more from his wish to make the American contribution to victory as prominent as possible in order to maximize American influence in defining the peace.

As American troops began to trickle into France, the Central Powers seemed close to victory. French offensives in April 1917 had failed, and a British summer effort in Flanders produced enormous casualties but little gain. The Italians suffered a major defeat late in the year. A Russian drive in mid-summer proved disastrous. Russia withdrew from the war late in 1917, and German commanders

shifted troops moved from east to west (see Map 22.2). Hoping to win the war before many American troops could reinforce the Allies' battered lines, the Germans planned a massive offensive for spring 1918.

The German thrust came in Picardy with sixty-four divisions smashing into the French and British lines and attempted to advance along the Marne River. AEF units were hurried to the front to block their advance. In mid-May, an AEF officer described trench life in a letter to his sister:

> *We have to lay low all day to escape observation. . . . At nine P.M. we emerge and do various work all night: digging trenches, wiring, carrying ammunition, burying the dead. . . . It is scary . . . when the shelling begins, the rockets and flares all along the near horizon lighting up the weird scene, the Boche*

American Expeditionary Force   American army commanded by General John J. Pershing that served in Europe during World War I.

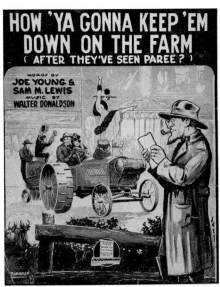

A black bandleader, James Reese Europe (left) went to France as a lieutenant, commanding a machine-gun company, and saw frontline action. When he and other black musicians were reassigned to present musical entertainment behind the lines, they were among the first to play jazz in France. Upon returning to the United States in 1919, he and his band recorded "How 'Ya Gonna Keep 'Em Down on the Farm After They've Seen Paree?" (right). Many groups recorded the popular song, but black musicians may have given it a different emphasis: how can black soldiers be kept "down" after they experienced less oppressive racial patterns in France? *Europe: Howard University Museum Archives, Moorland-Springarn Research Center; sheet music: The John Hay Library, Brown University, photo by Brooke Hammerle.*

flashlights [German searchlights] simulating the aurora, the everlasting crack and roar of our own artillery . . . and the whine of the innumerable shells passing overhead, the sputtering of the machine guns, and in the midst of it all the persistent singing of a nightingale down in the ravine.

By late May, the Germans were within 50 miles of Paris. As French officials considered evacuating the capital, all available troops were rushed to the front. At Chateau-Thierry and at Belleau Wood, AEF units took 8,000 casualties during a month-long battle over a single square mile of wheat fields and woods. Of 310,000 AEF troops who fought in the Marne River region, 67,000 were killed or wounded.

The Allies launched a counteroffensive in July as American troops poured into France, topping the million mark. The American command insisted on having its own sector of the front, and in September Pershing successfully launched a stunning one-day offensive against the St. Mihiel **salient** (see Map 22.2). AEF forces then joined a larger Allied offensive in the Meuse River-Argonne Forest region, the last major assault of the war and one of the fiercest battles in American military history. In the Argonne Forest on October 8, Alvin York became the most heroic American of the war, but his courage and coolness were not unique among the Americans who fought in the Meuse-Argonne campaign—

Harry J. Adams, with only an empty pistol, captured 300 prisoners; Hercules Korgia, captured by the Germans, persuaded his captors to become his prisoners; and Samuel Woodfill single-handedly took out five machine guns. By October, German military leaders were urging their government to seek an armistice. Fighting ended at 11 A.M., November 11 (the eleventh hour of the eleventh day of the eleventh month), 1918. By then, more than 2 million American soldiers were in France, giving the Allies an advantage of about 600,000 men.

By the time of the armistice, thirty-two nations had declared war on one or more of the Central Powers. Nearly 9 million men in uniform died: Germany lost 1.8 million, Russia 1.7 million, France 1.4 million, Austria-Hungary 1.2 million, the British Empire 908,400. France lost half its men between the ages of 20 and 32. More than 20 million combatants suffered wounds, producing many permanent disabilities. American losses were small in comparison—115,000 casualties, including 48,000 killed in action. Millions of people worldwide, including

---

salient   A part of a battle line where the enemy has launched an offensive and pushed the line forward; a projection of the line.

civilians, died from starvation and disease, especially during a global **influenza** epidemic in 1918 and 1919 that killed 500,000 Americans.

Some white Americans, including some military officers, worried that experiences in France might cause African-American soldiers to resist segregation at home. Many black units were assigned to menial tasks behind the lines, although some saw action. In August 1918, AEF headquarters secretly requested that the French not prominently commend black units. The grateful French, however, awarded the **Croix de Guerre** to several all-black units that had distinguished themselves in combat and presented awards to individual soldiers for acts of bravery and heroism. When the Allies staged a grand victory parade down Paris's Champs Elysées, the British and French contingents included all races and ethnicities, but American commanders directed that no African-American troops take part.

WILSON AND THE PEACE CONFERENCE

- What were the American war objectives, and what factors influenced Wilson as he defined them?

- Do you consider that Wilson was successful at the peace conference? On what basis?

- What caused the defeat of the treaty in the Senate? Who was responsible—Wilson, Lodge, or the irreconcilables?

When the war ended, Wilson hoped that the peace process would not sow the seeds of future wars. He hoped, too, to create an international organization to keep the peace. Most of the Allies, however, were more interested in grabbing territory and punishing Germany.

Bolshevism, the Secret Treaties, and the Fourteen Points

In March 1917, war-weary and hungry, Russians deposed their **tsar** and created a provisional government. In November, a group of radical socialists, the **Bolsheviks**, seized power. Soon renamed Communists, the Bolsheviks condemned capitalism and imperialism and sought to destroy them. **Vladimir Lenin**, the Bolshevik leader, immediately began peace negotiations. The **Treaty of Brest-Litovsk**, in March 1918, was harsh and humiliating, requiring Russia to surrender vast territories—Finland, its Baltic provinces, parts of Poland and the Ukraine—in all, a third of its population, half of its industries,

its most fertile agricultural land, and a quarter of its territory in Europe.

Condemning the war as nothing more than a scramble for imperial spoils, the Bolsheviks in December 1917 published secret treaties by which the Allies agreed to strip colonies and territories from the Central Powers and divide those spoils among themselves. These exposés strengthened Wilson's intent to separate American war aims from those of the Allies and to impose his war objectives on the Allies.

On January 8, 1918, Wilson spoke to Congress. Elaborating on the war objectives he had presented earlier, he directly challenged the secret treaties and tried to seize the initiative in defining a basis for peace. He stressed that American goals derived from "the principle of justice to all peoples and nationalities, and their right to live on equal terms of liberty and safety with one another, whether they be strong or weak." Wilson presented fourteen objectives, soon called the **Fourteen Points**. Points one through five provided a general context for lasting peace: no secret treaties, freedom of the seas, reduction of barriers to trade, reduction of armaments, and adjustment of colonial claims based partly on the interests of colonial peoples. Point six dealt with Russia, calling for other nations to withdraw from Russian territory and to welcome Russia "into the society of free nations." Points seven through thirteen addressed particular situations:

---

influenza Contagious viral infection characterized by fever, chills, congestion, and muscular pain, nicknamed "the flu"; an unusually deadly strain, usually called "Spanish flu," swept across the world in 1918 and 1919.

Croix de Guerre French military decoration for bravery in combat; in English, "the Cross of War."

tsar The monarch of the Russian empire; also spelled czar.

Bolsheviks Radical socialists, later called Communists, who seized power in Russia in November 1917.

Vladimir Lenin Leader of the Bolsheviks and of the Russian Revolution of 1917 and head of the Soviet Union until 1924.

Treaty of Brest-Litovsk Humiliating treaty with Germany that Russia signed in 1918 in order to withdraw from the World War I; it required Russia to surrender vast territories along its western boundary.

Fourteen Points President Wilson's program for maintaining peace after World War I, which called for arms reduction, national self-determination, and a league of nations.

return of territories France had lost to Germany in 1871 and self-determination in Central Europe and the Middle East. The fourteenth point called for "a general association of nations" that could afford "mutual guarantees of political independence and territorial integrity to great and small states alike."

The Allies reluctantly accepted Wilson's Fourteen Points as a starting point for discussion but expressed little enthusiasm for them. The Germans were more interested. When they asked for an end to the fighting, they made clear that their request was based on the Fourteen Points.

The World in 1919

In December 1918, Wilson sailed for France—the first time that an American president in office had gone to Europe and the first time that a president had personally negotiated with other world leaders. Wilson brought along some two hundred experts on European history, culture, ethnology, and geography. In France, Italy, and Britain, huge welcoming crowds paid homage to the great "peacemaker from America."

Delegates to the peace conference assembled amid far-reaching change. The Austro-Hungarian Empire had crumbled, producing the new nations of Poland and Czechoslovakia and the republics of Austria and Hungary. The German monarch, Kaiser Wilhelm, had **abdicated**, and a republic was being formed. In January 1919, Berlin witnessed an unsuccessful communist uprising. Throughout the ruins of the Russian Empire, ethnic groups were proclaiming independent republics (most of which were eventually incorporated into the Soviet Union, often through intervention by the Bolsheviks' **Red Army**). The Ottoman Empire was collapsing too as Arabs, with aid from Britain and France, revolted. Throughout Europe and the Middle East, national **self-determination** and government by the consent of the governed—part of Wilson's design for the postwar world—seemed to be stumbling into reality. Nor were the British and French colonial empires immune, for both faced growing independence movements among their many possessions.

In Russia, civil war raged between the Bolsheviks' and their opponents. When the Bolsheviks left the world war, the Allies pushed Wilson to join them in intervening in Russia, ostensibly to protect war supplies from falling into German hands. In mid-1918, Wilson included American troops in Allied expeditions to northern Russia and eastern Siberia. In Siberia, his intent was primarily to head off a

Japanese grab of territory. Lenin initially accepted the intervention in northern Russia as necessary to block a German advance. However, the purpose of the Allied intervention soon changed, to support for the foes of the Bolsheviks. By late 1918, despite his Sixth Point, Wilson had begun to express concern over what he called "mass terrorism" directed by the Bolsheviks toward "peaceable Russian citizens." Before the last American troops were withdrawn—from northern Russia in May 1919 and from eastern Siberia in early 1920—they had engaged in conflict with units of the Red Army.

Wilson at Versailles

The peace conference opened on January 18, 1919, just outside Paris, at the glittering Palace of Versailles, once home to French kings. Representatives attended from all nations that had declared war against the Central Powers, but the major decisions were made by the Big Four: Wilson, David Lloyd George of Britain, Georges Clemenceau of France, and Vittorio Orlando of Italy. Germany was excluded. Terms of peace were to be imposed, not negotiated. Russia, too, was absent, on the grounds that it had withdrawn from the war earlier and made a separate peace with Germany. Although Russia was barred from Versailles, the specter of Bolshevism was present throughout the proceedings, affecting decisions about eastern Europe especially.

Wilson quickly learned that the European leaders were far more interested in pursuing their own national interests than in his Fourteen Points. Clemenceau, nicknamed "the Tiger," could recall Germany's humiliating defeat of France in 1871 and intended to disable Germany so thoroughly that it could never again threaten his nation. Lloyd George agreed in principle with many of Wilson's proposals but came to Paris with a mandate from British voters

---

abdicate   To relinquish a high office; usually said only of monarchs.

Red Army   The army created by the Bolsheviks to defend their communist government in their civil war and to re-establish control in parts of the Russian Empire that tried to create separate republics in 1917 and 1918; the Red Army was the army of the Soviet Union throughout its existence.

self-determination   The freedom of a given people to determine their own political status.

The "big three" of the Versailles Conference—from the left, David Lloyd George, the British prime minister; Georges Clemenceau, the French prime minister; and Woodrow Wilson, president of the United States. They are on their way to one of the meetings of the peace conference. ©*Hulton Getty/Liaison.*

with Alsace-Lorraine (which Germany had taken from France in 1871), and other European territories (see Map 22.3.) The treaty also deprived Germany of its navy and merchant marine and limited its army to one hundred thousand men. German representatives signed on June 28, 1919.

Wilson reluctantly agreed to the massive reparations but insisted that colonies taken from Germany should not go to the Allies. Called **mandates**, they were to be administered by one of the Allies on behalf of the League of Nations. Mandates were intended to move toward self-government and independence. In nearly every case, however, the mandate went to the nation slated to receive the territory under the secret treaties. Wilson blocked Italy's most extreme territorial demands but gave in on others. The peace conference recognized the new nations of central Europe, thereby creating a so-called quarantine zone between Russian Bolshevism and western Europe. But the treaty ignored other matters of self-determination. No one gave a hearing to people—from Ireland to Vietnam—seeking the right of self-determination in colonies held by one of the victorious Allies. Japan failed to secure a statement supporting racial equality.

In the end, Wilson compromised on nearly all of his Fourteen Points, but every compromise intensified his commitment to the League of Nations. The League, he hoped, would not only resolve future controversies without war but also solve problems created by the compromises. Even so, Wilson had to threaten a separate peace with Germany before the Allies agreed to incorporate the **League Covenant** into the treaty. Wilson was especially pleased with Article 10 of the League Covenant—he called it the League's "heart."

to exact heavy **reparations** from Germany. Orlando insisted on the territorial gains promised when Italy joined the Allies in 1915. Other war aims had been spelled out in the secret treaties, so various Allies were expecting to gain territory at the expense of Germany, Austria-Hungary, and the Ottoman Empire. In addition, the European Allies feared the spread of Bolshevism and were intent on setting up buffers to keep it at bay.

Facing the insistent and acquisitive Allies, Wilson had no choice but to compromise. He did secure the creation of a **League of Nations**. Instead of "peace without victory," however, the **Treaty of Versailles** imposed harsh victors' terms, requiring Germany to accept the blame for starting the war, to pay reparations to the Allies (the exact amount to be determined later), and to surrender all its colonies along

---

reparations   Payments required as compensation for damage or injury.

League of Nations   A world organization proposed by President Wilson and created by the Versailles peace conference; it worked to promote peace and international cooperation.

Treaty of Versailles   Treaty signed in 1919 ending World War I; it imposed harsh terms on Germany, created several territorial mandates, and set up the League of Nations.

mandate   A territory that the League of Nations authorized one of its member nations to administer, with the understanding that the region would move toward self-government.

League Covenant   The constitution of the League of Nations, which was incorporated in the 1919 Treaty of Versailles.

MAP 22.3 Postwar Boundary Changes in Central Europe and the Middle East This map shows the boundary changes in Europe and the Middle East that resulted from the defeat of the four large, multiethnic empires—Austria-Hungary, Russia, Germany, and the Ottoman Empire.

It specified that League members agreed to protect one another's independence and territory against external attacks and to take joint economic and military action against aggressors.

The Senate and the Treaty

While Wilson was in Paris, opposition to his plans was percolating at home. The Senate, controlled by Republicans since the 1918 elections, had to approve any treaty. In response to concerns of some senators, Wilson added several provisions to the League Covenant.

Presented with the treaty, the Senate split into three groups. **Henry Cabot Lodge**, chairman of the Senate Foreign Relations Committee, led the largest faction, called reservationists after the *reservations*, or amendments, to the treaty that Lodge developed. Article 10 of the League Covenant especially bothered Lodge, for he feared it might be used to commit American troops to war without congressional approval. A small group, mostly Republicans, were called irreconcilables because they opposed any American involvement in European affairs. A third Senate group, nearly all Democrats, supported the president and his treaty.

Wilson decided to appeal directly to the American people. In September 1919, he undertook an arduous speaking tour—9,500 miles with speeches in twenty-nine cities. The effort proved too demanding for his fragile health, and he collapsed in Pueblo, Colorado. Soon after, he suffered a serious stroke.

Half-paralyzed and weak, Wilson could fulfill few of his duties. His wife, Edith Bolling Wilson, whom he had married in 1915, exercised what she later called a "stewardship," strictly limiting her ailing husband's contact with the outside world. Lodge now proposed that the Senate accept the treaty with fourteen reservations, his retort to the Fourteen Points. Some of his amendments were minor, but others would have permitted Congress to block action under Article 10. Wilson refused to compromise. On November 19, 1919, the Senate defeated the treaty with the Lodge reservations by votes of 39 to 55 and 41 to 50, with the irreconcilables joining the president's supporters in opposition. Then the Senate defeated the original version of the treaty by 38 to 53, with the irreconcilables joining the reservationists in voting no. The treaty with reservations came to a vote again in March 1920. By then, some treaty supporters had concluded that the League could never be approved without Lodge's reservations, so they joined the reservationists to produce a vote of 49 in favor to 35 opposed—still seven votes short of the two-thirds majority required for any treaty ratification. Enough Wilson loyalists—following their stubborn leader's order not to compromise—joined the irreconcilables to defeat the treaty once again. The United States did not join the League of Nations.

Legacies of the Great War

Roosevelt, Wilson, and most other prewar leaders had projected the progressive mood of optimism and confidence. Wilson invoked this tradition in claiming that the United States was going to war to make the world "safe for democracy." One of his supporters even described World War I as the "war to end war." Just as progressives defined their domestic policies in terms of progress, democracy, and social justice, so Wilson had tried to invest his foreign policy with similarly enlightened values. In doing so, however, he fostered unrealistic expectations that world politics might be transformed overnight.

Many Americans became disillusioned by the contrast between Wilson's lofty idealism and the Allies' cynical opportunism at Versailles. The war to make the world "safe for democracy" turned out to be a chance for Italy to annex Austrian territory and for Japan to seize German concessions in China. In addition, the "war to end war" spun off several wars in its wake. Romania invaded Hungary in 1919, Poland invaded Russia in 1920, the Russian civil war continued until 1921, and Greece and Turkey battled until 1923.

The peace conference left unresolved many problems. Wilson's promotion of self-government and self-determination encouraged aspirations for independence throughout the colonial empires retained by the Allies. Some of the new nations of Central Europe, supposedly based on ethnic self-determination, actually included different and sometimes antagonistic ethnic groups. Above all, the war and the treaty helped to produce economic and political instability in much of Europe, making it a breeding ground for totalitarian and nation-

> **Henry Cabot Lodge** Prominent Republican senator from Massachusetts and chair of the Senate Foreign Relations Committee, who led congressional opposition to Article 10 of the League of Nations.

alistic movements that eventually generated another world war.

AMERICA IN THE AFTERMATH OF WAR, NOVEMBER 1918–NOVEMBER 1920

• How did Americans react to the outcome of the war and the events of 1919? How did the war contribute to conflict within the nation in 1919?

• How did the events of 1917–1920 affect the 1920 presidential election? What was unusual about that contest?

Almost as soon as French church bells pealed for the armistice, the United States began to demobilize. By November 1919, nearly 4 million men and women were out of uniform. Industrial demobilization occurred even more quickly, as officials canceled war contracts with no more than a month's notice. The year 1919 saw not only the return of American troops from Europe but also raging inflation, massive strikes, bloody race riots, widespread fear of radical **subversion**, violations of civil liberties, and at the same time, two new constitutional amendments that embodied important elements of progressivism—prohibition and woman suffrage.

"HCL" and Strikes

Inflation—described in newspapers as "HCL" for "High Cost of Living"—was the most pressing single problem Americans faced after the war. Between 1913 and 1919, prices almost doubled. Inflation contributed to labor unrest. The armistice ended unions' no-strike pledge, and organized labor made wage demands to match the soaring cost of living. In 1919, however, employers were ready for a fight.

Many companies wanted to return labor relations to prewar patterns. They blamed wage increases for inflation, and some linked unions to "dangerous foreign ideas" from Bolshevik Russia. In February 1919, Seattle's Central Labor Council called out all the city's unions in a five-day general strike to support striking shipyard workers. Seattle's mayor claimed the strike was a Bolshevik plot. Boston's police struck in September 1919 after the city's police commissioner fired nineteen policemen for joining an AFL union. The governor of Massachusetts, Calvin Coolidge, refused to negotiate and instead activated the state guard to maintain

At the end of the war, the federal Employment Service tried to help returning soldiers and sailors to find jobs. Unemployment for 1918 and 1919 was less than 2 percent, but it rose above 5 percent in 1920 and to nearly 12 percent in 1921. *Picture Research Consultants & Archives.*

order and break the union. "There is no right to strike against the public safety by anybody, anywhere, anytime," he proclaimed. By mid-1919, many

---

subversion Efforts to undermine or overthrow an established government.

unionists concluded with dismay that conservative politicians had joined with business leaders in an effort to block further union organizing and to roll back the wartime gains.

The largest and most dramatic strike came against the United States Steel Corporation. Few steelworkers were represented by unions after the 1892 Homestead strike. Steel companies often hired recent immigrants, keeping the work force divided by language and culture. Most steelworkers put in twelve-hour workdays. Wages had not increased as fast as inflation—or as fast as company profits. In 1919 the AFL launched an ambitious unionization drive in the steel industry, and many steelworkers responded eagerly.

The men who ran the steel industry firmly refused to deal with the new organization. The workers went on strike in late September, demanding union recognition, collective bargaining, the eight-hour workday, and higher wages. United States Steel blamed the strike on radicals and effectively mobilized public opinion against the strikers. Company guards protected strikebreakers, and U.S. military forces moved into Gary, Indiana, to help round up what they called "the Red element." By January 1920, after eighteen workers had been killed and hundreds beaten, the strike was over and the unions were ousted.

Red Scare

The steel industry's charges of Bolshevism to discredit strikers came at a time when many government and corporate leaders vied in their depictions of the dangers of Bolshevism at home and abroad. And a few anarchist bombers contributed their part in stirring up a widespread frenzy aimed at rooting out subversive radicals.

In late April 1919, thirty-four bombs addressed to prominent Americans—including J. P. Morgan, John D. Rockefeller, and Supreme Court justice Oliver Wendell Holmes—were discovered in various post offices after the explosion of two others addressed to a senator and to the mayor of Seattle. In June, bombs in several cities damaged buildings and killed two people. The explosions helped produce a panic over a supposed nationwide conspiracy to overthrow the government.

Attorney General A. Mitchell Palmer now organized an anti-Red campaign, hoping that success might enhance his chances for the 1920 presidential nomination. "Like a prairie fire," Palmer claimed, "the blaze of revolution was sweeping over

every American institution." In August 1919, he appointed **J. Edgar Hoover**, a young lawyer, to head a new antiradical division in the Justice Department, the predecessor of the Federal Bureau of Investigation. In November, Palmer launched the first of what came to be called the **Palmer raids** to arrest suspected radicals. Authorities rounded up some five thousand people between November and January 1920. Although officials found only a few firearms and no explosives, the raids led to the **deportation** of several hundred aliens who had some tie to a radical organization.

In May 1919, a group of veterans formed the American Legion, which not only lobbied on behalf of veterans but also condemned radicals and endorsed the deportations. Committing itself "to foster and perpetuate a one hundred percent Americanism," the Legion signed up a million members by the end of the year. Some of its branches gained a reputation for vigilante action against suspected radicals.

State legislatures joined in with their own antiradical measures, including **criminal syndicalism laws**—measures criminalizing the advocacy of Bolshevik or IWW ideologies. In January 1920, the assembly of the New York state legislature expelled five members elected as Socialists, solely because they were Socialists. However, after a wide range of respected public figures denounced the assembly action as undemocratic, public opinion regarding the **Red Scare** began to shift. With the approach of May 1, the major day of celebration for radicals, Palmer issued dramatic warnings for the public to be on guard against leftist activity, including a gen-

---

J. Edgar Hoover Official appointed to head a new antiradical division in the Justice Department in 1919; he served as head of the FBI from its official founding in 1924 until his death in 1972.

Palmer raids Government raids on individuals and organizations in 1919 and 1920 to search for political radicals and to deport foreign-born activists.

deportation Expulsion of an undesirable alien from a country.

criminal syndicalism laws State laws that made membership in organizations that advocated communism or anarchism subject to criminal penalties.

Red Scare Wave of anticommunism in the United States in 1919 and 1920.

On September 16, 1920, a bomb went off at the corner of Wall and Broad Streets in New York City—the symbolic center of American capitalism, opposite the headquarters of J. P. Morgan and the New York Stock Exchange. Thirty-three people died and some two hundred were injured. The bomb came as the Red Scare was subsiding. Like the bombs of 1919, the person responsible has never been positively identified. *Brown Brothers.*

eral strike and more bombings. When nothing happened, many concluded that the radical threat might have been overstated.

As the Red Scare sputtered to an end, in May 1920, police in Massachusetts arrested **Nicola Sacco and Bartolomeo Vanzetti**, both Italian-born anarchists, and charged them with robbery and murder. Despite inconclusive evidence and the accused men's protestations of innocence, a jury found them guilty, and they were sentenced to death. Many Americans argued that the two had been convicted because of their political beliefs and Italian origins. Further, many doubted that they had received a fair trial because of the nativism and antiradicalism that infected the judge and jury. Over loud protests at home and abroad and after long appeals, both men were executed in 1927. (Historians continue to

debate the evidence in the case. Several have concluded that Sacco was probably guilty and Vanzetti innocent; others insist that both were innocent and that the state police concealed evidence.)

Race Riots and Lynchings

The racial tensions of the war years continued into the postwar period. Black soldiers encountered more

---

Nicola Sacco and Bartolomeo Vanzetti   Italian anarchists convicted in 1921 of the murder of a Braintree, Massachusetts, factory paymaster and theft of a $16,000 payroll; in spite of public protests on their behalf, they were electrocuted in 1927.

acceptance and less discrimination in Europe than they had ever known at home. In May 1919, the NAACP journal *Crisis* expressed what the more militant returning soldiers felt:

> We return. We return from fighting. We return fighting. Make way for Democracy! We saved it in France, and by the Great Jehovah, we will save it in the U.S.A., or know the reason why.

Some whites, North and South, greeted homecoming black troops with furious violence intended to restore prewar race relations. Southern mobs lynched ten returning black soldiers, some still in uniform. Rioters lynched more than seventy blacks in the first year after the war and burned eleven victims alive.

Rioting also struck outside the South. In July violence reached the nation's capital, where white mobs, many of them soldiers and sailors, attacked blacks throughout the city for three days, killing several. Unprotected, the city's African Americans organized their own defense, sometimes arming themselves. In Chicago in late July, war raged between white and black mobs for nearly two weeks, despite peacekeeping efforts by the militia. The rioting caused thirty-eight deaths (fifteen white, twenty-three black). More than a thousand families—nearly all black—were burned out of their homes. In Omaha in September, a mob tried to hang the mayor when he bravely stood between them and a black prisoner accused of rape. Police saved the mayor but not the prisoner.

By the end of 1919, race riots had flared in more than two dozen places. The year saw not only rampant lynchings, but also the appearance of a new Ku Klux Klan (see page 470). Despite violence and coercion directed at African Americans, some things had changed. As W. E. B. Du Bois observed, black veterans "would never be the same again. You cannot ask them to go back to what they were before. They cannot, for they are not the same men."

Amending the Constitution: Prohibition and Woman Suffrage

In the midst of the turmoil at the end of the war, two of the great crusades of the Progressive Era finally realized their goals. Both had roots deep in the nineteenth century, and both had attracted numerous and diverse supporters during the Progressive Era. Prohibition was adopted as the Eighteenth Amendment to the Constitution, and woman suffrage as the Nineteenth Amendment. In some ways, these two measures marked the last gasp of the reforming zeal that had energized much of progressivism.

Spearheaded by the Anti-Saloon League (see page 644), prohibition advocates convinced Congress to pass a temporary prohibition measure in 1917, as a war measure to conserve grain. A more important victory for the "dry" forces came later that year, when Congress adopted and sent to the states the Eighteenth Amendment, prohibiting the manufacture, sale, or transportation of alcoholic beverages. Intense and single-minded lobbying by dry advocates persuaded three-fourths of the state legislatures to ratify the amendment in 1919, and it took effect in January 1920.

In June 1919, by a narrow margin, Congress proposed the Nineteenth Amendment, to enfranchise women over 21, and sent it to the states for ratification. After a grueling, state-by-state battle, ratification came in August 1920. Though many women by then already exercised the franchise, especially in western states, ratification meant that the electorate for the 1920 elections was significantly expanded.

The Election of 1920

Republicans confidently expected to regain the White House in 1920. The Democrats had lost their congressional majorities in the 1918 elections, and the postwar confusion and disillusionment often focused on Wilson. One reporter described the stricken president as the "sacrificial whipping boy for the present bitterness."

The reaction against Wilson almost guaranteed election for any competent Republican nominee. Several candidates attracted significant support, notably former army chief of staff General Leonard Wood, Illinois governor Frank Lowden, and California senator Hiram Johnson. However, no candidate could muster a majority of the convention delegates. Harry Daugherty, campaign manager for Ohio senator Warren G. Harding, had foreseen such a deadlock months earlier and had predicted that it would be broken by a compromise candidate, chosen at about "eleven minutes after two o'clock on Friday morning," by about "fifteen or twenty men, bleary-eyed and perspiring profusely from the heat." And so it was. A small group of party leaders met late at night in a smoke-filled hotel room and picked Harding. Even some of his supporters were unenthusiastic—one called him "the best of the second-raters." For vice president, the Republicans nominated

Calvin Coolidge, the Massachusetts governor who had broken the Boston police strike.

The Democrats also suffered severe divisions. After forty-four ballots, they chose James Cox, the governor of Ohio, as their presidential candidate. For vice president, they nominated Wilson's assistant secretary of the navy, Franklin D. Roosevelt, a remote cousin of Theodore Roosevelt.

Usually described as good-natured and likable—and sometimes as bumbling—Harding had published a small-town newspaper in Marion, Ohio, until his wife Florence and some of his friends pushed him into politics. He eventually won election to the Senate. Unhappy with his marriage, Harding apparently found contentment with a series of mistresses. The press knew of Harding's liaisons but never reported them.

An uproar arose, however, over a claim by an Ohio professor that Harding's ancestry included African Americans. The story spread rapidly, and a reporter soon asked Harding, "Do you have any Negro blood?" Harding replied mildly, "How do I know, Jim? One of my ancestors may have jumped the fence." The allegation, and Harding's response to it, apparently did not hurt his cause. Most of Harding's campaign reflected his promise to "return to normalcy," and the voters responded with enthusiasm to the notion of returning to "normal" after the stress of the war and the immediate postwar years.

Republicans won in a landslide. Harding took thirty-seven of the forty-eight states and 60 percent of the popular vote—the largest popular majority up to that time. Wilson had hoped the election might be a "solemn referendum" on the League of Nations, but it proved more a reaction to the war and its aftermath—a war launched with lofty ideals that turned sour at Versailles, the high cost of living, the strikes and riots of 1919. Americans, it seemed, had tasted enough idealism and sacrifice for a while.

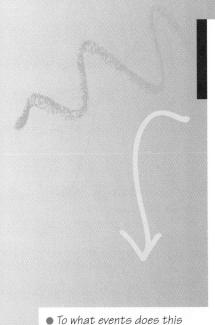

INDIVIDUAL VOICES

Examining a Primary Source

Woodrow Wilson Proposes His Fourteen Points

President Woodrow Wilson spoke to a joint session of Congress on January 8, 1918, and presented his objectives for peace, including his Fourteen Points. This is a condensed version of that speech.

● *To what events does this passage refer? To whom is it directed?*

. . . It will be our wish and purpose that the processes of peace, when they are begun, shall be absolutely open . . . . The day of conquest and aggrandizement is gone by; so is also the day of secret [treaties] . . . . ●

We entered this war because violations of right had occurred which touched us to the quick and made the life of our own people impossible unless they were corrected and the world secure once and for all against their recurrence. What we demand in this war, therefore, is nothing peculiar to ourselves. It is that the world be made fit and safe to live in; and particularly that it be made safe for every peace-loving nation which, like our own, wishes to live its own life, determine its own institutions, be assured of justice and fair dealing by

● How do these statements compare with the outcome of the peace conference?

● What are the connections between Points I through V and the causes of the war in general, and the reasons for America's entrance into the war in particular?

● Was Wilson creating unrealistic expectations with statements such as these?

● Compare Wilson's reasons, as stated here, for committing America to war with Alvin York's reasons, as he understood them, for his going to war.

the other peoples of the world as against force and selfish aggression. All the peoples of the world are in effect partners in this interest ● . . . . The program of the world's peace, therefore, is our program; and that program, the only possible program, as we see it, is this:

I. Open covenants of peace, openly arrived at, after which there shall be no private international understandings of any kind but diplomacy shall proceed always frankly and in the public view.

II. Absolute freedom of navigation upon the seas, outside territorial waters. . . .

III. The removal, so far as possible, of all economic barriers and the establishment of an equality of trade conditions among all the nations. . . .

IV. Adequate guarantees given and taken that national armaments will be reduced to the lowest point consistent with domestic safety.

V. A free, open-minded, and absolutely impartial adjustment of all colonial claims, based upon a strict observance of the principle that . . . the interests of the populations concerned must have equal weight with the equitable claims of the government whose title is to be determined. . . . ●

[Points VI–XIII laid out specific territorial restorations or adjustments.]

XIV. A general association of nations must be formed under specific covenants for the purpose of affording mutual guarantees of political independence and territorial integrity to great and small states alike. . . .

For such arrangements and covenants we are willing to fight and to continue to fight until they are achieved; but only because we wish the right to prevail and desire a just and stable peace such as can be secured only by removing the chief provocations to war. . . .

An evident principle runs through the whole program I have outlined. It is the principle of justice to all peoples and nationalities, and their right to live on equal terms of liberty and safety with one another, whether they be strong or weak. . . . ●

The people of the United States could act upon no other principle. . . . The moral climax of this the culminating and final war for human liberty has come. . . . ●

SUMMARY

Woodrow Wilson took office expecting to focus on domestic policy, not foreign affairs. He fulfilled some Democratic Party commitments to anti-imperialism but intervened extensively in the Caribbean. He also intervened in Mexico but failed to accomplish all of his objectives there.

When war broke out in Europe in 1914, Wilson declared the United States to be neutral, and most Americans agreed. German submarine warfare and British restrictions on commerce, however, threat-ened traditional definitions of neutrality. Wilson secured a German pledge to refrain from unrestricted submarine warfare. He was re-elected in 1916 on the argument that "he kept us out of war." Shortly after he won re-election, however, the Germans violated their pledge, and in April 1917 Wilson asked for war against Germany.

The war changed nearly every aspect of the nation's economic and social life. To overcome inefficiency, the federal government developed a high degree of centralized economic planning. Fearing that opposition to the war might limit mobilization, the Wilson administration tried to mold public opinion and to restrict dissent. When the federal government backed collective bargaining, unions registered important gains. In response to labor shortages, more women and African Americans entered the industrial work force, and many African Americans moved to northern and midwestern industrial cities.

Germany launched a major offensive in early 1918, expecting to achieve victory before American troops could make a difference. However, the AEF helped to break the German advance, and the Germans requested an armistice.

In his Fourteen Points, Wilson expressed his goals for peace. Facing opposition from the Allies, Wilson compromised at the peace conference but hoped that the League of Nations would be able to maintain the peace. Fearing the obligations that League membership might place on the United States, enough senators opposed the treaty to defeat it. Thus, the United States did not become a member of the League.

In the United States, the end of the war brought disillusionment and a year of high prices, costly strikes, a Red Scare, and race riots and lynchings. In 1920 the nation returned to its Republican preference when it elected Warren G. Harding, a mediocre conservative, to the White House.

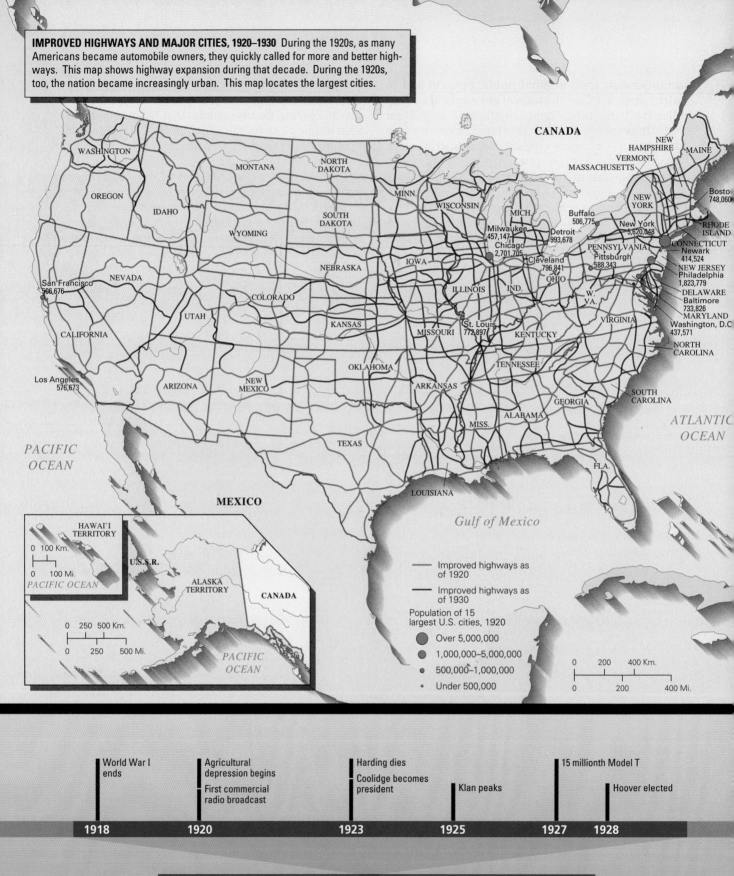

IMPROVED HIGHWAYS AND MAJOR CITIES, 1920–1930 During the 1920s, as many Americans became automobile owners, they quickly called for more and better highways. This map shows highway expansion during that decade. During the 1920s, too, the nation became increasingly urban. This map locates the largest cities.

CANADA

NEW HAMPSHIRE
MAINE
VERMONT
MASSACHUSETTS

WASHINGTON

MONTANA

NORTH DAKOTA

MINN.

WISCONSIN

NEW YORK

Bosto
748,060

OREGON

IDAHO

SOUTH DAKOTA

WYOMING

MICH.

Buffalo
506,775

New York
5,620,048

RHODE ISLAND

CONNECTICUT

Milwaukee
457,147

Detroit
993,678

Newark
414,524

Chicago
2,701,705

Cleveland
796,841

PENNSYLVANIA
Pittsburgh
588,343

NEW JERSEY
Philadelphia
1,823,779

San Francisco
506,676

NEVADA

IOWA

OHIO

DELAWARE
Baltimore
733,826

MARYLAND

COLORADO

NEBRASKA

ILLINOIS

IND.

W. VA.

Washington, D.C
437,571

UTAH

KANSAS

MISSOURI

St. Louis
772,897

KENTUCKY

VIRGINIA

NORTH CAROLINA

CALIFORNIA

OKLAHOMA

TENNESSEE

Los Angeles
576,673

ARIZONA

NEW MEXICO

ARKANSAS

SOUTH CAROLINA

GEORGIA

ALABAMA

MISS.

TEXAS

LOUISIANA

FLA.

ATLANTIC OCEAN

PACIFIC OCEAN

MEXICO

Gulf of Mexico

HAWAI'I TERRITORY

0 100 Km.
0 100 Mi.

PACIFIC OCEAN

U.S.S.R.

ALASKA TERRITORY

CANADA

0 250 500 Km.
0 250 500 Mi.

PACIFIC OCEAN

— Improved highways as of 1920

— Improved highways as of 1930

Population of 15 largest U.S. cities, 1920

⬤ Over 5,000,000

● 1,000,000–5,000,000

• 500,000–1,000,000

· Under 500,000

0 200 400 Km.
0 200 400 Mi.

World War I ends

Agricultural depression begins

First commercial radio broadcast

Harding dies

Coolidge becomes president

Klan peaks

15 millionth Model T

Hoover elected

1918 1920 1923 1925 1927 1928

1850 1900 1950 2000

Prosperity Decade, 1920–1928

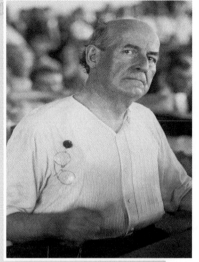

WILLIAM JENNINGS BRYAN

William Jennings Bryan is pictured here in the courtroom in Dayton, Tennessee, where the Scopes Trial was being held on July 15, 1925. The weather was very warm, and the crowded courtroom magnified the heat, so Bryan and Darrow took the lead in shedding their coats and ties. The photograph captures the intensity of Bryan's commitment to his cause of opposing the teaching of evolution. ©*Bettmann/Corbis.*

William Jennings Bryan

William Jennings Bryan, the three-time Democratic candidate for president, wrote to his son in 1925 to urge him to join in a court case. "The trial will become one of the greatest trials in history," Bryan predicted, and he was right.

Bryan, aged 65, had been an enthusiastic spokesman for several causes since resigning as secretary of state in 1915. He had opposed American entry into the war, advocated prohibition and woman suffrage, and defended the League of Nations. And he'd moved to Florida and earned some extra income by promoting Florida real estate.

Bryan also became actively engaged in seeking to restore Protestant Christianity to its "fundamentals." Where Christian "modernists" tried to reconcile religious belief with science, fundamentalists rejected anything— including science—that they found incompatible with the Bible. For Bryan and many others, the central issue was evolution. "You may trace your ancestry back to the monkey if you find pleasure or pride in doing so," he said, but added, "You shall not connect me to your family tree without more evidence." Bryan blamed the teaching of evolution for a loss of faith among many people, especially those who had attended college, and he attributed many of the problems of his day—materialism, social conflict, war—to a loss of faith. At base, Bryan knew very little about science, and he often fell back on rhetorical flourishes rather than reasoned analysis: "It is better to trust in the Rock of Ages," he repeatedly proclaimed, "than to know the age of rocks."

The trial he described to his son was that of John Scopes, a high school teacher in Dayton, Tennessee. When the governor of Tennessee signed a new state law that prohibited the teaching of evolution in Tennessee public schools, the American Civil Liberties Union (ACLU) offered legal counsel to any teacher who challenged the state. Urged on by local citizens, Scopes admitted to teaching evolution and was charged with violating the law. Bryan joined the prosecution, at its request. The ACLU defense team was headed by Clarence Darrow, aged 68, the nation's most famous defense attorney and a liberal war-horse for many progressive causes that Bryan had also backed. Dayton itself became a circus of journalists, movie cameramen, radio crews, traveling evangelists, and, as Scopes put it, "screwballs."

That Scopes broke the law was never in question. What was on trial was the law itself. For some, the case was even more basic: the Bible versus science. For Bryan, the issue was simple enough: "the *right* of the *people*, speaking through the legislature, to control the schools which they *create* and *support*." The defense lawyers, however, argued that, in the words of Thomas Jefferson, "to attempt to compel people to accept a religious doctrine by act of law was to make not Christians but hypocrites." Darrow was more blunt: his purpose, he

said, was "preventing bigots and ignoramuses from controlling the education of the United States."

The high point of the trial came when Darrow put Bryan on the witness stand as an expert on the Bible. After that confrontation, the verdict was anticlimactic. Scopes was found guilty, but his conviction was reversed on a technicality. The Tennessee law against teaching evolution was repealed in 1967, and similar laws were in force in other states until a Supreme Court decision in 1968. As recently as 1999, the Kansas State Board of Education deleted evolution from that state's science curriculum, but it was restored two years later after voters ousted two of the anti-evolution board members.

INTRODUCTION

Called the "Jazz Age" and the "Roaring Twenties," the 1920s sometimes seem to be a swirl of conflicting images. Prohibition marked an ambitious effort to preserve the values of nineteenth-century America while "flappers" were flaunting new freedoms for women. The booming stock market promised prosperity to all with money to invest even as thousands of farmers were abandoning the land because they could not survive financially. Business leaders celebrated the expansion of the economy while many wage earners in manufacturing endured the destruction of their unions and saw their legal protections evaporate. White-sheeted Klansmen marched as self-proclaimed defenders of Protestant American values and white supremacy, as African Americans' cultural expression in art, literature, and music was flowering.

Amid these seeming paradoxes, the economy roared along like a shiny new roadster, fueled by easy credit and consumer spending, virtually unregulated.

PROSPERITY DECADE

- What was the basis for the economic expansion of the 1920s?
- What weaknesses existed within the economy?

By 1920, the industrialization of America was substantially achieved—the foundations of the corporate economy were in place, controlled by large industrial corporations, most of them run by professional managers. During the 1920s, the rise and growth of the automobile industry dramatized the new prominence of industries producing **consumer goods**. This significant change in direction carried implications for advertising, banking, and even the stock market.

The Economics of Prosperity

The end of the war in 1918 brought cancellation of orders for war supplies from ships to uniforms. At the same time, large numbers of recently discharged military and naval personnel swelled the ranks of job seekers. Such postwar conditions often bring on a recession or depression. At the end of World War I, however, no immediate economic collapse ensued. Given wartime shortages and overtime pay, many Americans had been earning more than they could spend. At the end of the war, their eagerness to spend helped to delay the postwar slump until 1920 and

---

consumer goods   Products such as clothing, food, automobiles, and radios, intended for purchase and use by individuals or households, as opposed to products such as steel beams, locomotives, and electrical generators, intended for purchase and use by corporations.

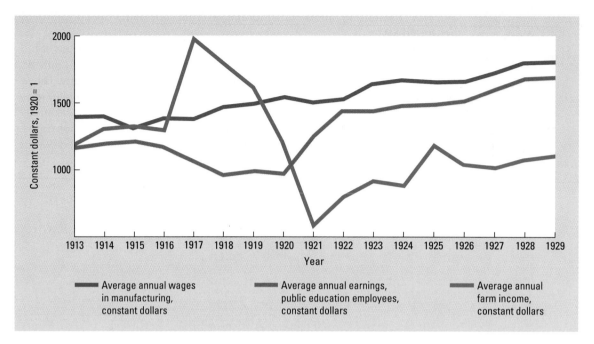

FIGURE 23.1 **Patterns of Annual Income for Three Groups of Americans, 1913–1929** This graph depicts the patterns of annual income for three different groups of Americans. Income as been converted to constant dollars, meaning that the dollar amounts are adjusted for changes in the purchasing power of the dollar. In this case, 1920 is used as the base year for calculating the value of the dollar. Wages for manufacturing workers rose steadily during the war years, leveled during the recession of the early 1920s, then rose again. For public education employees—mostly teachers—real earnings fell dramatically with the inflation of the war years and the postwar recession, then rose to parallel those of manufacturing workers. Farmers, in 1913, had a boom in income during the war, but then saw their real earnings plunge at the end of the war with only a modest recovery after the recession of the early 1920s. *Source:* U.S. Department of Commerce, Bureau of Census, *Historical Statistics of the United States, Colonial Times to 1970*, Bicentennial Edition, 2 vols. (Washington: Government Printing Office, 1975). I:167, 170, 483.

1921. The **gross national product** (GNP) dropped by only 4.3 percent between 1919 and 1920, then fell by 8.6 percent between 1920 and 1921. During the war, unemployment affected only about 1 percent of the work force. The jobless rate increased to 5 percent in 1920 and 12 percent in 1921. Some employers also cut hours and wages. Figure 23.1 presents earnings for three groups of Americans and indicates the impact of recession in the early 1920s. However, reduced earnings, unemployment, and declining demand halted the rampaging inflation of 1918 and 1919. In fact, consumer prices fell from 1920 to 1921, led by a 24 percent drop in the price of food.

The economy quickly rebounded. The gross national product increased by more than 15 percent between 1921 and 1922, a bigger jump than during the booming war years. Unemployment remained at 2–5 percent from 1923 through 1929, and prices for most manufactured goods remained relatively sta-

ble. Income for many increased. Thus many Americans seemed slightly better off by 1929 than in 1920: they earned more (at least in constant dollars) and paid somewhat less for necessities.

Targeting Consumers

By the 1920s, many business leaders understood that persuading Americans to consume an array of products was crucial to keeping the economy healthy. In 1921 General Foods Company invented Betty Crocker to give its baking products a wom-

gross national product The total market value of all goods and services that a nation produces during a specified period; now generally referred to as gross domestic product.

chronology

America in the 1920s

1908	Henry Ford introduces Model T General Motors formed
1914	Universal Negro Improvement Association founded War breaks out in Europe
1915	D. W. Griffith's *Birth of a Nation* Ku Klux Klan revives
1918	World War I ends
1920	Eighteenth Amendment (instituting Prohibition) takes effect Nineteenth Amendment (granting women the vote) takes effect Sinclair Lewis's *Main Street* Warren G. Harding elected president First commercial radio broadcasts
1920–1921	Nationwide recession Agricultural depression begins
1921	Temporary immigration quotas Halitosis sells Listerine Farm Bloc formed
1921–1922	Washington Naval Conference
1922	Fordney-McCumber Tariff Nine Power Pact Sinclair Lewis's *Babbitt* T. S. Eliot's *The Waste Land*
1923	Harding dies Calvin Coolidge becomes president Marcus Garvey convicted of mail fraud Jean Toomer's *Cane* American Indian Defense Association formed France occupies Ruhr Valley
1923–1927	Harding administration scandals revealed
1924	National Origins Act Coolidge elected First disposable handkerchiefs Wheaties marketed as "Breakfast of Champions" Crossword puzzle fad Full citizenship for American Indians Dawes Plan U.S. forces withdraw from Dominican Republic
1925	Scopes trial Bruce Barton's *The Man Nobody Knows* F. Scott Fitzgerald's *The Great Gatsby* Ku Klux Klan claims 5 million members Klan leader convicted of murder One automobile for every three residents in Los Angeles Chrysler Corporation formed
1926	Florida real-estate boom collapses Ernest Hemingway's *The Sun Also Rises* Gertrude Ederle swims English Channel United States intervenes in Nicaragua
1927	Coolidge vetoes McNary-Haugen bill Charles Lindbergh's transatlantic flight Duke Ellington conducts jazz at Cotton Club Peace of Titiapa Augusto Sandino begins guerilla war in Nicaragua
1928	Coolidge vetoes McNary-Haugen again Ford introduces Model A Kellogg-Briand Pact Herbert Hoover elected
1930	Rafael Trujillo seizes power in Dominican Republic
1931	Al Capone convicted and imprisoned
1934	U.S. forces withdraw from Haiti

anly, domestic image. In 1924 General Mills first advertised Wheaties as the "Breakfast of Champions," thereby tying consumption of cold cereal to the popularity of sports. Americans responded by buying those products and others with similarly creative pitches. "We grew up founding our dreams on the infinite promises of American advertising," Zelda Sayre Fitzgerald later wrote.

Advertising promised that those who used Listerine to eliminate halitosis would gain friends and even romance. *Courtesy Warner-Lambert Company.*

The marketing of Listerine demonstrates a new dimension in advertising. Listerine had been devised as a general antiseptic, but in 1921 Gerard Lambert devised a more persuasive—and profitable—approach when he plucked the obscure term *halitosis* from a medical journal. Through aggressive advertising using the word, he fostered anxieties about the impact of bad breath on popularity and made millions by selling Listerine to combat the offensive condition. Until then, few Americans had been concerned about freshening their breath. Afterward, other entrepreneurs also sought to sell products to meet needs that consumers had not identified before being alerted to them by advertising.

Changes in fashion also encouraged increased consumption. The chic new look of short hairstyles for women, for example, led to the development of hair salons and stimulated sales of the recently invented **bobby pin**. Cigarette advertisers began to target women, as when the American Tobacco Company advised women to "Reach for a Lucky instead of a sweet" to attain a fashionably slim figure. Style and

technology combined to create disposable products, thereby promoting regular, recurring consumer buying of throwaway items. Technological advances in the processing of wood cellulose fiber led in 1921 to the marketing of Kotex, the first manufactured disposable sanitary napkin, and in 1924 to the first disposable handkerchiefs, later known as Kleenex tissues.

Technological advances contributed in other ways to the growth of consumer-oriented manufacturing. In 1920 about one-third of all residences had electricity. By the end of the decade, electrical power had reached nearly all urban homes (but fewer than 10 percent of farm homes). As the number of residences with electricity increased, advertisers stressed the time and labor that housewives could save by using electric washing machines, irons, vacuum cleaners, and toasters. Between 1919 and 1929, consumer expenditures for household appliances grew by more than 120 percent.

Increased consumption encouraged a change in people's spending habits. Before the war, most families saved their money until they could pay cash for what they needed, but in the 1920s many retailers urged buyers to "Buy now, pay later." And many consumers responded, taking home a new radio today and worrying about paying for it tomorrow. By the late 1920s, about 15 percent of all retail purchases were made through the installment plan, including most furniture, phonographs, washing machines, and refrigerators. Charge accounts in department stores also became popular, and **finance companies** (which made loans) grew rapidly.

The Automobile: Driving the Economy

The automobile epitomized the new consumer-oriented economy of the 1920s. Early automobiles were luxuries, but **Henry Ford** developed a mass-production system that drove down production costs.

---

bobby pin   Small metal hair clip with ends pressed tightly together, designed for holding short or "bobbed" hair in place.

finance company   Business that makes loans to clients based on some form of collateral, such as a new car, thus allowing a form of installment buying when sellers do not extend credit.

Henry Ford   Inventor and manufacturer who founded the Ford Motor Company in 1903 and pioneered mass production in the auto industry.

"How did he ever get the money to buy a car"

Perhaps he *doesn't* make as much as you do—but he took
advantage of this quick, easy, sure way to own an automobile

Ford Weekly Purchase Plan

Henry Ford constantly worked to reduce car prices on his
cars. He also promoted installment buying, promising in
this ad that "with even the most modest income, [every
family] can now afford a car of their own." This ad also
encouraged impulse buying: "You live but once and the
years roll by quickly. Why wait for tomorrow for things
that you rightfully should enjoy today?" *Library of Congress.*

Ford, a former mechanic, built his success on the
Model T, introduced in 1908. A Model-T Ford was a
dream come true for many middle-income Americans, and families came to love their ungraceful but
reliable "Tin Lizzies" (so named because of their
lightweight metal bodies). By 1927, Ford had produced more than 15 million of them, dominating the
market by selling the largest possible number of
cars at the lowest possible price. "Get the prices
down to the buying power," Ford ordered. His dictatorial style of management combined with technological advances and high worker productivity to
bring the price of a new Model T as low as $290 by
1927 (equivalent to about $2,900 today). Cheap to
buy, the Model T sacrificed style and comfort for
durability, ease of maintenance, and the ability to
handle almost any road. It made Henry Ford into
a folk hero—a wealthy one. By 1925, Ford Motor
Company showed a daily profit of some $25,000.

Ford's company provides an example of efforts
by American entrepreneurs to reduce labor costs
by improving efficiency. In the process, however,
work on Ford's assembly line became a thoroughly
dehumanizing experience. Ford workers were prohibited from talking, sitting, smoking, singing, or

even whistling while working. As one critic put it,
workers were to "put nut 14 on bolt 132, repeating,
repeating, repeating until their hands shook and
their legs quivered."

Ford, however, paid his workers well, and they
could increase their pay more by completing the
company's Americanization classes. Ford workers
earned enough, in fact, to afford their own Model
T's. Ford's high wages pushed other automakers to
increase pay for their workers as well, to keep their
best workers from defecting to Ford. Auto workers
thus came to enjoy some of the consumer buying
previously restricted to middle- and upper-income
groups.

Not only streamlined production but also competition helped to keep auto prices low. Other automobile companies challenged Ford's predominance,
notably General Motors (GM), founded by William
Durant in 1908, and Chrysler Corporation, created
by Walter Chrysler in 1925. GM and Chrysler
adopted many of Ford's production techniques, but
their cars also offered more comfort and style than
the Model T. Ford only ended production of the
Model T in 1927, when Chevrolet passed Ford in
sales. The next year, Ford introduced the Model A,
which incorporated some features touted by his
competitors.

The automobile came to symbolize not only the
ability of many Americans to acquire material goods
but also technology, progress, and the freedom of
the open road. The industry worked to promote this
heady image. One car salesman remarked in 1926,
"When I sold a car, I sold it with the honest conviction that I was doing the buyer a favor in helping
him to take his place in a big forward movement."
American consumers were receptive. By the late
1920s, about 80 percent of the world's registered
vehicles were in the United States. By then, America's roadways sported nearly one automobile for
every five people.

The automobile industry in the 1920s often led
the way in devising new sales techniques. Installment buying became so widespread that by 1927
two-thirds of all American automobiles were sold
on credit. GM led the way in introducing new models every year. This practice enticed owners to trade

Model T   Lightweight automobile that Ford produced
from 1908 to 1927 and sold at the lowest possible price
on the theory that an affordable car would be more
profitable than an expensive one.

Pictured here is the assembly line at Ford's main assembly plant in 1928. Model-A Fords are under production, as assembly line workers quickly perform the same task on car after car, as the chassis moves past them at the rate of six feet per minute. Ford pioneered the assembly line as a way to reduce both cost and dependence on skilled workers. He paid the highest wages in Detroit but required complete obedience from his workers, even to the point of prohibiting whistling while at work. *From the Collections of Henry Ford Museum & Greenfield Village.*

in their cars just to keep up with new fashions in design, color, and optional features. Dozens of small automakers closed when they could not compete with Chrysler, Ford, and GM—the Big Three. By 1929, the Big Three were making 83 percent of all cars manufactured in the country. The industry had become an **oligopoly**.

Changes in Banking and Business

Just as Henry Ford helped to bring automobiles within reach of most Americans, so did **A. P. Giannini** revolutionize banking. The son of Italian immigrants, Giannini founded the Bank of Italy in 1904 as a bank for shopkeepers and workers in the Italian neighborhood of San Francisco. Until then, most banks had only one location, in the center of a city, and limited their services to businesses and substantial citizens with hefty accounts. Giannini not only based his bank on dealings with ordinary people but also opened branches throughout California, near people's homes and workplaces. Called the greatest innovator in twentieth-century American banking, Giannini broadened the base of banking by encouraging working people not only to open small checking and savings accounts but also to borrow for such investments as car purchases. In the process, his bank—later renamed the Bank of America—became the third largest in the nation by 1927.

Giannini's bank and Ford's auto factory survived as relics of family management in a new world of modern corporations with large bureaucracies. Ownership and control continued to grow apart, as salaried managers came to run most big businesses.

The number of corporations increased steadily throughout the 1920s, but a great corporate merger wave also accelerated as the 1920s progressed. These mergers continued earlier patterns toward greater economic concentration. By 1930, 5 percent of American corporations were receiving 85 percent of all net corporate income, up from 78 percent in 1921.

Leading entrepreneurs emerged as popular and respected public figures. Perhaps the ultimate glorification of the entrepreneur came in 1925, in a book entitled *The Man Nobody Knows*. The author, Bruce Barton (later founder of a leading advertising agency), suggested that Jesus Christ could best be understood as a business executive who "had picked up twelve men from the bottom ranks of business and forged them into an organization that conquered

oligopoly   An industry or market dominated by a few firms.

A. P. Giannini   Italian American who changed the banking industry by opening multiple branches and encouraging the use of banks for small accounts and personal loans.

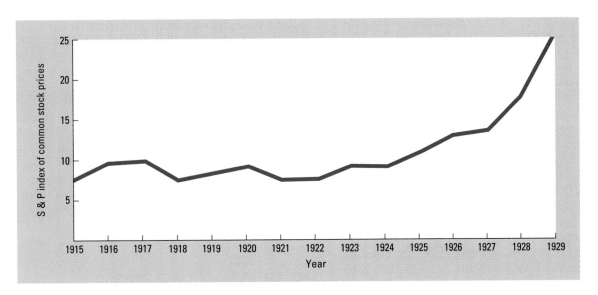

FIGURE 23.2 Stock Prices, 1915–1929   This graph shows the Standard and Poor index of common stock prices. This index is based on the years 1941–1942 as the base years (the index = 10 for those years). The figures for other years show stock prices in comparison to the base year. The Great Bull Market began in late 1924/early 1925 and roared upward until late 1929. *Source:* U.S. Department of Commerce, Bureau of Census, *Historical Statistics of the United States, Colonial Times to 1970,* Bicentennial Edition, 2 vols. (Washington: Government Printing Office, 1975). II:10-4.

the world." Portraying Jesus' parables as "the most powerful advertisements of all time," Barton's book led the nonfiction bestseller lists for two years.

"Get Rich Quick"— Speculative Mania

More than ever before, the stock market captured people's imagination as the fast track to riches. Stock market speculation—buying a stock with the expectation of making money by selling it at a higher price—ran rampant. Articles in popular periodicals proclaimed that everyone could participate and get rich in no time, even with a small investment. By 1929, 4 million Americans owned stock, equivalent to about 10 percent of American households.

Just as Americans purchased cars and radios on the installment plan, some also bought stock on credit. It was possible to purchase stock listed at $100 a share with as little as $10 down and the other $90 "on margin"—that is, owed to the stockbroker. If the stock price advanced to $150, the investor could sell, pay off the broker, and gain a profit of $50 (500 percent!) on the $10 investment. Unfortunately, if the stock price fell to $50, the investor would still owe $90 to the broker. Actually, fewer than 1 percent

of those who bought stocks did so on margin, and the size of the margin rarely exceeded 45 or 50 percent. A larger number of people borrowed money to buy stocks. Buying stocks with borrowed money, however, carried the same potential for disaster as buying on margin.

Driven partly by real economic growth and partly by speculation, stock prices rose higher and higher (see Figure 23.2). Standard and Poor's index of common stock prices tripled between 1920 and 1929. As long as the market stayed **bullish** and stock prices kept climbing, prosperity seemed endless.

The ease of borrowing funds and the ever-rising stock prices and corporate dividends of the 1920s encouraged the creation of holding companies (see page 534)—organizations designed not to sell actual goods or services but to keep dividends flowing to investors. Samuel Insull created a vast empire of electrical utilities companies. Much of his enterprise— and others like it—consisted of holding companies,

---

bullish   Optimistic or confident; when referring to the stock market, a bull market is when stock prices are going up, and a bear market is when stock prices come down.

which existed solely to own the stock of another company, some of which existed primarily to own the stock of yet another company. The entire structure rested on the dividends that the underlying **operating companies** produced. Those dividends enabled the holding companies to pay dividends on their bonds. Any interruption in the flow of dividends from the operating companies was likely to bring the collapse of the entire pyramid, swallowing up the investments of speculators.

Although the stock market held the nation's attention as the most popular path to instant riches, other speculative opportunities abounded. One of the most prominent was a land boom in Florida. During the early 1920s, people poured into Florida, especially Miami, attracted by the climate, the beaches, and the ease of travel from the cities of the chilly Northeast. Speculators began to buy land—almost any land—amid predictions that its value would soar. Stories circulated of land whose value had increased 1,500 percent over ten years. Like stocks, land was bought with borrowed money, to be resold at a profit. Early in 1926, however, the population influx slowed, and the boom began to falter. It collapsed completely when a hurricane slammed into Miami in September 1926. By 1927, many Florida land speculators were facing bankruptcy.

Agriculture: Depression in the Midst of Prosperity

The prosperity never extended to agriculture, and farmers still made up nearly 30 percent of the work force in 1920. During the war, many farmers expanded their operations in response to government demands for more food, and exports of farm products nearly quadrupled. After the war, as European farmers resumed production, a glut of agricultural goods on world markets caused prices to fall. Exports of farm products dropped by half. Throughout the 1920s, American farmers consistently produced more than the domestic market could absorb, and this **overproduction** caused prices to fall.

The average farm's net income for the years 1917 to 1920 ranged between $1,196 and $1,395 per year (see Figure 23.1, which is calculated in constant dollars rather than current dollars). Farm income fell to a dreadful $517 in 1921, then slowly began to rise but never reached the levels of 1917 to 1920 until World War II. Although farmers' income fell, their mortgage payments more than doubled from prewar levels, partly because of debts that farmers had

incurred to expand production during the war. Tax increases, purchases of tractors and trucks—now necessities on most farms—and the growing cost of fertilizer and other essential supplies bit further into farmers' meager earnings.

As the farm economy continued to hemorrhage, the average value of an acre of farmland, in constant dollars, fell by more than half between 1920 and 1928. The average farm was actually less valuable in 1928 than in 1912. Thousands of people left farming each year, and the proportion of farmers in the work force fell from nearly 30 percent to less than 20 percent. The 1920s were not the prosperity decade for rural America.

THE "ROARING TWENTIES"

- What groups most challenged traditional social patterns during the 1920s? Why?
- What role did technology play in social change during the 1920s?

"The world broke in two in 1922 or thereabouts," wrote novelist Willa Cather, and she indicated her distaste for much that came after. F. Scott Fitzgerald, another novelist, agreed with the date but embraced the change. He believed 1922 marked "the peak of the younger generation," who brought about an "age of miracles"—that, he admitted, became an "age of excess." For most Americans, evidence of sudden and dramatic social change was easy to see, from automobiles, radios, and movies to a new youth culture and an impressive cultural outpouring by African Americans in northern cities.

Putting a People on Wheels: The Automobile and American Life

The automobile profoundly changed American patterns of living. Highways significantly shortened the traveling time from rural areas to cities, reducing the isolation of farm life. One farm woman, when asked

---

operating company   A company that exists to sell goods or services, as opposed to a holding company that exists to own other companies, including operating companies.

overproduction   Production that exceeds consumer need or demand.

why her family had an automobile but no indoor plumbing, responded, "Why, you can't go to town in a bathtub." Trucks allowed farmers to take more products to market more quickly and conveniently than ever before. Tractors significantly expanded the amount of land that one family could cultivate. Because the spread of gasoline-powered farm vehicles reduced the need for human farm labor, they stimulated migration to urban areas.

If the automobile changed rural life, it made an even more profound impact on life in the cities. The 1920 census, for the first time, recorded more Americans living in urban areas (defined as places having 2,500 people or more) than in rural ones. As the automobile freed suburbanites from their dependence on commuter rail lines, new suburbs mushroomed and streetcars steadily declined. Most of the new suburban growth was in the form of single-family houses. From 1922 through 1928, construction began on an average of 883,000 new homes each year. New home construction rivaled the auto industry as a major driving force behind economic growth.

As early as 1913, the automobile demonstrated its ability to strangle urban traffic. One response was the development of traffic lights. Various versions were tried, but the four-directional, three-color traffic light first appeared in Detroit in 1920. Traffic lights spread rapidly to other large cities, but traffic congestion nonetheless worsened. By 1920, more than 250,000 cars entered Manhattan each day; by 1926, cars in the evening rush hour in Manhattan crawled along at less than 3 miles per hour—slower than a person could walk—and many commuters had returned to trains and subways.

Los Angeles: Automobile Metropolis

Most of Manhattan was not designed to handle automobile traffic, but the fastest-growing major city of the early twentieth century—Los Angeles—was. The population of Los Angeles increased tenfold between 1900 and 1920, then more than doubled by 1930, reaching 2.2 million. Expansion of citrus fruit raising, major oil discoveries, and the development of the motion-picture industry laid an economic foundation for rapid population growth in southern California. Manufacturing also expanded—during the 1920s, the city moved from twenty-eighth to ninth place among American cities based on manufacturing. Lack of sufficient water threatened to limit growth until city officials diverted the Owens River to Los Angeles through a

In the 1920s, civic leaders in Los Angeles cultivated an image of perpetual sunshine, warm weather the year-round, and abundant water. This photo from the late 1920s includes some of these and more—the personal automobile, and, in this case, a sporty touring car with its top down, and wide boulevards lined with palm trees and other semitropical vegetation to emphasize the warm climate. *Los Angeles Public Library.*

233-mile-long aqueduct, opened in 1913. Throughout the 1920s, southern California promoters attracted hundreds of thousands of people by presenting an image of perpetual summer, tall palm trees lining wide boulevards filled with automobiles, fountains gushing water into the sunshine, and broad sandy beaches.

The growth of Los Angeles came as the automobile industry was promoting the notion of a car for every family and real-estate developers were propounding the ideal of the single-family home. By 1930, about 94 percent of all residences in Los Angeles were single-family homes, an unprecedented level for a major city, and Los Angeles consequently had the lowest urban population density in the nation.

Life in Los Angeles came to be organized around the automobile in ways unknown in most other major cities. The first modern supermarket, offering "one-stop shopping," appeared in Los Angeles, and the "Miracle Mile" along Wilshire Boulevard was the nation's first large shopping district designed for the automobile. Such innovations set the pace for new urban development everywhere. The *Los Angeles*

Times put it this way in 1926: "Our forefathers in their immortal independence creed set forth 'the pursuit of happiness' as an inalienable right of mankind. And how can one pursue happiness by any swifter and surer means . . . than by the use of the automobile?" By then, Los Angeles had one automobile for every three residents, twice the national average.

A Homogenized Culture Searches for Heroes

As the automobile cut traveling time and more people moved to urban areas, restrictive immigration laws were closing the door to immigrants from abroad. These factors, together with the new technologies of radio and film, began to **homogenize** the culture—that is, to make it increasingly uniform by breaking down cultural differences based on region or ethnicity.

The first commercial radio station began broadcasting in 1920. Within six years, 681 were operating. By 1930, 40 percent of all households had radios. By the mid-1920s, too, most towns of any size boasted at least one movie theater. Movie attendance increased rapidly, from a weekly average of 40 million people in 1922 to 80 million in 1929—the equivalent of two-thirds of the total population. As Americans all across the country tuned in to the same radio broadcast, and families in rural villages as well as urban neighborhoods laughed or wept at the same movie, radio and film did their part to homogenize life in the United States.

Radio and film joined newspapers and magazines in creating and publicizing national trends and fashions as Americans pursued one fad after another. After the opening of the fabulous tomb of the Egyptian pharaoh Tutankhamen in 1922, Americans developed a passion for things Egyptian. In 1924, crossword puzzle books captured the attention of many Americans, and contract bridge, a card game, became the rage soon after, in 1926. Such fads created markets for new consumer goods, from Egyptian-style furniture to crossword dictionaries to folding card tables.

The media also helped to create national sports heroes. In the 1920s, spectator sports became an obsession. Baseball had long been the pre-eminent national sport, and radio now began to broadcast baseball games nationwide. Other sports vied with baseball for national favor and for fans' dollars. Most Americans were familiar with the exploits of Lou Gehrig and Babe Ruth on the baseball diamond, Jack Dempsey and Gene Tunney in boxing, and

Rudolph Valentino, the leading male movie star of the 1920s, starred in such costume epics as *The Sheik* and *Son of the Sheik*. This poster advertises *Son of the Sheik*, which appeared after Valentino's death in 1926, at the age of 31, from complications following the removal of his appendix. *Billy Rose Theatre Collection, The New York Public Library.*

Bobby Jones, a golfer. Gertrude Ederle won national acclaim in 1926 when she became the first woman to swim the English Channel and did so two hours faster than any previous man. Fame extended even to racehorses, notably Man o' War.

The rapid spread of movie theaters created a new category of fame—the movie star. Charlie Chaplin,

homogenize To make something uniform throughout.

Charles Lindbergh chose photo settings in which he was alone with his plane, thereby emphasizing the individual nature of his flights. This photo was taken before his solo flight across the Atlantic. *Culver Pictures, Inc.*

Buster Keaton, Harold Lloyd, and others brought laughter to the screen. Tom Mix was the best known of those introducing the western as a rugged dramatic genre. Sex, too, sold movie tickets and made stars of Theda Bara, the **vamp**, and Clara Bow, the "It" girl. Rudolph Valentino soared to fame as a male sex symbol, with his most famous film, *The Sheik*, set in a fanciful Arabian desert.

The greatest popular hero of the 1920s, however, was neither an athlete nor an actor but a small-town airmail pilot named **Charles Lindbergh**. At the time, aviation was barely out of its infancy. The earliest regular airmail deliveries in the United States began in 1918, and night flying did not become routine until the mid-1920s. A few transatlantic flights had been logged by 1926, but the longest nonstop flight to date was from San Diego to New York— 2,500 miles.

Lindbergh, in 1927, decided to collect the prize of $25,000 offered by a New York hotel owner to the pilot of the first successful nonstop flight between New York and Paris—3,500 miles. His plane, *The Spirit of St. Louis*, was a stripped-down, one-engine craft. In a sleepless, $33\frac{1}{2}$-hour flight, Lindbergh earned both the $25,000 and the adoration of crowds on both sides of the Atlantic. In an age devoted to materialism and dominated by a corporate mentality, Lindbergh's accomplishment suggested that old-fashioned individualism, courage, and self-reliance could still triumph over odds and adversity.

Alienated Intellectuals

Lindbergh flew to Paris and became a living legend. Other Americans, too, went to Paris and other European cities in the 1920s, but for different reasons. These **expatriates** left the United States to escape what they considered America's intellectual shallowness, dull materialism, and spreading uniformity. As Malcolm Cowley put it in *Exile's Return* (1934), his memoir of his life in France, "by expatriating himself, by living in Paris, Capri or the South of France, the artist can break the puritan shackles, drink, live freely, and be wholly creative." He added that Paris in the 1920s "was a great machine for stimulating the nerves and sharpening the senses."

Though **Sinclair Lewis** and H. L. Mencken did not move to Paris, they were among the leading critics of middle-class materialism and uniformity. Lewis, in *Main Street* (1920), presented small-town, middle-class existence as not just boring but stifling. In *Babbitt* (1922), Lewis presented a suburban businessman (George F. Babbitt) as materialistic, narrow-minded, and complacent, speaking in clichés and buying every gadget on the market. H. L. Mencken, the influential editor of *The American Mercury*, relentlessly pilloried the "booboisie," jeered at all politicians (reformers and conservatives alike), and celebrated only those writers who shared his disdain for most of American life.

---

vamp   A woman who uses her sexuality to entrap and exploit men.

Charles Lindbergh   American aviator who made the first solo transatlantic flight in 1927 and became an international hero.

expatriate   A person who takes up long-term residence in a foreign country.

Sinclair Lewis   Novelist who satirized middle-class America in works such as *Babbitt* (1922) and became the first American to win the Nobel Prize for literature.

By the time this 1923 photo was taken, F. Scott Fitzgerald had soared to fame as author of two novels and two collections of short stories, most of them depicting the hedonistic youth culture of the Jazz Age. Zelda, a writer, too, was best known as the beautiful and tormented wife of the handsome author. *Papers of F. Scott Fitzgerald, Manuscript Division. Department of Rare Books and Special Collections, Princeton University Libraries.*

Other writers celebrated the seeking of pleasure and excitement. Edna St. Vincent Millay, a prominent poet, captured some of this spirit in 1920:

My candle burns at both ends;
It will not last the night;
But ah, my foes, and oh, my friends—
It gives a lovely light!

Where Millay celebrated social rebellion, F. Scott Fitzgerald, in *The Great Gatsby* (1925), revealed a grim side of the hedonism of the 1920s as he portrayed the pointless lives of wealthy pleasure seekers and their careless disregard for life and values. Ernest Hemingway, in *The Sun Also Rises* (1926), depicted disillusioned and frustrated expatriates. Others expatriates extended the theme of hopelessness. In

The Waste Land (1922), T. S. Eliot, a poet who had fled to England in 1915, presented the barrenness of modern life. Some writers even predicted the end of Western civilization.

Renaissance Among African Americans

For the most part, feelings of despair and disillusionment troubled white writers and intellectuals. Such sentiments were rarely apparent in the striking outpouring of literature, music, and art by African Americans in the 1920s.

Many blacks moved to northern cities in the 1920s, continuing patterns begun earlier. Harlem emerged as the largest black neighborhood in New York City and quickly came to symbolize the new urban life of African Americans. The term **Harlem Renaissance**, or Negro Renaissance, refers to a literary and artistic movement in which black artists and writers insisted on the value of black culture and drew upon African and African-American traditions in their writing, painting, and sculpture. Alain Locke, a leading black author, likened it to "a spiritual emancipation." Black actors, notably **Paul Robeson**, began to appear in serious theaters and earn acclaim for their abilities. Earlier black writers, especially Locke, James Weldon Johnson, and Claude McKay, encouraged and guided the novelists and poets of the Renaissance.

Among the movement's poets, Langston Hughes became the best known. His poetry rang with the voice of the people, for he sometimes used folk language to convey powerful images. Born in Joplin, Missouri, in 1902, Hughes began to write poetry in high school, briefly attended college, then worked and traveled in Africa and Europe. By 1925, he was a significant figure in the Harlem Renaissance, sometimes reading his poetry to the musical accompaniment of jazz. Some of his works present images from black history, such as "The Negro Speaks of Rivers"

Harlem Renaissance Literary and artistic movement in the 1920s, centered in Harlem, in which black writers and artists described and celebrated African-American life.

Paul Robeson African-American singer and actor prominent from the early 1920s through the 1950s, when he was driven from public life by repeated accusations that he was a Communist.

(1921), and others, such as "Song for a Dark Girl" (1927), vividly depict racism. Some of his poems look to the future with an expectation for change and for new choices, as in "I, Too" (1925):

> *I, too, sing America.*
> *I am the darker brother.*
> *They send me*
> *To eat in the kitchen*
> *When company comes,*
> *But I laugh,*
> *And eat well,*
> *And grow strong.*
> *Tomorrow*
> *I'll sit at the table*
> *When company comes.*
> *Nobody'll dare*
> *Say to me,*
> *"Eat in the kitchen,"*
> *Then.*
> *Besides*
> *They'll see*
> *How beautiful I am*
> *And be ashamed.*
> *I, too, am America.*

Other important writers included Zora Neale Hurston, who came from a poor southern family, won a scholarship to Barnard College, and began her long writing career with several short stories in the 1920s. Jean Toomer's novel *Cane* (1923), dealing with African Americans in rural Georgia and Washington, D.C., has been praised as "the most impressive product of the Negro Renaissance."

The 1920s have sometimes been called the Jazz Age. **Jazz** developed in the early twentieth century, drawing from several strains in African-American music, particularly the blues and ragtime (see page 669). Created and nurtured by African-American musicians in southern cities, especially New Orleans, jazz had been introduced to northern and white audiences by 1917. Jazz influenced leading white composers, notably George Gershwin, whose *Rhapsody in Blue* (1924) brought jazz into the symphony halls. Some attacked the new sound, claiming it encouraged people to abandon self-restraint, especially with regard to sex. But despite—or perhaps because of—such condemnation, the wail of the saxophone became as much a part of the 1920s as the roar of the roadster and the flicker of the movie projector.

The great black jazz musicians of the 1920s—Louis "Satchmo" Armstrong, Bessie Smith, Fletcher Henderson, Ferdinand "Jelly Roll" Morton, and

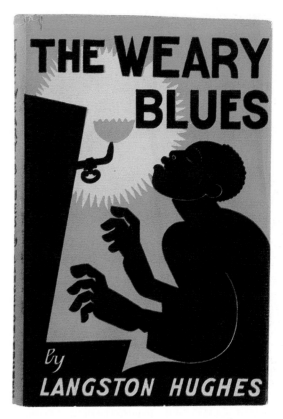

This is the original cover for *The Weary Blues*, the first book of poetry by Langston Hughes, published in 1926. Hughes later wrote that the book included some of the first blues that he had ever heard, dating to his childhood in Lawrence, Kansas. Both the reference to the blues in Hughes's poetry and the cover design for the book evoke the connection between music and poetry that was part of the Harlem Renaissance. *Picture Research Consultants & Archives.*

others—drew white audiences into black neighborhoods to hear them. Harlem came to be associated with exotic nightlife and glittering jazz clubs, with the Cotton Club the best known. There Edward "Duke" Ellington came in 1927 to lead the club band, and there he began to develop the works that made him one of the most respected American composers.

The fanfare of the Cotton Club was remote from the experience of most African Americans, but one

---

jazz   Style of music developed in America in the early twentieth century, characterized by strong, flexible rhythms and improvisation on basic melodies.

This was the cover of a special issue of *Survey Graphic* in March 1925. A popular magazine of the period, *Survey Graphic* devoted the entire issue to Harlem and the emergence of a new consciousness among its African-American residents. *Survey Graphic 1925.*

Louis Armstrong, born in 1900, first began to play the trumpet in New Orleans but emerged as a leading innovator in jazz after 1924, when he joined Fletcher Henderson's orchestra in New York. Some of his recordings from the 1920s are among the most original and imaginative contributions to jazz. *Frank Driggs Collection.*

Harlem black leader affected black people throughout the country and beyond. **Marcus Garvey**, born in Jamaica, advocated a form of **black separatism**. His organization, the Universal Negro Improvement Association (UNIA), founded in 1914, stressed racial pride, the importance of Africa, and racial solidarity across national boundaries. Garvey supporters urged blacks from around the world to help Africans overthrow colonial rule and build a strong African state—which, they hoped, would become a powerful symbol of black accomplishment. Garvey established a steamship company, the Black Star Line, which he envisioned would carry African Americans to Africa, and he promoted other black enterprises. The UNIA message of racial pride and solidarity attracted wide support among African Americans, especially in the cities. However, black integrationist leaders, especially W. E. B. Du Bois of the NAACP, opposed Garvey's separatism and argued that the first task facing blacks was integration and equality in the United States. Garvey and Du Bois each labeled the other a traitor to his race.

Federal officials eventually charged Garvey with irregularities in his fundraising, and he was convicted of mail fraud in 1923. He spent two years in jail and then was deported to his native Jamaica. Garvey continued to lead UNIA, but the organization lost members and influence.

"Flaming Youth"

Although African Americans created jazz, those who danced to it, in the popular imagination of the 1920s, were white—a male college student, clad in a stylish raccoon-skin coat with a hip flask of illegal liquor in

Marcus Garvey   Jamaican black nationalist active in America in the 1920s.

black separatism   A strategy of creating separate black institutions, based on the assumption that African Americans can never achieve equality within white society.

On the one hundred fiftieth anniversary of the Declaration of Independence, *Life* presented this cover parodying the famous painting, the "Spirit of '76," by depicting the "Spirit of '26"—an uninhibited flapper, a jazz saxophonist and drummer, and banners with the snappy sayings of the day. The caption reads: "One Hundred and Forty-three Years of LIBERTY and Seven Years of PROHIBITION." *Private Collection.*

his pocket, and his female counterpart, the uninhibited **flapper** with bobbed hair and a daringly short skirt. This stereotype of "flaming youth," the title of a popular novel, reflected far-reaching changes among many white, college-age youths of middle- or upper-class background.

In the 1920s adolescence emerged as a separate subculture. The prosperity of the 1920s allowed many middle-class families to send their children to college. On the eve of World War I, just over 3 percent of the population aged 18 to 24 were enrolled in college. By 1930, that proportion had more than doubled, with larger increases among women, and women were receiving 40 percent of all bachelor's degrees. On campus, students reshaped colleges into youth centers, where football games and dances assumed as much significance as examinations and term papers.

For some young women—especially college students but also others from urban backgrounds—the changes of the 1920s seemed especially dramatic. Called "flappers" because of the flapping sound made by their fashionably unfastened galoshes, many young women scandalized their elders with skirts that stopped at the knee, stockings rolled below the knee, short hair often dyed black, and generous amounts of rouge and lipstick. Many observers assumed that this outrageous look reflected outrageous behavior and that young women were abandoning their parents' moral values. In fact, women's sexual activity outside marriage had begun to increase before the war, especially among working-class women and radicals. In the 1920s, such changes affected college and high school students from middle-class families. About half of the women who came of age during the 1920s had intercourse before marriage, a marked increase from prewar patterns.

Such changes in behavior were often linked to the automobile. It brought greater freedom to young people, for behind the wheel they had no chaperone and could go where they wanted. Sometimes they went to a **speakeasy** (a place where illegal alcohol was sold). Before Prohibition, few women entered saloons, but Prohibition seemed to glamorize drinking. Men and women alike began to go to speakeasies, to drink and smoke together, and to dance to popular music derived from jazz. While some adults criticized the frivolities of the young, others emulated them, launching the first American youth culture. F. Scott Fitzgerald later called the years after 1922 "a children's party taken over by elders."

TRADITIONAL AMERICA ROARS BACK

- Why and how did some Americans try to restore traditional social values during the 1920s?
- What were some of the results of their efforts?

Americans embraced cars, electric appliances, movies, and radios, but many apparently felt threatened by

flapper In the 1920s, a young woman with short hair and short skirts who discarded old-fashioned standards of dress and behavior.

speakeasy A place that illegally sells liquor and sometimes offers entertainment.

the pace of change and the upheaval in social values that seemed centered in the cities. However, it is not accurate to see the 1920s as a time of cultural warfare between rural and urban values. In nearly every case, efforts to stop the tide of change were strong in cities as well as in rural areas, and many of those efforts dated to the prewar era. In the 1920s, several movements seeking to restore elements of an older America came to fruition at the same time as Fitzgerald's "age of excess."

Prohibition

The **Eighteenth Amendment** (Prohibition) took effect in January 1920, and it came to epitomize many of the cultural struggles of the 1920s to preserve white, old-stock, Protestant values. However, many Americans simply ignored the Eighteenth Amendment, and it grew less popular the longer it lasted. By 1926, a poll indicated that only 19 percent of Americans supported Prohibition, 50 percent wanted the amendment modified, and 31 percent favored outright **repeal**. Prohibition, however, remained the law, if not the reality, from 1920 until 1933, when the Twenty-first Amendment finally did repeal it.

Prohibition did reduce drinking somewhat, and it apparently produced a decline in drunkenness and in the number of deaths from alcoholism. It was never well enforced anywhere, however, partly because of the immensity of the task and partly because Congress never provided enough money for more than token federal enforcement. In 1923 a federal agent visited major cities to see how long it took to find an illegal drink: it took only 35 seconds in New Orleans, 3 minutes in Detroit, and 3 minutes and 10 seconds in New York City.

Prohibition produced unintended consequences. Neighborhood saloons had often functioned as social centers for working-class and lower-middle-class men, but the new speakeasies were often more glamorous, attracting an upper- and middle-class clientele, women as well as men. **Bootlegging**—production and sale of illegal beverages—flourished. Some bootleggers brewed only small amounts of beer and sold it to their neighbors. In the cities, however, the thirst for alcohol provided criminals with a fresh and lucrative source of income, part of which they used to buy influence in city politics and protection from police.

In Chicago, the gang led by **Al Capone** counted nearly a thousand members and, in 1927, took in more than $100 million (equivalent to more than a billion dollars today)—$60 million of it from bootlegged liquor. The scar-faced Capone systematically eliminated members of competing gangs through violence unprecedented in American cities. Gang warfare raged in Chicago throughout the 1920s, producing some five hundred slayings. In 1931 federal officials finally managed to convict Capone—of income-tax evasion—and send him to prison.

The blood-drenched mobs of Chicago had their counterparts elsewhere, as other gangsters—many of recent immigrant background, including Italians, Irish, Germans, and Jews—followed similar paths to wealth. Gangs also found riches in gambling, prostitution, and **racketeering**. Through racketeering they gained power in some labor unions. The gangs, killings, and corruption confirmed other Americans' long-standing distrust of cities and immigrants, and they clung to the vision of a dry America as the best hope for renewing traditional values.

Fundamentalism and the Crusade Against Evolution

Another effort to maintain traditional values came with the growth of fundamentalist Protestantism. **Fundamentalism** emerged from a conflict between Christian modernism and traditional beliefs. Modernists tried to reconcile their religious beliefs with modern science. Fundamentalists, however, rejected anything—including science—that they considered to be incompatible with a literal reading of the Scriptures. Every word of the Bible, they argued, is

---

Eighteenth Amendment   Constitutional amendment, ratified in 1919, that forbade the manufacture, sale, or transportation of alcoholic beverages.

repeal   Annulment of an official act; repeal of a constitutional amendment requires a new amendment.

bootlegging   Illegal production, distribution, or sale of liquor.

Al Capone   Italian-born American gangster who ruthlessly ruled the Chicago underworld until he was imprisoned for tax evasion in 1931.

racketeering   Commission of crimes such as extortion, loansharking, and bribery, sometimes behind the front of a seemingly legitimate business or union.

fundamentalism   A religious movement emphasizing the literal truth of the Bible and opposing religious modernists who seek to reconcile the Bible with science.

the revealed word of God. The fundamentalist movement grew throughout the first quarter of the twentieth century, led by figures such as Billy Sunday, a baseball player turned evangelist.

In the early 1920s, some fundamentalists focused on **evolution** as contrary to the Bible. Biologists cite the theory of evolution to explain how living things have developed over millions of years, but the Bible states that God created the world and all living things in six days. Fundamentalists saw in evolution not just a challenge to the Bible's account of creation but also a challenge to religion itself. William Jennings Bryan, the former Democratic presidential candidate and secretary of state, provided fundamentalists with their greatest champion from about 1920 until his death a few days after the **Scopes trial** ended (see Individual Choices, page 710). His eloquence, and enormous following—especially in the rural South—guaranteed that opposition to the teaching of evolution received wide attention.

Nativism and Immigration Restriction

Prohibition and laws against teaching evolution were efforts to use government to define individual behavior and beliefs. Laws designed to restrict immigration had a similar origin, resulting largely from nativist antagonism against immigrants, especially those from southern and eastern Europe (see page 607). After a hiatus in immigration during the war, 430,000 immigrants arrived in 1920 and 805,000 in 1921, more than half from southern and eastern Europe.

Efforts to cut off immigration were not new. However, the presence of so many German Americans during the war with Germany, the Red Scare and fear of foreign radicalism, and the continued influx of poor immigrants at a time of growing unemployment all combined in 1921 to win greater support for restriction. The result was an emergency act to limit immigration from any country to 3 percent of the number of people from that country living in the United States at the time of the 1910 census.

The act of 1921 slowed the arrival of immigrants, but advocates of restriction considered it temporary. In 1924 a permanent law, the **National Origins Act**, limited total immigration to 150,000 people each year. Quotas for each country were to be based on 2 percent of the number of Americans whose ancestors came from that country, but the law

completely excluded Asians. While statisticians worked at determining the ancestry of all Americans, quotas were based on the 1890 census (before the largest wave of immigrants from southern and eastern Europe). In attempting to freeze the ethnic composition of the nation, the law reflected the arguments of those nativists who contended that immigrants from southern and eastern Europe and Asia made less desirable citizens than people from northern and western Europe. The law did permit unrestricted immigration from Canada and Latin America.

Throughout the 1920s, nativism and discrimination flourished, sometimes taking violent forms. In West Frankfort, Illinois, for example, during three days in August 1920, rioting townspeople beat and stoned Italians, pulling them out of their homes and setting the houses on fire. Other times, discrimination took more subtle forms. **Restrictive covenants** attached to real-estate titles prohibited the future sale of the property to particular groups, typically African Americans and Jews. Exclusive eastern colleges placed quotas on the number of Jews admitted each year, and some companies refused to hire Jews. In 1920 Henry Ford, in a magazine for Ford dealers, accused Jewish bankers of controlling the American economy and then broadened his attack to suggest an international Jewish conspiracy to control virtually everything from baseball to bolshevism. After Aaron Sapiro, an attorney, sued Ford for defamation and challenged him to prove his claims, Ford retracted his charges and apologized in 1927.

evolution The central organizing theorem of the biological sciences, which holds that organisms change over generations, mainly as a result of natural selection; it includes the concept that humans evolved from nonhuman ancestors.

Scopes trial Trial in 1925 in which John Scopes, a high school biology teacher, was prosecuted for teaching evolution in violation of Tennessee law.

National Origins Act Law passed by Congress in 1924, establishing quotas for immigration to the United States; it limited immigration from southern and eastern Europe, permitted larger numbers of immigrants from northern and western Europe, and prohibited immigration from Asia.

restrictive covenant Provision in a property title that prohibits the sale of property to specified groups of people, especially people of color and Jews.

This image is from a Ku Klux Klan pamphlet published in the mid-1920s, when the Klan claimed as many as five million members nationwide. The Klan portrayed itself as defending traditional, white, Protestant America against Jews, Catholics, and African Americans. *Private collection.*

The Ku Klux Klan

Nativism, anti-Catholicism, anti-Semitism, and fear of radicalism all contributed to the spectacular growth of the Ku Klux Klan in the early 1920s. The original Klan, created during Reconstruction to intimidate former slaves, had long since died out, but D. W. Griffith's hugely popular film *The Birth of a Nation*, released in 1915, glorified the old Klan.

The new Klan portrayed itself as a patriotic order devoted to traditional American values, old-fashioned Protestant Christianity, and white supremacy. Attacking Catholics, Jews, immigrants, and blacks, along with bootleggers, corrupt politicians, and gamblers, the Klan fed on the insecurities of the day. Growth came slowly at first, to only five thousand members by 1920, but then a new recruiting scheme offered local organizers $4 out of every $10

initiation fee. This incentive combined with the postwar wave of nativism and antiradicalism to produce 5 million members nationwide by 1925.

The Klan was strong in the South, Midwest, West, and Southwest, and it mushroomed in towns and cities as well as in rural areas. The organization participated actively in local politics. Its leaders sometimes exerted powerful political influence in communities and in state governments, notably in Texas, Oklahoma, Kansas, Oregon, and Indiana. In Oklahoma, the Klan led a successful impeachment campaign against a governor who tried to restrict its activities. In Oregon, the Klan claimed responsibility for a 1922 law aimed at eliminating Catholic schools. (The Supreme Court ruled the law unconstitutional.) Many local and state elections in 1924 divided along pro- and anti-Klan lines.

Although Klan members in 1923 hailed themselves as "the return of the Puritans in this corrupt, and jazz-mad age," extensive corruption underlay the Klan's self-righteous rhetoric. Some Klan leaders joined primarily for the profits, both legal (from recruiting) and illegal (mostly from political payoffs). Some shamelessly violated the morality they preached. In 1925, D. C. Stephenson, Grand Dragon of Indiana and one of the most prominent Klan leaders, was convicted of second-degree murder after the death of a woman who had accused him of raping her. When the governor refused to pardon him, Stephenson produced records proving the corruption of many Indiana officials, including the governor, a member of Congress, and the mayor of Indianapolis. Klan membership fell sharply amid factional disputes and further evidence of fraud and corruption.

PATTERNS OF ETHNICITY, RACE, CLASS, AND GENDER

• How did race relations during the 1920s show continuities with earlier patterns? What new elements appeared?

• Is it appropriate to describe the 1920s as "the lean years" for working people?

• How did gender roles and definitions change in the 1920s?

The "spiritual emancipation" that Alain Locke ascribed to the Harlem Renaissance, on the one hand, and the terror of Klan nightriders, on the other, represent the polar extremes of race relations in the 1920s. For most people of color, the realities of daily life fell somewhere in between. For working people, the 1920s represented what Irving Bernstein, a labor historian, has termed "the lean years," when

African Americans intensified their efforts to put an end to lynching. This protest parade was held in Washington, D.C., in 1922. The NAACP's efforts to secure a federal antilynching law, however, were repeatedly defeated by southerners in Congress. *UPI/Bettmann.*

gains from the Progressive Era and World War I were lost and unions remained largely on the defensive. For women, the 1920s opened with a political victory in the form of suffrage, but the unity mustered in support of that measure soon broke down.

Ethnicity and Race:
North, South, and West

Discrimination against Jews, violence against Italians, and the Klan's appeal to white Protestants all point to the continuing significance of ethnicity in American life during the 1920s. Throughout the decade, racial relations remained deeply troubled at best, violent at worst.

Although the Harlem Renaissance helped to produce greater appreciation for black music and other accomplishments, racial discrimination continued to confront most African Americans, no matter where they lived. A few gained better jobs by moving north, but many found work only in low-paying service occupations. In nearly every city, social pressures and restrictive covenants limited access to desirable housing. Those who did succeed sometimes found themselves the targets of racial hostil-

ity, like the black physician whose home was attacked by a white mob when he moved into a white Detroit neighborhood in 1925. A race riot devastated Tulsa, Oklahoma, in 1921, leaving nearly 40 confirmed dead (with blacks outnumbering whites by more than two to one), rumors of hundreds more buried in mass graves, hundreds injured, and 1,400 black business and homes burned.

Throughout the 1920s, the NAACP tried to secure a federal antilynching law, but southern legislators defeated each attempt, arguing against any federal interference in the police power of the states. As part of its efforts to combat lynching, the NAACP tried to educate the public by publicizing crimes against blacks.

In the eastern United States, North and South, race relations usually meant black-white relations. In the West, race relations were always more complex, and became even more so in the years preceding and following World War I, when Filipinos began to arrive in Hawai`i and on the West Coast, most of them working in agriculture and aboard ships. In 1920 some eight thousand workers on Hawaiian sugar plantations, most of them Japanese and Filipino, went on strike for higher wages. After six months, however, most of the strikers gave up in defeat. Sikhs from India also entered the West Coast work force, mainly as agricultural laborers.

California had long led the way among western states in passing laws discriminating against Asian Americans. Westerners, especially Californians, had also compiled a lengthy record of violence aimed at Asians. By the 1920s, other western states had copied California laws forbidding Asian immigrants to own or lease land.

Some Asian immigrants and Asian Americans responded to discriminatory actions through court actions, but with little success. In the early 1920s, the U.S. Supreme Court affirmed that only white persons and persons of African descent could become naturalized citizens, denying persons born in Japan or India. The U.S. Supreme Court also ruled that Mississippi could require a Chinese-American schoolchild to attend the segregated school established for African Americans.

Beginnings of Change in Federal Indian Policy

Although Asian Americans made few gains in the 1920s, American Indians had more success, thanks in part to persistent and persuasive advocates. In the early 1920s, Interior Secretary Albert Fall tried to lease parts of reservations to white developers and to extinguish Pueblo Indians' title to lands along the Rio Grande. In the face of significant opposition, Fall's proposals were dropped or modified. The Pueblo land question led directly to the organization of the **American Indian Defense Association (AIDA)**, created in 1923 by John Collier, an eastern social worker, to support the Pueblos.

Collier and AIDA soon emerged as leading voices calling for changes in federal Indian policy. They sought better health and educational services on the reservations, creation of tribal governments, tolerance of Indian religious ceremonies and other customs, and an end to land allotments—all in all, a major policy change, from assimilation to recognition of Indian cultures and values. The political pressure that the AIDA and similar groups applied, as well as political efforts by Indians themselves, secured several new laws favorable to Indians, including one in 1924 extending full citizenship to all Indians.

In 1926 Secretary of the Interior Hubert Work ordered a comprehensive study of Indian life. Completed in 1928, the report described widespread poverty and health problems among Indians, demonstrated the lack of adequate healthcare and education on the reservations, and condemned allotment as the single most important cause of Indian hardship. The efforts to support and extend Indian rights, especially the work of Collier, laid the basis for a significant shift in federal policy in the 1930s.

Mexican Americans

California and the Southwest, home to many Mexican and Mexican-American families since the region was part of Mexico, attracted growing numbers of Mexican immigrants in the 1920s. Many Mexicans went north, most of them to Texas and California, to escape the revolution and civil war that devastated their nation from 1910 into the 1920s. Nearly seven hundred thousand Mexicans legally fled to the United States between 1910 and 1930, and probably the same number came illegally.

The agricultural economies of the Southwest were also changing. In south Texas, some cattle ranches were converted to farms, especially for cotton but for fruit and vegetables too. By 1925, the Southwest was relying on irrigation to produce 40 percent of the nation's fruits and vegetables, crops that were highly labor-intensive. In the late 1920s, Mexicans made up 80 to 85 percent of farm laborers in that region. At the same time, the southwestern states also experienced large increases in their Anglo populations. These changes in population and economy reshaped relations between Anglos and Mexicans.

In south Texas, many Anglo newcomers looked on Mexicans as what one Anglo called a "partly colored race," and white newcomers tried to import elements of southern black-white relations including disfranchisement and segregation. Disfranchisement was unsuccessful, but some schools and other social institutions were segregated despite Mexican opposition. Efforts organized through the League of United Latin American Citizens (LULAC) occasionally halted discrimination by businesses—but only occasionally.

In California, Mexican workers' efforts to organize and strike for better pay and working conditions often sparked violent opposition. Strikes in the early 1920s

---

American Indian Defense Association
Organization founded in 1923 to defend the rights of American Indians; it pushed for an end to allotment and a return to tribal government.

This photo, taken around 1920, depicts Mexican-American workers laying irrigation pipe in Ventura County, California. Immigration from Mexico increased significantly during the 1910s and 1920s, due to improvements in transportation within Mexico and to the social and economic dislocations produced by revolution and civil war in Mexico. By the 1920s, Mexicans made up much of the workforce in California agriculture. *Los Angeles Public Library.*

were broken quickly and brutally. Local authorities arrested and often beat strikers, and growers' private guards beat or kidnapped them. Leaders were likely to be deported. Nevertheless, Mexican labor had become vital to agriculture, and growers opposed any proposals to restrict immigration from Mexico. The landowners made certain that the revised immigration law of 1924 permitted unlimited immigration from the Western Hemisphere. In Lemon Grove, a small town near San Diego, in 1931, Mexican-American parents mounted the first successful court challenge to school segregation.

Not all immigrants from Mexico stayed in the Southwest. As the doors to European immigration closed with the new immigration law, midwestern manufacturers began to recruit Mexican workers to work in steel mills, meatpacking plants, and auto factories. By 1930, significant numbers of Mexican

Americans were to be found in such industrial cities as Chicago, Detroit, and Gary.

Labor on the Defensive

Difficulties in establishing unions among Mexican workers mirrored a larger failure of unions in the 1920s. When unions tried to recover lost purchasing power by striking in 1919 and 1920, nearly all failed. After 1921, employers took advantage of the conservative political climate to challenge Progressive-era legislation benefiting workers. The Supreme Court responded by limiting workers' rights, voiding laws that eliminated child labor, and striking down minimum wages for women and children.

Many companies undertook anti-union drives. Arguing that unions were not necessary and had become either corrupt or radical, some employers used the term **American Plan** to describe their refusal to recognize unions as representing employees. At the same time, many companies began to provide workers with benefit programs such as insurance, retirement pensions, cafeterias, paid vacations, and stock purchase plans, an approach sometimes called **welfare capitalism**. Such innovations stemmed both from genuine concern about workers' well-being and from the expectation that such improvements would increase productivity and discourage unionization.

The 1920s marked the first period of prosperity since the 1830s when union membership declined, falling from 5 million in 1920 to 3.6 million in 1929, a 28 percent decline at a time when the total work force increased by 15 percent. Some unions lost members for reasons in addition to hostile government policies, the American Plan, and lost strikes. Prohibition devastated once-strong unions of brewery workers and bartenders. AFL leaders, holding fast to their concept of separate unions for each different skill group, made no serious effort to organize the great mass-production industries. Some unions suffered from internal battles—the International Ladies' Garment Workers' Union lost two-thirds of its members during power struggles between Socialists and Communists.

The Communists sought influence and power within other unions, but the membership of the **American Communist Party** (CP) never approached the numbers claimed by the Socialist Party before World War I. In 1929 the CP counted only ninety-three hundred members. Always closely tied to the leadership of the Soviet Union, the CP labored strenuously to organize workers throughout the 1920s, first by working within AFL unions and then by creating separate unions. CP operatives tried to organize the unskilled, people of color, women, and others outside AFL craft unions, but they had little success.

Changes in Women's Lives

The attention given to the flapper in accounts of the 1920s should not detract from important changes in women's gender roles during those years. Significant changes occurred in two arenas: family and politics.

Marriage among white middle-class women and men came increasingly to be valued as companionship between two partners. Although the ideal of marriage was often expressed in terms of man and woman taking equal responsibility for a relationship,

the actual responsibility for the smooth functioning of the family typically fell on the woman. In addition, many women in the 1920s seem to have increased their control over decisions about childbearing.

Usually in American history, prosperity brings increases in the birth rate. In the 1920s, however, changing social values together with more options for birth control resulted in fewer births. Women who came of childbearing age in the 1910s and 1920s are distinctive in three ways, when compared with women of both earlier and later time periods: (1) they had fewer children on the average, (2) more of them had no children at all, and (3) far fewer had very large families (see Figure 23.3).

The declining birth rate in the 1920s reflected, in part, some degree of success for earlier efforts to secure wider availability of birth-control information and devices, for example, diaphragms. Margaret Sanger continued to carry the banner in the battle to extend birth-control information (see page 642), and she persuaded more doctors to join her efforts. As the birth-control movement gained the backing of male physicians, it became a more respectable, middle-class reform movement. By 1925, the American Medical Association, the New York Academy of Medicine, and the New York Obstetrical Society had all declared their support for birth control, and the Rockefeller Foundation began to fund medical research into contraception methods. Nevertheless, until 1936, federal law restricted public distribution of information about contraception.

Throughout the 1920s, working-class women still struggled to stretch their finances to cover their families' needs. As before, some women and children worked outside the home because the family needed additional income. The proportion of women working for wages remained quite stable during the 1920s, at about one in four. The proportion of married women working for wages increased, though, from 23 percent of the female labor force in 1920 to 29 percent in 1930.

American Plan Term that some employers in the 1920s used to describe their policy of refusing to negotiate with unions.

welfare capitalism Program adopted by some employers to provide to their employees benefits such as lunchrooms, paid vacations, bonuses, and profit-sharing plans.

American Communist Party Party organized in 1919, devoted to destroying capitalism and private property and replacing them with a system of socialism.

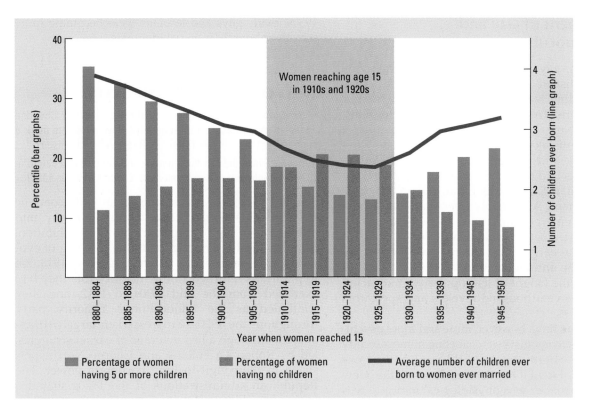

FIGURE 23.3 Changing Patterns of Childbearing Among Women   This figure depicts three different choices regarding family size: (1) the number of children born to women ever married, (2) the percentage of women having large families, and (3) the percentage of women having no children at all. Childbearing ages are considered to be between 15 and 45. *Sources:* For women born in 1914 and before, Series B42–48, Percent Distribution of Ever-Married Women (Survivors of Birth Cohorts of 1835–39 to 1920–24) by Race and By Number of Children Ever Born, as Reported in Censuses of 1910, 1940, 1950, 1960, and 1970, U.S. Bureau of the Census, *Historical Statistics of the United States, Colonial Times to 1970*, Bicentennial Edition, 2 vols. (Washington, D.C.: U.S. Government Printing Office, 1975), I:53. For women born in 1916 and after, Table 270, Children Ever Born and Marital Status of Women by Age, Race, and Spanish Origin: 1980, U.S. Bureau of the Census, *1980 Census of Population: Detailed Population Characteristics: United States Summary* (Washington, D.C.: U.S. Government Printing Office, 1984), pp. 1–103.

With the implementation of the **Nineteenth Amendment** (woman suffrage) in 1920, the unity of the suffrage movement disintegrated in disputes over the proper role for women voters. Both major political parties welcomed women as voters and modified the structure of their national committees to provide that each state be represented by both a national committeeman and a national committeewoman. Some suffrage activists joined the League of Women Voters, a nonpartisan group committed to social and political reform. The Congressional Union, led by Alice Paul (see page 643), converted itself into the National Woman's party and, after 1923, focused its efforts largely on securing an **Equal Rights Amendment** to the Constitution. The League of Women Voters disagreed, arguing that such an amendment would endanger laws that provided special rights and protections for women. In the end, woman suffrage seemed not to have dramatically changed either women or politics.

Nineteenth Amendment   Constitutional amendment, ratified in 1919, that prohibited federal or state governments from restricting the right to vote on account of sex.

Equal Rights Amendment   Proposed constitutional amendment, first advocated by the National Woman's Party in 1923, to give women in the United States equal rights under the law.

Development of Gay and Lesbian Subcultures

In the 1920s, gay and lesbian subcultures became more established and relatively open in some cities, including New York, Chicago, New Orleans, and Baltimore. *The Captive*, a play about lesbians, opened in New York in 1926, and some movies included unmistakable homosexual references. Novels with gay and lesbian characters circulated in the late 1920s and early 1930s. In Chicago, the Society for Human Rights was organized to advocate equal treatment. A relatively open gay and lesbian community emerged in Harlem, where some prominent figures of the Renaissance were gay or bisexual. In the early 1930s, the nation's largest gay event was the annual Hamilton Lodge drag ball in Harlem—at the height of its popularity, it attracted as many as seven thousand revelers and spectators of all races.

At the same time, however, more and more psychiatrists and psychologists were labeling homosexuality a **perversion**. Shortly before World War I, as the work of **Sigmund Freud** became well known, the view that homosexuality was physiological in origin was replaced by a different explanation. Most psychiatrists and psychologists now labeled homosexuality a sexual disorder that required a cure, though no "cure" ever proved viable. Thus Freud's theories may have been a liberating influence with regard to heterosexual relations, but they proved harmful for same-sex relations.

The new medical definitions were slow to work their way into the larger society. The armed forces, for example, continued previous practices, making little effort to prevent homosexuals from enlisting and taking disciplinary action only against behavior that clearly violated the law.

The late 1920s and early 1930s brought increased suppression of gays and lesbians. New state laws gave police greater authority to prosecute open expressions of homosexuality. In 1927 New York City police raided *The Captive* and other plays with gay or lesbian themes, and the New York state legislature banned all such plays. In 1929 Adam Clayton Powell, a leading Harlem minister, launched a highly publicized campaign against gays. Motion-picture studios instituted a morality code that, among its wide-ranging provisions, prohibited any depiction of homosexuality. The end of Prohibition after 1933 brought increased regulation of businesses selling liquor, and local authorities used this regulatory power to close establishments that tolerated gay or lesbian customers. Thus, by the

1930s, many gays and lesbians were becoming more secretive about their sexual identities.

THE POLITICS OF PROSPERITY

- What was the basic attitude of the Harding and Coolidge administrations toward the economy? How does this mark a change from the administrations of Roosevelt and Wilson?
- In what ways did the third-party candidacy of La Follette in 1924 resemble that of Roosevelt in 1912 and Weaver in 1892?

Sooner or later, nearly all the social and economic developments of the 1920s found their way into politics, from highway construction to prohibition, from immigration restriction to the teaching of evolution, from farm prices to lynching. After 1918, the Republicans returned to the majority role they had exercised from the mid-1890s to 1912, and they continued as the unquestioned majority party throughout the 1920s. Progressivism largely disappeared, although a few veterans of earlier struggles, led by Robert La Follette and George Norris, persisted in their vigil to limit corporate power. The Republican administrations of the 1920s shared a faith in the ability of business to establish prosperity and benefit the American people. Those in power considered government the partner of business, not its regulator.

Harding's Failed Presidency

Elected in 1920, Warren G. Harding looked presidential—handsome, gray-haired, dignified, warm, and outgoing—but had little intellectual depth. For some of his appointments, he chose the most respected leaders of his party, including Charles Evans Hughes for secretary of state, Andrew Mellon for secretary of the treasury, and Herbert Hoover for secretary of commerce. Harding, however, was most at home in smoke-filled rooms, drinking whiskey and playing poker with friends, and he gave hundreds of government jobs to his cronies and political supporters. They turned his administration into one

---

perversion Sexual practice considered abnormal or deviant.

Sigmund Freud Austrian who played a leading role in developing the field of psychoanalysis, known for his theory that the sex drive underlies much individual behavior.

In 1924, the Democrats tried to capitalize on the Republicans' embarrassment over the Teapot Dome scandal. They received little response because the death of Harding brought Calvin Coolidge to the presidency, and Coolidge's personal honesty and morality were unquestioned. *Collection of David J. and Janice L. Frent.*

of the most corrupt in American history. As their misdeeds began to come to light, Harding put off taking action until after a trip to Alaska. During his return, on August 2, 1923, he died when a blood vessel burst in his brain.

The full extent of the corruption became clear after Harding's death. Albert Fall, Secretary of the Interior, accepted huge bribes from oil companies for leases on federal oil reserves at Elk Hills, California, and Teapot Dome, Wyoming. Attorney General Harry Daugherty and others pocketed payoffs to approve the sale of government-held property for less than its value, and Daugherty may also have protected bootleggers. The head of the Veterans Bureau swindled the government out of more than $200 million. In all, three cabinet members resigned, four officials went to jail, and five men committed suicide. As if the financial dishonesty were not enough, in 1927 Nan Britton published a book claiming that she had been Harding's mistress, bore his child, and carried on trysts with him in the White House.

In the midst of these scandals, hard-pressed and debt-ridden farmers turned to the federal government for help. In 1921 farm organizations worked with a bipartisan group of senators and representatives to form a congressional **Farm Bloc**, which promoted legislation to assist farmers. The bloc enjoyed a substantial boost in the 1922 elections, when distraught farmers across the Midwest turned out conservatives

and elected candidates who voiced sympathy for farmers' problems. Congress passed a few assistance measures in the early 1920s, but none addressed the central problems of overproduction and low prices. By 1922, some farm organizations joined with unions, especially unions of railroad workers, to form the Conference for Progressive Political Action and agitate for a new Progressive Party.

The Three-Way Election of 1924

When Harding died, Vice President Calvin Coolidge became president. Fortunately for the Republican Party, the new president exemplified honesty, virtue, and sobriety. In 1924 Republicans quickly chose Coolidge as their candidate for president.

The Democratic convention, however, sank into a long and bitter deadlock. Since the Civil War, the party had divided between southerners (mostly Protestant and committed to white supremacy) and northerners (often city-dwellers and of recent immigrant descent, including many Catholics). In 1924 the Klan was approaching its peak membership and exercised significant influence among many Democratic delegates from the South and Midwest.

Northern Democrats tried to nominate **Al Smith** for president. Highly popular as governor of New York, Smith epitomized urban America. Catholic and the son of immigrants, he was everything the Klan—and most of the southern convention delegates—hated. His chief opponent for the nomination, William G. McAdoo of California, boasted progressive credentials but had done legal work for an oil company executive tainted by the Elk Hills scandal. After nine hot days of stalemate and 103 ballots, the exhausted Democrats turned to a compromise candidate, John W. Davis. Davis had served in the Wilson administration and then became a leading corporate lawyer. All in all, the convention seemed to confirm the observation by the contemporary humorist Will Rogers: "I belong to no organized political party. I am a Democrat."

Farm Bloc   Bipartisan group of senators and representatives formed in 1921 to promote legislation to assist farmers.

Al Smith   New York governor who unsuccessfully sought the Democratic nomination for president in 1924 and was the unsuccessful Democratic candidate for president in 1928; his Catholicism and desire to repeal Prohibition were political liabilities.

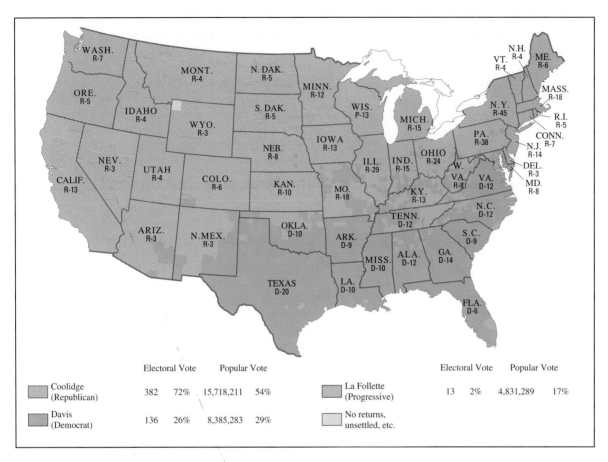

MAP 23.1 Election of 1924 The presidential election of 1924 was complicated by the campaign of Senator Robert La Follette of Wisconsin, who ran as a Progressive. As you can see, much of his support came from Republicans living in the north-central and northwestern regions where the agricultural economy was most hard hit.

Americans committed to progressivism welcomed the independent candidacy of Senator Robert M. La Follette as a Progressive. La Follette was nominated at a convention that expressed the concerns of farmers, unions, and an assortment of reformers dating back as far as the Populist Party of the 1890s. The La Follette Progressives attacked big business and promoted collective bargaining, reform of politics, public ownership of railroads and water power resources, and a public referendum on questions of war and peace. La Follette was the first presidential candidate to be endorsed by the American Federation of Labor, and the Socialist Party of America threw him its support as well.

Republican campaigners largely ignored Davis and focused on portraying La Follette as a dangerous radical. Coolidge claimed the key issue was "whether America will allow itself to be degraded into a communistic or socialistic state" or "remain American."

Coolidge won with nearly 16 million votes and 54 percent of the total, as voters seemed to champion the status quo. Davis held on to most traditional Democratic voters, especially in the South, receiving 8 million votes and 29 percent. La Follette carried only his home state of Wisconsin but garnered almost 5 million votes, 17 percent, and did well both in urban working-class neighborhoods and in parts of the rural Midwest and Northwest (see Map 23.1).

The Politics of Business

Committed to limited government and content to let problems work themselves out, Coolidge tried to reduce the significance of the presidency—and succeeded. Having once announced that "the business of America is business," he believed that the free market and free operation of business leadership would best sustain economic prosperity for all. As

This cartoon depicts Coolidge playing the praises of big business. Big business, dressed up like a flapper, responds by dancing the Charleston with wild abandon and singing a paraphrase of a popular song, "Yes Sir, He's My Baby." *Library of Congress.*

president, he set out to prevent government from interfering in the operation of business.

Firmly favoring an unfettered market economy, Coolidge had little sympathy for efforts to secure federal help for the faltering farm economy. Congress tried to address the related problems of low prices for farm products and persistent agricultural surpluses with the **McNary-Haugen bill**, which would have created federal price supports and authorized the government to buy farm surpluses and sell them abroad at prevailing world prices. The Farm Bloc finally pushed the bill through Congress in 1927, only to have Coolidge veto it. The same thing happened in 1928. By contrast, the **Railway Labor Act of 1926** drew on wartime experiences to establish collective bargaining for railroad employees. By meeting most of the railway unions' demands, the act effectively removed them from politics.

Andrew Mellon, an aluminum magnate and one of the wealthiest men in the nation, served as secre-

tary of the treasury throughout the Republican administrations of the 1920s. Acclaimed by Republicans and business leaders as the greatest secretary of the treasury since Alexander Hamilton, Mellon argued that high taxes on the wealthy stifled the economy. He secured substantial tax breaks for the affluent, arguing that they would bring economic benefits to all as a result of the "productive investments" that the wealthy would make. Herbert Hoover, secretary of commerce during the Harding and Coolidge administrations, urged Coolidge to regulate the increasingly wild use of credit, which inflated stock values and produced rampant stock market speculation, but Coolidge refused.

Coolidge cut federal spending and staffed federal agencies with people who shared his distaste for too much government. Unlike Harding, Coolidge found honest and competent appointees. Like Harding, he named probusiness figures to regulatory commissions and put conservative, probusiness judges in the courts. The *Wall Street Journal* described the outcome: "Never before, here or anywhere else, has a government been so completely fused with business."

The 1928 Campaign and the Election of Hoover

In August 1927, President Coolidge, on vacation in South Dakota, told reporters, "I do not choose to run in 1928." Coolidge's announcement stunned the country and his party. Secretary of Commerce Herbert Hoover immediately declared his candidacy, and Republicans found him an ideal candidate, representing what most Americans believed was best about the United States: individual effort and honestly earned success.

Son of a Quaker blacksmith from Iowa, Hoover was orphaned at ten and raised by uncles. He grew up among thrifty farmers who believed that hard work was the only way to success. Graduating from Stanford University, he traveled the world as a mining engineer. By 1914 his fortune was more than $4 million. Having succeeded in business, Hoover

---

McNary-Haugen bill Farm relief bill that provided for government purchase of crop surpluses during years of large output; Coolidge vetoed it in 1927 and in 1928.

Railway Labor Act of 1926 Federal law that guaranteed collective bargaining for railroad employees, the first peacetime federal law to extend this guarantee to any group of workers.

turned to public service. When World War I broke out, he offered his organizational skills and energy to help provide relief to Belgium through the Committee for the Relief of Belgium. Hoover traveled across war-torn Europe seeking funds and supplies for Belgium. "This man is not to be stopped anywhere under any circumstance," the Germans noted on his passport. When the United States entered the war, President Wilson named Hoover to head the U.S. Food Administration (see page 689). By the end of the war, Hoover was an international hero. He served as Secretary of Commerce under Harding and Coolidge, and attracted wide support in the business community for his efforts to encourage economic growth through associationalism—voluntary cooperation among otherwise competing groups.

In launching his campaign before thousands of supporters gathered in the Stanford football stadium, Hoover sounded the theme of his candidacy: prosperity. "We in America today are nearer to the final triumph over poverty than ever before. . . . The poorhouse is vanishing among us," he boldly announced.

The Democrats nominated Al Smith, four-time governor of New York. Like Hoover, Smith was a self-made man. But unlike his opponent, who had gone to Stanford, Smith had received his education on the streets of the Lower East Side of New York City and as part of Tammany Hall, the Democratic machine that ran the city. As a reform-minded, progressive governor, Smith had streamlined state government, improved its efficiency, and supported legislation to set a minimum wage and maximum hours of work and to establish state ownership of hydroelectric plants.

In many places, Smith became the main issue in the campaign. Opponents attacked his Catholic religion, his big-city background, his opposition to Prohibition, his Tammany connections, and even his New York accent. Anti-Catholic sentiment burned hotly in many parts of the country, often fanned by the remnants of the Klan, whose fiery crosses marked the route of Smith's campaign train in some areas. Evangelist Billy Sunday called Smith supporters "damnable whiskey politicians, bootleggers, crooks, pimps and business-men who deal with them." Thus, for many voters, the choice in 1928 seemed to be between a candidate who represented hard work and the pious values of small-town, old-stock, Protestant America and a candidate who represented Catholics, foreigners, machine politics, and the ugly problems of the cities.

Hoover won easily, with 58 percent of the popular vote. Prosperity and the nation's long-term Republican majority probably would have spelled victory for any competent Republican. Smith's religion and anti-Prohibition stance cost him support in the South, where Hoover carried some areas that had not voted Republican since the end of Reconstruction. Smith, however, helped Democrats make important gains in northern cities. In 1920 and 1924, the total vote in the twelve largest cities had been Republican by a large margin, but in 1928 Smith won a slim majority overall in those cities, partly by drawing to the polls Catholic women of immigrant descent who had not previously voted. As you can see in Figure 20.2 (page 622), voter participation spiked upward in 1928, temporarily interrupting a long-term downward trend.

The first president born west of the Mississippi River, Hoover came to the presidency with definite ideas about both domestic and foreign policy. More than Harding and Coolidge, he set out to be an active president at home and overseas. The role of government, he believed, was to promote cooperation without resorting to punitive measures like antitrust laws. He warned that once government, especially the federal government, stepped in to solve problems directly, the people gave up some of their freedom and government became part of the problem. Hoover recognized that the federal government had a responsibility to help find solutions to social and economic problems, but the key word was *help*: Hoover looked to the government to help but not to solve problems by itself.

THE DIPLOMACY OF PROSPERITY

- What is "independent internationalism"?
- What role did the United States play in Latin America and Europe during the 1920s?
- What were Hughes's goals for the Washington Naval Conference? How successful was he?

Two realities shaped American foreign policy in the 1920s: the rejection of Woodrow Wilson's internationalism following World War I and the continuing quest for economic expansion by American business. As president, Harding dismissed any American role in the League of Nations and refused to accept the **Treaty of Versailles** (see page 698). Undamaged by

---

Treaty of Versailles Treaty signed at Versailles in France in 1919 that ended the war with Germany and created the League of Nations.

the war, American firms outproduced and outtraded the rest of the world. U.S. trade amounted to 30 percent of the world's total, and American firms produced more than 70 percent of the world's oil and almost 50 percent of the world's coal and steel. American bankers loaned billions of dollars to other nations, expanding the global economy.

Because neither Harding nor Coolidge had any expertise or interest in foreign affairs, they deferred making and implementing policy to their secretaries of state: Charles Evans Hughes and Frank Kellogg, respectively. Both were capable men interested in developing American business and influence abroad through "independent internationalism." Independent (or unilateral) internationalism had two central thrusts: avoidance of multilateral commitments—sometimes called **isolationism**—and expansion of economic opportunities overseas. The Commerce and State Departments promoted American business activities worldwide and encouraged private American investments in Japan and China. American officials also worked to make it possible for U.S. oil companies to drill in Iran, Iraq, the Persian Gulf region, and Saudi Arabia. Successes in Asia and the Middle East were limited, but efforts to expand the American economic position in Latin America and Europe were quite successful. As president, Hoover and his secretary of state, Henry L. Stimson, followed the approach that had characterized the earlier 1920s.

The United States and Latin America

When Harding took office in 1921, the United States had troops stationed in Panama, Haiti, the Dominican Republic, and Nicaragua (see Map 23.2). During the presidential campaign, Harding had criticized Wilson's "bayonet rule" in Haiti and the Dominican Republic and expressed his intention to end the occupation of those nations. To ensure continued American dominance in the Caribbean, however, U.S. officials wanted local governments that could keep order. Therefore, American administrators maintained some control over national finances and trained national guards as each nation's police force. American troops left the Dominican Republic in 1924, Nicaragua in 1932, and Haiti in 1934. In the Dominican Republic and in Haiti, however, the United States kept control of the customhouse—and tariff revenues—until the 1940s.

When American troops withdrew from the Dominican Republic and Haiti, they left better roads, improved sanitation systems, governments favorable to the United States, and well-equipped national guards. But years of occupation had not advanced the educational systems, the national economies, or the standard of living for most residents. Nor did the United States do much to promote the cause of democracy, favoring stability over freedom even if it meant accepting dictators such as Rafael Trujillo, who seized power in the Dominican Republic in 1930 and ruled brutally until his death in 1961.

In Nicaragua, American forces left in 1925, only to be reintroduced in mid-1926 to protect the pro-American government when civil war broke out. Coolidge sent Henry L. Stimson to negotiate a peace agreement. The **Peace of Titiapa** (1927) ended most of the fighting, leaving only followers of **Augusto Sandino** continuing the war. Sandino, a nationalist who wanted to rid Nicaragua of American influence, rejected the Peace of Titiapa and continued guerilla warfare.

When the United States withdrew from Nicaragua in 1933, it left an American-equipped and trained national guard to maintain order. In 1934 the Nicaraguan president, Juan Bautista Sacasa, and **Anastasio Somoza**, his nephew and commander of the Guardia Nacional, arranged a peace conference with Sandino. Somoza, however, ordered Sandino and his aides seized and executed. Later Somoza turned against Sacasa and in 1936, using the national guard as a political weapon, secured election as president. Somoza ruled either directly or through puppet presidents until his assassination in 1956. His family remained in power until 1979, when rebels calling themselves Sandinistas—after their hero Sandino—took power in Nicaragua.

---

isolationism   The notion that the United States should avoid political, diplomatic, and military entanglements with other nations.

Peace of Titiapa   Agreement negotiated by Henry L. Stimson in 1927 that sought to end factional fighting in Nicaragua.

Augusto Sandino   Nicaraguan guerrilla leader who resisted Nicaraguan and American troops in a rebellion from 1925 to 1933; he was murdered at the orders of Anastasio Somoza following a peace conference in 1934.

Anastasio Somoza   General who established a military dictatorship in Nicaragua in 1933, deposed his uncle to become president in 1934, and ruled the country for two decades, amassing a personal fortune and suppressing all opposition.

CANADA

ATLANTIC

OCEAN

UNITED
STATES

Havana, Cuba
U.S. upholds right of intervention at
Pan American Conference, 1928

Cuba
Platt Amendment, 1902–1934
U.S. troops, 1906–1909, 1912, 1917–1922
U.S. companies invest in sugar

Haiti
U.S. troops, 1915–1934
U.S. financial supervision, 1916–1941

MEXICO

*Gulf
of
Mexico*

THE BAHAMAS
(BR.)

Dominican Republic
U.S. troops, 1916–1924
U.S. financial supervision, 1905–1941
Trujillo era, 1930–1961

Mexico
U.S. companies' investments, including railroads
and oil
Constitution of 1917 challenges U.S. interests
Nationalization of foreign oil companies, 1938

CUBA
JAMAICA
(BR.)

DOMINICAN
REP.

HAITI

VIRGIN IS. (US,UK)

PUERTO
RICO (US)

Virgin Islands
U.S. possession since 1916

Guatemala
United Fruit Company, coffee
investments

BRITISH HONDURAS
HONDURAS

Caribbean Sea

Puerto Rico
U.S. possession since 1898
Jones Act grants U.S. citizenship, 1917

GUATEMALA

NICARAGUA
COSTA
RICA

El Salvador
U.S. companies invest in coffee

EL SALVADOR

PANAMA

VENEZUELA

BRITISH GUIANA
DUTCH GUIANA
FRENCH GUIANA

Honduras
United Fruit Company investments

COLOMBIA

Nicaragua
U.S. financial supervision, 1911–1925
U.S. troops, 1912–1925, 1927–1933
War against Sandino, 1925–1933
Somoza era, 1936–1979

ECUADOR

U.S. companies
invest in oil

Panama
U.S. control of Canal Zone
since 1904

PERU

BRAZIL

BOLIVIA

PACIFIC

U.S. companies invest
in copper mining

CHILE

PARAGUAY

OCEAN

URUGUAY

ARGENTINA

0   500   1000 Km.

0   500   1000 Mi.

MAP 23.2 The United States and Latin America   As this map indicates, during the 1920s, the United States continued to play an active role throughout Central America and the Caribbean and, to a lesser extent, in South America. In some cases, as in Nicaragua in the 1920s, this included military intervention. But during the 1920s and after,
political and economic pressures largely replaced military force as the primary means for protecting U.S. interests.

During the 1920s, American businesses greatly expanded their operations overseas. In Latin America, corporations such as United Fruit Company oversaw a wide-range of enterprises, from running shiplines to growing bananas. Here, recently picked bananas begin their journey from the field to American homes. *Benson Latin American Collection, University of Texas at Austin.*

Elsewhere in Latin America, the 1920s saw American interventions of another sort—not military but commercial. Throughout Central America, American firms such as the United Fruit Company purchased thousands of acres of land for plantations on which to grow tropical fruit, especially bananas and coffee. In Venezuela and Colombia, American oil companies, with State Department help, negotiated profitable contracts for drilling rights, outmaneuvering European oil companies. U.S. investments in Latin America rose from nearly $2 billion in 1919 to over $3.5 billion in 1929.

Oil also played a key role in American relations with Mexico. Following the Mexican Revolution (see page 680), the Mexican constitution of 1917 limited foreign ownership, and Mexico moved to **nationalize** all of its subsurface resources, including oil. The United States, supported by American businessmen, strongly objected, especially to nationalization of oil. By 1925, American oilmen and some members of the Coolidge administration were calling for military action to protect American oil interests in northern Mexico from "bolshevism." Coolidge sent Dwight W. Morrow—a college friend—as ambassador to Mexico with instructions "to keep us out of war with Mexico." Morrow understood Mexican nationalism and pride, knew some Spanish, and appreciated Mexico and its people. He cultivated a personal relationship with Mexican president Plutarco Calles, which reduced tensions and delayed Mexico's nationalization of oil properties until 1938.

In 1928, at a Pan-American Conference in Havana, American intervention in Latin America came under sharp challenge in a resolution introduced by the Argentine delegate. Secretary of State Hughes was prepared, and he handled the issue through a combination of accommodation and rebuttal. He supported some mild proposals but staunchly defended "taking action—I would call it interposition of a temporary character—for the purpose of protecting the lives and property of its nationals." And the anti-intervention resolution was voted down. Soon after, following the election of 1928, president-elect Hoover undertook a good-will tour of eleven Latin American countries, seeking to build better relations.

America and the European Economy

While World War I was shattering much of Europe physically and economically, the American economy soared to unprecedented heights, and the United States became the world's leading creditor nation. After the war, Republican leaders joined with business figures to expand exports and restrict imports. In 1922 the **Fordney-McCumber Tariff** set the highest rates ever for most imported industrial goods. The tariff had the effect of not only limiting European imports but also making it difficult for Europeans to acquire the dollars needed to repay their war debts to the United States.

While Harding and Coolidge sought debt repayment, Secretary of State Hughes and Secretary of Commerce Hoover worked to expand American economic interests in Europe, especially Germany. They believed that, if Germany recovered economically and paid its $33 billion war reparations, other European nations would also recover and repay their debts. With government encouragement, over $4 billion in American investments flowed into Europe, doubling American investments there. General Motors purchased Opel, a German automobile firm. Ford built the largest automobile factory outside the United States, in England, and constructed a tractor factory in the Soviet Union.

nationalize To convert an industry or enterprise from private to government ownership and control.

Fordney-McCumber Tariff Tariff passed by Congress in 1922 to protect domestic production from foreign competitors; it raised tariff rates to record levels and provoked foreign tariff reprisals.

Even with the infusion of American capital, Germany could not keep up its reparation payments, defaulting in 1923 to France and Belgium. France responded by sending troops to occupy Germany's **Ruhr Valley**, a key economic region, igniting an international crisis. Hughes sent Charles G. Dawes, a Chicago banker and prominent Republican, to resolve the situation. Under the **Dawes Plan**, American bankers loaned $2.5 billion to Germany for economic development, and the Germans promised to pay $2 billion in reparations to the European Allies, who, in turn, were to pay $2.5 billion in war debts to the United States. This circular flow of capital was the butt of jokes at the time, but the remedy worked fairly well until 1929, when the Depression ended nearly all loans and payments.

Encouraging International Cooperation

Although committed to independent internationalism, the Republican policymakers of the 1920s also understood that some international cooperation was necessary to achieve policy goals and solve international problems. On such issues, they were willing to cooperate with other nations and enter into international agreements, but only with the understanding that the United States was not entering any alliance or otherwise agreeing to commit resources or troops in defense of another nation.

Disarmament was such an issue. The destruction caused by World War I had spurred pacifism and calls for disarmament. Disarmament, advocates urged, was necessary—it would reduce the number of weapons and military spending, and might allow lower taxes. In the United States, support for arms cuts was widespread and vocal, as proponents pressed Harding to trim military budgets. In early 1921, Senator William E. Borah of Idaho suggested an international conference to reduce the size of the world's navies. Fearing that naval expenditures would prevent desirable tax cuts, Treasury Secretary Mellon and many members of Congress joined the disarmament chorus. In November 1921, Harding invited the major naval powers to Washington to discuss reducing "the crushing burdens of military and naval establishments."

There were other reasons for American interest in disarmament, notably concerns about Japan. Tied for first in naval strength, the United States and Britain had no desire to expand their navies. Japan, the third-place naval power, seemed inclined to continue its naval buildup. Americans worried about growing Japanese pressures on China that could endanger Chinese territory and the Open Door policy (see page 632). To block the Japanese, Harding and Hughes were willing to host international discussions aimed at limiting the size of navies and ensuring the status quo in China.

When the naval powers assembled for the **Washington Naval Conference**, Hughes shocked delegates with a radical proposal to scrap nearly 2 million tons of warships, primarily battleships. He also called for a ten-year ban on naval construction and for limits to the size of navies that would keep the Japanese navy well behind the British and American fleets. Hughes suggested a ratio of 5 to 5 to 3 for the United States, Britain, and Japan. Italy and France were allocated smaller ratios—1.67 each. Hughes's plan gained immediate support among the American public and most of the nations attending—but not Japan. The Japanese called it a national insult and demanded equality. Discussions dragged on for two months, but the Japanese finally agreed. U.S. intelligence had broken the Japanese diplomatic code, so Hughes knew that the Japanese delegates had orders to concede, if he held firm.

By the end of the conference, in February 1922, the United States, Britain, Japan, France, and Italy agreed to build no more **capital ships** for ten years and to abide by the 5:5:3:1.7:1.7 ratio for future shipbuilding. A British observer commented that Hughes had sunk more British ships in one speech "than all the admirals of the world have sunk in . . . centuries." In other treaties, the powers agreed to prohibit the use of poison gas and not to attack one another's Asian possessions. The **Nine-Power Pact**

Ruhr Valley Region surrounding the Ruhr River in northwestern Germany, which contained many major industrial cities and valuable coal mines.

Dawes Plan Arrangement for collecting World War I reparations from Germany; it scheduled annual payments and stabilized German currency.

Washington Naval Conference International conference that in 1921–1922 produced a series of agreements to limit naval armaments and prevent conflict in the Far East and the Pacific.

capital ships Generally, a navy's largest, most heavily armed ships; at the Washington Naval Conference, ships weighing over 10,000 tons and using guns with at least an 8-inch bore were classified as capital ships.

Nine-Power Pact Agreement signed in 1922 by Britain, France, Italy, Japan, the United States, China, the Netherlands, Portugal, and Belgium to recognize China and affirm the Open Door policy.

In an era of isolationism, the United States hosted its first major international conference, the Washington Naval Conference, to limit the naval arms race and protect its interests in China. At the center of the conference was Secretary of State Charles Evans Hughes (pictured here), who shocked everyone by asking for major reductions in naval strength. *Brown Brothers.*

affirmed the sovereignty and territorial boundaries of China and guaranteed equal commercial access to China—the Open Door remained open.

Hughes considered the meetings successful, although critics complained that the agreements included no provisions for enforcement and no mention of smaller naval ships, including submarines. As it turned out, the Washington Naval Conference was the only successful disarmament conference of the 1920s. Other attempts to reduce naval and land forces had mixed outcomes. After a failure in 1927 to limit the number of smaller naval vessels, Britain, the United States, and Japan established a series of ratios at the 1930 London Conference similar to those of the Washington Naval Conference—but for cruisers and destroyers. Thereafter, competition reigned: by the mid-1930s, Japan's demands for naval equality ended British and American cooperation and spurred renewed naval construction by all three sea powers.

Many Americans and Europeans applauded the achievements of the Washington Naval Conference but wanted to go further, seeking a repudiation of war. In 1923 Senator Borah introduced a resolution in the Senate to outlaw war, and in 1924 La Follette campaigned for a national referendum as a requirement for declaring war. In 1927 the French Foreign Minister, Aristide Briand, suggested a pact formally outlawing war between the two nations, privately hoping that such an agreement would commit the United States to aid France, if attacked. Secretary of State Kellogg deflected the proposal by suggesting a multinational statement opposing war. Kellogg thereby removed any hint of an American commitment to any specific

nation. On August 27, 1928, the United States and fourteen other nations, including Britain, France, Germany, Italy, and Japan, signed the Pact of Paris, or **Kellogg-Briand Pact**. By doing so, they renounced war "as an instrument of national policy" and agreed to settle disputes peacefully. Eventually sixty-four nations signed, but the pact included no enforcement provisions, and nearly every **signatory** reserved its right to defend itself and its possessions.

Thus, late in 1928, American independent internationalism seemed a success. Investments and loans by American businesses were fueling an expansive world economy and contributing to American prosperity. Avoiding entangling alliances, the United States had protected its Asian and Pacific interests against Japan, while protecting China and promoting disarmament and world peace. In Latin America, the United States had moderated its interventionist image by withdrawing American troops from the Caribbean, avoiding intervention in Mexico, and trying to broker a peace in Nicaragua. Foreign policies based on economic expansion and noncoercive diplomacy appeared to be establishing a promising era of cooperation and peace in world affairs.

Kellogg-Briand Pact Treaty signed in 1928 by fifteen nations, including Britain, France, Germany, the United States, and Japan, renouncing war as a means of solving international disputes.

signatory One who has signed a treaty or other document.

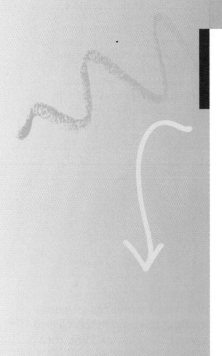

Examining a Primary Source

Parties in the Scopes Trial Pinpoint the Issues

A 1925 Tennessee law prohibited "any teacher in any of the Universities, Normals and all other public schools of the State which are supported in whole or in part by the public school funds of the State, to teach any theory that denies the story of the Divine Creation of man as taught in the Bible." When the American Civil Liberties Union offered to defend any teacher challenging the law, John Scopes stepped forward. He was immediately arrested and prosecuted. In the following excerpts, reprinted from the trial transcript, the opposing sides define the issues.

Dudley Field Malone, defending Scopes: The defense denies that it is part of any movement or conspiracy on the part of scientists to destroy the authority of Christianity or the Bible. The defense denies that any such conspiracy exists except in the mind and purpose of the evangelical leader of the prosecution [Bryan]. The defense maintains that the book of Genesis is in part a hymn, in part an allegory and work of religious interpretations written by men who believed that the earth was flat and whose authority cannot be accepted to control the teachings of science in our schools. . . . The Bible is a work of religious aspiration and rules of conduct which must be kept in the field of theology. The defense maintains that there is no more justification for imposing the conflicting views of the Bible on courses of biology than there would be for imposing the views of biologists on courses of comparative religion. We maintain that science and religion embrace two separate and distinct fields of thought and learning. ●

● How does this statement relate to the guilt or innocence of the defendant? Why do you think Malone introduced this argument?

Ben G. McKenzie, Assistant Attorney General of Tennessee, for the prosecution: There is but one issue before this court and jury, and that is, did the defendant violate the statute. ●

● What was McKenzie's purpose in defining the issues in this way?

Defendant John Scopes, upon being found guilty: Your honor, I feel that I have been convicted of violating an unjust statute. I will continue in the future, as I have in the past, to oppose this law in any way I can. Any other action would be in violation of my ideal of academic freedom—that is, to teach the truth as guaranteed in our constitution of personal and religious freedom. ●

● How does this constitutional argument compare with Bryan's argument about the right of the people to control their schools (the final excerpt)?

Clarence Darrow, attorney for the defense, at the end of the trial: We have done our best to turn back the tide . . . of testing every fact in science by a religious dictum.

William Jennings Bryan, chief prosecutor, in a speech made immediately after the trial: Science is a magnificent force, but it is not a teacher of morals. It can perfect machinery, but it adds no moral restraints to protect society from the misuse of the machine. . . . Science has made war so hellish that civilization

> *What does this argument have to do with Scopes's guilt or innocence? Compare the approaches of Malone and Bryan.*

was about to commit suicide. . . . If civilization is to be saved from the wreckage threatened by intelligence not consecrated by love, it must be saved by the moral code of the meek and lowly Nazarene [Jesus Christ]. His teachings, and His teachings, alone, can solve the problems that vex [the] heart and perplex the world. . . . It is for the jury to determine whether this attack upon the Christian religion shall be permitted in the public schools of Tennessee by teachers employed by the state and paid out of the public treasury. This case [is] between unbelief that attempts to speak through so-called science and the defenders of the Christian faith, speaking through the legislators of Tennessee. ●

SUMMARY

The 1920s were a decade of prosperity: unemployment was low, productivity grew steadily, and many Americans fared well. Sophisticated advertising campaigns created bright expectations, and installment buying freed consumers from having to pay cash. Many consumers bought more and bought on credit—stimulating manufacturing and expanding personal debt. Expectations of continuing prosperity also encouraged speculation. The stock market boomed, but agriculture did not share in this prosperity.

During the Roaring Twenties, Americans experienced significant social change. The automobile, radio, and movies, abetted by immigration restriction, produced a more homogeneous culture. Many American intellectuals, however, rejected the consumer-oriented culture. During the 1920s, African Americans produced an outpouring of significant art, literature, and music. Some young people rejected traditional constraints, and one result was the emergence of a youth culture.

Not all Americans embraced change. Some tried instead to maintain or restore earlier cultural values. The outcomes were mixed. Prohibition was largely unsuccessful. Fundamentalism grew and prompted a campaign against the teaching of evolution. Nativism helped produce significant new restrictions on immigration. The Ku Klux Klan, committed to nativism, traditional values, and white supremacy, experienced nationwide growth until 1925, but membership declined sharply thereafter.

Discrimination and occasional violence continued to affect the lives of people of color. Federal Indian policy had long stressed assimilation and allotment, but some groups successfully promoted different policies based on respect for Indian cultural values. Immigration from Mexico greatly increased the Latino population in California and the Southwest, and some Mexicans working in agriculture tried, in vain, to organize unions. Nearly all unions faced strong opposition from employers. Some older women's roles broke down as women gained the right to vote and exercised more control over the choice to have children. An identifiable gay and lesbian subculture emerged, especially in cities.

The politics of the era were marked by greater conservatism than before World War I. Warren G. Harding was a poor judge of character, and some of his appointees accepted bribes and disgraced their chief. Harding and his successor, Calvin Coolidge, expected government to act as a partner with business, and their economic policies minimized regulation and encouraged speculation. With some exceptions, progressive reform disappeared from politics, and efforts to secure federal assistance for farmers fizzled. The federal government was strongly conservative, staunchly probusiness, and absolutely unwilling to intervene in the economy. Herbert Hoover defeated Al Smith in the 1928 presidential election, in which the values of an older rural America seemed to be pitted against those of the new, urban, immigrant society.

During the 1920s, the United States followed a policy of independent internationalism that stressed voluntary cooperation among nations, while at the same time enhancing opportunities for American business around the world. Relations with Latin America improved somewhat, and the Washington Naval Conference held out the hope for preventing a naval arms race.

THE GREAT DEPRESSION AND UNEMPLOYMENT As Herbert Hoover confronted Franklin D. Roosevelt and the Great Depression in the race for the presidency in 1932, the nation was experiencing historically high unemployment. This map shows the percentage of the work force unemployed by state, and how much unemployment jumped in some cities during a ten-month period.

CANADA

WASHINGTON
23%
9%
Seattle

OREGON

MONTANA

IDAHO

NORTH DAKOTA

MINN.
21%
9%
Minneapolis

WISCONSIN

MICH.
35%
35%
15%
Buffalo

NEW YORK

MAINE
27%
11%

VT.
N.H.
MASS.
Boston

RHODE ISLAND
CONNECTICUT
NEW JERSEY

NEVADA

UTAH

WYOMING

SOUTH DAKOTA

IOWA

NEBRASKA

COLORADO
19%
9%
Denver

CALIFORNIA
19%
9%
Los Angeles

ARIZONA

NEW MEXICO

KANSAS

DUST BOWL

OKLAHOMA

TEXAS
23%
8%
Houston

ILLINOIS
25%
10%
Chicago

MISSOURI
13%
St. Louis

ARKANSAS

LOUISIANA
24%
11%
New Orleans

IND.

KENTUCKY

TENNESSEE
25%
7%
Birmingham

MISS.

ALABAMA

OHIO
31%
12%
Cleveland
Pittsburgh

PENNSYLVANIA
11%
33%

W. VA.

VIRGINIA

NORTH CAROLINA

SOUTH CAROLINA

GEORGIA

FLA.

DELAWARE
MARYLAND

PACIFIC OCEAN

ATLANTIC OCEAN

HAWAI'I TERRITORY
0 100 Km.
0 100 Mi.
PACIFIC OCEAN

MEXICO

U.S.S.R.

ALASKA TERRITORY

CANADA

PACIFIC OCEAN

0 250 500 Km.
0 250 500 Mi.

Gulf of Mexico

State unemployment in 1930
- 25–30%
- 20–25%
- 15–20%
- Under 15%

Urban unemployment
January 1931
25%
April 1930
8%
— 20%
— 10%
— 0

0 200 400 Km.
0 200 400 Mi.

Hoover elected

Kellogg-Briand Pact

Stock market crash

Roosevelt elected

First Hundred Days

Second Hundred Days

"Black Cabinet"

Court-packing plan

Sit-down strikes

Fair Labor Standards Act

1928 1929 1932 1933 1935 1936 1937 1938

1850 1900 1950 2000

The Great Depression and the New Deal, 1929–1939

Frances Perkins

FRANCES PERKINS

Beginning in 1911, Frances Perkins sought to improve working conditions for the nation's men, women, and children. Perkins was the first woman cabinet member, and as Secretary of Labor, she tirelessly worked to create the Social Security system, establish a minimum wage for workers, and limit the number of hours people could be required to work. *New York Historical Society.*

On February 1, 1933, responding to a month-long flurry of rumors in the press and among "those in the know" that she was to be chosen secretary of labor, Frances Perkins wrote President-elect Franklin D. Roosevelt saying that she "honestly" hoped that the rumors were false. Informed of the letter and fearful that Perkins might reject a cabinet position, Mary Dewson, director of the Women's Division of the Democratic National Committee, visited Perkins. Dewson had recommended Perkins to Roosevelt for the labor post and went to convince her that as a high-ranking member of the administration she could make a difference in establishing a better life for the American worker. She reminded Perkins of the many years she had spent fighting to establish unemployment compensation and a minimum wage and to abolish child labor. "You want these things done," Dewson argued. "You have ideas. Nobody else will do it." She told Perkins, "You owe it to the women. Too many people count on what you do."

On February 22, Roosevelt asked Frances Perkins to be secretary of labor. A hesitant Perkins replied, only if she could push for the abolition of child labor, the establishment of unemployment insurance, old-age pensions, a minimum wage, and a limit on the maximum hours of work. Roosevelt agreed but told her that she would "have to invent the way to do these things" and that she should not "expect too much help from" him. She accepted the nomination. Confirmed by the Senate, Frances Perkins became "Madam Secretary," the first woman to serve in a president's cabinet.

She had arrived at the position through hard work and a commitment to improving workers' lives. The daughter of a conservative middle-class family, she had been introduced to her life's mission while taking an economics class at Mount Holyoke College. She quickly immersed herself in the spirit of the Progressive Era, participating in the settlement house movement and investigating working conditions as part of the New York Factory Commission following the tragic fire at the Triangle Shirtwaist Company in 1911. Impressed by her work on the commission and with the Consumers' League, Governor Al Smith appointed her to the state's Industrial Commission, which sought to improve the lives of workers. When Franklin D. Roosevelt replaced Smith as governor in 1929, he named her industrial commissioner, a state cabinet-level position—making her the first woman to hold such a position.

As secretary of labor, she threw herself into the first hundred days, seeking means to improve the life of the average American. She played key roles in supporting programs to provide jobs and relief, including the creation of the Civilian Conservation Corps and the Federal Emergency Relief Administration. She worked tirelessly for more public works and was instrumental in merging the Public Works Administration with the National Industrial Recovery Act. But these programs were temporary, and by 1934 she was forging an agenda to provide permanent benefits. As the chair of the newly created Committee on Economic Security, she began to draft a social security bill that would provide workers with a retirement plan, increase unemployment compensation, and include support for children. An encouraging Roosevelt told her: "You care about this thing. You believe in it. Therefore I know you will put your back to it more than anyone else, and you'll drive it through."

The Social Security Act of 1935 was the outcome of many choices, most of which involved Perkins, Harry Hopkins, and Roosevelt. It was decided, for fiscal and political reasons, to have workers pay into the system as opposed to having the government pay for benefits out of taxes. Perkins had wanted to include medical coverage, but that option was excluded from the social security package, doused in large part by a hostile medical profession. To convince Congress to pass the bill, she made hundreds of public speeches and testified before countless congressional committees. With its enactment on August 14, 1935, the relationship between the federal government and the people fundamentally and permanently changed.

Frances Perkins took pride in the passage of the Social Security Act, but she was overjoyed when the Fair Labor Standards Act became law in 1938. "A self-supporting and self-respecting democracy," she testified, "can plead no justification for the existence of child labor, no economic reason for chiseling workers' wages or stretching workers' hours." The bill was attacked as allowing too much government intrusion. Conservatives called it a form of socialism, while a few union leaders argued that collective bargaining—not the government—should gain wage and hour benefits for workers. Nevertheless, in the closing months of the New Deal, the bill became law on June 25, 1938. More than 12 million workers felt its effect. It immediately raised the pay of 300,000 people and shortened the workday for a million more. Equally important to Perkins, it barred industrial child labor under 16. Together, the Social Security Act and the Fair Labor Standards Act recast the economic and social values of the nation and established a new caretaker role for the government.

Frances Perkins continued to serve Roosevelt and his successor Harry S Truman as an advocate of government support of workers and their families. Retiring in 1953, she wrote, lectured, and joined the faculty at Cornell University. She died in 1965, and her tombstone reflects the fateful choice she made in 1933:

FRANCES PERKINS WILSON
1880–1965
SECRETARY OF LABOR OF U.S.A.
1933–1945

INTRODUCTION

The Great Depression stretched across the thirties and affected all Americans, rich, poor, and in between. No segment of American society was untouched: lives were changed, traditions were challenged, and the function of the federal government was forever altered. When Herbert Clark Hoover became president, most Americans assumed that the United States would enjoy continued economic growth. Some even projected that domestic poverty would nearly disappear. Those optimistic voices were wrong. Before the start of the 1930s, the American and world economy had collapsed and the Great Depression had begun.

Hoover faced the new challenges of the Depression with ideas he had expected would produce continued growth. He found that they had little effect. He shifted policy but failed to change the course of the Depression. By 1932, the Depression had thwarted Hoover's hopes and ruined his political career as the American people chose a new path in the election of Franklin D. Roosevelt and a Democratic Congress.

Roosevelt, who would dominate American history for the next thirteen years, had few qualms about using the power of the government to combat the Depression and reform society. With a program called the "New Deal," the new administration unleashed a barrage of legislation along three paths: economic recovery, relief, and reform. By 1938, however, the New Deal was sputtering to an end. It had not rescued the economy, but it had totally transformed the role and function of government.

Against the backdrop of economic disaster, presidential actions, and partisan politics, Americans faced economic insecurity for the first time as the number of the underemployed and unemployed dramatically increased. Some feared that social values might be fundamentally changed, but their fears proved to be unfounded. The American people and society proved resilient, making do with less—getting by—many made new economic and social choices, and an increasing number looked for government intervention to ease their hardships and restore the economy. Most supported Roosevelt and the New Deal, although critics warned about the expanding power of government and the moving down the path toward socialism. By the end of the 1930s, most Americans had accepted a new activist role for government. Workers, farmers, women, and minorities had found new avenues of expression; and thousands of African Americans had joined the Democratic Party. Roosevelt and the New Deal had changed the definition of "liberalism" and had expanded the responsibilities and power of the federal government. Roosevelt would be both revered and reviled, but no one could deny his impact.

HOOVER AND ECONOMIC CRISIS

• What were Americans' expectations when they elected Herbert Hoover president in 1928?

• What was the impact of the stock market crash on the American economy, and what major economic weaknesses contributed to the crash and the Great Depression?

• What choices did Hoover make in dealing with the problems created by the Depression, and why were Hoover's efforts to fight the Depression unsuccessful?

Campaigning for the presidency, Herbert Hoover had promised a "New Day" for America, but his sweeping victory was more a vote for the status quo. The United States had seen almost a decade of economic growth and rising standards of living, and people had voted for Hoover expecting that trend to continue under Republican leadership. Hoover believed it could be accomplished by promoting **associationalism**—that is, by fostering voluntary cooperation among competing groups within American society. It was an approach soon tested by economic and social trauma.

The Great Crash and the Depression

Hoover assumed office as ever-rising stock prices, shiny new cars, and rapidly expanding suburbs seemed to verify his observation about "the final triumph over poverty." But behind the rush for radios, homes, and vacuum cleaners were economic weaknesses, overproduction, poor distribution of income, excessive credit buying, and weak and weakening sectors of the economy. Eight months later, on October 24, 1929, those hidden weaknesses became visible as the stock market crashed and the American economy stumbled and then fell. It was business as usual that Thursday morning as Americans went to work, most unconcerned about the rise and fall of stock prices on Wall Street. But on that day, later called **Black Thursday**, the bottom suddenly fell out of the stock market and nearly everyone's lives turned upside-down. The value of stocks plummeted and by noon the ticker-tape that relayed stock prices across the nation was running nearly two and a half hours behind. Brokerage offices across the country were in a frenzy as brokers rushed to place sell orders. No place was untouched by the panic. In the mid-Atlantic, on board the passenger liner *Berengaria*, Helena Rubenstein watched stock prices fall and finally sold 50,000 shares of Westinghouse Company. She had lost more than a million dollars in a few hours.

The market rebounded, holding its own on Friday, but it slipped again on Monday. Then, on October 29—Black Tuesday—prices plunged and would con-

---

associationalism President Hoover's theory that government could foster economic and social progress by promoting voluntary cooperation among competing groups and interests.

Black Thursday October 24, 1929, when the stock market fell dramatically in what proved to be the beginning of the Great Depression; over 12.8 million shares changed hands that day, but the worst day for the market was the following Tuesday, October 29, when nearly 16.5 million shares changed hands.

chronology

Depression and New Deal

1928	Herbert Hoover elected president
1929	Stock market crash
1929–1933	Depression deepens 4,000 U.S. banks fail 90,000 American businesses fail Unemployment rises from 9 to 25 percent
1930	Hawley-Smoot Tariff
1931	Mexican repatriation begins Scottsboro Nine convicted
1932	Glass-Steagall Banking Act Federal Home Loan Bank Act Reconstruction Finance Corporation Emergency Relief Division of Reconstruction Finance Corporation created Milo Reno forms Farmers' Holiday Association Bonus Army marches to Washington Franklin D. Roosevelt elected president
1933	Drought turns Midwest into Dust Bowl Franklin D. Roosevelt inaugurated New Deal begins National Bank Holiday First fireside chat First Hundred Days (March 9–June 16) Civilian Conservation Corps created Agricultural Adjustment Administration created Tennessee Valley Authority created Home Owners' Loan Corporation (HOLC) created National Industrial Recovery Act passed (NIRA and PWA) Twenty-first Amendment (repealing Prohibition) ratified

1934	Huey Long's Share the Wealth plan Father Charles Coughlin forms National Union for Social Justice Indian Reorganization Act Securities and Exchange Commission (SEC) created American Liberty League established Dr. Francis Townsend's movement begins
1935	Second Hundred Days Works Progress Administration created NRA ruled unconstitutional in *Schechter* case Rural Electrification Administration formed National Youth Administration created National Labor Relations Board created (Wagner Act) Social Security Act passed Long assassinated Congress for Industrial Organization established
1936	AAA ruled unconstitutional in *Butler* case Roosevelt reelected "Black Cabinet" organized Sit-down strikes begin
1937	Court-packing plan "Roosevelt's recession" U.S. unemployment climbs to 19 percent
1938	Works Progress Administration rolls double Fair Labor Standards Act AAA re-established Republican victories in congressional elections
1939	Marian Anderson's concert at Lincoln Memorial John Steinbeck's *The Grapes of Wrath*
1940	Richard Wright's *Native Son*

tinue to fall throughout the year. By mid-November, the *New York Times* **industrials** (selected industrial stocks chosen as indicators of trends in the economy) had declined from 469 to 221. Quality stocks plummeted—RCA from 101 to 28, Montgomery Ward from 138 to 49, and Union Carbide from 138 to 59. Hundreds of brokers and speculators were ruined. Stories circulated of New York hotel clerks asking guests whether they wanted rooms for sleeping or jumping.

industrials Industrial stocks identified as indicators of trends in the economy.

The day the stock market crashed, the entire nation suddenly became aware of Wall Street. The collapse of the stock market historically signals the beginning of the greatest depression in American history. Despite the efforts of Hoover and Roosevelt, it was only the economic activity generated by World War II that revived the economy. *"Black Friday: Richard Whitney and the Stock Exchange," 1939 by Edward Laning. Collection of John P. Axelrod.*

The crash is a convenient starting point for the **Great Depression**, but it was not its cause. The Depression was a product of overproduction, poor distribution of income, too much credit buying, and uneven economic growth. The prosperity of the 1920s had in part rested on robust, expanding industries—chemical, automobile, and electronics, among others—that pushed the rest of the economy forward. But by 1927, even these industries were seeing a slowing of growth. Construction starts fell from 11 billion to 9 billion units between 1926 and 1929. Furniture companies, like many other producers of consumer merchandise, expecting an unlimited market, had by 1927 produced too many goods and by 1928 were reducing their labor forces to shave production costs. The impact of a slowing economy was even worse in less robust sectors of the economy. Throughout the 1920s older industries such as railroads, textiles, and iron

and steel had barely made a profit while agriculture and mining suffered steady losses. Workers in those jobs saw little increase in wages or standard of living. Agriculture was especially weak. The postwar economic expansion had totally bypassed agriculture, as farmers watched their incomes and property values slip to about half of their wartime highs. Compounding these problems, credit had virtually dried up in rural America because five thousand banks had closed between 1921 and 1928. By the end of 1928, thousands of people had left their farms, and agriculture was approaching an economic crisis.

Another weakness of the economy was a maldistribution of wealth. The nation had over 513 millionaires, but that concentration of wealth represented too much money in too few hands to maintain consumer spending. The **Brookings Institute** judged that an annual salary of $2,500 provided an American family a comfortable standard of living. It also found that 70 percent of American families earned less than that amount. When Hoover took office, most people were exhausting nearly all of their monthly incomes on food, housing, and a variety of consumer products and were supplementing their wages with credit buying. Increasingly, Americans were in debt. Americans had spent about $100 million in credit buying in 1919, but ten years later that amount had soared to over $7 billion. Credit buying not only contributed significantly to consumer spending but had helped to generate the stock boom as well. Anxious to invest in the stock market, many individuals were borrowing money to buy stocks (see page 714), and their speculative fervor had pushed stock prices higher and higher until by 1929 the price of many stocks had little relationship to dividends the stocks paid or the actual worth of the issuing companies. Still, few worried about debt as long as the economy seemed stable, unemployment remained low, and Americans had confidence in the economy. All that changed with the stock market crash.

Great Depression   The years 1929 to 1941 when the economy of the United States suffered its greatest decline, millions of people were unemployed, and thousands of businesses went bankrupt; President Hoover used the term *depression* rather than the more traditional *panic* in hopes that it would reduce the public's fears.

Brookings Institute   A nonprofit, nonpartisan organization founded by Robert Brookings in 1916 that studies government, economic, and international issues.

Suddenly, when the market crashed, economic confidence was undermined and the weaknesses of the economy were highlighted. Americans had viewed the soaring stock market as a symbol of the vigor of the economy and nation. When the market continued to fall following Black Tuesday and the economy slumped, investors became wary to invest. Corporations were more likely to cut production and lay off workers, who could ill afford any reduction in wages. Consumers were hesitant to spend their money. Banks were less willing to lend money and increasingly wanted existing loans to be paid. The economy spiraled downward. And in the months following the crash, problems in the banking system became painfully obvious.

The Federal Reserve was designed to provide uniformity and stability to the banking system, but by 1928 only about one-third of the nation's banks had joined the system. Many of those outside the system were undercapitalized, had made too many loans and questionable investments, and were vulnerable to a slowing economy. **"Runs"** on banks, as customers lined up at teller windows to empty their accounts, were growing before the stock market crash and intensified afterward. With few available funds to satisfy their depositors' demands, banks foreclosed on mortgages and recalled loans, which contributed to the economic panic. Unable to meet their obligations, more and more banks went into bankruptcy, as in the case of the New York Bank of the United States. It had held over $280 million in savings accounts, and in December 1930 it closed its doors and thousands of people lost all their money. The failure of the nation's banks forecast a serious economic crisis for the growing number of unemployed and jarred the well-being of many upper- and middle-class families who suddenly found they had little or no savings—no buffer against hard times. Across the nation, Americans faced a deepening depression, the result of the stock market crash, too much credit, loss of economic confidence, and the existing weaknesses within the economy.

The effect of the stock market crash and the declining American economy had an international dimension as well. The European economy had never fully recovered from the destruction of the First World War and was partly dependent on American loans and markets. Following the crash, loans by American banks declined, as did purchases by American corporations. To protect American business from foreign competition, in 1930 Congress passed the **Hawley-Smoot Tariff**. Though a victory for American economic nationalism, it was a catastrophe abroad.

Angered by American actions, twenty-three foreign governments raised their tariffs on American goods, further stifling world trade.

By 1933, the world and American economies were in shambles. American exports were at their lowest level since 1905, nearly ninety thousand businesses had failed, corporate profits were down 60 percent, and nine thousand banks closed, with depositors losing $2.5 billion. As the money supply shrank, dropping by a third between 1930 and 1933, the average expenditure for goods plummeted by 45 percent. Purchases of automobiles dropped by 75 percent. At the same time, unemployment rose from 3 percent in 1929, to 9 percent in 1930, to an unheard-of 25 percent by 1933.

Hoover and the Depression

The most common and immediate response to the plunge in stock prices was voiced by Secretary of Treasury Andrew Mellon, who stated that the economy remained strong and that the plunge of the market was temporary and would in fact strengthen the economy. Most experts believed the government should let the economy heal itself. Hoover disagreed, however. He thought the government should take a more active role to ensure that a panic did not follow. Reflecting his vision of leadership, he summoned the nation's economic leaders. He asked industries to absorb the economic shock by reducing profits rather than the work force and wages. At the same time he worked with the Federal Reserve System to expand credit and urged Congress, states, and cities to increase spending on **public works projects**, including buildings, highways, government facilities, and, in particular, the **Boulder Dam**. At first there was some corporate compliance, and federal, state, and local governments

run Informal term describing a rush by depositors to withdraw their funds from a bank.

Hawley-Smoot Tariff Tariff passed by Congress in 1930 in response to the Depression, setting the highest tariff rates in U.S. history and thus undermining world trade.

public works projects Highways, dams, and other construction projects financed by public funds and carried out by the government.

Boulder Dam Dam on the Colorado River between Nevada and Arizona, begun during Hoover's administration and completed in 1935.

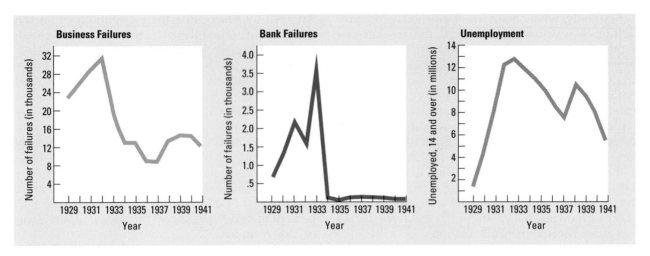

FIGURE 24.1 **Charting the Economics of the Depression** Between 1929 and 1933, the number of people unemployed and of banks and businesses shutting down steadily increased. By 1933, over 4,000 banks had failed, unemployment had reached 24.9 percent, and over 100,000 firms had closed. As the New Deal began, not only did the statistics improve, but for most Americans a new sense of hope also emerged.

doubled their spending on public works. But it did not last long. With fewer goods being sold, businesses faced declining profits and bankruptcy, and in desperation they cut production and wages and laid off workers. By the end of 1932, ninety thousand businesses and nine thousand banks had failed. Workers' incomes had dropped 40 percent and unemployment had raced to 25 percent (see Figure 24.1).

With the country slipping further into the Depression, in 1931 Hoover took new steps. He asked Congress for banking reforms, financial support for home mortgages, the creation of the **Reconstruction Finance Corporation** (RFC), and higher taxes to pay for it all. Congress responded with the **Glass-Steagall Banking Act**, which increased bank reserves to encourage lending, and the **Federal Home Loan Act**, which allowed homeowners to re-mortgage their homes at lower rates and payments. But it was through the RFC that Hoover intended to fight the depression by pumping money into the economy. Using federal funds, the RFC was to provide loans to banks, **savings and loan associations**, railroads, and large corporations to prevent their collapse and encourage expanded operations. Hoover and his advisers believed the money would "trickle down" to workers and the unemployed through higher wages and new jobs. Approved by Congress, within five months of operation, the RFC had loaned over $805 million, but little money seemed to be trickling down to workers. Liberal critics branded the program "welfare for the rich" and insisted Hoover do

more for the poor and unemployed through **direct relief payments**.

Hoover opposed direct federal relief, the "dole," to the poor, believing that it would be too expensive and, worse, would erode the work ethic. But with unemployment reaching nearly 25 percent and mounting pressure from Congress and the public, Hoover accepted an Emergency Relief Division within the RFC. It was to provide $300 million in loans to states to pay for relief. Yet little money was used because the RFC loaned funds too cautiously

Reconstruction Finance Corporation Organization established at Hoover's request in 1932 to promote economic recovery; it provided emergency financing for banks, life insurance companies, railroads, and farm mortgage associations.

Glass-Steagall Banking Act Law passed by Congress in 1932 that expanded credit through the Federal Reserve System in order to counteract foreign withdrawals and domestic hoarding of money.

Federal Home Loan Act Law passed by Congress in 1932 that established twelve banks across the nation to supplement lending resources to institutions making home loans in an effort to reduce foreclosures and to stimulate the construction industry.

savings and loan associations Cooperative mutual financial institutions that use funds from members to finance long-term real-estate mortgages.

direct relief payments Payments that government agencies make directly to the poor and unemployed.

The Great Depression produced large-scale unemployment, reaching 25 percent in 1933. This picture, titled "Unemployed," painted by Reginald Marsh effectively captured the despair of men and women seeking jobs. *"Unemployed" by Reginald Marsh, 1932. Library of Congress.*

and few states wanted to borrow and put themselves deeper in debt. By the end of 1932, 90 percent of the relief fund was still intact. Whether for relief or recovery, the RFC did not make enough funds available to relieve the economic crisis.

The onslaught of the Depression had changed Hoover's and the nation's fortunes. Many Americans blamed the president and the Republicans for the worsening economy and a callousness toward the hardships faced by many Americans. In the traditionally conservative farm belt, militant farmers joined the **Farmers' Holiday Association** led by **Milo Reno**. He accused the government of inaction and being in the "grip of Wall Street." Reno called on farmers to resist **foreclosures** and to destroy their crops. Farmers responded. On several occasions, they used numbers and threats of violence to force "penny auctions" that ensured that foreclosed farms were returned to their owners for a fraction of their value. In Ohio,

Walter Crozier, backed by a crowd of angry neighbors, regained his farm for a high bid of $1.90. Farmers were not alone. Across the nation, strikes, protest rallies, "bread marches," and rent riots took place as citizens demanded more jobs, higher wages, and relief payments. In Detroit, three workers died when a workers' demonstration against Ford was attacked by police and security guards.

A larger expression of protest took place in Washington, D.C., as thousands of World War I veterans, the **Bonus Army**, converged to support the "bonus bill," which would provide them with an early payment of their $1,000 veteran's bonus, scheduled to be paid in 1945. The marchers set up their **Hooverville** across from Congress at Anacosta Flats and picketed Congress and the White House demanding passage of the bill. When the bill failed in mid-June, most of the Bonus Marchers left Washington, but nearly 10,000 stayed behind. To remove the protesters, Hoover turned to the army, led by Army Chief of Staff General Douglas MacArthur. Using sabers, rifles, tear gas, and fixed bayonets, the army drove the "squatters" from their encampment. In a one-sided fight, the soldiers forced the veterans and their families from the huts and tents while the smell of smoke and tear gas hung over the city. Over one hundred veterans were injured, but rumors quickly swelled the number and added several fatalities, including the death of a baby who reportedly succumbed to tear gas. The rumors intensified the public's angry

Farmers' Holiday Association   Organization of farmers that called on members to take direct actions—such as destroying crops and resisting foreclosures—to protest the plight of agriculture and the lack of government support.

Milo Reno   Farm leader from Iowa who led the Farmers' Holiday Association and in 1932 called on farmers to strike, to "stay home, buy nothing, sell nothing"; he wanted government codes to control production but rejected President Roosevelt's farm program as a threat to independence and liberty; he died in 1936.

foreclosure   Confiscation of property by a bank when mortgage payments are delinquent.

Bonus Army   Unemployed World War I veterans who marched to Washington in 1932 to demand early payment of a promised bonus; Congress refused and the army evicted protesters who remained.

Hooverville   Crudely built camp set up by the homeless on the fringes of a town or city during the Depression; the largest Hooverville was outside Oklahoma City and covered over 100 square miles.

The sign in front of the "Bonus Dugout" reads, "We have come to collect the gratitude that was promised us for participating in the World War." They received neither gratitude nor the bonus. Instead, Hoover commented: "Thank God we still have a government that knows how to deal with a mob." *Library of Congress.*

reaction. Upon hearing of the forced eviction of the marchers, the governor of New York, Franklin D. Roosevelt, crowed, "This will elect me."

THE NEW DEAL

● How did the New Deal's "First Hundred Days" represent a change in the role of the federal government? In particular, what measures did it include, and how did they promote recovery?

● What were the sources of opposition to Roosevelt's First Hundred Days, and how did the Second One Hundred Days respond to those critics and differ from the first? Why did no Third Hundred Days follow Roosevelt's resounding victory in 1936?

● How did the New Deal change the structure of government and Americans' expectations about the role of government?

Nearly any Democratic candidate could have defeated Hoover in 1932, but the Democrats had nominated an exceptional politician in Franklin D. Roosevelt. Born into wealth and privilege, he had attended Groton Academy and Harvard University, schools popular with America's aristocracy. Neither academically nor athletically gifted, Roosevelt was nonetheless popular and after graduation, with a recognizable name, entered New York politics. Tall, handsome, charming, glib, he quickly moved up the political ladder, being nominated for vice president in 1920. Even though he and James Cox were defeated, his future looked bright. Suddenly, in 1921, it appeared his political career was over when he was stricken with polio and paralyzed from the waist down. Greatly aided by his wife Eleanor, he

In the 1932 election, Roosevelt campaigned across the nation, always appearing confident and cheerful. Some said that his smile was the biggest political weapon he had—not only against Hoover but the Depression. *FPG.*

kept his political career alive and in 1928 ran for governor of New York. Al Smith lost his bid for the presidency, but Roosevelt won.

As governor of New York, Roosevelt was one of the few governors to mobilize his state's limited resources to help the unemployed and poor. While making little headway against the Depression, his efforts projected an image of a more caring and energetic leader than Hoover. His valiant struggle to overcome polio combined with his actions as governor and cheery disposition earned him a reputation as the champion of the "forgotten man" and made him appear the opposite of Hoover, who seemed to have little concern for the 11 million unemployed Americans.

When nominated for president, showing dynamic flair, Roosevelt broke with the tradition and flew to Chicago, site of the national convention. He emphasized two points in his acceptance speech: he was a man of action who promoted change, and his health was good and his paralysis in no way hindered his activity. He also established a theme for the coming campaign. Pointing to his tradition-breaking trip to the convention, Roosevelt emphatically announced that he and the Democratic Party had no fear of breaking "all foolish traditions." He closed by promising a "new deal for the American people." The media quickly picked up on the term, handing Roosevelt a memorable slogan for his campaign: the **New Deal**. Although the acceptance speech offered no concrete solutions to the problems facing the country, it stirred the desire for hope and instilled the belief that Roosevelt would move the nation along new paths.

During the campaign, Roosevelt tried to avoid any commitments and policies that might offend voters or blocs within the Democratic Party. He supported direct federal relief while promising to balance the budget, but mostly he stressed hope and the prospect of change. Hoover, trying to overcome his opponent's popularity, emphasized their philosophical differences. He claimed that the campaign, "more than a contest between two men," was "a contest between two philosophies of government." The election was a huge success for the Democratic Party and Roosevelt. Across the nation, people voted for Democrats at every level from local to national. Roosevelt won in a landslide, burying Hoover with 22.8 million votes, 57.4 percent of over 39.7 million votes cast. Hoover carried only six states—the rest belonged to Roosevelt (see Map 24.1).

Roosevelt Confronts the Depression

In the four months between the election and inauguration day, the people eagerly waited for the New

New Deal   Term applied to Roosevelt's policies to attack the problems of the Depression, which included relief for poor and unemployed, efforts to stimulate economic recovery, and social security; the term was coined by Roosevelt's adviser Raymond Moley.

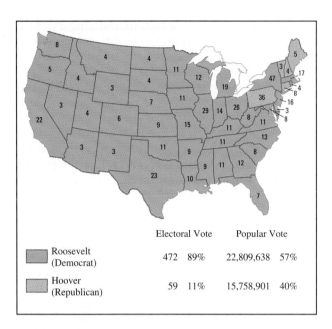

	Electoral Vote		Popular Vote	
Roosevelt (Democrat)	472	89%	22,809,638	57%
Hoover (Republican)	59	11%	15,758,901	40%

MAP 24.1 Election of 1932   In the election of 1932, Herbert Hoover faced not only Franklin D. Roosevelt but also the Great Depression. With many Americans blaming Hoover and the Republicans for the economic catastrophe and with Roosevelt promising a New Deal, the outcome was not close. Roosevelt won 42 of 48 states.

Deal to start even as the economy worsened. To many, it appeared that Roosevelt and his advisers, labeled by the press as the **Brain Trust**, were developing a clear plan to restore prosperity. It was an illusion. There was no plan, and in fact the Brain Trust and Roosevelt's other advisers were frequently at odds about which path of follow. Some, like Rexford Tugwell and Raymond Moley, supported a collective approach, working with big businesses through increased regulation and joint economic planning. Others, like Harry Hopkins, Eleanor Roosevelt, and Felix Frankfurter, advocated social programs and a more competitive economic system. All agreed, however, that the worst path was doing nothing and that federal power must be used.

Riding a wave of popular support and great expectations, Roosevelt faced a unique political climate of almost total bipartisanship. The result was that within its first hundred days in office, the Roosevelt administration passed more legislation than any president before or since and forever changed the public's vision of the role of the federal government. Roosevelt took office on March 4, as the

nation faced the possible collapse of its banking system. Nearly all the country's banks were closed, and the economy faced paralysis. The country waited anxiously to see how the new president would act. They were not disappointed. On inauguration day, Franklin D. Roosevelt spoke reassuring words to the American public and let the nation know that he was taking action. Millions listened to the radio as the president calmly stated that Americans had "nothing to fear but fear itself" and promised that the economy would revive. "We must act quickly," he added, announcing that he would ask Congress for sweeping powers to deal with the crisis. On March 6, Roosevelt declared a national **Bank Holiday** that closed all the country's banks. Three days later, as freshmen congressmen were still finding their seats, the president presented Congress with the **Emergency Banking Bill**. Without even seeing a written version of the bill, Democrats and Republicans gave Roosevelt what he wanted in less than four hours. It allowed the Federal Reserve and the Reconstruction Finance Corporation (which had outlasted Hoover) to support the nation's banks by providing funds and buying stocks of preferred banks. On Sunday evening, March 12, in the first of his **fireside chats**, the president said that that the federal government was solving the banking crisis and banks would be safe again. He joked, "It is safer to keep your money in a re-opened bank than under the mattress." Over 60 million Americans listened to the speech, and most believed in their leader. Confidence had been restored, and within a month nearly 75 percent of the nation's banks were operating again. In Atlanta

Brain Trust   Group of specialists in law, economics, and social welfare who, as advisers to President Roosevelt, helped develop the social and economic principles of the New Deal.

Bank Holiday   Temporary shutdown of banks throughout the country by executive order of President Roosevelt in March 1933.

Emergency Banking Bill (Act)   Law passed by Congress in 1933 that permitted sound banks in the Federal Reserve System to reopen and allowed the government to supply funds to support private banks.

fireside chats   Radio talks in which President Roosevelt promoted New Deal policies and reassured the nation; Roosevelt delivered twenty-eight fireside chats.

on the day following the fireside chat, deposits outnumbered withdrawals by over 3 to 1. The New Deal had begun. Roosevelt signed fifteen major pieces of legislation over the next one hundred days. The legislation, he explained in another fireside chat, was moving along three paths: recovery, relief, and reform.

Seeking Recovery

Among the first bills Roosevelt offered Congress, on March 16, was the **Agricultural Adjustment Act**. With the National Farmers' Holiday Association threatening to call a strike, Secretary of Agriculture Henry A. Wallace drafted a bill that used national planning and government payments to raise farm prices and provide a profit for agriculture. Passed by Congress on May 12, the Agricultural Adjustment Administration (AAA) encouraged farmers to reduce production by paying them *not* to plant. Focusing on wheat, cotton, field corn, rice, tobacco, hogs, and milk and milk products, a planning board set a domestic allotment and determined the amount to be removed from production. To pay for the program, a special tax on the industrial food processors was levied. Some critics argued that the AAA gave too much power to the government, calling it a form of socialism. Milo Reno, who still led the National Farmers' Association, rejected the AAA, charging that it would set up a "bureaucratic, autocratic, and dictatorial government." He called on farmers to strike. Others complained that the AAA did nothing to help small farmers, sharecroppers, and tenant farmers; they wanted the government to make the surplus food available for the needy.

Despite Reno's call for a strike, farmers and most of the nation put their trust in Roosevelt and the AAA. By 1935, it appeared that the program was working. Farm prices were climbing and the purchasing power of farmers was increasing (see Figure 24.2). Farmer approval of the AAA remained high even as the Supreme Court ruled that it was unconstitutional in *Butler v. the United States*. In its 1936 decision the Court ruled that the federal government could not set production quotas and that the special tax on processing food was illegal. Undeterred, the administration used other programs, such as the **Soil Conservation Act**, to reduce production. Nature also helped take land out of production as high winds swept across the drought-plagued Midwest creating what became known as the **Dust Bowl**. Dust storms sometimes stretched more than

Dorothea Lange became one of the most famous photographers of the Depression. Her photo of a migrant mother and her children at a migrant camp in Nipomo, California captured the human tragedy of the Depression. Seeking jobs and opportunities, over 350,000 people traveled to the state, most finding few opportunities. *Library of Congress.*

Agricultural Adjustment Act Law passed by Congress in 1933 to reduce overproduction by paying farmers not to grow crops or raise livestock.

Butler v. the United States Supreme Court decision (1936) declaring the Agricultural Adjustment Act invalid on the grounds that it unconstitutionally extended the powers of the federal government.

Soil Conservation Act Legislation by Congress that established an agency for the prevention of soil erosion; by paying farmers to cut back on soil-depleting crops, it also reduced overproduction.

Dust Bowl Name given to the Great Plains region devastated by drought and dust storms during the 1930s; the worst years (1936–1938) saw over sixty major storms per year, seventy-two in 1937.

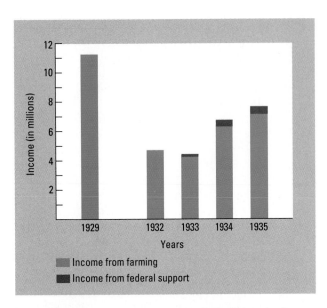

FIGURE 24.2 Farm Income, 1929–1935 Prices for farm products fell rapidly as the Depression set in (see Table 24.1), but by 1933, with support from New Deal programs like the Agricultural Adjustment Act, some farm incomes were rising. Note, however, that some of the increase was a direct result of government payments. *Source:* U.S. Department of Commerce, *Historical Statistics of the United States, Colonial Times to 1970* (2 parts) (Washington, D.C.: U.S. Government Printing Office), pp. 483–484, part 1.

MAP 24.2 The Dust Bowl Throughout the 1930s, sun and wind eroded millions of acres of crop land, sending tons of topsoil into the air, generating tidal waves of dust—and the Dust Bowl. This map shows the regions most affected by the Dust Bowl and decreases in population, and Route 66, which many chose to travel, hoping that it would lead to a better life in California.

200 miles across and over 7,000 feet high. In 1938 alone, over 850 million tons of topsoil were lost to wind erosion (see Map 24.2).

As the Dust Bowl reached its worst point, Congress approved a second Agricultural Adjustment Act that re-established the principle of federally set commodity quotas, acreage reduction, and **parity** payments. A year later, farm income had more than doubled since 1932, with the government providing over $4.5 billion in aid to farmers. Initially intended as a short-term measure, federal support for farm prices would last over fifty years and significantly changed the relationship between agricultural producers and the federal government.

The AAA addressed the problem of agriculture, and in May 1933, the administration offered Congress a program for dealing with the problem of industrial recovery. The Tugwell-Moley group favored stimulating industrial production through national economic planning and controls to stabilize production, prices, employment, and wages. Others favored expanding consumption and jobs through public works programs and a 30-hour workweek. The result was the **National Industrial Recovery**

Act (NIRA), introduced in May 1933 and approved a month later. Roosevelt called it the "most important and far reaching legislation passed by the American Congress." The act created two agencies, the National Recovery Administration (NRA) for long-term economic revival and the **Public Works Administration** (PWA) for more immediate work

parity The fair value of something compared with its market value; the parity ratio established by the government was the ratio between the price received for a basket of goods sold compared with its purchase price and was set at a ratio that existed from 1914–1920.

National Industrial Recovery Act Law passed by Congress in 1933 establishing the National Recovery Administration to supervise industry and the Public Works Administration to create jobs.

Public Works Administration Agency that the NIRA established to increase employment and to stimulate economic recovery by putting people to work to expand consumer buying power; it spent more than $4.25 million on 34,000 public works projects.

The National Recovery Administration was Roosevelt's main vehicle to restore industrial recovery during his First One Hundred Days. Headed by General Hugh Johnson, the NRA's goal was to mobilize management, workers, and consumers under the symbol of the Blue Eagle; establish national production codes; and get America moving again. *Collection of David J. and Janice L. Frent.*

relief. The goal of the **National Recovery Administration** (NRA), led by **General Hugh "Ironpants" Johnson**, was to implement national economic planning by establishing national boards to write "industrial codes." The codes established prices, production levels, and wages. Business supported the NRA because it allowed **price fixing** that raised both prices and profits. Labor was attracted by pro-labor codes—in Section 7a—that gave workers the right to organize and bargain collectively, outlawed child labor, and established minimum wages and maximum hours of work. With the Blue Eagle as its symbol and "We Do Our Part" as its motto, the NRA **juggernaut** rolled forward. A determined Johnson

exhorted the American public: "Nothing can stop the President's program, nothing will even hamper the President's program. . . . The power of this people, once aroused and united in a fixed purpose, is the most irresistible force in the world."

His efforts were amazingly successful. Nearly overnight, the Blue Eagle appeared everywhere. By the beginning of 1935, over 700 industries and 2.5 million workers were covered by the codes. But almost from the beginning, dissatisfaction brewed and critics dubbed it the "National Run Around." Workers complained that wages were too low, hours too long, and that employers resisted unionization. Consumers grumbled that prices rose without any noticeable growth in wages or jobs. Farmers griped that NRA-generated price increases ate up any AAA benefits they received. As production and profitability increased, businesses soon chafed under federal restrictions and regulations and questioned the government's right to impose such controls. Many opponents called the NRA unconstitutional and on May 27, 1935, the Supreme Court agreed. In **Schechter Poultry Corporation v. the United States**, the Court held that the government could not set national codes or set wages and hours in local plants. Roosevelt was furious at the Court, saying it had a "horse and buggy" mentality.

Perhaps the most innovative and successful recovery program was the **Tennessee Valley Authority** (TVA). The goal was to showcase federally directed regional planning and development of a rural and impoverished 40,000 square mile region. Passed midway through the First Hundred Days, the TVA cut across the lines of recovery and relief. The most

National Recovery Administration   Agency that the NIRA created to draft national industrial codes and supervise their implementation.

General Hugh Johnson   Head of the National Recovery Administration; consumer and labor advocates accused him of being too favorable to business interests.

price fixing   The artificial setting of commodity prices.

juggernaut   An overwhelming, advancing force that crushes or seems to roll over everything in its path.

Schechter Poultry Corporation v. the United States   Supreme Court decision (1935) declaring the NRA unconstitutional because it regulated companies not involved in interstate commerce.

Tennessee Valley Authority   Independent public corporation created by Congress in 1933 and authorized to construct dams and power plants in the Tennessee River valley region.

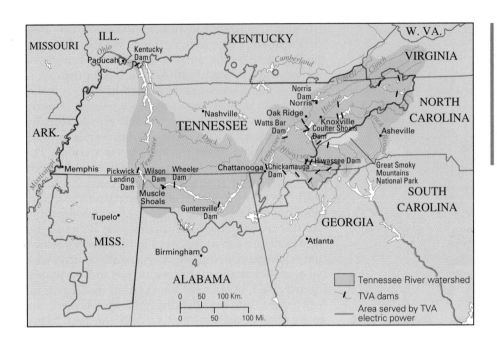

MAP 24.3 The Tennessee Valley Authority One of the most ambitious New Deal projects was developing the Tennessee Valley by improving waterways, building hydroelectric dams, and providing electricity to the area. This map shows the various components of the TVA and the region it changed.

immediate benefit was new jobs, as flood controls were improved and dams repaired and built. But the TVA was much more. Hundreds of miles of river and lakes were made more navigable, soil erosion reduced, and the TVA dams provided electricity through federally owned and operated hydroelectric systems (see Map 24.3). Critics opposed government-owned agencies that operated factories and power companies, blasting it as socialism. Despite fierce opposition, the Roosevelt administration successfully reshaped water and electrical power usage in the West. The Central Valley Project in central California harnessed the Sacramento River and its tributaries, while a series of dams and hydroelectric plants along the Columbia River, including the massive Grand Coulee Dam, provided water and power throughout Washington and Oregon.

The TVA's electrification program provided a precedent, and in 1935, the Roosevelt administration committed itself to the electrification of rural America through the **Rural Electrification Administration** (REA). Utility companies had argued that rural America was too isolated and poor to make service profitable, and in the early 1930s only about 30 percent of farms had electricity. The REA bypassed opposition from private utilities companies and state power commissions by aiding in the formation of rural and farmer electrical cooperatives. Twelve years later, electricity powered 45 percent of rural homes and farms. The electrification of

rural America helped integrate those areas with the culture of modern urban America. It lessened the drudgery of farm life, giving families running water and access to a variety of electrical appliances. Electricity improved education, health, and sanitation, and encouraged the diversification of agriculture and the introduction of new industries.

Remembering the "Forgotten Man"

Recovery was only one thrust of Roosevelt's offensive against the Depression. He had campaigned on the slogan of helping the "forgotten man." In March 1933, unemployment was at a historic high, 25 percent of the population, nearly 12 million people. In industrial states such as New York, Ohio, Pennsylvania, and Illinois, unemployment pushed toward 33 percent. Recognizing that state and private relief sources were unable to cope with people's needs, the administration accepted responsibility. During his First Hundred Days, Roosevelt proposed and Congress enacted four major relief programs. Though all were temporary measures, they estab-

Rural Electrification Administration Government agency established in 1936 for the purpose of loaning money to rural cooperatives to produce and distribute electricity in isolated areas.

Here, Civilian Conservation Corps workers plant seedlings to reforest a section of forest destroyed by fire. Before its demise in 1942, the CCC enrolled over 2.75 million young men. In addition to its work in conservation, the CCC also taught around thirty-five thousand men how to read and write. *UPI/Bettmann.*

lished a permanent new role for the federal government. By the end of the decade, about 46 million people had received some form of relief support.

The first was the **Civilian Conservation Corps** (CCC), passed on March 31, 1933. It established over 2,650 army-style camps to house and provide a healthy, moral environment for unemployed urban males aged 18 to 25. Within months it had enrolled over 300,000 men, paying them $30 a month, $25 of which had to be sent home. By 1941, enrollment was over 2 million men. The "Conservation Army" swept across the nation building, developing, and improving national park facilities, constructing roads and firebreaks, erecting telephone poles, digging irrigation ditches, and planting trees. In the camps, 35,000 men were taught to read. But the CCC touched only a small percentage of those needing relief. To widen the range of assistance, the Roosevelt administration created the **Federal Emergency Relief Administration** (FERA), the **Civil Works Administration** (CWA), and Public Works Administration (PWA). The FERA provided states with money for their relief needs, even though some governors rejected the idea of relief and federal aid. Oregon's governor, for example, opposed payments to anyone able to work and thought the elderly and feeble-minded who were unable to work should be **chloroformed**.

But the FERA did more. Like the CWA, it instituted federally administered programs that bypassed state and local government. One such FERA program opened special centers to provide housing, meals, and medical care for many of the homeless roaming the nation. In the program's first year of operation, it cared for as many as 5 million people. Ed Paulson was one. Riding the rails, he and other hobos were pulled off a train in Omaha and forced into trucks by deputies. "You're not going to jail," they assured him. "You're going to the Transient Camp." There, Paulson was deloused, given a bath, a bed, and "a spread with scrambled eggs, bacon, bread, coffee, and toast." "We ate a great meal," he recalled years later. "We thought we'd gone to heaven." In other programs, over half a million people attended literacy classes and 1 million received vaccinations and immunizations.

Civilian Conservation Corps   Organization created by Congress in 1933 to hire young unemployed men for conservation work, such as planting trees, digging irrigation ditches, and maintaining national parks.

Federal Emergency Relief Administration   Agency created in May 1933 to provide direct grants to states and municipalities to spend on relief.

Civil Works Administration   Emergency unemployment relief program in 1933 and 1934; it hired 4 million jobless people for federal, state, and local work projects.

chloroform   Used as an anesthetic for surgery; used here as a verb to mean to painlessly end a person's life (euthanasia).

The Public Works Administration, directed by Secretary of Interior **Harold Ickes**, paid 45 cents for unskilled labor and $1.10 for skilled workers, regardless of race, and eventually provided over $4 billion to state and local governments for more than 34,000 projects, including sidewalks, roads, schools, and community buildings. PWA funds also constructed two aircraft carriers, the *Yorktown* and *Enterprise*. In November, when unemployment still seemed too high, the CWA was created to put millions of people to work. Some objected to "make-work" projects, but the CWA provided much needed support during the winter before the program ended in February 1934. It paved over a half-million miles of road, built forty thousand schools, and paid the salaries of over fifty thousand teachers.

Not all relief programs were aimed at the homeless and poor. Two aided homeowners. The **Home Owners' Loan Corporation** (HOLC), established in May 1933, permitted homeowners to refinance their mortgages at lower interest rates through the federal government. Before it stopped making loans in 1936, the HOLC had refinanced 1 million homes, including 20 percent of all mortgaged urban homes. The National Housing Act, passed in June 1933, created the **Federal Housing Administration** (FHA), which still provides federally backed loans for home mortgages and repairs.

Interspersed among the recovery and relief programs were a number of reforms that sought to prevent the recurrence of the events that had triggered the Depression and to place more constraints on the unfair practices of business. To correct problems within the banking and securities industries, the 1933 Bank Act gave more power to the Federal Reserve System and created the **Federal Deposit Insurance Corporation** (FDIC). The act provided federal insurance for those who had deposited money in member banks. In less than six months, 97 percent of all commercial banks had joined the system. The **Securities and Exchange Commission** (SEC) passed in 1934 more closely regulated stock market activities.

Changing Focus

The New Deal started with almost total support in Congress and among the people. But as proposals flowed from the White House and the economy improved, opposition emerged. By mid-1933, most Republicans actively opposed relief programs, federal spending, and increased governmental controls over business. Conservatives fumed that Roosevelt threatened free enterprise, if not capitalism. The Hearst newspaper chain instructed its editors to tell the public that the New Deal was a "raw deal" and that Roosevelt planned to "Soak the Successful" and lead the nation down the path to socialism.

For the majority of the American people, however, Roosevelt and the New Deal still spelled hope and faith in the future. State and congressional elections held in 1934 showed Democrats gaining overwhelming victories. Supported by congressional Democrats and public opinion, Roosevelt continued to add to the New Deal and became less willing to cooperate with conservatives and business. The president was also aware that recovery was not progressing as rapidly as desired and that criticism was growing about the New Deal's failure to help the common man.

Three critics were especially popular: **Father Charles Coughlin**, Senator **Huey Long**, and **Dr. Francis Townsend**. At three o'clock every Sunday afternoon, Father Coughlin, a Roman Catholic priest,

Harold Ickes Secretary of the interior and director of the Public Works Administration who gained a reputation as an efficient administrator who opposed racial discrimination.

Home Owners' Loan Corporation Government agency created in 1933 that refinanced home mortgage debts for nonfarm homeowners and allowed them to borrow money from the agency to pay property taxes and make repairs.

Federal Housing Administration Agency created by the National Housing Act (1934) to insure loans made by banks and other institutions for new home construction, repairs, and improvements.

Federal Deposit Insurance Corporation Agency created by the Banking Act of 1933 to insure deposits up to a fixed sum in member banks of the Federal Reserve System and state banks that chose to participate.

Securities and Exchange Commission Agency created by Congress to license stock exchanges and supervise their activities, including the setting of margin rates.

Father Charles Coughlin Roman Catholic priest whose influential radio addresses in the 1930s at first emphasized social justice but eventually became anti-Semitic and profascist.

Huey Long Louisiana governor, then U.S. senator, who ran a powerful political machine and whose advocacy of redistribution of income was gaining him a national political following at the time of his assassination in 1935.

Dr. Francis Townsend California public health physician who proposed the Townsend Plan in 1933, under which every retired person over 60 would be paid a $200 monthly pension to be spent within the month.

In 1934, Huey Long, a fiery Populist politician from Louisiana, claimed that Roosevelt was not helping the common man enough. A dramatic and flamboyant speaker, Long proclaimed his support for the "little man" with the slogan, "Every Man a King" and the Share the Wealth program that would tax the rich and "spread the wealth among all our people." Before Long could become a real political threat to Roosevelt, he was assassinated in September 1935. *Corbis-Bettmann.*

incomes over $1 million to be taxed at 100 percent. Crying "Soak the Rich!" **Share the Wealth** societies mushroomed to over 4 million followers.

Coughlin's and Long's plans were broadly based, whereas Dr. Francis Townsend focused on the elderly. Once a public health doctor in Long Beach, California, Townsend advocated a federal old-age pension plan that would provide every American, age 60 and older, a monthly pension check for $200. To qualify, individuals could not work and had to spend the money within a month. A national sales tax of 2 percent on business transactions would finance the system. In support of Townsend's idea, thousands of clubs were created with an estimated membership of several million, including sixty members of Congress.

Roosevelt and his advisers were also aware of a growing pressure from workers and unions to initiate legislation to promote unionization and help industrial laborers. The national codes of the NRA had raised workers' expectations by promoting unions and establishing higher wages. Workers had responded positively. Union membership doubled, with the fastest growing unions in the mass-production industries, like Walter Reuther's **United Automobile Workers** (UAW). In 1935 leaders of the industrial unions formed the Committee of Industrial Organizations (CIO), which in 1938 became the **Congress of Industrial Organizations**. As workers became more dissatisfied with the application of NRA codes, a more militant and political worker emerged. They launched strikes, more than 1800 in 1934, and union leaders increasingly asked their members to support, with votes and contributions, those politicians who were friends of labor and willing to promote workers' goals.

Responding to these pressures, Roosevelt announced a change in priorities in business profits. He

used the radio to preach to nearly 30 million Americans. The "radio priest" had strongly supported Roosevelt, but in mid-1934, he turned his influential voice against the New Deal and Roosevelt. His organization, the National Union for Social Justice, which he called the "people's lobby," advocated a guaranteed annual income, the redistribution of wealth, tougher antimonopoly laws, and the nationalization of banking. Within a year the organization claimed more than 5 million members. Senator Huey Long of Louisiana suggested more radical programs to help the average American. His "Share the Wealth" plan included tempting provisions: every family would receive an annual check for $2,000, a home, a car, a radio, and a college education for each child. It would be funded by taxing the rich, with

Share the Wealth Movement that sprang up around the nation in the 1930s urging the redistribution of wealth through government taxes or programs; launched by Huey Long, its slogan was "Every man a king."

United Automobile Workers Union of workers in the automobile industry; it used sit-down strikes in 1936 and 1937 to end work speed-ups and win recognition for the fledgling labor organization.

Congress of Industrial Organizations Labor organization established in 1938 by a group of powerful unions that left the AFL to unionize workers by industry rather than by trade.

The Works Progress Administration not only built roads and buildings, but also provided employment for teachers, writers, and artists. A common theme among WPA artists and writers was the strength and dignity of common people as they faced their difficult lives. Here, a Michigan WPA artist sketches WPA workers. *National Archives.*

asked Congress to provide more **work relief**, to develop an old-age and unemployment insurance program, and to pass legislation regulating holding companies and utilities. A solidly Democratic and largely liberal Congress responded with a Second Hundred Days of legislation. In April 1935, Congress allocated nearly $5 billion for relief and created a new agency, the **Works Progress Administration** (WPA), led by **Harry Hopkins**. The WPA's goal was to put people to work, and it did. Between 1935 and 1938, the WPA employed over 2.1 million people a year. Most did manual labor, building roads, schools, and other public facilities. In its actions, the WPA established a maximum 140-hour work month and sought to pay wages higher than relief payments but lower than local wages. Wages for nonwhites and women were the exception—these generally exceeded the local rate. But the WPA went further than duplicating the PWA; it also created jobs for professionals, white-collar workers, writers, artists, actors and actresses, photographers, songwriters, and musicians. Historians conducted oral interviews, including those of ex-slaves, and wrote state and local histories and guidebooks. The WPA's Writers Project provided jobs for established and new novelists, including Saul Bellow and African-American writer Richard Wright, author of *Native Son*. Professional theater groups toured towns and cities, performing Shakespeare and other plays. By 1939 an estimated 30 million people had watched WPA productions.

"Art for the Millions" was a program designed to help artists and to elevate the public's awareness of art. It provided positive themes and images of American society, including over 2,500 murals—most adorn-

ing public buildings. Some objected to actors, artists, and writers receiving aid, arguing that their labor was not real work. But Hopkins bluntly responded, "Hell, they got to eat just like other people."

The WPA also made special efforts to help women, minorities, students, and young adults. Prodded by Eleanor Roosevelt, the WPA employed between 300,000 and 400,000 women a year. Although some were hired as teachers and nurses, the majority, especially in rural areas, worked on sewing and canning projects. Efforts to ensure African-American employment met with success in the northeastern states but were less successful in the South. The **National Youth Administration** (NYA), directed by Aubrey Williams, developed a successful program that provided aid for college and high school students and programs for young people not in school.

---

work relief   A system of governmental monetary support that provided work for the unemployed, who were usually paid a limited hourly or daily wage.

Works Progress Administration   Agency established in 1935 and headed by Harry Hopkins that hired the unemployed for construction, conservation, and arts programs.

Harry Hopkins   Head of several New Deal agencies, first organizing emergency relief and then administering public works; he remained a close adviser to Roosevelt during World War II.

National Youth Administration   Program established by executive order in 1935 to provide employment for young people and to help needy high school and college students continue their educations.

Mary McLeod Bethune, an African-American educator, directed the NYA's Office of Negro Affairs and through determination and constant, skillfully applied pressure obtained support for black schools and colleges and increased the number of African Americans enrolled in vocational and recreational programs.

The WPA reasserted Roosevelt's support for the common American, but it was the establishment of a federal old-age and survivor insurance program that set the tone of the Second Hundred Days and significantly modified the government's role in society. Frances Perkins (see Individual Choices, page 748) was a driving force behind the **Social Security Act** of 1935. Passed by Congress in August, the act's most controversial element was a pension plan for retirees 65 or older. The program would begin in 1937, and initial benefits would range from $10 to $85 per month, depending on how much the individual had paid into the system. Compared with Townsend's plan and many existing European systems, the U.S. social security system was limited and conservative. It required payments by workers, failed to cover domestic and agricultural laborers, and provided no health insurance. Nonetheless, it represented a major change in government's responsibility toward society.

Less controversial parts of the act provided federal aid to families with dependent children and the disabled, and helped fund state-run systems of unemployment compensation. Within two years, every state was part of the unemployment compensation system, paying between $15 and $18 a week in unemployment compensation and supplying support to over 28 million people.

The Second Hundred Days also supported organized labor with the passage of the National Labor Relations Act and quieted "Long's thunder" by raising taxes on corporations and the wealthy. Largely the work of Senator Robert Wagner, and called the **Wagner Act**, the National Labor Relations Act strengthened the unions by putting the power of government behind the workers' right to organize and to bargain with employers for wages and benefits. It created the National Labor Relations Board to ensure workers' rights, conduct elections to determine union representation, and prevent unfair labor practices such as firing or **blacklisting** workers for union activities. The act had its limitations. For example, it excluded many nonunionized workers as well as those in agriculture and service industries. Despite its limitations, the NLRA altered the relationships among business, labor, and the government and created a source of support for workers within the executive branch.

Waning of the New Deal

By the end of 1935, Roosevelt had effectively reasserted his leadership and popularity. The chances of a successful Republican or third-party challenge to the president were remote. In a less than enthusiastic convention, Republicans nominated **Alfred Landon** of Kansas, the only Republican governor re-elected in 1934. As governor, he had accepted and used most New Deal programs, but in keeping with party wishes he reluctantly attacked Roosevelt and the New Deal as destroying the values of America. As for Roosevelt's liberal critics, Huey Long was assassinated in 1935, and while Townsend and Coughlin continued to protest and formed a third party, the Union Party, they were no longer any threat to his re-election. Roosevelt followed a wise path, reminding voters of the New Deal's achievements and denouncing big business as greedy. It worked and Roosevelt won in a landslide. Landon carried only two states, Maine and Vermont.

The Democratic victory demonstrated not only the personal appeal of Roosevelt but also the re-alignment of political forces accepting the concept of an activist New Deal that could provide social and economic gains. Roosevelt's second inaugural address, sometimes referred to as the "One-third speech," raised expectations of a Third Hundred Days. "I see millions of families trying to live on incomes so meager that the pall of family disaster hangs over them day by day," he announced. "I see one-third of a nation ill-housed, ill-clad, ill-nourished." The words seemed to promise new legislation aimed at helping the poor and the working class. But the Third Hundred Days failed to materialize.

Mary McLeod Bethune African-American educator who founded Bethune College and who, as director of the Office of Minority Affairs within the National Youth Administration, was a strong and vocal advocate for equality of opportunity for African Americans during the New Deal.

Social Security Act Law passed by Congress in 1935 to create systems of unemployment, old-age, and disability insurance and to provide for child welfare.

Wagner Act The National Labor Relations Act, a law passed by Congress in 1935 that defined unfair labor practices and protected unions against coercive measures such as blacklisting.

blacklisting Practice in which businesses share information to deny employment to workers known to belong to unions.

Alfred Landon Kansas governor who ran unsuccessfully for president on the Republican ticket in 1936.

Roosevelt did not have a good year in 1937, and the once-sprinting New Deal slowed to a crawl. Several factors contributed to the waning of public and political support for new programs. Roosevelt's mishandling of the economy and the Supreme Court were two of the most important. Instead of promoting new social legislation, Roosevelt pitched his popularity against the Supreme Court—and lost. The president's anger at the High Court had been growing since the *Schechter* case, and as 1937 began, legal challenges to the Wagner Act and the Social Security Act were on the Court's docket. Roosevelt feared the Court was determined to undo the New Deal and sought to prevent it. Without consulting congressional leaders or close advisers, Roosevelt planned to enlarge the Court. His rationale was that the Court was overburdened and its elderly judges unable to meet the demands of the bench. He wanted the authority to add a new justice for every one over age 70 who had served more than ten years on the Court. Although changing the Court was a congressional power, many thought Roosevelt's "court-packing plan" threatened the checks-and-balances system of government as established by the Constitution. The scheme was a major political miscalculation. Several Democrats, especially those in the South, saw an opportunity to safely break with the president and led opposition in the Senate. Roosevelt's effort was further weakened when the Court upheld a state's minimum wage law, the Wagner Act, and the social security system. After conservative Justice Willis Van Devanter announced his retirement, Roosevelt dropped the issue and happily appointed Hugo Black, a southern New Dealer, to the Court. Justice Black was followed to the Court by eight other Roosevelt appointments.

Roosevelt now had a Court that accepted the philosophy of the New Deal, but he had lost valuable political control within his own party. Another setback that snagged the Roosevelt agenda was a recession, dubbed **Roosevelt's recession** by critics. Secretary of the Treasury Henry Morganthau pointed out that the economy was steady—industrial outputs had reached their 1929 levels and unemployment had fallen to 14 percent—and he urged Roosevelt to reduce government spending. Hoping to move toward a more balanced budget, Roosevelt agreed and cut back programs. Relief programs were targeted, and nearly 1.5 million workers were released from the WPA. But the economy was not strong enough to cope with thousands of people seeking jobs and reduced government spending. Advocates thought that the private sector could absorb the released workers, but it could not and unemployment rapidly soared to 19 percent.

The recovery collapsed and in April 1938, Roosevelt restored spending. The WPA and other agencies subsequently rehired those released. But Roosevelt's sterling image of being able to manage recovery was tarnished. It was not just the Court-packing scheme and the recession that weakened the New Deal. People were also reacting to higher taxes, including payments to social security (FICA), and labor strife. The public's mood had changed. The American people, Hopkins observed, were now "bored with the poor, the unemployed, and the insecure."

Despite waning support for New Deal-style legislation, the administration managed to pass two more significant pieces of legislation (see Table 24.1). A second Agricultural Adjustment Act that re-established the principle of federally set quotas on specific commodities, acreage reduction, and parity payments was approved over conservative opposition. Frances Perkins considered passage of the **Fair Labor Standards Act** in 1938 as one of her major accomplishments. It addressed causes she had long championed, establishing a standard workweek (forty-four hours), setting a minimum wage (25 cents an hour), and outlawing child labor (under age 16). With its minimum wage provision, the act was especially beneficial to unskilled, nonunion, and minority workers. It was also the last piece of New Deal legislation. In the November 1938 congressional elections, Roosevelt failed in his effort to get New Deal supporters elected. The new Congress was more conservative and determined to derail any more of the president's "socialistic" ideas. Roosevelt recognized political reality and asked for no new domestic programs. The legislative New Deal was over, but the changes it generated would remain part of the American social, economic, and political culture. By 1939, the economy was recovering, reaching the point where it had been in 1929 and 1937, before the "Roosevelt recession." Full "recovery" and economic growth would result from the vast demand for American goods generated by the outbreak of another world war, in 1939. It was spending connected with the war, not New Deal programs, that propelled the American economy to new levels of prosperity.

Roosevelt's recession Economic downturn that occurred when Roosevelt, responding to improving economic figures, cut $4 billion from the federal budget, mostly by reducing relief spending.

Fair Labor Standards Act Law passed by Congress in 1938 that established a minimum wage and a maximum workweek and forbade labor by children under 16.

| table 24.1 | **Relief, Recovery, Reform, 1933–1938** |

Relief	Recovery	Reform
1933		
Civilian Conservation Corps (CCC)	Emergency Banking Relief Act	Beer and Wine Revenue Act
Federal Emergency Relief Act (FERA)	Tennessee Valley Authority Act (TVA)	Banking Act, 1933 (guaranteed deposits)
Home Owner's Loan Corporation (HOLC)	Agricultural Adjustment Act (AAA)	Federal Securities Act
Public Works Administration (PWA)	National Recovery Administration (NRA)	Glass-Steagall Banking Act
Civil Works Administration (CWA)		
1934		
National Housing Act	Gold Reserve Act	Securities and Exchange Act
Federal Housing Administration (FHA)		Reciprocal Trade Agreements
1935		
Frazier-Lemke Farm Bankruptcy Act		National Labor Relations Act
Resettlement Administration		Rural Electrification Administration
National Youth Administration (NYA)		Social Security Act
Works Progress Administration (WPA)		Publc Utility Holding Company Act
Soil Conservation and Domestic Act		Revenue Act
1937		
Farm Security Administration		U.S. Housing Authority
1938		
	Second Agricultural Adjustment Act	Fair Labor Standards Act

SURVIVING THE DEPRESSION

• Amid the sweeping social changes taking place during the Depression, how did Americans manage to hold onto social and cultural values?

• What opportunities opened for women and minorities— African Americans, Hispanics, Asians, and Native Americans—and what challenges faced these groups as an outcome of the Depression?

One reason the New Deal was able to establish new paths of government responsibility was that the Depression touched every segment of American life. Poverty and hardship were no longer reserved for those viewed as unworthy or relegated to remote areas and inner cities. Now poverty included blue- and white-collar workers, and even some of the once-rich. American industry, according to *Fortune*, suffered 46 percent unemployment, but in many areas it

table 24.2   Consumer Prices, 1931

Food		Other goods	
Rye Bread	$ .05 a loaf	Eastman Camera	$6.95
Apples	.25 for 4 lbs	Philco Baby Grand Radio	79.95
Bananas	.19 for 4 lbs	Sears Refrigerator	139.50
Round Steak	.28 a pound	Men's Dress Shirt	.50
Chicken Broilers	.39 a pound	DeSoto Six (Automobile)	695.00
Ground Beef	.29 for 2 lbs		
Shredded Wheat	.19 for 2 boxes		
Clorox	.16 a bottle		
Cigarettes	.27 for 2 packs		
Coffee	.69 for 2 lbs		
Butter	.59 for 2 lbs		
Sugar	1.25 for 25 lbs		
Flour	.79 for 25 lbs		
Lifebuoy Soap	.25 for 4 cakes		
Milk	.10 for a quart		

Source: Data from *Observer Reporter* (Washington, PA), July, 1931.

table 24.3   Depression Menu, 1932

Breakfast	Lunch	Dinner
Oatmeal with milk	Macaroni and cheese	Salmon croquettes
Scrambled eggs	Cole slaw	Creamed potatoes
Toast	Corn bread	Stewed tomatoes
Milk	Baked apples	Bread
Coffee	Milk	Milk

Cost $1.72

Source: Data from Susan F. West, "Low Cost Diets Planned According to Different Standards," *Journal of Home Economics* (February 1932): 113–118.

was much worse. In Gary, Indiana, nearly the entire working class was out of a job by 1932. Average annual income dropped 35 percent, from $2,300 to $1,500, by 1933. Although income rose after 1933, most Americans worried about their futures and economic insecurity. Would the next day bring a reduction in wages, the loss of a job, or the closing of a business? Some saw their businesses go bankrupt and found new careers. E. Y. Harburg lost his family's hardware store, borrowed $500 from a friend, and started writing songs—striking a common plea with "Brother, Can You Spare a Dime?" Others worked for less, lost and found other jobs, or, disheartened, accepted relief.

To help those facing economic insecurity, magazines and newspapers provided useful hints and "Depression recipes" that stretched budgets and included information about nutrition. According to trained home economists, a careful shopper could feed a family of five on as little as $8 a week (see Tables 24.2 and 24.3). This was comforting news for those with that much to spend, but for many families and for relief agencies $8 a week for food was beyond possibility. To feed his family of seven, Angelos Douvitos received work relief from Ann Arbor, Michigan, at 30 cents an hour and took home a mere $4.20 a week. New York City provided only $2.39 a

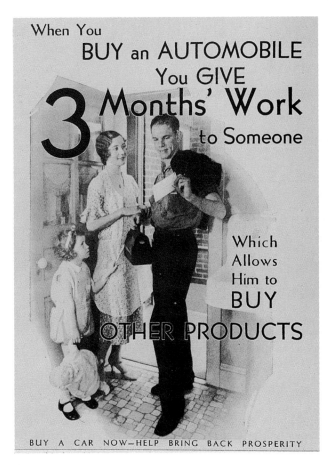

When You BUY an AUTOMOBILE You GIVE 3 Months' Work to Someone

Which Allows Him to BUY OTHER PRODUCTS

BUY A CAR NOW—HELP BRING BACK PROSPERITY

Recognizing the connection between sales and jobs, this ad asked readers to purchase an automobile and keep workers working so that they too could spend and stimulate the economy. Unfortunately, the number of people with enough money to spend was never enough to rekindle the economy and the Depression continued. *Private collection.*

homes, stimulated urban and suburban growth, and restored local tax bases. Federal relief agencies, especially the PWA and the WPA, not only provided civic improvements—constructing schools, post offices, and hospitals and repairing roads and bridges—but also through its jobs reduced local relief responsibilities. Chicago's Mayor Edward Kelly credited New Deal funds for saving Chicago. "Roosevelt is my religion," he announced during his campaign. In rural towns and city neighborhoods in the West, a variety of federal programs kept crumbling communities together. In North Dakota it was estimated that two-thirds of the people drew some form of federal relief. Use of the New Deal drastically altered the relationship between local and national government. Increasingly people saw the national government as having an obligation to support families and communities against economic adversity.

"Making Do"—Families and the Depression

With or without governmental aid, "Use it up, wear it out, make it do, or do without" became the motto of most American families. In many working-class and middle-class neighborhoods, "making do" meant many homes sprouted signs announcing a variety of services—household beauty parlors, kitchen bakeries, rooms for boarders. A Milwaukee wife recalled, "I did baking at home to supplement our income. I got 9 cents for a loaf of bread and 25 cents for an apple cake. . . . I cleared about $65 a month." A Singer sewing machine salesman commented that he was selling more and more machines to people who in the past would not have sewn. Feed sacks became a source of material. "I grew up in a small, exclusive suburb," recalled Florence Davis, who remembered her mother making a pretty new school dress out of one sack that had "a sky-blue background with gorgeous mallard ducks on it."

Still, even with "making do," many families—especially in the working class—failed, losing first jobs, then homes. Once evicted, fortunate families moved in with relatives. Don Blincoe remembered that during the Depression most households were like his, "where father, mother, children, aunts, uncles and grandma lived together." Approximately one-sixth of America's urban families "doubled up." Millions of others took to the road. Over 3 million, as in John Steinbeck's *Grapes of Wrath*, loaded their meager possessions on their jalopies and traveled across the country looking for jobs. Many trekked toward California, whose

week for each family. Things were bad, comedian Groucho Marx joked, when "pigeons started feeding people in Central Park."

Like New York, most towns and cities by 1933 had little ability to provide more than the smallest amount of relief and were unsuccessfully struggling to maintain basic city services. Experiencing a shrinking tax base, local, county, and state governments were forced to lay off teachers, policemen, and other workers. The city commissioner of Birmingham, Alabama, was typical when he said, "I am as much in favor of relief . . . as anyone, but I am unwilling to continue this relief at the expense of bankrupting . . . Birmingham." The New Deal provided relief for cities like Birmingham as programs such as the HOLC and the FHA saved

Throughout the Depression, the most popular form of entertainment was the movies, providing escape from daily hardships into a prosperous world of fantasy. At twenty cents a ticket, movies attracted as many as seventy-five million people a week. In this photo, taken at a movie theatre in San Diego, children display door prizes given during the matinee. *San Diego Historical Society, Photograph Collection.*

population by the end of the decade had jumped by over a million. Others found their families and lives torn apart. Those called "hobos" rode the rails, hitching rides in boxcars, living in shantytowns—"Hoovervilles"—begging and scrounging for food and supplies along the road. Records show increased numbers of suicides, people admitted to state mental hospitals, and children placed in orphanages. Some worried about the psychological problems created as women and children replaced husbands and fathers as breadwinners. A social worker wrote: "I used to see men cry because they didn't have a job."

Despite the hardships and migrations, American society did not collapse, as some had predicted. The vast majority of Americans clung tightly to traditional social norms and even expanded family togetherness. Economic necessity kept families at home. They played board games and cards, read books and magazines, and tended vegetable and flower gardens. The game of *Monopoly* was introduced, allowing players to fantasize about becoming millionaires. Church attendance rose and the number of divorces declined. Fewer people got married and the birth rate fell. But marriages were only delayed and the lower birth rate resulted not so much from economic fears as from the increased availability of birth control devices.

Movies and radio provided a break from the woes of the Depression. On a national average, 60 percent of the people saw a movie a week. Movies offered not only escape from the daily routine; some also reflected the social and political changes of the decade. The musical *Golddiggers of 1933* delighted audiences with its cheerful music, lavish sets, and attractive chorus line, but it also contained social commentary. As unemployed men march across the stage, a singer reminds viewers,

Remember my forgotten man,
You put a rifle in his hand,
You sent him far away,
You shouted, "Hip Hooray!"
But look at him today.

Gangster films remained popular but underwent a change as Roosevelt entered office. In the early thirties, the popular actors frequently played heroic but doomed gangsters, but by mid-thirties many of those stars now played the brave government officials who brought villains to justice. James Cagney underwent such a character change in *G-Men*, abandoning his usual tough-guy mobster image to portray a dedicated FBI agent protecting average citizens. The plots of romantic comedies revolved around romances between people of opposite social and economic backgrounds, comparing the wisdom and honesty of the common American to the snobbish, selfish values of the upper class. Inevitably love and common sense prevailed.

Novels, however, were frequently more critical of American society, culture, and politics. Many authors stressed the immorality of capitalism and the inequities caused by racism and class differences. They focused on the plight of workers, minorities, and the poor and found heroes among those who refused to break under the strain of the Depression and society's inhumanity. Steinbeck's *The Grapes of Wrath*, Erskine Caldwell's *Tobacco Road*, and Richard Wright's *Native Son* featured "losers" but showed that their misery was not of their own making but society's fault. In these and similar novels, writers assailed the rich and powerful and praised the humanitarian spirit and fair play of the poor.

The largest audience was reached by radio, which was heard in nearly 90 percent of American households. It mostly provided another avenue of escape from the concerns of the Depression. Crooners like Rudy Vallee and Bing Crosby, afternoon soap operas, quiz shows, and "gloom chasers"—comedians such as the Marx Brothers and George Burns and Gracie Allen—filled the airways. Crime fighters like the Green Hornet, Dick Tracy, and the Lone Ranger and Tonto proved again and again that truth, justice, honor, and courage triumphed. Comic strip heroes Superman (1938) and Batman (1939) also protected downtrodden workers and minorities from harm and oppression. Radio was also a powerful means for both Franklin and Eleanor Roosevelt to reach huge audiences with their visions of government, the New Deal, and hopes for America.

Women and Minorities in the Depression

The Depression and the New Deal provided mixed experiences for women and minorities. As unemployment rose, so too did pressures not to hire women or minorities. Emphasizing traditional roles in American society, public opinion polls consistently found that as unemployment rose, most people, including women, believed that men, not women, should have jobs. This was particularly true of married women, and in many cases companies chose not to hire married women, especially in professional and higher paying jobs. The number of women in the professions declined from 14.2 to 12.3

percent during the Depression years. Teachers were particularly vulnerable. One survey found that of 1,500 school districts, 77 percent did not hire married women and 63 percent had fired women when they married. By 1932, 2 million women were out of work and an estimated 145,000 women were homeless, wandering across America. But employment patterns were uneven. Women in low-paying and low-status jobs were less likely to be laid off and more likely to find employment. In Detroit, automakers preferred to hire women at 4 cents an hour rather than pay a man at 10 cents an hour. White women also took jobs away from minorities, especially in domestic service.

Few working women, however, found that bringing home the paycheck changed their status or role within the family. Husbands still maintained authority and dominance in the home, even if unemployed. Rarely did husbands help with work around the house. One husband agreed to help with the laundry but refused to hang the wash outside for fear that neighbors might see him. At home women renewed and reaffirmed traditional roles: they sewed, baked bread, and canned fruits and vegetables. As wives and mothers, if not workers, women were praised as pillars of stability in a changing and perilous society. Reflecting on her own steadiness, one woman remembered, "I did what I had to do. I seemed to always find a way to make things work."

While the Depression's economic impact on women was mixed, it only intensified the economic and social difficulties for minorities. African Americans, Hispanics, and Asians faced increased racial hostility and demands that they give up their jobs to whites. In Tucson, Arizona, "Mexicans" were accused of "taking the bread out of our white children's mouths." Low-paying, frequently temporary jobs and high unemployment made life in the *colonias* deplorable, where according to one observer, mothers and children went "up and down alleys, searching . . . for cast-off food." Throughout the Southwest, the United States Immigration Bureau worked with local authorities to facilitate repatriation of Mexican nationals to Mexico. To encourage returning to Mexico, many local and state agencies gave free transportation to the border

---

colonia Village settlements of Mexicans and Mexican Americans, frequently constructed by or for migrant citrus workers in southern California.

for those willing to leave. In some cities, such as Los Angeles, as early as 1931, the Immigration Bureau conducted sweeps of Mexican-American communities intended to scare Mexicans into leaving. Facing a lack of jobs and Anglo pressure, more than half a million Mexicans did leave the United States by 1937. Those who remained found fewer jobs and lower pay. On farms in California, the average yearly wage for Latinos was $289—about a third of what the government estimated it took to maintain a subsistence budget.

Officials made no effort to repatriate Asians living on the West Coast, but Asian immigrants and Asian Americans remained isolated, ignored in their ethnic enclaves, and received inadequate relief. In San Francisco, where nearly one-sixth of the Asian population picked up benefits, they got from 10–20 percent less than whites because relief agencies somehow concluded that Asians could subsist on a less-expensive diet. Hoping to remove economic and social barriers, some sought to assimilate, becoming "200 percent Americans." The Japanese-American Citizens League was organized in 1930 to overcome discrimination and oppose anti-Asian legislation, but by 1940 the group had made little headway.

Before 1929, African Americans working as sharecroppers, farm hands, and tenant farmers in the South already were experiencing depression conditions, earning only about $200 a year. Their lives worsened as farm prices continued to fall and as the number of evictions rose during the Depression. Many decided to leave and migrated to urban areas, seeking more economic security. Cities, however, provided few opportunities because whites were taking jobs previously held by African Americans, including low-paying and low-status domestic service jobs typically held by black women. In most cases, joblessness among African Americans in urban areas averaged 20 to 50 percent higher than for whites. Compounding the high unemployment, across the nation blacks faced increased racial hostility, violence, and intimidation. In 1931 the attention of the nation was drawn to Scottsboro, Alabama, where nine black men had been arrested and charged with raping two white prostitutes. Although no physical evidence linked the men to any crime, a jury of white males did not question the testimony of the women and quickly found the so-called **Scottsboro Nine** guilty. Eight were sentenced to death; the ninth, a minor, escaped the death penalty. Through appeals, intervention by the Supreme Court, retrials, parole, and escape, all those convicted were free by 1950.

Giving Her a Lift to Town — — — — — — **—By Knott**

Read editorial "The Unemployed Woman."

President Franklin D. Roosevelt campaigned on helping the "forgotten man." As shown in this political cartoon, as First Lady, Eleanor Roosevelt did not forget women. She worked diligently to ensure that they benefited from the New Deal and had access to government and the Democratic Party. *Franklin D. Roosevelt Library.*

A New Deal for Women and Minorities

Like the Depression, the New Deal impacted women and minorities in different ways, but gener-

> **Scottsboro Nine** Nine African Americans convicted of raping two white women in a freight train in Alabama in 1931; their case became famous as an example of racism in the legal system.

In 1935 Mary McLeod Bethune (front center), became the first African-American woman to hold a high-ranking government position, serving as the head of the Office of Minority Affairs in the National Youth Administration. Here, she is shown with the Council of Negro Women, which she helped organize in 1935 to focus on the problems faced by African Americans at the national level. *New York Public Library, Schomburg Center for Research in Black Culture.*

ally it inspired a belief that the Roosevelt government cared and was trying to improve their lives. Eleanor Roosevelt was at center of this image of compassion. She frequently acted as the social conscience of the administration and prodded her husband and other New Dealers not to forget women and minorities. "I'm the agitator," she said, "he's the politician." She crossed the country meeting and listening to people. She received thousands of letters that described people's hardships and asked for help. Rarely able to provide any direct assistance, her replies emphasized hope and pointed to the changes being made by the New Deal.

Within the White House, she helped convene a special White House conference on the needs of women in 1933 and, with the help of Frances Perkins, Ellen Woodward, and other women in the administration, worked to ensure that women received more than just token consideration from New Deal agencies. Woodward, who served as assistant director of the FERA and WPA, was especially successful in promoting women's programs, headed by women. With Eleanor Roosevelt as role model and advocate, the

New Deal provided more opportunities for women in government and politics than at any other time in American history.

Yet the New Deal developed only a few programs for women and frequently paid women less than men for the same work. Women made up only 10 percent of the WPA's work force and most of them were placed in programs that focused on traditional women's skills, such as sewing, which was the largest WPA program for women. In Texas, the state legislature mandated that women, especially minority women, were to be trained only in cooking, cleaning, and sewing. Passage of the Social Security Act and the Fair Labor Standards Act also ignored the needs of many women. Both acts excluded coverage of domestic workers and waitresses, professions largely composed of women.

For African Americans and Hispanics, the Roosevelts and the New Deal provided a large amount of hope and a lesser amount of change. More African Americans than ever before were appointed to government positions. Educator Mary Bethune headed the Office of Minority Affairs within the National

Youth Administration and organized African Americans in the administration into a **"Black Cabinet"** that met in her home and acted as a semiofficial advisory commission on racial relations. "We must think in terms of a 'whole' for the greatest service of our people," she said. Among the most pressing needs, the "Black Cabinet" concluded, was access to relief and jobs. The New Deal provided both, but never to the extent needed. Some New Deal administrators, notably Ickes and Hopkins, took steps to ensure that the PWA, WPA, and other New Deal agencies included minorities, especially African Americans. In northern cities, the WPA and the PWA nearly eliminated discrimination from their programs, but they had less success in other parts of the nation where skilled African-American workers were given menial minimum-wage jobs. Other agencies were less supportive. The Civilian Conservation Corps and the Tennessee Valley Authority practiced segregation and wage discrimination. Still, by 1938, nearly 30 percent of African Americans were receiving some federal relief, with the WPA alone supporting almost a million African-American families. But even in the best of cases, it was not enough. In Cleveland, 40 percent of PWA jobs were reserved for African Americans, but there as across the nation black unemployment and poverty remained higher than for whites.

The Roosevelt administration also shrank from supporting civil rights legislation. When confronted by black leaders for his refusal to promote an anti-lynching law, Roosevelt explained, "If I come out for the anti-lynching bill now, they will block every bill I ask Congress to pass . . . I just can't take that risk." Again, acting as an advocate, Eleanor Roosevelt was willing to take more risks and visibly supported equality for minorities. In 1939, when the Daughters of the American Revolution refused to allow renowned black opera singer Marian Anderson to sing at their concert hall in Washington, the First Lady resigned her membership and helped arrange a public concert on the steps of the Lincoln Memorial. Anderson's performance before Lincoln's statue attracted more than 75,000 people.

Hispanics benefited from the New Deal in much the same way as African Americans—indirectly. In New Mexico and other western states, the Depression curtailed much of the migratory farm work for Mexican-American workers, devastating local economies. New Deal agencies such as the CCC, PWA, and WPA provided welcome jobs and income. A worker in a CCC camp in northern New Mexico remembered, "I had plenty to eat, . . . I had brand new

In San Antonio, Texas, many Mexican Americans held jobs as pecan shellers and were among the worst paid in the nation—sometimes working a 54-hour week for only $3. *Benson Latin American Collection, University of Texas at Austin.*

clothes when I went to the CCC camps." Throughout the Southwest, federal relief agencies not only included Mexican Americans but also sometimes paid wages that exceeded what they received in the **private sector**. The WPA paid $8.54 a week for unskilled

---

Black Cabinet Semiofficial advisory committee on racial affairs made up of African-American members of the Roosevelt administration and organized by Mary McLeod Bethune.

private sector Businesses run by private citizens rather than by the government.

labor, whereas a comparable job in the private sector would have yielded an average of $6.02 or less. Discrimination, however, was still practiced, and enhanced by language differences.

New Deal legislation also helped union organizers trying to assist Hispanic workers throughout the West. San Antonio's Mexican-American pecan shellers, mostly women, were among the lowest-paid workers in the country, earning less than 4 cents per pound of shelled pecans, which amounted to an annual wage of less than $180. In 1934, 1935, and again in 1938, CIO organizers, including local activist "Red" Emma Tenayuca, led the pecan shellers in strikes, finally gaining higher wages and union recognition in 1938. However, not every New Deal administrator or agency was committed to aiding minorities. In the fields of central California, local authorities supported growers, and Mexican-American unions had little success and received negligible support from the federal government. Nor did the New Deal lessen efforts to repatriate Mexicans to Mexico.

Despite its limitations, the New Deal provided hope and support for many women and minorities, who in turn praised Roosevelt. "The WPA came along and Roosevelt came to be a god," said one African American. "You worked, you got a paycheck, and you had some dignity." Politically, such sentiments were more than praise because where they could vote, minorities voted for Roosevelt and the Democratic Party. Blacks bolted the Republican Party and enlisted in extraordinary numbers in the Democratic Party. In the 1936 presidential election, Roosevelt carried every black ward in Cleveland and nationally received nearly 90 percent of the black vote.

While most minorities benefited only indirectly from the New Deal, that was not the case for Native Americans. Native Americans had two strong supporters in Secretary of Interior Ickes and Commissioner of Indian Affairs John Collier. Both opposed existing Indian policies that since 1887 had sought to destroy the reservation system and eradicate Indian cultures. At Collier's urging, Congress passed the **Indian Reorganization Act** in 1934. The act returned land and community control to tribal organizations. It provided Indian self-rule on the reservations and prevented individual ownership of tribal lands. To improve the squalid conditions found on most reservations and to provide jobs, Collier organized a CCC-type agency for Indians and ensured that other New Deal agencies played a part in improving Indian lands and providing jobs. He also promoted Native American culture. Working with tribal leaders, Collier took measures to protect, preserve, and encourage

John Collier worked to ensure the passage of the Indian Reorganization Act. Designed to restore tribal sovereignty under federal authority, each tribe had to ratify the act to participate. Not all tribes did; seventy-seven rejected it, including the Navajos, the nation's largest tribe. This photo shows a group of Navajos meeting with Collier to discuss government-imposed limitations on the number of sheep each Navajo could own. *Wide World Photos.*

Indian customs, languages, religions, and folkways. Reservation school curricula incorporated Indian languages and customs, and Native Americans could once more openly and freely exercise their religions. While a positive effort, Collier's New Deal for Native Americans did little to improve the standard of living for most American Indians. Funds were too few, and the problems created by years of poverty and government neglect were too great. At best, Collier's programs slowed a long-standing economic decline and allowed Native Americans to regain some control over their cultures and societies.

Indian Reorganization Act   Law passed by Congress in 1934 that ended Indian allotment and returned surplus land to tribal ownership; it also sought to encourage tribal self-government and improve economic conditions on reservations.

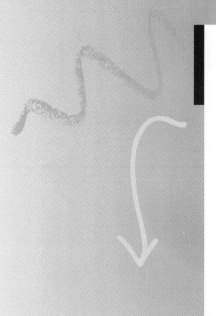

Examining a Primary Source

Frances Perkins Explains the Social Security Act

On September 2, 1935, Secretary of Labor Frances Perkins spoke over the radio to countless Americans to explain the importance of the recently passed Social Security Act. As the Social Security bill was being drafted and considered by Congress, it had come under attack from the right and the left. Conservatives argued that the bill imposed "big government" into an area best served by private and individual efforts. Liberals objected that it was not inclusive enough, leaving out large segments of the work force and providing no health benefits. Perkins's speech was for many Americans the first explanation they had heard of how the new act would change their lives. In this excerpt from her radio address, Madam Secretary Perkins underscores not only what the new law will accomplish for those participating in the program, but also how the milestone legislation charts new territory for the federal government.

● *What type of worker is most likely to receive an old-age pension? What type of worker would be less likely?*

● *A Mississippi newspaper in 1935 argued that the social security plan was a bad one because it would provide a pension to African Americans who would then live idly on their benefits "while cotton and corn crops are crying for workers." How do you think Perkins would have answered this charge?*

● *The Roosevelt administration believed that the social security program was an important reform in preventing another depression. Why would they believe that?*

● *In what ways does Perkins's speech respond to the criticisms of conservatives? of liberals?*

People who work for a living in the United States . . . can join with all other good citizens . . . in satisfaction that the Congress has passed the Social Security Act. . . . It provides for old-age pensions which mark great progress over the measures upon which we have hitherto depended in caring for those who have been unable to provide for the years when they no longer can work. It also provides security for dependent and crippled children, mothers, the indigent disabled and the blind.

Old-age benefits in the form of monthly payments are to be paid to individuals who have worked and contributed to the insurance fund in direct proportion to the total wages earned by such individuals in the course of their employment subsequent to 1936. The minimum monthly payment is to be $10, the maximum $85. These payments will begin in the year 1942 and will be to those who have worked and contributed. ●

Because of difficulty of administration not all employments are covered in this plan at this time . . . but it is sufficiently broad to cover all normally employed industrial workers. . . . It is a sound and reasonable plan . . . . It does not represent a complete solution to the problems of economic security, but it does represent a substantial, necessary beginning. ●

This is truly legislation in the interest of the national welfare . . . its enactment into law would not only carry us a long way toward the goal of economic security for the individual, but also a long way toward the promotion and stabilization of mass purchasing power without which the present economic system cannot endure. . . . ●

. . . The passage of this act . . . with so much intelligent public support is deeply significant of the progress which the American people have made in . . . using cooperation through government to overcome social hazards against which the individual alone is inadequate. ●

SUMMARY

From 1929 to 1939, the Great Depression brought about significant changes in the nature of American life, altering expectations of government, society, and the economy. When Hoover assumed the presidency, most Americans believed that the economy and the quality of life would continue to improve. The Depression changed that. The flaws in the economy, largely hidden by the apparent prosperity of the 1920s, were suddenly exposed as the stock market crashed and legions of banks and businesses closed. Unemployment soared and people lost their homes and their hope in the future.

More than previous presidents, Hoover expanded the role of the federal government to meet the economic and social crises. He initiated a series of measures, including the Reconstruction Finance Corporation, which tried to stimulate the economy. But Hoover's philosophy of limited government undermined the effort, and the economy continued to worsen. Losing faith in Hoover, most Americans put their faith instead in Roosevelt and his 1932 campaign promise of a New Deal. Roosevelt won easily and took office amid widespread expectations for a major shift in the role of government. The New Deal was launched, working to regenerate economic growth, aid millions of needy Americans, and institute reforms that further regulated the economy and ensured a more equitable society. The First Hundred Days witnessed a barrage of legislation, most dealing with the immediate problems of unemployment and economic collapse. The AAA and NRA were designed to restore the economy while a variety of relief programs such as the CCC and PWA put people to work.

In 1935, assailed by both liberals and conservatives, Roosevelt responded with a second burst of legislation that focused more on social legislation and putting people to work than on programs for business-oriented recovery. The overwhelming Democratic victory in 1936 confirmed the popularity of Roosevelt and the changes brought by his New Deal, and raised expectations of further social and economic regulatory legislation. A Third Hundred Days, however, never materialized. The Court-packing scheme, an economic downturn, labor unrest, and growing conservatism generated more political opposition than New Deal forces could overcome. The outcome was that the New Deal wound down after 1937.

The Depression affected all Americans, as they had to adjust their values and lifestyles to meet the economic and psychological crisis. People worried about economic insecurity, but industrial workers and minorities were the most likely to face hard times and carried the extra burdens of discrimination and loss of status. Lives were disrupted, homes and businesses lost, but most people learned to cope with the Great Depression and hoped for better times.

Roosevelt and the New Deal provided new reasons for hope and made coping easier. Farmers, blue-collar workers, women, and minorities directly and indirectly benefited from the New Deal. The HOLC and FHA saved thousands of homes; the Social Security Act provided some with retirement funds and established a national network of unemployment compensation; and the Fair Labor Standards Act guaranteed a minimum wage. But more than specific programs, the New Deal provided a sense of hope and a growing expectation about government's role in promoting the economy and providing for the welfare of those in need.

The New Deal never fully restored the economy, but it engineered a profound shift in the nature of government and in society's expectations about the federal government's role in people's lives. After the New Deal, neither the economy, nor society, nor government and politics would ever be the same.

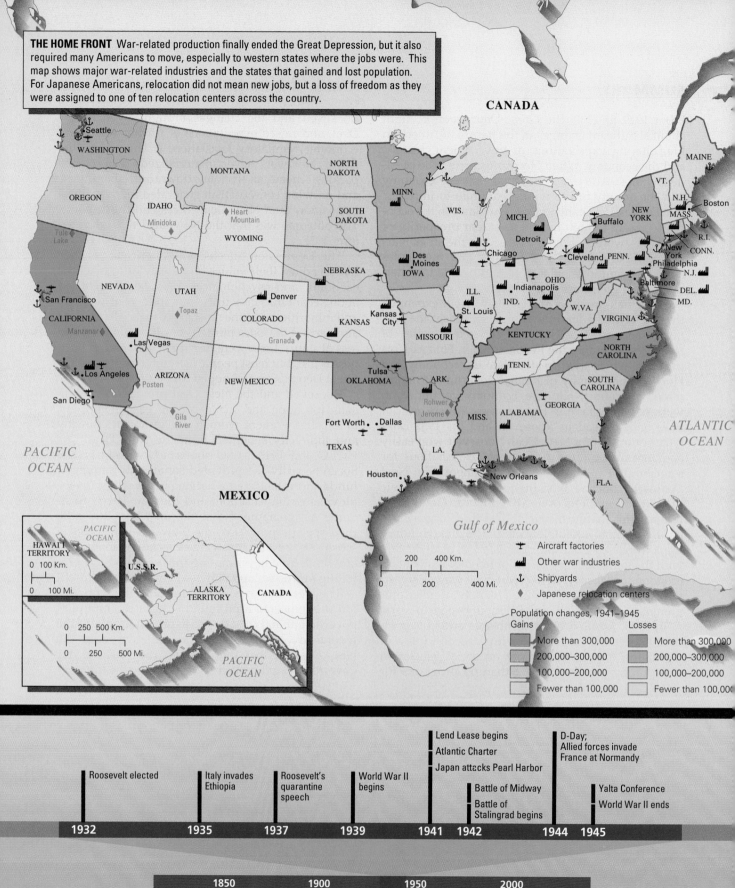

THE HOME FRONT War-related production finally ended the Great Depression, but it also required many Americans to move, especially to western states where the jobs were. This map shows major war-related industries and the states that gained and lost population. For Japanese Americans, relocation did not mean new jobs, but a loss of freedom as they were assigned to one of ten relocation centers across the country.

CANADA

Seattle
WASHINGTON
OREGON
MONTANA
IDAHO
Minidoka
NORTH DAKOTA
SOUTH DAKOTA
MINN.
WIS.
MICH.
Buffalo
MAINE
VT.
N.H.
Boston
MASS.
NEW YORK
R.I.
CONN.
New York
Detroit
Cleveland
PENN.
Heart Mountain
WYOMING
NEVADA
Tule Lake
UTAH
Topaz
CALIFORNIA
Manzanar
San Francisco
Las Vegas
Los Angeles
San Diego
COLORADO
Denver
Granada
NEBRASKA
Des Moines
IOWA
KANSAS
Kansas City
MISSOURI
St. Louis
ILL.
IND.
OHIO
Indianapolis
W.VA.
KENTUCKY
VIRGINIA
NORTH CAROLINA
Philadelphia
N.J.
DEL.
MD.
Baltimore
ARIZONA
Posten
NEW MEXICO
Gila River
OKLAHOMA
Tulsa
ARK.
Rohwer
Jerome
TENN.
MISS.
ALABAMA
GEORGIA
SOUTH CAROLINA
Fort Worth
Dallas
TEXAS
Houston
LA.
New Orleans
FLA.

PACIFIC OCEAN

MEXICO

Gulf of Mexico

ATLANTIC OCEAN

PACIFIC OCEAN
HAWAI'I TERRITORY
0   100 Km.
0   100 Mi.

U.S.S.R.
ALASKA TERRITORY
CANADA
PACIFIC OCEAN
0   250   500 Km.
0   250   500 Mi.

0   200   400 Km.
0   200   400 Mi.

✈ Aircraft factories
🏭 Other war industries
⚓ Shipyards
◆ Japanese relocation centers

Population changes, 1941–1945

Gains		Losses	
	More than 300,000		More than 300,000
	200,000–300,000		200,000–300,000
	100,000–200,000		100,000–200,000
	Fewer than 100,000		Fewer than 100,000

Roosevelt elected	Italy invades Ethiopia	Roosevelt's quarantine speech	World War II begins	Lend Lease begins		D-Day; Allied forces invade France at Normandy	
				Atlantic Charter			
				Japan attacks Pearl Harbor			
					Battle of Midway		Yalta Conference
					Battle of Stalingrad begins		World War II ends
1932	**1935**	**1937**	**1939**	**1941**	**1942**	**1944**	**1945**

| **1850** | **1900** | **1950** | **2000** |

America's Rise to World Leadership, 1929–1945

Sybil Lewis

SYBIL LEWIS

World War II caused a massive migration of African Americans to the West Coast, looking for jobs and a better life. Facing the possibility of a segregated life as a domestic worker, Sybil Lewis, like thousands of other black women, took the opportunity created by war. She found work in the defense industries of Southern California, learning skills that before the war were denied to most, if not all, women. Echoing the views of Sybil Lewis, another African American stated, "Hitler was the one that got us out of the white folks' kitchen." For Sybil Lewis and others, the war provided an opportunity for a profound change in their lives—Sybil Lewis never returned to the kitchen. In this picture a pair of riveters work on a section of an airplane—both contributing to the war effort and changing American society. *Courtesy of the Boeing Company.*

Sybil Lewis chose California. Out of 340,000 Americans who came to Los Angeles during the Second World War, she was among the over 140,000 African Americans. She, like others, had heard that California was a better place—a place with jobs for blacks and women, a place *without* segregation. Indeed, jobs were available, at first primarily for domestic workers, but by 1943 more and more wartime industries looked to African Americans to fill their labor shortages. Employers frequently preferred to hire black women for these industrial jobs instead of men. Reflecting the racism of the day, employers believed that hiring black men would threaten existing racial lines and set a worrisome precedent: African-American men would no doubt seek similar employment once the war was finished. But women, everyone understood, clearly were only temporary hires and could be easily dismissed at war's end. The same was true of residential patterns. Although Los Angeles endorsed no legal segregation, African Americans found housing available only in a few areas of town and encountered white hostility if they sought to live outside those sections. Consequently, most blacks lived in the central part of Los Angeles, in areas like Watts and "Bronzeville." Bronzeville had been "Little Tokyo" before the war and had housed nearly 30,000 Japanese Americans. Following Japanese removal, Bronzeville became home to nearly 80,000 African Americans.

Sybil Lewis came from a small, segregated town in Oklahoma where she had worked as a maid, doing ironing and washing and earning $3.50 a week. Arriving in California, she saw both sides of Los Angeles. She noted that African Americans, especially women, were working in occupations unavailable to them in the South. She also observed white and "black people in the school system." It seemed a much more open society, where blacks had better opportunities and lives. But she also experienced prejudice and segregation, not only because she was black and a woman but because she was also an "Okie."

Vowing never to be a maid again, she searched the want ads for a job. Bending under federal pressure and the need for workers, Lockheed Aircraft was willing to hire and train minorities and women to work in their plant. Sybil Lewis applied and after several attempts—"You had to be pretty persistent"—she was hired. Along with other women, she received a quick training program that taught her how to rivet. Riveting was a two-person operation. The riveter operated the rivet gun while another, the "bucker," used a heavy bar on the opposite side to expand and smooth the rivets as they came through. Sybil was selected to be a riveter and considered it a skilled position, unlike that of the bucker, which required more muscle than skill.

The new job not only provided Sybil a skill, but it placed her and others into a new environment that broke old patterns. She was paired with a white woman from Arkansas. Both had been raised in segregated societies and now found themselves working side by side as a team. It was a new experience. At first both were uncomfortable, but each learned to adapt. "I feel that the experience was meaningful to me and meaningful to her," Sybil wrote. "She learned that Negroes were people too, and I saw her as a person also, and we both gained from it." Another new experience was the pay, more money than she would ever have made in Oklahoma. She recalled, "When I got my first paycheck, I'd never seen that much money before." Overwhelmed to have made more than $350 in one month, she immediately treated herself to new clothes and shoes.

Sybil enjoyed working at Lockheed despite the occasional taunts, mostly from men, about her color and sex. Then, for no apparent reason, the foreman told her that she and her bucker were going to switch positions. "I wasn't failing as a riveter," she remembered. "In fact, the other girl learned to rivet from me." Although told that it was company policy to cross-train workers, she believed that "they gave me the job of bucker because I was black." Unwilling to accept what she considered a demotion, Sybil quit.

Next, Sybil Lewis became an arc welder in a shipyard. Arc welding was a higher skill and welders made more money ($1.20 an hour) than riveters. Again, she liked her job and her pay, but at the shipyards she encountered a form of discrimination that had been less obvious at Lockheed. Male welders made more money for doing the same job. While differential pay was a common practice, Sybil Lewis considered it unfair and asked why. "You'd ask about this," she said, "but they'd say . . . 'The men have to lift some heavy pieces of steel and you don't have to.'" She rejected that logic: "I had to help lift steel too." Not only was she getting less pay, but also she noticed that she got less respect when she wore slacks. Confronting a male worker, she asked why. The response was, "You have a man's job and you're getting paid almost the same, so we don't have to give you a seat anymore, or show the common courtesies that men show women." That too, she thought, did not seem right. Less troublesome to Sybil Lewis was the knowledge that her position was temporary. "We were trained to do this kind of work because of the war . . . . We were all told that when the war was over we would not be needed anymore."

When Japan surrendered in September 1945, Sybil Lewis, like millions of other Americans, celebrated and cheered herself hoarse. When the cheering stopped, she planned her next move. "I realized that the good jobs, all of the advantages that had been offered because of the war . . . were over." She knew what she wanted to do, and with her savings to support her, she enrolled in college. Graduating, she found a position in the California civil service where she worked until retirement. Looking back on her experiences, she stated, "The war changed my life, gave me an opportunity to leave my small town and discover there was another way of life. It . . . opened my eyes to opportunities I could take advantage of when the war was over." Sybil Lewis was not alone in having her life changed by the war. It had touched every American, altering their lives and society, but it also drastically changed the role of the United States in world affairs.

INTRODUCTION

The Great Depression was not only an American disaster—it impacted the entire world causing governments and the international system to collapse.

Three nations especially seemed intent on changing the international system and almost eager to use military force to achieve their goals. Japan, seeking raw materials and markets, began the process of dismantling the uneasy peace that had existed since

1918. Seeking an empire in Asia, Japan annexed Manchuria in 1931 and threatened China. In Germany, Adolf Hitler and the National Socialist (Nazi) Party assumed power determined to make their country a major military power again. To the south in Italy, Benito Mussolini was using Italian nationalism to expand his imperial designs. When Hoover left office in 1933, the cheery optimism of a prosperous world at peace that had greeted him had vanished.

Between 1933 and 1939, Roosevelt wrestled with two problems: how to improve U.S. economic and political positions abroad while protecting economic and political interests at home. As an internationalist he wanted the country to take a more active role in world affairs. Roosevelt the politician understood that there were strong isolationist views among the public and in Congress, and American economic recovery was his first priority. Focusing on the Depression, the president deferred to an isolationist Congress as world peace evaporated. The onslaught of the war in Europe in 1939 provided Roosevelt with new opportunities to chart a path toward international activism. Deciding that the United States must help Britain defeat Hitler, Roosevelt provided economic and military assistance to Britain. To check Japanese expansion, he used trade restrictions. Japan's attack on Pearl Harbor in December 1941 drew the United States into World War II.

The war managed to do what the New Deal had not—restore American prosperity. The full mobilization of the United States' resources resulted in full employment and unparalleled cooperation among business, labor, and government. As over 15 million Americans marched off to war, those at home, like Sybil Lewis, faced new challenges and opportunities. The result for women and minorities was mixed: they experienced greater opportunities, but they also were expected by most to relinquish their newfound status once the war ended.

In planning for a European and Pacific war, Roosevelt chose to allocate most of the nation's resources to defeat Hitler. Victory over Japan would have to wait. Allied with Britain and the Soviet Union, the United States began its efforts to liberate Europe by invading North Africa and Italy before invading France. In the Pacific, the victory at Midway gave the United States a naval and air advantage that allowed American forces to close the circle on Japan. By the end of May 1945, Hitler's Third Reich was in ruins and American forces were on the verge of victory over Japan. Roosevelt had died.

President Harry S Truman, wanting to end the war as soon as possible and facing the prospect of huge casualties with an invasion of Japan, decided to use the atomic bomb. The destruction of Hiroshima and Nagasaki led to Japan's surrender. It also announced the beginning of a new age of atomic power, the United States' emergence as a superpower, and what many called "America's century."

THE ROAD TO WAR

• How did Roosevelt's policies reflect those of Hoover, especially in Latin America? How was the Good Neighbor policy a change from previous American policies toward Latin America?

• What obstacles did Roosevelt face in trying to implement a more interventionist foreign policy from 1933 to 1939?

• Following the outbreak of World War II in 1939, how did Roosevelt reshape American neutrality?

When Herbert Hoover became president in 1928, the world appeared stable, peaceful, and increasingly prosperous. He saw no reason to change the policies of his predecessors. The United States would remain aloof from the political and diplomatic bickering of the world while expanding its trade and continuing to use economic and noncoercive policies to promote American interests. Supporting Hoover's international policies was a powerful economy that was the world's number one energy producer, supplied 46 percent of the world's industrial output, and led all nations in exports and foreign investments. The global Depression made a mockery of Hoover's foreign policy expectations.

The initial response of the United States was reflected in the views of Senator George W. Norris (R.–Nebraska), who proclaimed that the United States should look out for its own interests and not to worry about Europe. Blaming Europe for a large part of the country's economic woes, Hoover and Congress adopted policies that sought to protect American business by raising tariffs and cutting back on foreign trade and investments. As president, Franklin D. Roosevelt did not blame Europe for America's troubles and initially appeared to implement a policy of working with Europe. He sent his secretary of state, Cordell Hull, to the London Economic Conference to help shore up international currencies and facilitate world trade. But even while Hull argued for increased trade, Roosevelt adopted a Hoover-like policy of economic nationalism. He announced that the United States

chronology

A World at War

1929	Herbert Hoover becomes president
1931	Japan seizes Manchuria

1933	Franklin D. Roosevelt becomes president
	London Economic Conference
	Gerardo Machado resigns as president
	    of Cuba
	United States recognizes Soviet Union
	Hitler and Nazi party take power in
	    Germany

1934	Fulgencio Batista assumes power in Cuba
1935	Italy invades Ethiopia First Neutrality Act
1936	Germany reoccupies the Rhineland Spanish Civil War begins Second Neutrality Act
1937	Third Neutrality Act Roosevelt's quarantine speech Sino-Japanese War begins Japanese aircraft sink the *Panay*
1938	Germany annexes Austria Munich Conference
1939	Germany invades Czechoslovakia German-Soviet Nonaggression Pact World War II begins as Germany invades Poland Soviets invade Poland Neutrality Act of 1939 Soviets invade Finland
1940	Germany occupies most of Western Europe U.S. economic sanctions against Japan Burke-Wadsworth Act Destroyers-for-bases agreement Roosevelt reelected

1941	Lend-Lease Act Fair Employment Practices Commission created U.S. forces occupy Greenland and Iceland Germany invades Soviet Union Atlantic Charter U-boats attack U.S. warships Manhattan Project begins Japan attacks Pearl Harbor United States enters World War II
1942	War Production Board created Japanese conquer Philippines Japanese Americans interned Battles of Coral Sea and Midway Congress of Racial Equality founded U.S. troops invade North Africa
1943	U.S. forces capture Guadalcanal Soviets defeat Germans at Stalingrad Smith-Connally War Labor Disputes Act Detroit race riot U.S. and British forces invade Sicily and Italy Tehran Conference
1944	Operation Overload Allies reach Rhine River G.I. Bill becomes law U.S. forces invade the Philippines Roosevelt reelected Soviet forces liberate Eastern Europe Battle of the Bulge
1945	Yalta Conference Roosevelt dies Harry S Truman becomes president United Nations created Soviets capture Berlin Germany surrenders U.S. forces capture Iwo Jima and Okinawa Potsdam Conference United States drops atomic bombs on Hiroshima and Nagasaki Japan surrenders

would seek economic recovery "by means of a policy of **unilateralism**." Without American cooperation, the conference collapsed and the global economy worsened.

unilaterialism   A policy of acting alone, without consultation or agreement of others.

Diplomacy in a Dangerous World

Roosevelt also followed Hoover's so-called **Good Neighbor policy** toward Latin America. Hoover had vowed that the United States would respect the interests of the nations of the hemisphere and affirmed that the Monroe Doctrine did not give the United States the right to intervene in regional affairs. Latin Americans applauded Hoover's policies but asked that the United States explicitly renounce all forms and reasons for intervention in their affairs. On assuming office, Roosevelt's commitment to being a good neighbor and to noninterventionism was soon tested in Cuba and Mexico. Social and political unrest swept across Cuba in 1933 fed by opponents of oppressive president, Gerardo "the Butcher" Machado. Seeking to stabilize Cuba and protect American interests, Roosevelt sent special envoy Sumner Welles to encourage Machado to resign. Bending under American pressure, Machado left office and was replaced by Ramon Grau San Martin. It was not the change of government that Welles wanted. He considered the new Cuban leader too "communistic" and wanted the United States to use military force to remove him. Roosevelt rejected armed intervention and instead continued political maneuvers. The United States' refusal to recognize the new government allowed Welles to argue that a more acceptable government was needed. Without too much effort, he convinced **Colonel Fulgencio Batista** to oust Grau and establish a new government. Batista's regime was immediately recognized by the United States and received a favorable trade agreement. Batista would control the island nation until the end of 1958.

Mexico also tested Roosevelt's commitment to nonintervention in 1938 by **nationalizing** foreign-owned oil properties. American oil interests, supported by Hull, argued that Mexico had no right to seize their properties, demanded their return, and asked that Roosevelt intervene with military force if necessary. Roosevelt rejected the idea and instead accepted the principle of nationalization and sought a fair monetary settlement for the American companies. Not until 1941 did Mexico and the United States agree on the proper amount of compensation, but throughout, American relations with Mexico remained cordial. The Good Neighbor policy was also enhanced as the United States moved away from supporting the right to intervene, announcing at the Pan-American Conference in 1938 that there were no acceptable reasons for armed intervention.

While Hoover's and Roosevelt's Latin American policies greatly enhanced the United States' image in the Western Hemisphere, elsewhere in the world the ongoing Depression led to international crises that threatened peace. Japan acted first. Japan relied heavily on international trade for its economic growth and its food supply, and as shrinking world trade weakened its economy, calls arose for action to protect the economy and national interests. Rejecting most Western values and free trade, many nationalists advocated a Japanese sphere of influence, or empire, and looked toward Manchuria. Situated north and west of Japanese-controlled Korea, Manchuria was rich in iron and coal, accounted for 95 percent of Japanese overseas investment, and also supplied large amounts of vital foodstuffs. Most important, a Japanese military presence in Manchuria protected Japanese interests there. In September 1931, a small group of army officers executed a plan to establish Japanese rule over the region. A section of track of the Japanese-owned Southern Manchurian Railroad was destroyed. Local Japanese officials blamed the Chinese and, without informing their government, used the Japanese army to seize control of the province.

World reaction was one of shock and condemnation, but little else. The League of Nations sheepishly called for peace. From Washington, Hoover's secretary of state Henry Stimson denounced the Japanese aggression and asked the Chinese and Japanese governments to halt the fighting. American humorist Will Rogers sarcastically wrote that world leaders would run out of stationery writing their protests before Japan would run out of soldiers. Japan's successful conquest of Manchuria magnified the power of its pro-imperial factions as many Japanese spoke openly of establishing a Japanese dominance in Asia, a **Greater East Asian Co-Prosperity Sphere**.

Good Neighbor policy   An American policy toward Latin America that stressed nonintervention begun under Hoover but associated with Roosevelt.

Colonel Fulgencio Batista   Dictator who ruled Cuba from 1934 through 1958; his corrupt, authoritarian regime was overthrown by Fidel Castro's revolutionary movement.

nationalize   To convert an industry or enterprise from private to government ownership and control.

Greater East Asian Co-Prosperity Sphere   Japan's plan to create and dominate an economic and defensive union in East Asia, using force if necessary.

Roosevelt and Isolationism

In Europe, two nations were also seeking to alter the international status quo and expand their influence and power: Germany and Italy. Adolf Hitler had come to power in 1933, based on a promise to improve the economy and Germany's role in the world. Benito Mussolini argued that Italy needed to expand its influence abroad and to protect its interests in Africa. Caught between Germany and Japan, the Soviet Union's Joseph Stalin sought to improve relations with the United States, western European states, and China. Roosevelt, seeking trade possibilities and hoping to stiffen Soviet resolve in the face of possible Japanese or German aggression, also sought improved relations. The result was minimal: American recognition of the Soviet Union in November 1933, but no expansion of U.S.-Soviet trade, nor any attempt to bridge the ideological gap and the decade of distrust that separated the two nations.

Within the United States, Roosevelt's decision to establish relations with the Soviets prompted protests that he was abandoning isolationism. By 1934, isolationists were in full cry, even repudiating U.S. entry into World War I and suggesting that the "true origins" of that war had been greed and British propaganda. A congressional investigation chaired by Senator Gerald P. Nye of North Dakota alleged that America's entry into the war had been the product of arms manufacturers, bankers, and war profiteers—"the merchants of death." Novelists such as Ernest Hemingway (*A Farewell to Arms*, 1929) and John Dos Passos (*Three Soldiers*, 1921) added to antiwar and isolationist sentiments with their powerful stories depicting the senseless horror of war. As college students called for arms limitations and peace, a Gallup poll revealed that 67 percent of Americans believed that the nation's intervention in World War I had been wrong.

By 1935, tensions in Asia, Africa, and Europe combined with American isolationism to generate neutrality laws that many hoped would prevent American involvement in future foreign wars. In August 1935, Congress passed the **Neutrality Act of 1935** prohibiting the sale of arms and munitions to any nation at war. It also permitted the president to warn Americans traveling on ships of belligerent nations that they sailed at their own risk. If Roosevelt vetoed the legislation, announced Senator Key Pittman, he was "riding for a fall." Anxious to see the Second Hundred Days successfully through Congress, Roosevelt gave up his preference for **discriminatory neutrality** and accepted political reality. Isolationist Senator Hiram Johnson of

"GERMANY SHALL NEVER BE ENCIRCLED."

Despite Hitler's assurances about the limited territorial goals of Nazi Germany, following the invasion of Poland, most people quickly realized that his true goal was world domination. *Frank Wood Collection.*

California cheered the Neutrality Act as the means to keep the United States "out of European controversies, European wars, and European difficulties."

Most Americans thought that the Neutrality Act came just in time. On October 3, Benito Mussolini's Italian troops invaded the African nation of Ethiopia. Roosevelt immediately announced American neutrality toward the Ethiopian conflict, denying the sale of war supplies to either side. Aware that Italy was

---

Neutrality Act of 1935   Law passed by Congress prohibiting arms shipments to nations at war and authorizing the president to warn U.S. citizens against traveling on belligerents' vessels; known as the First Neutrality Act.

discriminatory neutrality   The ability to withhold aid and trade from one nation at war while providing it to another.

buying increasing amounts of American nonwar goods, including coal and oil, Roosevelt asked Americans to apply a "moral embargo" on Italy. The request had no effect. American trade continued, as did Italian victories. On May 9, 1936, Italy formally annexed Ethiopia.

The end of the Italian-Ethiopian war did not reduce international tensions. In March German troops violated the Treaty of Versailles by occupying the **Rhineland**, and in July civil war broke out in Spain. Roosevelt proclaimed that the remilitarization of the Rhineland was of no concern to the United States and then left on a planned fishing trip. Likewise, most Americans agreed when Roosevelt applied neutrality legislation to both sides of the Spanish Civil War. Taking no chances, Congress modified the neutrality legislation (the Second Neutrality Act) to require noninvolvement in civil wars and to forbid making loans to countries at war—whether victim or aggressor.

With the Italian conquest of Ethiopia, German remilitarization, and the war in Spain as background, both American political parties entered the 1936 elections as champions of neutrality. Roosevelt told an audience at Chautauqua, New York, that he hated war and if it came to "the choice of profits over peace, the nation will answer—must answer—'We choose peace.'" Alf Landon and the Republicans were equally adamant that they were the party best able to keep the nation out of war. Roosevelt easily defeated Landon and, with strong public support, approved the **Neutrality Act of 1937**. It required warring nations to pay cash for all "nonwar" goods and to carry them away on their own ships, and it barred Americans from sailing on belligerents' ships. Roosevelt would have liked a more flexible law, but because he was involved in his Supreme Court struggle, he signed the act. He did, however, appreciate a provision that allowed him to determine which nations were at war and which goods were nonwar goods.

Roosevelt used the provision in late July 1937, following a Japanese invasion of northern China. Ignoring reality and disregarding protests, he refused to recognize that China and Japan were fighting a war and allowed unrestricted American trade to continue with both nations. Hoping that isolationist views had softened, on October 5 Roosevelt suggested that the United States and other peace-loving nations should quarantine "bandit nations" that were contributing to "the epidemic of world lawlessness." The so-called quarantine speech was applauded in many foreign capitals, but not in Berlin, Rome, or Tokyo, and not at home. Within the United States, it only heightened

cries for isolationism while Japan continued gobbling up Chinese territory. On December 12, 1937, Japanese aircraft strafed, bombed, and sank the American gunboat *Panay*. Two Americans died and over thirty were wounded. Roosevelt was outraged and wanted to take some retaliatory action, but public opinion and Congress insisted otherwise. Within forty-eight hours of the *Panay* assault, isolationists in the House of Representatives pushed forward a previously proposed constitutional amendment drafted by Louis Ludlow of Indiana that would require a public referendum before Congress could declare war. Public opinion polls indicated that 70 percent of Americans supported the idea. Only after Roosevelt had expended a great deal of political effort did the House vote 209 to 188 to return the amendment to committee, effectively killing it. Understanding that he had no support for initiating any action against Japan, Roosevelt had no choice but to accept Japan's apology and payment of damages for the *Panay* attack.

World peace was crumbling fast as 1938 started. Fighting raged on in China and Spain with increased intensity. From Berlin, Hitler pronounced his intentions to unify all German-speaking lands and create a new German empire, or *Reich*. He first annexed Austria and then incorporated the Sudeten region of western Czechoslovakia into the German Reich (see Map 25.1). With a respectable military force and defense treaties with France and the Soviet Union, the Czechoslovakian government was prepared to resist. However, France, the Soviet Union, and Britain wanted no confrontation with Hitler. Choosing to negotiate, in late September, Britain's prime minister, Neville Chamberlain, met with Hitler in Munich. Hitler agreed to seek no further territory, and Chamberlain accepted Germany's annexation of the Sudetenland. France concurred. Chamberlain returned to England smiling and promising that he had secured "peace for our time." Privately, Roosevelt was angry with the British and French, but publicly he congratulated them on defusing the crisis.

Within Germany, Hitler stepped up the persecution of the country's nearly half a million Jews. In 1938 he

---

Rhineland   Region of western Germany along the Rhine River, which under the terms of the Versailles Treaty was to remain free of troops and military fortifications.

Neutrality Act of 1937   Law passed by Congress requiring warring nations to pay cash for "nonwar" goods and barring Americans from sailing on their ships; known as the Third Neutrality Act.

MAP 25.1 German and Italian Expansion, 1933–1942 By the end of 1942, the Axis nations of Italy and Germany, through conquest and annexation, had occupied nearly all of Europe. This map shows the political and military alignment of Europe as Germany and Italy reached the limit of their power.

launched government-sponsored violence against the German-Jewish population. Synagogues and Jewish businesses and homes were looted and destroyed. Detention centers—concentration camps—at Dachau and Buchenwald soon confined over fifty thousand Jews. Thousands of German and Austrian Jews fled to other countries. Many applied to enter the United States, but most were turned away. American anti-Semitism was strong, and the State Department, citing immigration requirements that no one be admitted to the country that would become "a public charge," routinely denied entry to German Jews whose property and assets had been seized by the German government. Advocates of changing the immigration rules found Congress and the public uninterested. Opinion polls consistently indicated

that large majorities objected to more Jewish immigration. One survey found that 85 percent of Protestants, 84 percent of Catholics, and even 25.8 percent of Jews in the United States opposed opening the door wider to more Jewish refugees. Roosevelt expressed concern but, like most politicians, did not translate that concern into any significant change in policy. In all, only about 60,000 Jewish refugees entered the United States between 1933 and 1938—many of them scientists, academics, and musicians. Even so, Roosevelt was convinced that Hitler was a threat to humanity and sounded a dire warning to Americans in his 1939 State of the Union address. "Events abroad have made it increasingly clear to the American people that the dangers within are less to be feared than dangers without," he cautioned. "This generation will nobly

In September 1939, Germany introduced the world to a new word and type of warfare, *blitzkrieg*—lightning war. Combining the use of tanks, aircraft, and infantry, German forces quickly overran first Poland then most of Western Europe. This picture shows a German victory parade in Warsaw, Poland. *Hugo Jaeger/LIFE Magazine. ©Time Warner, Inc.*

save or meanly lose the last best hope of earth." He then asked Congress to increase military spending for the construction of aircraft and to repeal the arms embargo section of the 1937 Neutrality Act. Congress approved aircraft construction but rejected changing neutrality laws. In quick succession, events seemed to verify Roosevelt's prediction of danger. Hitler ominously concluded a military alliance with Italy and a nonaggression pact with the Soviet Union. He seized what remained of Czechoslovakia and demanded that Poland turn over to Germany the Polish Corridor that connected Poland to the Baltic Sea. Incensed by Warsaw's refusal and no longer worried about a Soviet attack, Hitler invaded Poland on September 1, 1939. Two days later, Britain and France declared war on Germany. Within a matter of days, German troops had overrun nearly all of Poland. On September 17, Soviet forces entered the eastern parts of Poland as they had secretly agreed to do in their **German-Soviet Nonaggression Pact**.

War and American Neutrality

As hostilities began in Europe, isolationism remained strong in the United States, with public opinion polls showing little desire to become involved. Just weeks before the invasion of Poland, in a poll taken by *Fortune* magazine, 54 percent of the respondents believed that no international question was important enough to involve the United States in a war. Sixty-six percent opposed the United States going to war to save France and Britain from defeat by an unnamed dictatorship. Roosevelt, however, was determined to do everything possible, short of war, to help those nations opposing Hitler.

After proclaiming neutrality, he called Congress into special session and asked that the cash-and-carry policy of the Neutrality Act of 1937 be modified to allow the sale of any goods, including arms, to any nation, provided the goods were paid for in cash and carried away in ships belonging to the purchasing country. A "peace bloc" argued that the request was a ruse to aid France and Britain and would certainly drag America into the war. Responding to the rapid collapse of Poland, Congress yielded to the president and passed the **Neutrality Act of 1939** in November. Any nation could now buy weapons from the United States. Roosevelt also worked with Latin American neighbors to establish a 300-mile neutrality zone around the Western Hemisphere, excluding Canada and other British and French possessions. Within the zone, patrolled by the U.S. Navy, warships of the belligerent nations were forbidden.

Although neutral in appearance, both acts were designed to help France and England. While any nation could now theoretically buy weapons from the United States, German ships would be denied access to American ports by the British Royal Navy. The neutrality zone had to allow French and British

German-Soviet Nonaggression Pact Agreement in which Germany and the USSR in 1939 pledged not to fight one another and secretly arranged to divide Poland after Germany conquered it.

Neutrality Act of 1939 Law passed by Congress repealing the arms embargo and authorizing cash-and-carry exports of arms and munitions even to belligerent nations.

warships to reach their Western Hemisphere possessions; therefore, it was only German warships that would be stopped by the navy. If the navy happened to sink any German submarines, Roosevelt joked to his cabinet, he would apologize like "the Japs do, 'So sorry. Never do it again.' Tomorrow we sink two."

As Roosevelt shaped American neutrality, Hitler in April 1940 unleashed his forces on Denmark and Norway, which quickly fell under Nazi domination. On May 10 the German offensive against France began with an invasion of Belgium and the Netherlands (see Map 25.1). On May 26 Belgian forces surrendered while French and British troops began their remarkable evacuation to England from the French port of Dunkirk. That 350,000 British and French forces avoided total defeat at Dunkirk was the only bright spot in an otherwise dismal showing by Britain and France. On June 10 Mussolini entered the war on Germany's side and invaded France from the southeast. Twelve days later, France surrendered.

Germany and Italy, called the **Axis powers**, controlled almost all of western and central Europe, leaving Britain to face the seemingly invincible German army and air force alone. England's new prime minister, **Winston Churchill**, pledged never to surrender until the Nazi scourge was destroyed. On August 8 the **Battle of Britain** began with the German air force bombing targets throughout England in preparation for an invasion of the island. Britain's Royal Air Force outfought the German *Luftwaffe* and denied them air superiority. Hitler eventually cancelled the invasion. To defend England and defeat Hitler, Churchill turned to Roosevelt for aid. His ultimate goal was to bring the United States into the war, but his first request was for war supplies. He needed forty or fifty destroyers and a huge number of aircraft. Roosevelt promised to help. He convinced Congress to increase the military budget, placed orders for the production of more than fifty thousand planes a year, and ordered National Guard units to active federal duty. In September he signed the **Burke-Wadsworth Act**, creating the first peacetime military draft in American history, and by executive order, he exchanged fifty old, mothballed destroyers for ninety-nine-year leases of British military bases in Newfoundland, the Caribbean, and British Guiana. By the end of the year, Congress had approved over $37 billion for military spending, more than the total cost of World War I.

As both parties prepared for the 1940 presidential election, opinion polls on American foreign policy showed public confusion. Ninety percent of those asked said they hoped the United States would stay out of the war, but 70 percent approved giving Britain

Hitler ordered the German air force to attack British cities in an effort to break the will of the British people. London, like the British people, suffered tremendous damage but withstood the onslaught. By the end of 1942, the small British airforce was winning the battle against Germany for the air space over Britain. *William Vandivert ©Time Warner Inc.*

the destroyers, and 60 percent wanted to support England, even if doing so led to war. Determined to prevent support for Britain from diminishing, Roosevelt chose to run for an unprecedented third term. Guided

Axis powers   Coalition of nations that opposed the Allies in World War II, first consisting of Germany and Italy and later joined by Japan.

Winston Churchill   Prime minister who led Britain through World War II; he was known for his eloquent speeches and his refusal to give in to the Nazi threat. He would be voted out of office in July 1945.

Battle of Britain   Series of battles between British and German planes fought over Britain from August to October 1940, during which English cities suffered heavy bombing.

Burke-Wadsworth Act   Law passed by Congress in 1940 creating the first peacetime draft in American history.

by their isolationist positions, Republicans, to the surprise of nearly everyone, bypassed leading Republicans such as Robert Taft of Ohio and Arthur Vandenberg of Michigan and nominated **Wendell Willkie**, an ex-Democrat from Indiana. Initially, Willkie accepted the bulk of the New Deal, supported aid to Britain and increased military spending, and focused on the issue of Roosevelt's third term. With Willkie trailing in the preference polls, Republican leaders convinced Willkie to be more critical of the New Deal and to attack Roosevelt for pushing the nation toward war. Willkie's popularity surged upward. Roosevelt countered with a promise to American mothers: "Your boys are not going to be sent into any foreign wars." Hearing of the speech, Willkie remarked, "That is going to beat me." He was right. Roosevelt won easily, but his victory did not sweep other Democrats into office; Republicans gained seats in both the Senate and House of Representatives.

The Battle for the Atlantic

While Roosevelt relaxed during a post-election vacation in the Caribbean, he received an urgent message from Churchill. Britain was out of money to buy American goods, as required by the 1939 Neutrality Act. Churchill needed credit to pay for supplies. He also asked Roosevelt to allow American ships to carry goods to England and for American help to protect merchant ships from German submarines. Roosevelt agreed, but knowing that both requests would face tough congressional and public opposition, he turned to his powers of persuasion. In his December fireside chat, he told his audience that if England fell, Hitler would surely attack the United States next. He urged the people to make the nation the "arsenal of democracy" and to supply Britain with all the material help it needed to defeat Hitler. He then presented Congress with a bill allowing the president to lend, lease, or in any way provide goods to any country considered vital to American security. The request drew the expected fire from isolationists. Senator Burton K. Wheeler called it a military Agricultural Adjustment Act that would "plow under every fourth American boy." Supporters countered with "Send guns, not sons." On March 11, 1941, the 60-year-old president breathed a sigh of relief when the **Lend-Lease Act** passed easily.

For a while it appeared that Lend-Lease might have come too late. German submarines were sinking so much cargo and so many irreplaceable ships that not even Britain's minimal needs were reaching its ports. In March 1941, Churchill warned Roosevelt that Germany's foes could not afford to lose the battle for the Atlantic. In response, Roosevelt sent part of the Pacific fleet to the Atlantic and extended the neutrality zone to include Greenland. By the summer of 1941, the United States Navy's patrols of the neutrality zone overlapped Hitler's Atlantic war zone. It was only a matter of time until American and German ships confronted each other.

Meanwhile, German forces plowed into Yugoslavia and Greece, heading toward the Mediterranean and North Africa. The nonaggression pact having served its role, Hitler planned to crush the Soviets with the largest military force ever assembled on a single front. On June 22, 1941, German forces, supported by allied Finnish, Hungarian, Italian, and Romanian armies, opened the eastern front. Claiming he would join even with the devil to defeat Hitler, Churchill made an ally of Stalin, while Roosevelt extended credits and lend-lease goods to the Soviet Union. Many worried that the Red Army would not last more than three months and that German troops would soon occupy Moscow. Yet despite initial crushing victories in which German soldiers surrounded Leningrad and advanced within miles of Moscow, by November it was becoming clear that the Soviets were not going to collapse.

With the battle for the Atlantic reaching a turning point and Germany rolling through Russia, Roosevelt and Churchill met secretly off the coast of Newfoundland (the Argentia Conference, August 9–12, 1941). They discussed strategies, supplies, and future prospects. Churchill pleaded for an American declaration of war, but Roosevelt's main concern was more political than strategic. He urged Churchill to support the formation of a postwar world that subscribed to the goals of self-determination, freedom of trade and the seas, and the establishment of a "permanent system of general security" in the form of a new world organization. Roosevelt wanted the **Atlantic Charter**

Wendell Willkie Business executive and Republican presidential candidate who lost to Roosevelt in 1940; during the campaign, Roosevelt never publicly mentioned Willkie's name.

Lend-Lease Act Law passed by Congress in 1941 providing that any country whose security was vital to U.S. interests could receive arms and equipment by sale, transfer, or lease from the United States.

Atlantic Charter Joint statement issued by Roosevelt and Churchill in 1941 to formulate American and British postwar aims of international economic and political cooperation.

From the beginning of World War II, Roosevelt was determined to help defeat the forces of fascism. Meeting with Churchill, on board a cruiser off the coast of Newfoundland in August 1941, the two leaders signed the Atlantic Charter as a prelude to the United States waging war against Germany. *FDR Library.*

to highlight the distinctions between the open multilateral world of the democracies and the closed self-serving world of fascist expansion. Such a contrast, he believed, would help Americans support entry into the war. Churchill agreed to support the Atlantic Charter, but reminded Roosevelt that Britain could not fully accept the goals of self-determination and free trade within its Commonwealth and the British Empire. Roosevelt, who saw the Atlantic Charter as a domestic tool and not a blueprint for foreign policy, had no objection to the prime minister's exceptions. Returning to London, Churchill told his ministers that Roosevelt meant to "wage war, but not declare it, and that he would become more and more provocative . . . to force an incident . . . which would justify him in opening hostilities."

On September 4, 1941, an incident occurred that allowed the United States to step closer to officially ending its neutrality. In the North Atlantic, near Iceland, a German U-boat fired two torpedoes at the American destroyer *Greer*. Both missed and the *Greer* counterattacked. Neither ship was damaged, but Roosevelt used the skirmish to get Congress to

amend the neutrality laws to permit armed U.S. merchant ships to sail into combat zones. In October, following an attack on the U.S.S. *Kearney* and the sinking of the U.S.S. *Reuben James*, Congress rescinded all neutrality laws. As American ships were being attacked, the War Department sent its war plan, "the Victory Program," to the president. It concluded that the United States would have to fight a two-front war, one against Germany and another against Japan. It also stated that Hitler needed to be defeated before the Japanese, and that July 1943 was about the earliest date that American troops could be ready for any large-scale operation.

Pearl Harbor

Since 1937, Japanese troops had seized more and more of coastal China, while the United States did little but protest. By 1940, popular sentiment favored not only beefing up American defenses in the Pacific but also using economic pressure to slow Japanese aggression. In July 1940, Roosevelt began placing restrictions on Japanese-American trade, forbidding the sale and shipment of aviation fuel, steel, and scrap iron. Many Americans believed the action was too limited and pointed out that Japan was still allowed to buy millions of gallons of American oil, which it was using to "extinguish the lamps of China."

The situation in East Asia soon worsened. The **Vichy** French government, knuckling under to German and Japanese pressure, allowed Japanese troops to enter French Indochina (see Map 25.2), and Japan signed a defense treaty with Germany and Italy. America promptly strengthened its forces in the Philippines, tightened trade restrictions on Japan, and sent long-range bombers to the Philippines to "set the paper cities of Japan on fire" as a deterrent. Within the Japanese government of Prime Minister Fumimaro Konoye, those fearful of confrontation with the United States sought to negotiate. The subsequent discussions between Hull and Admiral Kichisaburo Nomura, Japan's ambassador to the United States, were confused and nonproductive. The lack of progress in the negotiations convinced many in the Japanese government that war was unavoidable

> **Vichy**   City in central France that was the capital of unoccupied France from 1940 to 1942; the Vichy government continued to govern French territories and was sympathetic to the fascists.

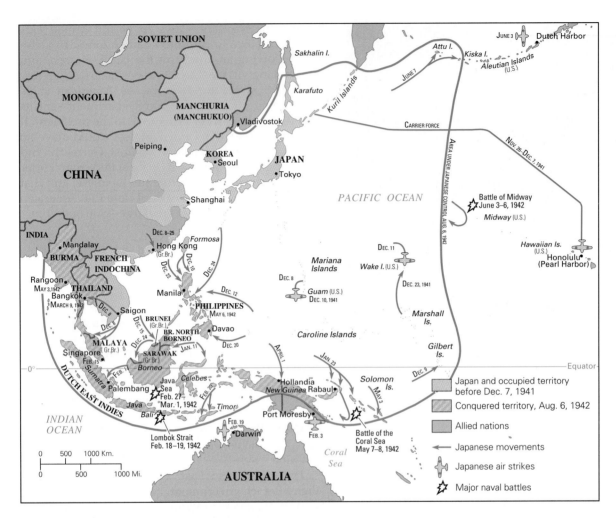

MAP 25.2 Japanese Advances, December 1941–1942 Beginning on December 7, 1941, Japanese forces began carving out a vast empire, the East Asian Co-Prosperity Sphere, by attacking American, British, Dutch, and Australian forces from Pearl Harbor to the Dutch East Indies. This map shows the course of Japanese expansion until the critical naval battles of the Coral Sea and Midway in the spring of 1942 that halted Japanese advances in the Pacific.

to break the "circle of force" that denied Japan its interests. High on the list of interests was Japanese control over Malaysia and the Dutch East Indies (Indonesia), sources of vital raw materials including oil. Seizing those regions, they concluded, would probably involve fighting the United States.

For Minister of War Hideki Tojo, the choice had become simple: either submit to American demands, giving up the achievements of the last ten years and accepting a world order defined by the United States, or safeguard the nation's honor and achievements by initiating a war. In his mind, war could be averted only if the United States, which had frozen Japanese assets in July, agreed to suspend aid to China, cap its

military presence in the Pacific, and resume full trade with Japan. If these concessions did not occur, Tojo decided, Japan would begin military operations in the first week of December. Naval aircraft would strike the American fleet at Pearl Harbor, in Hawai`i, while the army would invade the Philippines, Malaya, Singapore, and the Dutch East Indies. Negotiations remained stalled until November 26, when Hull made it clear that the United States would make no concessions and insisted that Japan withdraw from China. The die was cast.

On November 26, Admiral Isoroku Yamamoto dispatched part of the Japanese fleet, including six aircraft carriers, toward Hawai`i. American observers,

Roosevelt called it "A Day of Infamy"—December 7, 1941, when Japanese planes attacked Pearl Harbor, Hawai`i, without warning and before a declaration of war. In this photo, U.S.S. *West Virginia* sinks in flames, one of eight battleships sunk or badly damaged in the attack. *National Archives.*

however, focused on the activity of a larger part of the Japanese fleet, which joined troop ships in sailing on December 5 toward the South China Sea and the Gulf of Siam. At 7:49 A.M. December 7 (Hawaiian time), before Japan's declaration of war had been received in Washington, Japanese planes struck the American fleet anchored at Pearl Harbor. By 8:12 seven battleships of the American Pacific fleet lined up along Battleship Row were aflame, sinking, or badly damaged. Eleven other ships had been hit, nearly two hundred American aircraft had been destroyed, and 2,500 Americans had lost their lives. Fortunately, U.S. aircraft carriers were not at Pearl Harbor, and Admiral Chuichi Nagumo decided to withdraw without launching further attacks that would have targeted the important support facilities—repair shops, dry docks, and oil storage tanks. These incurred only light damages.

The attack on Pearl Harbor, however, was only a small part of Japan's strategy. Elsewhere that day Japanese planes struck Singapore, Guam, the Philip-

pines, and Hong Kong. Everywhere, British and American positions in the Pacific and East Asia were being overwhelmed. With the final collapse of Filipino and American forces in the Philippines in early May, Japan had occupied most of Southeast Asia and Burma. Seeing the defeat as temporary, upon evacuating the Philippines in March, General Douglas MacArthur vowed to return. Roosevelt declared that the unprovoked, sneak attack on Pearl Harbor made December 7 "a day which will live in infamy" and asked Congress for a declaration of war against Japan. Only the vote of Representative Jeannette Rankin of Montana, a pacifist, kept the December 8 declaration of war from being unanimous. Three days later, Germany and Italy declared war on the United States. Americans were angry and full of fight. In England Churchill "slept the sleep of the saved and thankful." He knew that with the economic and human resources of the United States finally committed to war, the Axis would be "ground to powder."

AMERICA RESPONDS TO WAR

• What actions did Roosevelt take to mobilize the nation for war? How did new wartime necessities affect the relationship between business and government?

• What new social and economic choices did Americans confront as the nation became the "arsenal of democracy"? In particular, what doors opened and closed for women and minorities?

• How were the military experiences of the Nisei, Mexican Americans, African Americans, and Indians different, and why?

The attack on Pearl Harbor unified the nation as no other event had done. Afterward, it was almost impossible to find an isolationist. Thousands of young men rushed to enlist, especially into the navy and marines. On December 8, 1,200 applicants besieged the navy recruiting station in New York City, some having waited outside the doors all night. Eventually over 16.4 million Americans would serve in the armed forces during World War II.

The shock of Japan's attack on Pearl Harbor raised fears of further attacks, especially along the Pacific Coast. On the night of December 7 and throughout the next week, West Coast cities reported enemy planes overhead and practiced blackouts. Phantom Japanese planes were spotted above San Francisco and Los Angeles. In Seattle, crowds hurled rocks at an offending blue neon light that defied the blackout and then, venting both fear and rage, rioted across the city. The Rose Bowl game between Oregon State and Duke was moved from the Bowl's home in Pasadena to Duke's stadium in Durham, North Carolina. Stores everywhere removed "made in Japan" goods from shelves. Alarm and anger were focused especially on Japanese Americans. Rumors circulated wildly that they intended to sabotage factories and military installations, paving the way for the invasion of the West Coast. Within a week, the FBI had arrested 2,541 citizens of Axis countries: 1,370 Japanese, 1,002 Germans, and 169 Italians. Attorney General Francis Biddle announced that he did not believe it would be necessary to arrest more. Biddle soon changed his mind as anti-Japanese hysteria spread.

Japanese-American Internment

The feelings against Japanese Americans were a product of long-standing racist attitudes and an immediate reaction to the war. Of the nearly 125,000 Japanese Americans in the country, about three-fourths were *Nisei*, who had been born in the United States. The remaining, *Issei*, were officially

In February 1942, President Roosevelt signed an order sending all Japanese Americans living on the West Coast to internment camps. This photo taken at a staging area for transportation to the internment camps, shows the quiet dignity of those waiting to be interned. *National Archives.*

citizens of Japan, although nearly all had lived in the United States more than eighteen years.

Fueling the hatred following Pearl Harbor were the actions of General John L. De Witt, commanding general of the Western Defense District. On December 7, he had seen Japanese planes over San Francisco where none existed, and he believed that everyone of Japanese heritage was a threat. Except for individual cases, the nation did not need to worry about Americans of Italian or German ancestry, he pronounced, but the Japanese were a different matter. "We must

Nisei   A person born in America of parents who emigrated from Japan.

Issei   A Japanese immigrant to the United States.

worry about the Japanese all the time," De Witt stated, "until he is wiped off the map." Unable to discover any acts of espionage or sabotage, California attorney general Earl Warren nonetheless concluded that a plot existed, and it was only a matter of time until "zero hour," when the enemy within would carry out its sinister plans. Echoing long-standing anti-Japanese feelings, California moved to "protect" itself. Japanese Americans were fired from state jobs and had their law and medical licenses revoked. Banks froze Japanese-American assets, stores refused service, and loyal citizens vandalized Nisei and Issei homes and businesses.

Although some doubted the reality of any threat from the Japanese-American community, few came forward to speak on its behalf or to protest the growing cry to relocate those of Japanese ancestry away from the coast. President Roosevelt was no exception. On February 19, 1942, he signed **Executive Order #9066**, which allowed the military to remove anyone deemed a threat from official military areas. When the entire West Coast was declared a military area, the eviction of the Japanese Americans from the region began. By the summer of 1942, over 110,000 Nisei and Issei had been transported to ten **internment camps** (see chapter-opening map). When tested in court, the Executive Order was upheld by the Supreme Court in *Korematsu v. the United States* (1944).

The orders to relocate gave Japanese-Americans almost no time to prepare. Families had to pack the few personal possessions they were allowed to take and to store or sell the rest of their property, including homes and businesses. Some had two weeks, others had two days, but it did not matter. Finding storage facilities was nearly impossible, and most families had to liquidate their possessions at ridiculously low prices. "It is difficult to describe the feeling of despair and humiliation experienced," one man recalled, "as we watched the Caucasians coming to look over all our possessions and offering such nominal amounts knowing we had no recourse but to accept." A twenty-six-room hotel was sold for $500; a pickup truck went for $25; farms sold for a fraction of what they were worth. When denied a few additional days to harvest his strawberry crop, one bitter farmer plowed it under. The FBI promptly arrested him for sabotage. Japanese-American families lost an estimated $810 million to $2 billion in property and goods.

If having to dispose of a lifetime of possessions almost overnight was not bad enough, the process of internment produced a feeling of helplessness and isolation. Tags with numbers were issued to every

family to tie to luggage and coats—no names, only numbers. "From then on," wrote one woman, "we were known as family #10710." Going to the camp, she had lost her identity, dignity, and privacy. In camps, the Nisei and Issei were surrounded by barbed wire and watched over by guards in towers mounted with machine guns pointing inward. Photographers were not allowed to take pictures of the wire or the guard towers. Families and individuals were assigned to apartments of 20 by 25 feet in long barracks of plywood covered with tarpaper. An average of eight people were assigned to each apartment. Cots, straw-filled mattresses, and three army blankets were furnished each person. Between rows of barracks were communal bathrooms and eating areas. Within each camp, the internees were expected to create a community complete with farms, shops, and small factories. And within a remarkably short period of time, they did. Making the desert bloom, the internees at Manzanar by 1944 were producing more than $2 million worth of agricultural products.

Some internees were able to leave the camps by working outside, supplying much-needed labor, especially farm work. By the fall of 1942, one-fifth of all males had left the camps to work. Others volunteered for military service. Japanese-American units served in both the Pacific and European theaters, the most famous being the four-thousand-man 442nd Regimental Combat Team that saw action in Italy, France, and Germany. The men of the 442nd would be among the most decorated in the Army. Years later, in 2000, the federal government, citing racial bias during the war for the delay, awarded the Medal of Honor to twenty-one Asian Americans—most belonging to the 442nd Regiment. Included in the group was **Daniel Ken Inouye**, who was elected senator from Hawai`i in 1960.

Executive Order #9066   Order of President Roosevelt in 1942 authorizing the removal of "enemy aliens" from military areas; it was used to isolate Japanese Americans in internment camps.

internment camps   Camps to which more than 110,000 Japanese Americans living in the West were moved soon after the attack on Pearl Harbor; Japanese Americans in Hawai`i were not confined in internment camps.

Daniel Ken Inouye   A Japanese American from Hawai`i who served in the 422nd Regimental Combat Team and was badly wounded in Italy; he later became a U.S. senator from Hawai`i and received the Congressional Medal of Honor for his valor.

Aware of rabidly anti-Japanese public opinion, Roosevelt waited until after the off-year 1943 elections to allow internees who passed a loyalty review to go home. A year later, the camps were empty, each internee having been given train fare home and $25. Returning home, the Japanese-Americans discovered that nearly everything was gone. Stored belongings had been stolen. Land, homes, and businesses had been confiscated by the government for unpaid taxes. Denied even an apology from the government, Japanese Americans nevertheless began to re-establish their homes and businesses. Decades later, in 1988, and after several lawsuits on behalf of victims, a semi-apologetic federal government paid $20,000 in compensation to each of the surviving sixty thousand internees.

Mobilizing the Nation for War

When President Roosevelt made his first fireside chat following Pearl Harbor, "Dr. New Deal" became "Dr. Win the War." He called on Americans to produce the goods necessary for victory—factories were to run twenty-four hours a day, seven days a week. Gone was every trace of the antibusiness attitude that had characterized much New Deal rhetoric, and in its place was the realization that only big business could produce the vast amount of armaments and supplies needed. Secretary of War Stimson noted: "You have to let business make money out of the process or business won't work." Overall, the United States paid over $240 billion in defense contracts, with 82 percent of them going to the nation's top hundred corporations. At the same time more than half a million small businesses collapsed. Every part of the nation benefited from defense-based prosperity, but the South and the coastal West saw huge economic gains. The South experienced a remarkable 40 percent increase in its industrial capacity, and the West did even better.

The New Deal had provided the West with economic growth and important resources such as electricity, experience in large-scale production projects, and a growing population. The war greatly intensified this economic expansion, as government contracts flowed into the region. Billions of dollars flooded into the area. A corridor from San Diego to Los Angeles emerged as the country's "largest urban military-industrial complex." Wrote one observer, "It was [as] if someone had tilted the country: people, money, and soldiers all spilled west."

Among the contractors, few outdid Henry J. Kaiser, "Sir Launchalot." He took the expertise gained in

THE SUPREME TEST

The ability to wage war rests on a nation's resources, not only of men, but of raw materials and production. In this political cartoon, the challenge is given, and over the next four years the United States easily produced more of the machines of war than either Germany or Japan. *Chicago Historical Society.*

building Boulder Dam and transformed the shipbuilding industry by constructing massive shipyards in California. By using **prefabricated** sections, he cut the time it took to build a merchant ship from about three hundred days prior to the war to an average of eighty days in 1942. To supply his plants with steel, he utilized federal resources to build a new steel mill in nearby Fontana, California. With men like Kaiser leading the way, by the end of 1942, one-third of all production was geared to the war, and the government had allocated millions of dollars to improve productivity by upgrading factories and generating new industries. When the war cut off some supplies of raw rubber, government and business cooperated to develop and produce synthetic rubber. By the end

---

prefabricated Manufactured in advance in standard sections that are easy to ship and assemble when and where needed.

of the war, the United States had pumped more than $320 billion into the American economy, and the final production amounts exceeded almost everyone's expectations: U.S. manufacturers had built over 300,000 aircraft, 88,140 tanks, and 86,000 warships.

Aiding contractors in another way, the government also built towns to house workers. To house workers at Kaiser's three shipyards along the Columbia River, the government constructed Vanport, Oregon. Construction began on September 14, 1942 and in ninety days "Vanport . . . the war metropolis appeared on the map." The Portland paper called it "a triumph of American enterprise. Born of the national emergency, it will shelter 40,000 residents . . . becoming the most extensive mass housing experiment of all time." Vanport contained apartments and homes, schools, fire and police stations, a movie theater, a library, an infirmary, and icehouses. Couples lived in one-room apartments that were furnished with "a 'daveno' (also used as a bed), two . . . chairs and a dining table." Kitchens had a sink, an electric hot plate, small oven, and an icebox. Seven years old while living in Vanport, Earl Washington recalled: "If you had a wagon . . . people would ask you to go and get ice for them, you know, because everybody had iceboxes. So you could make a lot of money as a kid in Vanport. . . . You didn't get rich but if you went and got somebody a twenty-five pound block of ice they gave you a quarter. A quarter would go a long way in those days." Completed by August 12, 1943, Vanport was a robust "24-hour city," with a population of 40,000, including nearly 15,000 African Americans. Vanport barely survived the war: when the shipyards closed, most people moved away, and in 1948 a major flood destroyed what was left of the city.

Millions of dollars were also spent on research and development (R&D) to create and improve a variety of goods from weapons to medicines. In "science cities" constructed by the government in New Mexico and Oregon, researchers and technicians of the Manhattan Project harnessed atomic energy and built an atomic bomb. Hundreds of colleges and universities and private laboratories, such as Bell Labs, received research and development grants that created new technologies or enhanced the operation of a variety of products. Improved radar and sonar allowed American forces to detect and destroy enemy planes and ships, and new, more effective medicines, including penicillin, and medical techniques saved millions of lives. Potent pesticides fought insects that carried typhus, malaria, and other diseases at home and overseas. In Van-

port, after residents complained of fleas, bed bugs, mice, and cockroaches, an experimental fumigation process that used a pint of DDT spray per apartment "yielded excellent results" with no further complaints. Some even boasted that insecticides such as DDT would be the "biggest contribution of military medicine to the civilian population" following the war.

As the economy retooled to provide the machines of war, Roosevelt acted to provide government direction and planning. His first steps were to establish an **Office of Price Administration** (OPA) to control prices, a War Production Board (WPB), and the War Labor Board (WLB). Working together, these boards plus the OPA were to coordinate and plan production, establish the allotment of materials, and ensure harmonious labor relations. When the agencies failed to resolve problems and create a smoothly working economy, Congress, in the fall of 1942, passed the Stabilization Act. It expanded the powers of the OPA and regulated agricultural prices. Still seeking a workable system to direct the war economy, in 1943 Roosevelt added a new umbrella agency—the Office of Economic Stabilization (OES)—and created the **Office of War Mobilization**. To direct both agencies, he appointed former Supreme Court Justice **James F. Byrnes**. Armed with extensive powers and the president's trust, Byrnes, nicknamed the "Assistant President," controlled a far-flung economic empire of policies and programs that touched every American and produced the machinery to win wars. "If you want something done, go see Jimmie Byrnes" became the watchword. By the fall of 1943, production was booming, jobs were plentiful, wages and family incomes were rising, and inflation was under control. Even farmers were climbing out of debt as farm income had tripled since 1939.

Office of Price Administration Agency established by executive order in 1941 to set prices for critical wartime commodities.

Office of War Mobilization Umbrella agency used to coordinate the production, procurement, and distribution of civilian and military supplies.

James F. Byrnes Left the Supreme Court to direct the nation's economy and war production; known as the "Assistant President," he directed the Office of Economic Stabilization and Office of War Mobilization and later became secretary of state under President Truman.

Mobilization for war provided full employment and new opportunities for both labor and its opponents. Unions, especially the CIO, grew rapidly during the war, and by 1945 union membership had reached a high of 15 million workers. Union leaders hoped its voluntary agreements not to strike during wartime would persuade industry to agree to union recognition, collective bargaining, **closed shops**, and increased wages. Opponents argued that unions should be forbidden to strike or otherwise hinder war production and accept the open shop. In 1941, even before the United States entered the war, four thousand strikes had stopped work on defense production and had forced the government on one occasion, a strike at North American Aviation, to seize the plant and threaten the strikers with induction into the military if they did not return to work. Roosevelt hoped his war production agencies could find a middle ground between union advocates and opponents. In 1942 OPA, the WLB, and other agencies hammered out a compromise promoting union membership and accepting the closed shop and collective bargaining, but also expecting unions to control wages and oppose strikes. While most workers and employers accepted the guidelines, others did not and strikes consistently plagued the administration. Every year nearly 3 million workers went on strike or conducted work slowdowns, but most lasted only a brief time and did not jeopardize production. Several strikes were more serious, generating the wrath of the president, Congress, and the public and prompting government intervention. The most serious confrontation occurred in 1943 when CIO president and head of the United Mine Workers, John L. Lewis, led a strike demanding higher wages and safer working conditions. An angry president threatened to take over the mines. Congress wanted Lewis jailed as a traitor and pushed through, over the president's veto, the **Smith-Connally War Labor Disputes Act**. It gave the president the power to seize and operate any strike-bound industries considered vital for war production. Eventually, the parties in the mine strike compromised, giving higher wages to the miners. By the end of the war, American workers had not only produced a massive amount of material but were receiving higher wages than ever before. Moreover, unions represented 35 percent of the labor force. Union leaders had gained unprecedented influence during the war and expected that it would continue into the postwar period. Unions, especially the CIO with its political action committee (PAC), intended to continue its key political role, especially within the Democratic Party.

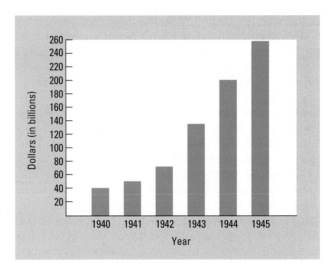

FIGURE 25.1 The Cost of War, 1940–1945 As the United States fought to defeat the Axis nations, its national debt soared. Rather than further raise taxes, the government chose to borrow about 60 percent of the cost, adding to a $259 billion national debt.

Taxes were also up, reflecting Roosevelt's desire to fund the war through taxes. The 1942 and 1943 Revenue Acts increased the number of people paying taxes and raised rates. In 1939, 4 million Americans paid income taxes; by the end of the war more than 40 million did so. Individuals making $500,000 or more a year paid 88 percent in taxes. Corporate taxes averaged 40 percent, with a 90 percent tax on excess profits.

These tax changes moderately altered the basic distribution of income by reducing the proportion held by the upper two-fifths of the population—but tax revenues paid for only about half of the cost of the war. The government borrowed the rest. The national debt jumped from $40 billion to $260 billion by 1945 (see Figure 25.1). The most publicized borrowing effort encouraged the purchase of **war bonds**. Movie stars and other celebrities asked Americans to "do their part" and buy bonds, especially Series E

closed shop   A business or factory whose workers are required to be union members.

Smith-Connally War Labor Disputes Act   Law passed by Congress in 1943 authorizing the government to seize plants in which labor disputes threatened war production; it was later used to take over the coal mines.

war bond   Bonds sold by the government to finance the war effort.

bonds worth $25 and $50. The public responded by purchasing more than $40 billion in individual bonds, but the majority of bonds—$95 billion—were bought by corporations and financial institutions.

Wartime Politics

As Roosevelt mobilized the nation for war, Republicans and conservative Democrats moved to bury what was left of the New Deal. People secure in their jobs were no longer as concerned about social welfare programs. They griped about higher taxes, rents, and prices, the scarcity of some goods, and government inefficiency. Business-oriented publications like *Fortune* and the *Wall Street Journal* renewed their attacks on New Deal **statism**, especially social welfare programs. Congressional elections in November 1942 continued the trend started in 1937 and returned more Republicans to Congress. A more conservative Congress axed the CCC, WPA, and NYA and slashed the budgets of other government agencies.

Roosevelt, seeking an unprecedented fourth term in 1944, hoped to recapture some social activism and called for the passage of an economic bill of rights that included government support for higher wage jobs, homes, and medical care, but his plea fell on deaf ears. Instead Congress passed a smaller version that would reward veterans of the war. In June the **G.I. Bill** became law. It guaranteed a year's unemployment compensation for veterans while they looked for "good" jobs, provided economic support if they chose to go to school, and offered low-interest home loans.

Roosevelt brushed aside concerns about his age and health, but responding to conservatives in the Party, he agreed to drop the too liberal vice president Henry Wallace and replace him with a more conservative running mate. The choice was Senator **Harry S Truman** from Missouri. Roosevelt campaigned on a strong wartime economy, his record of leadership, and by November 1944, a successful war effort.

Republicans nominated Governor Thomas Dewey of New York as their candidate, who attacked government inefficiency and waste and argued that his youth, 42, made him a better candidate than Roosevelt. A Republican-inspired "whispering campaign" hinted that at 62 Roosevelt was ill and close to death. Voters ignored the rumors and re-elected Roosevelt, whose winning totals, although not as large as in 1940, were still greater than pollsters had predicted and proved that FDR still generated widespread support.

A People at Work and War

America's entry into the war changed nearly everything about everyday life. Government agencies set prices and froze wages and rents. Cotton, silk, gasoline, and items made of metal, including hair clips and safety pins, became increasingly scarce. A rationing system was introduced, and by the end of 1942, most Americans had a ration book with an array of different colored and valued coupons that limited their purchases of such staples as meat, sugar, and gasoline. Explaining why most Americans received only 3 gallons of gasoline a week, Roosevelt explained that a bomber required nearly 1,100 gallons of fuel to bomb Naples, the equivalent of about 375 gasoline ration tickets. Also, the War Production Board changed fashion to conserve fabrics. Men's suits narrowed lapels and eliminated vests and pant cuffs. The amount of fabric in women's skirts was also reduced, and the two-piece bathing suit was introduced as "patriotic chic." Families collected scrap metals, paper, and rubber to be recycled for the war effort and grew **victory gardens** to support the war. When people complained about shortages and inconveniences, more would challenge, "Don't you know there's a war on?"

Even with rationing, most Americans were experiencing a higher than ever standard of living. Meat consumption increased to nearly 129 pounds a year, despite rationing that limited weekly consumption to 28 ounces. Consumer spending rose by 12 percent, and Americans were spending more than ever on entertainment from books, to movies, to horse racing. Included in those discovering prosperity were women and minorities, who by 1943 were being hired because of severe labor shortages. Even the Nisei were allowed to leave their relocation

---

statism The concept or practice of placing economic planning and policy under government control.

G.I. Bill Law passed by Congress in 1944 to provide financial and educational benefits for American veterans after World War II; G.I. stands for "government issue."

Harry S Truman Democratic senator from Missouri whom Roosevelt selected in 1944 to be vice president; in 1945, on Roosevelt's death, Truman became president.

victory garden Small plot cultivated by a patriotic citizen during World War II to supply household food and allow farm production to be used for the war effort.

WE'RE SCRAPPERS TOO

Across the nation, Americans contributed to the war effort by cutting back on using rubber, tin cans, and hundreds of other products. And as illustrated in this poster, they also collected scrap materials that could be recycled into the machines of war. It was a way for even children to contribute to the war effort. *Chicago Historical Society.*

camps when their labor was needed. To gain access to new jobs, 15 million Americans relocated between 1941 and 1945. Two hundred thousand people, many from the rural South, headed for Detroit, but more went west where defense industries beckoned. Shipbuilding and the aircraft industry sparked boomtowns that could not keep pace with the growing need for local services and facilities. San Diego, California, once a small retirement community with a quiet naval base, mushroomed into a major military and defense industrial city almost overnight. Nearly 55,000 people flocked there each year of the

war, with thousands living in small travel trailers leased by the federal government for $7 a month. Mobile, Alabama; Norfolk, Virginia; Seattle, Washington; Denver, Colorado—all experienced similar rapid growth (see chapter-opening map).

With the expanding populations, war industrial cities experienced massive problems providing homes, water, electricity, and sanitation. Crime flourished. Marriage, divorce, family violence, and juvenile delinquency rates soared. Twelve thousand sailors and soldiers looking for a good time gave Norfolk a reputation as a major sin city. Police estimated that from two to three thousand prostitutes worked in its alleys, taxis, clubs, and restaurants. Contributing to the social problems of the booming cities were those posed by many unsupervised teenage children. Juvenile crime increased dramatically during the war, much of it blamed on lockout and latchkey children whose working mothers left them alone during their job shifts. In Mobile, authorities speculated that two thousand children a day skipped school, some going to movies but most just hanging out looking for something to do.

Particularly worrisome to authorities were those nicknamed "V-girls." Victory girls were young teens, sometimes called "khaki-wacky teens," who hung around gathering spots like bus depots and drugstores to flirt with GIs and ask for dates. Wearing "sloppy-joe" sweaters, hair ribbons, bobby sox, and saddle shoes, their young faces thick with makeup and bright red lipstick, V-girls traded sex for movies, dances, and drinks. Seventeen-year-old Elvira Taylor of Norfolk took a different approach—she became an "Allotment Annie." She simply married the soldiers, preferably pilots, and collected their monthly **allotment checks**. Eventually, two American soldiers at an English pub showing off pictures of their wives discovered they had both married Elvira! It turned out she had wed six servicemen.

New Opportunities and Old Constraints

Mobilization forced the restructuring and redirecting of economic and human resources. Families had to adjust to new challenges. Minorities and women confronted new roles and accepted new responsi-

---

allotment checks   Check that a soldier's wife received from the government, amounting to a percentage of her husband's pay.

More than 350,000 women served in the military during the war, including Lt. Hazel Ying Lee, a Women's Airforce Service Pilot. WASPs flew "noncombat," ferrying planes and supplies across the United States and Canada. Already an experienced pilot in China, Lt. Lee is seated here in the cockpit of a trainer. Lt. Lee died in 1943, when her plane crashed. *Texas Woman's University.*

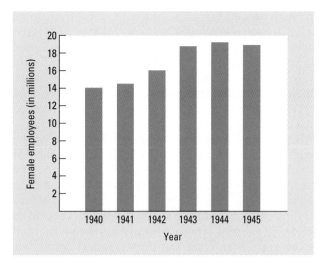

FIGURE 25.2 Women in the Work Force, 1940–1945 As men went to war, the nation turned increasingly to women to fill vital jobs. With government's encouragement, the number of women in the work force swelled from 14 million to nearly 20 million. With the war's end, however, many women left the workplace and returned to home.

bilities, both on the home front and in the military. Like men, many women were anxious to serve in the military. But the armed forces did not employ women except as nurses. To expand women's roles, Congresswoman Edith Norse Rogers prodded Congress and the Army, in March 1942, to create the Women's Auxiliary Army Corps (WAAC), which became the Women's Army Corps (WAC) a year later. The other services—with differing levels of enthusiasm—followed suit by creating the navy's Women Appointed for Volunteer Emergency Service (WAVES) and the marines' Women's Reserve. Relegated to noncombat roles, most women served as nurses and clerical workers, but there were notable exceptions. Women's Airforce Service Pilots (WASPS) tested planes, ferried planes across the United States and Canada, and trained male pilots. At the marine flight-training center at Cherry Point, North Carolina, all the flight instructors were women. By war's end, over 350,000 women had donned uniforms, earned equal pay with men who held the same rank, and provided a new female image.

Women serving in the military were not the only break with tradition. With over 10 million men marching off to war, employers increasingly turned to women. Until 1943, employers did not actively recruit women, preferring to hire white males. But as the labor shortage deepened, they turned to women and minorities to work the assembly lines. The federal government applauded the move and

conducted an emotional campaign, suggesting that women could shorten the war if they joined the work force. The image of Rosie the Riveter became the symbol of the patriotic woman doing her part. As more jobs opened, women did fill them—some because of patriotism, but most because they wanted both the job and the wages. Leaving home, Peggy Terry worked in a munitions plant and considered it "an absolute miracle. . . . We made the fabulous sum of $32 a week. . . . Before, we made nothing." Other women left menial jobs for better-paying positions with industries and the federal government. By 1944, 37 percent of all adult women were working, almost 19.4 million (see Figure 25.2). Of these, the majority (72.2 percent) were married and over half were 35 or older. Despite the number of women entering the work force, most stayed home. They supported the war effort in their homes and communities, providing volunteer efforts to organizations such as the Red Cross and Civil Defense.

Whether working or volunteering, however, women faced familiar constraints. Professional and supervisory positions were still dominated by men, and not all was rosy at work. Male workers resented and harassed women, who were generally paid lower wages than men, and constantly reminded them that their jobs were temporary. Employers and most men expected that when the war was over, women would happily return to their traditional roles at home. Without adequate childcare and nursery facilities, worried about abandoning traditional family roles and their families, some women found it difficult to balance family needs and work. Feeling regret or guilt, many gave up their jobs.

With the end of the war, the government reversed itself and pronounced that patriotism lay at home with the family. By the summer of 1945, many of the women who entered the work force during the war found themselves unemployed. Shipyards and the aircraft plants dismissed nearly three-fourths of their women employees. In Detroit, the automobile industry executed a similar cut in women workers, from 25 to 7.5 percent. Those who managed to remain at work were frequently transferred to less attractive, poorly paying jobs. Thus, for most women, the war experience was a mixed one of new choices cut short by changing circumstances.

Like the war experiences of women, those of minorities were mixed. New employment and social opportunities existed, but they were accompanied by racial and ethnic tensions and the knowledge that, when the war ended, the opportunities were likely to vanish. Initially, the war provided few opportunities for African Americans. Shipyards and other defense contractors wanted white workers. North American Aviation Company spoke for the aircraft industry when, in early 1942, it announced that it would not hire blacks "regardless of their training."

The antiblack bias began to change by mid-1942 as businesses felt pressure from the worsening labor shortage, especially in the West, the growing unwillingness of African Americans to be denied the equality and rights due all Americans, and the efforts of the federal government. **A. Philip Randolph**, leader of the powerful Brotherhood of Sleeping Car Porters union, in early 1941 declared that without direct pressure Roosevelt and the government would never provide legal, social, or economic justice for blacks. He proposed that African Americans march en masse on Washington to demand equality in jobs and the armed forces. Roosevelt tried to stop the march first by sending envoys to Randolph and then by meeting with him in person. In every case, Randolph held firm: either the president issue an executive order to open jobs to minorities or 100,000 marchers would be at his doorstep. Seeing no other resolution, in June Roosevelt issued Executive Order #8802 that created the **Fair Employment Practices Commission** (FEPC) and forbade racial job discrimination by the government and companies holding government contracts.

In California, these pressures dissolved the color line by the end of 1942. West Coast shipyards were the first to integrate. When Lockheed Aircraft broke the color barrier in August, even North American Aviation grudgingly complied. Word soon spread to the South that blacks could find work in California, and between the spring of 1942 and 1945, more than 340,000 African Americans moved to Los Angeles. Overall, nearly 400,000 African Americans abandoned the South for the West. Thousands of others went north to cities such as Chicago and Detroit.

The FEPC and increased access to jobs did not mean that segregation and discrimination ended. Black wages, although rising from an average of $457 to $1,976 a year, were still only about 65 percent of white wages. On the job, many African Americans were kept in unskilled positions and segregated from white workers. At North American Aviation, Don Gaunt asked his general foreman to switch him to the draftsman's department, "since I am a professional in that line." The foreman told him the truth: "I'll come out plain and tell you they are not taking any Negroes in the drafting department." Gaunt, in turn, said, "I quit." Gaunt's action was not unique. . . . Across the nation, blacks supported the "Double V" campaign: victory over racist Germany and victory over racism at home. Membership of the NAACP and Urban League increased as both turned to public opinion, the courts, and Congress to attack segregation, lynching, the poll tax, and discrimination. In 1942 the newly formed **Congress of Racial Equality** (CORE) adopted the sit-in tactic to attempt to integrate public facilities. Successes were minor but still noteworthy. Led by James Farmer, CORE integrated some public facilities in Chicago and Washington, although it failed in the South, where many CORE workers were badly beaten. Elsewhere patterns of hostility, discrimination, and violence hardened as the population of African Americans increased. In Detroit, real-estate and property-owner associations ensured that blacks

---

A. Philip Randolph   African-American labor leader who organized the 1941 march on Washington that pressured Roosevelt to issue an executive order banning racial discrimination in defense industries.

Fair Employment Practices Commission   Commission established in 1941 to halt discrimination in war production and government.

Congress of Racial Equality   Civil rights organization founded in 1942 and committed to using nonviolent techniques, such as sit-ins, to end segregation.

Captain William Campbell served in the 99th Pursuit Squadron, which was commanded by General Benjamin O. Davis. During the war, about 700,000 African Americans served in segregated units in all branches of the military and faced discrimination at all levels. At one air base in Arizona, the barracks were color-coded; those for whites were painted white and those for African Americans were covered with black tar paper. *"William Ayers Campbell" by Betsy Graves Reyneau, 1994. National Portrait Gallery. Gift of the Harmon Foundation.*

were tightly restricted to certain residential areas. White workers went on strike when three black workers were promoted, harping, "We'd rather see Hitler and Hirohito win than work beside a nigger on the assembly line." A Justice Department examination reported, "White Detroit seems to be a particularly hospitable climate for native fascist-type movements." On a hot summer Sunday, June 20, 1943, the tensions in Detroit erupted into a major race riot. Before federal troops arrived on June 21 and restored order, twenty-five blacks and nine whites were dead.

The opportunities and difficulties of African Americans in uniform paralleled those of black civilians. Prior to 1940, blacks served at the lowest ranks and in the most menial jobs in a segregated army and navy. The Army Air Corps and the Marines Corps refused to accept blacks at all. Compounding the problem, most in the military openly agreed with Secretary of War Henry L. Stimson when he asserted, "Leadership is not embedded in the Negro race." The manpower needs of war changed the role of the black soldier, opening up new ranks and occupations. In April 1942, Secretary of the Navy James Forrestal permitted black **noncommissioned officers** in the U.S. Navy, although blacks would wait until 1944 before being commissioned as officers. With only a small number of African-American officers, in 1940 the army began to encourage the recruitment of black officers and promoted **Benjamin O. Davis, Sr.**, from colonel to brigadier general. By the beginning of 1942, the Army Air Corps had an all-black unit, the 99th Pursuit Squadron. Eventually six hundred African Americans were commissioned as pilots. The army also organized other African-American units that fought in both the European and Pacific theaters of operations, such as the 371st Tank Battalion that battled its way across France and into Germany and liberated the concentration camps of Dachau and Buchenwald.

Higher ranks and better jobs for a few still did not disguise that for most blacks, even officers, military life was often demeaning and brutal and almost always segregated. In Indiana, more than a hundred black officers were arrested for trying to integrate an officers club. Across the country, blacks objected to the Red Cross's practice of segregating its blood supply. In Salinas, Kansas, German prisoners could eat at any local lunch counter and go to any movie theater, but their black guards could not. One dismayed soldier wrote, "The people of Salinas would serve these enemy soldiers and turn away black American GIs. . . . If we were . . . in Germany, they would break our bones. As 'colored' men in Salinas, they only break our hearts." In truth, many black soldiers had their bones broken, and their lives taken, on the home front. As in the civilian world, blacks in the military resisted discrimination and called on Roosevelt and the government for help. But their requests accomplished little.

noncommissioned officer   Enlisted member of the armed forces who has been promoted to a rank such as corporal or sergeant, conferring leadership over others.
Benjamin O. Davis, Sr.   Army officer who in 1940 became the first black general in the U.S. Army.

Latinos, too, found new opportunities during the war while encountering continued segregation and hostility. Like other Americans, Latinos, almost invariably called "Mexicans" by their fellow soldiers, rushed to enlist as the war started. More than 300,000 Latinos served—the highest percentage of any ethnic community—and seventeen won the nation's highest award for valor, the Medal of Honor. Although they faced some institutional and individual prejudices in the military, Latinos, unlike African Americans and most Nisei, served in integrated units and generally faced less discrimination in the military than in society.

For those remaining at home, more jobs were available, but still Latinos almost always worked as common laborers and agricultural workers. In the Southwest, it was not until 1943 that the FEPC attempted to open semiskilled and skilled positions to Mexican Americans. Jobs drew Mexican Americans to cities, creating a serious shortage of farm workers. After having deported Mexicans during the Depression repatriation program, the government had to ask Mexico to supply agricultural workers. Mexico agreed but insisted that the *braceros* (Spanish for "helping arms") receive fair wages and adequate housing, transportation, food, and medical care. In practice, whatever guarantees promised in *bracero* contracts mattered little. Most ranchers and farmers paid low wages and provided substandard facilities. The average Mexican American family earned about $800 a year, well below the government-established $1,130 annual minimum standard for a family of five.

Many young Mexican Americans, known as *pachucos*, expressed their rejection of Anglo culture and values by wearing **zoot suits**—long jackets with wide lapels and padded shoulders over pleated trousers, pegged and cuffed at the ankle—topped off by a pancake hat and gold chains. In the summer of 1943, tensions between Anglos and Mexican Americans were running high in Los Angeles, which had a history of discrimination in housing, jobs, and education toward its large Mexican-American population. Newspapers fanned racial tensions with articles highlighting a Mexican crime wave and depicting the "zooters" as dope addicts and draft dodgers. Anglo mobs, including several hundred servicemen, descended on East Los Angeles for three successive nights. They dragged zoot suiters out of movies, stores, even houses, beating them, and tearing apart their clothes. When the police acted, it was to arrest the victims—over six hundred Mexican-American youths were taken into "preventive custody." The riot lasted a week. Afterward, the Los Angeles city council outlawed the wearing of zoot suits.

Like other disadvantaged groups, American Indians took advantage of new job opportunities and served gallantly during the war in the military. The availability of jobs and higher wages lured more than 40,000 American Indians away from their reservations, many of whom never returned following the war. In addition, over 25,000 Indians served in the military. Among the most famous were three hundred Navajos who served as **code talkers** for the Marine Corps, using their native language as a secure means of communication. Although often called "chief," the American Indian, unlike other minorities, met little discrimination in the military. Whether in the armed forces or in the domestic work force, those who left the reservations saw their families' average incomes rise from $400 a year in 1941 to $1,200 in 1945, and many chose to assimilate into American culture and abandoned for good their old patterns of life.

Less visible in the military than women and minorities were homosexuals. Even though the military services had an official policy of not enlisting homosexuals, *Newsweek* complained that too many "inverts managed to slip through" an ineffective screening process that only asked if a person was a homosexual and looked for obvious effeminate behavior. In the military, many gays and lesbians discovered they could manage both military and personal needs, and that the military generally tolerated them—provided they were not caught in a sexual act. In a circular letter sent to military commanders, the surgeon general's office asked that homosexual relationships be overlooked as long as they did not disrupt the unit. During the war, gays' war records were much like other soldiers. "I was super patriotic," said one combat veteran.

---

braceros Mexican nationals who worked on U.S. farms beginning in 1942 because of the labor shortage during World War II.

pachucos/**zoot suiters** A Spanish term originally meaning "bandit," it became associated with juvenile delinquents of Mexican-American/Latino heritage; zoot suiters were those wearing the distinctive zoot suit that to many reflected racial or ethnic identity.

code talkers Navajos serving in the U.S. Marine Corps who communicated by radio in their native language, undecipherable by the enemy.

Secure communications on the battle field are a necessity, and no communications were more secure than those provided by the code talkers—American Indians, who spoke in their native languages. Here Henry Bake, Jr. and George H. Kork, Navajos, "talk code" in the jungle of Bougainville in the Solomon Islands. *National Archives.*

WAGING WORLD WAR

- What factors did Roosevelt consider in shaping America's strategy for global conflict?

- What stresses strained the Grand Alliance?

- Why did Truman and his advisers choose to use the atomic bomb?

The War Department's Victory Program, written prior to the Japanese attack on Pearl Harbor, argued that "the first major objective of the United States ought to be the complete military defeat of Germany." In the days that followed the attack, many Americans were convinced that defeating Japan should be the country's first priority. To Churchill's and Stalin's relief, Roosevelt remained committed to victory in Europe as the first priority. But the question remained, What was the best strategy to defeat Hitler? The Soviets, with 3.3 million Germans fighting within their borders, argued that opening a northern European second front as soon as possible was crucial. American military planners also supported a cross-channel attack, and Roosevelt told the Soviets that a second front would occur in 1942. However, the British vigorously opposed a cross-channel invasion. They considered it too risky and

calculated that a year was not nearly enough time to assemble sufficient troops and supplies. Instead, the British promoted the idea of an Allied landing in western North Africa—Operation Torch. It would be an easier, safer venture that also would help the British army fighting in western Egypt. Believing the people needed a victory anywhere, Roosevelt ignored his chiefs of staff opposition and approved the operation. Head of the **Joint Chiefs of Staff**, General George C. Marshall selected **General Dwight David Eisenhower** to command American forces in Europe and North Africa. Impressed with his planning and organizational ability, Marshall had chosen Eisenhower over 366 more senior general officers.

As planning began for the invasion of North Africa in 1942, the course of the war darkened for the Allies. German forces were advancing toward Egypt, while a renewed German offensive was penetrating deeper into the Soviet Union. In the Atlantic, German U-boats were sinking ships at an appalling rate. In April and May, the majority of American forces in the Philippines surrendered, and elsewhere in the Pacific, Japanese successes continued. General Patrick Hurley admitted, "We were out-shipped, out-planed, out-manned, and out-gunned by the Japanese."

Halting the Japanese Advance

Despite the commitment to defeating Germany, the nation's first victory came in the Pacific on May 7, at the **Battle of the Coral Sea** (see Map 25.3). Having deciphered secret Japanese codes, American military planners were aware that Japan was preparing to invade Port Moresby, New Guinea. They sent the aircraft carriers *Lexington* and *Yorktown* to intercept the invasion fleet. The *Lexington* was sunk, but the Japanese invasion was halted. The success in the Coral Sea was soon duplicated in June at Midway. Again, reading top-secret Japanese messages, the

---

Joint Chiefs of Staff   Military advisory group to the president that consists of the chiefs of the army, navy, air force, and marine corps; General George C. Marshall served in that position during World War II.

Dwight David Eisenhower   Supreme commander of Allied forces in Europe during World War II; he directed the D-day invasion and later became president of the United States.

Battle of the Coral Sea   U.S. victory in the Pacific in May 1942; it prevented the Japanese from invading New Guinea and thus isolating Australia.

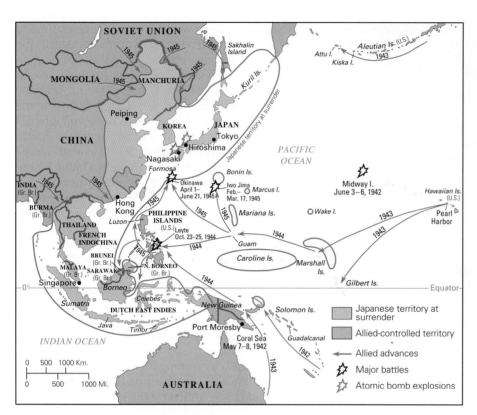

MAP 25.3 Closing the Circle on Japan, 1942–1945 Following the Battle of Midway, with the invasion of Guadalcanal (August 1942), American forces began the costly process of island hopping. This map shows the paths of the American campaign in the Pacific, closing the circle on Japan. After the Soviet Union entered the war and Hiroshima and Nagasaki were destroyed by atomic bombs, Japan surrendered on August 15, 1945.

United learned of a Japanese thrust aimed at **Midway Island**.

The Battle of Midway, June 4, 1942, helped change the course of the war in the Pacific. The air-to-sea battle was several hours old when a flight of thirty-seven American dive-bombers attacked the Japanese carriers in the middle of rearming and refueling their planes. The result was cataclysmic. Their decks cluttered with planes, fuel, and bombs, the Japanese carriers suffered staggering casualties and damage. Three immediately sank, a fourth sank later in the battle. Although the *Yorktown* was lost, the carriers and the air superiority of the Japanese had been destroyed. In the war of machines, the United States quickly replaced the *Yorktown* and by the end of the war had constructed fourteen additional large carriers—Japan was able to build only six.

With the victories at Coral Sea and Midway, the next step was to retake lost territory. General Douglas MacArthur and the army would take primary responsibility for an offensive beginning in New Guinea and advancing toward the Philippines from the south. The navy, under the direction of Admiral Chester Nimitz, would seize selected islands and atolls in the Solomon, Marshall, Gilbert, and Mariana island groups, approaching the Philippines from the east. Eventually, both forces would join for the final attack on Japan. On August 7, 1942, soldiers of the 1st Marine

Midway Island Strategically located Pacific island that the Japanese navy tried to capture in June 1942; warned about Japanese plans by U.S. naval intelligence, American forces repulsed the attack and inflicted heavy losses on Japanese planes and carriers.

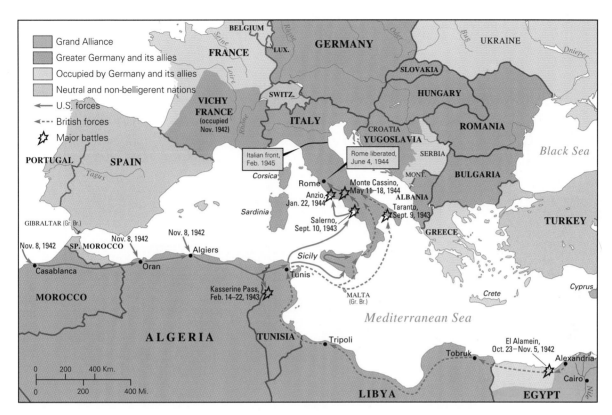

MAP 25.4 The North African and Italian Campaigns Having rejected a cross-channel attack on Hitler's "Atlantic Wall," British and American forces in 1942 and 1943 invaded North Africa and Italy, where victory seemed more assured. This map shows the British and American advances across North Africa and the invasions of Sicily and Italy. German forces fought stubbornly in Italy, slowing Allied advances up the peninsula. By February 1945, Allied forces were still advancing toward the Po Valley.

Division waded ashore on **Guadalcanal Island** in the Solomons (see Map 25.3). Japan, considering the invasion to be "the fork in the road that leads to victory for them or for us," furiously defended the island. Fierce fighting continued through November, but after heavy losses at sea and on land, Japan withdrew its last troops from Guadalcanal in early February. In the horrendous face-to-face combat that characterized the war in the Pacific, both sides suffered significant losses, but Japanese casualties far outnumbered American. The tide had been turned against Japan.

The Tide Turns in Europe

While American marines sweated in the jungles of Guadalcanal, British and American forces were closing in on German forces in North Africa (see Map 25.4). The British had halted the German advance at

El Alamein in August and had begun an offensive driving the Germans west toward Tunisia. In November, Operation Torch had successfully landed American troops in Morocco, who began to push eastward toward the British. Although temporarily halted by German forces at the Kasserine Pass, by early May the Americans had linked up with the British, forcing the last German forces in North Africa to surrender on May 13, 1943.

German losses in North Africa were light compared with those in Russia, where Soviet and German forces were locked in a titanic struggle. Through the summer and fall of 1942, German armies advanced steadily, but during the winter, the Soviet army drove them from

Guadalcanal Island Pacific island secured by U.S. troops in February 1943 in the first major U.S. offensive action in the Pacific.

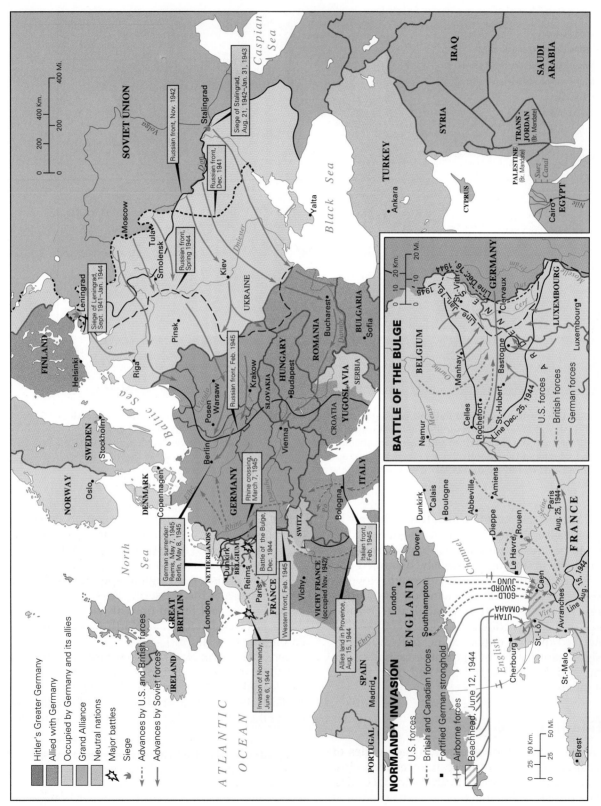

MAP 25.5 The Fall of the Third Reich In 1943 and 1944, the war turned in favor of the Allies. On the Eastern front, Soviet forces drove German forces back toward Germany. On June 6, 1944, D-Day, British, Canadian, and American forces landed on the coast of Normandy to begin the liberation of France. This map shows the course of the Allied armies as they fought their way toward Berlin. On May 7, 1945, Germany surrendered.

the Caucasus oil fields and trapped them at Stalingrad. On February 2, 1943, after a three-month Soviet counteroffensive in the dead of winter, 300,000 German soldiers surrendered, their 6th Army having lost more than 140,000 men. As German strength in Russia ebbed, Soviet strength grew. Although it was hard to predict in February, the tide of the war had turned in Europe. Soviet forces would continue to grind down the German army all the way to Berlin (see Map 25.5). But in February, Stalin knew only that the **Battle of Stalingrad** had cost the Russians dearly and that German strength was still formidable. He again demanded a second front in Western Europe. Again, he would be disappointed. Churchill meeting with Roosevelt at Casablanca (January 14–24, 1943) once more had overcome American desires for a cross-channel attack. Roosevelt agreed instead to invade Sicily and Italy, targets that Churchill called the "soft underbelly of the Axis." General Albert Wedemeyer expressed the U.S. military reaction to the Casablanca deal: "We lost our shirts . . . we came, we listened, and we were conquered."

The invasion of Sicily—Operation Husky—took place in early July, and in a month the Allies controlled the island (see Map 25.4). In response, the Italians overthrew Mussolini and opened negotiations with Britain and the United States to change sides. Italy surrendered unconditionally on September 8, just hours before Allied troops landed at Salerno in Operation Avalanche. Immediately, German forces assumed the defense of Italy and halted the Allied advance just north of Salerno. Not until late May 1944 did Allied forces finally break through the German defenses. On June 4, U.S. forces under General Mark Clark entered Rome. Two days later, the world's attention turned toward Normandy along the west coast of France. The second front demanded by Stalin had, at long last, begun (see Map 25.5).

Approval for the cross-channel attack was affirmed at the **Tehran Conference** (November 27 to December 1, 1943). In the Iranian capital, Roosevelt and Churchill met with Stalin to discuss strategy and to consider the process of establishing a postwar settlement. Confident that he could handle that "old buzzard" Stalin, Roosevelt wanted to establish Soviet support for a new world organization and to obtain a Soviet commitment to declare war against Japan. Roosevelt left Tehran pleased. Stalin had agreed to support a world organization and to enter the Japanese war once the battle with Hitler was over. Militarily, the three agreed on plans to coordinate a Soviet offensive with the Allied landings at Normandy.

The invasion of Normandy, France—**Operation Overlord**—was the grandest amphibious assault ever assembled: 6,483 ships, 1,500 tanks, and 200,000 men. Opposing the Allies were thousands of German troops behind the Atlantic Wall they had constructed along the coast to stop such an invasion. On D-day, June 6, 1944, American forces landed on Utah and Omaha beaches, while British and Canadian forces hit Sword, Gold, and Juno beaches (see Map 25.5 inset). At the landing sites, German resistance varied: the fiercest fighting was at Omaha Beach, where the American 1st Division suffered heavy casualties. One soldier from Arizona wrote:

Let the thunder roll,
Smoke and flame, will show th' way.
I am the Beach at Omaha.
The gates of hell, are open wide.
For all who come to play,
The stakes are high,
The game is death,
No winners here today.

After a week of attacks and counterattacks, the five beaches finally were linked, and British and American forces coiled to break through the German positions blocking the roads to the rest of France. On July 25, American soldiers under General Omar Bradley pierced the stubbornly held German defensive lines at St.-Lô. Paris was liberated on August 23, and in early November, the German city of Aachen on the west side of the Rhine River fell to the Allies. From November to March, American forces readied themselves to attack across the Rhine. While the British and Americans advanced across France, Allied bombers and fighter-bombers were

---

Battle of Stalingrad   Battle for the Russian city that was besieged by the German army in 1942 and recaptured by Soviet troops in 1943; regarded by many as the key battle of the European war.

Tehran Conference   Meeting in Iran in 1943 at which Roosevelt, Churchill, and Stalin discussed the invasion of Western Europe and considered plans for a new international organization; Stalin also renewed his promise to enter the war against Japan.

Operation Overlord   The Allied invasion of Europe on June 6, 1944—D-day—across the English Channel to Normandy; D-day is short for "designated day."

doing what they had been doing since the spring of 1942: bombing German-held Europe night and day. They destroyed vital industries and transportation systems as well as German cities. In one of the worst raids, during the night of February 13–14, 1945, three flights of British and American bombers set Dresden aflame, creating a firestorm that killed more than 135,000 civilians. Nearly 600,000 German civilians would die in Allied air raids, with another 800,000 injured.

Stresses in the Grand Alliance

As Allied forces struggled to move eastward toward the Rhine, the Soviets advanced rapidly westward, pushing the last German troops from Russia by the end of June. Behind Germany's retreating eastern armies, the Soviets occupied parts of Poland, Romania, Bulgaria, Hungary, and Czechoslovakia. Following the Red Army were Soviet officials and Eastern European Communists who had lived in exile in the Soviet Union before and during the war. The Soviet goal was to establish new Eastern European governments that would be "friendly" to the Soviet Union. A Communist Lublin government (named after the town where the government was installed) was established in Poland, while in Romania and Bulgaria **"popular front"** governments, heavily influenced by local and returning Communist Party members, took command. Only Czechoslovakia and Hungary managed to establish non–Communist-dominated governments as the German occupation collapsed.

On February 4, 1945, the Big Three met at the Black Sea resort of **Yalta** amid growing apprehension about Soviet territorial and political goals in Eastern Europe. Confident that he could work with Stalin, Roosevelt wanted to ensure the USSR would enter the war against Japan and maintain its support for a new United Nations. He also wanted the Soviets to show some willingness to modify their controls over Eastern Europe. Stalin's goals were Western acceptance of a Soviet sphere of influence in Eastern Europe, the weakening of Germany, and the economic restoration of the Soviet Union. Central to Allied differences over Eastern Europe was the nature of the Polish government. The Soviet Union supported the Lublin government, whereas Roosevelt and Churchill supported a London-based government-in-exile. They considered the Lublin regime to be undemocratic and a puppet of the Soviet Union. Stalin labeled the London-based government hostile to the Soviet Union and demanded

As allied armies fought their way closer to Berlin, Roosevelt, Churchill, and Stalin met at the Black Sea resort of Yalta, in February 1945, to discuss military strategy and postwar concerns. Among the most important issues were the Polish government, German reparations, and the formation of the United Nations. Two months later, Roosevelt died and Harry S Truman assumed the presidency. *National Archives.*

a friendly government in Poland. After considerable acidic haggling, the powers agreed on a compromise phrased in language that Admiral William Leahy, one of Roosevelt's primary advisers, ruefully noted was so vague that its meaning could be "stretched from Yalta to Washington" without breaking. Roosevelt reluctantly but realistically concluded that it was the best he could do for Poland at the moment. The Yalta Conference also

---

popular front   An organization or government composed of a wide spectrum of political groups; popular fronts were used by the Soviet Union in forming allegedly non-Communist governments in Eastern Europe.

Yalta   Site in the Crimea of the last meeting, in 1945, between Roosevelt, Churchill, and Stalin; they discussed the final defeat of the Axis powers and the problems of postwar occupation.

left control over Eastern Europe firmly in Soviet hands.

Roosevelt was extremely tired and seriously ill with high blood pressure and a bad heart throughout the Yalta meetings. Nevertheless, he had negotiated well, achieving two of his major goals. He had maintained Soviet support in defeating Japan and supporting a new world organization. Although disappointed over the continued Soviet domination of Eastern Europe, Roosevelt realized that little could be done to prevent the USSR from keeping what it already had, or could easily take. He hoped that his good will would encourage Stalin to respond in kind, maintaining at least a semblance of representative government in Eastern Europe and continuing to cooperate with the United States.

Roosevelt understood that postwar stability and security were impossible without Soviet cooperation, and he was especially hopeful that the "spirit of Yalta" would contribute to the formation of an effective **United Nations**. Roosevelt died shortly after his return from Yalta, thrusting Truman into the presidency. Truman brought a more assertive tone to American foreign policy but, like Roosevelt, was determined to see the creation of the world organization. Building on a series of high-level discussions in April 1945, a conference in San Francisco finished the task: the United Nations was born. The charter of the United Nations established an organization composed of the **General Assembly** and a **Security Council**. Composed of all member nations, the General Assembly was the weaker body having the authority only to discuss issues but not to resolve them. More important was the smaller Security Council composed of eleven nations. Six were elected by the General Assembly, but the real power was held by five permanent members: the United States, the Soviet Union, the United Kingdom, China, and France. The Security Council established and implemented policies and could apply economic and military pressures against other nations. To protect their interests, each of the five permanent nations could veto Security Council decisions. The United Nations represented the concept of peace through world cooperation, but its structure clearly left the future of peace in the hands of the major powers.

Defeating Hitler

With his forces crumbling in the east, Hitler approved a last-ditch attempt to halt the Allied advance late in 1944. Taking advantage of bad weather that grounded Allied aircraft, German forces launched an attack through the Ardennes Forest that drove 50 miles into Belgium. If successful, the attack would have split American forces. It was a desperate gamble that failed. Although surprised by the attack, not all American forces were pushed aside. At Bastogne, a critical crossroads, the 101st Airborne Division refused to retreat, and when invited to surrender, General A. C. McAuliffe simply told the Germans, "Nuts." After ten days, the weather improved, the German offensive slowed and halted, and a relief column reached Bastogne (see Map 25.5 inset). The **Battle of the Bulge** delayed Eisenhower's eastward assault briefly, but by costing Germany valuable reserves and equipment, it hastened the end of the war. Also by the end of 1944, the war in Italy was about over as Allied forces pushed through the Po Valley.

On March 7, 1945, American forces crossed the Rhine at Remagen and began to battle their way into the heart of Germany. While American and British troops moved steadily eastward, Russian soldiers began the bloody, house-to-house conquest of Berlin. On April 25, American and Soviet infantrymen shook hands at the Elbe River 60 miles south of Berlin. Inside the city, unwilling to be captured, Hitler committed suicide on April 30 and had aides burn his body. On May 8, 1945, German officials surrendered. The war in Europe was over.

Although Roosevelt had worked since 1939 to ensure Hitler's defeat, he did not live to see it. On April 12, while relaxing and recovering from the

United Nations International organization established in 1945 to maintain peace among nations and foster cooperation in human rights, education, health, welfare, and trade.

General Assembly Assembly of all members of the United Nations; it debates issues but neither creates nor executes policy.

Security Council The executive agency of the United Nations; it includes five permanent members with veto power (China, France, the United Kingdom, Russia, and the United States) and six members selected by the General Assembly for two-year terms.

Battle of the Bulge The last major Axis counteroffensive, in December 1944, against the Allied forces in Western Europe; German troops gained territory in Belgium but were eventually driven back.

Hitler ordered the "Final Solution"—the extermination of Europe's Jews—soon after the United States entered the war. In this picture, German troops arrest residents of the Warsaw ghetto for deportation to concentration camps. Few would survive the camps where over six million Jews died. *YIVO Institute for Jewish Research.*

strains of Yalta, he died of a massive cerebral hemorrhage at Warm Springs, Georgia. Nor did Roosevelt live to know the full horror of what came to be called the **Holocaust**. No atrocity of war could equal what advancing Allied armies found as they fought their way toward Berlin. In 1941 the Nazi political leadership had decided on what was called the **Final Solution** to rid German-occupied Europe of Jews. In concentration camps, Jews, along with homosexuals, gypsies, and the mentally ill, were brutalized, starved, worked as slave labor, and systematically exterminated. At Auschwitz, Nazis used gas chambers—disguised as showers—to execute twelve thousand victims a day. When the camps and their remaining inmates were liberated in 1945, 6 million Jews had been slaughtered in the death camps, nearly two-thirds of prewar Europe's Jewish population.

Closing the Circle on Japan

Victory in Europe—**V-E Day**—touched off parades and rejoicing in the United States. But Japan still had to be defeated. Japan's defensive strategy was simple: force the United States to invade a seem-

> **Holocaust** Mass murder of European Jews and other groups systematically carried out by the Nazis during World War II.
>
> **Final Solution** German plan to eliminate Jews through mass executions by isolating them in concentration camps; by the end of the war, the Nazis had killed 6 million Jews.
>
> **V-E Day** May 8, 1945, the day marking the official end of the war in Europe, following the unconditional surrender of the German armies.

On November 21, 1943, marines stormed ashore on the atoll of Tarawa, soon to be called "Bloody Tarawa." The marines secured the island, but the cost was high. Of the 5,000 marines who fought in the battle, more than 1,000 were killed and another 2,000 wounded. Nearly all of the 5,000 Japanese defenders died, many in a final "death charge." *U.S. Marine Corps Museum.*

ingly endless number of Pacific islands before it could launch an invasion against Japan—with each speck of land costing the Americans dearly in lives and materials. The American military, however, realized that it had to seize only the most strategic of islands. With carriers providing mobile air superiority, the Americans could bypass and isolate others.

Throughout 1943, General MacArthur advanced up the northern coast of New Guinea, while the navy and marines fought their way through the Solomon Islands. By mid-1944, MacArthur was ready to fulfill his promise to return to the Philippines. At the same time, far to the northeast, the U.S. Navy and the Marines Corps were establishing footholds in the Gilbert and Marshall islands. Exemplifying the bitter fighting was "bloody Tarawa," where marines fought their way ashore on November 21, 1943. Overcoming five thousand well-entrenched Japanese troops, nearly all of whom fought to the death, American marines suffered nearly three thousand casualties. With the Gilbert and Marshall islands neutralized, Admiral Nimitz approached Guam and Saipan in the Mariana Islands (see Map 25.3). In their effort to halt

the American invasion of Saipan, the Japanese lost 243 planes and three more aircraft carriers. On Saipan itself, the Japanese defenders, including 22,000 Japanese civilians, expended all their ammunition and then committed suicide rather than surrender. Marines next seized the nearby islands of Tinian (August 1) and Guam (August 11). By July 1944, the southern and eastern approaches to the Philippines were in American hands. From airfields on Tinian, Saipan, and Guam, long-range American bombers, the B-29s, began devastating raids against the homeland of Japan. In October, American forces landed on Leyte in the center of the Philippine archipelago. Again, the Japanese navy acted to halt the invasion, and with the same results. In the largest naval battle in history, the **Battle of Leyte Gulf** (October 23–25, 1944), American naval forces shattered what remained of

Battle of Leyte Gulf Naval battle in October 1944 in which American forces near the Philippines crushed Japanese air and sea power.

Japanese air and sea power. On October 23, wading ashore with an escort of subordinates and at least one photographer, General MacArthur returned to the Philippines.

After the Battle of Leyte Gulf, the full brunt of the American Pacific offensive bore down on Iwo Jima and **Okinawa**, only 750 miles from Tokyo. To defend the islands, Japan resorted to a new tactic: the *kamikaze*—suicide attacks by pilots in explosive-laden airplanes. The American assault on Iwo Jima began on February 19 and became the worst experience faced by U.S. Marines in the war. Virtually all of the 21,000 Japanese defenders fought to the death, and American losses approached one-third of the landing force: 6,821 dead and 20,000 wounded.

On Okinawa, the carnage was even worse. While American forces took heavy losses along Japanese defensive lines, nine hundred Japanese planes, including three hundred *kamikazes*, rained terror and destruction on the American fleet. Throughout May and June, the Japanese air onslaughts continued but became weaker each month as Japan ran out of planes and pilots. By the end of June, Okinawa was in American hands, but at a fearful price: 12,000 Americans, 110,000 Japanese soldiers, and 160,000 Okinawan and Japanese civilians dead.

Entering the Nuclear Age

Okinawa proved a painful warning for those planning the invasion of Japan. Fighting for their homeland, the Japanese could be expected to resist until death. American casualties would be extremely high, perhaps as many as a million. But by the summer of 1945, the United States had an alternative to invasion: a new and untried weapon—the atomic bomb. The A-bomb was the product of years of British-American research and development, the **Manhattan Project**. From the beginning of the conflict, science had played a vital role in the war effort by developing and improving the tools of combat. Among the outcomes were radar, sonar, flamethrowers, rockets, and a variety of other useful and frequently deadly products. But the most fearsome and secret of the projects was the drive started in 1941 to construct a nuclear weapon. Between then and 1945, the Manhattan engineers, led by J. Robert Oppenheimer and Edward Teller, controlled a chain reaction involving uranium and plutonium to create the atomic bomb. By the time Germany surrendered, the project had consumed more than $2 billion, but the bomb had been born. When it was tested at Alamogordo, New Mexico, on July 16, the results were spectacular. In the words of

On August 6, 1945 the world entered the atomic age when the city of Hiroshima was destroyed by an atomic bomb. "We had seen the city when we went in," said the pilot of the Enola Gay, "and there was nothing to see when we came back." The city and most of its people had died. *National Archives.*

General Leslie Groves: "The effect could well be called unprecedented, magnificent, beautiful, stupendous and terrifying. . . . The whole country was lighted by a searing light. . . . Thirty seconds after the explosion came . . . the air blast . . . followed almost immediately by the strong, sustained, awesome roar which warned of doomsday and made us feel that we puny things were blasphemous to dare tamper with the forces heretofore reserved to The Almighty." Word of the successful test was quickly relayed to Truman, who had assumed the presidency when Roosevelt died in April. Truman was meeting with Churchill and Stalin at Potsdam, outside Berlin.

Truman traveled to Potsdam with a new secretary of state, James F. Byrnes. Before leaving for Germany, they agreed not to tell Stalin any details about the atomic bomb (although both knew about a Soviet spy ring within the Manhattan Project) and to use the

Okinawa   Pacific island that U.S. troops captured in the spring of 1945 after a grueling battle in which over a quarter-million soldiers and civilians were killed.

Manhattan Project   A secret scientific research effort begun in 1941 to develop an atomic bomb; much of the research was done in a secret community of scientists and workers near Oak Ridge, Tennessee.

table 25.1 War Dead

Country	Dead
Soviet Union	13.5 million
China	7.4 million
Poland	6.0 million
Germany	4.6 million
Japan	1.2 million
Britain and Commonwealth	430,000
United States	220,000

bomb as quickly as possible against Japan. Using the atomic bomb, Truman and Byrnes hoped, would serve two purposes. It would force Japan to surrender without an invasion, and it would impress the Soviets and, just maybe, make them more amenable to American views on the postwar world order.

Soon after his arrival at the summit, Truman met privately with Stalin and received the Soviet dictator's promise to enter the Japanese war in mid-August. Later, in a major understatement, Truman informed Stalin that the United States had a new and powerful weapon to use against Japan, never mentioning that it was an atomic bomb. Stalin appeared uninterested and told Truman to go ahead and use the weapon. Then, with Prime Minister Clement Attlee of Britain, Truman released the **Potsdam Declaration**, which called on Japan to surrender by August or face total destruction. The declaration reflected two developments—one Japan knew about, the other it was soon to learn. Japanese officials had asked the "neutral" Soviets to try to persuade the Americans to consider negotiating a Japanese surrender. Stalin, Attlee, and Truman agreed instead to insist on unconditional surrender. In the Potsdam Declaration, the Japanese could read the rejection of their overture, but they had no way of knowing that the utter destruction referred to in the declaration meant the A-bomb. On July 25, Truman ordered the use of the atomic bombs as soon after August 3 as possible, provided the Japanese did not surrender.

On the island of Tinian, B-29s were readied to carry the two available bombs to targets in Japan; a third was waiting to be assembled. A B-29 bomber named the *Enola Gay* dropped the first bomb over **Hiroshima** at 9:15 A.M. on August 6. Japan's eighth-largest city, Hiroshima had a population of over 250,000 and had not to that point suffered heavy bombing. In the atomic blast and fireball, almost a hundred thousand

Japanese were killed or terribly maimed. Another hundred thousand would eventually die from the effects of radiation. The United States announced that unless the Japanese surrendered immediately, they could "expect a rain of ruin from the air, the like of which has never been seen on this earth."

In Tokyo, peace advocates in the Japanese government again sought to use the Soviets as an intermediary. They wanted some guarantee that Emperor Hirohito would be allowed to remain as emperor and a symbol of Japan. The Soviet response was to declare war and advance into Japanese-held Manchuria on August 8, exactly three months after V-E Day. On August 9, as a high-level Japanese council considered surrender, a second atomic bomb destroyed **Nagasaki**. Nearly sixty thousand people were killed. Although some within the Japanese army argued for continuing the fight, Emperor Hirohito, watching the Red Army slice through Japanese forces and afraid of losing more cities to atomic attacks, made the final decision. Japan must "bear the unbearable," he said, and surrender. On August 14, 1945, Japan officially surrendered, and the United States agreed to leave the position of emperor intact.

World War II was over, but much of the world now lay in ruins. Some 50 million people, military and civilian, had been killed (see Table 25.1). The United States was spared most of the destruction. It had suffered almost no civilian casualties, and its cities and industrial centers stood unharmed. In many ways, in fact, the war had been good to the United States. It had decisively ended the Depression, and although some economists predicted an immediate postwar recession, the overall economic picture was bright. Government regulation and planning for the economy that had their beginnings in the New Deal took root and flourished during the war. As the war ended, only a few wanted a return to the laissez-faire–style government that had characterized the 1920s. Big government was here to stay, and at the center of big government was a powerful presidency ready to direct and guide the nation.

Potsdam Declaration   The demand for Japan's unconditional surrender, made after the July 1945 Potsdam Conference.

Hiroshima   Japanese city that was the target on August 6, 1945, of the first atomic bomb, called "Little Boy."

Nagasaki   City in western Japan devastated on August 9, 1945, by the second atomic bomb, called "Fat Man."

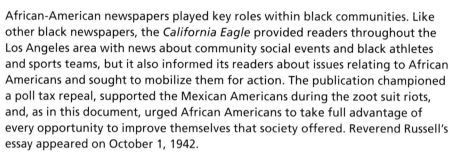

INDIVIDUAL VOICES

Examining a Primary Source

Rev. Clayton D. Russell Advocates Union Membership for Black Women

African-American newspapers played key roles within black communities. Like other black newspapers, the *California Eagle* provided readers throughout the Los Angeles area with news about community social events and black athletes and sports teams, but it also informed its readers about issues relating to African Americans and sought to mobilize them for action. The publication championed a poll tax repeal, supported the Mexican Americans during the zoot suit riots, and, as in this document, urged African Americans to take full advantage of every opportunity to improve themselves that society offered. Reverend Russell's essay appeared on October 1, 1942.

Many of the women who are now going into industry have never worked before and if they did the majority . . . were engaged in that form of work which was open to them, namely, domestic work. They experienced a paternal relationship with employers. . . . In industry the boss will never be seen. . . . This is a new relationship and Negro women who face it, many of them will have difficulty.

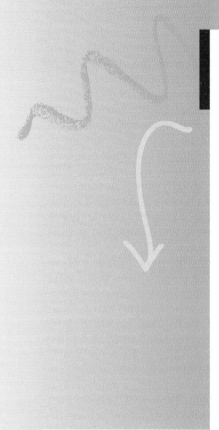

● *Sybil Lewis (see Individual Choices) joined the industrial work force. How closely did her experience follow the path Reverend Russell describes? How did she gain from her experiences?*

● *Why does Russell push union membership, and how does he suggest that joining a union is a commitment of freedom?*

● *What "war to be won" do you think Russell is referring to?*

● *What expectations do you think African Americans might have had about working in defense plants?*

I have no doubt as to the ability of Negro women to adjust to these new situations. Their whole history has been one of adjustment, but I raise these problems to show that the role of Negro women in this new field will not be an easy one and that there may be many who will fall by the wayside, both because of the new adjustments . . . and secondary because of racial discrimination that will be present in industry. ●

There will be many things of a racial nature that Negro women actually experienced [sic]. This will call for great broadness on the part of our women.

There is a way to beat racial discrimination. It cannot be broken down by individual effort. Racial discrimination can only be broken down by gradual every day organized action. In industry, the best weapon against racial discrimination, against all things undemocratic . . . is the trade union. Negro women must get into the new trade unions that will be formed of women workers. ●

Where the CIO is organized, Negro women must join, where the AFL is organized, Negro women must join. They must demand the right to join side by side with their white sister.

All over the country, CIO anti-discrimination committees have been active: white workers have left jobs because of discrimination against Negroes and have refused to return to work until these social injustices have been corrected.

. . . Today is the day of the industrial workers, the strength and the freedom of any people in America will depend on the amount of integration of that people in industry and the labor movement. Get into industry, there is a war to be won and much depends on you. ● *. . . If you do not have a skill, you will be in an unskilled position or relegated to domestic work. But if you have a skilled position, you will be able to get a higher graded position. Now is the time to get the training and the training is free.* ●

SUMMARY

As Herbert Hoover assumed office, he expected continued prosperity and peace. While he was able to further improve American relations with Latin America, he also sadly watched the global Depression destroy prosperity and peace. Both he and Franklin Roosevelt faced the collapse of the international system as Japan, Italy, and German sought to increase their territories, influence, and power. Japan seized Manchuria in 1931 and invaded China in 1937. Meanwhile Italy's Benito Mussolini conquered Ethiopia, and Adolph Hitler annexed Austria and sought to create a new German empire. In the lengthening shadow of world conflict, the majority of Americans maintained isolationism, and Congress passed neutrality laws designed to keep the nation from involvement in the faraway conflicts. Roosevelt wanted to take a more active role in world affairs but found himself hobbled by isolationist sentiment and by his own decision to fight the Depression at home first. Even as Germany invaded Poland in September 1939, the majority of Americans were still anxious to remain outside the conflict. Roosevelt, however, reshaped American neutrality to aid those nations fighting Germany, linking the United States' economic might first to England and then to the Soviet Union.

Roosevelt also increased economic and diplomatic pressures on Japan to halt its conquest of China and occupation of Indochina. But the pressure only heightened the crisis, convincing many in the Japanese government that the best choice was to attack the United States before it grew in strength. Japan's attack on Pearl Harbor on December 7, 1941, brought a fully committed American public and government into World War II.

Mobilizing the nation for war ended the Depression and increased government intervention in the economy. Another outcome of the war was a range of new choices for women and minorities in the military and the workplace. Japanese Americans, however, suffered a loss of freedom and property as the government placed them in internment camps.

Fighting a two-front war, American planners gave first priority to defeating Hitler. The British and American offensive to recover Europe began in North Africa and expanded to Italy in 1943, and to France in 1944. By the beginning of 1945, Allied armies were threatening Nazi Germany from the west and the east, and on May 8, 1945, Germany surrendered. In the Pacific theater, the victory at Midway in mid-1942 checked Japan's offensive and allowed the use of aircraft carriers to begin tightening the noose around the enemy. To bring the war to a close without a U.S. invasion, Truman elected to use the atomic bomb. Following the destruction of Hiroshima and Nagasaki, Japan surrendered, ending the war and for many Americans ushering in the beginning of "America's century."

POSTWAR AMERICA, 1947–1953 Postwar America was characterized by a growing affluency as many Americans enjoyed the fruits of a booming economy, rising wages, and a large variety of consumer goods. But as this map indicates, amid the prosperity and growth of metropolitan areas, there was a deep-seated fear generated by the Cold War and the possibility of nuclear war.

CANADA

Seattle
WASHINGTON
Portland
OREGON
MONTANA
IDAHO
WYOMING
NEVADA
UTAH
CALIFORNIA
San Francisco-Oakland
Los Angeles
San Diego
ARIZONA
NEW MEXICO

NORTH DAKOTA
SOUTH DAKOTA
NEBRASKA
COLORADO
Denver
KANSAS
Kansas City
OKLAHOMA
TEXAS
San Antonio
Houston
Dallas

MINN.
Minneapolis-St. Paul
WIS.
Milwaukee
IOWA
Chicago
ILL.
MISSOURI
St. Louis
ARK.
LA.
New Orleans

MICH.
Detroit
Cleveland
OHIO
Columbus
Indianapolis
IND.
Cincinnati
Louisville
KENTUCKY
TENN.
Birmingham
MISS.
ALABAMA
Atlanta
GEORGIA

PENN.
Youngstown
Pittsburgh
W. VA.
Washington
VIRGINIA
NORTH CAROLINA
SOUTH CAROLINA
FLA.

NEW YORK
Buffalo
Albany
New York
Philadelphia
Baltimore
MAINE
VT.
N.H.
Boston
MASS.
Providence
R.I.
CONN.
N.J.
DEL.
MD.

PACIFIC OCEAN

MEXICO

ATLANTIC OCEAN

Gulf of Mexico

CUBA

PACIFIC OCEAN
HAWAI'I
0   100 Km.
0   100 Mi.

U.S.S.R.
CANADA
ALASKA TERRITORY
PACIFIC OCEAN
0   250   500 Km.
0   250   500 Mi.

0   200   400 Km.
0   200   400 Mi.

Median family income, 1949
Under $2,000
$2,000–$2,500
$2,500–$3,000
Over $3,000

Standard metropolitan areas of 100,000 or more inhabitants

Targets of Soviet nuclear attack
First priority
Second priority

Churchill's "iron curtain" speech
First Levittown

Truman Doctrine
HUAC investigation of Hollywood begins

World War II ends
Berlin airlift
Truman defeats Dewey

Korean War
Rosenbergs convicted of treason
Korean armistice

1945   1946   1947   1948   1950   1951   1953

1850   1900   1950   2000

Truman and Cold War America, 1945–1952

GEORGE F. KENNAN

Following his graduation from Princeton University, George F. Kennan was trained by the State Department to be an expert on the Soviet Union. As such, he provided the Truman administration with evaluations of Soviet foreign policy that became the foundation of American foreign policy throughout the Cold War. He left the State Department in 1952 and became a respected historian, writer, and lecturer on foreign policy issues. *National Portrait Gallery.*

George Frost Kennan

It was a case, he concluded, "where nothing but the whole truth would do. They had asked for it. Now, by God, they would have it." Thus it was with a sense of urgency and expectation, that George Frost Kennan, the American chargé d'affairs to the Soviet Union, sat down to write a reply to a request from the State Department. President Harry S Truman and other high-level American policymakers were re-examining American policy toward the Soviet Union and wondering what factors determined Soviet foreign policy. They decided to ask their expert on Russia stationed in Moscow. Kennan's reply, called the "Long Telegram," written and dispatched to Washington on February 22, 1946, had a staggering impact among the inner circles of the Truman administration. The telegram contained a lucid, informative, and instructive evaluation of the motives behind Soviet policy and a positive suggestion about what course U.S. policy should take.

Kennan had entered the path that brought him to this critical juncture when, fresh from Princeton University, he joined the Foreign Service in 1926. He decided to become an expert on the Soviet Union and was sent to Riga, Latvia, to sharpen his Russian language skills and further his knowledge of Russia and the Soviet Union. His conversations with Russian exiles who had fled the Communist Revolution reinforced and sharpened his generally negative views about the Soviet Union and its leaders. When the United States established official relations with the Soviets in 1933, Kennan, who longed to be assigned to Moscow, was overjoyed to be part of the embassy's staff. Full of curiosity and enthusiasm, he was among the first contingent of Americans to arrive in Moscow. He would remain in the Soviet Union until 1937, when he returned to Washington. In those four years, he reached conclusions about the Soviet Union and its leaders that would shape his vision in the years to come and that were evident in his "Long Telegram." He rejected the view that revolutionary Communists would transform Russia. Communism, he wrote, "was not a turning point in history, but only another name, another milepost along the road of Russia's wasteful, painful" path toward an unknown future. Stalin and other leaders were copies of those who had ruled Russia for centuries—despotic, ruthless, and constantly beset by rivals who sought to topple them from power. Nor did Kennan hold out much optimism for positive Soviet-American relations, noting that their fundamental differences were too great.

Kennan returned to Moscow in 1944 at the request of William Averell Harriman, whom Roosevelt had appointed ambassador. Harriman wanted to draw on Kennan's expertise on the Soviet Union. Although Kennan appreciated the Soviets' key role in defeating Germany and understood the necessity of supplying the USSR with material aid, he disliked President Roosevelt's willingness to befriend and trust the Soviets. In memoranda and messages to Harriman and officials in the State Department, he repeated his fears of Soviet domination over Eastern and Central Europe and warned against a wrong-headed American policy. Moscow was determined "to have an extensive sphere of influence," he wrote, while the United States was "wandering about with our heads in the clouds of Wilsonian idealism." Although he liked President Harry S Truman's harsher view of the Soviets than Roosevelt's, Kennan was frustrated that his opinions seemed to have little or no impact on policymakers. He considered resigning. Then came the request from Washington for his analysis of Soviet policy and his response, the "Long Telegram."

The eight-thousand-word telegram catapulted Kennan from a minor voice in American foreign policy to a major player. His lengthy analysis described Soviet policy as driven by traditional Russian goals and the need for Soviet leaders to maintain their control over the people and the state. He argued that there could be no permanent truce with the Soviets and that the United States should use its power to contain Russian expansionism. Secretary of State James Byrnes called the analysis "splendid." Secretary of the Navy James Forrestal made copies of the telegram and distributed it around Washington. For American policymakers already angry with and suspicious of the Soviet Union, the report provided a clear, understandable, and logical explanation of Soviet behavior. The Soviets, not the United States, were responsible for the ominous hostility between the two nations, and the United States should take action to limit the growth of Soviet power and influence.

Kennan returned to the United States and was placed in charge of the Policy Planning Staff, whose task it was to formulate long-range policies, including the Marshall Plan. In July 1947, using the pen name "Mr. X," Kennan caught the attention of a wider national audience when he reformulated his views on the Soviet Union in an article, "The Sources of Soviet Conduct," published in the prestigious journal *Foreign Affairs*. Again he argued that the Soviets were expansionistic and that the United States needed to use "adroit and vigilant . . . counter-force" to contain Moscow's advances. He also speculated that American containment efforts, if applied correctly, would erode Soviet power.

Regarded by many as the "Father of Containment," Kennan left government service in 1953 to write, teach, and lecture. In 1975 he founded the Kennan Institute for Advanced Russian Studies in Washington, D.C. When the Soviet Union collapsed in 1991, many credited the policies advocated by George Kennan as the root cause, and he again enjoyed great popularity for his foreign policy wisdom and insight.

INTRODUCTION

When World War II ended, Americans hoped for world peace and expected to experience the "American dream" of having a good job, owning a home, and enjoying the benefits of a consumer society. George Kennan's "Long Telegram" reflected one of the harsh realities of postwar America: there would not be world peace. Instead, the United States entered into a Cold War with the Soviet Union that would last nearly fifty years and affect every aspect of American life. The *Los Angeles Times* expressed the desire of most Americans: the United States would lead the postwar world because it had "no other direct interest" except a lasting and just peace. Seeking this lasting peace, Truman worked to forge an American vision of world affairs, but by the close of 1947 American and Soviet differences ended their wartime cooperation and produced a bitter rivalry—the Cold War. Reflecting Kennan's recommendations, the United States began to implement a policy to contain Soviet influence, first in Western Europe and then in Asia. The isolationism that had existed after the First World War was now replaced by an expanded global role. When North Korea invaded South Korea, the Cold War suddenly became "hot" as Truman committed American troops to halt Communist aggression.

The Cold War not only changed American foreign policy, but it also had an important impact on domestic life and politics, creating a second Red Scare and what some have called "an age of anxiety." Aided by a growing concern over communism abroad and at home, conservatives and others found it easier to reverse the economic and social strides made by minorities, women, and workers. Women, many argued, should give up their jobs and greater independence and return full-time to the roles of wife and mother. Postwar America, nearly everyone thought, would provide a prosperous economy with good-paying jobs, homes in newly constructed suburban communities, and stable families. These prospects, however, seemed out-of-reach to most African Americans and other minorities. They were expected to leave their wartime gains behind and return to their customary place at the foot of American society. Yet many remained optimistic about the future. The skills, experiences, and self-confidence gained by the war could not be taken away. The possibility loomed that President Truman's efforts to expand on the New Deal might bring increased opportunities for minorities, and, as evidence, by 1947 an African-American athlete was playing professional baseball in what had been an all-white league.

For minorities and others, the key political question was whether Truman would indeed expand on the New Deal. Would he provide support for minorities, workers, and women in their quests for continued opportunity? Or would he buckle under conservative opposition that increasingly used the fears of the Cold War and New Deal socialism to press for fewer government controls and a retreat to traditional norms? Truman steered a middle course known as "politics of the possible," an agenda that pleased neither ardent liberals nor staunch conservatives. It reflected what some called the "vital center" of American politics—an acceptance of, and even some expansion on, existing government activism but little political or public support for any new programs.

But the growing fear of communism had uses other than merely political and soon became a weapon to use against social, cultural, and political foes, who could be accused of being too liberal. Conservatives and businessmen asserted that unions had become too powerful—they needed to be restrained and purged of their socialist and communist members. Southern whites charged that civil rights advocates were tainted with socialistic values. Across the nation, change and diversity were increasingly suspect. Spearheading America's defense against the dangers of communism were the House Un-American Activities Committee (HUAC) and Senator Joseph McCarthy. Both claimed that American institutions were rife with disloyal Americans whose values threatened the existence and soul of the nation. By the end of the Truman administration, "McCarthyism" had exposed a fearful and dark side of American society and politics—a paranoic intolerance that limited civil liberties, dissent, and social change.

THE COLD WAR BEGINS

• What were Americans' expectations for the postwar world and U.S.-Soviet relations?

• How was the containment theory applied to Western Europe between 1947 and 1951?

• Outside Western Europe, how did the Truman administration promote and protect American interests? What changes in policy did NSC-68 represent?

Germany, Italy, and Japan had been defeated, and the world hoped that an enduring peace would follow. But could the cooperative relationship of the victorious Allies continue into the postwar era without a common enemy to unite them? Suspicion and distrust had already surfaced when Britain and the United States objected to the establishment of pro-Soviet governments in Eastern Europe. President Franklin D. Roosevelt believed he could work with the Soviets and had deemed their cooperation more important than the composition of the Eastern European government. But Roosevelt's death in April 1945 left Harry S Truman the imposing tasks of finishing the war and creating the peace. Winning the war was mostly a matter of following existing policies and listening to the military planners, but establishing a new international system required new ideas and original policies. Unlike Roosevelt, Truman took a harsher position toward the Soviets. It was his opinion that "the Soviet Union needs us more than we need them." Truman loved history and especially the notion that great individuals shaped it. Lazy men caused trouble, he wrote, and those who "worked hard had the job of rectifying their mistakes." A plaque on his desk proclaimed, "THE BUCK STOPS HERE." Truman had read history; now he hoped to shape it.

chronology

From World War to Cold War

1945 Yalta Conference
President Roosevelt dies
Harry S Truman becomes president
Soviets advance across Eastern Europe
United Nations formed
Germany surrenders
Potsdam Conference
Japan surrenders

1946 Kennan's "Long Telegram"
Churchill's "iron curtain" speech
Iran crisis
Strikes by coal miners and railroad workers
Construction begins on first Levittown

1947 Truman Doctrine
Truman's employee loyalty program
Taft-Hartley Act
House Un-American Activities Committee begins
 investigation of Hollywood
Jackie Robinson joins Brooklyn Dodgers
Marshall Plan announced
To Secure These Rights issued
Rio Pact organized

1948 Communist coup in Czechoslovakia
Western zones of Germany unified
State of Israel founded
Congress approves Marshall Plan
Berlin blockade begins
Truman defeats Dewey

1949 North Atlantic Treaty Organization created
Allied airlift causes Stalin to lift Berlin blockade
West Germany created
Soviet Union explodes atomic bomb
Communist forces win civil war in China
Alger Hiss convicted of perjury

1950 U.S. hydrogen bomb project announced
McCarthy's announcement of Communists
 in the State Department
NSC–68
Korean War begins
Rosenbergs arrested for conspiracy to
 commit espionage
Inchon landing
North Korean forces retreat from South Korea
UN forces cross into North Korea
China enters Korean War

1951 General MacArthur relieved of command
Korean War peace talks begin
Rosenbergs convicted of espionage
Dennis et al. v. the United States

1953 Korean War armistice signed

Truman and the Soviets

Truman and other American leaders identified two overlapping paths to peace: international cooperation and **deterrence** based on military strength. They concluded that the United States must continue to field a strong military force with bases in Europe, Asia, and the Middle East and maintain its atomic monopoly. But deterrence alone could not guarantee peace and a stable world. Policymakers needed to address the underlying causes of war. Drawing on lessons learned from World War II, American planners formulated a new international system. Aggressors would have to be halted, democratic governments supported, and a prosperous world economy created. These were the

ideals of the Atlantic Charter, and most Americans saw them as fundamental values on which to construct peace. To achieve these ends required that the United States assume a leadership role and work with individual nations or through regional organizations or the United Nations.

Not all nations accepted the American vision for peace and stability. The Soviets, given their different

deterrence Measures that a state takes to discourage attacks by other states, often including a military buildup.

In July 1945, Truman met with Stalin and Churchill at Potsdam on the outskirts of Berlin. Meeting with Churchill and Stalin for the first time, Truman was surprised that the Soviet leader was shorter than he, and thought Churchill talked too much, giving him "a lot of hooey." Later, Truman wrote, "you never saw such pig-headed people as are the Russians." Here, Stalin and Truman (*left*) and advisers Byrnes and Molotov (*right*) pose for photographers. *Truman Library.*

political and economic systems and historical experiences—two invasions from Western Europe in thirty years—had markedly different postwar objectives: they wanted to be treated as a major power, to have Germany reduced in power, and to see "friendly" governments in neighboring states, especially in Eastern Europe. Truman, having little knowledge of diplomatic affairs or of Roosevelt's policies toward the Soviet Union, sought the counsel of experienced advisers on how to deal with the Soviets. Providing his recommendations, W. Averell Harriman, ambassador to the Soviet Union, pictured the Soviet advance across Eastern and Central Europe as a threat to peace and Western civilization. He was not alone. Others surrounding Truman agreed and noted that in Eastern Europe the Soviets were violating principles of the Atlantic Charter and the Yalta agreements.

Determined to be decisive, Truman quickly confronted Soviet foreign minister V. M. Molotov and berated the Soviet Union for not fulfilling its Yalta promises to allow self-determination in Eastern Europe. Although he moderated his toughness toward the Soviets during the next few months, it was clear that Truman was less willing to consider Soviet "needs" than Roosevelt had been. During his face-to-face meeting with Stalin at the Potsdam Conference, Truman wrote: "You never saw such pig-headed peoples as are the Russians."

By early 1946, it appeared that neither the Soviets nor the United States was much interested in cooperation. Truman said that he was "tired of babying the Soviets" and believed that it was time for them to prove their peaceful intentions. At the same time, the Soviet officials and the press warned of "capitalist encirclement" and accused the United States of poisoning Soviet-American relations. In Eastern Europe, the United States worried about signs of tightening Soviet controls that denied economic, political, and civil freedoms. Alarmed, the State Department concluded that the Soviets were following an "ominous course" and asked George Kennan to evaluate Soviet policy. He described Soviet totalitarianism as internally weak. Soviet leaders, he said, held communist ideology secondary to remaining in power, needing Western capitalism to serve as an enemy. But, he argued, Soviet leaders were not fanatics who wanted war and would retreat when met with opposition. He recommended a policy of **containment**, meeting head-on any attempted expansion of Soviet power. His eight-thousand-word report, the "Long Telegram," immediately received praise from Washington's official circles. Soon thereafter, Truman adopted a policy designed to "set will against will, force against force, idea against idea . . . until Soviet expansion is finally worn down."

containment   The U.S. policy of checking the expansion or influence of the Soviet Union by making strategic alliances, aiding friendly nations, and supporting weaker states in areas of conflict.

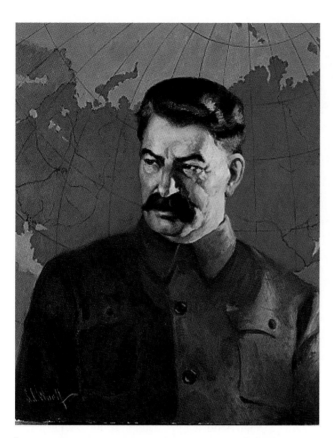

Joseph Stalin controlled the Soviet Union from 1926 until his death in 1955. During World War II, the popular image of the Soviet dictator was that of "Uncle Joe." By the time the Truman Doctrine was signed in March 1947, his image had changed to resemble Hitler's. At the Potsdam conference in July 1945, Truman's first impression of Stalin was that he was "dishonest but smart as hell" and they could work together. One of Truman's closest advisers bluntly stated that Stalin was "a liar and a crook." *National Portrait Gallery, Smithsonian Institution, Gift of Muriel Woolf Hobson/Art Resource, N.Y.*

Fear of Soviet expansion immediately became a bipartisan issue. Both Democrats and Republicans tried to educate the public about the Soviet threat—ending any possibility of a return to isolationism. One of the most dramatic warnings, however, came from Winston Churchill on March 5, 1946, at Westminster College in Fulton, Missouri. With President Truman sitting beside him, the former prime minister of Britain decried Soviet expansionism and stated that an **"iron curtain"** had fallen across Europe (see Map 26.1). He called for a "fraternal association of the English-speaking peoples" to halt the Russians. Truman thought it was a wonderfully eloquent speech

and would do "nothing but good." Churchill, *Time* magazine pronounced, had spoken with the voice of a "lion."

As Churchill spoke, it appeared that an "American lion" was needed in Iran. During World War II, the Big Three had stationed troops in Iran to ensure the safety of lend-lease materials going by that route to the Soviet Union. The troops were to be withdrawn by March 1946, but as that date neared, Soviet troops remained in northern Iran. Suddenly, on March 2, reports flashed from northern Iran that Soviet tanks were moving toward Tehran, the Iranian capital, as well as toward Iraq and Turkey. Some believed that war was imminent. Britain and the United States sent harshly worded telegrams to Moscow and petitioned the United Nations to consider an Iranian complaint against the Soviet Union. War did not break out and Soviet forces soon evacuated Iran. The crisis was over, but it convinced many Americans that the Soviets were aggressive and would retreat only if confronted with firmness.

Throughout the rest of 1946, the United States hardened its resolve in Europe, making postwar credits and loans available on the basis of ideology and geography. Thus, Britain received a $3.8 billion loan and France a $650 million loan, but the Soviet Union and Soviet-influenced Czechoslovakia received nothing. In Allied-occupied Germany, the United States promised that American troops would remain as long as necessary to protect the German people.

The Division of Europe

As the crisis in Iran receded, events in Europe assumed priority. Turkey was being pressured by the neighboring Soviets to permit them some control over the Dardanelles, the straits linking the Black Sea to the Mediterranean. A civil war between Communist-backed rebels and the British-supported conservative government raged in Greece. All of Europe seemed on the verge of economic exhaustion and political turmoil. Feeding on the economic and social problems, Communist and Socialist parties were gaining in popularity. In Italy, Communists represented one-third of the electorate while in France nearly a quarter of the voters went Communist.

iron curtain   Name given to the military, political, and ideological barrier established between the Soviet bloc and Western Europe after World War II.

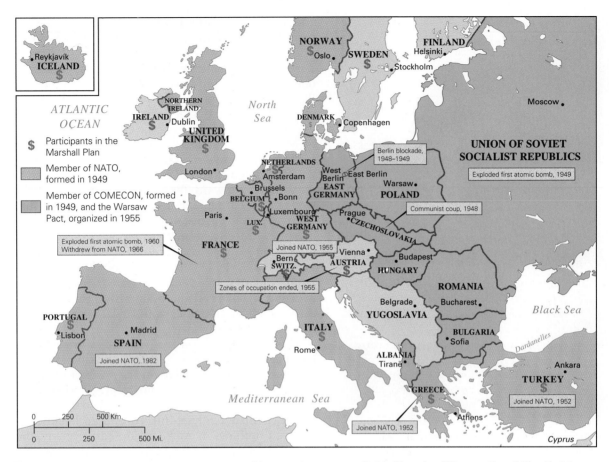

MAP 26.1 Cold War Europe Following World War II, Europe was divided by what Winston Churchill called the "iron curtain," which divided most of the continent politically, economically, and militarily into an eastern bloc (the Warsaw Pact) led by the Soviet Union and a western bloc (NATO) supported by the United States. This postwar division of Europe lasted until the collapse of the Soviet Union in the early 1990s.

Seeking to gain support for American intervention, Truman asked Congress for $400 million to support Greece and Turkey. Truman's request was a direct result of Britain's inability to supply those nations with continued economic and military aid. London had asked Washington to take its place. The Truman administration was eager to take on the "job of world leadership with all of its burdens and all of its glory."

To convince Congress and gain public support, Truman overstated the "crisis" and presented an image of the world under attack from the forces of evil. On March 12, 1947, he set forth the **Truman Doctrine**, offering an ideological, black-and-white view of world politics and blamed almost every threat to peace and stability on an unnamed but obvious villain: the Soviet Union. He said it was the duty of the United States "to support free people" who resisted subjugation "by armed minorities or by outside pressure." Congress accepted the president's request and provided aid for Greece and Turkey. Bolstered by American support, Turkey resisted Soviet pressure and retained control over the straits, and the Greek government was able to defeat the Communist rebels in 1949.

Truman Doctrine Anti-Communist foreign policy that Truman set forth in 1947; it called for military and economic aid to countries whose political stability was threatened by communism.

Although the Truman administration asked Congress only to support Greece and Turkey, officials admitted among themselves that the request was just the beginning. "It happens that we are having a little trouble with Greece and Turkey at the present time," stated a War Department official, "but they are just one of the keys on the keyboard of this world piano."

On June 5, 1947, in a commencement address at Harvard, Secretary of State George Marshall uncovered more of the keyboard. He offered Europe a program of economic aid, the **Marshall Plan**, to restore stability and prosperity. For the Truman administration, the difficult question was not whether to provide Western Europe with aid but whether to include the Soviets and Eastern Europeans. To allow the Soviets and their satellites to participate seemed contrary to the intent of the Truman Doctrine. Would a Congress that had just spent $400 million to keep Greece and Turkey out of Soviet hands be willing to provide millions of American dollars to the Soviet Union? But if the Soviets were excluded, the United States might seem to be encouraging the division of Europe, an image the State Department wanted to avoid. Chaired by Kennan, the State Department planning staff recommended that the United States take "a hell of a big gamble" and offer economic aid to all Europeans. Kennan was certain that the Soviets would reject the offer because it involved economic and political cooperation with capitalists. Thus, when Marshall spoke at Harvard, he invited all Europeans to work together and write a program "designed to place Europe on its feet economically."

The gamble worked. At a June 26, 1947, meeting in Paris of potential Marshall Plan participants, Soviet foreign minister Molotov rejected a British and French written proposal for an economically integrated Europe, joint economic planning, and a requirement to purchase mostly American goods. At first the Marshall Plan looked like a "tasty mushroom," commented one Soviet official, but on closer examination it turned out to be a "poisonous toadstool." Unwilling to participate in any form of economic integration, the Soviets and the Eastern Europeans left the conference. Over the next ten months the Soviet Union took steps to solidify their control over their satellite states. In July 1947, Moscow announced the Molotov Plan that further incorporated Eastern European economies into the Soviet system. Throughout the region non-Communist elements were expelled from governments, an effort that culminated in February

The goal of the Marshall Plan was to provide American economic support for the rebuilding of Europe's economy. By the time the plan ended, the United States had provided over $12.5 billion dollars to those European nations participating in the European Recovery Program. This poster demonstrated that with cooperation, Europe would soon be moving forward again. *Courtesy, George C. Marshall Foundation.*

1948 in a Soviet-engineered **coup** that toppled the Czechoslovakian government. "We are faced with exactly the same situation with which Britain and France were faced in 1938 and 1939 with Hitler," Truman announced. The Czech coup helped convince Congress to approve $12.5 billion in Marshall aid to Western Europe.

The "sovietization" taking place in Eastern Europe prompted the United States, Britain, and

---

Marshall Plan Program launched in 1948 to foster economic recovery in Western Europe in the postwar period through massive amounts of U.S. financial aid.

coup Sudden overthrow of a government by a group of people, usually with military support.

France to move to unify their German occupation zones economically and politically. In March 1948, the United States announced that the western zones were eligible for Marshall Plan aid, would hold elections to select delegates to a constitutional convention, and would utilize a standard currency. The meaning of these actions seemed clear: a West German state was being formed. Faced with the prospect of a pro-Western, industrialized, and potentially remilitarized Germany, Stalin reacted. On June 24, the Russians blockaded all land traffic to and from Berlin, which had been divided into British-, French-, Soviet-, and U.S.-controlled zones after the war. With a population of more than 2 million, West Berlin lay isolated 120 miles inside the Soviet zone of Germany (see Map 26.2). The Soviet goal was to force the West either to abandon the creation of West Germany or to face the loss of Berlin. Americans viewed the blockade simply as further proof of Soviet hostility and were determined not to back down. Churchill affirmed the West's stand. We want peace, he stated, "but we should by now have learned that there is no safety in yielding to dictators, whether Nazi or Communist." "We are very close to war," Truman wrote in his diary.

American strategists confronted the dilemma of how to stay in Berlin without starting a shooting war. Although some in the army recommended fighting their way across the Soviet zone to the city, Truman chose another option, one that would not violate Soviet occupied territory or any international agreements. Marshaling a massive effort of men, provisions, and aircraft, British and Americans flew supply planes to three Berlin airports on an average of one flight every three minutes, month after month. To drive home to the Soviets the depth of American resolve, Truman ordered a wing of B-29 bombers, the "atomic bombers," to Britain. These planes carried no atomic weapons, but the general impression was that their presence lessened the likelihood of Soviet aggression.

The **Berlin airlift** was a victory for the United States in the Cold War. The increasing flow of airplanes and supplies into West Berlin's three airports testified not only to America's economic and military power but also to America's resolve to stand firm against the Soviets and protect Western Europe. In May 1949, Stalin, finding no gains from the blockade, without explanation ended it and allowed land traffic to cross the Soviet zone to Berlin. Berlin was saved, but the crisis bore other fruit too. It swept away most congressional opposition to the Marshall Plan and the creation of West

MAP 26.2 Cold War Germany   This map shows how Germany and Berlin were divided into occupation zones. Meant as temporary divisions, they became permanent, transformed by the Cold War into East and West Germany. In 1948, with the Berlin airlift, and again in 1961, with the erection of the Berlin Wall, Berlin became the flash point of the Cold War. With the end of the Cold War, the division of Germany also ended. In 1989, the Berlin Wall was torn down, and in 1990 the two Germanies were re-unified.

> **Berlin airlift**   Response to the Soviet blockade of West Berlin in 1948 involving tens of thousands of continuous flights by American and British planes to deliver supplies.

When the Soviets blockaded the western zones of Berlin, in one of the first confrontations of the Cold War, the United States replied by staging one of the most successful logistical feats of the twentieth century, Operation Vittles, in which vital supplies were flown into the city. The airlift lasted 321 days and American planes flew more than 272,000 missions. *Walter Sanders LIFE Magazine ©Time, Inc.*

power there, but it did not ignore the rest of the world. Called one part humanitarianism and one part imperialism by a British official, U.S. foreign policy worked to expand American economic and political interests in Latin America, the Middle East, and Asia. Reflecting the United States's desire to remove barriers to trade and people, the State Department actively promoted the "Fifth Freedom," freedom of air travel, and worked to expand air routes for U.S. airlines such as Pan American Airways. To the south, the Truman administration rejected requests from Latin Americans for a Marshall Plan–style program. Instead, it encouraged private firms to develop the region through business and trade. To ensure that the Western Hemisphere remained under the American eagle's wing, however, the United States organized the **Rio Pact** of 1947. It established the concept of collective security for Latin America and created a regional organization—the **Organization of American States**—to coordinate common defense, economic, and social concerns.

In the Middle East, fear of future oil shortages led the United States to promote the expansion of American petroleum interests. In Saudi Arabia, Kuwait, and Iran, the goal was to replace Britain as the major economic and political influence. At the same time, the United States became a powerful supporter of a new Jewish state. Truman's support for such a nation, to be created in **Palestine**, arose from several considerations—moral, political, and

Germany and silenced those who had protested a permanent American military commitment to Western Europe. In June 1949, Congress approved American entry into the **North Atlantic Treaty Organization** (NATO). Membership in the alliance ensured that American forces would remain in the newly created West Germany and that Western Europe would be eligible for additional American economic and military aid. The Mutual Defense Assistance Act passed in 1949 provided $1.5 billion in arms and equipment for NATO member nations. By 1952, 80 percent of American assistance to Europe was military aid.

A Global Presence

American foreign policy from 1945 to 1950 focused on rebuilding Western Europe and containing Soviet

North Atlantic Treaty Organization   Mutual defense alliance formed in 1949 among most of the nations of Western Europe and North America in an effort to contain communism.

Rio Pact   Considered the first Cold War alliance, it joined Latin American nations, Canada, and the United States in an agreement to prevent Communist inroads in and to improve political, social, and economic conditions among Latin American nations; it created the Organization of American States.

Organization of American States   An international organization composed of most of the nations of the Americas, including the Caribbean, which deals with the mutual concerns of its members; Cuba is not currently a member.

Palestine   Region on the Mediterranean that was a British mandate after World War I; the UN partitioned the area in 1948 to allow for a Jewish state (Israel) and a Palestinian state, which was never established.

international. As early as August 1945, he had asked that at least a hundred thousand displaced European Jews be allowed to migrate to Palestine, then a World War I–era mandate under British rule (see page 698). Considering the Nazi terror against Jews, he believed that the Jews should have their own nation—a view strongly supported by the well-organized, pro-Jewish lobbying effort across the United States.

In May 1947, Britain announced it no longer had the resources or the desire to maintain control over Palestine. The stage was therefore set for the United Nations to divide the region into two nations: one Arab and one Jewish. When the United Nations voted to **partition** Palestine into Arab and Jewish states on May 14, 1948, Truman recognized the nation of Israel within fifteen minutes. And when war quickly broke out between Israel and the surrounding Arab states—which refused to accept partition—Truman and most Americans applauded the victories of Israeli armies.

If Americans were pleased with events in Latin America and the Middle East, Asia provided several disappointments. Under American occupation, Japan's government had been reshaped into a democratic system and placed safely within the American orbit, but success in Japan was offset by diplomatic setbacks in China and Korea. During World War II, the **Nationalist Chinese government** of Jiang Jieshi (Chiang Kai-shek) and the Chinese Communists under Mao Zedong (Mao Tse-tung) had collaborated to fight the Japanese. But when the war ended, old animosities quickly resurfaced and the truce between the two forces collapsed. By February 1946, civil war flared in China, and American supporters of Jiang were recommending that the United States increase its economic and military support for the Nationalist government. Especially vocal in promoting the cause of the Nationalists was the "China Lobby," led by *Time* and *Life* publisher Henry R. Luce and others who argued that Soviet power threatened China and the rest of Asia as much as it did Europe. Truman and Marshall (who was now secretary of state), aware of limited American resources, were of a different opinion. Though dreading Communist success in China, they questioned that the corrupt and inefficient Nationalist government under Jiang could ever effectively rule the vast country. While willing to continue some political, economic, and military support, neither wanted to commit American power to an Asian war. Providing more aid would be like "throwing money down a rat hole," Truman told his cabinet.

Faced with an efficient and popular opponent, unable to mobilize the Chinese people and resources, and denied additional American support, Jiang's forces steadily lost the civil war. In 1949 his army disintegrated, and the Nationalist government fled to the island of Taiwan. Conservative Democrats and Republicans labeled the rout of Jiang as a humiliating American defeat and complained that the Truman administration was too soft on communism. To quiet critics and to protect Jiang, Truman refused to recognize the People's Republic of China on the mainland and ordered the U.S. 7th Fleet to the waters near Taiwan.

Increasingly, Truman was feeling pressure to expand the containment policy to areas beyond Europe. The pressure intensified in late August 1949, when the Soviets detonated their own atomic bomb, shattering the American nuclear monopoly. Suddenly, it seemed to many Americans that the United States was losing the Cold War. Calls came from inside and outside the administration for a more global and aggressive policy against communism. David Lilienthal, one of Truman's atomic advisers and head of the Atomic Energy Commission, in 1950 recommended building a **hydrogen bomb**. A joint Pentagon–State Department committee, headed by Paul Nitze, concluded that the Soviets were driven by "a new fanatic faith, antithetical to our own," whose objective was to dominate the world. The group speculated that the Soviets would be able to launch a nuclear attack on the United States as early as 1954. The committee's report, NSC Memorandum #68, issued by the **National Security Council** (NSC), called for global containment and a massive buildup of American military force. In fact, NSC–68 called for an almost 400 percent increase in

---

partition   To divide a country into separate, autonomous nations.

Nationalist Chinese government   The government of Jiang Jieshi, who fought the Communists for control of China in the 1940s; Jiang and his supporters were defeated and retreated to Taiwan in 1949, where they set up a separate government.

hydrogen bomb   Nuclear weapon of much greater destructive power than the atomic bomb.

National Security Council   Executive agency established in 1947 to coordinate the strategic policies and defense of the United States; it includes the president, vice president, and four cabinet members.

military spending for the next fiscal year, which would have raised military expenditures to nearly $50 billion. Truman studied the report but worried about the impact of such large-scale military production on the manufacturing of domestic goods. A separate report concluded that the projected mobilization of industry for the Cold War would reduce automobile construction by nearly 60 percent and cut production of radios and television sets to zero. Truman eventually agreed to a "moderate" $12.3 billion military budget for 1950 that included building the hydrogen bomb. Proponents of NSC–68 won the final argument on June 25, 1950, when North Korean troops stormed across the 38th parallel.

THE KOREAN WAR

• As the North Koreans invaded South Korea, what choices did Truman face, and why did he decide to refer the issue to the United Nations?

• What were Truman's and MacArthur's goals in Korea? What was the consequence of China's entry into the war?

When World War II ended, Soviet forces occupied Korea north of the **38th parallel** (see Map 26.3), and American forces remained south of it. The division of Korea was expected to be temporary, but like the division of Germany it produced two nations. By mid-1946, an American-supported government led by Syngman Rhee existed in the south and a Communist-backed government headed by Kim Il Sung in the north. Having established two Koreas, in 1949 the Soviet and American forces were removed, leaving behind two hostile regimes. Both Koreas claimed to be Korea's rightful government and launched raids across the border. The raids accomplished little except to kill more than one hundred thousand Koreans and to expand their military capabilities.

Having received approval from the Soviets, on June 25, 1950, Kim Il Sung launched a full-scale invasion of the south. Overwhelmed by superior forces, South Korean (ROK) forces rapidly retreated. Apprised of the invasion, Truman drew parallels to Manchuria and Ethiopia in the 1930s and quickly announced that Korea was vital to American interests and needed protection from Communist aggression. Fearful that a congressional declaration of war against North Korea might trigger a Chinese and Soviet response, Truman instead asked the UN Security Council to intervene. The Security Council complied and called for a cease-fire and asked member nations to provide assistance to South Korea.

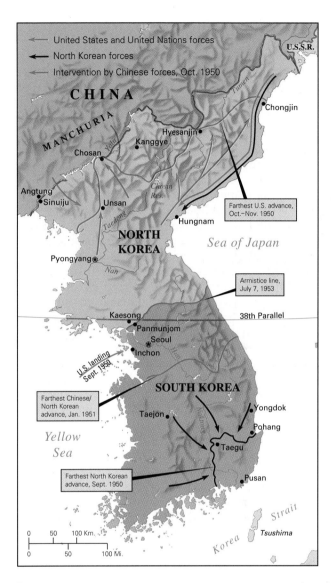

MAP 26.3 The Korean War, 1950–1953 Seeking to unify Korea, North Korean forces invaded South Korea in 1950. To protect South Korea, the United States and the United Nations intervened. After driving North Korean forces northward, Truman sought to unify Korea under South Korea. But as United Nations and South Korean forces pushed toward the Chinese border, Communist China intervened, forcing UN troops to retreat. This map shows the military thrusts and counterthrusts of the Korean War as it stalemated roughly along the 38th parallel.

38th parallel Negotiated dividing line between North and South Korea; it was the focus of much of the fighting in the Korean War.

Halting Communist Aggression

To blunt the invasion, Truman ordered **General Douglas MacArthur** to ready American naval and air units for deployment south of the 38th parallel. Two days later (June 27), as North Koreans captured Seoul, the South Korean capital, the Security Council approved an international military force to defend South Korea—that is, to push the invaders back into North Korea and restore peace. General MacArthur was named commander of the United Nations forces. As a member of the Security Council, the Soviet Union could have blocked these actions with its veto, but at the time of the invasion the Russians were boycotting the council for its refusal to recognize the People's Republic of China. The Soviets returned to the Security Council in August.

Although more than 70 percent of Americans polled supported Truman's decision to intervene, recruitment offices saw no rush to arms as they had in World War II. National guard and reserve forces had to be called to active duty to fill the ranks, and the draft was again used to ensure a monthly quota of fifty thousand soldiers. General Lewis B. Hershey, head of the Selective Service, noted, "Everyone wants out; nobody wants in." On July 1, the first American soldiers, officially under United Nations control, arrived in Korea. Anxious not to provoke the Chinese and Russians with a formal declaration of war against North Korea, Truman never sought one. American troops served in Korea under United Nations resolutions and followed Truman's orders as commander in chief. For the record the war was called the "Korean Conflict," a "police action" to defeat a "bandit raid." Few in Congress objected, and with little dissent the House and Senate approved large-scale expansions of the military and its budget.

The infusion of American troops did not halt the North Korean advance, and by the end of July, North Korean forces were occupying most of South Korea. United Nations forces, including nearly 122,000 Americans and the whole South Korean army, held only the southeastern corner of the peninsula—the Pusan perimeter—and prepared for a last-ditch offensive. A bold maneuver on September 15 turned the tide. Seventy thousand American troops landed at Inchon, near Seoul, nearly 200 miles north of the Pusan defensive perimeter (see Map 26.3). MacArthur's brilliant tactical move surprised the enemy and not only threatened North Korean supply and communication lines but also potentially blocked the retreat of North Korean troops. Eleven days later, UN forces advancing north from Pusan joined forces driving east from Inchon.

Their army collapsing, the North Koreans fled back across the 38th parallel. Seoul was liberated on September 27. The police action had achieved its purpose: the South Korean government was saved, and the 38th parallel was again a real border.

Seeking to Liberate North Korea

Now, however, restoring the conditions that had prevailed before the invasion was not enough. The South Korean leadership, MacArthur, Truman, and most Americans wanted to unify the peninsula under South Korean rule. Bending under American pressure, the United Nations approved the new goal on October 7, to "liberate" North Korea from Communist rule. MacArthur ordered UN and South Korean forces to cross the 38th parallel. With North Korean forces in disarray, by mid-October United Nations forces moved quickly northward toward the Korean-Chinese border at the Yalu River. The Chinese threatened intervention if the invaders approached the border, and some UN units had already encountered Chinese "volunteer" troops. Nevertheless, based on intelligence estimates, UN commander General MacArthur was supremely confident. If Chinese forces did cross the border, he explained to Truman, they would number less than fifty thousand and easily could be defeated. Not entirely convinced, Truman ordered MacArthur to use only South Korean forces in approaching the Yalu River. The overconfident general, however, bridled at being restrained by his civilian commander, and on November 24, in violation of his orders, MacArthur moved American, British, and Korean forces to within a few miles of the Yalu. He also publicly promised to have victorious American soldiers home by Christmas. Two days later, nearly three hundred thousand Chinese soldiers entered the Korean Conflict.

With their bugles blowing, the Chinese attacked in waves, hurling grenades, taking massive casualties, and encircling and nearly trapping several American and South Korean units in the most brutal fighting of the war. MacArthur had assumed that vastly superior American air and firepower would stop any Chinese invaders. He had not foreseen the arrival of hundreds of thousands of Chinese sol-

---

General Douglas MacArthur Commander of Allied forces in the southwest Pacific during World War II, of occupation forces in Japan, and of UN forces in Korea until a dispute over strategy led Truman to dismiss him.

The Korean War was one of ebb and flow, advances and retreats—the movement of troops up and down the rugged Korean peninsula. Here, American troops advance while Korean women and children march in the opposite direction hoping to avoid the destruction of war. Over 33,000 Americans lost their lives in Korea during the conflict. *Corbis-Bettmann.*

diers, the bitter winter weather, or night battles that severely limited the role of American aircraft. Across northern North Korea, UN forces fell back in bitter combat. The U.S. 1st Marine Division, nearly surrounded at the Chosin Reservoir, battled its way to the port of Hungnam by leap-frogging units to clear the road in front of them. During the Communist offensive, American casualties exceeded twelve thousand, but the Chinese lost more than three times as many, lending grim proof to General O. P. "Slam" Smith's statement about the "retreat" from Chosin: "Gentlemen, we are not retreating. We are merely advancing in another direction."

Within three weeks, the North Koreans and Chinese had shoved the UN forces back to the 38th parallel. During the retreat, General MacArthur asked for permission to bomb bridges on the Yalu River and Chinese bases across the border. He also urged a naval blockade of China and the possible use of Nationalist Chinese forces against the mainland. Believing such escalation could trigger World War III, Truman allowed only the Korean half of the bridges

to be targeted and flatly rejected MacArthur's other suggestions. In the face of the new military reality, Truman abandoned the goal of a unified pro-Western Korea and sought a negotiated settlement to end the conflict even if it would leave two Koreas. The decision was not popular. Americans wanted victory. Encouraged by public opinion polls and vocal Republican critics of Truman, in March and April 1951, General MacArthur publicly took exception to the limitations his commander in chief had placed on him. He put it simply: there was "no substitute for victory." Already displeased by MacArthur's arrogance, Truman used the general's direct challenge to presidential power as grounds to relieve him of his command. General Matthew Ridgeway replaced the fired MacArthur.

The decision unleashed a storm of protest. Some called for Truman's impeachment and MacArthur's nomination for president. Congressional hearings to investigate the conduct of the war followed in June 1951, with MacArthur testifying that an expanded war could achieve victory. The administration responded by projecting nuclear world war alarmism and effectively made the case for a limited war and the need for civilian authority over the military. In the face-off between MacArthur and Truman there was no winner. Polls showed Truman's public approval rating continuing to fall, reaching a dismal 24 percent by late 1951. At the same time, MacArthur's hopes for a presidential candidacy collapsed because most Americans feared his aggressive policies might indeed result in World War III. By the beginning of 1952, frustrated by the war, the vast majority of Americans were simply tired of the "useless" conflict and wanted it to end.

The Korean front, meanwhile, stabilized along the 38th parallel. Four-power peace talks among the United States, South Korea, China, and North Korea began on July 10, 1951, amid sharp and ugly fighting. The negotiations did not go smoothly. For two years, the powers postured and argued about prisoners, cease-fire lines, and a multitude of lesser issues while soldiers fought and died over scraps of territory. UN casualties exceeded 125,000 during the two years of peace negotiations. When the Eisenhower administration finally concluded the cease-fire on July 26, 1953, the Korean Conflict had cost more than $20 billion and 33,000 American lives, but left South Korea intact.

The "hot war" in Korea had far-reaching military and diplomatic results for the United States. The expansion of military spending envisioned by NSC–68 had proceeded rapidly after the North Korean invasion. In Europe, Truman moved forward with plans to rearm West Germany and Italy and, in the name of anticommunism, improved relations with Spain's dictator, Francisco Franco. Throughout Asia and the Pacific, a large American presence was made permanent. In 1951 the United States concluded a settlement with Japan that kept American forces in Japan and Okinawa. The Australian–New Zealand–United States (ANZUS) treaty of 1951 promised American military protection to Australia and New Zealand. At the same time, the United States was increasing its military aid and commitments to Nationalist China and French **Indochina**. The containment policy that George Kennan had envisioned to protect Western Europe had been expanded—formally and financially—to cover East Asia and the Pacific. Kennan objected to the growing number of commitments, but his arguments were more than offset by policymakers stressing the global struggle against the forces of communism. According to the philosophy of the day, a Communist victory anywhere threatened the national security of the United States.

POSTWAR POLITICS

• In what ways did Truman attempt to maintain and expand the New Deal? How did the fear of Communism strengthen conservative opposition to his programs?

• Why did Truman win the 1948 election?

When Roosevelt died, many wondered if Truman would continue the Roosevelt–New Deal approach to domestic policies. Would he work to protect the social and economic gains that labor, women, and minorities had earned during the Depression and the war? Conservatives and some of Truman's friends predicted that the new president was "going to be quite a shock to those who followed Roosevelt—that the New Deal is as good as dead . . . and that the 'Roosevelt nonsense' was over." But Truman had no intention of extinguishing the New Deal.

Truman and Liberalism

In September he presented to Congress what one Republican critic called an effort to "out–New Deal the New Deal." Truman set forth an ambitious program designed to ease the transition to a peacetime economy and re-energize the New Deal. To prevent inflation and a recession, he wanted Congress to continue wartime economic agencies such as the Office of Price Administration that would help control wages and prices. To protect wartime gains by

minorities, he asked that the Fair Employment Practices Commission be renewed. Furthering the New Deal, he recommended an expansion of Social Security coverage and benefits, an increase in the minimum wage to 65 cents an hour, the development of additional housing programs, and a national health system to ensure medical care for all Americans.

Opposing Truman's proposals was Congress. Since 1937, a coalition of Republicans and conservative Democrats had successfully blocked extensions of the New Deal liberalism, and they were determined to continue their efforts. They embarked on a campaign to persuade the American public of the dangers of socialism and communism and of the benefits of a return to business-directed free enterprise. The effectiveness of linking liberalism and social change to socialism and communism became an even more powerful weapon as the Cold War developed. Consequently, Truman's call for an extension of the New Deal was met with cries of "New Deal socialism." Political opponents of Truman's programs were not alone in using the image of communism to gain public support and to tar their opponents. Tobacco giant R. J. Reynolds conducted a multimillion-dollar public ad campaign to defeat union efforts in Operation Dixie to organize southern workers. Unionization was characterized as a step toward socialism. The National Association of Manufacturers spent nearly $37 million on such propaganda in one year. "Public sentiment is everything," wrote an officer of Standard Oil. "He who molds public sentiment goes deeper than he who enacts statutes or pronounces decisions." A Truman official sadly agreed: "The consuming fear of communism fostered a widespread belief that change was subversive and that those who supported change were Communists or **fellow-travelers**." Verifying that opinion was a public confrontation in 1950 that occurred when blacks and white supporters in Pittsburgh attempted to integrate a public swimming pool: the local paper labeled those trying to change the system "Commies."

Warning that Truman's "socialistic" program involved too much government, threatened private

---

Indochina   French colony in Southeast Asia, including present-day Vietnam, Laos, and Cambodia; it began fighting for its independence in the mid-twentieth century.

fellow-traveler   Individual who sympathizes with or supports the beliefs of the Communist Party without being a member.

Workers march in New York City in support of unions and worldwide worker solidarity. As the war ended, business and government assumed a more hostile attitude toward organized labor—many claiming that unions were socialistic or communistic. The outcome of this attitude was laws, including the Taft-Hartley Act, that restricted union activities and contributed to a decline in union membership. *UPI/Bettmann Archives.*

enterprise, and endangered existing class and social relations, Congress rejected or severely scaled back nearly all of his proposals. The Fair Employment Practices Commission faded away, allowing industries to return to prewar hiring practices that excluded minorities. Congress spurned any idea of a national health program and instead substituted a federal program to build hospitals. Congress also attacked any attempt to maintain controls on prices, wages, and production. As controls expired in 1946, the nation experienced rapidly rising prices and further declining wages. Purchasing power dropped by over 30 percent for many working families as prices rose—25 percent during the first eighteen months after the war. Seeking to protect wages and protest rising prices, especially on food, nearly 4.5 million workers staged more than five thousand strikes.

Congress and state and local governments responded to strikes and agitation with anti-labor measures designed to weaken unions and end work stoppages. Right-to-work laws banned compulsory union membership and in some cases provided legal and police protection for workers crossing picket lines. In the spring of 1946, Truman joined the attack on strikes, squaring off against the coal miners' and railroad unions. In April 1946, he faced down John L. Lewis and four hundred thousand striking United Mine Workers. Considering Lewis "a Hitler at heart, a demagogue in action, and a traitor in fact," the president seized the mines, ordered miners back to work, and applauded when a federal court fined Lewis and

the union $3.5 million. "Lewis folded up on Saturday," he wrote in his diary after the miners had returned to work. "He is, as all bullies are, as yellow as a dog pound pup." When locomotive engineers walked off the job in May, Truman asked Congress for power to draft the strikers. The railroad strike was settled before Congress responded, but momentum mounted in Congress to take legislative action to control strikes and disable unions.

Amid strikes, soaring inflation, divisions within Democratic ranks, and widespread dissatisfaction with Truman's leadership—"to err is Truman" was a common quip—Republicans asked the public, "Had enough?" Voters responded affirmatively, filling both houses of the Eightieth Congress with more Republicans and anti–New Deal Democrats. Refusing to retreat, Truman opened 1947 by presenting Congress with a restatement of many of the programs he had offered in 1945. The political battle between the president and Congress fired up again. Congress rejected Truman's proposals, Truman vetoed 250 bills, and Congress overrode 12 of Truman's vetoes. Among the most critical vetoes cast by Truman and overridden by Congress was the **Taft-Hartley Act**. The Taft-Hartley Act, passed in June 1947, was a clear victory for

> **Taft-Hartley Act**   Law passed by Congress in 1947 banning closed shops, permitting employers to sue unions for broken contracts, and requiring unions to observe a cooling-off period before striking.

management over labor. It banned the closed shop, prevented industry-wide collective bargaining, and legalized state-sponsored right-to-work laws that hindered union organizing. It also required that union officials sign affidavits that they were not communists. Echoing Truman's actions in the coal strike, the law also empowered the president to use a court injunction to force striking workers back to work for an eighty-day cooling-off period. Privately, Truman supported much of the bill and cast his veto knowing it would be overridden. He also knew his veto would help "hold labor support" for his 1948 run for the presidency.

Truman's veto of Taft-Hartley was an easy political decision. In contrast, the issue of civil rights was extremely complex and politically dangerous. Democrats were clearly divided on civil rights. Southern Democrats were opposed to any mention of civil rights, while African Americans and liberals, including Eleanor Roosevelt, demanded that he "speak" to the issue. Truman was cautious but supportive of civil rights and aware of Soviet criticism of American segregation. Confessing that he did not know how bad conditions were for African Americans and that, "[t]he top dog in a world . . . ought to clean his own house," Truman agreed in December 1946 to create a committee on civil rights to examine race relations in the country. The October 1947 report, *To Secure These Rights*, described the racial inequalities in American society and called on the government to take steps to correct the imbalance. Among its recommendations were the establishment of a permanent commission on civil rights, the enactment of anti-lynching laws, and the abolition of the **poll tax**. The committee also called for integration of the U.S. armed forces and support for integrating housing programs and education. Truman asked Congress in February 1948 to act on the recommendations but provided no direction or legislation. Nor did the White House make any effort to fully integrate the armed forces until black labor leader A. Philip Randolph once again threatened a march on Washington (see page 804). Faced with the prospect of an embarrassing mass protest only months before the 1948 election, Truman issued an executive order instructing the military to integrate its forces. The navy and air force complied, but the army resisted until high casualties in the summer of 1950 in Korea forced the integration of black replacements into previously white combat units. Despite his caution, Truman had done more in the area of civil rights than any president since Lincoln, a record that ensured African-American and liberal

Many considered Harry S Truman's 1948 victory over Thomas E. Dewey a major political upset—nearly all of the major polls had named the Republican an easy winner. Here Truman holds up the *Chicago Tribune's* incorrect headline announcing Dewey's triumph. *UPI/Bettmann Archives.*

support for his 1948 bid to be elected president in his own right.

The 1948 Election

Republicans' hopes were high in 1948. They had done well in congressional elections in 1946 and 1947. To take on Truman they chose New York's governor **Thomas E. Dewey.** In his loss to Roosevelt in 1944, Dewey had earned a respectable 46 percent of the popular vote, and Truman was not Roosevelt. The Democrats were also mired in bitter infighting over

poll tax   A tax imposed by many states that required a fee be paid as a prerequisite to voting and was used to exclude the poor, especially minorities, from voting.

Thomas E. Dewey   New York governor who twice ran unsuccessfully for president as the Republican candidate, the second time against Truman in 1948.

the direction of domestic policy. Many Democratic liberals and minorities were dissatisfied that Truman had not worked harder to sell his New Deal–type programs to the public and to push them through Congress. Truman was concerned that some liberals might switch their votes to Henry A. Wallace, the former vice president, who was running as a Progressive Party candidate. Southern Democrats, convinced that Truman was too liberal, opposed any efforts to support organized labor or civil rights. When a civil rights plank was inserted into the party's platform, many of them stalked out of the convention waving Confederate flags. Unwilling to support a Republican, they met in Birmingham and organized the States' Rights Democratic Party, better known as the **Dixiecrat Party**, nominating South Carolina's governor J. Strom Thurmond for president.

With the Democratic Party so splintered and public opinion polls showing a large Republican lead, Dewey, not known for his charm or speaking ability, conducted a low-key campaign almost devoid of debate on issues and contact with the public. In contrast, "Give 'Em Hell" Harry, running for his political life, crossed the nation by train, making hundreds of speeches that stressed the gains made under the progressive policies of the Democrats. He attacked the "do-nothing" Eightieth Congress and its business allies. He told one audience, "Wall Street expects its money to elect a Republican administration that will listen to the gluttons of privilege first and not to the people at all." Touting the Berlin crisis, Truman also emphasized his expertise in foreign policy and his experience in standing up to Stalin.

Confounding the pollsters, Truman defeated Dewey. His margin of victory was the smallest since 1916—slightly over 2 million votes. Nevertheless, Truman's victory was a triumph for Roosevelt's New Deal coalition. Despite the Dixiecrat candidate, most southerners did not abandon the Democratic Party. Thurmond carried only four southern states; Wallace carried none (see Map 26.4). Democrats also won majorities in Congress, and Truman hoped that in 1949 he would succeed with his domestic program, which he called the **Fair Deal**.

In his inaugural address, Truman again held up the images of the New Deal. He asked for increases in Social Security, public housing, and the minimum wage, the repeal of the Taft-Hartley Act, and the creation of a national health program. He also gave civil rights and federal aid to education a place on the national agenda. Rewarding farmers for their role in his victory, Truman submitted the Brannan Plan, which included federal benefits for small farmers.

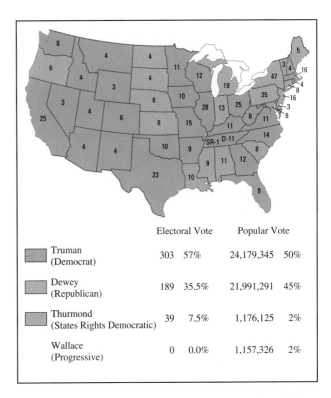

	Electoral Vote		Popular Vote	
Truman (Democrat)	303	57%	24,179,345	50%
Dewey (Republican)	189	35.5%	21,991,291	45%
Thurmond (States Rights Democratic)	39	7.5%	1,176,125	2%
Wallace (Progressive)	0	0.0%	1,157,326	2%

MAP 26.4 Election of 1948 In the 1948 presidential election, Harry S Truman confounded the polls and analysts by upsetting his Republican opponent Thomas Dewey, earning 50 percent of the popular vote and 57 percent of the electoral vote.

COLD WAR POLITICS

• What fears and events heightened society's worries about internal subversion, and how did politicians respond to the public's concerns?

• Why and how did Joseph McCarthy become so powerful by 1952?

Congress responded favorably to Truman's programs in areas already well established by the New Deal: a 65-cent minimum hourly wage, funds for low- and moderate-income housing, and increases

Dixiecrat Party Party organized in 1948 by southern delegates who refused to accept the civil rights plank of the Democratic platform; they nominated Strom Thurmond of South Carolina for president.

Fair Deal President Truman's plan for legislation on civil rights, fair employment practices, and educational appropriations.

in Social Security coverage and payments. Proposals going beyond the scope of the New Deal, however, encountered entrenched, organized opposition. Attacks on the Fair Deal revolved around a time-honored objection: so much government intrusion would move the country down a communistic path. Conservatives emphasized the "Communist" nature of a national health system and government intervention in education. Civil rights legislation was held captive by the southern wing of the Democratic Party, which considered it part of a Communist conspiracy to undermine American unity. Agribusiness leaders and conservatives attacked the Brannan Plan as socialistic and class oriented.

The Red Scare

Even before the 1948 election, responding to fears of Communists within the government—fears that Republicans exploited—Truman had moved to beef up the existing loyalty program. Nine days after his Truman Doctrine speech (March 12, 1947), the president issued Executive Order #9835, establishing the Federal Employee Loyalty Program. The order stated that, after a hearing, a federal employee could be fired if "reasonable grounds" existed for believing he or she was disloyal in belief or action. Attorney General Tom Clark provided a lengthy list of subversive organizations, and government administrators screened their employees for membership. Soon supervisors and workers also began to accuse one another of "un-American" thoughts and activities. Between 1947 and 1951, the government discharged more than three thousand federal employees because of their supposed disloyalty. In almost every case, the accused had no right to confront the accusers or to refute the evidence. Few of those forced to leave government service were Communists. Fewer still were threats to American security.

Truman's loyalty program, despite all the discharges, intensified rather than calmed hysteria about an "enemy within." And among those stepping forward to protect the nation from the insidious internal enemy, none were more vicious than the **House Un-American Activities Committee** (HUAC) and **Joseph McCarthy**, Wisconsin's Republican senator. Working with FBI director J. Edgar Hoover, HUAC in 1947 announced its intention to root out communism within the government and society. The committee targeted State Department officials, New Dealers, labor activists, entertainers, writers, educators, and individuals known to espouse liberal philosophies. Director Hoover proclaimed that there was one

"FIRE!"

HERBLOCK ©1949 THE WASHINGTON POST CO.
June 17, 1949

During the Red Scare, many people—in the name of security—seemed willing to accept limitations placed on individual rights and freedoms. In his June 1949 political cartoon, Herblock suggests that the panic over the fear of Communists was in reality a threat to extinguish the fire of American freedom. *From* Herblock: A Cartoonist's Life *(Time Books, 1998)*.

American Communist for every 1,814 loyal citizens, and Attorney General Clark warned that Communists were everywhere, "in factories, offices, butcher shops, on street corners, in private businesses," carrying "the germs of death for society."

HUAC made its first Cold War splash with its investigation of Hollywood. The committee's goals

House Un-American Activities Committee
Congressional committee, created in 1938, that investigated suspected Communists during the McCarthy era and that Richard Nixon used to advance his career.

Joseph McCarthy Senator from Wisconsin who in 1950 began a Communist witch-hunt that lasted until his censure by the Senate in 1954; *McCarthyism* is a term associated with attacks on liberals and others often based on unsupported assertions and carried out without regard for basic liberties.

were to grab headlines, remove people with liberal, leftist viewpoints from the entertainment industry, and ensure that the mass media promoted American capitalism and traditional American values. Just as World War II had required mobilization of the film industry, committee supporters reasoned, the Cold War necessitated that movies continue to promote the "right" images. With much fanfare, HUAC called Hollywood notables to testify about Communist influence in the industry. Many of those called used the opportunity to strut their patriotism and denounce communism. Actor Ronald Reagan, president of the Screen Actors Guild, denounced Communist methods that "sucked" people into carrying out "red policy without knowing what they are doing" and testified that the Conference of Studio Unions was full of Reds.

Not all witnesses were cooperative. Some who were or had been members of the Communist Party, including the "Hollywood Ten," took the Fifth Amendment and lashed out at the activities of the committee. Soon labeled "Fifth Amendment Communists," the ten were jailed for contempt of Congress and blacklisted by the industry. Eric Johnson, president of the Motion Picture Association, announced that no one would be hired who did not cooperate with the committee. He also stated that Hollywood would produce no more films like *The Grapes of Wrath* featuring the hardships of poor Americans or "the seamy side of American life." Moviemakers soon issued a new code—*A Screen Guide for Americans*—that demanded, "Don't Smear the Free Enterprise System"; "Don't Deify the Common Man"; "Don't Show That Poverty Is a Virtue."

Anticommunism proved to be a useful weapon for a variety of causes. Manufacturers used it to weaken unions, politicians to discredit opponents, and white southerners to squelch the civil rights movement. Neighborhoods and communities organized "watch groups," which screened books, movies, and public speakers and questioned teachers and public officials, seeking to ban or dismiss those considered suspect.

Just before the election of 1948, HUAC zeroed in on spies within the government, bringing forth a number of informants who had once been Soviet agents and were now willing to name other Americans who allegedly had sold out the United States. The most sensational revelation came from one of the editors of *Time*, a repentant ex-Communist named Whittaker Chambers. Chambers accused **Alger Hiss**, a New Deal liberal and one-time State Department official who had been with Roosevelt at Yalta, of being a Communist. At first Hiss denied even know-

ing Chambers, but under interrogation by HUAC members, especially Congressman Richard M. Nixon of California, Hiss admitted an acquaintance with Chambers in the 1930s but denied he was or had been a Communist. When Hiss sued Chambers for libel, Chambers escalated the charges. He stated that Hiss had passed State Department secrets to him in the 1930s, and he produced rolls of microfilm that he said Hiss had delivered to him. In a controversial and sensationalized trial, Hiss was found guilty of **perjury** (the statute of limitations on espionage had expired) and was sentenced to five years in prison.

As the nation followed the Hiss case, news of the Communist victory in China and the Soviet explosion of an atomic bomb heightened American fears. Many people believed that such Communist successes could have occurred only with help from American traitors. Congressman Harold Velde of Illinois proclaimed, "Our government from the White House down has been sympathetic toward the views of Communists and fellow-travelers, with the result that it has been infiltrated by a network of spies." Congress responded in 1950 by passing, over Truman's veto, the **McCarran Internal Security Act**. The law required all Communists to register with the attorney general and made it a crime to conspire to establish a totalitarian government in the United States. The following year the Supreme Court upheld the **Smith Act** (passed in June 1940) in *Dennis et al. v. the United States*, ruling that membership in the Communist Party was equivalent to conspiring to overthrow the American government and that no specific act of treason was necessary for conviction.

Congressman Velde's observation about spies seemed vindicated in February 1950, when English authorities arrested British scientist Klaus Fuchs for passing technical secrets to the Soviet Union. (A

Alger Hiss   State Department official accused in 1948 of being a Communist spy; he was convicted of perjury and sent to prison.

perjury   The deliberate giving of false testimony under oath.

McCarran Internal Security Act   Law passed by Congress in 1950 requiring Communists to register with the U.S. attorney general and making it a crime to conspire to establish a totalitarian government in the United States.

Smith Act   The Alien Registration Act, passed by Congress in 1940, which made it a crime to advocate or to belong to an organization that advocates the overthrow of the government by force or violence.

physicist, Fuchs had worked at Los Alamos, New Mexico, on the Manhattan Project.) Fuchs named an American accomplice, Harry Gold, who in turn named David Greenglass, an army sergeant at Los Alamos. Greenglass then claimed that his sister Ethel and her husband Julius Rosenberg were part of the Soviet atomic spy ring. In a controversial trial, the prosecution alleged that the information obtained and passed to the Soviets by **Ethel and Julius Rosenberg** was largely responsible for the successful Soviet atomic bomb. The Rosenbergs professed innocence but were convicted of espionage on the basis of Gold's and Greenglass's testimony. During the trial, J. Edgar Hoover asked that the death penalty not be considered for Ethel Rosenberg, but both she and her husband were executed in 1953. Soviet documents indicate that Julius Rosenberg was engaged in espionage but that Ethel was probably guilty only of being loyal to him.

Joseph McCarthy and the Politics of Loyalty

Feeding on the furor over the enemy within, Senator Joseph McCarthy of Wisconsin emerged at the forefront of the anti-Communist movement. He had entered the public arena as a candidate for Congress following World War II. Running for the Senate in 1946, he invented a glorious war record for himself that included the nickname "Tail-gunner Joe" and several wounds—he even walked with a fake limp—to help himself win the election. Some regarded him as among the worst senators in Washington—available to lobbyists, totally lacking moral principles, and absent most of the time. In February 1950, he was looking for an issue on which to peg his re-election bid. After conferring with friends, he settled on the internal Communist threat as an issue "with sex appeal."

The senator tried his gambit first in Wheeling, West Virginia. He announced to a Republican women's group that the United States was losing the Cold War because of traitors within the government. He claimed to know of 205 Communists working in the State Department. The senator next told a few curious reporters that in reality he had a list of "207 bad risks" in the State Department. McCarthy kept changing the number of people on his list but continued to hammer away at security risks, traitors who he could prove were employed by the State Department. He never produced his list of names for reporters.

McCarthy's charges were quickly examined by a Senate committee and shown to be at best inaccurate.

When the chair of the committee, Democrat Millard Tydings of Maryland, pronounced McCarthy a hoax and a fraud, the Wisconsin senator countered by accusing Tydings of questionable loyalty. During Tydings's 1950 re-election campaign, McCarthy worked for his defeat, spreading false stories and pictures that supposedly showed connections to American Communists, including a faked photograph of the Democrat talking to Earl Browder, head of the American Communist Party. When Tydings lost by forty thousand votes, McCarthy's stature soared. Republicans and conservative Democrats rarely opposed him and frequently supported his wild allegations. The Senate's most powerful Republican, Robert Taft of Ohio, slapped McCarthy on the back saying, "Keep it up, Joe," and sent him the names of State Department officials who merited investigation. Taft encouraged him: "If one case doesn't work out, bring up another."

The outbreak of the Korean War and the reversals at the hands of the Chinese only increased the senator's popularity. Supported by Republican political gains in the 1950 elections, McCarthyism became a powerful political and social force. Politicians flocked to the anti-Communist bandwagon, making it ever more difficult for Truman to push his Fair Deal. Federal Trade Commissioner John Carson despaired that liberals "were on the run" and that reactionaries were "winning the fight."

By 1952, Truman's popularity was almost nonexistent: only 24 percent of those who were asked said they approved of his presidency. The Korean Conflict was stalemated, and Republicans were having a field day attacking "cowardly containment" and calling for victory in Korea. The Fair Deal was dead, and Truman had lost control over domestic policy. Compounding his problems, a probe of organized crime by a congressional committee chaired by Tennessee senator Estes Kefauver had found scandal, corruption, and links to the mob within the government. Presidential aide Harry Vaughan and other administration appointees were accused of accepting gifts and selling their influence.

When Truman lost the opening presidential primary in New Hampshire to Kefauver, he withdrew from the race, leaving the Democrats with no clear

> **Ethel and Julius Rosenberg** Wife and husband who were arrested and tried for conspiracy to commit espionage in 1951 after being accused of passing atomic bomb information to the Soviets; they were executed in 1953.

As World War II ended, Americans flocked to the suburbs, creating a demand for new housing—a demand matched by developers of planned communities like Levittown, Pennsylvania. Developers kept the cost of the homes down using uniformity of style and of prefabricated materials. *Van Bucher/ Photo Researchers.*

choice for a candidate. As in 1948, Republicans looked to the November election with great anticipation. At last, they were sure, voters would elect a Republican president—someone who, in Thomas Dewey's opinion, would "save the country from going to Hades in the handbasket of paternalism-socialism-dictatorship."

HOMECOMING AND SOCIAL ADJUSTMENTS

• What social and economic expectations did most Americans have as the Second World War ended?

• What was the nature of suburban America?

• What adjustments did women and minorities have to make in postwar America?

Even before the war against Japan was over, Americans were returning home eager to resume normal lives. Organized "Bring Daddy Back" clubs flooded Washington with letters demanding a speedy return of husbands and fathers. With the defeat of Japan, soldiers in the Pacific sent letters and telegrams to their congressmen saying, "No boat; no vote." Twelve

million men and women were still in uniform and they wanted out. Despite protests from the military and the State Department, and against Truman's own better judgment, by November 1945, 1.25 million GIs were returning home each month. For Americans entering the postwar world, the homecoming was buoyed with expectations and fraught with anxieties. The United States had won the war and would oversee a peace, but would it last? The nation had experienced dramatic wartime economic growth and prosperity, but remembering the Depression, they wondered if the postwar economy would remain strong. Still, most were optimistic that any recession would be short-lived and they would be able to spend savings, find jobs, and enjoy the American dream. "Consumption is the frontier of the future," chirped one economic forecast.

Rising Expectations

Owning a home was for many the symbol of the American dream. Before 1945 the housing industry had focused on building custom homes or multi-family dwellings. But the postwar demand replaced custom homes with standardized ones. What people wanted were the charming "dream homes" in new planned communities that were advertised in popular magazines. To meet the demand, by mid-1946, William Levitt and other developers supplied mass-produced, prefabricated houses—the suburban **tract homes**. Using building techniques developed during the war, timber from his own forests, and nonunion workers, Levitt boasted that he could construct an affordable house on an existing concrete slab in sixteen minutes. Standardized, with few frills, the house was a two-story Cape Cod with four and a half rooms. Built on generous 60-by-100-foot lots, complete with a tree or two, Levitt homes cost slightly less than $8,000 and still provided Levitt with a $1,000 profit per house. The price was attractive and hopeful buyers formed long lines as soon as the homes went on sale. The first Levittown sprang up in Hempstead, Long Island, and had more than seventeen thousand homes, seven village greens, fourteen playgrounds, and nine swimming pools. Hundreds of look-alike suburban neighborhoods were soon built across the nation, contributing to a growing migration from rural and urban America to the suburbs.

Nowhere were tract homes more prominent than in southern California. Fostered since the 1920s by the automobile, Los Angeles's development was different from urban development in eastern and midwestern cities. During and after the war, networks of roads extended out from southern California cities, which developed several "satellite" economic centers, pulling businesses, homes, and industries away from the central cities. Continuing the process, Governor Earl Warren in 1947 allocated nearly $300 million over a ten-year period to build 105 miles of freeways in southern California—most crisscrossing the Los Angeles area. Statewide gasoline taxes and registration fees paid for the new roads. At the same time, in downtown Los Angeles and across the country, public transportation, especially streetcars and interurban rail systems, were vanishing and being replaced by bus lines that frequently provided only limited service to the poorer neighborhoods. The fate of downtown Los Angeles was not unique as it experienced a 50 percent loss in sales and revenues. Those still living and working in cities witnessed a parallel loss of jobs and wages.

Suburbs were not for everyone, and widespread discrimination kept some out by design. Whether it was the official policy of developers like Levitt, neighborhood covenants, or lack of home loans, almost every suburb in the nation was predominately white and Christian. Even though the Supreme Court ruled in *Shelly v. Kraemer* (1948) that restrictive housing covenants written to exclude minorities could not be enforced by lower courts, the decision failed to have much impact. Neither did the Court's decision to prevent banks and the FHA from rejecting home loan applications from minorities trying to buy houses in typical white neighborhoods. Real-estate agents also continued to abide by the Realtors' Code of Ethics, which called it unethical to permit the "infiltration of inharmonious elements" into a neighborhood. Across the nation, fewer than 5 percent of suburban neighborhoods provided nonwhites access to the American dream house. In the San Francisco Bay Area, not even 1 percent of the more than 100,000 homes built between 1945 and 1950 were sold to nonwhites.

For many veterans a cozy home was only part of the postwar dream—so too was going to college. Armed with economic support through the G.I. Bill in September 1946, nearly 1 million veterans enrolled in college. New Jersey's Rutgers University saw its enrollment climb from 7,000 to 16,000. At Lehigh University in Pennsylvania, 940 veteran students outnumbered the 396 "civilians" and refused to don the traditional freshman beanie. Faculty and administrators soon discovered that veterans made exceptional students and rarely needed disciplinary action. Nonveteran students, however, complained that because of the veterans they had to work harder and "slave to keep up." Schools scrambled to respond to the influx of students, not only hiring more faculty and building more facilities, but also providing special housing, day care centers, and expanded health clinics for married students. By the time the G.I. Bill expired in 1952, over 2 million veterans, including 64,000 women, had earned their degrees under its umbrella.

Veterans expected jobs, too, and most figured that wartime workers, especially minorities and women, would relinquish their jobs and return to traditional roles. At first jobs seemed scarce. The cancellation of wartime contracts and the nationwide switch to

tract homes One of numerous houses of similar design built on small plots of land.

Shelly v. Kraemer Supreme Court ruling (1948) that barred lower courts from enforcing restrictive agreements that prevented minorities from living in certain neighborhoods; it had little impact on actual practices.

domestic production resulted in 2.7 million workers being dismissed from their jobs within a month of Japan's surrender. Fortunately for veterans, the G.I. Bill provided unemployment compensation for a year until a job was found. And within a year, jobs were becoming more and more available. By 1947, 60 million people working, 7 million more than at the peak of wartime production. But the work force had changed, with noticeably fewer women and minorities as industries and businesses resumed their prewar hiring habits.

From Industrial Worker to Homemaker

Across the nation in a variety of ways, women were told that they were no longer wanted in the workplace and that they would be most fulfilled by being wives and mothers again. A *Fortune* poll in the fall of 1945 revealed that 57 percent of women and 63 percent of men believed that married women should not work outside the home. Psychiatrists and marriage counselors argued that men wanted their wives to be feminine and submissive, not their fellow workers. Yet many women resist these social pressures and rejected a return to the routine of housework. They wanted to keep their jobs. Despite their hopes, however, women experienced a rapid decline in employment, particularly in manufacturing. In the aircraft industry, women had comprised 40 percent of the work force, but by 1948 they were only 12 percent and most of those were now holding clerical positions. Women's wages declined too, from about $50 to $35 a week. Still, a significant majority of those women looking for work, 75 percent, found it, although in a more gender segregated workplace than before the war. Rosie the Riveter had become Fran the File Clerk, and by 1950 the number of women working reached 29 million—a million less than at their wartime peak.

At work or at home, Americans witnessed a renewed social emphasis on femininity, family, and a woman's proper role. Fashion designers, such as Christian Dior in his "New Look," lengthened skirts and accented waists and breasts to emphasize femininity. Marriage was more popular than ever: by 1950, two-thirds of the population were married and having children. Factors contributing to the rush to the altar were fears of "male scarcity" caused by war losses and a new attitude that viewed marriage as the ideal state for young people. Many women's magazines and marriage experts championed the

"*She's a gem—she used to work for Lockheed!*"

Following World War II, a majority of women left the industrial work force and returned to the home and more "traditional" occupations. In this cartoon, a more affluent homemaker benefits from the wartime skills her new domestic servant acquired. Many women, like Sybil Lewis, were determined never to return to traditional roles. *Ellen Kaiper Collection.*

idea that men should marry at around age 20 and women at age 18 or 19. With veterans returning home, with society celebrating family, and with prosperity increasing multifold came the **"baby boom"** that would last for nearly twenty years. From a Depression level of under 19 births per 1,000 women per year, the birth rate rose to over 25 per 1,000 by 1948 (see Figure 26.1).

baby boom   Sudden increase in the birth rate that occurred in the United States after World War II and lasted until roughly 1961.

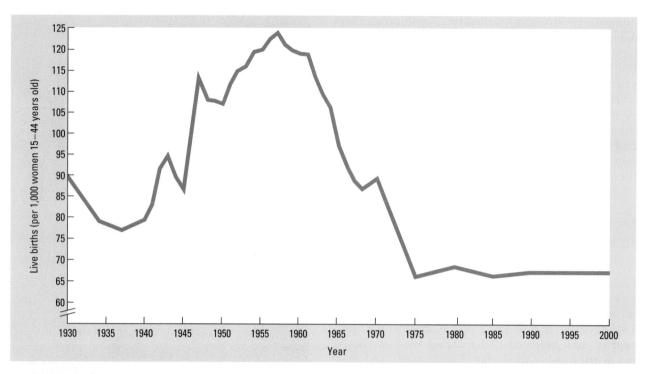

FIGURE 26.1 Birth Rate, 1930–2000   Between 1946 and 1957, rebounding from the low birth rate of the Depression, families choose to have more children. This increase is often called the "baby boom." Since around 1960, the birth rate has slowed, and since the mid-1970s, it has remained fairly constant.

Not all women accepted the role of contented, submissive wives or homemakers—the war experience had changed relationships. When one veteran informed his wife that she could no longer handle the finances because doing so was not "woman's work," she indignantly reminded him that she had successfully balanced the checkbook for four years and that his return had not made her suddenly stupid. Reflecting such tensions and too many hasty wartime marriages, the divorce rate jumped dramatically. Twenty-five percent of all marriages were ending in divorce in 1946, and by 1950 over a million G.I. marriages had dissolved. As the number of female heads of household rose, so also did the poverty and social stigma attached to single parenthood. Following her divorce, one suburban resident recalled that her neighbors "avoided" her and made remarks like "why don't you get a job" instead of taking tax monies. She also noted that her children were singled out at school because they did not have a father at home.

Restrained Expectations

Like Sybil Lewis (see Chapter 25, Individual Choices, page 782), nonwhites expected their wartime

advances would dissipate as society forced them to return to prewar social and economic patterns. Most still lived in a distinctly segregated world. From housing to jobs, from healthcare to education, white society continued to deny nonwhites full participation in the American dream. Still, minorities looked eagerly toward the postwar period. Despite ongoing discrimination, they had achieved social and economic gains during the war, and despite immediate postwar adjustments, more progress seemed possible. In 1945, for example, Jackie Robinson broke the color barrier in professional baseball when team owner Branch Rickey signed him to play for the Brooklyn Dodgers' farm team, the Montreal Royals. Robinson joined the Dodgers in 1947 as the first African-American player in the previously all-white major leagues and that season was voted the National League's Rookie of the Year.

Minorities also pursued activism to gain equality. Having fought for democracy overseas, Latino and African-American veterans insisted that democracy be practiced at home. W. E. B. Du Bois echoed their feelings, stating that the real problems facing the United States came not from Stalin and Molotov but from racists like Mississippi's Senator Theodore

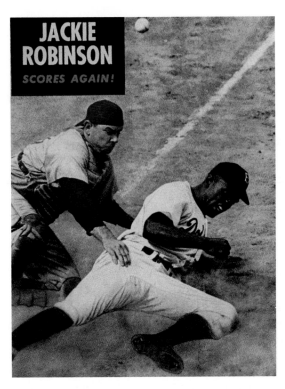

JACKIE ROBINSON
SCORES AGAIN!

Jackie Robinson broke the color barrier in major league baseball in 1947, when he joined the Brooklyn Dodgers. After serving as a lieutenant in the army during the war, Robinson, an All-American in football and baseball at UCLA, played with the Kansas City Monarchs of the Negro American Baseball League until he was signed by the Dodgers in 1945. Moved from the minors to the majors in 1947, he earned "Rookie of the Year" honors and later was inducted into the Baseball Hall of Fame. *Collection of Michael Barson/Past Perfect.*

Bilbo and Congressman John Rankin. "Internal injustice done to one's brother," Du Bois warned, "is far more dangerous than the aggression of strangers from abroad." Confronting restrictions on the right to vote, some black veterans like Medgar Evers attempted to register to vote. Most failed, including Evers who was barred from registering by armed whites, but some succeeded, especially in the Upper South and in urban areas. In several northern cities, while housing and race riots were one result of continuing black migration from the South, another was a growing political voice as African-American neighborhoods elected black representatives such as Adam Clayton Powell to Congress.

While they cheered every at-bat and stolen base of Jackie Robinson, the reality for most African Americans was unchanged. They watched "fair employment" vanish as employers favored white males once the war was over. "Last hired, first fired" reflected job reality, especially in skilled and industrial jobs. In 1943 more than a million African Americans were employed in the aircraft industry. By 1950, the number had shrunk to 237,000. The decline was less marked in the automobile, rubber, and shipbuilding industries, but minority job levels dropped there too, as employers routinely chose to exclude nonwhites from many of the skilled and higher-paying positions.

Latinos, too, had limited expectations because of discrimination and limited job and educational opportunities. Anxious to gain the benefits of democracy, existing organizations such as the League of Latin American Citizens (LULAC) worked with new ones such as the **American GI Forum** to attack discrimination throughout the West and Southwest. The GI Forum, organized in Texas in early 1948, worked to secure for Mexican-American veterans the benefits provided by the G.I. Bill and to develop leadership within the Mexican-American population. In California and Texas, LULAC and the GI Forum successfully used federal courts to attack school systems that segregated Latino from white children. In the *Mendez v. Westminster* (1946) and in *Delgado v. Bastrop School District* (1948), federal courts ruled that school systems could not educate Mexican American separately from Anglos. Despite these rulings, throughout the Southwest and West, Latino students remained in predominantly "Mexican" schools and classrooms, perpetuating the lack of educational opportunities and contributing to high dropout rates.

For women and minorities, the immediate postwar period saw significant loss of incomes and status as society expected the "underclass" to return to its prewar existence. But the war had energized those left outside white suburbia and the nation's expanding affluence. Women, African Americans, Hispanics, and other minority groups had their own vision of the American dream, one that included not only growing prosperity but also a full and unfettered role in society and an unmuzzled voice in politics.

American GI Forum   Organization formed in Texas in 1948 by Mexican-American veterans to overcome discrimination and provide support for veterans and all Hispanics; it led the court fight to end the segregation of Hispanic children in school systems in the West and Southwest.

Mendez v. Westminster and *Delgado v. Bastrop School District*   Two federal court cases that overturned the establishment of separate schools for Mexican-American children in California and Texas.

INDIVIDUAL VOICES

Examining a Primary Source

George F. Kennan Analyzes the Soviets' Worldview

Kennan's "Long Telegram" is one of the most important documents in American foreign policy. It provided the Truman administration with an intellectual understanding of what drove the Soviet Union as the two superpowers inched toward a Cold War that would last nearly fifty years. Sent to the State Department on February 22, 1946, the document—excerpted here—was widely read within the administration and was instrumental in shaping U.S. policy toward the USSR.

At the bottom of the Kremlin's neurotic view of world affairs is traditional and instinctive Russian sense of insecurity. . . . Russian rulers have invariably sensed that their rule was . . . fragile and . . . unable to stand comparison or contact with political systems of Western countries. For this reason they have always feared foreign penetrations, feared direct contact between Western world and their own.

. . . Marxist dogma . . . became the perfect vehicle for the sense of insecurity with which Bolsheviks, even more than previous Russian rulers, were afflicted. In this . . . they found justification for the dictatorship without which they did not know how to rule, for cruelties they . . . dare not to inflict, for sacrifices they . . . demand. . . . Today they cannot dispense without it [Marxism]. It is a fig leaf of their moral and intellectual respectability. Without it they would stand before history . . . as only the last of that long succession of cruel and wasteful Russian rulers. . . . ●

● *How does Kennan see both history and Marxism at work shaping Soviet foreign policy? Which seems more important?*

Soviet policy . . . is conducted on two planes: (1) official . . . and (2) subterranean. . . .

On official plane we must look for the following:

(a) Internal policy devoted to increasing in every way strength and prestige of Soviet state. . . .

(b) Wherever it is considered timely and promising, efforts will be made to advance official limits of Soviet Power. . . .

(c) Russians will participate . . . in international organizations where they see opportunity of extending Soviet power or of inhibiting or diluting power of others. . . .

[On the] Subterranean Plane . . .

(d) In foreign countries Communists will . . . work toward destruction of all forms of personal independence, economic, political, or moral. . . .

(e) Everything possible will be done to set major Western Powers against each other. . . .

● *What tactics do the Soviets have at their disposal to implement their foreign policy goals? What events during the Truman administration might counter their tactics?*

(f) In general, all Soviet efforts on unofficial . . . plane will be negative and destructive . . . designed to tear down sources of strength beyond reach of Soviet control. . . . ●

In summary, we have . . . a political force committed fanatically to the belief that with US there can be no permanent modus vivendi, *that it is desirable and*

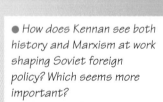

necessary that the internal harmony of our society be disrupted, our traditional way of life be destroyed, the international authority of our state be broken. . . .

Problem of how to cope with this force [is] undoubtedly greatest task our diplomacy has ever faced and probably greatest it will ever . . . face. . . . I cannot attempt to suggest all answers here. But I would like to record my conviction that . . .

(1) Soviet power is neither schematic nor adventuristic. It does not work by fixed plans. It does not take unnecessary risks. Impervious to logic of reason, and it is highly sensitive to logic of force. For this reason it can easily withdraw—and usually does—when strong resistance is encountered. . . .

(2) Gauged against Western World . . . Soviets are still by far the weaker force. Thus their success will really depend on . . . firmness and vigor which Western World can muster.

(3) Much depends on health and vigor of our own society. World communism is like malignant parasite which feeds only on diseased tissue. . . .

(4) We must formulate and put forward . . . a much more positive and constructive picture of world we would like to see than we have put forward in the past. . . . Many foreign peoples . . . are seeking guidance. . . . We should be better able than Russians to give them this. ●

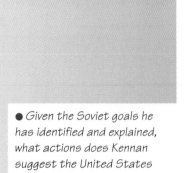

● *Given the Soviet goals he has identified and explained, what actions does Kennan suggest the United States take? Why?*

SUMMARY

People hoped that the end of World War II would usher in a period of international cooperation and peace. This expectation vanished as the world entered the Cold War, a period of armed and vigilant suspicion. To protect the country and the world from Soviet expansion, the United States asserted a primary economic, political, and military role around the globe. The Truman administration developed a containment policy that was first applied to Western Europe, but eventually included Asia. By the end of Truman's presidency, the United States had begun to view its national security in global terms and vowed to use its resources to combat the spread of Communist power.

At home the Cold War had its impact as well, acting to curb the expansion of liberalism. Truman sought to expand on the New Deal but found success difficult. While existing New Deal programs such as Social Security, farm supports, and a minimum wage were extended, a conservative Congress blocked new programs, including national health care. Linking liberal ideas and programs with communism, moderates and conservatives alike promoted their own political, social, and economic interests. They often successfully attacked liberals, unions, and civil rights advocates as too radical and their proposals as smacking of com-

munism. Ultraconservative groups such as the House Un-American Activities Committee and zealous individuals—especially Joseph McCarthy—led the way in promoting a Red Scare that not only attacked liberals in government but also deeply disturbed society.

Most Americans expected to enjoy the fruits of an expanding postwar economy that would bring increased prosperity and more consumer goods. For many the vision of the suburbs with its stable family structure and new-model car in every garage seemed obtainable and desirable. Women were encouraged to return to "domestic" life and raise a family. Postwar America saw a rise in marriages and births, the start of a baby boom. But alongside these trends were an increasing number of divorces and women dissatisfied with their traditional roles.

While jobs and homeownership multiplied for white males and white families seemed poised to achieve the American dream, minorities seemed hemmed in, or nudged out, by discrimination that turned back many of the economic and social gains they had made during the war. Though ousted from the work force or into lesser jobs, and still living in a socially segregated society, many minorities held their own more limited hopes for a future that would bring economic and educational improvement as well as full political and civil rights.

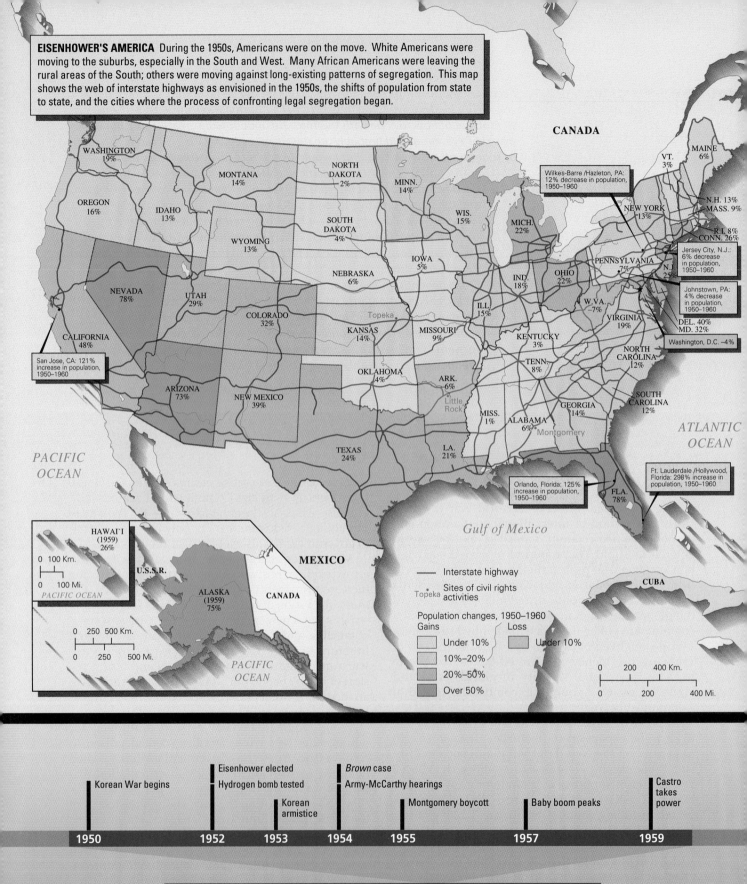

EISENHOWER'S AMERICA During the 1950s, Americans were on the move. White Americans were moving to the suburbs, especially in the South and West. Many African Americans were leaving the rural areas of the South; others were moving against long-existing patterns of segregation. This map shows the web of interstate highways as envisioned in the 1950s, the shifts of population from state to state, and the cities where the process of confronting legal segregation began.

CANADA

WASHINGTON 19%

OREGON 16%

IDAHO 13%

MONTANA 14%

NORTH DAKOTA 2%

MINN. 14%

WIS. 15%

MICH. 22%

NEW YORK 13%

VT. 3%

MAINE 6%

N.H. 13%
MASS. 9%
R.I. 8%
CONN. 26%

Wilkes-Barre/Hazleton, PA: 12% decrease in population, 1950–1960

Jersey City, N.J.: 6% decrease in population, 1950–1960

Johnstown, PA: 4% decrease in population, 1950–1960

PENNSYLVANIA 7%

N.J. 25%

WYOMING 13%

SOUTH DAKOTA 4%

IOWA 5%

NEBRASKA 6%

ILL. 15%

IND. 18%

OHIO 22%

W. VA. –7%

VIRGINIA 19%

DEL. 40%
MD. 32%

Washington, D.C. –4%

NEVADA 78%

UTAH 29%

COLORADO 32%

Topeka

KANSAS 14%

MISSOURI 9%

KENTUCKY 3%

NORTH CAROLINA 12%

CALIFORNIA 48%

San Jose, CA: 121% increase in population, 1950–1960

ARIZONA 73%

NEW MEXICO 39%

OKLAHOMA 4%

ARK. 6%

Little Rock

TENN. 8%

MISS. 1%

ALABAMA 6%

Montgomery

GEORGIA 14%

SOUTH CAROLINA 12%

ATLANTIC OCEAN

PACIFIC OCEAN

TEXAS 24%

LA. 21%

Orlando, Florida: 125% increase in population, 1950–1960

FLA. 78%

Ft. Lauderdale/Hollywood, Florida: 298% increase in population, 1950–1960

Gulf of Mexico

CUBA

HAWAI`I (1959) 26%

0   100 Km.
0   100 Mi.
PACIFIC OCEAN

U.S.S.R.

MEXICO

ALASKA (1959) 75%

CANADA

0   250 500 Km.
0   250   500 Mi.

PACIFIC OCEAN

——— Interstate highway

Topeka   Sites of civil rights activities

Population changes, 1950–1960
Gains   Loss

Under 10%   Under 10%

10%–20%

20%–50%

Over 50%

0   200   400 Km.
0   200   400 Mi.

Korean War begins

Eisenhower elected
Hydrogen bomb tested

Korean armistice

Brown case
Army-McCarthy hearings

Montgomery boycott

Baby boom peaks

Castro takes power

1950   1952   1953   1954   1955   1957   1959

1850   1900   1950   2000

ALLEN GINSBERG

Allen Ginsberg was born in Paterson, New Jersey, in 1926. He graduated from Columbia University, then moved to San Francisco. Dissatisfied with his traditional job and lifestyle, he chose to stop working and start writing poetry. Eventually, he became one of the leading Beat poets and voices of his generation. *Robert Kelley, LIFE magazine, ©Time Warner, Inc.*

Allen Ginsberg

"Your Honor, how far are we going to license the use of filthy, vulgar, obscene and disgusting language? How far can we go?" It was early October 1957 in a San Francisco court, and District Attorney Robert McIntosh was making his closing statement in an obscenity trial revolving around a poem written by Allen Ginsberg entitled *Howl*.

Ginsberg was not on trial for writing the poem. Instead, the defendants were Lawrence Ferlinghetti and Shig Murao, the poem's publisher and the bookstore owner who had sold a copy of the *Howl* to an undercover policeman. If convicted, they could have received a six-month prison sentence and been fined $500. But many people believed that the trial was much more than just about fines or jail time. To some it was yet another sign, like Hugh Hefner's *Playboy* and Elvis Presley's gyrating hips, that the traditional values and visions of American society were under attack. The prosecutors hoped that a successful trial would be the first of a salvo of court attacks across the nation on obscene materials that would enhance the right of local authorities to protect the public by imposing censorship. Supporters of Ferlinghetti and *Howl* argued that it was an assault on the First Amendment and secured the legal assistance of Jake Ehrlich, one of the nation's best-known and most flamboyant attorneys. In a letter to his friend Ferlinghetti, Ginsberg voiced confidence that his poem would not be found obscene but that a real problem might exist if the court ruled that the police could determine what was obscene. "I guess . . . [a] showdown was inevitable," Ginsberg wrote.

Howl was the product of two choices made by Ginsberg. The first was to leave New York and move to San Francisco. "I had passed one session of my life," he remembered, "and it was time to start all over again." In the San Francisco area, he took a job with a small market-research firm and explored poetry, but he was not personally satisfied. He sought psychotherapy, and psychiatrist Philip Hicks asked him what he would like to do. "Doctor, I don't think you're going to find this very healthy," Ginsberg responded, "but I really would like to stop working forever . . . and do nothing but write poetry and have leisure to spend the day outdoors and go to museums and see friends. And I'd like to keep living with someone—maybe even a man—and explore relationships." Hicks said, "Do it," and Ginsberg made his second choice.

Ginsberg established a long-term relationship with Peter Orlovsky, left work, overcame a writer's block, and wrote *Howl*. Pounding out a stream of ideas on his used typewriter, he completed the first and longest part of the poem in one sitting. "I began typing," he wrote, "not with the idea of writing a formal poem, but stating my imaginative sympathies. . . . I had nothing to gain, only the pleasure of enjoying on paper those sympathies most intimate to myself." *Howl* has three parts. Parts I and III he wrote at that first sitting, the second part came after a walk through San Francisco and was jotted down in a cafeteria. Following several revisions, the three sections were read aloud by Ginsberg at a poetry festival and soon published in a booklet by Ferlinghetti. In part because of the trial, which had attracted national and international media coverage, *Howl* had exploded on American society and by 1957 was in its fourth printing.

Arguing for the state, McIntosh charged that some of the poem's language was vulgar and obscene and should be banned. Ehrlich countered by emphasizing the artistic and literary merits of the poem and argued that words should not be taken out of context. In response to McIntosh's closing statement, he simply stated, "You can't think common, rotten things just because you read something in a book, unless it is your purpose to read common, rotten things and apply a common, rotten purpose to what you read." Judge Clayton Horn, who taught Sunday school Bible classes at his church, agreed with Ehrlich. The poem, he stated, had social value and therefore was not obscene.

Howl and other Ginsberg poems jarred the nation's consciousness, and despite those who sought to dismiss him and his fellow Beats as outcasts of society, Ginsberg believed he had opened ways for people to lift their voices in a society that sought to marginalize them. Interviewed by the *Village Voice* newspaper in 1959, he described recent history as "a vast conspiracy to impose . . . a level of mechanical consciousness" on humankind and suggested that the "suppression of contemplative individuality" was nearly complete. Fortunately, according to Ginsberg, "a few individuals, poets, have had the luck and courage . . . to glimpse something new through the crack of mass consciousness" and "have entered the world of Spirit" to battle "an America gone mad with materialism, a police-state America, a sexless and soulless America."

As the fifties dissolved into the sixties, Ginsberg and his apartment in San Francisco's Haight-Ashbury neighborhood became a center of the counterculture. He coined the term "flower power" while advocating spirituality and individual freedom induced by using psychedelic drugs and practicing Asian philosophies and Buddhism. Opposed to the war in Vietnam, he asked antiwar protesters to demonstrate for peace, but peacefully, arguing that flowers, bells, and chants would overcome jeers and oppression. In 1967 he organized the first "Gathering of the Tribes for a Human Be-In" in San Francisco. It was the first of hundreds of counterculture festivals.

As a poet, Ginsberg wrote about his political and social concerns, attacking what he described as the evil forces in society. His 1973 work, *The Fall of America, 1965–1971*, identified those evils as the war in Vietnam, nuclear energy, threats to the environment, and America's rampant materialism. It won a National Book Award. Allen Ginsberg died in 1997. According to one literary critic, beginning with *Howl* Ginsberg had changed what poetry could accomplish, how it could speak and articulate—he single-handedly gave poetry a new, powerful political and cultural impact. His was a literary Horatio Alger story about a "dirty" Beat poet—a hipster predicted to self-destruct—who became one of the country's best and best-known modern poets, "the biographer of his time," and even a professor of English at Brooklyn College.

INTRODUCTION

In his lifestyle and writings, Allen Ginsberg scoffed at the consensus of the 1950s and asked Americans and people everywhere to save themselves and the nation by rejecting conventionality and discovering their true talents and spirits. As a member of the "Beat Generation," his views were not well accepted by the majority of Americans. At the Republican convention in 1960, FBI director J. Edgar Hoover branded the "beatniks" as one of the major threats to the nation. Hoover and many others advocated a consensus around a new patriotism that arose from a growing fear generated by the Cold War. It praised conformity and tradition and feared the eccentric and assertive. It idolized the American family and its home and rejected those whose values were different.

In 1952 Republicans claimed that they best represented American values and the new patriotism. A victory by Dwight David Eisenhower would end twenty years of Democratic control of the White House and reverse two "dangerous" trends: creeping socialism in the form of New Deal–style programs and appeasement of communism in the guise of containment. Eisenhower and a Republican Congress wanted to reduce government intervention in social and economic affairs, expand prosperity by supporting capitalism, conclude the war in Korea, and win victories in the Cold War. But most of all, Americans expected the government to foster and protect the values of America and allow them to live their lives to the fullest, in the strongest, most democratic, and most prosperous nation in the world.

The United States of the 1950s was experiencing one of the longest periods of sustained economic growth in its history, one that in most people's opinion offered every citizen an opportunity to live free from the fear of economic want. This portrait of an affluent America meshed with the image of a gentle, quiet president who presided over a prosperous, stable nation.

Yet for Eisenhower and many other Americans, defining the consensus was not all that simple. Eisenhower himself was an example. Like the decade, President Eisenhower was more complex than commonly realized at the time. On the surface "Ike" seemed to live up to the popular joke: "What happens when you wind up an Eisenhower doll? Absolutely nothing!" But the real Eisenhower was an effective behind-the-scenes leader who recognized that a political and social consensus accepted the structure of government as shaped by the New Deal. Faced with this constraint on dismantling New Deal–style programs, he chose to modify some by cutting spending and to rein in government controls where possible, but he also increased social security and the minimum wage and initiated a massive highway building project and federal aid to public education. Rather than roll back the principles of the New Deal, Eisenhower's inability to change served only to confirm and strengthen them.

In foreign policy, Eisenhower made similar choices. He decided to maintain the basic strategy of containment, placing new areas of the globe under an American nuclear umbrella. Desiring at the same time to balance the budget, he adopted the New Look, stressing use of atomic weapons, the air force, alliances, and covert activities as foreign policy tools. Thus, responding to political and international constraints established by the Great Depression, World War II, and the Truman years, Eisenhower shaped a modified—not a re-invented—foreign policy.

While Eisenhower sought to establish a political and international consensus, a large segment of the population thought that they lived in the best of times. Social and economic trends begun after the war continued. Unemployment was low, wages and spending were reaching new highs, and it seemed to many that all Americans, even those not living in the suburbs, had the chance to live prosperous, happy, stable, and fulfilling lives. The focus of that fulfilling life centered on the suburban nuclear family, Dad at work, Mom at home.

Yet, that image of consensus was only partially valid. Many men and women were dissatisfied with their roles as husband and father, wife and mother. Dissatisfaction also struck many American youths, who rejected en masse the values of suburban culture, turning to the driving rhythms of rock 'n' roll and displaying antisocial behavior. At the same time, intellectual and cultural critics condemned the sameness and staleness of the suburban culture. The outcome was an American society fragmented by social realities that fed into, or starved, differing expectations.

Nor did prosperity touch all Americans. For minorities in 1950, the obstacles blocking their access to the American dream appeared insurmountable. Poverty, prejudice, and segregation remained the norm. Nevertheless, some groups nurtured expectations of change that would open new choices. By mid-decade, African Americans were tearing down barriers that excluded and isolated them. The outcome was a civil rights movement that attacked existing social and legal restrictions and forced government, political parties, and society to confront long-standing contradictions in the country's democratic image.

POLITICS OF CONSENSUS

• What were the popular images of Eisenhower, and how did they compare with reality?

• What were the goals of conservatives and Eisenhower as they sought to roll back the programs of the New Deal?

• What programs were successful under Eisenhower's "Dynamic Conservatism"?

chronology

The Fifties

1948 Alfred Kinsey's *Sexual Behavior in the Human Male*

1950 Korean War begins
David Riesman's *The Lonely Crowd*

1951 J. D. Salinger's *Catcher in the Rye*
Mattachine Society formed
Alan Freed's "Moondog's Rock 'n' Roll Party"

1952 Dwight David Eisenhower elected president
Eisenhower visits Korea
United States tests hydrogen bomb

1953 Korean armistice at Panmunjom
Mohammed Mossadegh overthrown in Iran
Joseph Stalin dies
Senator McCarthy investigates USIA
Kinsey's *Sexual Behavior in the Human Female*
Termination policy for American Indians implemented
Earl Warren appointed chief justice of Supreme Court
Father Knows Best debuts on television
Playboy begins publication

1954 *Brown v. Board of Education*
St. Lawrence Seaway Act
Federal budget balanced
Army-McCarthy hearings
Jacobo Arbenz overthrown in Guatemala
Gamal Nasser assumes power in Egypt
Battle of Dienbienphu
Geneva Agreement (Vietnam)
SEATO founded

1955 Montgomery bus boycott
Salk vaccine approved for use
AFL-CIO merger
Warsaw Pact formed
McDonald's opens in California
Baghdad Pact formed
Geneva Summit
Eisenhower's Open Skies proposal

1956 Federal Highway Act
Gayle et al. v. Browser
Southern Christian Leadership Conference formed
Eisenhower reelected
Suez crisis
Soviets invade Hungary
Allen Ginsberg's *Howl*
Grace Metalious's *Peyton Place*
Elvis Presley records "Heartbreak Hotel"

1957 Little Rock crisis
Civil Rights Act
Eisenhower Doctrine
United States joins Baghdad Pact
Soviets launch *Sputnik I*
Jack Kerouac's *On the Road*
Nevil Shute's *On the Beach*
Baby boom peaks at 4.3 million births

1958 Anti-U.S. demonstrations in Latin America
Berlin crisis
United States sends troops to Lebanon
National Defense Education Act
NASA established
Nuclear test moratorium

1959 Fidel Castro takes control in Cuba
CENTO formed
Alaska and Hawai`i become states
Nikita Khrushchev visits the United States
Cooper v. Aaron

1960 Soviets shoot down U-2 and capture pilot
Paris Summit

It was "time for a change," cried Republicans in 1952. Stigmatized by the lingering war in Korea and the soft-on-communism label, plus recent revelations of government corruption, the Democrats' twenty-year hold on the White House would finally be ended. Initially, the leading Republican candidate for the presidency was Senator Robert Taft, an ardent opponent of Roosevelt and the New Deal and a pre-war isolationist. Many moderate Republicans, though, feared that Taft was too conservative and would resume a more isolationist policy. They sought an alternative and found one in General Dwight David Eisenhower. While politically inexperienced, "Ike" appeared to be the perfect candidate. He was well known, revered as a war hero, and carried the image of an honest man thrust into public service. Skillfully gaining the nomination at the Republican convention, Eisenhower chose Richard M. Nixon of California as his vice-presidential running mate. Nixon was young and had risen rapidly in the party because of his outspoken anticommunism and his aggressive role in the investigation of Alger Hiss. Democrats nominated a liberal New Dealer, Illinois governor **Adlai E. Stevenson**. He not only carried political handicaps of being a liberal and "losing" the Cold War, but he also had been recently divorced.

Eisenhower Takes Command

The Republican campaign took two paths. One concentrated on the popular image of Eisenhower. Republicans introduced "spot commercials" on television and used them to stress Ike's honesty, integrity, and "American-ness." In public Eisenhower crusaded for high standards and good government and posed as another George Washington. A war-weary nation applauded his promise to go to Korea "in the cause of peace." McCarthy, Nixon, and others who brutally attacked the Democrats' Cold War and New Deal records took the second campaign path. They blasted the Democrats as representing "plunder at home and blunder abroad." Proudly they boasted of "no Communists in the Republican Party." Nixon and others called the containment policy cowardly and promised to roll back communism. They also vowed to end the liberal spending of the Democrats and dismantle the New Deal.

The campaign's only tense moment came with an allegation that Nixon had accepted gifts from and used a secret cash fund provided by California business friends. To counter the accusations and keep Eisenhower from dropping him from the ticket, Nixon explained his side of the story on television. In the "Checkers speech," a teary-eyed Nixon denied the fund existed and that the only gift his family had ever received was a puppy, Checkers. His daughter loved the puppy, Nixon stated, and he would not make her give it back, no matter what it did to his career. It was an overly sentimental speech, but the public and

In this picture, the triumphant Republican nominees for the White House pose with smiles and wives—Pat Nixon and Mamie Eisenhower. Seen as a statesman and not a politician during the campaign, Eisenhower worked hard to ensure his nomination over Robert Taft, and then chose Richard Nixon to balance the ticket because he was a younger man, a westerner, and a conservative. *UPI Bettmann Archives.*

Eisenhower rallied behind Nixon and they easily won the election. Eisenhower buried Stevenson in popular (55 percent) and electoral (442 to 89) votes (see Map 27.1). Ike's broad political coattails also swept a Republican majority into Congress. Four years later, the 1956 presidential election was a repeat of 1952, with Eisenhower receiving 457 electoral votes and again swamping Stevenson. But in 1956, the Republican victory was Eisenhower's alone, as Democrats maintained the majorities in both houses of Congress they had won in the 1954 midterm races.

During both of his administrations, to the public Eisenhower was Ike, a warm, friendly, slightly bumbling grandfather figure who projected middle-class values and habits. Critics complained that he seemed almost an absentee president, often leaving the government in the hands of Congress and his cabinet while he played golf or bridge. But to those

Adlai E. Stevenson Illinois governor who became the Democratic candidate for president in 1952 and 1956 and lost both times to Eisenhower.

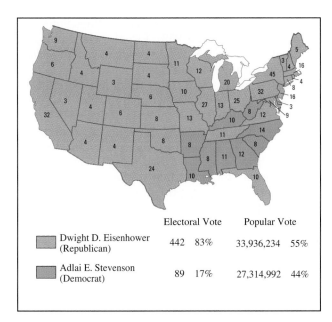

	Electoral Vote		Popular Vote	
Dwight D. Eisenhower (Republican)	442	83%	33,936,234	55%
Adlai E. Stevenson (Democrat)	89	17%	27,314,992	44%

MAP 27.1 Election of 1952 Dwight David Eisenhower and the Republicans swept into office in 1952. Leading the ticket, Eisenhower swamped his Democratic opponent Adlai Stevenson with 83 percent of the electoral vote and 55 percent of the popular vote. Republicans also won majorities in both houses of Congress. In the 1956 presidential election, Eisenhower beat Stevenson by even larger margins, but Democrats regained majority status in Congress.

who knew him and worked with him, he was far from bumbling or an absentee president. In military fashion, Eisenhower relied on his staff to provide a full discussion of any issue. We had a "good growl," he would say after especially heated cabinet talks, but he made the final decisions, and he expected them to be carried out.

Dynamic Conservatism

Eisenhower called himself a modern Republican and wanted to follow a "middle course" that was "conservative when it comes to money and liberal when it comes to human beings." He believed that government should be run efficiently, like a successful business, and he staffed the majority of his cabinet with businessmen, most of whom were millionaires. Among the president's key priorities was to reduce spending and the presence of the federal government. Federal controls over business and the economy would be limited and the authority of the states increased. Yet, like Truman's attempts to

expand the New Deal, Eisenhower's plan to rein in government met with only partial success.

Seeking to balance the budget, Eisenhower used a "meat axe" on Truman's projected budgets. He dismissed 200,000 workers from the government's payroll, cut domestic spending by 10 percent, and slashed the military budget. He succeeded in balancing the budget in 1954 and considered that and the balanced budget of 1960 among his greatest White House achievements.

Balancing the budget gave Eisenhower the means to reverse the "creeping socialism" of the New Deal and to return power and control to local and state governance. Among those areas he sought to remove from federal authority were energy, agriculture, and federal trusteeship for Indian reservations. Advocating private ownership and control, Congress approved—over Democratic opposition—private ownership of nuclear power plants and reduced federal controls. Congress also supported the return of much of the nation's offshore oil sources to state authority. Citing costs and expanding opportunities for Native Americans, Congress passed a resolution establishing a termination policy, which began the elimination of federal economic support to tribes and the liquidation of selected reservations. Before the policy was reversed in the 1960s, sixty-one tribes were involved, with some losing valuable lands and resources. The Klamath tribe in Oregon sold much of their ponderosa pine lands to lumber companies. For many individuals in the affected tribes, the economic gains from such sales proved short-lived, and by the end of the decade conditions for Native Americans worsened. By 1960 nearly half of all American Indians had abandoned their reservations.

But Eisenhower's efforts and desires to roll back the New Deal were limited. Initially hopeful of removing the New Deal legacy of farm subsidies, Eisenhower was forced to accept only minor modifications and watch the cost of subsidies increase. Other programs he regarded as too popular to attack. He told his brother that any political party that tried to "abolish social security and eliminate labor laws" would never be heard from again. The Democrats' return to power in Congress in 1954 also added to the president's willingness to accept and even expand such programs. Not wanting to preside over the demise of the Republican Party, Eisenhower accepted the addition of 10 million Americans to Social Security rolls and a raise in the minimum wage from 75 cents to $1 an hour. He also oversaw increased spending for urban housing and slum clearance and liberalized rules for FHA loans.

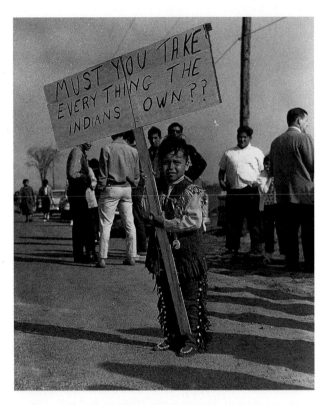

One of Eisenhower's goals was to reduce federal spending and controls. In line with this policy, he tried to turn Indian affairs over to the states and liquidate federal services and reservations. Between 1954 and 1960, sixty-one tribes were affected. This picture shows a 4-year-old Tuscarora boy protesting state and federal policies that attacked Indian rights. *Wide World.*

Recognizing the government's role in public policy, Eisenhower created the Department of Health, Education, and Welfare—directed by Oveta Culp Hobby, who had commanded the WACs during World War II. Rather than undo the New Deal, Eisenhower's action proved that the legacy of federal intervention had become part of the national consensus.

Although he sought a balanced budget, Eisenhower also committed the nation to significant spending, usually explained as economic and security needs. He signed into law the St. Lawrence Seaway Act (1954), which committed U.S. support for building an inland waterway to connect the Great Lakes with the Atlantic. He justified this act on the grounds that the seaway would benefit the nation by increasing trade. He approved the **Federal Highway Act** (1956) to meet the needs of an automobile-driven nation and to provide the military with a usable nationwide transportation network. After the

Soviet Union launched the space satellites *Sputnik I* (1957) and *Sputnik II* (1957), Eisenhower pointed to national security needs as grounds for increased federal spending on education.

The successful orbiting of the Soviet satellites—*Sputnik II* actually carried a dog into space—created a multilevel panic across the United States. Not only did the nation seem vulnerable to Soviet missiles, but also *Sputnik* seemed to underscore basic weaknesses in the American educational system. American schools, many critics argued, stressed soft subjects and social adjustment rather than hard subjects: science, languages, and mathematics. *Sputnik* spurred Eisenhower and Congress to pass the National Defense Education Act of 1958 to approve grants to schools developing strong programs in those areas. The act also provided $295 million in **National Defense Student Loans** for college students. Congress's creation in 1958 of the National Aeronautics and Space Administration (NASA) immediately made manned flight its major priority, unveiling Project Mercury with the goal of lifting an astronaut into space.

The Problem with McCarthy

While Eisenhower accepted much of the New Deal, he also sought to diminish the impact of Joseph McCarthy, whom he personally disliked and whose activities, now that the election was over, he deplored. With Ike in the White House and Republicans controlling Congress, many Republicans, including Eisenhower, hoped that McCarthy would quietly disappear. But the senator from Wisconsin enjoyed the spotlight, relished his power, and had no intention of fading from view. He continued his search for subversives within the government and even criticized the administration for not conducting an

---

Federal Highway Act Law passed by Congress in 1956, appropriating $32 billion for the construction of interstate highways.

Sputnik I The first artificial satellite launched into space, it weighed 184 pounds; this feat by the Soviet Union in October 1957 marked the beginning of the space race. A month later, the larger *Sputnik II* was launched, weighing 1,120 pounds and carrying a dog named Laika.

National Defense Student Loans Loans established by the U.S. government in 1958 to encourage the teaching and study of science and modern foreign languages.

At the heart of the Red Scare was Senator Joseph McCarthy. Using inquisition-style tactics to destroy opponents and bolster his own power, McCarthy became one of the most powerful politicians in the nation by 1952. In his televised efforts to discredit the United States Army, McCarthy lost the public's approval, which hastened his censorship by Congress in 1954 and his ultimate fall from power. ©1954/Time Inc.

aggressive foreign policy against communism. In particular, McCarthy took aim at the State Department and the **United States Information Agency** (USIA). Those government workers considered security risks were discharged or pressured to resign. The USIA cleaned its library shelves of questionable titles, including classics by Mark Twain.

But when McCarthy, furious at the army for drafting his aide David Schine, threatened to "expose" army favoritism toward known Communists, anti-McCarthy forces in Congress, quietly supported by Eisenhower, concluded that the time had come to silence the senator. Charging that he was trying to blackmail the U.S. Army, the Senate

investigated McCarthy. The American Broadcasting Company's telecast of the 1954 **Army-McCarthy hearings** allowed more than 20 million viewers to see McCarthy's ruthless bullying firsthand. Public and congressional opposition to the senator rose, and when the army's lawyer, Joseph Welch, asked the brooding McCarthy, "Have you no sense of decency?" the nation burst into applause. Several months later, with Republicans evenly divided, the Senate voted 67 to 22 to censure McCarthy's "unbecoming conduct." Drinking heavily, shunned by his colleagues, and ignored by the media, McCarthy died in 1957. But for years McCarthyism, refined and tempered, remained a potent political weapon against liberal opponents.

EISENHOWER AND A HOSTILE WORLD

• What considerations contributed to the New Look?

• What were the weaknesses of "massive retaliation," and how did Eisenhower address them?

• What tactics did the Eisenhower administration pursue in the Middle East and Latin America to protect American interests?

During the 1952 campaign, part of Eisenhower's popularity reflected the widely held view that he and the Republicans would conduct a more forceful foreign policy. Truman's containment was denounced and Republican spokesmen promised the rollback of communism and the liberation of peoples under Communist control. In a very popular move, Eisenhower promised—if elected—to go to Korea, "in the cause of peace." He went—for three days. Many expected him to find a means to win the conflict, but after visiting the front lines, he was convinced that a negotiated peace was the only solution. The problem was how to persuade the North Koreans and Chinese that such a settlement would be in their best interests. Eisenhower came to the presidency well qualified to lead American

United States Information Agency   Agency established by Congress in 1953 to distribute information about U.S. culture and political policies and gain support for American international goals.

Army-McCarthy hearings   Congressional investigation of Senator Joseph McCarthy televised in 1954; the hearings revealed McCarthy's villainous nature and ended his popularity.

foreign policy. His years in the military and as commander of NATO had made him not only an internationalist but also a realist, wary of too assertive and simplistic solutions to international problems. Despite the campaign rhetoric of liberation and roll-back, Eisenhower embraced the principle of containment and sought to modify it to match what he believed to be the nation's capabilities and needs. His new policy was called the **New Look**.

The New Look

The linchpin of the New Look was nuclear deterrence—an enhanced arsenal of nuclear weapons and delivery systems, and the threat of **massive retaliation** to protect American international interests. In explaining the shift to more atomic weapons, Vice President Nixon stated, "Rather than let the communists nibble us to death all over the world in little wars, we will rely . . . on massive mobile retaliation." Secretary of Defense Charles E. Wilson, noting that the nuclear strategy was cheaper than conventional forces, quipped that the policy ensured "more bang for the buck." Demonstrating the country's nuclear might, the United States exploded its first hydrogen bomb in November 1952 (the Soviets tested theirs in August 1953).

The New Look was sold to the public as more positive than Truman's defensive containment policy, but insiders recognized that it had several flaws. The central problem was where the United States should draw the massive-retaliation line: What if the enemy calls our bluff? "How do you convince the American people and the U.S. Congress to declare war?" asked one planner. The answer was to make the bluff so convincing that it would never be called. Potential aggressors had to be convinced that the United States would strike back, raining nuclear destruction not only on the attackers but also on the Soviets and Chinese, who obviously would be directing any aggression. This policy was called **brinksmanship** because it required the administration to be willing to take the nation to the brink of war, trusting that the opposition would back down. Thus Secretary of State **John Foster Dulles** and Eisenhower indulged in dramatic speeches explaining that nuclear weapons were as usable as conventional ones. It was necessary "to remove the taboo" from using nuclear weapons, Dulles informed the press.

To prod the North Koreans and Chinese to sign a Korean truce agreement, Eisenhower used the aggressive images of liberation and through public and private channels suggested that the United States might use atomic weapons. By July 1953, it seemed the strategy had worked. A truce signed at Panmunjom ended the fighting, brought home almost all the troops, but left Korea divided by a **demilitarized zone**. It seemed to many that the nuclear threat, "atomic diplomacy," had worked. In reality Stalin's death and the resolution of the prisoner of war issue were the deciding factors. Even so, Americans praised Eisenhower's new approach.

To strengthen the rationale for "going nuclear" and make the possibility of World War III less frightening, the administration introduced efforts related to surviving a nuclear war. Public and private underground **fallout shelters**—well stocked with food, water, and medical supplies—could, it was claimed, provide safety against an attack. A 32-inch-thick slab of concrete, *U.S. News and World Report* reported, could protect people from an atomic blast "as close as 1,000 feet away." Across the nation, civil defense drills were established for factories, offices, and businesses. "Duck-and-cover" drills were held in schools: when their teachers shouted, "Drop!" students immediately got into a kneeling or prone position, and placed their hands behind their necks.

While educators and government agencies worked to convince people that they could survive a nuclear war, movies and novels showed the horror of nuclear

---

New Look   National security policy under Eisenhower that called for reductions in the size of the army, development of tactical nuclear weapons, and the buildup of strategic air power employing nuclear weapons.

massive retaliation   Term that John Foster Dulles used in a 1954 speech implying that the United States was willing to use nuclear force in response to Communist aggression anywhere.

brinksmanship   Practice of seeking to win disputes in international politics by creating the impression of being willing to push a highly dangerous situation to the limit.

John Foster Dulles   Secretary of state under Eisenhower; he used the threat of nuclear war to deter Soviet aggression.

demilitarized zone   An area from which military forces, operations, and installations are prohibited.

fallout shelter   Underground shelter stocked with food and supplies that was intended to provide safety in case of atomic attack; *fallout* refers to the irradiated particles falling through the atmosphere after a nuclear attack.

As the Cold War intensified and the Soviets became a nuclear power, the government began to consider methods to survive a nuclear war. One "solution" was to encourage people to build backyard bomb shelters. Pictured here is one family's atomic bomb shelter that slept six. The cost was $1,250 in 1951. *Corbis-Bettmann.*

death and destruction. Nevil Shute realistically portrayed the extinction of humankind in his novel *On the Beach* (1957). In *Them!* (1954) and dozens of other B movies, giant ants and other hideous creatures mutated by atomic fallout threatened the world.

Despite the massive retaliation talk, Eisenhower recognized the limits of American power—areas under Communist control could not be liberated, and a thermonuclear war would yield no winners. Consequently, the administration sought ways to avoid a nuclear solution to international problems. Alliances and **covert operations** seemed logical alternatives. Alliances would identify areas protected by the American nuclear umbrella, and they would protect the United States from being drawn into limited,

"brushfire" wars. When small conflicts erupted, the ground forces of regional allies, perhaps supported with American naval and air strength, would snuff them out.

Mindful of existing tensions in Asia, Eisenhower concluded **bilateral** defense pacts with South Korea (1953) and Taiwan (1955) and a **multilateral** agreement, the Southeast Asia Treaty Organization (SEATO, 1954), that linked the United States, Australia, Thailand, the Philippines, Pakistan, New Zealand, France, and Britain. In the Middle East, the United States officially joined Britain, Iran, Pakistan, Turkey, and Iraq in the **Baghdad Pact** in 1957, later called the Central Treaty Organization (CENTO) after Iraq withdrew in 1959. In Europe, the United States helped to rearm West Germany and welcomed it into NATO. The Soviet bloc responded to that last move with the formation of a military alliance between Eastern European nations and the Soviet Union, the Warsaw Pact, in 1955. In all, the Eisenhower administration signed forty-three pacts to help defend regions or individual countries from Communist aggression (see Map 27.2).

Brinksmanship was also of little use in dealing with Soviet and Chinese efforts to enlist the support of emerging nations. Throughout the 1950s, the European colonial empires were disintegrating in the face of nationalism and decolonization. In 1953 the Soviets stopped their denunciation of non-Communist nations and announced their willingness to help nonaligned nations. Trade and economic agreements followed as Moscow improved relations with nations such as India, Egypt, Guinea, and Guatemala. No longer could the United States ignore developing parts of the world or rely on its European allies to provide stability. As Dulles explained: "In the old days we used to be able to let South America go through the wringer of bad times . . . but the trouble is, now, when you put it through the wringer, it comes out red." To prevent every state experiencing social change from "coming out red," Eisenhower relied on economic and political pressures and on

covert operation   A program or event carried out not openly but in secret.

bilateral   Involving two parties.

multilateral   Involving more than two parties.

Baghdad Pact   A regional defensive alliance signed between Turkey and Iraq in 1955; Great Britain, Pakistan, and Iran soon joined; the United States supported the pact but did not officially join until mid-1957.

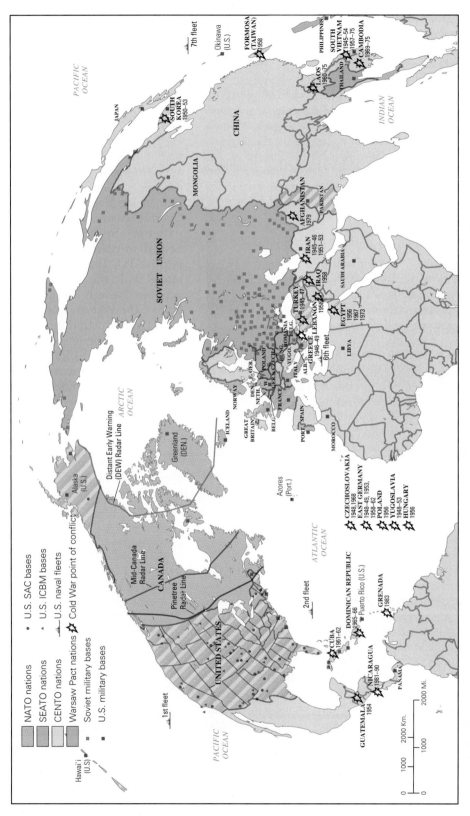

MAP 27.2 The Global Cold War During the Cold War, the United States and the Soviet Union faced each other as enemies. The United States attempted to construct a ring of containment around the Soviet Union and its allies, while the Soviets worked to expand their influence and power. This map shows the nature of this military confrontation—the bases, alliances, and flash points of the Cold War.

the **Central Intelligence Agency** (CIA). It seemed a never-ending task. "While we are busy rescuing Guatemala or assisting Korea and Indochina," Eisenhower observed, the Communists "make great inroads in Burma, Afghanistan, and Egypt."

Turmoil in the Middle East

In the Middle East, Arab nationalism, fired by anti-Israel and anti-Western attitudes, posed a serious threat to American interests. Iran and Egypt offered the greatest challenges. In Iran, Prime Minister Mohammed Mossadegh had nationalized British-owned oil properties and seemed likely to sell oil to the Soviets. Eisenhower considered him to be "neurotic and periodically unstable" and, along with the British, favored forcing him from power. Eisenhower gave the CIA the green light to overthrow the Iranian leader and replace him with a pro-Western government. On August 18, 1953, a mass demonstration funded and orchestrated by the CIA toppled the Mossadegh government. Quickly, millions in American money flowed into Iran to support the new regime. A thankful Iranian government, headed by **Shah Mohammed Reza Pahlevi**, awarded the United States 40 percent of Iranian oil production.

Like Mohammed Mossadegh, Egyptian leader Gamal Nasser, an army colonel who assumed power in 1954, was attempting to develop his nation's economic resources independent of European controls and influence. At first the United States supported Nasser, hoping to woo him with loans, cash, arms, and an offer to help build the Aswan Dam on the Nile. Eventually Nasser rejected the American offers, in large part because Americans pushed an Egyptian-Israeli peace and closer ties with Britain. Nasser then looked to the Soviet Union for support. When he bought Soviet-bloc weapons, Eisenhower concluded that he was an "evil influence" in the region and canceled the Aswan Dam project (July 1956). Days later, claiming the need to finance the dam, Nasser nationalized the Anglo-French–owned Suez Canal, through which the majority of European-bound oil passed. Some within the administration suggested that Nasser be assassinated, but Eisenhower rejected that option. Egypt had, he explained, no suitable replacement.

Israel, France, and Britain, however, responded with military action to regain control of the canal. On October 29, Israeli forces sliced through the Sinai Desert toward Egypt. Over the next week, French and British forces bombed Egyptian targets and seized the canal zone. Eisenhower was furious. He

disliked Nasser but could not approve of armed aggression. Joined by the Soviets, Eisenhower sponsored a UN General Assembly resolution (November 2, 1956) calling for an end to the fighting, the removal of foreign troops from Egyptian soil, and the assignment of a United Nations peacekeeping force there. Faced with worldwide opposition and intense pressure from the United States—including a threat to withhold oil shipments—France, Britain, and Israel withdrew their forces. Nasser regained control of the canal and, as Eisenhower had feared, emerged as the uncontested leader of those opposing Western influence in Arab countries.

Nasser's prestige and the growth of Soviet influence in the Middle East forced the Eisenhower administration to affirm American interests in the region and to support a regional anti-Soviet alliance with the northern tier of Middle Eastern states: the Baghdad Pact/CENTO. Eisenhower also redoubled his effort to contain Nasser's **pan-Arab movement** and an expanding Soviet presence. To protect Arab friends from Communist-nationalist revolutions, Eisenhower asked Congress for permission to commit American forces, if requested, to resist "armed attack from any country controlled by internationalism" (by *internationalism* Eisenhower meant the forces of communism). Congress agreed in March 1957, establishing the so-called **Eisenhower Doctrine** and providing $200 million in military and economic aid to improve military defenses in the nations of the Middle East.

It did not take long for Eisenhower to use his powers. When an internal revolt threatened Jordan's King Hussein in 1957, the White House announced Jordan was "vital" to American interests, moved

---

Central Intelligence Agency   Agency established by Congress in 1947 to gather data and organize intelligence operations in foreign countries; it has also conducted more active covert operations in some countries, including fomenting rebellions and assassinations.

Shah Mohammed Reza Pahlevi   Iranian ruler who received the hereditary title *shah* from his father in 1941 and with CIA support helped to oust the militant nationalist Mohammed Mossadegh in 1953.

pan-Arab movement   Attempts to politically unify the Arab nations of the Middle East; its followers advocated freedom from Western control and opposition to Israel.

Eisenhower Doctrine   Policy formulated by Eisenhower of providing military and economic aid to Arab nations in the Middle East to help defeat Communist-nationalistic rebellions.

Implementing the Eisenhower Doctrine, American forces landed troops in Lebanon in July 1958. The intervention and withdrawal was without incident, but not before some soldiers enjoyed the warm waters of the Mediterranean. American forces in Beirut in 1983 were not so lucky. *Paul Schutzer/Timepix.*

the U.S. 6th Fleet into the eastern Mediterranean, and supplied more than $10 million in aid. King Hussein put down the revolt, dismissed parliament and all political parties, and instituted authoritarian rule. In 1958, when Lebanon's Christian president Camile Chamoun ignored his country's constitution and ran for a second term, opposition leaders—including Muslim nationalistic, anti-West elements—rebelled. Chamoun requested American intervention, and Eisenhower committed nearly fifteen thousand troops to protect the pro-American government.

The U.S. Army arrived at the Beirut airport amid hordes of tourists, while U.S. Marines waded ashore in full battle gear as beachgoers watched from the sand. The American forces left in three months—after Chamoun had stepped down and, with American approval, been replaced by General Fuad Chehab. Eisenhower had demonstrated his willingness to protect American interests but had done little to resolve the problems that plagued Lebanon and the rest of the Middle East.

A Protective Neighbor

During the 1952 presidential campaign, Eisenhower charged Truman with following a "Poor Neighbor policy" toward Latin America, allowing the development of economic problems and popular uprisings that had been "skillfully exploited by the Communists." He was most concerned about Guatemala, disapproving of the reformist president, Jacobo Arbenz, who had instituted agrarian reforms by nationalizing thousands of acres of land, much of it owned by the American-based United Fruit Company. These radical actions convinced the administration to use the CIA to remove Arbenz. The CIA organized and supplied a rebel army in Honduras, led by Guatemalan Colonel Carlos Castillo Armas. Colonel Armas launched the effort to "liberate" Guatemala on June 18, 1954, and within two weeks a new, pro-American government was installed in Guatemala City. On July 8, 1954, a military **junta** named Colonel Armas president. Eisenhower had created a pro-American government in Guatemala but had failed to reduce social and economic inequalities, blunt the cry for revolution, or foster good will toward the United States among Latin Americans. When Vice President Nixon toured Latin America in 1958, demonstrators in Lima, Peru, stoned his car, and an angry mob in Caracas, Venezuela, almost overturned it. Nixon called the demonstrators "Communist thugs." And while Nixon toured Latin America, Fulgencio Batista, who had controlled Cuba through the 1940s and 1950s, was beset by a rebellion led by **Fidel Castro**.

junta   Group of military officers ruling a country after seizing power.

Fidel Castro   Cuban revolutionary leader who overthrew the corrupt regime of dictator Fulgencio Batista in 1959 and established a communist state.

For nearly four decades, Fidel Castro has plagued American presidents and policymakers. Gaining power in a popular revolution against the dictator Batista in 1959, Castro quickly moved Cuba into the Soviet bloc. Eisenhower sought to use a CIA-trained army to overthrow Castro, but left office before the plan could be executed. Kennedy implemented the plan, but it failed miserably. *Andrew St. George/Magnum Photos.*

The corrupt and dictatorial Batista had become an embarrassment to the United States, and many Americans believed that Castro could be a pro-American reformist leader. By 1959, rebel forces had control of the island, but by midyear many of Castro's economic and social reforms were endangering American investments and interests. American interests dominated Cuba's economy, controlling 40 percent of Cuba's sugar industry, 90 percent of Cuba's telephone and electric companies, 50 percent of its railroads, and 25 percent of its banking. In addition, 70 percent of Cuba's imports came from the United States. Concerned about Castro's political leanings, Washington tried to push Cuba in the right direction by applying economic pressure. In February 1960, Castro reacted to the American arm-twisting by signing an economic pact with the Soviet Union. Eisenhower seethed: Castro was a "madman . . . going wild and harming the whole American struc-

ture." In March Eisenhower approved a CIA plan to prepare an attack against Castro. Actual implementation of the plot to overthrow the Cuban leader, however, was left to Eisenhower's successor.

The New Look in Asia

When Eisenhower took office, Asia was the focal point of Cold War tensions. Fighting continued in Korea, and in Indochina the Communist **Viet Minh** directed by Ho Chi Minh was fighting a "war of national liberation" against the French. Truman had supported France, and Eisenhower saw no reason to alter American policy. By 1954, the United States had dispatched more than three hundred advisers to Vietnam, was paying nearly 78 percent of war's cost, and was watching the French military position worsen. A believer in the **domino theory**, Eisenhower warned that if Indochina fell to communism, the loss "of Burma, of Thailand, of the [Malay] Peninsula, and Indonesia" would certainly follow, endangering Australia and New Zealand.

In Vietnam, the Viet Minh forces led by General Vo Nguyen Giap encircled the French fortress at Dienbienphu and launched murderous attacks on the beleaguered garrison. Asserting, "My God, we must not lose Asia," Eisenhower transferred forty bombers and detailed two hundred air force mechanics to bolster the French in Vietnam. The French—and some members of the Eisenhower administration—wanted a more direct American role, but Eisenhower believed that "no military victory is possible in that kind of theater" and rejected such options. After a fifty-five-day siege, Dienbienphu fell on May 7, 1954, and Eisenhower was left no option but to try to salvage a partial victory at an international conference in Geneva.

But the West could piece together no victory at Geneva either. The **Geneva Agreement** "temporarily" partitioned Vietnam along the 17th parallel and created the neutral states of Cambodia and Laos.

Viet Minh Vietnamese army made up of Communist and other nationalist groups, which fought from 1946 to 1954 for independence from French rule.

domino theory The idea that if one nation came under Communist control, then neighboring nations would also fall to the Communists.

Geneva Agreement Truce signed at Geneva in 1954 by French and Viet Minh representatives, dividing Vietnam along the 17th parallel into the Communist North and the anti-Communist South.

Within two years, the two Vietnams were to hold elections to unify the nation, and neither was to enter into military alliances or allow foreign bases on its territory. American strategists called the settlement a "disaster"—half of Vietnam was lost to communism. Showing its displeasure, the United States refused to sign the agreement. Eisenhower rushed advisers and aid to the government of South Vietnam's prime minister, Ngo Dinh Diem, to ensure an anti-Communist South Vietnam. With American blessings, Diem ignored the Geneva-mandated unification elections, quashed his political opposition, and in October 1955 staged a **plebiscite** that created the Republic of Vietnam and elected him president. As will be seen in Chapters 30 and 31, the predicament of Vietnam was just beginning.

The Soviets and Cold War Politics

Eisenhower feared and opposed the spread of Communist influence. At the same time, he realized that improving American-Soviet relations would reduce the expanding arms race and limit points of conflict throughout the world. Both Eisenhower and Dulles, however, questioned the Soviets' commitment to peace and their willingness to keep agreements, and both knew that adversaries in the U.S. military and Congress and among the American public would condemn any softening of U.S. policy toward the Soviets. Still, growing Soviet nuclear capabilities and the death of Stalin in 1953 provided the need and the opportunity to reduce tensions.

Soon after Stalin's death, the new Soviet leader, Georgii Malenkov, called for "peaceful coexistence." Dulles dismissed the suggestion, but Eisenhower, with an eye on world opinion, called on the Soviets to demonstrate openly a change of policy and their willingness to cooperate with the West. Malenkov complied. He agreed to consider some form of on-site inspection to verify any approved arms reductions. Eisenhower responded by asking the Soviets in December 1953 to join him in the **Atoms for Peace plan** and to work toward universal disarmament.

Both countries by then were testing hydrogen **thermonuclear** bombs hundreds of times more powerful than atomic bombs. And world concern was growing not only about the threat of nuclear war but about the dangers of radiation from the testing. Throughout 1954, worldwide pressure grew for a summit meeting to deal with the "balance of terror." In 1955 Eisenhower agreed to a summit meeting in Geneva with the new Soviet leadership team of Nikolai Bulganin and **Nikita Khrushchev**, who had replaced Malenkov.

In this cartoon, an American suburban family sits contently next to their cozy home with little concern about the delicate Cold War balance between peace and destruction. By 1953, both the United States and the Soviet Union had tested hydrogen bombs and seemed willing to use it to protect national interests. *Granger Collection.*

Eisenhower expected no resolution of the two major issues—disarmament and Berlin—and instead saw the meeting as good public relations. He intended to make a bold disarmament initiative—the Open Skies

plebiscite Special election that allows people to either approve or reject a particular proposal.

Atoms for Peace plan Eisenhower's proposal to the United Nations in 1953 that the United States and other nations cooperate to develop peaceful uses of atomic energy.

thermonuclear Relating to the fusion of atomic nuclei at high temperatures, or to weapons based on fusion, such as the hydrogen bomb (as distinct from weapons based on fission).

Nikita Khrushchev Soviet leader who denounced Stalin in 1956 and improved the Soviet Union's image abroad; he was deposed in 1964 after six years as premier for his failure to improve the country's economy.

Freedom Has a New Sound!

CONVAIR

Promoting its new fighter, the F-102 Delta Dagger, Convair provided this image of the American way of life being protected by its newest jet. Rather than be annoyed by the sonic booms produced by the fighter, Convair asked Americans to hear the noise as "the New Sound of Freedom." *Gaslight Advertising Archives.*

proposal—that would certainly earn broad international support. In a dramatic presentation, highlighted by a sudden thunderstorm that momentarily blacked out the conference room, Eisenhower asked the Soviets to share information about military installations and to permit aerial reconnaissance to verify the information while work began on general disarmament. Bulganin voiced official interest, but Khrushchev, speaking privately, called the proposal a "very transparent espionage device."

Eisenhower recognized that Khrushchev represented the real power in the Soviet Union and that his disapproval meant rejection of the proposal. Thus the Geneva Summit went as expected: the Americans and Soviets agreed to disagree. Nevertheless, Eisenhower was pleased. The Open Skies proposal was popular, and the meeting had generated a "spirit of Geneva" that reduced East-West tensions without appeasing

the Communist foe. Besides, he knew that the United States would soon have in service a new high-altitude jet plane, the U-2, which it was thought could safely fly above Soviet anti-aircraft missiles while taking close-up photographs of Soviet territory. This was Cold War gamesmanship at its best.

The spirit of Geneva quickly vanished when Soviet forces invaded Hungary in November 1956 to put down a nationalistic, anti-Soviet revolt. Many Americans favored supporting the Hungarian freedom fighters, but facing the Suez crisis and seeing no way to send aid to the Hungarians without risking all-out war, the administration could only watch as the Soviets crushed the revolt.

After the Hungary crisis, Soviet-American relations cooled and rivalry intensified. Seeking to gain an advantage while gathering worldwide public support, Eisenhower and Khrushchev jousted with each other over nuclear testing and disarmament. First one and then the other, with little belief in success, offered to end nuclear testing and eliminate nuclear weapons if certain provisions were met. In the spring of 1958, both sides temporarily ended nuclear testing, but when discussion on how to implement and verify a test-ban treaty failed, the race resumed.

The simmering issue of Berlin was also aggravating tensions. In November 1958, the Soviets reported that they would soon sign a treaty with East Germany terminating the West's right to occupy West Berlin and unifying the city under East German control. For Eisenhower this was unthinkable. Supported by the British and French, he declared that the Western Allies would remain in West Berlin, and American and NATO forces made plans for the defense of the city. Faced with unflinching Western determination, Khrushchev noted a permanent delay in the treaty and suggested that he and Eisenhower exchange visits and hold a summit meeting. During Khrushchev's twelve-day tour of the United States in September 1959, the Soviet leader and Eisenhower announced that they would attend a summit in Paris in May and that Eisenhower would later visit the Soviet Union.

Neither event fully materialized. On May 1, 1960, the Soviets shot down an American U-2 spy plane over the Soviet Union and captured its pilot, Major Francis Gary Powers. At first, the United States feebly denied the purpose of the flight, saying the U-2 was a weather plane that had strayed from its Turkish flight plan. Khrushchev then showed pictures of the plane's wreckage and presented Major Powers, clearly proving the American spy mission.

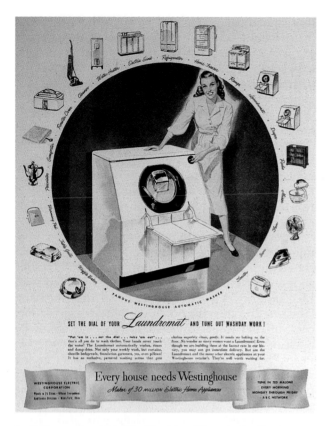

In September 1959, Vice President Nixon in the "kitchen debates" argued with Soviet Premier Nikita Khrushchev about the types of appliances the average working family in America had in their kitchens. This advertisement showing the range of consumer products made by Westinghouse clearly supports Nixon's claim that American families were affluent enough to furnish their homes with a wide range of products. *Picture Research Consultants.*

In Paris, Eisenhower took full responsibility but refused to apologize for such flights, which he contended were necessary to prevent a "nuclear Pearl Harbor." Khrushchev withdrew from the summit, and Eisenhower canceled his trip to the Soviet Union. The Cold War thaw was over.

Eisenhower returned home a hero, having stood up to the Soviets. But public support was temporary. The loss of the U-2, Soviet advances in missile technology and nuclear weaponry, and a Communist Cuba only 90 miles from Florida provided the Democrats with strong reasons to claim that the Republicans and Eisenhower had been deficient in meeting Soviet threats. In 1960, turning the Republicans' tactics of 1952 against them, Democrats cheerfully accused their opponents of endangering the United States by being too soft on communism.

THE BEST OF TIMES

- What factors contributed to prosperity in the 1950s, and what was new about the "new economics"?

- Why did Americans embrace suburban culture? What stresses were at work beneath the placid surface of suburbia?

- Who were some of the critics of suburban culture, and what were their complaints? Why were rock 'n' roll and rebellious teens seen as threats to social norms?

According to the middle-class magazine *Reader's Digest*, in 1954 the average American male stood 5 feet 9 inches tall and weighed 158 pounds. He liked brunettes, baseball, bowling, and steak and french fries. In seeking a wife, he could not decide if brains or beauty was more important, but he definitely wanted a wife who could run a home efficiently. The average female was 5 feet 4 inches tall and weighed 132 pounds. She preferred marriage to career, but she wanted to remove the word *obey* from her marriage vows. Both were enjoying life to the fullest, according to the *Digest*, and buying more of just about everything. The economy appeared to be bursting at the seams, providing jobs, good wages, a multitude of products, and profits. Table 27.1 shows a range of these products and the average prices consumers paid for them in 1955.

The Web of Prosperity

The nation's "easy street" was a product of big government, big business, cheap energy, and an expanding population. World War II and the Cold War had created military-industrial-governmental linkages that primed the economy through government spending. National security needs by 1955 accounted for half of the U.S. budget, equaling about 17 percent of the gross national product, and exceeded more than the total net incomes of all American corporations. The connection between government and business went beyond spending, however. Government officials and corporate managers moved back and forth in a vast network of jobs and directorships. Few saw any real conflict of interest. Frequently, people from the businesses to be regulated staffed cabinet positions and regulatory agencies. Secretary of Defense Wilson, who had been the president of General Motors, voiced the common view: "What was good for our country was good for General Motors and vice versa." It was an era of "new economics," in which, according to a 1952 ad in the *New York Times*, industry's "efforts are not in the selfish interest" but "for the good of many . . . the American way."

table 27.1 Consumer Prices, July 1955

Rye bread	$ .20 a loaf
Apples	.19 for 2 pounds
Bananas	.15 a pound
Round steak	.70 a pound
Chicken fryers	.49 a pound
Wheaties	.43 for two boxes
Clorox	.19 a bottle
Coffee	.91 a pound
Margarine (oleo)	.45 for 2 pounds
Sugar	.49 for 5 pounds
Flour	.95 for 10 pounds
Frozen orange juice	1.00 for 8, 6-ounce cans
Lifebuoy soap	.28 for 3 cakes
Milk	.23 a quart
Kodak Brownie camera	13.65
Portable, B & W 14-inch television set	120.00
Refrigerator	519.95
Oldsmobile 88 automobile	2,381.62
"Scrabble" game	2.39

Source: Data from *Observer-Reporter,* Washington, PA, July 1955.

Direct military spending was only one aspect of government involvement in the economy. Federal research and development (R&D) funds flowed into colleges and industries, producing not only new scientific and military technology but also a variety of marketable consumer goods. Production of plastics had increased during the war and by the mid-1950s, a variety of goods made of plastic had invaded the home. Stressing style, colors, and washability, vinyl floors and Formica countertops became standard features of new kitchens. In 1953 *McCall's* magazine published an entire issue on the wonders of plastic throughout the home. Monsanto, one of the nation's largest plastics producers, constructed and furnished a "home of the future" featuring nearly everything made of plastic in "Tomorrowland," one section of a new theme park named Disneyland. Plastics and another wartime invention called the transistor joined together to make radios smaller and portable.

Technological advances also increased profits and productivity. Profits doubled between 1948 and 1958, with 574 of the largest corporations making nearly 53 percent of all business income. Many small companies, however, could not afford to keep up with technology and **automation**. During the 1950s, more than four thousand mergers took place as large cor-

porations swallowed up less-well-off competitors. By 1960 only 5 percent of American corporations were generating 90 percent of corporate income. Meanwhile, the number of American multinational corporations increased as American firms constructed plants overseas, closer to growing markets, raw materials, and cheaper labor.

Expanding prosperity and productivity and the growth of the service sector characterized the work force. While salaries for industrial workers increased steadily from about $55 a week in 1950 to nearly $80 in 1960, their numbers declined. More and more jobs were created in the public and service sectors, and by 1956 white-collar workers outnumbered blue-collar workers for the first time. Unions responded to these changes and to the accusations made in the late 1940s of being too communistic by altering their goals. Wishing to avoid strikes and confrontation, they focused on negotiating better pensions,

automation A process or system designed so that equipment functions automatically; one outcome of automation is the replacement of workers with machines.

cost-of-living raises, and paid vacations for their members while giving up efforts to gain some control over the workplace and production. Despite favorable contracts, however, union membership as a percentage of the work force fell from about 35.5 percent to about 31 percent by 1960. Although the AFL and the CIO merged in 1955, they made little effort to organize agricultural workers, the growing number of white-collar workers, or people working in the **Sunbelt**.

Suburban and Family Culture

Across the Sunbelt a new economy centered on sprawling metropolitan areas that continued to develop from their wartime origins. Rather than a center city, towns, suburbs, and industrial parks were linked by an ever-growing system of roads and highways. The economy boomed in these hubs of businesses, shopping and entertainment, homes, administrative centers, and industry. In northern California, Stanford University, specialized firms, and federal grants combined to open new industrial areas—which became Silicon Valley—that focused on developing technology, especially electronics. By 1960 electronics was the fifth-largest industry in the United States.

In the metropolitan areas and across the country, people continued the postwar desire to live in the suburbs, and by 1960 more than 214 million single-family homes had been built. By the 1950s, Levitt's original Cape Cod–style home had given way to the "ranch" or California-style home. Levitt's new ranch-style developments also helped reshape home life by including a television in each "living" room and by relocating the kitchen to a central place in the house. Other developers followed his example. A California builder was the first to install a garbage disposal in each kitchen sink. His Lakewood, California, was advertised as the "perfect place to raise children." Planners provided not only homes with large back-yards, but also elementary schools, parks, swimming pools, and small shopping areas for each neighborhood. Unifying the neighborhoods were the high school and a major shopping center. When in 1960 "the Center" scored a major success by opening an upscale department store, the high school's band and cheerleaders highlighted the opening ceremony. For the residents of Lakewood, it seemed that life could only get better year after year.

The brand-new developments represented a fresh start, a commitment to community and the American dream and increasingly "classless" society. "We were thrilled to death," recalled one newly arrived suburbanite, "Everyone else was moving in at the same time. . . . It was a whole new adventure for us. Everyone was arriving with a sense of forward momentum. Everyone was taking courage from the sight of another orange moving van pulling in next door, a family just like us, unloading pole lamps and cribs and Formica dining tables like our own, reflections of ourselves multiplying around us. . . ." Glorying in the new postwar culture, *Harper's* noted that in these developments, "no wrong side of the tracks" existed and that a new informal "patio society" had emerged.

At the center of this view of America rested an expanding consumer economy, the modern ranch home, the nuclear, homeowning family, and the church. Religion, with an emphasis on family life, enjoyed new popularity. Church attendance rose to 59.5 percent in 1953, a historic high. Religious leaders were rated as the most important members of society, especially those who used television to reach huge audiences. Such preachers stressed positive, religious, and patriotic themes. In 1954 the **Reverend Norman Vincent Peale** was named one of the nation's ten most successful salesmen. In keeping with the spirit of the times, Congress added "under God" to the Pledge of Allegiance in 1954 and "In God We Trust" to the American currency in 1955.

Increasingly, television invaded American society and redefined America in its suburban, middle-class image. Developed in the 1930s, it was not until World War II ended that televisions became available to the consumer, and at first they were very expensive. As demand and production increased, prices fell, and more and more people regarded "the box" as a necessity. In 1950 only about 9 percent of homes had a television, but at the end of the decade that percentage had risen to nearly 90, and most people watched for five hours a day. As Levitt had understood, television would be at the heart of the home, in the living room, and would shape American society.

Every evening, families by the millions watched domestic situation comedies in which the home

---

Sunbelt   A region stretching from Florida in a westward arc to the state of Washington.

Reverend Norman Vincent Peale   Minister who told his congregations that positive thinking could help them overcome all their troubles in life; his book *The Power of Positive Thinking* was an immediate bestseller.

was invariably the center of togetherness. As defined in 1954 by *McCall's* magazine, "togetherness" reflected the popular vision of family life in the suburbs. There, husband and wife shared responsibilities from housekeeping and shopping to decision-making and fulfilling the needs and desires of their children. In popular television shows like *The Donna Reed Show* (1958), *Leave It to Beaver* (1957) and *Father Knows Best* (1953), the ideal middle-class TV families were white and had hardworking, earnest fathers and attractive, savvy mothers who shared household chores. Their children, usually numbering between two and four, did well in school, were not overly concerned about the future, and provided the usually humorous dilemmas that Mom's common sense and sensitivity untangled. During the day, soap operas, most also set in middle-class settings, revolved around personal problems that eventually were worked out in a manner that affirmed family values.

Families were seen as the strength of the nation, and the number of American families was growing. As the divorce rate slowed, the numbers of marriages and births climbed, the baby boom continued, peaking at 403 million births in 1957. Popular images of the family focused on the wife managing the house and raising the children, while the husband worked in an office and directed weekend events. "There was this pressure to be the perfect housekeeper. I mean now I had this home I *had* to be Donna Reed," remembered one Levittown resident. For guidance on how to raise babies and children, millions of Americans turned to Dr. Benjamin Spock's popular book, *Baby and Child Care*. A mother's love and positive parental guidance were keys to healthy and well-adjusted children. Strict rules and corporal punishment were to be avoided. And to ensure proper gender identity, boys should participate in sports and outdoor activities, whereas girls should concentrate on their appearance and domestic skills. Toy guns and doctor bags were for boys; dolls, tea sets, and nurse kits were for girls. Conforming—being part of the group—was as important for parents as for children. Those unwilling to fulfill those roles, especially women, were suspected of being homosexual, neurotic, emotionally immature, too involved in a career, or simply irresponsible.

Consumerism

Another dimension of suburbia was consumerism. Radio and television bombarded their audiences with images not only of the average American but of the products those Americans used. Commercials provided the average television watcher with over five hours a week of ads that enticed viewers to indulge themselves, enjoy life, and own more.

And Americans were in a buying mood, especially the suburbanite. New goods were a sign of progress and a matter of status. Moving into a new housing development involved buying more than a new house: often it required the purchase of a variety of household furnishings and appliances and, of course, a new car. One resident noted, "Our old car just didn't cut it . . . a car was a real status symbol and who didn't want to impress the neighbors." Those producing the goods responded by emphasizing style and "the latest model." The automobile industry was especially effective in upgrading and changing the styles of their cars. Market research showed that it was mostly the middle and upper classes that bought new cars and encouraged the automobile makers to close the gap between luxury and nonluxury cars. Cadillac introduced fins in 1948, and by the mid-1950s nearly every car had fins and dealer showrooms were waging a fin-war.

The automobile industry also benefited from and contributed to the development of both roads and suburbs. By 1960, 75 percent of all Americans had at least one car, increasing the pressure on all levels of government to build new roads and highways. Eisenhower's greatest spending program, the Federal Highway Act of 1956, allocated over $32 billion to begin a federal interstate highway system. New industries arose to service the needs of the automobile driving family—motels, amusement parks, drive-in theaters, and fast-food restaurants. Walt Disney opened Disneyland in 1955, in a televised extravaganza, with the intention of providing family entertainment in a sparkling, clean-cut setting that reflected the spirit of America. In a similar vein, McDonald's standardized 15-cent hamburger changed the nation's eating habits while providing "Mom a Night Off," in a clean and wholesome environment without cigarette machines, jukeboxes, and beer.

To sell cars and hamburgers and other products, advertisers continued to use images of youth, glamour, sex appeal, and sophistication. In the forefront of the advertising onslaught was the tobacco industry, persuading people that smoking cigarettes was a stylish way to relax from the rigors of work and family. When medical reports surfaced about health risks connected to smoking, the tobacco giants intensified their advertising and stressed that new, longer, filtered cigarettes were milder and posed no

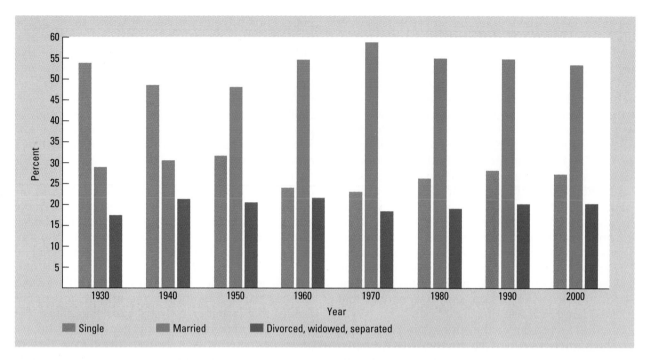

FIGURE 27.1 Marital Status of Women in the Work Force, 1930–2000   This figure shows the percentage of women in the work force from the Great Depression through 2000. While the number of women who fall into the category of divorced, widowed, and separated remained fairly constant, there was a significant shift in the number of single and married women in the work force, with the number of single women declining as the number of married women increased.   *Source:* U.S. Department of Commerce, *Historical Statistics of the United States, Colonial Times to 1970*, Vol. I (Washington, D.C.: U.S. Government Printing Office, 1970), pp. 20–21, 131–132; and U.S. Department of Commerce, *Statistics of the United States, 1993* (Washington, D.C.: U.S. Government Printing Office, 1993), pp. 74, 399.

health hazard. Cigarette advertising increased 400 percent between 1945 and 1960, whereas advertising in general increased "only" a little more than 250 percent.

Helping to pay for cars, televisions, washing machines, toys, and "Mom's night out" were increasing wages and credit. Why pay cash when consumer credit was available? The Diner's Club credit card made its debut in 1950 and was soon followed by American Express and a host of other plastic cards. Credit purchases leaped from $8.4 billion in 1946 to more than $44 billion in 1958.

Another View of Suburbia

Unlike the wives shown on television, more and more married women were working outside the home even though they had young children (see Figure 27.1). Some desired careers, but the majority worked to safeguard their family's existing **standard of living**. The percentage of middle-class women who worked for wages rose from 7 percent in 1950 to 25 percent

in 1960. Most held part-time jobs or sales clerk and clerical positions that paid low wages and provided few benefits. Women represented 46 percent of the banking work force—filling most secretary, teller, and receptionist slots—but held only 15 percent of upper-level positions.

Togetherness and suburban expectations did not make all homemakers happy. A study found that of eighteen household chores, men were willing to do three—lock up at night, do yard work, and make repairs. Other surveys discovered that more than one-fifth of suburban wives were unhappy with their marriages and lives. Many women complained of the drudgery and boredom of housework and the lack of understanding and affection from their husbands. Women were also more sexually active than

standard of living   Level of material comfort as measured by the goods, services, and luxuries currently available.

generally thought, shattering the image of loyal wife and pure mother. Research on women's sexuality conducted by **Alfred Kinsey** and described in his book *Sexual Behavior in the Human Female* (1953) indicated that a majority of American women had had sexual intercourse before marriage and 25 percent were having affairs while married.

Reflecting the shadier side of middle-class life in fiction, the best-selling novel *Peyton Place* (1956), by Grace Metalious, set America buzzing over the licentious escapades of the residents of a quiet town in New England. Hollywood kept pace with stars like Marilyn Monroe. Starting in 1952, the "blonde bombshell" was repeatedly cast in slightly dumb but very sexy roles in which older, more worldly men usually romanced her.

Rejecting Consensus

Americans seemed to consider sex symbols in the movies and men's magazines as a minor threat to the image of family, community, and nation. Homosexuality, however, was another matter. Many people believed it damaged the moral and social fabric of society. Kinsey's 1948 study of male sexuality shocked readers by claiming that nearly 8 percent of the population lived a gay lifestyle and that homosexuality existed throughout American society. An increasingly open gay subculture that centered around gay bars in every major city seemed to support his findings.

In a postwar society that emphasized the traditional family and feared internal subversion, homosexuals represented a double menace. A Senate investigating committee concluded that because of sexual perversions and lack of moral fiber, one homosexual could "pollute a Government office." Responding to such views, the Eisenhower administration barred homosexuals from most government jobs. Taking their cue from the federal government, state and local authorities intensified their efforts to control homosexuals and, if possible, purge them from society. **Vice squads** made frequent raids on gay and lesbian bars, and newspapers often listed the names, addresses, and employers of those arrested. In response to the virulent attacks, many took extra efforts to hide their homosexuality, but some organized to confront the offensive. In Los Angeles, Henry Hay formed the Mattachine Society in 1951 to fight for homosexual rights, and in San Francisco in 1955 Del Martin and Phyllis Lyon organized a similar organization for lesbians, the Daughters of Bilitis.

Also viewed as extreme were the **Beats**, or "beatniks," a group of often controversial artists, poets, and writers. Allen Ginsberg (see Individual Choices, page 852) in his poem *Howl* (1956) and Jack Kerouac in his novel *On the Road* (1957) denounced American materialism and sexual repression and glorified a freer, natural life.

A minority, especially among young college students, found the beatnik critique of "square America" meaningful. Most, however, had few qualms about rejecting the Beats' message and lifestyles. In an article in *Life* magazine in 1959, Paul O'Neil described beatniks as smelly, dirty people in beards and sandals, who were "sick little bums" and "hostile little females."

Most Americans could justify the suppression of beatniks and homosexuals because they appeared to mock traditional values of family and community. Other critics of American society, however, were more difficult to dismiss. Several respected writers and intellectuals claimed that the suburban and consumer culture was destructive—stifling diversity and individuality in favor of conformity. Mass-produced homes, meals, toys, fashions, and the other trappings of suburban life, they said, created a gray sameness about Americans. Sociologist David Riesman argued in *The Lonely Crowd* (1950) that postwar Americans, unlike earlier generations, were "outer-directed"—less sure of their values and morals and overly concerned about fitting into a group. Peer pressure, he suggested, had replaced individual thinking, and he urged readers to reassert their own identities. Serious literature also highlighted a sense of alienation from the conformist society. Much of Sylvia Plath's poetry and her novel *The Bell Jar* (1963) reflect those forces, especially as they affected women torn between the demands of society and the quest for individual freedom. Similar themes were central to many contemporary novels,

Alfred Kinsey   Biologist whose studies of human sexuality attracted great attention in the 1940s and 1950s, especially for his conclusions on infidelity and homosexuality.

vice squad   Police unit charged with the enforcement of laws dealing with vice—that is, immoral practices such as gambling and prostitution.

Beats   Group of American writers, poets, and artists in the 1950s, including Jack Kerouac and Allen Ginsberg, who rejected traditional middle-class values and championed nonconformity and sexual experimentation.

including J. D. Salinger's *Catcher in the Rye* (1951), whose hero, Holden Caulfield, concludes that the major features of American life are all phony.

The Trouble with Kids

While a small percentage of the nation's youth adopted the views of the Beats or turned their backs on middle-class values and consumerism, many parents and adults were concerned about teenagers, their behavior, and juvenile delinquency. Juvenile crime and gangs were not new topics, but for the first time many people worried that it was taking hold outside of the city and the urban poor and minorities. To the suburban middle-class parent, the violent crime associated with inner-city gangs was not the concern; instead, it was the behavior of their own teens as they seemed to flaunt traditional values and behavior. At the center of the problem, many believed, was a developing youth culture characterized by the car, rock 'n' roll, and disrespect for adults. One study of middle-class delinquency concluded that the automobile not only allowed teens to escape adult controls but also provided "a private lounge for drinking and for petting or sex episodes." Critics also blamed misbehavior on **rock 'n' roll**, comic books, television, and lack of proper family upbringing. In the film *Rebel Without a Cause* (1955), which featured soon-to-be teen idol James Dean, the rebellious characters came from atypical suburban homes where gender roles were reversed. Audiences saw a dominating mother and a father who cooked and assumed many traditional housewifely duties. To the adult audience, the message was clear: an "improper" family environment bred juvenile delinquents.

The problem with kids also seemed wedded to rock 'n' roll. Cleveland disc jockey Alan Freed coined the term in 1951. He had noticed that white teens were buying rhythm-and-blues (R&B) records popular among African Americans, but he also knew that few white households would listen to a radio program playing "black music." Freed decided to play the least sexually suggestive of the R&B records and call the music rock 'n' roll. His radio program, "Moondog's Rock 'n' Roll Party," was a smash hit. Quickly the barriers between "black music" and "white music" began to blur as white singers copied and modified R&B songs to produce **cover records**.

Cover artists like Pat Boone and Georgia Gibbs sold millions of records that avoided suggestive lyrics and were heard on hundreds of radio stations that had refused to play the original versions created by black artists. By mid-decade, African-American

In 1954, Elvis Presley's first record was released and within a year a new rock'n'roll star had burst onto the music scene. Elvis's style blended rhythm and blues, country, and gospel into a unique sound that, along with his body language, created an American icon. *Michael Barson Collection/Past Perfect.*

artists like Chuck Berry, Little Richard, and Ray Charles were successfully "crossing over" and being heard on "white" radio stations. At the same time, white artists, including the 1950s' most dynamic star, **Elvis Presley**, were making their own contributions.

---

rock 'n' roll   Style of music that developed out of rhythm-and-blues in the 1950s, with a fast beat and lyrics appealing to teenagers.

cover record   A new version of a song already recorded by an original artist.

Elvis Presley   Immensely popular rock 'n' roll musician from a poor white family in Mississippi; many of his songs and concert performances were considered sexually suggestive.

Beginning with "Heartbreak Hotel" in 1956, Presley recorded fourteen gold records within two years. In concerts, he drove his audiences into frenzies with sexually suggestive movements that earned him the nickname "Elvis the Pelvis."

Some sociologists argued that because of its roots in lower-class society, especially among African Americans, rock 'n' roll glamorized behavior that led to crime and delinquency. Blaming rock 'n' roll for a decline in morals, if not civilization, a Catholic Youth Center newspaper asked readers to "smash" rock 'n' roll records because they promoted "a pagan concept of life." But such opponents were waging a losing battle. Rock 'n' roll continued to surge in popularity, and by the end of the decade Dick Clark's *American Bandstand*, a weekly television show featuring teens dancing to rock 'n' roll, was one of the nation's most-watched and most-accepted programs.

OUTSIDE SUBURBIA

• What groups existed outside of the popular image of the nation?

• How did African Americans attack de jure segregation in American society during the 1950s?

• What role did the federal government play in promoting civil rights?

The average American depicted by *Reader's Digest* was a white, middle-class suburbanite. This portrait excluded a huge part of the population, especially minorities and the poor. Although the percentage of those living below the poverty line—set during the 1950s at around $3,000 a year—was declining, it was still over 22 percent and included large percentages of the elderly, minorities, and women heads of households. Even with Social Security payments, as 1959 ended nearly 31 percent of those over 65 lived below the poverty line, with 8 million receiving less than $1,000 a year. Women heads of households constituted about 23 percent of those making less than $3,000 annually. Throughout rural America, especially among small farmers and farm workers, poverty was common with most earning a $1,000 below the national average of about $3,500. In rural Mississippi, the annual per capital income was less than $900.

Poverty also increased in major cities as minorities continued to migrate seeking jobs and a less segregated society. Blacks continued their exodus from the rural South, and by 1960 half of African Americans lived in urban areas. Latinos also flocked to urban areas; only 20 percent of all Latinos did not live in cities by the end of the 1950s. New York's Puerto Rican community, for example, increased more than 1,000 percent. In some cities, including Atlanta and Washington, D.C., minorities became the majority, but they rarely exercised any political power proportionate to their numbers. No matter what the city, minority job seekers still found few openings and little economic opportunity, and it was common for nonwhite unemployment in cities to reach 40 percent.

At the same time, cities were less able or willing to provide services. Cities lost tax revenues and deteriorated at an accelerating rate as white middle- and working-class families moved into the suburbs and were followed by shopping centers and businesses. When funds were available for urban renewal and development, many city governments, like Miami and Los Angeles, used those funds to relocate and isolate minorities in specific neighborhoods away from developing entertainment, administrative, and shopping areas and upscale apartments. Cities also chose to build wider roads connecting them to the suburbs rather than invest in mass transit within the city. In south and east-central Los Angeles, freeway interchanges gobbled up 10 percent of the housing space and divided neighborhoods and families. For nearly all minorities, discrimination and **de facto** segregation put upward mobility and escaping poverty even farther out of reach.

Integrating Schools

For many African Americans, poverty was just one facet of life. They also faced a legally sanctioned segregated society. Legal, or **de jure,** segregation existed not only in the South but also in the District of Columbia and several western and midwestern states. Changes had occurred, but most African Americans regarded them as minor victories, indicating no real shift in white America's racial views. By 1952 the NAACP had won cases permitting African-American law and graduate students to attend white colleges and universities, even though the separate-but-equal ruling established in 1896 by the Supreme Court in *Plessy v. Ferguson* (see page 618) remained intact.

---

de facto Existing in practice, though not officially established by law.

de jure According to, or brought about by, law, such as "Jim Crow" laws that separated the races throughout the South until passage of the 1964 Civil Rights Act.

A step toward more significant change came in 1954 when the Supreme Court considered the case of *Brown v. Board of Education*, *Topeka, Kansas*. The *Brown* case had started four years earlier, when Oliver Brown sued to allow his daughter to attend a nearby white school rather than the black school across town. The Kansas courts had rejected his suit, pointing out that the availability of a school for African Americans fulfilled the Supreme Court's separate-but-equal ruling. The NAACP appealed. In addressing the Supreme Court, NAACP lawyer **Thurgood Marshall** argued that the concept of "separate but equal" was inherently self-contradictory. He used statistics to show that black schools were separate and *un*equal in financial resources, quality and number of teachers, and physical and educational resources. He also read into the record a psychological study indicating that black children educated in a segregated environment suffered from low self-esteem. Marshall stressed that segregated educational facilities, even if physically similar, could never yield equal results.

In 1952 a divided Court was unable to make a decision, but two years later the Court heard the case again. Now sitting as chief justice was **Earl Warren**, the Republican former governor of California, regarded by most as a legal conservative. Appointed to the Court by Eisenhower in 1953, the new chief justice made the difference. To the dismay of many, Warren moved the Court away from its long-time preoccupation with economic and regulatory issues and down new judicial paths. Rejecting social and political consensus, the activism of the Supreme Court promoted new visions of society as it deliberated racial issues and individual rights. Reflecting the opinion of a unanimous Court, the *Brown* decision stated that "separate educational facilities are inherently unequal." In 1955, in addressing how to implement *Brown*, the Court gave primary responsibility to local school boards. Not expecting integration overnight, the Court ordered school districts to proceed with "all deliberate speed." The justices instructed lower federal courts to monitor progress according to this vague guideline.

Reactions to the case were predictable. African Americans and liberals hailed the decision and hoped that segregated schools would soon be an institution of the past. Southern whites vowed to resist integration by all possible means. Virginia passed a law closing any integrated school. Southern congressional representatives issued the **Southern Manifesto**, in which they proudly pledged to oppose the *Brown* ruling. Eisenhower, who believed the Court had erred, refused to support the decision publicly.

As Elizabeth Eckford approached Little Rock's Central High School, the crowd began to hurl curses, yelling "Lynch her! Lynch her!" and a national guardsman blocked her entrance into the school with his rifle. Terrified, she retreated down the street away from the threatening mob. A week later, with army troops protecting her, Elizabeth Eckford finally attended—and integrated—Central High School. *Francis Miller, LIFE Magazine ©Time Warner Inc.*

While both political parties carefully danced around school integration and other civil rights

Brown v. Board of Education   Case in 1954 in which the Supreme Court ruled that separate educational facilities for different races were inherently unequal.

Thurgood Marshall   Civil rights lawyer who argued thirty-two cases before the Supreme Court and won twenty-nine; he became the first African-American justice of the Supreme Court in 1967.

Earl Warren   Chief justice of the Supreme Court from 1953 to 1969, under whom the Court issued decisions protecting civil rights, the rights of criminals, and First Amendment rights.

Southern Manifesto   Statement issued by one hundred southern congressmen in 1954 after the *Brown v. Board of Education* decision, pledging to oppose desegregation.

issues, school districts in Little Rock, Arkansas, moved forward with "all deliberate speed." Central High School was scheduled to integrate in 1957. Opposing integration were the parents of the school's students and Governor Orval Faubus, who ordered National Guard troops to surround the school and prevent desegregation. When Elizabeth Eckford, one of the nine integrating students, walked toward Central High, national guardsmen blocked her path as a hostile mob roared, "Lynch her! Lynch her!" Spat on by the jeering crowd, she retreated to her bus stop. Central High remained segregated.

For three weeks the National Guard prevented the black students from enrolling. Then on September 20 a federal judge ordered the integration of Central High School. Faubus complied and withdrew the National Guard. But the crisis was not over. Segregationists remained determined to block integration and were waiting for the black students on Monday, September 23, 1957. When they discovered that the nine had slipped into the school unnoticed, the mob rushed the police lines and battered the school doors open. Inside the school, Melba Patella Beaus thought, "We were trapped. I'm going to die here, in school." Hurriedly, the students were loaded into cars and warned to duck their heads. School officials ordered the drivers to "start driving, do not stop. . . . If you hit somebody, you keep rolling, 'cause [if you stop] the kids are dead."

With the black students safely away, the crowd's rampage quieted. Integration had lasted almost three hours. The following morning angry throngs began looting and burning part of the city, and the mayor asked for federal troops. Faced with insurrection, Eisenhower, on September 24, nationalized the Arkansas National Guard and dispatched a thousand troops of the 101st Airborne Division to Little Rock. Speaking to the nation, the president emphasized that he had sent the federal troops not to integrate the schools but to uphold the law and to restore order. The distinction was lost on most white southerners, who fumed as soldiers protected the nine black students for the rest of the school year.

In the school year that followed (1957–1958), the city closed its high schools rather than integrate them. To prevent such actions, the Supreme Court ruled in *Cooper v. Aaron* (1959) that an African American's right to attend school could not "be nullified openly and directly by state legislators or state executive officials nor nullified indirectly by them by evasive schemes for segregation." Little Rock's high schools reopened, and integration slowly spread to the lower grades. But in Little Rock, as in other communities, many white families fled the integrated public schools and enrolled their children in private schools that were beyond the reach of the federal courts. With no endorsement from the White House and entrenched southern opposition, "all deliberate speed" amounted to a snail's pace. By 1965, less than 2 percent of all southern schools were integrated.

The Montgomery Bus Boycott

In Montgomery, Alabama, African Americans confronted another form of white social control: segregation on the city bus line. The confrontation began almost imperceptibly on December 1, 1955, when **Rosa Parks** refused to give up her seat on the bus so that a white man could sit. At 42, Mrs. Parks, a high school graduate who earned $23 a week as a seamstress, had not boarded the bus with the intention of disobeying the law, although she strongly opposed it. But that afternoon, her fatigue and humiliation were suddenly too much. She refused to move and was arrested.

Hearing of her arrest, local African-American leaders Jo Ann Robinson and Edward Nixon felt they had found the right person committed enough to contest segregation. African-American community leaders called for a boycott of the buses to begin on the day of Mrs. Parks's court appearance. Accordingly, they submitted a list of proposals to city and bus officials calling for courteous drivers, the hiring of black drivers, and a more equitable system of bus seating.

On December 5, 1955, the night before the boycott was to begin, nearly four thousand people filled and surrounded Holt Street Baptist Church to hear **Martin Luther King, Jr.**, the newly selected leader

---

Cooper v. Aaron   Supreme Court decision (1959) that barred state authorities from interfering with desegregation either directly or through strategies of evasion.

Rosa Parks   Black seamstress who refused to give up her seat to a white man on a bus in Montgomery, Alabama, in 1955, triggering a bus boycott that stirred the civil rights movement.

Martin Luther King, Jr.   Ordained Baptist minister, brilliant orator, and civil rights leader committed to nonviolence; he led many of the important protests of the 1950s and 1960s.

On December 1, 1955, Rosa Parks made a fateful choice—she refused to give up her seat to a white man on a Montgomery, Alabama bus. She was arrested and fined $14 as a result of her decision. Her courageous act of defiance ignited a grassroots effort by African Americans to eliminate discrimination, and with it Martin Luther King, Jr. emerged as a national leader for civil rights. "I had no idea history was being made," she stated later, "I was just tired of giving in." *Corbis-Bettmann.*

of the boycott movement—now called the Montgomery Improvement Association. The 26-year-old King firmly believed that the church had a social justice mission and that violence and hatred, even when considered justified, brought only ruin. In shaping that evening's speech, he wrestled with the problem of how to balance disobedience with peace, confrontation with civility, and rebellion with tradition—and won. His words electrified the crowd: "We are here this evening to say to those who have mistreated us so long that we are tired of being segregated and humiliated, tired of being kicked about by the brutal feet of oppression." King asked the

crowd to boycott the buses, urging his listeners to protest "courageously, and yet with dignity and Christian love," and when confronted with violence, to "bless them that curse you."

On December 6, Rosa Parks was tried, found guilty, and fined $10, plus $4 for court costs. She appealed, and the boycott, 90 percent effective, stretched into days, weeks, and finally months. Police issued basketfuls of traffic tickets to drivers taking part in the car pools that provided transportation for the boycotters. Insurance companies canceled their automobile coverage, and acid was poured on the cars. On January 30, 1956, a stick of dynamite was thrown onto King's front porch, destroying it and almost injuring King's wife and a friend. King nevertheless remained calm, reminding supporters to avoid violence and persevere. Finally, as the boycott approached its first anniversary, the Supreme Court ruled in *Gayle et al. v. Browser* (1956) that the city's and bus company's policy of segregation was unconstitutional. "Praise the Lord. God has spoken from Washington, D.C.," cried one boycotter.

The Montgomery bus boycott shattered the traditional white view that African Americans accepted segregation, and it marked the beginning of a pattern of nonviolent resistance. King himself was determined to build on the energy generated by the boycott and fight segregation throughout American society. In 1956 he and other black leaders had formed a new civil rights organization, the **Southern Christian Leadership Conference** (SCLC), and across the South thousands of African Americans were ready and eager to take to the streets and use the federal courts to achieve equality.

Ike and Civil Rights

As the Montgomery boycott steamrolled into the headlines month after month, from the White House came either silence or carefully selected platitudes. When asked, Eisenhower gave elusive replies: "I believe we should not stagnate. . . . I plead for understanding, for really sympathetic consideration of a problem. . . . I am for moderation, but I am for progress; that is exactly what I am for in this thing." Personally, Eisenhower believed that government, especially the executive branch, had little role in integration. Max Rabb, the president's adviser on minority affairs, thought the "Negroes were being too aggressive." On a political level, cabinet members and Eisenhower were disappointed in the low number of blacks who had voted Republican in 1952 and 1956.

But not all within the administration were so unsympathetic toward civil rights. Attorney General Herbert Brownell drafted the first civil rights legislation since Reconstruction. The **Civil Rights Act of 1957** passed Congress after a year of political maneuvering, having gained the support of Democratic majority leader Lyndon B. Johnson of Texas. A moderate law, it provided for the formation of a Civil Rights Commission and opened the possibility of using federal lawsuits to ensure voter rights. The SCLC had hoped to enroll 3 million new black vot-

ers in the South but fell far short of the goal, enrolling only 160,000 between 1958 and 1960. Ella Baker, who headed the underfunded and understaffed effort, faced effective opposition from southern whites and local and state officials. In 1960 Congress passed a voting rights act that offered little help. To remove the barriers to black voting, the act mandated the use of the cumbersome and expensive judiciary system—again placing the burden of forcing change on African Americans. Critics acknowledged that Eisenhower had sent troops to Little Rock and signed two civil rights acts, but they argued that the president had provided little political or moral leadership. If the nation was to commit itself to civil rights, such leadership was imperative.

The activism of the civil rights movement and the Warren Court was at odds with the popular image of 1950s, a picture of consensual solutions, political inaction, and Eisenhower's blandness. By the end of the decade an increasing number of people were calling for more activism and decisive direction from the White House. As the 1960 presidential election neared, Democrats and other critics of the Eisenhower years called for a new, involved government that would protect American interests abroad and solve social problems at home.

Southern Christian Leadership Conference
 Group formed by Martin Luther King, Jr., and others after the Montgomery bus boycott; it became the backbone of the civil rights movement in the 1950s and 1960s.

Civil Rights Act of 1957 Created the U.S. Commission on Civil Rights and the Civil Rights Division of the Department of Justice; the Commission on Civil Rights primarily investigated restrictions on voting.

Examining a Primary Source

Allen Ginsberg Howls Against the Establishment

The publication of *Howl* brought Allen Ginsberg instant celebrity, or notoriety. The first section of the poem is an angry indictment of American industrial society, which is crushing the free spirits and creativity of "angleheaded hipsters" in a modern hell. "I saw the best minds of my generation destroyed by madness, starving hysterical naked, / dragging themselves through the negro streets at dawn," the lament begins. Part II describes and denounces "Moloch," the cause of the hipsters' sufferings and deaths. According to the ancient Hebrews, Moloch was a Canaanite god who demanded the sacrifice of children. Ginsberg's Moloch—in the guise of modern industrial society—also demands sacrifice and spews forth destruction of the soul. In the third and shortest section of the poem, Ginsberg expresses support for a friend, Carl Solomon, who was confined to a mental hospital, in Ginsberg's mind a victim of society. The poem created howls of both protest and applause, depending on the reader's view of poetry, the Beats, and America.

Howl, a portion of which is printed here, has been called a "volcanic eruption" that broke through the nation's "cultural crust" and was a turning point in American literature. This excerpt, from Part II, describes the fearful Moloch.

What sphinx of cement and aluminum bashed open their skulls and ate up their brains and imagination? . . .

Moloch! Moloch! Nightmare of Moloch! Moloch the loveless! Mental Moloch! Moloch the heavy judger of men! ●

● *What images does Ginsberg use to describe Moloch, and what does Moloch represent to Ginsberg?*

Moloch the incomprehensible prison! Moloch the crossbone soulless jailhouse and Congress of sorrows! Moloch whose buildings are judgment! Moloch the vast stone of war! Moloch the stunned governments!

Moloch whose mind is pure machinery! Moloch whose blood is running money! Moloch whose fingers are ten armies! Moloch whose breast is a cannibal dynamo! Moloch whose ear is a smoking tomb!

Moloch whose eyes are a thousand blind windows! Moloch whose skyscrapers stand in the long streets like endless Jehovahs! Moloch whose factories dream and croak in the fog! Moloch whose smokestacks and antennae crown the cities! ●

● *Why do you think Ginsberg titled the poem* Howl?

Moloch whose love is endless oil and stone! Moloch whose soul is electricity and banks! . . .

. . . Moloch who frightened me out of my natural ecstasy! Moloch whom I abandon! Wake up in Moloch! Light streaming out of the sky!

● *In what ways does the poem reflect the Beats' criticism of America?*

Moloch! Moloch! Robot apartments! invisible suburbs! skeleton treasuries! blind capitals! demonic industries! spectral nations! invincible mad houses! . . . monstrous bombs! ●

SUMMARY

"Had enough?" Republicans asked voters in 1952, offering the choice of a new vision of domestic and foreign policy. Americans answered by electing Eisenhower. Though promising change, Eisenhower in practice chose foreign and domestic policies that continued the basic patterns established by Roosevelt and Truman. Republican beliefs, pervasive anticommunism, and budget concerns allowed reductions in some domestic programs, but public acceptance of existing federal responsibilities prevented any large-scale dismantling of the New Deal. The New Look relied on new tactics, but Cold War foreign policies did not change significantly. Using alliances, military force, nuclear deterrence, and covert activities, Eisenhower continued containment and expanded American influence in southern Asia and the Middle East. Meanwhile, relations with the Soviet Union deteriorated with the launching of *Sputnik*, another Berlin crisis, Castro's victory in Cuba, and the U-2 incident. By the end of the decade, many questioned the effectiveness of the administration, especially the president, to lead in the fight against communism and solve what seemed to be a growing number of social and political problems at home.

Reflecting the image of Ike in the White House, the 1950s spawned comforting, if not entirely accurate, images of America centered on affluent suburbs and a growing consumer culture. To be sure, many white, working-class and middle-class Americans fulfilled their expectations by moving to the suburbs and living the American dream. Suburbs continued to expand and a society shaped by cars, expanded purchasing power, and middle-class values seemed to be what America "was about." Critics of this benign vision stated that such a consensual society bred a social grayness and stifled individualism. They argued that rather than trying to conform to society, individuals should work to change society. Yet life in suburbia did not necessarily fit either the popular or the critics' image. Many men, women, and children behaved contrary to the supposed norms of family and suburban culture. Teens and young adults, especially, turned to forms of expression that seemed to reject established norms and values.

Outside the suburbs another America existed, where economic realities, social prejudices, and old-fashioned politics blocked equality and upward mobility. Although declining, poverty still persisted, especially in rural America and among minorities living in urban areas. While poverty remained largely ignored, it became increasingly difficult to ignore the actions taken by African Americans to overturn decades of segregation. By the end of the decade, civil rights had emerged as an issue that neither political party nor white, suburban America could avoid.

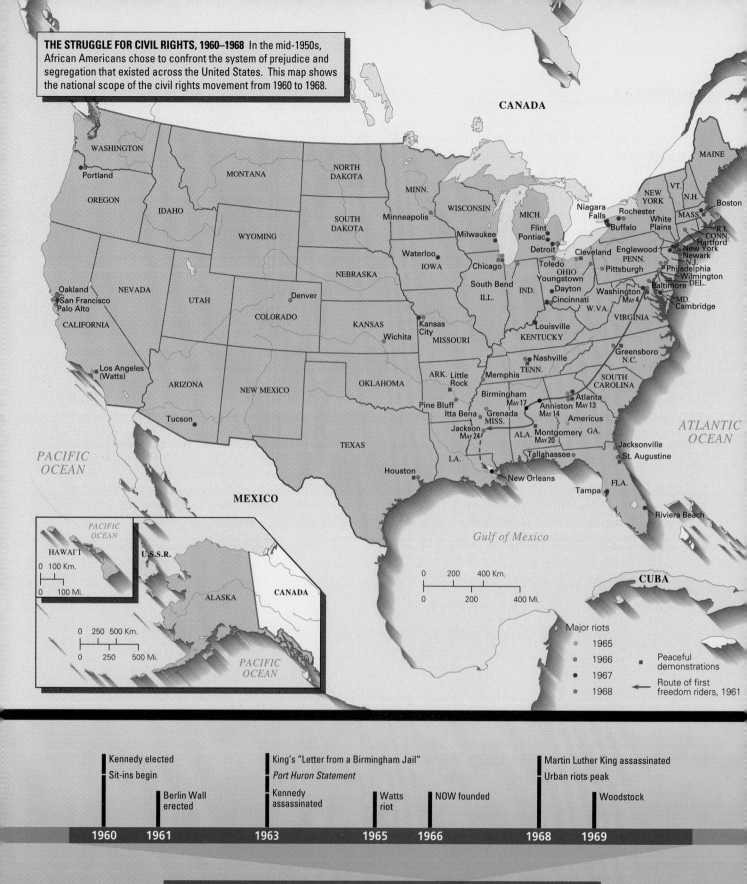

THE STRUGGLE FOR CIVIL RIGHTS, 1960–1968 In the mid-1950s, African Americans chose to confront the system of prejudice and segregation that existed across the United States. This map shows the national scope of the civil rights movement from 1960 to 1968.

CANADA

WASHINGTON
Portland
OREGON

MONTANA

NORTH DAKOTA

MINN.
Minneapolis

WISCONSIN

MICH.
Flint
Pontiac
Detroit

Niagara Falls
Rochester
Buffalo
White Plains

MAINE

VT.
N.H.
NEW YORK
Boston
MASS.
R.I.
CONN.
Hartford

IDAHO

WYOMING

SOUTH DAKOTA

Milwaukee
Waterloo
IOWA
Chicago
South Bend
ILL.
IND.

Toledo
OHIO
Youngstown
Dayton
Cincinnati

Cleveland
Englewood
PENN.
Pittsburgh

New York
Newark
N.J.
Philadelphia
Wilmington
DEL.

NEVADA
Oakland
San Francisco
Palo Alto
CALIFORNIA

UTAH

COLORADO
Denver

NEBRASKA

KANSAS
Wichita

Kansas City
MISSOURI

KENTUCKY
Louisville

Washington
MAY 4
W.VA.
VIRGINIA

Baltimore
MD.
Cambridge

Greensboro
N.C.

Los Angeles
(Watts)

ARIZONA

NEW MEXICO

OKLAHOMA

ARK. Little Rock
Pine Bluff
Itta Bena
Jackson
MAY 24

Memphis
Nashville
TENN.

Birmingham
MAY 17
Grenada
MISS.
Montgomery
MAY 20
ALA.

Anniston
MAY 14
Americus
GA.

Atlanta
MAY 13

SOUTH CAROLINA

Tucson

TEXAS

LA.

Jacksonville
St. Augustine
Tallahassee
FLA.

ATLANTIC OCEAN

Houston

New Orleans

Tampa

Riviera Beach

PACIFIC OCEAN

MEXICO

Gulf of Mexico

CUBA

PACIFIC OCEAN
HAWAI'I
0 100 Km.
0 100 Mi.

U.S.S.R.
ALASKA
CANADA
0 250 500 Km.
0 250 500 Mi.
PACIFIC OCEAN

0 200 400 Km.
0 200 400 Mi.

Major riots
- 1965
- 1966
- 1967
- 1968

■ Peaceful demonstrations

← Route of first freedom riders, 1961

Kennedy elected
Sit-ins begin

Berlin Wall erected

King's "Letter from a Birmingham Jail"
Port Huron Statement
Kennedy assassinated

Watts riot

NOW founded

Martin Luther King assassinated
Urban riots peak

Woodstock

1960   **1961**   **1963**   **1965**   **1966**   **1968**   **1969**

1850   1900   1950   2000

Great Promises, Bitter Disappointments, 1960–1968

STOKELY CARMICHAEL

Stokely Carmichael was one of the most influential African-American leaders of the 1960s and 1970s. Born in Trinidad in 1941, Carmichael attended Howard University where he immersed himself in the civil rights movement. He participated in one of the first freedom rides and was arrested the first of thirty-five times for civil rights activism. He graduated with a degree in philosophy in 1964, and two years later became nationally recognized as an advocate of "Black Power." Black Power was, he told a London newspaper, "the coming together of black people to fight for their liberation by any means necessary." *Marc Vignes/ Timepix.*

Stokely Carmichael (Kwame Ture)

It was an idea whose time had come. That was the decision of Stokely Carmichael and other leaders of the Student Nonviolent Coordinating Committee (SNCC) in the summer of 1966. Participating in the James Meredith march on June 16, Carmichael was arrested by Greenwood, Mississippi, police following a rally—it was his twenty-seventh arrest. Later that day, following his release, he spoke to a crowd of about 3,000 assembled marchers and local blacks. In a fiery speech, he called to the crowd to move away from the passive disobedience associated with Dr. Martin Luther King, Jr.'s "Freedom Now" crusade and adopt a more militant and separatistic vision of "Black Power." "The only way we gonna stop them white men from whuppin' us is to take over," he roared to the crowd. "We been saying freedom for six years—and we ain't got nothin'. What we gonna start saying now is 'Black Power.'" The crowd roared back, "Black Power!" Carmichael's call did more than energize a crowd of demonstrators. It also defiantly challenged the leadership and tactics of King and the Southern Christian Leadership Council. The nation suddenly was aware of another dimension of the civil rights movement. A white civil rights marcher listening to the thundering demand for Black Power reflected, "[S]uddenly I was a 'honky'" rather than a comrade.

The idea of Black Power had been building in Carmichael since his arrival in the United States at age 11. Born in Trinidad where blacks held positions of power, he discovered the reverse was true in America when he moved to Harlem in 1952. Graduating from high school in 1960, he was motivated by the sit-in students to join the Congress of Racial Equality on picket lines. As a freshman at Howard University, he joined one of the first "freedom rides," and in Mississippi he was arrested—the first of thirty-five times. Graduating from Howard in 1964, he helped organize SNCC and launch a voter registration drive in Lowndes County, Alabama.

Lowndes was a rural, impoverished county dominated by the Klan and white supremacy. The white minority—fewer than 1,000 of the total 13,000—owned 90 percent of the land. Over 12,000 African Americans lived in Lowndes, and in January of 1965, none were registered to vote. SNCC decided to organize a voters movement there, and Carmichael arrived to implement the effort, which included founding a new black political party and power base. The goal was "to register as many Blacks as we could . . . and take over the county." The effort moved at a crawl until passage of the 1965 Voting Rights Act and the arrival of federal registrars to oversee the end of the literacy test. Blacks surged forward to register and despite increased jailings and beatings—and one murder—formed a political organization in March 1966, the Lowndes County Freedom Organization. The goal of the new party and its symbol reflected Carmichael's growing sense of black power. The goal was to gain power; the symbol was the black panther, selected because, according to one organizer, it was "a vicious animal, who if he was attacked, would not back up. It said we would fight back if we had to." Soon afterward, in a contested election, SNCC members elected Carmichael as their chairman.

Under Carmichael's direction, SNCC reshaped itself along new, more militant, Black Nationalist, Black Power lines. The organization purged itself of white membership, abandoned nonviolence, promoted Black Nationalism, and clarified the term *Black Power*. While Carmichael had first used the term in Mississippi, he recognized it had a more significant impact in northern urban areas where Black Nationalism and militancy had exploded in the mid-1960s. A spokesman for Black Power and Black Nationalism, Carmichael directed SNCC for a year, leaving it in 1968. He became the honorary prime minister of the Black Panther Party and traveled overseas, speaking out against social, political, and economic repression and American imperialism, denouncing the Vietnam War. Under FBI surveillance and feeling harassed by efforts to neutralize the movement, Carmichael left the United States in 1969 and moved to Guinea, West Africa. He became deeply involved in African politics helping to establish the All-African People's Revolutionary Party, an international organization dedicated to Pan-Africanism and the worldwide plight of Africans. In 1978 he changed his name to Kwame Ture in honor of two African leaders and supporters of Pan-Africanism, Ghana's Kwame Nkrumah and Guinea's Sekou Ture. Carmichael died of cancer in Guinea in November in 1998.

INTRODUCTION

The 1960s appears as a unique decade in American history, unlike that which preceded and followed it. It invokes visions of change, of protest marches, demonstrations, and governmental intervention, of New Frontiers and Great Societies. It seemed to Stokely Carmichael and thousands of others that the sixties provided an opportunity to generate change through individual, group, and governmental activism. The election of John F. Kennedy symbolized a new level of youth and vigor in government that raised expectations and created the "politics of hope." He represented a more interventionist government in both foreign and domestic affairs. Per-

haps the activity found in the streets would be joined by that of government—and real change would occur.

Indeed, President Kennedy called for a New Frontier that promised a better society for all Americans and, especially among the poor and minorities, raised expectations that his administration would stimulate the economy, reduce poverty and discrimination, and improve education. But he faced political opposition from conservatives in Congress who objected to an expansion of liberal programs and obstructed civil rights legislation. The economy grew, but faced with Republican and southern Democratic opposition, Kennedy's legislative record generally expanded on existing programs. Policies that charted new paths such as civil rights, health care, and aid to education were delayed or abandoned. Still among many, especially minorities and women, there remained a heightened level of activism and expectations.

Finding fewer political obstacles in foreign policy, Kennedy preferred being a foreign policy president than a domestic one. He promised to overcome the "missile gap" and regain ground lost to communism. He chose "flexible response" over massive retaliation to confront the global Communist threat. As part of the Cold War he placed new emphasis on developing regions of the world, especially Latin America and South Vietnam. To fund new foreign aid and military spending, Kennedy loosened constraints on the military budget, entering both an arms race and a space race with the Soviets. Yet despite his administration's self-confidence and bold efforts, the outcome was not a safer and less divided world. The erection of the Berlin Wall, the Cuban missile crisis, and events in Vietnam heightened Cold War tensions while stretching American commitments.

Lyndon Johnson inherited two broad issues from Kennedy: completion of the New Frontier and continuation of the struggle against communism, especially in Vietnam. He attacked the domestic agenda immediately while postponing foreign policy decisions. He called on Congress to pass the civil rights bill and to fund a broad anti-poverty campaign. In the months before and after the 1964 presidential election, Johnson presented the nation with his proposals for a Great Society. In an onslaught of legislation, he waged war on poverty and discrimination, developed federal welfare programs, increased federal support for education, and created a national system of healthcare for the aged and poor. But 1965 was the high tide for Johnson and the politics of hope. Unfulfilled expectations, an expanding war in Vietnam, and controversial social and political issues drained away faith in the politics of hope and the effectiveness of the Great Society.

A wave of angry voices—including Stokely Carmichael's—began to challenge the assumptions of the Democratic social and political agenda. Black Power leaders chose confrontation over compromise. Urban riots and violence drove wedges between African-American leaders and some white supporters. The emergence of a youth-centered counterculture that rejected traditional social and moral values and stressed personal freedoms also worked to

fragment American society. The result was a decade that began with great optimism but ended with diminished expectations.

THE POLITICS OF ACTION

• What images did John Kennedy and his advisers project, and how did those images contribute to the flavor of the 1960s?

• What were the domestic goals of the Kennedy administration? How successful was the president on the home front, and why?

• What form of African-American activism pushed the civil rights movement forward, and how did Kennedy respond to those efforts?

Republicans had every reason to worry as the 1960 presidential campaign neared. The last years of the 1950s had not been kind to the Republican Party. The White House generated little or no leadership. Domestically neither the president nor Republicans in Congress appeared able to deal with the problems of the country—civil rights agitation, a slowing economy, and a soaring national debt that had reached $488 billion. The United States also saw few Cold War victories as the Soviets downed an American spy plane over the Soviet Union, launched *Sputnik* into space, and supported Castro in Cuba. Democratic gains in the congressional elections of 1958 signaled that the Democrats were again the majority, if not the dominant, party. Vice President Richard Nixon calculated that for a Republican presidential victory the "candidate would have to get practically all Republican votes, more than half of the independents—and, in addition the votes of five to six million Democrats."

The 1960 Campaign

On the Democratic side stood John Fitzgerald Kennedy, a youthful, vigorous senator from Massachusetts. A Harvard graduate, Kennedy came from a wealthy, Catholic family. Some worried about his young age (43) and lack of experience. Others worried about his religion—no Catholic had ever been elected president. To offset these possible liabilities, Kennedy had astutely added the politically savvy Senate majority leader Lyndon Johnson of Texas to the ticket, called for a new generation of leadership, and suggested that those who were making religion an issue were bigots. Drawing on the legacy of

chronology

New Frontiers

1960 Sit-ins begin
SNCC formed
Students for a Democratic Society formed
Boynton v. Virginia
John F. Kennedy elected president

1961 Peace Corps formed
Alliance for Progress
Bay of Pigs invasion
Freedom rides begin
Vienna summit
Berlin Wall erected

1962 Michael Harrington's *The Other America*
SDS's *Port Huron Statement*
James Meredith enrolls at the University
of Mississippi
Cuban missile crisis
Rachel Carson's *Silent Spring*

1963 *Report on the Status of Women*
Betty Friedan's *The Feminine Mystique*
Equal Pay Act
Martin Luther King's "Letter from a
Birmingham Jail"
Limited Test Ban Treaty
March on Washington
Diem assassinated
Kennedy assassinated; Lyndon Baines Johnson
becomes president
16,000 advisers in Vietnam

1964 War on Poverty begins
Freedom Summer in Mississippi
Civil Rights Act
Office of Economic Opportunity created
Johnson elected president

1965 Malcolm X assassinated
Selma march
Elementary and Secondary Education Act
Medicaid and Medicare
Voting Rights Act
Immigration Act

1966 Black Panther Party formed
National Organization for Women founded
Stokely Carmichael announces Black Power
Model Cities Act

1967 Urban riots in one hundred twenty-seven cities

1968 Kerner Commission Report
Martin Luther King, Jr., assassinated
Open Housing Law

1969 Woodstock
Stonewall Riot

Franklin Roosevelt, he challenged the nation to enter a **New Frontier**, to improve the overall quality of life of all Americans, and to re-energize American foreign policy to stand fast against the Communist threat. He offered action, empowerment to the government, people, and institutions.

Facing Kennedy was Eisenhower's vice president, Richard M. Nixon. Trying to distance himself from the image of Eisenhower's elderly leadership, Nixon promised a forceful, energetic presidency and emphasized his executive experience and history of anticommunism. He, too, vowed to improve the quality

of life, support civil rights, and defeat international communism. Several political commentators called the candidates "two peas in a pod" and speculated that the election would probably hinge on appearances more than on issues.

New Frontier   Program for social and educational
reform put forward by John F. Kennedy; though
charismatically presented, it was largely resisted by
Congress.

The 1960 presidential race was the closest in recent history, with many people believing that the outcome hinged on the public's perception of the candidates during their nationally televised debates. The majority of viewers believed that Kennedy won the debates and looked more in control and presidential than Nixon. Kennedy won the election by fewer than 120,000 votes. *UPI/Bettmann Archives.*

Trailing in the opinion polls and hoping to give his campaign a boost, Nixon agreed to televised debates with Kennedy. He was proud of his debating skills and thought he could adapt them successfully to radio and television. Kennedy seized the opportunity, recognizing that the candidate who appeared most calm and knowledgeable—more "presidential"— would "win" each debate. Before the camera's eye, in the war of images, Kennedy appeared fresh and confident, while Nixon, having been ill, appeared tired and haggard. The contrasts were critical. Unable to see Nixon, the radio audience believed he won the debates, but to the 70 million television viewers the winner was the self-assured and sweat-free Kennedy.

The televised debates helped Kennedy, but victory depended on his ability to hold the Democratic coalition together, maintaining southern Democratic support while wooing African-American and liberal voters. The Texan Johnson used his political clout to keep the South largely loyal while Kennedy blasted the lack of Republican leadership on civil rights. Martin Luther King, Jr., had been arrested for civil rights activities in Atlanta, and in a grand gesture, Kennedy telephoned Coretta Scott King to express his concern about her husband's jailing. Kennedy's brother Robert used his influence to get King freed, convincing even the staunchest Protestant black ministers, including Martin Luther King, Sr., to overlook Kennedy's religion and endorse him. Every vote was critical. When the ballots were counted, Kennedy had scored the slimmest of victories (see Map 28.1). Nixon carried more states, 25 to 21, but Kennedy had a narrow margin over Nixon in popular votes and won the electoral count, 303 to 219. (Independent southern candidate Harry Byrd earned 15 electoral votes.)

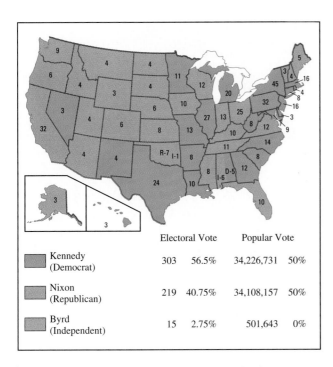

Electoral Vote   Popular Vote

		Electoral Vote		Popular Vote	
■	Kennedy (Democrat)	303	56.5%	34,226,731	50%
■	Nixon (Republican)	219	40.75%	34,108,157	50%
■	Byrd (Independent)	15	2.75%	501,643	0%

MAP 28.1 Election of 1960   Although Richard Nixon won in more states than John F. Kennedy, in the closest presidential election in the twentieth century, Kennedy defeated his Republican opponent by a slim 84 electoral votes and fewer than 19,000 popular votes.

The New Frontier

The weather in Washington was frigid when Kennedy gave his inaugural address, but his speech fired the imagination of the nation. Speaking in idealistic terms, avoiding any mention of specific programs, he pledged to march against "the common enemies of man: tyranny, poverty, disease, and war itself." He invited all Americans to participate, exhorting them to "ask not what your country can do for you; ask what you can do for your country." In this speech and throughout the campaign, Kennedy had tapped into a growing sense that activism and change were to be embraced and not avoided. This optimistic view was a product of the country's growing affluence and a youthful confidence that science and technology could solve whatever ills faced society. "Science and technology are making the problems of today irrelevant . . . the basic miracle of modern technology . . . is a magic wand that gives us what we desire," stated Adlai

Stevenson. Most national problems were "technical" and "administrative," Kennedy believed, and would be solved by experts. In keeping with his view, he selected for his cabinet and advisers those with "know-how," people who were willing to take action to get the nation moving again. Kennedy chose Rhodes scholars, successful businessmen, and Harvard professors. Harvard supplied economist John Kenneth Galbraith (a personal adviser) and Dean Rusk (secretary of state). The successful Ford Motor Company president Robert McNamara was tapped for secretary of defense. In a controversial move, Kennedy named his younger brother Robert as attorney general. Many hailed Kennedy's choices as representing "the best and the brightest." But not everyone thought so. Referring to the lack of political background among appointees, Speaker of the House Sam Rayburn remarked that he would "feel a whole lot better . . . if just one of them had run for sheriff once."

Rayburn had noted a critical point. Kennedy and his staff wanted to be activists leading the nation along new paths, but as political novices they would not be able to convince Congress to budge. Democrats dominated Congress, but since 1937 a powerful coalition of conservative, southern Democrats had voted with Republicans to prevent any notable expansion of the New Deal. Knowing it would be "very difficult" to pass controversial legislation, Kennedy decided to focus on legislation within the "vital center"—neither overly liberal nor overly conservative—that would improve the economy and the services provided under existing New Deal–style programs.

Like Truman, Kennedy asked Congress for a wide range of domestic programs, but he received only a modest, Eisenhower-like result. By 1963, Congress had approved small increases in Social Security coverage and benefits and in the minimum wage (to $1.25 an hour), an extension of unemployment insurance, a housing and **urban renewal** bill, and manpower and aid-to-depressed-areas bills. Bills for national health coverage, education, and civil rights remained bottled up in Congress.

urban renewal   Effort to revitalize rundown areas of cities by providing federal funding for the construction of apartment houses, office buildings, and public facilities.

Kennedy had better luck in spurring economic recovery. He turned to the **"new economics"** advocated by Walter Heller, his chairman of the Council of Economic Advisers. Heller called for a more **Keynesian** direction in the economy, including more spending and cuts in business and income taxes. With little opposition in the face of a seemingly more aggressive Soviet Union, Congress raised the defense budget by almost 20 percent ($6 billion) and funded an expensive space program, providing direct stimulation that helped expand the economy. Unemployment fell by 2 percent from a 1960 high of nearly 7 percent, but a new problem, inflation, arose. Hoping to stem inflation and demonstrating vigorous economic management, Kennedy established informal price and wage guidelines for businesses and labor unions.

Most accepted the president's formulas, but in early 1962 United States Steel Corporation and a few other steel makers raised their prices above Kennedy's ceiling. He denounced United States Steel for acting contrary to the public interest and threatened to reduce its government contracts. Facing an angry president and the prospect of being undersold by competitors, U.S. Steel surrendered and lowered prices. As 1962 ended, the White House boasted that the economy was strong and effectively managed. Although Kennedy failed to provide new domestic spending programs, his administration placed great trust in the ability of government and a healthy economy to solve social problems. Heller wrote that "modern economics can . . . deliver the goods" and that economists "can meet a crisis and help carry an expansion." Other economists and social scientists confidently argued that eliminating poverty was "within the means of Federal, state, and local governments."

Kennedy and Civil Rights

It was not only Kennedy and his advisers who believed that through their actions society might be improved and problems resolved, but it was a hope held by many other individuals and groups as well. The consensus that had dominated the vision of the 1950s was decaying as the decade ended. "Beats," intellectuals, and many of the young clamored for change. Exulting in individuality and despising social norms, they argued that individuals, especially if joined together into groups, had the potential to change the world. The ongoing civil rights movement provided proof and acted as a model for others.

Although their hopes had been raised by Kennedy's promises of executive action, most African Americans knew that progress depended on their

As Kennedy took office, the sit-in movement was spreading across the South as students from colleges and universities sought to integrate places of public accommodation. In this picture, whites harass students from Tougaloo College as they "sit-in" at a Woolworth lunch counter in Jackson, Mississippi. *State Historical Society of Wisconsin.*

own actions, that the movement must be generated at the grassroots level and could not wait for or depend on government. Even as Kennedy campaigned, a new wave of black activism swept across the South in the form of sit-ins. The **sit-ins** began when four freshmen at North Carolina Agricultural and Technical College in Greensboro, North Carolina, decided to integrate the public lunch counter at the local F. W. Woolworth store. On February 1, 1960, they entered the store, sat down at the counter, and ordered a meal. A black waitress told them she could not serve them, but still they sat and waited for

---

new economics Planning and shaping the national economy through the use of tax policies and federal spending as recommended by Keynesian economics.

Keynesian (KANE-zee-an) Refers to economic theories of Lord John Maynard Keynes, who in the 1920s and 1930s argued for government intervention in the economy; he believed that government expansion of the money supply could stimulate economic growth during periods of recession and depression.

sit-in The act of occupying the seats or an area of a segregated establishment to protest racial discrimination; CORE had used the tactic in the 1940s to integrate places of public accommodation.

service until the store closed. They were not served, but no one tried to remove or arrest them. The next day twenty A&T students sat at the lunch counter demanding service. The movement quickly spread to more than 140 cities, including some outside the South, in Nevada, Illinois, and Ohio. In some cities, including Greensboro, integration was achieved with a minimum of resistance. But elsewhere, particularly in the Deep South, whites resisted violently in order to protect segregation. Thousands of participants in sit-ins were beaten, blasted with high-pressure fire hoses, and jailed. Most of those taking part were young and initially unorganized, but as the movement grew, organized civil rights groups moved to incorporate the new tactic and its practitioners. In April 1961, SCLC official Ella Baker helped form the **Student Nonviolent Coordinating Committee** (SNCC, pronounced "snick"), a new civil rights organization built around the sit-in movement. Although its statement of purpose emphasized **nonviolence**, SNCC members were more militant than other civil rights activists. As one stated, "We do not intend to wait placidly for those rights which are already legally and morally ours." SNCC workers quickly spread across the South, emphasizing community solidarity and action, efforts they believed would prompt the new administration to take action.

The new administration was not rushing to action, not rushing to ask Congress for civil rights legislation. With southern Democrats entrenched in Congress, Kennedy saw little reason to "raise hell" and waste legislative efforts on civil rights. Instead, he relied on limited executive action. He appointed more African Americans to federal positions than any previous president, including over forty to major posts, and named NAACP lawyer **Thurgood Marshall** to the U.S. circuit court, although Congress delayed his appointment for over a year. But Kennedy also took until November 1962 to fulfill a campaign pledge to lift his pen to ban segregation in federal housing.

Seeking to stimulate executive action, James Farmer of the Congress of Racial Equality (CORE; see page 804) announced a series of **"freedom rides"** to force integration in southern bus lines and stations. The Supreme Court had ruled in *Boynton v. Virginia* that all interstate buses, trains, and terminals were to be desegregated, and Farmer intended to make that decision a reality. The buses of riders left Washington, D.C., in May 1961, headed toward Alabama and Mississippi. Trouble was anticipated and in Anniston, Alabama, angry whites attacked the buses, smashing their windows and setting them on fire and severely

Anniston, Alabama was the end of the line for this bus of freedom riders. As riders got off the bus, they were pelted by stones and savagely beaten by a white mob. The bus was fire-bombed and its tires slashed. A second bus continued on to Montgomery. *UPI/Bettmann Archives.*

beating several freedom riders. The savagery continued in Birmingham, where one freedom rider needed fifty-three stitches to close his head wound. As expected, the violence forced a response by the administration. Having failed to stop the ride for a "cooling-off" period, U.S. Attorney General Robert Kennedy negotiated state and local protection for the riders through Alabama and placed federal agents on the buses. It did little good. When the buses arrived in Montgomery, the police and National Guard escorts vanished, and a large mob attacked the riders again.

Student Nonviolent Coordinating Committee
Organization formed to give young blacks a greater voice in the civil rights movement; it initiated black voter registration drives, sit-ins, and freedom rides.

nonviolence The rejection of violence in favor of peaceful tactics as a means of achieving political objectives.

Thurgood Marshall African-American lawyer who argued the *Brown* case before the Supreme Court; appointed to the federal court system by Kennedy, he became the first African-American Supreme Court justice.

freedom riders Civil rights protesters who rode buses throughout the South in 1961 to press for integration in bus terminals.

Furious, the attorney general deputized local federal officials as marshals and ordered them to escort the freedom riders to the state line, where Mississippi forces would take over. Battered and bloodied, the riders continued to the state capital, Jackson. There they were peacefully arrested for violating Mississippi's recently passed **public order laws**. The jails quickly filled as more freedom riders arrived and were arrested—328 by the end of the summer. The freedom rides ended in September 1961 when the administration declared that the Interstate Commerce Commission would uphold the Supreme Court decision prohibiting segregation. Faced with direct federal involvement, most state and local authorities desegregated bus and train terminals.

Hoping to steer the activism away from freedom rides and sit-ins, the Kennedy administration argued that efforts should focus on voter registration drives. Thus was born the Voter Education Project, a federally protected cooperative movement among the major civil rights organizations that would put ballots in the hands of a population who had been disfranchised since Reconstruction. The results of the project, which ended in 1964, seemed impressive: black voters in the South increased from 29.4 to 43.1 percent. But most of the success came in urban areas, where white opposition was less pronounced than in rural areas. In addition, many of those involved in voter registration were brutally attacked and jailed. The reality was that the federal government provided minimal protection and preferred to work through the court system. The Justice Department was not, one official commented, a national police force.

In some instances, Robert Kennedy hoped to prevent racial violence by a show of federal force. When **James Meredith** sought to integrate the University of Mississippi by enrolling in 1962, the attorney general sent a hundred federal marshals to guard Meredith. The tactic did not work. Thousands of white students and nonstudents attacked Meredith and the marshals. Two people were killed and 166 marshals were wounded before five thousand army troops arrived and restored order. Protected by federal forces, Meredith finished the year. In May 1963, the University of Mississippi had its first African-American graduate.

In 1963 Martin Luther King, Jr., focused his attention on overturning segregation in Birmingham, Alabama. He scheduled a series of protest marches in carefully selected locations, places where he expected a violent white reaction, which would force federal intervention and raise national awareness and support. On Good Friday, 1963, King led the first march. He was quickly arrested and, from his cell, wrote a nineteen-page "letter" defending his confrontational tactics aimed at those who denounced his activism in favor of patience. The "Letter from a Birmingham Jail" called for immediate and continuous, peaceful civil disobedience. Freedom was "never given voluntarily by the oppressor," King asserted, but "must be demanded by the oppressed." Smuggled out of jail and read aloud in churches and printed in newspapers across the nation, the letter rallied support for King's efforts. In Birmingham the marches continued, and on May 3 young and old alike filled the city's streets. Sheriff "Bull" Connor's police attacked the marchers with nightsticks, attack dogs, and high-pressure fire hoses. Television caught it all, including the arrest of more than thirteen hundred battered and bruised children. Connor's brutality not only horrified much of the American public but also caused many Birmingham blacks to reject the tactic of nonviolence. The following day, many African Americans fought the police with stones and clubs. Fearing more violence, King and Birmingham's business element met on May 10, and white business owners agreed to hire black salespeople. Neither the agreement nor King's pleading, however, halted the violence, and two days later President Kennedy ordered three thousand troops to Birmingham to maintain order and to uphold the integration agreement. "The sound of the explosion in Birmingham," King observed, "reached all the way to Washington."

Indeed, Birmingham had helped Kennedy conclude that the time had come to fulfill his campaign promise to make civil rights a priority. In June 1963, he announced that America could not be truly free "until all its citizens were free" and that he would send Congress civil rights legislation that would mandate integration in places of public accommodation.

To pressure Congress to act on the bill, King and other civil rights leaders organized a **March on Washington**. The August 28 march, with upward of 250,000

---

public order laws   Laws passed by many southern communities to discourage civil rights protests; they allowed the police to arrest anyone suspected of intending to disrupt public order.

James Meredith   Black student admitted to the University of Mississippi under federal court order in 1962; in spite of rioting by racist mobs, he finished the year and graduated in 1963.

March on Washington   Meeting of a quarter of a million civil rights supporters in Washington in 1963, at which Martin Luther King, Jr., delivered his "I Have a Dream" speech.

On August 28, 1963, one-quarter of a million people gathered in Washington, D.C. to support racial equality. Martin Luther King, Jr. electrified the crowd by saying "I have a dream that my four little children will one day live . . . where they will not be judged by the color of their skin but the content of their character." *Francis Miller, LIFE Magazine ©Time Warner Inc.*

people, was the largest crowd that had ever assembled in American history. King capped the day with an address that electrified the throng. He promised to continue the struggle until justice flowed "like a mighty stream," and he warned about a "whirlwind of revolt" if black rights were denied. "I have a dream," he offered, "that even Mississippi could become an oasis of freedom and justice" and that "all of God's children, black men and white men, Jews and Gentiles, Protestants and Catholics, will be able to join hands and sing . . . 'Free at last! Free at last! Thank God almighty, we are free at last!'" It was a stirring speech, but it did not move Congress to act. The bill stalled in committee, while in the South whites vowed to maintain segregation and racial violence continued. In Birmingham, within weeks of King's "I Have a Dream" speech, a church bombing killed four young black girls attending Sunday school.

FLEXIBLE RESPONSE

- How did the Cold War shape Kennedy's foreign policy?
- What actions did Kennedy take in Latin America and Vietnam to promote American interests?

From day one President Kennedy favored foreign over domestic policy. In his inaugural address, he dropped most of the material on domestic policy and concentrated on foreign policy, generating the powerful lines: "We shall pay any price, bear any burden, meet any hardship, support any friend, oppose any foe to assure the survival and success of liberty." Advised by his close circle of "action intellectuals," Kennedy was anxious to meet whatever challenges the United States faced, from the arms race, to the space race, to winning the allegiance of third world countries.

To back up his foreign policies, Kennedy instituted a new defense strategy called **flexible response** and significantly expanded military spending to pay for it. Flexible response involved continuing support for NATO and other multilateral alliances, plus further development of nuclear capabilities and intercontinental ballistic missiles (ICBMs). Hand in hand with this technology initiative came a renewed commitment to a civilian-based space program. When the Soviets hurled the first human being, cosmonaut Yuri Gagarin, into space in April 1961, Kennedy challenged them to "race to the moon." Alan Shepard's flight into space a month later was a beginning, and in 1969, after spending nearly $33 billion, Neil Armstrong won

flexible response   Kennedy's strategy of considering a variety of military and nonmilitary options when facing foreign policy decisions.

the race and became the first human to step on the surface of the moon.

Another aspect of flexible response centered on conventional, non-nuclear, warfare. With increased budgets, each branch of the service sought new weapons and equipment and developed new strategies for deploying them. Of special urgency was how to win the Cold War in the world's developing, "third world," nations. In that volatile arena of political instability, economic inequalities, and social conflicts, the opportunity was ripe for the West and the Communist bloc to expand their influence. It was a struggle that Kennedy meant to win. To strengthen pro-Western governments with advisers and to combat revolutionaries and insurgents, special counterinsurgency forces, such as the Green Berets, were developed. The military commitment, though, was second to wider economic strategies that provided direct government aid and private investment to "friendly" nations. This effort also included the personal involvement of American volunteers participating in the **Peace Corps**. Beginning in March 1961, more than ten thousand idealistic young Americans enrolled for two years to help win the "hearts and minds" of what Kennedy called "the rising peoples" around the world, staffing schools, constructing homes, building roads, and making other improvements.

Confronting Castro and the Soviets

Like the rest of the developing world, Kennedy saw Latin America as a place that, like plastic, could be molded and whose future was "unlimited." Taking action, in 1961 he introduced the **Alliance for Progress**, a foreign-aid package, promising more than $20 billion to show that "liberty and progress walk hand in hand." In return, Latin American governments were to introduce land and tax reforms and commit themselves to improving education and their people's standard of living. Overall, it was a plan that, Kennedy noted, could "successfully counter the Communists in the Americas." Results fell short of expectations. The United States granted far less than proposed, and Latin American governments implemented few reforms and frequently squandered the aid. Throughout the 1960s in Latin America, the gap between rich and poor widened, and the number of military dictatorships increased.

The Alliance for Progress, however, would not deal with the problem of Castro. Determined to remove the Cuban dictator, Kennedy decided to implement the Eisenhower administration's covert plan to topple

the Cuban leader (see page 865). In March 1960, the Central Intelligence Agency began training Cuban exiles and mercenaries for an invasion of Cuba, which included a scheme to assassinate Castro.

The invasion of Cuba began on April 17, 1961. More than fourteen hundred Cuban exiles landed at the Bahia de Cochinos, the **Bay of Pigs**. The strike was a failure, and within three days Castro's forces had captured or killed most of them. Kennedy took responsibility for the fiasco but indicated no regrets for his aggressive policy and the violation of Cuban territory, vowing to continue the "relentless struggle" against Castro and communism. Responding to Kennedy's orders to disrupt Cuba, **Operation Mongoose** was devised. It and other operations sponsored CIA-backed raids that destroyed roads, bridges, factories, and crops, and about thirty attempts to assassinate Castro.

After the Bay of Pigs disaster, in early June 1961, Kennedy met with Soviet leader Nikita Khrushchev in Vienna. Both men were eager to show their toughness. Kennedy stressed American determination to protect its interests and fulfill its international commitments. The issue of Berlin was especially worrisome because Khrushchev was threatening to sign a peace treaty with East Germany that would give it full control of all four zones of the city.

Returning home, Kennedy asked for massive increases in military spending, tripled the draft, and called 51,000 reservists to active duty. Back in Moscow, Khrushchev renewed atmospheric nuclear weapons testing and reaffirmed his commitment to East Germany and his determination to oust the Allies from Berlin. Kennedy responded by beginning American

---

Peace Corps   Program established by President Kennedy in 1961 to send young American volunteers to other nations as educators, health workers, and technicians.

Alliance for Progress   Program proposed by Kennedy in 1961 through which the United States provided aid for social and economic programs in Latin American countries; Congress trimmed appropriations following Kennedy's death.

Bay of Pigs   Site of a 1961 invasion of Cuba by Cuban exiles and mercenaries sponsored by the CIA; the invasion was crushed within three days and embarrassed the United States.

Operation Mongoose   Mission authorized by President Kennedy in November 1961, and funded with a $50 million budget, to create conditions for the overthrow of Castro.

Soviet leader Nikita Khrushchev met with John Kennedy at the Vienna Summit in June 1961. After their first meetings, Kennedy, who had been warned that Khrushchev's style ranged from "cherubic to choleric," was convinced that the Soviet leader had bested him, and that he had appeared to be a man "with no guts." Following the Vienna summit, Kennedy was determined to be tougher with the Soviets. "If Khrushchev wants to rub my nose in the dirt, it's all over," Kennedy stated after their meeting. *Wide World Photos.*

nuclear testing and voicing his strong support for West Berlin. Some within the administration advocated the use of force if the East Germans or the Soviets interfered with West Berlin. With both sides posturing, many feared armed confrontation over Berlin.

In August, the tension finally broke. The Soviets and East Germans suddenly erected a wall between West and East Berlin to choke off the flow of refugees fleeing East Germany and Eastern Europe. Although the Berlin Wall challenged Western ideals of freedom, it did not directly threaten the West's presence in West Berlin.

Far more serious than the Berlin crisis was the possibility of nuclear confrontation over Cuba in October 1962. On October 14, an American U-2 spy plane flying over the island discovered that medium-range nuclear missile sites were being built there. Launched from Cuba, such missiles would drastically reduce the time for mobilizing a U.S. counterattack on the Soviet Union. Kennedy promptly decided on a showdown with the Soviets and mustered a small crisis staff.

Negotiations were out of the question until the missiles were removed or destroyed. The military offered a series of recommendations ranging from a military invasion to a "surgical" air strike to destroy the missiles. All were rejected as too dangerous, possibly inviting a Soviet attack on West Berlin or on American nuclear missile sites in Turkey. President Kennedy, supported by his brother, the attorney general, decided to impose a naval blockade around Cuba until Khrushchev met the U.S. demand to remove the missiles. On Monday, October 22, Kennedy went on television and radio to inform the public of the missile sightings and his decision to quarantine Cuba. As 180 American warships got into position to stop Soviet ships carrying supplies for the missiles, army units converged on Florida. The **Strategic Air Command** (SAC) kept a fleet of nuclear-armed B-52s in the air at all times. On Wednesday, confrontation and perhaps war seemed imminent as two Soviet freighters and a Russian submarine approached the quarantine line. Robert Kennedy recalled, "We were on the edge of a precipice with no way off." Voices around the world echoed his anxiety.

The Soviet vessels, however, stopped short of the blockade. Khrushchev had decided not to test Kennedy's will. After a series of diplomatic maneuvers,

---

Strategic Air Command   Military unit formed in March 1946 to conduct long-range operations anywhere in the world; its first strategic plan, completed in 1949, projected nuclear attacks on seventy Soviet cities; it was abolished in 1992, becoming U.S. Strategic Command.

the two sides reached an agreement based on an October 26 message from Khrushchev: if the United States agreed not to invade Cuba, the Soviets would remove their missiles. Khrushchev sent another letter the following day that called for the United States to remove existing American missiles in Turkey. Kennedy chose to ignore the second message, and the Soviets agreed to remove their missiles without the United States publicly linking the agreement to withdrawing missiles in Turkey. Privately, the Soviets told Washington that they expected the United States to uphold its agreement to remove American missiles in Turkey. The world breathed a collective sigh of relief. Kennedy basked in what many viewed as a victory, but he recognized how near the world had come to nuclear war and concluded that it was time to improve Soviet-American relations. A "hot line" telephone link was established between Moscow and Washington to allow direct talks in case of another East-West crisis.

In a major foreign-policy speech in June 1963, Kennedy suggested an end to the Cold War and offered that the United States, as a first step toward improving relations, would halt its nuclear testing. By July, American-Soviet negotiations produced the **Limited Test Ban Treaty**, which forbade those who signed to conduct nuclear tests in the atmosphere, in space, and under the seas. Underground testing, with its verification problems, was still allowed. By October 1963, one hundred nations had signed the treaty, although the two newest atomic powers, France and China, refused to participate and continued to test in the atmosphere.

Vietnam

South Vietnam represented one of the most challenging issues Kennedy faced. Like Eisenhower, Kennedy saw it as a place where the United States' flexible response could stem communism and develop a stable, democratic nation. But by 1961, President **Ngo Dinh Diem** was losing control of his nation. South Vietnamese Communist rebels, the **Viet Cong**, controlled a large portion of the countryside, having battled Diem's troops, the Army of the Republic of Vietnam (ARVN), to a standstill. Military advisers argued that the use of American troops was necessary to turn the tide. Kennedy was more cautious. "The troops will march in, the bands will play," he said privately, "the crowds will cheer; and in four days everyone will have forgotten. Then we will be told we have to send in more troops. It's like taking a drink. The effect wears off and you have to

take another." The South Vietnamese forces would have to continue to do the fighting, but the president agreed to send more "advisers." By November 1963, the United States had sent $185 million in military aid and had committed sixteen thousand advisers to Vietnam—compared with only a few hundred in 1961.

The Viet Cong was only part of the problem. Diem's administration was unpopular, out of touch with the people, and unwilling to heed Washington's pleas for on political and social reforms. Some were even concerned that Diem might seek an accord with North Vietnam, and by autumn of 1963, Diem and his inner circle seemed more a liability than an asset. American officials in Saigon secretly informed several Vietnamese generals that Washington would support a change of government. The army acted on November 1, killing Diem and installing a new military government. The change of government, however, brought neither political stability nor improvement in the ARVN's capacity to fight the Viet Cong.

Death in Dallas

With his civil rights and tax cut legislation in limbo in Congress, a growing military commitment shackling the country to Vietnam, and the economy languishing, Kennedy in late 1963 watched his popularity rating drop below 60 percent. He decided to visit Texas in November to try to heal divisions within the Texas Democratic Party. He was assassinated there on November 22, 1963. The police quickly captured the reputed assassin, Lee Harvey Oswald. The next day a local nightclub owner and gambler, Jack Ruby, shot Oswald to death in the basement of the police station.

Many wondered whether Kennedy's assassination was the work of Oswald alone or part of a larger conspiracy. To dispel rumors, the government

---

Limited Test Ban Treaty Treaty signed by the United States, the USSR, and nearly one hundred other nations in 1963, banning nuclear weapons tests in the atmosphere, in outer space, and underwater.

Ngo Dinh Diem President of South Vietnam (1954–1963) who jailed and tortured opponents of his rule; he was assassinated in a coup in 1963.

Viet Cong Vietnamese Communist rebels in South Vietnam.

hastily formed a commission headed reluctantly by Chief Justice Earl Warren to investigate the assassination and determine if others were involved. The commission hurriedly examined most, but not all, of the available evidence and announced that Oswald was a psychologically disturbed individual who had acted alone. No other gunmen were involved nor was there any conspiracy. While many Americans accepted the conclusions of the Warren Commission, others continued to find errors in the report and to suggest other theories about the assassination.

Kennedy's assassination traumatized the nation. Many people canonized the fallen president as a brilliant, innovative chief executive who combined vitality, youth, and good looks with forceful leadership and good judgment. Lyndon B. Johnson, sworn in as president as he flew back to Washington on the plane carrying Kennedy's body, did not appear to be cut from the same cloth. Kennedy had attended the best eastern schools, enjoyed the cultural and social life associated with wealth, and liked to surround himself with intellectuals. Johnson, a product of public schools and a state college of education, distrusted intellectuals. Raised in the hill country of Texas, his passion was politics. By 1960, his congressional experiences were unrivaled: he had served from 1937 to 1948 in the House of Representatives and from 1949 to 1961 in the Senate, where he had become Senate majority leader. Johnson knew how to wield political power and get things done in Washington.

DEFINING A NEW PRESIDENCY

- How did Johnson's programs build on those started by Kennedy?

- In what ways did the legislation associated with the Great Society differ from New Deal programs?

- How did Johnson's War on Poverty and Great Society further the civil rights movement?

As president, Johnson made those around him aware that he was a liberal. He described himself as a New Dealer and told one adviser that Kennedy was "a little too conservative to suit my taste." Johnson wanted to build a better society, "where progress is the servant of the neediest." Recognizing the political opening generated by the assassination, Johnson immediately committed himself to Kennedy's agenda, and in January 1964 he expanded on it by announcing an "unconditional war on poverty."

Old and New Agendas

Throughout the next year, Johnson transformed Kennedy's quest for action into his own quest for social reform. Wielding the political skill for which he was renowned, he moved Kennedy's tax cut and civil rights bill out of committee and toward passage. The Keynesian tax cut, designed to generate more economic growth, became law in February. The civil rights bill moved more slowly, especially in the Senate, where it faced a stubborn southern **filibuster**. Johnson traded political favors for Republican backing to silence the fifty-seven-day filibuster, and the **Civil Rights Act of 1964** became law on July 2. The act made it illegal to discriminate for reasons of race, religion, or gender in places and businesses that served the public. Putting force behind the law, Congress established a federal Fair Employment Practices Committee (FEPC) and empowered the executive branch to withhold federal funds from institutions that violated its provisions.

By August, the War on Poverty had begun, aimed at benefiting the 20 percent of the population who were classified as poor. In 1962 social critic Michael Harrington had alerted the public to widespread poverty in America with his book, *The Other America*, which indicated that 35 million people lived in poverty. His findings were confirmed by a government study that defined the poverty line at $3,130 for an urban household of four, $1,925 for a rural family, and discovered that among the poor almost 40 percent of them (15.6 million) were under the age of 18.

The **War on Poverty** was to be fought on two fronts: expanding opportunities and improving the social environment. In March, after having selected Sargent Shriver to direct the offensive, the administration introduced to Congress the Economic Opportunities bill. Passed in August, the act established a variety of programs to be coordinated by an Office of Economic Opportunity. The cornerstones of the effort were education and job training.

> **filibuster**   An obstructionist tactic of prolonged speechmaking used in the legislature to prevent a vote or stall discussion on a bill.
>
> **Civil Rights Act of 1964**   Law that barred segregation in public facilities and forbade employers to discriminate on the basis of race, religion, sex, or national origin.
>
> **War on Poverty**   Lyndon Johnson's program to help Americans escape poverty through education, job training, and community development.

Johnson wanted to be remembered for his domestic programs, especially his effort to reduce poverty. During his presidency, Congress passed a variety of new programs, including Medicaid and Head Start, that targeted the 35 million Americans living below the poverty line. *Richard Wallmeyer/LBJ Library.*

civil rights bill, and his War on Poverty. By August Congress had approved all three, and public opinion polls showed significant support for the president in all parts of the nation, except the South. They also indicated that he would win easily against any Republican opponent. Conservative Republicans made his election even more likely by nominating **Barry Goldwater**. To some it appeared that conservatives were more interested in promoting their ideology than in winning the White House, and one prominent Democrat noted that the Republicans were "going on a Kamakaze mission."

Plainspoken and direct, Goldwater had voted against the 1964 Civil Rights Act and was an outspoken opponent of "Big Government" and New Deal–style programs. On the world stage, the Arizona Republican promised a more intense anti-Communist crusade and appeared willing not only to commit American troops in Vietnam, but also to use nuclear weapons against Communist nations, including Cuba and North Vietnam. The Democrats presented Goldwater as a dangerous radical. Meanwhile, Johnson promoted his Great Society and promised that "American boys" would not "do the fighting for Asian boys." Johnson won easily in a lopsided election.

Implementing the Great Society

Not only did Goldwater lose, but so too did many Republicans—moderates and conservative—as more than forty new Democrats entered Congress. Armed with a seeming mandate for action and reform, Johnson pushed forward legislation to enact his **Great Society**. He told aides that they must hurry before the natural opposition of politics returned. Between 1965 and 1968, more than sixty programs were put in place (see Table 28.1). Most sought to provide better economic and social opportunities by removing barriers thrown up by health, education, region, and race.

One of Johnson's Great Society goals was to further equality for African Americans. Within months of his election, he signed an executive order that, like the old Fair Employment Practices Commission, required

Improved "training and . . . job opportunities," he stated, would "help more Americans, especially young Americans, to escape from squalor and misery." Johnson was, according to Vice President Hubert Humphrey, "a nut on education . . . he just believed in it, just like some people believe in miracle cures." Under Shriver's direction, the Job Corps, Head Start, and the Work Incentive Program provided new educational and economic opportunities for the disadvantaged. Job Corps branches enrolled unemployed teens and young adults (16 to 21) lacking skills, while Head Start reached out to prekindergarten children to provide disadvantaged preschoolers an opportunity to gain important thinking and social skills. Another program called Volunteers in Service to America (VISTA), modeled after the Peace Corps, sent service-minded Americans to help improve life in regions of poverty.

To assure his election in November, Johnson figured he needed passage of Kennedy's tax cuts, the

> **Barry Goldwater** Conservative Republican senator from Arizona who ran unsuccessfully for president in 1965.
>
> **Great Society** Social program that Johnson announced in 1965; it included the War on Poverty, protection of civil rights, and funding for education.

table 28.1 Great Society Programs, 1964–1966

1964	1965	1966
Tax Reduction Act	Elementary and Secondary Education Act	Demonstration Cities and Metropolitan Development Act
Civil Rights Act	Voting Rights Act	Motor Vehicle Safety Act
Economic Opportunity Act	Medical Care Act (Medicare and Medicaid)	Truth in Packaging Act
Equal Employment Opportunity Commission	Head Start	Model Cities
Twenty-fourth Amendment	Upward Bound	Clean Water Restoration Act
Job Corps	Water Quality Act and Air Quality Act	Department of Transportation
Legal Services for the Poor	Department of Housing and Urban Development	
VISTA	National Endowment for the Arts and Humanities	
	Immigrations and Nationality Act	

government contractors to practice nondiscrimination in hiring and on the job. He also appointed the first African American to the cabinet, Secretary of Housing and Urban Development Robert Weaver; the first African-American woman to the federal courts, Judge Constance Baker Motley; and the first African American to the Supreme Court, Justice Thurgood Marshall.

Blacks applauded the president's actions but vowed to continue their activism, realizing that passage of a civil rights act did not end discrimination or poverty and all too aware that large pockets of active opposition to civil rights remained—especially in Alabama and Mississippi. To keep up the pressure, Martin Luther King, Jr., explained, African Americans would peacefully press for change and would be physically attacked, and Americans, "in the name of decency," would demand federal intervention and "remedial legislation."

A major goal was to expand black voting in the South. For nearly one hundred years, most southern whites had viewed voting as an activity for whites only and, through the poll tax and their control of the ballot, had maintained their political power and a segregated society. The ratification of the Twenty-fourth Amendment (banning the poll tax) in January 1964 was a major step toward dismantling that system, and by mid-1964 plans were underway to gain access to the ballot. One effort was led by Bob Moses of SNCC, who organized a **Freedom Summer** in Mississippi. Whites and blacks opened "Freedom Schools" to teach literacy and black history, stress black pride and achievements, and help residents register to vote. In Mississippi, as in several other southern states, a voter literacy test

Freedom Summer Effort by civil rights groups in Mississippi to register black voters and cultivate black pride during the summer of 1964.

President Johnson's Great Society greatly expanded the role of society in the lives of Americans through passage of civil rights, welfare, and education legislation. In this picture, President Johnson signs legislation establishing Medicare. His wife, Lady Bird and Vice President Hubert Humphrey watch in the background. *Lyndon B. Johnson Presidential Library.*

required that all questions be answered to the satisfaction of a white registrar. Thus a question calling for "a reasonable interpretation" of an obscure section of the state constitution could be used to block blacks from registering.

In the face of white hostility, voter registration was dangerous work. "You talk about fear," an organizer told recruits. "It's like the heat down there, it's continually oppressive. You think they're rational. But, you know, you suddenly realize, they want to kill you." Indeed, from June through August of 1964, Mississippi was rocked by more than thirty-five shooting incidents, and thirty buildings, many of them churches, were bombed. Hundreds were beaten and arrested, and three Freedom Summer workers were murdered. But the crusade drew national support and registered nearly sixty thousand new African-American voters.

Keeping up the pressure, King announced that a voter registration drive was to take place in Selma,

Alabama, where only 2.1 percent of eligible black voters were registered. As expected, the police, led by sheriff Jim Clark, who wore mirrored sunglasses and a helmet and carried a swagger stick, confronted protesters, arresting nearly two thousand. King then called for a **freedom march** from Selma to Montgomery. On March 7, 1965, as scores of reporters watched, hundreds of freedom marchers faced fifty Alabama state troopers and Clark's mounted forces at Pettus Bridge. After ordering the marchers to halt and firing tear gas, Clark's men, brandishing clubs and whips, chased them down.

---

freedom march   Civil rights march from Selma to Montgomery, Alabama, in March 1965; the violent treatment of protesters by local authorities helped galvanize national opinion against segregationists.

The summer of 1964 was called "Freedom Summer," as hundreds of civil rights volunteers—many of them college students—converged on Alabama and Mississippi to conduct voter registration drives, often facing violent opposition. Many were beaten, some were jailed, and some lost their lives, but as Anne Moody wrote in her autobiography, *Coming of Age in Mississippi*, "threats did not stop them." *Art and Artifacts Division, Schomburg Center for Research in Black Culture, the New York Public Library, Astor, Lenox, and Tilden Foundations.*

Television coverage of the assault stirred nationwide condemnation of Clark's tactics and support for King and the marchers. When staunch segregationist Governor George Wallace told President Johnson that he could not provide protection for the marchers, Johnson ordered the National Guard, two army battalions, and 250 federal marshals to escort the protesters. The march began on March 21 with about 3,200 marchers. When it arrived in Montgomery, more than 25,000 had joined.

Johnson used the violence in Selma to pressure Congress to pass the **Voting Rights Act**, which he signed into law in August 1965. It banned a variety of methods that states had been using to deny blacks

the right to vote, including Mississippi's literacy test, and had immediate effect. Across the South, the percentage of African Americans registered to vote rose about 30 percent by 1968 (see Map 28.2). In Mississippi, it went from 7 to 67 percent, and in Selma, more than 60 percent of qualified African Americans voted in 1968, stopping Sheriff Clark's bid for re-election.

But civil rights legislation was only one of many facets of the Great Society. The Appalachian Regional Development Act (1965), Public Works and Development Act (1965), and Model Cities Act (1966) focused on developing economic growth in cities and long-depressed regional areas. An Omnibus Housing Bill (1965) provided $8 billion for constructing low- and middle-income housing and supplementing low-income rent programs. In a related move, a cabinet-level Department of Housing and Urban Development was created. Mass-transit laws (1964 and 1966) provided needed funds for the nation's bus and rail systems, and consumer protection legislation established new and higher standards for product safety and truth in advertising. Immigration laws also underwent major modification. The Immigration Return Act of 1965 dropped the racial and ethnic discrimination that had been established in the 1920s by setting a uniform yearly limit on immigration from any one nation.

Responding to his own concerns and rising voices, Johnson also worked to have environmental law enacted. It was increasingly clear that many of the products developed during the war and commonly used by the 1950s, such as plastics, fertilizers, and pesticides, carried with them health problems. In 1962 biologist Rachel Carson's book *Silent Spring* alerted readers to the health dangers of DDT and helped fuel a growing movement to protect the environment. Johnson, in 1965, stated that he wanted not only to clean up the water and clear the air but also to impose national standards to prevent environmental pollution. The proposals met stiff opposition from industry and underwent modifications in Congress. Still when Johnson signed the Water Quality and Air Quality acts in October, it was only a beginning and he knew it. Over the next three years, he would guide through Congress the Clean Water Restoration Act,

Voting Rights Act Law passed by Congress in 1965 that outlawed literacy and other voting tests and authorized federal supervision of elections in areas where black voting had been restricted.

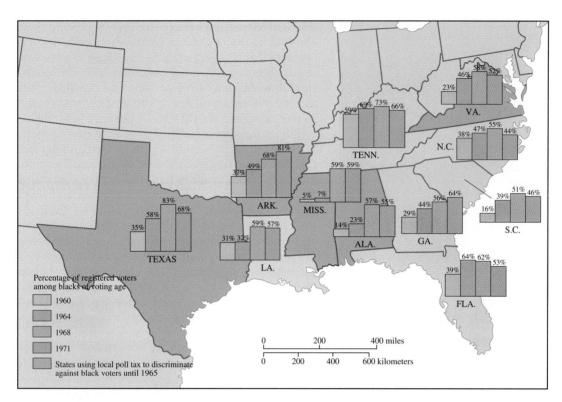

MAP 28.2 **African Americans and the Southern Vote, 1960–1971** An important part of the civil rights movement was to re-establish the African-American vote that had been stripped away in the South following Reconstruction. Between 1960 and 1971, with the outlawing of the poll tax and other voter restrictions, African-American voter participation rose significantly across the South.

expanding wilderness areas and a highway beautification program aimed at removing billboards from federal highways.

At the top of Johnson's priorities, however, were health and education. Above all, he wanted those two "coonskins on the wall." The Elementary and Secondary Education Act (1965) was the first general educational funding act by the federal government. It granted more than a billion dollars to public and parochial schools for textbooks, library materials, and special education programs. Poor and rural school districts were supposed to receive the highest percentage of federal support. But, as with many Great Society programs, implementation fell short of intention, and much of the money went to affluent suburban school districts. Johnson's biggest "coonskin" was the Medical Care Act (1965) which established **Medicaid** and **Medicare** to help pay healthcare costs for the elderly and individuals on welfare. In 1966 Democrats were calling the Eighty-ninth Congress "the Congress of accomplished hopes."

NEW VOICES

• How do the urban riots and the emergence of the Black Power movement reflect a new agenda for the civil rights movement? In what ways were the voices of Black Power new?

• What limitations on equality did women face and how did they organize to overcome those barriers? What was the critique of American values made by some women and homosexuals?

• What changes did the youth movement seek? How did the counterculture reject traditional social norms?

Medicaid Program of health insurance for the poor established in 1965; it provides states with money to buy healthcare for people on welfare.

Medicare Program of health insurance for the elderly and disabled established in 1965; it provides government payment for healthcare supplied by private doctors and hospitals.

By the end of 1965, legislation had ended **de jure** segregation and voting restrictions. Equality, however, depended on more than laws. Neither the Civil Rights Act nor the Voting Rights Act guaranteed justice, removed oppressive poverty, provided jobs, or ensured a higher standard of living. **De facto** discrimination and prejudice remained, and African-American frustrations—born of raised expectations—poverty, prejudice, and violence soon changed the nature of civil rights protest and ignited northern cities. During the 1960s, more than a million mostly poor and unskilled African Americans left the South each year. Most sought a better life in northern and western cities, but they mostly found soaring unemployment and cities unable or unwilling to provide adequate social services. Economics not segregation was the key issue: "I'd eat at your lunch counter—if only I had a job," spelled out the problem for many urban blacks. By the mid-1960s, the nation's cities were primed for racial trouble. Minor race riots occurred in Harlem and Rochester, New York, during the summer of 1964, but it was the Watts riot and the militant new voices that shook the nation.

Urban Riots and Black Power

In Los Angeles, African Americans earned more per capita and owned more homes than African Americans in any other American city. Within Los Angeles, most African Americans lived in a 50-square-mile area called **Watts**. To most outside observers, Watts did not look like a ghetto. It was a community of well-maintained single-family homes and duplexes. But looks were deceptive. With a population exceeding 250,000, Watts had a population density more than four times higher per block than the rest of the city. Schools were overcrowded, and male unemployment hovered at 34 percent. Patrolling Watts was the nearly all-white L.A. police force, which had a reputation for racism and brutality.

In this climate, on August 11, 1965, what began as a simple drunk driving arrest became a scuffle, and then a riot. Stores were looted and set on fire, cars were overturned and set ablaze, firefighters and police were attacked and unable to either put out the flames or restore order. Thirty-six hours passed until sixteen thousand poorly trained and equipped members of the California National Guard, along with police and sheriff's deputies, began to calm the storm. The costs of the Watts riot were high: 34 dead, including 28 African Americans, more than 900 injured, and $45 million in property destroyed.

The Watts riot also signaled a change in attitude among African Americans and shattered the complacency of many whites who thought civil rights was just a southern problem. In addition, the riot demonstrated a growing willingness of African Americans to reject nonviolence. The debate about goals and tactics intensified, with concrete goals gaining favor over "dreams" and force becoming the tool of choice. In 1964 Martin Luther King, Jr., had received the Nobel Peace Prize, but in 1965, when he spoke to the people of Watts after the rioting, he discovered they had little use for his "dreams." He was shouted down and jeered. "Hell, we don't need no damn dreams," one skeptic remarked. "We want jobs." Another civil rights leader noted that while the riot was unfortunate, it had brought numerous politicians to Watts offering grants and asking what programs needed to be implemented. Thus increasing numbers of blacks leaned toward a more militant response to racial and economic injustices. The new voices called on blacks to seek power through solidarity, independence, and, if necessary, violence. They called for **Black Power**.

African Americans needed to use the same means as whites, argued one veteran of the battle to integrate Mississippi: "If he pose with a smile, meet him with a smile, and if he pose with a gun, meet him with a gun." Many in SNCC and CORE agreed, and in the summer of 1965 they changed tactics to embrace Black Power. The new leader of SNCC was **Stokely Carmichael** (see Individual Choices, page 884), who exalted Black Power: "I'm not going to beg the white man for anything I deserve," he announced

---

de jure Latin term meaning "by law"; in this case, refers to laws that had segregated the South, also called Jim Crow laws.

de facto Latin term meaning "by fact"; in this case, refers to ways in which society, regardless of the law, discriminated against African Americans.

Watts Predominantly black neighborhood of Los Angeles where race riots in August 1965 did $45 million in damage and took the lives of twenty-eight blacks.

Black Power Movement begun in 1966 that rejected the nonviolent, coalition-building approach of traditional civil rights groups and advocated black control of black organizations; the self-determination approach was adopted by Latinos (Brown Power) and Native Americans (Red Power) as well.

Stokely Carmichael Civil rights activist who led SNCC and popularized the term "Black Power" to describe the need for blacks to use militant tactics to force whites to accept political change.

in 1966. "I'm going to take it." SNCC and CORE quickly changed from biracial, nonviolent organizations to Black Power resistance movements that stressed Black Nationalism. The insistence on independence from white allies and the violent rhetoric widened the gap between moderates and radicals.

The new voices also found advocates among the Nation of Islam, or **Black Muslims**. Founded by Elijah Muhammad in the 1930s, the movement attracted mostly young males and demanded adherence to a strict moral code that prohibited the use of drugs and alcohol. Black Muslims preached black superiority and separatism from an evil white world. By the early 1960s, there were nearly a hundred thousand Black Muslims, including **Malcolm X**.

A life of hard drugs, pimping, and burglary landed Malcolm Little in prison by the age of 20. Behind bars, his intellectual abilities blossomed. He devoured the prison library, took correspondence courses, and converted to the Nation of Islam—becoming Malcolm X. On his release in 1952, he quickly became one of the Black Muslims' most powerful and respected leaders. A mesmerizing speaker, he rejected integration with a white society that, he said, emasculated blacks by denying them power and personal identity. "Our enemy is the white man!" he roared. But in 1964 he re-evaluated his policy. Though still a Black Nationalist, he admitted that to achieve their goals Black Muslims needed to cooperate with other civil rights groups and with some whites. He broke with Elijah Muhammad, and the defection cost him his life. On February 21, 1965, three Black Muslims assassinated him in Harlem. After his death, Malcolm X's *Autobiography* (1965), chronicling his personal triumph over white oppression, became a revered guide for many blacks.

Carmichael and Malcolm X represented only two of the strident African-American voices advocating direct and, if necessary violent, action. Adopting the name and symbol of Loundes County (Alabama) Freedom Organization, Huey P. Newton, Eldridge Cleaver, and Bobby Seale organized the **Black Panthers** in Oakland, California, in 1966. Although they pursued community action, such as developing school lunch programs, they were more noticeable for being well-armed and willing to use their weapons. FBI director J. Edgar Hoover called them "the most dangerous . . . of all extremist groups."

The militant black nationalism and calls for self-defense by a new wave of black leaders appeared to fuel a growing number of race riots that shook more than three hundred cities between 1965 and 1968. The summer of 1967 marked the worst year with

Dropping his "slave name," Malcolm Little took the name Malcolm X—the letter "X" representing the stolen identities of African slaves. A member of the Black Muslims, he became one of the most recognized and controversial African-American nationalist leaders. He was assassinated in 1965 by members of the Nation of Islam after forming a rival organization. *Wide World Photos.*

more than seventy-five major riots. The deadliest occurred in Detroit. With its mayor strongly sup-

Black Muslims Popular name for the Nation of Islam, an African-American religious group founded by Elijah Muhammad, which professed Islamic religious beliefs and emphasized black separatism.

Malcolm X Black activist who advocated black separatism as a member of the Nation of Islam; in 1963 he converted to orthodox Islam and two years later was assassinated.

Black Panthers Black revolutionary party founded in 1966 that endorsed violence as a means of social change; many of its leaders were killed in confrontations with police or imprisoned.

porting civil rights and working closely with civil rights organizations, Detroit appeared to be a stable city. It received more than $200 million in federal grants for urban renewal, job training, and schools. Yet, as in Watts, tensions simmered beneath the surface. Jobs were few, urban renewal projects and a new highway system were breaking apart black neighborhoods, and the police were widely seen as racist. When in July the police raided an after-hours bar, the black neighborhoods exploded. In the five days it took the army to quell the riot, thirty-four people died, seven thousand were arrested, and millions of dollars' worth of property was destroyed.

Responding to the riots in Detroit and elsewhere, Johnson created a special commission chaired by Governor Otto Kerner of Illinois to investigate their causes. The commission report, issued in March 1968, put the primary blame on the racist attitudes of white America. The study described two Americas, one white and one black, and concluded: "Pervasive discrimination and segregation in employment, education, and housing have resulted in the continuing exclusion of great numbers of Negroes from the benefits of economic progress."

Just a month later, a new wave of riots spread across the United States following the assassination of Martin Luther King, Jr., by a white racist. King had worked hard to regain his leadership of the civil rights movement after the Watts riot and the emergence of Black Power. Shifting from legal rights to economic rights, he had become a champion of the black urban **underclass**, criticizing the capitalistic system that relegated millions of people to poverty. Still an advocate of nonviolence, King called for mass demonstrations to compel economic and social justice. He was in Memphis supporting striking black sanitation workers when, on April 4, 1968, he was killed by James Earl Ray. Spontaneously, African Americans took to the streets in 168 cities, including Washington, D.C.

Before long, the flames engulfing American cities and the fiery cries of "Burn, baby, burn!" and "Black Power!" sparked a white backlash. Many Americans, fearful of Black Power advocates and increasing urban violence, backed away from supporting civil rights. Republican politicians were especially vocal. Governor of California Ronald Reagan argued the "riff-raff" theory of urban problems: "mad dogs" and "lawbreakers" were the sole cause of the trouble. Most Americans applauded as the FBI and police cracked down on the radicals, especially the Black Panther Party, many of whose members were arrested or killed in battles with authorities. Others, including Cleaver and Carmichael, left for Africa.

From King to Carmichael, African Americans confronted the old order. But they were not alone. The 1960s found many other individuals and groups arguing and protesting for change. Young adults questioned social and cultural values and voiced demands for a more liberated society, one that placed few barriers on individual actions. Women in increasing numbers were seeking to alter the status quo and were rejecting the notion that they were fulfilled by running their homes and serving their families. For some, what began as an effort to gain equality resulted in a larger critique of traditional American views about sexuality and gender.

Rejecting the Feminine Mystique

The willingness of women to question their popular image was partially a response to the changing reality of society and the workplace. Since the 1950s, more women were entering the work force, graduating from college, getting divorced, and becoming heads of households. Households headed by single women were among the most impoverished group in America. Women complained that gender stereotyping denied them access to better-paying career jobs. The Kennedy administration's 1963 report of the *Presidential Commission on the Status of Women* confirmed in stark statistics that women constituted a social and economic underclass. They worked for less pay than white males (on average 40 percent less), were more likely to be fired or laid off, and rarely reached top career positions. It was not solely in the workplace that women faced discrimination. Throughout the country, divorce, credit, and property laws generally favored men, and in several states women were not even allowed to serve on juries.

The president's commission provided statistics, but it was **Betty Friedan's** 1963 bestseller, *The Feminine Mystique*, that many regard as the beginning of the women's movement. After reviewing the responsibilities of the housewife (making beds, grocery

---

underclass The lowest economic class; the term carries the implication that members of this class are so disadvantaged by poverty that they have little or no chance to escape it.

Betty Friedan Feminist who wrote *The Feminine Mystique* in 1963 and helped found the National Organization for Women in 1966.

In 1972, Title IX of the Education Amendments required gender equality in school and college sports, dramatically changing the nature of women's athletics by igniting a women's sports boom. In this 1967 picture, the first woman to attempt the running of the Boston Marathon—a previously all male event—is attacked by a race official and was prevented from finishing the race. Today, the Boston Marathon celebrates both men and women marathon runners. *Corbis-Bettmann.*

shopping, driving children everywhere, preparing meals and snacks, and pleasing her husband), Friedan asked: "Is this all?" She concluded it was not enough. Women needed to overcome the "feminine mystique" that promised them fulfillment in the domestic arts. She called on women to set their own goals and seek careers outside the home. Her book, combined with the presidential report, provided new perspectives to women and contributed to a renewed women's movement. Also engendering more activism was the passage of the 1964 Civil Rights Act with the inclusion of **Title VII**. The original version of the bill made no mention of discrimination on account of sex, but Representative Martha Griffins (D.-Michigan) joined with conservative Democrat Howard Smith of Virginia to add the word *sex* to the civil rights act—she to strengthen the bill, he thinking the addition would kill it. As finally approved, Title VII prohibited discrimination on the basis of race, religion, creed, national origin, or sex.

Many people hoped Title VII marked the beginning of a serious effort by government to provide gender equality. But when the Equal Employment Opportunity Commission, established to support the law, and the Johnson administration showed little interest in dealing with gender discrimination, they formed organizations to promote women's interests and to persuade the government to enforce Title VII. Many organizers, like Mary King and Casey Hayden of SNCC, were experienced civil rights activists and anxious to push women's rights. In "the black movement," a female civil rights worker wrote, "I had been fighting for someone else's oppression and now there

was a way I could fight for my own freedom and I was going to be much stronger than I ever was." The most prominent women's organization to emerge was the **National Organization for Women** (NOW) formed in 1966. With Betty Friedan as president, NOW launched an aggressive campaign to draw attention to sex discrimination and redress wrongs. It demanded an Equal Rights Amendment to the Constitution to ensure gender equality and pushed for easier access to birth control devices and the right to have an abortion. NOW grew rapidly from about 300 in 1966 to 175,000 in 1968. But the women's movement was larger than NOW and represented a variety of voices.

Rejecting Gender Roles

By the end of the decade, some of those seeking change went beyond economics and politics in their critique of American society, taking aim at existing norms of sex and gender roles. Radical feminists, for example, called for a redefinition of sexuality and repudiated America's enchantment with family,

Title VII   Provision of the Civil Rights Act of 1964 that guarantees women legal protection against discrimination.

National Organization for Women   Women's rights organization founded in 1966 to fight discrimination against women, to improve educational, employment, and political opportunities for women, and to fight for equal pay for equal work.

marriage, and male-dominated society. "We identify the agents of our oppression as men, ... We are exploited as sex objects, breeders, domestic servants and cheap labor," declared the Redstocking Manifesto in 1969. The New York group that issued the manifesto was among the first to use **"consciousness-raising"** groups to educate women about the oppression they faced because of the sex gender system. Rita Mae Brown went further, leaving the Redstockings in order to advocate lesbian rights. In 1973 she published her first acclaimed novel, *Rubyfruit*, which presented lesbianism in a positive light and provided a literary basis for discussion of lesbian life and attitudes.

By the late 1960s, Rita Brown and radical feminists were not the only ones asking society to reconsider its traditional views toward sexuality and gender. Since the 1950s, organizations such as the Daughters of Bilitis and the Mattachine Society had worked quietly to promote new attitudes toward homosexuality and to overturn laws that punished homosexual activities. But most homosexuals remained "in the closet," fearful of reprisals by the "straight" community and its institutions. The Stonewall Riot in 1969, however, brought increased visibility and renewed activism to the homosexual community.

The police raid on the Stonewall Inn in New York City resulted in an unexpected riot as gay patrons fought the police and were joined by other members of the community. A Gay Manifesto called for gays and lesbians to raise their consciousness and rid their minds of "garbage" poured into them by old values. "Liberation . . . is defining for ourselves how and with whom we live." "We are only at the beginning."

It was a beginning and success came slowly. Polls indicated that the majority of Americans still considered homosexuality immoral and even a disease. But by the mid-1970s, those polls indicated a shift as a slight majority of Americans opposed job discrimination based on sexual orientation and seemed willing to show more toleration of gay lifestyles. Responding to gay rights pressure in 1973, the American Psychiatric Association ended its classification of homosexuality as a mental disorder.

The Youth Movement

Within the civil rights, feminist, and gay rights movements, young college-age adults were among the loudest and most militant calling for change. Across the nation during the 1960s, the impact of an activist youth culture was instrumental in shaping the decade. The "youth culture" was a product of the baby boom as the leading edge of that generation went off to college. More than ever, Americans were attending post–high school education—and postponing full-time employment and marriage.

In 1965 more than 40 percent of the nation's high school graduates were attending college, a leap of 13 percent from 1955 and of nearly 30 percent since World War II. Graduate and professional schools were churning out record numbers of advanced degrees. Although the majority of young adults remained quite traditional, an expanding number chose alternative careers and values. Some joined the Peace Corps and VISTA, others led sit-ins, protested injustices, and joined organizations like SNCC and NOW, but all believed that the actions of one person or group could make a difference in transforming society and the world. As they enrolled in colleges in record numbers, some began to question the role of the university and the goals of education. Particularly at huge institutions like the University of California at Berkeley and at Los Angeles and the University of Michigan, students complained that humanism and concern for individuals were missing from education. Education seemed sterile, an assembly line producing standardized products, not a crucible of ideas creating independent, thinking individuals. Paul Goodman, in *Growing Up Absurd* (1960), argued that schools destroyed natural creativity and replaced it with a highly structured system that stressed order, conformity, and pragmatism. Education was designed to meet the needs of administrators and teachers, not students, he charged. Reflecting Goodman's view, many students demanded freedom of expression and a new, more flexible attitude from college administrators and faculty.

Campus activists denounced course requirements and restrictions on dress, behavior, and living arrangements. On some campuses they led protests and staged sit-ins in campus buildings demanding changes and more student freedoms. By the end of the decade, many colleges and schools had relaxed or eliminated dress codes. Long hair was accepted for males, and casual clothes like faded blue jeans and shorts were common dress for both sexes on most college campuses. Colleges also lifted dorm curfews, visitation restrictions, and other residence

---

consciousness-raising   Achieving greater awareness of the nature of political or social issues through group interaction.

rules. Some dorms became coed. Academic departments reduced the number of required courses. By the beginning of the 1970s, many colleges and even some high schools had introduced programs in nontraditional fields such as African-American, Native American, and women's studies.

Setting their sights beyond the campus community, some student activists urged that the campus should be a haven for free thought and a marshaling ground for efforts to change society significantly. At the University of Michigan in 1960, Tom Hayden and Al Haber organized **Students for a Democratic Society** (SDS). SDS members insisted that Americans recognize that their affluent nation was also a land of poverty and want and that business and government chose to ignore social inequalities. In 1962 SDS issued its *Port Huron Statement*, which maintained, "The search for truly democratic alternatives to the present, and a commitment to social experimentation with them, is a worthy and fulfilling human enterprise, one which moves us and, we hope, others today." Hayden argued that the country should reallocate its resources according to social need and strive to build "an environment for people to live in with dignity and creativeness."

The youth movement's discontent with social and cultural norms also found expression in what was called the **counterculture**. Many young people spurned the traditional moral and social values of their parents and the 1950s. "Don't trust anyone over 30" was the motto of the young generation. Counterculture thinking grated at conformity and glorified freedom of the spirit and self-knowledge. A large number of teens and young adults began to accuse American society of being "plastic" in its materialism and blind to change, and they sought ways to express their dissatisfaction.

Music was one of the most prominent forms of defiance. Some musicians, like Bob Dylan and Joan Baez, challenged society with protest and antiwar songs rooted in folk music and aimed at specific problems. For the majority, however, rock 'n' roll, which took a variety of forms, remained dominant. Performers like the **Beatles**, an English group that exploded on the American music scene in 1964, were among the most popular, sharing the stage with other British imports such as the Rolling Stones and the Animals, whose behavior and songs depicted a life of pleasure and lack of social restraints. Other musicians, like the Grateful Dead and Jimi Hendrix, turned rock 'n' roll into a new form of music, psychedelic **acid rock**, which acclaimed an uninhibited drug culture.

The Counterculture

The message of much music of the 1960s was that drugs offered another way to be free of the older generation's values. For many coming of age in the 1960s, marijuana, or "pot," was the primary means to get "stoned" or "high." Marijuana advocates claimed that it was nonaddictive and that, unlike the nation's traditional drug—alcohol—it reduced aggression and heightened perception. Thus, they argued, marijuana reinforced the counterculture's ideals of peace, serenity, and self-awareness. A more dangerous and unpredictable drug also became popular with some members of the counterculture: LSD, lysergic acid diethylamide, or "acid," a hallucinogenic drug that alters perception. Harvard psychology professor **Timothy Leary** argued that by "tripping" on LSD people could "turn on, tune in, and drop out" of the rat race that was American society. Although most youths did not use drugs, drugs offered some within the counterculture and the nation a new experience that many believed was liberating. Drugs also proved to be destructive and deadly, contributing to the deaths of several counterculture figures, including musicians Jimi Hendrix, Jim Morrison, and Janis Joplin.

Another realm of traditional American values the counterculture overturned was sex. Some young

---

Students for a Democratic Society   Left-wing student organization founded in 1962 to criticize American materialism and work for social justice.

Port Huron Statement   A 1962 critique of the Cold War and American materialism and complacency by Students for a Democratic Society; it called for "participatory democracy" and for universities to be centers of free speech and activism.

counterculture   A subculture espousing values or lifestyles in opposition to those of the established culture; prominent in the 1960s as members adopted lifestyles that stressed communal living, drugs, Asian religions, and free sexual expression.

Beatles   English rock group that gained international fame in 1964 and disbanded in 1970; they were known for the intelligence of their lyrics and their sophisticated instrumentation.

acid rock   Rock music having a driving, repetitive beat and lyrics that suggest psychedelic drug experiences.

Timothy Leary   Harvard professor and counterculture figure who advocated the expansion of consciousness through the use of drugs such as LSD.

To many, the counterculture was defined by "hippie" communes, where groups of young people left conventional society to establish alternative life styles, often close to nature, like the setting shown. *John Olsen/Timepix.*

people appalled their parents and society by questioning, if not rejecting, the values that placed restrictions on sexual activities. Sex was a form of human expression, they argued, and if it felt good, why stifle it? New openness about sexuality and relaxation of the stigma on extramarital sex turned out to be significant legacies of the 1960s. But the philosophy of **free love** also had a negative side as increased sexual activity contributed to a rapid rise in cases of sexually transmitted diseases. The notion of free love also exposed women to increased sexual assault as some men assumed that all "liberated" women desired sexual relations.

Perhaps the most colorful and best-known advocates of the counterculture and its ideals were the **"hippies."** Seeking a life of peace, love, and self-awareness—governed by the law of "what feels good" instead of by the rules of traditional behavior—hippies tried to distance themselves from traditional society. They flocked in large numbers to northern California, congregating especially in the Haight-Ashbury neighborhood of San Francisco, where they frequently carried drug abuse and free love to excess. Elsewhere, some hippie groups abandoned the "old-fashioned" nuclear family and lived together as extended families on communes. Hippies expressed their nonconformity in their appearance, favoring long unkempt hair and ratty blue jeans or long flowered dresses. Although the number of hippie dropouts was small, their style of dress and grooming greatly influenced young Americans.

The influence of the counterculture peaked, at least in one sense, in the summer of 1969, when an army of teens and young adults converged on **Woodstock**, New York, for the largest free rock concert in history. For three days, through summer rains and deepening mud, more than four hundred thousand came together in a temporary open-air community, where many of the most popular rock 'n' roll bands performed day and night. Touted as three days of peace and love, sex, drugs, and rock 'n' roll, Woodstock symbolized the power of counterculture values to promote cooperation and happiness.

The spirit of Woodstock was fleeting. For most people, at home and on campus, the communal ideal was impractical, if not unworkable. Nor did the vast majority of young people who took up some counterculture notions completely reject their parents' society. Most stayed in school and continued to participate in the society they were criticizing. To be sure, the counterculture had a lasting impact on American society—on dress, sexual attitudes, music, and even personal values—but it did not reshape America in its image.

> **free love** Popular belief among members of the counterculture in the 1960s that sexual activities should be unconstrained.
>
> **hippies** Members of the counterculture in the 1960s who rejected the competitiveness and materialism of American society and searched for peace, love, and autonomy.
>
> **Woodstock** Free rock concert in Woodstock, New York, in August 1969, which attracted 400,000 people and was remembered as the classic expression of the counterculture.

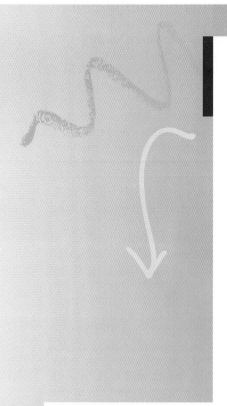

INDIVIDUAL VOICES

Examining a Primary Source

Stokely Carmichael Justifies Black Power

The pivotal catchphrase that redefined race relations in the sixties burst onto the front pages on June 16, 1966, when Stokely Carmichael renewed the call for "Black Power." Black Power conjured up a variety of images, depending on who said it. To many whites the term seemed threatening; to many African Americans it signaled the need to understand the race issue in a different way and to consider new choices. In the speech excerpted below, entitled "Toward Black Liberation," Carmichael defines *Black Power* and distinguishes its goals from those of other civil rights organizations.

Negroes are defined by two forces, their blackness and their powerlessness. There have been traditionally two communities in America. The White community, which controlled and defined the forms that all institutions within the society would take, and the Negro community, which has been excluded from participation in the power decisions that shaped the society, and has traditionally been dependent upon, and subservient to the White community. ●

● According to Carmichael, how is power shared in the United States, and what steps must the African-American population take to gain power?

● How does Carmichael differentiate personal from institutional racism? How might these two kinds of racism mirror de jure and de facto discrimination?

This has not been accidental. . . . This has not been on the level of individual acts of discrimination between individual whites against individual Negroes, but as total acts by the White Community against the Negro community. . . .

Let me give an example of the difference between individual racism and institutionalized racism, and the society's response to both. When . . . White terrorists bomb a Negro Church and kill five children, that is an act of individual racism, widely deplored by . . . society. But when in that same city . . . not five but 500 Negro babies die each year because of a lack of proper food, shelter, and medical facilities . . . that is a function of institutionalized racism. ● *But the society either pretends it doesn't know of this situation, or is incapable of doing anything meaningful about it. And, the resistance to do anything meaningful . . . is . . . a product of . . . forces and special interests in the White community, and the groups that have . . . resources and power to change that situation benefit, politically and economically, from the existence of that ghetto. . . . The people of the Negro community do not control the resources of that community, its political decisions, its law enforcement, its housing standards, and even the physical ownership of the land, houses and stores lie outside that community. . . .*

In recent years the answer to these questions which has been given by the most articulate groups of Negroes and their white allies . . . has been in terms of something called "integration" . . . social justice will be accomplished by "integrating the Negro into the mainstream institutions of the society . . . ."

This concept . . . had to be based on the assumption that there was nothing of value in the Negro community and that little of value could be created among Negroes, so the thing to do was to siphon off the "acceptable" Negroes into the surrounding middle-class white communities. . . . It is true . . . SNCC . . . had a

● *How do you think Carmichael might, in a few words, define Black Power?*

similar orientation. But while it is hardly a concern of a black sharecropper, dishwasher, or welfare recipient whether a certain fifteen-dollar-a-day motel offers accommodations to Negroes, the overt symbols of white superiority . . . had to be destroyed. Now, black people must look beyond these goals, to the issue of collective power. ●

SUMMARY

Kennedy's election generated a renewed wave of activism and optimism. Many hoped that the nation's and the world's problems could be solved by combinations of individual, institutional, and governmental actions. It fueled the heart of the New Frontier, the War on Poverty, and the Great Society and raised the expectations of a nation. Heightened expectations were clearly visible among the African Americans who looked to Kennedy, and later to Johnson, for legislation to end segregation and discrimination. As Kennedy took office, African-American leaders launched a series of sit-ins and freedom marches designed to keep the pressure on American society and the government. Kennedy's domestic options, however, were limited by a narrow Democratic margin in Congress, and a comprehensive civil rights bill was not introduced until mid-1963. It was quickly mired in congressional politics as were several other pieces of Kennedy's domestic agenda, including aid to education and a tax cut. Like Eisenhower, Kennedy had to settle for modest legislative successes that merely expanded existing programs and entitlements.

Hampered by congressional opposition, Kennedy favored foreign policy. In implementing flexible response, Kennedy adopted a more comprehensive strategy to confront communism. Confrontations over Berlin and Cuba, an escalating arms and space race, and an expanded commitment to Vietnam were accepted as part of the United States' global role and passed intact to Johnson.

As president, Johnson expanded on the slain president's agenda, announcing a War on Poverty and the implementation of a Great Society. Between 1964 and 1966 Johnson pushed through Congress a series of acts that extended New Deal liberalism into new areas of public policy. The 1964 Civil Rights Act and the 1965 Voting Rights Act reshaped society and politics. Other Great Society legislation tackled poverty and discrimination, expanded educational opportunities, and created a national system of health insurance for the poor and elderly.

The decade's emphasis on activism, the New Frontier, and the Great Society encouraged more Americans to seek equality and raise new agendas. Within the African-American movement, more emphasis was centered on economic and social issues. Some African-American activists rejected assimilation and expressed more militant demands for basic institutional social and economic changes. Drawing from the civil rights movement, consciousness-raising efforts, and the inclusion of gender in the civil rights act, the decade also saw a re-emergence of a women's movement. Many women also began to question the framework of gender roles in a male-dominated society as they sought economic, legal, and social equality. Within the civil rights and feminist movements, much of the activism came from young adults. The nation's youth, too, seemed unwilling to accept the traditional values of society and demanded change.

Some Americans, as the decade drew to a close, recoiled from the incessant demands for change. Disturbed by race riots and other attacks on the status quo, an increasing number of people were questioning government programs that appeared to favor the poor and minorities at the majority's expense. The result was that a decade that had begun with great promise produced, for many, disappointment and disillusionment.

MOVING TO THE SUNBELT From the 1960s on, many Americans have moved to the Sunbelt — a region, shown in this map, stretching from Florida in a westward arc to the state of Washington. Pushed by harsh winters and declining economic opportunities in the North and the East, thousands have sought warmer climates and jobs in states like California, Florida, and Arizona.

CANADA

WASHINGTON
44.8% 21.1%

OREGON
48.9% 25.9%

MONTANA
16.5%

NORTH DAKOTA
3.4%

MINN.
19.4%

CANADA

Jersey City, New Jersey:
8% decrease in
population, 1970–1980

Buffalo, New York:
8% decrease in
population, 1970–1980

VT.
31.2%
21.6% 24.8%

MAINE
16.1%

IDAHO
32.4% 41.5%

WYOMING
41.3% 42.1%

SOUTH DAKOTA
1.4%

WIS.
19.1%

Cleveland, Ohio:
8% decrease in
population, 1970–1980

N.H.
51.8%

NEW YORK
4.7%

MASS.
19.3%

NEBRASKA
11.2%

IOWA
5.6%

MICH.
18.4%

PENNSYLVANIA
4.8%

R.I.
10.3%

CONN.
22.6%

NEVADA
71.6% 63.8%
181.1%

UTAH
64% 37.9%

COLORADO
64.8% 26% 30.8%

OHIO
11.2%

22.9% 26.5%

N.J.
21.4%

DEL.
33.2%

CALIFORNIA
50.6% 27.1%

ILL.
13.3%

IND.
17.7%

W.VA.
5%

VIRGINIA
34.7%

MD.
36%

Washington, D.C.:
−16.4%

Las Vegas, Nevada:
70% increase in
population, 1970–1980

ARIZONA
108.7% 53.1%
36.3%

NEW MEXICO
36.9% 28.1%

KANSAS
8.5%

MISSOURI
13.8%

KENTUCKY
20.5%

TENN.
28.7%

NORTH CAROLINA
29.1%

SOUTH CAROLINA
31%

20.5%

OKLAHOMA
19.2%

ARK.
28%

GEORGIA
38.6%

ATLANTIC OCEAN

PACIFIC OCEAN

MEXICO

TEXAS
48.6% 27.1%

MISS.
15.7%

ALABAMA
19.2%

LA.
29.1%

FLA.
96.7% 43.5%
37.1%

Fort Lauderdale/
Hollywood, Florida:
64% increase in
population, 1970–1980

West Palm Beach, Florida:
65% increase in
population, 1970–1980

Gulf of Mexico

PACIFIC OCEAN

HAWAI'I
52.4% 21.0% 25.3%

U.S.S.R.

34.1% 32.8%

CANADA

ALASKA
78.1%

0   100 Km.
0   100 Mi.

0   250   500 Km.
0   250   500 Mi.

PACIFIC OCEAN

0   200   400 Km.
0   200   400 Mi.

CUBA

Increase in population,
1960–1980

Over 40%
30–40%
20–30%
10–20%
5–10%
Under 5%

State population increases
of 20% or more

1970–1980
1960–1970

20%

Kennedy assassinated

Johnson becomes president

Gulf of Tonkin Resolution

Escalation in
Vietnam begins

Tet offensive

Indians seize Alcatraz

EPA created

Nixon visits
China and
Soviet Union

Nixon
resigns

Fall of
South Vietnam

1963   **1964**   **1965**   **1968**   **1969**   **1970**   **1972**   **1974**   **1975**

1850   **1900**   **1950**   **2000**

CHAPTER

29

America Under Stress, 1967–1976

JESSIE LOPEZ DE LA CRUZ

Having worked in the fields picking crops for nearly forty years, in 1962 Jessie Lopez de la Cruz made a choice that changed her life and the lives of many farm workers. She became a union organizer, the first and one of the few women organizers whose role was to recruit workers in the fields. In her efforts to achieve a better life and dignity for farm workers, she also focused on the status of Latinas and became a forceful leader in efforts to improve the quality of life for women and children. *AP/Wide World Photos.*

Jessie Lopez de la Cruz

Jessie Lopez de la Cruz had always been a farm worker. As a child in the 1920s, she worked alongside her family in the fields of central California, picking prunes off the ground for $4 a ton. By the time she was in her teens, she was pulling 100-pound bags of picked cotton behind her 95-pound frame, lifting them, and dumping them into a bin for weighing. Married in her teens, she at first accepted the traditional role of wife in a Mexican family—"the women couldn't do anything" without permission, she observed later. But gradually she expanded her role and freedoms, including learning how to drive a car.

Economic necessity required entire families to work in the fields, and for Jessie de la Cruz, as wife and mother, life continued in the fields. "We always went where . . . the women and the men were going to work because if it were just the men . . . we wouldn't earn enough to support a family." Infant children did not alter the pattern. "I started taking Ray with me," she recalled, "when he wasn't a year old yet. I'd carry one of those wash tubs and put it under a vine and sit him in it. . . . I would move the tub . . . as we worked." Work in the fields, especially with a short-handled hoe, was exhausting, but like most picker wives, she knew that her workday did not end in the fields. Returning home, she was expected to keep the house, cook the meals, and care for the children.

In 1962 Jessie Lopez de la Cruz made a choice that changed not only her life but the lives of many others as well. Cesar Chavez had just organized the National Farm Workers Association and was recruiting members. He shocked many men when he argued that women should participate fully in union activities. Jessie agreed. Women worked in the fields as well as men, and in many cases their working conditions were worse than those of men. Sexual harassment was common, and bathrooms were always a problem. Frequently there were none. This forced women to wait as long as ten hours, until they could go home and have privacy. Jessie Lopez de la Cruz and her husband joined the union. Chavez's organization, however, was more than just a union interested in getting better pay and working conditions for farm workers. It was also a movement, *La Causa*, that stressed pride and dignity, political and self-awareness, and demanded respect and equality for all Latinos, not just men.

"Women can no longer be taken for granted—that we're just not going to stay home and do the cooking and cleaning," Jessie Lopez de la Cruz told other women farm workers. "It's way past the time when our husbands could say 'You stay home! . . . You have to do as I say.'" She convinced other women to attend union meetings and express their concerns. Quickly, she rose from the rank and file to become the first woman organizer in the fields. In her activities, she merged union messages with feminist language—providing one of the bases of the Chicana movement. She urged others to break old patterns: "You know we're not back in the 20s. We can stand up! We can talk back . . . we want a share of the money . . . [made] of our sweat and our work."

Like all organizers, she faced opposition from the growers, who frequently attacked union leaders and those picketing the fields during strikes. During a strike in Kern County, growers sprayed picketers with pesticides. She also faced opposition from male farm workers. Men, she stated, "gave us the most trouble. . . . They were for the union, but they were not taking orders from women." Still, she and others continued their efforts. Eventually, some growers agreed to sign contracts, and some men agreed to be led by women.

Jessie Lopez de la Cruz's union activities and support for *La Causa* made her aware of larger issues that affected families and women. She worked for the inclusion of Latina women on school and community service boards. She pressured school boards to consider the needs of Latino children, especially those of migrant farm workers. She fought for bilingual education and social services for poor families, including access to food stamps for farm workers. Because of her emergence as a spokesperson for women and the poor, Jessie Lopez de la Cruz was selected to be a member of the California Commission on Women.

But despite some successes, the lives of Latina women—living within a traditional machismo culture and strapped by poverty—remain largely unchanged. Chicano historian Rodolfo Acuña argues that although the Chicana represents half of the Chicano population, she remains part of a nearly "invisible" minority.

INTRODUCTION

The 1960s began with a wave of optimism and confidence in the ability of individuals and the national government to improve society and promote American interests abroad. Like other activists, Jessie Lopez de la Cruz believed that her efforts could make a difference. For her and others, the African-American civil rights movement provided a model. It showed how grassroots activism could promote change by mobilizing public opinion and pressuring government to take action. Of the three branches of government, the Supreme Court needed the least pressure. Throughout the 1960s, the Warren Court, in a series of controversial decisions, expanded the rights of individuals while limiting the power of the state. Its rulings protected those accused of crimes, separated church and state, and expanded privacy. Hispanic and Indian activists not only used the federal court system but organized and demonstrated to push state and federal government to recognize their needs. To varying degrees, the Kennedy and Johnson administrations not only responded, but also through its actions encouraged further activism.

In 1963 President Kennedy's assassination brought Lyndon Baines Johnson to the White House. As described in the previous chapter, Johnson's political skills enabled him to go beyond the New Frontier and fight a war on poverty and formulate his Great Society. Johnson was comfortable dealing with domestic affairs, but foreign affairs were a different matter. In that arena Johnson seemed content to continue Kennedy's policies as he understood them, especially in Vietnam, where he was determined that the United States would not be beaten by a "two-bit" nation like North Vietnam. Johnson agreed with his advisers that the commitment of American forces was the only effective solution to defeat the Communists.

Certain political circumstances initially made that commitment difficult. A sudden buildup could weaken support for Johnson's domestic program and might drive the Chinese and the Soviets to increase their support of North Vietnam. To Johnson, the best choice seemed a carefully controlled, gradual escalation of American force, which would convince the North Vietnamese that the cost of the war was too high. The administration expected the North Vietnamese would then abandon their efforts to unify Vietnam, and an American-supported South Vietnam would prevail.

The strategy failed miserably. North Vietnam chose to meet escalation with escalation until many Americans turned against both the war and Johnson. In 1968, watching opposition to the war mount, Johnson chose to break the momentum of escalation and started peace negotiations with North Vietnam. Unexpectedly, he also announced his withdrawal from the presidential campaign. The turbulent 1968 Democratic convention symbolized the outcome of Johnson's presidency—a divided nation and an end to liberal optimism.

Republicans rallied behind Richard Nixon, who, they said, would provide the leadership necessary to restore national unity and global prestige and reassert the traditions and values that had made the nation strong. Nixon's call for unity played on the uneasy expectations of a society that was fragmented by the Vietnam War, urban and campus unrest, and an array of groups clamoring for political, economic, and social changes. After the mid-1960s, the African-American civil rights movement competed with feminist, Latino, and American Indian activist groups for government and public recognition, but conservative and most moderate Americans declined to support their calls for change.

Despite their unity rhetoric, Nixon and Republicans inflamed social divisions to ensure their victories in 1968 and in 1972. They wanted to construct a solid political base around a Silent Majority, composed largely of middle-class, white Americans living in suburbs, the South, and the West, who supported the war, opposed antiwar protesters and "hippies," and rejected justifications for urban riots and campus demonstrations. Promising a new, pragmatic conservatism that accepted legitimate government activism, Nixon's first administration achieved generally successful results. Nixon improved relations with the Soviet Union and the People's Republic of China and withdrew American forces from Vietnam. Domestically, his policy choices showed flexibility, expanding some Great Society programs and following Keynesian guidelines to confront inflation and a sluggish economy.

Nixon, despite his successes, was not satisfied. He wanted his political enemies ruined, and this desire contributed to the illegal activities surrounding the Watergate break-in. Watergate produced a bitter harvest: not only the unprecedented resignation of a president but a nationwide wave of disillusionment with politics and government.

Gerald Ford assumed the presidency after Nixon's resignation. The first unelected president, he faced a floundering economy and a cynical public disgusted with politics. Regarded by many, even fellow Republicans, as an interim president, Ford gained few domestic or foreign policy victories. Nevertheless, after a sharp challenge from within his own party, he won the Republican Party nomination at their 1976 presidential convention.

LIBERAL FORCES AT WORK

• In what ways did the Supreme Court work to expand and protect rights of individuals during the 1960s? How did its decisions restrict the actions of local and state governments?

• What problems did Hispanics and American Indians face in American society, and how did they organize to bring about change?

• How did the federal government respond to the needs of Hispanics and American Indians?

The sixties provided many groups in American society with hope that they, together with the federal government, might successfully challenge inequities and expand their rights in American society. The civil rights movement demonstrated how grassroots activism could gain support from the federal government, especially from the Supreme Court and the executive branch, to achieve change.

The Warren Court

Until joined in the 1960s by the executive branch, the Supreme Court—the **Warren Court**—was at the

---

Warren Court   Term applied to the Supreme Court under Chief Justice Earl Warren; during this period the Court was especially active in expanding individual rights, often at the expense of state and local governments.

chronology

From Camelot to Watergate

1960	Kennedy elected president
1962	Cesar Chavez forms National Farm Workers Association *Baker v. Carr* *Engel v. Vitale*
1963	*Abington v. Schempp* *Gideon v. Wainright* *Jacobvellis v. Ohio* *La Raza Unida* formed in Texas John F. Kennedy assassinated Lyndon B. Johnson becomes president
1964	*Griswold v. Connecticut* *Escobedo v. Illinois* Civil Rights Act Gulf of Tonkin Resolution Johnson elected president
1965	U.S. air strikes against North Vietnam begin American combat troops arrive in South Vietnam Anti-Vietnam "teach-ins" begin *Miranda v. Arizona* Dominican Republic intervention National Farm Workers Association begins strike Voting Rights Act
1967	Antiwar march on Washington
1968	Tet offensive My Lai massacre Johnson withdraws from presidential race Peace talks begin in Paris Robert Kennedy assassinated Mexican-American student walkouts American Indian Movement founded Richard Nixon elected president

1969	Secret bombing of Cambodia Warren Burger appointed chief justice of Supreme Court Nixon Doctrine Anti-Vietnam march on Washington First American troop withdrawals from Vietnam *Alexander v. Holmes* American Indians occupy Alcatraz
1970	U.S. troops invade Cambodia Kent State and Jackson State killings Earth Day observed Harry Blackmun appointed to Supreme Court Environmental Protection Agency created Clean Air and Water Quality Improvement Act
1971	Nixon enacts price and wage controls *New York Times* publishes *Pentagon Papers* *Swann v. Charlotte-Mecklenburg* William Rehnquist and Lewis Powell appointed to Supreme Court
1972	Nixon visits China and Soviet Union Bombing of North Vietnam resumes Watergate break-in Nixon re-elected SALT I treaty
1973	Vietnam peace settlement "Second Battle of Wounded Knee" Watergate hearings Salvador Allende overthrown in Chile War Powers Act
1974	Nixon resigns Gerald Ford becomes president Brezhnev-Ford Summit at Vladivostok
1975	South Vietnam government falls to North Vietnamese Helsinki Summit

forefront of liberalism, altering the obligations of the government and the rights of citizens. The Court's decisions in the 1950s redefined race relations and contributed a legal base to the 1964 Civil Rights Act. Also in the 1950s, the Court's *Yates v. the United States* (1957) ruling began a reversal of earlier decisions about the rights of those accused of crimes and started to require that states accept many of the protections accorded individuals under the Bill of Rights. The liberal nature of the Court was intensified when Kennedy appointed Arthur Goldberg to replace retiring justice Felix Frankfurter in 1962. For the next decade and a half, the Court expanded freedom of expression, separated church and state, redrew voting districts, and increased protection to those accused of violating the law.

In the *Yates* case, the Court released American Communist Party officials from prison who had advocated the overthrow of the American government but had not taken any actions to support their rhetoric: actions not words constituted a crime. Between 1961 and 1969, the Court issued over two hundred criminal justice decisions that, according to critics, hampered law enforcement. Among the most important were *Gideon v. Wainwright* (1963), *Escobedo v. Illinois* (1964), and *Miranda v. Arizona* (1966). In those rulings the Court declared that all defendants have a right to an attorney, even if the state must provide one, and that those arrested must be informed of their right to remain silent and to have an attorney present during questioning (the *Miranda* warning).

The Warren Court's actions involving church and state also angered many. In *Engel v. Vitale* (1962) and *Abington v. Schempp* (1963), the Court applied the First Amendment—separation of church and state—to state and local actions that allowed prayer and the reading of the Bible in public schools. Both decisions produced outcries of protest across the nation and from Democrats and Republicans in Congress. Governor George Wallace of Alabama stated, "We find the court ruling against God." Congress introduced over 150 resolutions demanding that reading the Bible and praying aloud be permitted in schools. Still, the Court's decisions remained the law and communities and classrooms complied.

Critics also complained that the Court's actions not only undermined the tradition of religion but, perhaps worse, condoned and promoted immorality. The Court's weakening of "community standards" in favor of broader ones regarding "obscene" and sexually explicit materials in *Jacobvellis v. Ohio* (1963) was compounded in the 1964 *Griswold v. Connecticut* decision. In that case the Court attacked the state's responsibility to establish moral standards by overturning Connecticut's laws that forbid the sale of contraceptives, arguing that individuals have a right to privacy that the state cannot abridge.

The Court's rejection of statewide gerrymandering, or redrawing voting districts so as to favor one party, was less controversial but equally lasting in importance. It was the 1962 *Baker v. Carr* ruling that established the goal of making congressional districts "as nearly as practicable" equal in population—"one person, one vote." Two years later in *Reynolds v. Sims* the Court applied the same rule to state election districts. Still, by 1966, the Court's judicial activism had earned growing opposition. One poll found that 52 percent of the public considered the Court was doing a poor job. But for minorities and women and other groups outside the economic, social, and political mainstream, the Court remained a valuable ally.

The Emergence of *La Causa*

With varying degrees of success, Hispanic organizations such as the League of Latin American Citizens and the American GI Forum turned to the government and the court system to gain political, economic, and social legitimacy. Still they remained a generally ignored minority mired near society's lowest levels of income and education (see Table 29.1). Kennedy's candidacy, however, brought hope. Kennedy had initiated the "Viva Kennedy" movement to mobilize the Hispanic, especially the Mexican-American, vote. The effort increased Hispanic activism and resulted in new organizations, like the Political Association of Spanish-Speaking Organizations (PASO), that worked to increase Hispanic political representation and recognition of Hispanic issues. Initially expectant, Hispanic leaders soon were disappointed. The new administration named few Hispanics to government positions and seemed little interested in listening to their voices or promoting their civil rights.

Unwilling to rely on Anglo politics or the federal government, many Mexican Americans turned to more direct action. For many the beginning of the "revolution" came in 1963 when the Mexican-American majority in Crystal City, Texas, toppled the established Anglo political machine and elected an all Mexican-American slate to the city council. Democratic Texas governor Dolph Briscoe called those demanding Mexican-American political power Communists who wanted to create a "little Cuba" in South Texas. Briscoe was wrong: the growing militancy among Mexican Americans was a grassroots movement that by the mid-sixties was spreading throughout the Southwest.

table 29.1	Whites, African Americans, and Latinos, 1992		
	Whites	**African Americans**	**Latinos**
Average income	$30,513	$18,676	$22,330
Female-headed households	11.4%	47.8%	19.1%
High school education	80.5%	66.7%	51.3%
College	22.5%	11.5%	9.7%
Unemployment	6.9%	12.4%	10.0%
Below poverty	12.1%	31.9%	28.1%

Source: Congressional Quarterly Researcher, October 30, 1992, p. 936.

Among the most active were young adults, who called themselves **Chicanos**. They stressed pride in their heritage and Latino culture and called for resistance to the dictates of Anglo society.

Still most Hispanics looked to Washington for support—first to Kennedy and then to Johnson. Johnson was seen as an "amigo" and had a record of concern for the Mexican-American population. He claimed an understanding of their needs and aspirations. He quickly gained praise for appointing several prominent Mexican Americans to the administration and guaranteeing that programs established under the War on Poverty and the Great Society reached into Hispanic communities. The praise became muted by 1966 as many Mexican Americans believed they were still being ignored, particularly in the West and Southwest. There, federal agencies and power appeared to defer to local and state governments that frequently opposed increased Mexican-American political power and activism. Despite being the largest minority in western states (see Map 29.1), stated one Mexican-American leader, they were still the "invisible minority."

Seeking visibility, many Mexican Americans were calling for more direct action. Leaders like Rodolfo "Corky" Gonzales left federal service and formed the Crusade for Justice in Colorado to work for social justice for Mexican Americans, to integrate Colorado's schools, and to foster pride in Mexican heritage. In New Mexico, Reies Lopez Tijerina demanded that Mexican Americans enjoy the rights, including land grants, promised under the Treaty of Guadalupe Hidalgo (which had ended the Mexican War in 1848) and to that end formed the *Alianza Federal de Mer-*

cedes (the Federal Alliance of Land Grants). The nationalistic Brown Berets that formed in Los Angeles in 1967 expressed a militant view that rejected assimilation into the Anglo world: "We're not in the melting pot. . . . Chicanos don't melt."

For most Mexican Americans, however, it was education, jobs, and wages—not assimilation or land grievances—that were key issues. They argued that discrimination and segregation still barred their children from a decent education; school districts needed to provide better education opportunities for Hispanics and offer programs that would meet special needs of Hispanic students, including bilingual education. Raul Ruiz mobilized Mexican-American students in Los Angeles in 1967: "If you are a student you should be angry! You should demand! You should protest! You should organize for a better education! This is your right!" He called for students to walk out of class if schools did not meet their demands. "Walkouts" spread in California and Texas.

In November 1968, Mexican-American students walked out of the high school in the small south Texas school district of Edcouch-Elsa. The activists demanded dignity, respect, and an end to "blatant discrimination," including corporal punishment—paddling—for speaking Spanish outside Spanish

Chicano/Chicana   Terms that many Mexican Americans adopted during the late 1960s to signify their ethnic identity; it was associated with the promotion of Mexican-American heritage and rights.

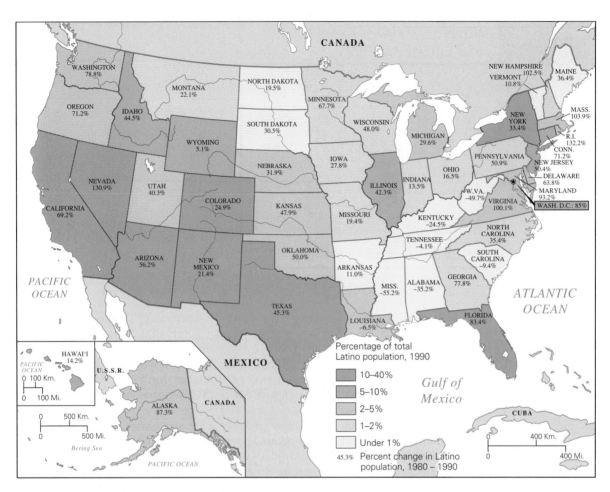

MAP 29.1 Changing Latino Population Growing rapidly, the Latino population became the largest minority population in the United States by 2000, reaching 12.5 percent of the total population.

class. The school board blamed "outside agitators" and suspended more than 150 students. But, as in other school districts, the protests brought results. The Edcouch-Elsa school district implemented Mexican-American studies and bilingual programs, hired more Mexican-American teachers and counselors, and created programs to meet the peculiar needs of migrant farm worker children, who moved from one school to another during picking season.

Cries for dignity, better working conditions, and a living wage were also heard in the fields, where many of the poorest Mexican Americans worked as laborers. Trapped at the bottom of the occupational ladder, not covered by Social Security or minimum wage and labor laws, unskilled and uneducated farm laborers toiled long hours for little wages under often deplorable conditions. Drawing from a traditional

base of farm worker organizations, especially in Texas and California, in 1962 **Cesar Chavez** created the **National Farm Workers Association** (NFWA) in the fields of central California. With a membership of seventeen hundred, Chavez's union gained national

Cesar Chavez Labor organizer who founded the National Farm Workers Association; he believed in nonviolence and used marches, boycotts, and fasts to bring moral and economic pressure to bear on growers.

National Farm Workers Association Migrant workers' union organized in 1962 by Cesar Chavez, originally named United Farm Workers Association; it changed its name again in 1972, becoming the United Farm Workers of America.

worker unions and to improve the wages and conditions of work for field workers, but agricultural workers, especially migrants, remain among the lowest paid workers in the nation.

American Indian Activism

American Indians, responding to poverty, federal and state termination policies, and efforts by state government to seize land for development, also organized and asserted their rights with new vigor in the 1960s. In 1961 reservation and nonreservation Indians, including those not officially recognized as tribes, held a convocation in Chicago to discuss problems and consider plans of action (see Map 29.2). They agreed on a "Declaration of Indian Purpose" that called for a reversal of termination policies and better education, economic, and health opportunities. "What we ask of America is not charity, not paternalism . . . we ask only that . . . our situation be recognized and be made a basis . . . of action."

The National Indian Youth Council, founded shortly after the Chicago conference, called for "Red Power"—that is, for Indians to use all means possible to resist further loss of their lands, rights, and traditions. They organized "fish-ins" when the Washington state government, in violation of treaty rights and a Supreme Court decision, barred Indians from fishing in certain areas. Protests, arrests, and violence continued until 1975 when the state complied with another federal court decision (*the United States v. Washington*) upholding treaty rights. Indian leaders also demanded the protection and restoration of their water and timber rights and ancient burial grounds. Museums were asked to return for proper burial the remains and grave goods of Indians on display. But for most, the crucial issue was self-determination, which would allow Indians control over their lands and over federal programs that served the reservations.

In 1969 a group of San Francisco Indian activists, led by **Russell Means**, gained national attention by seizing **Alcatraz Island** and holding it until 1971, when, without bloodshed, federal authorities

Cesar Chavez organized the first successful farm workers union in America in 1962, the National Farm Workers Association. Choosing to confront opponents by using the non-violent tactics of the Civil Rights movement, Chavez sought to give power and dignity to Mexican-American workers. *Bob Fitch/Black Star.*

recognition three years later when its charismatic leader called a strike against the grape growers. The "whole fight, if you're poor, and if you're a minority group," Chavez argued, "is economic power." Farm workers had none, and NFWA leaders, including Jessie Lopez de la Cruz (see Individual Choices, page 914), demanded a wage of $1.40 an hour and asked the public to buy only union-picked grapes. After five years, the strike and the nationwide boycott forced most of the major growers to accept unionization and to improve wages and working conditions. Chavez emerged as a national figure promoting *La Causa* not only for farm workers but for all Latinos and other exploited minorities. Eventually, California and other states passed legislation to recognize farm

Russell Means   Indian activist who helped organize the seizures of Alcatraz in 1969 and Wounded Knee in 1973.

Alcatraz Island   Rocky island, formerly a federal prison, in San Francisco Bay that was occupied in 1969 by Native American activists who demanded that it be made available to them as a cultural center.

In 1973, two hundred Sioux organized by the American Indian Movement (AIM) took over Wounded Knee, South Dakota, the site of the 1890 massacre, holding out for seventy-one days against state and federal authorities. The confrontation ended after one protester was killed and the government agreed to examine the treaty rights of the Oglala Sioux. In this picture, AIM leader Russell Means receives a blessing and symbolic red paint during the siege. *Dirck Halstead, TIME Magazine.*

visions, protect rights, and restore Indian lands. In 1974 Congress passed the **Indian Self-Determination and Education Assistance Act**, which gave tribes control and operation of many federal programs on their reservations. Other significant Indian victories included the Alaska Native Land Claims Act (1971), which returned 40 million acres to Eskimos and other native peoples. The Passamaquoddy and Penobscot tribes in Maine were compensated in 1980 with 300,000 acres and the establishment of a $27 million trust fund for more than 12.5 million acres they claimed had been stolen. Also in 1980, the Supreme Court decided that the federal government owed in excess of $106 million to the Lakotas for the Black Hills of South Dakota, taken from them in the 1870s. Leaders applauded these gains but lamented the slow pace of change and insisted that the Bureau of Indian Affairs and federal authorities still controlled too much of reservation life.

As federal courts asserted Indian treaty rights in the 1970, an increasing number of tribes found new economic resources in commercial and industrial ventures operated on reservations. Among the most lucrative and controversial were casinos, which started to open in the 1990s. The profits from such enterprises greatly improved the conditions of life of those involved. As Native Americans enter the twenty-first century, they remain among the nation's most impoverished and poorly educated minority, but there are reasons for optimism. Disease and mortality rates are declining, and Indian populations are increasing. Tribal and pan-Indian movements have sparked cultural pride and awareness; Indian languages are being revived and taught to the younger generations. "We're a giant that's been asleep because we've been fed through our veins by the federal government," stated a Navajo leader. "But now that's ending, and we're waking up and flexing muscles we never knew we had. And no one knows what we're capable of."

regained control. Two years later, in a more violent confrontation, **American Indian Movement** (AIM) leaders Means and Dennis Banks led an armed occupation of Wounded Knee, South Dakota, the site of the 1890 massacre of the Lakotas by the army (see page 578). AIM controlled the town for seventy-one days before surrendering to federal authorities. Two Indians were killed, and over 230 activists arrested, in the "Second Battle of Wounded Knee." Although the effort brought no change in federal policy, it did publicize Indian grievances and problems.

Taken as a whole, though, the wave of Indian activism did bring some results as federal courts and government agencies began to uphold treaty pro-

American Indian Movement   Militant Indian movement willing to use confrontation to obtain social justice and Indian treaty rights; organized the seizure of Wounded Knee.

Indian Self-Determination and Education Assistance Act   Law passed by Congress in 1974 giving Indian tribes control over federal programs carried out on their reservations and increasing their authority in reservation schools.

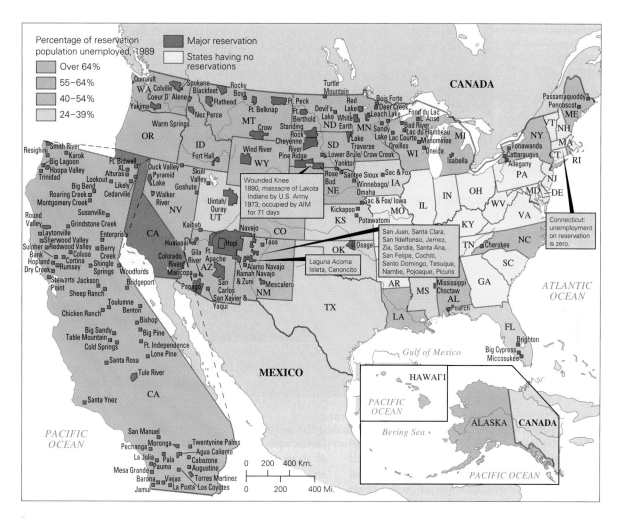

MAP 29.2 American Indian Reservations   In the seventeenth century, American Indians roamed over an estimated 1.9 billion acres, but by 1990 that area had shrunk to about 46 million acres spread across the United States. This area constitutes the federal reservation system. Composing about 1 percent of the population, American Indians are among the most impoverished people in society, facing a life expectancy of about twenty fewer years than the average non-Indian American. This map shows the location of most of the federal Indian reservations and highlights the high unemployment found on nearly every reservation. (*Note:* California is enlarged to show the many small reservations located there.)

JOHNSON AND THE WAR

• How did foreign policy decisions made by Kennedy influence Johnson's decisions regarding Latin America and Southeast Asia? In what ways were Johnson's policies different from Kennedy's?

• What considerations led Johnson to escalate America's role in Vietnam in 1965?

• What were the political, social, and military outcomes of the Tet offensive?

Suddenly thrust into the presidency by Kennedy's assassination, Lyndon Johnson moved quickly to breathe life into Kennedy's domestic program and to launch the more extensive Great Society. He was comfortable dealing with domestic issues and politics. In foreign policy, however, Johnson relied more heavily on his advisers—the "wise men," as he called them. Johnson was determined not to deviate significantly from past policies or allow further erosion of American power. Two regions of special concern were Latin America and Vietnam, where, like his predecessors, Johnson was determined to prevent further Communist inroads.

In the Western Hemisphere, Castro and his determination to export revolution remained the biggest issue. Johnson agreed to continue Kennedy's economic boycott of Cuba and the CIA's efforts to destabilize the Castro regime. Concerned about instability in Latin America and the growth of communism, Johnson refocused Kennedy's Alliance for Progress. Stability became more important than reform. Assistant Secretary of State Thomas Mann told Latin American leaders that political, social, and economic reforms were no longer a central requirement for American aid and support. This new perspective, labeled the **Mann Doctrine**, resulted in increased amounts of American military equipment and advisers in Latin America to aid various regimes to suppress those disruptive elements they labeled "Communist." The new policy led to direct military intervention in the Dominican Republic in 1965. There, supporters of deposed, democratically elected president Juan Bosch rebelled against a repressive, pro-American regime. Johnson and his advisers decided that the pro-Bosch coalition was dominated by Communists, asserted the right to protect the Dominican people from an "international conspiracy," and sent in twenty-two thousand American troops. They restored order, monitored elections that elected a pro-American president, Joaquin Balaguer, and left the island in mid-1966. Johnson claimed to have saved the Dominicans from communism, but many Latin Americans saw it only as an example of Yankee arrogance and the intrusive uses of its power.

Americanization of the Vietnam War

Kennedy had left Johnson a crisis in Vietnam. The South Vietnamese government remained unstable, its army ineffective, and the Viet Cong, supported by men and supplies from North Vietnam, were winning the conflict. Without a larger and more direct American involvement, Johnson's advisers saw little hope for improvement. Johnson felt trapped: "I don't think it is worth fighting for," he told an adviser, "and I don't think we can get out." "I am not going to be the President who saw Southeast Asia go the way China went," he asserted. But in 1964 he placed a higher priority on domestic events than on Vietnam. He needed to pass the civil rights bill and win the presidential election. Rather

than commit American forces to Vietnam, Johnson emphasized strategic planning, increased covert raids against North Vietnam, and began a massive public awareness campaign to generate support for a larger American role in defending South Vietnam. Encouraged by the White House and the **Pentagon**, throughout the spring and summer of 1964, newspapers and magazines printed articles and stories stressing the Communist threat to South Vietnam, Southeast Asia, and the Pacific. Fixed on the domino theory, the White House awaited a chance to ask Congress for permission to use whatever force would be necessary to defend South Vietnam.

The chance came in August 1964 off the coast of North Vietnam. Following a covert attack on its territory, North Vietnamese torpedo boats skirmished with the American destroyer *Maddox* in the Gulf of Tonkin on August 2 (see Map 29.3). On August 4, experiencing rough seas and poor visibility, radar operators on the *Maddox* and another destroyer, the *C. Turner Joy*, concluded that the patrol boats were making another attack. Confusion followed. Both ships fired wildly at targets shown only on radar screens. Johnson immediately ordered retaliatory air strikes on North Vietnam and prepared a resolution for Congress. Although within hours he learned that the second incident had probably not been an attack, Johnson told the public and Congress that Communist attacks against "peaceful villages" in South Vietnam had been "joined by open aggression on the high seas against the United States of America." On August 7, Congress approved the **Gulf of Tonkin Resolution**, allowing the United States "to take all necessary measures to repel" attacks against American forces and "to prevent further aggression." It was, in Johnson's terms, "like Grandma's nightgown, it covered everything." Public opinion polls showed strong support for the president, and only two senators opposed the

---

Mann Doctrine   U.S. policy outlined by Thomas Mann during the Johnson administration that called for stability in Latin America rather than economic and political reform.

Pentagon   U.S. military establishment, so named because its central offices are located in a five-sided building in Arlington, Virginia, called the Pentagon.

Gulf of Tonkin Resolution   Decree passed by Congress in 1964 authorizing the president to take any measures necessary to repel attacks against U.S. forces in Vietnam.

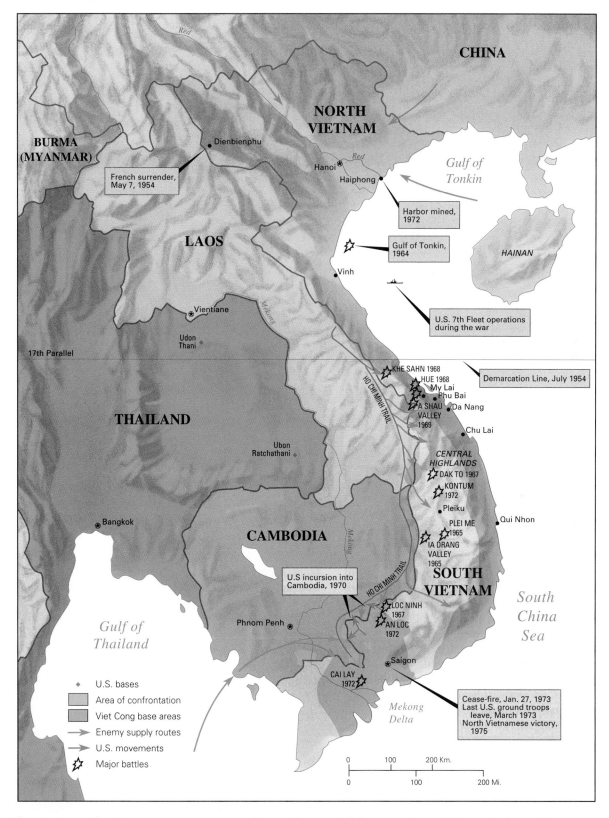

MAP 29.3 The Vietnam War, 1954–1975 Following the French defeat at Dienbienphu, the United States became increasingly committed to defending South Vietnam. This map shows some of the major battle sites of the Vietnam War from 1954 to the fall of Saigon and the defeat of the South Vietnamese government in 1975.

resolution: Wayne Morse of Oregon and Ernest Gruening of Alaska.

The resolution gave Johnson freedom to take whatever measures he wanted in Vietnam, but he remained unsure about what course of action to take and when. His advisers recommended committing American combat troops and bombing North Vietnam. To do nothing, Secretary of Defense Robert McNamara warned, was the "worst course of action" and would "lead only to a disastrous defeat." Johnson listened to his "wise men" and agreed to both proposals, with the first priority being the air war. A Viet Cong attack on the American base at Pleiku on February 7, 1965, that killed eight Americans provided a hoped-for provocation for unleashing the air assault.

Operation Rolling Thunder began on March 2. On March 8, the 3rd Marine Division arrived to take up positions around the American base at Da Nang. By July, American planes were flying more than nine hundred missions a week, and a hundred thousand American ground forces had reached Vietnam. Near their bases, American infantry and armored units patrolled aggressively, searching out the enemy. Johnson's strategy soon showed its flaws. As the United States escalated the war, so too did the enemy, which committed units of the North Vietnamese army (NVA) to the fighting in South Vietnam. The U.S. commanding general in Vietnam, **William Westmoreland**, and others insisted that victory required taking the offensive, which necessitated even more American soldiers. Reluctantly, Johnson gave the green light. Vietnam had become an American war.

Westmoreland's plan was to use overwhelming numbers and firepower to destroy the enemy. The first major American offensive was a large-scale sweep of the Ia Drang Valley in November 1965. Ten miles from the Cambodian border, the Ia Drang Valley contained no villages and was a long-time sanctuary for Communist forces. The goal was to airlift in units of the air cavalry and search out and destroy the enemy.

The initial landing went without incident, but soon the Americans came under fierce attack from North Vietnamese troops. One soldier recalled that his "assault line [that] had started out erect went down to . . . a low crawl." The battle raged for three days with air and artillery supporting the outnumbered Americans. "There was very vicious fighting," North Vietnamese commander Nguyen Huu noted. The "soldiers fought valiantly. They had no

Unlike previous wars, Vietnam was a war without fixed front lines. In this picture, marines work their way through the jungle south of the demilitarized zone (DMZ) trying to cut off North Vietnamese supplies and reinforcements moving into South Vietnam. *Larry Burrows/Timepix.*

choice, you were dead if not." Both sides claimed victory and drew different lessons from the engagement. Examining the losses, 305 Americans versus 3,561 Vietnamese, American officials embraced the strategy of search and destroy—the enemy would be ground down. *Time* magazine named Westmoreland "Man of the Year" for 1965. Hanoi concluded that its "peasant army" had withstood America's best firepower and had fought U.S. troops to a draw. The North Vietnamese were confident: the costs would be great, but they would wear down the Americans. Both sides, believing victory was possi-

William Westmoreland Commander of all American troops in Vietnam from 1964 to 1968.

ble, committed more troops and prepared for a lengthy war.

Thus the war spiraled upward in 1966 and 1967. The United States and the North Vietnamese committed more troops, while American aircraft rained more bombs on North Vietnam and supply routes, especially the **Ho Chi Minh Trail** (see Map 29.3). While the Viet Cong and North Vietnamese suffered heavy losses of men and supplies, their determination and capacity to continue the struggle was unchanged. By mid-1966, it appeared to some in Washington that the war had reached a stalemate with neither side able to win nor willing to lose. Some speculated that any victory would be a matter of will, and feared that growing opposition to the war in the United States might be a deciding factor.

The Antiwar Movement

Throughout 1964, support at home for an American role in Vietnam was widespread. Most Americans accepted the domino theory and predictions that horrible reprisals against non-Communists would follow a Communist victory. The escalation of the war in 1965 saw a largely college-based opposition to the war arise—with Students for a Democratic Society (SDS) the prime instigators. The University of Michigan held the first Vietnam "teach-in" to mobilize opposition to American policy on March 24, 1965. In April, SDS organized a protest march of nearly twenty thousand past the White House, and by October its membership had increased by 400 percent. But by mid-1966, SDS was losing its leadership of the movement and was only one of many groups and individuals demonstrating against the expanding war.

Those opposing the war fell into two major types who rarely agreed on anything other than that the war should be ended. Pacifists and radical liberals on the political left opposed the war for moral and ideological reasons. Others, as the American military commitment grew and the military draft claimed more young men, opposed the war for more pragmatic reasons: the draft, the loss of lives and money, and the inability of the United States to either defeat the enemy or create a stable, democratic South Vietnam. In 1966 high school students hardly mentioned Vietnam or the draft as a problem facing their lives. Three years later, 75 percent of those polled listed both as major worries. By 1967, the possibility of being sent to Vietnam was becoming a concern of many college students. A Univer-

Those opposing the war in Vietnam not only demonstrated against the war but also encouraged young men to resist the draft. Here, singer and activist Joan Baez (left) and her sisters suggest one "benefit" those who say "no" to the draft might expect. *National Museum of American History, Smithsonian Institution, Washington, D.C.*

sity of Michigan student complained that if he was drafted and spent two years in the army, he would lose more than $16,000 in income. "I know I sound selfish," he explained, "but . . . I paid $10,000 to get this education."

Yet college students and graduates were not the most likely to be drafted or go to Vietnam. Far more

---

Ho Chi Minh Trail   Main infiltration route for North Vietnamese soldiers and supplies into South Vietnam; it ran through Laos and Cambodia.

often, minorities and the poor served in Vietnam, especially in combat roles. African Americans constituted about 12 percent of the population but in Vietnam sometimes made up to 50 percent of frontline units and accounted for about 25 percent of combat deaths. Stokely Carmichael and SNCC had supported SDS actions against the war as early at 1965, but it was Martin Luther King's denouncement of the war in 1967 that made international headlines and shook the administration. King called the war immoral and preached that "the Great Society has been shot down on the battlefields of Vietnam." He stated that it was wrong to send young blacks to defend democracy in Vietnam when they were denied it in Georgia. He asked all Americans to oppose the war. Johnson labeled King a "crackpot" and insisted that war protesters represented a small fringe element, that the bulk of the American people supported a winnable war.

Privately, he knew he had to win the struggle at home to successfully win the war in Vietnam. Watching the antiwar movement grow and public opinion polls register increasing disapproval of the war effort, the administration responded with **COINTELPRO** and with **Operation Chaos**, in which federal agents infiltrated, spied on, and tried to discredit antiwar groups. FBI reports showing antiwar groups in league with Communists were leaked to the press and counterdemonstrations planned. Nevertheless, opposition to the war swelled. A "Stop-the-Draft Week" in October 1967 prompted more than ten thousand demonstrators to block the entrance of an induction center in Oakland, California, while over two hundred thousand people staged a massive protest march in Washington against "Lyndon's War."

The administration itself was torn by increasing disagreement about the course of the war. On the one hand, General Westmoreland informed Washington that the enemy was "largely confined to the periphery of South Vietnam" and that half of the enemy's forces were no longer capable of combat. The American military presence increased to 542,000 and more were needed. Yet, despite official positive reports and evaluations, by late 1967 awareness was growing among Johnson's advisers that the United States might not be able to win. In November, Secretary of War Robert McNamara recommended a sharp reduction in the war effort, including a permanent end to the bombing of North Vietnam. Johnson rejected his position and within months McNamara left the administration. Instead, Johnson focused on a "withdrawal strategy" that

would reduce American support while the South Vietnamese assumed a larger and larger role. First, however, it was necessary to commit more troops, intensify the bombing, and put more pressure on the South Vietnamese to make domestic reforms. "The clock is ticking," he said.

TET AND THE 1968 PRESIDENTIAL CAMPAIGN

- What were the political, social, and military outcomes of the Tet offensive?
- What key issues shaped the 1968 campaign? What strategy did Richard Nixon use to win?

Johnson was correct: the clock was ticking—not only for the United States but also for North Vietnam. As Westmoreland reported success, North Vietnamese leaders were planning an immense campaign to capture South Vietnamese cities during **Tet**, the Vietnamese new year holiday, a maneuver that would catch American intelligence agencies totally off guard.

The Tet Offensive

In January 1968, the Viet Cong struck forty-one cities throughout South Vietnam, including the capital, Saigon. In some of the bloodiest fighting of the war, American and South Vietnamese forces recaptured the lost cities and villages. It took twenty-four days to oust the Viet Cong from the old imperial city of Hue, leaving the city in ruins and costing more than 10,000 civilian, 5,000 Communist, 384 South Vietnamese, and 216 American lives.

COINTELPRO FBI counterintelligence program begun in 1956 and continued until 1971 that sought to expose, disrupt, and discredit groups considered radical political organizations; it targeted various antiwar groups during Vietnam War.

Operation Chaos CIA operation within the country from 1965 to 1973 that collected information on and disrupted anti–Vietnam War elements; though it is illegal for the CIA to operate within the United States, it collected files on over 7,000 Americans.

Tet The lunar new year celebrated as a huge holiday in Vietnam; the Viet Cong–North Vietnamese attack on South Vietnamese cities during Tet in January 1968 was a military defeat for North Vietnam, but it seriously undermined U.S. support for the war.

The Tet offensive was a military defeat for North Vietnam and the Viet Cong. It provoked no popular uprising against the South Vietnamese government, the Communists held no cities or provincial capitals, and they suffered staggering losses. More than forty thousand Viet Cong were killed. Tet was, nevertheless, a "victory" for the North Vietnamese, for it seriously weakened American support for the war. Amid official pronouncements of "victory just around the corner," Tet destroyed the Johnson administration's credibility and inflamed a growing antiwar movement. The highly respected CBS news anchor Walter Cronkite had supported the war, but Tet changed his mind. Unable to reconcile the administration's claims of impending victory with the fierce Communist offensive, he went on a personal fact-finding tour of Vietnam. On his return, Cronkite announced that there would be no victory in Vietnam and that the United States should make peace. "If I have lost Walter Cronkite, then it's over. I have lost Mr. Average Citizen," Johnson lamented.

By March, Johnson and most of his "wise men" had also concluded that the war was not going to be won. The new secretary of defense Clark Clifford admitted that four years of "enormous casualties" and "massive destruction from our bombing" had not weakened "the will of the enemy." The emerging strategy was to place more responsibility on South Vietnam, send fewer troops than Westmoreland had asked for, and seek a diplomatic end to the war.

Changing of the Guard

Two months after Tet came the first presidential primary in New Hampshire. There, Minnesota senator **Eugene McCarthy** was campaigning primarily on the antiwar issue. At the heart of his New Hampshire effort were hundreds of student volunteers who, deciding to "go clean for Gene," cut their long hair and shaved their counterculture beards. Newly respectable, they knocked on thousands of doors and distributed bales of flyers and pamphlets touting their candidate and condemning the war. Johnson had considered not running as early as mid-1967 but had refrained from making any official statement. In part this nondecision rested on a desire to ensure passage of Great Society bills in Congress and to see the war through. It also stemmed from reluctance to turn the presidency over to a liberal like McCarthy or Robert Kennedy.

Johnson had not entered the March 18 New Hampshire primary, but as McCarthy's antiwar candidacy strengthened, Johnson's political advisers organized a **write-in campaign** for the president. Johnson won, but by only 6 percent of the votes cast. Political commentators promptly called McCarthy the real winner. New York senator **Robert Kennedy's** announcement of his candidacy and his surging popularity in the public opinion polls added to the pressure on Johnson. Quietly, Johnson decided to not run for the presidency.

On March 31, 1968, a haggard-looking president delivered a major televised speech announcing changes in his Vietnam policy. The United States was going to seek a political settlement through negotiations with the Viet Cong and North Vietnamese. The escalation of the ground war was over, and the South Vietnamese would take a larger role in the war. The bombing of northern North Vietnam was going to end, and a complete halt of the air war would follow the start of negotiations. At the end of his speech, Johnson calmly made this announcement: "I have concluded that I should not permit the presidency to become involved in the partisan divisions that are developing in this political year. . . . Accordingly, I shall not seek, and I will not accept, the nomination of my party for another term as president." Listeners were shocked. Lyndon B. Johnson had thrown in the towel. Although he later claimed that his fear of having a heart attack while in office was the primary reason for his decision not to run, nearly everyone agreed that the Vietnam War had ended Johnson's political career and undermined his Great Society.

The Election of 1968

There were now three Democratic candidates. McCarthy campaigned against the war and the "imperial presidency." Kennedy opposed the war but not

---

Eugene McCarthy   Senator who opposed the Vietnam War and made an unsuccessful bid for the 1968 Democratic nomination for president.

write-in campaign   An attempt to elect a candidate in which voters are urged to write the name of an unregistered candidate directly on the ballot.

Robert Kennedy   Attorney general during the presidency of his brother John F. Kennedy; elected to the Senate in 1964, his campaign for the presidency was gathering momentum when he was assassinated in 1968.

Violence erupted during the 1968 Democratic National Convention in Chicago. Using nightsticks, police attacked antiwar and anti-establishment protesters that surrounded the convention hotel. The violent confrontations in Chicago did little to quell similar protests, unify the Democratic Party, or help Hubert Humphrey's chances for election. *Wide World Photos.*

executive and federal power, and he called on the government to better meet the needs of the poor and minorities. Vice President **Hubert H. Humphrey**, running in the shadow of Johnson, stood behind the president's foreign and domestic programs. He relied on party regulars and White House clout, rather than the primaries, to gain the nomination.

By June, Kennedy was winning the primary race, drawing heavily from minorities and urban Democratic voters. In the critical California primary, Kennedy gained a narrow victory over McCarthy, 46 to 41 percent, but the victory was all too short. As the winner left his election headquarters, he was shot by Sirhan Sirhan, a Jordanian immigrant. Kennedy died the next day. His death stunned the nation and ensured Humphrey's nomination. McCarthy continued his campaign but did not generate much support among party regulars. By the time of the national convention in Chicago in August, Humphrey had enough pledged votes to guarantee his nomination. Nevertheless, the convention was dramatic. Inside

and outside the convention center, antiwar and anti-establishment groups demonstrated for McCarthy, peace in Vietnam, and social justice. Radical factions within the Students for a Democratic Society promised physical confrontation and threatened to contaminate the water supply with drugs. Chicago mayor Richard Daley, determined to maintain order, called in twelve thousand police. By August 24, the second day of convention, clashes between the police and protesters started and grew more belligerent every day. Protesters threw eggs, bottles, rocks, and balloons filled with water, ink, and urine at the police, who responded with tear gas and nightsticks. On August 28, the police responded with force

Hubert H. Humphrey Vice president under Lyndon Johnson; he won the Democratic nomination for president in 1968 but lost the election to Richard Nixon.

indiscriminately attacking protesters and bystanders alike as television cameras recorded the scene. The violence in Chicago's streets overshadowed Humphrey's nomination and acceptance speech—and much of his campaign.

Many Americans were disgusted by the chaos in Chicago and saw it as typical of the general disruption that was plaguing the nation. The politics of hope that had begun the 1960s was losing its appeal by 1968. From both the political left and the right came criticisms of the social policies of the Great Society and the foreign policies that mired the nation in the war in Vietnam. The 1968 election saw the liberal center occupied by Kennedy and Johnson come under attack not only from Republicans but also from disgruntled Democrats.

Representing growing dissatisfaction with liberal social policies within Democratic ranks, Governor **George Wallace** of Alabama left the Democratic Party and ran for president as the American Independent Party's candidate. He aimed his campaign at southern whites, blue-collar workers, and low-income white Americans, all of whom deplored the "loss" of traditional American values and society. On the campaign trail, Wallace called for victory in Vietnam and took special glee in attacking the counterculture and the "rich-kid" war protesters, who avoided serving in Vietnam while the sons of working-class Americans died there. He also opposed federal civil rights and welfare legislation. Two months before the election, Wallace commanded 21 percent of the vote, according to national opinion polls. "On November 5," he confidently predicted, "they're going to find out there are a lot of rednecks in this country."

Richard Nixon was the Republican candidate, having easily won his party's nomination at an orderly convention. He also intended to tap the general dissatisfaction but without the antagonism of the Wallace campaign. He and **Spiro Agnew**, his vice-presidential running mate, focused the Republican campaign on the need for effective international leadership and law and order at home, while denouncing pot, pornography, protesters, and permissiveness. Nixon announced that he would "end the war and win the peace in Vietnam" but refused to comment further. Nixon won with a comfortable margin in the Electoral College, although he received only 43.4 percent of the popular vote (see Map 29.4). Conservatives were pleased. Together, Nixon and Wallace attracted almost 57 percent of the vote, which conservatives interpreted as wide public support for an end to liberal social programs and a return to traditional values.

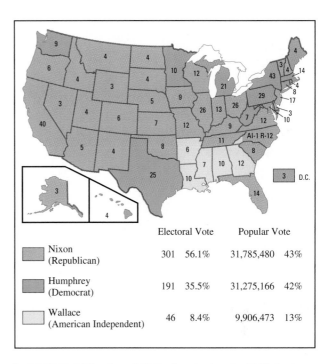

	Electoral Vote		Popular Vote	
Nixon (Republican)	301	56.1%	31,785,480	43%
Humphrey (Democrat)	191	35.5%	31,275,166	42%
Wallace (American Independent)	46	8.4%	9,906,473	13%

MAP 29.4 Election of 1968 In winning the 1968 election against Hubert Humphrey, Richard Nixon received fewer popular votes than he did in 1960, when he won more than 34 million votes. But in the all-important electoral vote, Nixon easily defeated his Democratic rival. As they did in the 1960 election, some southerners opted for a third choice, unwilling to vote for a Republican or a liberal Democrat. The third choice was George Wallace.

NIXON CONFRONTS THE WORLD

• How did Richard Nixon plan to achieve an "honorable" peace in Vietnam?

• How did Nixon's Cold War policies differ from those favored by earlier administrations?

As 1969 started, Nixon declared himself a happy man. He had achieved the dream that had been denied him in 1960. As president, he was determined to

George Wallace Conservative Alabama governor who opposed desegregation in the 1960s and ran unsuccessfully for the presidency in 1968 and 1972.

Spiro Agnew Vice president under Richard Nixon; he resigned in 1973 amid charges of illegal financial dealings during his governorship of Maryland.

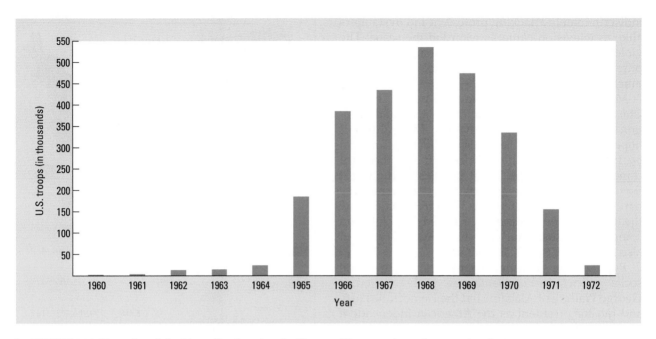

FIGURE 29.1 Troop Levels by Year For America, the Vietnam War went through two major phases: Americanization from 1960 to 1968 and Vietnamization from 1969 to 1972.

be the center of decision making, using a few close and loyal advisers to make policy. For domestic affairs, he relied on John Mitchell, his choice for attorney general, and long-time associates H. R. "Bob" Haldeman and John Ehrlichman. In foreign affairs, he tapped Harvard professor **Henry Kissinger**, as his national security adviser, and later made him secretary of state.

Repeating his campaign pledges, President Nixon promised to work for national unity and to promote minority rights. But he also wanted to consolidate a new conservative majority that linked long-term Republicans with those recently dissatisfied with protests, the Great Society, and the "liberal" attacks on traditional American society. While he presented himself as a pragmatic politician who could balance liberal and conservative views, his close circle of advisers knew that Nixon had little desire to incorporate liberal views with his own. Instead, he would court what he called the **"Silent Majority."**

Vietnamization

Nixon took office and faced not only a Democratic Congress but the looming specter of Vietnam. Vietnam influenced nearly all other issues: the budget, public and congressional opinion, foreign policy,

and domestic stability, and Nixon needed a solution before he could move ahead on other fronts. No one in the administration questioned whether American troops would be withdrawn, but there was considerable debate over the exit speed and how to ensure the government of Nguyen Van Thieu remained intact.

Connected to the Vietnam problem was the ongoing Cold War, which Nixon and Kissinger sought to restructure. They believed that too much of American foreign policy was based on ideology and morality; the thrust needed to be changed to reflect military and geopolitical realities. Among those realities were concerns that the Soviets might soon have military parity and a widening Soviet-Chinese split. With Congress unwilling to expand the budget to regain clear military superiority, Nixon concluded that efforts should

Henry Kissinger German-born American diplomat who was President Nixon's national security adviser and secretary of state; he helped negotiate the cease-fire in Vietnam.

Silent Majority Name given to the majority of Americans who supported the government and did not protest or riot; a typical member of the Silent Majority was believed to be white, middle class, average in income and education, and moderately conservative in values and attitudes.

Together Richard Nixon and Secretary of State Henry Kissinger (shown here) sought to refocus American foreign policy by ending the war in Vietnam and improving relations with the Soviet Union and the People's Republic of China. *Camera Press/Retna, Ltd.*

be made to improve relations with both Communist **superpowers**.

Nixon had no intention of being labeled the president who lost a war, and those who expected him to push for a quick peace and withdrawal, noted Haldeman, misunderstood the president's will. Nixon and Kissinger intended to negotiate an end to the war, but from a position of strength. "A nation cannot remain great, if it betrays its allies and lets down its friends," Nixon explained. To achieve their goals, they were willing to escalate the air war, to bomb targets outside of South Vietnam. At the same time, they would announce the policy of **Vietnamization**, which would withdraw American troops and return the responsibility of the war to the Thieu government (see Figure 29.1). Changing the "color of bodies" and bringing American soldiers home, Nixon believed, would rebuild public support and diminish the crowds of protesters. Expanding the theme of limiting American involvement, in July Nixon developed the **Nixon Doctrine**: countries warding off communism would have to shoulder most of the military burden, with the

United States providing political and economic support and limited naval and air support.

Nixon publicly announced Vietnamization in the spring of 1969, telling the public that twenty-five thousand American soldiers were coming home. At the same time, he convinced some in the media to alter their coverage of the war. ABC's news director instructed his staff to downplay the fighting and emphasize "themes and stories under the general

> **superpower**   Term applied to the United States, China, and the Soviet Union during the Cold War because all three were powerful and heavily armed and dominated their allies in international politics.
>
> **Vietnamization**   The U.S. policy of scaling back American involvement in Vietnam and helping Vietnamese forces fight their own war.
>
> **Nixon Doctrine**   Nixon's policy of requiring countries threatened by communism to shoulder most of the military burden, with the United States offering mainly political and economic support.

heading: We are on our way out of Vietnam." By the end of the year, American forces in Vietnam had declined by over 110,000, and public opinion polls indicated support for Nixon's policy.

The other dimensions of Nixon's Vietnam policy, however, were unknown to either the public or the press. Quietly, Kissinger and Nixon began work to improve relations with the Soviets and Chinese and to encourage them to reduce their support for North Vietnam. More significantly, the United States expanded its air war, in two directions: targeting enemy bases inside Cambodia and Laos and resuming the bombardment of North Vietnam. The secret attacks on Communist sanctuaries inside Cambodia (Operation Menu) began in March, with air force records being falsified to aid in official denials of stories about any such strikes. The intense air assault was part of a "madman strategy" that Nixon designed to convince the North Vietnamese to negotiate. Nixon said he wanted Hanoi "to believe that I've reached the point where I might do anything to stop the war." "We'll just slip the word," Nixon told his advisers, "that 'for God's sake, you know Nixon. . . . We can't restrain him when he's angry—and he has his hand on the nuclear button.'"

The strategy did not work. The North Vietnamese appeared unconcerned about Nixon's "madness," the increased bombing, or decreasing support from China and the Soviet Union. They believed that victory was only a matter of patiently waiting until America was fed up with the war. Consequently, talks between Kissinger and the North Vietnamese in Paris produced only bitter feelings. Despite such setbacks, Nixon continued his strategy and in 1970, he ordered American troops to cross the border into Cambodia and destroy Communist bases and supply areas. Nearly eighty thousand American and South Vietnamese troops entered Cambodia and demolished enemy bases and large amounts of supplies. The mission, however, failed to halt the flow of supplies or weaken North Vietnam's resolve.

News about the invasion also fueled antiwar protests across the United States, especially on college campuses. Demonstrations at Kent State University in Ohio and at Jackson State University in Mississippi resulted in the deaths of six protesters. Outraged, students shut down more than a hundred campuses, while thousands of antiwar demonstrators again marched through Washington. The mood in the White House was hopeful that the outcry would not last long. Nixon explained that the United States, if it had not invaded Cambodia, would seem like a "pitiful helpless giant." Haldeman

On May 4, 1970, Ohio National Guard troops opened fire on a crowd of Kent State students protesting the American incursion into Cambodia, killing four of them. Here, a student screams in horror as she hovers over the body of one of the dead students. In outrage, campuses throughout the nation closed and students flocked to Washington to protest the war. *John Filo.*

wrote five days following the killings at Kent State that the "major test" would come with Sunday's papers. "If we get by those, we can move with the next week in pretty good shape." When Sunday's results were positive, Nixon argued that the students had "overplayed their hands" and that he could mobilize the "blue collar group against them."

Despite the administration's hopes and mobilization of the "real majority," antiwar demonstrations continued. As the last American troops returned from Cambodia, an angry Senate repealed the Gulf of Tonkin Resolution and forbade the further use of American troops in Laos or Cambodia. But neither this action nor the outrage over revelations of American atrocities around the village of **My Lai**—a massacre of over three hundred men, women and children—shook Nixon's determination to swerve from his policies. As the air war continued and intensified, he told Kissinger "I have the will in spades."

> **My Lai** Site of a massacre of three hundred fifty South Vietnamese villagers by U.S. infantrymen in 1968, an event that added to antiwar sentiment in the United States.

As North Vietnamese forces entered Saigon in April 1975, the last American evacuees left by helicopter. Here, they scramble to the roof of Pittman apartments in Saigon; others left from the roof of the American embassy. Henry Kissinger asked the nation "to put Vietnam behind us." *©Bettmann/Corbis.*

Nixon's will seemed equally matched by North Vietnam. Peace discussions in Paris were still stalemated, and in March 1972, a Communist offensive demonstrated the frailty of Vietnamization. As North Vietnamese and Viet Cong forces drove toward Saigon, a livid Nixon responded with force. "I'm going to show the bastards," he told Kissinger. "Unless they deal with us I'm going to bomb the hell out of them." He ordered massive bombing raids against North Vietnam and Communist forces in South Vietnam. By mid-June 1972, American air power had stalled the offensive and enabled ARVN forces to regroup and drive back the North Vietnamese. With their cities under almost continuous air attacks, the North Vietnamese became more flexible in negotiations. By October, with both sides offering some concessions, a peace settlement was ready. "Peace is at hand," Kissinger announced—just in time for the 1972 presidential election.

South Vietnamese president Nguyen Van Thieu, however, rejected the plan. Reluctantly, Nixon supported Thieu and ordered the Christmas bombing of Hanoi and North Vietnam. One goal was to put additional pressure on Hanoi. Another was to convince Thieu that the United States would use its air power to protect South Vietnam. After eleven days, the bombing stopped and Washington advised Thieu that if he did not accept the next peace settlement, the United States would leave him to fend for himself. Thieu thereupon accepted a peace settlement that did

not differ significantly from the one offered in October. Nixon and Kissinger proclaimed peace with honor, and Kissinger shared the 1973 Nobel Peace Prize with his North Vietnamese counterpart.

The peace settlement imposed a cease-fire, required the removal of the twenty-four thousand remaining American troops but not North Vietnamese troops, and promised the return of American prisoners of war. The peace terms permitted the United States to complete its military and political withdrawal, but the pact did little to ensure the continued existence of Thieu's government or South Vietnam. The cease-fire, everyone expected, would be temporary. When Haldeman asked Kissinger how long the South Vietnamese government could last, Kissinger answered bluntly, "If they're lucky, they can hold out for a year and a half."

As expected, the cease-fire soon collapsed. North Vietnam continued to funnel men and supplies to the south, but substantial American air and naval support for South Vietnam never arrived. Neither Congress nor the public was eager to help Thieu's government. Instead, Congress cut aid to South Vietnam and in November 1973 passed the **War Powers Act**. The law

---

War Powers Act   Law passed by Congress in 1973 to prevent the president from involving the United States in war without authorization by Congress.

table 29.2	The Vietnam Generation, 1964–1975	
	Men	**Women**
Total in military service	8,700,000	250,000
Served in Vietnam	2,700,000	6,431
Killed in Vietnam	46,000	9
Wounded	300,635*	
Missing in action	2,330	—
Draft resisters (estimate)	570,000	—
Accused	210,000	—
Convicted	8,750	—

Source: Department of Defense and Veterans Administration.
*Combined men and women

requires the president to inform Congress within forty-eight hours of the deployment of troops overseas and to withdraw those troops within sixty days if Congress fails to authorize the action. In March 1975, North Vietnam began its final campaign to unify the country. A month later, North Vietnamese troops entered Saigon as a few remaining Americans and some South Vietnamese were evacuated by helicopter—some dramatically from the roof of the American embassy. The Vietnam War ended as it had started, with Vietnamese fighting Vietnamese (see Table 29.2).

Modifying the Cold War

Ending the Vietnam War was a political and diplomatic necessity for Nixon and part of his plan to reshape the Cold War. In his first inaugural address, Nixon urged that an "era of confrontation" give way to an "era of negotiation." To this end, he pursued **détente**, a policy that reduced tensions with the two Communist superpowers. China, with which the United States had had virtually no diplomatic contact since the end of the Chinese civil war in 1949, was the key to the Nixon-Kissinger strategy. The Soviets and Chinese had already engaged in several bloody clashes along their common border, and the Chinese feared a border war. Believing that better relations with the United States would help deter Soviet aggression, the Chinese were ready to open diplomatic discussions with Nixon.

Nixon believed that American friendship with the Chinese would encourage the Soviets to improve their relations with the United States and lead to détente on that front. Sending a signal to China, Nixon lowered restrictions on trade, and in April 1971 the Chinese responded by inviting an American Ping-Pong team to tour China. A few months later, Kissinger secretly flew to Beijing to meet with Premier Zhou Enlai. The result would, as Kissinger phrased it, "send a shock wave around the world": Nixon was going to China. In February 1972, Nixon arrived in Beijing and met with Communist Party chairman Mao Zedong and Zhou. Suddenly the "Red Chinese" were no longer the enemy but "hard-working, intelligent . . . and practical" people. The Cold War was thawing a little in the East.

Nixon's China policy, as hoped, did contribute to détente with the Soviet Union. Kissinger followed his secret visit to China with one to Moscow, where he discussed improving relations with President **Leonid Brezhnev**. Nixon flew to Moscow in May 1972 and told Brezhnev, "I know that my reputation

détente Relaxing of tensions between the superpowers in the early 1970s, which led to increased diplomatic, commercial, and cultural contact.

Leonid Brezhnev Leader of the Soviet Union (first as Communist Party secretary, and then also as president) from 1964 to his death in 1982; he worked to foster détente with the United States during the Nixon era.

In efforts to redirect the Cold War, Nixon became the first president to visit China, meeting with Mao Zedong and Zhou Enlai in 1972. With regard to Chinese–Soviet relations, Nixon confided to Zhou that if Moscow marched either East or West, he was ready to "turn like a cobra on the Russians." Nixon's visit to China began the process of normalizing relations with the People's Republic of China that was finalized under Carter. *John Dominis, LIFE Magazine ©Time Warner, Inc.*

is one of being a very hard-line, Cold War–oriented, anti-Communist," but now, he said, he believed that the two nations should "live together and work together." Needing to reduce military spending, develop the Soviet domestic economy, and increase American trade, Brezhnev agreed. The meeting was a success. Brezhnev obtained increased trade with the West, including shipments of American grain, and the superpowers announced the **Strategic Arms Limitation agreement** (SALT I), which restricted antimissile sites and established a maximum number of **intercontinental ballistic missiles** (ICBMs) and submarine-launched missiles (SLBMs) for each side. It seemed as if détente had arrived and Nixon was reshaping world affairs.

But in some areas, America's traditional Cold War stance was unwavering. In Latin America, Nixon followed closely in Johnson's footsteps, working to isolate Cuba and prevent any additional Communist-style leaders from gaining power. Borrowing from Eisenhower's foreign policy, he used covert operations to disrupt the democratically elected socialist-Marxist government of **Salvador Allende** in Chile. For three years the CIA squeezed the Chilean economy "until it screamed," producing food riots, numerous strikes, and massive inflation. Finally, in September 1973, Chilean armed forces bombed and stormed the presidential palace, killing Allende. Kissinger denied any direct American role in the coup and quickly recognized the repressive military government of General Augusto Pinochet, who promptly reinstated a free market economy.

NIXON AND THE PRESIDENCY

● How did Nixon's choices in dealing with welfare reform, the economy, and the environment reflect traditional Republican policies?

● What led to Nixon's success in the 1972 election? How did Nixon expect to create a new conservative base for the Republican Party, and what actions did he take to accomplish that goal?

● What actions led to the Watergate investigation and Nixon's impeachment? What success did Gerald Ford have in continuing the policies of the Nixon administration?

In his foreign policy, Nixon followed new paths in dealing with the Chinese and Soviets that did not reflect traditional Republican policies. This was also true in domestic affairs. Nixon had complex views of a new Republican domestic agenda that needed to be more receptive to social responsibility and executive activism. Nixon wanted to reassert law and order, improve the economy, change welfare, return some power to the states, develop an energy plan, and restructure the Republican Party. Domestic adviser Daniel Patrick Moynihan agreed, but

Strategic Arms Limitation agreement   Treaty between the United States and the Soviet Union in 1972 to limit offensive nuclear weapons and defensive antiballistic missile systems; known as SALT I.

intercontinental ballistic missile   Missiles that can travel from one continent to another.

Salvador Allende   Chilean president who was considered the first democratically elected Marxist to head a government; he was killed in a coup in 1973.

noted that without funding and with the Democrats controlling Congress, such an agenda was problematic. It was "time," he suggested, "to consolidate, not innovate." Nonetheless, Nixon told his advisers to plan new initiatives; he wanted "game plans" and not reactions.

Nixon as Pragmatist

For most of his first term, Nixon played **pragmatic** politics. Without fanfare, his administration increased welfare support and approved legislation that enhanced the regulatory powers of the federal government. Food stamps became more accessible, the elderly and handicapped received direct federal support, and Social Security, Medicare, and Medicaid payments were increased. In October 1969, Nixon established a new approach to affirmative action with the "Philadelphia Plan," which required construction unions in that city working under government contracts to hire black apprentices. The following year, the plan became national in scope involving all government hiring and contracting, setting aside jobs for minorities. Nixon also supported subsidized housing for low- and middle-income families, expanded the Job Corps, and oversaw the formation of the Occupational Safety and Health Administration (OSHA).

But there were also White House–sponsored innovations. Nixon sought to restructure the welfare system. He believed the existing system robbed people of their self-esteem, contributed to the breakup of nuclear families, and punished people for working. The Family Assistance Plan introduced in 1969 offered to replace existing programs and agencies with a simple direct payment, provided the recipient accepted work or job training. It was an innovative plan, but neither conservatives nor liberals adopted the idea and it was defeated in the Senate in 1969 and 1971. Despite that defeat, Nixon did not abandon what he saw as the political need for federal social responsibility.

Nixon believed that the Republican Party could not afford to ignore social needs and public concerns in the name of conservatism. The environmental issue was a case in point. When Nixon took office in 1969, the environment was not a major concern. Few Americans thought about ecology. Almost overnight, however, the environment became a serious public issue. The ever-present Los Angeles smog, an oil slick off Santa Barbara, California, the declaration that Lake Erie was ecologically dead, and growing

On April 22, 1970, the nation celebrated the first national Earth Day. Part of the environmental movement, Earth Day emphasized the things that ordinary people could do to improve the environment. A few days later, President Nixon created the Environmental Protection Agency. *Ken Regan/Regan Pictures, Inc.*

mountains of garbage everywhere provided graphic reminders of the ecological dangers facing the nation. Though comprising less than 6 percent of the world's population, environmentalists complained, Americans consumed 40 percent of the globe's resources and created 50 percent of the world's trash. During the first celebration of Earth Day, in April 1970, nearly every community in the nation and more than ten thousand schools and two thousand colleges hosted some type of Earth Day activities, emphasiz-

pragmatic Concerned with facts and actual events; in this case, refers to a willingness to adopt policies that could be either liberal or conservative, depending on the need.

ing a national call for government action to improve environmental quality.

Nixon was not an environmentalist, but he recognized a new national agenda topic. Seizing the opportunity, two days after Earth Day 1970, he proposed the creation of the **Environmental Protection Agency** (EPA). Congress joined in, approving five major environmental acts before the year was finished, including the Clean Air Act and the Water Quality Improvement Act. Both acts directed the EPA, which was rapidly growing into the third-largest government agency, to establish standards on the amount of pollutants that business and industry could discharge. Conservatives grumbled that the standards placed too great a burden on business, and liberals objected that the guidelines did not go far enough to protect the environment. But few denied that Nixon had moved quickly to expand government regulations in an area in which most people agreed intervention was appropriate.

Nixon also proved flexible in economic matters. When he took office, he faced a budget deficit of nearly $25 billion and a climbing rate of inflation. Nixon cut spending, increased interest rates, and balanced the budget in 1969. But economic recovery failed to follow, and inflation rose as economic growth slowed—giving rise to a new phenomenon, **stagflation**. By 1971, the economy was in its first recession since 1958. Unemployment and bankruptcies increased, but inflation still climbed, approaching 5.3 percent. Fearing that economic woes would erode his support, Nixon radically shifted his approach. In April 1971, he asked for increased federal spending to boost recovery and for wage and price controls to stall advancing inflation. Conservatives were shocked and complained bitterly at the betrayal of their values. The public and the economy responded positively, however, as inflation and unemployment declined. At the end of ninety days, Nixon replaced the wage and price freeze with recommended guidelines. Freed from federal restrictions, wages and prices began to climb again.

Nixon's battle with inflation was a losing one, in part because of events over which he had no control. A global drought pushed up farm prices, while Arab nations raised oil prices and limited oil sales in response to the devaluation of the American dollar and continued U.S. support for Israel. After the October 1973 Arab-Israeli Yom Kippur War, Arab nations instituted an oil boycott of the United States that, before it was over in 1974, nearly doubled gasoline prices and forced many Americans to wait in long lines to gas up their cars. Increases in food and oil prices pushed the 1974 inflation rate over 10 percent. That same year, 85 percent of those asked said not only that the economy was the nation's most pressing problem but also that they expected the situation to get worse.

Building the Silent Majority

During the 1968 campaign, Nixon had presented himself as the law-and-order candidate who would use the resources and power of government to combat crime and restore social stability. Nixon also hoped to use this issue to build a new, broader conservative base for the Republican Party. An aide to Attorney General **John Mitchell**, Kevin Phillips, argued in *The Emerging Republican Majority* (1969) that the future of the Republican Party rested on the support of people living in suburbs, working-class neighborhoods, the South, and the **Sunbelt**. In those areas, Phillips asserted, there was little sympathy for student activists, antiwar protesters, welfare recipients, or civil rights advocates. The parts of the new coalition of southern and other disaffected Democrats and Republicans could, in Nixon's terms, gain control of Congress by realignment rather than election.

Zealously, Vice President Spiro Agnew denounced antiwar protesters for aiding the enemy and undermining the nation's social and patriotic values, and he challenged the Silent Majority to reassert traditional values and restore stability to America. In many areas, blue-collar and middle-class America responded to Agnew's plea. Fearing integration and experiencing a

---

Environmental Protection Agency Agency created in 1970 to consolidate all major government programs controlling pollution and other programs to protect the environment.

stagflation Persistent inflation combined with stagnant consumer demand and relatively high unemployment.

John Mitchell Nixon's attorney general, who eventually served four years in prison for his part in the Watergate scandal.

Sunbelt Region of the United States that extends from Washington, D.C., to Florida and from Texas to California and the Pacific coast; during the 1960s, its population grew dramatically because of its climate and economic opportunities.

slowing of economic gains, more and more of suburban America voted Republican. In southern California, residents of Lakewood felt threatened by a seeming "invasion" of blacks and Latinos, who used "their" parks and swimming pools, encroaching on what had once been a model, modern, and upwardly mobile suburb.

As part of an ongoing **"southern strategy"**—an attempt to lock up the once solidly Democratic South for Republicans—the Nixon administration opposed busing to achieve school integration. In response to a 1969 request from Mississippi to postpone court-ordered integration of several school systems, Attorney General John Mitchell petitioned the Supreme Court for a delay. At the same time, the administration lobbied Congress for a revision of the 1965 Voting Rights Act that would have weakened southern compliance. Neither effort was successful. In October 1969, the Supreme Court unanimously decreed in *Alexander v. Holmes* that it was "the obligation of every school district to terminate dual school systems at once." The White House suffered another loss in 1971 when the Court reaffirmed the use of busing to achieve integration in a North Carolina case, *Swann v. Charlotte-Mecklenburg*. The Nixon administration criticized the decisions but agreed to "carry out the law." By 1973, most African-American children in the South were attending integrated public schools. Even though Nixon was unable to slow the process of integration, he won increasing political support among white southerners.

A second part of Nixon's southern strategy was to alter the composition of the Supreme Court. He wanted a more conservative Court that would more narrowly interpret the Constitution and move away from the social interventionism of the Warren Court. His first opportunity came in 1969 when Chief Justice Earl Warren retired. To take Warren's place, Nixon nominated Warren Burger, a respected, conservative federal judge, who was easily confirmed by the Senate. The resignation of liberal justice Abe Fortas soon after gave Nixon a second chance to alter the Court.

For political reasons, Nixon nominated Clement Haynesworth of South Carolina. Haynesworth's history of antilabor and anti–civil rights statements and decisions raised predictable trouble in the Senate. Democrats and several Republicans joined forces to deny his confirmation. The rejection incensed Nixon, who was determined to force a southerner down the Senate's throat. His second choice was worse than the first. Not only was G. Harrold Carswell of Florida opposed to civil rights and labor, but his ratings as a

lawyer and judge were below average. Carswell, too, failed confirmation. On his third try, Nixon stopped looking for a southerner and selected Harry Blackmun, a conservative from Minnesota. Blackmun was confirmed easily. In 1971 Nixon appointed two more justices, Lewis Powell of Virginia and William Rehnquist of Arizona, creating a more conservative Supreme Court.

An Embattled President

By the end of Nixon's first term, Republicans had every reason to gloat. Nearly 60 percent of respondents in national opinion polls said they approved of Nixon's record. The efforts on behalf of southern whites had ensured growing support in what had once been the "solid Democratic South." The law-and-order campaign appealed to so-called Middle America, and protesters and activists were losing strength. The economy, though still a worry, seemed under control: unemployment was dropping and inflation was being held in check. Diplomatically, Nixon had scored major successes: the opening of relations with China, détente with the Soviets, the reduction of American forces in Vietnam, and the possibility of a peace agreement in Paris. Nixon projected that his second term would hold few obstacles, especially since he did not have to run for office again.

The 1972 campaign was marked by a confident Republican Party and the continued disarray of the Democratic Party. Most of the enthusiastic Democrats had migrated to the two wings of the party, led by the liberal **George McGovern** and the conservative George Wallace. Moderate Democrats, led by Hubert Humphrey and Edmund Muskie, seemed unable to energize the voters, especially the new group of first-time voters—those between 18 and 21. The newest category of voter was a result of the Twenty-sixth Amendment ratified in 1971, which had lowered the voting age to 18.

Senator McGovern of South Dakota gained the presidential nomination after several bruising primaries and a divided nominating convention. Many

---

southern strategy A plan to entice southerners into the Republican Party by appointing white southerners to the Supreme Court and resisting the policy of busing to achieve integration.

George McGovern South Dakota senator who opposed the Vietnam War and was the unsuccessful Democratic candidate for president in 1972.

As the Watergate investigation uncovered a host of "dirty tricks" and other unethical and illegal activities by the Nixon administration, cartoonist Edward Sorell drew the "Watergate Shootout," showing Nixon, Mitchell, and others involved in the Watergate scandal as a band of mobsters holding off the police. *"Watergate Shootout" by Edward Sorell.*

Democrats believed he was too liberal and refused to support him. George Wallace—confined to a wheelchair following an assassination attempt that left him paralyzed—again bolted the party to run as a third-party candidate on the American Independent ticket.

Despite almost certain victory, as he had been since taking office, Nixon was convinced that enemies surrounded him: bureaucrats, Democrats, social activists, liberals, most of the press, and even some members of his own staff and party. Repeatedly, he spoke about "screwing" his domestic enemies before they got him. He kept an "enemies list," used illegal wiretaps and infiltration to spy on suspect organizations and people, and instructed the FBI, the Internal Revenue Service, and other government organizations to intimidate and punish his opponents.

Nixon and his campaign coordinators longed to humiliate the Democrats. To achieve this, Nixon's staff and the **Committee to Re-elect the President** (CREEP), directed by John Mitchell, stepped outside the normal bounds of election behavior. They turned to a Special Investigations Unit, known informally as the "Plumbers," who conducted "dirty tricks" to disrupt the Democrats. They sponsored hecklers to attack Democratic candidates who

supported McGovern. Seeking inside information on the opposition, CREEP approved a burglary of Democratic National Committee headquarters in the **Watergate** building in Washington, D.C., to copy documents and tap phones.

On June 17, 1972, a Watergate security guard detected the burglars and notified the police, who arrested five men carrying "bugging" equipment. Soon the burglars were linked to the Plumbers and then to CREEP. CREEP and the White House denied any connection to the burglars, while Mitchell and White House staffers destroyed documents indicating the opposite and encouraged the FBI to limit its

---

Committee to Re-elect the President   Nixon's campaign committee in 1972, which enlisted G. Gordon Liddy and others to spy on the Democrats and break into the offices of the Democratic National Committee.

Watergate   Apartment-office complex in Washington, D.C., that housed the headquarters of the Democratic National Committee; its name became synonymous with the scandal over the Nixon administration's involvement in a break-in there and the president's part in the cover-up that followed.

investigation. "I want you all to stonewall it," he told John Mitchell. "Cover it up." The furor passed and in November, Nixon buried McGovern in an avalanche of electoral votes, winning every state except Massachusetts. It was a personal victory, however, as Democrats still held majorities in Congress.

Nixon was overjoyed with the results. He had demolished his enemies and claimed a public mandate for his policies. Within the White House, however, the cheers were tempered with concerns about the trial of the Watergate burglars. The cover-up was unraveling. James McCord, who led the burglary team, had implicated key Republicans as having taken part in planning the operation and paying "hush money" to the burglars. *Washington Post* reporters Bob Woodward and Carl Bernstein investigated the suspicious payments and found a path leading to John Mitchell, CREEP, and the White House. To investigate allegations of White House involvement, the Senate convened a special committee to investigate the break-in, chaired by a Democrat, Senator Sam Ervin, Jr., of North Carolina. Among those testifying was White House staffer John Dean, who implicated top White House officials, including Nixon, in the cover-up.

Adding to Nixon's troubles were accusations he had improperly taken tax deductions and that Vice President Agnew was guilty of income-tax evasion and influence peddling. "I am not a crook," Nixon announced, as both denied any wrongdoing. Nevertheless, Nixon agreed that he had made errors in his income-tax deductions and that he owed the government an additional half-million dollars. Agnew, certain to be convicted, pleaded no contest to the charges against him and resigned. In October 1973, Nixon named Representative **Gerald R. Ford** of Michigan to be vice president.

As Ford assumed office, the cover-up rapidly disintegrated. The revelation that Nixon had secretly recorded meetings in the Oval Office, including those with John Dean, raised demands for the release of the tapes. Responding to public pressure, Nixon appointed Archibald Cox as special Justice Department prosecutor to investigate Watergate, promising full cooperation. But when Cox demanded the Oval Office tapes, Nixon ordered him fired. Following the October 20, 1973, **"Saturday Night Massacre,"** Nixon's popularity shrank to 30 percent, and calls for his resignation or impeachment intensified.

In March 1974, the grand jury investigating the Watergate break-in indicted Mitchell, Haldeman, and Ehrlichman and named Nixon as an "unindicted co-conspirator." Nixon, under tremendous pressure, released transcripts of selected tapes. The outcome was devastating. The transcripts contradicted some official testimony, and Nixon's apparent callousness, lack of decency, and profane language shocked the nation. By the end of July, the House Judiciary Committee had charged Nixon with three impeachable crimes: obstructing justice, abuse of power, and defying subpoenas. Nixon's remaining support evaporated, and once-loyal Republicans told him that he could either resign or face impeachment. Nixon resigned on August 9, 1974, making Gerald Ford an unelected president. Eventually, twenty-nine people connected to the White House were convicted of crimes related to Watergate and the 1972 campaign. Ex-president Nixon was spared from any further legal actions by a presidential pardon granted by Ford upon assuming office.

An Interim President

Most saw Gerald Ford as an honest man, a good administrator, a compassionate person to heal a nation, but only an interim president. Rejecting the activism of the Nixon, Republicans and Democrats in Congress saw an opportunity to reassert themselves. The most contentious issue was the economy. Nixon had faced and coped with the first recession in a decade, but the economy was not improving. Ford approached the problem from a traditional Republican perspective. The solution rested with cutting business taxes and federal spending, while raising interest rates. Democrats rejected the formula and instead introduced legislation to create jobs and to increase spending for social and educational programs. Ford vetoed the bills and conducted a public opinion campaign to mobilize support for his program. The result was a political stalemate. In two years, Ford successfully blocked thirty-seven bills but never generated enough public support to advance his own programs. At the same time the economy continued to worsen when

---

Gerald R. Ford   Michigan congressman whom Nixon appointed vice president when Spiro Agnew resigned and who became president in 1974 when Nixon resigned.

Saturday Night Massacre   Events on October 20, 1973, when Nixon ordered the firing of Watergate special prosecutor, Archibald Cox; two Justice Department officials resigned, rather than carry out his order.

oil prices rose 350 percent as the **Organization of Petroleum Exporting Countries** (OPEC) used its economic power to modify American support to Israel during the Yom Kippur War.

Ford fared only slightly better in conducting foreign policy. Relying heavily on Henry Kissinger, who was now national security adviser and secretary of state, Ford attempted to continue Nixon's policies. He managed some success in the Middle East, in ending the Yom Kippur War. Kissinger had shuttled between Egypt and Israel to broker an agreement to remove Israeli forces from Arab territory. His efforts paid off in September 1975, when Israel and Egypt signed a pact whereby Israeli troops withdrew from some occupied areas and Egypt resigned from the anti-Israeli Arab coalition. An added benefit of the agreement was that it convinced OPEC to increase oil production and lower prices. Other foreign policy efforts, however, produced few positive results, in part due to opposition from the right and the left in Congress.

Ford's efforts to maintain economic and military support for South Vietnam also met with congressional opposition and delays. When Saigon fell to Communist forces in April 1975, he blamed Congress for the defeat. Trying to maintain the Nixon-Kissinger effort to arrive at détente with Moscow, he met with Soviet premier Brezhnev at Vladivostok, in Siberia, and in Helsinki, Finland. At the summits he made progress toward strategic arms limitation and improved East-West relations but received little credit at home. In Congress and his own party. Ford's actions drew fire from those who wanted a tougher, more traditional Cold War policy toward the Soviet Union. Among the most forceful Republican critics was presidential hopeful Ronald Reagan. Embarrassing a sitting president, Reagan sought the Republican nomination in 1976 and won several primaries in the West and South. The ex-governor of California represented the conservative wing of the party and attacked the Ford-Kissinger policy of détente as well as Ford's political ineffectiveness. Ford managed to eke out a victory at the convention, embracing a conservative agenda that called for smaller government and tougher policies toward communism. Few expected the interim president would win the election.

Organization of Petroleum Exporting Countries
Economic alliance of oil-producing countries, mostly Arab, formed in 1960, powerful enough to influence the world price of oil by controlling oil supplies; in 1973 its members placed an embargo on the sale of oil to countries allied with Israel.

INDIVIDUAL VOICES

Examining a Primary Source

Striking Grape Workers Proclaim Their Goals

In 1965 Cesar Chavez called a strike of the National Farm Workers Association against the grape growers in Delano, California. When traditional labor protests such as picket lines failed to work, he moved to mobilize public opinion. He fasted, held parades and rallies, and called on consumers to buy only union-picked grapes. This document, which appeared in the NFWA newspaper, *El Malcriado* ("The Unruly One") in May 1969, was printed in Spanish and English to rally those supporting *la huelga*, the strike, and to explain in revolutionary terms the efforts of the strikers. The strike was settled in 1970.

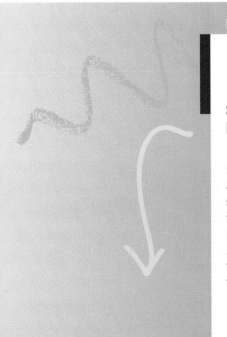

We the striking grape workers of California join . . . with consumers across the continent in planning the steps that lie ahead on the road to our liberation. . . .

We have been farm workers for hundreds of years and pioneers for seven. Mexicans, Filipinos, Africans, and others, our ancestors were among those who founded this land and tamed its wilderness. But we are still pilgrims on this land, and we are pioneers who blaze a trail out of the wilderness of hunger and deprivation. . . . ● *If this road we chart leads to the rights and reforms we demand, if it leads to just wages, humane working conditions, protection from the misuse of pesticides, and to the fundamental right of collective bargaining, if it changes the social order that relegates us to the bottom reaches of society, then in our wake will follow thousands of American farm workers.* ● *Our example will make them free. But if our road does not bring us victory and social change, it will not be because . . . our resolve is too weak, but only because our bodies are mortal and our journey hard. For we are in the midst of a great social movement, and we will not stop struggling 'til we die, or win!*

We have been farm workers for hundreds of years and strikers for four. It was four years ago that we threw down our plowshares and pruning hooks. These Biblical symbols of peace and tranquility to us represent too many lifetimes of unprotesting submission to a degrading social system that allows us no dignity, no comfort, no peace. . . . So we went and stood tall outside the vineyards where we had stooped for years. But the tailors of national labor legislation left us naked . . . our picket lines crippled by injunctions and harassed by growers; our strike was broken by imported scabs; our overtures to our employers were ignored. Yet we knew the day must come when they would talk to us as equals.

We have been farm workers for hundreds of years and boycotters for two. We did not choose the grape boycott, but we had chosen to leave our peonage, poverty, and despair behind. Though our first bid for freedom, the strike, was weakened, we would not turn back. The boycott was the only way forward the growers left to us. ● *We called upon our fellow men and were answered by consumers who said—as all men of conscience must—that they would no longer allow their tables to be subsidized by our sweat and our sorrow. They shunned the grapes, fruit of our affliction.*

. . . The grapes grow sweet and heavy on the vines, but they will have to wait while we reach out first for our freedom. The time is ripe for our liberation. ●

● What do the writers of the proclamation mean when they call themselves "pilgrims"?

● What changes in society are the strikers seeking?

● According to the document, why did the traditional tool of labor, the strike, fail, and why did the strikers turn to using a boycott?

● How do the sentiments in this document compare with Jessie Lopez de la Cruz's activism for La Causa?

SUMMARY

When President Johnson assumed the presidency in 1963, the forces of liberalism that had given substance to the Kennedy administration continued their efforts to reform society. Encouraged by Johnson's Great Society and War on Poverty, Hispanics and American Indians organized, demonstrated, and turned to the government—especially the federal courts—to further their causes. The activism associated with the Warren Court intensified as it continued to issue controversial decisions that expanded individual rights and protections. By the mid-1960s, however, liberals increasingly were divided and critical of the Johnson administration. At the heart of a growing disillusionment was the war in Vietnam.

Johnson continued Kennedy's foreign policies, expanding commitments to oppose communism around the world. Unable to find options that would save South Vietnam and reduce the American role, Johnson eventually implemented a series of planned escalations that Americanized the war. The expectation that American military superiority would defeat Ho Chi Minh's Communists proved disastrous. As the United States escalated its efforts, they kept pace and showed no slackening of resolve or resources. Within the United States, however, as the American commitment grew, a significant antiwar movement developed. The combination of the Tet offensive and presidential politics cost Johnson his presidency, divided the Democratic Party, and compounded the divisions in American society.

But more than the debate over the war divided the nation. By 1968, the country was aflame with riots in urban centers, and an increasing number of groups were seeking better social, economic, and political choices. Those advocating social reforms, however, faced a resurgence of conservatism that helped elect Nixon. Hoping to find a strategy for withdrawing from Vietnam, Nixon implemented a policy of Vietnamization. He also wanted to restructure international relations by working to improve relations with the Soviet Union and China. At home, Nixon charted an uneven course, switching between maintaining government activism and reducing the power of government. Though opposed to government intervention, he created the Environmental Protection Agency. Politically, he sought a broader base for the Republican Party by pursuing a southern strategy that curtailed federal support for civil rights. Despite Nixon's domestic and foreign policy successes, however, his desire to crush his enemies led to the Watergate scandal and his downfall. Facing impeachment, the president resigned. President Ford tried to restore confidence in government but faced too many obstacles to be successful. At the nation approached the 1976, bicentennial election, many wondered if the optimism that began the 1960s would ever return. The nation seemed mired in a slowing economy and a public cynicism toward government and politics generated by Vietnam and Watergate.

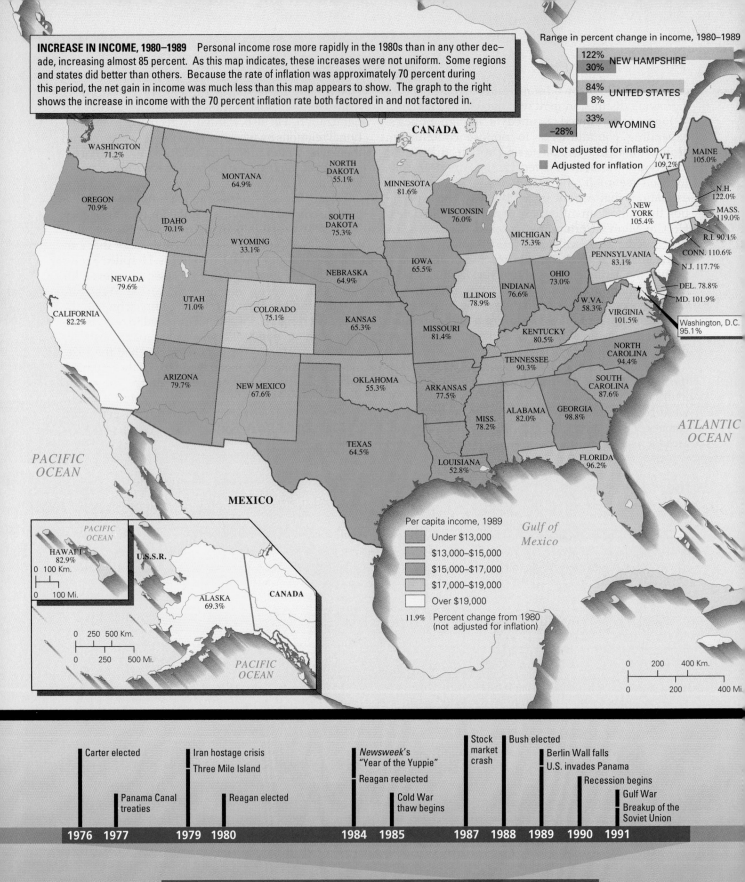

INCREASE IN INCOME, 1980–1989   Personal income rose more rapidly in the 1980s than in any other dec–ade, increasing almost 85 percent. As this map indicates, these increases were not uniform. Some regions and states did better than others. Because the rate of inflation was approximately 70 percent during this period, the net gain in income was much less than this map appears to show. The graph to the right shows the increase in income with the 70 percent inflation rate both factored in and not factored in.

Range in percent change in income, 1980–1989

122% NEW HAMPSHIRE
30%

84% UNITED STATES
8%

33% WYOMING
−28%

Not adjusted for inflation
Adjusted for inflation

CANADA

WASHINGTON
71.2%

OREGON
70.9%

MONTANA
64.9%

NORTH DAKOTA
55.1%

MINNESOTA
81.6%

IDAHO
70.1%

WYOMING
33.1%

SOUTH DAKOTA
75.3%

WISCONSIN
76.0%

MICHIGAN
75.3%

MAINE
105.0%

VT.
109.2%

NEW YORK
105.4%

N.H.
122.0%

MASS.
119.0%

NEVADA
79.6%

UTAH
71.0%

NEBRASKA
64.9%

IOWA
65.5%

PENNSYLVANIA
83.1%

R.I. 90.1%

CONN. 110.6%

N.J. 117.7%

CALIFORNIA
82.2%

COLORADO
75.1%

KANSAS
65.3%

ILLINOIS
78.9%

INDIANA
76.6%

OHIO
73.0%

W.VA.
58.3%

VIRGINIA
101.5%

DEL. 78.8%

MD. 101.9%

Washington, D.C.
95.1%

MISSOURI
81.4%

KENTUCKY
80.5%

NORTH CAROLINA
94.4%

ARIZONA
79.7%

NEW MEXICO
67.6%

OKLAHOMA
55.3%

ARKANSAS
77.5%

TENNESSEE
90.3%

SOUTH CAROLINA
87.6%

MISS.
78.2%

ALABAMA
82.0%

GEORGIA
98.8%

TEXAS
64.5%

LOUISIANA
52.8%

FLORIDA
96.2%

ATLANTIC OCEAN

PACIFIC OCEAN

MEXICO

Gulf of Mexico

PACIFIC OCEAN

HAWAII
82.9%

0   100 Km.
0   100 Mi.

U.S.S.R.

ALASKA
69.3%

CANADA

PACIFIC OCEAN

0   250 500 Km.
0   250 500 Mi.

Per capita income, 1989

Under $13,000
$13,000–$15,000
$15,000–$17,000
$17,000–$19,000
Over $19,000

11.9%   Percent change from 1980
        (not adjusted for inflation)

0   200   400 Km.
0   200   400 Mi.

Carter elected

Panama Canal treaties

Iran hostage crisis
Three Mile Island

Reagan elected

Newsweek's "Year of the Yuppie"
Reagan reelected

Cold War thaw begins

Stock market crash

Bush elected

Berlin Wall falls
U.S. invades Panama

Recession begins

Gulf War

Breakup of the Soviet Union

1976 1977   1979 1980   1984 1985   1987 1988 1989 1990 1991

1850   1900   1950   2000

Facing Limits, 1976–1992

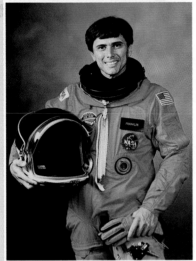

FRANKLIN CHANG-DIAZ

Born in Costa Rica, Franklin Chang-Diaz grew up wanting to travel into space. To fulfill his dream, he immigrated to the United States after finishing high school to continue his education. Eventually he received a Ph.D. from the Massachusetts Institute of Technology and became a scientist-astronaut. *NASA.*

Franklin Chang-Diaz

Twenty-one years separated the young child looking into space from a mango tree in Venezuela and the young man who looked down toward Latin America from space. Franklin Chang-Diaz's wish had come true—he was an astronaut. It was January 1986 and he was on board the space shuttle *Columbia*, chasing Halley's comet.

Born in Costa Rica in 1950, Franklin Chang-Diaz was living in Venezuela with his parents when the Soviets launched *Sputnik* in 1957. His mother told him that man had placed a new star in the heavens and someday man would explore the stars. Like other children around the world, Franklin dreamed of exploring space.

His family returned to Costa Rica, where his Chinese grandfather had settled, seeking a better life in the late nineteenth century. Growing up in Costa Rica, "I was a normal boy, living a normal life," he later recounted. In school, he was successful at both athletics and academics. He especially liked doing science experiments, and at home, he experimented with model rockets, using gunpowder as fuel. His fascination with space continued as he watched the Soviets and the Americans send astronauts into space. He too wanted to go into space, but that was impossible in Costa Rica. When he told his friends he planned to go to the United States, they said he was crazy. Pursuing his goal, he worked in a bank after high school each day to save money for his journey to America.

In nine months, he had saved $50.00 and had convinced his parents to buy him an airline ticket to the United States. He arrived in Hartford in 1968 and moved in with relatives but faced a major hurdle in trying to enter the local high school. Finally, he convinced school officials to place him in the senior class as a regular student. He initially failed his classes, but soon his English and his grades improved significantly. The second hurdle was to get into college. He knew it would be impossible to become an astronaut with just a high school diploma.

With superior grades and support from his teachers, Franklin Chang-Diaz received a scholarship to attend the University of Connecticut. Disappointment soon followed, however, for the scholarship was for citizens of the United States. His application had been read incorrectly; the scholarship board thought he was Puerto Rican. The scholarship was then withdrawn. But university officials and other supporters petitioned the Connecticut legislature to grant him a waiver of citizenship. In the fall of 1969, he entered the university intending to major in science, engineering, or mathematics. He chose mechanical engineering and graduated in 1973. The next step was to attend graduate school. Chang-Diaz determined that if he were a scientist, he would have a better chance of joining the National Aeronautics and Space Administration (NASA). Receiving a scholarship from the Massachusetts Institute of Technology, he entered the doctoral program. His area of interest and research was applied plasma physics and fusion technology. Watching space probes being sent to Mars and deeper into space, he concluded that nuclear power would be needed for long-range voyages and that "plasma physics would play a key role." Degree in hand, an optimistic Dr. Franklin Chang-Diaz applied to the astronaut program. "All of a sudden the space program was so close, I felt I could touch it."

The space program was in a period of limited funding and support and accepted only a handful of candidates into the program. Franklin Chang-Diaz was rejected; again, not being an American citizen had worked against him. He continued his scientific research, contributing to the concepts of how to make a fusion reactor. Two years later, now a naturalized U.S. citizen, he applied again to the NASA program, one of four thousand applicants for nineteen open slots. This time, he made the program and in 1981 earned his astronaut status. Still, however, there was disappointment. Chang-Diaz wanted to participate in space flights, but NASA kept finding other duties for him. He served as part of the support team for other missions, and he continued to conduct research on nuclear propulsion, developing a new technology for manned missions to Mars. Finally, in January 1986, his dream came true. The space shuttle *Columbia* lifted off from the Kennedy Space Center with Dr. Franklin Chang-Diaz on board for a six-day flight.

Since his first flight in 1986, he has made five additional flights, tying the record for flights (six) by one astronaut and logging more than 1,269 hours in space, including several space walks. He is currently preparing for his seventh flight to take place in 2002, and he serves as the director of the Advanced Space Propulsion Laboratory at the Johnson Space Center in Houston, Texas. Recently asked about his upcoming flight and his journey from Costa Rica to Houston, he replied: "I cannot think of a better job . . . I'm just having the time of my life. This is what I planned for all my life and I'm really enjoying it, and to me, I guess I feel I have the best of both worlds because I also continue my research, and so I am able to be a scientist at the same time that I am also an astronaut, and that is to me the perfect combination."

INTRODUCTION

As the nation celebrated its two-hundredth birthday in 1976, television networks showed 30-second clips of proud moments in American history. Watching those clips, Franklin Chang-Diaz was full of optimism about his future in America. In a year, he would graduate and apply to be an astronaut. His optimism, and the dreams of many Americans and immigrants, seemed overblown, though, as limits seemed to loom everywhere. A sluggish economy, increasing intolerance, and rising unemployment appeared to make achieving—or even maintaining—the American dream more difficult. Support for the liberalism that had attacked racism and poverty was waning, challenged by the belief that an activist government was part of the nation's problems. Even James Earl Carter, the Democratic candidate for the presidency in 1976, argued that government could not solve every problem. He urged Americans to make sacrifices to overcome problems at home and abroad.

Arriving in Washington as a political outsider, President Carter failed to lead the Democratic Congress and proved ineffective in reversing the slowing economy. His administration also failed to match the expectations of those seeking an activism government to support their goals. Carter's efforts to refocus American foreign policy fared only slightly better and to many Americans resulted in a near-eclipse of American prestige abroad.

A resurgent conservatism led by the New Right and Ronald Reagan defeated Carter in the 1980 presidential contest. Reagan had gained high public approval ratings by promising a renewed America, powerful and prosperous. He attacked liberal economic and social policies and re-emphasized a Cold War–style foreign policy that would "stand tall" against the Soviet "evil empire." During his administration, the economy was revitalized and government spending directed away from social programs toward military spending. Many Americans believed that his conservative values had freed businesses of many needless government controls and reasserted traditional social and family values. Reagan's foreign policy, supporters argued, promoted American interests in Central America and weakened the Soviet Union, which was ending the Cold War with an American victory.

Not everyone agreed that Reagan's choices produced favorable results. Critics argued that he placed too much emphasis on satisfying the wealthy and too little on the needs of minority groups, the less well off, and the poor. Others pointed to a massive national debt and the growing trade deficit as serious economic problems. Despite Reagan's personal popularity, as the Reagan administration ended, more and more Americans were uncertain about the ultimate outcome of Reagan's economic and social policies.

Running in the shadow of Reagan in 1988, Vice President George Bush gained the Republican presidential nomination in a nation that seemed dissatisfied but unable to pinpoint what was wrong or how to fix it. He offered the nation experienced leadership and promised to maintain American strength abroad. At home he would institute a "kinder, gentler nation" that would show more concern for minorities, the poor, education, and the environment. He easily defeated Democratic candidate Michael Dukakis, but as president, he showed little desire to implement domestic policy changes. Instead, he chose to focus on foreign policy. Taking office as the Soviet Union collapsed, he charted foreign policy in a new international setting with

the United States as the only superpower. Bush cautiously supported democratic change in Eastern Europe and Central America. To promote American interests he committed American military forces in Panama and Kuwait. As Bush prepared for his re-election, he was confident that his foreign policy success and Operation Desert Storm would carry him to victory.

THE CARTER PRESIDENCY

● What new directions in foreign policy did Carter take, and how did his policies toward Central America reflect that direction?

● What successes and failures did Carter experience in dealing with the Middle East?

● What domestic problems did Carter face on assuming the presidency? How did Carter's status as an "outsider" shape his goals and leadership?

The United States celebrated the two-hundredth anniversary of its independence in 1976. Amid the festivities and praise for its institutions and accomplishments, however, lurked a deepening sense of cynicism, uneasiness, and uncertainty. The social activism and turmoil of the 1960s, Vietnam, and Watergate had shaken the nation's belief in government's ability to solve problems. President Ford's efforts to restore faith in government had not succeeded as indicated by responses to a 1975 survey: most people said they believed that politicians consistently lied to them. Other surveys found that the same lack of faith had spread to other institutions. Americans were now questioning the motives and credibility of the medical and legal professions, business leaders, and even educators. The public's lack of trust and confidence was heightened by a slowing economy that raised concerns about the future. For the first time since the Depression, many parents worried that their children would not enjoy a higher standard of living. The optimism that had characterized the 1960s had faded into frustration and apathy, and a sense that the nation no longer shaped events but reacted to them.

To many Americans the political forecast did not look especially promising as the two presidential contenders began their race for the White House. Gerald Ford had his party's nomination for the presidency, after overcoming a stiff challenge from the more conservative Ronald Reagan. Polls showed that people liked Ford but considered him an ineffective president. His Democratic opponent, James Earl Carter, boasted about his lack of political expe-

chronology

New Directions, New Limits

1976	Jimmy Carter elected president
1977	Department of Energy created Panama Canal treaties SALT I treaty expires
1978	Camp David Accords Revolution in Iran topples shah
1979	Ayatollah Khomeini assumes power in Iran United States recognizes People's Republic of China Nuclear accident at Three Mile Island, Pennsylvania Egyptian-Israeli peace treaty signed in Washington, D.C. SALT II treaty signed in Vienna Hostages seized in Iran Soviet Union invades Afghanistan
1980	Carter applies sanctions against Soviet Union SALT II treaty withdrawn from Senate Carter Doctrine Iran-Iraq War begins Ronald Reagan elected president
1981	Iran releases American hostages Economic Recovery Tax Act
1982	United States sends marines to Beirut
1983	Congress funds Strategic Defense Initiative Marine barracks in Beirut destroyed United States invades Grenada
1984	Withdrawal of U.S. forces from Lebanon Boland Amendment Reagan reelected *Newsweek*'s "Year of the Yuppie"
1985	Gramm-Rudman-Hollings Act Mikhail Gorbachev assumes power in Soviet Union Secret arms sales to Iran in exchange for U.S. hostages Gorbachev-Reagan summit in Geneva
1986	U.S. bombing raid on Libya Gorbachev-Reagan summit in Iceland
1987	Iran-Contra hearings Stock market crash Intermediate Nuclear Force Treaty
1988	George Bush elected president
1989	Chinese government represses democracy movement in Tiananmen Square Berlin Wall pulled down United States invades Panama Gorbachev-Bush summit on Malta
1990	Recession begins Free elections in Nicaragua Clean Air Act Iraq invades Kuwait Americans with Disabilities Act
1991	Breakup of the Soviet Union Gorbachev resigns Persian Gulf War

rience, aside from being a one-time governor of Georgia. People seemed to like Carter's nonpolitical, folksy background but wondered if he had the political strength to lead Congress and the nation. Both men seemed full of good intentions, but neither appeared up to the task of implementing them.

The presidential contest between Ford and Carter lacked drama, even with nationally televised debates, in which Ford blundered and said that there was no Soviet domination of Eastern Europe. In the debates and throughout the campaign, the candidates were vague on issues but expansive on smiles and photo sessions. One political observer noted that on any issue Carter seemed "to have more positions than the *Kama Sutra*." The result was a very close election. Ford won more states than Carter but lost the electoral count by 56 votes. Reflecting the political apathy of the nation, only 54.4 percent of eligible voters cast their ballots. One Californian explained that he had not voted because he did not want "to force a second-class decision on my neighbors."

Jimmy Carter arrived in the nation's capital in January 1977 brimming with enthusiasm and stressing that he was free of Washington politics and the lures of special interests. On Inauguration Day he led the people from Capitol Hill to the White House by walking rather than riding in a limousine. As president, he pledged honesty, simplicity, and hard work. Anxious to get started, he wrote in his diary: "It's almost impossible for me to delay something that I see needs to be done."

New Directions in Foreign Policy

In international relations, Carter saw a lot that needed to be done. First and foremost, American foreign policy needed to be redirected. It was too European and Cold War–oriented, shaped too much by an "inordinate fear of communism." He sought a more open and moral diplomacy that would pay greater attention to the economic and social problems of the non-European world, including abuses of **human rights**.

Latin America seemed a good place to set the new tone in American policy. The United States would abandon its paternalism and consider the interests of each Latin American nation. Carter believed that the Panama Canal presented an excellent opportunity to chart a fresh Latin American policy. The Panama Canal Zone lay like an affluent, foreign-occupied island within Panama. To Panamanians it was a reminder of the inequalities between themselves and the United States. Panama wanted control over the canal, and for years negotiations on the issue had stalled because of American opposition. Carter made reaching an agreement with Panama one of his highest priorities, and within a year two treaties were complete. They laid the groundwork for transferring ownership and control of the canal to Panama by 1999 and guaranteeing its neutrality.

Carter was pleased, but almost 80 percent of the American public were not and opposed giving up the canal. Most agreed with Republicans (and many Democrats) that the canal was American-built and American-run and should remain that way. Republican senator Jesse Helms of North Carolina promised to kill the treaties in the Senate. He failed (by a single vote), but only after an amendment was added that gave the United States the right and responsibility to intervene if an outside force threatened the canal.

Carter's emphasis on moral governments and human rights also drew widespread opposition. Critics warned that letting human rights drive American policy might undermine pro-American but abusive governments, especially in developing countries. Some liberals and moderates also expressed concern that the human rights issue might harm improving relations with the Soviets and Chinese. Both were correct. In Nicaragua, Carter's emphasis on human rights contributed to the United States halting military and economic aid, which in turn was a factor in the ouster of Anastasio Somoza, who had ruled the nation with an iron hand for years. Fulfilling some Americans' worst fears, replacing Somoza in power was the largely Marxist **Sandinista Liberation Front**, led by Daniel Ortega.

Carter's criticism of Soviet and Eastern European violations of human rights led to an almost immediate cooling of relations with the Soviets that threatened the continuation of détente and efforts at arms limitations. Yet the talks continued, and despite chilly relations and difficult discussions, the two superpowers agreed to place some limits on long-range missiles, bombers, and nuclear warheads. Carter and Leonid Brezhnev signed the second **strategic arms limitation treaty** (SALT II) during their Vienna summit in June 1979. The agreement

human rights Basic rights and freedoms to which all human beings are entitled, such as the right to life and liberty, to freedom of thought and expression, and to equality before the law.

Sandinista Liberation Front Leftist guerrilla movement that overthrew Anastasio Somoza in Nicaragua in 1979 and established a revolutionary government under Daniel Ortega.

strategic arms limitation treaty Agreement, known as SALT II, between the United States and the Soviet Union in 1979 to limit the number of strategic nuclear missiles in each country; Congress never approved the treaty.

encountered stubborn, and bipartisan, congressional opposition. Conservatives concluded it gave too many advantages to the Soviets while liberals argued that it was not encompassing enough. Hopes that the Senate would approve the treaty faded quickly after the Soviet invasion of Afghanistan in early 1980. Calling the Soviet incursion the "gravest threat to peace since 1945," Carter withdrew the treaty from consideration, imposed **economic sanctions** on the Soviet Union, and boycotted the 1980 Olympic Games held in Moscow. He also provided aid to the **mujahedeen**, who were fighting the Soviets and announced the **"Carter Doctrine."** Any nation that attempted to take control of the **Persian Gulf**, Carter stated, would "be repelled by any means necessary, including the use of force." Relations with the other Communist superpower, however, got progressively better as Carter worked with China's new leader, Deng Xiaoping, and restored full diplomatic relations with the People's Republic of China in January 1979.

Middle Eastern Crises

Carter credited the Panama Canal treaty to his ability to take a new approach to an old issue. He believed that such a tactic would also move Israel and its Arab neighbors toward a peace settlement (see Map 30.1). To this end, Carter invited Egypt's president Anwar Sadat and Israel's prime minister Menachem Begin for talks at the presidential retreat at Camp David in Maryland. Surprisingly both accepted.

Meeting in September 1978, Sadat and Begin did not get along well, and Carter shuttled between the two leaders, smoothing relations and stressing his personal commitment to both nations. Personally friendly with Sadat, he frequently exchanged harsh words with Begin. But he carefully negotiated agreements by which Egypt would recognize Israel's right to exist and Israel would return the Israeli-occupied Sinai Peninsula to Egypt. It took several months to finalize the **Camp David Accords**, but in a ceremony at the White House on March 26, 1979, acting like a proud midwife, Carter watched Begin and Sadat sign the first peace treaty between an Arab state and Israel. Although the treaty was a major diplomatic achievement for Carter, Arab leaders and most of the Arab world condemned it.

The Soviet intervention in Afghanistan and Carter's announcement of the Carter Doctrine were responses to more than just events in Afghanistan. Both the Americans and the Soviets were reacting to the revolution in Iran, which had toppled the pro-

One of President Carter's greatest triumphs was the signing of the 1978 peace accords between President Anwar Sadat of Egypt (*left*) and Prime Minister Menachem Begin of Israel (*right*). The agreement followed days of personal diplomacy by Carter at the Camp David presidential retreat. Both Sadat and Begin received the Nobel Peace Prize for their efforts. *Jimmy Carter Presidential Library.*

American ruler, Shah Reza Pahlavi in early 1979. Led by **Ayatollah Ruhollah Khomeini**, the revolution established Islamic fundamentalism diametrically opposed to Western ideas and values as a powerful force in Middle Eastern politics.

economic sanctions   Trade restrictions imposed on a country that has violated international law.

mujahedeen   Afghan resistance group supplied with arms by the United States to assist in its fight against the Soviets following their 1979 invasion of Afghanistan.

Carter Doctrine   Carter's announced policy that the United States would use force to repel any nation that attempted to take control of the Persian Gulf.

Persian Gulf   Arm of the Arabian Sea and location of the ports of several major oil-producing Arab countries; its security is crucial to the flow of oil from the Middle East to the rest of the world.

Camp David Accords   Treaty, signed at Camp David in 1978, under which Israel returned territory captured from Egypt and Egypt recognized Israel as a nation.

Ayatollah Ruhollah Khomeini   Religious leader of Iran's Shiite Muslims; the Shiites toppled the shah in 1979, and the ayatollah established a new constitution giving himself supreme powers (*ayatollah* is a political/religious title).

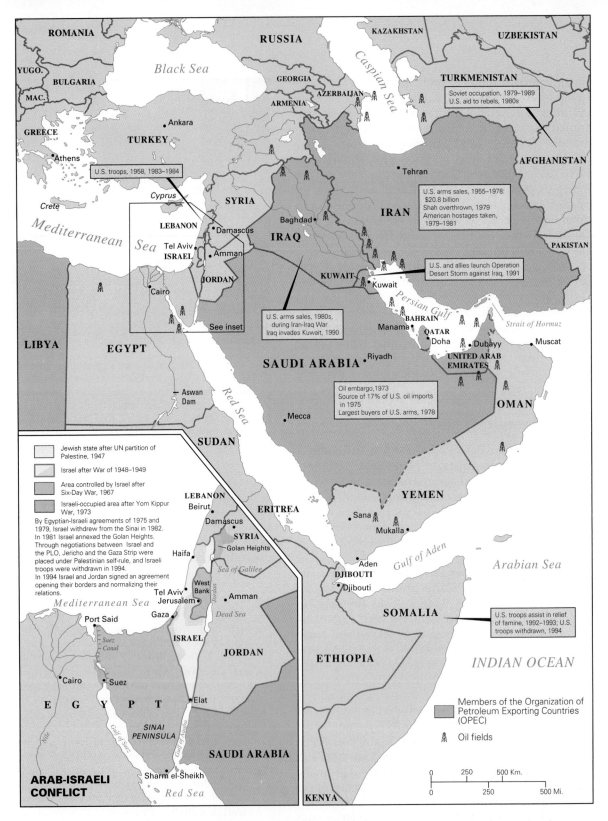

MAP 30.1 The Middle East Since 1946, the United States has tried to balance strong support for Israel with its need for oil from the Arab states. To support U.S. interests in this volatile region, the United States has funneled in large amounts of financial and military aid and used overt and covert force to shape regional governments. Agreements signed in Washington in 1993 and 1994 between Israel and the Palestine Liberation Organization and between Israel and the kingdom of Jordan reduced tensions in the region.

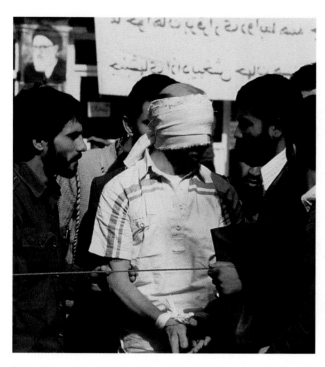

In November 1979, Iranians seized the American Embassy in Tehran and took seventy-one people hostage. Blindfolded and handcuffed, the hostages were paraded through the streets as crowds jeered. Held more than a year, the hostages were released as Ronald Reagan was being sworn in as president. *Alain Mingam/Gamma Liaison.*

Tensions between Iran and the United States increased as the revolutionary government called the United States the main source of evil in the world. Carter cut off economic and military aid to Iran, ordered Americans home, and reduced the embassy staff in Tehran. On October 22, the exiled shah, who was dying, entered a New York hospital to receive cancer treatments, amid warnings of Iranian reprisals. On November 4 an angry mob stormed the American embassy in Tehran and abducted the remaining staff. The sixty-six American hostages were paraded through the streets and subjected to numerous abuses, as the Iranians demanded the return of the shah for trial. The press quickly dubbed the crisis "America Held Hostage," and television accounts flooded American homes.

Carter's foreign policy advisers, Secretary of State **Cyrus Vance** and National Security Adviser **Zbigniew Brzezinski**, offered conflicting options. Brzezinski wanted to use military force to free the hostages. Vance argued for negotiation, hoping that Iranian moderates would find a way to release the captives.

Carter sided with Vance and was able to negotiate freedom for thirteen hostages, mostly women and African Americans. As further discussions failed, American frustration and anger grew, and Carter's popularity ratings fell to near 30 percent. It was time to "lance the boil," concluded Brzezinski. Carter ordered a military rescue mission. It was a disaster. After losing three helicopters in a violent dust storm in Iran, Carter scrapped the mission.

Diplomatic efforts through the Canadians and the Algerians eventually resulted in an agreement in late 1980 to release the hostages. By that time the shah had died of cancer, and Iran was at war against Iraq and needed the assets that Carter had frozen. Seen by many as a personal insult to Carter, Iran released the hostages on January 20, 1981, the day he left the presidency, ending 444 days of captivity.

Domestic Priorities

Domestically, Carter immediately faced two significant problems: a resurgent Congress anxious to exert leadership and the declining economy. Compounding the problems, Carter and his staff frequently ignored Congress and its leaders. Relations with the Democratic Congress quickly deteriorated. "I don't see this Congress rolling over and playing dead," announced one Democratic leader. "Carter is going to set up his priorities and we are going to set up ours. We'll see where we go from there." The divisions between the president and Congress became apparent as the White House presented its budget and Carter's economic recovery plan. Angry Democrats joined Republicans to attack the budget and oppose parts of the president's program to reduce energy costs and stimulate the sluggish economy. In turn, Carter opposed many of the proposals passed by a Democratic Congress. By the end of his term, he had vetoed nineteen bills.

A large part of the problem was that Carter was fiscally conservative, wanting to balance the budget and to energize the economy without additional government spending. Central to his plan was reducing the nation's dependency on foreign sources of oil.

Cyrus Vance   Carter's secretary of state, who wanted the United States to defend human rights and promote economic development of lesser developed nations.

Zbigniew Brzezinski   Carter's national security adviser, who favored confronting the Soviet Union with firmness.

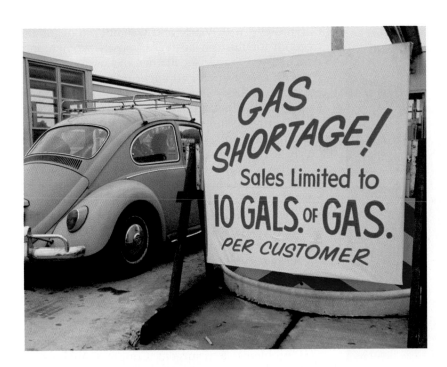

When OPEC reduced production in 1973 and drove up gas prices by 350 percent, the impact on the American economy and motorists was staggering, as a gas and oil shortage swept across the nation. Lucky were those who drove fuel-efficient cars. *Owen Franklin/Corbis.*

He concluded that the economy could not improve and unemployment be reduced until the United States stopped consuming more energy than it produced—the nation was importing about 60 percent of its oil. Solving the **energy crisis** was the "moral equivalent of war" and the only road to economic recovery, Carter told the American people. He offered Congress 113 energy proposals, including the creation of a cabinet-level Department of Energy, support for research and development of fuels other than oil, and special regulations and taxes to prevent the energy industry from reaping excess profits. He also asked individuals to reduce their energy consumption by wearing sweaters, using public transportation, and lowering their thermostats.

Few liked Carter's solutions. Almost everyone, including industry and Congress, favored increasing the production of domestic gas and oil. Buoyed by the potential of new oil fields in Alaska, Congress found it easy to dismiss most of Carter's recommendations. Only fragments of his plan were passed in 1977, including the formation of the Department of Energy, a few incentives for conservation, and deregulation of the natural-gas industry. When the Iranian government pushed up oil prices after 1978, Congress agreed to approve funds for **alternative fuels** (including nuclear energy) and an excess-profits tax on the oil and gas industry.

Nuclear power was an alternative source that many argued would be the most successful in reducing dependency on gas and oil. Advocates argued it was cheap and environmentally safe and called for funds to build new and larger facilities. Opponents replied that nuclear energy was expensive and potentially dangerous. On March 28, 1979, the critics' case was clinched when a serious accident at a nuclear power plant at **Three Mile Island** in central Pennsylvania released a cloud of radioactive gas and nearly caused a **meltdown**. Fortunately, no one was injured in the accident, but it took two weeks to shut down the reactor, and more than a hundred

energy crisis Vulnerability to dwindling oil supplies, wasteful energy consumption, and potential embargoes by oil-producing countries.

alternative fuels Sources of energy other than coal, oil, and natural gas, such as solar, geothermal, hydroelectric, and nuclear energy.

Three Mile Island Site of a nuclear power plant near Harrisburg, Pennsylvania; an accident at the plant in 1979 led to a release of radioactive gases and almost caused a meltdown.

meltdown Severe overheating of a nuclear reactor core, resulting in the melting of the core and the escape of life-threatening radiation.

thousand people were evacuated from the surrounding area. Suddenly, nuclear power became a less attractive energy source, as more than thirty energy companies canceled their nuclear energy projects. The nation remained dependent on natural gas, oil, and coal for most of its energy.

Most of Carter's other domestic efforts, especially those dealing with the economy, produced similar fights with Congress and similarly diluted results. Many in Congress objected to Carter's efforts to use higher interest rates, reduced federal spending, and price and wage controls to stem inflation, which by 1980 stood at 14 percent—the highest rate since 1947. Congress also rejected Carter's attempt to raise the minimum wage by only 20 cents and pushed through an increase—to be implemented by 1981—of 95 cents, to $3.25 an hour. Losing the fight against inflation was only part of Carter's problems. Unemployment rose to nearly 7.6 percent and many, especially liberals, denounced his lack of leadership. Carter admitted he had not provided enough leadership but also blamed the public's unwillingness to sacrifice for much of the nation's woes. The public, in turn, gave Carter only a 19 percent approval rating.

A SOCIETY IN TRANSITION

- What changes were taking place in the American economy, and what was their impact on American families and communities?

- Why did women, minorities, and liberals criticize Carter's social policies?

- Who were the "new immigrants," and what problems did they face?

More than a leadership deficit, however, caused Carter's political problems. He and the American people were caught in a changing economy and society. The period from the end of World War II to the 1970s had been the longest period of consistent economic growth in the history of the United States. Despite occasional recessions and setbacks, the gross national product and productivity rose at a rate slightly higher than 2.5 percent. In personal terms, it meant that wages increased, as did the American standard of living and homeownership. A college education for their children seemed possible for nearly every American who held a steady job. But during the 1970s, the economy grew at a slower rate, dipping to slightly over 1 percent, while the cost of living increased over 200 percent. In personal terms, this meant higher prices, fewer jobs, and less optimism.

Economic Slowdown

The problems with the economy varied, but many were the product of what was being called **globalization**, a changing world and American economy over which there seemed little control. Economically, the changes had started in the late 1960s with the expanding economies of West Germany, Japan, Korea, and Taiwan cutting into American domestic and foreign markets—reducing American profits and prosperity. In the new global economy, many American industries were unable to match the production costs, retail prices, or quality of goods produced overseas. Aggravating the situation were the high oil prices set by the **Organization of Petroleum Exporting Countries** (OPEC) that added to inflation and unemployment and threatened the nation's industrial base, which depended on inexpensive fuels. As a result of these pressures, many of the nation's primary industries (iron and steel, rubber, automobiles and their parts, clothing, coal), especially those located in the Great Lakes region, cut back production, laid off workers, and closed plants. Corporate profits fell from highs of 10 percent in the mid-1960s to under 5 percent by the end of the 1970s.

Adjusting to globalization and what some called the **postindustrial economy**, corporations devised new strategies for survival and profitability. One tactic was to refocus resources. Many corporations rid themselves of less profitable manufacturing operations and invested more heavily in service industries. Implementing these strategies, during the 1970s and 1980s General Electric, one of the largest American manufacturing firms, sold off most of its manufacturing divisions and moved its resources into the service sector by buying the entertainment giant RCA as well as a number of investment and insurance firms.

---

globalization   The process of opening national borders to the free flow of trade, capital, ideas and information, and people.

Organization of Petroleum Exporting Countries   Organization created in 1960 by eleven oil-producing nations in Africa, the Middle East, Latin America, and Asia to coordinate the price and level of production of their oil.

postindustrial society   A society whose economic base is no longer driven by manufacturing but by service and information industries.

At the same time, many companies shifted their production sites to locales where operating costs were lower and closed less-productive plants. Some companies kept their plants in the United States, moving their factories to southern and western states, but an increasing number moved their operations overseas, where expenses were even lower than in the Sunbelt. A so-called **Rust Belt** formed in the Northeast out of what had been the vibrant industrial center of the United States. Philadelphia from 1969 to 1981, for example, lost 42 percent of its factory jobs and 14 percent of its population, and its crime rate jumped by nearly 200 percent. Japanese goods, once the joke of international commerce, were gobbling up the electronics industry and cutting deeply into the American automobile market as Americans decided to purchase more gas-efficient Japanese automobiles. Many of those facilities that did not close or move overseas cut production costs by becoming more automated.

As the higher paying manufacturing jobs declined, the number of service jobs—which paid about one-third less and used more part-time help—increased. McDonald's became one of the largest employers in the nation. The changes were felt everywhere. Lakewood, California, which had seen great economic success in the three decades after World War II, underwent significant economic and social changes. By the 1980s wages were falling as jobs in defense-related and other nearby industries disappeared. Individuals who landed service-related jobs found that they paid less and provided few benefits. As the economic vitality of the community declined, the largest department store in Lakewood's central mall closed, and discount stores like Kmart and Wal-Mart took its place. It seemed to many of Lakewood's residents that their town had been transformed almost overnight from an optimistic middle-class community into a depressed lower-class one. Fear and anger replaced hope. A local minister observed that the combination of economic decline, growth in minority residents, and the expanding permissiveness of society had generated a "feeling of being encroached upon . . . overwhelmed." Politically, Lakewood shifted from moderate and generally Democratic to more conservative and mostly Republican.

Social Divisions

The problems of the changing economic structure were matched by the social and political problems of a disillusioned and diverse society. The late 1960s and 1970s saw a blunting of New Deal–Great Society liberalism. Nixon's election, in part, was a politi-

cal reaction to the activism, protests, and policies of the Kennedy and Johnson administrations. Nixon had left the political scene, but the political successes of Reagan, Wallace, and other conservative politicians demonstrated that many Americans, especially working- and middle-class whites, thought that too many governmental programs favored minorities over the majority.

Domestically, Carter's problem arose from the interaction of the changing economy, calls for more governmental social intervention, and the limits, especially financial, he saw on the ability of government to correct social problems. "Government cannot eliminate poverty or provide a bountiful economy," he stated, "or save our cities or cure literacy." Liberalism, he argued, had its limits. Liberal Democratic critics disagreed. Senator Edward Kennedy and others thought that Carter had unwisely put the brakes on needed social programs, that he was not liberal enough. Many minorities and women echoed Kennedy's view, even while acknowledging that Carter had appointed more minorities and women to government and judicial positions than any other president.

Hispanic and African-American leaders pointed to the lack of legislation and funding for housing, job training, and other social programs. Economically, they pointed out, minorities were experiencing the negative effects of the changing economy, higher unemployment, declining wages, and general lack of jobs. As one African-American spokesman put it, "It's not whether there is equal opportunity to get a job, but whether there's a job to be got." It seemed that minority social needs were being sacrificed for the cause of fiscal stringency. The Reverend Jesse Jackson called Carter's domestic program "a domestic neutron bomb" that destroyed people but not buildings. Harry Edwards, a black sociologist, commenting on the changing economy, noted: "What happens to African Americans eventually happens to all Americans. It just happens to African Americans first."

Another concern worrying liberals and minorities was the growing campaign against **affirmative action**

Rust Belt   Industrialized Middle Atlantic and Great Lakes region whose old factories are barely profitable or have closed.

affirmative action   Policy that seeks to redress past discrimination through active measures to ensure equal opportunity, especially in education and employment.

and the *Bakke* case, which had made its way to the Supreme Court. **Alan Bakke** was suing the University of California at Davis Medical School for reverse discrimination. Since the mid-1960s, in an effort to provide more opportunities, many businesses and colleges had established affirmative action slots for minorities. But as the economy slowed, a growing number of middle-class and blue-collar whites believed that these programs limited their own job and educational opportunities and constituted preferential treatment for minorities. Bakke claimed that he had been denied admission because he was white and that in his place the medical school had accepted less-qualified black students. Supporters of affirmative action pleaded with Carter to support the university. Eventually, the White House petitioned the Court to uphold affirmative action, but not after Carter had publicly stated, "I hate to endorse the proposition of quotas." In 1978, despite the Justice Department's brief, the Supreme Court, in a 5-to-4 decision, found in Bakke's favor and ruled that the university should admit him to the medical school.

Carter's lack of zeal in promoting minority needs, many feminists argued, was equally true when it came to the abortion issue. They applauded the president's support for extending the time needed to ratify the **Equal Rights Amendment** but thought he should be more supportive on the abortion issue. The ERA was needed, advocates argued, to overcome state and local practices that blocked equality for women. Congress in 1972 drafted a proposed amendment and sent it to the states for ratification. Thirty-eight states needed to approve the amendment to make it law, and at first, ratification appeared almost certain. Thirty-three states had approved it by 1974. But opposition stiffened under the leadership of conservative **Phyllis Schlafly**, and when the deadline for ratification expired in 1979, the amendment had only thirty-five states in its corner. Carter joined with Congress to extend the ratification deadline to 1982 but it did no good. In 1982 the amendment remained three states short of the thirty-eight required for ratification.

Part of the "Stop-ERA" movement's success was a growing conservative reaction to a variety of social issues that appeared, in Schlafly's words, to diminish the rights and status of women and to alter the "role of the American woman as wife and mother." Foremost among these issues was the acrid debate over abortion. In 1973, in a 5-to-2 decision, the Supreme Court in *Roe v. Wade* invalidated a Texas law that prevented abortion. Justice Harry

By the mid-1970s, the antifeminist movement was gathering strength as protests against the Equal Rights Amendment and the *Roe v. Wade* decision increased. Here, Phyllis Schlafly leads a Stop-ERA rally in the rotunda of the Illinois State Capitol to convince state legislators to reject the Equal Rights Amendment. Illinois failed to ratify the amendment. ©*Bettmann/Corbis*.

Alan Bakke   Rejected applicant who filed a law suit against the University of California at Davis for reverse discrimination; he claimed that he was denied admittance to medical school because of school policy that set aside admissions for lesser qualified minorities; the Supreme Court agreed in 1978.

Equal Rights Amendment   Proposed constitutional amendment giving women equal rights under the law; Congress approved it in 1972, but it failed to achieve ratification by the required thirty-eight states.

Phyllis Schlafly   Leader of the movement to defeat the Equal Rights Amendment; she believed that the amendment threatened the domestic role of women.

Roe v. Wade   Supreme Court ruling (1973) that women have an unrestricted right to choose an abortion during the first three months of pregnancy.

Blackmun, writing for the majority, held that "the right to privacy" gave women the freedom to choose to have an abortion during the first three months of pregnancy. The controversial ruling struck down laws in forty-six states that had made abortions nearly impossible to obtain except in cases of rape or to save the life of the mother. As the number of legal abortions rose from about 750,000 in 1973 to nearly a million and a half by 1980, so too did opposition.

Although most public opinion polls indicated that a majority of Americans favored giving women the right to choose an abortion, at least under some circumstances, Catholics, Mormons, some Orthodox Jews, and many Protestant churches worked with conservative groups to organize a "Right to Life" campaign to oppose abortion rights on moral and legal grounds. The **Right to Life movement** easily merged with the conservative critique of American society and liberalism. Responding to conservative and anti-abortion pressure, Congress in 1976 passed the Hyde Amendment, which prohibited the use of federal Medicaid funds to pay for abortions. In 1980 the Supreme Court upheld Hyde in *Harris v. McRae*. Feminists had lobbied Carter to oppose the Hyde Amendment, and when he refused, some within the NOW camp argued that their organization should support anyone but Carter in the forthcoming 1980 election.

New Immigrants

As American society became less tolerant and government less supportive of social programs, a new wave of immigrants started to arrive in the United States. The 1965 Immigration Act ended the national quota system for immigration and opened access to the United States from areas other than Europe. In 1960 three of every four immigrants had come from Europe, but that quickly changed as increasing numbers arrived from Mexico, Latin America, the Caribbean, and Asia. Within two decades more than half of all immigrants arrived from Latin America and nearly a fourth from Asia. San Francisco's Asian population reached over 30 percent by the end of the 1990s, while in Honolulu, Hawai`i, Asians constituted over 70 percent of the population. In the border city of Laredo, Texas, the Latino population exceeded 95 percent compared with 63 percent in Miami, Florida, and 40 percent in Los Angeles.

They came to the United States mostly for the traditional reasons: jobs and security. As one immigrant stated simply: "It was better in America." Many immigrants were uneducated and unskilled,

Latinos, Asians, and people from the Caribbean comprise the majority of immigrants arriving in the United States today. Critics of immigration worry that these groups will not assimilate easily and want to limit further immigration. Supporters argue that assimilation is taking place and point to increased rates of nationalization and citizenship. Here, a Vietnamese family participates in the all-American sport of baseball (T-Ball). *Bob Daemmrich.*

especially those who were refugees or from Latin America. But because immigration law favored professionals, many others were highly educated and skilled. Whether skilled or not, new immigrants fit nicely into the structure of the postindustrial economy. Those with few skills found jobs in the service and agriculture sectors, whereas the skilled newcomers filled the ranks of professionals and technicians.

The Asian population grew rapidly—40 percent of all immigrants by the mid-1970s. Most came as families and clustered in ethnic communities in major urban areas, especially along the Pacific Coast. Those who were well educated and had marketable skills found economic success as medical professionals, engineers, and owners of small businesses. This was

---

Right to Life movement Anti-abortion movement that favors a constitutional amendment to prohibit abortion; some adherents grew increasingly militant during the 1980s and 1990s; also called the pro-life movement.

especially true of those from Japan, China, Korea, and India. Many considered these populations the "model minority."

This view ignored the very different experiences of many other Asians, particularly those from Vietnam, Laos, and Cambodia. Coming as refugees, they arrived with few possessions, little education, and few skills. Mired in poverty and having difficulty assimilating into American society, they faced growing intolerance and hostility. The slowing economy contributed to the problem along the Gulf coast, where whites, objecting to the employment competition, attacked Vietnamese fishermen.

Tensions also rose in inner cities between Asians and other minorities when they competed for jobs, housing, public resources, and political influence. This was the case in south central Los Angeles, as it became a multiracial area with significant African-American, Hispanic, and Asian populations. When a riot swept through the community in 1992, many of the rioters targeted Asians, especially Koreans. Latino and African-American rioters justified their attacks by claiming Asian landlords and shop owners discriminated against and exploited them. "We hate [the Koreans,]" one rioter explained. "Everyone does."

If some Asians were regarded as model immigrants, the opposite was true of most immigrants from Mexico, Latin America, and the Caribbean. Coming as both legal and illegal immigrants, Hispanics represented the largest number of the new immigrants. Like Franklin Chang-Diaz, most came for new and better opportunities while speaking little or no English. Franklin Chang-Diaz fulfilled his dream of becoming an astronaut, but for most Hispanic immigrants the outcome was vastly different. Arriving with few skills and little education, most immigrants from the Caribbean, Mexico, and Latin America found themselves taking one or more low-paying jobs just to survive. Even with two jobs, stated one Mexican American activist, the social and economic "ladder isn't there" for most Latino immigrants.

Illegal immigration, primarily from Mexico, added to the growing hostility toward Hispanics and calls for immigration limits. Attempting to stem the flood of "illegals" into the United States, the **Immigration Reform and Control Act** was passed in 1986. It provided amnesty to illegal aliens who had been in the United States before 1982 and made them eligible for citizenship. It also provided criminal punishment for those who hired illegal aliens and strengthened controls to prevent illegal entry

into the United States. The crackdown did not work: the flow of immigrants entering the country illegally was unaffected. As the 1980s ended, demands for immigration restrictions increased—in a 1991 poll, 69 percent of those asked believed there were too many Latinos in the country.

RESURGENT CONSERVATISM

● What issues and forces contributed to the emergence of the New Right? How did the New Right shape American politics?

● How did the candidacy and goals of Ronald Reagan match those of the New Right?

● What is "Reaganomics," and what were the consequences of Reagan's economic policies?

Traditional liberals criticized Carter for his lack of zeal and continued to espouse government activism as a means to promote social equality and cultural pluralism. But their voices found little support as growing numbers of people began to argue that government activism was not the solution. "Liberalism is no longer the answer—it is the problem," insisted Ronald Reagan. Conservatives like Reagan argued that government was inefficient and that liberal programs made victims of middle-class Americans who worked hard, saved their money, and believed in strong, traditional family values. The activism of the 1960s, they believed, had made the nation a collection of interest groups clamoring for rights and power and produced a loss of national identity and a moral breakdown. Conservatives argued that liberal views threatened "to destroy everything that is good and moral here in America."

Conservatives had no trouble pinpointing the problems: a hedonistic society, the decline of marriage and the break down of the traditional family, the rise in abortions and divorces. To support their concerns, they pointed to a 1973 public television (PBS) program that followed the disintegration of the Loud family. In a series of installments, a twenty-year marriage broke apart due to incompatibility, a son announced his homosexuality, and

---

Immigration Reform and Control Act   Law passed by Congress in 1986 that prohibits the hiring of illegal aliens; it offered amnesty and legal residence to any who could prove that they had entered the country before January 1, 1982.

teenage children went their own aimless ways. By the mid-1970s, many conservatives had grouped around the **New Right**.

The New Right

The New Right emerged as a highly centralized alliance of political and social conservatives. Economically and politically, it embraced a retreat from government activism and reduction of taxes. By 1979, lowering taxes had become a hot national issue. A movement had sprung up in 1978 when Californians led a tax revolt by passing **Proposition 13**, which placed limits on property taxes and state spending. Recognizing the importance of the movement, a Carter aide confided: it "isn't just a tax revolt, it is a revolution against government." But the New Right's passion came from rejecting "liberal" moral and social values that advocated abortion and homosexuality. The nation's schools, it charged, had retreated from teaching a positive work ethic and moral habits and needed to return to the basics: reading, writing, arithmetic, and traditional values. To mobilize support, the New Right pioneered the effective political use of **direct mail** aimed at specific segments of the population.

Highly visible among New Right groups were evangelical Christian sects, many of whose ministers were **televangelists**—preachers who used radio and television to spread the gospel. Receiving donations that exceeded a billion dollars a year, they did not hesitate to mix religion and politics. Jerry Falwell's **Moral Majority** promoted conservative and New Right views on more than five hundred television and radio stations. Reaching millions of Americans, Falwell called on his listeners to wage political war against politicians whose views on the Bible, homosexuality, prayer in school, abortion, and communism were too liberal. Falwell told his religious colleagues to get people "saved, baptized, and registered."

The conservative resurgence aided Ronald Reagan more than any other Republican candidate. He promised to restore America by reducing government involvement and freeing American ingenuity and competitiveness, and he embraced the social positions of the New Right. Carter, according to Republicans, was a failure. He had failed to free the hostages, and he had failed to restore the nation's economy. Reagan, on the other hand, smacked of success: he was an effective campaigner who communicated confidence and a sense of humor. "A recession," he quipped, "is when your neighbor

In the 1970s and into the 1990s, the "electronic church" developed an audience of over 100 million viewers. With fancy, high-tech showmanship, televangelists like Jerry Falwell pictured here, damned liberalism, feminism, sex education, homosexuality, and the teaching of evolution, while demanding a return to traditional Christian values and prayer in school. Praising the power of the modern, media pulpit, Falwell stated, "You can explain the issues. . . . And you can endorse candidates, right there in church on Sunday morning." *Steve McCurry/Magnum Photos.*

New Right Conservative movement opposing the political and social reforms that developed in the late 1960s and demanding less government intervention in the economy and a return to traditional values; it was a major political force by the 1980s.

Proposition 13 Measure adopted by referendum in California in 1978 cutting local property taxes by more than 50 percent.

direct mail Advertising or promotional matter mailed directly to potential customers or audiences chosen because they are likely to respond favorably.

televangelist Protestant evangelist minister who conducts televised worship services; many such ministers used their broadcasts as a forum for promoting conservative values.

Moral Majority Right-wing religious organization led by televangelist Jerry Falwell; it had an active political lobby in the 1980s promoting such issues as opposition to abortion and to the Equal Rights Amendment.

loses his job. A depression is when you lose yours. A recovery is when Jimmy Carter loses his." Reagan presented himself as the "citizen politician, speaking out for the ideas, values, and common sense of everyday Americans." A vote for Reagan, his supporters claimed, would restore American pride, power, and traditions.

Reagan's message was welcome news not only to those who routinely voted Republican but also to many living in the Sunbelt. By 1980, the region's population exceeded that of the industrial North and East. Politically, the Sunbelt was more conservative and opposed the intrusive power of the federal government. White southerners equated "liberal" government with altering traditional racial norms, and a **"sagebrush rebellion"** in the western Sunbelt contested federal control and regulation of land and natural resources. Many westerners argued that federal environmental and land-use regulations blocked growth and economic development in the West. Throughout the Sunbelt, Reagan found enthusiastic voters ready to reject liberal, activist government. Further contributing to Republican totals were younger voters attracted by the economic goals and social stability Republicans represented. Except for the size of Reagan's majority and how many Republicans his **political coattails** would carry into office, the outcome of the election of 1980 was never in doubt.

When the voting ended, Reagan had 51 percent of the popular vote and an impressive 91 percent of the electoral count—489 to 49. Republicans held their majority in the Senate and substantially narrowed the Democratic majority in the House of Representatives. Many political observers believed the election of 1980 was the beginning of a new conservative era.

Reaganism

Reagan brought to the White House two distinct advantages lacked by Nixon, Ford, and Carter: he had a clear and simple vision of the type of America he wanted and an unusual ability to convey that image to the American public. Called the "Great Communicator" by the press, Reagan expertly presented images and visions, but he did not create the policies to bring them about. Secretary of the Treasury Donald Regan once commented, "The President's mind is not cluttered with facts." A hands-off president, Reagan delegated authority to the cabinet and executive staff while he set the grand agenda.

A former movie star and host of television shows, Ronald Reagan used television and radio very effectively to outline his visions of American domestic and foreign policies. Because of his communication style, he was called "the Great Communicator." *UPI/Bettmann Archives.*

His lieutenants assumed the blame when policies failed or were defeated.

Reagan rode to the presidency on a wide domestic platform promising not just prosperity and less government but also morality, tapping the New Right's political strength on issues of family and gender. In office, however, he virtually ignored the New Right's

sagebrush rebellion   A 1980s political movement in western states opposing federal regulations governing land use and natural resources, seeking state jurisdiction instead.

political coattails   Term referring to the ability of a presidential candidate to attract voters to other office seekers from the same political party.

social agenda and concentrated on the economic crisis of inflation, high interest rates, and unemployment. The administration's plan was deceptively simple: cut the number and cost of social programs, increase military spending, and reduce taxes and government restrictions. "If we can do that, the rest will take care of itself," Reagan's chief of staff James A. Baker III argued.

Much of the administration's formula for restoring economic vitality rested with the monetary policies of the Federal Reserve System and **supply-side economics**. To combat inflation, the Federal Reserve kept interest rates high, bringing about a substantial increase in foreign investments in the United States and a decline in American products sold overseas. While the Fed squeezed inflation, Reagan intended to stimulate growth by cutting personal and business taxes. The 1981 **Economic Recovery Tax Act** cut income taxes and most business taxes by an average of 25 percent—upper income levels received the largest tax reduction. Reagan's budget, supported by conservative Democrats in the House, raised military spending and slashed $25 billion from federal spending on social programs. Among the programs affected were food stamps, **Aid to Families with Dependent Children**, jobs and housing programs, and Medicare and Medicaid. Nixon's federal revenue-sharing programs were ended, forcing some states to raise their own taxes.

Cutting taxes and domestic spending was only part of the Reagan agenda for economic growth. Another aim of **Reaganomics** was deregulation—freeing businesses and corporations from restrictive regulation. Appointees to regulatory agencies were selected because of their support for deregulation and for business. Among the areas affected by deregulation were banking, transportation, and communications, but its impact was most visible in the area of environmental regulation. Secretary of the Interior James Watt sought to open federally controlled land, coastal waters, and wetlands to mining, lumber, oil, and gas companies—a policy strongly advocated by many in the West. The Environmental Protection Agency relaxed enforcement of federal guidelines for reducing air and water pollution and cleaning up toxic waste sites.

Reagan's economic policies were not immediately effective. Inflation fell from 14 to 4 percent by 1982, but economic growth failed to materialize. Unemployment rose to over 10 percent, and small businesses and farms faced bankruptcy in increasing numbers. Also troubling was a soaring **trade deficit**, the amount by which the value of imports exceeds the value of exports. From a surplus in 1975, the deficit has grown steadily, reaching over $240 billion by 1998. Also, growing at an alarming rate was the **federal deficit**, pushed by declining tax revenues and increases in military spending. Reagan called for patience, assuring the public that his economic programs eventually would work.

Suddenly in 1983, the recession ended, oil prices fell, and the economy surged. Inflation dropped to 4 percent and unemployment fell to 7.5 percent. Reagan's economic policies and his support of a positive business culture now received widespread praise. Corporate leaders especially cheered, applauding fewer government controls, more industries deregulated, and increased defense spending—most of which had gone to firms located in the Sunbelt. The deregulating of financial institutions was seen as especially positive because it spurred investment and speculation, which drove the stock market upward—the Great Bull Market. "I think we hit the jackpot," Reagan announced when he signed the Garn-St. Germain Act in 1982 that deregulated the **savings and loan industry** (S&Ls). In the opinion of deregu-

supply-side economics   Theory that reducing taxes on the wealthy and increasing the money available for investment will stimulate the economy and eventually benefit everyone.

Economic Recovery Tax Act   Law passed by Congress in 1981 that cut income taxes by 25 percent across the board and even further reduced taxes on the wealthy.

Aid to Families with Dependent Children   A program created by the Social Security Act of 1935; it provided states with matching federal funds and became one of the states' main welfare programs.

Reaganomics   Economic beliefs and policies of the Reagan administration, including the belief that tax cuts for the wealthy and deregulation of industry benefit the economy.

trade deficit   Amount by which the value of a nation's imports exceeds the value of its exports.

federal deficit   The total amount of debt owed by the national government.

savings and loan industry   Network of financial institutions originally founded to provide home mortgage loans; deregulation during the Reagan era allowed them to speculate in risky ventures and led to many S&L failures.

lation proponents, everyone would benefit by allowing S&Ls to enter into all forms of investment rather than just single-family homes. Quickly, S&Ls were adding to an expanding economy by making loans for the construction of office buildings, shopping malls, and industrial parks.

Reflecting the continuing postindustrial economy and the loosening antimonopoly restrictions, the 1980s witnessed an increase in corporate diversification, often through mergers. Within three years, twenty-one mergers had been completed, each worth over $1 billion. Business opportunities also multiplied as technological developments opened new fields, especially in the communications and electronics fields. In those two fields, advances in miniaturization, satellite transmissions, videocassette recorders (VCRs), and computers touched almost every American—and provided new avenues of wealth. With Apple and IBM leading the way, office and personal computers restructured the process of handling information and communications, spawning a new wave of "tech" companies and a new crop of millionaires like Bill Gates. Gates dropped out of Harvard to develop software for IBM's entry into the new field of personal computers and became America's youngest billionaire and founder of Microsoft.

Gates was not alone. It seemed that thousands of people were riding the expanding economy to wealth and power, from inventors to financial "wizards" who brokered mergers. Stories of economic success filled newspapers, magazines, television, and movies, creating a money culture. "Buy high, sell higher," *Fortune* magazine proclaimed. The pursuit of wealth and the goods that it could buy became a lifestyle sought after by many young Americans, particularly the baby boomers who were reaching peak earning and spending levels. *Money* magazine saw its circulation jump from 800,000 in 1980 to 1.85 million in 1987.

Some called the 1980s the "Me Decade," in which acquiring money and state-of-the-art high-tech gadgetry mattered very much and led to self-satisfaction. In 1974 only 46 percent of college freshmen and high school seniors listed being "financially successful" as the first priority in their lives. Twelve years later, in 1986, 73 percent of college freshmen considered being "very well off financially" as their number one priority. Income-conscious college graduates hoping to become highly paid, aggressive professionals eagerly applied to law, business, and other postgraduate schools. The number of doctors and lawyers swelled, executive salaries quickly broke $40 million, and everyone needed to have cell phones, Walkmans, videos, computers, and fax machines. Social critic and historian Christopher Lasch lamented the loss of the activism of the 1960s and thought that Americans had returned to purely personal preoccupations. *Newsweek*, however, expressed no such lament when it declared 1984 the "Year of the **Yuppie**"—the young, upwardly mobile, urban professional, who was on the leading edge of the new economic vitality.

A Second Term

Having engineered an expanding economy, Republicans faced the 1984 election with great anticipation. Reagan was popular with the people, even when they objected to administration policies. Using the theme "Morning in America," Reagan's re-election campaign projected continued economic growth and affirmed his commitment to a strong, upright America. Democrats nominated a traditional liberal, Walter Mondale, who selected Representative Geraldine Ferraro of New York as his vice-presidential candidate. It was liberalism versus conservatism. Reagan promised less government, Mondale promised more. When Mondale called for expanded social programs and higher taxes, Republican hopes for a political landslide and public repudiation of liberalism soared.

President Reagan won an overwhelming victory, taking 59 percent of the popular vote and carrying every state except Mondale's Minnesota. A postelection analysis showed that all that remained of the once-powerful Democratic voting coalition were the poor, African Americans, and Hispanics. A majority of organized labor, women, Catholics, white southerners, farmers, and the middle and upper classes all had voted for Reagan's Republican vision of "Morning in America."

However, dark clouds were growing on the horizon. Some economists warned of serious weaknesses in the economy—revenues had shrunk while spending continued to expand, creating an alarming federal deficit. Since 1980 the annual deficit had gone from $73.8 billion to more than $200 billion. Adding to the problem, Americans now imported

---

Yuppie Young urban resident with a high-paying professional job and a materialistic lifestyle.

more goods than they exported. What had once been a creditor nation had now become a debtor nation. Experts also argued that lax federal regulation and deregulation in the financial sector allowed investors too much of a free hand, contributing to stock and real-estate prices escalating far beyond actual value.

Beyond agreeing that the federal deficit had to be reduced, Democrats and Republicans found little common ground. Democrats generally called for cuts in military spending, while protecting social programs. Most Republicans held the opposite view. Finding some room for agreement, in late 1985, a coalition of Republicans and Democrats passed the Gramm-Rudman-Hollings Act. It established a maximum debt level and ordered across-the-board cuts if the budget failed to match the level set. But the plan never worked effectively as Congress and the White House found ways to circumvent and modify the law. By 1989, federal expenditures had climbed to $1,065 billion a year, and the national debt stood at nearly $3 trillion, requiring an annual interest payment of $200 million.

Critics of Reagan's economic policies also pointed out that the economic boom was selective. Regionally, the West Coast and Sunbelt seemed to be doing well, but the Northeast—the Rust Belt—was still rusting. Socially, the gap between rich and poor was widening as the percentage of the nation's wealth held by the top 10 percent of American families climbed from 67 to 73 percent between 1980 and 1988. At the same time many American workers found their wages and employment opportunities declining; thus the number of people living below the poverty line of $9,885 increased. Across the country the number of homeless increased, placing more pressure on social programs that found their budgets declining. With 15 percent blue-collar unemployment in Los Angeles, Juan Sanchez was happy to have a good job at a furniture factory, although he and his wife and three children were unable to afford a home and had to live in his brother-in-law's garage.

Those who asserted that the Reagan boom rested on a foundation of shaky credit and fast profits and did not generate real economic growth appeared correct in 1987: October 19, "Black Monday," the stock market crashed, losing 22 percent of its value in one day. The Federal Reserve quickly lowered interest rates, which slowed the panic selling. But confidence never recovered as people not only worried about the stock market but watched a slowing economy and tumbling property values. Beginning in 1987, many S&Ls started to feel the impact of the declining economy and poor investments. A year later, the S&L industry neared total collapse. Lincoln Savings and Loan in California had lost more than $2.6 billion of depositors' money. Responding to the crisis and to save the S&L industry, the federal government provided more than $500 billion to cover the losses. By the end of 1988, many people questioned the reality of Reaganomics, the administration's concern for the less privileged, and the ethics of many within the administration—over a hundred members of the administration were found guilty of unethical or illegal behavior. Throughout it all, Reagan, who was suffering from Alzheimer's disease, remained popular with the public, causing some to refer to him as the "Teflon President."

ASSERTING WORLD POWER

- What did the Reagan administration view as the main source of trouble in world affairs?

- In what ways did the Reagan administration attempt to implement a more assertive foreign policy?

- How did Reagan shift U.S.-Soviet policy during his second term?

Reagan's victories in 1980 and 1984 resulted not only from the popularity of his domestic agenda but also from public support for his views on the role of the United States in world affairs. Throughout the 1980 presidential campaign, the Republicans had hammered at Carter's ineffective foreign policy and at slipping American prestige in the world. As president, Reagan promised to restore American power and influence. With little expertise in foreign policy, Reagan set the broad patterns of American policy but left the specifics to his foreign policy staff, especially CIA director William Casey and Secretary of State George Shultz.

Cold War Renewed

At the center of Reagan's view of the world were two threats, the Soviet Union and nuclear war. The Soviet Union, he stated, constituted an "evil empire" and was the "focus of evil in the modern world." He believed that America's grand role was to defend the world from the Soviets and communism. Large increases in the military budget were necessary to back up the nation's diplomacy and to close the "window of vulnerability" that Carter had opened by allowing the Soviets to pull ahead in the arms race.

Congress quickly funded Reagan's military budget, which added more than $100 billion a year in appropriations, going from $164 billion in 1980 to $228 billion by 1985. By 1985, a million dollars was being spent on weapons every minute. Seeking a method to move from "assured destruction to one of assured survival," Reagan asked Congress to fund a controversial system of defense against Soviet missiles: the **Strategic Defense Initiative** (SDI). Between 1983 and 1989, Congress provided more than $17 billion for SDI research amid complaints that the concept was conceptually and technologically flawed. Critics pointed out that even if the system could work and was 95 percent effective, the 5 percent of Soviet warheads that would hit the United States would still destroy the nation, if not civilization.

With a stronger military and Cold War commitment, Reagan was determined to confront the Soviet menace and to roll back communism, especially in the third world. The Reagan Doctrine promised economic and military aid, including covert operations funded by the CIA, to those fighting Communist tyranny. Quickly, the United States initiated or increased support and funding for "freedom fighters" opposing communism in Afghanistan, Angola, Ethiopia, and several Central American countries. In the Caribbean, Reagan approved a military strike against the island nation of **Grenada**. There the Marxist government posed a direct threat to nearly five hundred American students attending medical school on the island and a potential threat to American interests by working with Cuba to build a large airport runway. On October 25, 1983, more than two thousand American soldiers quickly overcame minimal opposition, brought home the American students, and installed a pro-American government on the island. The administration basked in the light of public approval.

The nation applauded the administration for its action in Grenada, but some were concerned about American policies in Central America (see Map 30.2). They worried about the disturbing reports of human rights violations by "death squads" linked to the Salvadoran military and feared that Central America might become another Vietnam, with American troops following the aid and advisers

already being sent. Concern turned to opposition when the press uncovered large-scale American covert aid to the **Contras**, including the CIA's mining of Nicaraguan harbors in 1984. Congress passed legislation, the **Boland Amendment** in 1984, which allowed only humanitarian aid to the Contras. Reagan and CIA director William Casey quickly sought ways to continue to arm the Contras without Congress's knowledge. One plan involved a complicated system of secretly selling arms to the Iranians and then using the money to fund the Contras. The operation also involved securing Iran's help in gaining the release of American hostages held in Lebanon. One was freed but soon other Americans were seized and held hostage.

When the press broke word of the so-called Iran-Contra arms-for-hostages deal fourteen months later, a special White House commission and a congressional committee began separate investigations in 1987. Both discovered that members of the CIA and the National Security Council (NSC) had acted independently, without the knowledge or approval of Congress, and had lied to Congress to hide their operation. Fourteen people were charged with committing crimes, and eleven—including several top-level advisers to Reagan—were convicted of violating a variety of federal laws and were sentenced to prison terms. Investigators found no direct proof of Reagan's involvement in the undercover arrangement but concluded that he had set the stage for others' illegal activities by encouraging and, in general terms, ordering support for the Contras. Reagan protested, "I just didn't know." The Iran-Contra investigations showed a president out of touch with what was happening, and for once the image of Reagan was tarnished.

Strategic Defense Initiative   Research program to create an effective laser-based defense against nuclear missile attack.

Grenada   Country in the West Indies that achieved independence from Britain in 1974 and was invaded briefly by U.S. forces in 1983.

Contras   Nicaraguan rebels, many of them former followers of Somoza, fighting to overthrow the Sandinista government.

Boland Amendment   Motion, approved by Congress in 1984, that barred the CIA from using funds to give direct or indirect aid to the Nicaraguan Contras.

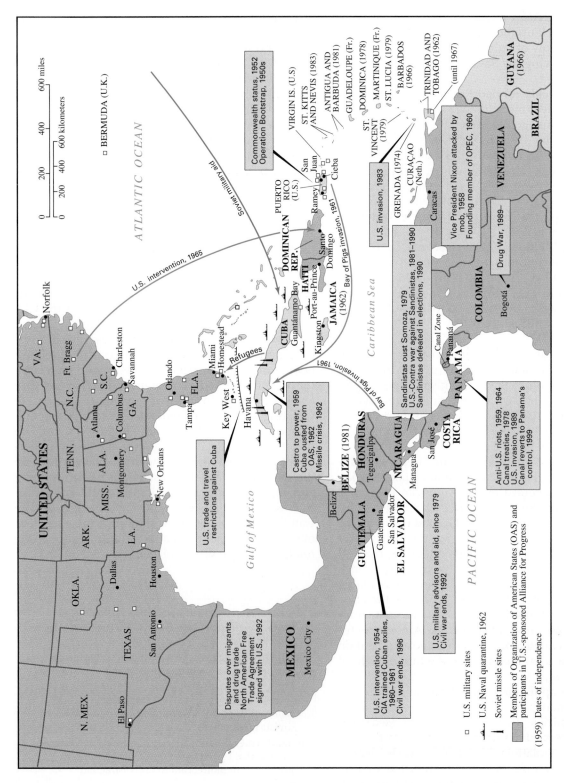

MAP 30.2 The United States and Central America and the Caribbean Geographical nearness, important economic ties, security needs, and the drug trade continue to make Central America and the Caribbean a critical region for American interests. This map shows some of the American economic, military, and political actions taken in the region since the end of World War II.

Like Eisenhower twenty years before, President Reagan in 1983 committed American troops to Beirut, Lebanon as part of a peacekeeping operation. This intervention, however, was not successful. In October, terrorists blew up the marine barracks, killing 241 soldiers. "Too few to fight and too many to die," said one Congressional critic, as four months later Reagan withdrew the remaining American forces from the war-torn nation. *UPI/Bettmann Archives.*

Terrorism

The hope of using Iran to help obtain the release of two Americans held hostage by terrorists reflected one of the most difficult problems complicating American policy—how to deal with terrorism directed against the United States. In 1985 over 800 terrorist attacks around the world killed over 900 people, including 23 Americans. The rise in terrorism was largely a product of the struggle between Israel and the **Palestine Liberation Organization** (PLO) and its Arab supporters. By the late 1970s, shadowy militant Islamic groups that had previously confined their assaults to Israel were launching campaigns of terrorism against Israel's Western supporters. Throughout the Mediterranean region, pro-Palestinian terrorists kidnapped and killed Americans and Europeans, hijacked planes and ships, and attacked airports and

other public places. American troops became a target in April 1983, when Muslim terrorists attacked the American embassy in Beirut and killed sixty-three people. In October a suicide driver rammed a truck filled with explosives into the marine barracks at the Beirut airport, killing 241 marines, who were part of a peacekeeping effort. Reagan vehemently denounced the terrorist attacks but found no solution to the problem except to remove American troops in January 1984. The Reagan administration came up with a more satisfying response two years later when it bombed targets in Libya. The attack was in retribution for a terrorist bombing of a disco in West Berlin that killed an American soldier. Intelligence sources linked the terrorists to the anti-American ruler of Libya, **Moamar Qaddafi**. Reagan condemned Qaddafi as the "mad dog of the Middle East" and, calling Libya a "rogue" nation, ordered a reprisal raid. American navy and air force planes hit several targets in Libya, including Qaddafi's quarters, killing his daughter. Qaddafi remained anti-American and continued to support the PLO and terrorist groups, but one American official bragged that they had shown Qaddafi "that we could get people close to him." To terrorists Reagan declared, "You can run but you can't hide." Neither the declaration of the president nor the attack on Libya deterred the terrorists, who continued their activities.

Reagan and Gorbachev

Until 1985, Reagan's foreign policy had focused on combating the power of the Soviet Union around the globe. Then, unexpectedly, the president executed a reversal of policy toward the Soviet Union. He called for the resumption of arms limitation talks and invited the Soviet leader, **Mikhail Gorbachev**, to the United States. Gorbachev appeared different from previous Soviet leaders. He was younger and

---

Palestine Liberation Organization   Political and military organization of Palestinians, originally dedicated to opposing the state of Israel through terrorism and other means.

Moamar Qaddafi   Political leader who seized power in a 1969 military coup and imposed a socialist regime and Islamic orthodoxy on Libya.

Mikhail Gorbachev   Soviet leader who came to power in 1985; he introduced political and economic reforms and then found himself presiding over the breakup of the Soviet Union.

After declaring the Soviet Union an "evil empire" responsible for nearly all the world's problems, President Reagan reversed course in 1988 and opened productive discussions with Soviet reformer Mikhail Gorbachev. The outcome was an intermediate-range nuclear-forces treaty that helped to end the Cold War as well as to reduce the overall number of nuclear missiles. Here, the two superpower leaders pose in front of the St. Basil cathedral in Moscow. *UPI/Bettmann Archives.*

seemed committed to change, wanting to breathe new life into an economy that was stagnating under the weight of military spending. He also sought to institute reforms that would provide more political and civil rights to the Soviet people.

Gorbachev declined Reagan's invitation but agreed to a summit meeting in Geneva in November 1985. The two leaders at first jousted with each other. Reagan condemned the Soviets for human rights abuses, their involvement in Afghanistan, and their aid to Communist factions fighting in Angola and Ethiopia. Gorbachev attacked the proposed development of SDI. But both were concerned over the possibility of nuclear war and slowly they gained a respect and fondness for each other. Soviet-American negotiations on arms limitations continued with new optimism. A year later, in October 1986, the two leaders met again

in Iceland to discuss reductions of strategic weapons. They reached no accord but agreed to keep working on arms limitations. Both leaders left the meeting more trusting of the other and increasingly determined to reduce the possibility of nuclear war. In December 1987, a breakthrough occurred. During a Washington summit, Reagan and Gorbachev signed the **Intermediate Nuclear Force Treaty** that removed their intermediate-range missiles from Europe.

Throughout 1988, Soviet-American relations continued to improve. Gorbachev withdrew Soviet forces from Afghanistan, the Senate approved the Intermediate Nuclear Force Treaty, and Reagan visited Moscow. Assessing the changes in Russia and Soviet policy, Secretary Shultz noted that the Cold War "was all over but the shouting."

IN REAGAN'S SHADOW

- What new foreign-policy choices did the United States face as a result of the collapse of the Soviet Union?

- How did Reagan's domestic policies affect expectations and outcomes for the Bush administration?

"Was it all over but the shouting?" could have been a question that many Republicans were asking by 1988. The Reagan presidency was coming to an end, and as Nancy Reagan said of 1987, "It's not been a great year." Despite the apparent thaw in the Cold War, for the first time in the Reagan administration, a combination of events had dented the image of Reagan and Republican leadership. The stock market collapse in October and the Iran-Contra revelations created the impression that the administration was not in control of events or of itself and that the president had little grasp of what was happening. Still, most Republicans believed that their conservative revolution was still strong, that they would defeat Democrats and continue to strengthen the nation.

Bush Assumes Office

Republicans passed the torch to Vice President George Bush, although some worried that he was not conservative enough to push the New Right's social agenda. Nonetheless, Bush had been the loyal vice

> **Intermediate Nuclear Force Treaty** Treaty (1987) that provided for the destruction of all U.S. and Soviet medium-range nuclear missiles and for verification with on-site inspections.

president and had served the party faithfully, holding important posts under Presidents Nixon and Ford: ambassador to the United Nations, chairman of the Republican National Committee, ambassador to China, and director of the Central Intelligence Agency. Several Democrats eagerly contended to confront Bush, whose popularity seemed a faint shadow of Reagan's. Eventually, Governor Michael Dukakis of Massachusetts gained the nomination.

The 1988 campaign was dull. Both candidates lacked flair, and neither was unable to energize the voters. Both candidates avoided most social and international issues, while claiming that they were the best suited to fight crime and drugs. While both vowed not to raise taxes, Bush's promise, "Read my lips, no new taxes," was best received. To motivate voters, the candidates relied on television and negative campaigning, which aimed at discrediting the opponent rather than addressing issues and policies. Republican ads were more effective and, combined with falling unemployment and inflation rates, contributed to Bush's easy victory. With 79.2 percent of the electoral vote and 54 percent of the popular vote, he became the first sitting vice president to be elected president since Martin Van Buren in 1836. Although Bush trounced Dukakis, the victory was not as sweet as Bush had hoped. Democrats controlled the House and the Senate.

Bush and a New International Order

Bush's own preferences and international events dictated that foreign affairs would consume most of his attention. The world was changing rapidly, and Bush considered the management of international relations to be one of his strengths. Unlike Reagan, he focused on specific policies. The immediate problems were those resulting from Gorbachev's reforms, which had produced significant political and economic changes through the Communist world. His withdrawal of Soviet forces from Afghanistan and Eastern Europe, combined with his announcement that the Soviets would not intervene to prevent political change in Eastern Europe, unleashed a series of events that undermined Communist systems that had operated since the end of World War II.

Communism was in retreat throughout Eastern Europe by 1989. Poland had a new constitution, a free market economy, and a non-Communist government. In Berlin the symbol of the Cold War, the **Berlin Wall**, was torn down by jubilant Germans.

With the collapse of the Soviet Union and communism across Eastern Europe, the symbol of the iron curtain and the Cold War came tumbling down in Berlin. Jubilant Berliners sit atop the Berlin Wall that had divided the city from 1962 to November 1989. *R. Bossu/Corbis Sygma.*

As the wall crumbled, so too did the Communist governments of East Germany, Hungary, Bulgaria, Czechoslovakia, and Romania (see Map 30.3). In December, Gorbachev met with Bush on the island of Malta in the Mediterranean Sea and declared that the Cold War was over. A year later, Germany had been unified and the Baltic states—Latvia, Estonia, and Lithuania—had declared their independence from the Soviet Union.

Throughout most of the Eastern bloc the change in governments was accompanied with little violence or territorial adjustments, but not in the case of Yugoslavia and the Soviet Union. When Yugoslavia's Communist regime collapsed in 1991, ethnic separatist movements demanded independence for the regions of Slovenia, Croatia, Bosnia-Herzegovina, and Macedonia. Serbian leader Slobodan Milosevic attempted to use the army to maintain unity under Serbian hegemony. Warfare ignited and quickly spread across the

---

Berlin Wall   Barrier that the Communist East German government built in 1961 to divide East and West Berlin; it was torn down in 1989 as the Cold War ended.

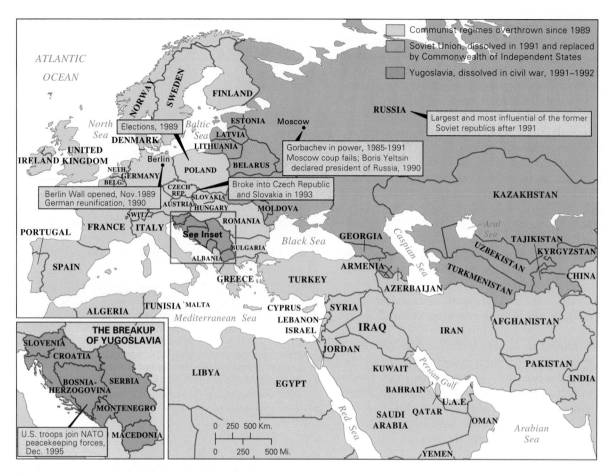

MAP 30.3 The Fall of Communism As the Soviet Union collapsed and lost its control over the countries of Eastern Europe, the map of Eastern Europe and Central Asia changed. The Soviet Union disappeared into history, replaced by fifteen new national units. In Eastern Europe, West and East Germany merged, Czechoslovakia divided into two nations, and Yugoslavia broke into five feuding states.

region. Slovenia, Croatia, and Macedonia gained independence by 1992. But in Bosnia-Herzegovina the fighting continued to rage as Serb forces instituted a policy of "ethnic cleansing" to remove the Muslim Bosnians from the country. By 1995 more than two hundred thousand people were dead and nearly 2 million left homeless.

The demise of the Soviet Union was almost as dramatic but less violent. Gorbachev's policies that permitted Eastern Europe to break free also caused the republics of the Soviet Union to demand greater autonomy and even independence. In August 1991, Communist hard-liners attempted a coup to topple Gorbachev. It failed in large part due to the actions of **Boris Yeltsin**, who declared the coup illegal and called on the Russian people to resist. Faced with popular opposition in Moscow and other cities, the coup

collapsed within seventy-two hours. The aborted coup accelerated the Soviet republics' movement toward independence. Pleas by Gorbachev to maintain Soviet unity were rejected, and by the end of 1991, the Soviet Union had ceased to exist. In its place was the **Commonwealth of Independent States** (CIS), a

Boris Yeltsin   Russian parliamentary leader who was elected president of the new Russian Republic in 1991 and provided increased democratic and economic reforms.

Commonwealth of Independent States   Weak federation of the former Soviet republics; it replaced the Soviet Union in 1992 and soon gave way to total independence of the member countries.

weak federation led by Yeltsin, the president of the Russian Republic.

The forces that promoted change in the Soviet bloc were alive throughout the globe. University students in China lead a series of demonstrations in 1989 demanding democracy and economic and governmental reform. In Beijing that June, thousands of protesters filled the massive expanse of Tiananmen Square. China's leaders chose to restore order by using force, killing hundreds as the world watched on television. Under political and public pressure to impose sanctions against China for their action, President Bush merely condemned Beijing. He argued that harsh action toward China would further isolate its leadership and make it even more brutal.

Criticized by some for his lenient China policy, Bush's policies in Central America gained widespread support. There he reduced American military support, pushed for political negotiations, and supported the **Contadora Plan**, a formula for peace in Nicaragua negotiated by a coalition of Central American nations. These actions contributed to the Contras halting military operations and the Marxist Ortega government accepting free elections. Those elections, in February 1990, saw opposition candidate Violeta de Chamorro defeat Daniel Ortega. In neighboring El Salvador, American-supported peace negotiations also ended the civil war.

Protecting American Interests Abroad

Promoting democracy and free trade were still clearly in the interests of the United States, but with the collapse of the Soviet Union, many wondered what goals and interests would now shape American foreign and military policies. Some called for a "peace dividend," asking that the United States reduce its global role and the military's budget. Bush resisted these suggestions and warned that the world was still a dangerous place. The bloody conflict in the Balkans, continued tensions in the Middle East, and the ever-present threat of nuclear weapons each demanded a strong, activist U.S. foreign policy. Less traditional foreign policy concerns included the drug trade, terrorism, and a variety of issues related to the global economy.

President Bush had made drugs a key issue during his campaign and had promised to crack down on the flow of cocaine into the United States. In December 1989, he ordered American troops into Panama, in Operation Just Cause, to arrest Pana-

manian dictator Manuel Noriega on drug-related charges. Once praised by Reagan and Bush, Noriega had been implicated in the torture and murder of his political enemies and the shipment of drugs from Colombia through Panama to the United States. Within seventy-two hours, American forces had accomplished their mission and had Noriega in custody. American casualties were light (only twenty-three lost their lives), but more than three thousand Panamanians, almost all civilians, died. A Miami court later found Noriega guilty of drug-related offenses and sentenced him to prison in 1992. Panama, however, remained a major route in the smuggling of drugs into the United States.

In the fall of 1990, President Bush faced a more traditional and serious threat. Iraq's Saddam Hussein invaded the oil-rich sheikdom of Kuwait and overran the country. Many worried that Hussein intended to dominate the Persian Gulf and thus gain control over the flow of more than 40 percent of the world's oil supply. Within hours of the invasion, Bush warned, "This will not stand," and he organized a United Nations response. A multinational force of more than 700,000, including 500,000 Americans, went to Saudi Arabia in Operation Desert Storm to protect Saudi borders and oil sources and to pressure Iraq to withdraw from Kuwait. Nearly 80 percent of the American public supported protecting Saudi Arabia, but most wanted to avoid war by using economic and diplomatic sanctions to force Iraq to leave Kuwait. Bush thought otherwise. He worked with other coalition nations to set a deadline for Iraqi withdrawal. If by January 15, 1991, Iraq still occupied Kuwait, the allies would use force.

Eighteen hours after the deadline expired, with Iraq making no move to pull out, aircraft of the UN coalition began devastating attacks on Iraqi positions in Kuwait and on Iraq itself. American public support immediately rallied behind the **Persian Gulf War**. After nearly forty days of air attacks, United Nations ground forces prepared to push Saddam Hussein's forces out of Kuwait (see

Contadora Plan Pact signed by the presidents of five Central American nations in 1987 calling for a cease-fire in conflicts in the region and for democratic reforms.

Persian Gulf War War in the Persian Gulf region in 1991, triggered by Iraq's invasion of Kuwait; a U.S.-led coalition defeated Iraqi forces and freed Kuwait.

In Operation Desert Storm, regarded by many as Bush's most successful action as president, United Nations forces led by the United States successfully pushed back the Iraqi army and liberated Kuwait. In this picture, U.S. Marines and their "humvees" prepare for action in Saudi Arabia, along the Kuwait border. *Bill Gentile/SIPA.*

Map 30.4). Saddam had promised that the ground war would be the "mother of all battles," but General Norman Schwarzkopf, coalition force commander, was confident of victory. He ridiculed the Iraqi leader's military ability: Hussein is "neither a strategist, nor is he schooled in the operational arts, nor is he a tactician, nor is he a general, nor is he a soldier. Other than that he is a great military man."

The ground offensive, called Operation Desert Storm, started the night of February 23. Within a hundred hours, coalition forces liberated Kuwait, where thousands of demoralized Iraqi soldiers, many of whom had gone without food and water for days, surrendered to advancing coalition forces. Estimates of Iraqi losses ranged from 70,000 to 115,000 killed. The United States lost fewer than 150. It was the "mother of all victories," quipped many Americans as President Bush's popularity momentarily soared above 90 percent. Some, less euphoric, speculated that the offensive had ended too soon and should have continued until all, or nearly all, of the Iraqi army had been destroyed and Hussein ousted from power.

By the summer of 1991, the United States could claim victory in two wars, the Persian Gulf War and the Cold War, and was clearly the diplomatic and military leader of the world. Riding a wave of popularity and foreign-policy successes, the White House looked hopefully toward the forthcoming presidential campaign.

A Kinder, Gentler Nation

Bush had entered the White House in 1989 promising a "kinder, gentler nation," an administration concerned about the nation's social problems. But the Bush administration made no move to improve America's society or economy. The goal was not "to remake society" but to manage the presidency, avoid "stupid mistakes," and "see that government doesn't get in the way." More government and more money were not always the best solutions to the country's ills, Bush frequently reminded his listeners. The message echoed Reagan's, but Bush was not as effective a communicator—he liked talking to people over the phone rather than face to face. Without Reagan's stage presence, Bush seemed to lack vision.

By the end of his first year in office, Bush and his advisers were confident they were managing well. They pointed to successful legislation that protected disabled Americans against discrimination (the Americans with Disabilities Act, 1990) and reduced smokestack and auto emissions and acid rain (the Clean Air Act, 1990). Bush also noted that under his administration the minimum wage had risen from $3.35 to $4.25 an hour and more funding had been provided for the Head Start program. Only two problem areas seemed to exist: the sluggish economy and his broken pledge on taxes.

In mid-1990, in part because of oil-price increases caused by Iraq's invasion of Kuwait, the nation entered into a recession. The recession, plus the growing federal deficit, had convinced Bush to work with Congress to raise taxes, despite his "no new taxes" pledge. Bush believed that by 1992 the recession would be over, the national debt would be reduced, and forgiving or forgetful voters would happily re-elect him. The recession, however, continued into 1992.

For several reasons, the recession lasted longer than Bush had expected. The world economy was slowing, and one result was that fewer American

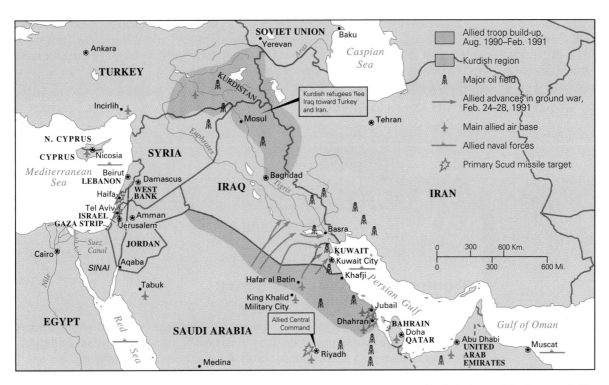

MAP 30.4 **The Gulf War**   On August 2, 1990, Iraq invaded Kuwait, threatening Saudi Arabia and the Persian Gulf region. In response, the United States and other nations formed an international coalition to restore Kuwait's independence. In January 1991, the coalition forces of Operation Desert Storm began to attack the forces of Saddam Hussein. The outcome was the destruction of most of the Iraqi army and Kuwait's liberation, but Saddam Hussein maintained control of Iraq.

goods were being sold overseas. A restructuring of the American economy forced many businesses to declare bankruptcy or downsize, releasing both blue-collar and white-collar workers. Between July 1990 and July 1993, more than 1.9 million people lost their jobs, and 63 percent of American corporations cut their staffs. IBM and General Motors were among those that faced huge losses and dismissed thousands of workers. "I don't see the United States regaining a substantial percentage of the jobs lost for five to ten years," said one chief executive.

Sharply rising federal spending and the ever-swelling deficit helped to lengthen and deepen the recession. Despite Bush's pledges to hold down federal spending and reduce the deficit, the budget skyrocketed during his term, reaching $1.5 trillion in 1992. At the same time, family income dropped below 1980 levels, to $37,300 from a 1980 high of $38,900. Consumers—caught between rising unemployment, falling wages, and nagging inflation—saw their savings shrink, and their confidence in the economy followed suit.

Bush did little to respond to the economic slide. Apart from saying that the American economy would rebound, Bush relied on raising interest rates and promoted globalization by reducing trade barriers to allow foreign trade to expand. Negotiations went forward to establish a North American free trading zone with Mexico and Canada and to eliminate Japanese barriers to American trade, but these negotiations had little impact on the economy. As the recession wore on, Democrats called for tax cuts on the middle class, increased and extended unemployment benefits, and other social programs. Bush responded with the veto. When House majority leader Richard Gephardt was asked to define Bush's domestic program, he icily commented that it was "the veto pen." Congressional Democrats replied by blocking Bush's attempts to reduce **capital gains taxes**. The result was political gridlock. As 1992 began,

capital gains tax   Tax on profits resulting from the sale of assets such as securities and real estate.

Bush faced his lowest approval rating ever in public opinion polls—around 40 percent. Political observers noted, and Republicans lamented, that Bush, unlike Reagan, seemed unable to project the image of an effective leader who had a vision of where the nation or the world should be going. Still, as a sitting president with important foreign policy successes, most observers believed he would have little problem winning the next presidential election.

INDIVIDUAL VOICES

Examining a Primary Source

Diameng Pa Tells His Story

The patterns of immigration that began with the passage of the 1965 Immigration Act continued throughout the 1990s, with increasing numbers of Asians and Latin Americans migrating to the United States. Amid growing calls for limitations on immigration, a Senate subcommittee held hearings on Ellis Island, New York, to hear testimonies from those supporting the idea that America should remain a nation of immigrants. On August 11, 1997, a senior from Wakefield High School in Arlington, Virginia, Diameng Pa, was one of several people to testify before the Senate's Judicial Committee's Subcommittee on Immigration. Among others presenting their views were the mayor of New York, Rudolph Giuliani, and the governor of New York, George Pataki, both of whom pointed out that their families too were once immigrants.

I would like to thank the Committee on Immigration for giving me this opportunity to tell . . . my strong belief that America should continue to be a nation of immigrants. This institution is hope for those still seeking a new beginning similar to the one I received.

I was born in Batdambang, Cambodia, on November 23, 1978 . . . a rural village . . . several miles from the Thai border. . . . This period produced a Cambodian Communist faction known as the Khmer Rouge, who killed more than 400,000 Cambodians and forced many more to flee to refugee camps in Thailand, including my family.

To acquire a better life for their family, my parents fled to a refugee camp in Thailand, fortunately able to escape from the constant threat of guerrilla attacks by the Khmer Rouge . . . and then to escape to the United States. . . . By coming to the United States of America, we were traveling to a land that was foreign to us and whose language we did not speak. However, it would be a place that we would receive new identities and a new chance of a better life. It is a land that would take time to adapt to, however, it is a land of opportunity. ●

My family initially settled in a minority neighborhood of south Arlington, Virginia, not far from Strayer College where my father, Mong Pa, pursued a degree in business administration. However, unfortunately, he abandoned his goals to support the family. My father would also mention the importance of

● In what ways were Diameng Pa's experiences and goals similar to those of Franklin Chang-Diaz?

education and its correlation with success. Though quite young, I realized that my father sacrificed his opportunity to pursue his business degree so that the family was financially stable. He encouraged me to reach out and to appreciate one of the many precious gifts that America offered—formal education.

Two years after I started school, I settled into the language thanks to my teachers and the miracle of TV. I remember adopting a few phrases here and there and soon enough I became accustomed to the English language and American culture. Bugs Bunny's "What's up, Doc" was my most favorite phrase during that time.

. . . [W]hile attending Thomas Jefferson Middle School . . . I accelerated in my studies and took the most demanding courses possible . . . I developed an interest in science activities. ●

As a sophomore at Wakefield High School I was privileged to be the first student in Wakefield history to attend the international Science and Engineer Fair in . . . Canada and to win second place in the category of environmental science.

As an immigrant, valedictorian of my senior class and now a proud American citizen, I realize that becoming an American took time. I feel that pursuing a dream takes dedication and will to strive and succeed. Only in America are you given this generous privilege. A world-renowned . . . researcher by the name of David Da-I Ho states, "Success is a result of immigrant drive. People get in this new world, they want to carve out their place in it. . . . You always retain a bit of underdog mentality. And if they work assiduously and lie low long enough, even underdogs will have their day." ●

● What key obstacle did both Pa and Chang-Diaz have to overcome, and what was the role of education in their lives?

● Do you agree with the statement that immigrants are underdogs and have a special drive for success? In your opinion, are the success stories of Pa and Chang-Diaz proof that America is a land of opportunity, or are these two immigrants exceptions to the rule?

SUMMARY

The years between Carter's inauguration and Bush's farewell were ones of changing expectations based in part on the health of the American economy. The economic growth that had characterized the postwar period was slowing, making the American dream harder and harder to attain. During Carter's presidency the nation seemed beset by blows to its domestic prosperity and international status. Carter seemed unable to lead Congress and unsure of the government's ability to solve the country's social and economic problems. In his foreign policy, Carter de-emphasized Cold War relationships and gave more attention to human rights and third world problems. Many believed the result was a weakening of America's international status, exemplified by the hostage crisis in Iran.

Reagan rejected Carter's notion that the nation was being held in check by some ill-defined limits. Instead, he argued that the only constraint on American greatness was government's excessive regulation and interference in society. He promised to reassert American power and renew the offensive in the Cold War. It was a popular message and contributed to a conservative resurgence that elevated Reagan to the presidency. As president, Reagan fulfilled many conservative expectations by reducing support for some social programs, easing and eliminating some government regulations, and exerting American power around the world—altering the structure of Soviet-American relations. Supporters claimed that the outcome of Reagan's choices was a prosperous nation that faced few constraints. They applauded Reagan's assessment that his administration had chosen to "change a nation, and instead . . . changed a world."

Bush inherited the expectations that the Reagan administration had generated. But unlike Reagan he could not project an image of strong and visionary leadership. Finding fewer constraints in conducting foreign policy, Bush directed most of his attention to world affairs. As the Soviet Union and communism in Eastern Europe collapsed, Bush gained public approval for his foreign policies, also demonstrating American strength and resolve in Panama and the Persian Gulf. His foreign-policy successes, however, only highlighted his weakness in domestic economic policy as the nation found itself mired in a nagging recession that sapped the public's confidence in Republican leadership and the economy.

LIVING PATTERNS, 2000 In 1900, the population of the United States was around 73 million people. One hundred years later, the population was 281.4 million people. In 1900, less than half of the population lived in urban areas. In 2000, about 80 percent of the population lives in urban areas. This map shows population density—the number of people living per square mile in each state. It also shows the poverty rate in each state.

U.S. population by age, 2000

- 65 and over 12.3%
- 55–64 9.6%
- 35–54 29.4%
- 19 and under 28.6%
- 20–34 20.9%

CANADA

WASHINGTON 10.2%
OREGON 11.6%
MONTANA 15.5%
IDAHO 13%
NORTH DAKOTA 12.5%
MINN. 8.9%
WIS. 9.2%
MICH. 11.5%
SOUTH DAKOTA 14%
WYOMING 12%
NEVADA 10.7%
UTAH 10%
IOWA 9.9%
NEBRASKA 9.6%
CALIFORNIA 16%
COLORADO 10.2%
KANSAS 10.9%
ILL. 11.3%
IND. 9.9%
OHIO 11%
MISSOURI 15.5%
KENTUCKY 16%
ARIZONA 15.5%
NEW MEXICO 19.3%
OKLAHOMA 16.3%
ARK. 17.5%
TENN. 13.6%
W.VA. 16.8%
VIRGINIA 11.6%
NORTH CAROLINA 12.6%
SOUTH CAROLINA 14.9%
GEORGIA 14.7%
MISS. 18.1%
ALABAMA 16.2%
TEXAS 16.7%
LA. 18.4%
FLA. 14.4%

MAINE 10.7%
VT. 9.7%
N.H. 7.5%
MASS. 10.7%
NEW YORK 15.6%
R.I. 11.2%
CONN. 8.9%
PENNSYLVANIA 10.9%
N.J. 9.3%
DEL. 10%
MD. 9.5%
Washington, D.C. 19.3%

PACIFIC OCEAN

MEXICO

ATLANTIC OCEAN

Gulf of Mexico

CUBA

Population per square mile, 1990

- 1,200–9,400
- 500–1,200
- 100–500
- 50–100
- 10–50
- 1–10

15.5% Percentage of state population living at poverty level in 2000

0   200   400 Km.
0   200   400 Mi.

PACIFIC OCEAN
HAWAI'I 11.1%
0 100 Km.
0 100 Mi.

U.S.S.R.
CANADA
ALASKA 11.2%
PACIFIC OCEAN

0   250   500 Km.
0   250   500 Mi.

Stephen Breyer appointed to Supreme Court

Clinton elected
NAFTA
Contract with America
Dayton Agreement
Clinton reelected
Balanced budget proposed
Bush elected President
Bush declares war on terrorism

1992   1993   1994   1995   1996   1998   2000   2001

1850   1900   1950   2000

Entering a New Century, 1992–2002

31

FATHER MYCHAL JUDGE

In 1996 Father Mychal Judge became a symbol for those seeking solace and reconciliation after a great tragedy—the crash of TWA flight #800 into Long Island Sound that killed all passengers on board. He told relatives of those lost: "Open your hearts, and let their spirit and life keep you going." Little did he know at the time that on September 11, 2001, his actions and words would provide meaning to a whole nation. Father Mychal Judge, who had grown up on the streets of New York, became the first "official" casualty of the terrorist attack that destroyed the World Trade Center. *Ed Betz/Wide World*.

Father Mychal Judge

In 1868 Horatio Alger wrote the first of his many works about young men with few prospects finding the road to success and respectability. In that novel, Ragged Dick, a vagabond shoeshine boy on the streets of New York, eventually found a sponsor, gained an education, and got a responsible job—fame and fortune were within reach. Mychal Judge followed a similar path but discovered a very different fame and fortune. Born of Irish immigrant parents in 1933, he grew up in Brooklyn during the Great Depression, and money was scarce. Things got worse when, in 1936, his father became gravely ill and was unable to work. When his father died three years later, Judge's childhood ended. "I never had a father growing up, someone I would play catch with or go for a walk with," he remembered. Instead of playing, he went to work as a shoeshine boy, earning money for his mother and family. He considered being a fireman when he grew up. Working the streets of Brooklyn and Manhattan, he would sometimes duck into neighboring Catholic churches to rest and find solace. He later recalled that he liked going to church—"I just felt good there." Despite his mother's favorite saying, "Too much religion is no good for anybody, " he found himself drawn to a religious life. At one of the churches he used to visit, St. Francis of Assisi in lower Manhattan, he met Father Teddy, who took him under his wing and became his mentor. "Watching him," Judge remembered, "I realized that I didn't care for material things all that much."

For a poor Irish boy, the church provided a path to a different world, and at the age of 14 Mychal Judge took it. He joined the Franciscan seminary and in 1958 became Friar Judge, officially entering the order. Three years later, he was ordained as a priest and was assigned to a parish in East Rutherford, New Jersey. It was a learning experience. "In seminary, you can get all the theology and Scripture in the world, and you land in your first parish," he recalled, "and you find out it's you—the personality and the gifts that God gave you."

Almost immediately the new priest became known for his "snappy laugh," charismatic personality, and "hands-on" concern for people. He would put his big Irish hand on you and give you a blessing, even if you didn't ask for one, recalled a friend. In 1974 he received national attention for helping talk a man into surrendering who was holding his wife and children at gunpoint. He also displayed a unique talent for being a peacemaker and helping people cope with grief. Recalled a colleague, "Mychal was really intuitive by diagnosing people's pain, their confusion, and guiding them to inner peace and inner strength. . . ."

In 1986 "Father Mike" returned to his roots—St. Francis of Assisi Church in Manhattan—and immersed himself in a wide variety of ministries, including working in local hospitals and among the poor, and running an AIDS ministry when many in society condemned and avoided people with AIDS. As an advocate of gay rights, he worked with gay organizations in New York, even marching in a gay St. Patrick's' Day Parade.

Father Mike gained recognition for his ability to build bridges between opposing parties and to bring comfort to the bereaved. In New York he became a close friend and confessor to Steven McDonald, a New York police detective who was shot and paralyzed in 1986, helping him to accept his condition and forgive his assailant. Later, on three occasions the two became involved in peace missions to Northern Ireland trying to reconcile Protestants and Catholics, meeting with leaders on both sides, including the prime minister of Ireland. In 1996 Father Mike received national attention for working with the relatives and friends of the victims of TWA flight 800, which had crashed into Long Island Sound. "What a beacon of light," recalled Senator Hillary Clinton, remembering a time when Mychal Judge and other clergy were invited to Washington. "He lit up the White House."

In 1992 Father Mike chose to become the chaplain to the New York Fire Department. According to one fireman, "He was a real fire buff. . . . He just loved firemen and their jobs." He became part of the firefighters' families, marrying (by one account 2,500 weddings), burying, and baptizing them. He lived in the Franciscan friary, sleeping on an old couch in a sparsely furnished room with a fire/police scanner. Across the street was his firehouse, Engine Company 1 and Ladder Company 24.

On September 11, 2001, he was with his squad as they responded to news that an airplane had just crashed into the World Trade Center's North Tower. There was orderly panic as people fled the towers and as firemen and police rushed inside to facilitate the evacuation and help the injured. As Father Mike headed to the North Tower, he passed Rudolph Giuliani, mayor of New York, who shouted, "Pray for us, Mychal." "I always do," he yelled back. A few minutes later, as Father Mike knelt and removed his helmet to administer last rites to a fallen firefighter, he was struck in the head by a falling piece of debris. He died instantly, "doing," Senator Clinton said later, "what he was called to do."

INTRODUCTION

When the 1990s began, it appeared in many ways that the country was divided and unsure of the future—the American vision needed to be rediscovered or redefined. Trends that had started two decades earlier were continuing to change the society, politics, and economy of the nation. The industrial economy that had characterized the United States for most of the twentieth century was shifting toward postindustrialism, in which service jobs and information-based technology—not manufacturing—shaped the economy. Globalization, too, provided new realities for society and the economy, as nations loosened their restrictions on the flow of goods, services, capital, ideas, and people.

These changes, as they had for the previous two decades, provided new opportunities for some while also aggravating growing disparities of wealth. At the same time, the numbers of people living near or at the poverty level grew while the middle class shrank slightly. Geographically, the Sunbelt, suburbs, and the new "boomburbs," continued to accumulate population, political power, and wealth. Many cities, especially those in the industrial states, continued to decline and sought to redefine their images and economies.

Throughout the 1990s, American population growth accelerated as many Asian and Latino immigrants continued to arrive. Newcomers with technical and professional skills often moved into the suburbs. But most settled in the cities, frequently joined the ranks of the underclass, finding few full-time, well-paying jobs and frequently making do with public assistance and part-time employment. Whether in suburbs or cities, many new immigrants experienced growing intolerance and sometimes ethnic and racial violence.

Across the nation, the discussions about the economy, poverty, and society frequently revolved around redefining the nation's social and political vision. A resurgent conservatism challenged New Deal and Great Society visions of social policy. Staunch liberals argued that government remained the prime force for improving American society and that social programs needed to be expanded and effectively funded. Conservatives disagreed. They maintained that policies supported by liberals were not only too expensive but were destroying the nation's basic value system. The product of liberal activism, they charged, was not a better, more stable society, but the breakdown of values, which resulted in increasing rates of divorce, abortion, crime, drug abuse, and violence. Many American social problems could be reduced, they insisted, by a return to traditional two-parent-family values.

Conservatives predicted that the 1992 presidential election would be a clash between liberal and conservative values, a cultural and social war for the soul of the nation. Running for re-election, President George Bush counted on the strong support of conservatives and expected that his foreign policy achievements would attract more than enough moderates to ensure his success. But that expectation faded quickly when it became obvious that the public was most interested in economic issues. Whereas Bush offered few answers to troubling economic issues, his main opponent—the Democratic governor of Arkansas, William Jefferson (Bill) Clinton—focused on the economy and promised to support social needs, while making the hard choices necessary to control the federal budget and reduce the national debt. Clinton pulled ahead of Bush in the public opinion polls and won the election.

The new president assumed office anxious to accomplish social reforms, but his efforts to enact major domestic legislation ran into obstacles. In 1994 Republicans gained control of Congress and announced a "Contract with America" to capture the legislative initiative. Clinton, however, proved politically adept, shedding liberal trappings and establishing himself as a centrist. He adopted the issue of welfare reform, oversaw an improvement of the economy, and proved successful in foreign policy. As Americans headed into the polls in 1996, the United States was at peace and the economy was prospering. It was an unbeatable combination, and Clinton easily defeated Robert Dole.

Clinton's second term politically polarized America and nearly saw the removal of a president through the process of impeachment. The central issue revolved around a sexual affair between Clinton and an ex-White House intern, Monica Lewinsky. Special prosecutor Kenneth Starr led the investigation and recommended to the House of Representatives that Clinton be impeached. He charged that the president had perjured himself and obstructed justice. After heated and partisan debate, the Republican-controlled House impeached Clinton and recommended to the Senate that he be removed from office. In February 1999, the Senate voted not to remove Clinton from office. Basking in an expanding economy, Clinton left office with high approval ratings and credit for balancing the budget.

Following Clinton's example, the 2000 presidential candidates, Republican governor of Texas George W. Bush and Democratic vice president Albert Gore, worked to occupy the center of the political spectrum. It produced a close campaign and an even closer vote. Gore won the popular vote, but Bush, in a decision facilitated by the Supreme Court, won the Electoral College count. With Republican and a few Democratic votes, Bush pushed through a broad tax cut and an education reform act, but most of the rest of his agenda fell victim to Democratic roadblocks. Partisan debate on Bush's domestic agenda was eclipsed on September 11, 2001 when nineteen terrorists hijacked domestic airliners and used them to attack the World Trade Center in New York City and the Pentagon in Washington, D.C.

The attacks killed over three thousand people, including Father Mychal Judge, but unified a nation determined to pursue justice and punish the terrorists. Investigations quickly linked the terrorists to Al-Qaeda, a terrorist organization led by Osama bin Laden, who directed operations from Afghanistan. After the Afghanistan (Taliban) government rejected an American demand to surrender bin Laden, the United States launched military actions against Al-Qaeda and the Taliban. To provide increased secu-

chronology

A New Century with New Challenges

1992 Riots in south-central Los Angeles
U.S. troops sent to Somalia
Bill Clinton elected president
*Planned Parenthood of Southeastern
Pennsylvania v. Casey*

1993 North American Free Trade Agreement
ratified
Clinton introduces national healthcare
package
Harris v. Forklift Systems

1994 Withdrawal of U.S. troops from Somalia
U.S. troops sent to Haiti
Violence Against Women Act
"Contract with America"

1995 Bombing of Oklahoma federal building
Dayton Agreement

1996 Welfare reform passed
Clinton re-elected

1997 Madeleine Albright confirmed as secretary of state
Reno v. ACLU

1998 Clinton proposes balanced budget
House of Representatives votes to impeach
Clinton
Terrorists attack U.S. embassies in Kenya and
Tanzania

1999 NATO bombs Serbia over Kosovo crisis
Senate votes not to remove Clinton from office
Columbine High School shooting

2000 Terrorists attack U.S.S. *Cole*
George W. Bush elected president
Nation experiences longest economic expansion
in its history

2001 Bush's tax cut bill passed
Terrorists associated with Al-Qaeda attack
World Trade Towers and Pentagon
Office of Homeland Security established
U.S. launches Operation Enduring Freedom
against Al-Qaeda and Taliban government of
Afghanistan
Economy in a recession
USA Patriot Act
Taliban regime collapses and is replaced by
interim government

rity within the United States, Bush established an Office of Homeland Security and asked for broader powers in dealing with suspected terrorists. In October Congress approved the USA Patriot Act that provided law enforcement agencies stronger means to investigate and detain individuals suspected of terrorist activities.

In Afghanistan, the war against terrorism—Operation Just Cause—continued successfully. By mid-November, the bombing campaign and American Special Forces teams working with anti-Taliban forces had ended most resistance and caused the collapse of the Taliban government. Osama bin Laden, however, eluded capture and vanished from sight. Looking forward, President Bush promised to continue the global fight against terrorism and to kill or capture bin Laden.

The war against terrorism provided the president with a new agenda that solidified public and political support, but some wondered if he would be able to transfer that support to domestic issues. By the start of 2002, it appeared that partisan politics, at least on domestic issues, was returning to normal and that the public was beginning to separate their support for Bush's campaign against terrorism from their opinion of his domestic agenda.

OLD VISIONS AND NEW REALITIES

• What changes were taking place in the American economy during the 1990s? How did the slowing economy affect people's lives and expectations?

• What debates surrounded issues faced by women and minorities, and what were the political implications?

As the two major political parties readied themselves for the 1992 presidential election, they presented two distinct visions of the critical issues and the condition of American society. Republicans hoped that the alignment of voters that had elected Reagan and Bush would continue to reject liberal activism and big government in favor of the conservative social values of the New Right. The party platform forcefully attacked permissiveness in American society, opposed abortion and alternative lifestyles, advocated less government, and stressed the "traditional American values" that emphasized family and religion. Pat Buchanan roused the convention by calling for a "cultural war . . . for the soul of the nation." Confident in their agenda, conservatives rallied around President George Bush. Bush accepted the social agenda but preferred to emphasize his experience, bask in the afterglow of Operation Desert Storm and the fall of communism, and call for tax cuts and reduced government spending to stimulate the economy. Republicans expected Bush to win easily.

Many prominent Democrats agreed with the Republican assessment and decided not to compete for their party's presidential nomination. This left the door open for Governor William (Bill) Clinton of Arkansas, 46-year-old baby boomer, who easily won the nomination. In his campaign, Clinton and his young team of political advisers focused on a different vision of American society and its needs. Unlike Republicans, they saw a vital need for an activist government to deal with social problems. They avoided "cultural war" slogans, targeting instead the slowing economy's impact on society. James Carville, Clinton's chief political adviser, tacked reminders over his desk reading, "It's the Economy, Stupid," "Change vs. More of the Same" and "Don't Forget Healthcare."

The Shifting Economy

While Republicans and Democrats honed their political messages about who could best solve America's problems, many people grew ever more concerned over their economic futures. The conventional vision of an American economy resting on industrial growth and robust sales of U.S. goods in foreign markets was giving way to a new reality. The postindustrial economy was replacing the nation's manufacturing firms with service and technology companies as the driving force behind the economy. Compounding the shift to a new economy was the impact of globalization. As the economy changed, so too did many of the nation's social, cultural, and economic underpinnings.

To many, the globalization of trade, information, services, and people provided a variety of benefits to the United States and the world. Advocates believed it reduced world poverty, promoted the spread of knowledge, improved international understanding, and provided solutions for global problems such as world hunger, human rights, and environmental threats. An expanding Internet used by over 250 million people around the world to communicate with a simple "point and click," supporters argued, was just one example of the benefits of new technology supporting globalization and the lowering of barriers between nations. Another aspect of globalization was the reduction of barriers to trade and the establishment of regional free trade areas. Such areas in North America began under President Reagan, who in 1988 signed a treaty with Canada to remove trade barriers, and continued by President Bush, who sought to include Mexico in an expanded free trade community. His efforts generated strong opposition from labor unions, environmentalists, and various American businesses that feared Mexico's participation. By the end of Bush's administration, the **North American Free Trade Agreement** existed, although opposition in Congress prevented the United States from ratifying the treaty.

Opponents of globalization, while accepting that some of its ideals were positive, argued that in practice its consequences were negative. Some were convinced that it primarily benefited rich multinational corporations, which relocated their factories to less developed nations where wages were low and laws

---

North American Free Trade Agreement Agreement approved by the Senate in 1993 that eliminated most tariffs and other trade barriers between the United States, Mexico, and Canada.

Opponents of globalization argue that the primary benefactors of the new economy are the industrialized nations and big business and that among the victims are the environment and the poor. Many antiglobalization protestors took to the streets in Seattle, Washington in November 1999, protesting the meeting of the World Trade Organization. *Karie Hamilton/CorbisSygma.*

to protect the environment and workers' rights were absent. Emphasizing the threats to human rights, the exploitation of workers, loss of jobs, and harm to the environment, in the 1990s antiglobalization organizations targeted the symbols of globalization—meetings of the leaders of the industrial nations, the **G-8 nations**, and the **World Trade Organization**. In November 1999, fifty thousand protesters carried out a massive demonstration against the WTO and globalization at a conference in Seattle, Washington. Less concerned with global issues, others fear that open borders invited more narcotics, diseases, terrorism, and immigrants, thus weakening the United States' ability to protect its economy, interests, and culture.

The shift from an industrial base to a more global, postindustrial economy had a significant

impact on where people worked and lived. As the economy became increasingly based on service and information technology (IT) industries, blue-collar

G-8 nations   Term given to the leading industrial nations (Canada, China, France, Germany, Italy, Japan, the United Kingdom and the United States) that meet periodically to deal with major economic and political problems facing their countries and the international community; the first summit in 1975 only had six members, as Canada and China were not yet members.

World Trade Organization   Geneva-based organization that oversees world trading systems; founded in 1995 by 135 countries to replace the 1948 General Agreement on Tariffs and Trades (GATT).

The globalization of technology and trade are central parts of the new world economy. Few developments better reflect the globalization of communications and technology than the spread of the Internet. In Ho Chi Minh City, Internet access is available in public offices, while the Vietnamese government has a five-year plan to develop high-tech industrial parts to attract software industries. *Hoang Dinh Man-AFP.*

Many of those classified as technical and professional workers were part of the fastest growing segment of the economy, the information-based industries associated with computers and global networking. Almost overnight, companies associated with computer technology, software, and the Internet proliferated and saw the value of their stocks skyrocket—pushing the stock market and the **Nasdaq** indexes that listed many of the new hi-tech companies to record highs. Suddenly, the ranks of the rich included large numbers of new millionaires—"dot-com millionaires"—men and women who owned businesses focused on the exchange of services, information, and goods over the Internet or who invested in those businesses. The Silicon Valley in northern California, a center for the microprocessing industry, boasted the greatest concentration of new wealth in the nation.

New Faces of the Economy

Throughout the Sunbelt and West the new economy pushed wealth and population upward. Phoenix became the nation's sixth-largest city, acquiring professional football and baseball teams. But surrounding Phoenix and many other western cities, the suburbs grew even faster. By the end of the 1990s, many suburbs had a population larger than traditional cities, becoming **"boomburbs."** In 2000 there were fifty-three boomburbs, each with populations larger than 100,000, and four larger than 300,000, including Mesa, Arizona, and Arlington, Texas. No longer bedroom communities, these boomburbs have the same functions and offer the same facilities as traditional cities, while matching the needs of a drive-through society. Like traditional urban areas, the expanding suburbs have a

manufacturing jobs declined, while jobs in the service sector rose. In 1960 factories accounted for about 19 percent of the work force, whereas only about 11 percent of the work force was defined as technical or professional workers. By mid 1990, those numbers had reversed: 18 percent of the work force was classified as technical or professional, and only 10 percent still labored in factories (see Figure 31.1). In the larger service industry the numbers were similar, employing only about 15 percent of the work force in the early 1960s but about 25 percent by 1997.

Nasdaq   A stock index, launched in 1971, that focuses on companies in technological fields; *Nasdaq* stands for National Association of Securities Dealers Automated Quotation.

boomburbs   Term used to describe suburban cities with populations of over 100,000 and double-digit growth every decade since they first exceeded a population of 2,500; other terms for this new classification of city are "fringe cities" and "technoburbs."

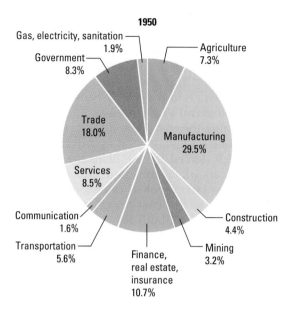

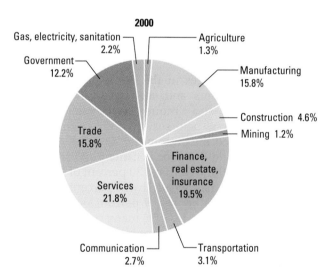

FIGURE 31.1 Main Sectors of U.S. Economy   A comparison of the 1950 and 2000 graphs shows that many of the economic sectors that deal with the production and marketing of goods, such as manufacturing, agriculture, transportation, and trade, have declined, while those sectors that mainly provide services have increased, especially government, services, and finance.

Throughout much of urban America, especially in factory cities, the decline in population, industrial jobs, and financial resources continued. Those who could afford to leave frequently moved to the suburbs, including many middle-class African Americans and Latinos. With fewer resources and shrinking tax bases, city services and infrastructures deteriorated, schools decayed, and public and private aid services were overwhelmed. In urban schools, the dropout rates rose—among African Americans to more than 50 percent—as did membership in gangs. One expert on gangs noted that "gangs don't have membership drives" and that "kids drift toward gangs . . . where there are no [other] programs."

The proliferation of gangs and the scourge of drugs, especially **crack cocaine**, were thought by many to be chief contributors to urban violence. FBI statistics showed that while incidents of violent crime dropped nationally, they remained high in the city. By 1991, murder was the leading cause of death for urban black males under the age of 35, and a fourth of all urban school districts used metal detectors to try to prevent students from bringing weapons to school.

Replacing those who left for the suburbs were larger numbers of minorities, including the unskilled immigrants from Mexico, Central America, and Asia. In Los Angeles the largest immigrant groups were Mexicans, Iranians, Salvadorans, Japanese, Chinese, and Filipinos. Commenting on Los Angeles, one writer wrote that it was an ethnic and cultural borderland "on a frontier between Europe and Asia and between Anglo and Hispanic cultures." Urban cultural borderlands were also places of increased ethnic and racial tensions, which at times erupted into large-scale violence. Miami witnessed clashes between Hispanics, mostly Cuban, and African Americans, and in April 1992, tensions among black, whites, Hispanics, and Asians contributed to an explosive multiethnic riot in south-central Los Angeles. The immediate cause of the riot was the acquittal of three white Los Angeles policemen accused of excessive violence (one policeman was found guilty) during the arrest of

growing minority population. In many cases, suburban minorities—as they had in the city—cluster in communities within the suburb that are poorer and more likely to have less effective facilities and higher crime rates.

crack cocaine   Highly potent form of cocaine that is smoked through a glass pipe and is extremely addictive.

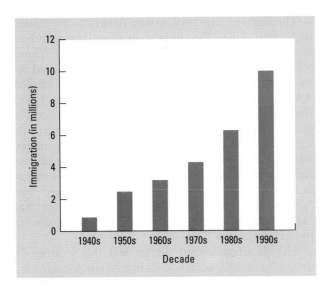

FIGURE 31.2 Immigration to the United States since 1940 Since the 1940s, the number of immigrants coming to the United States has grown steadily. Changes in immigration laws in 1965 and 1990 not only allowed more immigrants to enter the country, but also changed the point of departure for most of those immigrants from Europe to Latin America and Asia.

Rodney King, an African American. Caught on videotape by an eyewitness, four policemen beat King after he had seemingly been subdued. For many African Americans, the officers' actions were further proof of white, and especially white police, racism. When an all-white jury returned the verdict, a five-day riot began, resulting in more than 16,000 arrests, the destruction of 4,000 businesses, 60 deaths and 2,300 injuries, and between $750 million and $1 billion in property damage. Forty-five percent of those arrested were Latino compared with 41 percent African American, while stores owned by Asians were among the most damaged.

Throughout the 1990s the number of legal immigrants had risen by nearly 4 million more people than had arrived in the previous decade (see Figure 31.2). One of the causes was the **Immigration Act of 1990**, which increased the number of immigrants who could come to the United States each year to nearly 700,000. The swelling numbers of immigrants combined with census projections to indicate that by 2050, if not sooner, the percentage of "minorities" in the United States would equal that of whites. This reality prompted increased calls for

immigration restrictions, limits on affirmative action and welfare, and protection of "the American culture." Conservative spokesman and Republican candidate for the presidency in 1992, Pat Buchanan sounded the alarm: "The melting pot is in need of repair. . . . If America is to survive as 'one nation, one people,' we need to call a time out on immigration." Californians, citing the costs that illegal immigrants added to the state budget, in 1994 approved Proposition 187, which denied illegal aliens access to all but emergency social, health, and education services. The act was later revoked as unconstitutional but served notice to the country of growing concerns about immigrants, both legal and illegal. By 2001, the growth of the Hispanic, especially Mexican, population had caused nearly thirty states to take steps to approve "English only" legislation. Even Iowa, with about 13,000 Hispanics out of a total population of nearly 200,000, considered such legislation.

Rich and Poor

The ongoing changes in the economy produced a three-level economy and society. At the top were highly trained and frequently transient professionals, while low-paid service and assembly plant workers peopled the bottom tier. The rich were getting richer, while the poor became poorer. Between 1979 and 1995, the wealthiest 20 percent of the population increased their wealth by 26 percent, while the poorest 20 percent became 9 percent poorer. Put in more dramatic terms, by 1996 many company executives received 209 times more income than a factory worker. Between the two tiers was a shrinking middle class, whose incomes were barely holding steady (see Figure 31.3 and Table 31.1). Middle- and working-class families not only saw their economic status

Rodney King African American whose beating by Los Angeles police officers was captured on videotape; the acquittal of the officers in 1992 triggered rioting in which sixty people were killed.

Immigration Act of 1990 Law passed that reformed the Immigration Act of 1965; it increased the number of immigrants allowed annually into the United States to around 700,000 and gave preference to skilled workers and those with families already living in the country.

table 31.1 Consumer Prices, January 1998

Rye bread	$	1.59 a loaf
Apples		1.29 a pound
Bananas		0.49 a pound
Round steak		3.49 a pound
Chicken fryers		1.29 a pound
Wheaties		2.29 a box
Clorox		1.15 a bottle
Coffee		3.69 for 13 ounces
Margarine (oleo)		0.69 a pound
Sugar		2.09 for 5 pounds
Flour		1.69 for 5 pounds
Frozen orange juice		1.00 for 12 ounces
Dial soap		2.09 for 3 cakes
Milk		0.69 a quart
Kodak disposable camera		9.96
19-inch color television set		199.99
Refrigerator		599.99
Oldsmobile 88 automobile		20,273.00
"Scrabble" game		9.86

Source: Data from *Observer-Reporter*, Washington, Pa., January 1998.

jeopardized, but many doubted that the Social Security system would be able to provide them an adequate retirement. As baby boomers were getting older, approaching retirement age, fewer and fewer younger workers were paying into the Social Security system. Many worried that, without a major overhaul, both Social Security and Medicare would go broke before the boomer generation could benefit from them. In the 1980s, a 25 percent increase in Social Security taxes helped make the system more solvent, but the tax increase also had drawn down take-home wages. Even more worrisome, medical costs were among the fastest rising in the country.

Concerns about retirement were not in the minds of more than 15 percent of the population who lived below the official poverty line of $14,335 (for a family of four) in 1995. Among the poorest were those called an underclass, unemployed or underemployed people with little education and very little hope of escaping poverty. The underclass included at least a half-million homeless living on the streets in metropolitan centers across the country. The homeless were a cross-section of the nation's poorest: 51 percent were African American, 35 percent white; 46 percent single men, 36 percent families with children, 14 percent single women, 4 percent unaccompanied children. Similar percentages applied for the nonhomeless poor, whose numbers had climbed since the late 1960s.

The increasing numbers of women heads of households among the poor, a "feminization of poverty," was of particular concern. Nationally, over 30 percent of single women were living in poverty, contributing to an alarming increase in the percent of children living in poverty—26.3 percent by 1993. The causes were varied. Lack of skills was a general cause for the poverty, forcing people into service industry jobs, where wages were low and benefits scarce. But, especially for women, there were other reasons: more children were being born to unwed mothers, more marriages were ending in divorce, less money was being paid in alimony and child support. Changes in divorce laws eliminated or reduced alimony, and child support payments were often not paid. In 1990, for example, more than a fourth of spouses, mostly men, who owed child support paid nothing. Another problem faced by women, not only those living in poverty, was that women still encountered pay inequality. For the same or comparable jobs, women made about 27 cents less per dollar than men.

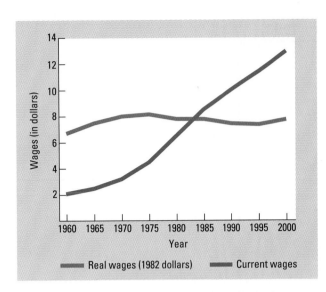

FIGURE 31.3 Real Versus Current Wages Reflecting the growing economic uneasiness that many Americans began to feel in the mid-1980s, purchasing power generated by wages began to decline, even though wages themselves continued to climb. In 1999 the average wage of about $13.00 an hour was worth only about $7.80, based on the amounts of goods that a dollar in 1982 could buy. Adjusted for inflation, the increase in wages from 1960 to the present has remained fairly constant.

Women and Family Values

Throughout American history people and politicians have expressed concern about the poor and about social change. The liberal activism of the 1960s provided one vantage point, and the conservative reaction on the New Right provided another. For the past two decades, conflict between the two views has raged around issues of economic and social opportunity, welfare, sexuality, and family values. Connecting several of the issues, Kate O'Beirne of the conservative Heritage Foundation stressed the importance of the traditional American family. "Why experiment with new antipoverty programs," she asked, "when the most important indicator of poverty is whether there are two parents at home?" She and others firmly advocated what they labeled strong family values and blamed feminism for many of society's problems.

O'Beirne's antifeminist attitude seemed by the 1990s to be gaining acceptance as a backlash against feminism gained momentum. By 1995, only 20 percent of women college freshmen accepted the label

"feminist," and in an article titled "What Happened to the Women's Movement?" *Newsweek* suggested the death of feminism. Central to the conservative attack on feminism was that it presented women as victims of a heterosexual, male-dominated culture. Unwilling to make a distinction between the radical **"gender feminists"** and the feminist movement, conservative groups like Concerned Women of America, in large part, blamed the women's movement for the decline in moral values and "traditional" families. As one antifeminist explained: "It all comes down to values. Traditional values work because they are the guidelines most consistent with human nature."

Abortion remained one of the most divisive issues. Since *Roe v. Wade*, pro-choice supporters had worried that the growing power of the New Right and an increasingly conservative Supreme Court might restrict access to abortions. In 1992 the Supreme Court's decision in *Planned Parenthood of Southeastern Pennsylvania v. Casey* (1992) confirmed a woman's right to have an abortion. But it had offset that affirmation with the condition that, in some cases, the state could modify that right. Advocates of a "woman's right to choose" also worried about the violent tactics that some opponents were adopting.

Opponents of abortion, on the other hand, were more and more frustrated and angered by the inability of the Court and Congress to ban, or at least limit, abortions. Acting on their anger, a minority within the **Right to Life movement** decided to take more direct and forceful tactics. Abortion clinics' doctors, staff, and patients became targets. By 1994, more than half of all abortion clinics reported varied cases of intimidation and violence, and a hundred clinics had been targets of arson or bombings. In an effort to prevent these occurrences, in 1994 the federal government passed the Freedom of Access to Clinic Entrances Act. It restricted the tactics of intimidation that pro-life supporters such

---

gender feminists Term applied to those within the feminist movement who focus on the subordination of women and on the need for radical changes in gender-related roles and traditions.

Right to Life movement Anti-abortion movement that favors a constitutional amendment to prohibit abortion; some segments grew increasingly militant during the 1980s and 1990s; also called the pro-life movement.

Ever since the controversial *Roe v. Wade* decision in 1973, opponents of abortion have asked the Supreme Court, lobbied Congress, and demonstrated to ban abortions. In January 1990, with President Bush's encouragement, thousands of participants in the March for Life rallied outside the White House, demanding an end to abortions. Some radical pro-life supporters have even advocated violence against and murder of those performing abortions as a moral choice in the "war" against abortion. *Reuters/Bettmann/Corbis.*

as **Operation Rescue** could use. Nonetheless, opponents vowed to maintain the struggle against abortion and feminism.

Many feminist leaders, however, asserted that the women's movement was alive and well, despite internal tensions. They pointed out that most within the women's movement disagreed with the views held by gender feminists and that a "new wave" of more inclusive and less ideological feminism was emerging. Most women, they said, including the vast majority who worked, wanted to "fit their new gains at work and in the public world into . . . the story of marriage and family that they . . . inherited from their mothers." They wanted to keep the gains women had made, while strengthening marriage and family, reducing sexual permissiveness, and softening the impact on young children whose mothers worked. As signs of the movement's continuing achievements, they pointed to efforts to combat **sexual harassment**, changes in the workplace, breaking the **"glass ceiling,"** and the growing number of women in the professions.

The problem of sexual harassment caught the nation's attention in 1991 when Anita Hill, a University of Oklahoma law professor, testified that she had been sexually harassed by Supreme Court nominee Clarence Thomas ten years earlier when they had been associates on the Equal Employment Opportunity Commission. Thomas denied the charges and was confirmed. The problem of sexual harassment was how it was defined and what was needed for proof. One poll at the time of the

Operation Rescue   A militant anti-abortion group that advocates intimidation and physical confrontation as a means to stop abortion.

sexual harassment   Unwanted sexual advances, sexually derogatory remarks, gender-related discrimination, or the existence of a sexually hostile work environment.

glass ceiling   Term used to express an intangible barrier within the hierarchy of a company that prevents women or minorities from rising to upper-level positions.

hearings revealed that 42 percent of women had been sexually harassed, and the National Organization for Women claimed that physical abuse of women was a cultural norm. Responding to sexual harassment lawsuits, courts began to define its legal dimensions. In 1993 the Supreme Court decided in *Harris v. Forklift Systems* (1993) that sexual harassment not only constituted "verbal and physical conduct" but also created a "hostile environment." Congress, the following year, passed the **Violence Against Women Act**. Part of a larger anticrime bill, it provided funds and federal support for efforts to more harshly punish sexual violence and other attacks on women and to provide resources to aid victims and prevent future attacks.

Supporters of the women's movement also stated that their efforts to fight harassment were only one part of a continuing effort to improve the workplace for women. The gap between salaries for men and women was narrowing, and more women were entering the professions, but more needed to be done to adjust the workplace to suit the needs of women with families. Programs such as flextime and flexplace, job sharing, and family leave should be more widely adopted and more accessible day care provided. The editor of *Ms.* magazine noted that the central issues were recognizing choices and their consequences and promoting a "woman-friendly family and a family-friendly workplace."

While feminists listed their accomplishments on behalf of women, their critics remained focused on the "threats" to the family and the need for a moral society. They argued that even "mommy-friendly" workplaces were not a replacement for full-time mothers and an environment that respected moral values. Echoing the concerns of many in the public, they pressed for more controls to ban pornography and to limit the amount of sex and violence in the media. During the 1980s, sexual content had become standard fare in books, magazines, music, movies, television, and on the Internet. In 1987 it was estimated that more than sixty-five thousand sexual references were broadcast each year on prime-time television programs. During the day, sex and sex-related issues became more daring and numerous on the soaps, and talk-show hosts probed guests for intimate details about their sex lives. Violence, too, seemed everywhere, including on video games. A 1997 study indicated that 44 percent of all network programming had violent content, 73 percent of which went unpunished in the storyline. On cable and satellite television, another study concluded, it was worse, with 85 percent of the programming having violent content.

The impact of a climate of sex and violence, some believed, was especially detrimental to children and contributed to increasingly violent incidents involving children, citing tragedies such as the April 1999 shooting at Columbine High School in Colorado. Admitting that these problems existed, as expected, the nation responded differently. Many conservatives wanted tougher laws and more stringent enforcement. Some proposed that juveniles who committed violent crimes be tried as adults. Others believed more controls on guns were the best means to reduce crime and violence. To some, the best way to combat the amount of sex and violence in society was to curb the amount of sex and violence in the media. But efforts to impose censorship usually were rejected by the courts, as in 1997 when the Supreme Court declared unconstitutional an effort to censor the Internet in *Reno v. ACLU*. Rather than governmental censorship, others supported technology allowing individual or parental control within the home and rating systems that indicated the level of sex and violence in songs, music videos, movies, and television shows.

THE CLINTON YEARS

• How did Clinton redefine himself politically during his two terms? What was the effect on his administration of an improving economy? What was the impact of his personal life on his presidency?

• What did the "Contract with America" represent, and in what ways have the decisions of the Rehnquist Court supported its agenda?

• What policies did Clinton promote to expand democracy and the globalization of trade?

As the 1992 presidential campaign began, it appeared that the two candidates epitomized the visions of the country projected by their political parties. Republicans were fond of saying that

---

Violence Against Women Act Law passed by Congress in 1994 that provided federal funds and support to judicial and law-enforcement agencies to prevent violence against women, to aid victims, and to punish those convicted of sexual violence and attacks on women.

Even though Bush, Clinton, and Perot dressed alike in the 1992 presidential debates, many observers believed Clinton emerged the strongest. Although a candidate for the presidency again in 1996, Perot was not invited to participate in the presidential debates between Clinton and Dole—a decision upheld by a federal court that concluded he did not have enough support to be a credible candidate. *Wide World Photos.*

Clinton had opposed the war in Vietnam, avoided military service, used drugs, and was a womanizer. He represented the moral weakness that infected America. George Bush had served gallantly in World War II, had the needed experience and maturity to be president, and was a family man. Clinton ignored most of the attacks on his character and focused on the economy and the need to revitalize the nation. In typical Democratic fashion, he promised welfare reform, support of minority goals, a national healthcare system, and a smaller federal deficit. In February, a new contender entered the battle when **H. Ross Perot** launched his campaign as a third-party candidate. Perot's message was simple: politicians had messed up the nation, and control had to be returned to the people. "It's time to take out the trash and clean up the barn," he told listeners. His antipolitician stance and determination to fix the

economy and end the deficit struck a responsive chord with many Americans.

The campaign culminated in three televised debates among three candidates. An estimated 88 million people watched the third debate. Both Bush and Perot gained in the public opinion polls following the head-to-head encounters, but they could not overtake the front-running Clinton. In a three-way race, Clinton earned 43 percent of the popular vote, compared with Bush's 37.4 percent and Perot's 18.9 percent (see Map 31.1). Clinton swept to victory with 370 votes in the Electoral College, 100 more than he needed to win. Clinton's victory, however, provided no Democratic gains in Congress, while the Republicans gained nine seats in the House of Representatives. In both parties, a record number of women and minorities were elected to Congress.

Clinton and Congress

From the start it was clear that Clinton relished being president and was eager to begin. "I want to get something done," he told a press conference. Setting an ambitious agenda, he dove into producing an economic recovery plan, welfare reform, and national healthcare system. Setting a liberal tone to his administration, he signed into law the Family and Medical Leave Act, which had previously been vetoed by Bush, and asked Congress to lift the ban against homosexuals in the military. Although public opinion polls showed that many Americans tolerated homosexuality as a lifestyle, there seemed much less support for broad antidiscriminatory laws that favored gay rights. The proposal met immediate and irresistible opposition from both political parties, the military, and the public. Faced with such opposition, Clinton retreated and accepted a compromise. The armed forces were not to ask recruits about sexual preferences, and gays and lesbians in the service were expected to refrain from homosexual activities. It was a system that did not work and failed to please either side of the debate. Gay-rights activists continued their efforts to gain antidiscriminatory laws that

H. Ross Perot   Texas billionaire who used large amounts of his own money to run as an Independent candidate for president in 1992 and who created the Reform Party for his 1996 bid for the presidency.

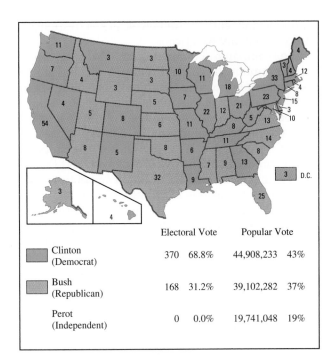

	Electoral Vote		Popular Vote	
Clinton (Democrat)	370	68.8%	44,908,233	43%
Bush (Republican)	168	31.2%	39,102,282	37%
Perot (Independent)	0	0.0%	19,741,048	19%

MAP 31.1 Election of 1992 Bill Clinton received almost 69 percent of the electoral votes—almost double the electoral votes received by George Bush. Nevertheless, Clinton received only 43 percent of the popular vote—the lowest popular vote percentage since Wilson's victory in 1912 over Theodore Roosevelt and William Taft. Third-party candidate Ross Perot drew votes from both Democrats and Republicans in equal numbers and had no impact on the electoral vote.

would protect jobs, provide work-related benefits for partners, and allow same-sex marriages.

On a related issue, Clinton and Congress supported more funds to fight the AIDS epidemic. AIDS, or **acquired immune deficiency syndrome**, began to be noticed in American cities in the early 1980s. Because the disease mostly infected gays and drug users, and seemed confined to the inner cities, official and public response was largely apathetic. Linking AIDS to the "morality battle," some, like Pat Buchanan and Senator Jesse Helms (R.–NC), even suggested that those with the disease were being punished for their unnatural perversions. Responding to conservative pressure, the Reagan administration did little to fight the disease. As the number of victims climbed and the disease spread to the heterosexual populations, the public's fear of AIDS grew rapidly, and in the 1990s federal support became available for education and prevention programs and for research. By the mid-1990s, the disease had claimed more than 280,000 American lives and had infected 20 million

people around the world, especially in Africa. At the same time, significant advances were being made in research toward controlling AIDS. Combinations of drugs seemed to have a positive effect in slowing the advance and death rate of the disease but their experimental nature and high costs severely limited their availability.

The AIDS crisis dramatized Americans' uneven access to healthcare. Studies showed that large segments of the population, especially among the working poor who did not qualify for Medicaid, were virtually unprotected should disease or serious injuries occur. During the campaign, Clinton had made a national healthcare system a priority of his administration. Soon after assuming office, he announced a task force chaired by First Lady Hillary Clinton to draft legislation. After months of testimony, in September 1993, President Clinton asked Congress to write a "new chapter in the American story" and "guarantee every American comprehensive health benefits that can never be taken away." The initial public response to the legislation was favorable, but soon it withered as nearly everyone found some fault in the complex plan. Many congressional Democrats, angry at not being included in the drafting stages, pronounced the plan too complicated. One Democratic Congressional leader dubbed the bill "Godzilla." Republicans attacked the bill with gusto, saying that it affirmed that Clinton was an advocate of big government and big spending. After a year of public and congressional hearings and debate, President Clinton admitted defeat and abandoned the effort.

Clinton also struggled with Congress over his economic programs. Having made the economy the focal point of his campaign, he introduced a number of initiatives to fulfill his campaign promises. One part of the plan was to increase international trade by selectively lowering trading barriers. Continuing initiatives started by Bush, Clinton pushed for congressional approval of the North American Free Trade Agreement (NAFTA) and the General Agreement on Tariffs and Trade (GATT). Both were part of the trend toward globalization and were designed to reduce or eliminate trade barriers and to increase

acquired immune deficiency syndrome Gradual and eventually fatal breakdown of the immune system caused by the virus HIV; it is transmitted by the exchange of body fluids through such means as sexual intercourse or needle sharing.

Efforts to create the North American Free Trade Agreement began under the George Bush administration. But it was the Clinton administration that obtained Senate approval for the agreement over the objections of many within the Democratic Party. *Collection of Janice L. and David J. Frent.*

international trade—NAFTA for the United States, Mexico, and Canada; GATT for most of the world. Opponents claimed that both would harm the American economy by encouraging U.S. companies to relocate their factories to nations with lower environmental, worker, and product standards. Organized labor was especially vocal about the potential loss of jobs. Unable to convince many Democrats to support the bills, Clinton was forced to rely on Republican votes for their passage.

While Republicans supported NAFTA, they staunchly opposed most of Clinton's budget and economic recovery plan. Based on his conviction that reducing the deficit was necessary to end the recession and promote future growth, Clinton's plan raised taxes on the wealthiest Americans, made major spending cuts throughout the budget, and expanded tax credits for low-income families. Republicans denounced the budget as a typical liberal Democratic "tax and spend" measure that would create a "job-killing recession" and put the nation's economy in the "gutter." Six months later, with Vice President Albert Gore casting the tie-breaking vote in the Senate, the Clinton budget passed without the votes of any Republican senators.

The fights over the budget, healthcare, and gays in the military, combined with allegations of wrongdoing in land investments **(Whitewater)** and his womanizing, by the end of 1993 had eroded the president's popularity. Republicans led by Newt Gingrich, a conservative representative from Georgia, seized the opportunity to regain the political initiative and drafted a political agenda called the **"Contract with America."** It called for reduced federal spending (especially for welfare), a balanced budget by 2002, and support for family values. The "revolt of angry white men," as some dubbed the Republican effort, was hugely successful. The 1994 elections elected nine new Republican senators and fifty-two new Republican representatives, establishing a Republican majority in both houses of Congress for the first time in forty years. Gingrich, the new Republican Speaker of the House, predicted that the conservative majority was "going to change the world."

Judicial Restraint and the Rehnquist Court

Part of the Republican hopes for reconstructing government rested with the Supreme Court under Chief Justice William Rehnquist. Since the Nixon administration, Republican presidents had made an effort, not always successful, to appoint Supreme Court justices who rejected the social and political activism of the Warren Court. They believed that, since the New Deal, the Court had worked to strengthen the power of the federal government over areas that had traditionally been reserved for state and local controls. It was a trend that conservatives and most Republicans believed needed to be reversed. What was needed was a Court that practiced **judicial restraint**, restricting federal authority and returning executive power to individuals and

Whitewater   A scandal involving a failed real-estate development in Arkansas in which President Clinton invested.

Contract with America   Pledge taken in 1994 by some three hundred Republican candidates for the House, who promised to reduce the size and scope of the federal government and to balance the federal budget by 2002.

judicial restraint   Refraining from using the courts as a forum for implementing social change but instead deferring to Congress, the president, and the consensus of the people.

state and local governments. Using those criteria, Presidents Reagan and Bush had appointed six justices to the Court, constituting a narrow but not always stable conservative majority.

By 1992, the Rehnquist Court had modified many of the principles behind the Warren Court's decisions that had promoted forced desegregation and affirmative action. During the 1980s, the Reagan and Bush administrations had backed away from supporting court-ordered busing to integrate schools. "We aren't going to compel children who don't want to have an integrated education to have one," said a Reagan Justice Department official. In 1992 the Court agreed in the *DeKalb County, Georgia*, case, stating that busing should not be used to integrate schools segregated by de facto housing patterns.

Similarly, the Reagan and Bush administrations had echoed increasingly popular opposition to **affirmative action**, saying that it undermined freedom of action and merit-based achievement. Reflecting that view, in 1989, in the *Croson* decision, the Supreme Court ruled that state and local government affirmative action guidelines that set aside jobs and contracts for minorities were unconstitutional. Six years later in the *Adarand* decision, the Court reaffirmed its decision and further limited the criteria for providing "set-asides" for minorities. The Court's 1995 decision matched public opinion poll results: 77 percent of those surveyed, including 66 percent of African Americans, believed that affirmative action discriminated against whites. The debate over affirmative action surfaced as a political issue in a heated California election in 1997, when voters approved a measure forbidding any consideration of racial or gender preferences in hiring, college admissions, or contracting. Those critical of affirmative action announced that the Court's decisions and the California vote represented a true step forward in creating a "color-blind society."

The Rehnquist Court also chipped away at the federal government's power to make state and local governments comply with its directives. In several cases throughout the 1990s, the Court upheld state sovereignty by deciding that states and municipalities could resist implementing executive and congressional directives. In *Printz v. the United States* (1997), the Court declared unconstitutional certain provisions in the so-called Brady Bill requiring state police to do a background search of anyone wanting to buy a handgun. Continuing the pattern, in 2000 a divided Court invalidated provisions in the Violence Against Women Act that permitted suits in federal courts by victims of gender-motivated

Those supporting affirmative action were overwhelmed by California voters in 1997, who voted to eliminate consideration of race or gender in state hiring and contracting, and in admission to the state's colleges and universities. *Lou Dematteis/The Image Works.*

crimes. In writing for the majority, Chief Justice Rehnquist announced that distinctions must be made between "what is truly national and what is truly local."

Although it has placed limitations on affirmative action, criminal rights, and federal power, the Court has not delivered the judicial revolution sought by many conservatives and continues to uphold the right to an abortion, sexual harassment laws, and separation of church and state.

---

affirmative action Policy that seeks to redress past discrimination through active measures to ensure equal opportunity, especially in education and employment.

Clinton's Comeback

The 1994 election results were a blow to Democrats and Clinton. Disoriented about which direction to take, Democrats watched as Republicans, led by Gingrich and eager to do battle with Clinton, assumed the political offensive. Assured of their mandate, Republicans saw no need to try and compromise with the White House. Their key strategy was to balance the budget. "You cannot sustain the old welfare state" with a balanced budget, Gingrich proclaimed. Immediately, Republicans began work on an economic plan that would slash government spending on education, welfare, Medicare and Medicaid, and the environment, while reducing taxes—especially for the more affluent. Taking advice from his political adviser, Dick Morris, Clinton began an effort to carve out a centrist position between "slash programs" Republicans and "tax and spend" Democrats. He called himself the "dynamic center."

As Clinton redefined himself and sought to regain political leadership, on April 19, 1995, Americans were stunned by an act of "home-grown terrorism" that destroyed a federal building in Oklahoma City. The explosion killed 168 people, 19 of them children. Many initially concluded that the powerful bomb was the work of Islamic terrorists, but it soon became clear that the terrorist was Timothy McVeigh, an American extremist who believed that the federal government was a threat to the freedom of the American people. His heinous crime seemed to symbolize the depth of division and the dangers of extremism in the nation, and it brought forth cries for national unity. While the disaster did nothing to bridge the gap between the White House and congressional Republicans, it did provide Clinton an opportunity to reassert his presidential leadership and to appeal to moderates to reject extremism. Public opinion polls again gave the president positive numbers.

Establishing a strategy, the "battle of the budget," to defeat Gingrich, Clinton accepted the need to reduce the deficit, reduce taxes, and achieve a balanced budget, but he also insisted that it was necessary to protect spending for education, Medicare, Social Security, and the environment. He also moved to break the image of a Republican monopoly over family-value issues. In a series of "common ground" speeches, Clinton affirmed his commitment to passing anticrime legislation, finding methods to limit sex and violence on television, reforming welfare, and fixing affirmative action.

The battle over welfare reform was one example of Clinton's successful strategy. Critics of the Repub-

On April 19, 1995 a terrorist truck-bomb exploded in front of the federal building in Oklahoma City, killing 168 people. Here, a fireman carries the lifeless body of one of the nineteen children that lost their lives in a day-care center housed in the building. *Charles H. Porter IV/Sygma.*

lican plan questioned whether the private sector would be able to hire all those shaved from the welfare rolls. Conservatives argued that welfare programs created a class of welfare-dependent people, "welfare mothers" with little integrity and no work ethic who represented "spiritual and moral poverty." Clinton and other Democrats denounced such statements as mean-spirited and blind to the reality of those on welfare—especially regarding the number of children on welfare. They argued that to replace relief with jobs, it was vital to increase funds for training, educational programs, and daycare. Clinton's efforts brought success. By the fall when the battle over the budget began in earnest, Clinton had moved to a center position and had been able to portray aspects of the Republican's program as too extreme.

The battle came over the Republicans' 1995–1996 budget, which slashed funds for many social programs. Clinton refused to accept it, sending it back to Congress. Overconfident, Republicans in turn refused to pass a temporary measure to keep the government operating unless the president accepted their budget. Unmoved, and with no operating funds, Clinton shut down all nonessential functions of the government. It was a twenty-one-day stand-off that Clinton won. Most of the nation blamed Gingrich and his followers for the budget impasse and the government shutdown.

Having won the battle of the budget, Clinton solidified his position in the center. He publicly stated that the "era of big government was over" and committed himself to balancing the budget by 2002, reforming welfare, supporting family issues, and fighting crime. As the 1996 presidential election approached, one political observer noted that Clinton had effectively negated the conservative-inspired image of a liberal as someone who would "tax me and send the money to a welfare mother whose son will mug my wife at the shopping mall." In its place, he had tagged Republicans as people who would "take the money away from my parents' Medicare and send it as tax breaks to polluters who downsize me out of work." One disgruntled Republican commented that Clinton had stolen their agenda—all that was left was to claim that Clinton's big spending had "sucked the life out of the economy, eaten up the American workers' pay and given money to the government instead." The problem with that approach was that the economy was beginning to boom and Clinton was boasting that his administration had created 10 million new jobs.

A Revitalized Economy

Almost as Clinton took office, the economy started to climb out of the recession (see Figure 31.4). It would improve for almost a decade before slowing again in 2001, one of the longest periods of sustained economic growth in the nation's history. The revitalized economy was in large part the product of the transition to an information and service economy. American leadership in computer software, microprocessing, and telecommunications industries, as well as growth in the retail markets at home and overseas, sparked the economy boom. Beginning in 1992, the economy grew at about 3 percent per year, the strongest showing since World War II. The rapid growth of technology stocks spurred the stock market to reach new heights. The S&P 500, an index of the five hundred largest American companies, averaged unprecedented increases of 33 per-

cent per year between 1994 and 1998. Stories about individual investors becoming overnight millionaires by investing in Internet-connected stocks, the "dot-coms," convinced many to invest. In 1999 the number of Americans participating in the stock market reached 43 percent, whereas in 1965 only about 10 percent of the public owned stock.

The surging stock market seemed matched by increasing prosperity and wages and falling unemployment and inflation rates. In 1996 national prosperity matched that of the peak year of 1989 and continued upward as take-home pay mushroomed. Average wages for men grew at about 4 percent beginning in 1997, with low-income workers' incomes growing by 6 percent between 1993 and 1998. The median household income in 2000 was $42,148, with Hispanic and black incomes reaching new highs ($33,447 and $30,439). Unemployment shrank throughout the 1990s, declining to only 4.1 percent in 1999, the lowest figure since 1968. Minority unemployment rates also recorded new lows, 7.2 percent for Hispanics and 8.9 percent for African Americans. With more jobs and higher wages, the number of Americans living in poverty (incomes below $17,603 for a family of four) fell to 11.3 percent, the lowest rate since 1979. Hidden within the income gains, however, lurked the reality that the income gap between the poor and the upper class continued to widen, and that middle-class incomes, when adjusted for inflation, stayed the same or declined slightly.

Clinton's Second Term

Despite the improving economy and Clinton's shrewd shift to the center, Republicans were confident that they could regain the presidency. Conservative Republicans dominated the convention and once again declared a "cultural war" and focused on Clinton's moral shortcomings. Robert Dole, the Republican candidate, generally avoided the cultural war issues and stressed the economy and ethics. The moral issues—Paula Jones's accusation of sexual harassment by Clinton when he was governor of Arkansas, and Whitewater—drew headlines but had little impact on the election. Public opinion polls found that 54 percent of those asked thought Clinton was not "honest" or "trustworthy" but few said it would change their vote.

Facing Clinton's popularity, Dole would have to run an energizing campaign if Republicans hoped to win the election. It did not happen. The Dole cam-

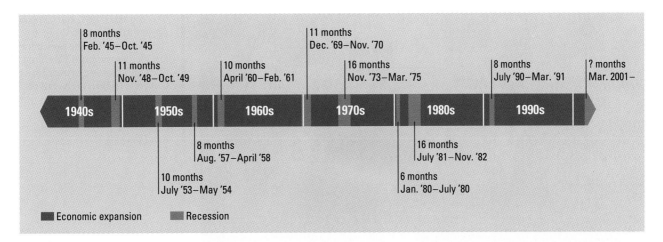

FIGURE 31.4 Expansion and Recession, 1940 to 2001 Economists define a recession as a contraction in the economy that is characterized by rising unemployment and decreasing production. Since the end of World War II, the average recession has lasted about ten months. As this figure shows, the period of economic expansion that ended in March 2001 was the longest period of growth since the end of World War II. *Source: The New York Times, Nov. 27, 2001, p. C-18.*

paign lacked energy from the start, and more than a few Americans regarded him, at 73, as too old for the office. Perot ran again too, but with no more than a shadow of the momentum he had in 1992. In an election marked by low voter turnout, Clinton became the first Democratic president to be re-elected since Franklin D. Roosevelt. He captured 379 electoral votes and 49 percent of the popular vote.

As Clinton started his second term, he enjoyed the highest approval ratings in his presidency at over 60 percent. Believing that the considerable public support reflected satisfaction with the status quo, Clinton set his political goal at finding common ground with the Republican majority. In his State of the Union address, he focused on the economic strength of the nation and projected the first balanced budget in thirty years. The balanced budget, he stated, marked "an end to decades of deficits that have shackled our economy, paralyzed our policies, and held our people back." To set a political agenda and to stifle Republican calls for an immediate tax cut, he said that any surplus should be set aside to ensure the viability of Social Security. "Let's save Social Security first," he told Congress and urged them to support him in promoting a "smart government." Calling for an end to "bickering and extreme partisanship," he asked Congress to approve programs to improve education, daycare, Medicare, and Medicaid. Finding some common ground, Republicans and Democrats managed to approve the budget and pass the Balanced Budget Act and the Taxpayer's Relief Act.

Beyond those agreements, however, few Republicans were interested in collaborating with Clinton or ending bipartisanship. Those most interested in challenging the president soon found a suitable issue, a sex scandal that involved Clinton and a White House intern, **Monica Lewinsky**. Their affair, including meetings in the Oval Office, had occurred between 1995 and 1997. When the allegations arose in January 1998, Clinton denied them as ugly rumors, telling the nation that he had not had "sexual relations with that woman, Miss Lewinsky." His denial drew heavy doses of public and Republican skepticism. Kenneth Starr knew better and had proof. Starr had been appointed by the Justice Department as an independent counsel to investigate the Whitewater matter, but by 1998 his powers had been broadened to include allegations of Clinton's relationship with Lewinsky. Starr's proof included a series of recordings secretly taped by a friend of Lewinsky. In the tapes, the young intern discussed her sexual relations with the president. In August, Clinton admitted he had inappropriate relations with Lewinsky and that he had "misled" the public.

Within weeks, Starr submitted his 445-page report, which identified eleven possible grounds

Monica Lewinsky White House intern who had a two-year sexual affair with President Clinton; Clinton's misleading testimony about the affair contributed to his impeachment.

On August 5, 1997, Bill Clinton signed the Balanced Budget Act. Applauding the president are Vice President Albert Gore (left) and House Speaker Newt Gingrich (right). In the fall of 1998, Clinton announced a budget surplus of $70 billion, the first surplus since 1969. *Ron Edmonds/World Wide.*

for impeaching the president. As momentum for impeachment grew, many of Clinton's supporters argued that the Lewinsky affair was a private matter that in no way obstructed his running of the government. Public opinion polls confirmed that a majority of Americans agreed and continued to give Clinton high marks as president, even as they gave him low marks for integrity. The November congressional elections also indicated that most Americans did not see politics as revolving solely around Clinton. Republicans had projected large gains in Congress because of Clinton's behavior but were disappointed: no Senate seats changed hands and they lost five seats in the House. Undeterred by the polls and election results, and anxious to continue the attack on Clinton, Republicans in the House of Representatives—in a purely partisan vote—agreed in December to vote for impeachment. Believing that while the sexual indiscretions were minor, the lies were major, they cited two offenses, perjury and attempting to obstruct justice. Clinton was the second president to face trial in the Senate, which with a two-thirds vote could remove him from office.

Senate Republicans had a 55 to 45 majority, but it was not be enough to ensure Clinton's removal from office. The trial consumed five weeks and, to many, confirmed the view that Republicans were more interested in destroying Clinton politically than in governing. It was a position echoed by the president in his January 1999 State of the Union message. In it he asked Congress to move beyond politics and address in "a spirit of civility" the real issues facing the nation. With the economy continuing to set records, Clinton called for using the surplus to guarantee the effectiveness of Social Security and Medicare in the future. On February 19, the Senate voted and acquitted. On the issue of perjury, ten Republicans voted with the Democrats to defeat the charge 55 to 44. The vote on obstruction of justice was closer, 50 to 50, but nowhere near a two-thirds majority. Following the Senate's decision, Clinton expressed his sorrow for the burden he had placed on the nation.

With the high drama and low tragedy of impeachment over, politics returned to government spending and tax cuts, how best to "save" Social Security and improve education and the environment, the role of the military in foreign affairs, and jockeying for position in the upcoming 2000 election.

Clinton's Foreign Policy

When Clinton assumed control of America's foreign policy, it still was not clear what general policy would replace that of the Cold War. Americans wanted to maintain status and influence as a superpower but were divided over what situations warranted American attention or intervention. Inexperienced in foreign affairs, Clinton proceeded cautiously and followed the general outline set by President Bush.

Seeking to expand the American economy, Clinton worked to reduce trade barriers and enhance global economic stability. Congress passed the NAFTA and GATT agreements, while Clinton worked to improve trade with China and to encourage Japan to buy more American goods. To promote global economic stability, the Clinton administration provided loans and used the International Monetary Fund to support the economies of several countries, including Mexico, Russia, and Indonesia.

Clinton also continued efforts in the Middle East to ease tensions and resolve disputes between Israel and the Palestinians. The Clinton state department played a role in reaching an accord that established Palestinian self-rule in some Israeli-occupied areas and a treaty in which Jordan and Israel pledged cooperation. Despite the administration's efforts, however, solutions to differences between the PLO and Israel deteriorated as hard-liners on each side opposed peace initiatives and violence escalated.

Clinton's efforts to promote democracy in Haiti proved more successful. A 1991 military coup had ousted the democratically elected government headed by President Jean Bertrand Aristide. When isolation and economic pressure failed to convince the ruling junta, which was brutally repressing its opponents, to restore democracy, Clinton in 1994 obtained UN support for an invasion. Under this threat, the junta opened discussions in October with a delegation led by former president Jimmy Carter. The resulting agreement allowed the junta members to leave the country and Aristide to return. Elections followed, and U.S. troops left after helping Haiti make the transition back to democracy.

Clinton also inherited two additional, and highly controversial, foreign policy commitments from Bush. One was in the East African nation of Somalia and the other dealt with Bosnia, once part of Yugoslavia. United States troops had intervened in Somalia in 1992 as part of a United Nations undertaking to provide humanitarian aid and to keep the peace between factions in a civil war. In October

1993, eighteen American soldiers were ambushed and killed. Seeing little direct American interest in Somalia and responding to public outrage and congressional pressure, Clinton withdrew American forces in April 1994.

In Bosnia, Clinton faced a similar problem: how to justify and use American forces in a region where few Americans believed the United States had a direct interest. During the 1992 campaign, Clinton had chided Bush for not promoting peace in Bosnia more assertively. Once in office, however, he too became cautious and moved slowly in supporting UN peacekeeping and relief efforts. As the carnage increased, however, the Clinton administration agreed to allow American forces to participate in a UN campaign to establish and protect "safe areas" for refugees displaced by the fighting. In the fall of 1995, the United States sponsored talks between the warring elements—the Serbs, the Muslim Bosnians, and the Croats. The resulting **Dayton Agreement** partitioned the country into a Bosnian-Croat federation and Serbia, and called for UN forces, including twenty thousand Americans, to police the peace. By the summer of 1996, when most American forces were withdrawn, much had been accomplished to rebuild the shattered region. Although Clinton assured Americans that efforts in Bosnia had been successful, in December 1997 he announced that a continued American presence in that nation was necessary to continue with the task of nation building.

Clinton's commitment to peace in the Balkans was soon tested again. President Slobodan Milosevic of Serbia was intent on crushing dissent and insurgent forces in the province of Kosovo. The conflict that had erupted in 1998 involved ancient hostilities between Serbian Orthodox Christians and Muslim ethnic Albanians, who made up 90 percent of the province's population. When the Kosovo Liberation Army (KLA) began to fight for independence in 1998, Milosevic had responded with force—targeting both members of the KLA and the Muslim population. As the bloodshed increased, NATO leaders sought a diplomatic solution before it ignited another war in the Balkans. When negotiations with

---

Dayton Agreement   Agreement signed in Dayton, Ohio, in November 1995 by the three rival ethnic groups in Bosnia, which pledged to end the four-year-old civil war there.

American forces play a key role in the United Nations and NATO peacekeeping effort in Bosnia and Kosovo. In this picture, an American patrol greets Albanian children from a Kosovo village. *Andrew Testa.*

Milosevic proved unsuccessful, Secretary of State Madeleine Albright called for "humanitarian intervention" and the establishment of autonomy for Kosovo within Serbia. Unwilling to use ground forces, NATO began a bombing campaign in March 1999, with American air power providing the bulk of planes and bombs. The goal, the president announced, was to halt Serbian aggression.

Milosevic responded by sending more troops into Kosovo and stepping up his program of **"ethnic cleansing."** As the bombing intensified and expanded to include the Serbian capital of Belgrade, Milosevic agreed to withdraw his troops, recognize Kosovo's autonomy, and allow United Nations peacekeeping forces into the area to insure the peace. Clinton called it "a victory for a safer world, for our democratic values, and a stronger America." Later, investigations estimated that more than ten thousand ethnic Albanian civilians had been killed in ethnic cleansing since January 1998, and an international war crimes tribunal has charged Milosevic with crimes against humanity. Another consequence of the conflict was that in 2000 Milosevic was overthrown in a bloodless coup.

Also contributing to a safer world were American efforts to maintain sanctions against Iraq. In January 1998, Saddam Hussein refused to allow United Nation's inspection teams access to several sites where, some suspected, he was manufacturing or stockpiling biological and chemical weapons. Clinton stated that the United States was willing to attack Iraq to force compliance with the United Nations' mandate to eliminate all such weapons. As the United States moved military units into the Gulf region, one navy pilot was heard to say: "I don't think you can find a more powerful tool to make a statement than to park an airplane twenty miles off a guy's beach." No direct attack took place, but the Clinton administration worked with Britain and other allies to contain Hussein by maintaining the UN-sanctioned economic boycotts and patroling the skies over Iraq.

By 1999, Clinton believed he had moved well along the path of fulfilling his broad foreign policy goals of promoting peace, democracy, and economic globalization. In Haiti, Bosnia, and Kosovo, American

---

ethnic cleansing   An effort to eradicate an ethnic or religious group from a country or region, often through mass killings.

actions had helped establish democracy and restore stability. In the economic arena, Clinton pointed to NAFTA, improved trade with China and Japan, and the more than 270 trade agreements he had signed that had lowered trade barriers around the globe.

THE TESTING OF PRESIDENT BUSH

- To what degree did Bush and Gore represent the political centers of their respective parties? How did their solutions to America's problems differ?
- What were Democratic criticisms of President Bush's domestic and foreign policies?
- How did the events of September 11, 2001, affect politics, the public, and foreign policy?

Americans welcomed the twenty-first century with celebrations and optimism. The rumors of disaster that were to accompany the New Year had not materialized. The much discussed **Y2K** computer problem failed to cause any slowdown in the whirl of worldwide hard drives and Internet connections. With the economy growing and providing more jobs and prosperity, President Clinton was more popular than ever with a 63 percent approval rating in the polls. Thus it was an upbeat president who, on January 27, 2000, presented his State of the Union address: "We have restored the vital center, replacing outdated ideologies with a new vision anchored in basic enduring values: opportunity for all, responsibility from all, and a community for all Americans. . . . We begin the new century with over 20 million new jobs. The fastest economic growth in more than 30 years; the lowest unemployment rates in 30 years; the lowest poverty rates in 20 years; the lowest African-American and Hispanic unemployment rates on record. . . ." He called for improving Social Security, healthcare, and the quality of education. It seemed an agenda that Vice President Al Gore could expand on in his campaign for the presidency. Gore occupied the Democratic center, seeing a major role for government in solving national problems and advocating selected tax cuts.

The 2000 Election

Normally under such circumstances, Republicans would not have great expectations of successfully challenging the vice president. But 2000 was hardly an ordinary year, and many Republicans believed that Gore was vulnerable exactly *because* he was the vice president. Republicans were encouraged by several polls in mid-1999: as many as 52 percent of those asked said that they would be less likely to vote for Gore if Clinton actively campaigned for him. It appeared that Clinton was a liability for Gore, and Republicans focused their campaign not only on cutting taxes and the dangers of big-government, "tax-and-spend" Democrats, but on the Clinton-Gore connection and the need to restore integrity to the White House.

Leading the Republican hopefuls was George W. Bush, governor of Texas and son of the former president. Others challenged Bush, most importantly Senator John McCain from Arizona, but support from party regulars and money from a massive campaign fund allowed Bush to outdistance his rivals and win the nomination. To quiet those who thought he lacked enough national experience, especially in foreign policy, he selected a veteran Republican statesman, Dick Cheney, as his vice president. Some joked that Cheney would be the de facto president while Bush officiated over ceremonies and represented America at state funerals.

Running for the presidency, Bush announced a policy of "compassionate conservatism" that avoided the militancy of the culture war and moved away from opposing most government programs. Occupying the Republican center, he focused his efforts on suggesting how private initiatives could improve education, Social Security, and healthcare. He gave only scant attention to past controversial issues like abortion and prayer in schools. At the heart of this campaign was a promise to reduce taxes and restore dignity to the White House.

The campaign generated a lot of spending and almost no heated rhetoric or sharp debates between the two contenders. On the issues, their differences were largely matters of "how to," reflecting party ideologies. To improve education, Bush supported state initiatives and more stringent testing, whereas Gore wanted federal funds to hire more teachers and repair school facilities. Gore suggested using other government funds to support the Social Security

---

Y2K Term applied to a projected global computer problem when calendar software had to adjust to the year 2000; many people feared that computers would not be able to distinguish between 1900 and 2000.

The winner of the 2000 presidential election was determined by a disputed vote count in Florida that was later upheld by the Supreme Court. As the justices considered their decision, supporters of Gore and Bush confronted each other outside of the Supreme Court building. *Douglas Graham/Corbis Sygma.*

trust fund, whereas Bush considered allowing people to use part of their tax payments to invest in private retirement accounts. On how to spend the budget surplus, Bush advocated a tax cut to give money back to the people. Gore called the tax cut dangerous and unfair—it favored the rich, he insisted—and said he would use the surplus to reduce the national debt and fund government programs. Even the three televised debates failed to generate much excitement or change people's minds. When official campaigning began in August, polls had the candidates tied, and they stayed tied throughout the campaign, including on election day.

Nationally, the two candidates ran a dead heat, but the geography of support told a different story—of a confrontation between two nations. Bush ran strong in the less-populated states compared with Gore's strength in urban areas (he received over 70 percent of the vote in large metropolitan areas) and in the Northeast and Pacific Coast. Bush was particularly popular with white males, who voted for him 5 to 3. Gore, as expected, did exceedingly well among minorities, with Bush receiving fewer African-American votes than any Republican candidate since 1960. On election day Gore received a minuscule majority of votes, half a million more out of 10.5 million votes cast, but Bush won the Electoral College vote with 271 votes to 267, one vote more than necessary to win (see Map 31.2).

Before the final votes were in, the nation's attention was centered on the results in Florida, whose 25 electoral votes gave Bush the victory. Because of

Bush's narrow margin of less than a thousand votes, Florida state law required a recount. As the recount proceeded, Gore supporters alleged that voting irregularities in several counties needed to be reviewed and thought a hand count would be more accurate than the current machine count. They asked the Florida Supreme Court to set aside certification of the vote until hand counts were completed in several largely Democratic counties. The Court agreed to give those doing the hand count extra time to complete the slower process. Bush supporters protested that Gore was trying to "steal" the election by including in the count votes that had not been clearly marked or punched through the ballot. To halt the hand recount and certify existing totals that made Bush the victor, Bush supporters filed suit in federal court. On December 4, a month after the election, the federal district court set aside the Florida Supreme Court's decision—the existing count would be certified. But the legal struggle was not finished. There was the question of which court—the federal district court or the Florida Supreme Court—should decide the issue. The question of jurisdiction was heard by a special session of the Supreme Court. On December 4, the justices decided, 5 to 4, in favor of accepting the existing count and allowing Florida officials to certify that Bush had won Florida's electoral votes and the presidential election. Gore conceded and an hour later President-elect Bush stated, "Whether you voted for me or not, I will do my best to serve your interest, and I will work to earn your respect."

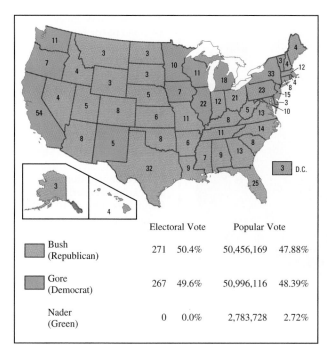

		Electoral Vote		Popular Vote	
▨	Bush (Republican)	271	50.4%	50,456,169	47.88%
▨	Gore (Democrat)	267	49.6%	50,996,116	48.39%
	Nader (Green)	0	0.0%	2,783,728	2.72%

MAP 31.2 Election of 2000 Democratic candidate Al Gore won the popular vote, but George W. Bush succeeded in gaining electoral victory by four votes. Among white males, Bush ran extremely well, while Gore won a majority of minority and women voters. Ralph Nader's Green Party won less than 3 percent of the national vote, but his votes in Florida may have detracted from the Gore tally, helping Bush win the critical electoral votes.

Establishing the Bush Agenda

George Walker Bush entered the presidency with the flimsiest national support, but as determined to implement his campaign promises as if he had received a clear mandate from the voters. In establishing his program, Bush expected to be able to work with a Republican majority in the House of Representatives and a 50-50 tie in the Senate (which, if necessary, could be broken by the vote of the vice president). Observing that Bush's administration was "more Reaganite than the Reagan administration," conservatives were anxious to shape the nation's new path. Bush made his first major address to Congress in February, setting out his legislative agenda and philosophy of government. "Government has a role and an important one," he stated. "Yet, too much government crowds out initiative and hard work, private charity and the private economy. . . . Our new governing vision says

that government should be active, but limited; engaged, but not overbearing." Among his highest priorities were tax cuts and education reform, two issues that had some degree of bipartisan support. Bush's tax cut called for reducing the federal government's revenue by $1.60 trillion over a six-year period. Such a reduction, most Republicans cheerfully reasoned, would limit government spending, especially for social programs.

Democrats voiced a willingness to work with the president on taxes, but most rejected the size of his projected tax cut. It was too large and favored the rich, they argued. But, finding it difficult to oppose a tax cut in a period of government surplus, several Democrats voted with the Republicans to approve a slightly smaller, $1.35 trillion, tax cut in June. Bush had succeeded in making good on one of his key campaign promises. Next, Bush pushed forward on his education bill. Many Republicans sought a major shake-up in the structure of education, supporting a system that provided a means for people to take their children out of "failing" public schools and enroll them in private and alternative schools, with some form of financial support from local, state, or federal educations funds. Democrats wanted more federal spending for additional teachers and improved schools. As the debate on education intensified, in June, Vermont senator James Jeffords shocked and angered his party by leaving the Republican fold and becoming an Independent. His switch gave the Democrats a one-vote majority in the Senate and, equally important, leadership over the Senate and all its committees.

Congressional gridlock followed. The Republican House would pass a bill along the lines that Bush requested, and the Democratic Senate would reject it and draft an alternative bill that Bush and the House generally opposed. Caught in the gridlock were the education reform package, an energy bill, and healthcare programs. In late June, public opinion polls indicated that Bush's popularity had fallen to around 50 percent, the lowest rating for a president in five years. Still, when in August President Bush evaluated his first six months in office, he was pleased with his performance. Saying that governmental "deadlock and drift" was ending, he gave himself and his staff an A. Democrats disagreed and provided different grades, an A for public statements but a D for proposed programs. As for Bush's support for bipartisanship, a Democratic senator scoffed, "He says, 'When you agree with me, you're bipartisan, but if you disagree with me you're partisan.'"

When George W. Bush assumed the presidency in 2001, many believed that domestic policy would dominate the agenda, but national security issues soon became the overriding priority. Among those most important in shaping U.S. national security policy are shown here with the president: Secretary of State Colin Powell, Secretary of Defense Donald Rumsfeld, and National Security Adviser Condoleezza Rice. *AP Photo/ J. Scott Applewhite.*

To many observers, most Democrats, and several heads of state, that statement also seemed to match the Bush administration's approach to foreign policy—telling countries they must live by American terms if they want U.S. support. The White House appeared too willing to back away from past agreements and treaty obligations, including efforts to fight global warming. In addition, critics argued that the president's determination to push forward with a missile defense system that violated a 1972 antiballistic missile pact with the Soviet Union might destabilize the international system and start a new arms race with Russia and China. Democratic leader Richard Gephardt warned that Bush's "go it alone policy" undermined national security. Administration officials denied the charges and said that the administration was practicing "a la carte multilateralism" sensitive to American interests. At the same time, some insiders spoke about divisions within the administration between such individuals as Secretary of State **Colin Powell**, who favored a more international role for the United States, and National Security Adviser Condoleezza Rice and Secretary of Defense Donald Rumsfeld, who preferred a more limited role for the United States in world affairs. It was, they thought, a struggle that Powell seemed to be losing.

Democrats were convinced that when Congress returned from its Labor Day recess and President Bush from his "working vacation" at his ranch in Texas, Capitol Hill would see little bipartisanship and a lot of heated debate about the economy and proposed legislation. The economy had once again cooled down, with the stock market experiencing huge declines and with companies announcing staggering layoffs. Democrats said the Bush tax cut had created an "alarming fiscal crisis" that would leave the government with too little revenue to fund needed programs. They attacked the administration for its willingness to tap into Social Security reserves to fund government programs—after both parties had solemnly vowed not to touch them. Republicans, in turn, blamed Democratic spending for the slump and stated that they would use the Social Security fund "only if the government was in a recession or at war."

An Assault Against a Nation

It was an event that no one thought possible. On the morning of September 11, 2001, the world changed for the United States as four hijacked airplanes became flying bombs aimed at symbols of American financial and military power. At 8:48 A.M., a group of five terrorists led by Mohammed Atta crashed American Airlines Flight 11 into the North Tower of the World Trade Center. As New York fire and police departments responded to the disaster, a

Colin Powell   First African American to hold the position of secretary of state; a career army officer, Powell served as national security adviser to President Reagan and chairman of the Joint Chiefs of Staff under the first President Bush.

second airliner, United Airlines Flight 175 struck the South Tower of the WTC at 9:06. With the second plane, Americans across the nation became aware that this was not an accident but a terrorist attack on the United States. The extent of the planned attack was further dramatized forty minutes later when a third hijacked plane, American Airlines Flight 77, slammed into the Pentagon, just outside Washington, at 9:45. A fourth plane, United Airlines Flight 93, was seized by four hijackers, altered course toward the nation's capital, and crashed in a field southeast of Pittsburgh, Pennsylvania. On that flight, passengers, having learned about the three other hijackings by cell phone, attempted to regain control of the plane—the struggle resulted in the crash of the plane short of its targeted destination.

In New York City the tragedy was soon magnified when the twin towers of the WTC, the tallest structures in the city, collapsed engulfing and killing thousands, including many of the firefighters and policemen who had rushed to the scene and had entered the towers to provide help. The first official casualty was Father Mychal Judge, the fire department chaplain who had accompanied the firefighters into "Ground Zero" (see Individual Choices, page 980). Earlier at morning prayer, he had called for "peace and joy in our city." He would be among the nearly three thousand people who died in the airliners, at the Pentagon, and in the WTC. On that morning, the United States had entered a new kind of war.

President Bush was in Florida promoting his education program when he heard the reports at 9:00. He was immediately whisked away on Air Force One to destinations in Louisiana and Nebraska before returning to Washington. Speaking to a stunned and concerned nation, he declared, "Freedom itself was attacked this morning by a faceless coward." America had witnessed "evil, the very worst of human nature." He vowed to defend freedom and to track down those responsible and bring them to justice. On the Capitol steps, congressional leaders, back after being evacuated from the city, promised support for the president and spontaneously sang a chorus of "God Bless America." Patriotism and support for the president swept across the country, American flags flew from homes and car antennas, and President Bush's approval rating soared to over 86 percent.

Among Democrats and Republicans, efforts were made to minimize political rhetoric and support the president. The battles over education, Social Security, missile defense, and the budget were set aside.

The September 11, 2001 attack on the World Trade Center by terrorists who hijacked two civilian airliners and used them as missiles against the twin towers, left the nation stunned, angry, and determined to bring those who had orchestrated the attack to justice. *Robert Clark/Aurora.*

"Everything has changed," stated the Democratic chair of the Senate budget committee. "We've been attacked." "The political war will cease," said Democrat John Breaux of Louisiana. "The war we have now is against terrorism. And that's going to be the No. 1, 2, and 3 priority for the rest of the year." Both parties stopped their direct mail campaign efforts. Forgetting their pledges not to tap into Social Security surpluses to fund government spending, Congress quickly appropriated $40 billion for disaster relief and support for the effort to fight terrorism.

Within days, the horrifying event had been linked to Al-Qaeda, a worldwide terrorist organization led by **Osama bin Laden**. The son of a wealthy

Osama bin Laden A military Muslim fundamentalist, whose terrorist organization, Al-Qaeda, has organized terrorist attacks on Americans, including those against the American embassies in Kenya and Tanzania in 1998.

Saudi Arabian family, bin Laden had fought against Soviet forces in Afghanistan, but after the Gulf War, angered by American forces remaining in his homeland, he dedicated himself to conducting a war of terror against the United States. At the root of his decision was his conversion to Muslim fundamentalism and his belief that U.S. forces in Saudi Arabia defiled the holy ground of Islam. By the early 1990s he and Al-Qaeda were linked to several terrorist attacks on the United States, including the 1993 attempt to car-bomb the World Trade Center, in which the terrorists were caught and eventually sentenced (October 2001) to life in prison. Three years later, his organization was involved in a truck-bombing of an apartment complex in Saudi Arabia that housed American servicemen and their families. Nineteen Americans had died in the explosion, a grievous loss, but even worse casualties were suffered when Al-Qaeda terrorists attacked the American embassies in Kenya and Tanzania in August 1998, killing 224 and wounding over 5,000. Following that attack, President Clinton ordered missile strikes against bin Laden and his training camps in Afghanistan. The attacks destroyed the camps but did not deter bin Laden or terrorism. Threats and rumors of schemes to attack American targets continued, and in October 2000 those associated with bin Laden damaged the American destroyer U.S.S. *Cole* while it was at anchor in a Yemen port. Seventeen sailors died and over thirty were injured. Unknown to American intelligence in 1999, a group of terrorists in Germany led by Atta were already formulating their plan to attack the United States. For more than a year, the nineteen known terrorists who hijacked the planes on September 11 lived openly in the United States, several of them taking lessons at U.S. flight schools to become airline pilots.

As the magnitude of the September 11 attacks unfolded, rumors and fears of further terrorism became part of American life. Warnings abounded from official sources that Americans should expect further terrorist attacks. Twice crop-dusters were grounded following rumors of a plot to use chemical and biological weapons sprayed from such planes. It seemed to many that terrorism had destroyed the American sense of safety and left in its place feelings of fear and vulnerability. Reflecting the fear of enemies within, the sales of guns, gas masks, and biological warfare detection kits increased. Attacks and threats against Arab Americans and those who looked Middle Eastern occurred, and the Justice Department initially

arrested over 1,200 immigrants, mostly from Arab nations.

Responding to the attacks, President Bush sought global support of American antiterrorism efforts. Most nations agreed to help in a variety of forms. For the first time in its history, NATO invoked Article 5, which stated that the attack against the United States was an attack against all members of the alliance. Inside the White House, planning had started on how best to fight global terrorism. Some in the administration called for an immediate military response against bin Laden and other supporters of terrorism throughout the Middle East, especially Iraq. Secretary of State Powell led another faction, urging the president to move more slowly and build an international coalition based on evidence of bin Laden's role in the September 11 attacks. "We can't solve everything with one blow," stated a White House supporter of Powell's position.

President Bush launched his own war, calling the terrorists "evildoers" and rallying support for a "crusade." He wanted Osama bin Laden and his associates brought in "dead or alive." At the same time, he reached out to over eighty nations talking personally to key leaders, forming a multitiered coalition to combat terrorism in general and bin Laden in particular. The first step was to convince as many foreign governments as possible to denounce terrorism and promise to root out terrorists and their support systems within their own countries. This basic tier of support included sharing intelligence, freezing bank accounts and other financial assets associated with terrorist groups, and accepting the possibility of American military retaliation. On a higher level, negotiations were started with other nations to allow the U.S. military to use or fly over their territories should force be necessary against bin Laden's resources and the **Taliban** government that sheltered him. Critical to this effort was convincing the governments of Pakistan, Tajikistan, and Uzbekistan to allow American forces to use bases in their nations for attacks against targets in Afghanistan. The topmost tier of the coalition effort was to find allies to join with the United States in any military actions against Afghanistan and Al-Qaeda.

Taliban An organization of Muslim fundamentalists that gained control over Afghanistan after the Soviets withdrew and established a strict Islamic government.

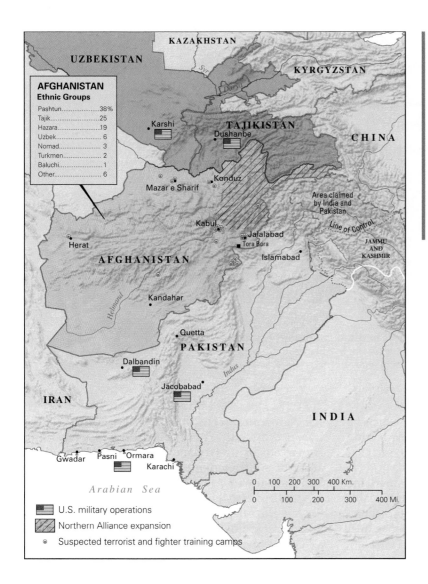

MAP 31.3 Afghanistan Following the terrorist attacks on American targets in September 2001, the Bush administration linked the terrorist organization Al-Qaeda to the attacks. It then asked the Taliban government of Afghanistan to take action against the Al-Qaeda, which used Afghanistan as a base of operations. When Taliban leaders refused to turn over the leaders of the Al-Qaeda, particularly Osama bin Laden, the United States and its allies joined with anti-Taliban forces in military action in Afghanistan. By the end of December 2001, the Taliban government and Al-Qaeda forces had collapsed, although leaders of both organizations eluded capture.

The coalition-building effort was extremely successful. Nearly every nation approached agreed to cooperate at the first level, including most Arab nations, Iran, and China. Building the second tier also produced positive results, especially as Pakistan, Tajikistan, and Uzbekistan agreed to allow American forces to use their territory for military operations (see Map 31.3). As expected, fewer nations agreed to participate in the military dimension of the war on terrorism. Without hesitation, Britain's prime minister Tony Blair offered direct military support to attack terrorist targets, noting that more than two hundred British citizens were killed in the attack on the World Trade Center. France, Germany, Australia, and Canada also agreed to supply some type of military support. As the coalition took shape, President Bush called up reserve and National Guard units and deployed military forces into positions around Afghanistan. On October 7, the United States and Britain launched bombing and missile attacks on selected targets in Afghanistan. Among those taking part in the attacks were women fighter pilots. Speaking about her mission that destroyed two anti-aircraft batteries, one naval aviator stated, "I was smiling . . . I had done my thing for the country." Along with the air bombardment, American Special Forces units were providing support to the anti-Taliban groups within Afghanistan, especially the Northern Alliance. The Northern Alliance held a section of northeast Afghanistan and provided the best internal military opposition to the Taliban government. In response to the air attacks,

In Operation Enduring Freedom, American forces joined with anti-Taliban forces in Afghanistan in attacking government and Al-Qaeda forces. In this picture, American Special Forces personnel work with members of the Northern Alliance in directing operations north of the capital city of Kabul. *Sigma/Corbis.*

Osama bin Laden released a videotape in which he praised the men who attacked the WTC as having the "Grace and gratitude of God" and promised that "America would not live in peace."

As the assault commenced, Bush reassured the world that this was not an attack on Islam but an attack on terrorists and those who harbored them. He told the American people that the war against terrorism, now called Operation Enduring Freedom, would be lengthy, multifaceted, and not limited to actions in Afghanistan. He also warned there could be more acts of terrorism against the United States and appointed Tom Ridge, the governor of Pennsylvania, to assume the new post of Director of Homeland Security. Ridge's job was to coordinate and direct various government agencies in efforts to prevent further acts of terrorism against the United States. The administration's efforts to deter and apprehend terrorists were improved on October 26, 2001, when Congress approved the **USA Patriot Act**. It provided law enforcement agencies wider discretion in dealing with those suspected of terrorism. It loosened restrictions on wiretaps, monitoring the Internet, and searches. It also allowed the attorney general's office to detain and deport noncitizens thought to be a security risk. The passage of the act and the decision to try noncitizens accused of terrorism in military courts caused some to protest that

the new rules were threats to civil liberties and unconstitutional. They pointed to cases of Arab Americans being targeted because of public anxiety and not solid evidence. In Houston, for example, two Palestinian Americans were detained for two months because their passports looked suspicious— they were released after tests showed that their passports were valid. Most Americans, however, agreed with the government and supported the new, tougher anti-terrorism measures.

Within days of the September 11, fears focused on biological terrorism following a diagnosis of **anthrax**. The first case occurred in Florida, when a media company that published tabloids received a letter, around September 17, that was tainted with anthrax spores. One person died and more were infected and exposed. Concern increased on October 12 when

USA Patriot Act Law passed by Congress in 2001 that reduced constraints on the Justice Department and other law enforcement agencies dealing with individuals with suspected links to terrorism.

anthrax An infectious disease usually associated with livestock but that can be deadly to humans; the disease can be contracted through touching or breathing anthrax spores.

another case was detected at NBC news in New York and an anthrax-laced letter was received in Senator Tom Daschle's office. Fears grew as more and more people showed signs of anthrax infection. Finally, on October 25, after weeks of downplaying the threat, Ridge announced that the nature of the anthrax was more deadly and more easily spread than previously thought. Raising concerns even higher, he warned that "a shadow enemy . . . people who have no regard for human life" were using anthrax was a weapon. By the end of October, three people had died of exposure to anthrax, thirteen others had been infected, and twenty-eight had tested positive for exposure. At the time, many people believed bin Laden was behind the anthrax attack, but investigators later concluded that it was more probably a case of domestic terrorism.

While the search for the source of the anthrax accomplished little, the battle for Afghanistan was producing very positive results. Coordinated air and ground attacks resulted in the capture of the major cities of Mazar-i-Sharif and Kabul by mid-November, and the disintegration of the Taliban government. By December 14, Kandahar surrendered to Alliance forces, and the training camps and bases of Al-Qaeda in the Tora Bora mountains were under relentless attack (see Map 31.3). By early January 2002, a new interim government for Afghanistan was established, and hundreds of Taliban and Al-Qaeda fighters had been captured. However, the whereabouts of Osama bin Laden remained unknown, with some speculating that he had successfully fled Afghanistan.

Despite the success in Afghanistan, President Bush reminded Americans that the war against terrorism had no quick ending and the search for Osama bin Laden, Al-Qaeda and other terrorist organizations would continue. In January, Bush dispatched American troops as advisers to the Philippines to help local forces destroy a terrorist rebel group and asked Congress to approve over $20 billion in additional spending for the military.

Congressional approval, though, appears unlikely as, by January 2002, domestic politics returned to normal. During the period between September and January, partisan politics had been tabled and Republican and Democratic leadership had taken special efforts to support the war effort and applaud each other. Showing bipartisanship, in December supporters of Bush's education proposal had worked with Senator Ted Kennedy (D.–MA) and other Democrats to fashion an education bill that Congress readily enacted. It instituted a series of competency tests for grades 1 through 8 and held

schools accountable for what their students learned or failed to learn. It also provided more funding to teachers and schools. Gone from the bill was the school voucher concept supported by many conservative Republicans. But soon after the harmonious passage of the education act, it became clear that in domestic politics things were returning to normal. Democrats began to attack Bush and Republicans for the once-again slowing economy that most agreed had slid into a recession.

The economy had showed signs of weakness before Bush assumed office as the stock market plummeted, led by heavy losses in high-tech stocks on the Nasdaq, and as sales of computer, Internet, and communications products fell, leading to widespread layoffs. The abrupt slowdown in the service and technological sectors, combined with higher oil prices, produced steep declines in the stock market and huge corporate losses. To combat the faltering economy, the Federal Reserve trimmed interest rates and Bush argued for his tax cut—both designed to put money into the hands of consumers. Before the effects of either remedy could be determined, September 11 occurred and consumers stopped buying. The economy declined and more companies laid off more employees: about a million workers lost their jobs in the last four months of 2001. Many of those now looking for work were college graduates and under 30, and 30 percent had worked for technology companies.

The budget surplus disappeared with the contracting economy and increased spending associated with the war on terrorism. Deficit spending and the use of Social Security revenues to pay for government programs resumed. Democrats blamed Bush's handling of the economy and his tax cut for deepening the recession. Democratic Senate Majority Leader Tom Daschle said it was a case of fiscal irresponsibility. Republicans responded that further tax cuts would help restore the economy and that they were more fiscally responsible than the tax-and-spend Democrats. Speaking to a crowd in California, President Bush sounded like his father in promising no new taxes: "Not over my dead body will they raise your taxes." Some chuckled about the president's verbal misstatement, but no one misunderstood what he meant. President Bush further clarified the new priorities of his administration in his January 2002 State of the Union address. Security was now the administration's priority: "America is no longer protected by vast oceans. We are protected from attack only by vigorous action abroad and increased vigilance at home."

Bush vowed that the United States would continue the war on terrorism, saying that the world was still full of "dangerous killers . . . set to go off without warning." Focusing on what he termed an "axis of evil," he referred to Iraq, Iran, and North Korea as nations that represented threats to world peace. To protect the nation, he asked for large increases in security spending for the military and for homeland defense. He admitted that such spending would result in a deficit, but maintained that the price of freedom was "never too high." Linking security to a sound economy, Bush said, "we'll prevail in the war, and we will defeat this recession. The way out of this recession, the way to create jobs, is to grow the economy by encouraging investment in factories and equipment, and by speeding up tax relief so people have more money to spend." Beyond asking Congress to pass additional tax cuts, there was little emphasis—only a fraction of the speech— on other domestic programs. "We have clear priorities," he told Americans. "History has called

America . . . to action, and it is both our responsibility and our privilege to fight freedom's fight."

As Americans entered the new millennium, they faced the future and drew on their understanding of the past. Much had changed: The Cold War was over, but a new and different type of war had begun, a war on terrorism. The economy was changing from its old national, industrial base to a more global, postindustrial one, but every day millions of Americans went to work and returned to their homes as usual. Society was becoming more and more diverse, but most Americans still had faith in assimilation and the future. Following September 11, 2001, many Americans felt less safe and secure, but nearly all Americans agreed not to let the catastrophic events of that day shape their lives and actions. The next decade would see more change and unforeseen challenges, and would pit new visions against new realities—and history will continue to provide continuity for the further making of America.

INDIVIDUAL VOICES

Examining a Primary Source

President George W. Bush Consoles a Nation

History is full of dates, but only a few have special meaning to a whole society. Such days usually are connected with a great tragedy or a thrilling triumph. September 11, 2001, will probably be one of those dates in American history— one that people will remember without the prompting of a history book. To commemorate that tragic day, on September 14 President George W. Bush spoke at the National Cathedral in Washington, D.C., joining millions of others who were observing a National Day of Prayer and Remembrance in churches, synagogues, mosques, and other places of worship all across the United States. In his remarks, he not only lamented a nation's sorrow, but also stated a nation's determination to exact justice on those who had attacked the soul of America.

On Tuesday, our country was attacked with deliberate and massive cruelty. We have seen the images of fire and ashes, and bent steel.

Now come the names, the list of casualties we are only beginning to read. They are the names of men and women who began their day at a desk or in an

airport, busy with life. They are the names of people who faced death, and in their last moments called home to say, be brave, and I love you. . . .

Just three days removed from these events, Americans do not yet have the distance of history. But our responsibility to history is already clear: to answer these attacks and rid the world of evil.

War has been waged against us by stealth and deceit and murder. This nation is peaceful, but fierce when stirred to anger. This conflict was begun on the timing and terms of others. It will end in a way, and at an hour, of our choosing. . . . ●

It is said that adversity introduces us to ourselves. This is true of a nation as well. In this trial, we have been reminded, and the world has seen, that our fellow Americans are generous and kind, resourceful and brave. We see our national character in rescuers working past exhaustion; in long lines of blood donors; in thousands of citizens who have asked to work and serve in any way possible.

And we have seen our national character in eloquent acts of sacrifice. Inside the World Trade Center, one man who could have saved himself stayed until the end at the side of his quadriplegic friend. A beloved priest died giving the last rites to a firefighter. Two office workers, finding a disabled stranger, carried her down sixty-eight floors to safety. . . . ●

In these acts, and in many others, Americans showed a deep commitment to one another, and an abiding love for our country. Today, we feel what Franklin Roosevelt called the warm courage of national unity. . . .

It has joined together political parties in both houses of Congress. It is evident in services of prayer and candlelight vigils, and American flags, which are displayed in pride, and wave in defiance. ●

Our unity is a kinship of grief, and a steadfast resolve to prevail against our enemies. . . .

America is a nation full of good fortune, with so much to be grateful for. But we are not spared from suffering. In every generation, the world has produced enemies of human freedom. They have attacked America, because we are freedom's home and defender. And the commitment of our fathers is now the calling of our time. . . . ●

● How does President Bush characterize the perpetrators of the September 11 attacks?

● If Father Mychal Judge had been able to address the crowd gathered in the cathedral, how might his speech have differed from the president's?

● How does President Bush want the American people to respond to the attacks?

● Who, according to President Bush, are the victims of the terrorist attacks?

SUMMARY

James Carville said during the 1992 election that the central issue was the economy, and he was right. Throughout the 1990s it was the economy that shaped political and social issues. At the beginning of the decade, a shifting and slowing economy provided new opportunities and old challenges; it underlined divisions within the nation, contributing to what some called an hourglass-shaped society. Those at the top of society continued to prosper while others, including the middle class, worried about their and their children's future. In urban areas, the changes in the economy, the continuing poverty, and the reduced social services created a volatile and dangerous environment. The debate over the causes and cures of social problems continued to divide liberals and conservatives, and provided the framework for political debate.

The 1992 presidential election, however, was more about economics than social values as people voted their pocketbooks. It was the economy that helped to elect Clinton, and it was the economy that helped re-elect him and saved him from being removed from office following his impeachment.

Clinton's first administration provided images of indecisiveness and ineffective leadership, as efforts to expand the welfare state by implementing a national healthcare system failed. Clinton's political problems worsened in 1994, when Republicans gained control of Congress and announced their "Contract with America" legislative agenda. Clinton, however, proved politically adept in moving toward the political center and painting Republicans as extremists. After facing down Republicans over the budget, Clinton shifted again and adopted aspects of the Republican Party's plans for the budget and welfare reform. His political shifts, a resurgent economy, and a successful foreign policy made his re-election over Bob Dole almost a sure thing.

The political momentum Clinton gained in the 1996 election was soon lost as he became entangled in the Monica Lewinsky scandal. In a partisan debate, the House of Representatives voted to impeach the president, but he survived the Senate trial, keeping office, and throughout it all, to the amazement of many, he remained popular with the public. Contributing to Clinton's popularity and high approval ratings was a booming economy that restored prosperity, reduced poverty, and resulted in a balanced budget and a smaller national debt.

Seeing the benefits Clinton had gained, during the 2000 presidential election both Gore and Bush moved to occupy the political center of their parties. The closeness of the election only seemed to strengthen the view of some political observers that, while the "age of the New Deal" was over, there was little

support for eliminating or reducing government programs. As President Bush implemented a tax cut and sought legislation on education and other agenda items, the nation was overwhelmed by the events of September 11, 2001.

Terrorists affiliated with Osama bin Laden had attacked the World Trade Center and the Pentagon, killing over three thousand people. Soon after that shock, anthrax-laced letters put the postal system on high alert. The nation was under siege, and the Bush administration responded with a military operation against the terrorists in Afghanistan and the creation of an Office for Homeland Defense. American efforts created a global coalition to fight terrorist organizations and joined forces with others, including anti-Taliban elements in Afghanistan, to conduct a successful war that brought down the Taliban government and much of the Al-Qaeda organization—although Osama bin Laden remained at large. Caught in a rapidly changing economy and society, many Americans looked into the future and found it a bleaker one than the new millennium had seemed to promise. But there was also optimism—terrorism would be defeated, the economy would again improve, and divisions in society would close. The past was history, and perhaps more than in previous decades, Americans knew that they were living as history was being made.

BIBLIOGRAPHY

CHAPTER 16 Reconstruction: High Hopes and Shattered Dreams, 1865–1877

Herman Belz, *A New Birth of Freedom: The Republican Party and Freedmen's Rights, 1861 to 1866* (2000); Michael Les Benedict, *The Impeachment and Trial of Andrew Johnson* (1973); Paul A. Cimbala and Randall M. Miller, eds., *The Freedmen's Bureau and Reconstruction* (1999); LaWanda C. Cox, *Freedom, Racism, and Reconstruction* (1997); David Donald, Jean Baker, and Michael Holt, *The Civil War and Reconstruction* (2001); W. E. B. Du Bois, *Black Reconstruction in America* (1935); Laura F. Edwards, *Gendered Strife and Confusion: The Political Culture of Reconstruction* (1997); John Hope Franklin, *Reconstruction: After the Civil War*, 2d ed. (1994); John Hope Franklin and Alfred A. Moss, Jr., *From Slavery to Freedom: A History of African Americans*, 8th ed. (2000); Eric Foner, *Reconstruction: America's Unfinished Revolution, 1863–1877* (1988); Herbert G. Gutman, *The Black Family in Slavery and Freedom* (1976); William C. Harris, *With Charity for All: Lincoln and the Restoration of the Union* (1997); James G. Hollandsworth, *An Absolute Massacre: The New Orleans Race Riot of July 30, 1866* (2001); Harold M. Hyman and William M. Wiecek, *Equal Justice Under Law: Constitutional Development, 1835–1875* (1982); Jacqueline Jones, *Labor of Love, Labor of Sorrow: Black Women, Work and the Family, from Slavery to the Present* (1985); David A. Lincove, *Reconstruction in the United States: An Annotated Bibliography* (2000); Leon F. Litwack, *Been in the Storm So Long: The Aftermath of Slavery* (1979); William S. McFeely, *Frederick Douglass* (1991); William S. McFeely, *Grant: A Biography* (1981); James M. McPherson, *Ordeal by Fire: Reconstruction* (1982); David Montgomery, *Beyond Equality: Labor and the Radical Republicans, 1862–1872* (1967); Scott Nelson, *Iron Confederacies: Southern Railways, Klan Violence, and Reconstruction* (1999); Michael Perman, *Emancipation and Reconstruction, 1862–1879* (1987); Michael Perman, ed., *Major Problems in the Civil War and Reconstruction*, 2d ed. (1998); Keith I. Polakoff, *The Politics of Inertia: The Election of 1876 and the End of Reconstruction* (1973); George P. Rawick, ed., *The American Slave*, 24 vols., 2 suppls. (1972–1979); Brooks D. Simpson, *The Reconstruction Presidents* (1998); John David Smith, *Black Voices from Reconstruction, 1865–1877* (1996); Hans Trefousse, *Andrew Johnson: A Biography* (1989); Allen W. Trelease, *White Terror: The Ku Klux Klan Conspiracy and Southern Reconstruction* (1971); C. Vann Woodward, *Reunion and Reaction: The Compromise of 1877 and the End of Reconstruction*, rev. ed. (1966).

CHAPTER 17 An Industrial Order Emerges, 1865–1880

Ralph Andreano, ed., *The Economic Impact of the Civil War*, rev. ed. (1967); Robert L. Beisner, *From the Old Diplomacy to the New, 1865–1900*, 2d ed. (1986); Richard F. Bensel, *The Political Economy of American Industrialization* (2000); Robert V. Bruce, *1877: Year of Violence* (1989, 1959); Alfred D. Chandler, Jr., with Takashi Hikino, *Scale and Scope* (1990); Alfred D. Chandler, ed., *The Railroads* (1965); Thomas C. Cochran and William Miller, *The Age of Enterprise*, rev. ed. (1961); Carl N. Degler, *In Search of Human Nature* (1991); Melvyn Dubofsky, *Industrialism and the American Worker*, 3d ed. (1996); Milton Friedman and Anna Jacobson Schwartz, *A Monetary History of the United States* (1963); Peter George, *The Emergence of Industrial America* (1982); Louis M. Hacker, *The World of Andrew Carnegie* (1968); Mike Hawkins, *Social Darwinism in European and American Thought* (1997); Samuel P. Hays, "Political Parties and the Community-Society Continuum," in W. N. Chambers and W. D. Burnham, eds., *The American Party Systems*, 2d ed. (1975); Robert L. Heilbroner and Aaron Singer, *The Economic Transformation of America Since 1865* (1994); Richard Hofstadter, *Social Darwinism in American Thought* (1944); Ari Hoogenboom, *Rutherford B. Hayes* (1995); Matthew Josephson, *The Robber Barons* (1962, 1934); Alice Kessler-Harris, *Out to Work* (1982); Edward Chase Kirkland, *Industry Comes of Age* (1961); Paul Kleppner, *The Third Electoral System* (1979); Bruce Laurie, *Artisans into Workers* (1989); Thomas M. Leonard, ed., *United States–Latin American Relations* (1999); Walter Licht, *Industrializing America* (1995); Harold C. Livesay, *Andrew Carnegie and the Rise of Big Business* (1975); Richard L. McCormick, *The Party Period and Public Policy* (1986); Thomas K. McCraw, ed., *The Essential Alfred Chandler* (1988); David Montgomery, *Citizen Worker* (1993); David Montgomery, *Workers' Control in America* (1979); Daniel Nelson, *Managers and Workers* (1975); Patrick K. O'Brien, *The Economic Effects of the American Civil War* (1988); Dexter Perkins, *The Monroe Doctrine, 1867–1901* (1966, 1937); Geoffrey Perret, *Ulysses S. Grant* (1997); Glenn Porter, *The Rise of Big Business*, 2d ed. (1992); Frank Roney, *An Autobiography*, ed. by Ira B. Cross (1976, 1931); Frank J. Scaturro, *President Grant Reconsidered* (1998); Fred A. Shannon, *The Farmer's Last Frontier: Agriculture, 1860–1897* (1945); David O. Stowell, *Streets, Railroads, and the Great Strike of 1877* (1999); Brooks D. Simpson, *The Reconstruction Presidents* (1998); Stephan Thernstrom, *Poverty and Progress* (1964); Harold G. Vatter, *The Drive to Industrial Maturity* (1975); Joseph F. Wall, *Andrew Carnegie* (1970); Joseph F. Wall, ed., *The Andrew Carnegie Reader* (1992); Thomas Weiss and Donald Schaefer, eds., *American Economic Development in Historical Perspective* (1994); Xi Wang, *The Trial of Democracy* (1997).

CHAPTER 18 Becoming an Urban Industrial Society, 1880–1890

Peter H. Argersinger, *Structure, Process, and Party* (1992); Paul Avrich, *The Haymarket Tragedy* (1984); Edward L. Ayers, *The Promise of the New South* (1992); Susan Porter Benson, *Counter Cultures: American Department Stores* (1986); Karen J. Blair, *The Clubwoman as Feminist* (1980); John E. Bodnar, *The Transplanted* (1985); Ruth Bordin, *Frances Willard* (1986); Vincent P. Carosso, *The Morgans* (1987); George Chauncy, *Gay New York* (1994); Ron Chernow, *Titan: The Life of John D. Rockefeller, Sr.* (1998); Robert W. Cherny, *American Politics in the Gilded Age, 1868–1900* (1997); Edward P. Crapol, *James G. Blaine* (2000); Lawrence Cremin, *American Education: The Metropolitan Experience* (1988); John D'Emilio and Estelle B. Freedman, *Intimate Matters* (1988);

Justus D. Doenecke, *The Presidencies of James A. Garfield and Chester A. Arthur* (1981); Rebecca Edwards, *Angels in the Machinery: Gender in American Party Politics* (1997); Leon Fink, *Workingmen's Democracy: The Knights of Labor* (1983); Eleanor Flexner, *Century of Struggle: The Woman's Rights Movement*, rev. ed., 1996; John A. Garraty, *The New Commonwealth, 1877–1890* (1968); Ellen Gruber Garvey, *The Adman in the Parlor* (1996); Lynn D. Gordon, *Gender and Higher Education in the Progressive Era* (1990); David F. Greenberg, *The Construction of Homosexuality* (1988); Melanie Gustafson et al., eds., *We Have Come to Stay: American Women and Political Parties* (1999); David C. Hammack, *Power and Society: Greater New York* (1982); Ari Hoogenboom, *Outlawing the Spoils* (1961); Noel Ignatiev, *How the Irish Became White* (1995); Kenneth T. Jackson, *Crabgrass Frontier: Suburbanization* (1985); Jonathan Ned Katz, ed., *Gay American History*, rev. ed. (1992); Paul M. Kennedy, *The Samoan Tangle* (1974); William Leach, *Land of Desire* (1993); Suzanne M. Marilley, *Woman Suffrage and the Origins of Liberal Feminism* (1996); Raymond A. Mohl, *The New City* (1985); Horace Samuel Merrill, *Bourbon Leader: Grover Cleveland* (1957); Eric H. Monkkonen, *America Becomes Urban* (1988); Regina Markell Morantz-Sanchez, *Sympathy and Science: Women Physicians* (1985); H. Wayne Morgan, ed., *The Gilded Age*, rev. ed. (1970); H. Wayne Morgan, ed., *Victorian Culture in America, 1865–1914* (1973); Orm Overland, *Immigrant Minds, American Identities* (2000); Nell Irvin Painter, *Standing at Armageddon* (1987); Milton Plesur, *America's Outward Thrust* (1971); E. Anthony Rotundo, *American Manhood* (1993); Lewis O. Saum, *The Popular Mood of America* (1990); Thomas J. Schlereth, *Victorian America* (1991); Louise L. Stevenson, *The Victorian Homefront* (1991); Jon C. Teaford, *The Unheralded Triumph: City Government* (1984); Kim Voss, *The Making of American Exceptionalism* (1993); David Ward, *Cities and Immigrants* (1971); Richard E. Welch, Jr., *The Presidencies of Grover Cleveland* (1988); Mark Wyman, *Round-trip to America* (1993).

CHAPTER 19   Conflict and Change in the West, 1865–1902

Armando C. Alonzo, *Tejano Legacy* (1998); Stephen E. Ambrose, *Nothing Like It in the World: The Men Who Built the Transcontinental Railroad* (2000); Gordon Morris Bakken and Brenda Farrington, eds., *The Gendered West* (2001); Paula Bartley and Cathy Loxton, *Plains Women* (1991); Ray Allen Billington, and Martin Ridge, *Westward Expansion*, 5th ed. (1982); Gray A. Brechin, *Imperial San Francisco* (1999); Dee Brown, *Bury My Heart at Wounded Knee: An Indian History of the American West* (1971); Anne M. Butler, *Uncommon Common Women* (1996); Albert Camarillo, *Chicanos in a Changing Society*, rev. ed. (1996); Sucheng Chan, *Asian Americans* (1990); Sucheng Chan, *Asian Californians* (1991); Yong Chen, *Chinese San Francisco* (2000); Gloria Heyung Chun, *Of Orphans and Warriors: Inventing Chinese American Culture and Identity* (2000); Sarah Deutsch, *No Separate Refuge: Culture, Class, and Gender on an Anglo-Hispanic Frontier in the American Southwest* (1987); Everett Dick, *The Sod-House Frontier* (1954); Robert R. Dykstra, *The Cattle Towns* (1968); Juan Gómez-Quiñones, *Roots of Chicano Politics* (1994); Erlinda Gonzales-Berry and David Maciel, eds., *The Contested Homeland: Chicano History of New Mexico* (2000); Richard Griswold del Castillo, *The Los Angeles Barrio* (1979); Andrew Gyory, *Closing the Gate: Race, Politics, and the Chinese Exclusion Act* (1998); Frederick E. Hoxie, *A Final Promise: The Campaign to Assimilate the Indians* (1984); Norris Hundley, Jr., *The Great Thirst: Californians and Water* (1992); Albert L. Hurtado, *Intimate Frontiers* (1999); William Issel and Robert W. Cherny, *San Francisco, 1865–1932* (1986); Peter Iverson, *When Indians Became Cowboys* (1994); Julie Roy Jeffrey, *Frontier Women*, rev. ed. (1998); William L. Kahrl, *Water and Power* (1982); Patricia Nelson Limerick, *The Legacy of Conquest* (1987); Clyde A. Milner II, ed., *A New Significance: Re-envisioning the History of the American West* (1996); Douglas Monroy, *Thrown Among Strangers: The Making of Mexican Culture in Frontier California* (1990); David Montejano, *Anglos and Mexicans in the Making of Texas* (1997); Sandra L. Myres, *Westering Women and the Frontier Experience* (1982); Donald Pisani, *From the Family Farm to Agribusiness* (1984); Leonard Pitt, *The Decline of the Californios* (1971); Earl Pomeroy, *The Pacific Slope* (1965); Francis Prucha, *The Churches and the Indian Schools* (1979); Francis Prucha, *American Indian Policy in Crisis* (1975); Glenda Riley, *The Female Frontier* (1988); Robert C. Ritchie and Paul Andrew Hutton, eds., *Frontier and Region* (1997); William G. Robbins, *Colony and Empire* (1994); Joseph G. Rosa, *Age of the Gunfighter* (1995); Carlos A. Schwantes, *The Pacific Northwest*, rev. ed. (1996); Fred A. Shannon, *The Farmer's Last Frontier* (1945); Neil L. Shumsky, *The Evolution of Political Protest and the Workingmen's Party of California* (1991); Ronald Takaki, *Strangers from a Different Shore* (1989); Quintard Taylor, *In Search of the Racial Frontier: African Americans in the American West* (1998); Robert M. Utley, *The Indian Frontier of the American West* (1984); Robert M. Utley, *The Lance and the Shield: The Life and Times of Sitting Bull* (1993); David Vaught, *Cultivating California* (1999); Walter Prescott Webb, *The Great Plains* (1931); Richard White, *"It's Your Misfortune and None of My Own": A History of the American West* (1991); Donald Worster, *Rivers of Empire: Water* (1985).

CHAPTER 20   Economic Crash and Political Upheaval, 1890–1900

Jane Addams, *Twenty Years at Hull House* (1910); Robert L. Beisner, *From the Old Diplomacy to the New*, 2d ed. (1986); Robert L. Beisner, *Twelve Against Empire: The Anti-Imperialists* (1968); Walter Dean Burnham, *Critical Elections and the Mainsprings of American Politics* (1970); Mina Julia Carson, *Settlement Folk* (1990); Robert W. Cherny, *A Righteous Cause: Life of William Jennings Bryan* (1985, rpt. 1995); Gene Clanton, *Populism* (1991); Roger Daniels, *Not Like Us: Immigrants and Minorities in America* (1997); Allen F. Davis, *American Heroine: Life and Legend of Jane Addams*, rev. ed. (2000); Gioia Diliberto, *A Useful Woman: Early Life of Jane Addams* (1999); John M. Dobson, *Reticent Expansionism: Foreign Policy of William McKinley* (1988); A. B. Feuer, *The Spanish-American War at Sea* (1995); Willard B. Gatewood, *Black Americans and the White Man's Burden* (1975); Mark T. Gilderhus, *The Second Century: U.S.–Latin American Relations Since 1889* (2000); Paul W. Glad, *McKinley, Bryan, and the People* (1964, rpt. 1991); Michael L. Goldberg, *An Army of Women* (1997); Robert M. Goldman, *"A free ballot and a fair count": The Department of Justice and the Enforcement of Voting Rights in the South, 1877–1893* (2001); Lewis L. Gould, *America in the Progressive Era* (2001); Lewis L. Gould, *The Presidency of William McKinley* (1980); Louis R. Harlan, *Booker T. Washington* (1972); David Healy, *U.S. Expansionism* (1970); John D. Hicks, *The Populist Revolt* (1931); John Higham, *Strangers in the Land*, 2d ed. (1994); Charles Hoffman, *The Depression of the Nineties* (1970); J. Rogers Hollingsworth, *The*

Whirligig of Politics (1963); Stanley L. Jones, *The Presidential Election of 1896* (1964); Michael Kazin, *The Populist Persuasion* (1995); Donald L. Kinzer, *An Episode in Anti-Catholicism: The American Protective Association* (1964); Walter LaFeber, *The New Empire* (1963); Gerald F. Linderman, *Mirror of War: American Society and the Spanish-American War* (1974); T. J. McCormick, *China Market* (1967); Robert C. McMath, Jr., *American Populism* (1993); Alfred Thayer Mahan, *The Influence of Sea Power upon History* (1890, rpt., 1983); Ernest R. May, *American Imperialism* (1968); Ernest R. May, *Imperial Democracy* (1961, rpt. 1973); Stuart C. Miller, *"Benevolent Assimilation": American Conquest of the Philippines, 1899–1903* (1982); H. Wayne Morgan, *America's Road to Empire* (1965); H. Wayne Morgan, *William McKinley and His America* (1963); John L. Offner, *An Unwanted War* (1992); Thomas J. Osborne, *"Empire Can Wait": American Opposition to Hawaiian Annexation* (1981); Thomas G. Paterson and Stephen G. Rabe, eds., *Imperial Surge* (1992); Louis A. Perez, *The War of 1898* (1998); Norman Pollack, ed., *The Populist Mind* (1967); Julius W. Pratt, *Expansionists of 1898* (1936); Edward J. Renehan, Jr., *The Lion's Pride: Theodore Roosevelt and his Family in Peace and War* (1998); Jacob A. Riis, *The Battle with the Slum* (1902); Jacob A. Riis, *How the Other Half Lives* (1890); Theodore Roosevelt, *The Rough Riders* (1899); Emily S. Rosenberg, *Spreading the American Dream: American Economic and Cultural Expansion* (1982); Nick Salvatore, *Eugene V. Debs* (1982); Peggy Samuels, *Teddy Roosevelt at San Juan* (1997); Richard Schneirov, Shelton Stromquist, and Nick Salvatore, eds., *The Pullman Strike and the Crisis of the 1890s* (1999); Carlos A. Schwantes, *Coxey's Army* (1985); Kathryn Kish Sklar, *Florence Kelley and the Nation's Work* (1995); Theda Skocpol, *Protecting Soldiers and Mothers* (1992); Joseph Smith, *The Spanish-American War* (1994); Homer E. Socolofsky and Allan B. Spetter, *The Presidency of Benjamin Harrison* (1987); Douglas W. Steeples, *Democracy in Desperation: The Depression of 1893* (1998); Shelton Stromquist, *A Generation of Boomers: Railroad Labor Conflict in Nineteenth-century America* (1993); E. Berkeley Tompkins, *Anti-Imperialism in the United States* (1970); David F. Trask, *The War with Spain in 1898* (1981, rpt. 1996); Richard E. Welch, Jr., *Response to Imperialism* (1979); R. Hal Williams, *Years of Decision: American Politics in the 1890s*

(1978); William Appleman Williams, *The Roots of the Modern American Empire* (1969); Marilyn Blatt Young, *The Rhetoric of Empire* (1968).

CHAPTER 21   The Progressive Era, 1900–1917

Jack S. Blocker, Jr., *Retreat from Reform: The Prohibition Movement in the United States, 1890–1913* (1976); John Morton Blum, *The Republican Roosevelt*, 2d ed. (1977); Christine E. Bose, *Women in 1900* (2001); H. W. Brands, *T.R.* (1997); David F. Burg, *Chicago's White City of 1893* (1976); Ellen Chesler, *Woman of Valor: Margaret Sanger* (1992); Elisabeth Clemens, *The People's Lobby: Organizational Innovation and the Rise of Interest Group Politics in the United States* (1997); Kendrick A. Clements, *The Presidency of Woodrow Wilson* (1992); Nancy F. Cott, *The Grounding of Modern Feminism* (1987); Richard H. Collin, *Theodore Roosevelt: Culture, Diplomacy, and Expansion* (1985); Steven J. Diner, *A Very Different Age: Americans of the Progressive Era* (1998); Ellen DuBois, *Harriot Stanton Blatch and the Winning of Woman Suffrage* (1997); Louis Filler, *Appointment at Armageddon: Muckraking and Progressivism in the American Tradition*, rev. ed. (1996); Noralee Frankel and Nancy S. Dye, eds., *Gender, Class, Race, and Reform in the Progressive Era* (1991); Peter Gammond, *Scott Joplin and the Ragtime Era* (1975); William H. Gerdts, *American Impressionism* (1984); Linda Gordon, *Woman's Body, Woman's Right: Birth Control in America*, rev. ed. (1990); Lewis L. Gould, *The Presidency of Theodore Roosevelt* (1991); Lewis L. Gould, *Reform and Regulation: American Politics from Roosevelt to Wilson*, 3d ed. (1996); Mark T. Gilderhus, *The Second Century: U.S.-Latin American Relations Since 1889* (2000); Louis R. Harlan, *Booker T. Washington: The Wizard of Tuskegee, 1901–1915* (1983); Samuel P. Hays, *Conservation and the Gospel of Efficiency* (1959); Samuel P. Hays, *The Response to Industrialism, 1885–1914*, 2d ed. (1995); Ari and Olive Hoogenboom, *A History of the ICC: From Panacea to Palliative* (1976); K. Austin Kerr, *Organized for Prohibition: A New History of the Anti-Saloon League* (1985); Alexander Keyssar, *The Right to Vote* (2000); Mark Kornbluh, *Why America Stopped Voting* (2000); David Levering Lewis, *W. E. B. Du Bois: Biography of a Race, 1868–1919* (1993); Lawrence W. Levine, *Highbrow/Lowbrow: The Emergence of Cultural Hierarchy in America* (1988); Arthur S. Link and Richard L. McCormick,

Progressivism (1983); Arthur S. Link, *Woodrow Wilson*, 5 vols. (1947–1965); Richard Coke Lower, *A Bloc of One: The Political Career of Hiram W. Johnson* (1993); David G. McCullough, *The Path Between the Seas: The Creation of the Panama Canal, 1870–1914* (1977); Michael E. McGerr, *The Decline of Popular Politics: The American North, 1865–1928* (1986); Linda O. McMurry, *To Keep the Waters Troubled: Life of Ida B. Wells* (1998); Manning Marable, *W. E. B. Du Bois: Black Radical Democrat* (1986); Ernest R. May, *Imperial Democracy: The Emergence of America as a Great Power* (1961, rpt. 1973); Sally M. Miller, *Victor Berger and the Promise of Constructive Socialism, 1910–1920* (1973); H. Wayne Morgan, ed., *Victorian Culture in America, 1865–1914* (1973); Robyn Muncy, *Creating a Female Dominion in American Reform, 1890–1935* (1991); Bradford Perkins, *The Great Rapprochement: England and the United States, 1895–1914* (1968); Bernard B. Perlman, *Painters of the Ashcan School* (1979); Steven Riess, *Sport in Industrial America, 1850–1920* (1995); Theodore Roosevelt, *An Autobiography* (1913); Emily S. Rosenberg, *Spreading the American Dream: American Economic and Cultural Expansion, 1890–1945* (1982); Robert Rydell, *All the World's a Fair: Visions of Empire at American International Expositions, 1876–1916* (1984); Nick Salvatore, *Eugene V. Debs: Citizen and Socialist* (1982); Stanley K. Schultz, *Constructing Urban Culture: American Cities and City Planning, 1880–1920* (1989); Upton Sinclair, *The Jungle* (1906); Martin J. Sklar, *The United States as a Developing Country: Studies in U.S. History in the Progressive Era and the 1920s* (1992); Melvin I. Urofsky, *Louis D. Brandeis and the Progressive Tradition* (1981); Ida B. Wells-Barnett, *Crusade for Justice: The Autobiography of Ida B. Wells*, ed. by Alfreda M. Duster (1970); Robert H. Wiebe, *The Search for Order, 1877–1920* (1967); William H. Wilson, *The City Beautiful Movement* (1989); Marilyn Blatt Young, *The Rhetoric of Empire: American China Policy, 1895–1901* (1968).

CHAPTER 22   The United States in a World at War, 1913–1920

Lloyd E. Ambrosius, *Wilsonian Statecraft* (1991); Lloyd E. Ambrosius, *Woodrow Wilson and the American Diplomatic Tradition* (1987); Arthur E. Barbeau and Florette Henri, *The Unknown Soldiers: Black American Troops in World War I* (1974); W. J. Breen, *Labor Market Politics and the*

Great War (1997); David Brody, *Labor in Crisis: The Steel Strike of 1919* (1965); John Whiteclay Chambers II, *To Raise an Army: The Draft Comes to Modern America* (1987); Kendrick A. Clements, *The Presidency of Woodrow Wilson* (1992); Kendrick A. Clements, *William Jennings Bryan: Missionary Isolationist* (1982); Edward M. Coffman, *The War to End All Wars* (1986); Jean Conner, *The National War Labor Board* (1983); John Milton Cooper, Jr., *The Vanity of Power: American Isolationism and World War I* (1969); Patrick Devlin, *Too Proud to Fight: Woodrow Wilson's Neutrality* (1974); Frances H. Early, *A World Without War: How U.S. Feminists and Pacifists Resisted World War I* (1997); Mark Ellis, *Race, War, and Surveillance: African Americans and the United States Government during World War I* (2001); Byron Farwell, *Over There* (1999); Robert H. Ferrell, *Woodrow Wilson and World War I* (1985); Frank Freidel, *Over There*, rev. ed. (1990); Mark T. Gilderhus, *Diplomacy and Revolution: U.S.-Mexican Relations Under Wilson and Carranza* (1977); Maurine Weiner Greenwald, *War and Work: The Impact of World War I on Women Workers* (1980); Edward Haley, *Revolution and Intervention: The Diplomacy of Taft and Wilson in Mexico* (1970); John M. Hart, *Revolutionary Mexico*, rev. ed. (1997); Ellis Hawley, *The Great War and the Search for a Modern Order*, 2d ed. (1997); D. Clayton James and Anne Sharp Wells, *America and the Great War* (1998); Robert Johnson, *The Peace Progressives and American Foreign Relations* (1995); Jennifer D. Keene, *Doughboys, the Great War, and the Remaking of America* (2001); Jennifer D. Keene, *The United States and the First World War* (2000); David M. Kennedy, *Over Here* (1986); Thomas J. Knock, *To End All Wars* (1992); David D. Lee, *Sergeant York* (1985); C. Roland Marchand, *The American Peace Movement and Social Reform* (1972); Ernest R. May, *The World War and American Isolation* (1959); Arno J. Mayer, *Politics and Diplomacy of Peacemaking* (1967); Joseph A. McCartin, *Labor's Great War* (1997); John A. Morello, *Selling the President, 1920* (2001); Paul L. Murphy, *World War I and the Origin of Civil Liberties in the United States* (1979); Robert E. Quirk, *An Affair of Honor: Woodrow Wilson and the Occupation of Veracruz* (1962); Robert K. Murray, *Red Scare* (1955); Francis Russell, *A City in Terror, 1919: The Boston Police Strike* (1975); Ronald Schaffer, *America in the Great War* (1991); Robert Freeman Smith, *The United States and Revolutionary*

Nationalism in Mexico (1972); Barbara W. Tuchman, *The Guns of August* (1962); William M. Tuttle, *Race Riot: Chicago in the Red Summer of 1919* (1970); Stephen Vaughn, *Holding Fast the Inner Lines: Democracy, Nationalism, and the Committee on Public Information* (1980); James Weinstein, *The Decline of Socialism in America* (1967); William C. Widenor, *Henry Cabot Lodge and the Search for an American Foreign Policy* (1980); William Young and David E. Kaiser, *Postmortem: New Evidence in the Case of Sacco and Vanzetti* (1985); Robert H. Zieger, *America's Great War* (2000); Susan Zeiger, *In Uncle Sam's Service: Women Workers with the American Expeditionary Force* (1999).

CHAPTER 23   Prosperity Decade, 1920–1928

Carl Abbott, *Urban America in the Modern Age* (1987); Frederick Lewis Allen, *Only Yesterday* (1931); William J. Barber, *From New Era to New Deal: Herbert Hoover, the Economists, and American Economic Policy* (1985); Elliott Barkan, *And Still They Come: Immigrants and American Society* (1996); Ray Batchelor, *Henry Ford, Mass Production, Modernism, and Design* (1994); Ronald Berman, *Fitzgerald, Hemingway, and the Twenties* (2001); Daniel H. Borus, ed., *These United States: Portraits of America from the 1920s* (1992); David Burner, *Politics of Provincialism: The Democratic Party in Transition* (1968); Paul A. Carter, *The Twenties in America*, 2d ed. (1987); Warren I. Cohen, *Empire Without Tears* (1987); Douglas B. Craig, *Fireside Politics: Radio and Culture in the United States* (2000); E. David Cronon, *Black Moses: Marcus Garvey and the Universal Negro Improvement Association*, 2d ed. (1981); Vincent Curcio, *Chrysler* (2000); Charles DeBenedetti, *Origins of the Modern American Peace Movement* (1978); Lyle W. Dorset, *Billy Sunday and the Redemption of Urban America* (1991); Martin Bauml Duberman, *Paul Robeson* (1989); Martin Bauml Duberman, Martha Vicinus, and George Chauney, Jr., eds., *Hidden From History: Reclaiming the Gay and Lesbian Past* (1989); Lynn Dumenil, *The Modern Temper: American Culture and Society in the 1920s* (1995); Paula Elder, *Governor Alfred E. Smith* (1983); Martin L. Fausold, *The Presidency of Herbert C. Hoover* (1985); Robert H. Ferrell, *The Presidency of Calvin Coolidge* (1998); Richard Wrightman Fox and T. J. Jackson Lears, eds., *The Culture of Consumption* (1983); David J. Goldberg, *Discontented America: The U.S. in the*

1920s (1999); Linda Gordon, *Woman's Body, Woman's Right: Birth Control in America,* rev. ed. (1990); Clarence Hooker, *Life in the Shadows of the Crystal Palace, 1910–1927: Ford Workers* (1997); Nathan Irvin Huggins, *Harlem Renaissance* (1971); Peter Iverson, *"We Are Still Here": American Indians in the Twentieth Century* (1998); Edward Jablonski, *Gershwin* (1987); Kenneth T. Jackson, *The Ku Klux Klan in the City* (1967); Harvey Klehr and John Earl Haynes, *The American Communist Movement* (1992); Lester D. Langley, *The Banana Wars: United States Intervention in the Caribbean* (1983); Edward J. Larson, *Summer for the Gods: The Scopes Trial and America's Continuing Debate over Science and Religion* (1997); Shawn Lay, ed., *The Invisible Empire in the West: The Ku Klux Klan* (1992); William E. Leuchtenburg, *The Perils of Prosperity, 1914–1932,* 2d ed. (1993); David L. Lewis, *When Harlem Was in Vogue* (1981); Robert S. Lynd and Helen M. Lynd, *Middletown* (1929); Neil Macauley, *The Sandino Affair* (1985); Roland Marchand, *Advertising the American Dream* (1985); Karen A. J. Miller, *Populist Nationalism: Republican Insurgency and American Foreign Policy Making* (1999); Gerald D. Nash, *A. P. Giannini and the Bank of America* (1992); Arnold Rampersad, *The Life of Langston Hughes,* 2 vols. (1986, 1988); Arnold Shaw, *The Jazz Age: Popular Music in the 1920's* (1987); Tom Sitton and William Deverell, eds., *Metropolis in the Making: Los Angeles in the 1920s* (2001); Robert Sobel, *The Great Bull Market: Wall Street in the 1920s* (1968); Ferenc Szasz, *The Divided Mind of Protestant America* (1982); Eugene R. Trani and David L. Wilson, *The Presidency of Warren G. Harding* (1977); Jules Tygiel, *The Great Los Angeles Swindle: Oil, Stocks, and Scandal During the Roaring Twenties* (1996); David L. Waterhouse, *The Progressive Movement of 1924 and the Development of Interest Group Liberalism* (1991); Bernard A. Weisberger, *The Dream Maker: William C. Durant, Founder of General Motors* (1979); Joan Hoff Wilson, *American Business and Foreign Policy* (1968); Joan Hoff Wilson, *Herbert Hoover* (1970); Cary D. Wintz, ed., *The Harlem Renaissance,* 7 vols. (1996); Robert H. Zieger, *American Workers, American Unions* (1986).

CHAPTER 24   The Great Depression and the New Deal, 1929–1939

Anthony Badger, *The New Deal: The Depression Years, 1933–1940* (1989); Francisco Balderrama and Raymond

Rodriguez, *Decade of Betrayal: Mexican Repatriation in the 1930s* (1995); Ann Banks, ed., *First Person America* (1980); William J. Barber, *Designs Within Disorder: Franklin D. Roosevelt, the Economists, and the Shaping of American Economic Policy* (1996); John Barnard, *Walter Reuther and the Rise of the Auto Workers* (1983); Edward D. Berkowitz, *America's Welfare State: From Roosevelt to Reagan* (1991); Irving Bernstein, *A Caring Society: The New Deal, The Worker, and the Great Depression* (1985); Gary D. Best, *Pride, Prejudice, and Politics: Roosevelt Versus Recovery, 1933–1938* (1990); Roger Biles, *A New Deal for the American People* (1991); Julia Kirk Blackwelder, *No Hiring: The Feminization of Work in the United States, 1900–1995* (1997); Julia Kirk Blackwelder, *Women of the Depression: Caste and Culture in San Antonio, 1929–1939* (1984); Alan Brinkley, *Voices of Protest: Huey Long, Father Coughlin, and the Great Depression* (1982); David Burner, *Herbert Hoover: The Public Life* (1978); Dan T. Carter, *Scottsboro* (1969); William U. Chandler, *The Myth of the TVA: Conservation and Development in the Tennessee Valley, 1933–1983* (1984); Kendrick A. Clement, *Hoover, Conservation, Consumerism: Engineering the Good Life* (2000); Blanche W. Cook, *Eleanor Roosevelt, Vol. 2: 1933–1938* (1999); Roger Daniels, *The Bonus March* (1971); Kenneth S. Davis, *FDR: Into the Storm, 1937–1940: A History* (1993); Kenneth S. Davis, *FDR: The New Deal Years, 1933–1937* (1986); Sidney Fine, *Sit-Down: The General Motors Strike of 1936–1937* (1969); Melvyn Dubofsky, *The State and Labor in Modern America* (1994); Milton Friedman and Anna Schwartz, *The Great Contraction, 1929–1933* (1965); John Kenneth Galbraith, *The Great Crash, 1929* (1961); Colin Gordon, *New Deals: Business, Labor, and Politics in America* (1994); Cheryl L. Greenberg, *"Or Does It Explode?" Black Harlem in the Great Depression* (1991); James Gregory, *American Exodus: The Dust Bowl Migration and the Okie Culture in California* (1989); Camille Gurin-Gonzalez, *Mexican Workers and American Dreams: Immigration, Repatriation, and California Farm Labor, 1900–1939* (1994); David Hamilton, *From New Day to New Deal: American Farm Policy from Hoover to Roosevelt, 1928–1933* (1991); Lois Rita Helmbold, "Beyond the Family Economy: Black and White Working-Class Women During the Great Depression," *Feminist Studies*, 13 (Fall 1987); Peter Iverson, *"We Are Still Here": American Indians in the Twentieth Century* (1998); Lawrence C. Kelley, *The Assault on Assimilation: John Collier and the Origins of Indian Policy Reform* (1983); David M. Kennedy, *Freedom From Fear: The American People in Depression and War, 1929–1945* (1999); Maury Klein, *Rainbow's End: The Crash of 1929* (2000); Donald L. Lisio, *Hoover, Blacks, and Lily-Whites* (1985); Roy Lubove, *The Struggle for Social Security* (1968); Robert S. McElvaine, ed., *Down and Out in the Great Depression: Letters from the Forgotten Man* (1983); George McJimsey, *Harry Hopkins* (1987); George McJimsey, *The Presidency of Franklin D. Roosevelt* (2000); Patrick J. Maney, *The Roosevelt Presence: A Biography of Franklin Delano Roosevelt* (1992); Jerre Mangione, *The Dream and the Deal: The Federal Writers' Project, 1935–1943* (1972); David Milton, *The Politics of U.S. Labor: From the Great Depression to the New Deal* (1980); William Mullins, *The Depression and the Urban West Coast, 1929–1933* (1991); James S. Olson, *Herbert Hoover and the Reconstruction Finance Corporation, 1931–1933* (1977); James T. Patterson, *Congressional Conservatism and the New Deal* (1967); Richard Pells, *Radical Visions and American Dreams: Culture and Social Thought in the Depression Years* (1973); Kenneth Philip, *John Collier's Crusade for Indian Reform, 1920–1945* (1977); Kenneth Philip, *Termination Revisited: American Indians on the Trail to Self-Determination, 1933–1954* (1999); David Plotke, *Building a Democratic Political Order: Reshaping American Liberalism in the 1930s and 1940s* (1996); Vicki Ruiz, *Cannery Women, Cannery Lives: Mexican Women, Unionization and the California Food Processing Industry, 1930–1950* (1987); Theodore Saloutos, *The American Farmer and the New Deal* (1982); Lois Schraf, *Eleanor Roosevelt: First Lady of American Liberalism* (1987); Louis Schraf, *To Work and to Wed: Female Employment and the Great Depression* (1980); Harvard Sitkoff, ed., *Fifty Years Later: The New Deal Evaluated* (1985); John Shover, *Cornbelt Rebellion: The Farmers' Holiday Association* (1965); Bernard Sternsher, ed., *Hitting Home: The Great Depression in Town and Country* (1989); Catherine Stock, *Main Street in Crisis: The Great Depression and the Old Middle Class on the Northern Plains* (1992); Patricia Sullivan, *Days of Hope: Race and Democracy in the New Deal Era* (1996); Peter Timim, *Did Monetary Forces Cause the Great Depression?* (1976); Susan Ware, *Holding Their Own: American Women in the Thirties* (1982); Devra Weber, *Dark Sweat, White Gold: California Farm Workers, Cotton, and the New Deal* (1994); Nancy J. Weiss, *Farewell to the Party of Lincoln: Black Politics in the Age of FDR* (1983); Donald Worster, *Dust Bowl: The Southern Plains in the 1930s* (1979).

CHAPTER 25 America's Rise to World Leadership, 1929–1945

David Alverez, *Secret Messages: Code Breaking and American Diplomacy, 1930–1945* (2000); Stephen E. Ambrose, *D-Day, June 6, 1944* (1994); Stephen E. Ambrose, *Citizen Soldiers: The U.S. Army from the Normandy Beaches to the Bulge to the Surrender of Germany, June 7, 1944–May 7, 1945* (1997); James Atleson, *Labor and the Wartime State: Labor Relations and Law During World War II* (1998); Allen Berube, *Coming Out Under Fire: The History of Gay Men and Women in World War II* (1990); Dorothy Borg and Shumpei Okamoto, eds., *Pearl Harbor as History* (1973); David Brinkley, *Washington Goes to War* (1988); Dominic J. Capeci, Jr., *Race Relations in Wartime Detroit: The Sojourner Truth Housing Controversy of 1942* (1984); Wayne Cole, *Roosevelt and the Isolationists* (1983); John Costello, *Virtue Under Fire: How World War II Changed Our Social and Sexual Attitudes* (1985); Lyn Crost, *Honor by Fire: Japanese Americans at War in Europe and the Pacific* (1994); Justus D. Doenecke, *Storm on the Horizon: The Challenge to American Intervention, 1939–1941* (2001); Thomas Doherty, *Projections of War: Hollywood, American Culture, and World War II* (1993); Paul J. Dosal, *Doing Business with the Dictators* (1993); Keith E. Eiler, *Mobilizing Americans: Robert P. Patterson and the War Effort, 1940–1945* (1997); Lewis A. Erenberg and Susan Hirsch, eds., *The War in American Culture: Society and Consciousness During World War II* (1996); Henry L. Feingold, *Bearing Witness: How America and Its Jews Responded to the Holocaust* (1995); Irwin F. Gellman, *The Good Neighbor Diplomacy: United States Policies in Latin America, 1933–1945* (1979); Susan Hartmann, *The Homefront and Beyond: American Women in the 1940s* (1982); Waldo H. Heinrichs, Jr., *Threshold of War* (1988); Akira Iriye, *Power and Culture: The Japanese-American War, 1941–1945* (1981); Nelson Lichtenstein, *Labor's War at Home: The CIO in World War II* (1983); Gerald D. Nash, *The American West Transformed: The Impact of the Second World War* (1985); Judy B. Litoff, *We're in This War Too: World*

War II Letters of American Women in Uniform (1994); Neil R. McMillen, ed., Remaking Dixie: The Impact of World War II on the American South (1997); Verne W. Newton, ed., FDR and the Holocaust (1995); William O'Neill, A Democracy at War: America's Fight at Home and Abroad in World War II (1993); Richard Polenberg, War and Society: The United States, 1941–1945 (1972); Richard Rhodes, The Making of the Atomic Bomb (1987); Eric Paul Roorda, The Dictator Next Door: The Good Neighbor Policy and the Trujillo Regime in the Dominican Republic, 1930–1945 (1998); Ronald Schaffer, Wings of Judgment: American Bombing in World War II (1985); Martin Sherman, A World Destroyed (1975); Michael Sherry, In the Shadow of War: The United States Since the 1930s (1995); John R. Skates, The Invasion of Japan: Alternative to the Bomb (1994); Gaddis Smith, American Diplomacy During the Second World War (1965); Mark Stoler, "A Half Century of Conflict: Interpretations of World War II Diplomacy," Diplomatic History 18 (Summer 1994): 375–403; Robert G. Spinney, World War II in Nashville: The Transformation of the Homefront (1998); Susan C. Taylor, Jewel of the Desert: Japanese American Internment at Topaz (1994); Studs Terkel, The Good War: An Oral History of World War Two (1984); Kenneth W. Townsend, World War II and the American Indian (2000); Jonathan Utley, Going to War with Japan (1985); Harold G. Vetter, The U.S. Economy in World War II (1985); Allen E. Winkler, Home Front U.S.A.: America During World War II (1986); David S. Wyman, The Abandonment of the Jews (1984); Neil A. Wynn, The Afro-American and the Second World War (1975); David K. Yoo, Growing Up Nisei: Race, Generation, and Culture among Japanese Americans of California, 1924–1949 (2000).

CHAPTER 26 Truman and Cold War America, 1945–1952

Jack S. Ballard, The Shock of Peace: Military and Economic Demobilization after World War II (1983); Rosalyn Baxandall and Elizabeth Ewen, Picture Window: How Suburbs Happened (2000); William C. Berman, The Politics of Civil Rights in the Truman Administration (1970); Dorothy Borg and Waldo Heinrichs, eds., Uncertain Years: Chinese-American Relations, 1947–1950 (1980); Paul Boyer, By the Bomb's Early Light: American Thought and Culture at the Dawn of the Atomic Age (1985); Kevin Boyle, The UAW and the Heyday of American Liberalism (1995); Richard M. Dalfiume, Desegregation of the U.S. Armed Forces (1969); Robert J. Donovan, The Tumultuous Years: The Presidency of Harry S Truman, 1949–1953 (1982); Norman Friedman, The Fifty-Year War: Conflict and Strategy in the Cold War (2000); John L. Gaddis, Strategies of Containment (1982); John L. Gaddis, We Now Know: Rethinking Cold War History (1997); Herbert J. Gans, The Levittowners (1967); William S. Graebner, The Age of Doubt: American Thought and Culture in the 1940s (1991); John Halliday and Bruce Cummings, Korea: The Unknown War (1987); Alonzo Hamby, Man of the People: A Life of Harry S Truman (1995); Susan Hartman, Truman and the 80th Congress (1971); Gregory Herken, The Winning Weapon (1981); Michael Hogan, The Marshall Plan (1987); Kenneth T. Jackson, Crabgrass Frontiers: The Suburbanization of the United States (1985); Landon Y. Jones, Great Expectations: America and the Baby Boom Generation (1980); Burton Kaufman, The Arab Middle East and the United States: Inter-Arab Rivalry and Superpower Diplomacy (1996); Donald Katz, Home Fires: An Intimate Portrait of One Middle-Class Family in Postwar America (1992); Barbara Kelly, Expanding the American Dream: Building and Rebuilding Levittown (1993); Melvyn Leffler, A Preponderance of Power (1991); George Lipsitz, A Rainbow at Midnight: Labor and Culture in the 1940s (1994); Allen J. Matusow, Farm Policies and Politics in the Truman Years (1967); Elaine Tyler May, Homeward Bound: American Families in the Cold War Era (1988); William O'Neil, American High: The Years of Confidence, 1945–1960 (1986); David M. Oshinsky, A Conspiracy So Immense: The World of Joseph McCarthy (1983); Thomas G. Paterson, On Every Front: The Making and Unmaking of the Cold War (1992); James T. Patterson, Grand Expectations: The United States, 1945–1974 (1996); Henry A. J. Ramos, The American GI Forum: In Pursuit of the Dream, 1948–1983 (1998); Arnold Rampersad, Jackie Robinson (1997); Gregory C. Randall, America's Original GI Town: Park Forest, Illinois (2000); Gary W. Reichard, Politics as Usual (1988); Stanley Sandler, The Korean War: No Victors, No Vanquished (1999); Michael Schaller, The American Occupation of Japan: The Origins of the Cold War in Asia (1985); Ellen W. Schrenker, The Age of McCarthyism (1994); Ellen Schrenker, Many Are the Crimes: McCarthyism in America (1998); W. R. Smyser, From Yalta to Berlin: The Cold War Struggle over Germany (1999); Athan Theoharis and John S. Cox, The Boss: J. Edgar Hoover and the Great American Inquisition (1988); Marc A. Trachtenberg, Constructed Peace: The Making of the European Settlement, 1945–1963 (1999).

CHAPTER 27 Quest for Consensus, 1952–1960

Charles C. Alexander, Holding the Line (1985); H. W. Brands, Jr., Cold Warriors (1988); Wini Breines, Young, White, and Miserable: Growing Up Female in the Fifties (1992); Taylor Branch, Parting the Water: America in the King Years, 1954–1963 (1988); Larry W. Burt, Tribalism in Crisis: Federal Indian Policy, 1953–1961 (1982); Willard W. Cochrane and Mary E. Ryan, American Farm Policy, 1948–1973 (1976); John D'Emilio and Estelle B. Freedman, Intimate Matters: A History of Sexuality in America (1988); Robert A. Devine, Blowing in the Wind: The Nuclear Test Ban Debate (1978); Robert A. Devine, The Sputnik Challenge (1993); Saki Dockrill, Eisenhower's New Look: National Security Policy, 1953–1961 (1996); Barbara Ehrenreich, Hearts of Men (1983); Robert Fishman, Bourgeois Utopias (1987); Donald I. Fixico, Termination and Relocation: Federal Indian Policy, 1945–1970 (1986); Lloyd Gardner, Approaching Vietnam (1988); William Graebner, Coming of Age in Buffalo (1990); Fred I. Greenstein, The Hidden-Hand Presidency (1982); Richard G. Hewlett and Jack M. Hall, Atoms for Peace and War (1989); Zachary Karabell, Architects of Intervention: The United States, The Third World, and the Cold War, 1946–1962 (1999); Alice Kessler-Harris, Out to Work: A History of Wage-Earning Women in the United States (1982); Chana Kai Lee, For Freedom's Sake: The Life of Fannie Lou Hamer (1999); Nicholas Lemann, The Promised Land (1991); George Lipsitz, Time Passages: Collective Memory and American Popular Culture (1991); Victory Marchetti and John D. Marks, The CIA and the Cult of Intelligence (1974); Karal Ann Marling, As Seen on TV: The Visual Culture of Everyday Life in the 1950s (1994); Waldo Martin, Jr., Brown v. Board of Education: A Brief History with Documents (1998); Martin E. Marty, Modern American Religion, Vol. 3: Under God, Indivisible, 1941–1960 (1996); Joan Meyerowitz, ed., Not June Cleaver: Women and Gender in Postwar America (1994); Thomas Paterson, Confronting Castro: The United States and the Triumph of the Cuban Revolution (1994); Richard H. Pells, The Liberal

Mind in a Conservative Age (1983); William Pickett, *Dwight David Eisenhower and American Power* (1995); Stephen G. Rabe, *Eisenhower and Latin America* (1988); Mark H. Rose, *Interstate* (1979); Michael Schumacher, *Dharma Lion: A Critical Biography of Allen Ginsberg* (1992); John W. Sloan, *Eisenhower and the Management of Prosperity* (1991); Jane Smith, *Patenting the Sun: Polio and the Salk Vaccine* (1990); Rennard Strickland, *Tonto's Revenge: Reflections on American Indian Culture and Policy* (1997); John C. Teaford, *The Twentieth Century City* (1993); Mark V. Tushnet, *Making Civil Rights Law: Thurgood Marshall and the Supreme Court, 1936–1961* (1995); John Tytell, *Naked Angels: The Lives and Literature of the Beat Generation* (1976); Steven Watts, *The Magic Kingdom: Walt Disney and the American Way of Life* (1997); Alan Winkler, *Life Under a Cloud: American Anxiety About the Atom* (1993).

CHAPTER 28 Great Promises, Bitter Disappointments, 1960–1968

Jervis Anderson, *Bayard Rustin: Troubles I've Seen* (1997); Terry Anderson, *The Movement and the Sixties* (1995); Irving Bernstein, *Guns or Butter: The Presidency of Lyndon Johnson* (1996); Alexander Bloom, ed., *"Takin' It to the Streets": A Sixties Reader* (1995); David Burner, *John F. Kennedy and a New Generation* (1988); Eric Burner, *And Gently He Shall Lead Them: Robert Parris Moses and Civil Rights in Mississippi* (1994); Claude Andrew Clegg III, *An Original Man: The Life and Times of Elijah Muhammad* (1997); David Farber, *The Age of Great Dreams: America in the 1960s* (1994); Fritz Fischer, *Making Them Like Us: Peace Corps Volunteers in the 1960s* (1998); Alexander Fursendo and Timothy Naftali, *"One Hell of a Gamble": Khrushchev, Castro, and Kennedy, 1958–1964* (1998); David Garrow, *Protest at Selma: Martin Luther King and the Voting Rights Act of 1965* (1978); Paula Giddings and Cornel West, *Regarding Malcolm X* (1994); James Giglio, *The Presidency of John F. Kennedy* (1991); Hugh Davis Graham, *The Civil Rights Era: Origins and Development of National Policy, 1960–1972* (1990); Maurice Isserman and Michael Kazin, *America Divided: The Civil War of the 1960s* (1999); Michael B. Katz, *The Undeserving Poor: From the War on Poverty to the War on Welfare* (1989); Richard D. Mahoney, *JFK: Ordeal in Africa* (1983); Allen Matusow, *The Unraveling of America: A History of Liberalism in the 1960s* (1984); James Miller, *"Democracy Is in the Streets"—From Port Huron to the Siege at Chicago* (1987); Charles Murray, *Losing Ground: American Social Policy, 1950–1980* (1984); Thomas Paterson, ed., *Kennedy's Quest for Victory: American Foreign Policy, 1961–1963* (1989); Stephen Rabe, *The Most Dangerous Area in the World: John F. Kennedy Confronts Communist Revolution in Latin America* (1999); Thomas C. Reeves, *President Kennedy: Profile of Power* (1994); Theodore Roszak, *The Making of the Counterculture* (1969); Thomas Schoenbaum, *Waging Peace and War: Dean Rusk in the Truman, Kennedy, and Johnson Years* (1988); Bernard Schwartz, *Super Chief: Earl Warren and His Supreme Court* (1983); John E. Schwartz, *America's Hidden Success: A Reassessment of Twenty Years of Public Policy* (1983); Jay Stevens, *Storming Heaven: LSD and the American Dream* (1987); Barbara L. Tischler, ed., *Sights on the Sixties* (1992); Irwin Unger, *The Movement: A History of the American New Left, 1959–1972* (1974); Melvin Urofsky, *The Continuity of Change: The Supreme Court and Individual Liberties, 1953–1986* (1991); William L. Van Deburg, ed., *Modern Black Nationalism: From Marcus Garvey to Louis Farrakhan* (1997); Elizabeth S. Watkins, *On the Pill: A Social History of Oral Contraception, 1950–1970* (1998); Robert Weisbrot, *Freedom Bound: A History of America's Civil Rights Movement* (1991).

CHAPTER 29 America Under Stress, 1967–1976

Rodolfo F. Acuna, *Community Under Seige: A Chronicle of Chicanos East of the Los Angeles River, 1945–1975* (1984); Stephen Ambrose, *Nixon: The Triumph of the Politician, 1962–1972* (1990); Larry Berman, *Lyndon Johnson's War* (1989); Robert Buzzanco, *Masters of War: Military Dissent and Politics in Vietnam* (1996); H. W. Brand, *The Wages of Globalism: Lyndon Johnson and the Limits of American Power* (1995); H. W. Brands, *Beyond Vietnam: The Foreign Policies of Lyndon Johnson* (1999); Robert Buzzanco, *Vietnam and the Transformation of American Life* (1999); Larry Cable, *Unholy Grail* (1991); Peter Carroll, *It Seemed Like Nothing Happened* (1982); Dan T. Carter, *Politics of Rage: George Wallace, the Origins of the New Conservatism, and the Transformation of American Politics* (1996); Robert Dallek, *Flawed Giant: Lyndon Johnson and His Times, 1961–1973* (1998); Vine Deloria, Jr., *Custer Died for Your Sins: An Indian Manifesto* (1969); Robert Devine, *The Johnson Years*, Vols. 1–3 (1981, 1987, 1994); W. D. Ehrhart, *Ordinary Lives: Platoon 1005 and the Vietnam War* (1999); Richard W. Etulain, ed., *Cesar Chavez* (2002); E. Garcia and Pablo De Greiff, *Hispanics/Latinos in the United States: Ethnicity, Race, and Rights* (2000); Juan Gomez-Quinones, *Chicano Politics: Reality and Promise, 1940–1990* (1990); Richard Griswold de Castillo and Richard A. Garcia, *Cesar Chavez: A Triumph of Spirit* (1995); John R. Greene, *The Presidency of Gerald R. Ford* (1995); Jose Angel Gutierrez, *The Making of a Chicano Militant: Lessons from Cristal* (1999); H. R. Haldeman, *The Haldeman Diaries: Inside the Nixon White House* (1994); Seymour Hersh, *The Price of Power: Kissinger in the Nixon White House* (1983); Troy R. Johnson, *The Occupation of Alcatraz Island: Indian Self-Determination and the Rise of American Activism* (1996); Dean J. Kotlowski, *Nixon's Civil Rights* (2001); Blanche Linden-Ward and Carol Hurd Green, *American Women in the 1960s* (1993); Fredrick Logevall, *Choosing War: The Lost Chance for Peace and the Escalation of War in Vietnam* (1999); Kim McQuaid, *The Anxious Years: America in the Vietnam and Watergate Era* (1989); Marguerite V. Marin, *Social Protest in an Urban Barrio: A Study of the Chicano Movement, 1966–1974* (1991); George D. Moss, *Vietnam: An American Ordeal* (1994); Carlos Munoz, Jr., *Youth, Identity, Power: The Chicano Movement* (1989); Armando Navarro, *Mexican American Youth Organization: Avant-Garde of the Chicano Movement in Texas* (1995); Richard Nixon, *RN: The Memoirs of Richard Nixon* (1978); James S. Olson and Randy Roberts, *My Lai: A Brief History with Documents* (1998); Herbert Parmet, *The World and Richard Nixon* (1990); Maria Perez y Gonzalez, *Puerto Ricans in the United States* (2000); Julie Pycior, *LBJ and Mexican Americans: The Paradox of Power* (1997); Vicki L. Ruiz, *From Out of the Shadows: Mexican Women in 20th Century America* (1997); Kirkpatrick Sales, *The Green Revolution: The American Environmental Movement, 1962–1992* (1996); Michael Schaller and George Rising, *The Republican Ascendancy: American Politics, 1968–2001* (2002); Deborah Shapely, *Promise and Power: The Life and Times of Robert McNamara* (1993); Neil Sheehan, *A Bright Shining Lie: John Paul Vann and America in Vietnam* (1988); Melvin Small, *Johnson, Nixon, and the Doves* (1988); Ronald Spector, *After Tet: The Bloodiest Year in Vietnam* (1992); Steven J. Spiegel, *The Other Arab-Israeli Conflict: Making America's Middle East Policy from Truman* to Reagan (1985); David E. Wilkins, *American Indian Politics* (2001); Bob Woodward and Carl Bernstein, *All the President's Men* (1974, rpt. 1994); Daniel Yergin, *The Prize* (1994).

CHAPTER 30   Facing Limits, 1976–1992

William Berman, *America's Right Turn: From Nixon to Bush* (1994); Kenneth S. Baer, *Reinventing Democrats: The Politics of Liberalism from Reagan to Clinton* (2000); John A. Booth and Thomas W. Walker, *Understanding Central America* (1989); Peter G. Bourne, *Jimmy Carter: A Comprehensive Biography from Plains to Post-Presidency* (1997); Paul Boyer, ed., *Reagan as President* (1990); Connie Bruck, *The Predator's Ball: The Junk Bond Raiders and the Man Who Staked Them* (1988); Dan Carter, *From George Wallace to Newt Gingrich: Race in the Conservative Counterrevolution, 1963–1994* (1996); Leslie W. Dunbar, ed., *Minority Report: What Has Happened to Blacks, Hispanics, American Indians, and Other Minorities in the Eighties* (1984); Michael Duffy and Daniel Goodgame, *Marching in Place: The Status Quo Presidency of George Bush* (1992); Paul Dukes, *The Last Great Game* (1989); John Dumbrell, *American Foreign Policy: Carter to Clinton* (1997); Carol Felsenthal, *The Sweetheart of the Silent Majority* (1981); Lawrence Freedman and Efraim Karsh, *The Gulf Conflict, 1990–1992* (1993); Raymond Gartoff, *The Great Transition: American-Soviet Relations and the End of the Cold War* (1994); Nathan Glazer, ed., *Clamor at the Gates: The New American Immigration* (1986); John R. Greene, *The Presidency of George Bush* (2000); William E. Griffth, ed., *Central and Eastern Europe: The Opening Curtain* (1989); Samuel P. Hays, *Beauty, Health, and Permanence: Environmental Politics in the United States, 1955–1985* (1987); Michael J. Hogan, *The Panama Canal in American Politics* (1986); Haynes Johnson, *Sleepwalking Through History: America in the Reagan Years* (1991); Charles O. Jones, *The Trusteeship Presidency: Jimmy Carter and the United States Congress* (1988); Harold H. Koh, *The National Security Constitution* (1990); Walter LaFeber, *The Panama Canal* (1989); Robert S. Leiken, ed., *Central America: Anatomy of Conflict* (1984); Robert C. Liberman and Robert Wuthnow, eds., *The New Christian Right* (1983); Theodore Lowi, *The End of the Republican Era* (1995); Donald Mabry, ed., *The Latin American Narcotics Trade* (1992); David Mervin, *George Bush and the Guardianship*

Presidency (1996); John Palmer and Elizabeth Sawmill, eds., *The Reagan Record* (1984); William B. Quandt, *Camp David* (1986); T. S. Reid, *The Chip* (1985); Herbert D. Rosenbaum and Alexi Ugrinsky, eds., *The Presidency and Domestic Policies of Jimmy Carter* (1993); Lillian Rubin, *Families on the Fault Line: America's Working Class Speaks about the Family, the Economy, Race, and Ethnicity* (1994); Robert Scheer, *With Enough Shovels* (1982); Peter Scott and Jonathan Marshall, *Cocaine Politics: Drugs, Armies, and the CIA in Central America* (1991); Laurence H. Shoup, *The Carter Presidency and Beyond* (1980); Allan P. Sindler, *Bakke, DeFunis, and the Minority Admissions* (1978); John W. Sloan, *The Reagan Effect: Economics and Presidential Leadership* (1999); Gaddis Smith, *Morality, Reason, and Power* (1986); James B. Stewart, *Den of Thieves* (1991); Robert A. Strong, *Working in the World: Jimmy Carter and the Making of American Foreign Policy* (2000); William Wei, *The Asian American Movement* (1993); John Kenneth White, *The New Politics of Old Values* (1988); Clyde Wilcox, *Onward Christian Soldiers: The Religious Right in American Politics* (1996); John Woodridge, *The Evangelicals* (1975).

CHAPTER 31   Entering a New Century, 1992–2002

Dan Balz and Ronald Brownstein, *Storming the Gates: Protest Politics and the Republican Revival* (1996); David Bender and Bruno Leane, *Abortion: Opposing Viewpoints* (1997); William C. Berman, *From the Center to the Edge: The Politics and Policies of the Clinton Presidency* (2001); Andrew J. Bracevich and Eliot A. Cohen, *War Over Kosovo* (2001); Susan K. Cahn, *Coming on Strong: Gender and Sexuality in 20th-Century Sport* (1994); Colin Campbell and Bert A. Rockman, eds., *The Clinton Legacy* (2001); Ruth Colker, *Abortion and Dialogue: Pro-Choice, Pro-Life, and American Law* (1992); Donald T. Crithlow, ed., *The Politics of Abortion and Birth Control in Historical Perspective* (1996); Margaret Cruikshank, *The Gay and Lesbian Liberation Movement* (1992); W. Avon Drake and Robert D. Holsworth, *Affirmative Action and the Stalled Quest for Black Progress* (1996); Thomas Friedman, *The Lexus and the Olive Tree: Understanding Globalization* (1999); Herbert Gans, *The War Against the Poor: The Underclass and Anti-Poverty Policy* (1995); Howard Gillman, *The Votes That Counted: How the Court Decided the 2000 Presidential

Election* (2001); Willman Greider, *One World, Ready or Not: The Manic Logic of Global Capitalism* (2000); James D. Hunter, *Culture Wars: The Struggle to Define America* (1991); Kathleen H. Jamieson and Paul Waldman, eds., *Electing the President, 2000: The Insiders' View* (2001); Michael Katz, *The Undeserving Poor: From the War on Poverty to the War on Welfare* (1989); Jonathan Kozol, *Rachael and Her Children: Homeless Families in America* (1988); Elliot Liebow, *Tell Them Who I Am: The Lives of Homeless Women* (1993); John Longone, *AIDS: The Facts* (1988); Manhattan Institute and Pacific Research Institute, *Strangers at Our Gate: Immigration in the 1990s* (1994); David Maraniss, *First In His Class: A Biography of Bill Clinton* (1995); Robert Morris, *Partners in Power: The Clintons and Their America* (1996); Gary Nash, Charlotte Crabtree, and Ross E. Dunn, *History on Trial: Culture Wars and the Lessons of the Past* (1998); Michael Nelson, ed., *The Elections of 1992* (1993); Gary Orfield and Susan Eaton, *Dismantling Desegregation: The Quiet Reversal of* Brown v. Board of Education (1996); Juan Perea, ed., *Immigrants Out! The New Nativism and the Anti-Immigrant Impulse in the United States* (1997); Robert Reich, *The Work of Nations: Preparing Ourselves for Twenty-First-Century Capitalism* (1991); Stanley Renshon, *High Hopes: The Clinton Presidency and the Politics of Ambition* (1996); Farley Reynolds and Walter R. Allen, *The Color Line and the Quality of Life in America* (1987); Lillian Rubin, *Families on the Fault Line: America's Working Class Speaks About the Family, the Economy, Race, and Ethnicity* (1994); Arthur Schlesinger, Jr., *The Disuniting of America* (1991); Steven E. Schier, *The Postmodern Presidency* (2001); Jan Aart Scholte, *Globalization: A Critical Introduction* (2000); Hilda Scott, *Working Your Way to the Bottom: The Feminization of Poverty* (1985); William Serrin, *Homestead: The Glory and Tragedy of an American Steel Town* (1992); Ruth Sildel, *Women and Children Last* (1986); James Simon, *The Center Holds: The Power Struggle Inside the Rehnquist Court* (1995); Christina Hoff Sommers, *Who Stole Feminism? How Women Have Betrayed Women* (1994); Chris Toulouse and Timothy W. Luke, *The Politics of Cyberspace* (1997); Lawrence Tribe, *Clash of Absolutes* (1992); Melvin Urofsky, *A Conflict of Rights: The Supreme Court and Affirmative Action* (1991); Dewayne Wickham, *Bill Clinton and Black America* (2002); William J. Wilson, *The Truly Disadvantaged* (1987).

Declaration of Independence in Congress, July 4, 1776

When, in the course of human events, it becomes necessary for one people to dissolve the political bonds which have connected them with another, and to assume, among the powers of the earth, the separate and equal station to which the laws of nature and of nature's God entitle them, a decent respect to the opinions of mankind requires that they should declare the causes which impel them to the separation.

We hold these truths to be self-evident: That all men are created equal; that they are endowed by their Creator with certain unalienable rights; that among these are life, liberty, and the pursuit of happiness; that, to secure these rights, governments are instituted among men, deriving their just powers from the consent of the governed; that whenever any form of government becomes destructive of these ends, it is the right of the people to alter or to abolish it, and to institute new government, laying its foundation on such principles, and organizing its powers in such form, as to them shall seem most likely to effect their safety and happiness. Prudence, indeed, will dictate that governments long established should not be changed for light and transient causes; and accordingly all experience hath shown that mankind are more disposed to suffer, while evils are sufferable, than to right themselves by abolishing the forms to which they are accustomed. But when a long train of abuses and usurpations, pursuing invariably the same object, evinces a design to reduce them under absolute despotism, it is their right, it is their duty, to throw off such government, and to provide new guards for their future security. Such has been the patient sufferance of these colonies; and such is now the necessity which constrains them to alter their former systems of government. The history of the present King of Great Britain is a history of repeated injuries and usurpations, all having in direct object the establishment of an absolute tyranny over these states. To prove this, let facts be submitted to a candid world.

He has refused his assent to laws, the most wholesome and necessary for the public good.

He has forbidden his governors to pass laws of immediate and pressing importance, unless suspended in their operation till his assent should be obtained; and, when so suspended, he has utterly neglected to attend to them.

He has refused to pass other laws for the accommodation of large districts of people, unless those people would relinquish the right of representation in the legislature, a right inestimable to them, and formidable to tyrants only.

He has called together legislative bodies at places unusual, uncomfortable, and distant from the depository of their public records, for the sole purpose of fatiguing them into compliance with his measures.

He has dissolved representative houses repeatedly, for opposing, with manly firmness, his invasions on the rights of the people.

He has refused for a long time, after such dissolutions, to cause others to be elected; whereby the legislative powers, incapable of annihilation, have returned to the people at large for their exercise; the state remaining, in the mean time, exposed to all the dangers of invasions from without and convulsions within.

He has endeavored to prevent the population of these states; for that purpose obstructing the laws for naturalization of foreigners; refusing to pass others to encourage their migration hither, and raising the conditions of new appropriations of lands.

He has obstructed the administration of justice, by refusing his assent to laws for establishing judiciary powers.

He has made judges dependent on his will alone, for the tenure of their offices, and the amount and payment of their salaries.

He has erected a multitude of new offices, and sent hither swarms of officers to harass our people and eat out their substance.

He has kept among us, in times of peace, standing armies, without the consent of our legislatures.

He has affected to render the military independent of, and superior to, the civil power.

He has combined with others to subject us to a jurisdiction foreign to our constitution, and unacknowledged by our laws, giving his assent to their acts of pretended legislation:

For quartering large bodies of armed troops among us;

For protecting them, by a mock trial, from punishment for any murders which they should commit on the inhabitants of these states;

For cutting off our trade with all parts of the world;

For imposing taxes on us without our consent;

For depriving us, in many cases, of the benefits of trial by jury;

For transporting us beyond seas, to be tried for pretended offenses;

For abolishing the free system of English laws in a neighboring province, establishing therein an arbitrary government, and enlarging its boundaries, so as to render it at once an example and fit instrument for introducing the same absolute rule into these colonies;

For taking away our charters, abolishing our most valuable laws, and altering fundamentally the forms of our governments;

For suspending our own legislatures, and declaring themselves invested with power to legislate for us in all cases whatsoever.

He has abdicated government here, by declaring us out of his protection and waging war against us.

He has plundered our seas, ravaged our coasts, burned our towns, and destroyed the lives of our people.

He is at this time transporting large armies of foreign mercenaries to complete the works of death, desolation, and tyranny already begun with circumstances of cruelty and perfidy scarcely paralleled in the most barbarous ages, and totally unworthy the head of a civilized nation.

He has constrained our fellow-citizens, taken captive on the high seas, to bear arms against their country, to become the executioners of their friends and brethren, or to fall themselves by their hands.

He has excited domestic insurrection among us, and has endeavored to bring on the inhabitants of our frontiers the merciless Indian savages, whose known rule of warfare is an undistinguished destruction of all ages, sexes, and conditions.

In every stage of these oppressions we have petitioned for redress in the most humble terms; our repeated petitions have been answered only by repeated injury. A prince, whose character is thus marked by every act which may define a tyrant, is unfit to be the ruler of a free people.

Nor have we been wanting in our attentions to our British brethren. We have warned them, from time to time, of attempts by their legislature to extend an unwarrantable jurisdiction over us. We have reminded them of the circumstances of our emigration and settlement here. We have appealed to their native justice and magnanimity; and we have conjured them, by the ties of our common kindred, to disavow these usurpations, which would inevitably interrupt our connections and correspondence. They, too, have been deaf to the voice of justice and of consanguinity. We must, therefore, acquiesce in the necessity which denounces our separation, and hold them, as we hold the rest of mankind, enemies in war, in peace friends.

We, therefore, the representatives of the United States of America, in General Congress assembled, appealing to the Supreme Judge of the world for the rectitude of our intentions, do, in the name and by the authority of the good people of these colonies, solemnly publish and declare, that these United Colonies are, and of right ought to be, FREE AND INDEPENDENT STATES; that they are absolved from all allegiance to the British crown, and that all political connection between them and the state of Great Britain is, and ought to be, totally dissolved; and that, as free and independent states, they have full power to levy war, conclude peace, contract alliances, establish commerce, and do all other acts and things which independent states may of right do. And for the support of this declaration, with a firm reliance on the protection of Divine Providence, we mutually pledge to each other our lives, our fortunes, and our sacred honor.

JOHN HANCOCK
and fifty-five others

Articles of Confederation

Whereas the Delegates of the United States of America in Congress assembled did on the fifteenth day of November in the Year of our Lord One Thousand Seven Hundred and Seventy seven, and in the Second Year of the Independence of America agree to certain articles of Confederation and perpetual Union between the States of Newhampshire, Massachusetts-bay, Rhode-island and Providence Plantations, Connecticut, New-York, New-Jersey, Pennsylvania, Delaware, Maryland, Virginia, North-Carolina, South-Carolina and Georgia in the Words following, viz. "Articles of Confederation and perpetual Union between the states of Newhampshire, Massachusetts-bay, Rhodeisland and Providence Plantations, Connecticut, New-York, New-Jersey, Pennsylvania, Delaware, Maryland, Virginia, North-Carolina, South-Carolina and Georgia.

Article I The Stile of this confederacy shall be "The United States of America."

Article II Each state retains its sovereignty, freedom and independence, and every Power, Jurisdiction and right, which is not by this confederation expressly delegated to the United States, in Congress assembled.

Article III The said states hereby severally enter into a firm league of friendship with each other, for their common defence, the security of their Liberties, and their mutual and general welfare, binding themselves to assist each other, against all force offered to, or attacks made upon them, or any of them, on account of religion, sovereignty, trade, or any other pretence whatever.

Article IV The better to secure and perpetuate mutual friendship and intercourse among the people of the different states in this union, the free inhabitants of each of these states, paupers, vagabonds and fugitives from Justice excepted, shall be entitled to all privileges and immunities of free citizens in the several states; and the people of each state shall have free ingress and regress to and from any other state, and shall enjoy therein all the privileges of trade and commerce, subject to the same duties, impositions and restrictions as the inhabitants thereof respectively, provided that such restriction shall not extend so far as to prevent the removal of property imported into any state, to any other state of which the Owner is an inhabitant; provided also that no imposition, duties or restriction shall be laid by any state, on the property of the united states, or either of them.

If any Person guilty of, or charged with treason, felony, or other high misdemeanor in any state, shall flee from Justice, and be found in any of the united states, he shall upon demand of the Governor or executive power, of the state from which he fled, be delivered up and removed to the state having jurisdiction of his offence.

Full faith and credit shall be given in each of these states to the records, acts and judicial proceedings of the courts and magistrats of every other state.

Article V For the more convenient management of the general interests of the united states, delegates shall be annually appointed in such manner as the legislature of each state shall direct, to meet in Congress on the first Monday in November, in every year, with a power reserved to each state, to recall its delegates, or any of them, at any time within the year, and to send others in their stead, for the remainder of the Year.

No state shall be represented in Congress by less than two, nor by more than seven Members; and no person shall be capable of being a delegate for more than three years in any term of six years; nor shall any person, being a delegate, be capable of holding any office under the united states, for which he, or another for his benefit receives any salary, fees or emolument of any kind.

Each state shall maintain its own delegates in a meeting of the states, and while they act as members of the committee of the states.

In determining questions in the united states, in Congress assembled, each state shall have one vote.

Freedom of speech and debate in Congress shall not be impeached or questioned in any Court, or place out of Congress, and the members of congress shall be protected in their persons from arrests and imprisonments, during the time of their going to and from, and attendance on congress, except for treason, felony, or breach of the peace.

Article VI No state without the Consent of the united states in congress assembled, shall send any embassy to, or receive any embassy from, or enter into any conference, agreement, or alliance or treaty with any King, prince or state; nor shall any person holding any office of profit or trust under the united states, or any of them, accept of any present, emolument, office or title of any kind whatever from any king, prince or foreign state; nor shall the united states in congress assembled, or any of them, grant any title of nobility.

No two or more states shall enter into any treaty, confederation or alliance whatever between them, without the consent of the united states in congress assembled, specifying accurately the purposes for which the same is to be entered into, and how long it shall continue.

No state shall lay any imposts or duties, which may interfere with any stipulations in treaties, entered into by the united states in congress assembled, with any king, prince or state, in pursuance of any treaties already proposed by congress, to the courts of France and Spain.

No vessels of war shall be kept up in time of peace by any state, except such number only, as shall be deemed necessary by the united states in congress assembled, for the defence of such state, or its trade; nor shall any body of forces be kept up by any state, in time of peace, except such number only, as in the judgment of the united states, in congress assembled, shall be deemed requisite to garrison the forts necessary for the defence of such state; but every state shall always keep up a well regulated and disciplined militia, sufficiently armed and accoutred, and shall provide and constantly have ready for use, in public stores, a due number of field pieces and tents, and a proper quantity of arms, ammunition and camp equipage.

No state shall engage in any war without the consent of the united states in congress assembled, unless such state be actually invaded by enemies, or shall have received certain advice of a resolution being formed by some nation of Indians to invade such state, and the danger is so imminent as not to admit of a delay, till the united states in congress assembled can be consulted: nor shall any state grant commissions to any ships or vessels of war, nor letters of marque or reprisal, except it be after a declaration of war by the united states in congress assembled, and then only against the kingdom or state and the subjects thereof, against which war has been so declared, and under such regulations as shall be established by the united states in congress assembled, unless such state be infested by pirates, in which case vessels of war may be fitted out for that occasion, and kept so long as the danger shall continue, or until the united states in congress assembled shall determine otherwise.

Article VII   When land-forces are raised by any state for the common defence, all officers of or under the rank of colonel, shall be appointed by the legislature of each state respectively by whom such forces shall be raised, or in such manner as such state shall direct, and all vacancies shall be filled up by the state which first made the appointment.

Article VIII   All charges of war, and all other expences that shall be incurred for the common defence or general welfare, and allowed by the united states in congress assembled, shall be defrayed out of a common treasury, which shall be supplied by the several states, in proportion to the value of all land within each state, granted to or surveyed for any Person, as such land and the buildings and improvements thereon shall be estimated according to such mode as the united states in congress assembled, shall from time to time direct and appoint. The taxes for paying that proportion shall be laid and levied by the authority and direction of the legislatures of the several states within the time agreed upon by the united states in congress assembled.

Article IX   The united states in congress assembled, shall have the sole and exclusive right and power of determining on peace and war, except in the cases mentioned in the sixth article—of sending and receiving ambassadors—entering into treaties and alliances, provided that no treaty of commerce shall be made whereby the legislative power of the respective states shall be restrained from imposing such imposts and duties on foreigners, as their own people are subjected to, or from prohibiting the exportation or importation of any species of goods or commodities whatsoever—of establishing rules for deciding in all cases, what captures on land or water shall be legal, and in what manner prizes taken by land or naval forces in the service of the united states shall be divided or appropriated.—

of granting letters of marque and reprisal in times of peace—appointing courts for the trial of piracies and felonies committed on the high seas and establishing courts for receiving and determining finally appeals in all cases of captures, provided that no member of congress shall be appointed a judge of any of the said courts.

The united states in congress assembled shall also be the last resort on appeal in all disputes and differences now subsisting or that hereafter may arise between two or more states concerning boundary, jurisdiction or any other cause whatever; which authority shall always be exercised in the manner following. Whenever the legislative or executive authority or lawful agent of any state in controversy with another shall present a petition to congress, stating the matter in question and praying for a hearing, notice thereof shall be given by order of congress to the legislative or executive authority of the other state in controversy, and a day assigned for the appearance of the parties by their lawful agents, who shall then be directed to appoint by joint consent, commissioners or judges to constitute a court for hearing and determining the matter in question: but if they cannot agree, congress shall name three persons out of each of the united states, and from the list of such persons each party shall alternately strike out one, the petitioners beginning, until the number shall be reduced to thirteen; and from that number not less than seven, nor more than nine names as congress shall direct, shall in the presence of congress be drawn out by lot, and the persons whose names shall be so drawn or any five of them, shall be commissioners or judges, to hear and finally determine the controversy, so always as a major part of the judges who shall hear the cause shall agree in the determination: and if either party shall neglect to attend at the day appointed, without shewing reasons, which congress shall judge sufficient, or being present shall refuse to strike, the congress shall proceed to nominate three persons out of each state, and the secretary of congress shall strike in behalf of such party absent or refusing; and the judgment and sentence of the court to be appointed, in the manner before prescribed, shall be final and conclusive; and if any of the parties shall refuse to submit to the authority of such court, or to appear to defend their claim or cause, the court shall nevertheless proceed to pronounce sentence, or judgment, which shall in like manner be final and decisive, the judgment or sentence and other proceedings being in either case transmitted to congress, and lodged among the acts of congress for the security of the parties concerned: provided that every commissioner, before he sits in judgment, shall take an oath to be administered by one of the judges of the supreme or superior court of the state, where the cause shall be tried, "well and truly to hear and determine the matter in question, according to the best of his judgment, without favour, affection or hope of reward:" provided also that no state shall be deprived of territory for the benefit of the united states.

All controversies concerning the private right of soil claimed under different grants of two or more states, whose jurisdictions as they may respect such lands, and the states which passed such grants are adjusted, the said grants or either of them being at the same time claimed to have originated antecedent to such settlement of jurisdiction, shall on the petition of either party to the congress of the united states, be finally determined as near as may be in the same manner as is before prescribed for deciding disputes respecting territorial jurisdiction between different states.

The united states in congress assembled shall also have the sole and exclusive right and power of regulating the alloy and value of coin struck by their own authority, or by that of the respective states—fixing the standard of weights and measures throughout the united states.—regulating the trade and managing all affairs with the Indians, not members of any of the states, provided that the legislative right of any state within its own limits be not infringed or violated—establishing and regulating post-offices from one state to another, throughout all the united states, and exacting such postage on the papers passing thro' the same as may be requisite to defray the expences of the said office—appointing all officers of the land forces, in the service of the united states, excepting regimental officers.—appointing all the officers of the naval forces, and commissioning all officers whatever in the service of the united states—making rules for the government and regulation of the said land and naval forces, and directing their operations.

The united states in congress assembled shall have authority to appoint a committee, to sit in the recess of congress, to be denominated "A Committee of the States," and to consist of one delegate from each state; and to appoint such other committees and civil officers as may be necessary for managing the general affairs of the united states under their direction—to appoint one of their number to preside, provided that no person be allowed to serve in the office of president more than one year in any term of three years; to ascertain the necessary sums of Money to be raised for the service of the united states, and to appropriate and apply the same for defraying the public expences—to borrow money, or emit bills on the credit of the united states,

transmitting every half year to the respective states an account of the sums of money so borrowed or emitted,—to build and equip a navy—to agree upon the number of land forces, and to make requisitions from each state for its quota, in proportion to the number of white inhabitants in such state; which requisition shall be binding, and thereupon the legislature of each state shall appoint the regimental officers, raise the men and cloath, arm and equip them in a soldier like manner, at the expence of the united states, and the officers and men so cloathed, armed and equipped shall march to the place appointed, and within the time agreed on by the united states in congress assembled: But if the united states in congress assembled shall, on consideration of circumstances judge proper that any state should not raise men, or should raise a smaller number than its quota, and that any other state should raise a greater number of men than the quota thereof, such extra number shall be raised, officered, cloathed, armed and equipped in the same manner as the quota of such state, unless the legislature of such state shall judge that such extra number cannot be safely spared out of the same, in which case they shall raise, officer, cloath, arm and equip as many of such extra number as they judge can be safely spared. And the officers and men so cloathed, armed and equipped, shall march to the place appointed, and within the time agreed on by the united states in congress assembled.

The united states in congress assembled shall never engage in a war, nor grant letters of marque and reprisal in time of peace, nor enter into any treaties or alliances, nor coin money, nor regulate the value thereof, nor ascertain the sums and expences necessary for the defence and welfare of the united states, or any of them, nor emit bills, nor borrow money on the credit of the united states, nor appropriate money, nor agree upon the number of vessels of war, to be built or purchased, or the number of land or sea forces to be raised, nor appoint a commander in chief of the army or navy, unless nine states assent to the same: nor shall a question on any other point, except for adjourning from day to day be determined, unless by the votes of a majority of the united states in congress assembled.

The congress of the united states shall have power to adjourn to any time within the year, and to any place within the united states, so that no period of adjournment be for a longer duration than the space of six Months, and shall publish the Journal of their proceedings monthly, except such parts thereof relating to treaties, alliances or military operations as in their judgment require secresy; and the yeas and nays of the delegates of each state on any question shall be entered on the Journal, when it is desired by any delegate; and the delegates of a state, or any of them, at his or their request shall be furnished with a transcript of the said Journal, except such parts as are above excepted, to lay before the legislatures of the several states.

Article X The committee of the states, or any nine of them, shall be authorised to execute, in the recess of congress, such of the powers of congress as the united states in congress assembled, by the consent of nine states, shall from time to time think expedient to vest them with; provided that no power be delegated to the said committee, for the exercise of which, by the articles of confederation, the voice of nine states in the congress of the united states assembled is requisite.

Article XI Canada acceding to this confederation, and joining in the measures of the united states, shall be admitted into, and entitled to all the advantages of this union: but no other colony shall be admitted into the same, unless such admission be agreed to by nine states.

Article XII All bills of credit emitted, monies borrowed and debts contracted by, or under the authority of congress, before the assembling of the united states, in pursuance of the present confederation, shall be deemed and considered as a charge against the united states, for payment and satisfaction whereof the said united states, and the public faith are hereby solemnly pledged.

Article XIII Every state shall abide by the determinations of the united states in congress assembled, on all questions which by this confederation are submitted to them. And the Articles of this confederation shall be inviolably observed by every state, and the union shall be perpetual; nor shall any alteration at any time hereafter be made in any of them; unless such alteration be agreed to in a congress of the united states, and be afterwards confirmed by the legislatures of every state.

AND WHEREAS it hath pleased the Great Governor of the World to incline the hearts of the legislatures we respectively represent in congress, to approve of, and to authorize us to ratify the said articles of confederation and perpetual union. Know Ye that we the under-signed delegates, by virtue of the power and authority to us given for that purpose, do by these presents, in the name and in behalf of our respective constituents, fully and entirely ratify and confirm each and every of the said articles of confederation and perpetual union, and all and singular the matters and things therein contained: And we do further solemnly

plight and engage the faith of our respective constituents, that they shall abide by the determinations of the united states in congress assembled, on all questions, which by the said confederation are submitted to them. And that the articles thereof shall be inviolably observed by the states we respectively represent, and that the union shall be perpetual. In Witness whereof we have hereunto set our hands in Congress. Done at Philadelphia in the state of Pennsylvania the ninth Day of July in the Year of our Lord one Thousand seven Hundred and Seventy-eight, and in the third year of the independence of America.

Constitution of the United States of America and Amendments*

Preamble

We the people of the United States, in order to form a more perfect union, establish justice, insure domestic tranquillity, provide for the common defense, promote the general welfare, and secure the blessings of liberty to ourselves and our posterity, do ordain and establish this Constitution for the United States of America.

Article I

Section 1 All legislative powers herein granted shall be vested in a Congress of the United States, which shall consist of a Senate and a House of Representatives.

Section 2 The House of Representatives shall be composed of members chosen every second year by the people of the several States, and the electors in each State shall have the qualifications requisite for electors of the most numerous branch of the State Legislature.

No person shall be a Representative who shall not have attained to the age of twenty-five years, and been seven years a citizen of the United States, and who shall not, when elected, be an inhabitant of that State in which he shall be chosen.

Representatives and direct taxes shall be apportioned among the several States which may be included within this Union, according to their respective numbers, *which shall be determined by adding to the whole number of free persons, including those bound to service for a term of years and excluding Indians not taxed, three-fifths of all other persons.* The actual enumeration shall be made within three years after the first meeting of the Congress of the United States, and within every

---

* Passages no longer in effect are printed in italic type.

subsequent term of ten years, in such manner as they shall by law direct. The number of Representatives shall not exceed one for every thirty thousand, but each State shall have at least one Representative; *and until such enumeration shall be made, the State of New Hampshire shall be entitled to choose three, Massachusetts eight, Rhode Island and Providence Plantations one, Connecticut five, New York six, New Jersey four, Pennsylvania eight, Delaware one, Maryland six, Virginia ten, North Carolina five, South Carolina five, and Georgia three.*

When vacancies happen in the representation from any State, the Executive authority thereof shall issue writs of election to fill such vacancies.

The House of Representatives shall choose their Speaker and other officers; and shall have the sole power of impeachment.

Section 3 The Senate of the United States shall be composed of two Senators from each State, *chosen by the legislature thereof,* for six years; and each Senator shall have one vote.

Immediately after they shall be assembled in consequence of the first election, they shall be divided as equally as may be into three classes. The seats of the Senators of the first class shall be vacated at the expiration of the second year, of the second class at the expiration of the fourth year, and of the third class at the expiration of the sixth year, so that one-third may be chosen every second year; *and if vacancies happen by resignation or otherwise, during the recess of the legislature of any State, the Executive thereof may make temporary appointments until the next meeting of the legislature, which shall then fill such vacancies.*

No person shall be a Senator who shall not have attained to the age of thirty years, and been nine years a citizen of the United States, and who shall not, when elected, be an inhabitant of that State for which he shall be chosen.

The Vice-President of the United States shall be President of the Senate, but shall have no vote, unless they be equally divided.

The Senate shall choose their other officers, and also a President *pro tempore*, in the absence of the Vice-President, or when he shall exercise the office of President of the United States.

The Senate shall have the sole power to try all impeachments. When sitting for that purpose, they shall be on oath or affirmation. When the President of the United States is tried, the Chief Justice shall preside: and no person shall be convicted with-out the concurrence of two-thirds of the members present.

Judgment in cases of impeachment shall not extend further than to removal from the office, and disqualification to hold and enjoy any office of honor, trust or profit under the United States: but the party convicted shall nevertheless be liable and subject to indictment, trial, judgment and punishment, according to law.

Section 4 The times, places and manner of holding elections for Senators and Representatives shall be prescribed in each State by the legislature thereof; but the Congress may at any time by law make or alter such regulations, except as to the places of choosing Senators.

The Congress shall assemble at least once in every year, and such meeting *shall be on the first Monday in December, unless they shall by law appoint a different day.*

Section 5 Each house shall be the judge of the elections, returns and qualifications of its own members, and a majority of each shall constitute a quorum to do business; but a smaller number may adjourn from day to day, and may be authorized to compel the attendance of absent members, in such manner, and under such penalties, as each house may provide.

Each house may determine the rules of its proceedings, punish its members for disorderly behavior, and with the concurrence of two-thirds, expel a member.

Each house shall keep a journal of its proceedings, and from time to time publish the same, excepting such parts as may in their judgment require secrecy; and the yeas and nays of the members of either house on any question shall, at the desire of one-fifth of those present, be entered on the journal.

Neither house, during the session of Congress, shall, without the consent of the other, adjourn for more than three days, nor to any other place than that in which the two houses shall be sitting.

Section 6 The Senators and Representatives shall receive a compensation for their services, to be ascertained by law and paid out of the treasury of the United States. They shall in all cases except treason, felony and breach of the peace, be privileged from arrest during their attendance at the session of their respective houses, and in going to and returning from the same; and for any speech or debate in either house, they shall not be questioned in any other place.

No Senator or Representative shall, during the time for which he was elected, be appointed to any civil office under the authority of the United States, which shall have been created, or the emoluments whereof shall have been increased, during such time; and no person holding any office under the United States shall be a member of either house during his continuance in office.

Section 7 All bills for raising revenue shall originate in the House of Representatives; but the Senate may propose or concur with amendments as on other bills.

Every bill which shall have passed the House of Representatives and the Senate, shall, before it become a law, be presented to the President of the United States; if he approve he shall sign it, but if not he shall return it with objections to that house in which it originated, who shall enter the objections at large on their journal, and proceed to reconsider it. If after such reconsideration two-thirds of that house shall agree to pass the bill, it shall be sent, together with the objections, to the other house, by which it shall likewise be reconsidered, and, if approved by two-thirds of that house, it shall become a law. But in all such cases the votes of both houses shall be determined by yeas and nays, and the names of the persons voting for and against the bill shall be entered on the journal of each house respectively. If any bill shall not be returned by the President within ten days (Sundays excepted) after it shall have been presented to him, the same shall be a law, in like manner as if he had signed it, unless the Congress by their adjournment prevent its return, in which case it shall not be a law.

Every order, resolution, or vote to which the concurrence of the Senate and House of Representatives may be necessary (except on a question of adjournment) shall be presented to the President of the United States; and before the same shall take effect, shall be approved by him, or being disapproved by him, shall be repassed by two-thirds of the Senate and House of Representatives, according to the rules and limitations prescribed in the case of a bill.

Section 8   The Congress shall have power

To lay and collect taxes, duties, imposts, and excises, to pay the debts and provide for the common defense and general welfare of the United States; but all duties, imposts and excises shall be uniform throughout the United States;

To borrow money on the credit of the United States;

To regulate commerce with foreign nations, and among the several States, and with the Indian tribes;

To establish an uniform rule of naturalization, and uniform laws on the subject of bankruptcies throughout the United States;

To coin money, regulate the value thereof, and of foreign coin, and fix the standard of weights and measures;

To provide for the punishment of counterfeiting the securities and current coin of the United States;

To establish post offices and post roads;

To promote the progress of science and useful arts by securing for limited times to authors and inventors the exclusive right to their respective writings and discoveries;

To constitute tribunals inferior to the Supreme Court;

To define and punish piracies and felonies committed on the high seas and offenses against the law of nations;

To declare war, grant letters of marque and reprisal, and make rules concerning captures on land and water;

To raise and support armies, but no appropriation of money to that use shall be for a longer term than two years;

To provide and maintain a navy;

To make rules for the government and regulation of the land and naval forces;

To provide for calling forth the militia to execute the laws of the Union, suppress insurrections, and repel invasions;

To provide for organizing, arming, and disciplining the militia, and for governing such part of them as may be employed in the service of the United States, reserving to the States respectively the appointment of the officers, and the authority of training the militia according to the discipline prescribed by Congress;

To exercise exclusive legislation in all cases whatsoever, over such district (not exceeding ten miles square) as may, by cession of particular States, and the acceptance of Congress, become the seat of government of the United States, and to exercise like authority over all places purchased by the consent of the legislature of the State, in which the same shall be, for erection of forts, magazines, arsenals, dockyards, and other needful buildings; — and

To make all laws which shall be necessary and proper for carrying into execution the foregoing powers, and all other powers vested by this Constitution in the government of the United States, or in any department or officer thereof.

Section 9   The migration or importation of such persons as any of the States now existing shall think proper to admit shall not be prohibited by the Congress prior to the year 1808; but a tax or duty may be imposed on such importation, not exceeding $10 for each person.

The privilege of the writ of habeas corpus shall not be suspended, unless when in cases of rebellion or invasion the public safety may require it.

No bill of attainder or ex post facto law shall be passed.

No capitation, or other direct, tax shall be laid, unless in proportion to the census or enumeration herein before directed to be taken.

No tax or duty shall be laid on articles exported from any State.

No preference shall be given by any regulation of commerce or revenue to the ports of one State over those of another; nor shall vessels bound to, or from, one State, be obliged to enter, clear, or pay duties in another.

No money shall be drawn from the treasury, but in consequence of appropriations made by law; and a regular statement and account of the receipts and expenditures of all public money shall be published from time to time.

No title of nobility shall be granted by the United States: and no person holding any office of profit or trust under them, shall, without the consent of the Congress, accept of any present, emolument, office, or title, of any kind whatever, from any king, prince, or foreign state.

Section 10 No State shall enter into any treaty, alliance, or confederation; grant letters of marque and reprisal; coin money; emit bills of credit; make anything but gold and silver coin a tender in payment of debts; pass any bill of attainder, ex post facto law, or law impairing the obligation of contracts, or grant any title of nobility.

No State shall, without the consent of Congress, lay any imposts or duties on imports or exports, except what may be absolutely necessary for executing its inspection laws: and the net produce of all duties and imposts, laid by any State on imports or exports, shall be for the use of the treasury of the United States; and all such laws shall be subject to the revision and control of the Congress.

No State shall, without the consent of Congress, lay any duty of tonnage, keep troops or ships of war in time of peace, enter into any agreement or compact with another State, or with a foreign power, or engage in war, unless actually invaded, or in such imminent danger as will not admit of delay.

Article II

Section 1 The executive power shall be vested in a President of the United States of America. He shall hold his office during the term of four years, and, together with the Vice-President, chosen for the same term, be elected as follows:

Each State shall appoint, in such manner as the legislature thereof may direct, a number of electors, equal to the whole number of Senators and Representatives to which the State may be entitled in the Congress; but no Senator or Representative, or person holding an office of trust or profit under the United States, shall be appointed an elector.

The electors shall meet in their respective States, and vote by ballot for two persons, of whom one at least shall not be an inhabitant of the same State with themselves. And they shall make a list of all the persons voted for, and of the number of votes for each; which list they shall sign and certify, and transmit sealed to the seat of government of the United States, directed to the President of the Senate. The President of the Senate shall, in the presence of the Senate and House of Representatives, open all the certificates, and the votes shall then be counted. The person having the greatest number of votes shall be the President, if such number be a majority of the whole number of electors appointed; and if there be more than one who have such majority, and have an equal number of votes, then the House of Representatives shall immediately choose by ballot one of them for President; and if no person have a majority, then from the five highest on the list said house shall in like manner choose the President. But in choosing the President the votes shall be taken by States, the representation from each State having one vote; a quorum for this purpose shall consist of a member or members from two-thirds of the States, and a majority of all the States shall be necessary to a choice. In every case, after the choice of the President, the person having the greatest number of votes of the electors shall be the Vice-President. But if there should remain two or more who have equal votes, the Senate shall choose from them by ballot the Vice-President.

The Congress may determine the time of choosing the electors and the day on which they shall give their votes; which day shall be the same throughout the United States.

No person except a natural-born citizen, *or a citizen of the United States at the time of the adoption of this Constitution,* shall be eligible to the office of President; neither shall any person be eligible to that office who shall not have attained to the age of thirty-five years, and been fourteen years a resident within the United States.

In cases of the removal of the President from office or of his death, resignation, or inability to discharge the powers and duties of the said office, the same shall devolve on the Vice-President, and the Congress may by law provide for the case of removal, death, resignation, or inability, both of the President and Vice-President, declaring what officer shall then act as President, and such officer shall act accordingly, until the disability be removed, or a President shall be elected.

The President shall, at stated times, receive for his services a compensation, which shall neither be increased nor diminished during the period for which he shall have been elected, and he shall not receive within that period any other emolument from the United States, or any of them.

Before he enter on the execution of his office, he shall take the following oath or affirmation:—"I do solemnly swear (or affirm) that I will faithfully execute the office of the President of the United States, and will to the best of my ability preserve, protect and defend the Constitution of the United States."

Section 2 The President shall be commander in chief of the army and navy of the United States, and of the militia of the several States, when called into the actual service of the United States; he may require the opinion, in writing, of the principal officer in each of the executive departments, upon any subject relating to the duties of their respective offices, and he shall have power to grant reprieves and pardons for offenses against the United States, except in cases of impeachment.

He shall have power, by and with the advice and consent of the Senate, to make treaties, provided two-thirds of the Senators present concur; and he shall nominate, and by and with the advice and consent of the Senate, shall appoint ambassadors, other public ministers and consuls, judges of the Supreme Court, and all other officers of the United States, whose appointments are not herein otherwise provided for, and which shall be established by law: but Congress may by law vest the appointment of such inferior officers, as they think proper, in the President alone, in the courts of law, or in the heads of departments.

The President shall have power to fill up all vacancies that may happen during the recess of the Senate, by granting commissions which shall expire at the end of their next session.

Section 3 He shall from time to time give to the Congress information of the state of the Union, and recommend to their consideration such measures as he shall judge necessary and expedient; he may, on extraordinary occasions, convene both houses, or either of them, and in case of disagreement between them, with respect to the time of adjournment, he may adjourn them to such time as he shall think proper; he shall receive ambassadors and other public ministers; he shall take care that the laws be faithfully executed, and shall commission all the officers of the United States.

Section 4 The President, Vice-President and all civil officers of the United States shall be removed from office on impeachment for, and on conviction of, treason, bribery, or other high crimes and misdemeanors.

Article III

Section 1 The judicial power of the United States shall be vested in one Supreme Court, and in such inferior courts as the Congress may from time to time ordain and establish. The judges, both of the Supreme and inferior courts, shall hold their offices during good behavior, and shall, at stated times, receive for their services a compensation which shall not be diminished during their continuance in office.

Section 2 The judicial power shall extend to all cases, in law and equity, arising under this Constitution, the laws of the United States, and treaties made, or which shall be made, under their authority;—to all cases affecting ambassadors, other public ministers and consuls;—to all cases of admiralty and maritime jurisdiction;—to controversies to which the United States shall be a party;—to controversies between two or more States;—*between a State and citizens of another State;*—between citizens of different States;—between citizens of the same State claiming lands under grants of different States, and between a State, or the citizens thereof, and foreign states, citizens or subjects.

In all cases affecting ambassadors, other public ministers and consuls, and those in which a State shall be party, the Supreme Court shall have original jurisdiction. In all the other cases before mentioned, the Supreme Court shall have appellate jurisdiction, both as to law and fact, with such exceptions, and under such regulations, as the Congress shall make.

The trial of all crimes, except in cases of impeachment, shall be by jury; and such trial shall be held in the State where said crimes shall have been committed; but when not committed within any State, the trial shall be at such place or places as the Congress may by law have directed.

Section 3 Treason against the United States shall consist only in levying war against them, or in adhering to their enemies, giving them aid and comfort. No person shall be convicted of treason unless on the testimony of two witnesses to the same overt act, or on confession in open court.

The Congress shall have power to declare the punishment of treason, but no attainder of treason shall work corruption of blood, or forfeiture except during the life of the person attainted.

Article IV

Section 1 Full faith and credit shall be given in each State to the public acts, records, and judicial proceedings of every other State. And the Congress may by general laws prescribe the manner in which such acts, records, and proceedings shall be proved, and the effect thereof.

Section 2 The citizens of each State shall be entitled to all privileges and immunities of citizens in the several States.

A person charged in any State with treason, felony, or other crime, who shall flee from justice, and be found in another State, shall on demand of the executive authority of the State from which he fled, be delivered up, to be removed to the State having jurisdiction of the crime.

No person held to service or labor in one State, under the laws thereof, escaping into another, shall, in consequence of any law or regulation therein, be discharged from such service or labor, but shall be delivered up on claim of the party to whom such service or labor may be due.

Section 3 New States may be admitted by the Congress into this Union; but no new State shall be formed or erected within the jurisdiction of any other State; nor any State be formed by the junction of two or more States, or parts of States, without the consent of the legislatures of the States concerned as well as of the Congress.

The Congress shall have power to dispose of and make all needful rules and regulations respecting the territory or other property belonging to the United States; and nothing in this Constitution shall be so construed as to prejudice any claims of the United States, or of any particular State.

Section 4 The United States shall guarantee to every State in this Union a republican form of government, and shall protect each of them against invasion; and on application of the legislature, or of the executive (when the legislature cannot be convened), against domestic violence.

Article V

The Congress, whenever two-thirds of both houses shall deem it necessary, shall propose amendments to this Constitution, or, on the application of the legislatures of two-thirds of the several States, shall call a convention for proposing amendments, which, in either case, shall be valid to all intents and purposes, as part of this Constitution, when ratified by the legislatures of three-fourths of the several States, or by conventions in three-fourths thereof, as the one or the other mode of ratification may be proposed by the Congress; provided *that no amendments which may be made prior to the year one thousand eight hundred and eight shall in any manner affect the first and fourth clauses in the ninth section of the first article;* and that no State, without its consent, shall be deprived of its equal suffrage in the Senate.

Article VI

All debts contracted and engagements entered into, before the adoption of this Constitution, shall be as valid against the United States under this Constitution, as under the Confederation.

This Constitution, and the laws of the United States which shall be made in pursuance thereof; and all treaties made, or which shall be made, under the authority of the United States, shall be the supreme law

of the land; and the judges in every State shall be bound thereby, anything in the Constitution or laws of any State to the contrary notwithstanding.

The Senators and Representatives before mentioned, and the members of the several State legislatures, and all executive and judicial officers, both of the United States and of the several States, shall be bound by oath or affirmation to support this Constitution; but no religious test shall ever be required as a qualification to any office or public trust under the United States.

Article VII

The ratification of the conventions of nine States shall be sufficient for the establishment of this Constitution between the States so ratifying the same.

Done in Convention by the unanimous consent of the States present, the seventeenth day of September in the year of our Lord one thousand seven hundred and eighty-seven and of the Independence of the United States of America the twelfth. In witness whereof we have hereunto subscribed our names.

GEORGE WASHINGTON
and thirty-seven others

Amendments to the Constitution[*]

Amendment I

Congress shall make no law respecting an establishment of religion, or prohibiting the free exercise thereof; or abridging the freedom of speech, or of the press; or the right of the people peaceably to assemble, and to petition the government for a redress of grievances.

Amendment II

A well-regulated militia being necessary to the security of a free State, the right of the people to keep and bear arms shall not be infringed.

Amendment III

No soldier shall, in time of peace, be quartered in any house without the consent of the owner, nor in time of war, but in a manner to be prescribed by law.

Amendment IV

The right of the people to be secure in their persons, houses, papers, and effects, against unreasonable searches and seizures, shall not be violated, and no warrants shall issue but upon probable cause, supported by oath or affirmation, and particularly describ-

---

[*] The first ten Amendments (the Bill of Rights) were adopted in 1791.

ing the place to be searched, and the persons or things to be seized.

Amendment V

No person shall be held to answer for a capital, or otherwise infamous crime, unless on a presentment or indictment of a grand jury, except in cases arising in the land or naval forces, or in the militia, when in actual service in time of war or public danger; nor shall any person be subject for the same offense to be twice put in jeopardy of life or limb; nor shall be compelled in any criminal case to be a witness against himself, nor be deprived of life, liberty, or property, without due process of law; nor shall private property be taken for public use without just compensation.

Amendment VI

In all criminal prosecutions, the accused shall enjoy the right to a speedy and public trial, by an impartial jury of the State and district wherein the crime shall have been committed, which district shall have been previously ascertained by law, and to be informed of the nature and cause of the accusation; to be confronted with the witnesses against him; to have compulsory process for obtaining witnesses in his favor, and to have the assistance of counsel for his defense.

Amendment VII

In suits at common law, where the value in controversy shall exceed twenty dollars, the right of trial by jury shall be preserved, and no fact tried by a jury shall be otherwise reexamined in any court of the United States, than according to the rules of the common law.

Amendment VIII

Excessive bail shall not be required, nor excessive fines imposed, nor cruel and unusual punishments inflicted.

Amendment IX

The enumeration in the Constitution, of certain rights, shall not be construed to deny or disparage others retained by the people.

Amendment X

The powers not delegated to the United States by the Constitution, nor prohibited by it to the States, are reserved to the States respectively, or to the people.

Amendment XI

[Adopted 1798]

The judicial power of the United States shall not be construed to extend to any suit in law or equity, commenced or prosecuted against one of the United States by citizens of another State, or by citizens or subjects of any foreign state.

Amendment XII

[Adopted 1804]

The electors shall meet in their respective States, and vote by ballot for President and Vice-President, one of whom, at least, shall not be an inhabitant of the same State with themselves; they shall name in their ballots the person voted for as President, and in distinct ballots the person voted for as Vice-President, and they shall make distinct lists of all persons voted for as President, and of all persons voted for as Vice-President, and of the number of votes for each, which lists they shall sign and certify, and transmit sealed to the seat of government of the United States, directed to the President of the Senate;—the President of the Senate shall, in the presence of the Senate and House of Representatives, open all the certificates and the votes shall then be counted;—the person having the greatest number of votes for President shall be the President, if such number be a majority of the whole number of electors appointed; and if no person have such majority, then from the persons having the highest numbers not exceeding three on the list of those voted for as President, the House of Representatives shall choose immediately, by ballot, the President. But in choosing the President, the votes shall be taken by States, the representation from each State having one vote; a quorum for this purpose shall consist of a member or members from two-thirds of the States, and a majority of all the States shall be necessary to a choice. And if the House of Representatives shall not choose a President whenever the right of choice shall devolve upon them, before the fourth day of March next following, then the Vice-President shall act as President, as in the case of the death or other constitutional disability of the President.

The person having the greatest number of votes as Vice-President shall be the Vice-President, if such number be a majority of the whole number of electors appointed; and if no person have a majority, then from the two highest numbers on the list the Senate shall choose the Vice-President; a quorum for the purpose shall consist of two-thirds of the whole number of Senators, and a majority of the whole number shall be necessary to a choice. But no person constitutionally ineligible to the office of President shall be eligible to that of Vice-President of the United States.

Amendment XIII

[Adopted 1865]

Section 1 Neither slavery nor involuntary servitude, except as a punishment for crime whereof the party shall have been duly convicted, shall exist within the United States, or any place subject to their jurisdiction.

Section 2 Congress shall have power to enforce this article by appropriate legislation.

Amendment XIV

[Adopted 1868]

Section 1 All persons born or naturalized in the United States, and subject to the jurisdiction thereof, are citizens of the United States and of the State wherein they reside. No State shall make or enforce any law which shall abridge the privileges or immunities of citizens of the United States; nor shall any State deprive any person of life, liberty, or property, without due process of law; nor deny to any person within its jurisdiction the equal protection of the laws.

Section 2 Representatives shall be apportioned among the several States according to their respective numbers, counting the whole number of persons in each State, excluding Indians not taxed. But when the right to vote at any election for the choice of Electors for President and Vice-President of the United States, Representatives in Congress, the executive and judicial officers of a State, or the members of the legislature thereof, is denied to any of the male inhabitants of such State, being twenty-one years of age and citizens of the United States, or in any way abridged, except for participation in rebellion, or other crime, the basis of representation therein shall be reduced in the proportion which the number of such male citizens shall bear to the whole number of male citizens twenty-one years of age in such State.

Section 3 No person shall be a Senator or Representative in Congress, or Elector of President and Vice-President, or hold any office, civil or military, under the United States, or under any State, who, having previously taken an oath, as a member of Congress, or as an officer of the United States, or as a member of any State legislature, or as an executive or judicial officer of any State, to support the Constitution of the United States, shall have engaged in insurrection or rebellion against the same, or given aid or comfort to the enemies thereof. Congress may, by a vote of two-thirds of each house, remove such disability.

Section 4 The validity of the public debt of the United States, authorized by law, including debts incurred for payment of pensions and bounties for services in suppressing insurrection or rebellion, shall not be questioned. But neither the United States nor any State shall assume or pay any debt or obligation incurred in aid of insurrection or rebellion against the United States, or any claim for the loss or emancipation of any slave; but

all such debts, obligations, and claims shall be held illegal and void.

Section 5 The Congress shall have power to enforce, by appropriate legislation, the provisions of this article.

Amendment XV

[Adopted 1870]

Section 1 The right of citizens of the United States to vote shall not be denied or abridged by the United States or by any State on account of race, color, or previous condition of servitude.

Section 2 The Congress shall have power to enforce this article by appropriate legislation.

Amendment XVI

[Adopted 1913]

The Congress shall have power to lay and collect taxes on incomes, from whatever source derived, without apportionment among the several States, and without regard to any census or enumeration.

Amendment XVII

[Adopted 1913]

Section 1 The Senate of the United States shall be composed of two Senators from each State, elected by the people thereof, for six years; and each Senator shall have one vote. The electors in each State shall have the qualifications requisite for electors of [voters for] the most numerous branch of the State legislatures.

Section 2 When vacancies happen in the representation of any State in the Senate, the executive authority of such State shall issue writs of election to fill such vacancies: Provided, that the Legislature of any State may empower the executive thereof to make temporary appointments until the people fill the vacancies by election as the Legislature may direct.

Section 3 This amendment shall not be so construed as to affect the election or term of any Senator chosen before it becomes valid as part of the Constitution.

Amendment XVIII

[Adopted 1919; Repealed 1933]

Section 1 After one year from the ratification of this article the manufacture, sale, or transportation of intoxicating liquors within, the importation thereof into, or the exportation thereof from the United States and all territory subject to the jurisdiction thereof, for beverage purposes, is hereby prohibited.

Section 2 The Congress and the several States shall have concurrent power to enforce this article by appropriate legislation.

Section 3 This article shall be inoperative unless it shall have been ratified as an amendment to the Constitution by the legislatures of the several States, as provided by the Constitution, within seven years from the date of the submission thereof to the States by the Congress.

Amendment XIX

[Adopted 1920]

Section 1 The right of citizens of the United States to vote shall not be denied or abridged by the United States or by any State on account of sex.

Section 2 The Congress shall have power to enforce this article by appropriate legislation.

Amendment XX

[Adopted 1933]

Section 1 The terms of the President and Vice-President shall end at noon on the 20th day of January, and the terms of Senators and Representatives at noon on the 3rd day of January, of the years in which such terms would have ended if this article had not been ratified; and the terms of their successors shall then begin.

Section 2 The Congress shall assemble at least once in every year, and such meeting shall begin at noon on the 3d day of January, unless they shall by law appoint a different day.

Section 3 If, at the time fixed for the beginning of the term of the President, the President-elect shall have died, the Vice-President-elect shall become President. If a President shall not have been chosen before the time fixed for the beginning of his term, or if the President-elect shall have failed to qualify, then the Vice-President-elect shall act as President until a President shall have qualified; and the Congress may by law provide for the case wherein neither a President-elect nor a Vice-President-elect shall have qualified, declaring who shall then act as President, or the manner in which one who is to act shall be selected, and such persons shall act accordingly until a President or Vice-President shall have qualified.

Section 4 The Congress may by law provide for the case of the death of any of the persons from whom the House of Representatives may choose a President whenever the right of choice shall have devolved upon them, and for the case of the death of any of the persons from whom the Senate may choose a Vice-President whenever the right of choice shall have devolved upon them.

Section 5 Sections 1 and 2 shall take effect on the 15th day of October following the ratification of this article.

Section 6 This article shall be inoperative unless it shall have been ratified as an amendment to the Constitution by the Legislatures of three-fourths of the several States within seven years from the date of its submission.

Amendment XXI

[Adopted 1933]

Section 1 The eighteenth article of amendment to the Constitution of the United States is hereby repealed.

Section 2 The transportation or importation into any State, Territory, or Possession of the United States for delivery or use therein of intoxicating liquors, in violation of the laws thereof, is hereby prohibited.

Section 3 This article shall be inoperative unless it shall have been ratified as an amendment to the Constitution by conventions in the several States, as provided in the Constitution, within seven years from the date of submission thereof to the States by the Congress.

Amendment XXII

[Adopted 1951]

Section 1 No person shall be elected to the office of President more than twice, and no person who has held the office of President, or acted as President, for more than two years of a term to which some other person was elected President shall be elected to the office of President more than once. But this article shall not apply to any person holding the office of President when this article was proposed by the Congress, and shall not prevent any person who may be holding the office of President, or acting as President, during the term within which this article becomes operative from holding the office of President or acting as President during the remainder of such term.

Section 2 This article shall be inoperative unless it shall have been ratified as an amendment to the Constitution by the legislatures of three-fourths of the several States within seven years from the date of its submission to the States by the Congress.

Amendment XXIII

[Adopted 1961]

Section 1 The District constituting the seat of Government of the United States shall appoint in such manner as the Congress may direct:

A number of electors of President and Vice-President equal to the whole number of Senators and Representatives in Congress to which the District would be entitled if it were a State, but in no event more than the least populous State; they shall be in addition to those appointed by the States, but they shall be considered for the purposes of the election of President and Vice-President, to be electors appointed by a State; and they shall meet in the District and perform such duties as provided by the twelfth article of amendment.

Section 2 The Congress shall have the power to enforce this article by appropriate legislation.

Amendment XXIV

[Adopted 1964]

Section 1 The right of citizens of the United States to vote in any primary or other election for President or Vice-President, for electors for President or Vice-President, or for Senator or Representative in Congress, shall not be denied or abridged by the United States or any State by reason of failure to pay any poll tax or other tax.

Section 2 The Congress shall have the power to enforce this article by appropriate legislation.

Amendment XXV

[Adopted 1967]

Section 1 In case of the removal of the President from office or of his death or resignation, the Vice-President shall become President.

Section 2 Whenever there is a vacancy in the office of the Vice-President, the President shall nominate a Vice-President who shall take office upon confirmation by a majority vote of both Houses of Congress.

Section 3 Whenever the President transmits to the President pro tempore of the Senate and the Speaker of the House of Representatives his written declaration that he is unable to discharge the powers and duties of his office, and until he transmits to them a written declaration to the contrary, such powers and duties shall be discharged by the Vice-President as Acting President.

Section 4 Whenever the Vice-President and a majority of either the principal officers of the executive departments or of such other body as Congress may by law provide, transmit to the President pro tempore of the Senate and the Speaker of the House of Representatives their written declaration that the President is un-able to discharge the powers and duties of his office, the Vice-President shall immediately assume the powers and duties of the office as Acting President.

Thereafter, when the President transmits to the President pro tempore of the Senate and the Speaker of the House of Representatives his written declaration that no inability exists, he shall resume the powers and duties of his office unless the Vice-President and a majority of either the principal officers of the executive department[s] or of such other body as Congress may by law provide, transmit within four days to the President pro tempore of the Senate and the Speaker of the House of Representatives their written declaration that the President is unable to discharge the powers and duties of his office. Thereupon Congress shall decide the issue, assembling within forty-eight hours for that purpose if not in session. If the Congress, within twenty-one days after receipt of the latter written declaration, or, if Congress is not in session, within twenty-one days after Congress is required to assemble, determines by two-thirds vote of both Houses that the President is unable to discharge the powers and duties of his office, the Vice-President shall continue to discharge the same as Acting President; otherwise, the President shall resume the powers and duties of his office.

Amendment XXVI

[Adopted 1971]

Section 1 The right of citizens of the United States, who are eighteen years of age or older, to vote shall not be denied or abridged by the United States or by any State on account of age.

Section 2 The Congress shall have power to enforce this article by appropriate legislation.

Amendment XXVII

[Adopted 1992]

No law, varying the compensation for the services of the Senators and Representatives, shall take effect, until an election of Representatives shall have intervened.

Territorial Expansion of the United States

Territory	Date Acquired	Square Miles	How Acquired
Original states and territories	1783	888,685	Treaty with Great Britain
Louisiana Purchase	1803	827,192	Purchase from France
Florida	1819	72,003	Treaty with Spain
Texas	1845	390,143	Annexation of independent nation
Oregon	1846	285,580	Treaty with Great Britain
Mexican Cession	1848	529,017	Conquest from Mexico
Gadsden Purchase	1853	29,640	Purchase from Mexico
Alaska	1867	589,757	Purchase from Russia
Hawai`i	1898	6,450	Annexation of independent nation
The Philippines	1899	115,600	Conquest from Spain (granted independence in 1946)
Puerto Rico	1899	3,435	Conquest from Spain
Guam	1899	212	Conquest from Spain
American Samoa	1900	76	Treaty with Germany and Great Britain
Panama Canal Zone	1904	553	Treaty with Panama (returned to Panama by treaty in 1978)
Corn Islands	1914	4	Treaty with Nicaragua (returned to Nicaragua by treaty in 1971)
Virgin Islands	1917	133	Purchase from Denmark
Pacific Islands Trust (Micronesia)	1947	8,489	Trusteeship under United Nations (some granted independence)
All others (Midway, Wake, and other islands)		42	

Admission of States into the Union

State	Date of Admission	State	Date of Admission
1. Delaware	December 7, 1787	26. Michigan	January 26, 1837
2. Pennsylvania	December 12, 1787	27. Florida	March 3, 1845
3. New Jersey	December 18, 1787	28. Texas	December 29, 1845
4. Georgia	January 2, 1788	29. Iowa	December 28, 1846
5. Connecticut	January 9, 1788	30. Wisconsin	May 29, 1848
6. Massachusetts	February 6, 1788	31. California	September 9, 1850
7. Maryland	April 28, 1788	32. Minnesota	May 11, 1858
8. South Carolina	May 23, 1788	33. Oregon	February 14, 1859
9. New Hampshire	June 21, 1788	34. Kansas	January 29, 1861
10. Virginia	June 25, 1788	35. West Virginia	June 20, 1863
11. New York	July 26, 1788	36. Nevada	October 31, 1864
12. North Carolina	November 21, 1789	37. Nebraska	March 1, 1867
13. Rhode Island	May 29, 1790	38. Colorado	August 1, 1876
14. Vermont	March 4, 1791	39. North Dakota	November 2, 1889
15. Kentucky	June 1, 1792	40. South Dakota	November 2, 1889
16. Tennessee	June 1, 1796	41. Montana	November 8, 1889
17. Ohio	March 1, 1803	42. Washington	November 11, 1889
18. Louisiana	April 30, 1812	43. Idaho	July 3, 1890
19. Indiana	December 11, 1816	44. Wyoming	July 10, 1890
20. Mississippi	December 10, 1817	45. Utah	January 4, 1896
21. Illinois	December 3, 1818	46. Oklahoma	November 16, 1907
22. Alabama	December 14, 1819	47. New Mexico	January 6, 1912
23. Maine	March 15, 1820	48. Arizona	February 14, 1912
24. Missouri	August 10, 1821	49. Alaska	January 3, 1959
25. Arkansas	June 15, 1836	50. Hawai`i	August 21, 1959

Presidential Elections

Year	Number of States	Candidates	Parties	Popular Vote	% of Popular Vote	Electoral Vote	% Voter Participation[a]
1789	11	**George Washington**	No party			69	
		John Adams	designations			34	
		Other candidates				35	
1792	15	**George Washington**	No party			132	
		John Adams	designations			77	
		George Clinton				50	
		Other candidates				5	
1796	16	**John Adams**	Federalist			71	
		Thomas Jefferson	Democratic-Republican			68	
		Thomas Pinckney	Federalist			59	
		Aaron Burr	Democratic-Republican			30	
		Other candidates				48	
1800	16	**Thomas Jefferson**	Democratic-Republican			73	
		Aaron Burr	Democratic-Republican			73	
		John Adams	Federalist			65	
		Charles C. Pinckney	Federalist			64	
		John Jay	Federalist			1	
1804	17	**Thomas Jefferson**	Democratic-Republican			162	
		Charles C. Pinckney	Federalist			14	
1808	17	**James Madison**	Democratic-Republican			122	
		Charles C. Pinckney	Federalist			47	
		George Clinton	Democratic-Republican			6	
1812	18	**James Madison**	Democratic-Republican			128	
		DeWitt Clinton	Federalist			89	
1816	19	**James Monroe**	Democratic-Republican			183	
		Rufus King	Federalist			34	
1820	24	**James Monroe**	Democratic-Republican			231	
		John Quincy Adams	Independent-Republican			1	
1824	24	**John Quincy Adams**	Democratic-Republican	108,740	30.5	84	26.9
		Andrew Jackson	Democratic-Republican	153,544	43.1	99	

Presidential Elections *(continued)*

Year	Number of States	Candidates	Parties	Popular Vote	% of Popular Vote	Electoral Vote	% Voter Participation[a]
		Henry Clay	Democratic-Republican	47,136	13.2	37	
		William H. Crawford	Democratic-Republican	46,618	13.1	41	
1828	24	**Andrew Jackson**	Democratic	647,286	56.0	178	57.6
		John Quincy Adams	National Republican	508,064	44.0	83	
1832	24	**Andrew Jackson**	Democratic	688,242	54.5	219	55.4
		Henry Clay	National Republican	473,462	37.5	49	
		William Wirt	Anti-Masonic	101,051	8.0	7	
		John Floyd	Democratic			11	
1836	26	**Martin Van Buren**	Democratic	765,483	50.9	170	57.8
		William H. Harrison	Whig			73	
		Hugh L. White	Whig			26	
		Daniel Webster	Whig	739,795	49.1	14	
		W. P. Mangum	Whig			11	
1840	26	**William H. Harrison**	Whig	1,274,624	53.1	234	80.2
		Martin Van Buren	Democratic	1,127,781	46.9	60	
1844	26	**James K. Polk**	Democratic	1,338,464	49.6	170	78.9
		Henry Clay	Whig	1,300,097	48.1	105	
		James G. Birney	Liberty	62,300	2.3		
1848	30	**Zachary Taylor**	Whig	1,360,967	47.4	163	72.7
		Lewis Cass	Democratic	1,222,342	42.5	127	
		Martin Van Buren	Free Soil	291,263	10.1		
1852	31	**Franklin Pierce**	Democratic	1,601,117	50.9	254	69.6
		Winfield Scott	Whig	1,385,453	44.1	42	
		John P. Hale	Free Soil	155,825	5.0		
1856	31	**James Buchanan**	Democratic	1,832,955	45.3	174	78.9
		John C. Frémont	Republican	1,339,932	33.1	114	
		Millard Fillmore	American	871,731	21.6	8	
1860	33	**Abraham Lincoln**	Republican	1,865,593	39.8	180	81.2
		Stephen A. Douglas	Democratic	1,382,713	29.5	12	
		John C. Breckinridge	Democratic	848,356	18.1	72	
		John Bell	Constitutional Union	592,906	12.6	39	
1864	36	**Abraham Lincoln**	Republican	2,206,938	55.0	212	73.8
		George B. McClellan	Democratic	1,803,787	45.0	21	
1868	37	**Ulysses S. Grant**	Republican	3,013,421	52.7	214	78.1
		Horatio Seymour	Democratic	2,706,829	47.3	80	
1872	37	**Ulysses S. Grant**	Republican	3,596,745	55.6	286	71.3
		Horace Greeley	Democratic	2,843,446	43.9	[b]	
1876	38	**Rutherford B. Hayes**	Republican	4,036,572	48.0	185	81.8

Presidential Elections *(continued)*

Year	Number of States	Candidates	Parties	Popular Vote	% of Popular Vote	Elec- toral Vote	% Voter Partici- pation[a]
		Samuel J. Tilden	Democratic	4,284,020	51.0	184	
1880	38	**James A. Garfield**	Republican	4,453,295	48.5	214	79.4
		Winfield S. Hancock	Democratic	4,414,082	48.1	155	
		James B. Weaver	Greenback- Labor	308,578	3.4		
1884	38	**Grover Cleveland**	Democratic	4,879,507	48.5	219	77.5
		James G. Blaine	Republican	4,850,293	48.2	182	
		Benjamin F. Butler	Greenback- Labor	175,370	1.8		
		John P. St. John	Prohibition	150,369	1.5		
1888	38	**Benjamin Harrison**	Republican	5,477,129	47.9	233	79.3
		Grover Cleveland	Democratic	5,537,857	48.6	168	
		Clinton B. Fisk	Prohibition	249,506	2.2		
		Anson J. Streeter	Union Labor	146,935	1.3		
1892	44	**Grover Cleveland**	Democratic	5,555,426	46.1	277	74.7
		Benjamin Harrison	Republican	5,182,690	43.0	145	
		James B. Weaver	People's	1,029,846	8.5	22	
		John Bidwell	Prohibition	264,133	2.2		
1896	45	**William McKinley**	Republican	7,102,246	51.1	271	79.3
		William J. Bryan	Democratic	6,492,559	47.7	176	
1900	45	**William McKinley**	Republican	7,218,491	51.7	292	73.2
		William J. Bryan	Democratic; Populist	6,356,734	45.5	155	
		John C. Wooley	Prohibition	208,914	1.5		
1904	45	**Theodore Roosevelt**	Republican	7,628,461	57.4	336	65.2
		Alton B. Parker	Democratic	5,084,223	37.6	140	
		Eugene V. Debs	Socialist	402,283	3.0		
		Silas C. Swallow	Prohibition	258,536	1.9		
1908	46	**William H. Taft**	Republican	7,675,320	51.6	321	65.4
		William J. Bryan	Democratic	6,412,294	43.1	162	
		Eugene V. Debs	Socialist	420,793	2.8		
		Eugene W. Chafin	Prohibition	253,840	1.7		
1912	48	**Woodrow Wilson**	Democratic	6,296,547	41.9	435	58.8
		Theodore Roosevelt	Progressive	4,118,571	27.4	88	
		William H. Taft	Republican	3,486,720	23.2	8	
		Eugene V. Debs	Socialist	900,672	6.0		
		Eugene W. Chafin	Prohibition	206,275	1.4		
1916	48	**Woodrow Wilson**	Democratic	9,127,695	49.4	277	61.6
		Charles E. Hughes	Republican	8,533,507	46.2	254	
		A. L. Benson	Socialist	585,113	3.2		
		J. Frank Hanly	Prohibition	220,506	1.2		
1920	48	**Warren G. Harding**	Republican	16,143,407	60.4	404	49.2
		James M. Cox	Democratic	9,130,328	34.2	127	

Presidential Elections *(continued)*

Year	Number of States	Candidates	Parties	Popular Vote	% of Popular Vote	Electoral Vote	% Voter Participation[a]
		Eugene V. Debs	Socialist	919,799	3.4		
		P. P. Christensen	Farmer-Labor	265,411	1.0		
1924	48	**Calvin Coolidge**	Republican	15,718,211	54.0	382	48.9
		John W. Davis	Democratic	8,385,283	28.8	136	
		Robert M. La Follette	Progressive	4,831,289	16.6	13	
1928	48	**Herbert C. Hoover**	Republican	21,391,993	58.2	444	56.9
		Alfred E. Smith	Democratic	15,016,169	40.9	87	
1932	48	**Franklin D. Roosevelt**	Democratic	22,809,638	57.4	472	56.9
		Herbert C. Hoover	Republican	15,758,901	39.7	59	
		Norman Thomas	Socialist	881,951	2.2		
1936	48	**Franklin D. Roosevelt**	Democratic	27,752,869	60.8	523	61.0
		Alfred M. Landon	Republican	16,674,665	36.5	8	
		William Lemke	Union	882,479	1.9		
1940	48	**Franklin D. Roosevelt**	Democratic	27,307,819	54.8	449	62.5
		Wendell L. Wilkie	Republican	22,321,018	44.8	82	
1944	48	**Franklin D. Roosevelt**	Democratic	25,606,585	53.5	432	55.9
		Thomas E. Dewey	Republican	22,014,745	46.0	99	
1948	48	**Harry S Truman**	Democratic	24,179,345	49.6	303	53.0
		Thomas E. Dewey	Republican	21,991,291	45.1	189	
		J. Strom Thurmond	States' Rights	1,176,125	2.4	39	
		Henry A. Wallace	Progressive	1,157,326	2.4		
1952	48	**Dwight D. Eisenhower**	Republican	33,936,234	55.1	442	63.3
		Adlai E. Stevenson	Democratic	27,314,992	44.4	89	
1956	48	**Dwight D. Eisenhower**	Republican	35,590,472	57.6	457	60.6
		Adlai E. Stevenson	Democratic	26,022,752	42.1	73	
1960	50	**John F. Kennedy**	Democratic	34,226,731	49.7	303	62.8
		Richard M. Nixon	Republican	34,108,157	49.5	219	
1964	50	**Lyndon B. Johnson**	Democratic	43,129,566	61.1	486	61.7
		Barry M. Goldwater	Republican	27,178,188	38.5	52	
1968	50	**Richard M. Nixon**	Republican	31,785,480	43.4	301	60.6
		Hubert H. Humphrey	Democratic	31,275,166	42.7	191	
		George C. Wallace	American Independent	9,906,473	13.5	46	
1972	50	**Richard M. Nixon**	Republican	47,169,911	60.7	520	55.2
		George S. McGovern	Democratic	29,170,383	37.5	17	
		John G. Schmitz	American	1,099,482	1.4		
1976	50	**Jimmy Carter**	Democratic	40,830,763	50.1	297	53.5
		Gerald R. Ford	Republican	39,147,793	48.0	240	
1980	50	**Ronald Reagan**	Republican	43,899,248	50.8	489	52.6
		Jimmy Carter	Democratic	35,481,432	41.0	49	
		John B. Anderson	Independent	5,719,437	6.6	0	
		Ed Clark	Libertarian	920,859	1.1	0	

Presidential Elections *(continued)*

Year	Number of States	Candidates	Parties	Popular Vote	% of Popular Vote	Electoral Vote	% Voter Participation[a]
1984	50	**Ronald Reagan**	Republican	54,455,075	58.8	525	53.1
		Walter Mondale	Democratic	37,577,185	40.6	13	
1988	50	**George Bush**	Republican	48,901,046	53.4	426	50.2
		Michael Dukakis	Democratic	41,809,030	45.6	111[c]	
1992	50	**Bill Clinton**	Democratic	44,908,233	43.0	370	55.0
		George Bush	Republican	39,102,282	37.4	168	
		Ross Perot	Independent	19,741,048	18.9	0	
1996	50	**Bill Clinton**	Democratic	47,401,054	49.2	379	49.0
		Robert Dole	Republican	39,197,350	40.7	159	
		Ross Perot	Independent	8,085,285	8.4	0	
		Ralph Nader	Green	684,871	0.7	0	
2000	50	**George W. Bush**	Republican	50,456,169	47.88	271	50.7
		Albert Gore, Jr.	Democratic	50,996,116	48.39	267	
		Ralph Nader	Green	2,783,728	2.72	0	

Candidates receiving less than 1 percent of the popular vote have been omitted. Thus the percentage of popular vote given for any election year may not total 100 percent.

Before the passage of the Twelfth Amendment in 1804, the Electoral College voted for two presidential candidates; the runner-up became vice president.

Before 1824, most presidential electors were chosen by state legislatures, not by popular vote.

[a]Percent of voting-age population casting ballots.

[b]Greeley died shortly after the election; the electors supporting him then divided their votes among minor candidates.

[c]One elector from West Virginia cast her Electoral College presidential ballot for Lloyd Bentsen, the Democratic Party's vice-presidential candidate.

Presidents, Vice Presidents, and Cabinet Members

The Washington Administration

President	George Washington	1789–1797
Vice President	John Adams	1789–1797
Secretary of State	Thomas Jefferson	1789–1793
	Edmund Randolph	1794–1795
	Timothy Pickering	1795–1797
Secretary of Treasury	Alexander Hamilton	1789–1795
	Oliver Wolcott	1795–1797
Secretary of War	Henry Knox	1789–1794
	Timothy Pickering	1795–1796
	James McHenry	1796–1797
Attorney General	Edmund Randolph	1789–1793
	William Bradford	1794–1795
	Charles Lee	1795–1797
Postmaster General	Samuel Osgood	1789–1791
	Timothy Pickering	1791–1794
	Joseph Habersham	1795–1797

The John Adams Administration

President	John Adams	1797–1801
Vice President	Thomas Jefferson	1797–1801
Secretary of State	Timothy Pickering	1797–1800
	John Marshall	1800–1801
Secretary of Treasury	Oliver Wolcott	1797–1800
	Samuel Dexter	1800–1801
Secretary of War	James McHenry	1797–1800
	Samuel Dexter	1800–1801
Attorney General	Charles Lee	1797–1801
Postmaster General	Joseph Habersham	1797–1801
Secretary of Navy	Benjamin Stoddert	1798–1801

The Jefferson Administration

President	Thomas Jefferson	1801–1809
Vice President	Aaron Burr	1801–1805
	George Clinton	1805–1809
Secretary of State	James Madison	1801–1809
Secretary of Treasury	Samuel Dexter	1801
	Albert Gallatin	1801–1809
Secretary of War	Henry Dearborn	1801–1809
Attorney General	Levi Lincoln	1801–1805
	Robert Smith	1805
	John Breckinridge	1805–1806
	Caesar Rodney	1807–1809
Postmaster General	Joseph Habersham	1801
	Gideon Granger	1801–1809
Secretary of Navy	Robert Smith	1801–1809

The Madison Administration

President	James Madison	1809–1817
Vice President	George Clinton	1809–1813
	Elbridge Gerry	1813–1817
Secretary of State	Robert Smith	1809–1811
	James Monroe	1811–1817
Secretary of Treasury	Albert Gallatin	1809–1813
	George Campbell	1814
	Alexander Dallas	1814–1816
	William Crawford	1816–1817
Secretary of War	William Eustis	1809–1812
	John Armstrong	1813–1814
	James Monroe	1814–1815
	William Crawford	1815–1817
Attorney General	Caesar Rodney	1809–1811
	William Pinkney	1811–1814
	Richard Rush	1814–1817
Postmaster General	Gideon Granger	1809–1814
	Return Meigs	1814–1817
Secretary of Navy	Paul Hamilton	1809–1813
	William Jones	1813–1814
	Benjamin Crowninshield	1814–1817

The Monroe Administration

President	James Monroe	1817–1825
Vice President	Daniel Tompkins	1817–1825
Secretary of State	John Quincy Adams	1817–1825
Secretary of Treasury	William Crawford	1817–1825
Secretary of War	George Graham	1817
	John C. Calhoun	1817–1825
Attorney General	Richard Rush	1817
	William Wirt	1817–1825
Postmaster General	Return Meigs	1817–1823
	John McLean	1823–1825
Secretary of Navy	Benjamin Crowninshield	1817–1818
	Smith Thompson	1818–1823
	Samuel Southard	1823–1825

The John Quincy Adams Administration

President	John Quincy Adams	1825–1829
Vice President	John C. Calhoun	1825–1829

Presidents, Vice Presidents, and Cabinet Members *(continued)*

Secretary of State	Henry Clay	1825–1829
Secretary of Treasury	Richard Rush	1825–1829
Secretary of War	James Barbour	1825–1828
	Peter Porter	1828–1829
Attorney General	William Wirt	1825–1829
Postmaster General	John McLean	1825–1829
Secretary of Navy	Samuel Southard	1825–1829

The Jackson Administration

President	Andrew Jackson	1829–1837
Vice President	John C. Calhoun	1829–1833
	Martin Van Buren	1833–1837
Secretary of State	Martin Van Buren	1829–1831
	Edward Livingston	1831–1833
	Louis McLane	1833–1834
	John Forsyth	1834–1837
Secretary of Treasury	Samuel Ingham	1829–1831
	Louis McLane	1831–1833
	William Duane	1833
	Roger B. Taney	1833–1834
	Levi Woodbury	1834–1837
Secretary of War	John H. Eaton	1829–1831
	Lewis Cass	1831–1837
	Benjamin Butler	1837
Attorney General	John M. Berrien	1829–1831
	Roger B. Taney	1831–1833
	Benjamin Butler	1833–1837
Postmaster General	William Barry	1829–1835
	Amos Kendall	1835–1837
Secretary of Navy	John Branch	1829–1831
	Levi Woodbury	1831–1834
	Mahlon Dickerson	1834–1837

The Van Buren Administration

President	Martin Van Buren	1837–1841
Vice President	Richard M. Johnson	1837–1841
Secretary of State	John Forsyth	1837–1841
Secretary of Treasury	Levi Woodbury	1837–1841
Secretary of War	Joel Poinsett	1837–1841
Attorney General	Benjamin Butler	1837–1838
	Felix Grundy	1838–1840
	Henry D. Gilpin	1840–1841
Postmaster General	Amos Kendall	1837–1840
	John M. Niles	1840–1841
Secretary of Navy	Mahlon Dickerson	1837–1838
	James Paulding	1838–1841

The William Harrison Administration

President	William H. Harrison	1841
Vice President	John Tyler	1841
Secretary of State	Daniel Webster	1841
Secretary of Treasury	Thomas Ewing	1841
Secretary of War	John Bell	1841
Attorney General	John J. Crittenden	1841
Postmaster General	Francis Granger	1841
Secretary of Navy	George Badger	1841

The Tyler Administration

President	John Tyler	1841–1845
Vice President	None	
Secretary of State	Daniel Webster	1841–1843
	Hugh S. Legaré	1843
	Abel P. Upshur	1843–1844
	John C. Calhoun	1844–1845
Secretary of Treasury	Thomas Ewing	1841
	Walter Forward	1841–1843
	John C. Spencer	1843–1844
	George Bibb	1844–1845
Secretary of Treasury	John Bell	1841
	John C. Spencer	1841–1843
	James M. Porter	1843–1844
	William Wilkins	1844–1845
Attorney General	John J. Crittenden	1841
	Hugh S. Legaré	1841–1843
	John Nelson	1843–1845
Postmaster General	Francis Granger	1841
	Charles Wickliffe	1841
Secretary of Navy	George Badger	1841
	Abel P. Upshur	1841
	David Henshaw	1843–1844
	Thomas Gilmer	1844
	John Y. Mason	1844–1845

The Polk Administration

President	James K. Polk	1845–1849
Vice President	George M. Dallas	1845–1849
Secretary of State	James Buchanan	1845–1849
Secretary of Treasury	Robert J. Walker	1845–1849
Secretary of War	William L. Marcy	1845–1849
Attorney General	John Y. Mason	1845–1846
	Nathan Clifford	1846–1848
	Isaac Toucey	1848–1849

Presidents, Vice Presidents, and Cabinet Members *(continued)*

Postmaster General	Cave Johnson	1845–1849
Secretary of Navy	George Bancroft	1845–1846
	John Y. Mason	1846–1849

The Taylor Administration

President	Zachary Taylor	1849–1850
Vice President	Millard Fillmore	1849–1850
Secretary of State	John M. Clayton	1849–1850
Secretary of Treasury	William Meredith	1849–1850
Secretary of War	George Crawford	1849–1850
Attorney General	Reverdy Johnson	1849–1850
Postmaster General	Jacob Collamer	1849–1850
Secretary of Navy	William Preston	1849–1850
Secretary of Interior	Thomas Ewing	1849–1850

The Fillmore Administration

President	Millard Fillmore	1850–1853
Vice President	None	
Secretary of State	Daniel Webster	1850–1852
	Edward Everett	1852–1853
Secretary of Treasury	Thomas Corwin	1850–1853
Secretary of War	Charles Conrad	1850–1853
Attorney General	John J. Crittenden	1850–1853
Postmaster General	Nathan Hall	1850–1852
	Sam D. Hubbard	1852–1853
Secretary of Navy	William A. Graham	1850–1852
	John P. Kennedy	1852–1853
Secretary of Interior	Thomas McKennan	1850
	Alexander Stuart	1850–1853

The Pierce Administration

President	Franklin Pierce	1853–1857
Vice President	William R. King	1853–1857
Secretary of State	William L. Marcy	1853–1857
Secretary of Treasury	James Guthrie	1853–1857
Secretary of War	Jefferson Davis	1853–1857
Attorney General	Caleb Cushing	1853–1857
Postmaster General	James Campbell	1853–1857
Secretary of Navy	James C. Dobbin	1853–1857
Secretary of Interior	Robert McClelland	1853–1857

The Buchanan Administration

President	James Buchanan	1857–1861
Vice President	John C. Breckinridge	1857–1861
Secretary of State	Lewis Cass	1857–1860
	Jeremiah S. Black	1860–1861
Secretary of Treasury	Howell Cobb	1857–1860
	Philip Thomas	1860–1861
	John A. Dix	1861
Secretary of War	John B. Floyd	1857–1861
	Joseph Holt	1861
Attorney General	Jeremiah S. Black	1857–1860
	Edwin M. Stanton	1860–1861
Postmaster General	Aaron V. Brown	1857–1859
	Joseph Holt	1859–1861
	Horatio King	1861
Secretary of Navy	Isaac Toucey	1857–1861
Secretary of Interior	Jacob Thompson	1857–1861

The Lincoln Administration

President	Abraham Lincoln	1861–1865
Vice President	Hannibal Hamlin	1861–1865
	Andrew Johnson	1865
Secretary of State	William H. Seward	1861–1865
Secretary of Treasury	Salmon P. Chase	1861–1864
William P. Fessenden	1864–1865	
Hugh McCulloch	1865	
Secretary of War	Simon Cameron	1861–1862
	Edwin M. Stanton	1862–1865
Attorney General	Edward Bates	1861–1864
	James Speed	1864–1865
Postmaster General	Horatio King	1861
	Montgomery Blair	1861–1864
	William Dennison	1864–1865
Secretary of Navy	Gideon Welles	1861–1865
Secretary of Interior	Caleb B. Smith	1861–1863
	John P. Usher	1863–1865

The Andrew Johnson Administration

President	Andrew Johnson	1865–1869
Vice President	None	
Secretary of State	William H. Seward	1865–1869
Secretary of Treasury	Hugh McCulloch	1865–1869
Secretary of War	Edwin M. Stanton	1865–1867
	Ulysses S. Grant	1867–1868

Presidents, Vice Presidents, and Cabinet Members *(continued)*

	Lorenzo Thomas	1868
	John M. Schofield	1868–1869
Attorney General	James Speed	1865–1866
	Henry Stanbery	1866–1868
	William M. Evarts	1868–1869
Postmaster General	William Dennison	1865–1866
	Alexander Randall	1866–1869
Secretary of Navy	Gideon Welles	1865–1869
Secretary of Interior	John P. Usher	1865
	James Harlan	1865–1866
	Orville H. Browning	1866–1869

The Grant Administration

President	Ulysses S. Grant	1869–1877
Vice President	Schuyler Colfax	1869–1873
	Henry Wilson	1873–1877
Secretary of State	Elihu B. Washburne	1869
	Hamilton Fish	1869–1877
Secretary of Treasury	George S. Boutwell	1869–1873
	William Richardson	1873–1874
	Benjamin Bristow	1874–1876
	Lot M. Morrill	1876–1877
Secretary of War	John A. Rawlins	1869
	William T. Sherman	1869
	William W. Belknap	1869–1876
	Alphonso Taft	1876
	James D. Cameron	1876–1877
Attorney General	Ebenezer Hoar	1869–1870
	Amos T. Ackerman	1870–1871
	G. H. Williams	1871–1875
	Edwards Pierrepont	1875–1876
	Alphonso Taft	1876–1877
Postmaster General	John A. J. Creswell	1869–1874
	James W. Marshall	1874
	Marshall Jewell	1874–1876
	James N. Tyner	1876–1877
Secretary of Navy	Adolph E. Borie	1869
	George M. Robeson	1869–1877
Secretary of Interior	Jacob D. Cox	1869–1870
	Columbus Delano	1870–1875
	Zachariah Chandler	1875–1877

The Hayes Administration

President	Rutherford B. Hayes	1877–1881
Vice President	William A. Wheeler	1877–1881
Secretary of State	William B. Evarts	1877–1881

Secretary of Treasury	John Sherman	1877–1881
Secretary of War	George W. McCrary	1877–1879
	Alex Ramsey	1879–1881
Attorney General	Charles Devens	1877–1881
Postmaster General	David M. Key	1877–1880
	Horace Maynard	1880–1881
Secretary of Navy	Richard W. Thompson	1877–1880
	Nathan Goff, Jr.	1881
Secretary of Interior	Carl Schurz	1877–1881

The Garfield Administration

President	James A. Garfield	1881
Vice President	Chester A. Arthur	1881
Secretary of State	James G. Blaine	1881
Secretary of Treasury	William Windom	1881
Secretary of War	Robert T. Lincoln	1881
Attorney General	Wayne MacVeagh	1881
Postmaster General	Thomas L. James	1881
Secretary of Navy	William H. Hunt	1881
Secretary of Interior	Samuel J. Kirkwood	1881

The Arthur Administration

President	Chester A. Arthur	1881–1885
Vice President	None	
Secretary of State	F. T. Frelinghuysen	1881–1885
Secretary of Treasury	Charles J. Folger	1881–1884
	Walter Q. Gresham	1884
	Hugh McCulloch	1884–1885
Secretary of War	Robert T. Lincoln	1881–1885
Attorney General	Benjamin H. Brewster	1881–1885
Postmaster General	Timothy O. Howe	1881–1883
	Walter Q. Gresham	1883–1884
	Frank Hatton	1884–1885
Secretary of Navy	William H. Hunt	1881–1882
	William E. Chandler	1882–1885
Secretary of Interior	Samuel J. Kirkwood	1881–1882
	Henry M. Teller	1882–1885

The Cleveland Administration

President	Grover Cleveland	1885–1889
Vice President	Thomas A. Hendricks	1885–1889
Secretary of State	Thomas F. Bayard	1885–1889

Presidents, Vice Presidents, and Cabinet Members *(continued)*

Secretary of Treasury	Daniel Manning	1885–1887
	Charles S. Fairchild	1887–1889
Secretary of War	William C. Endicott	1885–1889
Attorney General	Augustus H. Garland	1885–1889
Postmaster General	William F. Vilas	1885–1888
	Don M. Dickinson	1888–1889
Secretary of Navy	William C. Whitney	1885–1889
Secretary of Interior	Lucius G. C. Lamar	1885–1888
	William F. Vilas	1888–1889
Secretary of Agriculture	Norman J. Colman	1889

The Benjamin Harrison Administration

President	Benjamin Harrison	1889–1893
Vice President	Levi P. Morton	1889–1893
Secretary of State	James G. Blaine	1889–1892
	John W. Foster	1892–1893
Secretary of Treasury	William Windom	1889–1891
	Charles Foster	1891–1893
Secretary of War	Redfield Proctor	1889–1891
	Stephen B. Elkins	1891–1893
Attorney General	William H. H. Miller	1889–1891
Postmaster General	John Wanamaker	1889–1893
Secretary of Navy	Benjamin F. Tracy	1889–1893
Secretary of Interior	John W. Noble	1889–1893
Secretary of Agriculture	Jeremiah M. Rusk	1889–1893

The Cleveland Administration

President	Grover Cleveland	1893–1897
Vice President	Adlai E. Stevenson	1893–1897
Secretary of State	Walter Q. Gresham	1893–1895
	Richard Olney	1895–1897
Secretary of Treasury	John G. Carlisle	1893–1897
Secretary of War	Daniel S. Lamont	1893–1897
Attorney General	Richard Olney	1893–1895
	James Harmon	1895–1897
Postmaster General	Wilson S. Bissell	1893–1895
	William L. Wilson	1895–1897
Secretary of Navy	Hilary A. Herbert	1893–1897
Secretary of Interior	Hoke Smith	1893–1896
	David R. Francis	1896–1897
Secretary of Agriculture	Julius S. Morton	1893–1897

The McKinley Administration

President	William McKinley	1897–1901
Vice President	Garret A. Hobart	1897–1901
	Theodore Roosevelt	1901
Secretary of State	John Sherman	1897–1898
	William R. Day	1898
	John Hay	1898–1901
Secretary of Treasury	Lyman J. Gage	1897–1901
Secretary of War	Russell A. Alger	1897–1899
	Elihu Root	1899–1901
Attorney General	Joseph McKenna	1897–1898
	John W. Griggs	1898–1901
	Philander C. Knox	1901
Postmaster General	James A. Gary	1897–1898
	Charles E. Smith	1898–1901
Secretary of Navy	John D. Long	1897–1901
Secretary of Interior	Cornelius N. Bliss	1897–1899
	Ethan A. Hitchcock	1899–1901
Secretary of Agriculture	James Wilson	1897–1901

The Theodore Roosevelt Administration

President	Theodore Roosevelt	1901–1909
Vice President	Charles Fairbanks	1905–1909
Secretary of State	John Hay	1901–1905
	Elihu Root	1905–1909
	Robert Bacon	1909
Secretary of Treasury	Lyman J. Gage	1901–1902
	Leslie M. Shaw	1902–1907
	George B. Cortelyou	1907–1909
Secretary of War	Elihu Root	1901–1904
	William H. Taft	1904–1908
	Luke E. Wright	1908–1909
Attorney General	Philander C. Knox	1901–1904
	William H. Moody	1904–1906
	Charles J. Bonaparte	1906–1909
Postmaster General	Charles E. Smith	1901–1902
	Henry C. Payne	1902–1904
	Robert J. Wynne	1904–1905
	George B. Cortelyou	1905–1907
	George von L. Meyer	1907–1909
Secretary of Navy	John D. Long	1901–1902
	William H. Moody	1902–1904
	Paul Morton	1904–1905
	Charles J. Bonaparte	1905–1906
	Victor H. Metcalf	1906–1908
	Truman H. Newberry	1908–1909

Presidents, Vice Presidents, and Cabinet Members *(continued)*

Secretary of Interior	Ethan A. Hitchcock	1901–1907
	James R. Garfield	1907–1909
Secretary of Agriculture	James Wilson	1901–1909
Secretary of Labor and Commerce	George B. Cortelyou	1903–1904
	Victor H. Metcalf	1904–1906
	Oscar S. Straus	1906–1909
	Charles Nagel	1909

The Taft Administration

President	William H. Taft	1909–1913
Vice President	James S. Sherman	1909–1913
Secretary of State	Philander C. Knox	1909–1913
Secretary of Treasury	Franklin MacVeagh	1909–1913
Secretary of War	Jacob M. Dickinson	1909–1911
	Henry L. Stimson	1911–1913
Attorney General	George W. Wickersham	1909–1913
Postmaster General	Frank H. Hitchcock	1909–1913
Secretary of Navy	George von L. Meyer	1909–1913
Secretary of Interior	Richard A. Ballinger	1909–1911
	Walter L. Fisher	1911–1913
Secretary of Agriculture	James Wilson	1909–1913
Secretary of Labor and Commerce	Charles Nagel	1909–1913

The Wilson Administration

President	Woodrow Wilson	1913–1921
Vice President	Thomas R. Marshall	1913–1921
Secretary of State	William J. Bryan	1913–1915
	Robert Lansing	1915–1920
	Bainbridge Colby	1920–1921
Secretary of Treasury	William G. McAdoo	1913–1918
	Carter Glass	1918–1920
	David F. Houston	1920–1921
Secretary of War	Lindley M. Garrison	1913–1916
	Newton D. Baker	1916–1921
Attorney General	James C. McReynolds	1913–1914
	Thomas W. Gregory	1914–1919
	A. Mitchell Palmer	1919–1921
Postmaster General	Albert S. Burleson	1913–1921
Secretary of Navy	Josephus Daniels	1913–1921
Secretary of Interior	Franklin K. Lane	1913–1920
	John B. Payne	1920–1921
Secretary of Agriculture	David F. Houston	1913–1920
	Edwin T. Meredith	1920–1921
Secretary of Commerce	William C. Redfield	1913–1919
	Joshua W. Alexander	1919–1921
Secretary of Labor	William B. Wilson	1913–1921

The Harding Administration

President	Warren G. Harding	1921–1923
Vice President	Calvin Coolidge	1921–1923
Secretary of State	Charles E. Hughes	1921–1923
Secretary of Treasury	Andrew Mellon	1921–1923
Secretary of War	John W. Weeks	1921–1923
Attorney General	Harry M. Daugherty	1921–1923
Postmaster General	Will H. Hays	1921–1922
	Hubert Work	1922–1923
	Harry S. New	1923
Secretary of Navy	Edwin Denby	1921–1923
Secretary of Interior	Albert B. Fall	1921–1923
	Hubert Work	1923
Secretary of Agriculture	Henry C. Wallace	1921–1923
Secretary of Commerce	Herbert C. Hoover	1921–1923
Secretary of Labor	James J. Davis	1921–1923

The Coolidge Administration

President	Calvin Coolidge	1923–1929
Vice President	Charles G. Dawes	1925–1929
Secretary of State	Charles E. Hughes	1923–1925
	Frank B. Kellogg	1925–1929
Secretary of Treasury	Andrew Mellon	1923–1929
Secretary of War	John W. Weeks	1923–1925
	Dwight F. Davis	1925–1929
Attorney General	Henry M. Daugherty	1923–1924
	Harlan F. Stone	1924–1925
	John G. Sargent	1925–1929
Postmaster General	Harry S. New	1923–1929
Secretary of Navy	Edwin Derby	1923–1924
	Curtis D. Wilbur	1924–1929
Secretary of Interior	Hubert Work	1923–1928
	Roy O. West	1928–1929
Secretary of Agriculture	Henry C. Wallace	1923–1924
	Howard M. Gore	1924–1925
	William M. Jardine	1925–1929

Presidents, Vice Presidents, and Cabinet Members *(continued)*

Secretary of Commerce	Herbert C. Hoover	1923–1928
	William F. Whiting	1928–1929
Secretary of Labor	James J. Davis	1923–1929

The Hoover Administration

President	Herbert C. Hoover	1929–1933
Vice President	Charles Curtis	1929–1933
Secretary of State	Henry L. Stimson	1929–1933
Secretary of Treasury	Andrew Mellon	1929–1932
	Ogden L. Mills	1932–1933
Secretary of War	James W. Good	1929
	Patrick J. Hurley	1929–1933
Attorney General	William D. Mitchell	1929–1933
Postmaster General	Walter F. Brown	1929–1933
Secretary of Navy	Charles F. Adams	1929–1933
Secretary of Interior	Ray L. Wilbur	1929–1933
Secretary of Agriculture	Arthur M. Hyde	1929–1933
Secretary of Commerce	Robert P. Lamont	1929–1932
	Roy D. Chapin	1932–1933
Secretary of Labor	James J. Davis	1929–1930
	William N. Doak	1930–1933

The Franklin D. Roosevelt Administration

President	Franklin D. Roosevelt	1933–1945
Vice President	John Nance Garner	1933–1941
	Henry A. Wallace	1941–1945
	Harry S Truman	1945
Secretary of State	Cordell Hull	1933–1944
	Edward R. Stettinius, Jr.	1944–1945
Secretary of Treasury	William H. Woodin	1933–1934
	Henry Morgenthau, Jr.	1934–1945
Secretary of War	George H. Dern	1933–1936
	Henry A. Woodring	1936–1940
	Henry L. Stimson	1940–1945
Attorney General	Homer S. Cummings	1933–1939
	Frank Murphy	1939–1940
	Robert H. Jackson	1940–1941
	Francis Biddle	1941–1945
Postmaster General	James A. Farley	1933–1940
	Frank C. Walker	1940–1945
Secretary of Navy	Claude A. Swanson	1933–1940
	Charles Edison	1940
	Frank Knox	1940–1944
	James V. Forrestal	1944–1945

Secretary of Interior	Harold L. Ickes	1933–1945
Secretary of Agriculture	Henry A. Wallace	1933–1940
	Claude R. Wickard	1940–1945
Secretary of Commerce	Daniel C. Roper	1933–1939
	Harry L. Hopkins	1939–1940
	Jesse Jones	1940–1945
	Henry A. Wallace	1945
Secretary of Labor	Frances Perkins	1933–1945

The Truman Administration

President	Harry S Truman	1945–1953
Vice President	Alben W. Barkley	1949–1953
Secretary of State	Edward R. Stettinius, Jr.	1945
	James F. Byrnes	1945–1947
	George C. Marshall	1947–1949
	Dean G. Acheson	1949–1953
Secretary of Treasury	Fred M. Vinson	1945–1946
	John W. Snyder	1946–1953
Secretary of War	Robert P. Patterson	1945–1947
	Kenneth C. Royall	1947
Attorney General	Tom C. Clark	1945–1949
	J. Howard McGrath	1949–1952
	James P. McGranery	1952–1953
Postmaster General	Frank C. Walker	1945
	Robert E. Hannegan	1945–1947
	Jesse M. Donaldson	1947–1953
Secretary of Navy	James V. Forrestal	1945–1947
Secretary of Interior	Harold L. Ickes	1945–1946
	Julius A. Krug	1946–1949
	Oscar L. Chapman	1949–1953
Secretary of Agriculture	Clinton P. Anderson	1945–1948
	Charles F. Brannan	1948–1953
Secretary of Commerce	Henry A. Wallace	1945–1946
	W. Averell Harriman	1946–1948
	Charles W. Sawyer	1948–1953
Secretary of Labor	Lewis B. Schwellenbach	1945–1948
	Maurice J. Tobin	1948–1953
Secretary of Defense	James V. Forrestal	1947–1949
	Louis A. Johnson	1949–1950
	George C. Marshall	1950–1951
	Robert A. Lovett	1951–1953

The Eisenhower Administration

President	Dwight D. Eisenhower	1953–1961
Vice President	Richard M. Nixon	1953–1961

Presidents, Vice Presidents, and Cabinet Members *(continued)*

Secretary of State	John Foster Dulles	1953–1959
	Christian A. Herter	1959–1961
Secretary of Treasury	George M. Humphrey	1953–1957
	Robert B. Anderson	1957–1961
Attorney General	Herbert Brownell, Jr.	1953–1958
	William P. Rogers	1958–1961
Postmaster General	Arthur E. Summerfield	1953–1961
Secretary of Interior	Douglas McKay	1953–1956
	Fred A. Seaton	1956–1961
Secretary of Agriculture	Ezra T. Benson	1953–1961
Secretary of Commerce	Sinclair Weeks	1953–1958
	Lewis L. Strauss	1958–1959
	Frederick H. Mueller	1959–1961
Secretary of Labor	Martin P. Durkin	1953
	James P. Mitchell	1953–1961
Secretary of Defense	Charles E. Wilson	1953–1957
	Neil H. McElroy	1957–1959
	Thomas S. Gates, Jr.	1959–1961
Secretary of Health, Education, and Welfare	Oveta Culp Hobby	1953–1955
	Marion B. Folsom	1955–1958
	Arthur S. Flemming	1958–1961

The Kennedy Administration

President	John F. Kennedy	1961–1963
Vice President	Lyndon B. Johnson	1961–1963
Secretary of State	Dean Rusk	1961–1963
Secretary of Treasury	C. Douglas Dillon	1961–1963
Attorney General	Robert F. Kennedy	1961–1963
Postmaster General	J. Edward Day	1961–1963
	John A. Gronouski	1963
Secretary of Interior	Stewart L. Udall	1961–1963
Secretary of Agriculture	Orville L. Freeman	1961–1963
Secretary of Commerce	Luther H. Hodges	1961–1963
Secretary of Labor	Arthur J. Goldberg	1961–1962
	W. Willard Wirtz	1962–1963
Secretary of Defense	Robert S. McNamara	1961–1963
Secretary of Health, Education, and Welfare	Abraham A. Ribicoff	1961–1962
	Anthony J. Celebrezze	1962–1963

The Lyndon Johnson Administration

President	Lyndon B. Johnson	1963–1969
Vice President	Hubert H. Humphrey	1965–1969

Secretary of State	Dean Rusk	1963–1969
Secretary of Treasury	C. Douglas Dillon	1963–1965
	Henry H. Fowler	1965–1969
Attorney General	Robert F. Kennedy	1963–1964
	Nicholas Katzenbach	1965–1966
	Ramsey Clark	1967–1969
Postmaster General	John A. Gronouski	1963–1965
	Lawrence F. O'Brien	1965–1968
	Marvin Watson	1968–1969
Secretary of Interior	Stewart L. Udall	1963–1969
Secretary of Agriculture	Orville L. Freeman	1963–1969
Secretary of Commerce	Luther H. Hodges	1963–1964
	John T. Connor	1964–1967
	Alexander B. Trowbridge	1967–1968
	Cyrus R. Smith	1968–1969
Secretary of Labor	W. Willard Wirtz	1963–1969
Secretary of Defense	Robert S. McNamara	1963–1968
	Clark Clifford	1968–1969
Secretary of Health, Education, and Welfare	Anthony J. Celebrezze	1963–1965
	John W. Gardner	1965–1968
	Wilbur J. Cohen	1968–1969
Secretary of Housing and Urban Development	Robert C. Weaver	1966–1969
	Robert C. Wood	1969
Secretary of Transportation	Alan S. Boyd	1967–1969

The Nixon Administration

President	Richard M. Nixon	1969–1974
Vice President	Spiro T. Agnew	1969–1973
	Gerald R. Ford	1973–1974
Secretary of State	William P. Rogers	1969–1973
	Henry A. Kissinger	1973–1974
Secretary of Treasury	David M. Kennedy	1969–1970
	John B. Connally	1971–1972
	George P. Shultz	1972–1974
	William E. Simon	1974
Attorney General	John N. Mitchell	1969–1972
	Richard G. Kleindienst	1972–1973
	Elliot L. Richardson	1973
	William B. Saxbe	1973–1974
Postmaster General	Winton M. Blount	1969–1971
Secretary of Interior	Walter J. Hickel	1969–1970
	Rogers Morton	1971–1974
Secretary of Agriculture	Clifford M. Hardin	1969–1971
	Earl L. Butz	1971–1974

Presidents, Vice Presidents, and Cabinet Members (continued)

Secretary of Commerce	Maurice H. Stans	1969–1972
	Peter G. Peterson	1972–1973
	Frederick B. Dent	1973–1974
Secretary of Labor	George P. Shultz	1969–1970
	James D. Hodgson	1970–1973
	Peter J. Brennan	1973–1974
Secretary of Defense	Melvin R. Laird	1969–1973
	Elliot L. Richardson	1973
	James R. Schlesinger	1973–1974
Secretary of Health, Education, and Welfare	Robert H. Finch	1969–1970
	Elliot L. Richardson	1970–1973
	Casper W. Weinberger	1973–1974
Secretary of Housing and Urban Development	George Romney	1969–1973
	James T. Lynn	1973–1974
Secretary of Transportation	John A. Volpe	1969–1973
	Claude S. Brinegar	1973–1974

The Ford Administration

President	Gerald R. Ford	1974–1977
Vice President	Nelson A. Rockefeller	1974–1977
Secretary of State	Henry A. Kissinger	1974–1977
Secretary of Treasury	William E. Simon	1974–1977
Attorney General	William Saxbe	1974–1975
	Edward Levi	1975–1977
Secretary of Interior	Rogers Morton	1974–1975
	Stanley K. Hathaway	1975
	Thomas Kleppe	1975–1977
Secretary of Agriculture	Earl L. Butz	1974–1976
	John A. Knebel	1976–1977
Secretary of Commerce	Frederick B. Dent	1974–1975
	Rogers Morton	1975–1976
	Elliot L. Richardson	1976–1977
Secretary of Labor	Peter J. Brennan	1974–1975
	John T. Dunlop	1975–1976
	W. J. Usery	1976–1977
Secretary of Defense	James R. Schlesinger	1974–1975
	Donald Rumsfeld	1975–1977
Secretary of Health, Education, and Welfare	Casper Weinberger	1974–1975
	Forrest D. Mathews	1975–1977
Secretary of Housing and Urban Development	James T. Lynn	1974–1975
	Carla A. Hills	1975–1977
Secretary of Transportation	Claude Brinegar	1974–1975
	William T. Coleman	1975–1977

The Carter Administration

President	Jimmy Carter	1977–1981
Vice President	Walter F. Mondale	1977–1981
Secretary of State	Cyrus R. Vance	1977–1980
	Edmund Muskie	1980–1981
Secretary of Treasury	W. Michael Blumenthal	1977–1979
	G. William Miller	1979–1981
Attorney General	Griffin Bell	1977–1979
	Benjamin R. Civiletti	1979–1981
Secretary of Interior	Cecil D. Andrus	1977–1981
Secretary of Agriculture	Robert Bergland	1977–1981
Secretary of Commerce	Juanita M. Kreps	1977–1979
	Philip M. Klutznick	1979–1981
Secretary of Labor	F. Ray Marshall	1977–1981
Secretary of Defense	Harold Brown	1977–1981
Secretary of Health, Education, and Welfare	Joseph A. Califano	1977–1979
	Patricia R. Harris	1979
Secretary of Health and Human Services	Patricia R. Harris	1979–1981
Secretary of Education	Shirley M. Hufstedler	1979–1981
Secretary of Housing and Urban Development	Patricia R. Harris	1977–1979
	Moon Landrieu	1979–1981
Secretary of Transportation	Brock Adams	1977–1979
	Neil E. Goldschmidt	1979–1981
Secretary of Energy	James R. Schlesinger	1977–1979
	Charles W. Duncan	1979–1981

The Reagan Administration

President	Ronald Reagan	1981–1989
Vice President	George Bush	1981–1989
Secretary of State	Alexander M. Haig	1981–1982
	George P. Shultz	1982–1989
Secretary of Treasury	Donald Regan	1981–1985
	James A. Baker III	1985–1988
	Nicholas F. Brady	1988–1989
Attorney General	William F. Smith	1981–1985
	Edwin A. Meese III	1985–1988
	Richard L. Thornburgh	1988–1989
Secretary of Interior	James G. Watt	1981–1983
	William P. Clark, Jr.	1983–1985
	Donald P. Hodel	1985–1989

Presidents, Vice Presidents, and Cabinet Members *(continued)*

Secretary of Agriculture	John Block	1981–1986
	Richard E. Lyng	1986–1989
Secretary of Commerce	Malcolm Baldridge	1981–1987
	C. William Verity, Jr.	1987–1989
Secretary of Labor	Raymond J. Donovan	1981–1985
	William E. Brock	1985–1987
	Ann Dore McLaughlin	1987–1989
Secretary of Defense	Casper Weinberger	1981–1987
	Frank C. Carlucci	1987–1989
Secretary of Health and Human Services	Richard S. Schweiker	1981–1983
	Margaret Heckler	1983–1985
	Otis R. Bowen	1985–1989
Secretary of Education	Terrel H. Bell	1981–1984
	William J. Bennett	1985–1988
	Lauro F. Cavazos	1988–1989
Secretary of Housing and Urban Development	Samuel R. Pierce, Jr.	1981–1989
Secretary of Transportation	Drew Lewis	1981–1982
	Elizabeth Hanford Dole	1983–1987
	James H. Burnley IV	1987–1989
Secretary of Energy	James B. Edwards	1981–1982
	Donald P. Hodel	1982–1985
	John S. Herrington	1985–1989

The George Bush Administration

President	George Bush	1989–1993
Vice President	Dan Quayle	1989–1993
Secretary of State	James A. Baker III	1989–1992
	Lawrence Eagleburger	1992–1993
Secretary of Treasury	Nicholas F. Brady	1989–1993
Attorney General	Richard L. Thornburgh	1989–1992
	William P. Barr	1992–1993
Secretary of Interior	Manuel Lujan, Jr.	1989–1993
Secretary of Agriculture	Clayton K. Yeutter	1989–1991
	Edward Madigan	1991–1993
Secretary of Commerce	Robert A. Mosbacher	1989–1992
	Barbara Hackman Franklin	1992–1993
Secretary of Labor	Elizabeth Hanford Dole	1989–1991
	Lynn Martin	1991–1993
Secretary of Defense	Richard B. Cheney	1989–1993
Secretary of Health and Human Services	Louis W. Sullivan	1989–1993

Secretary of Education	Lauro F. Cavazos	1989–1991
	Lamar Alexander	1991–1993
Secretary of Housing and Urban Development	Jack F. Kemp	1989–1993
Secretary of Transportation	Samuel K. Skinner	1989–1992
	Andrew H. Card	1992–1993
Secretary of Energy	James D. Watkins	1989–1993
Secretary of Veterans Affairs	Edward J. Derwinski	1989–1993

The Clinton Administration

President	Bill Clinton	1993–2000
Vice President	Albert Gore, Jr.	1993–2000
Secretary of State	Warren M. Christopher	1993–1997
	Madeleine K. Albright	1997–2000
Secretary of Treasury	Lloyd Bentsen	1993–1995
	Robert E. Rubin	1995–2000
Attorney General	Janet Reno	1993–2000
Secretary of the Interior	Bruce Babbitt	1993–2000
Secretary of Agriculture	Mike Espy	1993–1995
	Daniel R. Glickman	1995–2000
Secretary of Commerce	Ronald H. Brown	1993–1996
	Mickey Kantor	1996–1997
	William Daley	1997–2000
Secretary of Labor	Robert M. Reich	1993–1997
	Alexis M. Herman	1997–2000
Secretary of Defense	Les Aspin	1993–1994
	William J. Perry	1994–1997
	William S. Cohen	1997–2000
Secretary of Health and Human Services	Donna E. Shalala	1993–2000
Secretary of Education	Richard W. Riley	1993–2000
Secretary of Housing and Urban Development	Henry G. Cisneros	1993–1996
	Andrew Cuomo	1997–2000
Secretary of Transportation	Federico F. Peña	1993–1997
	Rodney E. Slater	1997–2000
Secretary of Energy	Hazel O'Leary	1993–1997
	Federico F. Peña	1997–1998
Secretary of Veterans Affairs	Jesse Brown	1993–2000

Presidents, Vice Presidents, and Cabinet Members *(continued)*

The George W. Bush Administration

President	George W. Bush	2001–
Vice President	Richard Cheney	2001–
Secretary of State	Colin Powell	2001–
Secretary of Treasury	Paul O'Neill	2001–
Attorney General	John Ashcroft	2001–
Secretary of Interior	Gale Norton	2001–
Secretary of Agriculture	Ann Veneman	2001–
Secretary of Commerce	Donald Evans	2001–
Secretary of Labor	Elaine Chao	2001–
Secretary of Defense	Donald Rumsfeld	2001–
Secretary of Health and Human Services	Tommy Thompson	2001–
Secretary of Education	Rodney Paige	2001–
Secretary of Housing and Urban Development	Melvin Martinez	2001–
Secretary of Transportation	Norman Mineta	2001–
Secretary of Energy	Spencer Abraham	2001–
Secretary of Veterans Affairs	Anthony Principi	2001–

Party Strength in Congress, 1789–2000

Year	President and vice president	Party of president	Congress	House Majority party	House Minority party	Senate Majority party	Senate Minority party
1789–1797	George Washington John Adams	None	1st 2d 3d 4th	38 Admin 37 Fed 57 Dem-Rep 54 Fed	26 Opp 33 Dem-Rep 48 Fed 52 Dem-Rep	17 Admin 16 Fed 17 Fed 19 Fed	9 Opp 13 Dem-Rep 13 Dem-Rep 13 Dem-Rep
1797–1801	John Adams Thomas Jefferson	Federalist	5th 6th	58 Fed 64 Fed	48 Dem-Rep 42 Dem-Rep	20 Fed 19 Fed	12 Dem-Rep 13 Dem-Rep
1801–1809	Thomas Jefferson Aaron Burr (to 1805) George Clinton (to 1809)	Dem-Rep	7th 8th 9th 10th	69 Dem-Rep 102 Dem-Rep 116 Dem-Rep 118 Dem-Rep	36 Fed 39 Fed 25 Fed 24 Fed	18 Dem-Rep 25 Dem-Rep 27 Dem-Rep 28 Dem-Rep	13 Fed 9 Fed 7 Fed 6 Fed
1809–1817	James Madison George Clinton (to 1813) Elbridge Gerry (to 1817)	Dem-Rep	11th 12th 13th 14th	94 Dem-Rep 108 Dem-Rep 112 Dem-Rep 117 Dem-Rep	48 Fed 36 Fed 68 Fed 65 Fed	28 Dem-Rep 30 Dem-Rep 27 Dem-Rep 25 Dem-Rep	6 Fed 6 Fed 9 Fed 11 Fed
1817–1825	James Monroe Daniel D. Tompkins	Dem-Rep	15th 16th 17th 18th	141 Dem-Rep 156 Dem-Rep 158 Dem-Rep 187 Dem-Rep	42 Fed 27 Fed 25 Fed 26 Fed	34 Dem-Rep 35 Dem-Rep 44 Dem-Rep 44 Dem-Rep	10 Fed 7 Fed 4 Fed 4 Fed
1825–1829	John Quincy Adams John C. Calhoun	Nat-Rep	19th 20th	105 Admin 119 Jack	97 Jack 94 Admin	26 Admin 28 Jack	20 Jack 20 Admin
1829–1837	Andrew Jackson John C. Calhoun (to 1833) Martin Van Buren (to 1837)	Democratic	21st 22d 23d 24th	139 Dem 141 Dem 147 Dem 145 Dem	74 Nat Rep 58 Nat Rep 53 AntiMas 98 Whig	26 Dem 25 Dem 20 Dem 27 Dem	22 Nat Rep 21 Nat Rep 20 Nat Rep 25 Whig
1837–1841	Martin Van Buren Richard M. Johnson	Democratic	25th 26th	108 Dem 124 Dem	107 Whig 118 Whig	30 Dem 28 Dem	18 Whig 22 Whig
1841	William H. Harrison[*] John Tyler	Whig					
1841–1845	John Tyler (VP vacant)	Whig	27th 28th	133 Whig 142 Dem	102 Dem 79 Whig	28 Whig 28 Whig	22 Dem 25 Dem
1845–1849	James K. Polk George M. Dallas	Democratic	29th 30th	143 Dem 115 Whig	77 Whig 108 Dem	31 Dem 36 Dem	25 Whig 21 Whig

NOTES: Only members of two major parties in Congress are shown; omitted are independents, members of minor parties, and vacancies.

Party balance as of beginning of Congress.

Congresses in which one or both houses are controlled by party other than that of the president are shown in color.

During administration of George Washington and (in part) John Quincy Adams, Congress was not organized by formal parties; the split shown is between supporters and opponents of administration.

ABBREVIATIONS: **Admin** = Administration supporters; **AntiMas** = Anti-Masonic; **Dem** = Democratic; **Dem-Rep** = Democratic-Republican; **Fed** = Federalist; **Jack** = Jacksonian Democrats; **Nat-Rep** = National Republican; **Opp** = Opponents of administration; **Rep** = Republican; **Union** = Unionist; **Whig** = Whig.

[*]Died in office.

Party Strength in Congress, 1789–2000 *(continued)*

Year	President and vice president	Party of president	Congress	House Majority party	House Minority party	Senate Majority party	Senate Minority party
1849–1850	**Zachary Taylor**[*] Millard Fillmore	Whig	31st	112 Dem	109 Whig	35 Dem	25 Whig
1850–1853	**Millard Fillmore** (VP vacant)	Whig	32d	140 Dem	88 Whig	35 Dem	24 Whig
1853–1857	**Franklin Pierce** William R. King	Democratic	33d 34th	159 Dem 108 Rep	71 Whig 83 Dem	38 Dem 40 Dem	22 Whig 15 Rep
1857–1861	**James Buchanan** John C. Breckinridge	Democratic	35th 36th	118 Dem 114 Rep	92 Rep 92 Dem	36 Dem 36 Dem	20 Rep 26 Rep
1861–1865	**Abraham Lincoln**[*] Hannibal Hamlin (to 1865) Andrew Johnson (1865)	Republican	37th 38th	105 Rep 102 Rep	43 Dem 75 Dem	31 Rep 36 Rep	10 Dem 9 Dem
1865–1869	**Andrew Johnson** (VP vacant)	Republican	39th 40th	149 Union 143 Rep	42 Dem 49 Dem	42 Union 42 Rep	10 Dem 11 Dem
1869–1877	**Ulysses S. Grant** Schuyler Colfax (to 1873) Henry Wilson (to 1877)	Republican	41st 42d 43d 44th	149 Rep 134 Rep 194 Rep 169 Dem	63 Dem 104 Dem 92 Dem 109 Rep	56 Rep 52 Rep 49 Rep 45 Rep	11 Dem 17 Dem 19 Dem 29 Dem
1877–1881	**Rutherford B. Hayes** William A. Wheeler	Republican	45th 46th	153 Dem 149 Dem	140 Rep 130 Rep	39 Rep 42 Dem	36 Dem 33 Rep
1881	**James A. Garfield**[*] Chester A. Arthur	Republican	47th	147 Rep	135 Dem	37 Rep	37 Dem
1881–1885	**Chester A. Arthur** (VP vacant)	Republican	48th	197 Dem	118 Rep	38 Rep	36 Dem
1885–1889	**Grover Cleveland** Thomas A. Hendricks	Democratic	49th 50th	183 Dem 169 Dem	140 Rep 152 Rep	43 Rep 39 Rep	34 Dem 37 Dem
1889–1893	**Benjamin Harrison** Levi P. Morton	Republican	51st 52d	166 Rep 235 Dem	159 Dem 88 Rep	39 Rep 47 Rep	37 Dem 39 Dem
1893–1897	**Grover Cleveland** Adlai E. Stevenson	Democratic	53d 54th	218 Dem 244 Rep	127 Rep 105 Dem	44 Dem 43 Rep	38 Rep 39 Dem
1897–1901	**William McKinley**[*] Garret A. Hobart (to 1901) Theodore Roosevelt (1901)	Republican	55th 56th	204 Rep 185 Rep	113 Dem 163 Dem	47 Rep 53 Rep	34 Dem 26 Dem
1901–1909	**Theodore Roosevelt** (VP vacant, 1901–1905) Charles W. Fairbanks (1905–1909)	Republican	57th 58th 59th 60th	197 Rep 208 Rep 250 Rep 222 Rep	151 Dem 178 Dem 136 Dem 164 Dem	55 Rep 57 Rep 57 Rep 61 Rep	31 Dem 33 Dem 33 Dem 31 Dem

[*]Died in office.

Party Strength in Congress, 1789–2000 *(continued)*

Year	President and vice president	Party of president	Congress	House Majority party	House Minority party	Senate Majority party	Senate Minority party
1909–1913	**William Howard Taft** James S. Sherman	Republican	61st 62d	219 Rep 228 Dem	172 Dem 161 Rep	61 Rep 51 Rep	32 Dem 41 Dem
1913–1921	**Woodrow Wilson** Thomas R. Marshall	Democratic	63d 64th 65th 66th	291 Dem 230 Dem 216 Dem 240 Rep	127 Rep 196 Rep 210 Rep 190 Dem	51 Dem 56 Dem 53 Dem 49 Rep	44 Rep 40 Rep 42 Rep 47 Dem
1921–1923	**Warren G. Harding*** Calvin Coolidge	Republican	67th	301 Rep	131 Dem	59 Rep	37 Dem
1923–1929	**Calvin Coolidge** (VP vacant, 1923–1925) Charles G. Dawes (1925–1929)	Republican	68th 69th 70th	225 Rep 247 Rep 237 Rep	205 Dem 183 Dem 195 Dem	51 Rep 56 Rep 49 Rep	43 Dem 39 Dem 46 Dem
1929–1933	**Herbert Hoover** Charles Curtis	Republican	71st 72d	267 Rep 220 Dem	167 Dem 214 Rep	56 Rep 48 Rep	39 Dem 47 Dem
1933–1945	**Franklin D. Roosevelt*** John N. Garner (1933–1941) Henry A. Wallace (1941–1945) Harry S Truman (1945)	Democratic	73d 74th 75th 76th 77th 78th	310 Dem 319 Dem 331 Dem 261 Dem 268 Dem 218 Dem	117 Rep 103 Rep 89 Rep 164 Rep 162 Rep 208 Rep	60 Dem 69 Dem 76 Dem 69 Dem 66 Dem 58 Dem	35 Rep 25 Rep 16 Rep 23 Rep 28 Rep 37 Rep
1945–1953	**Harry S Truman** (VP vacant, 1945–1949) Alben W. Barkley (1949–1953)	Democratic	79th 80th 81st 82d	242 Dem 245 Rep 263 Dem 234 Dem	190 Rep 188 Dem 171 Rep 199 Rep	56 Dem 51 Rep 54 Dem 49 Dem	38 Rep 45 Dem 42 Rep 47 Rep
1953–1961	**Dwight D. Eisenhower** Richard M. Nixon	Republican	83d 84th 85th 86th	221 Rep 232 Dem 233 Dem 283 Dem	211 Dem 203 Rep 200 Rep 153 Rep	48 Rep 48 Dem 49 Dem 64 Dem	47 Dem 47 Rep 47 Rep 34 Rep
1961–1963	**John F. Kennedy*** Lyndon B. Johnson	Democratic	87th	263 Dem	174 Rep	65 Dem	35 Rep
1963–1969	**Lyndon B. Johnson** (VP vacant, 1963–1965) Hubert H. Humphrey (1965–1969)	Democratic	88th 89th 90th	258 Dem 295 Dem 247 Dem	177 Rep 140 Rep 187 Rep	67 Dem 68 Dem 64 Dem	33 Rep 32 Rep 36 Rep
1969–1974	**Richard M. Nixon**† Spiro T. Agnew†† Gerald R. Ford§	Republican	91st 92d	243 Dem 254 Dem	192 Rep 180 Rep	57 Dem 54 Dem	43 Rep 44 Rep

*Died in office.   †Resigned from the presidency.   ††Resigned from the vice presidency.   §Appointed vice president.

Party Strength in Congress, 1789–2000 *(continued)*

Year	President and vice president	Party of president	Congress	House		Senate	
				Majority party	Minority party	Majority party	Minority party
1974–1977	Gerald R. Ford Nelson A. Rockefeller[§]	Republican	93d 94th	239 Dem 291 Dem	192 Rep 144 Rep	56 Dem 60 Dem	42 Rep 37 Rep
1977–1981	Jimmy Carter Walter Mondale	Democratic	95th 96th	292 Dem 266 Dem	143 Rep 157 Rep	61 Dem 58 Dem	38 Rep 41 Rep
1981–1989	Ronald Reagan George Bush	Republican	97th 98th 99th 100th	243 Dem 269 Dem 253 Dem 257 Dem	192 Rep 165 Rep 182 Rep 178 Rep	53 Rep 54 Rep 53 Rep 54 Dem	46 Dem 46 Dem 47 Dem 46 Rep
1989–1993	George Bush Dan Quayle	Republican	101st 102d	262 Dem 267 Dem	173 Rep 167 Rep	55 Dem 56 Dem	45 Rep 44 Rep
1993–2000	Bill Clinton Albert Gore, Jr.	Democratic	103d 104th 105th 106th	258 Dem 230 Rep 228 Rep 223 Rep	176 Rep 204 Dem 206 Dem 211 Dem	57 Dem 53 Rep 55 Rep 54 Rep	43 Rep 47 Dem 45 Dem 46 Dem
2000	George W. Bush Richard Cheney	Republican	107th	220 Rep	215 Dem	49 Rep	51 Dem

[§]Appointed vice president.